Random House Webster's

Pocket American Dictionary

Third Edition

RANDOM HOUSE
NEW YORK

This book is available for special purchases in bulk by organizations and institutions, not for resale, at special discounts. Please direct your inquiries to the Random House Special Sales Department, toll-free 888-591-1200 or fax 212-572-4961.

Please address all inquiries about electronic licensing of this division's products, for use on a network or in software or on CD-ROM, to the Subsidiary Rights Department, Random House Reference & Information Publishing, fax 212-940-7370.

Library of Congress Catalog Card Number: 98-67042

Typeset and printed in the United States of America.

Visit the Random House Web site at www.randomhouse.com

Third Edition
0 9 8 7 6 5 4 3 2 1
August 1998
ISBN: 0-375-70353-5

New York   Toronto   London   Sydney   Auckland

Contents

Pronunciation Key

The symbol (′), as in **moth′er**, is used to mark primary stress; the syllable preceding it is pronounced with greater prominence than the other syllables in the word. The symbol (′), as in **grand′moth′er**, is used to mark secondary stress; a syllable marked for secondary stress is pronounced with less prominence than one marked (′) but with more prominence than those bearing no stress mark at all.

a	act, bat	**o͝o**	book, put
ā	able, cape	**o͞o**	ooze, rule
â	air, dare	**ou**	out, loud
ä	art, calm		
		p	page, stop
b	back, rub	**r**	read, cry
ch	chief, beach	**s**	see, miss
d	do, bed	**sh**	shoe, push
		t	ten, bit
e	ebb, set	**th**	thin, path
ē	equal, bee	**t͟h**	that, other
f	fit, puff	**u**	up, love
g	give, beg	**û**	urge, burn
h	hit, hear		
		v	voice, live
i	if, big	**w**	west, away
ī	ice, bite	**y**	yes, young
		z	zeal, lazy, those
j	just, edge	**zh**	vision, measure
k	kept, make		
l	low, all	**ə**	occurs only in unaccented syllables and indicates the sound of
m	my, him		a *in* along
n	now, on		e *in* system
ng	sing, England		i *in* easily
			o *in* gallop
o	box, hot		u *in* circus
ō	over, no		
ô	order, ball		
oi	oil, joy		

Abbreviations Commonly Used in This Book

adj.	adjective	*interj.*	interjection
adv.	adverb	*l.c.*	lower case
art.	article	*n.*	noun
aux.	auxiliary	*pl.*	plural
Brit.	British	*prep.*	preposition
cap.	capital	*pron.*	pronoun
conj.	conjunction	*pt.*	past tense
def.	definition	*sing.*	singular
esp.	especially	*usu.*	usually
fem.	feminine	*v.*	verb

New Words in English

The vocabulary of English, especially American English, is growing at a remarkable rate. Among all the varieties of English around the world, including British English, it is American English that changes the fastest, adding more new words each year. New words and phrases have entered the language mostly as a result of recent inventions or knowledge in the fields of science and technology. Social and cultural trends and fashions have also contributed to the great expansion of the English vocabulary. These new terms represent a variety of subject categories, both general and specialized.

Many new words and phrases are borrowed from other languages, such as *fajitas* (from Spanish) and *karaoke* (from Japanese). Others are formed by combining or blending two or more existing words, such as *camcorder* (from *camera* and *recorder*) and *control freak*. The creation of abbreviations is another common method of word formation in English. The abbreviation *ATM* is certainly more convenient to use than the full phrase "automated-teller machine"; the shortened form *PIN* is easier to pronounce and remember than the full form "personal identification number." New words are also commonly formed from existing words by the addition of a prefix or suffix, such as *microbrewery* (prefix *micro-*) and *cyberspace* (prefix *cyber-*).

Not only does the language add new vocabulary, but existing words change, broaden, or narrow their meanings over time. The new sense of *rocket scientist* (highly intelligent person) extends the original meaning (specialist in rocket design).

New words and phrases become popular and are given life in our newspapers, magazines, books, and electronic documents, not to mention radio and television shows, movies, and plays. Some new expressions last only for a few months and are forgotten soon after their introduction. Others are controversial because of their slang status, or because they are thought to be offensive. It is not possible to predict the future of a particular word. As for the future of English, the language is certain to continue its expansion in the course of the 21st century.

The Random House family of dictionaries has kept up with the remarkable growth of the English language by recording new words faster. A careful study of the following selection of words will reveal a great deal about our changing world. You will find many more new words in the A–Z dictionary.

ag/i·ta (aj/i ta) *n.* **1.** heartburn; indigestion. **2.** agitation; anxiety.

a-life (ā/līf/) *n.* artificial life.

an/ti·ox/i·dant (an/tē ok/si dant, an/tī-) *n.* organic substance countering oxidation damage in animal tissues.

artificial life, the simulation of any aspect of life, as through computers, robotics, or biochemistry.

bean counter, *Informal.* person who makes judgments chiefly on the basis of numerical calculations.

bi/o·di·ver/si·ty, *n.* diversity of plant and animal species in an environment.

brows/er, *n.* **1.** one that browses. **2.** computer program that allows users to examine encoded World Wide Web documents in form suitable for display.

challenged, *adj.* (used as a euphemism) disabled, handicapped, or deficient (usu. preceded by adverb).

chat room, branch of computer system in which participants can have live discussions with one another.

choc/o·hol/ic (chô/ka hôl/ik, -hol/ik) *n.* person who is excessively fond of chocolate.

chump change, *Slang.* small or insignificant amount of money.

co/de·pend/ent (kō/di pen/dant) *adj.* **1.** pertaining to a relationship in which one person is addicted and the other is psychologically dependent on the addict. —*n.* **2.** person in a codependent relationship.

comp time (komp) compensatory time off from work, granted to employee in lieu of overtime pay.

con·trar/i·an (kan trâr/ē an) *n.* person who takes opposing view, esp. one who rejects majority opinion in economic matters.

control freak, person having a strong need for control.

cy/ber·punk/, *n.* **1.** science fiction featuring human interaction with supercomputers in an urban setting. **2.** *Slang.* computer hacker.

dig/e·ra/ti (dij/ə rä/tē, -rä/-) *n.pl.* people skilled with or knowledgeable about computers.

dream team, group of highly skilled experts associated in a joint action.

DVD, optical disc that can store very large amount of digital data, as text, music, or images.

dweeb (dwēb) *n. Slang.* nerd; wimp.

ed/u·tain/ment (ej/ŏŏ tān/mant) *n.* TV programs, books, software, etc., that are both educational and entertaining.

eu/ro (yŏŏr/ō, yûr/-) *n., pl.* **-ros.** proposed single monetary unit for all European countries.

fa·ji/tas (fä hē/taz, fa-) *n.pl.* thin strips of marinated and grilled meat, served with tortillas.

family leave, unpaid leave of absence from work to take care of baby or ailing family member.

FAQ (fak, ef/ā/kyōō/) *n., pl.* **FAQs, FAQ's.** *Chiefly Computers.* frequently asked questions: a document that introduces newcomers to a topic.

food/ie, *n. Slang.* person keenly interested in food, esp. a gourmet.

401(k) (fôr/ō/wun/kā/, fôr/-) *n.* savings plan that allows employees to contribute fixed amount of income to retirement account.

gang/sta rap/ (gang/sta) *n.* type of rap music whose lyrics feature violence and sexual exploits.

ga·zil/lion (gə zil/yən) *n. Informal.* extremely large, indeterminate number.

geek (gēk) *n. Slang.* **1.** carnival performer who performs bizarre acts. **2.** peculiar or offensive person, esp. one who is overly intellectual. **3.** computer expert.

grunge (grunj) *n. Slang.* **1.** dirt; filth. **2.** movement in rock music characterized by aggressive songs, associated with fashion style of unkempt clothing.

hel/i·ski/ing (hel/ē skē/ing) *n.* skiing on remote mountains to which skiers are brought by helicopter.

hep·tath/lon (hep tath/lən, -lon) *n.* athletic contest for women comprising seven track-and-field events.

home/boy/, *n.* **1.** person from the same locality as oneself. **2.** *Slang.* close friend or fellow gang member. Also, **hom/ey.**

home office, 1. main office of a company. **2.** work or office space set up in a person's home and used regularly and exclusively for business.

home page, the initial page of a Web site.

hy/per·text/, *n.* computerized data in which pieces of text, pictures, etc., are linked to allow for nonsequential access.

in/tra·net/ (in/trə net/) *n.* computer network with restricted access, as within a corporation, that uses Internet technology.

ja/va (jä/və) *n.* **1.** *Slang.* coffee. **2.** (*cap.*) *Trademark.* programming language used to create interactive applications running on the Internet.

jel′lies n.pl. transparent polyurethane shoes.

Jet Ski, Trademark. jet-propelled boat ridden like a motorcycle.

Joe′ Six′pack, Slang. the average or typical blue-collar man. Also, **Joe′ Six′-pack.**

ken·te (ken′tā) n. colorful Ghanaian fabric, often worn as symbol of African-American pride.

level playing field, a state of equality; an equal opportunity.

life′-care′, adj. (of a facility or community) designed to provide for the basic needs of elderly residents.

Lyme disease (līm) tick-transmitted disease characterized esp. by joint pains and fatigue.

mi′cro-fi′ber, n. very fine polyester fiber, used esp. for clothing.

mi′cro-man′age, v., **-aged, -aging.** manage or control with excessive attention to minor details.

morph′ing, n. the smooth transformation of one image into another by computer, as in a motion picture.

mosh (mosh) v. Slang. engage in a form of frenzied, violent dancing.

muscle shirt, Slang. T-shirt having short sleeves or no sleeves.

net′i·quette (net′i kit, -ket′) n. the etiquette of computer networks, esp. the Internet.

network computer, computer with minimal processing power, designed primarily to provide access to networks.

new′bie (nōō′bē, nyōō′-) n. newcomer, esp. an inexperienced user of computers or the Internet.

news′group′, n. discussion group on specific topic, maintained on computer network.

PCS, Personal Communications Service: system of digital wireless communications, used esp. for mobile phones.

phat (fat), adj. Slang. great; terrific.

phone card, prepaid card or charge card used at public telephones instead of coins. Also, **calling card.**

phone tag, repeated unsuccessful attempts by two persons to reach each other by phone.

play date, appointment made by parents from separate families to have their young children play together.

propeller head, Slang. person obsessively devoted to a technical pursuit.

Pro′zac (prō′zak), n. Trademark. drug used as antidepressant.

quant (kwänt) n. Slang. expert in the use of quantitative or mathematical analysis to make business forecasts, decisions, etc.

ret′ro·nym (re′trə nim) n. term, such as acoustic guitar, coined to distinguish an original referent, such as guitar, from a later development, such as electric guitar.

right′siz′ing, v., **-sized, -sizing.** adjust to an appropriate size, as a work force.

road kill, the body of an animal killed on a road by a motor vehicle.

road warrior, Slang. person who travels extensively on business.

scrunch′y (skrun′chē) n., pl. **-ies.** round elasticized fabric band, used to fasten the hair.

shock jock, radio disc jockey who features offensive or controversial material.

skort (skôrt) n. women's garment resembling short skirt but having leg sections covered by front flap.

slam dunk, forceful, often dramatic dunk shot in basketball.

spam (spam) n. **1.** unwanted or inappropriate advertisement or other message that appears on computer netwo:k. **2.** to send spam.

stick′y n., pl. **-ies.** small sheet of paper on notepad, having an adhesive backing.

strip mall, stores or restaurants in adjacent spaces in one long building.

tech′no (tek′nō), n. style of disco music characterized by very fast synthesizer rhythms.

trans·gen′dered (trans jen′dərd, tranz-) adj. **1.** appearing or attempting to be a member of the opposite sex, as a transsexual. **2.** pertaining to transgendered people.

trophy wife, young, often second, wife of rich middle-aged man.

24-7 (twen′tē fôr′ sev′ən) adv. Slang. continually; constantly (alluding to twenty-four hours a day, seven days a week). Also, **twen′ty-four′ sev′en.**

Vi·ag′ra (vī ag′rə) n. Trademark. drug used to treat impotence.

Web site, group of pages on the World Wide Web devoted to one topic or several related topics. Also, **website.**

win-win, adj. advantageous to both sides, as in a negotiation.

wuss (wŏŏs) n. Slang. weakling; wimp.

ya′da-ya′da-ya′da (yä′də yä′də-yä′də) adv. and so on; and so forth. Also, **yad′da-yad′da-yad′da.**

A

A, a (ā) *n.* first letter of English alphabet.

a (ə; *when stressed* ā) *adj. or indef. art. before initial consonant sounds.* **1.** some. **2.** one. **3.** any.

a-, prefix indicating: **1.** not, as *atypical.* **2.** without, as *amorality.*

AA, 1. administrative assistant. **2.** Alcoholics Anonymous. **3.** antiaircraft.

A.A., Associate in Arts.

aard'vark' (ärd'värk') *n.* African ant-eating mammal.

A.B., Bachelor of Arts.

A.B.A., American Bar Association.

a·back' (ə bak') *adv.* by surprise.

ab'a·cus (ab'ə kəs) *n.* calculating device using rows of sliding beads.

a·ba·lo'ne (ab'ə lō'nē) *n.* edible mollusk with mother-of-pearl shell.

a·ban'don (ə ban'dən) *v.* **1.** leave completely; forsake. **2.** give up. —*n.* **3.** surrender to natural impulses. —**a·ban'don·ment,** *n.*

a·ban'doned, *adj.* **1.** forsaken or deserted. **2.** lacking in moral restraint.

a·base' (ə bās') *v.,* **abased, abasing.** lower; degrade.

a·bash' (ə bash') *v.* embarrass or shame.

a·bate' (ə bāt') *v.,* **abated, abating.** lessen or subside.

ab'at·toir' (ab'ə twär', ab'ə twär') *n.* slaughterhouse.

ab·bé' (a bā', ab'ā) *n.* abbot; priest.

ab'bess (ab'is) *n.* convent head.

ab'bey (ab'ē) *n.* monastery or convent.

ab'bot (ab'ət) *n.* monastery head.

abbr., abbreviation.

ab·bre'vi·ate' (ə brē'vē āt') *v.,* **-ated, -ating.** shorten. —**ab·bre'vi·a'tion,** *n.*

ABC, *n., pl.* **ABC's, ABCs. 1.** alphabet. **2.** (*pl.*) basics.

ab'di·cate' (ab'di kāt') *v.,* **-cated, -cating.** give up (power or office). —**ab'di·ca'tion,** *n.*

ab'do·men (ab'də mən) *n.* part of body between thorax and pelvis; belly. —**ab·dom'i·nal** (ab dom'ə nl) *adj.*

ab·dom'i·nals, *n.pl.* muscles of abdomen. Also, **abs.**

ab·duct' (ab dukt') *v.* kidnap. —**ab·duc'tion,** *n.* —**ab·duc'tor,** *n.*

a·bed' (ə bed') *adv.* in bed.

ab·er·ra'tion (ab'ə rā'shən), *n.* **1.** deviation from what is usual, normal, or right. **2.** mental unsoundness or disorder. —**ab·er'rant** (ə ber'ənt, ab'ər-), *adj.*

a·bet' (ə bet') *v.,* **abetted, abetting.** encourage in wrongdoing.

a·bey'ance (ə bā'əns) *n.* temporary inactivity.

ab·hor' (ab hôr') *v.,* **-horred, -horring.** loathe; find repugnant. —**ab·hor'rence,** *n.* —**ab·hor'rent,** *adj.*

a·bide' (ə bīd') *v.,* **abode** (ə bōd') **or abided, abiding. 1.** remain; stay. **2.** reside. **3.** wait for. **4.** agree; conform. **5.** *Informal.* tolerate; bear.

a·bid'ing, *adj.* steadfast; lasting.

a·bil'i·ty (ə bil'i tē) *n., pl.* **-ties. 1.** power or talent. **2.** competence.

ab'ject (ab'jekt, ab jekt') *adj.* **1.** humiliating. **2.** despicable.

ab·jure' (ab jŏŏr') *v.,* **-jured, -juring.** renounce or abstain from.

ab'la·tive (ab'lə tiv) *adj. Gram.* denoting origin, means, etc.

a·blaze' (ə blāz') *adj.* **1.** on fire. **2.** gleaming. **3.** excited.

a'ble (ā'bəl) *adj.,* **abler, ablest. 1.** having sufficient power or qualification. **2.** competent. —**a'bly,** *adv.*

-able, suffix indicating: **1.** able to be, as *readable.* **2.** tending to be, as *changeable.* **3.** worthy of, as *loveable.*

a'ble-bod'ied, *adj.* physically fit.

ab·lu'tion (ə blōō'shən) *n.* ritual washing.

ab'ne·gate' (ab'ni gāt') *v.,* **-gated, -gating.** deny to oneself.

ab·nor'mal (ab nôr'məl) *adj.* not normal; not usual or typical. —**ab'nor·mal'i·ty** (-mal'i tē) *n.* —**ab·nor'mal·ly,** *adv.*

a·board' (ə bôrd') *adv.* **1.** on a ship, train, etc. —*prep.* **2.** on.

a·bode' (ə bōd') *n.* **1.** home. **2.** stay.

a·bol'ish (ə bol'ish) *v.* do away with; annul.

ab'o·li'tion (ab'ə lish'ən) *n.* **1.** act of abolishing. **2.** end of slavery in the U.S. —**ab'o·li'tion·ist,** *n.*

A'-bomb' (ā'bom') *n.* atomic bomb.

a·bom'i·na·ble (ə bom'ə nə bəl) *adj.* hateful; loathesome.

a·bom'i·nate' (-nāt') *v.,* **-nated, -nating.** abhor or hate.

ab'o·rig'i·nal (ab'ə rij'ə nl) *adj.* **1.** original. —*n.* **2.** aborigine.

ab'o·rig'i·ne (-rij'ə nē) *n.* original inhabitant of a land.

a·bort' (ə bôrt') *v.* **1.** have or cause abortion. **2.** terminate prematurely. —**a·bor'tive,** *adj.*

a·bor'tion, *n.* end of pregnancy by

expulsion of fetus before it is viable. —**a·bor´tion·ist**, *n.*

a·bound´ (a bound´) *v.* be or have a lot of.

a·bout´ (a bout´) *prep.* **1.** concerning. **2.** near, in, on, or around. **3.** ready. —*adv.* **4.** approximately. **5.** almost. **6.** on all sides. **7.** oppositely. —*adj.* **8.** astir. —*Usage.* Both ON and ABOUT mean "concerning"; ABOUT is used when the information given is general and not too technical: *A novel* ABOUT *the Civil War.* ON is used when the information is particular, as by being scholarly or technical: *an important article* ON *the Civil War.*

a·bove´ (a buv´) *adv.* **1.** higher. **2.** previously. **3.** in or to heaven. —*prep.* **4.** higher or greater than. —*adj.* **5.** foregoing.

a·bove´board´, *adv., adj.* honest; fair.

ab´ra·ca·dab´ra (ab´rə kə dab´rə) *n.* word used in magic.

a·bra´sion (a brā´zhən), *n.* **1.** wearing or rubbing away. **2.** scraped area on skin. —**a·brade´**, *v.*

a·bra´sive (a brā´siv, -ziv) *adj.* **1.** abrading. **2.** annoying. —*n.* **3.** material used to grind or smooth. —**a·bra´sive·ly**, *adv.*

a·breast´ (a brest´) *adv., adj.* **1.** side by side. **2.** informed; aware.

a·bridge´ (a brij´) *v.*, **abridged**, **abridging.** shorten.

a·broad´ (a brôd´) *adv., adj.* **1.** out of one's own country. **2.** in circulation.

ab´ro·gate´ (ab´rə gāt´) *v.*, **-gated**, **-gating.** annul or repeal.

ab·rupt´ (a brupt´) *adj.* **1.** sudden; unexpected. **2.** steep. —**ab·rupt´ly**, *adv.* —**ab·rupt´ness**, *n.*

ab´scess (ab´ses) *n.* infected, pus-filled place on the body.

ab·scond´ (ab skond´) *v.* leave suddenly and secretly.

ab´sent (ab´sent) *adj.* **1.** not present. **2.** lacking. —*v.* (ab sent´) **3.** keep away. —**ab´sence**, *n.*

ab´sen·tee´ (ab´sən tē´) *n.* absent person.

ab´sent-mind´ed, *adj.* forgetful or preoccupied. —**ab´sent-mind´ed·ly**, *adv.* —**ab´sent-mind´ed·ness**, *n.*

ab´so·lute´ (ab´sə lōōt´) *adj.* **1.** complete; perfect. **2.** pure. **3.** unrestricted. **4.** despotic. **5.** definite. —**ab´so·lute´ly**, *adv.*

absolute zero, temperature (−273. 16° C or −459.69° F) at which molecular activity ceases.

ab·solve´ (ab zolv´) *v.*, **-solved**, **-solving.** pardon sins of. —**ab´so·lu´tion** (ab´sə lōō´shən) *n.*

ab·sorb´ (ab sôrb´, -zôrb´) *v.* **1.** take in. **2.** occupy completely; fascinate. —**ab·sorb´ent**, *adj., n.* —**ab·sorb´ing**, *adj.* —**ab·sorp´tion**, *n.*

ab·stain´ (ab stān´) *v.* refrain (from). —**ab·sten´tion** (-sten´shən) *n.*

ab·ste´mi·ous (ab stē´mē əs) *adj.* moderate in eating, drinking, etc.

ab·sti·nence (ab´stə nəns) *n.* forbearance; self-restraint.

ab·stract´ (adj. ab strakt´, ab´strakt) **1.** apart from specific objects. **2.** theoretical. **3.** hard to understand. **4.** (of art) not representing natural objects or forms. —*n.* (ab´strakt) **5.** summary. **6.** essence. —*v.* (ab strakt´) **7.** remove or steal. **8.** summarize. —**ab·strac´tion**, *n.*

ab·stract´ed, *adj.* preoccupied; absentminded.

ab·struse´ (ab strōōs´) *adj.* hard to understand.

ab·surd´ (ab sûrd´, -zûrd´) *adj.* ridiculous. —**ab·surd´ly**, *adv.* —**ab·surd´i·ty**, *n.*

a·bun´dance (ə bun´dəns) *n.* plentiful supply. —**a·bun´dant**, *adj.* —**a·bun´dant·ly**, *adv.*

a·buse´ *v.*, **abused**, **abusing**, *n.* —*v.* (ə byōōz´) **1.** use wrongly. **2.** treat badly. —*n.* (ə byōōs´) **3.** wrong use or treatment. **4.** insult. —**a·bu´sive**, *adj.*

a·but´ (ə but´) *v.*, **abutted**, **abutting.** touch at the edge.

a·bys´mal (ə biz´məl) *adj.* **1.** very deep. **2.** dreadful.

a·byss´ (ə bis´) *n.* **1.** very deep chasm. **2.** hell.

Ab´ys·sin´i·an (ab´ə sin´ē ən) *adj.* **1.** from ancient Ethiopia. —*n.* **2.** type of cat.

AC, **1.** air conditioning. **2.** Also, *ac., a.c., A.C.* alternating current.

a·ca´cia (ə kā´shə) *n.* small tree or shrub.

ac´a·dem´ic (ak´ə dem´ik) *adj.* **1.** of a school, college, etc. **2.** theoretical. —*n.* **3.** college student or teacher. —**ac´a·dem´i·cal·ly**, *adv.*

a·cad´e·my (ə kad´ə mē) *n., pl.* **-mies.** **1.** school. **2.** cultural society.

a´ cap·pel´la (ä´ kə pel´ə) *adj., adv. Music.* without instrumental accompaniment.

ac·cede´ (ak sēd´) *v.*, **-ceded**, **-ceding.** **1.** consent. **2.** assume.

ac·cel´er·ate´ (ak sel´ə rāt´) *v.*, **-ated**, **-ating.** speed up; hasten. —**ac·cel´er·a´tion**, *n.*

ac·cel´er·a´tor, *n.* pedal that controls vehicle's speed.

ac´cent (ak´sent) *n.* **1.** emphasis. **2.** characteristic pronunciation. **3.**

mark showing stress, etc. —v. (ak-sent/) **4.** emphasize.

ac·cen/tu·ate/ (ak sen/chŏŏ āt/) v., **-ated, -ating.** stress or emphasize.

ac·cept/ (ak sept/) v. **1.** receive willingly. **2.** agree to. **3.** believe. —**ac·cept/a·ble,** adj. —**ac·cept/ed,** adj. —**ac·cept/a·bil/i·ty,** n. —**ac·cept/a·bly,** adv. —**ac·cept/ance,** n.
—**Usage.** Because of similarity in pronunciation, ACCEPT and EXCEPT are sometimes confused in writing. ACCEPT is a verb meaning "to receive willingly": *Please accept my gift.* EXCEPT is usually a preposition meaning "other than": *Everybody came except you.* When EXCEPT is used as a verb, it means "to leave out": *Some students were excepted from taking the exam.*

ac/cess (ak/ses) n. **1.** right to enter or use. —v. **2.** gain access to. **3.** find in a computer.

ac·ces/si·ble, adj. easy to reach or influence. —**ac·ces/si·bil/i·ty,** n.

ac·ces/sion (-sesh/ən) n. **1.** attainment of an office, etc. **2.** increase.

ac·ces/so·ry (-ses/ə rē) n., pl. **-ries. 1.** something added for convenience, decoration, etc. **2.** one who helps another commit a felony.

ac/ci·dent (ak/si dənt) n. unexpected event, usually unfortunate. —**ac/ci·den/tal,** adj. —**ac/ci·den/tal·ly,** adv.

ac/ci·dent-prone/, adj. inclined to have accidents.

ac·claim/ (ə klām/) v. **1.** salute with applause, cheers, etc. —n. **2.** applause, cheers, etc.

ac/cli·mate/ (ak/lə māt/, ə klī/mit) v., **-ated, -ating.** accustom to new conditions. Also, **ac·cli/ma·tize/.**

ac/co·lade/ (ak/ə lād/, -läd/) n. award, honor, or applause.

ac·com/mo·date/ (ə kom/ə dāt/) v., **-dated, -dating. 1.** do a favor for. **2.** supply. **3.** provide with room, food, etc. **4.** adjust.

ac·com/mo·dat/ing, adj. helpful; obliging.

ac·com/mo·da/tion, n. **1.** act of accommodating. **2.** (pl.) space for lodging or travel.

ac·com/pa·ni·ment (ə kum/pə ni-mənt, ə kump/ni-) n. **1.** something added as decoration, etc. **2.** subsidiary music for performer.

ac·com/pa·ny, v., **-nied, -nying. 1.** go or be with. **2.** provide musical accompaniment for. —**ac·com/pa·nist,** n.

ac·com/plice (ə kom/plis) n. partner in crime.

ac·com/plish (ə kom/plish) v. do or finish.

ac·com/plished, adj. expert.

ac·com/plish·ment, n. **1.** completion. **2.** skill or learning.

ac·cord/ (ə kôrd/) v. **1.** agree; be in harmony. **2.** cause to agree. **3.** grant; allow. —n. **4.** agreement; harmony. —**ac·cord/ance,** n.

ac·cord/ing·ly, adv. therefore.

according to, 1. in keeping with or proportion to. **2.** on authority of.

ac·cor/di·on (ə kôr/dē ən) n. musical instrument with keyboard and bellows.

ac·cost/ (ə kôst/) v. approach or confront.

ac·count/ (ə kount/) n. **1.** report. **2.** reason. **3.** importance. **4.** money in bank. **5.** record of business transactions. —v. **6.** explain. **7.** consider.

ac·count/a·ble, adj. **1.** responsible. **2.** explainable. —**ac·count/a·bly,** adv.

ac·count/ant, n. person whose profession is accounting. —**ac·count/an·cy,** n.

ac·count/ing, n. organization and maintenance of financial records.

ac·cred/it (ə kred/it) v. **1.** attribute. **2.** authorize or approve. —**ac·cred/i·ta/tion,** n.

ac·crue/ (ə krōō/) v., **-crued, -cruing.** be added (to). —**ac·cru/al,** n.

ac·cul/tur·ate/ (ə kul/chə rāt/) v., **-ated, -ating.** adopt cultural traits of another group.

ac·cu/mu·late/ (ə kyōō/myə lāt/) v., **-lated, -lating.** gather; collect. —**ac·cu/mu·la/tion,** n. —**ac·cu/mu·la·tive** (-lə tiv) adj. —**ac·cu/mu·la·tor,** n.

ac/cu·rate (ak/yər it) adj. exact; correct. —**ac/cu·rate·ly,** adv. —**ac/cu·ra·cy,** n.

ac·curs/ed (ə kûr/sid, ə kûrst/) adj. **1.** cursed. **2.** hateful.

ac·cu/sa·tive (ə kyōō/zə tiv) adj. Gram. denoting verb's direct object.

ac·cuse/ (ə kyōōz/) v., **-cused, -cusing.** blame; charge. —**ac/cu·sa/tion** (ak/yŏŏ zā/shən) n. —**ac·cus/er,** n.

ac·cused/, n. person tried in court.

ac·cus/tom (ə kus/təm) v. make used to.

ac·cus/tomed, adj. **1.** usual; habitual. **2.** habituated.

ace (ās) n., v. **aced, acing.** —n. **1.** playing card with single spot. **2.** expert who excels at something. **3.** Tennis. serve opponent cannot touch. —v. **4.** score ace against. **5.** do very well on.

a·cer/bic (ə sûr/bik) adj. **1.** sour. **2.** sharp or severe. —**a·cer/bi·ty,** n.

a·ce/ta·min/o·phen (ə sē/tə min/ə-

fan) *n.* substance used to reduce pain or fever.

ac•e•tate (as′i tāt′) *n.* salt or ester of acetic acid.

a•ce′tic (ə sē′tik) *adj.* of or producing vinegar.

acetic acid, sharp-tasting acid found in vinegar.

ac•e•tone (as′i tōn′) *n.* flammable liquid used as a solvent.

a•cet′y•lene (ə set′l ēn′) *n.* gas used in welding, etc.

ache (āk) *v.,* **ached, aching,** —*v.* **1.** suffer dull pain. —*n.* **2.** dull pain.

a•chieve′ (ə chēv′) *v.,* **achieved, achieving.** accomplish; bring about. —**a•chieve′ment,** *n.*

A•chil′les heel (ə kil′ēz) vulnerable spot.

ac′id (as′id) *n.* **1.** chemical compound containing hydrogen replaceable by a metal to form a salt. **2.** sour substance. —*adj.* **3.** of acids. **4.** sour or sharp. —**a•cid′i•ty,** *n.*

acid rain, rain containing chemicals from industrial pollution.

ac•knowl′edge (ak nol′ij) *v.,* **-edged, -edging. 1.** recognize; admit. **2.** show appreciation for. —**ac•knowl′edg•ment,** *n.*

ac′me (ak′mē) *n.* highest point.

ac′ne (ak′nē) *n.* skin disorder.

ac′o•lyte′ (ak′ə līt′) *n.* **1.** altar attendant. **2.** follower.

a′corn (ā′kôrn, ā′kərn) *n.* fruit or nut of the oak.

a•cous′tic (ə kōō′stik) *adj.* of sound or hearing. —**a•cous′ti•cal•ly,** *adv.*

a•cous′tics, *n.* **1.** science of sound. **2.** sound qualities.

ac•quaint′ (ə kwānt′) *v.* make known or familiar.

ac•quaint′ance, *n.* **1.** someone personally known. **2.** personal knowledge.

ac′qui•esce′ (ak′wē es′) *v.,* **-esced, -escing.** agree or comply. —**ac′qui•es′cence,** *n.* —**ac′qui•es′cent,** *adj.*

ac•quire′ (ə kwīˀr′) *v.,* **-quired, -quiring.** get; obtain. —**ac•quire′ment,** *n.*

ac′qui•si′tion (ak′wə zish′ən) *n.* **1.** acquiring. **2.** something acquired.

ac•quis′i•tive (ə kwiz′i tiv) *adj.* eager to acquire.

ac•quit′ (ə kwit′) *v.,* **-quitted, -quitting. 1.** free of blame or guilt. **2.** behave or conduct. —**ac•quit′tal,** *n.*

a′cre (ā′kər) *n.* unit of land area (1/640 sq. mi. or 43,560 sq. ft.). —**a′cre•age,** *n.*

ac′rid (ak′rid) *adj.* sharp; biting.

ac′ri•mo′ny (ak′rə mō′nē) *n.* harsh-

ness or bitterness of manner or speech. —**ac′ri•mo′ni•ous,** *adj.*

ac′ro•bat′ (ak′rə bat′) *n.* performer on trapeze, tightrope, etc. —**ac′ro•bat′ic,** *adj.*

ac′ro•bat′ics, *n. (used with a pl. v.)* **1.** acrobat's feats. **2.** any feats requiring skill.

ac′ro•nym (ak′rə nim) *n.* word formed from successive initials or groups of letters, as NATO, UNICEF.

ac′ro•pho′bi•a (ak′rə fō′bē ə) *n.* fear of heights.

a•cross′ (ə krôs′) *prep.* **1.** from side to side of. **2.** on the other side of. —*adv.* **3.** from one side to another.

across-the-board, *adj.* applying to all members or categories.

a•cryl′ic (ə kril′ik) *n.* chemical used to make textile fibers and paints.

act (akt) *n.* **1.** something done. **2.** law or decree. **3.** part of a play or opera. —*v.* **4.** do something. **5.** behave. **6.** pretend. **7.** perform in play, movie, etc.

act′ing, *adj.* substitute.

ac•tin′i•um (ak tin′ē əm) *n.* radioactive metallic element.

ac′tion (ak′shən) *n.* **1.** state of being active. **2.** something done. **3.** behavior. **4.** combat. **5.** lawsuit.

ac′tion•a•ble, *adj.* providing grounds for a lawsuit.

ac′ti•vate′ (ak′tə vāt′) *v.,* **-vated, -vating.** make active; start. —**ac′ti•va′tion,** *n.*

ac′tive (ak′tiv) *adj.* **1.** in action; busy, nimble, or lively. **2.** indicating that the subject performs the action of the verb. —**ac′tive•ly,** *adv.*

ac′tiv•ism, *n.* vigorous action toward social or political goals. —**ac′tiv•ist,** *n.*

ac•tiv′i•ty (ak tiv′i tē) *n., pl.* **-ties. 1.** being active. **2.** busy action. **3.** specific occupation or pursuit.

ac′tor (ak′tər) *n.* performer in play or movie. —**ac′tress,** *n.fem.*

ac′tu•al (ak′chōō əl) *adj.* real. —**ac′tu•al•ly,** *adv.* —**ac′tu•al′i•ty** (-al′i tē) *n.*

ac′tu•ar′y (ak′chōō er′ē) *n., pl.* **-ar•ies.** calculator of insurance rates and risks. —**ac′tu•ar′i•al,** *adj.*

ac′tu•ate′ (ak′chōō āt′) *v.,* **-ated, -ating.** cause to act; effect.

a•cu′i•ty (ə kyōō′i tē) *n.* sharpness of perception.

a•cu′men (ə kyōō′mən) *n.* mental keenness.

ac′u•punc′ture (ak′yōō pungk′chər) *n.* Chinese art of healing by inserting needles into the body. —**ac′u•punc′tur•ist,** *n.*

a·cute' (ə kyo͞ot') adj. **1.** sharp; pointed. **2.** severe. **3.** crucial. **4.** keen, clever. **5.** high-pitched. **6.** (of an angle) less than 90 degrees. —**a·cute'ly,** adv. —**a·cute'ness,** n.

ad (ad) n. Informal. advertisement.

A.D., anno Domini: in the year of our Lord.

ad'age (ad'ij) n. proverb.

a·da'gio (ə dä'jō, -zhē ō') adj., adv. Music. slow.

ad'a·mant (ad'ə mənt) adj. insistent.

Ad'am's ap'ple (ad'əmz) projection of thyroid cartilage in front of neck.

a·dapt' (ə dapt') v. adjust to new requirements. —**a·dapt'a·ble,** adj. —**a·dapt'a·bil'i·ty,** n. —**ad·ap·ta'tion** (ad'ap tā'shən) n. —**a·dapt'er, a·dap'tor,** n.

add (ad) v. **1.** unite or join. **2.** find the sum (of). **3.** increase. **4.** say more.

ad·den'dum (ə den'dəm) n., pl. -da (-də). something to be added.

ad'der (ad'ər) n. small venomous snake.

ad'dict n. (ad'ikt) **1.** person dependent on a drug, etc. —v. (ə dikt') **2.** make dependent on. —**ad·dic'tion,** n. —**ad·dic'tive,** adj.

ad·di'tion (ə dish'ən) n. **1.** adding. **2.** anything added. **3. in addition to,** besides. —**ad·di'tion·al,** adj. —**ad·di'tion·al·ly,** adv.

ad'di·tive (ad'i tiv) n. added ingredient.

ad'dle (ad'l) v., -dled, -dling. confuse.

ad·dress' (ə dres') n. **1.** formal speech. **2.** place of residence. —v. **3.** speak or write (to). **4.** send. **5.** apply (oneself). —**ad·dress·ee'** (ad're sē') n.

ad·duce' (ə do͞os', ə dyo͞os') v., -duced, -ducing. present; cite.

ad'e·noid' (ad'n oid') n. mass of tissue between back of nose and throat.

a·dept', adj. (ə dept') **1.** skilled. —n. (ad'ept, ə dept') **2.** expert.

ad'e·quate (ad'i kwit) adj. sufficient; fit. —**ad'e·quate·ly,** adv. —**ad'e·qua·cy,** n.

ad·here' (ad hēr') v., -hered, -hering. **1.** stick or cling. **2.** be faithful or loyal. —**ad·her'ence,** n. —**ad·her'ent,** n., adj. —**ad·he'sion** (-hē'zhən) n.

ad·he'sive (ad hē'siv, -ziv) adj. **1.** coated with a sticky substance. **2.** sticky. —n. **3.** adhesive substance.

ad hoc (ad hok', hōk') for a specified purpose.

a·dieu' (ə do͞o', ə dyo͞o') interj., n. French. good-by; farewell.

ad in·fi·ni·tum (ad in'fə nī'təm) to infinity; endlessly.

adj., 1. adjective. **2.** adjustment. **3.** adjutant.

ad·ja'cent (ə jā'sənt) adj. near; adjoining.

ad'jec·tive (aj'ik tiv) n. word describing a noun. —**ad'jec·ti'val** (-tī'vəl) adj.

ad·join' (ə join') v. be next to.

ad·journ' (ə jûrn') v. suspend (meeting) till another time. —**ad·journ'ment,** n.

ad·judge' (ə juj') v., -judged, -judging. **1.** decree or decide. **2.** award.

ad·ju'di·cate' (ə jo͞o'di kāt') v., -cated, -cating. decide on as a judge. —**ad·ju'di·ca'tion,** n.

ad'junct (aj'ungkt) n. something added.

ad·just' (ə just') v. **1.** fit; adapt. **2.** regulate. **3.** settle. —**ad·just'a·ble,** adj. —**ad·just'er, ad·jus'tor,** n. —**ad·just'ment,** n.

ad'ju·tant (aj'ə tənt) n. military assistant to commandant.

ad-lib' (ad lib') v., -libbed, -libbing. improvise (speech, music, etc.). —**ad-lib',** adv.

Adm., admiral.

adm. or **admn.,** **1.** administration. **2.** administrative. **3.** administrator.

ad'man' (ad'man', -mən) n. advertising professional.

ad·min'is·ter (ad min'ə stər) v. **1.** manage; direct. **2.** dispense or give.

ad·min'is·tra'tion (-ə strā'shən) n. **1.** management. **2.** dispensing. **3.** executive officials. —**ad·min'is·tra'tive,** adj.

ad·min'is·tra'tor, n. manager.

ad'mi·ra·ble (ad'mər ə bəl) adj. worthy of admiration.

ad'mi·ral (ad'mər əl) n. **1.** high-ranking navy officer. **2.** brightly colored type of butterfly.

ad'mi·ral·ty, n., pl. -ties. navy department.

ad·mire' (ad mī[ə]r') v., -mired, -miring. regard highly. —**ad·mir'er,** n. —**ad·mi·ra'tion** (ad'mə rā'shən) n.

ad·mis'si·ble (ad mis'ə bəl) adj. allowable.

ad·mis'sion (-mish'ən) n. **1.** act of admitting. **2.** entrance price. **3.** confession or acknowledgment.

ad·mit' (-mit') v., -mitted, -mitting. **1.** allow to enter. **2.** permit. **3.** confess or acknowledge. —**ad·mit'tance,** n.

ad·mit'ted·ly, adv. without doubt.

ad·mon'ish (ad mon'ish) v. **1.** warn. **2.** reprove. —**ad·mo·ni'tion** (ad'mə nish'ən) n. —**ad·mon'i·to'ry,** adj.

ad nau/se·am (ad nô/zē əm) to a sickening degree.

a·do/ (ə dōō/) n. activity; fuss.

a·do/be (ə dō/bē) n. sun-dried brick.

ad/o·les/cence (ad/l es/əns) n. period between childhood and adulthood. —**ad/o·les/cent,** adj., n.

a·dopt/ (ə dopt/) v. take or accept as one's own. —**a·dop/tion,** n. —**a·dopt/ive,** adj.

a·dore/ (ə dôr/) v., **adored, adoring.** love; worship. —**a·dor/a·ble,** adj. —**ad/o·ra/tion** (ad/ə rā/shən) n.

a·dorn/ (ə dôrn/) v. decorate. —**a·dorn/ment,** n.

ad·re/nal (ə drēn/l) adj. of a pair of glands near the kidneys.

ad·ren/al·in (ə dren/l in) n. glandular secretion that speeds heart, etc.

a·drift/ (ə drift/) adv., adj. floating about, esp. helplessly.

a·droit/ (ə droit/) adj. expert; deft. —**a·droit/ly,** adv.

ad/u·la/tion (aj/ə lā/shən) n. excessive praise. —**ad/u·late/,** v.

a·dult/ (ə dult/) adj. **1.** full-grown; mature. —n. **2.** full-grown person. —**a·dult/hood,** n.

a·dul/ter·ate/ (ə dul/tə rāt/) v., **-ated, -ating.** make impure.

a·dul/ter·y, n., pl. **-teries.** marital infidelity. —**a·dul/ter·er,** n. —**a·dul/ter·ess,** n. —**a·dul/ter·ous,** adj.

adv. 1. advance. **2.** adverb. **3.** adverbial. **4.** advertisement.

ad·vance/ (ad vans/) v., **-vanced, -vancing. 1.** move forward. **2.** propose. **3.** raise in rank, price, etc. **4.** supply beforehand. —n. **5.** forward move. **6.** promotion. **7.** increase. **8.** loan. **9.** friendly gesture. —adj. **10.** early. —**ad·vance/ment,** n.

ad·vanced/, adj. **1.** progressive. **2.** relatively learned, old, etc.

ad·van/tage (ad van/tij) n. **1.** more favorable condition. **2.** benefit. —**ad/van·ta/geous,** adj.

ad/vent (ad/vent) n. **1.** arrival. **2.** coming of Christ. **3.** (cap.) month before Christmas.

ad/ven·ti/tious (ad/van tish/əs) adj. accidentally added.

ad·ven/ture (ad ven/chər) n., v., **-tured, -turing.** —n. **1.** risky undertaking. **2.** exciting event. —v. **3.** risk or dare. —**ad·ven/tur·er,** n. —**ad·ven/tur·ous,** adj.

ad/verb (ad/vûrb) n. word modifying a verb, verbal noun, or other adverb. —**ad·ver/bi·al,** adj.

ad/ver·sar/y (ad/vər ser/ē) n., pl. **-saries.** opponent.

ad·verse/ (ad vûrs/) adj. opposing; antagonistic. —**ad·verse/ly,** adv.

ad·ver/si·ty (-vûr/si tē) n., pl. **-ties.** misfortune.

ad/ver·tise/ (ad/vər tīz/) v., **-tised, -tising.** bring to public notice. —**ad/ver·tis/er,** n. —**ad/ver·tise/-ment,** n. —**ad/ver·tis/ing,** n.

ad·vice/ (ad vīs/) n. **1.** opinion offered. **2.** news.

ad·vis/a·ble (ad vī/zə bəl) adj. wise or desirable. —**ad·vis/a·bil/i·ty,** n.

ad·vise/ (ad vīz/) v. **-vised, -vising. 1.** offer an opinion. **2.** recommend. **3.** consult (with). **4.** give news. —**ad·vis/er, ad·vi/sor,** n.

ad·vis/ed·ly, adv. deliberately.

ad·vi/so·ry, adj. giving advice.

ad/vo·cate/, v., **-cated, -cating,** n. —v. (ad/və kāt/) **1.** urge; recommend. —n. (-kit) **2.** supporter of cause. **3.** lawyer. —**ad/vo·ca·cy,** n.

adz (adz) n. axlike tool.

ae/gis (ē/jis) n. sponsorship or protection.

ae/on (ē/an, ē/on) n. eon.

aer/ate (âr/āt) v., **-ated, -ating.** expose to air.

aer/i·al (âr/ē əl) adj. **1.** of or in air. **2.** lofty. —n. **3.** antenna.

aer/ie (âr/ē, ēr/ē) n, pl. **-ies.** eagle's nest.

aero-, prefix indicating: **1.** air. **2.** aircraft. Also, **aer-.**

aer·o/bic (â rō/bik) adj. **1.** needing oxygen to live. **2.** of aerobics.

aer·o/bics, n.pl. exercises designed to strengthen the heart and lungs.

aer/o·dy·nam/ics (âr/ō dī nam/iks) n. science of action of air against solids. —**aer/o·dy·nam/ic,** adj.

aer/o·naut/ (âr/ə nôt/) n. pilot.

aer/o·nau/tics, n. science of flight in aircraft. —**aer/o·nau/ti·cal,** adj.

aer/o·plane/ (âr/ə plän/) n. Brit. airplane.

aer/o·sol/ (âr/ə sôl/) n. **1.** liquid distributed through a gas. **2.** spray of such liquid.

aer/o·space/ (âr/ō spās/) n. **1.** earth's atmosphere and the space beyond. —adj. **2.** of missiles, aircraft, and spacecraft.

aes·thet/ic (es thet/ik) adj. **1.** of beauty. **2.** appreciating beauty. —**aes·thet/ics,** n. study of beauty.

a·far/ (ə fär/) adv. at a distance.

af/fa·ble (af/ə bəl) adj. friendly; cordial. —**af/fa·bil/i·ty,** n.

af·fair/ (ə fâr/) n. **1.** matter of business. **2.** event. **3.** amorous relationship.

af·fect/ (ə fekt/) v. **1.** produce an effect; act on. **2.** impress the feelings of; move. **3.** pretend to possess or feel. —**Usage.** Because of similarity in pronunciation, AF-

FECT and EFFECT are sometimes confused in writing. The verb AFFECT means "to act on" or "to move": *His words affected the crowd so deeply that many wept.* The verb EFFECT means "to bring about, accomplish": *The new taxes effected many changes in people's lives.* The noun EFFECT means "result, consequence": *the tragic effect of the hurricane.*

af·fec·ta/tion (af'ek tā'shən) *n.* pretense.

af·fect/ed (ə fek'tid) *adj.* **1.** vain; haughty. **2.** pretended.

af·fec/tion (ə fek'shən) *n.* love.

af·fec/tion·ate (-nit) *adj.* fondly tender; loving. —**af·fec/tion·ate·ly,** *adv.*

af·fi·da·vit (af'i dā'vit) *n.* written statement under oath.

af·fil/i·ate, *v.,* **-ated, -ating,** *n.* —*v.* (ə filē āt') **1.** join; connect. —*n.* (-ē it) **2.** associate.

af·fin/i·ty (ə fin'i tē) *n., pl.* **-ties. 1.** attraction. **2.** similarity.

af·firm/ (ə fûrm') *v.* **1.** state; assert. **2.** ratify. —**af·fir·ma/tion** (af'ər-mā'shən) *n.*

af·firm/a·tive, *adj.* saying yes; affirming.

affirmative action, policy to increase employment opportunities for women and minorities.

af·fix/ *v.* (ə fiks') **1.** attach. —*n.* (af'iks) **2.** added part.

af·flict/ (ə flikt') *v.* distress; trouble. —**af·flic/tion,** *n.*

af·flu·ent (af'lōō ənt) *adj.* rich; abundant. —**af·flu·ence,** *n.*

af·ford/ (ə fôrd') *v.* **1.** have resources enough. **2.** provide.

af·fray/ (ə frā') *n.* fight.

af·front/ (ə frunt') *n., v.* insult.

af·ghan (af'gən) *n.* knitted blanket.

a·field/ (ə fēld') *adv.* astray.

a·fire/ (ə fī″r') *adv., adj.* on fire.

a·flame/ (ə flām') *adv., adj.* in flames.

AFL-CIO, American Federation of Labor and Congress of Industrial Organizations.

a·float/ (ə flōt') *adv.* **1.** floating. **2.** in circulation. **3.** out of debt.

a·foot/ (ə fŏŏt') *adv., adj.* **1.** on foot. **2.** in existence.

a·fore·said/ (ə fôr'sed') *adj.* said before. Also, **a·fore/men/tioned** (-men'shənd).

a·fraid/ (ə frād') *adj.* feeling fear.

a·fresh/ (ə fresh') *adv.* anew.

Af·ri·can (af'ri kən) *n.* native of Africa. —**Af·ri·can,** *adj.*

Af·ri·can-A·mer/i·can, *n., adj.* black American.

Af·ri·kaans (af'ri käns', -känz') *n.*

language of South Africa, derived from Dutch.

Af·ri·ka/ner (-kä'nər, -kan'ər) *n.* white South African who speaks Afrikaans.

Af/ro (af'rō) *n.* full, bushy hairstyle.

Af/ro-A·mer/i·can, *n., adj.* African-American.

aft (aft) *adv.* Naut. at or toward the stern.

af/ter (af'tər) *prep.* **1.** behind. **2.** about. **3.** later than. **4.** in imitation of. —*adv.* **5.** behind. **6.** later.

af/ter·birth/, *n.* placenta and other matter expelled from uterus after childbirth.

af/ter·care/, *n.* care of recovering patient.

af/ter·glow/, *n.* glow after sunset. **2.** pleasant memory.

af/ter·life/, *n.* life after death.

af/ter·math/ (-math') *n.* results.

af/ter·noon/, *n.* period between noon and evening.

af/ter·thought/, *n.* later thought.

af/ter·ward (-wərd) *adv.* later. Also, **af/ter·wards.**

a·gain/ (ə gen') *adv.* **1.** once more. **2.** besides.

a·gainst/ (ə genst') *prep.* **1.** opposed to. **2.** in or into contact with.

a·gape/ (ə gāp') *adv., adj.* wide open.

ag/ate (ag'it) *n.* kind of quartz.

agcy., agency.

age (āj) *n., v.,* **aged, aging.** —*n.* **1.** length of time in existence. **2.** stage; period. **3.** legal maturity. —*v.* **4.** make or become older.

ag/ed (ā'jid for 1; ājd for 1–3) *adj.* **1.** having lived long. **2.** matured. —*n.pl.* **3.** elderly persons.

age/ism, *n.* discrimination against elderly persons. —**age/ist,** *n.*

age/less, *adj.* **1.** apparently not aging. **2.** not outdated.

a/gen·cy (ā'jən sē) *n., pl.* **-cies. 1.** office. **2.** action. **3.** means.

a·gen/da (ə jen'də) *n.* matters to be dealt with.

a/gent (ā'jənt) *n.* **1.** person acting for another. **2.** means. **3.** official.

ag·glom/er·ate/, *v.,* **-ated, -ating,** *adj.,* *n.* —*v.* (ə glom'ə rāt') **1.** collect into a mass. —*adj.* (-ər it) **2.** collected in a mass. —*n.* (-ər it) **3.** such a mass.

ag·gran/dize (ə gran'dīz, ag'rən-dīz') *v.,* **-dized, -dizing.** increase in size, rank, etc. —**ag·gran/dize·ment** (-diz mənt) *n.*

ag/gra·vate/ (ag'rə vāt') *v.,* **-vated, -vating. 1.** make worse. **2.** annoy. —**ag/gra·va/tion,** *n.* —**Usage.**

formal speech and writing, the meaning "to annoy" (*Stop aggravating me!*) is sometimes criticized and is used less often than the meaning "to make worse" (*His insulting words aggravated his tense situation*).

ag'gre·gate, *adj., n., v.,* **-gated, -gating.** —*adj.* (ag'ri git) 1. combined. —*n.* (-git) 2. whole amount. —*v.* (-gāt') 3. collect; gather.

ag·gres'sion (ə gresh'ən) *n.* hostile act; attack. —**ag·gres'sor,** *n.*

ag·gres'sive (ə gres'iv) *adj.* 1. boldly energetic. 2. hostile.

ag·grieve' (ə grēv') *v.,* **-grieved, -grieving.** wrong severely.

a·ghast' (ə gast') *adj.* shocked or horrified.

ag'ile (aj'əl) *adj.* quick; nimble. —**a·gil'i·ty** (ə jil'i tē) *n.*

ag'i·tate' (aj'i tāt') *v.,* **-tated, -tating.** 1. shake. 2. disturb; excite. —**ag'i·ta'tion,** *n.* —**ag'i·ta'tor,** *n.*

ag·nos'tic (ag nos'tik) *n.* one who believes God is beyond human knowledge. —**ag·nos'ti·cism** (-tə siz'əm) *n.*

a·go' (ə gō') *adj., adv.* in the past.

a·gog' (ə gog') *adj.* eagerly excited.

ag'o·nize' (ag'ə nīz') *v.,* **-nized, -nizing.** suffer anxiety.

ag'o·ny (-nē) *n., pl.* **-nies.** intense pain or suffering.

ag'o·ra·pho'bi·a (ag'ər ə fō'bē ə) *n.* fear of open spaces.

a·grar'i·an (ə grâr'ē ən) *adj.* of the land.

a·gree' (ə grē') *v.,* **agreed, agreeing.** 1. consent or promise. 2. be in harmony. 3. be similar.

a·gree'a·ble, *adj.* 1. pleasant. 2. willing. —**a·gree'a·bly,** *adv.*

a·gree'ment *n.* 1. harmony. 2. arrangement.

ag'ri·busi'ness (ag'rə biz'nis) large-scale business of growing, processing, and distributing farm products.

ag'ri·cul'ture, *n.* science of farming. —**ag'ri·cul'tur·al,** *adj.*

a·gron'o·my (ə gron'ə mē) *n.* science of farm management.

a·ground' (ə ground') *adv., adj. Naut.* onto the bottom or shore.

ah (ä) *interj.* (exclamation of pain, surprise, or satisfaction)

a·head' (ə hed') *adv.* 1. in front; forward. 2. winning.

a·hoy' (ə hoi') *interj. Naut.* (hey there!)

aid (ād) *v., n.* help.

aide (ād) *n.* assistant.

aide-de-camp (ād'də kamp') *n., pl.* **aides-de-camp.** military assistant.

AIDS (ādz) *n.* acquired immunity deficiency syndrome, a disease making one increasingly susceptible to infections and other diseases.

ail (āl) *v.* 1. trouble. 2. be sick.

ai'ler·on' (ā'lə ron') *n.* flap on airplane wing.

ail'ment, *n.* illness.

aim (ām) *v.* 1. point or direct. 2. intend. —*n.* 3. act of aiming. 4. target. 5. purpose. —**aim'less,** *adj.*

ain't (ānt) *v. Nonstandard or Dial.* am not; are not; is not. —**Usage.** AIN'T is more common in uneducated speech, though it occurs with some frequency in the informal speech of the educated: *I ain't going. He ain't so young anymore.* The question form "Ain't I...?" is sometimes substituted for "Aren't I ..?", which is considered to be ungrammatical. AIN'T also occurs in some humorous or set phrases, and it is sometimes used to give emphasis: *Ain't it the truth! It just ain't so!*

air (âr) *n.* 1. mixture of gases forming atmosphere of earth. 2. appearance; manner. 3. tune. —*v.* 4. expose to air. 5. broadcast.

air bag, bag that inflates automatically to protect passengers in a car collision.

air'borne', *adj.* carried by air; flying.

air'brush', *n.* 1. atomizer for spraying paint. —*v.* 2. paint with an airbrush.

air conditioning, control of interior air for temperature, humidity, etc. —**air-conditioned,** *adj.*

air'craft', *n.* vehicle or vehicles for flight.

air'field', *n.* ground area for airplanes to land on and take off from.

air' force', military branch for air operations.

air'head', *n. Slang.* scatterbrained or stupid person.

air'lift', *n.* 1. major transport by air. —*v.* 2. move by airlift.

air'line', *n.* air transport company.

air·lin'er, *n.* large passenger airplane operated by airline.

air'mail', *n.* 1. system of sending mail by airplane. 2. mail sent by airmail. —**air'mail',** *v.*

air'man, *n., pl.* **-men.** aviator.

air'plane', *n.* powered heavier-than-air craft with wings.

air'port', *n.* place where aircraft pick up passengers and cargo.

air raid, attack by aircraft.

air'ship', *n.* lighter-than-air aircraft.

air'sick/ness, n. nausea from motion in air travel. **—air'sick/,** adj.

air'space/, n. space above a nation, city, etc., over which it has control.

air'tight/, adj. **1.** impermeable to air. **2.** perfect; free of error.

air'waves/, n.pl. medium of radio and television broadcasting.

air'y, adj. **-ier, -iest. 1.** of or like air. **2.** delicate. **3.** well ventilated. **4.** light; lively. **—air'i•ly,** adv.

aisle (īl) n. passageway.

a•jar/ (ə jär/) adj., adv. partly open.

AK, Alaska.

a.k.a., also known as.

a•kim/bo (ə kim/bō) adj., adv. with hands at hips.

a•kin/ (ə kin/) adj. alike.

-al, 1. adjective suffix meaning: of or pertaining to, as *tribal;* characterized by, as *typical.* **2.** noun suffix meaning: act or process, as *refusal.*

AL, Alabama.

à la or **a la** (ä/ lä, ä/ lə) prep. in the manner or style of.

Ala., Alabama.

à la carte (ä/ lə kärt/) with each dish separately priced.

a•lac/ri•ty (ə lak/ri tē) n. quickness; readiness.

à la mode (ä/ lə mōd/) **1.** in the fashion. **2.** with ice cream.

a•larm/ (ə lärm/) n. **1.** fear of danger. **2.** sudden warning. **3.** call to arms. —v. **4.** fill with fear.

alarm clock, clock with device to awaken sleeper.

a•las/ (ə las/) interj. (cry of sorrow.)

al/a•tross/ (al/ə trôs/) n. large white sea bird.

al•be/it (ôl bē/it) conj. though.

al•bi/no (al bī/nō) n., pl. **-nos.** one lacking in pigmentation.

al/bum (al/bəm) n. **1.** blank book for pictures, stamps, etc. **2.** collection of recordings.

al•bu/men (al byōō/mən) n. egg white.

al•bu/min (-mən) n. water-soluble protein found in egg white, milk, blood, etc.

al/che•my (al/kə mē) n. medieval chemistry. **—al/che•mist,** n.

al/co•hol (al/kə hôl/) n. colorless intoxicating liquid.

al/co•hol/ic, 1. of alcohol. —n. **2.** one addicted to alcohol.

al/co•hol•ism, n. addiction to alcohol.

al/cove (al/kōv) n. recessed space.

al/der (ôl/dər) n. small tree, usually growing in moist places.

al/der•man (ôl/dər mən) n., pl. **-men.** city official.

ale (āl) n. dark, bitter beer.

a•lert/ (ə lûrt/) adj. **1.** vigilant. —n. **2.** air-raid alarm. —v. **3.** warn.

al•fal/fa (al fal/fə) n. forage plant also grown as food.

al•fres/co (al fres/kō) adv., adj. in the open air. Also, **al fres/co.**

al/ga (al/gə) n., pl. **-gae** (-jē). water plant; seaweed.

al/ge•bra (al/jə brə) n. branch of mathematics using symbols rather than specific numbers. **—al/ge•bra/ic** (-jə brā/ik) adj.

Al•gon/qui•an (al gong/kē ən, -kwē ən) n. member of a North American Indian people. Also, **Al•gon/ki•an.**

al/go•rithm (al/gə rith/əm) n. set of rules or steps to solve mathematical problem, program computer, etc. **—al/go•rith/mic,** adj.

a/li•as (ā/lē əs) adv. **1.** otherwise known as. —n. **2.** assumed name.

al/i•bi/ (al/ə bī/) n. **1.** defense by accused person of being elsewhere. **2.** excuse.

al/ien (āl/yən) n. **1.** foreigner. **2.** creature from outer space. —adj. **3.** foreign.

al/ien•ate/ (-yə nāt/) v., **-ated, -ating.** lose friendship of; repel. **—al/ien•a/tion,** n.

a•light/ (ə līt/) v. **1.** dismount after travel. **2.** descend to perch or sit. —adv., adj. **3.** lighted up.

a•lign/ (ə līn/) v. bring into line. **—a•lign/ment,** n.

a•like/ (ə līk/) adv. **1.** similarly. —adj. **2.** similar.

al/i•men/ta•ry (al/ə men/tə rē) adj. of or for food.

alimentary canal, tube in body for digestion of food.

al/i•mo/ny (al/ə mō/nē) n. money for support of a spouse after separation or divorce.

a•live/ (ə līv/) adj. **1.** living. **2.** active. **3.** lively. **4.** teeming.

al/ka•li/ (al/kə lī/) n. chemical that neutralizes acids to form salts. **—al/ka•line/,** adj.

al/ka•loid/ (-loid/) n. organic compound in plants, as morphine.

all (ôl) adj. **1.** the whole of. **2.** every. —n., pron. **3.** the whole; everything. —adv. **4.** entirely.

Al/lah (al/ə, ä/lə) n. Muslim name for God.

All/-Amer/ican, adj. **1.** best in the U.S., as in a sport. **2.** typically American. —n. **3.** all-American player or team.

all'-around', *adj.* **1.** versatile. **2.** having many uses.

al•lay' (ə lā') *v.* quiet or lessen.

al•lege' (ə lej') *v.*, **-leged, -leging.** state, often without proof. —**al'le•ga'tion** (al'ə gā'shən) *n.* —**al•leg'ed•ly** (-lej'id-) *adv.*

al•le'giance (ə lē'jəns) *n.* loyalty.

al'le•go•ry (al'ə gôr'ē) *n., pl.* **-ries.** symbolic story. —**al'le•gor'i•cal,** *adj.*

al•le'gro (ə lā'grō, ə leg'rō) *adv. Music.* fast.

al'le•lu'ia (al'ə lōō'yə) *interj.* (hallelujah.)

al'ler•gen (al'ər jən) *n.* substance that causes allergic reaction. —**al'ler•gen'ic** (-jen'ik) *adj.*

al'ler•gy (-jē) *n., pl.* **-gies.** bodily sensitiveness to certain substances. —**al•ler'gic** (ə lûr'jik) *adj.*

al•le'vi•ate (ə lē'vē āt') *v.*, **-ated, -ating.** lessen; relieve.

al'ley (al'ē) *n.* narrow street.

alley cat, stray cat.

al•li'ance (ə lī'əns) *n.* **1.** union. **2.** treaty. **3.** parties to treaty.

al•lied' (ə līd', al'īd) *adj.* **1.** joined by treaty. **2.** related.

al'li•ga'tor (al'i gā'tər) *n.* broadsnouted type of crocodile.

all'-in•clu'sive (ə lit'ə) *adj.* comprehensive.

al•lit'er•a'tion (ə lit'ə rā'shən) *n.* series of words starting with the same sound.

al'lo•cate' (al'ə kāt') *v.*, **-cated, -cating.** allot. —**al'lo•ca'tion,** *n.*

al•lot' (ə lot') *v.*, **-lotted, -lotting.** **1.** divide; distribute. **2.** assign. —**al•lot'ment,** *n.*

all'-out', *adj.* total; unrestricted.

al•low' (ə lou') *v.*, **1.** permit. **2.** give. **3.** admit. —**al•low'a•ble,** *adj.* —**al•low'ance,** *n.*

al'loy, *n.* **1.** mixture of metals. —*v.* (ə loi') **2.** mix (metals). **3.** adulterate.

all right, 1. yes; I agree. **2.** in a satisfactory way. **3.** safe; sound. **4.** acceptable; satisfactory. —**Usage.** The one-word spelling ALRIGHT is used in informal writing, probably by analogy with such words as *altogether* and *already.* However, the phrase ALL RIGHT is preferred in formal, edited writing.

All Saints' Day, church festival Nov. 1 in honor of saints.

all'spice', *n.* sharp, fragrant spice.

all'-star', *adj.* consisting of star performers.

all'-time', *adj.* never equaled or surpassed.

al•lude' (ə lōōd') *v.*, **-luded, -luding.** refer (to) in words. —**al•lu'sion,** *n.*

al•lure' (ə lōōr') *v.*, **-lured, -luring.** attract; tempt. —**al•lure'ment,** *n.*

al•lu'vi•um (ə lōō'vē əm) *n.* earth deposited by rivers, etc.

al•ly', *v.*, **-lied, -lying,** *n., pl.* **-lies.** —*v.* (ə lī') **1.** unite in an alliance. —*n.* (al'ī) **2.** person, nation, etc., bound to another, as by treaty.

al'ma ma'ter (äl'mə mä'tər; al'mə mä'tər) one's school.

al'ma•nac' (ôl'mə nak') *n.* calendar showing special events, etc.

al•might'y (ôl mī'tē) *adj.* **1.** having all power. —*n.* **2.** (*cap.*) God.

al'mond (ä'mənd) *n.* edible nut of the almond tree.

al'most (ôl'mōst, ôl mōst') *adv.* nearly.

alms (ämz) *n., pl.* charity.

a•loft' (ə lôft') *adv., adj.* high up.

a•lo'ha (ə lō'ə, ä lō'hä) *n., interj.* **1.** (hello). **2.** (farewell.)

a•lone' (ə lōn') *adj., adv.* **1.** apart. **2.** by oneself.

a•long' (ə lông') *prep.* **1.** through length of. —*adv.* **2.** onward. **3.** together; with one.

a•long'side', *adv.* **1.** to one's side. —*prep.* **2.** beside.

a•loof' (ə lōōf') *adv.* **1.** at a distance. —*adj.* **2.** reserved; indifferent.

a•lot' (ə lot') *n.* LOT (def. 4). —**Usage.** The spelling ALOT, though fairly common in informal writing such as memos and personal letters, is usually considered an error. The two-word spelling A LOT is the accepted form: *He has a lot of money. I like her a lot.* A LOT is itself considered informal; in formal speech or writing, the phrases "a great number," "a great amount," or "a great deal" are usually substituted for A LOT.

a•loud' (ə loud') *adv.* loudly.

al•pac'a (al pak'ə) *n.* South American sheep with soft, silky wool.

al'pha (al'fə) *n.* first letter of Greek alphabet.

al'pha•bet' (al'fə bet', -bit) *n.* letters of a language in order. —**al'pha•bet'i•cal,** *adj.* —**al'pha•bet•ize',** *v.*

al'pha•nu•mer'ic, *adj.* using both letters and numbers.

al'pine (al'pīn, -pin) *adj.* growing or found in high mountains.

al•read'y (ôl red'ē) *adv.* previously.

al•right' (ôl rīt') *adv., adj.* ALL RIGHT. —**Usage.** See ALL RIGHT.

al'so (ôl'sō) *adv.* in addition.

alt., **1.** alteration. **2.** alternate. **3.** altitude. **4.** alto.

al'tar (ôl'tər) *n.* **1.** platform for religious rites. **2.** communion table.

al′ter (ôl′tər) *v.* change.

al′ter·ca′tion (ôl′tər kā′shən) *n.* dispute.

alter ego, other side of one's personality.

al′ter·nate′, *v.,* -nated, -nating, *adj., n.* —*v.* (-nāt′) **1.** occur or do in turns. —*adj.* (-nit) **2.** being by turns. —*n.* (-nit) **3.** substitute.

alternating current, electric current that regularly reverses its direction.

al·ter′na·tive (-tûr′nə tiv) *n.* **1.** other choice. —*adj.* **2.** offering a choice.

al′ter·na′tor (-tər nā′tər) *n.* generator of alternating current.

al·though′ (ôl thō′) *conj.* even though.

al·tim′e·ter (al tim′i tər, al′tə mē′-tər) *n.* device for measuring altitude.

al′ti·tude′ (al′ti tōōd′, -tyōōd′) *n.* height.

al′to (al′tō) *n., pl.* -tos. lowest female voice.

al′to·geth′er (ôl′tə geth′ər) *adv.* entirely.

al′tru·ism′ (al′trōō iz′əm) *n.* devotion to others. —**al′tru·is′tic,** *adj.*

al′um (al′əm) *n.* astringent substance, used in medicine, etc.

a·lu′mi·num (ə lōō′mə nəm) *n.* light, silvery metal. Also, *Brit.,* **al·u·min′i·um** (al′yə mēr′ē əm).

a·lum′na (ə lum′nə) *n., pl.* -nae (-nē). female graduate.

a·lum′nus (-nəs) *n., pl.* -ni (-nī). graduate.

al′ways (ôl′wāz, -wēz) *adv.* **1.** all the time. **2.** every time.

Alz′hei·mer's disease (älts′hī marz, ôlts′-) disease marked by increasing memory loss and mental deterioration, usually in old age.

am (*unstressed* əm, m) *v.* 1st pers. sing. pres. indic. of **be.**

Am., **1.** America. **2.** American.

a.m., the period before noon. Also, **A.M.**

A.M.A., American Medical Association.

a·mal′gam (ə mal′gəm) *n.* mixture, esp. one with mercury.

a·mal′ga·mate′ (-gə māt′) *v.,* -mated, -mating. combine.

am′a·ret′to (am′ə ret′ō, ä′mə-) *n.* almond-flavored liqueur.

am′a·ryl′lis (am′ə ril′is) *n.* plant with large, lilylike flowers.

a·mass′ (ə mas′) *v.* collect.

am′a·teur′ (am′ə chōōr′, -chər) *n.* nonprofessional artist, athlete, etc. —**am′a·teur′ish,** *adj.*

am′a·to′ry (am′ə tôr′ē) *adj.* of love.

a·maze′ (ə māz′) *v.,* amazed,

amazing. astonish. —**a·maze′-ment,** *n.*

Am′a·zon′ (am′ə zon′, -zən) *n.* tall, powerful woman.

am·bas′sa·dor (am bas′ə dər, -dôr′) *n.* diplomat of highest rank.

am′ber (am′bər) *n.* **1.** yellowish fossil resin. —*adj.* **2.** yellowish.

am′ber·gris′ (-grēs′) *n.* secretion of sperm whale, used in perfumes.

am′bi·dex′trous (am′bi deks′trəs) *adj.* using both hands equally well.

am′bi·ence (-əns) *n.* surroundings; atmosphere. Also, **am′bi·ance.** —**am′bi·ent,** *adj.*

am·big′u·ous (am big′yōō əs) *adj.* unclear in meaning. —**am′bi·gu′i·ty,** *n.*

am·bi′tion (-bish′ən) *n.* **1.** desire for success, power, etc. **2.** object so desired. —**am·bi′tious,** *adj.*

am·biv′a·lent (-biv′ə lənt) *adj.* with conflicting emotions. —**am·biv′a·lence,** *n.*

am′ble (am′bəl) *v.,* -bled, -bling, *n.* go at an easy pace. —*n.* **2.** easy pace.

am·bro′sia (am brō′zhə) *n.* food of Greek and Roman gods.

am′bu·lance (am′byə ləns) *n.* vehicle for sick or wounded.

am′bu·la·to′ry (-lə tôr′ē) *adj.* able to walk.

am′bush (-bōōsh) *n.* **1.** concealment for a surprise attack. **2.** surprise attack. **3.** place of such concealment. —*v.* **4.** attack thus.

a·me′ba (ə mē′bə) *n., pl.* -bas or -bae (-bē). microscopic one-celled animal. Also, **a·moe′ba.**

a·mel′io·rate′ (ə mēl′yə rāt′) *v.,* -rated, -rating. improve.

a′men′ (ā′men′, ä′men′) *interj.* (so be it!)

a·me′na·ble (ə mē′nə bəl, ə men′ə-) *adj.* willing; agreeable.

a·mend′ (ə mend′) *v.* **1.** change or correct. **2.** improve.

a·mend′ment, *n.* change in a law.

a·mends′, *n.pl.* reparation.

a·men′i·ty (ə men′i tē) *n., pl.* -ties. pleasant feature, etc.

Am′er·a′sian (am′ə rā′zhən) *n.* person of mixed American and Asian descent.

A·mer′i·can (ə mer′i kən) *n.* **1.** citizen of the U.S. **2.** native of N. or S. America. —*adj.* **3.** of the U.S. or its inhabitants. **4.** of N. or S. America.

American Indian, member of the indigenous peoples of N. or S. America.

A·mer′i·can·ism′ (-kə niz′əm) *n.* **1.** devotion to the U.S. **2.** custom, etc., of the U.S.

A·mer′i·can·ize′ (-kə nīz′) *v.,*

make or become American in character.

American plan, payment of fixed hotel rate for room, service, and meals.

am•e•thyst (am′ə thist) *n.* violet quartz used in jewelry.

a′mi•a•ble (ā′mē ə bəl) *adj.* pleasantly kind or friendly.

am•i•ca•ble (am′i kə bal) *adj.* not hostile. —**am′i•ca•bly,** *adv.*

a•mid′ (ə mid′) *prep.* among. Also, **a•midst′.**

a•mi•go (ə mē′gō, ä mē′-) *n., pl.* -gos. *Spanish.* friend.

a•mi′no ac•id (ə mē′nō, am′ə nō) type of organic compound from which proteins are made.

a•miss′ (ə mis′) *adv.* **1.** wrongly. —*adj.* **2.** wrong.

am•i•ty (am′i tē) *n.* friendship.

am•me•ter (am′mē′tər) *n.* instrument for measuring current in amperes.

am•mo (am′ō) *n. Slang.* ammunition.

am•mo•ni•a (ə mōn′yə) *n.* colorless, pungent, water-soluble gas.

am•mu•ni•tion (am′yə nish′ən) *n.* bullets, shot, etc., for weapons.

am•ne•sia (am nē′zhə) *n.* loss of memory. —**am•ne′si•ac′** (-zhē ak′, -zē-), **am•ne′sic,** *adj.*

am•nes•ty (am′nə stē) *n.* pardon for political crimes.

am•ni•o•cen•te•sis (am′nē ō sen tē′ sis) *n., pl.* -ses (-sēz) surgical procedure of withdrawing fluid from pregnant woman for genetic diagnosis of fetus.

a•mok (ə muk′, ə mok′) *adv.* amuck.

a•mong (ə mung′) *prep.* **1.** in the midst of. **2.** in the group of. Also, **a•mongst′.** —*Usage.* See BETWEEN.

a•mor•al (ā môr′əl) *adj.* indifferent to moral standards.

am•o•rous (am′ər əs) *adj.* inclined to, or showing, love.

a•mor•phous (ə môr′fəs) *adj.* formless.

am•or•tize (am′ər tīz′, ə môr′tīz) *v.,* -tized, -tizing. pay off.

a•mount′ (ə mount′) *n.* **1.** sum total. **2.** quantity. —*v.* **3.** add up (to); equal. —*Usage.* AMOUNT refers to quantity that cannot be counted (*the amount of paperwork; the amount of energy*), while NUMBER refers to things that can be counted (*a number of songs; a number of days*).

a•mour′ (ə mŏŏr′) *n.* love affair.

am•per•age (am′pər ij, am pēr′-) *n.* strength of an electric current.

am•pere (am′pēr) *n.* unit measuring electric current.

am′per•sand′ (am′pər sand′) *n.* sign (&) meaning "and."

am•phet•a•mine (am fet′ə mēn′, -min) *n.* stimulating drug.

am•phib•i•an (-fib′ē ən) *n.* **1.** animal living both in water and on land. —*adj.* **2.** Also, **am•phib′i•ous.** operating on land or water.

am•phi•the•a•ter (am′fə thē′ə tar, -thē′ə-) *n.* theater with seats tiered around its center.

am•ple (am′pəl) *adj.,* -pler, -plest. **1.** sufficient. **2.** abundant.

am′pli•fy′ (am′plə fi′) *v.,* -fied, -fying. make larger or louder. —**am′ pli•fi′er** *n.* —**am′pli•fi•ca′tion,** *n.*

am′pli•tude′ (-tood′, -tyood′) *n.* **1.** extent. **2.** abundance.

am′pu•tate′ (am′pyoo tāt′) *v.,* -tated, -tating. cut off (limb). —**am′pu•ta′tion,** *n.* —**am′pu•tee′,** *n.*

a•muck′ (ə muk′) *adv.* violently; in an uncontrolled way.

am′u•let (am′yoo lit) *n.* magical charm.

a•muse′ (ə myōōz′) *v.,* amused, amusing. **1.** entertain. **2.** cause to laugh. —**a•muse′ment,** *n.*

amusement park, park with roller coasters or other recreational rides.

an (ən; *when stressed* an) *adj.* or *indef.* art. before initial vowel sounds. See **a.**

a•nach′ro•nism (ə nak′rə niz′əm) *n.* chronological discrepancy.

an′a•con′da (an′ə kon′də) *n.* large South American snake.

an′a•gram′ (an′ə gram′) *n.* word formed from letters of another.

a′nal (ān′l) *adj.* of the anus.

an′al•ge′sic (an′əl jē′zik) *n.* drug for relieving pain.

a•nal′o•gy (ə nal′ə jē) *n., pl.* -gies. similarity in some respects. —**a• nal′o•gous** (-gəs) *adj.*

a•nal′y•sis (-sis) *n., pl.* -ses (-sēz′). **1.** separation into constituent parts. **2.** summary. **3.** psychoanalysis. —**an′a•lyst** (an′l ist) *n.* —**an′a•lyt′ ic, an′a•lyt′i•cal,** *adj.* —**an′a•lyze′,** *v.,* -lyzed, -lyzing.

an•ar•chy (an′ər kē) *n.* lawless society. —**an′ar•chism,** *n.* —**an′ar• chist,** *n.*

a•nath•e•ma (ə nath′ə mə) *n.* **1.** solemn curse. **2.** thing or person detested.

a•nat′o•my (ə nat′ə mē) *n., pl.* -mies. **1.** structure of an animal or plant. **2.** science dealing with such structure. —**an′a•tom′i•cal** (an′ə tom′i kəl) *adj.*

-ance, suffix meaning: action, as *ap*-

pearance; state or quality, as *brilliance*; thing or object, as *contrivance*.

an·ces·tor (an'ses tar) *n.* person from whom one is descended. —**an·ces·try,** *n.* —**an·ces'tral,** *adj.*

an·chor (ang'kar) *n.* **1.** heavy device for keeping boats, etc., in place. **2.** broadcaster who coordinates TV or radio newscast. —*v.* **3.** fasten by an anchor. **4.** serve as anchor (for newscast).

an·chor·man/, *n.*, *pl.* **-men.** person who anchors a newscast. Also, *fem.*, **an'chor·wom'an;** *masc.* or *fem.*

an·cho·vy (an'chō vē) *n.*, *pl.* **-vies.** small herringlike fish.

an·cient (ān'shənt) *adj.* **1.** of long ago. **2.** very old. —*n.* **3.** person who lived long ago.

an·cil·lar·y (an'sə ler'ē) *adj.* subordinate; auxiliary.

and (and; *unstressed* ənd, ən, n) *conj.* **1.** with; also. **2.** *Informal.* (used in place of **to** in infinitive): *Try and stop me.*

an·dan·te (än dän'tā) *adv. Music.* at moderate speed.

and'i·rons (and'ī'ərnz) *n.pl.* metal supports for logs in fireplace.

an'dro·gen (an'drə jən) *n.* male sex hormone, as testosterone.

an·drog·y·nous (an droj'ə nəs) *adj.* having both masculine and feminine characteristics.

an'droid (an'droid) *n.* automaton in human form.

an·ec·dote/ (an'ik dōt') *n.* short story.

a·ne·mi·a (ə nē'mē ə) *n.* inadequate supply of hemoglobin and red blood cells. —**a·ne'mic,** *adj.*

a·nem'o·ne/ (ə nem'ə nē') *n.* buttercuplike plant with colorful flowers.

an·es·the·sia (an'əs thē'zhə) *n.* insensibility to pain, usually induced by a drug **(an'es·thet'ic)** (-thet'ik). —**an·es'the·tize/** (ə nes'thə tīz') *v.*, **-tized, -tizing.**

a·new/ (ə nōō', ə nyōō') *adv.* again.

an'gel (ān'jəl) *n.* **1.** spiritual being who is messenger of God. **2.** very kind and helpful person.

angel food cake, light, spongy cake made with egg whites.

an·ger (ang'gər) *n.* **1.** strong displeasure; outrage. —*v.* **2.** cause anger in.

an·gi'na pec'to·ris (an jī'nə pek'tə-ris) coronary attack.

an'gle (ang'gəl) *n.*, *v.*, **-gled, -gling.** —*n.* **1.** spread between converging lines or surfaces. —*v.* **2.**

fish with a hook on a line. **3.** try for something by artful means. **4.** bend in angles. —**an'gler,** *n.*

An'gli·can (ang'gli kən) *adj.* **1.** of the Church of England. —*n.* **2.** member of this church.

An'gli·cize/ (-sīz') *v.*, **-cized, -cizing.** make or become English in form or character.

An'glo-Sax'on (ang'glō sak'sən) *n.* **1.** person of English descent. **2.** inhabitant of England before 1066. —*adj.* **3.** of Anglo-Saxons.

An·go'ra (ang gôr'ə) *n.* **1.** cat, goat, or rabbit with long, silky hair. **2.** (*l.c.*) yarn or fabric from Angora goat or rabbit.

an'gry (ang'grē) *adj.*, **-grier, -griest. 1.** full of anger. **2.** inflamed. —**an'gri·ly,** *adv.*

angst (ängkst) *n.* feeling of dread, anxiety, or anguish.

an'guish (ang'gwish) *n.* intense pain or grief.

an·gu·lar (ang'gyə lər) *adj.* having angles. —**an·gu·lar'i·ty,** *n.*

an'i·mad·vert/ (an'ə mad vûrt') *v.* criticize. —**an'i·mad·ver'sion** (-vûr'zhən) *n.*

an'i·mal (an'ə məl) *n.* **1.** living thing that is not a plant. **2.** beast. —*adj.* **3.** of animals.

an'i·mate/ *v.*, **-mated, -mating,** *adj.* —*v.* (-māt') **1.** make alive or lively. **2.** make move. —*adj.* (-mit) **3.** alive.

an'i·ma'tion, *n.* **1.** liveliness. **2.** animated cartoon.

an'i·mism (-miz'əm) *n.* belief that animals and natural objects have souls. —**an'i·mist,** *n.*, *adj.*

an'i·mos'i·ty (ə mos'i tē) *n.*, *pl.* **-ties.** strong dislike or enmity.

an'i·mus (-məs) *n.* strong dislike; animosity.

an'ise (an'is) *n.* plant yielding aromatic seed **(an'i·seed/).**

an'kle (ang'kəl) *n.* joint between foot and leg.

an'klet (-klit) *n.* **1.** short, anklelength sock. **2.** ornament for ankle.

an'nals (an'lz) *n.pl.* historical record of events.

an·neal/ (ə nēl') *v.* to toughen or temper.

an·nex/, *v.* (ə neks') **1.** add; join. —*n.* (an' eks) **2.** attached building. —**an'nex·a'tion,** *n.*

an·ni'hi·late/ (ə nī'ə lāt') *v.*, **-lated, -lating.** destroy completely. —**an·ni'hi·la'tion,** *n.*

an·ni·ver·sa·ry (an'ə vûr'sə rē) *n.*, *pl.* **-ries.** annual recurrence of the date of a past event.

an'no·tate/ (an'ə tāt') *v.*, **-tated, -tating.** supply with notes.

an·nounce′ (ə nouns′) *v.*, **-nounced**, **-nouncing.** make known. —**an·nounce′ment**, *n.*

an·noy′ (ə noi′) *v.* irritate or trouble. —**an·noy′ance**, *n.*

an·nu·al (an′yoo əl) *adj.* yearly. **2.** living only one season. —*n.* **3.** annual plant. **4.** yearbook. —**an′nu·al·ly**, *adv.*

an·nu·i·ty (ə noo′i tē) *n., pl.* **-ties.** income in annual payments.

an·nul′ (ə nul′) *v.*, **-nulled, -nulling.** make void. —**an·nul′ment**, *n.*

An·nun′ci·a′tion (ə nun′sē ā′shən) *n.* announcement to Virgin Mary of incarnation of Christ (March 25).

an′ode (an′ōd) *n.* **1.** electrode with positive charge. **2.** negative terminal of a battery.

a·noint′ (ə noint′) *v.* to put oil on, as in consecration.

a·nom′a·ly (ə nom′ə lē) *n., pl.* **-lies.** something irregular or abnormal. —**a·nom′a·lous,** *adj.*

a·non′ (ə non′) *adv. Archaic.* soon.

anon., anonymous.

a·non′y·mous (ə non′ə məs) *adj.* by someone unnamed. —**an·o·nym′i·ty** (an′ə nim′i tē) *n.* —**a·non′y·mous·ly,** *adv.*

an′o·rak′ (an′ə rak′) *n.* hooded jacket; parka.

an·o·rex′i·a ner·vo′sa (nûr vō′sə). eating disorder marked by excessive dieting. —**an′o·rex′ic,** *adj., n.*

an·oth′er (ə nuth′ər) *adj.* additional. **2.** different. —*n.* **3.** one more. **4.** different one.

an′swer (an′sər) *n.* **1.** reply. **2.** solution. —*v.* **3.** reply to. **4.** suit. **5.** be responsible. **6.** correspond.

an′swer·a·ble, *adj.* **1.** able to be answered. **2.** responsible.

answering machine, device that answers telephone calls with recorded message and records messages from callers.

ant (ant) *n.* common small insect.

-ant, suffix meaning: one that performs or promotes, as *pollutant*; performing, promoting, or being, as *pleasant.*

ant·ac′id (ant as′id) *n.* medicine to counteract acids.

an·tag′o·nism′ (an tag′ə niz′əm) *n.* hostility. —**an·tag′o·nize′,** *v.*, **-nized, -nizing.**

ant·arc′tic (ant ärk′tik, -är′tik) *adj. (often cap.)* of or at the South Pole.

an′te (an′tē) *n.* **1.** (in poker) stake put in pot before cards are dealt. **2.** price or cost of something.

ante- prefix indicating: **1.** happening before, as *antediluvian.* **2.** in front of, as *anteroom.*

ant·eat′er, *n.* tropical American mammal having snout and feeding on ants and termites.

an′te·bel′lum (an′tē bel′əm) *adj.* before a war, esp. the American Civil War.

an·te·ced′ent (an′tə sēd′nt) *adj.* **1.** prior. —*n.* **2.** anything that precedes.

an′te·di·lu′vi·an (an′tē di loo′vē-ən) *adj.* before the Flood.

an′te·lope′ (an′tl ōp′) *n.* deerlike animal.

an·ten′na (an ten′ə) *n., pl.* **-nae** (-nē), *for* **1.** feeler on the head of an insect, etc. **2.** wires for transmitting radio waves, TV pictures, etc.

an·te′ri·or (an tēr′ē ər) *adj.* **1.** earlier. **2.** frontward.

an′te·room′ (an′tē room′, -room′) *n.* room before the main room.

an′them (an′thəm) *n.* patriotic or sacred hymn.

an′ther (an′thər) *n.* pollen-bearing part of stamen.

an·thol′o·gy (an thol′ə jē) *n., pl.* **-gies.** collection of writings.

an′thra·cite′ (an′thrə sīt′) *n.* hard coal.

an′thrax (an′thraks) *n.* cattle disease.

an′thro·poid′ (an′thrə poid′) *adj.* resembling a human or an ape.

an·thro·pol′o·gy (-pol′ə jē) *n.* science of humankind. —**an′thro·pol′o·gist,** *n.*

an·thro·po·mor′phic (ə môr′fik) *adj.* ascribing human qualities to a nonhuman thing or being. —**an′thro·po·mor′phism** (-fiz əm) *n.*

anti-, prefix indicating: **1.** against or opposed to, as *antisocial.* **2.** acting against, as *antihistamine.*

an′ti·bi·ot′ic (an′tī bī ot′ik) *n.* substance used to destroy microorganisms.

an′ti·bod′y, *n., pl.* **-bodies.** substance in the blood that destroys bacteria.

an′tic (an′tik) *n.* **1.** odd behavior. —*adj.* **2.** playful.

an·tic′i·pate′ (an tis′ə pāt′) *v.*, **-pated, -pating. 1.** expect and prepare for. **2.** foresee.

an′ti·cli′max (an′tē klī′maks, an′tī-) *n.* disappointing or undramatic outcome.

an′ti·de·pres′sant (an′tē di-pres′ənt, an′tī-) *n.* drug for relieving depression.

an′ti·dote′ (an′ti dōt′) *n.* medicine counteracting poison, etc.

an′ti·freeze′ (an′ti frēz′, an′tē-) *n.* liquid used in engine's radiator to prevent freezing of cooling fluid.

an′ti·his′ta·mine′ (an′tē hist′əmĕn′, -min) *n.* substance used esp. against allergic reactions.

an·ti·mat·ter (an′tē mat′ər, an′tī-) *n.* matter with charges opposite to those of common particles.

an·ti·mo·ny (an′tə mō′nē) *n.* brittle white metallic element.

an·ti·pas·to (an′ti pä′stō) *n., pl.* **-pas·tos, -pas·ti** (-pä′stē) Italian appetizer.

an·tip·a·thy (an tip′ə thē) *n., pl.* **-thies.** dislike; aversion.

an·ti·per·spi·rant (an′ti pûr′spər ənt) *n.* astringent product for reducing perspiration.

an·tip·o·des (an tip′ə dēz′) *n.pl.* places opposite each other on the globe.

an·ti·quar·i·an (an′ti kwâr′ē ən) *adj.* **1.** of the study of antiquities. —*n.* **2.** antiquary.

an·ti·quar·y (-kwer′ē) *n., pl.* **-ries.** collector of antiquities.

an·ti·quat·ed (-kwā′tid) *adj.* old or obsolete.

an·tique (an tēk′) *adj.* **1.** old or old-fashioned. —*n.* **2.** valuable old object.

an·tiq·ui·ty (-tik′wi tē) *n., pl.* **-ties. 1.** ancient times. **2.** something ancient.

an·ti-Sem·ite (an′tē sem′īt, an′tī-) *n.* person hostile to Jews. —**an′ti-Se·mit′ic** (-sə mit′ik) *adj.* —**an′ti-Sem′i·tism** (-sem′i tiz′əm) *n.*

an·ti·sep·tic (an′tə sep′tik) *adj.* **1.** destroying certain germs. —*n.* **2.** antiseptic substance.

an·ti·so·cial (an′tē sō′shəl, an′tī-) *adj.* **1.** hostile to society. **2.** not sociable.

an·tith·e·sis (an tith′ə sis) *n., pl.* **-ses.** direct opposite.

an·ti·tox·in (an′ti tok′sin) *n.* substance counteracting germ-produced poisons in the body.

ant·ler (ant′lər) *n.* horn on deer, etc.

an·to·nym (an′tə nim) *n.* word of opposite meaning.

a′nus (ā′nəs) *n.* opening at lower end of alimentary canal.

an·vil (an′vil) *n.* iron block on which hot metals are hammered into shape.

anx·i·e·ty (ang zī′i tē) *n., pl.* **-ties.** worried distress. —**anx′ious** (angk′shəs) *adj.* —**anx′ious·ly,** *adv.*

an·y (en′ē) *adj.* **1.** one; some. **2.** every. —*pron.* **3.** any person, etc. —**an′y·bod′y, an′y·one′,** *pron.* —**an′y·thing′,** *pron.* —**Usage.** See SOME.

an′y·how′, *adv.* in any way, case, etc. Also, **an′y·way′.**

an′y·place′, *adv.* anywhere.

an′y·time′, *adv.* at any time.

an′y·where′, *adv.* in, at, or to any place.

A′ one′ (ā′ wun′) *adj.* excellent. Also, **A′ 1′, A′-1′.**

a·or·ta (ā ôr′tə) *n., pl.* **-tas, -tae** (-tē). main blood vessel from heart.

a·pace′ (ə pās′) *adv.* quickly.

A·pach·e (ə pach′ē) *n., pl.* **A·pach·e, A·pach·es.** member of a group of American Indian peoples of the U.S. Southwest.

a·part′ (ə pärt′) *adv.* **1.** into pieces. **2.** separately.

a·part′heid (-hāt, -hīt) *n.* (formerly, in South Africa) separation of and discrimination against blacks.

a·part′ment (-mənt) *n.* set of rooms to live in in a building.

ap·a·thy (ap′ə thē) *n., pl.* **-thies.** lack of emotion or interest. —**ap′a·thet′ic** (-thet′ik) *adj.*

ape (āp) *n., v.,* **aped, ap·ing.** —*n.* **1.** large, tailless monkeylike animal. —*v.* **2.** imitate stupidly.

a·pé·ri·tif (ä per′i tēf′) *n.* liquor served before meal.

ap′er·ture (ap′ər chər) *n.* opening.

a′pex (ā′peks) *n.* tip; summit.

a′phid (ā′fid, af′id) *n.* plant-sucking insect.

aph′o·rism′ (af′ə riz′əm) *n.* brief maxim.

aph·ro·dis·i·ac′ (af′rə dēz′ē ak′, -diz′ē ak′) *adj.* **1.** sexually exciting. —*n.* **2.** aphrodisiac food, drug, etc.

a′pi·ar′y (ā′pē er′ē) *n., pl.* **-ries.** place where bees are kept.

a·piece′ (ə pēs′) *adv.* for each.

a·plen′ty (ə plen′tē) *adv., adv.* in generous amounts.

a·plomb (ə plom′, ə plum′) *n.* poise; self-possession.

A·poc′a·lypse (ə pok′ə lips) *n.* **1.** revelation of the apostle John. **2.** (*l.c.*) prophetic revelation. —**a·poc′a·lyp′tic,** *adj.*

A·poc′ry·pha (ə pok′rə fə) *n.* uncanonical parts of the Bible.

a·poc′ry·phal, *adj.* not verified; dubious.

ap′o·gee′ (ap′ə jē′) *n.* remotest point of satellite orbit.

a′po·lit′i·cal (ā′pə lit′i kəl) *adj.* not interested in politics.

a·pol′o·gist (ə pol′ə jist) *n.* advocate; defender.

a·pol′o·gize′, *v.,* **-gized, -gizing.** offer apology.

a·pol′o·gy, *n., pl.* **-gies. 1.** statement of regret for one's act. **2.** stated defense. —**a·pol′o·get′ic** (-jet′ik) *adj.*

ap′o·plex′y (ap′ə plek′sē) *n.* sudden loss of bodily function due to bursting of blood vessel.

a·pos'tate (ə pos'tāt, -tit) *n.* deserter of one's faith, cause, etc.

a' pos·te'ri·o'ri (ā' po stēr'ē ôr'ē, -ôr'ē) *adj.* **1.** from particular instances to a general principle. **2.** based on observation or experiment.

a·pos'tle (ə pos'əl) *n.* **1.** disciple sent by Jesus to preach gospel. **2.** moral reformer.

a·pos'tro·phe (ə pos'trə fē) *n.* **1.** sign (') indicating an omitted letter, the possessive, or certain plurals. **2.** words in passing to one person or group.

a·poth'e·car'y (ə poth'ə ker'ē) *n.,* *pl.* **-ries.** druggist.

a·poth'e·o'sis (ə poth'ē ō'sis, ap'ə thē'ə sis) *n., pl.* **-ses** (-sēz, -sēz'). **1.** elevation to the rank of a god. **2.** ideal example; epitome.

ap·pall' (ə pôl') *v.* fill with horror. Also, **ap·pal'.** —**ap·pall'ing,** *adj.*

ap'pa·ra'tus (ap'ə rat'əs, -rā'təs) *n.* **1.** instruments and machines for some task. **2.** organization.

ap·par'el (ə par'əl) *n.* clothes.

ap·par'ent (ə par'ənt, ə pâr'-) *adj.* **1.** obvious. **2.** seeming. —**ap·par'ent·ly,** *adv.*

ap'pa·ri'tion (ap'ə rish'ən) *n.* specter.

ap·peal' (ə pēl') *n.* **1.** call for aid, mercy, etc. **2.** request for corroboration or review. **3.** attractiveness. —*v.* **4.** make an appeal. **5.** be attractive.

ap·pear' (ə pēr') *v.* **1.** come into sight. **2.** seem.

ap·pear'ance (-əns) *n.* **1.** act of appearing. **2.** outward look.

ap·pease' (ə pēz') *v.,* **-peased, -peasing. 1.** placate. **2.** satisfy.

ap·pel'late (ə pel'it) *adj.* dealing with appeals.

ap·pend' (ə pend') *v.* add; join.

ap·pend'age (ə pen'dij) *n.* subordinate attached part.

ap'pen·dec'to·my (ap'ən dek'tə mē) *n., pl.* **-mies.** removal of the appendix.

ap·pen'di·ci'tis (ə pen'də sī'tis) *n.* inflammation of appendix.

ap·pen'dix (ə pen'diks) *n., pl.* **-dixes, -dices** (-də sēz'). **1.** supplement. **2.** closed tube from the large intestine.

ap'per·tain' (ap'ər tān') *v.* belong or pertain.

ap'pe·tite' (ap'i tīt') *n.* desire, esp. for food.

ap'pe·tiz'er (-tī'zər) *n.* portion of food or drink served before meal to stimulate appetite.

ap·plaud' (ə plôd') *v.* praise by clapping, cheers, etc. —**ap·plause'** (ə plôz') *n.*

ap'ple (ap'əl) *n.* round fruit with firm, white flesh.

ap'ple·jack', *n.* brandy made from fermented cider.

ap'ple·sauce', *n.* apples stewed to a pulp.

ap·pli'ance (ə plī'əns) *n.* special device or instrument.

ap'pli·ca·ble (ap'li kə bəl) *adj.* that can be applied.

ap'pli·cant (-kənt) *n.* one who applies.

ap'pli·ca'tion (-kā'shən) *n.* **1.** act of applying. **2.** use to which something is put. **3.** relevance. **4.** persistent attention.

ap'pli·ca'tor, *n.* device for applying a substance, as medication.

ap'pli·qué' (ap'li kā') *n., v.,* **-quéd, -quéing.** —*n.* **1.** cutout design of one material applied to another. —*v.* **2.** decorate with appliqué.

ap·ply' (ə plī') *v.* **-plied, -plying. 1.** put on. **2.** put into practice. **3.** use or devote. **4.** be relevant. **5.** make request.

ap·point' (ə point') *v.* **1.** choose; name. **2.** furnish.

ap·point'ment, *n.* **1.** act of choosing. **2.** prearranged meeting.

ap·por'tion (ə pôr'shən) *v.* divide into shares. —**ap·por'tion·ment,** *n.*

ap'po·site (ap'ə zit) *adj.* suitable.

ap·praise' (ə prāz') *v.,* **-praised, -praising.** estimate the value of. —**ap·prais'al,** *n.* —**ap·prais'er,** *n.*

ap·pre'ci·a·ble (ə prē'shē ə bəl) *adj.* noticeable; significant.

ap·pre'ci·ate' (-shē āt') *v.,* **-ated, -ating. 1.** value at true worth. **2.** increase in value.

ap'pre·hend' (ap'ri hend') *v.* **1.** take into custody. **2.** understand.

ap'pre·hen'sion (-hen'shən) *n.* **1.** anxiety. **2.** comprehension. **3.** arrest.

ap'pre·hen'sive (-siv) *adj.* worried.

ap·pren'tice (ə pren'tis) *n., v.,* **-ticed, -ticing.** —*n.* **1.** assistant learning a trade. —*v.* **2.** bind as such an assistant.

ap·prise' (ə prīz') *v.,* **-prised, -prising.** notify. Also, **ap·prize'.**

ap·proach' (ə prōch') *v.* **1.** come near to. **2.** make a proposal to. —*n.* **3.** coming near. **4.** access. **5.** method.

ap'pro·ba'tion (ap'rə bā'shən) *n.* approval.

ap·pro'pri·ate, *adj., v.,* **-ated, -ating.** —*adj.* (ə prō'prē it) **1.** suitable; proper. —*v.* (-prē āt') **2.** designate for a use. **3.** take possession of. —**ap·pro·pri·ate·ly,** adv. —**ap·pro·pri·ate·ness,** n. —**ap·pro·pri·a·tion,** n.

ap·prove (ə prōōv′) v., -**proved,** -**proving. 1.** think or speak well of. **2.** confirm. —**ap·prov·al,** n.

approx., approximately.

ap·prox·i·mate, adj., v., -**mated,** -**mating.** —adj. (ə prok′sə mit) **1.** near; similar. —v. (-māt′) **2.** come near to. —**ap·prox·i·mate·ly,** adv. —**ap·prox·i·ma·tion,** n.

ap·pur·te·nance (ə pûr′tn əns) n. accessory.

Apr., April.

a·pri·cot′ (ap′ri kot′, ā′pri-) n. small peachlike fruit.

A′pril (ā′prəl) n. fourth month of year.

a′ pri·o′ri (ā′ prē ôr′ī, -ôr′ē) adj. from a general law to a particular instance.

a′pron (ā′prən) n. protective garment for the front of one's clothes.

ap′ro·pos′ (ap′rə pō′) adv. **1.** opportunely. **2.** with reference. —adj. **3.** timely.

apse (aps) n. vaulted recess in a church.

apt (apt) adj. **1.** prone. **2.** likely. **3.** skilled; able. —**apt′ly,** adv.

apt., apartment.

ap′ti·tude′ (ap′ti tōōd′, -tyōōd′) n. skill; talent.

Aq′ua·lung′, Trademark. underwater breathing device.

aq′ua·ma·rine′, n. **1.** light greenish blue. **2.** gemstone of this color.

a·quar′i·um (ə kwâr′ē əm) n., pl. -**iums, -ia** (-ē ə). place for exhibiting aquatic animals and plants.

a·quat′ic (ə kwat′ik, ə kwot′-) adj. of living in water.

aq′ue·duct′ (ak′wi dukt′) n. artificial channel for conducting water.

a′que·ous (ā′kwē əs, ak′wē-) adj. of like water.

aq′ui·line′ (ak′wə lin′, -lin) adj. (of a nose) curved like a beak.

AR, Arkansas.

Ar′ab (ar′əb) n. **1.** member of a people living or originating in Arabia, a peninsula in SW Asia. **2.** of Arabs. Also, **A·ra′bi·an** (ə rā′bē ən).

Ar′a·bic (ar′ə bik) n. **1.** Semitic language spoken chiefly in S.W. Asia and N. Africa. —adj. **2.** of Arabic, Arabia, or Arabs.

Arabic numeral, any of the numerals 0, 1, 2, 3, 4, 5, 6, 7, 8, or 9.

ar′a·ble (ar′ə bəl) adj. plowable.

a·rach′nid (ə rak′nid) n. small eight-legged arthropod, as the spider.

A·rap·a·ho′ or **-hoe′** (ə rap′ə hō′)

n., pl. -**hos** or -**hoes** or **hoe.** member of a North American Indian people.

ar′bi·ter (ar′bi tər) n. judge.

ar·bi·trage′ (-träzh′) n. simultaneous security or commodity in different markets to profit from unequal prices. —**ar′bi·trag′er** n.

ar′bi·trar·y (ar′bi trer′ē) adj. **1.** subject to personal judgment. **2.** capricious. **3.** abusing powers. —**ar′bi·trar·i·ly,** adv.

ar′bi·trate′ (-trāt′) v., -**trated, -trating.** adjudicate as, or submit to, an arbiter. —**ar′bi·tra′tion,** n. —**ar′bi·tra′tor,** n.

ar′bor (ar′bər) n. tree-shaded walk or garden.

ar·bo·re·al (-bôr′ē əl) adj. of or living in trees.

ar′bo·re′tum (ar′bə rē′təm) n., pl. -**tums, -ta** (-tə). parklike area with trees or shrubs for study or display.

arc (ark) n. **1.** part of circle. **2.** luminous current between two electric conductors.

ar·cade′ (ar kād′) n. **1.** row of archways. **2.** covered passage with stores.

ar·cane′ (ar kān′) adj. known only to those with special knowledge.

arch (arch) n. **1.** upwardly curved structure. —v. **2.** cover with an arch. —adj. **3.** chief. **4.** roguish. —**arch′ly,** adv.

ar·chae·ol·o·gy (ar′kē ol′ə jē) n. study of past cultures from artifacts. Also, **ar′che·ol′o·gy.** —**ar′chae·o·log′i·cal** (-ə loj′i kəl) adj. —**ar′chae·ol′o·gist,** n.

ar·cha′ic (ar kā′ik) adj. **1.** no longer used. **2.** ancient.

arch′an·gel (ark′ān′jəl) n. chief angel.

arch′bish′op (arch′bish′əp) n. bishop of highest rank.

arch′di′o·cese (arch dī′ə sis, -sēz′, -sēs′) n. diocese of archbishop.

arch′duke′, n. royal prince.

arch′en′e·my, n., pl. -**mies.** chief enemy.

arch′er (ar′chər) n. one who shoots a bow and arrow. —**arch′er·y,** n.

ar′che·type′ (ar′ki tīp′) n. original pattern or model.

ar′chi·pel·a·go (ar′kə pel′ə gō′) n., pl. -**gos, -goes. 1.** body of water with many islands. **2.** the islands.

ar′chi·tect′ (ar′ki tekt′) n. designer of buildings. —**ar′chi·tec·ture,** n. —**ar′chi·tec′tur·al,** adj.

ar′chives (ar′kīvz) n.pl. **1.** documents. **2.** place for documents.

arch′way′ (arch′wā′) n. entrance covered by arch.

arc/tic (ärk'tik, är'tik) *adj.* (*often cap.*) of or at the North Pole.

ar/dent (är'dnt) *adj.* earnest; zealous. **—ar/dent•ly,** *adv.*

ar/dor (är'dər) *n.* zeal.

ar/du•ous (är'jōō əs) *adj.* **1.** difficult. **2.** steep. **3.** severe.

are (är; *unstressed är*) *v.* pres. indic. pl. of **be.**

ar/e•a (âr'ē ə) *n.* **1.** extent of surface; region. **2.** scope.

area code, three-digit number used in long-distance telephone dialing.

a•re/na (ə rē'nə) *n.* open space for contests, shows, etc.

aren't (ärnt, är'ənt) contraction of **are not.**

ar/got (är'gət, -gō) *n.* special vocabulary used by particular group of people.

ar/gue (är'gyōō) *v.,* **-gued, -guing. 1.** present reasons for or against something. **2.** dispute. **3.** persuade. **—ar/gu•ment,** *n.*

ar/gu•men/ta•tive (-men'tə tiv) *adj.* tending to dispute.

ar/gyle (är'gīl) *n.* (*often cap.*) diamond-shaped knitting pattern, as of socks.

a/ri•a (är'ē ə) *n.* operatic solo.

-arian, suffix indicating: **1.** one connected with, as *librarian.* **2.** one supporting or practicing, as *vegetarian.*

ar/id (ar'id) *adj.* dry.

a•right/ (ə rīt') *adv.* rightly.

a•rise/ (ə rīz') *v.,* **arose** (ə rōz'), **arisen** (ə riz'ən), **arising. 1.** move or get up. **2.** occur.

ar/is•toc/ra•cy (ar'ə stok'rə sē) *n., pl.* **-cies. 1.** state governed by nobility. **2.** nobility. **—a•ris/to•crat** (ə ris'tə krat') *n.* **—a•ris/to•crat/ic,** *adj.*

a•rith/me•tic (ə rith'mə tik) *n.* computation with figures. **—ar/ith•met/i•cal** (ar'ith met'i kəl) *adj.* **—ar/ith•met/i•cal•ly,** *adv.*

Ariz., Arizona.

ark (ärk) *n.* Archaic. large ship.

Ark., Arkansas.

arm (ärm) *n.* **1.** upper limb from hand to shoulder. **2.** weapon. **3.** combat branch. **4.** armlike part. **—v.** **5.** equip with weapons; outfit. **—n.** **6.** arm.

ar•ma/da (är mä'də) *n.* fleet of warships.

ar/ma•dil/lo (är'mə dil'ō) *n.* burrowing mammal covered with plates of bone and horn.

ar/ma•ged/don (är'mə ged'n) *n.* crucial or final conflict.

ar/ma•ment (är'mə mənt) *n.* military weapons.

arm/chair/, *n.* chair with supports for the arms.

armed forces, military, naval, and air forces.

ar/mi•stice (är'mə stis) *n.* truce.

ar/mor (är'mər) *n.* protective covering against weapons.

ar/mor•y (-mə rē) *n., pl.* **-ries.** storage place for weapons.

arm/pit/, *n.* hollow part under arm at shoulder.

ar/my (är'mē) *n., pl.* **-mies. 1.** military force for land combat. **2.** large group.

a•ro/ma (ə rō'mə) *n.* odor. **—ar/o•mat/ic** (ar'ə mat'ik) *adj.*

a•ro/ma•ther/a•py, *n.* use of fragrances to alter a person's mood and make them feel healthy.

a•round/ (ə round') *adv., prep.* **1.** on every side of. **2.** somewhere in or near. **3.** about.

a•rouse/ (ə rouz') *v.,* **aroused, arousing. 1.** awaken. **2.** stir to act. **—a•rous/al,** *n.*

ar•raign/ (ə rān') *v.* **1.** call to court. **2.** accuse. **—ar•raign/ment,** *n.*

ar•range/ (ə rānj') *v.,* **-ranged, -ranging. 1.** place in order. **2.** plan or prepare. **—ar•range/ment,** *n.*

ar•ray/ (ə rā') *v.* **1.** arrange. **2.** clothe. **—n.** **3.** arrangement, as for battle. **4.** clothes.

ar•rears/ (ə rērz') *n.pl.* overdue debt.

ar•rest/ (ə rest') *v.* **1.** seize (person) by law. **2.** stop. **—n.** **3.** seizure. **4.** stoppage.

ar•rest/ing, *adj.* attracting attention; engaging.

ar•rive/ (ə rīv') *v.,* **-rived, -riving.** reach a place. **—ar•riv/al,** *n.*

ar/ro•gant (ar'ə gənt) *adj.* insolently proud. **—ar/ro•gance,** *n.* **—ar/ro•gant•ly,** *adv.*

ar/ro•gate/ (-gāt') *v.,* **-gated, -gating.** claim presumptuously; appropriate. **—ar/ro•ga/tion,** *n.*

ar/row (ar'ō) *n.* pointed stick shot by a bow.

ar/row•head/, *n.* pointed tip of arrow.

ar/row•root/, *n.* edible starch from tropical plant root.

ar•roy/o (ə roi'ō) *n., pl.* **-os.** steep, dry gulch.

ar/se•nal (är'sə nl) *n.* military storehouse or factory.

ar/se•nic (är'sə nik) *n.* **1.** metallic element. **2.** poisonous powder.

ar/son (är'sən) *n.* malicious burning of a building.

art (ärt) *n.* **1.** production of something beautiful or extraordinary. **2.** skill; ability. **3.** cunning. **—art/ful,** *adj.*

art de•co/ (dek'ō) *n.* (*often caps.*)

1920s decorative art with geometric designs.

ar.te/ri.o.scle.ro/sis (är tēr'ē ō sklə rō'sis) *n.* hardening of arteries.

ar/ter.y (är'tə rē) *n., pl.* **-ies. 1.** blood vessel from the heart. **2.** main channel. **—ar.te/ri.al** (-tēr'ē əl) *adj.*

ar.thri/tis (är thrī'tis) *n.* inflammation of a joint.

ar/thro.pod/ (är'thrə pod') *n.* invertebrate with segmented body and jointed legs, as the lobster.

ar/ti.choke/ (är'ti chōk') *n.* plant with an edible flower head.

ar/ti.cle (är'ti kəl) *n.* **1.** literary composition. **2.** thing; item. **3.** the words *a, an,* or *the.*

ar.tic/u.late, *adj., v.,* **-lated, -lating.** **—***adj.* (är tik'yə lit) **1.** clear. **2.** able to speak. **3.** jointed. **—***v.* (-lāt') **4.** speak, esp. distinctly. **5.** joint. **—ar.tic/u.la/tion,** *n.*

ar/ti.fact/ (är'tə fakt') *n.* object made by human being or beings.

ar/ti.fice (är'tə fis) *n.* trick.

ar/ti.fi/cial (-ta fish'əl) *adj.* **1.** manufactured, esp. as an imitation. **2.** affected. **—ar/ti.fi/cial.ly,** *adv.* **—ar/ti.fi/ci.al/i.ty** (-fish'ē al'i tē) *n.*

artificial respiration, forcing of air into and out of lungs of a nonbreathing person.

ar.til/ler.y (är til'ə rē) *n.* large guns.

ar/ti.san (är'tə zən) *n.* person skilled in a practical art.

art/ist (är'tist) *n.* practitioner of fine art. **—ar.tis/tic,** *adj.* **—art/ist.ry,** *n.*

art/less, *adj.* natural.

art/y, *adj.,* **artier, artiest.** *Informal.* self-consciously artistic.

as (az; *unstressed* əz) *adv.* **1.** to such an extent. **—***conj.* **2.** in the manner, etc., that. **3.** while. **4.** because. **—***pron.* **5.** that.

ASAP (ā'es'ā'pē', ā'sap) **1.** as soon as possible. **2.** without delay. Also, **A.S.A.P., a.s.a.p.**

as.bes/tos (as bes'təs, az-) *n.* fibrous material formerly used in fireproofing.

as.cend/ (ə send') *v.* climb. **—as.cent/,** *n.*

as.cend/an.cy, *n.* domination; power. **—as.cend/ant,** *adj., n.*

As.cen/sion (ə sen'shən) *n.* bodily passing of Christ to heaven.

as/cer.tain/ (as'ər tān') *v.* find out.

as.cet/ic (ə set'ik) *n.* **1.** one who lives austerely. **—***adj.* **2.** austere or abstemious.

ASCII (as'kē) *n.* standardized code for computer storage and transmission.

as.cor/bic ac/id (ə skôr'bik) vitamin C.

as/cot (as'kət, -kot) *n.* tie or scarf with broad ends.

as.cribe/ (ə skrīb') *v.,* **-cribed, -cribing.** attribute.

a.sep/sis (ā sep'sis, ā sep'-) *n.* absence of certain harmful bacteria.

a.sex/u.al (ā sek'shōō əl) *adj.* **1.** without sex; sexless. **2.** having no sex organs.

ash (ash) *n.* **1.** (*pl.* **ashes**) residue of burned matter. **2.** a common tree. **—ash/y,** *adj.*

a.shamed/ (ə shāmd') *adj.* feeling shame.

ash/en (ash'ən) *adj.* pale gray.

a.shore/ (ə shôr') *adv.,* on or to shore.

ash/tray/, *n.* small dish for tobacco ashes.

A/sian (ā'zhən) *n.* native of Asia. **—Asian,** *adj.*

A/si.at/ic (ā'zhē at'ik) *adj., n. Offensive.* Asian.

a.side/ (ə sīd') *adv.* **1.** on or to one side. **2.** separate.

as/i.nine/ (as'ə nīn') *adj.* stupid.

ask (ask) *v.* **1.** put a question to. **2.** request. **3.** invite. **4.** inquire.

a.skance/ (ə skans') *adv.* with doubt or disapproval.

a.skew/ (ə skyōō') *adv., adj.* twisted.

a.sleep/ (ə slēp') *adj., adv.* sleeping.

a.so/cial (ā sō'shəl) *adj.* **1.** not sociable. **2.** selfish.

asp (asp) *n.* poisonous snake.

as.par/a.gus (ə spar'ə gəs) *n.* plant with edible shoots.

as/pect (as'pekt) *n.* **1.** appearance. **2.** phase. **3.** direction faced.

as/pen (as'pən) *n.* variety of poplar.

as.per/i.ty (ə sper'i tē) *n., pl.* **-ties.** roughness.

as.per/sion (ə spûr'zhən, -shən) *n.* derogatory remark.

as/phalt (as'fôlt) *n.* hard, black material used for pavements.

as.phyx/i.ate/ (as fik'sē āt') *v.,* **-ated, -ating.** affect by a lack of oxygen; choke or smother. **—as.phyx/i.a/tion,** *n.*

as.pire/ (ə spīr') *v.,* **-pired, -piring.** long, aim, or seek for. **—as/pi.ra/tion** (as'pə rā'shən) *n.*

as/pi.rin (as'pə rin, -prin) *n.* crystalline derivative of salicylic acid, used to reduce pain and fever.

ass (as) *n.* **1.** donkey. **2.** fool.

as.sail/ (ə sāl') *v.* attack. **—as.sail/ant,** *n.*

as.sas/sin (ə sas'in) *n.* murderer, esp. of an important person. **—as-**

sas'si·nate', v., **-nated**, **-nating**.
—**as·sas'si·na'tion**, n.

as·sault' (ə sôlt') n., v. attack.
—**as·sault'**, v.

as·say' (a sā') v. analyze or evaluate. —**as·say**, n. —**as·say'er**, n.

as·sem'blage (ə sem'blij) n. 1. group; assembly. 2. act of assembling.

as·sem'ble (ə sem'bəl) v., **-bled**, **-bling**. come or bring together.

as·sem'bly, n., pl. **-blies**. 1. group gathered together. 2. legislative body. 3. putting together of parts.

as·sem'bly·man, n., pl. **-men**. member of legislative assembly. Also, fem., **as·sem'bly·wom'an**.

as·sent' (ə sent') v. 1. agree. —n. 2. agreement.

as·sert' (ə sûrt') v. 1. state; declare. 2. claim. 3. present (oneself) boldly. —**as·ser'tion**, n. —**as·ser'tive**, adj.

as·sess' (ə ses') v. evaluate, as for taxes. —**as·sess'ment**, n. —**as·ses'sor**, n.

as·set (as'et) n. 1. item of property. 2. quality.

as·sid'u·ous (ə sij'ōō əs) adj. persistent; devoted. —**as·sid'u·ous·ly**, adv. —**as·si·du'i·ty**, n.

as·sign' (ə sīn') v. 1. give. 2. appoint. 3. transfer. —**as·sign'a·ble**, adj. —**as·sign'ment**, n.

as·sig·na'tion (as'ig nā'shən) n. appointment; rendezvous.

as·sim'i·late' (ə sim'ə lāt') v., **-lated**, **-lating**. absorb or become absorbed.

as·sist' (ə sist') v., n. help; aid. —**as·sist'ant**, n., adj. —**as·sist'ance**, n.

assn., association.

as·so'ci·ate', v., **-ated**, **-ating**, n., adj. —v. (ə sō'shē āt', -sē-) 1. connect or join. 2. keep company. —n. (-it) 3. partner; colleague. —adj. (-it) 4. allied. —**as·so'ci·a'tion**, n.

as·so'nance (as'ə nəns) n. similarity of sound in words or syllables.

as·sort'ed (ə sôr'tid) adj. of various kinds.

as·sort'ment a mixed collection.

asst., assistant.

as·suage' (ə swāj') v., **-suaged**, **-suaging**. lessen (pain, grief, etc.).

as·sume' (ə sōōm') v., **-sumed**, **-suming**. 1. take without proof. 2. undertake. 3. pretend. 4. take upon oneself.

as·sump'tion (ə sump'shən) n. 1. unverified belief. 2. undertaking. 3. (cap.) ascent to heaven of Virgin Mary.

as·sure' (ə shŏŏr') v., **-sured**, **-suring**. 1. affirm to. 2. guarantee. 3.

encourage. 4. insure. —**as·sur'ance**, n. —**as·sured'**, adj., n.

as'ter (as'tər) n. plant with many petals around a center disk.

as'ter·isk (as'tə risk) n. star (*) symbol used in writing as a reference mark. —**Pronunciation.** The word ASTERISK is pronounced (as'tə risk). Note that the final syllable is pronounced (-risk), with the (s) before the (k). Both (as'tə riks) and (as'tə rik), although occasionally heard among educated speakers, are considered nonstandard pronunciations.

a·stern' (ə stûrn') adv., adj. Naut. toward or at the rear.

as'ter·oid' (as'tə roid') n. planet-like body beyond Mars.

asth'ma (az'mə) n. painful respiratory disorder. —**asth·mat'ic** (az-mat'ik) adj., n.

a·stig'ma·tism (ə stig'mə tiz'əm) n. eye defect resulting in imperfect images.

a·stir' (ə stûr') adj., adv. active.

as·ton'ish (ə ston'ish) v. surprise greatly; amaze. —**as·ton'ish·ing**, adj. —**as·ton'ish·ing·ly**, adv. —**as·ton'ish·ment**, n.

as·tound' (ə stound') v. amaze greatly.

as'tral (as'trəl) adj. of the stars.

a·stray' (ə strā') adj., adv. straying.

a·stride' (ə strīd') adv., adj., prep. straddling.

as·trin'gent (ə strin'jənt) adj. causing constriction of skin tissue.

as·trol'o·gy (ə strol'ə jē) n. study of stars to determine their influence on human affairs. —**as'tro·log'i·cal** (as'trə loj'i kəl) adj. —**as·trol'o·ger**, n.

as'tro·naut' (as'trə nôt') n. traveler outside earth's atmosphere.

as'tro·nau'tics, n. science and technology of space travel.

as'tro·nom'i·cal (-nom'i kəl) adj. 1. of astronomy. 2. extremely great, etc. —**as'tro·nom'i·cal·ly**, adv.

as·tron'o·my (ə stron'ə mē) n. science of all the celestial bodies. —**as·tron'o·mer**, n.

as'tro·phys'ics (as'trō fiz'iks) n. branch of astronomy dealing with physical properties of celestial bodies. —**as'tro·phys'i·cist** (-ə sist) n.

as·tute' (ə stōōt', ə styōōt') adj. shrewd; clever. —**as·tute'ly**, adv.

a·sun'der (ə sun'dər) adv., adj. apart.

a·sy'lum (ə sī'ləm) n. 1. institution for care of ill or needy persons. 2. place of refuge; sanctuary.

a·sym'me·try (ā sim'i trē) n. lack

of symmetry. —a·sym·met·ric (ā'-
sə me'trik), a'sym·met'ri·cal, adj.

at (at; *unstressed* ət, it) *prep.* (word
used in indicating place, time, etc.)

at·a·vism (at'ə viz'əm) n. reappear-
ance of ancestral traits.

ate (āt; *Brit.* et) v. pt. of **eat.**

at·el·ier (at'l yā') n. studio, esp.
of an artist.

a·the·ism (ā'thē iz'əm) n. belief
that there is no God. —a'the·ist, n.

ath·lete (ath'lēt) n. one who partic-
ipates in sports or physical
exercises. —ath·let'ic (-let'ik) adj.
—ath·let'ics, n.

—**Pronunciation.** The word ATHLETE
is normally pronounced as a two-
syllable word: (ath'lēt). Similarly,
ATHLETIC has only three syllables:
(ath let'ik). Pronunciations of these
words that add an extra syllable,
with a weak vowel sound inserted
between the (th) and the (l), are
not considered standard.

athlete's foot, ringworm of the feet.

at·las (at'ləs) n. book of maps.

ATM, automated-teller machine,
which provides certain bank
services when an electronic bank
card is inserted.

at·mos·phere (at'məs fēr') n. 1.
air surrounding earth. 2. pervading
mood. —at·mos·pher·ic (-fer'ik)
adj.

at·oll (at'ôl) n. ring-shaped coral island.

at·om (at'əm) n. smallest unit
making up chemical element. —a·
tom'ic (ə tom'ik) adj. —a·tom'i·
cal·ly, adv.

atomic bomb, bomb whose force is
derived from nuclear fission of certain atoms, causing the conversion
of some mass to energy (**atomic energy**). Also, **atom bomb.**

at·om·iz·er (at'ə mī'zər) n. device
for making a fine spray.

a·ton·al (ā tōn'l) adj. lacking tonality. —a'to·nal'i·ty (-nal'i tē) n.

a·tone (ə tōn') v., **atoned, aton-
ing.** make amends (for). —a·tone'-
ment, n.

a·top (ə top') adj., adv., prep. on
or at the top of.

a·tri·um (ā'trē əm) n., pl. **atria,
atriums. 1.** enclosed court in building. **2.** either of two upper chambers of the heart.

a·tro·cious (ə trō'shəs) adj. **1.**
wicked. **2.** very bad. —a·troc'i·ty
(ə tros'i tē) n.

at·ro·phy (a'trə fē) n., v., **-phied,
-phying.** —n. **1.** wasting away of
the body. —v. **2.** cause or undergo
atrophy.

at·tach' (ə tach') v. **1.** fasten or
join. **2.** take by legal authority.

at·ta·ché (at'ə shā') n. embassy
official.

at·tach·ment (ə tach'mənt) n. **1.**
an attaching. **2.** something fastened
on. **3.** affection.

at·tack' (ə tak') v. **1.** act against
with sudden force **2.** do vigorously.
—n. **3.** an attacking; onset.

at·tain' (ə tān') v. **1.** reach; arrive
at. **2.** accomplish; fulfill. —at·tain'-
a·ble, adj. —at·tain'ment, n.

at·tempt' (ə tempt') v., n. try.

at·tend' (ə tend') v. **1.** be present
at. **2.** go with. **3.** take care of. **4.**
give heed to. —at·tend'ance, n.
—at·tend'ant, n.

at·ten·tion (ə ten'shən) n. **1.** act of
attending. **2.** careful notice. —at·
ten'tive, adj. —at·ten'tive·ly, adv.

at·ten·u·ate' (ə ten'yōō āt') v., -ated,
-ating. **1.** make thin. **2.** lessen.

at·test' (ə test') v. declare or cer-
tify as true, genuine, etc.

at·tic (at'ik) n. room under the
roof.

at·tire (ə tīr') v., -tired, -tiring. **1.**
—v. **1.** dress; adorn. —n. **2.**
clothes.

at·ti·tude' (at'i tōōd', -tyōōd') n. **1.**
feeling or opinion, esp. as expressed. **2.** posture.

attn., attention.

at·tor·ney (ə tûr'nē) n. lawyer.

attorney general, pl. **attorneys
general, attorney generals.** chief
law officer of a country or state.

at·tract' (ə trakt') v. **1.** draw toward. **2.** invite; allure. —at·trac'-
tion, n. —at·trac'tive, adj. —at·
trac'tive·ly, adv. —at·trac'tive·
ness, n.

at·trib·ute (v., ə trib'yōōt') **1.** ascribe; credit;
impute. —n. (a'trə byōōt') **2.** spe-
cial quality, aspect, etc.

at·tri·tion (ə trish'ən) n. wearing
down.

at·tune' (ə tōōn', ə tyōōn') v.,
-tuned, -tuning. harmonize.

atty., attorney.

ATV, n. all-terrain vehicle: small
motor vehicle with treads or wheels
for nonroad travel.

auc·tion (ôk'shən) n. **1.** sale of
goods to highest bidders. —v. **2.** sell
by auction. —auc'tion·eer', n., v.

au·da·cious (ô dā'shəs) adj. bold;
daring. —au·dac'i·ty (-das'i tē) n.

au·di·ble (ô'də bəl) adj. that can
be heard. —au'di·bly, adv.

au·di·ence (ô′dē əns) n. **1.** group of hearers or spectators. **2.** formal hearing or interview.

au·di·o (ô′dē ō′) adj. **1.** of sound reception or reproduction. —n. **2.** audible part of TV.

au·di·ol·o·gy (-ol′ə jē) n. study and treatment of hearing disorders.

au·di·om·e·ter (-om′i tər) n. instrument for testing hearing.

au·di·o·tape (ô′dē ō-) n. magnetic tape for recording sound.

au·di·o·vis·u·al, adj. using films, TV, and recordings, as for education.

au·dit (ô′dit) n. official examination of accounts. —aud′it, v. —au′di·tor, n.

au·di′tion (ô dish′ən) n. **1.** trial performance. —v. **2.** give an audition.

au·di·to·ri·um (-tôr′ē əm) n. large meeting room.

au·di·to·ry, adj. of hearing.

Aug., August.

au′ger (ô′gər) n. drill.

aught (ôt) n. **1.** anything. **2.** zero (0). —adv. **3.** at all.

aug·ment′ (ôg ment′) v. increase. —aug′men·ta′tion, n.

au′gur (ô′gər) v. predict; bode.

Au′gust (ô′gəst) n. eighth month of year.

au·gust′ (ə gust′) adj. majestic.

auk (ôk) n. northern diving bird.

auld lang syne (ōld′ lang zīn′) fondly remembered times.

aunt (ant, änt) n. **1.** sister of a parent. **2.** wife of an uncle.

au pair (ō pâr′) person, usu. young foreign visitor, who does household tasks in exchange for room and board.

au·ra (ôr′ə) n. **1.** atmosphere, quality, etc. **2.** radiance coming from the body.

au′ral (ôr′əl) adj. of or by hearing.

au·re·ole (ôr′ē ōl′) n. halo.

au′ re·voir′ (ō′ rə vwär′) French. good-by.

au′ri·cle (ôr′i kəl) n. **1.** outer part of ear. **2.** chamber in heart.

au·ro·ra (ə rôr′ə) n. display of bands of light in the night sky.

aus′pice (ô′spis) n. (usually pl.) patronage.

aus·pi′cious (ô spish′əs) adj. favorable. —aus·pi′cious·ly, adv.

aus·tere′ (ô stēr′) adj. **1.** harsh; stern. **2.** severely simple. —aus·ter′i·ty, n.

Aus·tral′ian (ô strāl′yən) n. native or citizen of Australia. —Australian, adj.

Aus′tri·an (ô′strē ən) n. native of Austria. —Austrian, adj.

au·then′tic (ô then′tik) adj. reliable; genuine. —au·then·tic′i·ty (-tis′i tē) n. —au·then′ti·cate′, v.

au′thor (ô′thər) n. writer or creator. —au′thor·ship′, n.

au·thor·i·tar·i·an (ə thôr′i târ′ē ən) adj. requiring total obedience.

au·thor·i·ta·tive (-tā′tiv) adj. to be accepted as true.

au·thor′i·ty, n., pl. **-ties. 1.** right to order or decide. **2.** one with such right. **3.** respected source of information.

au′thor·ize′ (ô′thə rīz′) v., **-ized, -izing.** permit officially.

au′tism (ô′tiz əm) n. disorder characterized by extreme self-absorption and detachment from reality. —au·tis′tic (ə tis′tik) adj.

au′to (ô′tō) n. automobile.

auto-, prefix meaning self or same, as autograph.

au·to·bi·og·ra·phy, n., pl. **-phies.** story of one's own life.

au·toc′ra·cy (ô tok′rə sē) n., pl. **-cies.** absolute political power.

au′to·di·dact (ô′tō dī′dakt) n. self-taught person.

au′to·graph (ô′tə graf′) n. **1.** signature. —v. **2.** sign.

au′to·im·mune (ô′tō i myōōn′) adj. of or relating to the body's immune response to its own components.

au′to·mat′ (ô′tə mat′) n. restaurant with coin-operated service.

au′to·mate′ (-māt′) v., **-mated, -mating.** make or become automatic.

au′to·mat′ic (-mat′ik) adj. **1.** self-acting. **2.** inevitably following. —au′to·mat′i·cal·ly, adv.

automatic pilot, automatic electronic control system for piloting aircraft.

au′to·ma′tion (-mā′shən) n. system of controlling a mechanical process automatically, as by electronic devices.

au·tom′a·ton (ô tom′ə ton′) n. mechanical device or figure; robot.

au′to·mo·bile′ (ô′tə mə bēl′) n. motorized passenger vehicle.

au·ton′o·my (ô ton′ə mē) n. self-government. —au·ton′o·mous, adj.

au′top·sy (ô′top sē) n., pl. **-sies.** examination of body for causes of death.

au′tumn (ô′təm) n. season before winter; fall. —au·tum′nal (ə tum′nl) adj.

aux·il′ia·ry (ôg zil′yə rē) adj., n., pl. **-ries.** —adj. **1.** assisting. **2.** subsidiary. —n. **3.** verb preceding other verbs to express tense, etc.

a·vail′ (ə vāl′) v. **1.** be of use,

value, etc. **2.** take to (oneself) advantageously. —*n.* **3.** benefit; advantage.

a•vail′a•ble, *adj.* present for use. —**a•vail′a•bil′i•ty,** *n.*

av′a•lanche′ (av′ə lanch′) *n.* mass of falling snow, ice, etc.

a•vant′-garde′ (ə vänt′gärd′, äv′änt-) *adj.* progressive, esp. in art.

a′va•rice (av′ər is) *n.* greed. —**av′a•ri′cious** (-rish′əs) *adj.*

ave., avenue.

a•venge′ (ə venj′) *v.,* **avenged, avenging.** take vengeance for.

av•e•nue′ (av′ə nyōō′) *n.* **1.** broad street. **2.** approach.

a•ver′ (ə vûr′) *v.,* **averred, aver-ring.** affirm; declare.

av′er•age (av′ər ij) *n., adj., v.,* **-aged, -aging.** —*n.* **1.** sum of a series of numbers divided by the number of terms in the series. —*adj.* **2.** of or like an average. **3.** typical. —*v.* **4.** find average of.

a•verse′ (ə vûrs′) *adj.* unwilling.

a•ver′sion (ə vûr′zhən) *n.* dislike.

a•vert′ (ə vûrt′) *v.* **1.** turn away. **2.** prevent.

avg., average.

a′vi•ar′y (ā′vē er′ē) *n., pl.* **-aries.** place in which birds are kept.

a′vi•a′tion (ā′vē ā′shən) *n.* science of flying aircraft. —**a′vi•a′tor,** *n.* —**a′vi•a′trix,** *n.fem.*

av′id (av′id) *adj.* eager. —**a•vid′i•ty,** *n.* —**av′id•ly,** *adv.*

av′o•ca′do (av′ə kä′dō, ä′va-) *n., pl.* **-dos.** tropical pear-shaped fruit.

av′o•ca′tion (av′ə kā′shən) *n.* hobby.

a•void′ (ə void′) *v.* shun; evade. —**a•void′a•ble,** *adj.* —**a•void′ance,** *n.*

av′oir•du•pois′ (av′ər də poiz′) *n.* system of weights with 16-ounce pounds.

a•vow′ (ə vou′) *v.* declare; confess. —**a•vow′al,** *n.* —**a•vowed′,** *adj.*

a•wait′ (ə wāt′) *v.* wait for.

a•wake′ (ə wāk′) *v.,* **awoke** (ə-wōk′) *or* **awaked, awaking,** *adj.* —*v.* **1.** Also, **a•wak′en.** rouse from sleep. —*adj.* **2.** not asleep.

a•wak′en, *v.* awake. —**a•wak′en-ing,** *n., adj.*

a•ward′ (ə wôrd′) *v.* **1.** bestow; grant. —*n.* **2.** thing bestowed.

a•ware′ (ə wâr′) *adj.* conscious (of). —**a•ware′ness,** *n.*

a•wash′ (ə wosh′) *adj.* flooded.

a•way′ (ə wā′) *adv.* **1.** from this or that place. **2.** apart. **3.** aside. —*adj.* **4.** absent. **5.** distant.

awe (ô) *n., v.,* **awed, awing.** —*n.* **1.** respectful fear. —*v.* **2.** fill with awe.

awe′some (ô′səm) *adj.* **1.** inspiring or characterized by awe. **2.** *Slang.* very impressive.

awe′struck′, *adj.* filled with awe.

aw′ful (ô′fal) *adj.* **1.** fearful. **2.** very bad. **3.** *Informal.* very.

aw′ful•ly, *adv.* **1.** very badly. **2.** *Informal.* very.

a•while′ (ə hwīl′) *adv.* for a short time. —**Usage.** The adverb AWHILE is always spelled as one word: *We rested awhile.* A WHILE is a noun phrase (an article and a noun) and is used after a preposition: *We rested for a while.*

awk′ward (ôk′wərd) *adj.* **1.** clumsy. **2.** embarrassing. **3.** difficult; risky. —**awk′ward•ly,** *adv.*

awl (ôl) *n.* tool for making holes.

awn′ing (ô′ning) *n.* canvas over-hang.

AWOL (*pronounced as initials or* ā′wôl) *adj., adv.* absent without leave.

a•wry′ (ə rī′) *adv., adj.* **1.** twisted. **2.** wrong.

ax (aks) *n.* small chopping tool. Also, **axe.**

ax′i•om (ak′sē əm) *n.* accepted truth. —**ax′i•o•mat′ic** (-ə mat′ik) *adj.*

ax′is (ak′sis) *n., pl.* **axes** (ak′sēz). line about which something turns.

ax′le (ak′səl) *n.* bar on which a wheel turns.

a′ya•tol′lah (ä′yə tō′lə) *n.* chief Muslim leader.

aye (ī) *adv.* **1.** yes.

a•zal′ea (ə zāl′yə) *n.* flowering shrub.

AZT, *n. Trademark.* drug used in AIDS treatment.

Az′tec (az′tek) *n.* American Indian people whose Mexican empire was conquered by Spaniards in 1521. —**Az′tec•an,** *adj.*

az′ure (azh′ər) *adj., n.* sky-blue.

B

B, b (bē) *n.* second letter of English alphabet.

B.A., Bachelor of Arts.

bab·ble (bab′əl) *v.,* **-bled, -bling. 1.** talk indistinctly or foolishly. **2.** murmur. **—bab′ble,** *n.*

babe (bāb) *n.* **1.** baby. **2.** innocent person.

ba·boon′ (ba bōōn′, bə-) *n.* large monkey of Africa and Arabia.

ba′by (bā′bē) *n., pl.* **-bies,** *v.,* **-bied, -bying. 1.** infant. **2.** childish person. **—v. 3.** pamper. **—ba′by·ish,** *adj.*

baby boom, period of increase in the rate of births. **—baby boomer.**

ba′by·sit′, *v.,* **-sat** (-sat′) **-sitting.** tend another's child for a few hours. **—ba′by·sit′ter,** *n.*

bac′ca·lau′re·ate (bak′ə lôr′ē it) *n.* bachelor's degree.

bac′cha·nal′ (bak′ə nal′) *n.* drunken reveler.

bach′e·lor (bach′ə lər) *n.* **1.** unmarried man. **2.** person holding first degree of a college.

ba·cil′lus (ba sil′əs) *n., pl.* **-cilli** (-sil′ī). type of bacteria.

back (bak) *n.* **1.** rear part of human and animal body. **2.** rear. **3.** spine. **—v. 4.** sponsor. **5.** move backward. **6.** bet in favor of. **7.** furnish or form a back. **—adj. 8.** being behind. **9.** in the past. **10.** overdue. **11.** at or toward the rear. **12.** toward original point or condition. **13.** in return. **—back′er,** *n.* **—back′ing,** *n.*

back′bite′, *v.,* **-bit** (-bit′), **-bitten,** **-biting.** discuss (someone) maliciously.

back′board′, *n.* in basketball, vertical board behind basket.

back′bone′, *n.* **1.** spine. **2.** strength of character. **—back′boned′,** *adj.*

back′break′ing, *adj.* fatiguing.

back′drop′, *n.* **1.** curtain at the back of a stage. **2.** background of an event; setting.

back′field′, *n.* football players behind the line.

back′fire′, *v.,* **-fired, firing. 1.** (of an engine) ignite prematurely. **2.** bring results opposite to those planned. **—back′fire′,** *n.*

back′gam′mon (bak′gam′ən) *n.* board game for two persons.

back′ground′, *n.* **1.** parts in the rear. **2.** distant portions in a picture. **3.** origins; antecedents.

back′hand′, *n.* **1.** in tennis and other sports, stroke made with back of hand facing direction of movement. **—adj. 2.** backhanded. **—v. 3.** hit with a backhand.

back′hand′ed, *adj.* **1.** with upper part of hand forward. **2.** ambiguous.

back′lash′, *n.* retaliatory reaction.

back′log′, *n.* reserve or accumulation, as of work.

back′pack′, *n.* **1.** knapsack. **—v. 2.** hike using backpack.

back′-ped′al, *v.,* **-aled, -aling. 1.** slow a bicycle by pressing backward on pedals. **2.** retreat from or reverse a previous stand or opinion.

back′side′, *n.* **1.** rear. **2.** rump.

back′slide′, *v.,* **-slid** (-slid′), **-slidden** or **-slid, -sliding.** relapse into bad habits. **—back′slid′er,** *n.*

back′stage′, *adv.* in theater wings or dressing rooms.

back′stroke′, *n.* swimming stroke performed while lying on back.

back talk, impertinent talk.

back′track′, *v.* retreat slowly.

back′up′, *n.* **1.** person or thing that supports or reinforces another. **2.** accumulation caused by a stoppage, as of traffic. **3.** alternate kept in reserve.

back′ward (-wərd) *adv.* Also, **back′wards. 1.** toward the back or rear. **2.** back foremost. **3.** toward or in the past. **—adj. 4.** toward the back or past. **5.** behind in time or progress. **6.** bashful.

back′wa′ter, *n.* place that is backward or stagnant.

back′woods′, *n.pl.* wooded or unsettled districts.

ba·con (bā′kən) *n.* cured back and sides of a hog.

bac·te′ri·a (bak tēr′ē ə) *n.pl.,* *sing.* **-um** (-əm). group of one-celled organisms, involved in fermentation, infectious disease, etc. **—bac·te′ri·al,** *adj.* **—bac·te′ri·al·ly,** *adv.*

bac·te′ri·ol′o·gy (-ol′ə jē) *n.* science dealing with bacteria. **—bac·te′ri·o·log′i·cal** (-ə loj′i kal) *adj.* **—bac·te′ri·ol′o·gist,** *n.*

bad (bad) *adj.,* **worse** (wûrs), **worst** (wûrst), *n.* **—adj. 1.** not good. **—n. 2.** bad thing, condition, or quality. **—bad′ly,** *adv.*

—Usage. The adjective BAD, meaning "unpleasant, unattractive, unfavorable, spoiled, etc.," is the usual form after such verbs as *sound, smell, look,* and *taste:* The music *sounds* bad. The locker room *smells* bad. You *look* pretty bad; are you sick? The water *tasted* bad. After the verb *feel,* the adjective BADLY may also be used (*She was feeling badly that day*), although BAD is more common in formal writing. BAD as an adverb appears mainly in informal situations: *He wanted to win pretty bad.*

bad blood, hostility.

badge (baj) *n.* emblem or insignia.

badg′er (baj′ər) *n.* **1.** burrowing mammal. —*v.* **2.** harass.

bad′min·ton (bad′min tn′) *n.* game similar to lawn tennis.

bad′-mouth′ (-mouth′, -mouth′) *v.* criticize. Also, **bad′mouth′.**

baf′fle (baf′əl) *v.,* **-fled, -fling.** —*v.* **1.** thwart; confuse. —*n.* **2.** obstacle; obstruction.

bag (bag) *n., v.,* **bagged, bagging.** —*n.* **1.** sack or receptacle of flexible material. **2.** purse. —*v.* **3.** bulge. **4.** put into a bag. **5.** kill or catch. —**bag′gy,** *adj.* —**bag′gi·ness,** *n.*

bag′a·telle′ (bag′ə tel′) *n.* article of small value.

ba′gel (bā′gəl) *n.* hard ringlike roll.

bag′gage (bag′ij) *n.* trunks, suitcases, etc., for travel.

bag′pipe′, *n.* (*often pl.*) musical instrument with windbag and two or more pipes. —**bag′pip′er,** *n.*

bah (bä, ba) *interj.* (exclamation of contempt or annoyance).

bail (bāl) *n.* **1.** security for the return of a prisoner to custody. **2.** person giving bail. **3.** release following payment of security. —*v.* **4.** give or obtain liberty by bail. **5.** dip water out of boat. **6.** bail out, make a parachute jump. —**bail′a·ble,** *adj.*

bail′iff (bā′lif) *n.* public officer similar to sheriff or deputy.

bail′i·wick (bā′lə wik′) *n.* person's area of authority, skill, etc.

bail′out′, *n.* rescue from financial problems.

bait (bāt) *n.* **1.** food used as lure in fishing or hunting. —*v.* **2.** prepare with bait. **3.** set dogs upon for sport.

bake (bāk) *v.,* **baked, baking.** **1.** cook by dry heat, as in oven. **2.** harden by heat. —**bak′er,** *n.*

baker's dozen, a dozen plus one; 13.

bak′er·y, *n., pl.* **-eries.** place for baking; baker's shop.

baking powder, white powder used as leavening agent in baking.

baking soda, sodium bicarbonate, white powder used as an antacid and in baking.

bal′ance (bal′əns) *n., v.,* **-anced, -ancing.** —*n.* **1.** instrument for weighing. **2.** equilibrium. **3.** harmonious arrangement. **4.** act of balancing. **5.** remainder, as of money due. —*v.* **6.** weigh. **7.** set or hold in equilibrium. **8.** be equivalent to. **9.** reckon or adjust accounts.

bal′co·ny (bal′kə nē) *n., pl.* **-nies.** **1.** platform projecting from wall of building. **2.** theater gallery.

bald (bôld) *adj.* **1.** lacking hair on scalp. **2.** plain; undisguised.

bal′der·dash′ (bôl′dər dash′) *n.* nonsense.

bale (bāl) *n., v.,* **baled, baling.** —*n.* **1.** large bundle or package. —*v.* **2.** make into bales. —**bal′er,** *n.*

bale′ful, *adj.* evil; menacing.

balk (bôk) *v.* **1.** stop or stop short. **2.** hinder; thwart. —*n.* **3.** hindrance. **4.** in baseball, illegal stop in pitcher's motion. —**balk′y,** *adj.*

ball (bôl) *n.* **1.** round or roundish object. **2.** game played with ball. **3.** social assembly for dancing. **4.** *Informal.* good time. —*v.* **5.** make or form into ball.

bal′lad (bal′əd) *n.* **1.** narrative folk song or poem. **2.** sentimental song.

bal′last (bal′əst) *n.* **1.** heavy material carried to ensure stability. —*v.* **2.** furnish with ballast.

ball bearing, bearing in which a moving part turns on steel balls.

bal′le·ri′na (bal′ə rē′nə) *n.* woman ballet dancer.

bal′let′ (ba lā′) *n.* theatrical entertainment by dancers.

ballistic missile (bə lis′tik) guided missile completing its trajectory in free fall.

bal·lis′tics, *n.* study of the motion of projectiles. —**bal·lis′tic,** *adj.*

bal·loon′ (bə lōōn′) *n.* **1.** bag filled with a gas lighter than air, designed to float in atmosphere. —*v.* **2.** go up in balloon. **3.** increase rapidly. —**bal·loon′ist,** *n.*

bal′lot (bal′ət) *n., v.,* **-loted, -loting.** —*n.* **1.** paper used in voting. **2.** vote. —*v.* **3.** vote by ballot.

ball′park′, *n.* baseball arena.

ball′room′, *n.* room for dancing.

bal′ly·hoo′ (bal′ē hōō′) *n. Informal.* exaggerated publicity.

balm (bäm) *n.* **1.** fragrant, oily substance obtained from tropical trees. **2.** aromatic ointment or fragrance.

balm′y, *adj.,* **balmier, balmiest. 1.** mild; refreshing. **2.** fragrant.

ba·lo′ney (bə lō′nē) *n. Informal.* **1.** bologna. **2.** false or foolish talk.

bal′sa (bôl′sə, bäl′-) *n.* tropical tree with light wood.

bal′sam (bôl′səm) *n.* **1.** fragrant substance exuded from certain trees. **2.** any of these trees. —**bal·sam/ic** (bôl sam/ik) adj.

bal/us·ter (bal/ə stər) n. pillarlike support for railing.

bal/us·trade/ (-ə strād/) n. series of balusters supporting a railing.

bam·boo/ (bam boo/) n., pl. **-boos.** treelike tropical grass having a hollow woody stem.

bam·boo/zle (bam boo/zəl) v., **-zled, -zling.** Informal. trick.

ban (ban) v., **banned, banning,** n. —v. **1.** prohibit. —n. **2.** prohibition.

ba·nal/ (bə nal/, -näl/, bän/l) adj. trite. —**ba·nal/i·ty,** n.

ba·nan/a (bə nan/ə) n. **1.** tropical plant. **2.** yellow fruit of this plant.

band (band) n. **1.** strip of material for binding. **2.** stripe. **3.** company of persons. **4.** group of musicians. —v. **5.** mark with bands. **6.** unite.

band/age (ban/dij) n., v., **-aged, -aging.** —n. **1.** strip of cloth for binding wound. —v. **2.** bind with bandage. —**band/ag·er,** n.

Band/-Aid/ n. Trademark. small adhesive bandage with gauze center.

ban·dan/na (ban dan/ə) n. colored handkerchief worn on head. Also, **ban·dan/a.**

ban/dit (ban/dit) n. robber; outlaw.

band/stand/, n. platform on which band performs.

band/wag/on, n. cause or movement that appears popular and successful.

ban/dy (ban/dē) v., **-died, -dying,** adj. —v. **1.** exchange (words) back and forth. —adj. **2.** bent outward. —**ban/dy-leg/ged** (-leg/id, -legd/) adj.

bane (bān) n. thing causing death or destruction.

bane/ful, adj. destructive.

bang (bang) n. **1.** loud, sudden noise. **2.** (often pl.) fringe of hair across forehead. —v. **3.** make loud noise. **4.** strike noisily.

ban/gle (bang/gəl) n. bracelet.

bang/-up/, adj. Informal. excellent.

ban/ish (ban/ish) v. **1.** exile. **2.** drive or put away. —**ban/ish·ment,** n.

ban/is·ter (ban/ə stər) n. **1.** baluster. **2.** (pl.) balustrade.

ban/jo (ban/jō) n., pl. **-jos, -joes.** musical instrument similar to guitar, with circular body. —**ban/jo·ist,** n.

bank (bangk) n. **1.** pile; heap. **2.** slope bordering stream. **3.** place or institution for receiving and lending money. **4.** store of something, such as blood, for future use. —v. **5.** border with or make into bank. **6.** cover fire to make burn slowly. **7.**

slope upward. **8.** deposit or keep money in bank. **9.** rely (on). —**bank/er,** n. —**bank/ing,** n.

bank/roll/, n. **1.** money possessed. —v. **2.** pay for; fund.

bank/rupt (-rupt) n. **1.** insolvent person. —adj. **2.** insolvent. **3.** lacking. —v. **4.** make bankrupt. —**bank/rupt·cy,** n.

ban/ner (ban/ər) n. flag.

banns (banz) n.pl. notice of intended marriage. Also, **bans.**

ban/quet (bang/kwit) n. **1.** feast. —v. **2.** dine or entertain at banquet.

ban/shee (ban/shē) n. female spirit of Irish folklore whose wailing means a loved one is about to die.

ban/tam (ban/təm) n. **1.** breed of small domestic fowl. —adj. **2.** tiny.

ban/ter (ban/tər) n. **1.** good-natured teasing. —v. **2.** use banter.

ban/yan (ban/yən) n. East Indian fig tree.

bap/tism (bap/tiz əm) n. immersion in or application of water, esp. as initiatory rite in Christian church. —**bap·tis/mal,** adj.

Bap/tist (-tist) n. Christian who undergoes baptism only after profession of faith.

bap·tize/ (bap tīz/, bap/tīz) v., **-tized, -tizing. 1.** administer baptism. **2.** christen. —**bap·tiz/er,** n.

bar (bär) n., v., **barred, barring,** prep. —n. **1.** long, evenly shaped piece, esp. of wood or metal. **2.** band; stripe. **3.** long ridge in shallow waters. **4.** obstruction; hindrance. **5.** line marking division between two measures of music. **6.** place where liquors are served. **7.** legal profession or its members. **8.** railing in courtroom between public and court officers. **9.** place in courtroom where prisoners are stationed. —v. **10.** provide or fasten with a bar. **11.** block; hinder. —prep. **12.** except for. —**barred,** adj.

barb (bärb) n. **1.** point projecting backward. —v. **2.** furnish with barb.

bar·bar/i·an (bär bâr/ē ən) n. **1.** savage or uncivilized person. —adj. **2.** uncivilized. —**bar·bar/ic,** adj. —**bar·bar/i·cal·ly,** adv.

bar/ba·rism (bär/bə riz/əm) n. barbarian state or act.

bar·bar/i·ty (-bâr/i tē) n., pl. **-ties. 1.** cruelty. **2.** crudity.

bar/ba·rous (-bər əs) adj. **1.** barbarian. **2.** harsh; harsh-sounding. —**bar/ba·rous·ly,** adv.

bar/be·cue/ (bär/bi kyoo/) v., **-cued, -cuing.** —n. **1.** outdoor meal at which foods are roasted over an open fire. —v. **2.** broil over an open fire. Also, **bar·be·que′.**

bar′ber (bär′bər) n. **1.** one who gives haircuts, shaves, etc. —v. **2.** shave or cut the hair.

bar·bi′tu·rate (bär bich′ər it, bär′bi tŏŏr′it, -tyŏŏr′-) n. sedative drug.

bar code, series of lines of different widths placed on item for identification by computer scanner.

bard (bärd) n. poet.

bare (bâr) adj., **barer, barest,** v., **bared, baring.** —adj. **1.** uncovered; unclothed. **2.** unfurnished. **3.** unconcealed. **4.** mere. —v. **5.** make bare. —**bare′foot′,** adj., adv.

bare′back′, adv., adj. without a saddle.

bare′faced′, adj. **1.** undisguised. **2.** impudent.

bare′ly, adv. no more than; only.

bar′gain (bär′gən) n. **1.** agreement. **2.** advantageous purchase. —v. **3.** discuss or arrive at agreement.

barge (bärj) n., v., **barged, barging.** —n. **1.** unpowered vessel for freight. —v. **2.** carry by barge. **3.** move clumsily. **4.** Informal. intrude.

bar′i·tone′ (bar′i tōn′) n. male voice or part between tenor and bass.

bar′i·um (bâr′ē əm, bar′-) n. metallic element.

bark (bärk) n. **1.** cry of a dog. **2.** external covering of woody plants. **3.** Also, **barque.** three-masted sailing ship. —v. **4.** sound a bark. **5.** utter with barking sound. **6.** strip from bark. **7.** scrape the skin of.

bark′er (bär′kər) n. person who stands at the entrance to a show, shouting out its attractions.

bar′ley (bär′lē) n. edible cereal plant.

bar mitz′vah (bär mits′və) Jewish religious ceremony recognizing manhood.

barn (bärn) n. farm building for storage and stabling. —**barn′yard′,** n.

bar′na·cle (bär′nə kəl) n. type of shellfish that clings to ship bottoms, etc. —**bar′na·cled,** adj.

barn′storm′, v. tour rural areas giving speeches or performing plays.

ba·rom′e·ter (bə rom′i tər) n. instrument for measuring atmospheric pressure.

bar′on (bar′ən) n. member of lowest nobility. Also, n.fem. **bar′on·ess.** —**bar′on·age,** n. —**ba·ro′ni·al** (bə rō′nē əl) adj.

bar′on·et (-ə nit, -net′) n. member of nobility ranking below baron. —**bar′on·et·cy,** n.

Ba·roque′ (bə rōk′) n. artistic style

marked by exuberant decoration and grotesque effects.

bar′rack (bar′ək) n. (usually pl.) building for lodging soldiers.

bar·ra·cu′da (bar′ə kōō′də) n. edible eellike fish.

bar·rage′ (bə räzh′) n. concentrated artillery fire.

bar′rel (bar′əl) n., v., **-reled, -reling.** —n. **1.** wooden cylindrical vessel with bulging sides. **2.** quantity held in such vessel. —v. **3.** put in barrel or barrels.

bar′ren (bar′ən) adj. **1.** sterile; unfruitful. **2.** dull. —**bar′ren·ness,** n.

bar·rette′ (bə ret′) n. clasp for hair.

bar′ri·cade′ (bar′i kād′, bar′i kād′) n., v., **-caded, -cading.** —n. **1.** defensive barrier. —v. **2.** block or defend with barricade.

bar′ri·er (bar′ē ər) n. obstacle; obstruction.

bar′ring (bär′ing) prep. excepting.

bar′ris·ter (bar′ə stər) n. in England, lawyer in higher courts.

bar′row (bar′ō) n. **1.** flat frame for carrying load. **2.** artificial mound, as over a grave.

bar′tend′er (bär′-) n. person mixing and serving drinks at a bar.

bar′ter (bär′tər) v. **1.** trade by exchange. —n. **2.** act of bartering.

ba·salt′ (bə sôlt′, bas′ôlt) n. dark, hard rock. —**ba·sal′tic,** adj.

base (bās) n., v., **based, basing,** adj., **baser, basest.** —n. **1.** bottom or foundation of something. **2.** fundamental principle. **3.** starting point. **4.** Mil. a. protected place from which operations proceed. **b.** supply installation. **5.** chemical compound which unites with an acid to form a salt. —v. **6.** make foundation for. —adj. **7.** despicable. **8.** inferior.

base′ball′, n. **1.** ball game played by two teams of nine players on diamond-shaped field. **2.** ball used.

base′board′, n. board or molding at the base of a room's walls.

base′less, adj. unfounded.

base′line′, n. **1.** line between bases on baseball diamond. **2.** line at each end of tennis court. **3.** basic standard or level; guideline.

base′ment, n. story of building below the ground floor.

base on balls, pl. **bases on balls,** awarding of first base to a batter after four pitches not strikes.

bash (bash) v. **1.** hit hard. —n. **2.** hard blow. **3.** big, lively party.

bash′ful, adj. shy; timid.

ba′sic (bā′sik) adj. **1.** rudimentary.

2. essential. —n. 3. (pl.) rudiments. —**ba/si·cal·ly,** adv.

BASIC (bā'sik) n. computer programming language using English words, punctuation, and algebraic notation.

bas/il (baz/əl, bā/zəl) n. aromatic mintlike herb.

ba·sil/i·ca (bə sil/i kə) n. 1. ancient church. 2. Roman Catholic church.

ba/sin (bā'sən) n. 1. circular vessel for liquids. 2. area drained by river.

ba/sis (bā'sis) n., pl. **-ses** (-sēz). 1. base (defs. 1, 2). 2. principal ingredient.

bask (bask) v. expose to warmth.

bas/ket (bas/kit) n. receptacle woven of twigs, strips of wood, etc.

bas/ket·ball/, n. 1. ball game played by two teams of five players on rectangular court. 2. ball used.

bas/-re·lief/ (bā'ri lēf') n. sculpture in which figures are raised slightly.

bass adj., n., (for 3) **basses, bass.** —adj. (bās) 1. of the lowest musical part or range. —n 2. (bās) bass part, voice, instrument, etc. 3. (bas) any of various edible, spiny fishes.

basset hound (bas/it) short-legged hound with drooping ears.

bas/si·net/ (bas'ə net') n. basket with hood, used as cradle.

bas·soon/ (ba sōōn', ba-) n. baritone woodwind instrument.

bas/tard (bas/tərd) n. 1. illegitimate child. 2. Slang. mean person. —adj. 3. illegitimate in birth. 4. not pure or authentic.

baste (bāst) v., basted, basting. 1. sew with temporary stitches. 2. moisten (meat, etc.) while cooking.

bas/tion (bas/chən) n. 1. fortified place. 2. something that preserves or protects.

bat (bat) n., v., batted, batting. —n. 1. stick or club, esp. as used in ball games. 2. nocturnal flying mammal. —v. 3. strike with bat. 4. take turn in batting. 5. blink; flutter.

batch (bach) n. material, esp. bread, prepared in one operation.

bat/ed (bā'tid) adj. (of breath) held back in suspense.

bath (bath) n., pl. baths. 1. washing of entire body. 2. water used. —bath/room/, n. —bath/tub/, n.

bathe (bā t h) v., bathed, bathing. 1. take a bath. 2. immerse in liquid; moisten. —bath/er, n.

bathing suit, garment worn for swimming; swimsuit.

ba/thos (bā'thos, -thōs) n. 1. ludicrous change in tone from lofty to commonplace. 2. false pathos; trite sentiment.

bath/robe/, n. robe worn going to and from bath.

ba·tik/ (bə tēk') n. cloth partly waxed to resist dye.

bat mitz/vah (bät mits/və) Jewish religious ceremony for a girl, paralleling the bar mitzvah.

ba·ton/ (bə ton', ba-) n. staff used by orchestral conductor.

bat·tal/ion (ba tal/yən) n. military unit of three or more companies.

bat/ten (bat/n) n. 1. strip of wood. —v. 2. fasten with battens.

bat/ter (bat/ər) v. 1. beat persistently. 2. damage by hard usage. —n. 3. semiliquid cooking mixture. 4. one who bats.

bat/ter·y, n., pl. -teries. 1. device for producing electricity. 2. combination of artillery pieces. 3. illegal attack by beating or wounding.

bat/tle (bat/l) n., v., -tled, -tling. —n. 1. hostile encounter. —v. 2. fight. —**bat/tle·field/,** n.

bat/tle·ment, n. indented parapet.

bat/tle·ship/, n. heavily armed warship.

bat/ty (bat/ē) adj., -tier, -tiest. Slang. crazy or eccentric.

baud (bôd) n. unit used to measure speed of a signal or data transfer, as in computers.

baux/ite (bôk/sīt, bō'zīt) n. principal ore of aluminum.

bawd/y (bô/dē) adj., bawdier, bawdiest. obscene.

bawl (bôl) v. 1. shout out. —n. 2. shout.

bay (bā) n. 1. inlet of sea or lake. 2. vertical section of window. 3. compartment or recess in a building. 4. deep, prolonged bark. 5. stand made by hunted animal or person. 6. reddish brown. 7. laurel tree. —v. 8. bark. 9. bring to bay (def. 5). —adj. 10. of the color bay.

bay/ber/ry, n., pl. -ries. fragrant shrub with berries.

bay leaf, dried leaf of the laurel, used in cooking.

bay/o·net (bā'ə net', bā'ə nit) n., 1. dagger attached to rifle muzzle. —v. 2. kill or wound with bayonet.

bay/ou (bī/ōō) n., pl. bayous. arm of river, etc.

ba·zaar/ (bə zär') n. 1. marketplace. 2. charity sale.

ba·zoo/ka (bə zōō'kə) n. hand-held rocket launcher.

BB (bē'bē') n., pl. BB's. small metal shot fired from an air rifle (BB gun).

B.C., before Christ.

B.C.E., before the Common (or Christian) Era.

be (bē; *unstressed* bĕ, bi) *v.* **1.** exist. **2.** occur.

beach (bēch) *n.* **1.** sand or pebbles of seashore. —*v.* **2.** run or pull a ship onto beach.

beach/comb/er, *n.* **1.** person who gathers salable jetsam or refuse on a beach. **2.** vagrant living on a beach.

beach/head/, *n.* part of beach landed on and seized by military force.

bea/con (bē/kən) *n.* signal, esp. a fire.

bead (bēd) *n.* **1.** small ball of glass, pearl, etc., designed to be strung. **2.** (*pl.*) necklace. —*v.* **3.** ornament with beads. —**bead/ing,** *n.*

bea/gle (bē/gəl) *n.* short-legged hunting dog.

beak (bēk) *n.* **1.** bill of bird. **2.** beaklike object.

beak/er, *n.* large glass.

beam (bēm) *n.* **1.** horizontal support secured at both ends. **2.** ray of light or other radiation. —*v.* **3.** emit beams. **4.** smile radiantly.

bean (bēn) *n.* **1.** edible seed of certain plants. **2.** plant producing such seed.

bear (bâr) *v.,* **bore** (bôr), **borne** (bôrn), **bearing,** *n.* *adj.* —*v.* **1.** support. **2.** carry. **3.** undergo; endure. **4.** move; go. **5.** give birth to. —*n.* **6.** large shaggy mammal. **7.** clumsy or rude person. **8.** speculator who counts on falling prices. —*adj.* **9.** marked by falling prices.

beard (bērd) *n.* **1.** hair on face of man. **2.** similar growth or part. —*v.* **3.** defy. —**beard/ed,** *adj.*

bear hug, tight embrace.

bear/ing, *n.* **1.** manner. **2.** reference; relation. **3.** *Mach.* part in which another part moves. **4.** (*often pl.*) position; direction.

beast (bēst) *n.* **1.** animal. **2.** coarse or inhuman person.

beast/ly, *adj.,* **-lier, -liest. 1.** brutish. **2.** nasty. —**beast/li-ness,** *n.*

beat (bēt) *v.,* **beat, beaten** or **beat, beating,** *n.* —*v.* **1.** strike repeatedly. **2.** dash against. **3.** mark time in music. **4.** defeat. **5.** throb. —*n.* **6.** blow. **7.** sound of a blow. **8.** habitual rounds. **9.** musical time.

be/a-tif/ic (bē/ə tif/ik) *adj.* blissful.

be-at/i-tude/ (bē at/i tōōd/, -tyōōd/) *n.* **1.** blessedness. **2.** (*often cap.*) declaration of blessedness made by Christ (Matthew 5).

beat/nik (bēt/nik) *n.* disillusioned,

unconventional person, esp. of the 1950s.

beau (bō) *n., pl.* **beaus, beaux. 1.** lover. **2.** fop.

beau/te-ous (byōō/tē əs) *adj.* beautiful.

beau/ti/cian (-tish/ən) *n.* person who works in beauty parlor.

beau/ti-ful (-tə fəl) *adj.* having beauty. —**beau/ti-ful-ly,** *adv.*

beau/ti-fy/ (-fī/) *v.,* **-fied, -fying.** make beautiful.

beau/ty, *n., pl.* **-ties. 1.** quality that excites admiration. **2.** beautiful thing or person.

beauty parlor, salon for women's haircuts and styling.

bea/ver (bē/vər) *n.* **1.** amphibious rodent. **2.** its fur.

be-cause/ (bi kôz/, -koz/, -kuz/) *conj.* **1.** for the reason that. —*adv.* **2.** by reason (of).

beck (bek) *n.* beckoning gesture.

beck/on (-an) *v.* signal by gesture.

be-cloud/ (bi kloud/) *v.* **1.** obscure with clouds. **2.** confuse.

be-come/ (bi kum/) *v.,* **became** (-kām/), **become, becoming. 1.** come to be. **2.** suit. —**be-com/ing,** *adj.*

bed (bed) *n.* **1.** piece of furniture on or in which a person sleeps. **2.** sleep. **3.** piece of ground for planting. **4.** foundation. —**bed/time/,** *n.*

bed/bug/, *n.* bloodsucking insect.

bed/ding, *n.* blankets, sheets, etc., for a bed.

be-dev/il (bi dev/əl) *v.,* **-iled, -il-ing. 1.** torment maliciously. **2.** confuse; confound.

bed/fel/low, *n.* **1.** sharer of bed. **2.** ally.

bed/lam (bed/ləm) *n.* **1.** scene of loud confusion. **2.** lunatic asylum.

Bed/ou-in (bed/ōō in) *n.* **1.** desert Arab. **2.** nomad.

bed/pan/, *n.* shallow pan used as toilet for bedridden person.

be-drag/gled (bi drag/əld) *adj.* soiled and wet.

bed/rid-den/, *adj.* confined to bed.

bed/rock/, *n.* **1.** continuous solid rock under soil. **2.** firm foundation.

bed/room/, *n.* sleeping room.

bed/sore/, *n.* skin ulcer caused by long confinement in bed.

bed/spread/, *n.* cover for bed.

bed/stead/ (-sted/, -stid) *n.* frame for bed.

bee (bē) *n.* **1.** four-winged, nectar-gathering insect. **2.** local gathering. —**bee/hive/,** *n.* —**bee/keep/er,** *n.*

beech (bēch) *n.* tree bearing small edible nuts (**beech/nuts/**).

beef (bēf) *n., pl.* **beeves. 1.** bull, cow, or steer. **2.** edible flesh of such an animal. **3.** brawn. —**beef′/steak′**, n.

bee′line′, n. direct course.

beep (bēp) n. **1.** short tone, usu. high in pitch, as from electronic device. —v. **2.** make a beep.

beep′er, n. small electronic device whose signal notifies person carrying it of telephone message.

beer (bēr) n. beverage brewed and fermented from cereals.

beet (bēt) n. plant with edible root.

bee′tle (bēt′l) v., **-tled, -tling**, n. —v. **1.** project. —n. **2.** insect with hard, horny forewings.

be·fall′ (bi fôl′) v., **-fell, -fallen, -falling**. happen to.

be·fit′ (bi fit′) v., **-fitted, -fitting.** be fitting for. —**be·fit′ting**, adj.

be·fore′ (bi fôr′) adv. **1.** in front. **2.** earlier. —prep. **3.** in front of. **4.** previously to. **5.** in preference to. **6.** in precedence of. **7.** in presence of. —conj. **8.** previously to time when.

be·fore′hand′, adv. in advance; ahead of time.

be·friend′ (bi frend′) v. act as friend toward.

be·fud′dle (bi fud′l) v., **-dled, -dling.** confuse thoroughly.

beg (beg) v., **begged, begging. 1.** ask for charity. **2.** ask humbly.

be·get′ (bi get′) v., **begot** (bi got′), **begotten** or **begot, begetting.** procreate. —**be·get′ter**, n.

beg′gar (beg′ər) n. **1.** one who begs alms. **2.** penniless person. —v. **3.** reduce to poverty.

beg′gar·ly, adj. very poor.

be·gin′ (bi gin′) v., **-gan** (-gan′), **-gun** (-gun′), **-ginning. 1.** start. **2.** originate. —**be·gin′ner**, n. —**be·gin′ning**, n.

be·gone′ (bi gôn′) interj. (depart!)

be·go′nia (bi gōn′yə) n. tropical flowering plant.

be·grudge′ (bi gruj′) v., **-grudged, -grudging. 1.** envy the good fortune or pleasure of. **2.** give or allow reluctantly.

be·guile′ (bi gīl′) v., **-guiled, -guiling. 1.** delude. **2.** charm; divert.

be·half′ (bi haf′) n. **1.** side; part. **2.** interest; favor.

be·have′ (bi hāv′) v., **-haved, -having. 1.** conduct oneself. **2.** act properly.

be·hav′ior (-yər) n. manner of behaving.

be·head′ (bi hed′) v. cut off the head of.

be·hest′ (bi hest′) n. urgent request.

be·hind′ (bi hīnd′) prep. **1.** at the back of. **2.** later than. —adv. **3.** at

the back. **4.** in arrears. —n. **5.** Informal. buttocks.

be·hold′ (bi hōld′) v., **beheld, beholding,** interj. —v. **1.** look at; see. —interj. **2.** look! —**be·hold′er,** n.

be·hold′en, adj. obliged.

be·hoove′ (bi hōōv′) v., **-hooved, -hooving.** be necessary for (someone).

beige (bāzh) n. light brown.

be′ing (bē′ing) n. **1.** existence. **2.** something that exists.

be·la′bor (bi lā′bər) v. **1.** discuss, etc., excessively. **2.** beat.

be·lat′ed (bi lā′tid) adj. late.

belch (belch) v. **1.** eject gas from stomach. **2.** emit violently. —n. **3.** act of belching.

be·lea′guer (bi lē′gər) v. beset with difficulties.

bel′fry (bel′frē) n., pl. **-fries.** bell tower.

be·lie′ (bi lī′) v., **-lied, -lying. 1.** misrepresent. **2.** show to be false.

be·lief′ (bi lēf′) n. **1.** thing believed. **2.** conviction. **3.** faith.

be·lieve′ (bi lēv′) v., **-lieved, -lieving. 1.** trust. **2.** accept as true. **3.** regard as likely. —**be·liev′a·ble,** adj. —**be·liev′er,** n.

be·lit′tle (bi lit′l) v., **-littled, -littling.** disparage.

bell (bel) n. **1.** metal instrument producing ringing sound. —v. **2.** put bell on. **3.** flare outward.

bel′la·don′na (bel′ə don′ə) n. poisonous plant yielding medicinal drug.

belle (bel) n. beautiful woman.

bell′hop′, n. person who carries luggage and runs errands in a hotel. Also, **bell′boy′.**

bel′li·cose (bel′i kōs′) adj. warlike.

bel·lig·er·ent (bə lij′ər ənt) adj. **1.** warlike. **2.** engaged in war. —n. **3.** nation at war. —**bel·lig′er·ence,** n. —**bel·lig′er·ent·ly,** adv.

bel·low (bel′ō) v. **1.** roar, as a bull. **2.** utter in deep, loud voice. —n. **3.** act or sound of bellowing.

bel·lows (bel′ōz, -əz) n.sing. and pl. collapsing device producing strong current of air.

bell pepper, plant yielding a mild, bell-shaped pepper.

bell′weth′er (bel′weth′ər) n. one that leads or marks a trend.

bel′ly (bel′ē) n., pl. **-lies,** v., **-lied, -lying.** —n. **1.** abdomen. —v. **2.** swell out.

bel′ly·ache′, n., v., **-ached, -aching.** —n. **1.** pain in the abdomen. —v. **2.** Informal. complain.

be·long′ (bi lông′) v. **1.** be a member of. **2.** belong to, be the property of.

be·long·ings, n.pl. possessions; effects.

be·lov·ed (bi luv'id, -luvd') adj. **1.** greatly loved. —n. **2.** object of love.

be·low' (bi lō') adv. **1.** beneath. **2.** in lower rank. —prep. **3.** lower than.

belt (belt) n. **1.** band for encircling waist. **2.** any flexible band. —v. **3.** put a belt around. **4.** hit hard.

belt'way', n. highway around perimeter of urban area.

be·moan' (bi mōn') v. lament.

be·mused' (bi myōōzd') adj. lost in thought; preoccupied.

bench (bench) n. **1.** long seat. **2.** judge's seat. **3.** body of judges. **4.** work table.

bench'mark', n. standard against which others can be measured.

bend (bend) v., **bent, bending,** —v. **1.** curve. **2.** become curved. **3.** turn or incline. —n. **4.** a bending. **5.** something bent.

be·neath' (bi nēth') adj. **1.** in a lower place, state, etc. —prep. **2.** under. **3.** lower than. **4.** unworthy of.

ben'e·dic'tion (ben'i dik'shən) n. blessing.

ben'e·fac'tor (-fak'tər) n. one who gives financial help. —**ben'e·fac'tress,** n.fem.

be·nef'i·cent (bə nef'ə sənt) adj. doing good. —**be·nef'i·cence,** n.

ben'e·fi'cial (ben'ə fish'əl) adj. helpful. —**ben'e·fi'cial·ly,** adv.

ben'e·fi'ci·ar·y (-fish'ē er'ē, -fish'ə-rē) n., pl. **-aries.** recipient of benefits or funds.

ben'e·fit (-fit) n., v., **-fited, -fiting.** —n. **1.** advantage. **2.** money from insurance, etc. **3.** entertainment for worthy cause. —v. **4.** do good to. **5.** gain advantage.

be·nev'o·lent (bə nev'ə lənt) adj. kind and charitable. —**be·nev'o·lence,** n.

be·night'ed (bi nī'tid) adj. ignorant.

be·nign' (bi nīn') adj. **1.** kind. **2.** favorable. —**be·nign'ly,** adv.

be·nig'nant (-nig'nənt) adj. **1.** kind. **2.** beneficial.

bent (bent) adj. **1.** curved. **2.** determined. —n. **3.** inclination.

be·numb' (bi num') v. **1.** make numb. **2.** make inactive; stupefy.

ben'zene (ben'zēn, ben zēn') n. inflammable liquid, used as solvent.

be·queath' (bi kwēth', -kwēth') v. dispose of by will.

be·quest' (bi kwest') n. legacy.

be·rate' (bi rāt') v., **-rated, -rating.** scold.

be·reaved' (bi revd') adj. suffering a loved one's death. —**be·reave',** v. —**be·reave'ment,** n.

be·reft' (-reft') adj. deprived of something.

be·ret' (bə rā') n. cloth cap.

ber'i·ber'i (berē berē) n. disease caused by vitamin deficiency.

ber'ry (berē) n., pl. **-ries,** v., **-ried, -rying.** —n. **1.** small juicy fruit. —v. **2.** produce or gather berries.

ber·serk' (bar sûrk', -zûrk') adj. wild; frenzied.

berth (bûrth) n. **1.** sleeping space for traveler. **2.** mooring space for vessel. —v. **3.** provide with a berth.

ber'yl (ber'əl) n. green mineral.

be·seech' (bi sēch') v., **-sought, -seeching.** implore; beg.

be·set' (bi set') v., **-set, -setting. 1.** attack on all sides. **2.** surround.

be·side' (bi sīd') prep. **1.** at the side of. **2.** compared with. **3.** in addition to. —adv. **4.** in addition.

be·sides', adv. **1.** moreover. **2.** otherwise. —prep. **3.** in addition to. **4.** other than.

be·siege' (bi sēj') v., **-sieged, -sieging.** lay siege to.

be·smirch' (bi smûrch') v. defile.

be·sot'ted (bi sot'id) adj. **1.** drunk. **2.** infatuated.

be·speak' (bi spēk') v., **-spoke** (-spōk), **-spoken** or **-spoke, -speaking. 1.** ask for in advance. **2.** imply.

best (best) adj. **1.** of highest quality. **2.** most suitable. —adv. **3.** most excellently. **4.** most fully. —n. **5.** best person or thing. —v. **6.** defeat.

bes'tial (bes'chal, bēs'-) adj. **1.** beastlike. **2.** brutal.

be·stir' (bi stûr') v., **-stirred, -stirring.** stir up.

best man, chief attendant at the bridegroom at a wedding.

be·stow' (bi stō') v. present.

be·strew' (bi strōō') v., **-strewed, -strewed** or **-strewn, -strewing. 1.** cover. **2.** scatter.

bet (bet) v., **bet** or **betted, betting,** n. —v. **1.** risk on a chance result. —n. **2.** thing or amount bet.

be·take' (bi tāk') v., **-took** (-tōōk'), **-taken, -taking.** betake oneself, go.

bête noire (bāt' nwär', bet') most dreaded person or thing.

be·tide' (bi tīd') v., **-tided, -tiding.** happen to.

be·to'ken (bi tō'kən) v. indicate.

be·tray' (bi trā') v. **1.** expose by treachery. **2.** be unfaithful to. **3.** reveal. **4.** deceive. **5.** seduce. —**be·tray'al,** n. —**be·tray'er,** n.

be·troth' (bi trōth', -trôth') v. promise to marry. —**be·troth'al,** n.

bet'ter (bet'ər) adj. **1.** of superior quality. **2.** healthier. —adv. **3.** in a more excellent way. **4.** more. —n. **5.** something or someone better. **6.** one's superior. —v. **7.** improve on.

be·tween' (bi twēn') prep. **1.** in the space separating. **2.** intermediate to. **3.** connecting. **4.** one or the other of. **5.** by the combined effect of. —adv. **6.** in the intervening space or time. —Usage. Traditionally, BETWEEN is used to show relationship involving two people or things (to decide between tea and coffee), while AMONG expresses more than two (The four brothers quarrelled among themselves). BETWEEN, however, is also used to express relationship of persons or things considered individually, no matter how many: Between holding public office, teaching, and raising a family, she has little free time.

be·twixt' (bi twikst') prep., adv. between.

bev'el (bev'əl) n., v., **-eled, -eling.** —n. **1.** surface cutting off a corner. —v. **2.** cut or slant at a bevel.

bev'er·age (bev'ər ij) n. drink.

bev'y (bev'ē) n., pl. **-ies.** group.

be·wail' (bi wāl') v. lament.

be·ware' (bi wâr') v., **-wared, -waring.** be wary of.

be·wil'der (bi wil'dər) v. confuse or puzzle. —**be·wil'der·ment,** n.

be·witch' (bi wich') v. enchant. —**be·witch'ing,** adj.

be·yond' (bē ond') prep. **1.** on the farther side of. **2.** farther, more, or later on. —adv. **3.** farther on.

bi-, prefix meaning twice or two, as bisect.

bi·an'nu·al (bī an'yōō əl) adj. occurring twice a year. —**bi·an'nu·al·ly,** adv.

bi'as (bī'əs) n. **1.** slant. **2.** prejudice. —v. **3.** prejudice.

bi·ath'lon (bī ath'lon) n. athletic contest comprising two consecutive events.

bib (bib) n. cloth to protect clothing while eating.

Bi'ble (bī'bəl) n. Old and New Testaments. —**Bib'li·cal** (bib'li kəl) adj. —**bib'li·cal·ly,** adv.

bib'li·og'ra·phy (bib'lē og'rə fē) n., pl. **-phies.** list of sources.

bi·cam'er·al (bī kam'ər əl) adj. composed of two legislative bodies.

bi·car'bo·nate of soda (bī kär'bə nit, -nāt) baking soda.

bi·cen·ten'ni·al (bī'sen ten'ē əl) n. two-hundredth anniversary. Also, **bi'cen·ten'a·ry.**

bi'ceps (-seps) n. muscle of upper arm.

bick'er (bik'ər) v. squabble.

bi·cus'pid, n. tooth having two cusps or points.

bi·cy·cle (bī'si kəl) n., v., **-cled, -cling.** —n. **1.** two-wheeled vehicle. —v. **2.** ride a bicycle. —**bi'cy·clist,** n.

bid (bid) v., **bade** (bad, bād) or **bid** (for 3), **bidden** or **bid, bidding,** n. —v. **1.** command. **2.** say. **3.** offer. —n. **4.** offer. —**bid'der,** n.

bide (bīd) v., **bided, biding.** bide one's time, await opportunity.

bi·det' (bē dā') n. tub for bathing genital areas.

bi·en'ni·al (bī en'ē əl) adj. occurring every two years. —**bi·en'ni·al·ly,** adv.

bier (bēr) n. stand for a coffin.

bi·fo'cal (bī fō'kəl, bī'fō'-) adj. **1.** having two focuses. **2.** (of eyeglass lens) having separate areas for near and far vision. —n. **3.** (pl.) eyeglasses with bifocal lenses.

big (big) adj., **bigger, biggest. 1.** large. **2.** important. —**big'ness,** n.

big'a·my (big'ə mē) n., pl. **-mies.** crime of marrying again while legally married. —**big'a·mist,** n.

big bang theory, theory that universe began with explosion of dense mass of matter and is still expanding.

big'horn' (big'hôrn') n. wild sheep of western U.S.

bight (bīt) n. **1.** loop of rope. **2.** deep bend in seashore.

big'ot (big'ət) n. bigoted person.

big'ot·ed, adj. intolerant of another's creed, belief, or opinion.

big shot, Informal. important person.

bike (bīk) n. **1.** bicycle or motorcycle. —v. **2.** ride a bike. —**bik'er,** n.

bi·ki'ni (bi kē'nē) n. woman's brief two-piece bathing suit.

bi·lat'er·al (bī lat'ər əl) adj. on or affecting two sides.

bile (bīl) n. **1.** digestive secretion of the liver. **2.** ill nature.

bilge (bilj) n. lowest inner part of ship bottom.

bi·lin'gual (bī ling'gwəl) speaking or expressed in two languages.

bil'ious (bil'yəs) adj. **1.** pertaining to bile or excess bile. **2.** peevish.

bilk (bilk) v. cheat; defraud.

bill (bil) n. **1.** account of money owed. **2.** piece of paper to pay. **3.** draft of proposed statute. **4.** written list. **5.** horny part of bird's jaw. **6.** poster. —v. **7.** charge.

bill/board/, *n.* large outdoor advertising display panel.

bil/let (bil/it) *n.*, *v.*, **-leted, -leting.** —*n.* **1.** lodging for a soldier. —*v.* **2.** provide with lodging.

bil/let-doux/ (bil/ā dōō/) *n.*, *pl.* **billets-doux** (-dōōz/). love letter.

bill/fold/, *n.* wallet.

bil/liards (bil/yərdz) *n.* game played with hard balls on a table.

bil/lion (bil/yən) *n.* thousand million. —**bil/lionth,** *adj., n.*

bil/lion·aire/ (-âr/) *n.* owner of a billion dollars or more.

bill of sale, document transferring personal property from seller to buyer.

bil/low (bil/ō) *n.* **1.** great wave. —*v.* **2.** surge. —**bil/low·y,** *adj.*

billy goat, male goat.

bim/bo (bim/bō) *n.*, *pl.* **-bos, -boes.** *Slang.* unintelligent young woman with loose morals.

bi·month/ly (bī munth/lē) *adv., adj.* every two months.

bin (bin) *n.*, *v.*, **binned, binning.** —*n.* **1.** box for storing grain, coal, etc. —*v.* **2.** store in bin.

bi/na·ry (bī/nə rē) *adj.* **1.** involving two parts, choices, etc. **2.** of a numerical system in which each place of a number is expressed as 0 or 1.

bind (bīnd) *v.*, **bound, binding. 1.** tie or encircle with band. **2.** unite. **3.** oblige. **4.** attach cover to book.

bind/ing, *n.* **1.** something that binds. —*adj.* **2.** obligatory.

binge (binj) *n.*, *v.*, **binged, binging.** —*n.* **1.** bout of excessive indulgence, as in eating. —*v.* **2.** go on binge.

bin/go (bing/gō) *n.* game of chance using cards with numbered squares.

bin/na·cle (bin/ə kəl) *n.* stand for ship's compass.

bin·oc/u·lars (bə nok/yə lərz, bī-) *n.pl.* field glasses.

bio-, prefix meaning life or living organisms, as *biodegradable.*

bi/o·chem/is·try (bī/ō kem/ə strē) *n.* chemistry of living matter. —**bi/o·chem/ist,** *n.*

bi/o·de·grad/a·ble, *adj.* decaying and being absorbed into environment.

bi/o·en/gi·neer/ing, *n.* **1.** application of engineering principles to problems in biology and medicine. **2.** application of biological principles to manufacturing or engineering processes.

bi/o·eth/ics, *n.* study of ethical implications of medical or biological procedures.

bi/o·feed/back/, *n.* method for achieving self-control through observation of one's brain waves, blood pressure, etc.

bi·og/ra·phy (bī og/rə fē) *n.*, *pl.* **-phies.** written account of person's life. —**bi·og/ra·pher,** *n.* —**bi/o·graph/i·cal** (-ə graf/i kəl) *adj.*

bi/o·haz/ard, *n.* anything used in or produced in biological research that poses a health hazard.

biol., biology.

biological clock, 1. natural mechanism regulating bodily cycles. **2.** this mechanism seen as the passage of one's child-bearing ability.

biological warfare, use of toxic organisms as weapons.

bi·ol/o·gy (bī ol/ə jē) *n.* science of living matter. —**bi/o·log/i·cal** (-ə loj/i kəl) *adj.* —**bi·ol/o·gist,** *n.*

bi·on/ics (bī on/iks) *n.* use of electronic devices to increase human strength or ability. —**bi·on/ic,** *adj.*

bi/op·sy (bī/op sē) *n.*, *pl.* **-sies.** examination of specimen of living tissue.

bi/o·rhythm (bī/ō-) *n.* natural, periodic bodily cycle, as sleeping and waking.

bi/o·sphere/ (bī/ə-) *n.* the part of the earth's surface and atmosphere that supports life.

bi/o·tech·nol/o·gy (bī/ō-) *n.* use of living organisms in making products or to manage the environment.

bi·par/ti·san (bī pär/tə zən) *adj.* representing two parties.

bi·par/tite (-pär/tīt) *adj.* **1.** having two parts. **2.** shared by two; joint.

bi/ped (-ped) *n.* **1.** two-footed animal. —*adj.* **2.** having two feet.

birch (bûrch) *n.* tree with light bark.

bird (bûrd) *n.* vertebrate with feathers and wings.

bird/ie, *n.* score of one under par on a golf hole.

bird's/-eye/ (bûrdz/ī/) *adj.* seen from above.

birth (bûrth) *n.* **1.** fact of being born. **2.** lineage. **3.** origin. —**birth/day/,** *n.* —**birth/place/,** *n.*

birth control, contraception.

birth/mark/, *n.* blemish on the skin at birth.

birth/rate/, *n.* number of births in given time and place.

birth/right/, *n.* hereditary right.

bis/cuit (bis/kit) *n.* small, soft, raised bread.

bi·sect/ (bī sekt/) *v.* cut into two parts. —**bi·sec/tion,** *n.*

bi·sex/u·al, *adj.* **1.** being both heterosexual and homosexual. —*n.* **2.** bisexual person. —**bi·sex/u·al/i·ty,** *n.*

bish/op (bish/əp) *n.* **1.** overseer of a diocese. **2.** piece in chess.

bish′op·ric (-rik) *n.* diocese or office of bishop.

bi′son (bī′sən) *n., pl.* bisons, bison. oxlike mammal.

bis′tro (bis′trō, bē′strō) *n.* French café.

bit (bit) *n., v.,* **bitted, bitting.** —*n.* **1.** mouthpiece of bridle. **2.** small amount. **3.** drill. **4.** unit of computer information. —*v.* **5.** restrain with a bit.

bitch (bich) *n.* **1.** female dog. **2.** *Slang.* mean woman. —*v.* **3.** *Slang.* complain.

bite (bīt) *v.,* **bit, bitten** or **bit, biting,** *n.* —*v.* **1.** cut or grip with teeth. **2.** sting. **3.** corrode. —*n.* **4.** act of biting. **5.** wound made by biting. **6.** sting. **7.** piece bitten off.

bit′ing, *adj.* **1.** harsh to the senses. **2.** severely critical. —**bit′ing·ly,** *adv.*

bit′ter (bit′ər) *adj.* **1.** of harsh taste. **2.** hard to bear. **3.** intensely hostile. —**bit′ter·ly,** *adv.* —**bit′ter·ness,** *n.*

bit′tern (bit′ərn) *n.* type of heron.

bit′ter·sweet′ *n.* **1.** tasting both bitter and sweet. **2.** being both painful and pleasant.

bi·tu′men (bī tōō′mən, -tyōō′-) *n.* asphalt or asphaltlike substance.

bituminous coal, soft coal that burns with a yellow, smoky flame.

bi′valve′, *n.* mollusk with two shells hinged together.

biv′ou·ac′ (biv′ōō ak′) *n., v.,* **-acked, -acking.** —*n.* **1.** temporary resting or assembly place for troops. —*v.* **2.** dispose or meet in bivouac.

bi·week′ly (bī-) *adv., adj.* **1.** every two weeks. **2.** twice a week.

bi·zarre′ (bi zär′) *adj.* strange.

blab (blab) *v.,* **blabbed, blabbing. 1.** talk idly. **2.** reveal secrets.

black (blak) *adj.* **1.** without brightness or color. **2.** having dark skin color. **3.** without light. **4.** gloomy. **5.** wicked. —*n.* **6.** member of a dark-skinned people, esp. of Africa or African ancestry. **7.** black clothing. **8.** something black. —*v.* **9.** make or become black.

black′-and-blue′, *adj.* discolored, as by bruising.

black′ball′, *n.* **1.** adverse vote. —*v.* **2.** ostracize.

black′ber′ry, *n., pl.* **-ries. 1.** dark-purple fruit. **2.** plant bearing it.

black′bird′, *n.* black-feathered American bird.

black′board′, *n.* dark board for writing on with chalk.

black′en, *v.* **1.** black (def. 9). **2.** defame.

black′guard (blag′ärd, -ərd) *n.* despicable person.

black′head′ (blak′-) *n.* small dark fatty mass in a skin follicle.

black hole, area in outer space whose great density prevents radiation of light.

black′jack′, *n.* **1.** short flexible club. **2.** game of cards; twenty-one. —*v.* **3.** strike with a blackjack.

black′list′, *n.* list of persons in disfavor. —**black′list′,** *v.*

black magic, sorcery.

black′mail′, *n.* **1.** extortion by intimidation. —*v.* **2.** extort by blackmail. —**black′mail′·er,** *n.*

black market, illegal buying and selling of goods in violation of laws.

black′out′, *n.* **1.** extinction of lights. **2.** loss of consciousness.

black sheep, person who causes embarrassment or shame to his or her family.

black′smith′, *n.* person who shoes horses or forges iron objects.

black′thorn′, *n.* thorny shrub with plumlike fruit.

black′top′, *n., v.,* **-topped, -topping.** —*n.* **1.** bituminous paving substance, as asphalt. —*v.* **2.** pave with blacktop.

black widow, poisonous spider.

blad′der (blad′ər) *n.* sac in body holding urine.

blade (blād) *n.* **1.** cutting part of knife, sword, etc. **2.** leaf. **3.** thin, flat part. **4.** dashing young man.

blame (blām) *v.,* **blamed, blaming,** *n.* —*v.* **1.** hold responsible for fault. **2.** find fault with. —*n.* **3.** censure. —**blame′less,** *adj.*

blanch (blanch) *v.* whiten.

bland (bland) *adj.* **1.** not harsh. **2.** not flavorful. —**bland′ly,** *adv.*

blan′dish·ment (blan′dish mənt) *n.* coaxing.

blank (blangk) *adj.* **1.** not written on. **2.** without interest or emotion. **3.** white. **4.** unrhymed. —*n.* **5.** place lacking something. **6.** space to be filled in. **7.** paper with such space. —*v.* **8.** make blank. —**blank′ly,** *adv.* —**blank′ness,** *n.*

blan′ket (blang′kit) *n.* **1.** warm bed covering. —*v.* **2.** cover.

blare (blâr) *v.,* **blared, blaring,** *n.* —*v.* **1.** sound loudly. —*n.* **2.** loud, raucous noise.

blar′ney (blär′nē) *n.* **1.** flattery. —*v.* **2.** flatter.

bla·sé′ (blä zā′) *adj.* bored; unimpressed.

blas·pheme′ (blas fēm′) *v.* speak impiously or evilly. —**blas′phe-**

mous (blas′fə məs) adj. —**blas′-phe•my,** n.

blast (blast) n. **1.** gust of wind. **2.** loud trumpet tone. **3.** explosion. **4.** charge of explosive. —v. **5.** blow. **6.** blight; destroy. **7.** explode.

blast furnace, forced-air furnace for smelting iron ore.

blast′off′, n. rocket launching.

bla′tant (blāt′nt) adj. brazenly obvious. —**bla′tan•cy,** n.

blaze (blāz) n., v., **blazed, blazing.** —n. **1.** bright flame. **2.** bright glow. **3.** brightness. **4.** mark cut on tree. **5.** white spot on animal's face. —v. **6.** burn or shine brightly. **7.** mark with blazes (def. 4).

blaz′er, n. sports jacket.

bldg., building.

bleach (blēch) v. **1.** whiten. —n. **2.** bleaching agent.

bleach′ers, n.pl. tiers of spectators' seats.

bleak (blēk) adj. **1.** bare. **2.** cold. **3.** dreary; depressing. —**bleak′ly,** adv. —**bleak′ness,** n.

blear′y (blēr′ē) adj. unclear.

bleat (blēt) v. **1.** cry, as sheep, goat, etc. —n. **2.** such a cry.

bleed (blēd) v., **bled** (bled), **bleeding.** lose or cause to lose blood.

bleep (blēp) v. delete (sound, esp. speech) from a broadcast.

blem′ish (blem′ish) v. **1.** mar. —n. **2.** defect.

blend (blend) v. **1.** mix. —n. **2.** mixture.

blend′er, n. electric appliance that purées or mixes food.

bless (bles) v., **blessed** or **blest, blessing. 1.** consecrate. **2.** request divine favor on. **3.** extol as holy. —**bless′ing,** n.

blight (blīt) n. **1.** plant disease. **2.** ruin. —v. **3.** wither. **4.** ruin.

blimp (blimp) n. small nonrigid airship.

blind (blīnd) adj. **1.** sightless. **2.** uncomprehending. **3.** hidden. **4.** without an outlet. **5.** without advance knowledge. —v. **6.** make blind. —n. **7.** window covering. **8.** ruse or disguise. —**blind′ly,** adv.

blind date, arranged date between two strangers.

blind′fold′, v. **1.** cover eyes. —n. **2.** covering over eyes. —adj. **3.** with covered eyes.

blind′side′, v., **-sided, -siding.** hit someone unawares.

blink (blingk) v. **1.** wink. —n. **2.** act of blinking. **3.** gleam.

blip (blip) n. **1.** point of light on radar screen, indicating an object. **2.** brief interruption or upward turn in a continuity.

bliss (blis) n. **1.** gladness. **2.** supreme happiness. —**bliss′ful,** adj.

blis′ter (blis′tər) n. **1.** swelling on the skin containing watery liquid. —v. **2.** raise blisters on.

blithe (blīth, blīth) adj. joyous; cheerful. —**blithe′ly,** adv.

blitz (blits) n. Also, **blitz′krieg′** (-krēg′). **1.** swift, violent war, waged by surprise. —v. **2.** attack by blitz.

bliz′zard (bliz′ərd) n. severe snowstorm.

bloat (blōt) v. swell.

blob (blob) n. **1.** small lump or drop. **2.** shapeless mass.

bloc (blok) n. political or economic confederation.

block (blok) n. **1.** solid mass. **2.** platform. **3.** obstacle. **4.** single quantity. **5.** unit of city street pattern. —v. **6.** obstruct. **7.** outline roughly. —**block′er,** n.

block•ade′ (blo kād′) n., v., **-aded, -ading.** —n. **1.** shutting-up of place by armed force. **2.** obstruction. —v. **3.** subject to blockade.

block′age, n. obstruction.

block′bust′er, n. highly successful movie, novel, etc.

block′head′, n. stupid person.

blond (blond) adj. **1.** light-colored. **2.** having light-colored hair, skin, etc. —n. **3.** blond person. —**blonde,** adj., n.fem.

blood (blud) n. **1.** red fluid in arteries and veins. **2.** bloodshed. **3.** extraction. —**blood′y,** adj.

blood count, number of red and white blood cells in specific volume of blood.

blood′cur′dling, adj. causing terror or horror.

blood′hound′, n. large dog with acute sense of smell.

blood′mo•bile′ (-mə bēl′) n. truck for receiving blood donations.

blood pressure, pressure of blood against inner walls of blood vessels.

blood′shed′, n. slaughter.

blood′shot′, adj. with eye veins conspicuous.

blood′stream′, n. blood flowing through the body's circulatory system.

blood′suck′er, n. **1.** leech. **2.** extortionist.

blood′thirst′y, adj. murderous.

blood vessel, artery, vein, or capillary.

bloom (blōōm) n. **1.** flower. **2.** healthy glow. —v. **3.** blossom. **4.** flourish. —**bloom′ing,** adj.

bloom′ers (blōō′mərz) n.pl. short loose trousers formerly worn as underwear by women.

bloop'er (blōō'par) n. embarrassing mistake.

blos'som (blos'am) n. **1.** flower. —v. **2.** produce blossoms. **3.** develop.

blot (blot) n., v., **blotted, blotting.** —n. **1.** stain. —v. **2.** spot. **3.** dry with absorbent material.

blotch (bloch) n. **1.** large spot. —v. **2.** stain; spot. —**blotch'y,** adj.

blot'ter, n. piece of paper for blotting.

blouse (blous, blouz) n. women's upper garment.

blow (blō) v., **blew** (blōō), **blown, blowing.** —v. **1.** (of air) move. **2.** drive by current of air. **3.** sound a wind instrument. **4.** shape by blowing. **5.** explode. **6.** Informal. bungle. —n. **7.** blast of air. **8.** sudden stroke. **9.** sudden shock, calamity, etc.

blow'-by-blow', adj. detailed.

blow'out', n. rupture of tire.

blow'torch', n. device producing hot flame.

blow'up', n. **1.** explosion. **2.** Informal. emotional outbreak. **3.** photographic enlargement.

blub'ber (blub'ar) n. **1.** fat of whales. —v. **2.** weep.

bludg'eon (bluj'an) n. **1.** heavy club. —v. **2.** strike with a bludgeon.

blue (blōō) n., adj., **bluer, bluest,** v., **blued, bluing** or **blueing.** —n. **1.** color of sky. —adj. **2.** (of skin) discolored by cold, etc. **3.** melancholy. —v. **4.** make blue.

blue'ber'ry, n. pl. **-ries.** edible berry, usually bluish.

blue'bird', n. small, blue North American bird.

blue blood, aristocrat.

blue chip', high-priced stock yielding regular dividends.

blue'-col'lar, adj. of or designating manual laborers.

blue'jay', n. crested North American jay.

blue jeans, trousers of blue denim.

blue law, law against certain practices, as business, on Sunday.

blue'print', n. **1.** white-on-blue photocopy of line drawing. **2.** plan of action.

blue ribbon, highest award.

blues, n.pl. **1.** melancholy. **2.** melancholy genre of jazz.

bluff (bluf) v. **1.** mislead by show of boldness. —n. **2.** act of bluffing. **3.** steep cliff or hill. —adj. **4.** vigorously frank. —**bluff'er,** n.

blu'ing, n. bleaching agent. Also, **blue'ing.**

blun'der (blun'dar) n. **1.** mistake. —v. **2.** err. **3.** move blindly.

blunt (blunt) adj. **1.** having a dull edge or point. **2.** abrupt in manner. —v. **3.** make blunt. —**blunt'ly,** adv.

blur (blûr) v., **blurred, blurring.** —v. **1.** obscure. **2.** make or become indistinct. —n. **3.** smudge. —**blur'ry,** adj.

blurb (blûrb) n. brief advertisement.

blurt (blûrt) v. utter suddenly.

blush (blush) v. **1.** redden. **2.** feel shame. —n. **3.** reddening. **4.** reddish tinge.

blush'er, n. cosmetic used to color cheeks.

blus'ter (blus'tar) v. **1.** blow violently. **2.** be noisy or swaggering. —n. **3.** tumult. **4.** noisy talk.

blvd., boulevard.

bo'a (bō'a) n. **1.** large snake. **2.** long scarf of silk or feathers.

boar (bōr) n. male of swine.

board (bōrd) n. **1.** thin flat piece of timber. **2.** daily meals. **3.** official controlling body. —v. **4.** cover with boards. **5.** furnish with food. **6.** take meals. **7.** enter (a ship, train, etc.). —**board'er,** n.

board'ing-house', n. house where one can get room and board for payment.

board'walk', n. wooden walk along beach.

boast (bōst) v. **1.** speak with pride; be proud of. —n. **2.** thing boasted.

boat (bōt) n. **1.** vessel. **2.** go or move in boat. —**boat'house',** n. —**boat'man,** n. —**boat'ing,** n.

boat'swain (bō'san) n. petty officer on ship.

bob (bob) n., v., **bobbed, bobbing.** —n. **1.** short jerky motion. **2.** short haircut. —v. **3.** move jerkily. **4.** cut short. —**bob'bin** (bob'in) n. reel; spool.

bob'by pin, flat metal hairpin.

bob'cat', n. pl. **-cats, -cat.** North American lynx.

bob'o·link' (-a lingk') n. meadow-dwelling songbird.

bob'sled', n., v., **-sledded, -sledding.** —n. **1.** long sled with two pairs of runners and a steering mechanism. —v. **2.** ride on a bobsled.

bob'tail', n. **1.** short tail. —v. **2.** cut short.

bob'white', n. North American quail.

bode (bōd) v., **boded, boding.** portend.

bod'ice (bod'is) n. top part of dress.

bod'y (bod'ē) n., pl. **bodies. 1.** animal's physical structure. **2.** corpse. **3.** main mass. **4.** collective group.

bod′y·guard′, *n.* guard for personal safety.

body language, communication through gestures or attitudes.

body piercing, piercing of a body part, as the navel, to insert ornamental ring or stud.

bog (bog) *n.*, *v.*, **bogged, bogging.** —*n.* swampy ground. —*v.* **2.** sink or catch in a bog. —**bog′gy**, *adj.*

bog′gle (bog′əl) *v.*, **-gled, -gling.** overwhelm or bewilder.

bo′gus (bō′gəs) *adj.* fake.

bo′gy (bō′gē, bŏŏg′ē, bōō′gē) *n.*, *pl.* **-gies.** hobgoblin. Also, **bo′gey, bo′gie.**

bo·he′mi·an (bō hē′mē ən) *n.* **1.** person who leads an unconventional life. —*adj.* **2.** unconventional.

boil (boil) *v.* **1.** heat to bubbling point. **2.** be agitated. **3.** cook by boiling. —*n.* **4.** act or state of boiling. **5.** inflamed sore. —**boil′er,** *n.*

bois′ter·ous (boi′stər əs) *adj.* rough; noisy.

bok′ choy′ (bok′ choy′) Asian plant whose leaves are used as a vegetable. Also, **bok′-choy′.**

bold (bōld) *adj.* **1.** fearless. **2.** conspicuous. —**bold′ly,** *adv.*

bo·le′ro (bə lâr′ō, bō-) *n.*, *pl.* **-ros. 1.** lively Spanish dance. **2.** waist-length, open vest.

boll (bōl) *n.* rounded seed pod.

boll weevil, beetle that attacks bolls of cotton.

bo·lo′gna (bə lō′nē) *n.* beef and pork sausage.

Bol′she·vik (bōl′shə vik) *n.*, *pl.* **-viks, -viki.** Russian communist. Also, **Bol′she·vist** (-vist).

bol′ster (bōl′stər) *n.* **1.** long pillow. —*v.* **2.** support.

bolt (bōlt) *n.* **1.** bar fastening a door. **2.** similar part in a lock. **3.** threaded metal pin. **4.** sudden flight. **5.** roll of cloth. **6.** thunderbolt. —*v.* **7.** fasten. **8.** swallow hurriedly. **9.** move or leave suddenly. **10.** sift.

bomb (bom) *n.* **1.** projectile with explosive charge. **2.** Slang. total failure. —*v.* **3.** attack with bombs. **4.** Slang. fail totally. —**bomb′-proof′,** *adj.*

bom·bard′ (bom bärd′) *v.* **1.** attack with artillery or bombs. **2.** assail vigorously. —**bom·bar·dier′** (-bər dēr′) *n.* —**bom·bard′ment,** *n.*

bom′bast (bom′bast) *n.* pompous words. —**bom·bas′tic, bom·bas′ti·cal,** *adj.*

bomb′er (bom′ər) *n.* **1.** airplane that drops bombs. **2.** one who plants bombs.

bomb′shell′, *n.* something or someone having a sensational effect.

bo′na fide′ (bō′nə fīd′) real.

bo·nan′za (bə nan′zə) *n.* **1.** rich mass of ore. **2.** good luck.

bon′bon′ (bon′bon′) *n.* piece of candy.

bond (bond) *n.* **1.** something that binds or unites. **2.** bondsman. **3.** written contractual obligation. **4.** certificate held by creditor. —*v.* **5.** put on or under bond. **6.** mortgage.

bond′age (bon′dij) *n.* slavery.

bond′man, *n.*, *pl.* **-men.** male slave. Also, **bond′wom·an,** *n.fem.*

bonds·man, *n.*, *pl.* **-men.** person who gives surety for another.

bone (bōn) *n.*, *v.*, **boned, boning.** —*n.* **1.** piece of the skeleton. **2.** hard substance composing it. —*v.* **3.** remove bones of. —**bon′y,** *adj.*

bon′er (bō′nər) *n. Slang.* stupid mistake.

bon′fire′ (bon′-) *n.* outdoor fire.

bon′go (bong′gō) *n.*, *pl.* **-gos, -goes.** small hand drum.

bon′kers (bong′kərz) *adj. Slang.* crazy.

bon′net (bon′it) *n.* hat formerly worn by women or children.

bo′nus (bō′nəs) *n.* extra payment.

boo (bōō) *interj.* (exclamation used to frighten or express contempt.)

boo′-boo′, *n. Slang.* **1.** stupid mistake. **2.** minor injury.

boo′by (bōō′bē) *n.*, *pl.* **-bies.** *Informal.* fool. Also, **boob.**

booby prize, prize given to worst player in contest.

booby trap, trap set for unsuspecting person.

book (bŏŏk) *n.* **1.** printed or blank sheets bound together. **2.** (*pl.*) accounts. **3.** division of literary work. —*v.* **4.** enter in book. **5.** engage beforehand. —**book′bind′er,** *n.* —**book′case′,** *n.* —**book′keep′er,** *n.* —**book′let,** *n.* —**book′sell′er,** *n.* —**book′store′, book′shop′,** *n.*

book′end′, *n.* prop for books.

book′ie, *n.* bookmaker.

book′ing, *n.* engagement of professional entertainer.

book′ish, *adj.* fond of reading.

book′mak′er, *n.* one who takes bets.

book′mark′, *n.* something for marking one's place in a book.

book′worm′, *n.* person who likes reading.

boom (bōōm) *v.* **1.** make a loud hollow sound. **2.** flourish vigorously. —*n.* **3.** loud hollow sound.

4. rapid development. **5.** spar extending sail. **6.** beam on derrick.

boom′er·ang′ (bŏŏ′ma rang′) *n.* **1.** Australian stick that returns when thrown. —*v.* **2.** cause harm to the originator; backfire.

boon (bŏŏn) *n.* benefit.

boon′docks′, *n.pl.* **1.** backwoods. **2.** remote rural area.

boon′dog′gle (-dôg′al) *n. Informal.* useless work paid for with public money.

boor (bŏŏr) *n.* unmannerly, rude person. —**boor′ish**, *adj.*

boost (bŏŏst) *v.* **1.** lift by pushing. **2.** praise; advocate. **3.** increase. —*n.* **4.** upward push. **5.** assistance.

boot (bŏŏt) *n.* **1.** covering for foot and leg. **2.** kick. —*v.* **3.** kick.

booth (bŏŏth) *n.* **1.** light structure for exhibiting goods, etc. **2.** small compartment.

boot′leg′, *n., v.*, **-legged, -legging**, *adj.* —*n.* **1.** illicit liquor. —*v.* **2.** deal in illicit goods. —*adj.* **3.** illicit. —**boot′leg′ger**, *n.*

boot′less, *adj.* futile; useless.

boo′ty (bŏŏ′tē) *n., pl.* **-ties.** plunder.

booze (bŏŏz) *n., v.*, **boozed, boozing.** *Informal.* —*n.* **1.** liquor. —*v.* **2.** drink liquor excessively.

bop (bop) *v.*, **bopped, bopping**, *n. Slang.* —*v.* **1.** hit. —*n.* **2.** a blow.

bo′rax (bôr′aks) *n.* white crystalline substance used as cleanser, in glassmaking, etc.

bor·del′lo (bôr del′ō) *n.* brothel.

bor′der (bôr′dar) *n.* **1.** edge; margin. **2.** frontier. —*v.* **3.** make a border. **4.** adjoin. —**bor′der·line′**, *n.*

bore (bôr) *v.*, **bored, boring**, *n.* —*v.* **1.** drill into. **2.** be uninteresting to. —*n.* **3.** bored hole. **4.** inside diameter. **5.** dull person. —**bore′dom**, *n.*

born (bôrn) *adj.* brought forth from the womb by birth.

born′-a·gain′, *adj.* recommitted to faith through an intensely religious experience.

bor′ough (bûr′ō, bur′ō) *n.* **1.** small incorporated municipality. **2.** division of city.

bor′row (bor′ō) *v.* **1.** take or obtain on loan. **2.** adopt. —**Usage.** Do not confuse BORROW and LEND. One way to keep the meanings distinct is to think of BORROW as "take," while LEND is "give." So you can *borrow* something you don't have, and you can *lend* something you do have.

bos′om (bŏŏz′am, bŏŏ′zam) *n.* **1.** breast. —*adj.* **2.** intimate. —**bos′om·y**, *adj.*

boss (bôs) *n.* **1.** employer. **2.** powerful politician. —*v.* **3.** control; manage. **4.** be domineering. —**boss′y**, *adj.*

bot′a·ny (bot′n ē) *n.* science of plant life. —**bo·tan′i·cal** (ba tan′i kal) *adj.* —**bot′a·nist**, *n.*

botch (boch) *v.* **1.** bungle. **2.** do clumsily. —*n.* **3.** botched work.

both (bōth) *adj., pron.* **1.** the two. —*conj., adv.* **2.** alike.

both′er (bo*th*′ar) *v.* **1.** annoy. **2.** trouble or inconvenience (oneself). —*n.* **3.** annoying or troublesome thing. —**both′er·some**, *adj.*

bot′tle (bot′l) *n., v.*, **-tled, -tling.** —*n.* **1.** sealed container for liquids. —*v.* **2.** put into bottle.

bot′tle·neck′, *n.* **1.** narrow passage. **2.** place of impeded progress.

bot′tom (bot′am) *n.* **1.** lowest or deepest part. **2.** underside. **3.** lowest rank. —*v.* **4.** reach the lowest level.

bot′tom·less, *adj.* without bottom. **2.** without limit.

bottom line, basic or decisive point.

bot′u·lism′ (boch′a liz′am) *n.* disease caused by eating spoiled foods.

bou′doir (bŏŏ′dwär, -dwôr) *n.* woman's bedroom.

bouf·fant′ (bŏŏ fänt′) *adj.* puffed out, as a hairdo.

bough (bou) *n.* branch of tree.

bouil′lon (bŏŏl′yon, -yan, bŏŏ′-) *n.* clear broth.

boul′der (bōl′dar) *n.* large rock.

boul′e·vard′ (bŏŏl′a värd′) *n.* broad avenue.

bounce (bouns) *v.*, **bounced, bouncing**, *n.* —*v.* **1.** spring back. —*n.* **2.** act of bouncing. —**boun′ci·ness**, *n.* —**bounc′y**, *adj.*

bounc′ing, *adj.* healthy.

bound (bound) *adj.* **1.** in bonds. **2.** made into book. **3.** obligated. **4.** going toward. —*v.* **5.** jump. **6.** limit. **7.** adjoin. —*n.* **8.** jump. **9.** (*usually pl.*) boundary.

bound′a·ry (boun′da rē, -drē) *n., pl.* **-ries.** borderline; limit.

bound′less, *adj.* unlimited.

boun′te·ous (boun′tē as) *adj.* generous. Also, **boun′ti·ful.**

boun′ty, *n., pl.* **-ties.** **1.** generosity. **2.** gift.

bou·quet′ (bō kā′, bŏŏ-) *n.* **1.** bunch of flowers. **2.** aroma.

bour′bon (bûr′ban) *n.* corn whiskey.

bour·geois′ (bŏŏr zhwä′) *n., pl.* **-geois.** **1.** one of the middle class. —*adj.* **2.** of the middle class.

bour·geoi·sie′ (-zē′) *n.* middle class.

bout (bout) n. **1.** contest. **2.** attack.

bou•tique′ (bōō tēk′) n. small shop with fashionable items.

bo′vine (bō′vīn, -vēn) adj. oxlike or cowlike.

bow (bou, for 1, 2, 3, 5, 9; bō, for 4, 6, 7, 8), v. **1.** bend down. **2.** bend in worship, etc. **3.** subdue. **4.** curve. —n. **5.** inclination of head or body. **6.** strip of bent wood for shooting arrow. **7.** looped knot. **8.** rod for playing violin. **9.** front of ship. —**bow′man,** n.

bow′el (bou′əl, boul) n. intestine. Also, **bow′els.**

bow′er (bou′ər) n. leafy shelter.

bowl (bōl) n. **1.** deep round dish. **2.** rounded hollow part. **3.** ball rolled at pins in various games. —v. **4.** roll a ball underhand. **5.** play bowling games. —**bowl′ing,** n.

bow′leg′ged (bō′leg′id) adj. having legs curved outward.

box (boks) n. **1.** receptacle of wood, metal, etc. **2.** compartment. **3.** blow with fist. **4.** Also, **box′wood′.** evergreen tree or shrub. —v. **5.** put into box. **6.** fight with fists. —**box′er,** n. —**box′ing,** n.

box′car′, n. completely enclosed railroad freight car.

box office, office at which tickets are sold.

boy (boi) n. male child. —**boy′hood,** n. —**boy′ish,** adj.

boy′cott (-kot) v. **1.** abstain from dealing with or using. —n. **2.** instance of boycotting.

boy′friend′, n. **1.** male sweetheart or lover. **2.** male friend.

Boy Scout, member of organization for boys (**Boy Scouts**) promoting self-reliance and service.

bra (brä) n. brassiere.

brace (brās) v., **braced, bracing.** —n. **1.** stiffening device. **2.** pair. **3.** character, {or}, used to connect words or lines to be considered together. **4.** (pl.) device to straighten teeth. —v. **5.** fasten with brace. **6.** make steady. **7.** stimulate.

brace′let (brās′lit) n. ornamental band for the wrist.

brack′et (brak′it) n. **1.** armlike support for ledge. **2.** mark, [or], for enclosing parenthetical words. —v. **3.** place within brackets.

brack′ish (brak′ish) adj. salty.

brad (brad) n. small wire nail.

brag (brag) v., **bragged, bragging,** n. boast. —**brag′gart** (-art) n.

braid (brād) v. **1.** weave together. —n. **2.** something braided.

braille (brāl) n. (often cap.) alphabet for the blind.

brain (brān) n. **1.** soft mass of nerves in cranium. **2.** intelligence. —v. **3.** dash out the brains.

brain death, complete ending of brain function, used as legal definition of death. —**brain′-dead,** adj.

brain drain, loss of trained professional personnel to another company, nation, etc.

brain′storm′, n. sudden idea.

brain′wash′, v. indoctrinate under stress. —**brain′wash′ing,** n.

braise (brāz) v., **braised, braising.** cook slowly in moisture.

brake (brāk) n., v., **braked, braking.** —**1.** device for stopping a vehicle. —v. **2.** slow or stop with a brake.

bram′ble (bram′bəl) n. prickly shrub. —**bram′bly,** adj.

bran (bran) n. husk of grain.

branch (branch) n. **1.** division of plant's stem. **2.** local office, store, etc. **3.** division of body, system, family, etc. —v. **4.** put forth or divide into branches.

brand (brand) n. **1.** kind; make. **2.** burned mark. **3.** burning piece of wood. —v. **4.** mark with a brand.

brand′ish (bran′dish) v. wave.

brand′-new′ (bran′-, brand′-) adj. extremely new.

bran′dy (bran′dē) n., pl. **-dies.** spirit from fermented grapes.

brash (brash) adj. **1.** impudent; tactless. **2.** rash; impetuous.

brass (bras) n. **1.** alloy of copper and zinc. **2.** musical instrument such as trumpet or horn. **3.** Informal. high-ranking officials. **4.** impudence. —**brass′y,** adj.

bras•siere′ (brə zēr′) n. undergarment supporting the breasts.

brass tacks, n.pl. basics.

brat (brat) n. spoiled or rude child.

brat′wurst′ (brat′wûrst, -vōōrst′, brät′-) n. pork sausage.

bra•va′do (brə vä′dō) n., pl. **-does, -dos.** boasting; swaggering.

brave (brāv) adj., **braver, bravest,** n., v., **braved, braving.** —adj. **1.** courageous. —n. **2.** North American Indian warrior. —v. **3.** meet courageously. **4.** defy. —**brave′ly,** adv. —**brave′ness, brav′er•y,** n.

bra′vo (brä′vō, brä vō′) interj. well done!

brawl (brôl) n. **1.** quarrel. —v. **2.** quarrel noisily. —**brawl′er,** n.

brawn (brôn) n. **1.** muscles. **2.** muscular strength. —**brawn′y,** adj.

bray (brā) n. **1.** cry of a donkey. —v. **2.** sound a bray.

bra′zen (brā′zən) adj. **1.** of or like

brass. **2.** shameless; impudent. —*v.* **3.** face boldly. —**bra′zen·ness,** *n.*

bra′zier (brā′zhər) *n.* receptacle for burning charcoal.

Bra·zil′ nut (brə zil′) three-sided edible seed of South American tree.

breach (brēch) *n.* **1.** a breaking. **2.** gap. **3.** infraction; violation. **4.** break. —*v.* **5.** make breach.

bread (bred) *n.* **1.** food of baked dough. **2.** *Slang.* money. —*v.* **3.** cover with breadcrumbs.

bread′crumb′, *n.* (*usually pl.*) a crumb of bread.

breadth (bredth, bretth) *n.* width.

bread′win′ner, *n.* main money earner in family.

break (brāk) *v.,* **broke** (brōk), **bro·ken, breaking,** *n.* —*v.* **1.** separate into parts. **2.** violate; dissolve. **3.** fracture. **4.** interrupt. **5.** disclose. **6.** fail; disable. **7.** (*pp.* **broke**) ruin financially. **8.** tame. —*n.* **9.** forcible disruption or separation. **10.** gap. **11.** attempt to escape. **12.** brief rest. **13.** *Informal.* opportunity. —**break′a·ble,** *adj.*

break′down′, *n.* **1.** failure to operate. **2.** nervous crisis. **3.** analysis of figures.

break′er, *n.* wave breaking on land.

break′fast (brek′fast) *n.* **1.** first meal of day. —*v.* **2.** eat breakfast.

break′-in′ (brāk′-) *n.* illegal forcible entry into home, office, etc.

break′neck′, *adj.* reckless or dangerous, esp. because of excessive speed.

break′through′, *n.* important discovery.

break′up′, *n.* **1.** dispersal or disintegration. **2.** ending of a personal relationship.

break′wa′ter, *n.* barrier against the force of waves.

breast (brest) *n.* **1.** chest. **2.** milk gland.

breast′bone′, *n.* sternum.

breast′stroke′, *n.* swimming stroke in which the arms move forward, outward, and rearward while the legs kick outward.

breath (breth) *n.* **1.** air inhaled and exhaled. **2.** ability to breathe. **3.** light breeze. —**breath′less,** *adj.*

breathe (brēth) *v.,* **breathed, breathing. 1.** inhale and exhale. **2.** blow lightly. **3.** live. **4.** whisper.

breath′er (brē′thər) *n. Informal.* short rest.

breath′tak′ing (breth′-) *adj.* awesome or exciting.

breech′es (brich′iz) *n.pl.* trousers.

breed (brēd) *v.,* **bred** (bred), **breed-**

ing, *n.* —*v.* **1.** produce. **2.** raise. —*n.* **3.** related animals. **4.** lineage.

breed′ing, *n.* **1.** ancestry. **2.** training. **3.** manners.

breeze (brēz) *n.* light current of air. —**breez′y,** *adj.*

breeze′way′, *n.* open-sided roofed passageway joining two buildings.

breth′ren (breth′rin) *n.* a *pl.* of brother.

bre·vi·ar·y (brē′vē er′ē, brev′ē-) *n., pl.* **-aries.** book of daily prayers and readings.

brev′i·ty (brev′i tē) *n.* shortness.

brew (broo) *v.* **1.** prepare beverage such as beer or ale. **2.** concoct. —*n.* **3.** quantity brewed. **4.** act or instance of brewing. —**brew′er,** *n.* —**brew′er·y,** *n.*

bri′ar (brī′ər) *n.* brier.

bribe (brīb) *n., v.,* **bribed, bribing.** —*n.* **1.** gift made for corrupt performance of duty. —*v.* **2.** give or influence by bribe. —**brib′er·y,** *n.*

bric′-a-brac′ (brik′ə brak′) *n.* trinkets.

brick (brik) *n.* **1.** building block of baked clay. —*v.* **2.** fill or build with brick. —**brick′lay′er,** *n.* —**brick′- lay′ing,** *n.*

brick′bat′, *n.* **1.** fragment of brick. **2.** caustic criticism.

bride (brīd) *n.* woman newly married or about to be married. —**brid′al,** *adj.*

bride′groom′, *n.* man newly married or about to be married.

brides′maid′, *n.* bride's wedding attendant.

bridge (brij) *n., v.,* **bridged, bridging.** —*n.* **1.** structure spanning river, road, etc. **2.** card game for four players. **3.** artificial replacement for teeth. —*v.* **4.** span.

bridge′work′, *n.* dental bridges.

bri′dle (brīd′l) *n., v.,* **-dled, -dling.** —*n.* **1.** harness at horse's head. **2.** anything that restrains. —*v.* **3.** put bridle on. **4.** restrain.

brief (brēf) *adj.* **1.** short. **2.** concise. —*n.* **3.** concise statement. **4.** outline of arguments and facts. —*v.* **5.** instruct in advance. —**brief′ly,** *adv.*

brief′case′, *n.* flat carrier for business papers, etc.

bri′er (brī′ər) *n.* **1.** prickly plant. **2.** plant with woody root.

brig (brig) *n.* **1.** two-masted square-rigged ship. **2.** ship's jail.

bri·gade′ (bri gād′) *n.* large military unit or body of troops.

brig′a·dier′ (brig′ə dēr′) *n.* military officer between colonel and major general. Also, **brigadier general.**

brig′and (brig′ənd) *n.* bandit.

bright (brīt) *adj.* **1.** shining. **2.** filled with light. **3.** brilliant. **4.** clever. —**bright'en,** *v.* —**bright'ly,** *adv.* —**bright'ness,** *n.*

bril'liant (bril'yant) *adj.* **1.** sparkling. **2.** illustrious. **3.** highly intelligent. —*n.* **4.** brilliant diamond. —**bril'liant·ly,** *adv.* —**bril'liance,** *n.*

brim (brim) *n.*, *v.*, **brimmed, brimming.** —*n.* **1.** upper edge; rim. —*v.* **2.** fill or be full to brim. —**brim'ful,** *adj.*

brim'stone', *n.* sulfur.

brin'dle (brin'dl) *n.* brindled coloring or animal.

brin'dled, *adj.* having dark streaks or spots.

brine (brīn) *n.*, *v.*, **brined, brining.** —*n.* **1.** salt water. **2.** sea. —*v.* **3.** treat with brine. —**briny,** *adj.*

bring (bring) *v.*, **brought** (brôt), **bringing. 1.** fetch. **2.** cause to come. **3.** lead.

brink (bringk) *n.* edge.

bri·quette' (bri ket') *n.* small block of compressed coal dust or charcoal used as fuel. Also, **bri·quet'.**

brisk (brisk) *adj.* **1.** lively. **2.** stimulating. —**brisk'ly,** *adv.*

bris'ket (bris'kit) *n.* animal's breast.

bris'tle (bris'al) *n.*, *v.*, **-tled, -tling.** —*n.* **1.** short, stiff, coarse hair. —*v.* **2.** rise stiffly. **3.** show indignation.

britch'es (brich'iz) *n.* (*used with a pl. v.*) breeches.

Brit'ish (brit'ish) *adj.* of Great Britain or its inhabitants.

British thermal unit, amount of heat needed to raise temperature of 1 lb. (0.4 kg) water 1°F. *Abbr.:* Btu, BTU

Brit'on (brit'n) *n.* native of Great Britain.

brit'tle (brit'l) *adj.* breaking readily.

broach (brōch) *v.* **1.** pierce. **2.** mention for first time.

broad (brôd) *adj.* **1.** wide. **2.** main. **3.** liberal. —**broad'ly,** *adv.*

broad'cast', *v.*, **-cast** or **-casted, -casting,** *n.* —*v.* **1.** send by radio or television. **2.** scatter widely. —*n.* **3.** something broadcast. **4.** radio or television program. —**broad'cast'er,** *n.*

broad'cloth', *n.* fine cotton material.

broad'en, *v.* widen.

broad jump, long jump.

broad'loom', *n.* carpet woven on wide loom.

broad'-mind'ed, *adj.* tolerant.

broad'side', *n.* **1.** simultaneous firing of all guns on one side of warship. **2.** verbal attack.

broad'-spec'trum, *adj.* (of antibiotics) effective against wide range of organisms.

bro·cade' (brō kād') *n.* woven fabric with raised design.

broc'co·li (brok'ə lē) *n.* green plant with edible flower heads.

bro·chure' (brō shŏŏr') *n.* pamphlet; booklet.

brogue (brōg) *n.* Irish accent.

broil (broil) *v.* cook by direct heat. —**broil'er,** *n.*

broke (brōk) *adj.* without money.

bro'ken (brō'kən) *v.* **1.** pp. of **break.** —*adj.* **2.** in fragments. **3.** fractured. **4.** incomplete. **5.** weakened. **6.** imperfectly spoken.

bro'ken·heart'ed, *adj.* sorrowing deeply.

bro'ker, *n.* commercial agent.

bro'mide (brō'mīd, -mid) *n.* soothing compound.

bro'mine (brō'mēn, -min) *n.* reddish, toxic liquid element.

bron'chi·al (brong'kē əl) *adj.* of the **bronchi,** two branches of the trachea.

bron·chi'tis (-kī'tis) *n.* inflammation in windpipe and chest.

bron'co (brong'kō) *n., pl.* **-cos.** pony or small horse of western U.S.

bronze (bronz) *n.*, *v.*, **bronzed, bronzing.** —*n.* **1.** alloy of copper and tin. **2.** brownish color. —*v.* **3.** make bronze in color.

brooch (brōch) *n.* clasp or ornament.

brood (brōod) *n.* **1.** group of animals born at one time. —*v.* **2.** hatch. **3.** think moodily.

brook (brŏŏk) *n.* **1.** small stream. —*v.* **2.** tolerate.

broom (brōom, brŏŏm) *n.* **1.** sweeping implement. **2.** shrubby plant.

broom'stick, *n.* handle of a broom.

bros., brothers.

broth (brôth) *n.* thin soup.

broth'el (broth'al) *n.* house of prostitution.

broth'er (bruth'ər) *n., pl.* **brothers, brethren. 1.** male child of same parents. **2.** member of same group. —**broth'er·hood',** *n.*

broth'er-in-law', *n., pl.* **brothers-in-law. 1.** husband's or wife's brother. **2.** sister's husband.

brou·ha·ha' (brōo'hä hä') *n., pl.* **-has.** uproar.

brow (brou) *n.* **1.** eyebrow. **2.** forehead. **3.** edge of a height.

brow'beat', *v.*, **-beat, -beaten, -beating.** bully.

brown (broun) *n.* **1.** dark reddish or yellowish color. —*adj.* **2.** of this color. —*v.* **3.** make or become brown.

brown/-bag/, v., -bagged, -bagging. bring (one's lunch) to work or school. —**brown/-bag/ger**, n.

brown/ie (brou/nē) n. 1. small, chewy chocolate cake. 2. (cap.) Girl Scout ages 6 to 8.

brown/out/, n. reduction of electric power to prevent a blackout.

browse (brouz) v., browsed, browsing. 1. graze; feed. 2. examine books, etc., at leisure.

bruise (brooz) v., bruised, bruising, n. —v. 1. injure without breaking. —n. 2. bruised injury.

bruis/er, n. Informal. strong, tough man.

brunch (brunch) n. meal that serves as both breakfast and lunch. —v. 2. eat brunch.

bru-net/ (broo net/) adj. dark brown, esp. of skin or hair.

bru-nette/ (broo net/) n. woman with dark hair and usu. dark skin. Also, adj.

brunt (brunt) n. main force.

brush (brush) n. 1. instrument with bristles. 2. bushy tail. 3. brief encounter. 4. dense bushes, shrubs, etc. —v. 5. use brush. 6. touch lightly.

brush/-off/, n. abrupt rebuff.

brusque (brusk) adj. abrupt; blunt. Also, **brusk**. —**brusque/ly**, adv.

Brus/sels sprouts (brus/əlz) plant with small, edible heads.

bru/tal (broot/l) adj. 1. cruel. 2. severe. —**bru-tal/i-ty**, n.

bru/tal-ize/ (-īzd, -izing), 1. make brutal. 2. treat brutally.

brute (broot) n. 1. beast. 2. beast-like person. —adj. 3. not human. 4. irrational. 5. like animals. 6. savage. —**bru/tal**, adj. —**brut/ish**, adj.

B.S., Bachelor of Science.

Btu, British thermal unit. Also, **BTU bu.**, bushel.

bub/ble (bub/əl) n., v., -bled, -bling. —n. 1. globule of gas, esp. in liquid. —v. 2. make or give off bubbles. —**bub/bly**, adj.

buc/ca-neer/ (buk/ə nēr/) n. pirate.

buck (buk) v. 1. leap to unseat a rider. 2. resist. —n. 3. male of the deer, rabbit, goat, etc.

buck/et (buk/it) n. deep, open-topped container; pail.

buck/le (buk/əl) n., v., -led, -ling. —n. 1. clasp for two loose ends. —v. 2. fasten with buckle. 3. bend. 4. set to work.

buck/ler, n. shield.

buck/ram (buk/rəm) n. stiff cotton fabric.

buck/shot/, n. large lead shot.

buck/skin/, n. skin of buck.

buck/tooth/, n., pl. -teeth. projecting tooth.

buck/wheat/, n. plant with edible triangular seeds.

bu-col/ic (byoo kol/ik) adj. rustic.

bud (bud) n., v., budded, budding. —n. 1. small bulge on plant stem, from which leaves or flowers develop. 2. small rounded part. —v. 3. produce buds. 4. begin to grow.

Bud/dhism (boo/diz əm, bood/iz-) n. Eastern religion based on teachings of Buddha. —**Bud/dhist**, n.

bud/dy (bud/ē) n., pl. -dies. Informal. friend; comrade.

budge (buj) v., budged, budging. move slightly.

budg/et (buj/it) n. 1. estimate of income and expense. 2. plan allotment of funds. 3. allot.

buff (buf) n. 1. thick light-yellow leather. 2. yellowish brown. 3. enthusiast. —adj. 4. made or colored like buff. —v. 5. polish brightly.

buf/fa-lo/ (buf/ə lō/) n., pl. -loes, -los, -lo. large bovine mammal.

buff/er, n. 1. cushioning device. 2. polishing device.

buf/fet n. 1. (buf/it) blow. 2. (bə-fā/) cabinet. 3. (bə fā/) food counter. 4. (bə fā/) meal where guests serve themselves. —v. (buf/it) 5. strike.

buf-foon/ (bə foon/) n. clown.

bug (bug) n., v., bugged, bugging. —n. 1. insect. 2. microorganism. 3. defect or imperfection. 4. hidden microphone. —v. 5. install secret listening device in. 6. Informal. pester.

bug/bear/, n. any source, real or imaginary, of fright or terror. Also, **bug/a-boo/** (bug/ə boo/).

bug/gy (bug/ē) n., pl. -gies. carriage.

bu/gle (byoo/gəl) n., v., -gled, -gling. —n. 1. cornetlike wind instrument. —v. 2. sound a bugle.

build (bild) v., built, building, n. —v. 1. construct. 2. form. 3. develop. —n. 4. manner or form of construction. —**build/er**, n.

build/ing, n. 1. structure with roof and walls. 2. construction business.

build/up/, n. Informal. 1. steady increase. 2. publicity.

built/-in/, adj. built as part of a structure.

built/-up/, adj. 1. made bigger or higher by addition. 2. filled in with buildings.

bulb (bulb) n. 1. underground bud. 2. rounded part. 3. electric lamp.

bulge (bulj) n., v., bulged, bulging. —n. 1. rounded projection. —v. 2. swell out. —**bulg/y**, adj.

bu-lim/i-a (byoo lim/ē ə, -lē/mē ə, boo-) n. disorder marked by eating binges followed by self-induced vomiting.

bulk (bulk) *n.* **1.** magnitude. **2.** main mass. —*v.* **3.** increase in size.

bulk'head', *n.* wall-like partition in a ship.

bulk'y, *adj.,* **bulkier, bulkiest.** of great bulk. —**bulk'i·ness,** *n.*

bull (bŏŏl) *n.* **1.** male bovine. **2.** bull-like person. **3.** speculator who depends on rise in prices. **4.** papal document. **5.** *Slang.* lying talk. —*adj.* **6.** male. **7.** marked by rise in prices. —**bull'ish,** *adj.*

bull'dog', *n.* breed of heavily built dog.

bull'doz'er, *n.* powerful earth-moving tractor.

bul'let (bŏŏl'it) *n.* projectile for firing from small guns.

bul'le·tin (bŏŏl'i tn, -tin) *n.* brief public statement, esp. late news.

bull'fight', *n.* combat between man and a bull. —**bull'fight'er**, *n.*

bull'frog', *n.* large frog.

bull'head'ed, *adj.* stubborn.

bul'lion (bŏŏl'yan) *n.* uncoined gold or silver.

bull'ock (bŏŏl'ak) *n.* castrated bull.

bull'pen', *n.* place where relief pitchers warm up.

bull's'-eye', *n.* center of target.

bul'ly (bŏŏl'ē) *n., pl.* **-lies,** *v.,* **-lied, -lying.** **—n. 1.** overbearing person who hurts smaller or weaker people. —*v.* **2.** intimidate.

bul'rush' (bŏŏl'rush') *n.* rushlike plant.

bul'wark (bŏŏl'wark, -wôrk) *n.* **1.** rampart. **2.** protection.

bum (bum) *n. Informal.* **1.** tramp or hobo. **2.** loafer; idler. —*v.* **3.** *Informal.* beg. —*adj.* **4.** of poor quality.

bum'ble (bum'bal) *v.,* **-bled, -bling.** **1.** blunder. **2.** bungle; botch.

bum'ble·bee', *n.* large bee.

bum'mer (bum'ər) *n. Slang.* frustrating or bad experience.

bump (bump) *v.* **1.** strike; collide. —*n.* **2.** act or shock of bumping. **3.** swelling. —**bump'y,** *adj.*

bump'er, *n.* **1.** device for protection in collisions. **2.** glass filled to brim. —*adj.* **3.** abundant.

bump'kin (bump'kin) *n.* awkward, simple person from rural area.

bun (bun) *n.* kind of bread roll.

bunch (bunch) *n.* **1.** cluster. **2.** group. —*v.* **3.** group; gather.

bun'dle (bun'dl) *n., v.,* **-dled, -dling.** —*n.* **1.** group bound together. **2.** package. —*v.* **3.** wrap in bundle. **4.** dress warmly.

bun'ga·low' (bung'gə lō') *n.* cottage.

bun'gle (bung'gal) *v.,* **-gled, -gling,**

n. —*v.* **1.** fail to do properly. —*n.* **2.** something bungled.

bun'ion (bun'yan) *n.* swelling on foot.

bunk (bungk) *n.* **1.** built-in bed. **2.** bunkum.

bunk'er (bung'kar) *n.* **1.** bin. **2.** underground refuge.

bun'kum (bung'kəm) *n.* nonsense. Also, **bunk.**

bun'ny (bun'ē) *n., pl.* **-nies.** *Informal.* rabbit.

bunt (bunt) *v.* push or tap forward.

bun'ting (bun'ting) *n.* **1.** fabric for flags, etc. **2.** flags. **3.** finchlike bird.

buoy (bōō'ē, boi) *n.* **1.** floating marker. —*v.* **2.** support. **3.** mark with buoy. **4.** raise the spirits of.

buoy'an·cy (boi'ʌn sē, bōō'yant) *adj.* **1.** tending to float. **2.** cheerful. —**buoy'an·cy,** *n.*

bur (bûr) *n.* prickly seed case.

bur'den (bûr'dn) *n.* **1.** load. —*v.* **2.** load heavily. —**bur'den·some,** *adj.*

bur'dock (bûr'dok) *n.* prickly plant.

bu'reau (byŏŏr'ō) *n., pl.* **-eaus, -eaux.** **1.** chest of drawers. **2.** government department.

bu·reauc'ra·cy (byŏŏ rok'rə sē) *n., pl.* **-cies.** **1.** government by bureaus. **2.** bureau officials.

bu'reau·crat' (byŏŏr'ə krat') *n.* official of a bureaucracy. —**bu'reau·crat'ic,** *adj.*

bur'geon (bûr'jan) *v.* **1.** grow quickly. **2.** begin to grow.

burg'er (bûr'gar) *n.* hamburger.

bur'glar (bûr'glar) *n.* thief who breaks and enters. —**bur'glar·ize',** *v.* —**bur'gla·ry,** *n.*

Bur'gun·dy (bûr'gan dē) *n., pl.* **-dies.** dry red wine.

bur'i·al (ber'ē al) *n.* act of burying.

bur'lap (bûr'lap) *n.* coarse fabric of jute, etc.

bur·lesque' (bar lesk') *n., v.,* **-lesqued, -lesquing.** —*n.* **1.** artistic travesty. **2.** sexually suggestive entertainment. —*v.* **3.** make a burlesque of.

bur'ly (bûr'lē) *adj.,* **-lier, -liest.** **1.** of great size. **2.** brusque.

burn (bûrn) *v.,* **burned** or **burnt, burning,** *n.* —*v.* **1.** be on fire. **2.** consume with fire. **3.** heat. **4.** glow. **5.** feel passion. —*n.* **6.** burned place.

bur'nish (bûr'nish) *v.* polish.

burn'out', *n.* **1.** point at which rocket engine stops because it runs out of fuel. **2.** fatigue and frustration from too much work and stress.

burp (bûrp) *n.* belch. —**burp,** *v.*

burr (bûr) *n.* bur.

bur′ro (bûr′ō, bŏŏr′ō, bur′ō) *n., pl.* -ros. donkey.

bur′row (bûr′ō) *n.* **1.** animal's hole in ground. —*v.* **1.** make or lodge in burrow.

bur′sar (bûr′sər, -sär) *n.* treasurer, esp. of a college.

bur•si′tis (bər sī′tis) *n.* inflammation of a bursa (sac containing fluid) in a joint.

burst (bûrst) *v.,* **burst, bursting.** —*v.* **1.** break open or issue forth violently. **2.** rupture. —*n.* **3.** act or result of bursting. **4.** sudden display.

bur′y (ber′ē) *v.,* **buried, burying. 1.** put into ground and cover. **2.** conceal.

bus (bus) *n., pl.* **buses, busses,** *v.,* **bused** or **bussed, busing** or **bussing.** —*n.* **1.** large passenger motor vehicle. —*v.* **2.** move by bus.

bus′boy′, *n.* helper of waiter.

bush (bŏŏsh) *n.* **1.** shrubby plant. **2.** land covered by bushes.

bushed, *adj. Informal.* exhausted.

bush′el (bŏŏsh′əl) *n.* unit of 4 pecks.

bush league, secondary baseball league. —**bush leaguer,** *n.*

busi′ness (biz′nis) *n.* **1.** occupation; profession. **2.** trade. **3.** trading enterprise. **4.** affair; matter. —**busi′ness•man′, busi′ness•wom•an,** *n.*

busi′ness•like′, *adj.* practical and efficient.

bus′ing (bus′ing) *n.* moving of pupils by bus to achieve racially balanced classes. Also, **bus′sing.**

bust (bust) *n.* **1.** sculpture of head and shoulders. **2.** bosom. —*v. Informal.* **3.** burst or break. **4.** become or make bankrupt. **5.** arrest. **6.** hit.

bus′tle (bus′əl) *v.,* **-tled, -tling. 1.** move or act energetically. —*n.* **2.** energetic activity.

bus′y (biz′ē) *adj.,* **busier, busiest,** *v.,* **busied, busying.** —*adj.* **1.** actively employed. **2.** full of activity. —*v.* **3.** make or keep busy.

bus′y•bod′y, *n., pl.* **-bodies.** meddler.

but (but; *unstressed* bət) *conj.* **1.** on the contrary. **2.** except. **3.** except that. —*prep.* **4.** except. —*adv.* **5.** only.

bu′tane (byōō′tān) *n. Slang.* gas used as fuel.

butch (bŏŏch) *adj. Slang.* **1.** (of a woman) having traits usu. associated with men. **2.** (of a man) having exaggerated masculine traits.

butch′er (bŏŏch′ər) *n.* **1.** dealer in meat. **2.** slaughterer. —*v.* **3.** kill for food. **4.** bungle. —**butch′er•y,** *n.*

but′ler (but′lər) *n.* chief male servant.

butt (but) *n.* **1.** thick or blunt end. **2.** object of ridicule. **3.** large cask. **4.** cigarette end. **5.** *Slang.* buttocks. —*v.* **6.** be adjacent; join. **7.** strike with head or horns.

but′ter (but′ər) *n.* **1.** solid fatty part of milk. —*v.* **2.** put butter on.

but′ter•cup′, *n.* plant with yellow cup-shaped flowers.

but′ter•fin′gers, *n., pl.* **-gers.** clumsy person.

but′ter•fly′, *n., pl.* **-flies.** insect with colorful wings.

but′ter•milk′, *n.* sour liquid remaining after butter is made.

but′ter•nut′, *n.* nut of walnutlike tree.

but′ter•scotch′, *n.* kind of taffy.

but′tock (but′ək) *n.* (*usually pl.*) one of two protuberances forming lower back part of human body.

but′ton (but′n) *n.* **1.** disk or knob for fastening. **2.** buttonlike object. —*v.* **3.** fasten with button.

but′ton•down′, *adj.* **1.** (of a collar) having buttonholes for attachment to shirt. **2.** conventional.

but′ton•hole′, *n., v.,* **-holed, -holing.** —*n.* **1.** slit through which a button is passed. —*v.* **2.** accost and detain in conversation.

but′tress (bu′tris) *n.* **1.** structure steadying wall. —*v.* **2.** support.

bux′om (buk′səm) *adj.* (of a woman) attractively plump.

buy (bī) *v.,* **bought** (bôt) **buying. 1.** acquire by payment. **2.** bribe.

buy′back′, *n.* repurchase by a company of its own stock.

buy′out′, *n.* purchase of a majority of shares in a company.

buzz (buz) *n.* **1.** low humming sound. —*v.* **2.** make buzz.

buz′zard (buz′ərd) *n.* carnivorous bird.

buzz′word′, *n. Informal.* fashionable cliché used to give specious weight to argument.

by (bī) *prep.* **1.** near to. **2.** through. **3.** not later than. **4.** past. **5.** using as means or method. —*adv.* **6.** near. **7.** past.

bye (bī) *n.* (in a tournament) automatic advancement to the next round.

by′-elec′tion, *n.* special election to fill vacancy.

by′gone′, *adj.* **1.** past. —*n.* **2.** something past.

by′law′, *n.* rule within corporation.

by′line′, *n.* line, as in a newspaper, giving the writer or reporter's name.

by′pass′, *n.* **1.** detour. **2.** surgical

procedure in which diseased or blocked organ is circumvented.
—v. 3. avoid through bypass.

by/-prod/uct, n. secondary product.

by/road/, n. side road; byway.

by/stand/er, n. chance looker-on.

byte (bīt) n. unit of computer information, larger than bit.

by/way/, n. little-used road.

by/word/, n. proverb.

Byz/an/tine/ (biz/ən tēn/, -tīn/) adj. (sometimes l.c.) **1.** complex; intricate. **2.** marked by intrigue.

C

C, c (sē) n. third letter of English alphabet.

C, Celsius, Centigrade.

c., 1. centimeter. **2.** century. **3.** copyright.

CA, California.

ca., circa.

cab (kab) n. **1.** taxicab. **2.** one-horse carriage. **3.** part of locomotive, truck, etc., where driver sits.

ca·bal/ (kə bal/) n. group of plotters.

ca·ban/a (kə ban/ə, -ban/yə) n. small structure at beach or pool.

cab/a·ret/ (kab/ə rā/) n. restaurant providing entertainment.

cab/bage (kab/ij) n. plant with edible head of leaves.

cab/in (kab/in) n. **1.** small house. **2.** room in a ship or plane.

cab/i·net (kab/ə nit) n. **1.** advisory council. **2.** cupboard.

ca/ble (kā/bəl) n., v., **-bled, -bling.** —n. **1.** thick, strong rope. **2.** cablegram. **3.** bundle of electrical wires. —v. **4.** send cablegram (to).

ca/ble·gram/, n. telegram sent by underwater wires.

cable TV, system of distributing television programs to subscribers over coaxial cables.

ca·boose/ (kə bōōs/) n. car for the crew at the end of a train.

ca·ca/o (kə kä/ō) n., pl. **-caos.** tropical tree whose seeds yield cocoa.

cache (kash) n., v., **cached, cach·ing.** —n. **1.** hiding place for treasure, etc. —v. **2.** hide.

ca·chet/ (ka shā/) n. **1.** official seal or sign. **2.** superior status; prestige.

cack/le (kak/əl) v., **-led, -ling.** —n. v. **1.** utter shrill, broken cry. —n. **2.** act or sound of cackling.

ca·coph/o·ny (kə kof/ə nē) n., pl. **-nies.** harsh, discordant sound.

cac/tus (kak/təs) n., pl. **-tuses, -ti** (-tī). leafless, spiny plant.

cad (kad) n. ungentlemanly person.

ca·dav/er (kə dav/ər) n. corpse.

CAD/CAM (kad/kam/) n. computer-aided design and computer-aided manufacturing.

cad/die (kad/ē) n., v., **-died, -dying.** —n. **1.** person who carries one's

golf clubs. —v. **2.** work as caddie. Also, **cad/dy.**

ca/dence (kād/ns) n. rhythmic flow or beat.

ca·det/ (kə det/) n. military student.

cadge (kaj) v., **cadged, cadging.** obtain by begging.

cad/mi·um (kad/mē əm) n. white metallic element used in plating.

ca/dre (kä/drā, kad/rē) n. highly trained group within organization.

Cae·sar/e·an (si zârē ən) n. Cesarean.

ca·fé/ (ka fā/) n. restaurant.

caf/e·te/ri·a (kaf/i tēr/ē ə) n. self-service restaurant.

caf/feine (ka fēn/) n. chemical in coffee, etc., used as stimulant. Also, **caf/fein.**

caf/tan (kaf/tan) n. long wide-sleeved garment.

cage (kāj) n., v., **caged, caging.** —n. **1.** barred box or room. —v. **2.** put in cage.

cag/ey, adj. **-ier, -iest.** shrewd; cautious. Also, **cag/y.** —**cag/i·ly,** adv. —**cag/i·ness,** n.

cais/son (kā/son, -sən) n. **1.** ammunition wagon. **2.** airtight underwater chamber.

ca·jole/ (kə jōl/) v., **-joled, -joling.** coax; wheedle. —**ca·jol/er·y,** n.

Ca/jun (kā/jən) n. Louisianan of Nova Scotia-French origin.

cake (kāk) n., v., **caked, caking.** —n. **1.** sweet baked dough. **2.** compact mass. —v. **3.** form into compact mass.

Cal., California. Also, **Calif.**

cal., 1. caliber. **2.** calorie.

cal/a·bash/ (kal/ə bash/) n. kind of gourd.

cal·a·ma/ri (kal/ə mär/ē, kä/lə-) n. cooked squid.

cal/a·mine/ (kal/ə mīn/) n. powder used in skin lotions.

ca·lam/i·ty (kə lam/i tē) n., pl. **-ties.** disaster. —**ca·lam/i·tous,** adj.

cal/ci·fy/ (kal/sə fī/) v. **-fied, -fying.** harden.

cal/ci·um (kal/sē əm) n. white metallic chemical element.

cal/cu·late/ (kal/kyə lāt/) v., **-lated, -lating.** compute or estimate by mathematics. —**cal/cu·la/tion,** n.

cal/cu·lat/ing, adj. shrewd.

calculator

cal′cu·la′tor, *n.* small electronic or mechanical device that performs mathematical calculations.

cal′cu·lus (kal′kyə ləs) *n.* a method of calculation by a system of algebraic notations.

cal′dron (kôl′drən) *n.* cauldron.

cal′en·dar (kal′ən dər) *n.* **1.** list of days, weeks, and months of year. **2.** list of events.

calf (kaf) *n., pl.* **calves. 1.** young of cow, etc. **2.** fleshy part of leg below knee.

cal′i·ber (kal′ə bər) *n.* **1.** diameter of bullet or gun bore. **2.** quality. Also **cal′i·bre.**

cal′i·brate′ (-brāt′) *v.,* **-brated, -brating.** mark for measuring purposes. **—cal′i·bra′tion,** *n.*

cal′i·co′ (kal′i kō′) *n., pl.* **-coes, -cos.** printed cotton cloth.

cal′i·per (kal′ə pər) *n.* (*usu. pl.*) compass for measuring.

ca′liph (kā′lif) *n.* former title of Islamic religious and civil ruler.

cal·is·then′ics (kal′əs then′iks) *n.pl.* physical exercises.

calk (kôk) *v.* caulk.

call (kôl) *v.* **1.** cry out loudly. **2.** announce. **3.** summon. **4.** telephone. **5.** name. **6.** visit briefly. **—n. 7.** cry or shout. **8.** summons. **9.** brief visit. **10.** need; demand. **—call′er,** *n.*

call girl, female prostitute who is called for services.

cal·lig′ra·phy (kə lig′rə fē) *n.* fancy penmanship; art of beautiful writing.

call′ing, *n.* **1.** trade. **2.** summons.

cal′lous (kal′əs) *adj.* unsympathetic. **—v. 2.** harden.

cal′low (kal′ō) *adj.* immature.

cal′lus (kal′əs) *n.* hardened part of the skin.

calm (käm) *adj.* **1.** undisturbed. **2.** not windy. **—n. 3.** calm state. **—v. 4.** make calm. **—calm′ly,** *adv.*

ca·lor′ic (kə lôr′ik) *adj.* **1.** of heat or calories. **2.** high in calories.

cal′o·rie (kal′ə rē) *n.* measured unit of heat, esp. of fuel or energy value of food.

ca·lum′ni·ate′ (kə lum′nē āt′) *v.,* **-ated, -ating.** slander. **—cal′um·ny** (kal′əm nē) *n.*

calve (kav, käv) *v.* give birth to calf.

ca·lyp′so (kə lip′sō) *n.* musical style of the West Indies.

ca′lyx (kā′liks) *n.* small leaflets around flower petals.

cam (kam) *n.* device for changing circular movement to straight.

ca′ma·ra·de·rie (kä′mə rä′də rē) *n.* comradeship; fellowship.

cam′ber (kam′bər) *n.* slight upward curve; convexity.

cam′bric (kām′brik) *n.* close-woven fabric.

came (kām) *v.* pt. of **come.**

cam′cord′er (kam′kôr′dər) *n.* handheld television camera with an incorporated VCR.

cam′el (kam′əl) *n.* large humped quadruped.

ca·mel′lia (kə mēl′yə) *n.* shrub with glossy leaves and roselike flowers.

cam′e·o′ (kam′ē ō′) *n., pl.* **-eos.** gem with head carved in relief.

cam′er·a (kam′ər ə) *n.* device for making photographs.

cam′i·sole′ (kam′ə sōl′) *n.* woman's sleeveless undershirt.

cam′o·mile′ (kam′ə mīl′) *n.* chamomile.

cam′ou·flage′ (kam′ə fläzh′) *n., v.,* **-flaged, -flaging. —n. 1.** deceptive covering. **—v. 2.** hide by camouflage.

camp (kamp) *n.* **1.** place of temporary lodging, esp. in tents. **2.** faction. **3.** something that amuses by being overdone or tasteless. **—adj. 4.** Also, **camp′y.** amusing as camp. **—v. 5.** form or live in camp. **—camp′er,** *n.* **—camp′site′,** *n.*

cam·paign′ (kam pān′) *n.* **1.** military operation. **2.** competition for political office, sales, etc. **—v. 3.** engage in campaign.

cam′phor (kam′fər) *n.* white crystalline substance used as moth repellent, medicine, etc.

cam′pus (kam′pəs) *n.* school grounds.

cam′shaft′, *n.* engine shaft fitted with cams.

can, *v.,* canned (could for def. 1), canning (for def. 2), *n.* **—v. 1.** (kan; *unstressed* kən) be able or qualified to. **2.** (kan) put in airtight container. **—n. 3.** (kan) cylindrical metal container. **—can′ner,** *n.*

Ca·na′di·an (kə nā′dē ən) *n.* citizen of Canada. **—Canadian,** *adj.*

ca·nal′ (kə nal′) *n.* **1.** artificial waterway. **2.** tube in animal or plant.

can′a·pé (kan′ə pē, -pā′) *n.* morsel of food served as appetizer.

ca·nar′y (kə nâr′ē) *n., pl.* **-ries.** yellow cage bird.

can′cel (kan′səl) *v.,* **-celed, -celing. 1.** cross out. **2.** make void. **—can′cel·la′tion,** *n.*

can′cer (kan′sər) *n.* malignant growth. **—can′cer·ous,** *adj.*

can′de·la′brum (kan′dl ä′brəm) *n., pl.* **-bra** (-brə). branched candlestick. Also, **can′de·la′bra,** *pl.* **-bras.**

can·did (kan'did) *adj.* frank or honest. —**can'did·ly,** *adv.*

can·di·da (kan'di da) *n.* disease-causing fungus.

can·di·date' (kan'di dāt', -dit) *n.* one seeking to be elected or chosen. —**can'di·da·cy,** *n.*

can·dle (kan'dl) *n.* waxy cylinder with wick for burning.

can'dor (kan'dər) *n.* frankness.

can·dy (kan'dē) *n., pl.* **-dies,** *v.,* **-died, -dying.** —*n.* **1.** sweet confection. —*v.* **2.** cover with sugar.

cane (kān) *n.* **1.** stick used in walking. **2.** long, woody stem. —*v.* **3.** beat with a cane.

ca·nine (kā'nīn) *adj.* **1.** of dogs. —*n.* **2.** animal of dog family.

canine tooth, one of the four pointed teeth next to the incisors.

can'is·ter (kan'ə stər) *n.* small box.

can'ker (kang'kər) *n.* ulcerous sore. —**can'ker·ous,** *adj.*

can·na·bis (kan'ə bis) *n.* hemp plant; marijuana, used as drug.

canned, *adj.* **1.** put into cans or sealed jars. **2.** *Informal.* recorded.

can'ner·y, *n., pl.* **-ies.** factory where foods are canned.

can'ni·bal (kan'ə bəl) *n.* person who eats human flesh.

can'ni·bal·ize', *v.,* **-ized, -izing.** strip of reusable parts.

can'non (kan'ən) *n.* large mounted gun. —**can'non·eer',** *n.*

can·non·ade' (-ə nād') *n.* long burst of cannon fire.

can'not (kan'ot, ka not', kə-) *v.* am, are, or is unable to.

can'ny (kan'ē) *adj.,* **-nier, -niest.** **1.** careful. **2.** shrewd.

ca·noe' (kə nōō') *n.* light boat propelled by paddles.

can'on (kan'ən) *n.* **1.** rule or law. **2.** recognized books of Bible. **3.** church official.

can'on·ize', *v.,* **-ized, -izing.** declare as saint.

can'o·py (kan'ə pē) *n., pl.* **-pies.** overhead covering.

cant (kant) *n.* **1.** insincerely virtuous talk. **2.** special jargon.

can't (kant) contraction of **cannot.**

can'ta·loupe' (kan'tl ōp') *n.* small melon with orange flesh.

can·tan·ker·ous (kan tang'kər əs) *adj.* ill-natured.

can·ta'ta (kan tä'tə) *n.* dramatic choral composition.

can·teen' (kan tēn') *n.* **1.** container for water, etc. **2.** cafeteria or entertainment place for soldiers, etc.

can'ter (kan'tər) *n.* **1.** easy gallop. —*v.* **2.** go at easy gallop.

can'ti·cle (kan'ti kəl) *n.* hymn.

can'ti·le'ver (kan'tl ē'vər) *n.* structure secured at one end only.

can'to (kan'tō) *n., pl.* **-tos.** section of a long poem.

can'ton (kan'tn, kan ton') *n.* small territorial district in Switzerland.

can'tor (kan'tər) *n.* synagogue official who sings certain prayers.

can'vas (kan'vəs) *n.* **1.** cloth used for sails, tents, etc. **2.** sails.

can'vas·back', *n., pl.* **-backs, -back.** wild duck with a whitish or grayish back.

can'vass (kan'vəs) *v.* **1.** investigate. **2.** solicit votes, etc. —**can'vass·er,** *n.*

can'yon (kan'yən) *n.* narrow valley.

cap (kap) *n., v.,* **capped, capping.** —*n.* **1.** brimless cap with visor. **2.** cover. —*v.* **3.** cover. **4.** surpass.

cap., **1.** capacity. **2.** capital.

capital letter.

ca·pa·ble (kā'pə bəl) *adj.* able; qualified. —**ca'pa·bil'i·ty,** *n.*

ca·pa'cious (kə pā'shəs) *adj.* roomy.

ca·pac'i·tor (kə pas'i tər) *n.* device for collecting and holding an electrical charge.

ca·pac'i·ty (kə pas'i tē) *n., pl.* **-ties.** **1.** volume. **2.** capability. **3.** role.

cape (kāp) *n.* **1.** sleeveless coat. **2.** projecting point of land.

ca'per (kā'pər) *v.* **1.** leap playfully. —*n.* **2.** playful leap. **3.** bud of shrub, used as seasoning.

cap·il·lar·y (kap'ə ler'ē) *adj., n., pl.* **-laries.** —*adj.* **1.** of or in a tube. —*n.* **2.** tiny blood vessel.

cap'i·tal (kap'i tl) *n.* **1.** city in which government is located. **2.** letter different from and larger than its corresponding lowercase letter. **3.** money available for business use. —*adj.* **4.** important or chief. **5.** excellent. **6.** uppercase. **7.** punishable by death.

capital gain, profit from the sale of an asset.

capital goods, *n.pl.* machines for production of goods.

cap'i·tal·ism, *n.* system of private investment in and ownership of business. —**cap'i·tal·ist,** *n.*

cap'i·tal·ize', *v.,* **-ized, -izing.** **1.** put in capital letters. **2.** use as capital. **3.** take advantage.

cap'i·tal·ly, *adv.* well.

cap'i·tol (kap'i tl) *n.* building used by legislature.

ca·pit'u·late' (kə pich'ə lāt') *v.,* **-lated, -lating.** surrender.

cap'let (kap'lit) *n.* oval medicinal tablet, coated for easy swallowing.

ca·pon (kā′pon, -pən) *n.* castrated rooster.

cap·puc·ci·no (kap′ə chē′nō) *n.* espresso coffee with steamed milk.

ca·price′ (kə prēs′) *n.* whim. —**ca·pri·cious** (-prish′əs, -prē′shəs) *adj.* overturn; upset.

cap·size (kap′sīz′) *v.*, **-sized**, **-sizing.** overturn; upset.

cap·stan (kap′stan, -stən) *n.* device turned to pull cables.

cap·sule (kap′səl) *n.* small sealed container. —**cap′su·lar,** *adj.*

capt., captain.

cap·tain (kap′tən) *n.* **1.** officer below major or rear admiral. **2.** ship master. **3.** leader of sports team. —**cap′tain·cy,** *n.*

cap·tion (kap′shən) *n.* heading.

cap·tious (kap′shəs) *adj.* noting trivial faults. —**cap′tious·ly,** *adv.*

cap·ti·vate (-tiv′) *v.*, **-vated**, **-vating.** charm.

cap·tive (-tiv) *n.* prisoner. —**cap·tiv′i·ty,** *n.*

cap·ture (-char) *v.*, **-tured**, **-turing.** *n.* —*v.* **1.** take prisoner. —*n.* **2.** act of capturing. —**cap′tor,** *n.*

car (kär) *n.* **1.** vehicle, esp. automobile. **2.** cage of elevator.

ca·rafe (kə raf′) *n.* broad-mouthed bottle for wine, water, etc.

car·a·mel (kar′ə mal, kär′məl) *n.* confection made of burnt sugar.

car·at (kar′ət) *n.* **1.** unit of weight for gems. **2.** karat.

car·a·van (kar′ə van′) *n.* group traveling together, esp. over deserts.

car·a·way (kar′ə wā′) *n.* herb bearing aromatic seeds.

car·bide (kär′bīd) *n.* carbon compound.

car·bine (kär′bēn, -bīn) *n.* short rifle.

car·bo·hy·drate (kär′bō hī′drāt, -bə-) *n.* organic compound group including starches and sugars.

car·bol·ic acid (kär bol′ik) brown germicidal liquid.

car·bon (kär′bən) *n.* chemical element occurring as diamonds, charcoal, etc. —**car·bon·if′er·ous,** *adj.*

car·bon·ate (kär′bə nāt′) *v.*, **-ated**, **-ating.** charge with carbon dioxide.

carbon dioxide, chemical compound of carbon and oxygen: a gas produced esp. by animal respiration.

carbon monoxide, chemical compound of carbon and oxygen: a poisonous gas produced esp. by automobile engines.

carbon paper, paper coated with a carbon pigment, used to make copies.

car·bun·cle (kär′bung kəl) *n.* painful inflammation under skin.

car·bu·re·tor (kär′bə rā′tər, -byə-) *n.* mechanism that mixes gasoline and air in motor.

car·cass (kär′kəs) *n.* dead body of an animal.

car·cin·o·gen (kär sin′ə jən) *n.* cancer-producing substance. —**car·cin·o·gen′ic** (-sə na jen′ik) *adj.*

car·ci·no·ma (kär′sə nō′mə) *n., pl.* **-mas, -mata.** malignant tumor.

card (kärd) *n.* **1.** piece of stiff paper, with one's name (**calling card**), marks for game purposes (**playing card**), etc. **2.** comb for wool, flax, etc. —*v.* **3.** dress (wool, etc.) with card. **4.** ask for proof of age.

card′board′, *n.* **1.** thin, stiff pasteboard. —*adj.* **2.** flimsy. **3.** seeming real.

car·di·ac′ (kär′dē ak′) *adj.* of the heart.

cardiac arrest, abrupt stopping of the heartbeat.

car·di·gan (kär′di gən) *n.* sweater that buttons down the front.

car·di·nal (kär′dn l) *adj.* **1.** main; chief. **2.** (of numbers) used to express quantities or positions in series, e.g., 3, 15, 45. **3.** deep red. —*n.* **4.** red bird. **5.** high official of Roman Catholic Church.

cardio-, prefix meaning heart, as *cardiology.*

car·di·o·graph (kär′dē ə graf′) *n.* instrument for recording movements of heart. —**car′di·o·gram′,** *n.*

car·di·ol·o·gy (-ol′ə jē) *n.* study of the heart and its functions.

car·di·o·pul·mo·nar·y (kär′dē ō-) *adj.* of the heart and lungs.

car·di·o·vas·cu·lar, *adj.* of the heart and blood vessels.

card′sharp′, *n.* person who cheats at card games. Also, **card shark.**

care (kâr) *n., v.,* **cared, caring.** —*n.* **1.** worry. **2.** caution. —*v.* **3.** be concerned. —**care′free′,** *adj.*

ca·reen′ (kə rēn′) *v.* tip; sway.

ca·reer′ (kə rēr′) *n.* **1.** profession followed as one's lifework. **2.** course through life. **3.** speed. —*v.* **4.** speed.

care′ful, *adj.* **1.** cautious. **2.** exact. —**care′ful·ly,** *adv.*

care′giv′er, *n.* person who cares for a child or an invalid.

care′less, *adj.* **1.** not paying attention. **2.** not accurate.

ca·ress′ (kə res′) *v., n.* touch in expressing affection.

car′et (kar′it) *n.* insertion mark (^).

care′tak′er (kâr′-) *n.* **1.** maintenance person. **2.** caregiver.

car′fare′ (kär′fâr′) *n.* cost of ride.

car·go (kär′gō) n., pl. **-goes, -gos**. goods carried by vessel.

car·i·bou (kar′ə bōō′) n. North American reindeer.

car·i·ca·ture (kar′i kə chər) n. mocking portrait. —**car·i·ca·ture**, v., **-tured, -turing.**

car·ies (kâr′ēz) n., pl. **-ies**. tooth decay.

car·il·lon (kar′ə lon′, -lən) n. musical bells.

car/jack·ing (kär′jak′ing) n. theft of car by force. —**car/jack·er**, n.

car·mine (-min) n., adj. crimson or purplish red.

car·nage (-nij) n. massacre.

car·nal (-nl) adj. of the body.

car·na·tion (kär nā′shən) n. common fragrant flower.

car·ni·val (kär′nə vəl) n. 1. amusement fair. 2. festival before Lent.

car·ni·vore (-vôr′) n. flesh-eating mammal. —**car·niv·o·rous** (-niv′ə rəs) adj.

car·ob (kar′əb) n. 1. tree bearing long pods. 2. pulp from the pods, used as chocolate substitute.

car·ol (kar′əl) n., v., **-oled, -oling.** —n. 1. Christmas song. —v. 2. sing joyously. —**car·ol·er**, n.

car·om (kar′əm) v. 1. hit and rebound. —n. 2. rebound.

ca·rot·id (kə rot′id) n. either of two large arteries in the neck.

ca·rouse (kə rouz′) n., v., **-roused, -rousing.** —n. 1. noisy or drunken feast. —v. 2. engage in a carouse.

carp (kärp) v. 1. find fault. —n. 2. large fresh-water fish.

car·pal (kär′pəl) adj. 1. of the carpus. —n. 2. wrist bone.

carpal tunnel syndrome, chronic wrist pain associated esp. with repetitive movements, as at a keyboard.

car·pel (kär′pəl) n. seed-bearing leaf.

car·pen·ter (-pən tər) n. builder in wood. —**car·pen·try**, n.

car·pet (-pit) n. 1. fabric covering for floors. —v. 2. cover with carpet.

car·pool′, n. 1. group of automobile owners who take turns to drive, for example, to work. —v. 2. participate in a carpool.

car·port′, n. roof that provides shelter for a car.

car·pus (kär′pəs) n., pl. **-pi** (pī). 1. wrist. 2. wrist bones as a group.

car·rel (kar′əl) n. small study space in a library. Also, **car/rell.**

car·riage (-ij) n. 1. wheeled vehicle. 2. posture. 3. conveyance.

car·ri·on (-ē ən) n. dead flesh.

car·rot (-ət) n. orange root vegetable.

car·rou·sel′ (kar′ə sel′) n. merry-go-round.

car·ry (kar′ē) v., **-ried, -rying. 1.** transport. 2. support; bear. 3. behave. 4. win. 5. extend. 6. have in stock. 7. carry out, accomplish.

car/ry-out′, adj., n. takeout.

car·sick′ (kär′-) adj. nauseated and dizzy from car travel.

cart (kärt) n. small wagon.

carte blanche (kärt′ blänch′, blänsh′) unconditional authority.

car·tel′ (kär tel′) n. syndicate controlling prices and production.

car/ti·lage (kär′tl ij) n. flexible connective body tissue.

car·tog/ra·phy (kär tog′rə fē) n. map production.

car·ton (kär′tn) n. cardboard box.

car·toon′ (kär tōōn′) n. 1. comic drawing. 2. design for large art work. —**car·toon′ist**, n.

car·tridge (kär′trij) n. 1. case containing bullet and explosive. 2. container with frequently replaced machine parts.

cart/wheel′, n. 1. sideways handspring. —v. 2. roll forward end over end.

carve (kärv) v., **carved, carving.** cut into shape. —**carv′er**, n.

cas·cade′ (kas kād′) n. waterfall.

case (kās), n., v., **cased, casing.** —n. 1. example. 2. situation. 3. event. 4. statement of arguments. 5. medical patient. 6. lawsuit. 7. category in inflection of nouns, adjectives, and pronouns. **8. in case,** if. **9.** container. —v. **10.** put in case.

ca·sein (kā′sēn) n. protein derived from milk, used in making cheese.

case/ment (kās′mənt) n. hinged window.

cash (kash) n. 1. money. —v. 2. give or get cash for.

cash/ew (kash′ōō, kə shōō′) n. small curved nut.

cash·ier′ (ka shēr′) n. 1. person in charge of money. —v. 2. dismiss in disgrace.

cash/mere (kazh′mēr, kash′-) n. soft wool fabric.

cas/ing (kā′sing) n. 1. outer covering. 2. framework, as of a door.

ca·si·no (kə sē′nō) n., pl. **-nos.** amusement or gambling hall.

cask (kask) n. 1. barrel for liquids.

cas/ket (kas′kit) n. coffin.

cas·sa·va (kə sä′və) n. tropical plant with starchy roots.

cas/se·role′ (kas′ə rōl′) n. covered baking dish.

cas·sette′ (kə set′) n. compact case that holds film or recording tape.

cas·sock (kas´ək) n. long ecclesiastical vestment.

cast (kast) v., **cast, casting.** —n. **1.** throw. **2.** deposit (vote). **3.** pour and mold. —n. **4.** act of casting. **5.** actors in play. **6.** form; mold. **7.** rigid surgical dressing. **8.** tinge.

cas·ta·net´ (kas´tə net´) n. pieces of shell, etc., held in the palm and struck together.

cast´a·way´, n. shipwrecked person.

caste (kast) n. hereditary social division of Hindu society.

cast´er, n. small swivel-mounted wheel. Also, **cast´or.**

cas´ti·gate´ (kas´ti gāt´) v., **-gated, -gating.** scold severely. —**cas´ti·ga´tion**, n.

cast iron, hard, brittle alloy of carbon, iron, and silicon.

cas·tle (kas´əl) n., v., **-tled, -tling.** —n. **1.** royal or noble residence, usually fortified. **2.** chess piece; rook. —v. **3.** Chess. transpose rook and king.

cas´tor oil (kas´tər) cathartic oil.

cas·trate (kas´trāt) v., **-trated, -trating.** remove testicles of.

cas´u·al (kazh´ōō əl) adj. **1.** accidental; not planned. **2.** not caring.

cas´u·al·ty, n., pl. **-ties.** **1.** person injurious to person. **2.** soldier missing in action, killed, wounded, or captured.

cas´u·ist·ry, n., pl. **-ries.** adroit, specious argument. —**cas´u·ist**, n.

cat (kat) n. common domestic animal. —**cat´like´**, adj.

cat´a·clysm´ (kat´ə kliz´əm) n. upheaval. —**cat´a·clys´mic**, adj.

cat´a·comb´ (-kōm´) n. underground cemetery.

cat´a·logue´ (kat´l ôg´) n., v., **-logued, -loguing.** —n. **1.** organized list. —v. **2.** enter in catalogue. Also, **cat´a·log´.**

ca·tal´pa (kə tal´pə) n. tree with bell-shaped white flowers.

cat´a·lyst (kat´l ist) n. **1.** substance that causes a chemical reaction without itself being affected. **2.** anything that precipitates an event.

cat´a·ma·ran´ (kat´ə mə ran´) n. two-hulled boat.

cat´a·mount´, n. cougar.

cat´a·pult´ (-pult´, -pŏŏlt´) n. **1.** device for hurling or launching. —v. **2.** hurl.

cat´a·ract´ (-rakt´) n. **1.** waterfall. **2.** opacity of eye lens.

ca·tarrh´ (kə tär´) n. **1.** inflammation of respiratory mucous membranes.

ca·tas´tro·phe (kə tas´trə fē) n. great disaster. —**cat´a·stroph´ic** (kat´ə strof´ik) adj.

cat´bird´, n. songbird with catlike call.

cat´call´, n. jeer.

catch (kach) v., **caught** (kôt), **catching**, n. —v. **1.** capture. **2.** trap or surprise. **3.** hit. **4.** seize and hold. **5.** be in time for. **6.** get or contract. **7.** be entangled. —n. **8.** act of catching. **9.** thing that catches. **10.** thing caught. **11.** snag.

Catch-22 (kach´twen´tē tōō´) n. frustrating situation involving contradictions.

catch´ing, adj. contagious.

catch´up, n. ketchup.

catch´word´, n. slogan.

catch´y, adj., **-ier, -iest.** memorable and pleasing.

cat´e·chism (kat´i kiz´əm) n. set of questions and answers on religious principles.

cat´e·gor´i·cal (-gôr´i kəl) adj. unconditional.

cat´e·go·ry (-gôr´ē) n., pl. **-ries.** division; class. —**cat´e·go·rize´** (-gə rīz´) v., **-rized, -rizing.**

ca´ter (kā´tər) v. **1.** provide food, etc. **2.** make special effort to provide what is needed. —**ca´ter·er**, n.

cat´er·cor´nered (kat´i-, katē´-, kat´ər-) adj. **1.** diagonal. —adv. **2.** diagonally.

cat´er·pil´lar (kat´ə pil´ər) n. **1.** wormlike larva of butterfly. **2.** type of tractor.

cat´er·waul´ (kat´ər wôl´) v. **1.** utter long wails, as cats in rut. —n. **2.** such a wail.

cat´fish´, n. fresh-water fish.

cat´gut´, n. string made from animal intestine.

ca·thar´sis (kə thär´sis) n. **1.** purging of emotions, as through art. **2.** evacuation of bowels.

ca·thar´tic, adj. **1.** effecting a catharsis. **2.** evacuating the bowels. —n. **3.** medicine doing this.

ca·the´dral (kə thē´drəl) n. main church of diocese.

cath´e·ter (kath´i tər) n. tube inserted into a body passage.

cath´ode (kath´ōd) n. **1.** electrode with negative charge. **2.** positive terminal of a battery.

cathode ray, beam of electrons coming from a cathode.

cathode-ray tube, vacuum tube generating cathode rays directed at screen, used to display images on receiver or monitor. Abbr.: CRT.

Cath´o·lic (kath´ə lik) adj. **1.** of Roman Catholic Church. **2.** (l.c.) universal. —n. **3.** member of Roman Catholic Church. —**Ca·thol´i·cism** (kə thol´ə siz´əm) n.

cat′kin (kat′kin) *n.* spike of bunched small flowers.

cat′nap′, *n.* **1.** short, light sleep. —*v.* **2.** sleep briefly.

cat′nip, *n.* plant with scented leaves.

CAT scan (kat) **1.** examination using x-rays at various angles to show cross section of body. **2.** image produced by CAT scan. —**CAT scanner** *n.*

cat′s′-paw′, *n.* person exploited by another.

cat′sup (kat′səp, kech′əp, kach′-) *n.* ketchup.

cat′tail′, *n.* tall spiky marsh plant.

cat′tle (kat′l) *n.* livestock.

cat′ty (kat′ē) *adj.,* **-tier, -tiest.** maliciously gossiping.

cat′walk′, *n.* narrow walkway.

Cau·ca′sian (kô kā′zhən) *adj.* **1.** of or characteristic of one of the racial divisions of humankind, marked by minimum skin pigmentation. —*n.* **2.** Caucasian person.

cau′cus (kô′kəs) *n.* political meeting.

caul′dron (kôl′drən) *n.* large kettle.

cau′li·flow′er (kô′lə flou′ər) *n.* plant with an edible head.

caulk (kôk) *v.* **1.** close seams of to keep water or air out. —*n.* **2.** Also, **caulk′ing.** material used to caulk.

cause (kôz) *n., v.,* **caused, causing.** —*n.* **1.** person or thing producing an effect. **2.** reason. **3.** aim; purpose. —*v.* **4.** bring about; produce. —**caus′al,** *adj.* —**cau·sa′tion,** *n.*

cause cé·lè·bres (kôz′ sə leb′) *n., pl.* **causes cé·lè·bres** (kôz′ sə leb′) controversy attracting attention.

cause′way′, *n.* raised road.

caus′tic (kô′stik) *adj.,* **1.** corroding. **2.** sharply critical.

cau′ter·ize′ (kô′tə rīz′) *v.,* **-ized, -izing.** burn. —**cau′ter·y,** *n.*

cau′tion (kô′shən) *n.* **1.** carefulness. **2.** warning. —*v.* **3.** warn. —**cau′tious,** *adj.*

cav′al·cade′ (kav′əl kād′) *n.* procession, esp. on horseback.

cav′a·lier′ (kav′ə lēr′) *n.* **1.** knight or horseman. **2.** courtly gentleman. —*adj.* **3.** haughty; indifferent. **4.** offhand.

cav′al·ry (kav′əl rē) *n., pl.* **-ries.** troops on horseback or in armored vehicles. —**cav′al·ry·man,** *n.*

cave (kāv) *n., v.,* **caved, caving.** —*n.* **1.** hollow space in the earth. —*v.* **2.** fall or sink.

cave man, **1.** Stone Age cave dweller. **2.** rough, brutal man.

cav′ern (kav′ərn) *n.* large cave.

cav′i·ar′ (-ē är′) *n.* roe of sturgeon, etc., eaten as a delicacy.

cav′il (-əl) *v.,* **-iled, -iling,** *n.* —*v.* **1.** find trivial faults. —*n.* **2.** trivial objection.

cav′i·ty (-i tē) *n., pl.* **-ties.** hollow.

ca·vort′ (kə vôrt′) *v.* prance about.

caw (kô) *n.* **1.** harsh call of a crow. —*v.* **2.** make a caw.

cay·enne′ (kī en′) *n.* hot pepper.

CB, citizens band: private two-way radio.

cc, **1.** carbon copy. **2.** cubic centimeter.

CCU, coronary-care unit.

CD, **1.** certificate of deposit. **2.** Civil Defense. **3.** compact disc.

CD-ROM (sē′dē′rom′) *n.* compact disc for storing digitized read-only data.

cease (sēs) *v.,* **ceased, ceasing.** stop; end. —**cease′less,** *adj.*

cease′-fire′, *n.* truce.

ce′dar (sē′dər) *n.* coniferous tree.

cede (sēd) *v.,* **ceded, ceding.** yield or give up.

ceil′ing (sē′ling) *n.* **1.** upper surface of room. **2.** maximum altitude.

cel′e·brate′ (sel′ə brāt′) *v.,* **-brated, -brating.** **1.** commemorate. **2.** act rejoicingly. **3.** perform ritually. **4.** extol. —**cel′e·bra′tion,** *n.*

ce·leb′ri·ty (sə leb′ri tē) *n., pl.* **-ties.** **1.** famous person. **2.** fame.

ce·ler′i·ty (sə ler′i tē) *n.* speed.

cel′er·y (sel′ə rē) *n.* plant with edible leaf stalks.

ce·les′tial (sə les′chəl) *adj.* of heaven or the sky.

cel′i·ba·cy (sel′ə bə sē) *n.* **1.** unmarried state. **2.** sexual abstinence.

cell (sel) *n.* **1.** a small room. **2.** microscopic biological structure. **3.** electric battery. **4.** organizational unit. —**cel′lu·lar,** *adj.*

cel′lar (sel′ər) *n.* basement.

cel′lo (chel′ō) *n., pl.* **-los.** large violinlike instrument. —**cel′list,** *n.*

cel′lo·phane′ (sel′ə fān′) *n.* transparent wrapping material.

cellular phone, mobile telephone. Also, **cell phone.**

cel′lu·lite′ (sel′yə līt′, -lēt′) *n.* lumpy fat deposits, esp. in thighs.

cel′lu·loid′ (-loid′) *n.* hard, flammable substance.

cel′lu·lose′ (-lōs′) *n.* carbohydrate of plant origin.

Cel′si·us (sel′sē əs) *n.* temperature scale in which water freezes at 0° and boils at 100°.

ce·ment′ (si ment′) *n.* **1.** clay-lime mixture that hardens into stonelike mass. **2.** binding material. —*v.* **3.** treat with cement. **4.** unite.

cem′e·ter′y (sem′i ter′ē) *n., pl.* **-ter·ies.** burial ground.

cen'o·taph' (sen'ə taf') *n.* monument for one buried elsewhere.

Ce'no·zo'ic (sē'nə zō'ik) *adj.* of the present geologic era.

cen'ser (sen'sər) *n.* incense burner.

cen'sor (sen'sər) *n.* 1. person eliminating undesirable words, pictures, etc. —*v.* 2. deal with as a censor. —**cen'sor·ship'**, *n.*

cen·so'ri·ous (-sôr'ē əs) *adj.* severely critical.

cen'sure (-shər) *n.*, *v.*, **-sured**, **-suring.** —*n.* 1. disapproval. —*v.* 2. rebuke.

cen'sus (sen'səs) *n.* count of inhabitants.

cent (sent) *n.* $\frac{1}{100}$ of a dollar; penny. **cent.,** century.

cen'taur (sen'tôr) *n.* mythological creature, half horse and half man.

cen·ten'ar·y (sen ten'ə rē, sen'tn-er'ē) *n.*, *pl.* **-aries.** 100th anniversary.

cen·ten'ni·al (-ten'ē əl) *n.* 1. 100th anniversary. —*adj.* 2. of 100 years.

cen'ter (sen'tər) *n.* 1. middle point, part, or person. —*v.* 2. place or gather at center. 3. concentrate. Also, **cen'tre.**

cen'ter·fold', *n.* page that folds out from magazine center.

cen'ter·piece', *n.* decoration for center of table.

cen'ti·grade' (sen'ti grād') *adj.* Celsius.

cen'ti·gram', *n.* $\frac{1}{100}$ of gram.

cen'ti·li'ter (-lē'tər) *n.* $\frac{1}{100}$ of liter.

cen'ti·me'ter, *n.* $\frac{1}{100}$ of meter.

cen'ti·pede' (-pēd') *n.* insect with many legs.

cen'tral (sen'trəl) *adj.* 1. of or at center. 2. main. —**cen'tral·ly**, *adv.*

cen'tral·ize', *v.*, **-ized**, **-izing.** 1. gather at a center. 2. concentrate control of. —**cen'tral·i·za'tion**, *n.*

cen·trif'u·gal (-trif'yə gal, -ə gal) *adj.* moving away from center.

cen'tri·fuge' (-fyōoj') *n.* high-speed rotating apparatus for separating substances of different densities.

cen'trist (sen'trist) *n.* 1. person with political views that are not extreme. —*adj.* 2. of views that are not extreme.

cen'tu·ry (sen'chə rē) *n.*, *pl.* **-ries.** period of one hundred years.

CEO, chief executive officer.

ce·ram'ic (sə ram'ik) *adj.* of clay and similar materials. —**ce·ram'ics**, *n.*

ce're·al (sēr'ē əl) *n.* 1. plant yielding edible grain. 2. food from such grain.

cer'e·bel'lum (ser'ə bel'əm) *n.* rear part of brain.

ce·re'bral (ser'ə brəl, sə rē'-) *adj.* 1. of brain. 2. intellectual.

cerebral palsy, paralysis due to brain injury.

cer'e·brum (sə rē'brəm, ser'ə-) *n.*, *pl.* **-brums, -bra** (-brə). front, upper part of brain.

cer'e·mo'ny (ser'ə mō'nē) *n.*, *pl.* **-nies.** formal act or ritual.

ce·rise' (sə rēs', -rēz') *adj.*, *n.* medium to deep red.

cer'tain (sûr'tn) *adj.* 1. without doubt; sure. 2. agreed upon. 3. definite but unspecified. —**cer'tain·ly**, *adv.* —**cer'tain·ty**, *n.*

cer·tif'i·cate (sər tif'i kit) *n.* document of proof.

cer'ti·fy' (sûr'tə fī') *v.*, **-fied**, **-fying.** 1. guarantee as certain. 2. vouch for in writing. —**cer·tif'i·ca'tion**, *n.*

cer'ti·tude' (-tōod', -tyōod') *n.* sureness.

ce·ru'le·an (sə rōo'lē ən) *adj.* deep blue.

cer'vix (sûr'viks) *n.*, *pl.* **cer·vixes, cer'vices** (sûr'və sēz', sər vī'sēz). necklike part, esp. lower end of uterus. —**cer'vi·cal** (-vi kəl) *adj.*

Ce·sar'e·an (si zâr'ē ən) *n.* delivery of baby by cutting through abdomen and uterus. Also, **Cesarean section, C-section, Cae·sar'e·an.**

ces·sa'tion (se sā'shən) *n.* stop.

ces'sion (sesh'ən) *n.* ceding.

cess'pool' (ses'pōol') *n.* receptacle for waste, etc., from house.

cf., compare.

cg., centigram.

ch., 1. chapter. 2. church.

Cha·blis' (sha blē') *n.* dry white wine. Also, **cha·blis'.**

chafe (chāf) *v.*, **chafed, chafing.** make sore by rubbing.

chaff (chaf) *n.* 1. grain husks. 2. worthless matter. —*v.* 3. tease.

chafing dish (chā'fing) device for warming food at table.

cha·grin' (sha grin') *n.* 1. shame or disappointment. —*v.* 2. cause chagrin to.

chain (chān) *n.* 1. connected series of links. 2. any series. 3. mountain range. —*v.* 4. fasten with chain.

chain reaction, process which automatically continues and spreads.

chain saw, power saw with teeth set on endless chain.

chair (châr) *n.* 1. seat with a back and legs. 2. position of authority. 3. chairperson. —*v.* 4. preside over.

chair'man, *n.*, *pl.* **-men.** presiding officer. Also, *fem.*, **chair'wom'an;** *masc. or fem.*, **chair'per'son.**

chaise longue (shāz' lông') type of couch.

cha·let' (sha lā') n. mountain house.

chal'ice (chal'is) n. cup for ritual wine.

chalk (chôk) n. 1. soft limestone used to write on chalkboards. —v. 2. mark with chalk. —**chalk'board'**, n.

chal·lenge (chal'inj) n., v., **-lenged, -lenging.** —n. 1. call to fight, contest, etc. 2. demand for identification. 3. objection to juror. —v. 4. make challenge to.

cham·ber (chām'bar) n. 1. room, esp. bedroom. 2. assembly hall. 3. legislative body. 4. space in gun for ammunition.

cham'ber·maid', n. maid who cleans bedrooms.

chamber music, music for performance by a small ensemble in a room or parlor.

cha·me·le·on (ka mē'lē an) n. lizard able to change color.

cham·ois (sham'ē) n. 1. European antelope. 2. soft leather from its skin.

cham'o·mile' (kam'ə mīl', -mēl') n. plant whose flowers are used as a tea. Also, **cam'o·mile'.**

champ¹ (champ). 1. Informal. champion. —v. (chomp, champ). 2. bite.

cham·pagne' (sham pān') n. sparkling white wine.

cham·pi·on (cham'pē an) n. 1. best competitor. 2. supporter. —v. 3. advocate. —adj. 4. best. —**cham'pi·on·ship'**, n.

chance (chans) n., v., **chanced, chancing,** adj. —n. 1. fate; luck. 2. possibility. 3. opportunity. 4. risk. —v. 5. occur by chance. 6. risk. —adj. 7. accidental.

chan·cel (chan'sal) n. space around church altar.

chan·cel·ler·y (-sə lə rē, -səl rē) n., pl. **-leries.** offices of chancellor.

chan·cel·lor (-lər) n. 1. high government official. 2. university head.

chan·cre (shang'kər) n., lesion, as of syphilis.

chanc'y (chan'sē) adj., **-cier, -ciest,** risky; uncertain.

chan·de·lier' (shan'dl ēr') n. hanging lighting fixture.

change (chānj) v., **changed, changing,** n. —v. 1. alter in condition, etc. 2. substitute for. 3. put on other clothes. —n. 4. alteration. 5. substitution. 6. novelty. 7. coins of low value. —**change'a·ble,** adj.

change of life, menopause.

change'o'ver, n. change from one system to another.

chan'nel (chan'l) n., v., **-neled, -neling.** —n. 1. bed of stream. 2. wide strait. 3. access; route. 4. broadcast frequency band. —v. 5. convey or direct in channel.

chant (chant) n. 1. song; psalm. —v. 2. sing, esp. slowly.

chant'ey (shan'tē) n., pl. **-eys, -ies.** sailors' song. Also, **chant'y.**

Cha'nu·kah (к҂ä'nə kə, hä'-) n. Hanukkah.

cha'os (kā'os) n. utter disorder. —**cha·ot'ic** (-ot'ik) adj.

chap (chap) v., **chapped, chapping,** n. —v. 1. roughen and redden. —n. 2. Informal. fellow.

chap., chapter.

chap·el (chap'əl) n. small church.

chap·er·on' (shap'ə rōn') n., v., **-oned, -oning.** —n. 1. escort of young unmarried woman for propriety. —v. 2. be a chaperon for or to. Also, **chap'er·one'.**

chap·lain (chap'lin) n. institutional clergyman.

chaps (chaps, shaps) n.pl. leather leg protectors worn by cowboys.

chap·ter (chap'tər) n. 1. division of book. 2. branch of society.

char (chär) v., **charred, charring.** burn slightly.

char·ac·ter (kar'ik tər) n. 1. personal nature. 2. reputation. 3. person in fiction. 4. written or printed symbol.

char·ac·ter·is·tic (-tə ris'tik) adj. 1. typical. —n. 2. special feature; trait.

char·ac·ter·ize' (-, -ized, -izing.** 1. distinguish. 2. describe. —**char'ac·ter·i·za'tion,** n.

char·ades' (shə rädz') n.pl. miming game.

char'broil' (chär'-) v. broil over charcoal fire.

char'coal', n. carbonized wood.

chard (chärd) n. plant with edible green leafy stalks.

Char·don·nay' (shär'dn ā') n. dry white wine.

charge (chärj) v., **charged, charging,** n. —v. 1. load or fill. 2. put electricity through or into. 3. command. 4. accuse. 5. ask payment of. 6. attack. —n. 7. load. 8. unit of explosive. 9. care. 10. command. 11. accusation. 12. expense. 13. price. 14. attack. —**charge'a·ble,** adj.

charg'er, n. battle horse.

char'i·ot (char'ē ət) n. ancient two-wheeled carriage. —**char'i·ot·eer',** n.

cha·ris'ma (kə riz'mə) n. power to charm and inspire people. —**char'is·mat'ic** (kar'iz mat'ik) adj.

char'i·ty (char'i tē) n., pl. **-ties.** 1.

aid to needy persons. **2.** benevolent institution. —**char′i•ta•ble,** adj.

char′la•tan (shär′lə tn) n. fraud.

charm (chärm) n. **1.** power to attract and please. **2.** magical object, verse, etc. —v. **3.** attract; enchant. —**charm′er,** n. —**charm′ing,** adj.

char′nel house (chär′nl) place for dead bodies.

chart (chärt) n. **1.** map. —v. **2.** make a chart of.

char′ter, n. **1.** document authorizing new corporation. —v. **2.** establish by charter. **3.** hire; lease.

char•treuse′ (shär trōōz′) adj., n. yellowish green.

char′wom•an (chär′-) n. woman who cleans floors, houses, etc.

char′y (châr′ē) adj., **charier, chariest.** careful.

chase (chās) v., **chased, chasing,** n. —v. **1.** go after. **2.** drive away. —n. **3.** instance of chasing.

chasm (kaz′əm) n. deep cleft in earth.

chas′sis (chas′ē, shas′ē) n. frame, wheels, and motor of vehicle.

chaste (chāst) adj., **chaster, chastest. 1.** virtuous. **2.** simple. —**chas′ti•ty** (chas′ti tē) n.

chas′ten (chā′sən) v. discipline.

chas•tise′ (chas tīz′) v., **-tised, -tising.** punish; beat.

chat (chat) v., **chatted, chatting,** n. —v. **1.** talk informally. —n. **2.** informal talk.

cha•teau′ (sha tō′) n., pl. **-teaux** (-tōz′). stately residence, esp. in France.

chat′tel (chat′l) n. article of property other than real estate.

chat′ter (chat′ər) v. **1.** talk rapidly or foolishly. **2.** click or rattle rapidly. —n. **3.** rapid or foolish talk.

chat′ter•box′, n. talkative person.

chat′ty (chat′ē) adj., **-tier, -tiest.** loquacious.

chauf′feur (shō′fər, shō fûr′) n. hired driver.

chau′vin•ism′ (shō′və niz′əm) n. **1.** blind patriotism. **2.** fanatic devotion to one's race, gender, etc. —**chau′vin•ist** (-və nist) n., adj.

cheap (chēp) adj. of low price or value. —**cheap′en,** v.

cheap′skate′, n. stingy person.

cheat (chēt) v. **1.** defraud; deceive. —n. **2.** fraud. **3.** one who defrauds.

check (chek) v. **1.** stop or restrain. **2.** investigate; verify. **3.** note with a mark. **4.** leave or receive for temporary custody. —n. **5.** stop; restraint. **6.** written order for bank to pay money. **7.** bill. **8.** identification tag. **9.** square pattern. **10.** Chess. direct attack on king.

check′er, n. **1.** piece used in checkers. **2.** (pl.) game played by two persons, each with 12 pieces.

check′er•board′, n. board with 64 squares on which checkers is played.

check′ered, adj. **1.** marked with squares. **2.** varied. **3.** dubious.

check′list′, n. list of items for comparison, verification, etc.

check′mate′ (-māt′) n., v., **-mated, -mating.** Chess. —n. **1.** inescapable check. —v. **2.** put into inescapable check.

check′out′, n. **1.** act of leaving and paying for hotel room. **2.** counter where customers pay for purchases.

check′point′, n. place, as at a border, where travelers are checked.

check′up′, n. physical examination.

ched′dar (ched′ər) n. sharp cheese.

cheek (chēk) n. **1.** soft side of face. **2.** Informal. impudence. —**cheek′i•ly,** adv. —**cheek′y,** adj.

cheer (chēr) n. **1.** shout of support. **2.** gladness. —v. **3.** shout encouragement to. **4.** gladden. —**cheer′ful,** adj. —**cheer′less,** adj. —**cheer′y,** adj.

cheese (chēz) n. solid, edible product from milk.

cheese′burg′er, n. hamburger with melted cheese.

cheese′cloth′, n. open cotton fabric.

chee′tah (chē′tə) n. wild cat resembling leopard.

chef (shef) n. professional cook.

chem′i•cal (kem′i kəl) adj. **1.** of chemistry. —n. **2.** substance in chemistry. —**chem′i•cal•ly,** adv.

chemical warfare, warfare with the use of chemicals.

che•mise′ (sha mēz′) n. woman's undershirt.

chem′is•try (kem′ə strē) n. science of composition of substances. —**chem′ist,** n.

che′mo•ther′a•py (kē′mō ther′ə pē) n. treatment of disease, esp. cancer, with chemicals.

cheque (chek) n. Brit. bank check.

cher′ish (cher′ish) v. treat as dear.

Cher′o•kee′ (cher′ə kē′) n., pl. **-kee, -kees.** member of an American Indian people.

cher′ry (cher′ē) n., pl. **-ries.** small red fruit of certain trees.

cher′ub (cher′əb) n. **1.** pl. **-ubim** (-ə bim). celestial being. **2.** pl. **-ubs.** angelic child.

chess (ches) n. board game for two, each using 16 pieces.

chest (chest) n. **1.** part of body between neck and abdomen. **2.** large box.

chest′nut′ (ches′nut′) *n.* **1.** edible nut. **2.** reddish brown.

chev′i·ot (shev′ē ət) *n.* sturdy worsted fabric.

chev′ron (shev′rən) *n.* set of stripes indicating military rank.

chew (chŏŏ) *v.* crush with teeth.

chew′y, *adj.,* **-ier, -iest.** not easily chewed.

Chey·enne′ (shī en′, -an′) *n., pl.* **-enne, -ennes.** member of an American Indian people.

Chi·an′ti (kē än′tē) *n.* dry red wine.

chic (shēk) *adj.* stylish.
—**Pronunciation.** The pronunciation (chik) for the word CHIC is considered nonstandard except when used jokingly.

chi·can′er·y (shi kā′nə rē, chi-) *n., pl.* **-ies.** deception; trick.

Chi·ca′no (chi kä′nō) *n., pl.* **-nos.** Mexican-American. Also, *n.fem.,* **Chi·ca′na.**

chick (chik) *n.* **1.** young chicken. **2.** *Slang.* young woman.

chick′a·dee′ (chik′ə dē′) *n.* small gray North American bird.

Chick′a·saw′ (chik′ə sô′) *n., pl.* **-saw, -saws.** member of an American Indian people.

chick′en (chik′ən) *n.* common domestic fowl.

chicken pox, viral disease marked by eruption of blisters.

chick′pea′ *n.* **1.** legume with pea-like seeds. **2.** its seed.

chic′o·ry (-ə rē) *n., pl.* **-ries.** plant with edible leaves and root.

chide (chīd) *v.,* **chided, chiding.** scold. —**chid′er,** *n.*

chief (chēf) *n.* **1.** leader. —*adj.* **2.** main; principal. —**chief′ly,** *adv.*

chief′tain (-tən) *n.* leader.

chif·fon′ (shi fon′) *n.* sheer silk or rayon fabric.

chif′fo·nier′ (shif′ə nēr′) *n.* tall chest of drawers.

chig′ger (chig′ər) *n.* larva of certain mites.

chil′blains′ (chil′blānz′) *n.pl.* inflammation caused by overexposure to cold, etc.

child (chīld) *n., pl.* **children** (chil′drən). **1.** baby. **2.** son or daughter. —**child′bear′ing,** *n., adj.* —**child′birth,** *n.* —**child′hood,** *n.* —**child′ish,** *adj.* —**child′less,** *adj.* —**child′like,** *adj.*

child′proof′, *adj.* designed to prevent child from being hurt.

chil′i (chil′ē) *n., pl.* **-ies.** pungent pod of a red pepper. **2.** dish made with these peppers. Also, **chil′e.**

chill (chil) *n.* **1.** coldness. —*adj.* **2.** cold. **3.** not cordial. —*v.* **4.** make or become cool. —**chill′ly,** *adv.*

chime (chīm) *n., v.,* **chimed, chiming.** —*n.* **1.** set of musical tubes, bells, etc. —*v.* **2.** sound harmoniously.

chi·me′ra (ki mēr′ə, kī-) *n.* **1.** (*often cap.*) mythical monster with lion's head, goat's body, and serpent's tail. **2.** dream.

chim′ney (chim′nē) *n.* passage for smoke.

chim·pan·zee′ (chim′pan zē′, chim pan′zē) *n.* large, intelligent African ape.

chin (chin) *n.* part of face below mouth.

chi′na (chī′nə) *n.* ceramic ware.

chin·chil′la (chin chil′ə) *n.* small rodent valued for its fur.

Chi·nese′ (chī nēz′, -nēs′) *n., pl.* **-nese.** native or language of China.

chink (chingk) *n.* **1.** crack. **2.** short ringing sound. —*v.* **3.** make such a sound.

Chi·nook′ (shi nŏŏk′, -nŏŏk′, chi-) *n., pl.* **-nook** or **nooks.** member of an American Indian people.

chintz (chints) *n.* printed cotton.

chintz′y, *adj.,* **-ier, -iest.** cheap-looking.

chip (chip) *n., v.,* **chipped, chipping.** —*n.* **1.** small flat piece. **2.** broken place. **3.** small plate carrying electric circuit. —*v.* **4.** cut or break off (bits). **5. chip in,** contribute.

chip′munk (-mungk) *n.* small striped rodent resembling squirrel.

chip′per, *adj. Informal.* lively.

chi·rop′o·dy (ki rop′ə dē, kī-) *n.* treatment of foot ailments.

chi′ro·prac′tor (kī′rə prak′tər) *n.* one who practices therapy based upon adjusting body structures.

chirp (chûrp) *n.* **1.** short, sharp sound of birds, etc. —*v.* **2.** make such sound. Also, **chir′rup** (chēr′əp, chûrp′).

chis′el (chiz′əl) *n.* **1.** tool with broad cutting tip. —*v.* **2.** cut with such tool. **3.** *Informal.* cheat.

chit′chat′ (chit′chat′) *n.* light talk.

chiv′al·ry (shiv′əl rē) *n., adj. pl.* **-ries. 1.** qualities such as courtesy and courage. **2.** knightly way of life. —**chiv′al·ric, chiv′al·rous,** *adj.*

chive (chīv) *n.* (*usually pl.*) onionlike plant with slender leaves.

chlo·rine (klōr′ēn, -in) *n.* green gaseous element. —**chlor′in·ate′** (-i nāt′) *v.,* **-ated. -ating.**

chlo′ro·form′ (klōr′ə fôrm′) *n.* **1.** liquid used as anesthetic. —*v.* **2.** administer chloroform to.

chlo·ro·phyll (-fil) *n.* green coloring matter of plants.

chock (chŏk) *n.* wedge; block.

choc·o·late (chô′kə lit) *n.* **1.** product made from cacao seeds. **2.** dark brown.

Choc·taw (chŏk′tô) *n.*, *pl.* **taw, -taws.** member of an American Indian people.

choice (chois) *n.* **1.** act or right of choosing. **2.** person or thing chosen. —*adj.* **3.** excellent.

choir (kwīr) *n.* group of singers.

choke (chōk) *v.*, **choked, choking,** *n.* —*v.* **1.** stop breath of. **2.** obstruct. **3.** be unable to breathe. —*n.* **4.** act of choking.

chol·er·a (kŏl′ər ə) *n.* acute, often deadly, disease.

cho·les·te·rol (kə les′tə rôl′) *n.* fatty, crystalline substance in animal tissues.

chomp (chŏmp) *v.* chew noisily.

choose (chōōz) *v.*, **chose** (chōz), **chosen, choosing.** take as one thinks best. —**choos′er,** *n.*

choos·y, *adj.*, **-ier, -iest.** hard to please; particular.

chop (chŏp) *v.*, **chopped, chopping,** *n.* —*v.* **1.** cut with blows. **2.** cut in pieces. —*n.* **3.** sharp blow. **4.** slice of meat with rib. **5.** jaw.

chop·per, *n.* **1.** thing that chops. **2.** *Informal.* helicopter.

chop·py, *adj.*, **-pier, -piest.** forming short waves.

chop·sticks′, *n.pl.* sticks used in eating, esp. in some Asian countries.

chop su·ey (sōō′ē) Chinese-style vegetable dish.

cho·ral (kôr′əl) *adj.* for chorus.

cho·rale′ (kə rāl′, -räl′) *n.* **1.** type of hymn. **2.** choir.

chord (kôrd) *n.* **1.** combination of harmonious tones. **2.** straight line across circle.

chore (chôr) *n.* routine job.

cho·re·og·ra·phy (kôr′ē og′rə fē) *n.* art of composing dances. —**cho′re·o·graph′** (-ə graf′) *v.* —**cho·re·og′ra·pher,** *n.*

chor·is·ter (kôr′ə stər) *n.* choir singer.

chor·tle (chôr′tl) *v.*, **-tled, -tling,** *n.* chuckle.

cho·rus (kôr′əs) *n.* **1.** group of singers. **2.** recurring melody.

chow (chou) *n.* *Slang.* food.

chow·der (chou′dər) *n.* vegetable soup usu. containing clams or fish.

chow mein (mān) Chinese-style dish served on fried noodles.

Christ (krīst) *n.* Jesus Christ; (in Christian belief) the Messiah.

chris·ten (kris′ən) *v.* baptize; name.

Chris·ten·dom (kris′ən dəm) *n.* all Christians.

Chris·tian (kris′chən) *adj.* **1.** of Jesus Christ, his teachings, etc. —*n.* **2.** believer in Christianity.

Chris·ti·an·i·ty (-chē an′i tē) *n.* religion based on teachings of Christ.

Christ·mas (kris′məs) *n.* festival in honor of birth of Christ.

chro·mat·ic (krō mat′ik, krə-) *adj.* **1.** of color. **2.** *Music.* progressing by semitones.

chro·mi·um (krō′mē əm) *n.* lustrous metallic element. Also, **chrome.**

chro·mo·some (krō′mə sōm′) *n.* part of cell carrying genes.

chron·ic (kron′ik) *adj.* constant; long-lasting; habitual.

chron·i·cle (kron′i kəl) *n.*, *v.*, **-cled, -cling.** —*n.* **1.** record of events in order. —*v.* **2.** record in chronicle.

chrono-, prefix meaning time, as *chronometer.*

chro·nol·o·gy (krə nol′ə jē) *n.*, *pl.* **-gies.** historical order of events. —**chron·o·log·i·cal** (kron′l oj′i kəl) *adj.*

chro·nom·e·ter (krə nom′i tər) *n.* very exact clock.

chrys·a·lis (kris′ə lis) *n.* pupa.

chry·san·the·mum (kri san′thə məm) *n.* large, colorful flower.

chub·by, *adj.*, **-bier, -biest.** plump.

chuck (chuk) *v.* **1.** pat lightly. —*n.* **2.** light pat. **3.** cut of beef.

chuck·le (chuk′əl) *v.*, **-led, -ling,** *n.* —*v.* **1.** laugh softly. —*n.* **2.** soft laugh.

chum (chum) *n.* close friend. —**chum′my,** *adj.*, **-mier, -miest.**

chump (chump) *n.* *Informal.* fool.

chunk (chungk) *n.* big lump.

chunk·y, *adj.*, **-ier, -iest.** **1.** thick or stout; stocky. **2.** full of chunks.

church (chûrch) *n.* **1.** place of Christian worship. **2.** sect.

churl·ish (chûr′lish) *adj.* boorish.

churn (chûrn) *n.* **1.** agitator for making butter. —*v.* **2.** agitate.

chute (shōōt) *n.* sloping slide.

chut·ney (chut′nē) *n.* East Indian relish.

chutz·pah (KHŎŌT′spə, hŏŌt′-) *n.* nerve; gall. Also, **chutz·pa.**

CIA, Central Intelligence Agency.

ci·ca·da (si kā′də) *n.* large insect with shrill call.

-cide, suffix indicating: **1.** killer, as *pesticide.* **2.** killing, as *homicide.*

ci·der (sī′dər) *n.* apple juice.

ci·gar (si gär′) *n.* roll of tobacco for smoking.

cig·a·rette′ (sig′ə ret′) *n.* roll of smoking tobacco in paper.

clandestine

cinch (sinch) n. **1.** firm hold. **2.** *Informal.* sure or easy thing.

cin'der (sin'dər) n. **1.** burned piece; ash.

cin'e·ma (sin'ə mə) n. **1.** motion pictures. **2.** movie theater.

cin'e·ma·tog'ra·phy (-tog'rə fē) n. art or technique of motion-picture photography.

cin'na·mon (sin'ə mən) n. brown spice from bark of Asian tree.

ci'pher (sī'fər) n. **1.** the symbol (0) for zero. **2.** secret writing, using code. —v. **3.** calculate.

cir'ca (sûr'kə) *prep.* approximately.

cir'cle (sûr'kəl) n., v., **-cled, -cling.** —n. **1.** closed curve of uniform distance from its center. **2.** range; scope. **3.** group of friends or associates. —v. **4.** enclose or go in circle.

cir'cuit (-kit) n. **1.** tour, esp. in connection with duties. **2.** electrical path or arrangement. —**cir'cuit·ry,** n.

circuit breaker, device that interrupts electrical circuit to prevent excessive current.

cir·cu'i·tous (sər kyōō'i təs) adj. roundabout. —**cir·cu'i·tous·ly,** adv.

cir'cu·lar (-kyə lər) adj. **1.** of or in circle. —n. **2.** advertisement distributed widely.

cir'cu·late' (-lāt') v., **-lated, -lating.** move or pass around. —**cir'cu·la'tion,** n. —**cir'cu·la·to'ry** (-lə tôr'ē) adj.

circum-, prefix indicating around or about, as *circumnavigate.*

cir'cum·cise' (sûr'kəm sīz') v., **-cised, -cising.** remove foreskin of. —**cir'cum·ci'sion** (-sizh'ən) n.

cir·cum'fer·ence (sər kum'fər əns) n. outer boundary of a circle.

cir'cum·flex' (sûr'kəm fleks') n. diacritical mark (`).

cir'cum·lo·cu'tion (-lō kyōō'shən) n. roundabout expression.

cir'cum·nav'i·gate' (-nav'i gāt') v., **-gated, -gating.** sail around.

cir'cum·scribe' (-skrīb') v., **-scribed, -scribing.** **1.** encircle. **2.** confine.

cir'cum·spect' (-spekt') adj. cautious. —**cir'cum·spec'tion** (-spek'shən) n.

cir'cum·stance' (-stans') n. **1.** condition accompanying or affecting event. **2.** existing condition, esp. with regard to finances. **3.** ceremony.

cir'cum·stan'tial (-stan'shəl) adj. of or from circumstances.

cir'cum·vent' (-vent') v. outwit or evade. —**cir'cum·ven'tion,** n.

cir'cus (sûr'kəs) n. show with animals, acrobats, etc.

cir·rho'sis (si rō'sis) n. chronic liver disease.

cir'rus (sir'əs) n. fleecy cloud.

cis'tern (sis'tərn) n. reservoir.

cit'a·del (sit'ə dl, -ə del') n. fortress.

cite (sīt) v., **cited, citing.** **1.** mention in proof, etc. **2.** summon. **3.** commend. —**ci·ta'tion,** n.

cit'i·zen (sit'ə zən, -sən) n. subject of a country. —**cit'i·zen·ship',** n.

citric acid (si'trik) white powder in citrus fruits.

cit'ron (si'trən) n. lemonlike fruit.

cit'ro·nel'la (si'trə nel'ə) n. pungent oil used esp. as insect repellent.

cit'rus (si'trəs) adj. of the genus including the orange, lemon, etc. —n.

cit'y (sit'ē) n., pl. **-ies.** large town.

civ'ic (siv'ik) adj. **1.** of cities. **2.** of citizens.

civ'ics, n. study of citizenship.

civ'il (-əl) adj. **1.** of citizens. **2.** civilized. **3.** polite. —**ci·vil'i·ty** (-vil'i·tē) n.

ci·vil'ian (si vil'yən) n. **1.** nonmilitary or nonpolice person. —adj. **2.** of such persons.

civ'i·li·za'tion (siv'ə lə zā'shən) n. **1.** process of civilizing. **2.** culture of a people or period.

civ'i·lize' (-līz') v., **-lized, -lizing.** bring out of savage state.

civil liberty, fundamental right guaranteed by law.

civil rights, rights of all people to freedom and equality.

civil servant, employee of civil service.

civil service, branches of governmental administration outside the armed services.

civil war, war between parts of same state.

cl., centiliter.

claim (klām) v. **1.** demand as one's right, property, etc. **2.** assert. —n. **3.** demand. **4.** assertion. **5.** something claimed. —**claim'ant,** n.

clair·voy'ant (klâr voi'ənt) adj. seeing beyond physical vision. —**clair·voy'ant,** n. —**clair·voy'ance,** n.

clam (klam) n. common mollusk.

clam'ber (klam'bər, klam'ər) v. climb awkwardly.

clam'my, adj., **-mier, -miest.** cold and moist. —**clam'mi·ness,** n.

clam'or (klam'ər) n. **1.** loud outcry or noise. —v. **2.** raise clamor. —**clam'or·ous,** adj.

clamp (klamp) n. **1.** clasping device. —v. **2.** fasten with clamp.

clan (klan) n. related families.

clan·des'tine (klan des'tin) adj. done in secret.

clang (klang) v. **1.** ring harshly. —n. **2.** Also, **clang/or.** harsh ring.

clank (klangk) v. **1.** ring dully. —n. **2.** dull ringing.

clap (klap) v., **clapped, clapping,** n. —v. **1.** hit together, as hands in applause. —n. **2.** act of clapping.

clap/board (klab′ərd) n. overlapping boards on exterior walls.

clap/trap/ (klap′-) n. empty speech.

clar/et (klar′it) n. dry red wine.

clar/i•fy/ (klar′ə fī′) v., **-fied, -fying.** make or become clear. —**clar/i•fi•ca/tion,** n.

clar/i•net/ (-ə net′) n. musical wind instrument.

clar/i•on (-ē ən) adj. clear and loud.

clar/i•ty (-i tē) n. clearness.

clash (klash) v. **1.** conflict. **2.** collide. —n. **3.** collision. **4.** conflict.

clasp (klasp) n. **1.** fastening device. **2.** hug. —v. **3.** fasten. **4.** hug.

class (klas) n. **1.** group of similar persons or things. **2.** social rank. **3.** group of students. **4.** division. **5.** Informal. elegance, grace, or dignity. —v. **6.** place in classes. —**class/mate/,** n. —**class/room/,** n.

class action, lawsuit on behalf of persons with complaint in common.

clas/sic (klas′ik) adj. Also, **clas/si•cal.** **1.** of finest or fundamental type. **2.** in Greek or Roman manner. —n. **3.** author, book, etc., of acknowledged superiority. —**clas/si•cism/** (klas′ə siz/əm) n.

clas/si•fied/ (klas′ə fīd′) adj. limited to authorized persons.

clas/si•fy/, v., **-fied, -fying.** arrange in classes. —**clas/si•fi•ca/tion,** n.

class•y, adj., **-ier, -iest.** Informal. stylish; elegant. —**class/i•ness,** n.

clat/ter (klat′ər) n. **1.** rattle.

clause (klôz) n. part of sentence with its own subject and predicate.

claus/tro•pho/bi•a (klô′strə fō′bē ə) n. dread of closed places. —**claus/tro•pho/bic,** adj., n.

clav/i•chord/ (klav′i kôrd′) n. early keyboard instrument.

clav/i•cle (klav′i kəl) n. collarbone.

claw (klô) n. **1.** sharp, curved nail on animal's paw. —v. **2.** dig or scratch roughly.

clay (klā) n. soft earth, used in making bricks, pottery, etc.

clean (klēn) adj. **1.** free from dirt. **2.** complete. —adv. **3.** completely. —v. **4.** make clean. —**clean/er,** n.

clean•ly (klen′lē) adj. keeping or kept clean. —**clean/li•ness,** n.

cleanse (klenz) v., **cleansed, cleansing.** make clean. —**cleans/er,** n.

clear (klēr) adj. **1.** bright. **2.** easily perceived. **3.** evident. **4.** unob-

structed. **5.** free of obligations. **6.** blameless. —v. **7.** in a clear manner. —v. **8.** make or become clear. **9.** pay in full. **10.** pass beyond. —**clear/ly,** adv.

clear/ance, n. **1.** space between objects. **2.** authorization.

clear/-cut/, adj. apparent; obvious.

clear/ing, n. treeless space.

cleat (klēt) n. metal piece to which ropes, etc., are fastened.

cleav/age (klē′vij), n. space between woman's breasts.

cleave (klēv) v., **cleft** (kleft) or **cleaved, cleaving.** split.

cleave (klēv) v., **cleaved, cleaving.** **1.** cling. **2.** remain faithful.

cleav/er, n. heavy knife.

clef (klef) n. musical symbol indicating pitch.

cleft (kleft) n. split.

cleft palate, birth defect involving fissure in the roof of the mouth.

clem/a•tis (klem′ə tis) n. flowering vine.

clem/ent (klem′ənt) adj. **1.** lenient. **2.** mild. —**clem/en•cy,** n.

clench (klench) v. close tightly.

cler/gy (klûr′jē) n., pl. **-gies.** religious officials. —**cler/gy•man,** n. —**cler/gy•wom•an,** n.fem.

cler/ic (kler′ik) n. member of the clergy.

cler/i•cal, adj. **1.** of clerks. **2.** of clergy.

clerk (klûrk) n. **1.** employee who keeps records, etc. **2.** sales person in store.

clev/er (klev′ər) adj. bright, witty, or creative. —**clev/er•ly,** adv.

CLI or **cli,** cost-of-living index.

cli•ché/ (klē shā′) n. trite expression.

click (klik) n. **1.** slight, sharp noise. —v. **2.** make a click. **3.** Slang. succeed.

cli/ent (klī′ənt) n. customer.

cli/en•tele/ (-an tel′) n. patrons.

cliff (klif) n. steep bluff.

cliff/-hang•er, n. suspenseful situation.

cli/mate (klī′mit) n. weather conditions. —**cli•mat/ic** (-mat′ik) adj.

cli/max (klī′maks) n. high point. —**cli•mac/tic** (-mak′tik) adj.

climb (klīm) v. **1.** ascend. **2.** climb down, a. descend. b. Informal. compromise. —n. **3.** ascent.

clinch (klinch) v. **1.** fasten (a nail) by bending the point. **2.** hold tightly. **3.** settle decisively. —n. **4.** act of clinching. —**clinch/er,** n.

cling (kling) v., **clung** (klung), **clinging.** hold firmly to.

clin/ic (klin′ik) n. hospital for nonresident or charity patients. —**clin′i‧cal,** adj.

clink (klingk) v. **1.** make light, ringing sound. —n. **2.** such a sound.

clink′er (kling′kər) n. fused mass of incombustible residue.

clip (klip) v., **clipped, clipping,** n. —v. **1.** cut with short snips. **2.** hit sharply. —n. **3.** act of clipping. **4.** clasp. **5.** cartridge holder.

clip′per (klip′ər) n. **1.** cutting device. **2.** fast sailing vessel.

clique (klēk) n. elitist group.

clit′o‧ris (klit′ər is) n., pl. **clitorises** or **clitorides** (kli tôr′i dēz′). erectile organ of vulva.

cloak (klōk) n. **1.** loose outer garment. —v. **2.** cover with cloak. **3.** hide.

cloak′-and-dag′ger, adj. of espionage or intrigue.

clob′ber (klob′ər) v. Informal. batter or defeat.

clock (klok) n. device for telling time.

clock′wise′, adv., adj. in direction that clock hands turn.

clock′work′, n. **1.** mechanism of a clock. **2.** perfectly regular function, like that of a clock.

clod (klod) n. piece of earth.

clog (klog) v., **clogged, clogging,** n. —v. **1.** hamper; obstruct. —n. **2.** obstruction, etc. **3.** heavy wooden shoe.

clois′ter (kloi′stər) n. **1.** covered walk. **2.** monastery or nunnery.

clone (klōn) n., v., **cloned, cloning.** —n. **1.** organism created by asexual reproduction. **2.** Informal. duplicate. —v. **3.** grow as clone.

close, v., **closed, closing,** adj., **closer, closest,** adv., n. —v. (klōz) **1.** shut, obstruct, or end. **2.** come to terms. —adj. (klōs) **3.** shut. **4.** confined. **5.** lacking fresh air. **6.** secretive. **7.** compact. **8.** near. **9.** intimate. —adv. (klōs) **10.** in a close manner. —n. (klōz) **11.** end. —**close′ly,** adv. —**clo′sure** (klō′zhər) n.

close call (klōs) narrow escape.

closed′-cap′tioned, adj. broadcast with captions usable only with decoding device.

closed shop, place where workers must belong to union.

close′out′ (klōz′-) n. sale at greatly reduced prices.

clos′et (kloz′it) n. **1.** cabinet for clothes, etc. —adj. **2.** clandestine.

close′up′ (klōs′-) n. photograph taken at close range.

clot (klot) n., v., **clotted, clotting.** —n. **1.** mass, esp. of dried blood. —v. **2.** form clot.

cloth (klôth) n. fabric of threads.

clothe (klōth) v., **clothed** or **clad** (klad), **clothing.** dress.

clothes (klōz, klōthz) n.pl. garments; apparel. Also, **cloth′ing.**

cloud (kloud) n. **1.** mass of water particles, etc., in the air. —v. **2.** grow dark or gloomy. **3.** lose or deprive of transparency. —**cloud′y,** adj.

clout (klout) n. **1.** blow from hand. **2.** influence. —v. **3.** hit with hand.

clove (klōv) n. **1.** tropical spice. **2.** section of plant bulb.

clo′ver (klō′vər) n. three-leaved plant.

clown (kloun) n. **1.** comic performer. **2.** prankster. **3.** fool. —v. **4.** act like a clown. —**clown′ish,** adj.

cloy (kloi) v. weary by excess, as of sweetness.

club (klub) n., v., **clubbed, clubbing.** —n. **1.** bat. **2.** organized group. **3.** (pl.) suit of playing cards. —v. **4.** beat with club.

club′foot′, n. deformed foot.

club soda, soda water.

cluck (kluk) n. **1.** call of hen. —v. **2.** utter such call.

clue (klōō) n. hint in solving mystery, etc.

clump (klump) n. cluster.

clum′sy (klum′zē) adj., **-sier, -siest.** awkward. —**clum′si‧ly,** adv.

clus′ter (klus′tər) n. **1.** group; bunch. —v. **2.** gather into cluster.

clutch (kluch) v. **1.** grasp. —n. **2.** grasp. **3.** (pl.) control. **4.** device for engaging or disengaging machinery.

clut′ter (klut′ər) v. **1.** litter untidily. —n. **2.** disorderly heap.

cm., centimeter.

CO, 1. Colorado. **2.** Commanding Officer.

co-, prefix indicating: **1.** together, as cooperate. **2.** joint or jointly, as coauthor.

Co., 1. Company. **2.** County.

c/o, care of.

coach (kōch) n. **1.** enclosed carriage, bus, etc. **2.** trainer. —v. **3.** instruct.

co‧ag′u‧late′ (kō ag′yə lāt′) v., **-lated, -lating.** thicken or clot.

coal (kōl) n. black mineral burned as fuel.

co′a‧lesce′ (kō′ə les′) v., **-lesced, -lescing.** unite or ally.

co‧a‧li′tion (kō′ə lish′ən) n. alliance.

coarse (kôrs) adj., **coarser, coarsest. 1.** rough or harsh. **2.** vulgar. —**coarse′ly,** adv. —**coars′en,** v.

coast (kōst) n. **1.** seashore. —v. **2.** drift easily. —**coast′al,** adj.

coast′er, *n.* object protecting surfaces from moisture.

coast guard, military service that enforces maritime laws, saves lives at sea, etc.

coat (kōt) *n.* **1.** outer garment. **2.** covering, as fur or bark. —*v.* **3.** cover or enclose.

coat′ing, *n.* outer layer.

coat of arms, emblems, motto, etc., of one's family.

co·au′thor (kō ô′thər, kō′ô′-) *n.* one of two or more joint authors. —**co·au′thor,** *v.*

coax (kōks) *v.* influence by persuasion, flattery, etc. —**coax′er,** *n.*

co·ax′i·al (kō ak′sē əl) *adj.* having a common axis, as **coaxial cables** for simultaneous long-distance transmission of radio or television signals.

cob (kob) *n.* corncob.

co′balt (kō′bôlt) *n.* silvery metallic element.

cob′ble (kob′əl) *v.,* **-bled, -bling,** *n.* —*v.* **1.** mend (shoes). —*n.* **2.** Also, **cob′ble·stone′.** round stone for paving, etc. —**cob′bler,** *n.*

COBOL (kō′bôl) *n.* computer language for writing programs to process large files.

co′bra (kō′brə) *n.* venomous snake.

cob′web′ (kob′-) *n.* spider web.

co·caine′ (kō kān′, kō′kān) *n.* narcotic drug.

cock (kok) *n.* **1.** male bird. **2.** valve. **3.** hammer in gun. **4.** pile of hay. —*v.* **5.** set cock of (a gun). **6.** set aslant.

cock·ade′ (ko kād′) *n.* hat ornament.

cock′a·too′ (kok′ə tōō′, kok′ə tōō′) *n.* colorful crested parrot.

cock′eyed′, *adj.* **1.** tilted to one side. **2.** absurd. **3.** drunk.

cock′le (kok′əl) *n.* **1.** mollusk with radially ribbed valves. **2.** inmost part.

cock′ney (-nē) *n.* **1.** resident of London, esp. East End. **2.** pronunciation of such persons.

cock′pit′, *n.* space for pilot.

cock′roach′, *n.* common crawling insect.

cock′tail′, *n.* **1.** drink containing mixture of liquors. **2.** mixed appetizer.

cock′y, *adj.,* **-ier, -iest.** too sure of oneself. —**cock′i·ness,** *n.*

co′coa (kō′kō) *n.* **1.** powdered seeds of cacao, used esp. in making a beverage. **2.** brown.

co′co·nut′ (kō′kə nut′, -nət) *n.* large, hard-shelled seed of the **co′co palm.**

co·coon′ (kə kōōn′) *n.* silky larval covering.

cod (kod) *n.* edible Atlantic fish.

C.O.D., cash, or collect, on delivery.

co′da (kō′də) *n.* final passage of a musical movement.

cod′dle (kod′l) *v.,* **-dled, -dling. 1.** pamper. **2.** cook in boiling water.

code (kōd) *n., v.,* **coded, coding.** —*n.* **1.** collection of laws or rules. **2.** system of signals or secret words. —*v.* **3.** put into code.

co′deine (kō′dēn) *n.* drug derived from opium.

codg′er (koj′ər) *n.* eccentric man.

cod′i·cil (kod′ə sil) *n.* supplement, esp. to a will.

cod′i·fy′ (kod′ə fī′, kō′də-) *v.,* **-fied, -fying.** organize into legal or formal code. —**cod′i·fi·ca′tion,** *n.*

co′ed′ (kō′ed′, -ed′) *n.* female student, esp. in coeducational school.

co·ed·u·ca′tion, *n.* education of both sexes in the same classes.

co·ef·fi′cient (kō′ə fish′ənt) *n.* number by which another is multiplied.

co·erce′ (kō ûrs′) *v.,* **-erced, -ercing.** force; compel. —**co·er′cion** (-ûr′shən) *n.* —**co·er′cive,** *adj.*

co·ex·ist′ (kō′ig zist′) *v.* **1.** exist simultaneously. **2.** exist together peacefully. —**co·ex·ist′ence,** *n.*

cof′fee (kô′fē) *n.* **1.** brown seeds of tropical tree. **2.** beverage made by roasting and grinding these seeds.

cof′fer (kô′fər) *n.* chest.

cof′fin (kô′fin) *n.* box for a corpse.

cog (kog) *n.* tooth on wheel (**cog′wheel′**), connecting with another such wheel.

co′gent (kō′jənt) *adj.* convincing. —**co′gen·cy,** *n.* —**co′gent·ly,** *adv.*

cog′i·tate′ (koj′i tāt′) *v.,* **-tated, -tating.** ponder. —**cog′i·ta′tion,** *n.*

co′gnac (kōn′yak) *n.* brandy.

cog′nate (kog′nāt) *adj.* related.

cog·ni′tion (-nish′ən) *n.* knowing.

cog′ni·zance (-nə zəns) *n.* notice, esp. official. —**cog′ni·zant,** *adj.*

co·gno·scen′ti (kon′yə shen′tē, kog′nə-) *n.pl., sing.* **-te** (-tā, -tē) those having superior knowledge.

co·hab′it (kō hab′it) *v.* live together, esp. as husband and wife without being married. —**co·hab′i·ta′tion,** *n.*

co·here′ (kō hēr′) *v.,* **-hered, -hering.** stick together. —**co·he′sion** (-hē′zhən) *n.* —**co·he′sive** (-siv) *adj.*

co·her′ent (-hēr′ənt, -her′-) *adj.* making sense. —**co·her′ence,** *n.*

co′hort (kō′hôrt) *n.* **1.** companion. **2.** group, esp. of soldiers.

coif·fure′ (kwä fyŏŏr′) n. arrangement of hair.

coil (koil) v. 1. wind spirally or in rings. —n. 2. ring. 3. series of spirals.

coin (koin) n. 1. piece of metal used as money. —v. 2. make metal into money. 3. invent. —**coin′age**, n.

co·in·cide′ (kō′in sīd′) v., -cided, -ciding. 1. occur at same time, place, etc. 2. match. —**co·in′ci·dence** (-si dans) n. —**co·in′ci·den′tal** (-den′tl) adj. —**co·in′ci·den′tal·ly**, adv.

co·i′tus (kō′i təs) n. sexual intercourse. —**co′i·tal**, adj.

coke (kōk) n. —n. 1. solid carbon produced from coal. 2. Slang. cocaine.

Col., 1. Colonel. 2. Colorado.

co′la (kō′lə) n. soft drink containing extract from kola nuts.

col′an·der (kul′ən dər, kol′-) n. large strainer.

cold (kōld) adj. 1. without warmth. 2. not cordial. —n. 3. absence of heat. 4. common illness marked by runny nose. —**cold′ly**, adv.

cold′-blood′ed, adj. 1. callous; unemotional. 2. with blood at same temperature as environment.

cold cream, preparation for cleansing or soothing the skin.

cold feet, Informal. lack of courage.

cold shoulder, deliberate show of indifference.

cold turkey, Informal. —n. 1. abrupt withdrawal from addictive substance. —adv. 2. impromptu.

cold war, rivalry between nations just short of armed conflict.

cole′slaw′ (kōl′slô′) n. sliced raw cabbage.

col′ic (kol′ik) n. pain in bowels.

col·i·se′um (kol′i sē′əm) n. large stadium.

co·li′tis (kə lī′tis, kō-) n. inflammation of the colon.

col·lab′o·rate′ (kə lab′ə rāt′) v., -rated, -rating. work together. —**col·lab′o·ra′tion**, n. —**col·lab′o·ra′tor**, n.

col·lage′ (kə läzh′) n. work of art made with various materials pasted on a surface.

col·lapse′ (kə laps′) v., -lapsed, -lapsing, n. —v. 1. fall in or together. 2. fail abruptly. —n. 3. a falling-in. 4. sudden failure. —**col·laps′i·ble**, adj.

col′lar (kol′ər) n. 1. part of garment around neck. —v. 2. seize by collar.

col′lar·bone′, n. slender bone connecting sternum and scapula; clavicle.

col·lat′er·al (kə lat′ər əl) n. 1. security pledged on loan. —adj. 2. additional. 3. on side.

col′league (kol′ēg) n. associate in work, etc.

col·lect′ (kə lekt′) v. 1. gather together. 2. take payment of. —adj., adv. 3. payable on delivery. —**col·lec′tion**, n. —**col·lec′tor**, n.

col·lect′i·ble, n. 1. object collected. —adj. 2. able to be collected.

col·lec′tive, adj. 1. by a group. —n. 2. socialist productive group.

collective bargaining, negotiation between union and employer.

col·lec′tiv·ism, n. principle of communal control. —**col·lec′tiv·ist**, n.

col′lege (kol′ij) n. school of higher learning. —**col·le′giate** (kə lē′jit) adj.

col·lide′ (kə līd′) v., -lided, -liding. strike together violently.

col′lie (kol′ē) n. kind of large, longhaired dog.

col′lier (kol′yər) n. 1. ship for carrying coal. 2. coal miner.

col·li′sion (kə lizh′ən) n. 1. crash. 2. conflict.

col·lo′qui·al (kə lō′kwē əl) adj. appropriate to casual rather than formal speech or writing.

col·lo′qui·um (-kwē əm) n., pl. -quiums, -quia (-kwē ə). conference of experts.

col′lo·quy (kol′ə kwē) n., pl. -quies. conversation.

col·lu′sion (kə lōō′zhən) n. illicit agreement.

Colo., Colorado.

co·logne′ (kə lōn′) n. perfumed toilet water.

co′lon (kō′lən) n. 1. mark of punctuation (:). 2. part of large intestine. —**co·lon′ic** (kə lon′ik) adj.

colo′nel (kûr′nl) n. military officer below general. —**colo′nel·cy**, n.

co·lo′ni·al·ism (kə lō′nē ə liz′əm) n. policy of extending national authority over foreign territories.

col′on·nade′ (kol′ə nād′) n. series of columns.

col′o·ny (kol′ə nē) n., pl. -nies. 1. group of people settling in another land. 2. territory subject to outside ruling power. 3. community. —**co·lo′ni·al** (kə lō′nē əl) adj., n. —**col′o·nist**, n. —**col′o·nize′**, v.t., -nized, -nizing.

col′or (kul′ər) n. 1. quality of light perceived by human eye. 2. pigment. 3. complexion. 4. vivid description. 5. (pl.) flag. 6. race. —v. 7. apply color to. Also, Brit., **col′our**. —**col′or·ing**, n.

col′o·ra·tu′ra (kul′ər ə tŏŏr′ə, -tyŏŏr′ə, kol′-) n. soprano specializing in music containing ornamental trills.

col'or-blind', *adj.* **1.** unable to distinguish certain colors. **2.** without racial bias.

col'ored, *adj. Often Offensive.* belonging to a race other than Caucasian.

col'or-ful, *adj.* **1.** full of color. **2.** vivid; interesting.

col'or-less, *adj.* **1.** without color. **2.** uninteresting. —**col'or-less-ly,** *adv.*

co-los'sal (kə los'əl) *adj.* huge.

co-los'sus (-los'əs) *n.* anything colossal.

colt (kōlt) *n.* young male horse.

col'umn (kol'əm) *n.* **1.** upright shaft or support. **2.** long area of print. **3.** regular journalistic piece. **4.** long group of troops, ships, etc. —**col'um-nist** (-əm nist) *n.*

com-, prefix indicating: **1.** with or together, as *commingle.* **2.** completely, as *commit.*

co'ma (kō'mə) *n.* unconscious state. —**com'a-tose'** (-tōs') *adj.*

Co-man'che (kə man'chē) *n., pl.* **-che, -ches.** member of an American Indian people.

comb (kōm) *n.* **1.** toothed object, for straightening hair or fiber. **2.** growth on a cock's head. —*v.* **3.** tidy with comb. **4.** search.

com-bat', *v.,* **-bated, -bating,** *n.* —*v.* (kəm bat', kom'bat) **1.** fight. —*n.* (kom'bat) **2.** battle. —**com-bat'ant,** *n.* —**com-bat'ive,** *adj.*

com'bi-na'tion (kom'bə nā'shən) *n.* **1.** act of combining. **2.** mixture. **3.** alliance. **4.** sets of figures dialed to operate a lock.

com-bine', *v.,* **-bined, -bining,** *n.* —*v.* (kəm bīn') **1.** unite; join. —*n.* (kom'bīn) **2.** combination. **3.** machine that cuts and threshes grain.

com'bo (kom'bō) *n., pl.* **-bos.** *Informal.* small jazz band.

com-bus'ti-ble (kəm bus'tə bəl) *adj.* **1.** inflammable. —*n.* **2.** inflammable substance.

com-bus'tion (-chən) *n.* burning.

come (kum) *v.,* **came, come, coming.** **1.** approach or arrive. **2.** happen. **3.** emerge.

come'back', *n.* **1.** return to former status. **2.** retort.

co-me'di-an (kə mē'dē ən) *n.* humorous actor or performer. —**co-me'di-enne',** *n.fem.*

com'e-dy (kom'i dē) *n., pl.* **-dies.** humorous drama.

come'ly (kum'lē) *adj.,* **-lier, -liest.** attractive. —**come'li-ness,** *n.*

com'er (kum'ər) *n. Informal.* one likely to have great success.

com'et (kom'it) *n.* celestial body orbiting around and lighted by sun, often with misty tail.

com'fort (kum'fərt) *v.* **1.** console or cheer. —*n.* **2.** consolation. **3.** ease. —**com'fort-a-ble,** *adj.* —**com'fort-a-bly,** *adv.*

com'fort-er, *n.* **1.** one who comforts. **2.** warm quilt.

com'ic (kom'ik) *adj.* **1.** of comedy. **2.** Also, **com'i-cal.** funny. —*n.* **3.** comedian. **4.** (*pl.*) comic strips.

comic strip, sequence of drawings relating comic incident or story.

com'ma (kom'ə) *n.* punctuation mark (,).

com-mand' (kə mand') *v.* **1.** order. **2.** control. —*n.* **3.** order. **4.** control. **5.** troops, etc., under command.

com'man-dant' (kom'ən dant', -dänt') *n.* commanding officer.

com'man-deer' (-dēr') *v.* seize for official use.

com-mand'er, *n.* **1.** chief officer. **2.** *Navy.* officer below captain.

com-mand'ment, *n.* **1.** command. **2.** precept of God.

com-man'do (kə man'dō) *n., pl.* **-dos, -does.** soldier making brief raids against enemy.

com-mem'o-rate' (kə mem'ə rāt') *v.,* **-rated, -rating.** honor memory of. —**com-mem'o-ra'tion,** *n.* —**com-mem'o-ra-tive** (-rə tiv) *adj.*

com-mence' (kə mens') *v.,* **-menced, -mencing.** start.

com-mence'ment, *n.* **1.** beginning. **2.** graduation day or ceremonies.

com-mend' (kə mend') *v.* **1.** praise. **2.** entrust. —**com-mend'a-ble,** *adj.* —**com'men-da'tion** (kom'ən dā'shən) *n.* —**com-mend'a-to'ry,** *adj.*

com-men'su-rate (-men'shə rit, -sə-) *adj.* equal or corresponding.

com'ment (kom'ent) *n.* **1.** remark or criticism. —*v.* **2.** make remarks.

com'men-tar'y (-ən ter'ē) *n., pl.* **-taries.** explanatory remarks.

com'men-ta'tor (-tā'tər) *n.* one who discusses news events, etc.

com'merce (kom'ərs) *n.* trade.

com-mer'cial (kə mûr'shəl) *adj.* **1.** of or in commerce. **2.** radio or television advertisement.

com-mer'cial-ize', *v.,* **-ized, -izing.** treat as a business.

com-min'gle (kə ming'gəl) *v.,* **-gled, -gling.** blend.

com-mis'er-ate' (kə miz'ə rāt') *v.,* **-ated, -ating.** sympathize.

com'mis-sar'y (kom'ə ser'ē) *n., pl.* **-ies.** store selling food, etc.

com-mis'sion (kə mish'ən) *n.* **1.** act of committing. **2.** document giving authority. **3.** group of persons with special task. **4.** usable condition. **5.** fee for agent's services.

—v. **6.** give commission to. **7.** authorize. **8.** put into service.

com·mis′sion·er, n. government official.

com·mit′ (kə mit′) v., **-mitted, -mitting. 1.** give in trust or custody. **2.** refer to committee. **3.** do. **4.** obligate. **—com·mit′ment,** n.

com·mit′tee (kə mit′ē) n. group assigned to special duties.

com·mode′ (kə mōd′) n. **1.** chest of drawers. **2.** stand with washbasin. **3.** toilet.

com·mo′di·ous (kə mō′dē əs) adj. roomy.

com·mod′i·ty (kə mod′i tē) n., pl. **-ties.** article of commerce.

com′mo·dore′ (kom′ə dôr′) n. officer below rear admiral.

com′mon (kom′ən) adj. **1.** joint. **2.** ordinary. **3.** vulgar. **4.** area of public land. **—com′mon·ly,** adv.

com′mon·er, n. one of common people.

common law, system of law based on custom and court decisions.

com′mon·place′ (-plās′) adj. **1.** ordinary; trite. **2.** commonplace remark.

com′mons, n. **1.** (cap.) elective house of certain legislatures. **2.** large dining room.

common sense, sound practical judgment. **—com′mon·sense′,** adj.

com′mon·weal′ (-wēl′) n. public welfare.

com′mon·wealth′ (-welth′) n. **1.** democratic state. **2.** people of a state.

com·mo′tion (kə mō′shən) n. disturbance.

com·mu′nal (kə myōōn′l, kom′yə-nl) adj. of or belonging to a community.

com·mune′, v., **-muned, -muning.** n. —v. (kə myōōn′) **1.** talk together. —n. (kom′yōōn) **2.** small community with shared property.

com·mu′ni·cate′, v., **-cated, -cating. 1.** make known. **2.** transmit. **3.** exchange news, etc. **—com·mu′ni·ca·ble** (-ni kə bəl) adj. **—com·mu′ni·ca′tion,** n. **—com·mu′ni·ca′tive** (-kā′tiv, -kə-) adj.

com·mun′ion (kə myōōn′yən) n. **1.** act of sharing. **2.** sacrament commemorating Jesus' last supper.

com·mu·ni·qué′ (kə myōō′ni kā′) n. official bulletin.

com′mu·nism (kom′yə niz′əm) n. **1.** social system based on collective ownership of property. **2.** (cap.) political doctrine advocating this. **—com′mu·nist** (-nist) n., adj.

com·mu′ni·ty (kə myōō′ni tē) n., pl. **-ties.** people with common culture living in one locality.

com·mute′ (kə myōōt′) v., **-muted, -muting. 1.** reduce (punishment). **2.** travel between home and work. **—com·mut′er,** n.

com·pact′, adj. (kəm pakt′, kom′pakt) **1.** packed together. **2.** pithy. —v. (kəm pakt′) **3.** pack together. —n. (kom′pakt) **4.** small cosmetic case. **5.** agreement.

compact disc, optical disc on which music, data, or images are digitally recorded. Also, **CD.**

com·pac′tor (kəm pak′tər, kom′-pak-) n. appliance that compresses trash into small bundles.

com·pan′ion (kəm pan′yən) n. **1.** associate. **2.** mate. **—com·pan′ion·a·ble,** adj. **—com·pan′ion·ship′,** n.

com′pa·ny (kum′pə nē) n., pl. **-nies. 1.** business organization. **2.** companionship. **3.** guests. **4.** military unit.

com·par′a·tive (kəm par′ə tiv) adj. **1.** of or based on comparison. —n. **2.** Gram. intermediate degree of comparison. **—com·par′a·tive·ly,** adv.

com·pare′ (kəm pâr′) v., **-pared, -paring.** consider for similarities. **—com′pa·ra·ble** (kom′pər ə bəl) adj. **—com·par′i·son** (kəm par′ə-sən) n.

com·part′ment (kəm pärt′mənt) n. separate room, space, etc. **—com·part·men′tal·ize′,** v., **-ized, -izing.**

com′pass (kum′pəs) n. **1.** instrument for finding direction. **2.** extent. **3.** tool for measuring circles.

com·pas′sion (kəm pash′ən) n. pity or sympathy. **—com·pas′sion·ate,** adj. **—com·pas′sion·ate·ly,** adv.

com·pat′i·ble (kəm pat′ə bəl) adj. congenial. **—com·pat′i·bil′i·ty,** n.

com·pa′tri·ot (kəm pā′trē ət) n. person from one's own country.

com·pel′ (kəm pel′) v., **-pelled, -pelling.** force.

com·pel′ling, adj. **1.** forceful. **2.** demanding attention.

com·pen′di·ous (kəm pen′dē əs) adj. concise.

com·pen′di·um (-dē əm) n., pl. **-diums, -dia** (-dē ə). summary.

com′pen·sate′ (kom′pən sāt′) v., **-sated, -sating. 1.** make up for. **2.** pay. **—com′pen·sa′tion,** n.

com·pete′ (kəm pēt′) v., **-peted, -peting.** contend; rival.

com′pe·tent (kom′pi tənt) adj. **1.** able enough. **2.** legally qualified **—com′pe·tence, com′pe·ten·cy,** n.

com·pe·ti′tion (kom′pi tish′ən) n. **1.** contest. **2.** rivalry. **—com·pet′i-**

tive (kəm pet'i tiv) *adj.* —**com•pet'i•tor,** *n.*

com•pile' (kəm pīl') *v.,* **-piled, -pil•ing.** put together; assemble. —**com•pil'er,** *n.* —**com'pi•la'tion** (kom'pə lā'shən) *n.*

com•pla•cen•cy (kəm plā'sən sē) *n., pl.* **-cies.** satisfaction, esp. with self. Also, **com•pla'cence.** —**com•pla'cent,** —**com•pla'cent•ly,** *adv.*

com•plain' (kəm plān') *v.* **1.** express pain, dissatisfaction, etc. **2.** accuse. —**com•plain'er,** —**com•plain'ant,** —**com•plaint',** *n.*

com•plai'sant (kəm plā'sənt) *adj.* obliging.

com•ple•ment (kom'plə mənt) **1.** that which completes. **2.** full amount. —*v.* **3.** complete. —**com'ple•men'ta•ry,** *adj.*

com•plete' (kəm plēt') *adj., v.,* **-pleted, -pleting.** **1.** entire. —*v.* **2.** make complete. —**com•plete'ly,** *adv.* —**com•ple'tion,** *n.*

com•plex' *adj.* (kəm pleks', kom'pleks) **1.** having many parts; intricate. —*n.* (kom'pleks) **2.** obsession. —**com•plex'i•ty,** *n.*

com•plex'ion (kəm plek'shən) *n.* color of skin.

com'pli•ca'ted (kom'pli kā'tid) *adj.* complex or difficult. —**com'pli•cate',** *v.*

com•plic'i•ty (kəm plis'i tē) *n., pl.* **-ties.** partnership in crime.

com'pli•ment *n.* (kom'plə mənt) **1.** expression of praise. —*v.* (-mənt') **2.** express praise.

com'pli•men'ta•ry, *adj.* **1.** of or being a compliment; praising. **2.** free.

com•ply' (kəm plī') *v.,* **-plied, -ply•ing.** act in accordance. —**com•pli'ance,** *n.* —**com•pli'ant,** *adj.*

com•po•nent (kəm pō'nənt) *adj.* **1.** composing. —*n.* **2.** part of whole.

com•port' (kəm pōrt') *v.* **1.** conduct (oneself). **2.** agree.

com•pose' (kəm pōz') *v.,* **-posed, -posing.** **1.** make by uniting parts. **2.** constitute. **3.** calm. **4.** create and write. **5.** set type. —**com'po•si'tion** (kom'pə zish'ən) *n.*

com•posed', *adj.* calm.

com•pos'er, *n.* writer, esp. of music.

com•pos'ite (kəm poz'it) *adj.* made of many parts.

com'post (kom'pōst) *n.* decaying mixture of leaves, etc.

com•po'sure (kəm pō'zhər) *n.* calm.

com'pote (kom'pōt) *n.* stewed fruit.

com'pound *adj.* (kom'pound) **1.** having two or more parts, functions, etc. —*n.* (kom'pound) **2.** something made by combining parts. **3.** enclosure with buildings. —*v.* (kəm pound') **4.** combine. **5.** make worse.

com•pre•hend' (kom'pri hend') *v.* **1.** understand. **2.** include. —**com'pre•hen'si•ble,** *adj.* —**com'pre•hen'sion,** *n.*

com'pre•hen'sive (-hen'siv) *adj.* inclusive.

com•press' *v.* (kəm pres') **1.** press together. —*n.* (kom'pres) **2.** pad applied to affected part of body. —**com•pres'sion,** *n.* —**com•pres'sor,** *n.*

com•prise' (kəm prīz') *v.,* **-prised, -prising.** consist of.

com'pro•mise' (kom'prə mīz') *n., v.,* **-mised, -mising.** —*n.* **1.** agreement to mutual concessions. **2.** something intermediate. —*v.* **3.** settle by compromise. **4.** endanger.

comp•trol'ler (kən trō'lər) *n.* controller.

com•pul'sion (kəm pul'shən) *n.* compelling force. —**com•pul'so•ry** (-sə rē) *adj.*

com•pul'sive, *adj.* due to or acting on inner compulsion.

com•punc'tion (kəm pungk'shən) *n.* remorse.

com•pute' (kəm pyōōt') *v.,* **-puted, -puting.** calculate; figure. —**com'pu•ta'tion** (kom'-) *n.*

com•put'er, *n.* electronic apparatus for processing data.

com•put'er•ize', *v.,* **-ized, -izing.** **1.** do by computer. **2.** automate by computer, as a business.

com'rade (kom'rad) *n.* companion. —**com'rade•ship,** *n.*

con (kon) *adv., n., v.,* **conned, con•ning.** —*adv.* **1.** opposed to a plan, etc. —*n.* **2.** argument against. —*v.* **3.** *Informal.* deceive; swindle.

con•cave' (kon kāv') *adj.* curved inward. —**con•cav'i•ty** (-kav'i tē) *n.*

con•ceal' (kən sēl') *v.* hide. —**con•ceal'ment,** *n.*

con•cede' (kən sēd') *v.,* **-ceded, -ceding.** **1.** admit. **2.** yield.

con•ceit' (kən sēt') *n.* **1.** excess self-esteem. **2.** fanciful idea. —**con•ceit'ed,** *adj.*

con•ceive' (kən sēv') *v.,* **-ceived, -ceiving.** **1.** form (plan or idea). **2.** understand. **3.** become pregnant. —**con•ceiv'a•ble,** *adj.*

con'cen•trate' (kon'sən trāt') *v.,* **-trated, -trating.** —*v.* **1.** bring to one point. **2.** intensify. **3.** give full attention. —*n.* **4.** product of concentration. —**con'cen•tra'tion,** *n.*

concentration camp, guarded compound where political prisoners, minorities, etc., are confined.

con·cen·tric (kən sen′trik) *adj.* having common center.

con·cept (kon′sept) *n.* notion.

con·cep·tion (kən sep′shən) *n.* 1. act of conceiving. 2. idea.

con·cep·tu·a·lize (–choo̅ ə līz′) *v.*, **-lized, -lizing.** 1. form a concept of. 2. think in concepts.

con·cern′ (kən sûrn′) *v.* 1. relate to. 2. involve. 3. worry. —*n.* 4. worry. 5. business firm.

con·cerned′ (–) 1. interested or affected. 2. troubled; anxious.

con·cern·ing, *prep.* concerning.

con·cert (kon′sûrt) *n.* 1. musical performance. 2. accord.

con·cert·ed (kən sûr′tid) *adj.* 1. planned together. 2. performed together or in cooperation.

con·cer·ti·na (kon′sər tē′nə) *n.* small accordion.

con·cer·to (kən cher′tō) *n., pl.* **-tos** or **-ti** (-tē). musical piece for principal instruments and orchestra.

con·ces·sion (kən sesh′ən) *n.* 1. act of conceding. 2. what is conceded. 3. grant conceded by authority.

conch (kongk, konch) *n.* spiral shell.

con·cil·i·ate (kən sil′ē āt′) *v.*, **-ated, -ating.** win over; reconcile. —**con·cil·i·a′tion,** *n.* —**con·cil′i·a·to′ry** (-ə tôr′ē) *adj.*

con·cise′ (kən sīs′) *adj.* brief; succinct. —**con·cise′ly,** *adv.*

con′clave (kon′klāv) *n.* private meeting.

con·clude′ (kən klōōd′) *v.*, **-cluded, -cluding.** 1. finish; settle. 2. infer. —**con·clu′sion** (-klōō′zhən) *n.* —**con·clu′sive,** *adj.*

con·coct′ (kon kokt′, kən-) *v.* make by combining. —**con·coc′tion,** *n.*

con·com′i·tant (kən kom′i tənt, kən-) *adj.* 1. accompanying. —*n.* 2. anything concomitant.

con′cord (kon′kôrd, kong′-) *n.* agreement.

con·cord′ance (kon kôr′dns, kən-) *n.* 1. concord. 2. index of key words of book.

con·cor′dat (kon kôr′dat) *n.* agreement, esp. between Pope and a government.

con′course (kon′kôrs, kong′-) *n.* place for crowds in motion.

con·crete′ (adj., n., v., –crēted, -creting. —adj.) (kon′krēt, kon krēt′) 1. real; objective. 2. made of concrete. —*n.* (kon′krēt) 3. material of cement and hard matter. —*v.* (kon′krēt′) 4. become solid. —**con·crete′ly,** *adv.* —**con·crete′ness,** *n.*

con′cu·bine (kong′kyə bīn′) *n.*

woman living with but not married to a man.

con·cur′ (kən kûr′) *v.*, **-curred, -curring.** 1. agree. 2. coincide. —**con·cur′rence,** *n.* —**con·cur′rent,** *adj.* —**con·cur′rent·ly,** *adv.*

con·cus′sion (kən kush′ən) *n.* injury to brain from blow, etc.

con·demn′ (kən dem′) *v.* 1. denounce. 2. pronounce guilty. 3. judge unfit. —**con′dem·na′tion** (kon′dem nā′shən, -dəm-) *n.*

con·dense′ (kən dens′) *v.*, **-densed, -densing.** 1. reduce to denser form. 2. make or become compact. —**con′den·sa′tion** (kon′den sā′shən) *n.* —**con·dens′er,** *n.*

condensed milk, thick, sweetened milk.

con′de·scend′ (kon′də send′) *v.* 1. pretend equality with an inferior. 2. deign. —**con′de·scen′sion,** *n.*

con′di·ment (kon′də mənt) *n.* seasoning.

con·di′tion (kən dish′ən) *n.* 1. state of being or health. 2. fit state. 3. requirement. —*v.* 4. put in condition. —**con·di′tion·al,** *adj.* —**con·di′tion·er,** *n.*

con·dole′ (kən dōl′) *v.*, **-doled, -doling.** sympathize in sorrow. —**con·do′lence,** *n.*

con′dom (kon′dəm, kun′-) *n.* contraceptive device worn over penis.

con′do·min′i·um (kon′də min′ē·əm) *n.* apartment house in which units are individually owned. Also, *Informal.* **con′do** (-dō).

con·done′ (kən dōn′) *v.*, **-doned, -doning.** excuse.

con′dor (kon′dər, -dôr) *n.* vulture.

con·du′cive (kən dōō′siv, -dyōō′-) *adj.* tending to.

con′duct (kon′dukt) *n.* 1. behavior. 2. management. —*v.* (kən dukt′) 3. behave. 4. manage. 5. lead or carry. 6. transmit, as electric current. —**con·duc′tion,** *n.*

con·duc′tor (kən duk′tər) *n.* 1. guide. 2. director of an orchestra. 3. official on trains. 4. substance that conveys electricity, heat, etc.

con′duit (kon′dwit) *n.* pipe for water, etc.

cone (kōn) *n.* 1. form tapering from round base to single point. 2. fruit of fir, pine, etc.

con′fab (kon′fab) *n.* conversation.

con·fec′tion (kən fek′shən) *n.* candy or other sweet preparation. —**con·fec′tion·er,** *n.* —**con·fec′tion·er·y,** *n.*

con·fed′er·a·cy (kən fed′ər ə sē) *n., pl.* **-cies.** 1. league. 2. (cap.) Confederate States of America.

con·fed′er·ate, *adj., n., v.*, **-ated,**

-ating. —*adj.* **1.** in league. **2.** (*cap.*) of **Confederate States of America,** separated from U.S. during Civil War. —*n.* (-ər it) **3.** ally. **4.** accomplice. **5.** (*cap.*) citizen of Confederate States of America. —*v.* (-ə rāt′) **6.** be allied. —**con·fed′er·a′tion,** *n.*

con·fer′ (kən fûr′) *v.,* **-ferred, -fer·ring. 1.** bestow. **2.** consult. —**con·fer′ment,** *n.*

con′fer·ence (kon′fər əns) *n.* **1.** meeting. **2.** discussion.

con·fess′ (kən fes′) *v.* **1.** admit. **2.** declare one's sins, as to priest. —**con·fes′sion,** *n.*

con·fess′ed·ly (-id lē) *adv.* by confession; admittedly.

con·fes′sion·al, *adj.* **1.** characteristic of confession. —*n.* **2.** place in church set apart for confession.

con·fes′sor, *n.* **1.** one who confesses. **2.** one who hears confessions.

con·fet′ti (kən fet′ē) *n.* bits of colored paper thrown at festive events.

con′fi·dant′ (kon′fi dant′, -dänt′) *n.* one to whom secrets are told. —**con′fi·dante′,** *n.fem.*

con·fide′ (kən fīd′) *v.,* **-fided, -fid·ing. 1.** trust with secret. **2.** entrust.

con′fi·dence (kon′fi dəns) *n.* **1.** full trust. **2.** assurance. —**con′fi·dent,** *adj.* —**con′fi·dent·ly,** *adv.*

con′fi·den′tial (-den′shəl) *adj.* **1.** entrusted as secret. **2.** private. —**con′fi·den′tial·ly,** *adv.*

con·fig′u·ra′tion (kən fig′yə rā′shən) *n.* external form.

con·fine′, *v.,* **-fined, -fining.** —*v.* (kən fīn′) **1.** keep within bounds. **2.** shut or lock up. —*n.* (pl.) (kon′fīnz) **3.** boundary.

con·fined′, *adj.* restricted.

con·fine′ment, *n.* **1.** imprisonment. **2.** childbirth.

con·firm′ (kən fûrm′) *v.* **1.** make sure. **2.** make valid. **3.** admit into church. —**con′fir·ma′tion** (kon′fər-) *n.*

con·firmed′, *adj.* habitual.

con′fis·cate (kon′fə skāt′) *v.,* **-cated, -cating.** seize by public authority. —**con′fis·ca′tion,** *n.*

con′fla·gra′tion (kon′flə grā′shən) *n.* fierce fire.

con·flict′, *v.,* (kən flikt′) **1.** oppose; clash. —*n.* (kon′flikt) **2.** battle. **3.** antagonism.

con′flu·ence (kon′flōō əns) *n.* act or place of flowing together. —**con′flu·ent,** *adj.*

con·form′ (kən fôrm′) *v.* **1.** adapt. **2.** make similar. —**con·form′ist,** *n.* —**con·form′i·ty,** *n.*

con·found′ (kon found′) *v.* **1.** confuse. **2.** perplex.

con·found′ed, *adj.* **1.** bewildered. **2.** damned.

con·front′ (kən frunt′) *v.* **1.** meet or set facing. **2.** challenge openly. —**con′fron·ta′tion** (kon′frun tā′-shən) *n.* —**con′fron·ta′tion·al,** *adj.*

con·fuse′ (kən fyōōz′) *v.,* **-fused, -fusing. 1.** throw into disorder. **2.** associate wrongly. **3.** disconcert. —**con·fu′sion,** *n.*

con·fute′ (-fyōōt′) *v.,* **-futed, -fut·ing.** prove to be wrong.

Cong., 1. Congregational. **2.** Congress. **3.** Congressional.

con·geal′ (kən jēl′) *v.* **1.** make solid or thick. —**con·geal′ment,** *n.*

con·gen′ial (kən jēn′yəl) *adj.* agreeable; suited. —**con·ge′ni·al′i·ty** (-jē′nē al′i tē) *n.*

con·gen′i·tal (kən jen′i tl) *adj.* innate. —**con·gen′i·tal·ly,** *adv.*

con·gest′ (kən jest′) *v.* **1.** fill to excess. —**con·ges′tion,** *n.*

con·glom′er·ate, *n., adj., v.,* **-ated, -ating.** —*n.* (kən glom′ər it) **1.** mixture. **2.** rock formed of pebbles, etc. **3.** company owning variety of other companies. —*adj.* (-ər it) **4.** mixed. —*v.* (-ə rāt′) **5.** gather into mass. —**con·glom′er·a′tion,** *n.*

con·grat′u·late (kən grach′ə lāt′) *v.,* **-lated, -lating.** express sympathetic joy. —**con·grat′u·la′tion,** *n.*

con′gre·gate (kong′gri gāt′) *v.,* **-gated, -gating.** assemble. —**con′gre·ga′tion,** *n.*

con′gre·ga′tion·al, *adj.* **1.** of congregations. **2.** (*cap.*) denoting church denomination wherein each church acts independently. —**con′gre·ga′tion·al·ism,** *n.*

con′gress (kong′gris) *n.* **1.** national legislative body, esp. (*cap.*) of the U.S. **2.** formal meeting. —**con·gres′sion·al** (kəng gresh′ə nl) *adj.* —**con′gress·man,** *n.* —**con′gress·per′son,** *n.* —**con′gress·wom′an,** *n.fem.*

con′gru·ent (kong′grōō ənt) *adj.* **1.** agreeing. **2.** (of geometric figures) coinciding at all points when superimposed. —**con·gru′ence,** *n.*

con·gru′i·ty (kən grōō′i tē) *n., pl.* **-ties.** agreement. —**con′gru·ous** (kong′grōō əs) *adj.*

con′ic (kon′ik) *adj.* of or like cone. Also, **con′i·cal.**

co′ni·fer (kō′nə fər, kon′ə-) *n.* tree bearing cones. —**co·nif′er·ous** (-nif′ər əs) *adj.*

con·jec′ture (kən jek′chər) *n., v.,* **-tured, -turing.** guess.

con·join′ (kən join′) *v.* join together.

con·ju·gal (kon′jə gəl) *adj.* of marriage. —**con·ju·gal·ly,** *adv.*

con·ju·gate (kon′jə gāt′), *v.,* -**gated,** -**gating.** give inflected forms of (verb). —**con·ju·ga′tion,** *n.*

con·junc′tion (kən jungk′shən) *n.* **1.** union; combination. **2.** *Gram.* word that joins words, phrases, clauses, or sentences. —**con·junc′tive,** *adj.*

con·junc·ti·vi·tis (kən jungk′tə vī′tis) *n.* inflammation of mucous membrane of the eye.

con·jure (kon′jər, kun′-) *v.,* -**jured,** -**juring.** invoke or produce by magic. —**con·jur·er,** *n.*

conk (kongk) *v. Slang.* **1.** strike on the head. **2. conk out. a.** break down. **b.** go to sleep. —*n.* **3.** blow on the head.

Conn. Connecticut.

con·nect′ (kə nekt′) *v.* join; link. —**con·nec′tion;** *Brit.* **con·nex′ion,** *n.* —**con·nec′tive,** *adj., n.*

con·nive (kə nīv′) *v.,* -**nived,** -**niving.** conspire. —**con·niv′ance,** *n.*

con·nois·seur (kon′ə sûr′) *n.* skilled judge.

con·note (kə nōt′) *v.,* -**noted,** -**noting.** signify in addition; imply. —**con·no·ta′tion** (kə′nə tā′shən) *n.*

con·nu·bi·al (kə nōō′bē əl, -nyōō′-) *adj.* matrimonial.

con′quer (kong′kər) *v.* **1.** acquire by force. **2.** defeat. —**con′quer·or,** *n.* —**con′quest,** *n.*

con·quis·ta·dor (kong kwis′tə dôr′, -kēs′-) *n.* -**quis·ta·dors, quis′· ta·do·res** (-kēs′tə dôr′ēz, -āz). 16th-century Spanish conqueror of the Americas.

con′science (kon′shəns) *n.* recognition of right or wrong in oneself.

con′sci·en′tious (-shē en′shəs), *adj.* hardworking.

conscientious objector, person who refuses to serve in military for moral reasons.

con′scious (kon′shəs) *adj.* **1.** in possession of one's senses. **2.** aware. **3.** deliberate. —**con′scious· ly,** *adv.* —**con′scious·ness,** *n.*

con′script, *adj.* (kon′skript) **1.** drafted. —*n.* (kon′skript) **2.** one drafted. —*v.* (kən skript′) **3.** draft for military service. —**con·scrip′· tion,** *n.*

con′se·crate (kon′si krāt′) *v.,* -**crated,** -**crating. 1.** make sacred. **2.** devote. —**con′se·cra′tion,** *n.*

con·sec′u·tive (kən sek′yə tiv) *adj.* successive.

con·sen′sus (kən sen′səs) *n.* agreement.

con·sent′ (kən sent′) *v.* **1.** agree; comply. **2.** assent.

con′se·quence (kon′si kwens′, -kwəns) *n.* **1.** effect. **2.** importance.

con′se·quent′, *adj.* following; resulting. —**con′se·quent·ly,** *adv.*

con·ser·va′tion (kon′sər vā′shən) *n.* preservation of resources. —**con·ser·va′tion·ist,** *n.*

con·ser′va·tive (kən sûr′və tiv) *adj.* **1.** favoring status quo. **2.** cautious. **3.** conservative person. —**con· serv′a·tive·ly,** *adv.* —**con·serv′a· tism,** *n.*

con·serv′a·to·ry (-tôr′ē) *n.,* pl. -**ries. 1.** school of music or drama. **2.** hothouse.

con·serve′, *v.,* -**served,** -**serving,** *n.* —*v.* (kən sûrv′) **1.** keep intact. —*n.* (kon′sûrv) **2.** preserves.

con·sid′er (kən sid′ər) *v.* **1.** think over. **2.** deem. **3.** respect. —**con· sid′er·ate,** *adj.* —**con·sid′er·ate·ly,** *adv.*

con·sid′er·a·ble, *adj.* important or sizable. —**con·sid′er·a·bly,** *adv.*

con·sid·er·a′tion (-ə rā′shən) *n.* **1.** thought. **2.** regard. **3.** fee.

con·sid′er·ing, *prep.* in view of.

con·sign′ (kən sīn′) *v.* **1.** deliver. **2.** entrust. —**con·sign′ment,** *n.*

con·sist′ (kən sist′) *v.* be composed.

con·sist′en·cy (-sis′tən sē) *n.,* pl. -**cies. 1.** firmness. **2.** density. **3.** adherence to principles, behavior, etc. —**con·sist′ent,** *adj.*

con·sole′, *v.,* -**soled,** -**soling.** *v.* —*v.* (kən sōl′) **1.** comfort. —*n.* (kon′sōl) **2.** control panel. —**con′· so·la′tion,** *n.* —**con·sol′a·ble,** *adj.*

con·sol′i·date (kən sol′i dāt′) *v.,* -**dated,** -**dating. 1.** make or become firm. **2.** unite. —**con·sol′i·da′tion,** *n.*

con·som·mé′ (kon′sə mā′) *n.* clear soup.

con′so·nant (kon′sə nənt) *n.* **1.** letter for sound made by obstruction of breath. —*adj.* **2.** in agreement. —**con′so·nant·ly,** *adv.*

con′sort, *n.* (kon′sôrt) **1.** spouse. —*v.* (kən sôrt′) **2.** associate.

con·sor′ti·um (kən sôr′shē əm, -tē-) *n., pl.* -**tia** (-shē ə, -tē ə). **1.** combination for business purposes. **2.** association.

con·spic′u·ous (kən spik′yōō əs) *adj.* **1.** easily seen. **2.** notable. —**con·spic′u·ous·ly,** *adv.*

con·spire′ (kən spīr′) *v.,* -**spired,** -**spiring.** plot together. —**con·spir′· a·cy** (-spir′ə sē) *n.* —**con·spir′a· tor,** *n.*

con′sta·ble (kon′stə bəl) *n.* police officer.

con·stab′u·lar·y (kən stab′yə ler′ē) *n., pl.* -**ies.** police.

con′stant (kon′stənt) *adj.* **1.** uni-

form. **2.** uninterrupted. **3.** faithful.
—n. **4.** something unchanging.
—con'stan•cy, n. —con'stant•ly, adv.

con'stel•la'tion (kon'stə lā'shən) n. group of stars.

con'ster•na'tion (kon'stər nā'shən) n. utter dismay.

con'sti•pate' (kon'stə pāt') v., -pated, -pating. cause difficult evacuation of bowels. —con'sti•pa'tion, n.

con•stit'u•ent (kən stich'σ̄o ant) adj. **1.** being part; composing. —n. **2.** ingredient. **3.** represented voter. —con•stit'u•en•cy, n.

con'sti•tute' (kon'sti tσ̄ot', -tyσ̄ot') v., -tuted, -tuting. **1.** compose. **2.** make.

con'sti•tu'tion, n. **1.** make-up. **2.** physical condition. **3.** system of governmental principles. —con'sti•tu'tion•al, adj.

con•strain' (kən strān') v. **1.** force or oblige. **2.** confine. —con•strained', adj. —con•straint', n.

con•strict' (kən strikt') v. draw together; shrink. —con•stric'tion, n.

con•struct' (kən strukt') v. build or devise. —con•struc'tion, n.

con•struc'tive, adj. **1.** of construction. **2.** helpful.

con•strue' (kən strōō') v., -strued, -struing. interpret.

con'sul (kon'səl) n. local diplomatic official. —con'su•lar, adj. —con'su•late (-sə lit) n.

con•sult' (kən sult') v. **1.** ask advice of. **2.** refer to. **3.** confer. —con•sult'ant, n. —con•sul•ta'tion, n.

con•sume' (kən sōōm') v., -sumed, -suming. **1.** use up. **2.** devour.

con•sum'er, n. **1.** one that consumes. **2.** purchaser of goods.

con•sum'er•ism, n. policies protecting consumers.

con'sum•mate', v., -mated, -mating, adj. —v. (kon'sə māt'), adj. (kan sum'it, kon'sə mit). complete or perfect. —con'sum•ma'tion, n.

con•sump'tion (kən sump'shən) n. **1.** act of consuming. **2.** amount consumed. **3.** wasting disease, esp. tuberculosis of lungs. —con•sump'tive, adj., n.

cont., continued.

con'tact (kon'takt) n. **1.** a touching. **2.** association. **3.** business acquaintance. —v. **4.** put or bring into contact. **5.** communicate with. **contact lens,** corrective lens put directly on eye.

con•ta'gion (kən tā'jən) n. spread of disease by contact. —con•ta'gious, adj.

con•tain' (kən tān') v. **1.** have within itself. **2.** have space for. —con•tain'er, n.

con•tam'i•nate' (kən tam'ə nāt') v., -nated, -nating. make impure.

contd., continued.

con•tem'plate' (kon'təm plāt', -təm-) v., -plated, -plating. **1.** consider. **2.** observe. —con•tem'pla'tion, n.

con•tem'po•rar'y (kən tem'pə rer'ē) adj., n., pl. -raries. —adj. **1.** Also, con•tem'po•ra'ne•ous (-rā'nē əs). of same age or period. —n. **2.** contemporary person.

con•tempt' (kən tempt') n. **1.** scorn. **2.** disgrace. **3.** disrespect of court. —con•tempt'i•ble, adj. —con•temp'tu•ous, adj.

con•tend' (kən tend') v. **1.** be in struggle. **2.** assert.

con•tent', adj. (kən tent') **1.** Also, con•tent'ed. satisfied. —v. (kən tent') **2.** make content. —n. (kən tent') **3.** Also, con•tent'ment. ease of mind. **4.** (kon'tent) (often pl.). what is contained. **5.** (kon'tent) capacity. —con•tent'ed•ly, adv.

con•ten'tion (kən ten'shən) n. controversy. —con•ten'tious, adj.

con•test', n. (kon'test) **1.** struggle; competition. —v. (kən test') **2.** fight for. **3.** dispute. —con•test'ant, n.

con'text (kon'tekst) n. surrounding words or circumstances.

con•tig'u•ous (kən tig'yōō əs) adj. **1.** touching. **2.** near.

con'ti•nent (kon'tn ənt) n. **1.** major land mass. —adj. **2.** self-restrained. —con'ti•nen'tal (-nen'tl) adj.

con•tin'gen•cy (kən tin'jən sē) n., pl. -cies. chance; event.

con•tin'gent (kən tin'jənt) adj. **1.** conditional; possible. —n. **2.** group. **3.** contingency.

con•tin'u•al (kən tin'yōō əl) adj. happening regularly or frequently. **2.** happening without interruption.
—**Usage.** Use CONTINUAL for actions that occur over and over again (especially actions that are annoying): *The dog's continual barking was driving me crazy.* The word CONTINUOUS is used for actions that keep going and do not stop: *We had continuous electricity during the big storm.*

con•tin'ue (kən tin'yōō) v. **1.** go or carry on. **2.** stay. **3.** extend. **4.** carry over. —con•tin'u•al•ly, adv.

con•ti•nu'i•ty (kon'tn σ̄oı̄ tē, -tn yōō'-) n., pl. -ties. **1.** continuous whole. **2.** script.

con•tin'u•ous (kən tin'yōō əs) adj.

going on without stop; uninterrupted. —**con·tin'u·ous·ly,** adv.
—*Usage.* See CONTINUAL.

con·tin'u·um (-yōō əm) n., pl. **-ua.** continuous extent, series, or whole.

con·tort' (kən tôrt') v. twist; distort. —**con·tor'tion,** n.

con·tor'tion·ist, n. person who can twist into unusual positions.

con'tour (kon'tŏŏr) n. outline.

contra-, prefix meaning against, opposite, or opposing, as *contradict.*

con'tra·band' (kon'trə band') n. goods prohibited from import. —**con'tra·band',** adj.

con'tra·cep'tion (-sep'shən) n. deliberate prevention of pregnancy. —v. (kən trakt') 3. shorten.

con'tract, n. (kon'trakt) 1. agreement. —v. (kən trakt') 2. shorten. 3. become ill. 4. agree. —**con·trac'tion,** n.

con'trac·tor (kon'trak tər) n. one who supplies work by contract.

con'tra·dict' (kon'trə dikt') v. deny as being correct. —**con'tra·dic'tion,** n. —**con'tra·dic'to·ry,** adj.

con·tral'to (kən tral'tō) n., pl. **-tos.** lowest female voice.

con·trap'tion (kən trap'shən) n. strange machine; gadget.

con'tra·ry (kon'trer ē) adj., n., pl. **-ries.** —adj. 1. opposite. 2. *(also kən trâr'ē)* perverse. —n. 3. something contrary. —**con'tra·ri·ly,** adv. —**con'tra·ri·wise,** adv.

con·trast', v. (kən trast') 1. show unlikeness. 2. compare. —n. (kon'trast) 3. show of unlikeness. 4. something unlike.

con'tra·vene' (kon'trə vēn') v., **-vened, -vening.** 1. oppose. 2. violate. —**con'tra·ven'tion** (-ven'shən) n.

con·trib'ute (kən trib'yŏŏt) v., **-uted, -uting.** give with others; donate. —**con'tri·bu'tion** (kon'trə-byŏŏ'shən) n. —**con·trib'u·tor,** n.

con·trite' (kən trīt') adj. penitent. —**con·tri'tion** (-trish'ən) n.

con·trive' (kən trīv') v., **-trived, -triving.** 1. plan; devise. 2. plot.

con·trol' (kən trōl') v., **-trolled, -trolling.** —v. 1. have direction over. 2. restrain. —n. 3. power of controlling. 4. restraint. 5. regulating device. —**con·trol'la·ble,** adj.

con·trol'ler, n. 1. officer who superintends finances. 2. regulator.

con'tro·ver'sy (kon'trə vûr'sē) n., pl. **-sies.** dispute or debate. —**con'tro·ver'sial** (-vûr'shəl) adj. —**con'tro·ver'sial·ly,** adv.

con'tro·vert' (kon'trə vûrt', kon'-trə vûrt') v. dispute.

con·tu·ma'cious (kon'tŏŏ mā'shəs, -tyŏō-) adj. stubbornly disobedient.

con'tu·me·ly (kon'tŏŏ mə lē, -tyŏō-) n., pl. **-lies.** contemptuous treatment.

con·tu'sion (kən tŏō'zhən, -tyŏō'-) n. bruise.

co·nun'drum (kə nun'drəm) n. riddle involving pun.

con'ur·ba'tion (kon'ər bā'shən) n. continuous mass of urban settlements.

con'va·lesce' (kon'və les') v., **-lesced, -lescing.** recover from illness. —**con'va·les'cence,** n. —**con'va·les'cent,** adj., n.

con·vec'tion (kən vek'shən) n. transference of heat by movement of heated matter.

con·vene' (kən vēn') v., **-vened, -vening.** assemble.

con·ven'ient (-vēn'yənt) adj. handy or favorable. —**con·ven'ience,** n. —**con·ven'ient·ly,** adv.

con'vent (kon'vent, -vənt) n. community of nuns.

con·ven'tion (kən ven'shən) n. 1. meeting. 2. accepted usage. —**con·ven'tion·al,** adj.

con·verge' (kən vûrj') v., **-verged, -verging.** meet in a point.

con·ver'sant (kən vûr'sənt) adj. acquainted.

con'ver·sa'tion (kon'vər sā'shən) n. informal discussion. —**con'ver·sa'tion·al,** adj.

con·verse', v., **-versed, -versing,** adj., n. —v. (kən vûrs') 1. talk informally. —adj., n. (kon'vûrs) 2. opposite. —**con·verse'ly,** adv.

con·vert', v. (kən vûrt') 1. change. 2. persuade to different beliefs. —n. (kon'vûrt) 3. converted person. —**con·ver'sion,** n. —**con·vert'er,** n.

con·vert'i·ble, adj. able to be converted. —n. 2. automobile with folding top.

con·vex' (kon veks') adj. curved outward. —**con·vex'i·ty,** n.

con·vey' (kən vā') v. 1. transport. 2. transmit.

con·vey'ance, n. 1. act of conveying. 2. vehicle. 3. transfer of property.

con·vict', v. (kən vikt') 1. find guilty. —n. (kon'vikt) 2. convicted person.

con·vic'tion, n. 1. a convicting. 2. firm belief.

con·vince' (kən vins') v., **-vinced, -vincing.** cause to believe. —**con·vinc'ing,** adj.

con·viv'i·al (kən viv'ē əl) adj. sociable. —**con·viv'i·al'i·ty** (-al'i tē) n.

con·voke′ (kən vōk′) v., **-voked,**
-voking. call together. —**con′vo·**
ca′tion (kon′vō kā′shən) n.

con′vo·lu′tion (kon′və lōō′shən) n.
coil. —**con′vo·lut′ed,** adj.

con′voy (kon′voi) v. **1.** escort for
protection. —n. **2.** group of ships.

con·vulse′ (kən vuls′) v., **-vulsed,**
-vulsing. shake violently. —**con·**
vul′sion, n. —**con·vul′sive,** adj.

co′ny (kō′nē, kun′ē) n., pl. **-nies.**
rabbit fur.

coo (kōō) v., **cooed, cooing.** murmur softly. —**coo,** n.

cook (kŏŏk) v. **1.** prepare by heating. —n. **2.** person who cooks.
—**cook′book′,** n. —**cook′er·y,** n.

cook′ie, n. small sweet cake.

cook′out′, n. outdoor gathering at
which food is cooked and eaten.

cool (kōōl) adj. **1.** moderately cold.
2. calm. **3.** not enthusiastic. **4.**
Slang. great; excellent. —v. **5.** make
or become cool. —**cool′ant,** n.
—**cool′er,** n. —**cool′ly,** adv.

coo′lie (kōō′lē) n. unskilled laborer,
esp. formerly in Far East.

coop (kōōp, kŏŏp) n. **1.** cage for
fowls. —v. **2.** keep in coop.

coop′er, n. barrel maker.

co·op′er·ate′ (kō op′ə rāt′) v.,
-ated, -ating. work or act together.
—**co·op′er·a′tion,** n.

co·op′er·a·tive (-ər ə tiv) adj. **1.**
involving cooperation. **2.** willing to
act with others. —n. **3.** Also, **co-op**
(kō′op′). jointly owned apartment
house or business.

co-opt′ (kō opt′) v. **1.** choose as
fellow member. **2.** win over into
larger group.

co·or′di·nate′, v., **-nated, -nating.**
adj., n. —v. (kō ôr′dn āt′) **1.** put
in order. **2.** adjust. —adj., n. (-dn-
it) **3.** equal. —**co·or′di·na′tion,** n.

coot (kōōt) n. aquatic bird.

cop (kop) n. Slang. police officer.

co′pay′ (kō′pā′) n. percentage of
fee, or fixed amount, paid by patient to health-care provider. Also,
co′pay′ment,

cope (kōp) v., **coped, coping.** n.
—v. **1.** deal with problems or duties. —n. **2.** cloak worn by priests.

cop′i·er (kop′ē ər) n. machine for
making copies.

co′pi·lot (kō′pī′lət) n. aircraft pilot
second in command.

cop′ing, n. top layer of
wall.

co′pi·ous (kō′pē əs) adj. abundant.

cop′per (kop′ər) n. soft reddish
metallic element.

cop′per·head′, n. venomous snake.

copse (kops) n. thicket. Also, **cop′**
pice.

cop′u·late′ (kop′yə lāt′) v., **-lated,**
-lating. have sexual intercourse.
—**cop′u·la′tion,** n.

cop′y (kop′ē) n., pl. **copies,** v., **cop-**
ied, copying. —n. **1.** reproduction
or imitation. **2.** material to be copied. —v. **3.** make copy of.

cop′y·cat′, n. imitator.

cop′y·right′, n. exclusive control
of book, picture, etc. —v. **2.** secure
copyright on. —adj. **3.** covered by
copyright.

co·quette′ (kō ket′) n. female flirt.
—**co·quet′tish,** adj.

cor′al (kôr′əl) n. **1.** substance
formed from skeletons of certain marine animals. **2.** yellowish pink.

cord (kôrd) n. **1.** small rope. **2.**
Elect. small insulated cable.

cor′dial (kôr′jəl) adj. **1.** hearty;
friendly. —n. **2.** liqueur. —**cor·**
dial′i·ty (-jal′i tē, -jē al′-) n.

cord′less, adj. (of electrical appliance) having self-contained power
supply.

cor′don (kôr′dn) n. line of police.

cor′do·van (kôr′də van) n. soft
leather.

cor′du·roy (kôr′də roi′) n. ribbed
fabric.

core (kôr) n., v., **cored, coring.**
—n. **1.** central part. —v. **2.** remove
core of.

co′ri·an′der (kôr′ē an′dər) n. herb
with pungent leaves and seeds.

cork (kôrk) n. **1.** bark of an oak
tree. **2.** stopper of cork, rubber, etc.
—v. **3.** close with a cork.

cork′screw′, n. spiral, pointed instrument for pulling corks.

cor′mo·rant (kôr′mər ənt) n. water
bird.

corn (kôrn) n. **1.** maize. **2.** any edible grain. **3.** horny callus, esp. on
toe. —v. **4.** preserve in brine.

corn bread, n. bread made with
cornmeal.

corn′cob′, n. core of an ear of corn
which holds grains.

cor′ne·a (kôr′nē ə) n. transparent
part of coat of the eye.

cor′ner (kôr′nər) n. **1.** place or
point where two lines or streets
meet. **2.** exclusive control. —v. **3.**
put into corner. **4.** gain exclusive
control of (stock or commodity).

cor′ner·stone′, n. **1.** stone representing start of building construction. **2.** something basic.

cor·net′ (kôr net′) n. wind instrument resembling trumpet.

cor′nice (kôr′nis) n. horizontal projection at top of a wall.

corn′meal′, n. meal made from
corn.

corn′starch′, *n.* starchy flour made from corn.

cor•nu•co′pi•a (kôr′nə kō′pē ə, -nyə-) *n.* horn-shaped container of food, etc.; horn of plenty.

corn′y, *adj.*, **-i•er**, **-i•est**. trite, sentimental, or old-fashioned.

co•rol′la (ka rol′ə, -rō′lə) *n.* petals of a flower.

cor′ol•lar′y (kôr′ə ler′ē) *n., pl.* **-ies**. logical deduction.

co•ro′na (kə rō′nə) *n., pl.* **-nas, -nae** (-nē) circle of light, esp. around sun or moon.

cor′o•nar′y (kôr′ə ner′ē) *adj., n., pl.* **-naries**. —*adj.* **1.** of arteries supplying heart. —*n.* **2.** heart attack.

cor•o•na′tion (kôr′ə nā′shən) *n.* crowning.

cor′o•ner (kôr′ə nər) *n.* official who investigates suspicious deaths.

cor′o•net (kôr′ə net′) *n.* small crown.

corp., corporation.

cor′po•ral (kôr′pər əl) *adj.* **1.** physical. **2.** *Mil.* officer below sergeant.

cor•po•ra′tion (-rā′shən) *n.* legally formed association for business, etc. —**cor′po•rate** (-pər it, -prit) *adj.*

cor•po′re•al (kôr pôr′ē əl) *adj.* tangible.

corps (kôr) *n., pl.* **corps. 1.** military unit. **2.** any group.

corpse (kôrps) *n.* dead body.

cor′pu•lent (kôr′pyə lənt) *adj.* fat.

cor′pus (kôr′pəs) *n., pl.* **-pora** (-pər ə) **1.** comprehensive collection of writings. **2.** body, esp. when dead.

cor′pus•cle (kôr′pə səl) *n.* blood cell.

cor•ral′ (kə ral′) *n.*, *v.*, **-ralled, -ralling.** —*n.* **1.** pen for stock. —*v.* **2.** keep in corral. **3.** corner or capture.

cor•rect′ (kə rekt′) *v.* **1.** mark or remove errors. **2.** rebuke or punish. —*adj.* **3.** right. —**cor•rec′tion,** *n.* —**cor•rec′tive,** *adj., n.*

cor′re•late (kôr′ə lāt′) *v.*, **-lated, -lating.** bring into mutual relation. —**cor′re•la′tion,** *n.*

cor′re•spond (kôr′ə spond′) *v.* **1.** conform or be similar. **2.** communicate by letters. —**cor′re•spond′ence,** *n.*

cor′re•spond′ent, *n.* **1.** letter writer. **2.** reporter. —*adj.* **3.** corresponding.

cor′ri•dor (kôr′i dər) *n.* passageway.

cor•rob′o•rate (kə rob′ə rāt′) *v.*, **-rated, -rating.** confirm. —**cor•rob′o•ra′tion,** *n.* —**cor•rob′o•ra′tive** (-ə rā′tiv, -ər ə tiv) *adj.*

cor•rode′ (kə rōd′) *v.*, **-roded, -rod-**

ing. eat away gradually. —**cor•ro′sion** (-rō′zhən) *n.* —**cor•ro′sive,** *adj., n.*

cor′ru•gate′ (kôr′ə gāt′) *v.*, **-gated, -gating.** bend into folds.

cor•rupt′ (kə rupt′) *adj.* **1.** dishonest. **2.** tainted. —*v.* **3.** make or become corrupt. —**cor•rup′tion,** *n.*

cor•sage′ (kôr säzh′) *n.* small bouquet to be worn.

cor′sair (kôr′sâr) *n.* pirate.

cor′set (kôr′sit) *n.* undergarment for shaping the body.

cor•tege′ (kôr tezh′) *n.* procession.

cor′tex (kôr′teks) *n.* **1.** bark. **2.** outer covering of brain or organ.

cor′ti•sone (kôr′tə zōn′, -sōn′) *n.* hormone used esp. in treating inflammatory diseases.

cor•vette′ (kôr vet′) *n.* small fast vessel.

cos•met′ic (koz met′ik) *n.* **1.** beautifying product. —*adj.* **2.** of cosmetics. **3.** superficial.

cos′mic (koz′mik) *adj.* **1.** of the cosmos. **2.** vast.

cos•mol′o•gy (-mol′ə jē) *n.* study of the origin and structure of the universe.

cos′mo•pol′i•tan (koz′mə pol′i tn) *adj.* worldly.

cos′mos (-məs, -mōs) *n.* ordered universe.

cost (kôst) *n.* **1.** price paid. **2.** loss or penalty. —*v.* **3.** require as payment. —**cost′ly,** *adj.*

cost′-ef•fec′tive, *adj.* producing optimum results for the expenditure.

cost of living, average amount paid for basic necessities.

cos′tume (kos′tōōm, -tyōōm) *n.* historical or theatrical dress.

co′sy (kō′zē) *adj.*, **-sier, -siest.** cozy.

cot (kot) *n.* light bed.

cote (kōt) *n.* shelter for pigeons, sheep, etc.

co′te•rie (kō′tə rē) *n.* group of social acquaintances.

co•til′lion (kə til′yən) *n.* **1.** elaborate dance. **2.** formal ball.

cot′tage (kot′ij) *n.* small house.

cottage cheese, soft, mild cheese made from skim milk.

cot′ton (kot′n) *n.* downy plant substance made into fabric.

cot′ton•mouth′ (-mouth′) *n.* venomous snake. Also, **water moccasin.**

cot′ton•seed′, *n.* seed of cotton plant, yielding an oil (**cottonseed oil**) used in cooking and medicine.

couch (kouch) *n.* **1.** bed. —*v.* **2.** express.

couch potato, *Informal.* person who watches a lot of television.

cou′gar (kōō′gər) n. large American wildcat.

cough (kôf) v. **1.** expel air from lungs suddenly and loudly. —n. **2.** act or sound of coughing.

cough drop, lozenge for relieving sore throat, etc.

could (kŏŏd; *unstressed* kəd) v. pt. of **can.**

coun′cil (koun′səl) n. deliberative or advisory body. —**coun′ci•lor, coun′cil•lor,** n.

coun′sel (koun′səl) n., v., **-seled, -seling.** —n. **1.** advice. **2.** consultation. **3.** lawyer. —v. **4.** advise. —**coun′se•lor, coun′sel•lor,** n.

count (kount) v. **1.** find total number. **2.** name numbers to. **3.** esteem. **4.** rely. **5.** be noticed. —n. **6.** a counting. **7.** total number. **8.** item in indictment. **9.** nobleman.

count′down′, n. backward counting in time units to scheduled event.

coun′te•nance (koun′tn əns) n., v., **-nanced, -nancing.** —n. **1.** appearance. —v. **2.** tolerate.

coun′ter (koun′tər) n. **1.** table or display case in store. **2.** one that counts. **3.** anything opposite. —v. **4.** oppose. **5.** return (blow). —adv., adj. **6.** contrary.

counter-, prefix indicating: **1.** against, as *counterinfluence.* **2.** in response to, as *counterattack.* **3.** opposite, as *counterclockwise.* **4.** complementary, as *counterbalance.*

coun′ter•act′, v. neutralize.

coun′ter•at•tack′, n., v. attack in response.

coun′ter•bal′ance, n., v., **-anced, -ancing.** —n. (koun′tər bal′əns) **1.** anything that balances another. —v. (koun′tər bal′əns) **2.** offset.

coun′ter•clock′wise′, adv., adj. opposite to direction of turning clock hands.

coun′ter•cul′ture, n. culture of those opposed to prevailing culture.

coun′ter•feit (-fit) adj. **1.** fake. —n. **2.** fraudulent imitation. —v. **3.** make counterfeits. feign.

coun′ter•in•tel′li•gence, n. thwarting of espionage of a foreign power.

coun′ter•mand′ (-mand′) v. revoke (command).

coun′ter•part′, n. match or complement.

coun′ter•point′, n. combining of melodies.

coun′ter•pro•duc′tive, adj. giving contrary results.

coun′ter•sign′, n. **1.** secret signal. —v. **2.** sign to confirm another signature.

count′ess (koun′tis) n. **1.** wife of count or earl. **2.** woman equal in rank to count or earl.

count′less, adj. innumerable.

coun′try (kun′trē) n., pl. **-tries. 1.** nation. **2.** rural districts. —**coun′try•side′,** n.

coun′ty (koun′tē) n., pl. **-ties.** political unit within state.

coup (kōō) n., pl. **coups.** daring and successful stroke.

coup d′é•tat′ (kōō′ dā tä′) pl. **coups d′état** (-dā täz′, -tä′). overthrow of a government.

coupe (kōōp) n. small, two-door car. Also, **cou•pé′** (kōō pā′).

cou′ple (kup′əl) n., v., **-pled, -pling.** —n. **1.** pair. —v. **2.** fasten or unite. —**cou′pler,** n.

—**Usage.** Do not confuse PAIR and COUPLE. Both words have the meaning "a group of two" but are used differently. PAIR is used when two things come as a set, with one not usually used without the other: *a pair of socks, a pair of gloves* or when there is one item that has two parts, as in *a pair of shorts, a pair of scissors.* COUPLE is used for things of the same kind that happen to be two in number: *a couple of books, a couple of chairs.*

cou′plet (kup′lit) n. pair of rhyming lines.

cou′pon (kōō′pon, kyōō′-) n. certificate entitling holder to a gift or discount.

cour′age (kûr′ij, kur′-) n. bravery. —**cou•ra′geous** (kə rā′jəs) adj. —**cou•ra′geous•ly,** adv.

cou′ri•er (kûr′ē ər) n. messenger.

course (kôrs) n., v., **coursed, coursing.** —n. **1.** continuous passage. **2.** route. **3.** series of lessons. **4.** one part of meal. —v. **5.** run.

court (kôrt) n. **1.** enclosed space. **2.** level area for certain games. **3.** palace. **4.** assembly held by sovereign. **5.** homage or attention. **6.** place where justice is dealt. **7.** judge or judges. —v. **8.** woo. —**court′house,** n. —**court′room′,** n. —**court′ship,** n. —**court′yard′,** n.

cour′te•san (kôr′tə zən) n. prostitute with noble or wealthy clients.

cour′te•sy (kûr′tə sē) n., pl. **-sies. 1.** good manners. **2.** indulgence. —**cour′te•ous** (-tē əs) adj.

cour′ti•er (kôr′tē ər) n. person in attendance at court.

court′ly, adj. elegant.

court′-mar′tial, n., pl. **courts-martial,** v., **-tialed, -tialing.** —n. **1.** military court. —v. **2.** try by court-martial.

cous′in (kuz′ən) n. child of uncle or aunt.

cou•tu'ri•er (kōō tŏŏr'ē ər, -ē ā') n. designer of stylish clothes.

cove (kōv) n. recess in shoreline.

cov'en (kuv'ən, kō'vən) n. assembly of witches.

cov•e•nant (kuv'ə nənt) n. solemn agreement; oath or pact.

cov'er (kuv'ər) v. **1.** be or put something over. **2.** include. **3.** have in range. **4.** meet or offset. —n. **5.** thing that covers.

cov'er•age (-ij) n. **1.** protection by insurance. **2.** reporting of news.

cov'er•let n. quilt.

cov'ert (kō'vərt) adj. secret.
—**cov'ert•ly,** adv.

cov'er-up', n. concealing of illegal activity, a blunder, etc.

cov'et (kuv'it) v. desire greatly or wrongfully. —**cov'et•ous,** adj.

cov'ey (kuv'ē) n., pl. -eys. small flock.

cow (kou) n. female of bovine or other large animal. —v. **2.** intimidate.

cow'ard (kou'ərd) n. person who lacks courage. —**cow'ard•ice** (-ar-dis) n. —**cow'ard•ly,** adj., adv.

cow'boy', n. cattle herder. Also, **cow'hand'; cow'girl',** n. fem.

cow'er (kou'ər) v. crouch in fear.

cowl (koul) n. hoodlike part.

cow'lick', n. tuft of hair growing in a different direction.

cow'slip', n. plant with yellow flowers.

cox'swain (kok'sən) n. person who steers boat or racing shell. Also, **cox.**

coy (koi) adj. affectedly shy.
—**coy'ly,** adv. —**coy'ness,** n.

coy•o'te (kī ōt'ē) n. wild animal related to wolf.

coz'en (kuz'ən) v. cheat or deceive.

co'zy (kō'zē) adj., -zier, -ziest. comfortable; snug. —**co'zi•ly,** adv. —**co'zi•ness,** n.

CPA, certified public accountant.

CPI, consumer price index.

CPR, cardiopulmonary resuscitation: a form of lifesaving.

CPU, central processing unit, the key component of a computer system.

crab (krab) n. crustacean with broad flat body.

crab apple, small tart apple.

crab'by, adj., -bier, -biest. grouchy.

crack (krak) v. **1.** make sudden, sharp sound. **2.** break without separating. —n. **3.** sudden, sharp sound. **4.** break without separation. **5.** smokable form of cocaine.

crack'down', n. stern enforcement of regulations.

crack'er, n. **1.** crisp biscuit. **2.** firecracker.

crack'le (krak'əl) v., -led, -ling, n. —v. **1.** crack repeatedly. —n. **2.** crackling sound.

crack'pot', n. person with irrational theories.

crack'up', n. breakdown.

cra'dle (krād'l) n., v., -dled, -dling. —n. **1.** bed for baby. —v. **2.** place in cradle. **3.** hold protectively.

craft (kraft) n. **1.** skill; skilled trade. **2.** cunning. **3.** vessels or aircraft. —**crafts'man,** n. —**crafts'wom•an,** n. fem. —**crafts'man•ship',** n.

craft'y, adj., -ier, -iest. cunning.

crag (krag) n. steep rough rock.

cram (kram) v., crammed, cramming. **1.** fill tightly. **2.** study hard.

cramp (kramp) n. **1.** involuntary muscular contraction. —v. **2.** affect with a cramp. **3.** hamper.

cramped (krampt) adj. confined or limited.

cran'ber•ry (kran'ber'ē) n., pl. -ries. red acid edible berry.

crane (krān) n. **1.** tall wading bird. **2.** lifting device or machine.

cra'ni•um (krā'nē əm) n., pl. -niums, -nia (-nē ə). skull.

crank (krangk) n. **1.** right-angled lever to operate machine. **2.** Informal. grouchy person. —v. **3.** turn with a crank.

crank'y (krang'kē) adj., -ier, -iest. ill-tempered. —**crank'i•ness,** n.

cran'ny (kran'ē) n., pl. -nies. cleft.

crap (krap) n. Slang. **1.** worthless material. **2.** false or meaningless statements.

crape (krāp) n. crepe (defs. 1, 2).

craps (kraps) n. dice game.

crash (krash) v. **1.** strike or collide noisily. **2.** land or fall with damage. —n. **3.** noise or act of crashing. **4.** collapse. **5.** act of crashing.

crass (kras) adj. insensitive; crude.

crate (krāt) n., v., crated, crating. —n. **1.** box or frame for packing. —v. **2.** put in crate.

cra'ter (krā'tər) n. cup-shaped hole, as in volcano or on moon.

cra•vat' (krə vat') n. necktie.

crave (krāv) v., craved, craving. yearn or beg for.

cra'ven (krā'vən) adj. **1.** cowardly. —n. **2.** coward.

crav'ing, n. intense yearning.

crawl (krôl) v. **1.** move slowly, as on stomach. —n. **2.** act of crawling. **3.** swimming stroke. —**crawl'er,** n.

cray'fish' (krā'fish') n. crustacean resembling a lobster. Also, **craw'fish'** (krô'-).

cray·on (krā′on) n. stick of colored wax or chalk for drawing.

craze (krāz) v., **crazed, crazing,** n. —v. 1. make insane. 2. mark with fine cracks, as glaze. —n. 3. mania.

cra·zy (krā′zē) adj., **-zier, -ziest.** 1. insane. 2. impractical.

creak (krēk) v. 1. squeak sharply. —n. 2. creaking sound.

cream (krēm) n. 1. fatty part of milk. 2. best part of anything. —v. 3. thick, smooth substance to put on skin. 4. make with cream. 5. mix until creamy. 6. Informal. defeat utterly. —**cream′y,** adj.

cream′er·y, n., pl. **-ies.** place where dairy goods are produced.

crease (krēs) n., v., **creased, creasing.** —n. 1. mark from folding. —v. 2. make creases in.

cre·ate (krē āt′) v., **-ated, -ating.** cause to exist. —**cre·a′tion,** n. —**cre·a′tive,** adj. —**cre·a′tor,** n.

crea′ture (krē′chər) n. 1. animate being. 2. anything created.

cre′dence (krēd′ns) n. belief.

cre·den′tial (kri den′shəl) n. (usually pl.) verifying document.

cre·den′za (kri den′zə) n. sideboard, esp. one without legs.

cred′i·ble (kred′ə bəl) adj. believable. —**cred·i·bil′i·ty,** n.

cred′it (kred′it) n. 1. belief. 2. honor. 3. time allowed for payment. 4. balance in person's favor. —v. 5. believe. 6. ascribe to. —**cred′it·a·ble,** adj. worthy.

credit card, card entitling holder to charge purchases.

cred′i·tor, n. person owed.

credit union, cooperative group that makes loans to its members at low interest rates.

cred′u·lous (krej′ə ləs) adj. too trusting. —**cre·du·li·ty** (krə dōō′li-tē, -dyōō′-) n.

creed (krēd) n. formula of belief.

creek (krēk, krik) n. brook.

creep (krēp) v., **crept** (krept) or **creeped, creeping,** n. —v. 1. move stealthily; crawl. —n. 2. Slang. disagreeable person.

creep′y, adj., **-ier, -iest.** causing uneasiness.

cre·mate (krē′māt) v., **-mated, -mating.** burn (corpse) to ashes. —**cre·ma′tion,** n. —**cre′ma·to′ry,** n.

Cre·ole (krē′ōl) n. 1. one of French and Spanish blood born in Louisiana. 2. (l.c.) pidgin that has become native language of a group.

cre′o·sote (krē′ə sōt′) n. oily liquid from tar.

crepe (krāp; for 3 also krep) n. 1. light crinkled fabric. 2. Also, **crepe paper,** thin, wrinkled paper used

for decorating. 3. thin, light pancake.

cre·scen′do (kri shen′dō) n., pl. **-dos.** Music. gradual increase in loudness.

cres′cent (kres′ənt) n. 1. moon in its first or last quarter. 2. object having this shape.

cress (kres) n. plant with pungent leaves, eaten in salads.

crest (krest) n. 1. tuft or plume. 2. figure above coat of arms.

crest′fal′len, adj. abruptly discouraged or depressed.

cre′tin (krēt′n) n. boorish person.

cre·tonne′ (kri ton′) n. heavily printed cotton.

cre·vasse′ (krə vas′) n. fissure, esp. in glacier.

crev′ice (krev′is) n. fissure.

crew (krōō) n. 1. group of persons working together, as on ship. —v. 2. form crew of.

crew cut, haircut in which the hair is cut close to the head.

crib (krib) n., v., **cribbed, cribbing.** —n. 1. child's bed. 2. rack or bin. —v. 3. put in a crib. 4. plagiarize.

crib′bage (krib′ij) n. card game using score-board with pegs.

crick (krik) n. muscular spasm.

crick′et (krik′it) n. 1. leaping, noisy insect. 2. British outdoor ballgame with bats and wickets.

cri′er (krī′ər) n. one who announces.

crime (krīm) n. 1. unlawful act. 2. sin. —**crim′i·nal** (krim′ə nl) adj., n. —**crim′i·nal·ly,** adv.

crimp (krimp) v. 1. make wavy. —n. 2. crimped form.

crim′son (krim′zən) n., adj. deep red.

cringe (krinj) v., **cringed, cringing.** shrink in fear or embarrassment.

crin′kle (kring′kəl) v., **-kled, -kling,** n. wrinkle. —**crin′kly,** adj.

crin′o·line (krin′l in) n. 1. stiff, coarse fabric. 2. petticoat.

crip′ple (krip′əl) n., v., **-pled, -pling.** —n. 1. Sometimes Offensive. lame or disabled person or animal. —v. 2. make lame; disable.

cri′sis (krī′sis) n., pl. **-ses** (-sēz). decisive stage or point.

crisp (krisp) adj. 1. brittle. 2. firm and fresh. 3. brisk. 4. cold and dry. —v. 5. make or become crisp. —**crisp′ly,** adv. —**crisp′ness,** n.

criss′cross′ (kris′krôs′) adj. 1. marked with crossed lines. —v. 2. mark with crossed lines. —n. 3. crisscross pattern. —v. 3. mark with crossed lines.

cri·te′ri·on (krī tēr′ē ən) n., pl. **-teria** (-tēr′ē ə). standard for judgment.

crit′ic (krit′ik) n. **1.** judge of art or literature. **2.** faultfinding person.

crit′i·cal, adj. **1.** severe in judgment. **2.** involving criticism. **3.** crucial.

crit′i·cize′ (-sīz′) v., -cized, -cizing. **1.** discuss as a critic. **2.** find fault with. —**crit′i·cism** (-siz′əm) n.

cri·tique′ (kri tēk′) n. critical article.

crit′ter (krit′ər) n. Dial. creature.

croak (krōk) v. utter a hoarse cry.

cro·chet′ (krō shā′) v. form thread into designs with hooked needle.

crock (krok) n. earthen jar. —**crock′er·y**, n.

croc′o·dile′ (krok′ə dīl′) n. large aquatic legged reptile with long, powerful jaws and tail.

cro′cus (krō′kəs) n. small bulbous plant blooming in early spring.

crois·sant′ (Fr. kwä sän′; Eng. krə sänt′) n. crescent-shaped pastry.

crone (krōn) n. witchlike old woman.

cro′ny (krō′nē) n., pl. -nies. close friend.

crook (krŏok) n. **1.** curved tool. **2.** dishonest person. —**crook′ed**, adj.

croon (krōon) v. sing softly.

crop (krop) n., v., cropped, cropping. —n. **1.** produce from the soil. **2.** short whip. **3.** pouch in gullet of bird. —v. **4.** remove ends. **5.** cut short. **6.** reap. **7. crop up**, appear.

cro·quet′ (krō kā′) n. game with wooden balls and mallets.

cro·quette′ (krō ket′) n. fried or baked piece of chopped food.

cro′sier (krō′zhər) n. staff of bishop.

cross (krôs) n. **1.** structure whose basic form has an upright with transverse piece. **2.** emblem of Christianity. **3.** figure resembling cross. **4.** mixture of breeds. —v. **5.** make sign of cross over. **6.** put, lie, or pass across. **7.** oppose or frustrate. **8.** mark (out). **9.** mix (breeds). —adj. **10.** transverse. **11.** ill-humored. —**cross′ly**, adv.

cross′bow′ (krôs′bō′) n. weapon consisting of a bow fixed on a stock like that of a rifle.

cross′ breed′, v., -bred, -breeding. n. —v. **1.** hybridize. —n. **2.** hybrid.

cross′-coun′try, adj. **1.** proceeding over fields, through woods, etc., rather than on a road or track. **2.** from one end of a country to the other. —n. **3.** sport of cross-country racing.

cross′-ex·am′ine, v., -ined, -ining. examine closely, as opposing witness. —**cross′-ex·am′in·a′tion**, n.

cross′-eye′, n. visual disorder. —**cross′-eyed′**, adj.

cross reference, reference to another part of book.

cross′roads′, n. **1.** intersection. **2.** decisive point.

cross section, **1.** section made by cutting across something. **2.** representative sample of a whole.

cross′walk′, n. place where people can cross the street.

cross′word puz′zle, puzzle in which words determined from numbered clues are fitted into pattern of horizontal and vertical squares.

crotch (kroch) n. place where something divides, as the human body between the legs.

crotch′et (kroch′it) n. whim.

crotch′et·y, adj. grumpy.

crouch (krouch) v. **1.** stoop or bend low. —n. **2.** act of crouching.

croup (krōop) n. inflammation of throat.

crou·pi·er (krōo′pē ər, -pē ā′) n. attendant who handles bets and money at gambling table.

crou′ton (krōo′ton) n. small cube of toasted bread.

crow (krō) v. **1.** cry, as cock. **2.** boast. —n. **3.** cry of cock. **4.** black, harsh-voiced bird. **5.** (cap.) member of an American Indian people.

crow′bar′, n. iron bar for prying.

crowd (kroud) n. **1.** large group of people. —v. **2.** throng.

crown (kroun) n. **1.** ornate headgear for sovereign. **2.** power of a sovereign. **3.** top. —v. **4.** put crown on. **5.** reward or complete.

crow′s′-foot′, n., pl. -feet. (usually pl.) tiny wrinkle at outer corner of the eye.

CRT, cathode-ray tube.

cru′cial (krōo′shəl) adj. decisive.

cru′ci·ble (krōo′sə bəl) n. vessel for melting metals, etc.

cru′ci·fix (krōo′sə fiks) n. cross with figure of Jesus crucified.

cru′ci·fy′ (-fī′) v., -fied, -fying. **1.** put to death on cross. **2.** persecute. —**cru′ci·fix′ion**, n.

crude (krōod) adj., cruder, crudest. n. **1.** unrefined. **2.** unfinished. —adj. **1.** Informal. unrefined petroleum. —**crude′ly**, adv.

cru′di·tés′ (krōo′di tā′) n.pl. cut-up raw vegetables served with a dip.

cru′el (krōo′əl) adj. disposed to inflict pains. **2.** causing pain. —**cru′el·ly**, adv. —**cru′el·ty**, n.

cru′et (krōo′it) n. stoppered bottle for vinegar, etc.

cruise (krōoz) v., cruised, cruising. n. —v. **1.** sail or fly at moderate speed. **2.** travel for pleasure. —n. **3.** cruising trip.

cruis·er, n. **1.** kind of warship. **2.** small pleasure boat.

crumb (krum) n. small bit of bread, cookie, etc.

crum·ble (krum′bəl) v., **-bled, -bling.** break into fragments; decay.

crum·my (krum′ē) adj., **-mier, -miest.** Informal. **1.** shabby. **2.** cheap. **3.** miserable.

crum·ple (krum′pəl) v., **-pled, -pling.** wrinkle; rumple.

crunch (krunch) v. **1.** chew or crush noisily. —n. **2.** crunching sound.

cru·sade (krōō sād′) n., v., **-saded, -sading.** —n. **1.** Christian expedition to recover Holy Land from Muslims. **2.** campaign for good cause. —v. **3.** engage in crusade. —**cru·sad′er,** n.

crush (krush) v. **1.** bruise or break by pressing. **2.** subdue. —n. **3.** dense crowd. **4.** infatuation.

crust (krust) n. **1.** hard outer part or covering. —v. **2.** cover with crust. —**crust′y,** adj.

crus·ta·cean (kru stā′shən) n. sea animal having hard shell.

crutch (kruch) n. **1.** stick fitting under the armpit for support in walking. **2.** Informal. temporary aid or prop.

crux (kruks) n., pl. **cruxes, cruces** (krōō′sēz). vital point.

cry (krī) v., **cried, crying,** n., pl. **cries.** —v. **1.** make sounds of grief, etc. **2.** utter characteristic sounds. **3.** shout. —n. **4.** act or sound of crying.

cry·o·gen·ics (krī′ə jen′iks) n. study or use of extremely low temperatures. —**cry·o·gen′ic,** adj.

crypt (kript) n. underground chamber.

cryp′tic, adj. mysterious.

crys·tal (kris′tl) n. **1.** clear transparent mineral. **2.** body with symmetrical plane faces. **3.** fine glass. —**crys′tal·line** (-tl in, -īn′) adj.

crys·tal·lize, v., **-lized, -lizing. 1.** form or cause to form into crystals. **2.** assume or cause to assume definite form. —**crys′tal·li·za′tion,** n.

C′-sec′tion, n. Cesarean.

CST, Central Standard Time.

CT, Connecticut.

Ct., 1. Connecticut. **2.** Count.

ct., 1. carat. **2.** cent. **3.** court.

cu., cubic.

cub (kub) n. young fox, bear, etc.

cub′by·hole′ (kub′ē-) n. small enclosed space.

cube (kyōōb) n., v., **cubed, cubing.** —n. **1.** solid bounded by six

squares. **2.** Math. third power of a quantity. —v. **3.** make into cubes. **4.** Math. raise to third power. —**cu′bic,** adj.

cu′bi·cle (kyōō′bi kəl) n. small room.

cub′ism, n. artistic style marked by reduction of natural forms to geometric shapes. —**cub′ist,** adj., n.

Cub Scout, Boy Scout aged 8 to 10.

cuck′old (kuk′əld) n. husband of unfaithful wife.

cuck′oo (kōō′kōō, kook′ōō) n. small bird.

cu·cum·ber (kyōō′kum bər) n. green-skinned cylindrical fruit.

cud (kud) n. food that cow returns to mouth for further chewing.

cud·dle (kud′l) v., **-dled, -dling.** hold tenderly. —**cud′dly,** adj.

cudg·el (kuj′əl) n., v., **-eled, -eling.** —n. **1.** short thick stick. —v. **2.** beat with cudgel.

cue (kyōō) n. **1.** (esp. on stage) something that signals speech or action. **2.** rod for billiards.

cuff (kuf) n. **1.** fold or band at end of sleeve or trouser leg. **2.** slap. —v. **3.** slap.

cui·sine (kwi zēn′) n. cookery.

cu·li·nar·y (kyōō′lə ner′ē, kul′ə-) adj. of cooking.

cull (kul) v. select best parts of.

cul′mi·nate (kul′mə nāt′) v., **-nated, -nating.** reach highest point. —**cul′mi·na′tion,** n.

cul·pa·ble (kul′pə bəl) adj. deserving blame. —**cul·pa·bil′i·ty,** n.

cul·prit (kul′prit) n. person arraigned for or guilty of an offense.

cult (kult) n. **1.** religious sect or system. —adj. **2.** popular with some people.

cul′ti·vate′ (kul′tə vāt′) v., **-vated, -vating. 1.** prepare and care for (land). **2.** develop possibilities of. —**cul′ti·va′tion,** n.

cul′ti·vat′ed, adj. educated.

cul′ture (kul′chər) n. **1.** raising of plants or animals. **2.** development of mind. **3.** state or form of civilization. —**cul′tur·al,** adj.

culture shock, distress of person exposed to new culture.

cul′vert (kul′vərt) n. channel under road, etc.

cum·ber·some (kum′bər səm) adj. clumsy or bulky.

cu·mu·la·tive (kyōō′myə lə tiv) adj. increasing by accumulation.

cu·mu·lus (kyōō′myə ləs) n., pl. **-li.** rounded cloud.

cu·ne·i·form′ (kyōō nē′ə fôrm′) adj. composed of wedge-shaped elements, as some ancient writing.

cun'ning (kun'ing) *adj.* **1.** clever. **2.** sly. —*n.* **3.** skill. **4.** guile.

cup (kup) *n., v.,* **cupped, cupping.** —*n.* **1.** small open drinking vessel. —*v.* **2.** shape like a cup.

cup'board (kub'ərd) *n.* closet for dishes, etc.

Cu'pid (kyōō'pid) *n.* Roman god of carnal love.

cu·pid'i·ty (-pid'i tē) *n.* greed.

cu'po·la (kyōō'pə lə) *n.* rounded dome.

cur (kûr) *n.* worthless dog.

cu'rate (kyōōr'it) *n.* clergyman assisting rector or vicar.

cu·ra'tor (kyŏŏ rā'tər, kyŏŏr'ā-) *n.* person in charge of museum.

curb (kûrb) *n.* **1.** strap for restraining horse. **2.** restraint. **3.** edge of sidewalk. —*v.* **4.** control.

curd (kûrd) *n.* **1.** substance formed when milk coagulates. —*v.* **2.** change into curd.

cur'dle (kûr'dl) *v.,* **-dled, -dling.** congeal, turn into curd.

cure (kyŏŏr) *n., v.,* **cured, curing.** —*n.* **1.** treatment of disease. **2.** restoration to health. —*v.* **3.** restore to health. **4.** preserve.

cur'few (kûr'fyōō) *n.* order to be home or off the streets by a certain time.

cu'ri·o (kyŏŏr'ē ō') *n., pl.* **-rios.** unusual valuable article.

cu·ri·os'i·ty (kyŏŏr'ē os'i tē) *n., pl.* **-ties.** **1.** desire to know. **2.** odd thing.

cu'ri·ous (-əs) *adj.* **1.** wanting to know. **2.** prying. **3.** strange.

curl (kûrl) *v.* **1.** form in ringlets. **2.** coil. —*n.* **3.** ringlet. —**curl'er,** *n.* —**curl'y,** *adj.*

cur'lew (kûr'lōō) *n.* shore bird.

curl'i·cue' (kûr'li kyōō') *n.* fancy curl.

cur·mudg'eon (kər muj'ən) *n.* bad-tempered, difficult person.

cur'rant (kûr'ənt) *n.* **1.** small seedless raisin. **2.** edible acid berry.

cur'ren·cy (kûr'ən sē) *n., pl.* **-cies.** **1.** money in use in a country. **2.** prevalence. **3.** circulation.

cur'rent (kûr'ənt) *adj.* **1.** present. **2.** generally known or believed. —*n.* **3.** stream; flow. **4.** water, air, etc., moving in one direction. **5.** movement of electricity.

cur·ric'u·lum (kə rik'yə ləm) *n., pl.* **-lums.** (-la). course of study.

cur'ry (kûr'ē, kur'ē) *n., pl.* **-ries,** *v.,* **-ried, -rying.** —*n.* **1.** East Indian hot dish or powder (**curry powder**). **2.** prepare with curry. **3.** rub and comb (horse, etc.). **4.** seek (favor) with servility.

cur'ry·comb', *n.* wire brush for horse.

curse (kûrs) *n., v.,* **cursed** or **curst, cursing.** —*v.* **1.** wish that evil befall someone. **2.** evil so invoked. **3.** profane oath. **4.** cause of evil. —*v.* **5.** wish evil upon. **6.** swear. **7.** afflict.

cur'sive (kûr'siv) *adj.* (of handwriting) in flowing strokes with letters joined together.

cur'sor (-sər) *n.* movable symbol on computer screen to indicate where data may be input.

cur·so·ry, *adj.* superficial.

curt (kûrt) *adj.* brief, esp. rudely so. —**curt'ly,** *adv.*

cur·tail' (kər tāl') *v.* cut short. —**cur·tail'ment,** *n.*

cur'tain (kûr'tn) *n.* **1.** piece of fabric hung to adorn, conceal, etc. —*v.* **2.** cover with curtains.

curt'sy (kûrt'sē) *n., pl.* **-sies,** *v.,* **-sied, -sying.** —*n.* **1.** bow by women. —*v.* **2.** make curtsy.

cur'va·ture (kûr'və chər) *n.* **1.** a curving. **2.** degree of curving.

curve (kûrv) *n., v.,* **curved, curving.** —*n.* **1.** bending line. —*v.* **2.** bend or move in a curve.

cush'ion (kŏŏsh'ən) *n.* **1.** soft bag of feathers, air, etc. —*v.* **2.** lessen the effects of.

cush'y (kŏŏsh'ē) *adj. Informal.* easy and profitable.

cusp (kusp) *n.* pointed end.

cus'pid (kus'pid) *n.* canine tooth.

cuss (kus) *v. Informal.* curse.

cus'tard (kus'tərd) *n.* cooked dish of eggs and milk.

cus'to·dy (kus'tə dē) *n., pl.* **-dies.** **1.** keeping; care. **2.** imprisonment. —**cus·to'di·al** (kə stō'dē əl) *adj.* —**cus·to'di·an,** *n.*

cus'tom (kus'təm) *n.* **1.** usual practice. **2.** set of such practices. **3.** (*pl.*) **a.** duties on imports. **b.** agency collecting these. —*adj.* **4.** made for the individual. —**cus'tom·ar'y,** *adj.*

cus'tom·er, *n.* **1.** purchaser or prospective purchaser. **2.** *Informal.* person.

cus'tom·ize', *v.,* **-ized, -iz·ing.** make to individual specifications.

cut (kut) *v.,* **cut, cutting,** *n.* —*v.* **1.** sever or penetrate as with knife. **2.** wound feelings of. **3.** reap or trim. **4.** shorten by omitting part. **5.** dilute. **6.** move or cross. **7.** be absent from. —*n.* **8.** a cutting. **9.** result of cutting. **10.** straight passage.

cu·ta'ne·ous (kyŏŏ tā'nē əs) *adj.* of the skin.

cut'back', *n.* reduction in rate, quantity, etc.

cute (kyōōt) *adj.*, **cuter, cutest.** pretty or pleasing.

cu'ti·cle (kyōō'ti kəl) *n.* epidermis, esp. around nails.

cut'lass (kut'ləs) *n.* short curved sword.

cut'ler·y (-lə rē) *n.* knives collectively.

cut'let (-lit) *n.* slice of meat for frying or broiling.

cut'off', *n.* **1.** point beyond which something is no longer effective or possible. **2.** road that leaves another to make a shortcut.

cut'-rate', *adj.* offered at reduced prices.

cut'ter, *n.* **1.** one that cuts. **2.** small fast vessel. **3.** sleigh.

cut'throat', *n.* **1.** murderer. —*adj.* **2.** ruthless.

cut'tle·fish' (kut'l fish') *n.*, *pl.* **-fish, -fish·es.** mollusk with ten arms and hard internal shell (**cut'tle·bone'**).

cy'a·nide' (sī'ə nīd') *n.* poisonous salt of hydrocyanic acid.

cyber-, prefix meaning computer, as *cyberspace.*

cy'ber·net'ics (sī'bər net'iks) *n.* study of control and communications systems.

cy'ber·space', *n.* **1.** realm of electronic communication. **2.** virtual reality.

cy'cle (sī'kəl) *n.*, *v.*, **-cled, -cling.** —*n.* **1.** recurring time or process. **2.** complete set. **3.** bicycle, etc. —*v.* **4.** ride bicycle.

cy'clone (sī'klōn) *n.* tornado. —**cy·clon'ic** (-klon'ik) *adj.*

cy'clo·pe'di·a (sī'klə pē'dē ə) *n.* encyclopedia.

cy'clo·tron' (-tron') *n.* device used in splitting atoms.

cyg'net (sig'nit) *n.* young swan.

cyl'in·der (sil'in dər) *n.* **1.** round elongated solid with ends that are equal parallel circles. **2.** machine part or opening in this form. —**cy·lin'dri·cal,** *adj.*

cym'bal (sim'bəl) *n.* brass plate used in orchestras.

cyn'ic (sin'ik) *n.* person who doubts or lacks approval of motive. —**cyn'i·cal,** *adj.* —**cyn'i·cism** (-ə siz'əm) *n.*

cy'no·sure' (sī'nə shŏŏr') *n.* object that attracts by its brilliance.

cy'press (sī'prəs) *n.* evergreen tree of pine family.

cyst (sist) *n.* abnormal sac containing matter formed in live tissue. —**cys'tic,** *adj.*

cys'tic fi·bro'sis (sis'tik fi brō'sis) hereditary disease marked by breathing difficulties and growth of excess fibrous tissue.

czar (zär) *n.* **1.** former emperor of Russia. Also, **tsar.**

cza·ri'na (zä rē'nə) *n.* wife of a czar.

Czech (chek) *n.* native or language of Czech Republic.

D

D, d (dē) *n.* fourth letter of English alphabet.

d. **1.** date. **2.** deceased. **3.** degree. **4.** diameter. **5.** dose.

D.A. District Attorney.

dab (dab) *v.*, **dabbed, dabbing. 1.** apply lightly. —*n.* **2.** small quantity.

dab'ble (dab'əl) *v.*, **-bled, -bling. 1.** splatter. **2.** be interested superficially. —**dab'bler,** *n.*

dachs'hund' (däks'hŏŏnt', -hŏŏnd') *n.* kind of long, short-legged dog.

Da'·cron (dā'kron, dak'ron) *n. Trademark.* strong synthetic fabric.

dad (dad) *n. Informal.* father.

dad'dy (dad'ē) *n.*, *pl.* **-dies.** *Informal.* father.

dad'dy-long'legs', *n.*, *pl.* **-legs.** spiderlike arachnid with long, slender legs. Also, **dad'dy long'legs'.**

daf'fo·dil (daf'ə dil) *n.* plant with yellow trumpet-shaped flowers.

daft (daft) *adj.* **1.** insane. **2.** foolish.

dag'ger (dag'ər) *n.* short knifelike weapon.

dahl'ia (dal'yə, däl'-) *n.* showy cultivated flowering plant.

dai'ly (dā'lē) *adj.* **1.** of or occurring each day. —*n.* **2.** daily newspaper.

dain'ty (dān'tē) *adj.*, **-tier, -tiest,** *n.*, *pl.* **-ties.** —*adj.* **1.** delicate. —*n.* **2.** delicacy. —**dain'ti·ly,** *adv.*

dair'y (dâr'ē) *n.*, *pl.* **-ies.** place for making or selling milk, butter, etc.

da'is (dā'is) *n.* raised platform.

dai'sy (dā'zē) *n.*, *pl.* **-sies.** flower with yellow center and white petals.

Da·ko'ta (də kō'tə) *n.*, *pl.* **-ta, -tas.** member of a North American Indian people.

dale (dāl) *n.* valley.

dal'ly (dal'ē) *v.*, **-lied, -lying. 1.** flirt. **2.** delay. —**dal'li·ance,** *n.*

Dal·ma'tian (dal mā'shən) *n.* large white-and-black dog.

dam (dam) *n.*, *v.*, **dammed, damming.** —*n.* **1.** barrier to obstruct water. **2.** female quadruped parent. —*v.* **3.** obstruct flow.

dam'age (dam'ij) *n., v.,* **-aged, -ag-ing.** —*n.* **1.** injury. **2.** (*pl.*) payment for injury. —*v.* **3.** injure.

dam'ask (dam'ask) *n.* **1.** woven figured fabric. —*adj.* **2.** pink.

dame (dām) *n.* **1.** woman of rank. **2.** *Slang (sometimes offensive).* any woman.

damn (dam) *v.* **1.** declare bad. **2.** condemn to hell. —**dam'na·ble** (-na bal) *adj.* —**dam·na'tion,** *n.*

damp (damp) *adj.* **1.** moist. —*n.* **2.** moisture. —*v.* Also, **damp'en. 3.** moisten. **4.** discourage. **5.** deaden. —**damp'ness,** *n.*

damp'er, *n.* **1.** control for air or smoke currents. **2.** discouraging influence.

dam'sel (dam'zal) *n.* maiden.

dam'son (dam'zan, -san) *n.* small plum.

dance (dans) *v.,* **danced, dancing,** *n.* —*v.* **1.** move rhythmically. —*n.* **2.** act of dancing. **3.** gathering or music for dancing. —**danc'er,** *n.*

dan'de·li'on (dan'dl ī'an) *n.* plant with yellow flowers.

dan'der (-dar) *n. Informal.* temper.

dan'dle (dan'dl) *v.,* **-dled, -dling.** move (a child) lightly up and down.

dan'druff (-draf) *n.* scales of dry skin on scalp.

dan'dy (-dē) *n., pl.* **-dies,** *adj.,* **-dier, -diest.** —*n.* **1.** fashionable dresser. —*adj.* **2.** fine.

Dane (dān) *n.* native of Denmark.

dan'ger (dān'jar) *n.* exposure to harm. —**dan'ger·ous,** *adj.* —**dan'ger·ous·ly,** *adv.*

dan'gle (dang'gal) *v.,* **-gled, -gling.** hang loosely.

Dan'ish (dā'nish) *adj.* **1.** of Denmark, the Danes, or their language. **2.** the language of the Danes. **3.** (*sometimes l.c.*) filled pastry.

dank (dangk) *adj.* unpleasantly damp. —**dank'ness,** *n.*

dap'per (dap'ar) *adj.* neat and well-dressed.

dap'ple (dap'al) *adj., v.,* **-pled, -pling.** —*adj.* **1.** mottled. Also, **dap'pled.** —*v.* **2.** mottle.

dare (dâr) *v.,* **dared** or **durst** (dûrst), **dared, daring,** *n.* —*v.* **1.** be bold enough. **2.** challenge. —*n.* **3.** challenge. —**dar'ing,** *adj., n.*

dare'dev'il *n.* **1.** recklessly daring person. —*adj.* **2.** recklessly daring.

dark (därk) *adj.* **1.** lacking light. **2.** blackish. **3.** gloomy. —*n.* **4.** absence of light. —**dark'en,** *n.* —**dark'ly,** *adv.* —**dark'ness,** *n.*

Dark Ages, Middle Ages, esp. from A.D. 476 to about 1000.

dark horse, unexpected winner.

dark'room', *n.* place for developing and printing films.

dar'ling (där'ling) *n.* **1.** loved one. **2.** favorite. —*adj.* **3.** cherished. **4.** charming.

darn (därn) *v.* mend with rows of stitches. —**darn'er,** *n.*

dart (därt) *n.* **1.** slender pointed missile. **2.** (*pl.*) game of throwing darts at target. **3.** tapered seam. —*v.* **4.** move swiftly.

dash (dash) *v.* **1.** strike or throw violently. **2.** frustrate. **3.** do something quickly. **4.** hurry. —*n.* **5.** violent blow. **6.** small quantity. **7.** punctuation mark (--) noting abrupt break. **8.** rush.

dash'board', *n.* instrument board on motor vehicle.

dash'ing, *adj.* **1.** lively. **2.** stylish.

das'tard (das'tard) *n.* coward. —**das'tard·ly,** *adj.*

da'ta (dā'ta, dat'a) *n.pl., sing.* **datum** (dā'tam, dat'am). facts or other information.

da'ta·base', *n.* collection of data, esp. one accessible by computer.

data processing, high-speed handling of information by computer.

date (dāt) *n., v.,* **dated, dating.** —*n.* **1.** particular month, day, and year. **2.** fleshy, edible fruit of **date palm. 3.** social engagement arranged beforehand, esp. one of a romantic nature. **4.** person with whom one has a date. —*v.* **5.** exist from particular time. **6.** fix date with.

dat'ed, *adj.* **1.** having or showing a date. **2.** out-of-date.

da'tive (dā'tiv) *adj.* denoting verb's indirect object.

daub (dôb) *v.* **1.** paint clumsily. —*n.* **2.** something daubed on.

daugh'ter (dô'tar) *n.* female child.

daugh'ter-in-law', *n., pl.* **daughters-in-law.** son's wife.

daunt (dônt, dänt) *v.* dishearten.

daunt'less, *adj.* bold; fearless.

dav'en·port' (dav'an pôrt') *n.* large sofa.

daw'dle (dôd'l) *v.,* **-dled, -dling.** waste time. —**daw'dler,** *n.*

dawn (dôn) *n.* **1.** break of day. —*v.* **2.** begin to grow light. **3.** become apparent.

day (dā) *n.* **1.** period between two nights. **2.** period (24 hours) of earth's rotation on its axis.

day'break', *n.* first appearance of light; dawn.

day care, supervised care for young children or the elderly, usu. in daytime and at a center outside the home. —**day′-care′**, adj.

day′dream′, n. **1.** reverie; fancy. —v. **2.** indulge in reveries. —**day′-dream′er**, n.

day′light′, n. **1.** light of day. **2.** openness. **3.** (pl.) wits; sanity.

daylight-saving time, time one hour later than standard time. Also, **daylight-savings time.**

day′time′, n. time from sunrise to sunset.

day′-to-day′, adj. routine.

daze (dāz) v., **dazed, dazing.** —v. **1.** stun. —n. **2.** dazed state.

daz′zle (daz′əl) v., **-zled, -zling.** overwhelm with light.

dba, doing business as.

dbl, **1.** decibel. **2.** double.

DC, **1.** direct current. **2.** District of Columbia.

D.D., Doctor of Divinity.

D.D.S., **1.** Doctor of Dental Science. **2.** Doctor of Dental Surgery.

DDT, strong insecticide, now banned from use.

de-, prefix indicating: **1.** reverse, as *deactivate.* **2.** remove, as *decaffeinate.* **3.** reduce, as *degrade.*

dea′con (dē′kən) n. **1.** cleric inferior to priest. **2.** lay church officer. —**dea′con·ess**, n.fem.

de·ac′ti·vate′ (dē ak′tə vāt′) v., **-vated, -vating.** make inactive.

dead (ded) adj. **1.** no longer alive or active. **2.** exhausted. **3.** absolute. —n. **4.** dead persons. **5.** darkest, coldest time. —adv. **6.** completely. **7.** directly. —**dead′en**, v.

dead′beat′, n. **1.** person who avoids paying. **2.** sponger.

dead end, **1.** street, corridor, etc., with no exit. **2.** position with no hope of progress. —**dead′-end′**, adj.

dead heat, race that finishes in a tie.

dead′line′, n. last allowable time.

dead′lock′, n. standstill.

dead′ly, adj., **-lier, -liest. 1.** fatal. **2.** dreary. **3.** extremely accurate. —adv. **4.** extremely.

dead′pan′, adj. without expression.

dead′wood′, n. **1.** useless or extraneous persons or things.

deaf (def) adj. unable to hear. —**deaf′en**, v. —**deaf′ness**, n.

deaf′-mute′, n. Often Offensive. person unable to hear or speak.

deal (dēl) v., **dealt** (delt), **dealing,** n. —v. **1.** be concerned with. **2.** do business. **3.** distribute. —n. **4.** transaction. **5.** quantity. —**deal′er**, n.

deal′ing, n. (usually pl.)

transactions or interactions with others.

dean (dēn) n. **1.** head of academic faculty. **2.** head of cathedral organization.

dear (dēr) adj. **1.** loved. **2.** expensive. —n. **3.** dear one. —**dear′ly**, adv.

dearth (dûrth) n. scarcity.

death (deth) n. end of life. —**death′ly**, adj., adv. —**death′bed′**, n.

death′less, adj. enduring.

de·ba·cle (də bä′kəl, -bak′əl, dā-) n. **1.** breakup; rout. **2.** utter failure.

de·bar′ (di bär′) v., **-barred, -barring.** exclude. —**de·bar′ment**, n.

de·bark′ (di bärk′) v. disembark. —**de′bar·ka′tion**, n.

de·base′ (di bās′) v., **-based, -basing.** reduce in quality.

de·bate′ (di bāt′) n., v., **-bated, -bating.** —n. **1.** controversial discussion. —v. **2.** argue; discuss. —**de·bat′a·ble**, adj.

de·bauch′ (di bôch′) v. corrupt; pervert. —**de·bauch′er·y**, n.

de·bil′i·tate′ (di bil′i tāt′) v., **-tated, -tating.** weaken.

de·bil′i·ty, n., pl. **-ties.** weakness.

deb′it (deb′it) n. **1.** recorded debt. **2.** account of debts. —v. **3.** charge as debt.

deb′o·nair′ (deb′ə nâr′) adj. **1.** suave; urbane. **2.** relaxed; calm.

de·brief′ (dē brēf′) v. gather information from someone about a completed mission.

de·bris′ (də brē′, dā′brē) n. rubbish; ruins.

debt (det) n. **1.** something owed. **2.** obligation to pay. —**debt′or**, n.

de·bug′ (dē bug′) v., **-bugged, -bugging. 1.** remove defects or errors from (computer program). **2.** remove electronic bugs from (room or building).

de·bunk′ (di bungk′) v. expose as false.

de·but′ (dā byōō′, di-, dā′byōō) n. first public appearance. —**deb′u·tante′**, n.fem.

Dec., December.

dec′ade (dek′ād) n. 10-year period.

dec′a·dence (dek′ə dəns, di kād′ns) n. decline in morality; corruption. —**dec′a·dent**, adj.

de·caf′fein·at·ed (dē kaf′ə nā′tad), adj. having the caffeine removed.

dec′a·he′dron (dek′ə hē′drən) n., pl. **-drons, -dra** (-drə). solid figure with 10 faces.

de′cal (dē′kal, di kal′) n. picture or design on specially prepared paper for transfer to wood, metal, etc.

Dec′a·logue′ (dek′ə lôg′) n. Ten Commandments.

de·camp′ (di kamp′) v. depart, esp. secretly.

de·cant′ (di kant′) v. pour off.

de·cant′er, (di kant′ər) n. ornamental bottle.

de·cap′i·tate′ (di kap′i tāt′) v., -tated, -tating. behead.

de·cath′lon (di kath′lon) n. contest of 10 events.

de·cay′ (di kā′) v., n. decline in quality, health, etc.

de·cease′ (di sēs′) n., v., -ceased, -ceasing. —n. **1.** death. —v. **2.** die. —**de·ceased′,** adj., n.

de·ceit′ (di sēt′) n. **1.** fraud. **2.** trick. —**de·ceit′ful,** adj.

de·ceive′ (di sēv′) v., -ceived, -ceiving. lead into error; mislead.

De·cem′ber (di sem′bər) n. 12th month of year.

de′cen·cy (dē′sən sē) n., pl. -cies. **1.** conformity to moral standards. **2.** respectability. **3.** adequacy. **4.** kindness or willingness to help. —**de′cent,** adj. —**de′cent·ly,** adv.

de·cen·tral·ize′ (dē sen′trə līz′) v., -ized, -izing. end central control of. —**de·cen′tral·i·za′tion,** n.

de·cep′tion (di sep′shən) n. **1.** act of deceiving. **2.** fraud. —**de·cep′tive,** adj.

dec′i·bel′ (des′ə bel′, -bəl) n. unit of intensity of sound.

de·cide′ (di sīd′) v., -cided, -ciding. settle; resolve.

de·cid′ed, adj. unambiguous; emphatic. —**de·cid′ed·ly,** adv.

de·cid′u·ous (di sij′ōō əs) adj. shedding leaves annually.

dec′i·mal (des′ə məl) adj. **1.** of tenths. **2.** proceeding by tens. —n. **3.** fraction in tenths, hundredths, etc., indicated by dot (**decimal point**) before numerator.

dec′i·mate′ (des′ə māt′) v., -mated, -mating. kill or destroy much of.

de·ci′pher (di sī′fər) v. find meaning of. —**de·ci′pher·a·ble,** adj.

de·ci′sion (di sizh′ən) n. **1.** something decided. **2.** firmness of mind.

de·ci′sive (-sī′siv) adj. **1.** determining. **2.** resolute. —**de·ci′sive·ly,** adv. —**de·ci′sive·ness,** n.

deck (dek) n. **1.** level on ship. **2.** pack of playing cards. —v. **3.** array.

de·claim′ (di klām′) v. speak rhetorically. —**de·claim′er,** n.

dec′la·ma′tion (dek′lə mā′shən) n. oratorical speech.

de·clare′ (di klâr′) v., -clared, -claring. **1.** make known. **2.** affirm. —**dec′la·ra′tion** (dek′lə rā′shən) n. —**de·clar′a·tive,** adj.

de·clen′sion (di klen′shən) n. grammatical inflection or set of inflections.

de·cline′ (di klīn′) v., -clined, -clining, n. —v. **1.** refuse. **2.** slant down. **3.** give grammatical inflections. **4.** fail; diminish. —n. **5.** downward slope. **6.** deterioration.

de·code′ (dē kōd′) v., -coded, -coding. decipher from code.

de′com·mis′sion (-kəm-) v. retire (vessel) from active service.

de′com·pose′ (-kəm pōz′) v., -posed, -posing. **1.** separate into constituent parts. **2.** rot. —**de′com·po·si′tion,** n.

de′con·ges′tant (dē′kən jes′tənt) adj. **1.** relieving congestion of the upper respiratory tract. —n. **2.** decongestant agent.

de′con·tam′i·nate (-nāt′) v., -nated, -nating. make safe by removing or neutralizing harmful contaminants.

dé·cor′ (dā kôr′, di-) n. style of decoration, as of a room. Also, **de·cor′.**

dec′o·rate′ (dek′ə rāt′) v., -rated, -rating. **1.** add something attractive to. **2.** honor. —**dec′o·ra′tion,** n. —**dec′o·ra·tive** (-ər ə tiv) adj. —**dec′o·ra′tor,** n.

de·co′rous, adj. proper; dignified. —**de·co′rum** (di kôr′əm) n. propriety.

de·coy′ (n. dē′koi, di koi′; v. di koi′, dē′koi) n., v. lure.

de·crease′ (di krēs′) v., -creased, -creasing, n. —v. (di krēs′) **1.** lessen. —n. (dē′krēs, di krēs′) **2.** lessening.

de·cree′ (di krē′) n., v., -creed, -creeing. —n. **1.** published command. —v. **2.** proclaim or command.

de·crep′it (di krep′it) adj. old and feeble. —**de·crep′i·tude′,** n.

de·cre·scen·do (dē′kri shen′dō, dā′-) adj., adv. Music. gradually decreasing in loudness.

de·crim′i·nal·ize′ (dē krim′ə nl īz′) v., -ized, -izing. cease to treat as a crime. —**de·crim′i·nal·i·za′tion,** n.

de·cry′ (di krī′) v., -cried, -crying. publicly disapprove of.

ded′i·cate′ (ded′i kāt′) v., -cated, -cating. **1.** set apart. **2.** devote. **3.** inscribe in honor of. —**ded′i·ca′tion,** n.

de·duce′ (di dōōs′, -dyōōs′) v., -duced, -ducing. derive logically.

de·duct′ (di dukt′) v. subtract. —**de·duct′i·ble,** adj.

de·duc′tion, n. **1.** subtraction. **2.** conclusion. —**de·duc′tive,** adj.

deed (dēd) n. **1.** act. **2.** written conveyance of property. —v. **3.** transfer by deed.

dee′jay′ (dē′jā′) n. disc jockey.

deem (dēm) v. think; estimate.

deep (dēp) adj. **1.** extending far

down or in. **2.** difficult to understand. **3.** intense. **4.** low in pitch. **6.** at great depth. —**deep′en,** *v.* —**deep′ly,** *adv.*

deep′-freeze′, *v.,* **-froze, -frozen, -freezing,** *n.* —*v.* **1.** freeze rapidly for preservation. —*n.* **2.** refrigerator that deep-freezes.

deep′-fry′, *v.,* **-fried, -frying.** cook in boiling fat.

deep′-seat′ed, *adj.* firmly fixed. Also, **deep′-root′ed.**

deep space, space beyond the solar system.

deer (dēr) *n., pl.* **deer.** hoofed, ruminant animal, the male of which usually has antlers.

de·face′ (di fās′) *v.* deface, spoil appearance of.

de fac′to (dē fak′tō, dā) **1.** in fact; in reality. **2.** actually existing, esp. without legal authority.

de·fame′ (di fām′) *v.,* **-famed, -faming.** attack the reputation of. —**def′a·ma′tion** (def′ə mā′shən) *n.* —**de·fam′a·to′ry** (-fam′ə tôr′ē) *adj.*

de·fault′ (di fôlt′) *n.* **1.** failure; neglect. —*v.* **2.** fail to meet obligation.

de·feat′ (di fēt′) *v.* **1.** overthrow. **2.** frustrate. —*n.* **3.** defeat.

de·feat′ist *n.* one who accepts defeat too easily. —**de·feat′ism,** *n.*

def′e·cate (def′i kāt′) *v.,* **-cated, -cating.** void feces from bowels. —**def′e·ca′tion,** *n.*

de·fect′ *n.* (dē′fekt, di fekt′) **1.** fault; imperfection. —*v.* (di fekt′) **2.** desert a cause, country, etc. —**de·fec′tive,** *adj.*

de·fec′tion, *n.* desertion of a cause, country, etc.

de·fend′ (di fend′) *v.* **1.** protect against attack. **2.** uphold. —**de·fend′er,** *n.*

de·fend′ant, *n.* person accused of a crime or sued in court.

de·fense′ (di fens′) *n.* **1.** resistance to attack. **2.** defending argument. —**de·fense′less,** *adj.* —**de·fen′sive,** *adj., n.*

de·fer′ (di fûr′) *v.,* **-ferred, -ferring. 1.** postpone. **2.** yield to someone's opinion. —**de·fer′ment,** *n.*

def′er·ence (def′ər əns) *n.* act of showing respect. —**def′er·en′tial** (-ə ren′shal) *adj.*

de·fi′ance (di fī′əns) *n.* **1.** bold resistance. **2.** disregard. —**de·fi′ant,** *adj.* —**de·fi′ant·ly,** *adv.*

de·fi′cien·cy (di fish′ən sē) *n., pl.* **-cies.** lack. —**de·fi′cient,** *adj.*

def′i·cit (def′ə sit) *n.* lack of funds.

de·file′ (di fīl′) *v.,* **-filed, -filing,** *n.* —*v.* **1.** dirty. **2.** desecrate. —*n.* **3.** narrow pass.

de·fine′ (di fīn′) *v.,* **-fined, -fining. 1.** state meaning of. **2.** determine precisely. —**def′i·ni′tion,** *n.*

def′i·nite (def′ə nit) *adj.* **1.** exact. **2.** with fixed limits. —**def′i·nite·ly,** *adv.*

de·fin′i·tive (di fin′i tiv) *adj.* conclusive. —**de·fin′i·tive·ly,** *adv.*

de·flate′ (di flāt′) *v.,* **-flated, -flating.** release gas from.

de·fla′tion, *n.* sharp fall in prices.

de·flect′ (di flekt′) *v.* turn from true course. —**de·flec′tion,** *n.*

de·fo′li·ate (dē fō′lē āt′) *v.,* **-ated, -ating. 1.** strip of leaves. **2.** clear of vegetation, as to expose hidden enemy forces. —**de·fo′li·a′tion,** *n.* —**de·fo′li·ant** (-ənt) *n.*

de·for′est (di fôr′ist) *v.* clear of trees. —**de·for′es·ta′tion,** *n.*

de·form′, *v.* distort. —**de·form′i·ty,** *n.*

de·fraud′, *v.* cheat. —**de·fraud′er,** *n.*

de·fray′, *v.* pay (expenses).

de·frost′, *v.* **1.** remove frost or ice from. **2.** thaw.

deft (deft) *adj.* quick and skillful.

de·funct′ (di fungkt′) *adj.* no longer in existence.

de·fuse′ (dē fyōoz′) *v.* **1.** remove detonating parts from. **2.** make less dangerous or tense.

de·fy′ (di fī′) *v.,* **-fied, -fying.** challenge; resist.

de·gen′er·ate, *v.,* **-ated, -ating,** *adj., n.* —*v.* (di jen′ə rāt′) **1.** decline; deteriorate. —*adj.* (-ər it) **2.** having declined. **3.** corrupt. —*n.* (-ər it) **4.** degenerate person.

de·grade′ (di grād′) *v.,* **-graded, -grading.** reduce in status. —**deg′ra·da′tion** (deg′ri dā′shən) *n.*

de·gree′ (di grē′) *n.* **1.** stage or extent. **2.** 360th part of a circle. **3.** unit of temperature. **4.** title conferred by college.

de·hu′man·ize′ (dē hyōō′mə nīz′; *often -yōo′-*) *v.,* **-ized, -izing.** treat as lacking human qualities or requirements.

de·hu·mid′i·fi′er, *n.* device for removing moisture from air. —**de·hu·mid′i·fy,** *v.*

de·hy′drate′ (-drāt) *v.,* **-drated, -drating.** deprive of moisture. —**de·hy·dra′tion,** *n.*

de·i·fy′ (dē′ə fī′) *v.,* **-fied, -fying.** make a god of. —**de·i·fi·ca′tion,** *n.*

deign (dān) *v.* condescend.

de·in·sti·tu′tion·al·ize′, *v.,* **-ized, -izing.** release from an institution to community care.

de·ism (dē′iz əm) (dē′iz əm) *n.* belief in the existence of a God based on reason and evidence in nature, rather than on divine revelation. —**de·ist,** *n.*

de·i·ty (dē′i tē) *n., pl.* **-ties.** god or goddess.

dé·jà vu′ (dā′zhä vōō′) feeling of having lived through same moment before.

de·ject′ed (di jek′tid) *adj.* disheartened. —**de·jec′tion,** *n.*

de ju′re (di jōōr′ē, dä jōōr′ā) by right or according to law.

Del. Delaware.

de·lay′ (di lā′) *v.* **1.** postpone. **2.** hinder. —*n.* **3.** act of delaying. **4.** instance of being delayed.

de·lec·ta·ble (di lek′tə bəl) *adj.* delightful or delicious.

del′e·gate *n., v.,* **-gated, -gating.** —*n.* (del′i git, -gāt′) **1.** deputy. **2.** legislator. —*v.* (-gāt′) **3.** send as deputy. **4.** give (powers) to another. —**del′e·ga′tion,** *n.*

de·lete′ (di lēt′) *v.,* **-leted, -leting.** cancel; erase. —**de·le′tion,** *n.*

del′e·te′ri·ous (del′i tēr′ē əs) *adj.* harmful.

del′i (del′ē) *n.* delicatessen.

de·lib′er·ate *adj., v.,* **-ated, -ating.** —*adj.* (di lib′ər it) **1.** intentional. **2.** unhurried. —*v.* (-ə rāt′) **3.** consider. **4.** confer. —**de·lib′er·a′tion,** *n.* —**de·lib′er·ate·ly,** *adv.*

del′i·ca·cy (del′i kə sē) *n., pl.* **-cies.** **1.** fineness. **2.** frailty. **3.** choice food.

del′i·cate (-kit) *adj.* **1.** fine. **2.** fragile. **3.** tactful. —**del′i·cate·ly,** *adv.*

del′i·ca·tes′sen (del′i kə tes′ən) *n.* store that sells prepared food.

de·li′cious (di lish′əs) *adj.* pleasing, esp. to taste. —**de·li′cious·ly,** *adv.*

de·light′ (di līt′) *n.* **1.** joy. —*v.* **2.** please highly. **3.** take joy. —**de·light′ed,** *adj.* —**de·light′ful,** *adj.*

de·lim′it (di lim′it) *v.* fix or mark limits of. —**de·lim′i·ta′tion,** *n.*

de·lin′e·ate′ (di lin′ē āt′) *v.,* **-ated, -ating.** sketch; outline.

de·lin′quent (di ling′kwənt) *adj.* **1.** neglectful; guilty. —*n.* **2.** delinquent one. —**de·lin′quen·cy,** *n.*

de·lir′i·um (di lēr′ē əm) *n.* mental disorder marked by excitement, visions, etc. —**de·lir′i·ous,** *adj.*

de·liv′er (di liv′ər) *v.* **1.** give up. **2.** hand over. **3.** utter. **4.** direct. **5.** give birth. **6.** assist at birth. —**de·liv′er·ance,** *n.* —**de·liv′er·y,** *n.*

dell (del) *n.* small, wooded valley.

del·phin′i·um (del fin′ē əm) *n., pl.* **-iums, -ia** (-ē ə). tall blue garden flower.

del′ta (del′tə) *n.* **1.** 4th letter of Greek alphabet. **2.** triangular area between branches of river mouth.

de·lude′ (di lōōd′) *v.,* **-luded, -luding.** mislead or deceive.

del′uge (del′yōōj) *n., v.,* **-uged, -uging.** —*n.* **1.** great flood. —*v.* **2.** flood. **3.** overwhelm.

de·lu′sion (di lōō′zhən) *n.* false opinion or conception.

de·luxe′ (də luks′) *adj.* of finest quality.

delve (delv) *v.,* **delved, delving.** search carefully for information.

Dem., 1. Democrat. **2.** Democratic.

dem′a·gogue′ (dem′ə gog′) *n.* unscrupulous popular leader. —**dem′a·gog′uer·y,** *n.*

de·mand′ (di mand′) *v.* **1.** claim. **2.** require. **3.** ask for in urgent or peremptory manner. —*n.* **4.** claim. **5.** requirement. **6.** desire for a product.

de·mar·cate (di mär′kāt, dē′mär kāt′) *v.,* **-cated, -cating.** set limits of. —**de·mar·ca′tion,** *n.*

de·mean′ (di mēn′) *v.* **1.** conduct (oneself). **2.** lower in dignity.

de·mean′or, *n.* conduct; behavior.

de·ment′ed (di men′tid) *adj.* crazed.

de·men′tia (-shə, -shē ə) *n.* severe mental impairment.

de·mer′it (di mer′it) *n.* **1.** fault. **2.** rating for misconduct.

demi-, prefix indicating half or lesser, as *demigod.*

dem′i·god′ (dem′ē god′) *n.* one partly divine and partly human.

de·mil′i·ta·rize′ (dē mil′i tə rīz′) *v.,* **-rized, -rizing.** free from military influence. —**de·mil′i·ta·ri·za′tion,** *n.*

de·mise′ (di mīz′) *n., v.,* **-mised, -mising.** —*n.* **1.** death. **2.** transfer of estate. —*v.* **3.** transfer.

dem′i·tasse′ (dem′i tas′, -täs′) *n.* small coffee cup.

dem′o (dem′ō) *n.* product displayed or offered for trial.

de·mo·bi·lize′ (dē mō′bə līz′) *v.,* **-lized, -lizing.** disband (army).

de·moc·ra·cy (di mok′rə sē) *n., pl.* **-cies. 1.** government in which the people hold supreme power. **2.** social equality. —**dem′o·crat′** (dem′ə krat′) *n.* —**dem′o·crat′ic,** *adj.*

Democratic Party, a major political party in the U.S.

dem′o·graph′ic (dem′ə graf′ik) *adj.* of statistics on population. —**dem′o·graph′i·cal·ly,** *adv.* —**dem·og′ra·phy,** *n.* —**dem′o·graph′ics,** *n.*

de·mol′ish (di mol′ish) *v.* destroy. —**dem′o·li′tion** (dem′ə lish′ən) *n.*

de′mon (dē′mən) *n.* evil spirit.

de·mon′ic (di mon′ik) *adj.* **1.** inspired. **2.** like a demon.

dem′on·strate′ (dem′ən strāt′) *v.,*

-strated, -strating. **1.** prove. **2.** describe and explain. **3.** display. **4.** parade in support or opposition. —**dem/on·stra/tor,** n.

de·mon/stra·ble (di mon/strable) adj. —**dem/on·stra/tion,** n.

de·mon/stra·tive (də mon/strə tiv) adj. expressive.

de·mor/al·ize/ (di môr/ə līz/) v., **-ized, -izing.** destroy confidence of.

de·mote/ (di mōt/) v., **-moted, -moting.** reduce in rank. —**de·mo/tion,** n.

de·mur/ (di mûr/) v., **-murred, -murring.** —v. object. —n. **2.** objection. —**de·mur/ral,** n.

de·mure/ (di myŏŏr/) adj. modest. —**de·mure/ly,** n.

den (den) n. **1.** cave of wild beast. **2.** room at home for relaxing.

de·na/ture (dē nā/chər) v., **-tured, -turing.** make (alcohol) unfit to drink.

de·ni/al (di nī/əl) n. **1.** contradiction. **2.** refusal to agree or give.

den/i·grate/ (den/i grāt/) v., **-grated, -grating.** speak badly of.

den/im (den/əm) n. **1.** heavy cotton fabric. **2.** (pl.) trousers of this.

den/i·zen (den/ə zən) n. inhabitant.

de·nom/i·nate/ (di nom/ə nāt/) v., **-nated, -nating.** name specifically.

de·nom/i·na/tion, n. **1.** name or designation. **2.** religious group. **3.** value of piece of money.

de·nom/i·na/tor, n. lower term in fraction.

de·note/ (di nōt/) v., **-noted, -noting.** **1.** indicate. **2.** mean.

de/noue·ment/ (dā/nōō mäN/) n. **1.** final resolution of plot or story. **2.** outcome of series of events. Also, **dé/noue·ment/.**

de·nounce/ (di nouns/) v., **-nounced, -nouncing.** **1.** condemn. **2.** inform against.

dense (dens) adj., **denser, densest.** **1.** compact. **2.** stupid. —**den/si·ty,** n. —**dense/ly,** adv.

dent (dent) n. **1.** hollow. —v. **2.** make a dent.

den/tal (den/tl) adj. of teeth.

den/ti·frice (-tə fris) n. teeth-cleaning substance.

den/tin (-tn, -tin) n. hard tissue that forms most of a tooth. Also, **den/tine** (-tēn).

den/tist (-tist) n. person who prevents and treats tooth disease. —**den/tist·ry,** n.

den/ture (-chər, -chŏŏr) n. artificial tooth.

de·nude/ (di nōōd/, -nyōōd/) v., **-nuded, -nuding.** make bare; strip.

de·nun/ci·a/tion (di nun/sē ā/shən) n. **1.** condemnation. **2.** accusation.

de·ny/ (di nī/) v., **-nied, -nying.** **1.** declare not to be true. **2.** refuse to agree or give.

de·o/dor·ant (dē ō/dər ənt) n. agent for destroying odors.

de·o/dor·ize/, v., **-ized, -izing.** rid of odors. —**de·o/dor·iz/er,** n.

de·part/ (di pärt/) v. **1.** go away. **2.** die. —**de·par/ture,** n.

de·part/ment, n. **1.** part; section. **2.** area. —**de/part·men/tal,** adj.

de·pend/ (di pend/) v. **1.** rely. **2.** be contingent. —**de·pend/ence,** n. —**de·pend/ent,** adj., n.

de·pend/a·ble, adj. reliable. —**de·pend/a·bil/i·ty,** n.

de·pict/ (di pikt/) v. **1.** portray. **2.** describe. —**de·pic/tion,** n.

de·pil/a·to/ry (di pil/ə tôr/ē) adj., n., pl. **-ries.** —adj. **1.** capable of removing hair. —n. **2.** depilatory agent.

de·plete/ (di plēt/) v., **-pleted, -pleting.** reduce in amount.

de·plore/, v. (di plôr/ -plōr/) **-plored, -ploring.** lament. —**de·plor/a·ble,** adj.

de·ploy/ (-ploi/) v. place strategically. —**de·ploy/ment,** n.

de·po·lit/i·cize/ (dē/pə lit/ə sīz/) v., **-cized, -cizing.** remove from realm of politics.

de·pop/u·late/ (dē pop/yə lāt/) v., **-lated, -lating.** reduce population of. —**de·pop/u·la/tion,** n.

de·port/ (di pôrt/) v. **1.** expel from country. **2.** conduct (oneself).

de/por·ta/tion (dē/pôr tā/shən) n. expulsion from country.

de·port/ment, n. conduct.

de·pose/ (di pōz/) v., **-posed, -posing.** **1.** remove from office. **2.** testify. —**dep/o·si/tion** (dep/ə zish/ən) n.

de·pos/it (di poz/it) v. **1.** place. **2.** place for safekeeping. —n. **3.** sediment. **4.** something deposited.

de·pos/i·to/ry (di poz/i tôr/ē) n., pl. **-ries.** place for safekeeping.

de/pot (dē/pō, Mil. or Brit. dep/ō) n. **1.** station. **2.** storage base.

de·prave/ (di prāv/) v., **-praved, -praving.** corrupt morally. —**de·praved/,** adj. —**de·prav/i·ty** (-prav/i tē) n.

dep/re·cate/ (dep/ri kāt/) v., **-cated, -cating.** **1.** disapprove of. **2.** belittle. —**dep/re·ca·to/ry,** adj.

de·pre/ci·ate/ (di prē/shē āt/) v., **-ated, -ating.** **1.** reduce or decline in value. **2.** belittle.

dep/re·da/tion (dep/ri dā/shən) n. plunder.

de·press/ (di pres/) v. **1.** deject. **2.**

weaken. **3.** press down. —**de·pressed/**, *adj.*

de·pres/sion, *n.* **1.** act of depressing. **2.** depressed state. **3.** depressed place. **4.** decline in business. —**de·pres/sive,** *adj.*

de·prive/ (-prīv/) *v.*, **-prived, -priving.** withhold from. —**dep/ri·va/tion,** *n.*

dept., 1. department. **2.** deputy.

depth (depth) *n.* **1.** distance down. **2.** intensity. **3.** lowness of pitch. **4.** deep part.

dep/u·ta/tion (dep/yə tā/shən) *n.* delegation.

dep/u·ty (-tē) *n., pl.* **-ties.** agent; substitute. —**dep/u·tize/** (-tīz/) *v.*, **-tized, -tizing.**

de·rail/ (dē rāl/) *v.* cause to run off rails. —**de·rail/ment,** *n.*

de·range/ (di rānj/) *v.*, **-ranged, -ranging.** make insane.

der/by (dûr/bē; *Brit.* där/-) *n., pl.* **-bies. 1.** stiff, rounded hat. **2.** race.

de·reg/u·late/ (dē reg/yə lāt/) *v.*, **-lated, -lating.** free of regulation.

der/e·lict/ (der/ə likt) *adj.* **1.** abandoned. **2.** neglectful. —*n.* **3.** something abandoned. **4.** vagrant.

der/e·lic/tion, *n.* neglect.

de·ride/ (di rīd/) *v.*, **-rided, -riding.** mock. —**de·ri/sion** (-rizh/ən) *n.* —**de·ri/sive** (-rī/siv) *adj.*

de·rive/ (di rīv/) *v.*, **-rived, -riving. 1.** get from source. **2.** trace. **3.** deduce. **4.** originate. —**der/i·va/tion** (der/ə vā/shən) *n.* —**de·riv/a·tive** (di riv/ə tiv) *n., adj.*

der/ma·ti/tis (dûr/mə tī/tis) *n.* inflammation of the skin.

der/ma·tol/o·gy (dûr/mə tol/ə jē) *n.* medical study and treatment of the skin. —**der/ma·tol/o·gist,** *n.*

der/o·gate/ (der/ə gāt/) *v.*, **-gated, -gating.** detract.

de·rog/a·to/ry (di rog/ə tôr/ē) *adj.* disparaging.

der/rick (der/ik) *n.* crane with boom pivoted at one end.

der/ri·ere/ (der/ē âr/) *n.* buttocks.

de·scend/ (di send/) *v.* **1.** move down. **2.** have as relative in the past. —**de·scent/,** *n.*

de·scend/ant, *n.* person descended from ancestor; offspring.

de·scribe/ (di skrīb/) *v.*, **-scribed, -scribing. 1.** put down in words. **2.** trace. —**de·scrip/tion** (-skrip/shən) *n.* —**de·scrip/tive,** *adj.*

de·scry/ (di skrī/) *v.*, **-scried, -scrying.** happen to see.

des/e·crate/ (des/i krāt/) *v.*, **-crated, -crating.** divest of sacredness; profane. —**des/e·cra/tion,** *n.*

de·seg/re·gate/ (dē seg/ri gāt/) *v.*, **-gated, -gating.** eliminate racial segregation in.

de·sen/si·tize/ (dē sen/si tīz/) *v.*, **-tized, -tizing.** make less sensitive.

des/ert (dez/ərt) arid region.

de·sert/ (di zûrt/) (*often pl.*) due reward or punishment. —*v.* **3.** (di zûrt/) abandon. —**de·sert/er,** *n.* —**de·ser/tion,** *n.*

de·serve/ (di zûrv/) *v.*, **-served, -serving.** be worthy of; merit.

des/ic·cate/ (des/i kāt/) *v.*, **-cated, -cating.** dry up.

de·sid/er·a/tum (di sid/ə rā/təm, -rä/-, -zid/-) *n., pl.* **-ta** (-tə). something wanted.

de·sign/ (di zīn/) *v.* **1.** plan. **2.** conceive form of. —*n.* **3.** sketch or plan. **4.** art of designing. **5.** pattern. **6.** purpose. —**de·sign/er,** *n.*

des/ig·nate/ (dez/ig nāt/) *v.*, **-nated, -nating. 1.** indicate. **2.** name. —**des/ig·na/tion,** *n.*

designated driver, person who does not drink alcohol at a gathering in order to drive companions home safely.

de·sign/ing, scheming.

de·sire/ (di zīər/) *v.*, **-sired, -siring.** **1.** wish for. **2.** request. —*n.* **3.** longing. **4.** request. **5.** thing desired. **6.** lust. —**de·sir/a·ble,** *adj.*

de·sist/ (di zist/, -sist/) *v.* stop.

desk (desk) *n.* **1.** table for writing. **2.** specialized section of organization, esp. in newspaper office.

desk/top/ publishing, design and production of publications using a microcomputer.

des/o·late *adj., v.*, **-lated, -lating.** —*adj.* (des/ə lit) **1.** barren. **2.** lonely. **3.** dismal. —*v.* (-ə lāt/) **4.** lay waste. **5.** make hopeless. —**des/o·la/tion,** *n.*

de·spair/ (di spâr/) *n.* **1.** hopelessness. —*v.* **2.** lose hope.

des/per·a/do (des/pə rä/dō, -rā/-) *n., pl.* **-does, -dos.** bold outlaw.

des/per·ate (des/pər it) *adj.* **1.** reckless from despair. **2.** despairing. —**des/per·a/tion,** *n.*

des/pi·ca·ble (des/pi kə bəl, di·spik/ə-) *adj.* contemptible.

de·spise/ (di spīz/) *v.*, **-spised, -spising.** scorn or hate.

de·spite/ (di spīt/) *prep.* in spite of.

de·spoil/ (di spoil/) *v.* plunder.

de·spond/ent (di spon/dənt) *adj.* in low spirits; dejected. —**de·spond/en·cy** *n.*

des/pot (des/pət, -pot) *n.* tyrant. —**des·pot/ic,** *adj.*

des·sert/ (di zûrt/) *n.* final course of meal, usually sweet.

des/ti·na/tion (des/tə nā/shən) *n.* goal of journey.

des/tine (-tin) *v.*, **-tined, -tining. 1.** set apart. **2.** predetermine by fate.

des·ti·ny, *n.,* *pl.* **-nies.** **1.** predetermined future. **2.** fate.

des·ti·tute' (-tōōt', -tyōōt') *adj.* **1.** very poor. **2.** deprived.

de·stroy' (di stroi') *v.* **1.** ruin. **2.** end. **3.** kill.

de·stroy'er, *n.* **1.** one that destroys. **2.** naval vessel.

de·struct' (di strukt') *v.* be destroyed automatically.

de·struc'tion, *n.* **1.** act or means of destroying. **2.** fact of being destroyed. —**de·struc'tive,** *adj.*

des·ul·to·ry (des'əl tôr'ē) *adj.* not methodical. —**des'ul·to·ri·ly,** *adv.*

de·tach' (di tach') *v.* take off or away. —**de·tach'a·ble,** *adj.*

de·tached', *adj.* **1.** separate. **2.** uninterested.

de·tach'ment, *n.* **1.** act of detaching. **2.** unconcern. **3.** impartiality. **4.** troops for special duty.

de·tail' (di tāl', dē'tāl) *n.* **1.** individual or minute part. **2. in detail,** with all details specified. **3.** troops or group selected for special duty. —*v.* **4.** relate in detail. **5.** assign.

de·tain' (di tān') *v.* **1.** delay. **2.** keep in custody. —**de·ten'tion,** *n.*

de·tect' (di tekt') *v.* **1.** discover. **2.** perceive. —**de·tec'tion,** *n.* **de·tec'tor,** *n.*

de·tec'tive, *n.* professional investigator of crimes, etc.

dé·tente (dā tänt') *n.* lessening of international hostility.

de·ter' (di tûr') *v.* **1.** terred, **-terring.** discourage or restrain.

de·ter'gent (di tûr'jənt) *adj.* **1.** cleansing. —*n.* **2.** cleansing agent.

de·te·ri·o·rate (di tēr'ē ə rāt') *v.,* **-rated, -rating.** make or become worse. —**de·te·ri·o·ra'tion,** *n.*

de·ter'mi·na·tion (-nā'shən) *n.* **1.** act of determining. **2.** firmness of purpose.

de·ter'mine (-min) *v.,* **-mined, -mining. 1.** settle; decide. **2.** ascertain. **3.** limit.

de·ter'mined, *adj.* resolved.

de·ter'rence (di tûr'əns) *n.* discouragement, as of crime or military aggression. —**de·ter'rent,** *adj.,* *n.*

de·test' (di test') *v.* **1.** hate or despise. —**de·test'a·ble,** *adj.*

de·throne' (dē thrōn') *v.,* **-throned, -throning.** remove from a throne.

det'o·nate (det'n āt') *v.,* **-nated, -nating.** explode. —**det'o·na'tion,** *n.*

de'tour (dē'tŏŏr, di tŏŏr') *n.* **1.** roundabout course. —*v.* **2.** make detour.

de'tox *n., v.,* **-toxed, -toxing.** *Informal.* —*n.* (dē'toks) **1.** detoxification. **2.** hospital unit for patients

undergoing detoxification. —*v.* (dē-toks') **3.** detoxify.

de·tox·i·fy, *v.,* **-fied, -fying.** rid of effects of alcohol or drug use. —**de·tox'i·fi·ca'tion,** *n.*

de·tract' (di trakt') *v.* take away quality or reputation.

det'ri·ment (de'trə mənt) *n.* damage or loss. —**det'ri·men'tal** (-men'tl) *adj.*

de·tri'tus (di trī'təs) *n.* rock particles worn away from a mass; debris.

deuce (dōōs, dyōōs) *n.* **1.** card or die with two pips. **2.** tie score as in tennis.

de·val·u·ate (dē val'yōō āt') *v.,* **-ated, -ating.** reduce in value; depreciate. —**de·val·u·a'tion,** *n.*

dev·as·tate' (dev'ə stāt') *v.,* **-tated, -tating.** lay waste. —**dev'as·ta'-tion,** *n.*

de·vel'op (di vel'əp) *v.* **1.** mature. **2.** elaborate. **3.** bring into being. **4.** make (images on film) visible. **5.** acquire. —**de·vel'op·ment,** *n.* —**de·vel'op·er,** *n.*

de·vi·ate (dē'vē āt') *v.,* **-ated, -ating. 1.** digress. **2.** depart from normal. —**de·vi·a'tion,** *n.* —**de·vi·ant,** *adj., n.*

de·vice' (di vīs') *n.* **1.** contrivance. **2.** plan. **3.** slogan or emblem.

dev'il (dev'əl) *n.* **1.** Satan. **2.** evil spirit or person. —**dev'il·ish,** *adj.* —**dev'il·try,** *n.*

dev'il-may-care', *adj.* reckless.

devil's advocate, person who takes opposing view for the sake of argument.

devil's food cake, rich chocolate cake.

de'vi·ous (dē'vē əs) *adj.* **1.** circuitous. **2.** not sincere.

de·vise' (di vīz') *v.,* **-vised, -vising. 1.** plan; contrive. **2.** bequeath.

de·vi·tal·ize (dē vīt'l īz') *v.,* **-ized, -izing.** remove vitality of.

de·void' (di void') *adj.* destitute.

de·volve' (di volv') *v.,* **-volved, -volving. 1.** transfer or delegate. **2.** fall as a duty.

de·vote' (di vōt') *v.,* **-voted, -voting. 1.** give up or apply to a certain pursuit, cause, etc. **2.** dedicate.

de·vot'ed, *adj.* **1.** zealous. **2.** dedicated.

dev·o·tee' (dev'ə tē') *n.* devoted one.

de·vo'tion (di vō'shən) *n.* **1.** consecration. **2.** attachment or dedication. **3.** (*pl.*) worship.

de·vour' (di vour') *v.* consume ravenously.

de·vout' (di vout') *adj.* pious.

dew (dōō, dyōō) *n.* atmospheric

moisture condensed in droplets at night. —**dew′y,** *adj.*

dex·ter′i·ty (dek ster′i tē) *n.* **1.** physical skill. **2.** cleverness. —**dex′ter·ous** (dek′star əs, -strəs) *adj.*

dex′trose (dek′strōs) *n.* type of sugar.

di·a·be′tes (dī′ə bē′tis, -tēz) *n.* disease characterized by high levels of glucose in the blood. —**di′a·bet′ic** (-bet′ik) *adj.*

di·a·bol′ic (dī′ə bol′ik) *adj.* fiendish. Also, **di·a·bol′i·cal.**

di·a·crit′ic (dī′ə krit′ik) *n.* mark added to a letter to give it a particular phonetic value.

di′a·dem′ (dī′ə dem′) *n.* crown.

di·ag·nose′ (dī′əg nōs′, -nōz′) *v.*, **-nosed, -nosing.** determine nature of (disease). —**di′ag·no′sis,** *n.* —**di′ag·nos′tic** (-nos′tik) *adj.*

di·ag′o·nal (dī ag′ə nl) *adj.* **1.** connecting two non-adjacent angles. **2.** oblique. —**di·ag′o·nal·ly,** *adv.*

di′a·gram′ (dī′ə gram′) *n.*, *v.*, **-gramed, -graming.** chart or plan.

di′al (dī′əl, dīl) *n.*, *v.*, **-aled, -aling.** —*n.* **1.** numbered face, as on a watch. —*v.* **2.** select or contact by using a dial.

di′a·lect′ (dī′ə lekt′) *n.* language of district or class.

di′a·lec′tic, *n.* art or practice of debate or conversation by which truth of theory or opinion is arrived at logically. Also, **di′a·lec′tics.** —**di′a·lec′ti·cal,** *adj.*

di′a·logue′ (dī′ə lôg′) *n.* conversation between two or more people. Also, **di′a·log′.**

di·al′y·sis (dī al′ə sis) *n.* process of removing waste products from blood of someone with kidney disease.

di·am′e·ter (dī am′i tər) *n.* straight line through center of a circle.

di′a·met′ri·cal (-ə me′tri kal) *adj.* **1.** of diameters. **2.** completely in contrast. —**di′a·met′ri·cal·ly,** *adv.*

di′a·mond (dī′mənd, dī′ə-) *n.* **1.** hard, brilliant precious stone. **2.** rhombus or square. **3.** (*pl.*) suit of playing cards. **4.** baseball field.

di′a·mond·back′, *n.* venomous rattlesnake.

di′a·per (dī′pər, dī′ə pər) *n.* **1.** infant's undergarment. —*v.* **2.** put diaper on.

di·aph′a·nous (dī af′ə nəs) *adj.* very sheer and light.

di′a·phragm′ (dī′ə fram′) *n.* **1.** muscle between chest and abdomen. **2.** vibrating membrane. **3.** contraceptive device.

di′ar·rhe′a (dī′ə rē′ə) *n.* intestinal disorder. Also, **di′ar·rhoe′a.**

di′a·ry (dī′ə rē) *n.*, *pl.* **-ries.** personal daily record. —**di′a·rist,** *n.*

di′a·tribe′ (-trīb′) *n.* denunciation.

dib′ble (dib′əl) *n.* pointed instrument for planting.

dice (dīs) *n.pl., sing.* **die,** *v.*, **diced, dicing.** —*n.* **1.** small cubes, used in games. —*v.* **2.** cut into small cubes.

dic′ey (dī′sē) *adj.* **-ier, -iest.** risky.

di·chot′o·my (dī kot′ə mē) *n.*, *pl.* **-mies.** division into two irreconcilable groups.

dick′er (dik′ər) *v.* bargain.

di·cot′y·le′don (dī kot′l ēd′n, dī′kot l-) *n.* plant having two embryonic seed leaves.

Dic′ta·phone′ (dik′tə fōn′) *n. Trademark.* brand name for machine that records and plays back dictated speech.

dic′tate (dik′tāt) *v.*, **-tated, -tating.** —*v.* **1.** say something to be written down. **2.** command. —*n.* **3.** command. —**dic·ta′tion,** *n.*

dic·ta′tor, *n.* absolute ruler. —**dic′ta·to′ri·al** (-tə tôr′ē əl) *adj.* —**dic·ta′tor·ship′,** *n.*

dic′tion (dik′shən) *n.* style of speaking.

dic′tion·ar′y (dik′shə ner′ē) *n.*, *pl.* **-aries.** book on meaning, spelling, pronunciation, etc., of words.

dic′tum (dik′təm) *n.*, *pl.* **-ta, -tums.** authoritative declaration.

di·dac′tic (dī dak′tik) *adj.* instructive.

did′n't (did′nt) contraction of **did not.**

die (dī) *v.*, **died, dying,** *n.*, (*for* **3**) **dies.** —*v.* **1.** cease to be. **2.** lose force; fade. —*n.* **3.** shaping device. **4.** *sing.* of **dice.**

die′hard′, *n.* defender of lost cause.

di·er·e·sis (dī er′ə sis) *n.*, *pl.* **-ses.** sign (¨) over a vowel indicating separate pronunciation, as in Noël.

die′sel (dē′zal, -sal) *n.* **1.** engine using air compression for ignition. **2.** machine powered by diesel engine. **3.** fuel used by diesel engine.

di′et (dī′it) *n.* **1.** food one eats. **2.** food specially chosen for health or weight control. **3.** formal assembly. —*v.* **4.** adhere to diet. —**di′e·tar′y** (-i ter′ē) *adj.* —**di′e·tet′ic** (-tet′ik) *adj.*

di′e·ti′tian (dī′i tish′ən) *n.* expert in nutrition and dietary requirements. Also, **di′e·ti′cian.**

dif′fer (dif′ər) *v.* **1.** be unlike. **2.** disagree.

dif′fer·ence (dif′ər əns, dif′rəns) *n.* **1.** unlikeness. **2.** disagreement. **3.**

amount separating two quantities. —**dif•fer•ent,** *adj.* —**dif•fer•ent•ly,** *adv.* —Usage. DIFFERENT FROM is more common today in introducing a phrase, but DIFFERENT THAN is also used: *New York speech is different from/than that of Chicago.* DIFFERENT THAN is usually used when a clause follows, especially when the word "from" would create an awkward sentence: *The stream followed a different course than the map showed.*

dif•fer•en'ti•ate' (-en'shē āt') *v.,* -ated, -ating. 1. alter. 2. distinguish. —**dif•fer'en•ti•a'tion,** *n.*

dif•fi•cult' (dif'i kult', -kalt) *adj.* 1. hard to do or understand. 2. unmanageable.

dif•fi•cul'ty, *n., pl.* -ties. 1. condition of being difficult. 2. difficult situation. 3. trouble. 4. disagreement.

dif•fi•dent (-dant) *adj.* timid; shy.

dif•frac'tion (di frak'shan) *n.* breaking up of rays of light to produce spectrum.

dif•fuse' *v.* -fused, -fusing, *adj.* —*v.* (di fyōoz') 1. spread or scatter. —*adj.* (-fyōos') 2. not to the point. 3. spread or scattered.

dig (dig) *v.,* dug (dug) or digged, digging, *n.* —*v.* 1. remove earth. 2. uncover by removing earth. 3. form by removing earth. 4. *Slang.* understand or appreciate. —*n.* 5. sarcastic remark. —**dig'ger,** *n.*

di•gest' *v* (di jest') 1. prepare (food) for assimilation. 2. assimilate mentally. —*n.* (dī'jest) 3. collection or summary, esp. of laws. —**di•ges'tion,** *n.* —**di•ges'tive,** *adj.*

dig'it (dij'it) *n.* 1. finger or toe. 2. any Arabic numeral.

dig'it•al (-i tl) *adj.* of, using, or expressing data in numerals.

dig'i•tize' (-tīz') *v.,* -tized, -tizing. convert (data) to digital form.

dig'ni•fied' (dig'na fīd') *adj.* marked by dignity; stately.

dig'ni•fy', *v.,* -fied, -fying. 1. honor. 2. honor more than is deserved.

dig'ni•tar'y (-ter'ē) *n., pl.* -ries. high-ranking person.

dig'ni•ty, *n., pl.* -ties. 1. nobility. 2. worthiness. 3. high rank, office, or title.

di•gress' (di gres', dī-) *v.* wander from main purpose, theme, etc. —**di•gres'sion,** *n.*

dike (dīk) *n.* 1. bank for restraining waters. 2. ditch.

di•lap'i•dat'ed (di lap'i dā'tid) *adj.* decayed.

di•lap'i•da'tion, *n.* ruin; decay.

di•late' (dī lāt') *v.,* -lated, -lating. expand. —**di•la'tion,** *n.*

dil'a•to•ry (dil'a tôr'ē) *adj.* delaying; tardy. —**dil'a•to'ri•ness,** *n.*

di•lem'ma (di lem'a) *n.* predicament.

dil'et•tante' (dil'i tänt', dil'i tänt') *n.* superficial practitioner.

dil'i•gence (dil'i jans) *n.* earnest effort. —**dil'i•gent,** *adj.*

dill (dil) *n.* herb with aromatic seeds and leaves.

dil'ly-dal'ly (dil'ē dal'ē) *v.,* -lied, -lying. waste time, esp. by indecision.

di•lute' (di lōōt', dī-) *v.,* -luted, -luting. thin, as with water; weaken. —**di•lu'tion,** *n.*

dim (dim) *adj.,* dimmer, dimmest, *v.,* dimmed, dimming. —*adj.* 1. not bright. 2. indistinct. —*v.* 3. make or become dim. —**dim'ly,** *adv.*

dime (dīm) *n.* coin worth 10 cents.

di•men'sion (di men'shan, dī-) *n.* 1. extension in a given direction. 2. magnitude. —**di•men'sion•al,** *adj.*

di•min'ish (di min'ish) *v.* lessen; reduce.

di•min'u•en'do (di min'yōō en'dō) *adj., adv. Music.* gradually reducing in loudness.

di•min'u•tive (di min'ya tiv) *adj.* 1. small. —*n.* 2. diminutive form, as of a word.

dim'i•ty (dim'i tē) *n., pl.* -ties. thin cotton fabric.

dim'ple (dim'pal) *n.* small hollow, esp. in cheek.

dim'wit', *n. Slang.* stupid person. —**dim'wit'ted,** *adj.*

din (din) *n.,* v., dinned, dinning. —*n.* 1. confused noise. —*v.* 2. assail with din.

dine (dīn) *v.,* dined, dining. eat dinner or another meal.

din'er, *n.* 1. person who dines. 2. railroad dining car. 3. restaurant.

di•nette' (-net') *n.* small area or alcove for dining.

din'ghy (ding'gē) *n., pl.* -ghies. small boat.

din'gy (din'jē) *adj.,* -gier, -giest. dark; dirty.

din'ner (din'ar) *n.* main meal.

di'no•saur' (dī'na sôr') *n.* any of various extinct reptiles.

dint (dint) *n.* 1. force. 2. dent.

di'o•cese' (dī'a sis, -sēz', -sēs') *n.* district under a bishop. —**di•oc'e•san** (-os'a san) *adj.*

di'o•ram'a (dī'a ram'a, -rä'ma) *n.* miniature three-dimensional scene against painted background.

di•ox'ide (dī ok'sīd, -sid) *n.* oxide with two atoms of oxygen.

di·ox′in (-ok′sin) *n.* toxic by-product of pesticide.

dip (dip) *v.,* **dipped, dipping,** *n.* —*v.* **1.** plunge temporarily in liquid. **2.** bail or scoop. **3.** slope down. —*n.* **4.** act of dipping. **5.** downward slope. **6.** substance into which something is dipped.

diph·the′ri·a (dif thēr′ē ə, dip-) *n.* infectious disease of air passages, esp. throat.

diph′thong (dif′thông, dip′-) *n.* sound containing two vowels.

di·plo′ma (di plō′ma) *n.* document of academic qualifications.

di·plo′ma·cy (-sē) *n., pl.* **-cies. 1.** conduct of international relations. **2.** skill in negotiation. —**dip′lo·mat′** (dip′lə mat′) *n.*

dip′lo·mat′ic, *adj.* **1.** of diplomacy. **2.** tactful.

dip′so·ma′ni·a (dip′sə mā′nē ə, -sō-) *n.* morbid craving for alcohol. —**dip′so·ma′ni·ac,** *n.*

dir., director.

dire (dīr) *adj.,* **direr, direst.** dreadful.

di·rect′ (di rekt′, dī-) *v.* **1.** guide. **2.** command. **3.** manage. **4.** address. —*adj.* **5.** straight. **6.** straightforward. —**di·rect′ly,** *adv.* —**di·rect′ness,** *n.* —**di·rec′tor,** *n.*

direct current, electric current flowing continuously in one direction.

di·rec′tion, *n.* **1.** act of directing. **2.** line along which a thing lies or moves. —**di·rec′tion·al,** *adj.*

di·rec′tive, *n.* order or instruction from authority.

di·rec′to·ry, *n., pl.* **-ries.** list of locations, telephone numbers, etc.

dirge (dûrj) *n.* funeral song.

dir′i·gi·ble (dir′i jə bəl, di rij′ə-) *n.* airship.

dirk (dûrk) *n.* dagger.

dirt (dûrt) *n.* **1.** filth. **2.** earth.

dirt′y, *adj.,* **-ier, -iest,** *v.,* **-ied, -ying.** —*adj.* **1.** soiled. **2.** indecent. —*v.* **3.** soil. —**dirt′i·ness,** *n.*

dis (dis) *v.,* **dissed, dissing,** *Slang.* —*v.* **1.** show disrespect for. **2.** disparage. —*n.* **3.** disparagement or criticism.

dis- prefix indicating: **1.** reversal, as *disconnect.* **2.** negation or lack, as *distrust.* **3.** removal, as *disbar.*

dis·a′ble (-ā′bəl) *v.,* **-bled, -bling.** damage capability of. —**dis′a·bil′i·ty,** *n.*

dis·a′bled, *adj.* handicapped; incapacitated.

dis·a·buse′ (-byōōz′) *v.,* **-bused, -busing.** free from deception.

dis′ad·van′tage, *n.* **1.** drawback; handicap. **2.** injury.

dis′ad·van′taged, *adj.* lacking economic and social opportunity.

dis′af·fect′, *v.* alienate.

dis′a·gree′, *v.,* **-greed, -greeing.** differ in opinion. —**dis′a·gree′ment,** *n.*

dis′a·gree′a·ble, *adj.* unpleasant.

dis′al·low′, *v.* refuse to allow.

dis′ap·pear′, *v.* **1.** cease to be seen. **2.** cease to exist. —**dis′ap·pear′ance,** *n.*

dis′ap·point′, *v.* fail to fulfill hopes of. —**dis′ap·point′ment,** *n.*

dis′ap·pro·ba′tion, *n.* disapproval.

dis′ap·prove′, *v.,* **-proved, -proving.** condemn; censure. —**dis′ap·prov′al,** *n.*

dis·arm′, *v.* **1.** deprive of arms. **2.** reduce one's own armed power.

dis′ar·range′, *n.* **-ranged, -ranging.** disorder.

dis′ar·ray′, *n.* lack of order.

dis·as·so′ci·ate′ (-āt′) *v.,* **-ated, -ating.** dissociate.

dis·as′ter (di zas′tər) *n.* extreme misfortune. —**dis·as′trous,** *adj.*

dis·a·vow′ (dis′ə vou′) *v.* deny responsibility for. —**dis′a·vow′al,** *n.*

dis·band′, *v.* break up (an organization). —**dis·band′ment,** *n.*

dis·bar′, *v.,* **-barred, -barring.** expel from law practice.

dis′be·lieve′, *v.,* **-lieved, -lieving.** reject as untrue. —**dis′be·lief′,** *n.*

dis·burse′ (dis bûrs′) *v.,* **-bursed, -bursing.** pay out.

disc (disk) *n.* **1.** disk. **2.** phonograph record.

dis·card′ *v.* (di skärd′) **1.** reject. —*n.* (dis′kärd) something discarded. **3.** discarded state.

dis·cern′ (di sûrn′, -zûrn′) *v.* **1.** see. **2.** distinguish. —**dis·cern′ible,** *adj.* —**dis·cern′ing,** *adj.* —**dis·cern′ment,** *n.*

dis·charge′ *v.,* **-charged, -charging,** *n.* —*v.* (dis chärj′) **1.** rid of load. **2.** send forth. **3.** shoot. **4.** end employment of. **5.** fulfill. —*n.* (dis′chärj) **6.** act of discharging. **7.** something discharged.

dis·ci′ple (di sī′pəl) *n.* follower.

dis′ci·pline (dis′ə plin) *n., v.,* **-plined, -plining. 1.** training in rules. **2.** punishment. **3.** subjection to rules. **4.** branch of instruction or learning. —*v.* **5.** train. **6.** punish. —**dis′ci·pli·nar′y,** *adj.*

disc jockey, person who plays and comments on recorded music on a radio program. Also, **disk jockey.**

dis·claim′ (dis klām′) *v.* disown.

dis·close′ (di sklōz′) *v.,* **-closed, -closing.** reveal. —**dis·clo′sure,** *n.*

dis′co (dis′kō) *n., pl.* **-cos. 1.** discotheque. **2.** rhythmic style of dance music.

dis·col·or (dis kul′ər) v. change in color. —**dis·col·or·a′tion,** n.

dis·com·bob·u·late′ (dis′kəm bob′yə lāt′) v., **-lated, -lating.** confuse or perturb.

dis·com·fit (dis kum′fit) v. defeat; thwart. —**dis·com′fi·ture,** n.

dis·com·fort (dis kum′fərt) n. lack of comfort.

dis·com·mode′ (dis′kə mōd′) v., **-moded, -moding.** cause inconvenience to.

dis·com·pose′, v., **-posed, -posing. 1.** upset the order of. **2.** disturb the composure of.

dis·con·cert′ (dis′kən sûrt′) v. perturb.

dis·con·nect′, v. break connection of.

dis·con·so·late (dis kon′sə lit) adj. sad. —**dis·con′so·late·ly,** adv.

dis·con·tent′ (-kən tent′) adj. Also **dis·con·tent′ed. 1.** not contented. —n. **2.** lack of contentment.

dis·con·tin′ue, v., **-tinued, -tinuing.** end; stop.

dis·cord (dis′kôrd) n. **1.** lack of harmony. **2.** strife. —**dis·cord′ance,** n. —**dis·cord′ant,** adj.

dis·co·theque (dis′kə tek′, dis′kə tek′) n. nightclub where recorded dance music is played.

dis·count (v. dis kount, dis kount′) **1.** deduct. **2.** advance money after deduction of interest. **3.** disregard. —n. (dis′kount) **4.** deduction.

dis·coun·te·nance, v., **-nanced, -nancing. 1.** disconcert regularly. **2.** show disapproval of.

dis·cour·age (di skûr′ij, -skur′-) v., **-aged, -aging. 1.** deprive of resolution. **2.** hinder.

dis·course, n., v., **-coursed, -coursing.** —n. (dis′kôrs) **1.** talk. **2.** formal discussion. —v. (dis kôrs′) **3.** talk.

dis·cour·te·sy, n., pl. **-sies. 1.** lack of courtesy. **2.** impolite act. —**dis·cour′te·ous,** adj.

dis·cov·er (di skuv′ər) v. learn or see for first time. —**dis·cov′er·y,** n. —**dis·cov′er·er,** n. —**Usage.** Do not confuse DISCOVER and INVENT, two words that deal with something new. DISCOVER is used when the object is an idea or place that existed before, but few people or no one knew about it. In the sentence *Columbus discovered the New World,* the New World clearly existed and was known to the people living there, but not to Columbus and the people of his time. INVENT is used when the object is a device or thing

built. In the sentence *Edison invented the light bulb,* the light bulb did not exist before Edison invented it, and it was not known by anyone.

dis·cred·it, v. **1.** defame. **2.** disbelieve. —n. **3.** lack of belief. **4.** disrepute.

dis·creet′ (di skrēt′) adj. wise; prudent. —**dis·creet′ly,** adv.

dis·crep·an·cy (di skrep′ən sē) n., pl. **-cies.** difference; inconsistency.

dis·crete′ (di skrēt′) adj. separate.

dis·cre′tion (di skresh′ən) n. **1.** freedom of choice. **2.** prudence.

dis·crim′i·nate, v., **-nated, -nating.** adj. —v. (di skrim′ə nāt′) **1.** distinguish accurately. **2.** show bias. —adj. (-ə nit) **3.** making distinctions. —**dis·crim′i·na′tion,** n.

dis·cur·sive (di skûr′siv) adj. rambling.

dis·cus (dis′kəs) n. disk for throwing in athletic competition.

dis·cuss′ (di skus′) v. talk about. —**dis·cus′sion,** n.

dis·dain′ (dis dān′, di stān′) n. scorn. —v. **2.** disdain. —**dis·dain′ful,** adj.

dis·ease′ (di zēz′) n., v., **-eased, -easing.** —n. **1.** ailment. —v. **2.** affect with disease. —**dis·eased′,** adj.

dis·em·bark′ (dis′em bärk′) v. leave airplane or ship. —**dis·em′bar·ka′tion,** n.

dis·em·bod′y (dis′em bod′ē) v., **-bodied, -bodying.** free from the body.

dis·en·chant′, v. free from enchantment or illusion.

dis·en·gage′, v., **-gaged, -gaging.** separate; disconnect.

dis·fa′vor, n., **1.** displeasure. **2.** disregard. —v. **3.** regard or treat with disfavor.

dis·fig′ure, v., **-ured, -uring.** spoil appearance of. —**dis·fig′ure·ment′,** n.

dis·fran′chise, v., **-chised, -chising.** deprive of franchise.

dis·gorge′ (dis gôrj′) v., **-gorged, -gorging.** vomit forth.

dis·grace′ (dis grās′) n., v., **-graced, -gracing.** —n. **1.** state or cause of dishonor. —v. **2.** bring shame upon. —**dis·grace′ful,** adj. —**dis·grace′ful·ly,** adv.

dis·grun′tle (dis grun′tl) v., **-tled, -tling.** make discontented.

dis·guise′ (dis gīz′, di skīz′) v., **-guised, -guising.** —v. **1.** conceal true identity of. —n. **2.** something that disguises.

dis·gust′ (dis gust′, di skust′) v. **1.** cause loathing in. —n. **2.** loathing. —**dis·gust′ed,** adj. —**dis·gust′ing,** adj.

dish (dish) *n.* **1.** open shallow container. **2.** article of food.

dis·ha·bille' (dis'ə bēl', -bē') *n.* state of being partially dressed.

dis·heart'en, *v.* discourage.

di·shev'el (di shev'əl) *v.,* **-eled, -el·ing.** let (hair, clothes) look messy.

dis·hon'est, *adj.* not honest.

dis·hon'or, *n.* **1.** lack of honor. **2.** disgrace. —*v.* **3.** disgrace. **4.** fail to honor. —**dis·hon'or·a·ble,** *adj.*

dish'wash'er, *n.* person or machine that washes dishes.

dis·il·lu'sion, *v.* free from illusion.

dis·in·cline', *v.,* **-clined, -clin·ing.** make or be averse.

dis·in·fect', *v.* destroy disease germs in. —**dis·in·fect'ant,** *n., adj.*

dis·in·for·ma'tion, *n.* false information released by a government to mislead rivals.

dis·in·gen'u·ous, *adj.* lacking frankness.

dis·in·her'it, *v.* exclude from inheritance.

dis·in'te·grate', *v.,* **-grated, -grat·ing.** break into parts. —**dis·in'te·gra'tion,** *n.*

dis·in·ter', *v.,* **-terred, -ter·ring.** take out of the place of interment.

dis·in'ter·est, *n.* indifference.

dis·in'ter·est'ed, *adj.* **1.** not partial or biased. **2.** not interested.
—**Usage.** Do not confuse DISINTERESTED and UNINTERESTED. DISINTERESTED usually means "able to act fairly; not partial or biased," while UNINTERESTED means "not taking an interest." But the second meaning listed here means the same as UNINTERESTED and many users of English consider this use of DISINTERESTED incorrect.

dis·joint'ed, *adj.* **1.** separated at joints. **2.** incoherent.

disk (disk) *n.* **1.** flat circular plate. **2.** phonograph record. **3.** device for storing electronic data. **4.** roundish, flat anatomical part, as in the spine. Also, **disc.**

disk·ette' (di sket') *n.* floppy disk.

disk jockey, disc jockey.

dis·like', *v.,* **-liked, -lik·ing,** *n.* —*v.* **1.** regard with displeasure. —*n.* **2.** distaste.

dis·lo'cate' (dis'lō kāt', dis lō'kāt) *v.,* **-cated, -cat·ing.** **1.** displace. **2.** put out of order.

dis·lodge', *v.,* **-lodged, -lodg·ing.** force from place.

dis·loy'al, *adj.* not loyal; traitorous.

dis·mal (diz'məl) *adj.* **1.** gloomy. **2.** terrible. —**dis·mal·ly,** *adv.*

dis·man'tle (dis man'tl) *v.,* **-tled, -tling.** **1.** deprive of equipment. **2.** take apart. —**dis·man'tle·ment,** *n.*

dis·may' (dis mā') *v.* **1.** dishearten. —*n.* **2.** consternation.

dis·mem'ber (dis mem'bər) *v.* remove limbs of.

dis·miss' (dis mis') *v.* **1.** direct or allow to go away. **2.** remove from service. **3.** reject. —**dis·mis'sal,** *n.*

dis·mount', *v.* **1.** get or throw down from saddle. **2.** take apart.

dis'o·be'di·ent, *adj.* not obedient. —**dis'o·be'di·ence,** *n.* —**dis'o·bey',** *v.*

dis·or'der, *n.* **1.** lack of order. **2.** illness or disease. —*v.* **3.** create disorder in. —**dis·or'der·ly,** *adj.*

dis·or'gan·ize', *v.,* **-ized, -iz·ing.** throw into disorder. —**dis·or'gan·i·za'tion,** *n.*

dis·o'ri·ent', *v.* **1.** cause to lose one's way. **2.** confuse.

dis·own', *v.* repudiate.

dis·par'age (di spar'ij) *v.,* **-aged, -ag·ing.** speak badly of; belittle.

dis'pa·rate (dis'pər it, di spar'-) *adj.* distinct in kind; dissimilar. —**dis·par'i·ty,** *n.*

dis·pas'sion·ate, *adj.* impartial; calm. —**dis·pas'sion·ate·ly,** *adv.*

dis·patch' (di spach') *v.* **1.** send off. **2.** transact quickly. **3.** kill. —*n.* **4.** act of sending off. **5.** killing. **6.** speed. **7.** message or report.

dis·pel' (di spel') *v.,* **-pelled, -pel·ling.** drive off; scatter.

dis·pen'sa·ry (di spen'sə rē) *n., pl.* **-ries.** place for dispensing medicines.

dis·pen·sa'tion (dis'pən sā'shən, -pen-) *n.* **1.** act of dispensing. **2.** divine order. **3.** relaxation of law.

dis·pense' (di spens') *v.,* **-pensed, -pens·ing.** **1.** distribute. **2.** make up (medicines). **3.** forgo. **4.** do away. —**dis·pens'er,** *n.*

dis·perse' (di spûrs') *v.,* **-persed, -pers·ing.** scatter. —**dis·per'sal,** *n.*

dis·pir'it·ed, *adj.* downhearted.

dis·place', *v.,* **-placed, -plac·ing.** **1.** put out of place. **2.** replace. —**dis·place'ment,** *n.*

dis·play' (di splā') *v.* **1.** exhibit. —*n.* **2.** exhibition.

dis·please', *v.,* **-pleased, -pleas·ing.** offend. —**dis·pleas'ure** (-plezh'ər) *n.*

dis·pose', *v.,* **-posed, -pos·ing.** **1.** arrange. **2.** incline. **3.** decide. **4.** get rid. —**dis·pos'a·ble,** *adj.,* *n.* —**dis·pos'al,** *n.*

dis·po·si'tion (dis'pə zish'ən) *n.* **1.** mood. **2.** tendency. **3.** disposal.

dis·pos·sess', *v.* deprive of possession. —**dis·pos·ses'sion,** *n.*

dis·pro·por'tion, *n.* lack of proportion. —**dis·pro·por'tion·ate,** *adj.*

dis·prove', *v.,* **-proved, -prov·ing.** prove false.

dis·pute′ (di spyōōt′) v., **-puted,**
-puting, n. —v. 1. argue or quarrel.
—n. 1. argument; quarrel. —**dis·**
put′a·ble, adj. —**dis′pu·ta′tion,** n.

dis·qual′i·fy′, v., **-fied, -fying.**
make ineligible. —**dis·qual′i·fi·ca′**
tion, n.

dis·qui′et, v. 1. disturb. —n. 2.
lack of peace.

dis′re·gard′, v. 1. ignore. —n. 2.
neglect.

dis′re·pair′, n. bad condition.

dis′re·pute′, n. ill repute. —**dis·**
rep′u·ta·ble, adj.

dis′re·spect′, n. lack of respect.
—**dis′re·spect′ful,** adj.

dis·robe′, v., **-robed, -robing.** un-
dress.

dis·rupt′ (dis rupt′) v. break up or
interrupt. —**dis·rup′tion,** n. —**dis·**
rup′tive, adj.

dis·sat′is·fy′, v., **-fied, -fying.** make
discontented. —**dis′sat·is·fac′tion**
(-fak′shən) n.

dis·sect′ (di sekt′, dī-) v. cut apart
for examination; analyze in detail.
—**dis·sec′tion,** n.

dis·sem′ble (di sem′bəl) v., **-bled,**
-bling. feign. —**dis·sem′bler,** n.

dis·sem′i·nate′ (di sem′ə nāt′) v.,
-nated, -nating. spread widely.

dis·sen′sion (di sen′shən) n. 1. disagreement; discord.

dis·sent′ (di sent′) v. 1. disagree.
—n. 2. difference of opinion.

dis′ser·ta′tion (dis′ər tā′shən) n.
formal essay or thesis.

dis·serv′ice, n. harm or injury.

dis′si·dent (dis′i dənt) adj. 1. refusing to agree or conform. —n. 2.
dissident person. —**dis′si·dence,** n.

dis·sim′i·lar, adj. not similar.
—**dis·sim′i·lar′i·ty** (-lar′ĭ tē) n.

dis·sim′u·late′ (di sim′yə lāt′) v.,
-lated, -lating. disguise; dissemble.

dis′si·pate′ (dis′ə pāt′) v., **-pated,**
-pating. 1. scatter. 2. squander. 3.
live dissolutely. —**dis′si·pa′tion,** n.

dis·so′ci·ate′ (di sō′shē āt′, -sē-) v.,
-ated, -ating. separate.

dis′so·lute′ (dis′ə lōōt′) adj. immoral; licentious.

dis·solve′ (di zolv′) v., **-solved,**
-solving. 1. make solution of. 2.
terminate. —**dis′so·lu′tion** (dis′ə-
lōō′shən) n.

dis′so·nance (dis′ə nəns) n. inhar-
monious or harsh sound.

dis·suade′ (di swād′) v., **-suaded,**
-suading. persuade against.

dist., 1. distance. 2. district.

dis′taff (dis′taf) n. 1. staff for holding wool, flax, etc., in spinning.
—adj. 2. of women.

dis′tance (dis′təns) n. 1. space between. 2. remoteness. 3. aloofness.

dis′tant, adj. 1. remote. 2. reserved. —**dis′tant·ly,** adv.

dis·taste′, n. dislike; aversion.
—**dis·taste′ful,** adj.

dis·tem′per (dis tem′pər) n. infectious disease of dogs and cats.

dis·tend′ (di stend′) v. expand abnormally. —**dis·ten′tion,** n.

dis·till′ (di stil′) v. 1. obtain by
evaporation and condensation. 2.
purify. 3. fall in drops. —**dis·till′er,**
n. —**dis·till′er·y,** n.

dis·tinct′ (di stingkt′) adj. 1. clear.
2. separate. —**dis·tinct′ly,** adv.

dis·tinc′tion, n. 1. act or instance
of distinguishing. 2. discrimination.
3. difference. 4. special honor.
—**dis·tinc′tive,** adj.

dis·tin′guish (di sting′gwish) v. 1.
identify as different. 2. perceive. 3.
make eminent.

dis·tin′guished, adj. dignified or elegant.

dis·tort′ (di stôrt′) v. 1. twist out
of shape. 2. hide true meaning of.
—**dis·tor′tion,** n.

dis·tract′ (di strakt′) v. divert attention of. —**dis·trac′tion,** n.

dis·traught′ (di strôt′) adj. crazed
with anxiety; agitated.

dis·tress′ (di stres′) n. 1. pain or
sorrow. 2. state of emergency. —v.
3. afflict with pain or sorrow.

dis·trib′ute (di strib′yōōt) v., **-uted,**
-uting. 1. divide in shares. 2.
spread. 3. sort. —**dis′tri·bu′tion,**
n. —**dis·trib′u·tor,** n.

dis′trict (dis′trikt) n. 1. political division. 2. region.

district attorney, attorney for the
government within a given district,
whose job is primarily prosecuting.

dis·trust′, v. 1. suspect. —n. 2.
suspicion; doubt.

dis·turb′ (di stûrb′) v. 1. interrupt
peace of. 2. unsettle. —**dis·turb′**
ance, n.

dis·use′ (dis yōōs′) n. lack of use.

ditch (dich) n. 1. trench; channel.
—v. 2. Slang. get rid of.

dith′er (dith′ər) n. 1. flustered excitement or fear. —v. 2. vacillate.

dit′to (dit′ō) n., pl. **-tos,** adv. —n.
1. the same. —adv. 2. as stated before.

ditto mark, mark (″) indicating
repetition.

dit′ty (dit′ē) n., pl. **-ties.** simple
song.

di′u·ret′ic (dī′ə ret′ik) adj. promoting urination. —**di·u·ret′ic,** n.

di·ur′nal (dī ûr′nl) adj. daily.

div., 1. dividend. 2. division. 3. divorced.

di′va (dē′və, -vä) n. prima donna
(def. 1).

di′van (di van′) n. sofa.

dive (dīv) v., **dived** or **dove** (dōv), **dived**, **diving**, n. —v. **1.** plunge into water. **2.** plunge deeply. —n. **3.** act of diving. —**div'er**, n.

di·verge' (di vûrj', dī-) v., **-verged**, **-verging**. **1.** move or lie in different directions. **2.** differ. —**di·ver'gence**, n. —**di·ver'gent**, adj.

di'vers (dī'vərz) adj. various.

di·verse' (di vûrs', dī-) adj. of different kinds. —**di·ver'si·fy'**, v., **-fied**, **-fying**. —**di·ver'si·ty**, n.

di·vert' (di vûrt', dī-) v. **1.** turn aside. **2.** amuse. —**di·ver'sion**, n.

di·vest' (di vest', dī-) v. deprive; dispossess.

di·vide' (di vīd') v., **-vided**, **-viding**, n. —v. **1.** separate into parts. **2.** apportion. —n. **3.** zone separating drainage basins. —**di·vid'er**, n.

div'i·dend' (div'i dend') n. **1.** number to be divided. **2.** share in profits.

di·vine' (di vīn') adj., n., v., **-vined**, **-vining**. —adj. **1.** of or from God or a god. **2.** religious. **3.** god-like. —n. **4.** theologian or clergyman. —v. **5.** prophesy. **6.** perceive. —**di·vine'ly**, adv.

divining rod, forked stick for finding water deposits.

di·vin'i·ty (-vin'i tē) n., pl. **-ties. 1.** divine nature. **2.** god.

di·vi'sion (di vizh'ən) n. **1.** act or result of dividing. **2.** thing that divides. **3.** section. **4.** military unit under major general. —**di·vis'i·ble**, adj. —**di·vi'sive** (-vī'siv) adj.

di·vi'sor (-vī'zər) n. number dividing dividend.

di·vorce' (di vôrs') n., v., **-vorced**, **-vorcing.** —n. **1.** legal dissolution of marriage. **2.** separation. —v. **3.** separate by divorce. —**di·vor'cee'** (-sē') n.fem.

div'ot (div'ət) n. turf gouged out by a golf club stroke.

di·vulge' (di vulj', dī-) v., **-vulged**, **-vulging.** disclose.

Dix'ie (dik'sē) n. southern states of the U.S., esp. those that joined Confederacy.

Dix'ie·land', n. style of jazz marked by accented four-four rhythm and improvisation.

diz'zy (diz'ē) adj., **-zier**, **-ziest. 1.** giddy. **2.** confused. **3.** Informal. foolish; silly. —**diz'zi·ly**, adv.

D.J. (dē'jā') disc jockey. Also, **DJ**, **deejay.**

DNA, deoxyribonucleic acid, substance that carries genes along its strands.

do (dō; unstressed dŏŏ, də) v., **did**, **done**, **doing**, n. —v. **1.** perform; execute. **2.** behave. **3.** fare. **4.** fin-ish. **5.** effect. **6.** render. **7.** suffice. —n. **8.** Informal. social gathering. **9.** (dō). first note of musical scale.

DOA, dead on arrival.

doc'ile (dos'əl) adj. **1.** readily taught. **2.** submissive.

dock (dok) n. **1.** wharf. **2.** place for ship. **3.** prisoner's place in court-room. —v. **4.** put into dock. **5.** cut off end of. **6.** deduct from (pay).

dock'et (dok'it) n. **1.** list of court cases. **2.** label.

doc'tor (dok'tər) n. **1.** medical practitioner. **2.** holder of highest academic degree. —v. **3.** treat medicinally. **4.** tamper with.

doc'tor·ate (-it) n. doctor's degree.

doctor's degree, degree of the highest rank awarded by universities.

doc'trine (-trin) n. **1.** principle. **2.** teachings. —**doc'tri·nal**, adj.

doc'u·dra'ma (dok'yə drä'mə, -dram'ə) n. fictionalized TV drama depicting actual events.

doc'u·ment, n. (-mənt) **1.** paper with information or evidence. —v. (-ment') **2.** support by documents. —**doc'u·men·ta'ry** (-men'tə rē) adj., n., pl. **-ries.** —adj. **1.** use of or derived from documents. —n. **2.** film on factual subject.

dod'der (dod'ər) v. shake; totter.

dodge (doj) v., **dodged**, **dodging**, n. —v. **1.** elude. **2.** trick. —n. **3.** trick. —**dodg'er**, n.

do'do (dō'dō) n., pl. **-dos**, **-does.** extinct bird.

doe (dō) n. female deer, etc.

does (duz) v. third pers. sing. pres. indic. of **do.**

does'n't (duz'ənt) contraction of **does not.**

doff (dof) v. remove.

dog (dôg) n., v., **dogged**, **dogging.** —n. **1.** domesticated carnivore. —v. **2.** follow closely.

dog'-ear', n. folded-down corner of book page. —**dog'-eared'**, adj.

dog'ged (dô'gid) adj. persistent.

dog'house', n. **1.** shelter for dog. **2.** place of disfavor.

dog'ma (-ma) n. system of beliefs.

dog·mat'ic (-mat'ik) adj. **1.** of dogma. **2.** opinionated.

dog'ma·tism', n. aggressive assertion of opinions.

dog'wood', n. flowering tree.

doi'ly (doi'lē) n., pl. **-lies.** small napkin.

dol'drums (dōl'drəmz, dol'-) n.pl. **1.** flat calms at sea. **2.** listless mood.

dole (dōl) n., v., **doled**, **doling.** —n. **1.** portion of charitable gift. —v. **2.** give out sparingly.

dole'ful, adj. sorrowful; gloomy.

doll (dol) *n.* **1.** toy representing baby or other human being. **2.** attractive or nice person.

dol·lar (dol′ər) *n.* monetary unit equal to 100 cents.

dol·lop (dol′əp) *n.* lump or blob of soft substance, as whipped cream.

dol·ly (dol′ē) *n., pl.* **-lies. 1.** low cart for moving heavy loads. **2.** movable platform for movie or TV camera.

dol·or·ous (dō′lər əs, dol′ər-) *adj.* grievous.

dol·phin (dol′fin) *n.* whalelike animal.

dolt (dōlt) *n.* fool. —**dolt′ish,** *adj.*

-dom, suffix indicating: **1.** domain, as *kingdom.* **2.** rank or station, as *dukedom.* **3.** general condition, as *freedom.*

do·main (dō mān′) *n.* **1.** ownership of land. **2.** realm.

dome (dōm) *n.* hemispherical roof.

do·mes·tic (da mes′tik) *adj.* **1.** of the home. **2.** not foreign. —*n.* **3.** household servant. —**do·mes·tic·i·ty** (dō′me stis′i tē) *n.*

do·mes·ti·cate′ (-kāt′) *v.,* **-cated, -cating.** tame.

domestic partner, unmarried person who cohabits with another.

dom·i·cile′ (dom′ə sīl′, -səl, dō′mə-) *n.* home.

dom·i·nate (dom′ə nāt′) *v.,* **-nated, -nating. 1.** rule. **2.** tower above. —**dom·i·na′tion, dom·i·nance,** *n.* —**dom′i·nant,** *adj.*

dom·i·neer′ (dom′ə nēr′) *v.* rule oppressively.

do·min·ion (də min′yən) *n.* **1.** power of governing. **2.** territory governed.

dom·i·no′ (dom′ə nō′) *n., pl.* **-noes.** oblong dotted piece used in game of dominoes.

don (don) *v.,* **donned, donning.** put on.

do′nate (dō′nāt, dō nāt′) *v.,* **-nated, -nating.** give.

don·key (dong′kē, dông-′, dung′-) *n.* **1.** ass. **2.** fool.

do′nor (dō′nər) *n.* giver.

doo·dle (dōōd′l) *v.,* **-dled, -dling.** scribble. —**doo′dler,** *n.*

doom (dōōm) *n.* **1.** fate. **2.** ruin. **3.** judgment. —*v.* **4.** condemn.

dooms′day′, *n.* day the world ends; Judgment Day.

door (dōr) *n.* **1.** movable barrier at entrance. **2.** Also, **door′way′.** entrance. —**door′step′,** *n.*

door′yard′, *n.* yard near front door of house.

dope (dōp) *n., v.,* **doped, doping.** —*n.* **1.** *Informal.* narcotic. **2.** *Slang.*

information; news. **3.** *Informal.* stupid person. —*v.* **4.** drug.

dop′ey, *adj.,* **-ier, -iest.** *Informal.* **1.** stupid. **2.** sluggish or confused, as from drug use. Also, **dop′y.**

dor′mant (dôr′mənt) *adj.* **1.** asleep. **2.** inactive. —**dor′man·cy,** *n.*

dor′mer (dôr′mər) *n.* vertical window projecting from sloping roof.

dor′mi·to·ry (dôr′mi tôr′ē) *n., pl.* **-ries.** group sleeping place. Also, **dorm.**

dor′mouse′ (dôr′mous′) *n., pl.* **-mice.** small rodent.

dor′sal (dôr′səl) *adj.* of or on the back.

do′ry (dōr′ē) *n., pl.* **-ries.** flat-bottomed rowboat.

DOS *n.* disk operating system for microcomputers.

dose (dōs) *n., v.,* **dosed, dosing.** —*n.* **1.** amount of medicine taken at one time. —*v.* **2.** give doses to.

dos·si·er (dos′ē ā′) *n.* file of documents.

dot (dot) *n., v.,* **dotted, dotting.** —*n.* **1.** small spot. —*v.* **2.** mark with or make dots.

do′tard (dō′tərd) *n.* senile person.

dote (dōt) *v.,* **doted, doting. 1.** be overfond. **2.** be senile. —**dot′age,** *n.*

dou′ble (dub′əl) *adj., n., v.,* **-bled, -bling.** —*adj.* **1.** twice as great, etc. **2.** of two parts. **3.** deceitful. —*n.* **4.** double quantity. **5.** duplicate. —*v.* **6.** make or become double. **7.** bend or fold. **8.** turn back.

double bass (bās) lowest-pitched instrument of violin family.

doub′le-cross′, *v.* cheat or betray.

dou′ble en·ten′dre (än tän′drə, -tänd′) *n., pl.* **-ten′dres** (-tän′drəz, -tändz′) saying with two meanings.

dou′ble-head′er, *n.* two games played on the same day in rapid succession.

double play, baseball play in which two players are put out.

double standard, standard that differs for different persons or groups.

double take, delayed response, as to something not immediately recognized.

doub′le-talk′, *n.* evasive talk.

doubt (dout) *v.* **1.** be uncertain about. —*n.* **2.** uncertainty.

doubt′ful, *adj.* **1.** having doubts. **2.** causing doubts or suspicion.

douche (dōōsh) *n., v.,* **douched, douching.** —*n.* **1.** jet of liquid applied to a body part or cavity. —*v.* **2.** apply a douche.

dough (dō) *n.* mixture of flour, liquid, etc., for baking.

dough'nut (dō'nət, -nut') n. ring-like cake of fried, sweet dough.

dour (door, dou³r, dou'ər) adj. sullen.

douse (dous) v., **doused, dousing. 1.** plunge; dip. **2.** extinguish.

dove (duv) n. pigeon.

dove'cote' n. structure for tame pigeons. Also, **dove'cot'.**

dove'tail', n. **1.** tenon-and-mortise joint. —v. **2.** join by dovetail. **3.** fit together harmoniously.

dow'a·ger (dou'ə jər) n. titled or wealthy widow. **2.** dignified elderly woman.

dow'dy (dou'dē) adj., **-dier, -diest.** not stylish or attractive.

dow'el (dou'əl) n. wooden pin fitting into hole.

dow'er (dou'ər) n. widow's share of husband's property.

down (doun) adv. **1.** to, at, or in lower place or state. **2.** on or to ground. **3.** on paper. —prep. **4.** in descending direction. —n. Also **5.** soft feathers. —v. **6.** subdue. —**down'wards,** adv. —**down'ward,** adv., adj.

down'cast', adj. dejected.

down'er, n. Informal. **1.** depressing experience or person. **2.** sedative drug.

down'fall', n. **1.** ruin. **2.** fall.

down'grade', v., **-graded, -grading,** n. —v. **1.** reduce in rank. —n. **2.** downward slope.

down'heart'ed, adj. dejected.

down'hill' (adv. -hil'; adj. -hil') adv., adj. **1.** in downward direction.

down'play', v. minimize.

down'pour', n. heavy rain.

down'right', adj. **1.** thorough. —adv. **2.** completely.

down'scale', adj. of or for people at lower end of economic scale.

down'size', v., **-sized, -sizing.** reduce in size or number.

down'stage', adv. at or toward front of stage.

down'stairs' (adv. -stârz'; adj. -stârz') adv., adj. to or on lower floor.

down'stream', adv., adj. with current of stream.

Down syndrome, genetic disorder characterized by mental retardation, a wide, flattened skull, and slanting eyes. Also, **Down's syndrome.**

down'-to-earth', adj. practical.

down'town', n. **1.** central part of town. —adj. **2.** of this part. —adv. **3.** to or in this part.

down'trod'den, adj. oppressed.

down'turn', n. downward trend.

down'y, adj. like soft feathers.

dow'ry (dou'rē) n., pl. **-ries.** bride's property given to husband.

dowse (dous) v., **dowsed, dowsing.** use divining rod.

doz., dozen.

doze (dōz) v., **dozed, dozing,** n. —v. **1.** sleep lightly. —n. **2.** light sleep.

doz'en (duz'ən) n., pl. **dozen, dozens.** group of 12.

Dr., 1. Doctor. **2.** Drive.

drab (drab) n., adj., **drabber, drabbest.** —n. **1.** dull brownish gray. —adj. **2.** uninteresting.

draft (draft) n. **1.** sketch. **2.** rough version. **3.** current of air. **4.** haul. **5.** swallow of liquid. **6.** selection for military service. **7.** written request for payment. —v. **8.** plan. **9.** write. **10.** enlist by draft. —**draft'y,** adj. —**draft·ee',** n.

drafts'man, n. person who draws plans, etc.

drag (drag) v., **dragged, dragging,** n. —v. **1.** draw heavily; haul. **2.** dredge. **3.** trail on ground. **4.** pass slowly. —n. **5.** thing used in dragging. **6.** hindrance.

drag'net', n. net for dragging in water. **2.** system for catching criminal.

drag'on (drag'ən) n. fabled reptile.

drag'on·fly', n., pl. **-flies.** large four-winged insect.

dra·goon' (drə gōōn') n. **1.** heavily armed mounted soldier, formerly common in European armies. —v. **2.** force; coerce.

drag race, race with cars accelerating from a standstill.

drain (drān) v. **1.** draw or flow off gradually. **2.** empty; dry. **3.** exhaust. —n. **4.** channel or pipe for draining. —**drain'age,** n.

drake (drāk) n. male duck.

dram (dram) n. **1.** apothecaries' weight, equal to $\frac{1}{8}$ ounce. **2.** small drink of liquor.

dra'ma (drä'mə, dram'ə) n. **1.** story acted on stage. **2.** vivid series of events.

dra·mat'ic (drə mat'ik) adj. **1.** of plays or theater. **2.** highly vivid.

dra·mat'ics, n. **1.** theatrical art. **2.** exaggerated conduct or emotion.

dram'a·tist (dram'ə tist, drä'mə-) n. playwright.

dram'a·tize', v., **-tized, -tizing.** put in dramatic form.

drape (drāp) v., **draped, draping,** n. —v. **1.** cover with fabric. **2.** arrange in folds. —n. **3.** draped hanging. —**drap'er·y,** n.

dras'tic (dras'tik) adj. extreme.

draught (draft) n. Brit. draft.

draw (drô) v., **drew** (drōō), **drawn,**

drawing, n. —v. **1.** pull; lead. **2.** take out. **3.** attract. **4.** sketch. **5.** take in. **6.** deduce. **7.** stretch. **8.** make or have as draft. —n. **9.** act of drawing. **10.** equal score. **11.** Informal. attraction to public.

draw′back′, n. disadvantage.

draw′bridge′, n. bridge that can be drawn up.

draw′er (drôr for 1, 2; drô′ər for 3) n. **1.** sliding compartment. **2.** (pl.) trouserlike undergarment. **3.** person who draws.

draw′ing, n. drawn picture.

drawl (drôl) v. **1.** speak slowly. —n. **2.** drawled utterance.

drawn (drôn) adj. tense; haggard.

dray (drā) n. low, strong cart.

dread (dred) v. **1.** fear. —n. **2.** fear. **3.** awe. —adj. **4.** feared. **5.** revered.

dread′ful, adj. **1.** very bad. **2.** inspiring dread.

dread′ful·ly, adv. Informal. very.

dread′locks′, n. hairstyle with many long, ropelike pieces.

dream (drēm) n. **1.** ideas imagined during sleep. **2.** reverie. —v. **3.** have dream (about). **4.** imagine.

drear′y, adj., **drearier, dreariest.** gloomy or boring. —**drear′i·ly,** adv.

dredge (drej) n., v., **dredged, dredging.** —n. **1.** machine for moving earth at the bottom of river, etc. —v. **2.** move with dredge. **3.** sprinkle with flour.

dregs (gregz) n.pl. sediment.

drench (drench) v. soak.

dress (dres) n. **1.** woman's garment. **2.** clothing. —v. **3.** clothe. **4.** ornament. **5.** prepare. **6.** treat (wounds).

dres·sage′ (drə säzh′, dre-) n. art of training a horse in obedience and precision of movement.

dress circle, semicircular division of seats in a theater.

dress′er, n. chest of drawers. **2.** person who dresses another.

dress′ing, n. **1.** sauce or stuffing. **2.** application for wound.

dress rehearsal, final rehearsal with costumes.

dress′y, adj., **-ier, -iest.** fancy; formal.

drib′ble (drib′əl) v., **-bled, -bling,** n. —v. **1.** fall in drops. **2.** bounce repeatedly. —n. **3.** trickle.

dri′er (drī′ər) n. dryer.

drift (drift) n. **1.** deviation from set course. **2.** tendency. **3.** something driven, esp. into heap. —v. **4.** carry or be carried by currents.

drift′er, n. person who moves frequently.

drill (dril) n. **1.** boring tool. **2.** me-

thodical training. **3.** furrow for seeds. **4.** sowing machine. **5.** strong twilled cotton. —v. **6.** pierce with drill. **7.** train methodically.

drink (dringk) v., **drank,** (drangk) **drunk** (drungk), **drinking.** —v. **1.** swallow liquid. **2.** swallow alcoholic liquids. —n. **3.** liquid for quenching thirst. **4.** alcoholic drink.

drip (drip) v., **dripped, dripping. 1.** fall or let fall in drops. —n. **2.** act or sound of dripping.

drive (drīv) v., **drove** (drōv), **driven, driving,** n. —v. **1.** send by force. **2.** control. **3.** convey or travel in vehicle. **4.** impel. —n. **5.** military offensive. **6.** strong effort. **7.** trip in vehicle. **8.** road for driving.

drive′-by′, n., pl. **-bys. 1.** action of driving by something specified. **2.** shooting that occurs from vehicle driving by. —**drive′-by′,** adj.

drive′-in′, adj. **1.** designed for persons in automobiles. —n. **2.** a drive-in bank, movie theater, etc.

driv′el (driv′əl) v., **-eled, -eling,** n. —v. **1.** drool. **2.** talk foolishly. —n. **3.** foolish talk.

drive′way′, n. road on private property.

driz′zle (driz′əl) v., **-zled, -zling,** n. rain in fine drops.

droll (drōl) adj. amusingly odd.

drom′e·dar′y (drom′i der′ē, drum′-) n., pl. **-daries.** one-humped camel.

drone (drōn) v., **droned, droning,** n. —v. **1.** make humming sound. **2.** speak dully. —n. **3.** monotonous tone. **4.** male of honeybee.

drool (drōōl) v. **1.** salivate. —n. **2.** saliva dripping from the mouth.

droop (drōōp) v. **1.** sink or hang down. **2.** lose spirit. —n. **3.** act of drooping. —**droop′y,** adj.

drop (drop) n., v., **dropped, dropping.** —n. **1.** small mass of liquid. **2.** small quantity. **3.** fall. **4.** steep slope. —v. **5.** fall or let fall. **6.** cease. **7.** visit. —**drop′per,** n.

drop kick, kick made by dropping ball to the ground and kicking it as it starts to bounce up.

drop′out′, n. student who quits before graduation.

dross (drôs) n. refuse.

drought (drout) n. dry weather.

drove (drōv) n. **1.** group of driven cattle. **2.** crowd.

drown (droun) v. suffocate by immersion in liquid.

drow′sy (drou′zē) adj. sleepy.

drub (drub) v. **1.** beat. **2.** defeat.

drudge (druj) n., v., **drudged,**

drudging. —*n.* person doing tedious work. —**drudg′er•y,** *n.*

drug (drug) *n., v.,* **drugged, drugging.** —*n.* **1.** therapeutic chemical. **2.** narcotic. —*v.* **3.** mix or affect with drug. —**drug′store′,** *n.*

drug′gist, *n.* **1.** pharmacist. **2.** person who operates drugstore.

dru′id (drōō′id) *n. (often cap.)* member of a pre-Christian religious order in Europe. —**dru′id•ism,** *n.*

drum (drum) *n., v.,* **drummed, drumming.** —*n.* **1.** percussion musical instrument. **2.** eardrum. —*v.* **3.** beat on or as on drum.

drum major, leader of marching band.

drum majorette, majorette.

drum′stick′, *n.* **1.** stick for beating a drum. **2.** leg of a cooked fowl.

drunk (drungk) *adj.* intoxicated.

drunk′ard (drung′kərd) *n.* **1.** habitually drunk person.

dry (drī) *adj.,* **drier, driest,** *v.,* **dried, drying.** —*adj.* **1.** not wet. **2.** rainless. **3.** not yielding liquid. **4.** thirsty. **5.** boring. **6.** not expressing emotion. **7.** not sweet. —*v.* **8.** make or become dry. —**dry′ly,** *adv.*

dry′ad (drī′ad, -ad) *n. (often cap.)* nymph of the woods.

dry′-clean′, *v.* clean with solvents. —**dry′-clean′er,** *n.*

dry′er, *n.* machine for drying.

dry ice, solid carbon dioxide, used esp. as a refrigerant.

dry run, rehearsal or trial.

DST, daylight-saving time.

du′al (dōō′al, dyōō′-) *adj.* twofold.

dub (dub) *v.,* **dubbed, dubbing. 1.** name formally. **2.** furnish with new sound track.

du′bi•ous (dōō′bē əs) *adj.* doubtful.

du′cal (dōō′kəl, dyōō′-) *adj.* of dukes.

duch′ess (duch′is) *n.* **1.** duke's wife. **2.** woman equal in rank to duke.

duch′y (duch′ē) *n., pl.* **duchies. 1.** territory of duke. **2.** small state.

duck (duk) *v.* **1.** plunge under water. **2.** stoop quickly. **3.** avoid. —*n.* **4.** act of ducking. **5.** type of swimming bird. **6.** heavy cotton fabric. —**duck′ling,** *n.*

duck′bill′, *n.* small, egg-laying mammal.

duct (dukt) *n.* tube or canal in body. —**duct′less,** *adj.*

duc′tile (duk′til, -til) *adj.* **1.** readily drawn out; malleable. **2.** pliable.

duct tape (duk, dukt) strongly adhesive cloth tape, used in plumbing, household repairs, etc.

dud (dud) *n. Informal.* failure.

dude (dōōd, dyōōd) *n.* **1.** man excessively concerned with his clothes. **2.** *Slang.* fellow; guy.

dudg′eon (duj′ən) *n.* indignation.

due (dōō, dyōō) *adj.* **1.** payable. **2.** proper. **3.** attributable. **4.** expected. —*n.* **5.** something due. **6.** *(sometimes pl.)* regularly payable fee for membership. —*adv.* **7.** in a straight line.

du′el (dōō′al, dyōō′-) *n., v.* **-eled, -eling.** —*n.* **1.** prearranged combat between two persons. —*v.* **2.** fight in duel. —**du′el•er, du′el•ist,** *n.*

du•et′ (dōō et′, dyōō-) *n.* music for two performers.

duf′fel bag (duf′al) cylindrical bag for carrying belongings.

duff′er (duf′ar) *n.* **1.** *Informal.* incompetent person. **2.** person inept at a specific sport, as golf.

dug′out′, *n.* **1.** boat made by hollowing a log. **2.** roofed structure where baseball players sit when not on the field. **3.** rough shelter dug in the ground, as by soldiers.

duke (dōōk, dyōōk) *n.* nobleman below prince. —**duke′dom,** *n.*

dul′ci•mer (dul′sə mar) *n.* musical instrument with metal strings.

dull (dul) *adj.* **1.** stupid. **2.** not brisk. **3.** tedious. **4.** not sharp. **5.** dim. —*v.* **6.** make or become dull.

du′ly (dōō′lē, dyōō′-) *adv.* **1.** properly. **2.** punctually.

dumb (dum) *adj.* **1.** temporarily unable to speak. **2.** *Often Offensive.* lacking the power of speech. **3.** *Informal.* stupid.

dumb′bell′, *n.* **1.** weighted bar for exercising. **2.** *Informal.* stupid person.

dumb•found′ (dum found′, dum′found′) *v.* astonish. Also, **dumb•found′.**

dumb′wait′er, *n.* small elevator for moving food, etc.

dum′my, *n., pl.* **-mies,** *adj.* —*n.* **1.** model or copy. **2.** *Informal.* **a.** *Offensive.* mute. **b.** stupid person. —*adj.* **3.** counterfeit.

dump (dump) *v.* **1.** drop heavily. **2.** empty. —*n.* **3.** place for dumping. **4.** *Informal.* dilapidated, dirty place.

dump′ling (-ling) *n.* mass of steamed dough.

dump′y, *adj.,* **-ier, -iest.** short and stout. —**dump′i•ness,** *n.*

dun (dun) *v.,* **dunned, dunning,** *n.* —*v.* **1.** demand payment of. —*n.* **2.** demand for payment. **3.** dull brown.

dunce (duns) *n.* stupid person.

dune (dōōn, dyōōn) *n.* sand hill formed by wind.

dung (dung) *n.* manure; excrement.

dun′ga•ree′ (dung′gə rē′) *n.* coarse

cotton fabric for work clothes (**dungarees**).

dun'geon (dun'jən) n. underground cell.

dunk (dungk) v. **1.** dip in beverage before eating. **2.** submerge briefly in liquid. **3.** thrust (basketball) downward through basket.

du'o (dōō'ō, dōō'ō) n. **1.** duet. **2.** couple or pair.

du'o·de'num (dōō'ə dē'nəm, dyōō'-; dōō od'n əm, dyōō-) n. uppermost part of small intestine.

dupe (dōōp, dyōōp) n., v., **duped**, **duping**. —n. **1.** deceived person. —v. **2.** deceive.

du'plex (dōō'pleks, dyōō'-) n. **1.** apartment with two floors. **2.** house for two families.

du'pli·cate, adj., n., v., **-cated**, **-cating**. —adj. (dōō'pli kit) **1.** exactly like. **2.** double. —n. (-kit) **3.** copy. —v. (-kāt') **4.** copy. **5.** double.

du·plic'i·ty (dōō plis'i tē, dyōō-) n., pl. **-ties**. deceitfulness.

du'ra·ble (dōōr'ə bəl, dyōōr'-) adj. enduring. —**du'ra·bil'i·ty,** n.

du·ra'tion (dōō rā'shən, dyōō-) n. continuance in time.

du·ress' (dōō res', dyōō-, dōōr'is, dyōōr'-) n. compulsion.

dur'ing (dōōr'ing, dyōōr'-) prep. in the course of.

du'rum (dōōr'əm, dyōōr'-) n. kind of wheat flour used in pasta.

dusk (dusk) n. twilight.

dust (dust) n. **1.** fine particles of earth, etc. —v. **2.** free from dust. **3.** sprinkle. —**dust'y,** adj.

Dutch (duch) n. people or language of the Netherlands.

Dutch uncle, mentor who criticizes very frankly.

du'ti·ful (dōō'tə fəl, dyōō'-) adj. doing one's duties.

du'ty (dōō'tē, dyōō'-) n., pl. **-ties**. **1.** moral or legal obligation. **2.** function. **3.** tax, esp. on imports.

dwarf (dwôrf) n. **1.** abnormally small person, etc. —v. **2.** make or make to seem small.

dwell (dwel) v., **dwelt** or **dwelled**, **dwelling**. **1.** reside. **2.** linger, esp. in words. —**dwell'ing,** n.

dwin'dle (dwin'dl) v., **-dled**, **-dling**. shrink; lessen.

dye (dī) n., v., **dyed**, **dyeing**. —n. **1.** coloring material. —v. **2.** color with dye. —**dye'ing,** n. —**dy'er,** n.

dyed'-in-the-wool', adj. uncompromising.

dyke (dīk) n. **1.** dike. **2.** Slang (often offensive) female homosexual.

dy·nam'ic (dī nam'ik) adj. **1.** of force. **2.** energetic. —**dy'na·mism** (dī'nə miz'əm) n.

dy'na·mite (dī'nə mīt') n., v., **-mited**, **-miting**. —n. **1.** explosive. —v. **2.** blow up with dynamite.

dy'na·mo' (dī'nə mō') n., pl. **-mos**. **1.** machine for generating electricity. **2.** energetic, forceful person.

dy'nas·ty (dī'nə stē) n., pl. **-ties**. rulers of same family.

dys-, prefix meaning ill or bad, as dysfunction.

dys'en·ter'y (dis'ən ter'ē) n. infectious disease of bowels.

dys·func'tion (dis fungk'shən) n. ineffective functioning.

dys·lex'i·a (dis lek'sē ə) n. impairment of ability to read. —**dys·lex'ic,** adj., n.

dys·pep'si·a (dis pep'shə, -sē ə) n. indigestion.

dz., dozen.

E

E, e (ē) n. fifth letter of English alphabet.

E, 1. east, eastern. **2.** English.

ea., each.

each (ēch) adj., pron. **1.** every one. —adv. **2.** apiece.

ea'ger (ē'gər) adj. ardent.

ea'gle (ē'gal) n. large bird of prey.

ea'gle-eyed', adj. having unusually sharp eyesight.

ear (ēr) n. **1.** organ of hearing. **2.** grain-containing part of cereal plant.

ear'drum', n. sensitive membrane in ear.

earl (ûrl) n. nobleman ranking below marquis. —**earl'dom,** n.

ear'ly (ûr'lē) adv., **-lier**, **-liest**, adj.

1. in first part of. **2.** before usual time.

ear'mark' (ēr'märk') n. **1.** identifying mark. —v. **2.** designate.

ear'muffs', n.pl. warm connected coverings for the ears.

earn (ûrn) v. gain by labor or merit.

ear'nest (ûr'nist) adj. very serious. —**ear'nest·ness,** n.

earn'ings, n.pl. profits.

ear'phone' (ēr'fōn') n. sound receiver held to the ear.

ear'ring' (ēr'ring', ēr'ing) n. ornament worn on ear lobe.

ear'shot', n. hearing range.

ear'split'ting, adj. extremely loud or shrill.

earth (ûrth) n. **1.** planet we inhabit. **2.** dry land. **3.** soil.

earth′en, *adj.* made of clay or earth. —**earth′en·ware′,** *n.*

earth′ly, *adj.,* **-lier, -liest.** of or in this world.

earth′quake′, *n.* vibration of earth's surface.

earth′work′, *n.* **1.** fortification formed of moved earth. **2.** work of art involving large land area.

earth′worm′, *n.* burrowing worm.

earth′y, *adj.,* **earth·i·est. 1.** practical; realistic. **2.** coarse; unrefined.

ease (ēz) *n., v.,* **eased, easing.** —*n.* **1.** freedom from work, pain, etc. **2.** facility. —*v.* **3.** relieve.

ea′sel (ē′zal) *n.* support stand, as for picture.

east (ēst) *n.* **1.** direction from which sun rises. **2.** (*sometimes cap.*) region in this direction. —*adj., adv.* **3.** toward, in, or from east. —**east′er·ly,** *adj., adv.* —**east′ern,** *adj.* —**east′ward,** *adj.* —**East′ern·er,** *n.*

East′er (ē′star) *n.* anniversary of resurrection of Christ.

eas′y (ē′zē) *adj.,* **easier, easiest. 1.** not difficult. **2.** at ease. **3.** moderate. —**eas′i·ly,** *adv.*

eas′y-go′ing, *adj.* **1.** casual; relaxed. **2.** lenient.

eat (ēt) *v.,* **ate** (āt), **eating, eaten. 1.** take into the mouth and swallow. **2.** wear away or dissolve.

eat′er·y, *n., pl.* **-eries.** *Informal.* restaurant.

eaves (ēvz) *n.pl.* overhanging edge of roof.

eaves′drop′, *v.,* **dropped, dropping.** listen secretly.

ebb (eb) *n.* **1.** fall of tide. **2.** decline. —*v.* **3.** flow back. **4.** decline.

eb′on·y (eb′ə nē) *n.* **1.** hard black wood. **2.** very dark.

e·bul′lient (i bul′yant, i bõol′-) *adj.* full of enthusiasm.

ec·cen′tric (ik sen′trik) *adj.* **1.** odd. **2.** off center. —*n.* **3.** odd person. —**ec·cen′tric′i·ty** (-tris′i tē) *n.*

ec·cle′si·as′tic (i klē′zē as′tik) *n.* **1.** member of the clergy. —*adj.* **2.** Also, **ec·cle′si·as′ti·cal.** of church or clergy.

ech′e·lon (esh′ə lon′) *n.* level of command.

ech′o (ek′ō) *n., pl.* **echoes,** *v.,* **echoed, echoing.** —*n.* **1.** repetition of sound, esp. by reflection. —*v.* **2.** emit or repeat as echo.

é·clair′ (ā klâr′) *n.* cream- or custard-filled pastry.

é·clat′ (ā klä′) *n.* **1.** brilliance, as of success. **2.** acclaim.

ec·lec′tic (i klek′tik) *adj.* chosen from various sources.

e·clipse′ (i klips′) *n., v.,* **eclipsed,**

eclipsing. —*n.* **1.** obscuring of light of sun or moon by passage of body in front of it. —*v.* **2.** obscure.

e·clip′tic (i klip′tik) *n.* apparent annual path of sun.

eco-, prefix meaning ecology, environment or natural habitat, as *eco-cide.*

e′co·cide′ (ek′ə sīd′, ē′kə-) *n.* widespread destruction of natural environment.

e·col′o·gy (i kol′ə jē) *n.* science of relationship between organisms and environment. —**e·col′o·gist,** *n.*

e·co·nom′i·cal (ek′ə nom′i kal, ē′-kə-) *adj.* thrifty.

ec′o·nom′ics, *n.* production, distribution, and use of wealth. —**ec′o·nom′ic,** *adj.* —**e·con′o·mist** (i kon′ə mist) *n.*

e·con′o·mize′ (i kon′ə mīz′) *v.,* **-mized, -mizing.** save; be thrifty.

e·con′o·my, *n., pl.* **-mies. 1.** thrifty management. **2.** system of producing and distributing wealth.

ec′o·sys′tem (ek′ō sis′təm, ē′kō-) *n.* distinct ecological system.

ec′ru (ek′rōō, ā′krōō) *adj.* light brown; beige. Also, **é·cru** (ā′krōō).

ec′sta·sy (ek′stə sē) *n., pl.* **-sies. 1.** overpowering emotion. **2.** rapture. —**ec·stat′ic** (ek stat′ik) *adj.*

-ectomy, suffix meaning surgical removal of, as *tonsillectomy.*

ec′u·men′i·cal (ek′yōō men′i kal) *adj.* **1.** universal. **2.** pertaining to movement for universal Christian unity.

ec′ze·ma (ek′sə mə, eg′zə-, ig zē′-) *n.* disease of skin.

E′dam (ē′dəm) *n.* mild yellow cheese.

ed′dy (ed′ē) *n., pl.* **-dies,** *v.,* **-died, -dying.** —*n.* **1.** current at variance with main current. —*v.* **2.** whirl in eddies.

e′del·weiss′ (ād′l vīs′, -wīs′) *n.* small, flowering Alpine plant.

e·de′ma (i dē′mə) *n.* abnormal accumulation of fluid in body tissue.

E′den (ēd′n) *n.* garden where Adam and Eve first lived; paradise.

edge (ej) *n., v.,* **edged, edging.** —*n.* **1.** border; brink. **2.** cutting side. —*v.* **3.** border. **4.** move sidewise. —**edge′wise′,** *adv.*

edg′y, *adj.,* **edgier, edgiest.** nervous or tense.

ed′i·ble (ed′ə bəl) *adj.* fit to be eaten. —**ed′i·bil′i·ty,** *n.*

e′dict (ē′dikt) *n.* official decree.

ed′i·fice (ed′ə fis) *n.* building.

ed′i·fy′, *v.,* **-fied, -fying.** instruct.

ed′it (ed′it) *v.* prepare for or direct publication of. —**ed′i·tor,** *n.*

e·di′tion (i dish′ən) *n.* one of various printings of a book.

ed′i·to′ri·al (ed′i tôr′ē əl) *n.* article in periodical presenting its point of view. —*adj.* 2. of or written by editor. —**ed′i·to′ri·al·ize′**, *v.*, **-ized, -izing.**

EDP, electronic data processing.

ed′u·cate′ (ej′ŏ͞o kāt′) *v.*, **-cated, -cating.** provide with knowledge or instruction. —**ed′u·ca′tion**, *n.* —**ed′u·ca′tion·al**, *adj.*

-ee, suffix denoting person who is the object, beneficiary, or performer of an act, as *addressee; grantee; escapee.*

EEG, electroencephalogram.

eel (ēl) *n.* snakelike fish.

e′er (âr) *adv.* Poetic. ever.

ee′rie (ēr′ē) *adj.*, **-rier, -riest.** weird; unsettling. —**ee′ri·ly**, *adv.*

ef·face′ (i fās′) *v.*, **-faced, -facing.** wipe out. —**ef·face′ment**, *n.*

ef·fect′ (i fekt′) *n.* 1. result; consequence. 2. power to produce results. 3. operation. 4. (*pl.*) personal property. —*v.* 5. bring about. —**Usage.** See AFFECT.

ef·fec′tive, *adj.* 1. producing intended results. 2. in force. **ef·fec′tive·ly**, *adv.* 1. in an effective way. 2. for all practical purposes.

ef·fec′tu·al (-chŏ͞o əl) *adj.* 1. capable; adequate. 2. valid or binding.

ef·fem′i·nate (i fem′ə nit) *adj.* (of a man) having feminine traits.

ef′fer·vesce′ (ef′ər ves′) *v.*, **-vesced, -vescing.** give off bubbles of gas. —**ef′fer·ves′cence**, *n.* —**ef′fer·ves′cent**, *adj.*

ef·fete′ (i fēt′) *adj.* worn out.

ef′fi·ca′cious (ef′i kā′shəs) *adj.* effective. —**ef′fi·ca·cy** (-kə sē) *n.*

ef·fi′cient (i fish′ənt) *adj.* acting effectively. —**ef·fi′cien·cy**, *n.*

ef′fi·gy (ef′i jē) *n., pl.* **-gies.** visual representation of person.

ef′flu·ent (ef′lŏ͞o ənt) *n.* something that flows out.

ef′fort (ef′ərt) *n.* 1. exertion of power. 2. attempt.

ef·fron′ter·y (i frun′tə rē) *n., pl.* **-teries.** impudence.

ef·fu′sion (i fyŏ͞o′zhən) *n.* free expression of feelings. —**ef·fu′sive**, *adj.*

e.g., for example.

e·gal′i·tar′i·an (i gal′i târ′ē ən) *adj.* having all persons equal in status.

egg (eg) *n.* 1. reproductive body produced by animals. —*v.* 2. encourage.

egg′head′, *n.* Slang. impractical intellectual.

egg′nog′ (-nog′) *n.* drink containing eggs, milk, etc.

egg′plant′, *n.* purple, egg-shaped fruit, eaten as a vegetable.

e′go (ē′gō) *n.* self.

e′go·cen′tric (-sen′trik) *adj.* self-centered.

e′go·ism, *n.* thinking only in terms of oneself. —**e′go·ist**, *n.*

e′go·tism, *n.* vanity. —**e′go·tist**, *n.* —**e′go·tis′tic, e′go·tis′ti·cal**, *adj.*

e·gre′gious (i grē′jəs) *adj.* flagrant.

e′gress (ē′gres) *n.* exit.

e′gret (ē′gret) *n.* kind of heron.

E·gyp′tian (i jip′shən) *n.* native or citizen of Egypt. —**E·gyp′tian**, *adj.*

eh (ā, e) *interj.* (exclamation of surprise or doubt).

ei′der duck (ī′dər) northern sea duck yielding eiderdown.

eight (āt) *n., adj.* seven plus one. —**eighth**, *adj., n.*

eight·een′ (ā′tēn′) *n., adj.* ten plus eight. —**eight·eenth′**, *adj., n.*

eight′y, *n., adj.* ten times eight. —**eight′i·eth**, *adj., n.*

ei′ther (ē′thər, ī′thər) *adj., pron.* 1. one or the other of two. —*conj.* 2. (introducing an alternative) —*adv.* 3. (after negative clauses joined by and, or, nor.) —**Pronunciation.** The pronunciations (ē′thər) for the word EITHER and (nē′thər) for the word NEITHER, with the vowel of *see*, are the usual ones in American English. The pronunciations (ī′thər) and (nī′thər), with the vowel of *sigh*, occur occasionally in the U.S., chiefly in the speech of the educated and in the standard English of radio and television. Since the 19th century, the (ī) has been the more common pronunciation in standard British usage.

e·jac′u·late′ (i jak′yə lāt′) *v.*, **-lated, -lating.** 1. exclaim. 2. eject; discharge. —**e·jac′u·la′tion**, *n.*

e·ject′ (i jekt′) *v.* force out.

eke (ēk) *v.*, **eked, eking. eke out,** 1. supplement. 2. make (a living) with difficulty.

EKG, 1. electrocardiogram. 2. electrocardiograph.

e·lab′o·rate, *adj., v.*, **-rated, -rating.** —*adj.* (i lab′ər it) 1. done with care and detail. —*v.* (-ə rāt′) 2. supply details; work out.

é·lan′ (ā län′, ā län′) *n.* dashing spirit.

e·lapse′ (i laps′) *v.*, **elapsed, elapsing.** (of time) pass; slip by.

e·las′tic (i las′tik) *adj.* 1. springy. —*n.* 2. material containing rubber.

e·late′ (i lāt′) *v.*, **elated, elating.** put in high spirits. —**e·la′tion**, *n.*

el•bow (el/bō) n. **1.** joint where arm bends. —v. **2.** jostle.

elbow grease, hard work.

el/bow•room/, n. space to move or work freely.

eld/er (el/dər) adj. **1.** older. —n. **2.** older person. **3.** small tree bearing clusters of **el/der•ber/ries.**

el/der•ly, adj. rather old.

eld/est (el/dist) adj. oldest.

e•lect/ (i lekt/) v. **1.** select by vote. —adj. **2.** selected. —n. **3.** (pl.) persons chosen. —**e•lec/tion,** n.

e•lec•tion•eer/, v. work for candidate in an election.

e•lec/tor•al college (-tər əl) body of special voters (**electors**) chosen to elect president and vice-president of U.S.

e•lec/tor•ate (-tər it) n. voters.

e•lec/tri/cian (i lek trish/ən, ē/lek-) n. one who installs or repairs electrical systems.

e•lec•tric/i•ty (-tris/i tē) n. **1.** agency producing certain phenomena, as light, heat, attraction, etc. **2.** electric current. —**e•lec/tric,** **e•lec/tri•cal,** adj. —**e•lec/tri•cal•ly,** adv. —**e•lec/tri•fy/,** v., -fied, -fying.

e•lec/tro•car/di•o•gram/ (i lek/trō-kär/dē ə gram/) n. graphic record of heart action.

e•lec/tro•car/di•o•graph/, instrument for making electrocardiograms.

e•lec/tro•cute/ (i lek/trə kyoot/) v., -cuted, -cuting. kill by electricity.

e•lec/trode (i lek/trōd) n. conductor through which current enters or leaves electric device.

e•lec/tro•en•ceph/a•lo•gram/ (i lek/trō en sef/ə lə gram/) n. graphic record of brain action.

e•lec/tro•en•ceph/a•lo•graph/, n. instrument for making electroencephalograms.

e•lec•trol/o•gist (i lek trol/ə jist) n. person trained in electrolysis for removing unwanted hair, moles, etc.

e•lec•trol/y•sis (-ə sis) n. **1.** decomposition by electric current. **2.** destruction by electric current.

e•lec/tro•lyte/ (-trə līt/) n. substance that conducts electricity when melted or dissolved.

e•lec/tro•mag/net (i lek/trō-) n. device with iron or steel core made magnetic by electric current in surrounding coil. —**e•lec/tro•mag•net/ic,** adj.

e•lec/tron (i lek/tron) n. minute particle containing a unit of negative electricity.

electronic mail, e-mail.

e•lec•tron/ics, n. science dealing with development of devices involving flow of electrons. —**e•lec•tron/ic,** adj. —**e•lec•tron/i•cal•ly,** adv.

el/e•gant (el/i gənt) adj. luxurious or refined. —**el/e•gance,** n.

el/e•gy (el/i jē) n., pl. -gies. poem of mourning. —**el/e•gi/ac** (-jī/ak), adj.

el/e•ment (el/ə mənt) n. **1.** part of whole. **2.** rudiment. **3.** suitable environment. **4.** (pl.) atmospheric forces. **5.** substance that cannot be broken down chemically. **6.** (pl.) bread and wine of the Eucharist.

el/e•men/ta•ry (-tə rē) adj. of or dealing with elements or rudiments.

elementary school, school giving elementary instruction in six or eight grades.

el/e•phant (el/ə fənt) n. large mammal with long trunk and tusks.

el/e•phan/tine (el/ə fan/tēn, -tīn) adj. **1.** huge. **2.** clumsy.

el/e•vate/ (el/ə vāt/) v., -vated, -vating. **1.** raise higher. **2.** exalt.

el/e•va/tion, n. **1.** high place. **2.** height. **3.** drawing of vertical face.

el/e•va/tor, n. **1.** platform for lifting. **2.** grain storage place.

e•lev/en (i lev/ən) n., adj. ten plus one. —**e•lev/enth,** adj., n.

elf (elf) n., pl. **elves.** tiny mischievous sprite. —**elf/in,** adj.

e•lic/it (i lis/it) v. draw forth; evoke.

e•lide/ (i līd/) v., -lided, -liding. omit in pronunciation.

el/i•gi•ble (el/i jə bəl) adj. fit to be chosen. —**el/i•gi•bil/i•ty,** n.

e•lim/i•nate/ (i lim/ə nāt/) v., -nated, -nating. get rid of.

e•lite/ (i lēt/, ā lēt/) n. **1.** chosen or regarded as finest. —n. **2.** (sing. or pl.) elite group of persons.

e•lit/ism, n. rule by an elite. —**e•lit/ist,** n., adj.

e•lix/ir (i lik/sər) n. preparation supposed to prolong life.

elk (elk) n. large deer.

el•lipse/ (i lips/) n. closed plane curve forming regular oblong figure.

el•lip/sis (i lip/sis) n., pl. -ses. omission of word or words.

elm (elm) n. large shade tree.

el/o•cu/tion (el/ə kyoo/shən) n. art of speaking in public.

e•lon/gate (i lông/gāt) v., -gated, -gating. lengthen. —**e•lon•ga/tion,** n.

e•lope/ (i lōp/) v., eloped, eloping. run off with lover to be married. —**e•lope/ment,** n.

el/o•quent (el/ə kwənt) adj. fluent and forcible. —**el/o•quence,** n.

else (els) adv. **1.** instead. **2.** in addition. **3.** otherwise.

else·where′, *adv.* somewhere else.

e·lu′ci·date′ (i loō′si dāt′) *v.,* -dated, -dating. explain. —**e·lu′ci·da′tion,** *n.* —**e·lu′ci·da′tor,** *n.*

e·lude′ (i loōd′) *v.,* eluded, eluding. **1.** avoid cleverly. **2.** baffle. —**e·lu′sive,** *adj.* —Usage. See ESCAPE.

e·ma′ci·ate′ (i mā′shē āt′) *v.,* -ated, -ating. make thin. —**e·ma′ci·a′tion,** *n.*

e′·mail, (ē′māl′) *n.* **1.** system for sending messages between computers. **2.** message sent by e-mail. —*v.* **3.** send message to by e-mail. Also, **E-mail.**

em′a·nate′ (em′ə nāt′) *v.,* -nated, -nating. come forth.

e·man′ci·pate′ (i man′sə pāt′) *v.,* -pated, -pating. liberate. —**e·man′ci·pa′tion,** *n.*

e·mas′cu·late′ (i mas′kyə lāt′) *v.,* -lated, -lating. **1.** castrate. **2.** weaken. —**e·mas′cu·la′tion,** *n.*

em·balm′ (em bäm′) *v.* treat (dead body) to prevent decay. —**em·balm′er,** *n.*

em·bank′ment (em bangk′mənt) *n.* long earthen mound.

em·bar′go (em bär′gō) *n., pl.* -goes. government restriction of movement of ships or goods.

em·bark′ (em bärk′) *v.* **1.** put or go on board ship. **2.** start. —**em·bar·ka′tion,** *n.*

em·bar′rass (em bar′əs) *v.* **1.** make self-conscious or ashamed. **2.** complicate. —**em·bar′rass·ment,** *n.*

em·bas′sy (em′bə sē) *n., pl.* -sies. **1.** ambassador and staff. **2.** headquarters of ambassador.

em·bat′tled (em bat′ld) *adj.* prepared for or engaged in conflict.

em·bed′ (em bed′) *v.,* -bedded, -bedding. fix in surrounding mass.

em·bel′lish (em bel′ish) *v.* decorate. —**em·bel′lish·ment,** *n.*

em′ber (em′bər) *n.* live coal.

em·bez′zle (em bez′əl) *v.,* -zled, -zling. steal (money entrusted). —**em·bez′zle·ment,** *n.*

em·bit′ter (em bit′ər) *v.* make bitter.

em·bla′zon (em blā′zən) *v.* decorate, as with heraldic devices.

em′blem (em′bləm) *n.* symbol.

em·bod′y (em bod′ē) *v.,* -bodied, -bodying. **1.** put in concrete form. **2.** comprise. —**em·bod′i·ment,** *n.*

em′bo·lism (em′bə liz′əm) *n.* closing off of blood vessel, as by gas bubble or fat globule.

em·boss′ (em bôs′) *v.* ornament with raised design.

em·brace′ (em brās′) *v.,* -braced, -bracing. *n.* —*v.* **1.** clasp in arms.

2. accept willingly. **3.** include. —*n.* **4.** act of embracing.

em·broi′der (em broi′dər) *v.* decorate with needlework. —**em·broi′der·y,** *n.*

em·broil′, *v.* involve in strife.

em′bry·o′ (em′brē ō′) *n., pl.* -bryos. organism in first stages of development. —**em′bry·on′ic,** *adj.*

em·cee′ (em′sē′) *n., v.,* -ceed, -ceeing. —*n.* **1.** master of ceremonies; person who conducts an event, as a banquet. —*v.* **2.** act as emcee.

e·mend′ (i mend′) *v.* correct.

em′er·ald (em′ər əld) *n.* **1.** green gem. —*adj.* **2.** of a clear, deep green.

e·merge′ (i mûrj′) *v.,* emerged, emerging. come forth or into notice. —**e·mer′gence,** *n.*

e·mer′gen·cy (i mûr′jən sē) *n., pl.* -cies. urgent situation requiring action.

em′er·y (em′ə rē) *n.* mineral used for grinding, etc.

e·met′ic (i met′ik) *n.* medicine that induces vomiting.

em′i·grate′ (em′i grāt′) *v.,* -grated, -grating. leave one's country to settle in another. —**em′i·gra′tion,** *n.*

é′mi·gré′ (em′i grā′) *n.* emigrant who flees esp. for political reasons.

em′i·nence (em′ə nəns) *n.* high repute. —**em′i·nent,** *adj.*

em·is·sar′y (em′ə ser′ē) *n., pl.* -saries. agent on mission.

e·mit′ (i mit′) *v.,* emitted, emitting. send forth. —**e·mis′sion,** *n.*

e·mol′lient (i mol′yənt) *adj.* **1.** softening; soothing. —*n.* **2.** emollient substance.

e·mol′u·ment (i mol′yə mənt) *n.* salary.

e·mote′ (i mōt′) *v.,* emoted, emoting. show emotion in or as if in acting. —**e·mot′er,** *n.*

e·mo′tion (i mō′shən) *n.* state of feeling. —**e·mo′tion·al,** *adj.*

em′pa·thy (em′pə thē) *n.* sensitive awareness of another's feelings. —**em′pa·thize′,** *v.*

em′per·or (em′pər ər) *n.* ruler of empire. **em′press,** *n.fem.*

em′pha·sis (em′fə sis) *n., pl.* -ses. greater importance; stress. —**em·phat′ic** (-fat′ik) *adj.* —**em·phat′i·cal·ly,** *adv.* —**em′pha·size′,** *v.*

em′phy·se′ma (em′fə sē′mə) *n.* chronic lung disease.

em′pire (em′pīr′) *n.* nations under one ruler.

em·pir′i·cal (em pir′i kəl) *adj.* drawing on experience or observation only.

em·ploy′ (em ploi′) *v.* **1.** use or hire. —*n.* **2.** employment. **em·**

ploy•ee, n. —**em•ploy•er,** n.
—**em•ploy•ment,** n.

em•po•ri•um (em pôr'ē əm) n.
large store.

em•pow•er, v. **1.** authorize to act
for one. **2.** enable. —**em•pow•er•
ment,** n.

emp•ty (emp'tē) adj., **-tier, -tiest,**
v., **-tied, -tying.** —adj. **1.** containing nothing. —v. **2.** deprive of
contents. **3.** become empty.

empty nest syndrome, depressed
state felt by some parents after
their children have grown up and
left home.

EMT, emergency medical technician.

e•mu (ē'myoō) n. large flightless
Australian bird.

em•u•late (em'yə lāt') v., **-lated,
-lating.** try to equal or surpass.

e•mul•si•fy (i mul'sə fī') v., **-fied,
-fying.** make into emulsion.

e•mul•sion (-shən) n. **1.** milklike
mixture of liquids. **2.** light-sensitive
layer on film.

en-, prefix meaning: **1.** put into or
on, as *enthrone.* **2.** cover or surround with, as *encircle.* **3.** make or
cause to be, as *enlarge.*

en•a•ble (en ā'bəl) v., **-bled, -bling.**
give power, means, etc., to.

en•act, v. **1.** make into law. **2.** act
the part of. —**en•act•ment,** n.

e•nam•el (i nam'əl) n., v., **-eled,
-eling.** —n. **1.** glassy coating fused
to metal, etc. **2.** paint giving a
glossy surface. **3.** surface of teeth.
—v. **4.** apply enamel to.

en•am•or (i nam'ər) v. fill with
love.

en•camp, v., settle in camp. —**en•
camp'ment,** n.

en•cap•su•late (en kap'sə lāt') v.,
-lated, -lating. summarize; condense.

en•case (en kās') v., **-cased, -cas-
ing.** enclose in or as if in a case.

-ence, suffix meaning: act or fact
(*abhorrence*); state or quality (*absence*).

en•ceph•a•li•tis (en sef'ə lī'tis) n.
inflammation of the brain.

en•chant' (en chant') v. **1.** bewitch;
charm. —**en•chant'ment,** n.

en•chi•la•da (en'chə lä'də) n. food
consisting of a tortilla rolled around
a filling, usu. with a chili-flavored
sauce.

en•cir•cle, v., **-cled, -cling.** surround.

encl., **1.** enclosed. **2.** enclosure.

en•clave (en'klāv, än'-) n. country,
etc., surrounded by alien territory.

en•close (en klōz') v., **-closed,
-closing.** **1.** close in on all sides. **2.**
put in envelope. —**en•clo'sure,** n.

en•code, v., **-coded, -coding.** convert into code.

en•co•mi•um (en kō'mē əm) n., pl.
-miums, -mia. praise; eulogy.

en•com•pass (en kum'pas) v. **1.** encircle. **2.** contain.

en•core (äng'kôr, än'-) interj. **1.**
again! bravo! —n. **2.** additional
song, etc.

en•coun•ter (en koun'tər) v. **1.**
meet, esp. unexpectedly. —n. **2.**
casual meeting. **3.** combat.

en•cour•age (en kûr'ij, -kur'-) v.,
-aged, -aging. inspire or help.
—**en•cour'age•ment,** n.

en•croach (en krōch') v. trespass.

en•cum•ber (en kum'bər) v. impede; burden. —**en•cum'brance,** n.

en•cyc'li•cal (en sik'li kəl) n. letter
from Pope to bishops.

en•cy•clo•pe•di•a (en sī'klə pē'dē ə)
n. reference book giving information on many subjects. —**en•cy•clo•
pe'dic,** adj.

end (end) n. **1.** extreme or concluding part. **2.** close. **3.** purpose. **4.**
result. —v. **5.** bring or come to an
end. **6.** result. —**end'less,** adj.

en•dan•ger (en dān'jər) v. expose
to danger.

en•dear (en dēr') v. make beloved.

en•deav•or (en dev'ər) n., v. attempt.

en•dem•ic (en dem'ik) adj. belonging to a particular people or place.

end'ing (en'ding) n. close.

en•dive (en'dīv, än dēv') n. plant
for salad.

en•do•crine (en'də krin, -krīn') adj.
secreting internally into the blood
or lymph.

en•dorse (en dôrs') v., **-dorsed,
-dorsing.** **1.** approve or support. **2.**
sign on back of (a check, etc.).

en•dow (en dou') v. **1.** give permanent fund to. **2.** equip.

en•dure (en dŏŏr', -dyŏŏr') v.,
-dured, -during. **1.** tolerate. **2.** last.
—**en•dur'ance,** n.

en•e•ma (en'ə mə) n. liquid injection into rectum.

en•e•my (en'ə mē) n., pl. **-mies.**
adversary; opponent.

en•er•gize (en'ər jīz') v., **-gized,
-gizing.** give energy to.

en•er•gy (-jē) n., pl. **-gies.** capacity
for activity; vigor. —**en•er•get'ic**
(-jet'ik) adj.

en•er•vate (en'ər vāt') v., **-vated,
-vating.** weaken.

en•fee•ble (en fē'bəl) v., **-bled,
-bling.** weaken.

en•fold (en fōld') v. wrap around.

en•force (en fôrs') v. **forced, forc-**

ing. compel obedience to. —en-
force'ment, n. —en-forc'er, n.

en-fran'chise (en fran'chīz) v.,
-chised, -chising. grant citizenship
to.

en-gage' (en gāj') v., -gaged, -gag-
ing. 1. occupy. 2. hire. 3. please.
4. betroth. 5. interlock with. 6. enter into conflict with. —en-gaged',
adj. —en-gage'ment, n.

en-gag'ing, adj. attractive.

en-gen'der (en jen'dar) v. cause.

en'gine (en'jan) n. 1. machine for
converting energy into mechanical
work. 2. locomotive.

en'gi-neer' (en'jə nēr') n. 1. expert
in engineering. 2. engine operator.
—v. 3. contrive.

en'gi-neer'ing, n. practical application of physics, chemistry, etc.

Eng'lish (ing'glish; often -lish) n.
language of the people of Great
Britain, Australia, the U.S., etc.
—Eng'lish, adj.

en-gorge' (en gôrj') v., -gorged,
-gorging. fill or congest, esp. with
blood. —en-gorge'ment, n.

en-grave' (en grāv') v., -graved,
-graving. cut into hard surface.
—en-grav'er, n. —en-grav'ing, n.

en-gross' (en grōs') v. occupy
wholly.

en-gulf' (en gulf') v. swallow up.

en-hance' (en hans') v., -hanced,
-hancing. improve.

e-nig'ma (a nig'ma) n. something
puzzling. —en-ig-mat'ic, en-ig-
mat'i-cal, adj.

en-join' (en join') v. command or
prohibit. —en-join'der, n.

en-joy' (en joi') v. find pleasure in
or for. —en-joy'a-ble, adj. —en-
joy'ment, n.

en-large' (en lärj') v., -larged, -lar-
ging. make or grow larger. —enlarge'ment, n.

en-light'en (en līt'n) v. impart
knowledge to.

en-list' (en list') v. enroll for service. —en-list'ment, n.

en-liv'en (en lī'vən) v. make active.

en masse' (än mas', än) in a mass;
all together.

en-mesh' (en mesh') v. entangle.

en'mi-ty (en'mi tē) n., pl. -ties. hatred.

en-nui' (än wē') n. boredom.

e-nor'mi-ty (i nôr'mi tē) n., pl.
-ties. 1. extreme wickedness. 2.
grievous crime; atrocity.

e-nor'mous (-mas) adj. huge.

e-nough' (i nuf') adj. 1. adequate.
—n. 2. adequate amount. —adv. 3.
sufficiently.

en-quire' (en kwīr') v., -quired,
-quiring. inquire. —en-quir'y, n.

en-rage' (en rāj') v., -raged, -rag-
ing. make furious.

en-rap'ture (en rap'char) v.,
-tured, -turing. delight.

en-rich' (en rich') v. make rich or
better. —en-rich'ment, n.

en-roll' (en rōl') v. take into group
or organization. —en-roll'ment, n.

en route (än rōōt') on the way.

en-sconce' (en skons') v., -sconced,
-sconcing. settle securely or snugly.

en-sem'ble (än säm'bəl) n. assem-
bled whole.

en-shrine' (en shrīn') v., -shrined,
-shrining. cherish.

en-shroud' (en shroud') v. conceal.

en'sign (en'sīn; Mil. -san) n. 1.
flag. 2. lowest commissioned naval
officer.

en-slave' (en slāv') v., -slaved,
-slaving. make slave of.

en-snare' (en snâr') v., -snared,
-snaring. entrap.

en-sue' (en sōō') v., -sued, -suing.
follow.

en-sure' (en shŏŏr') v., -sured,
-suring. make certain; secure.

-ent, suffix equivalent to -ant, as
president, insistent.

en-tail' (en tāl') v. involve.

en-tan'gle (en tang'gal) v., -gled,
-gling. involve; entrap.

en-tente' (än tänt') n. international
agreement on policy.

en-ter (en'tar) v. 1. come or go in.
2. begin. 3. record.

en-ter-i'tis (en'ta rī'tis) n. inflammation of the intestines.

en'ter-prise' (en'tar prīz') n. 1.
project. 2. initiative.

en'ter-pris'ing, adj. showing initiative.

en-ter-tain' (en'tar tān') v. 1.
amuse. 2. treat as guest. 3. hold in
mind. —en'ter-tain'er, n. —en'-
ter-tain'ment, n.

en-thrall' (en thrôl') v. 1. hold by
fascination; captivate. 2. enslave.

en-throne' (en thrōn') v., -throned,
-throning. place on or as if on a
throne. —en-throne'ment, n.

en-thuse' (en thōōz') v., -thused,
-thusing. show enthusiasm.

en-thu'si-asm (-thōō'zē az'am) n.
lively interest. —en-thu'si-ast', n.
—en-thu'si-as'tic, adj.

en-tice' (en tīs') v., -ticed, -ticing.
lure. —en-tice'ment, n.

en-tire' (en tīr') adj. whole. —entire'ly, adv. —en-tire'ty, n.

en-ti'tle (en tī'tl) v., -tled, -tling.
permit (one) to claim something.

en'ti-ty (en'ti tē) n., pl. -ties. real
or whole thing.

en-tomb' (en tōōm') v. bury.

en·to·mol·o·gy (en'tə mol'ə jē) *n.* study of insects.

en·tou·rage (än'tŏŏ räzh') *n.* group of personal attendants.

en·trails (en'trālz, -trəlz) *n.pl.* internal parts of body, esp. intestines.

en·trance, *n., v.,* **-tranced, -trancing.** —*n.* **1.** act of entering. **2.** place for entering. **3.** admission. —*v.* (en trans') **4.** charm.

en·trant (en'trant) *n.* person who enters competition or contest.

en·trap (en trap') *v.,* **-trapped, -trapping. 1.** catch in a trap. **2.** entice into guilty situation.

en·treat (en trēt') *v.* implore.

en·treat·y, *n., pl.* **-ies.** earnest request.

en·tree (än'trā) *n.* **1.** main dish of meal. **2.** access.

en·trench (en trench') *v.* fix in strong position.

en·tre·pre·neur (än'trə prə nûr') *n.* independent business manager. —**en'tre·pre·neur'i·al,** *adj.*

en·tro·py (en'trə pē) *n.* **1.** measure of the amount of energy unavailable for useful work in a thermodynamic process. **2.** tendency toward disorder in any system.

en·trust (en trust') *v.* give in trust.

en·try (en'trē) *n., pl.* **-tries. 1.** entrance. **2.** recorded statement, etc. **3.** contestant.

en·twine (en twīn') *v.,* **-twined, -twining.** twine around or together.

e·nu·mer·ate (i nōō'mə rāt', i nyōō'-) *v.,* **-ated, -ating.** list; count. —**e·nu'mer·a'tion,** *n.*

e·nun·ci·ate (i nun'sē āt') *v.,* **-ated, -ating.** say distinctly.

en·vel·op (en vel'əp) *v.* surround.

en·ve·lope (en'və lōp', än'-) *n.* covering for letter.

en·vi·ron·ment (en vī'rən mənt, -vī'ərn-) *n.* surrounding things, conditions, etc. —**en·vi'ron·men'tal** (-men'tl) *adj.*

en·vi·ron·men·tal·ist (-men'tl ist) *n.* person working to protect environment from pollution, etc.

en·vi·rons (en vī'rənz) *n.pl.* outskirts.

en·vis·age (en viz'ij) *v.,* **-aged, -aging.** form mental picture of. Also, **en·vi'sion.**

en·voy (en'voi, än'-) *n.* **1.** diplomatic agent. **2.** messenger.

en·vy (en'vē) *n., pl.* **-vies,** *v.,* **-vied, -vying.** —*n.* **1.** discontent at another's good fortune. **2.** thing coveted. —*v.* **3.** regard with envy. —**en'vi·ous,** *adj.* —**en'vi·ous·ly,** *adv.*

en·zyme (en'zīm) *n.* bodily substance capable of producing chemical change in other substances.

e·on (ē'ən, ē'on) *n.* long period of time.

EPA, Environmental Protection Agency.

ep·au·let (ep'ə let', -lit) *n.* shoulder piece worn on uniform. Also, **ep'au·lette'.**

e·phem·er·al (i fem'ər əl) *adj.* brief; transitory.

ep·ic (ep'ik) *adj.* **1.** describing heroic deeds. —*n.* **2.** epic poem.

ep·i·cen·ter (ep'ə sen'tər) *n.* point directly above center of earthquake.

ep·i·cure (ep'i kyŏŏr') *n.* connoisseur of food and drink.

ep·i·dem·ic (ep'i dem'ik) *adj.* **1.** affecting many persons at once. —*n.* **2.** epidemic disease.

ep·i·der·mis, *n.* outer layer of skin.

ep·i·glot·tis (-glot'is) *n., pl.* **-glottises, -glottides** (-glot'i dēz'). thin structure that covers larynx during swallowing.

ep·i·gram (ep'i gram') *n.* witty statement.

ep·i·lep·sy (ep'ə lep'sē) *n.* nervous disease often marked by convulsions. —**ep'i·lep'tic,** *adj., n.*

ep·i·logue (ep'i lôg') *n.* concluding part or speech.

e·piph·a·ny (i pif'ə nē) *n.* **1.** appearance. **2.** sudden realization. **3.** (*cap.*) festival, Jan. 6, commemorating the Wise Men's visit to Christ.

e·pis·co·pal (i pis'kə pəl) *adj.* **1.** governed by bishops. **2.** (*cap.*) designating Anglican Church. —**E·pis·co·pa'li·an** (-pā'lē ən) *n.*

ep·i·sode (ep'ə sōd') *n.* incident. —**ep'i·sod'ic,** (-sod'ik) *adj.*

ep·is·tle (i pis'əl) *n.* letter.

ep·i·taph (ep'i taf') *n.* inscription on tomb.

ep·i·thet (ep'ə thet') *n.* descriptive term for person or things.

e·pit·o·me (i pit'ə mē) *n.* **1.** summary. **2.** typical specimen. —**e·pit'o·mize',** *v.,* **-mized, -mizing.**

e plu·ri·bus u·num (ē plŏŏ'ri bŏŏs ŏŏ'nŏŏm; Eng. ē plŏŏr'ə bəs yŏŏ'nəm) *Latin.* out of many, one (motto of the U.S.).

ep·och (ep'ək) *n.* distinctive period of time. —**ep'och·al,** *adj.*

ep·ox·y (i pok'sē) *n., pl.* **-ies.** tough synthetic resin used in glues.

Ep'som salts (ep'səm) salt used esp. as a cathartic.

e·qua·ble (ek'wə bəl) *adj.* even.

e·qual (ē'kwəl) *adj., n., v.,* **equaled, equaling.** —*adj.* **1.** alike in quantity, rank, size, etc. uniform. **2.** adequate. —*n.* **4.** one that is equal to. —*v.* **5.** be equal to. —**e·qual'i·ty,** *n.* —**e'qual·ize',** *v.*

equal sign, symbol (=) indicating

equality between terms. Also, **equals sign.**

e'qua·nim'i·ty (ē'kwə nim'i tē) n. calmness.

e·quate' (i kwāt') v., **equated, equating.** make or consider as equal.

e·qua'tion (i kwā'zhən) n. expression of equality of two quantities.

e·qua'tor (-tər) n. imaginary circle around earth midway between poles. —**e·qua·to'ri·al,** adj.

e·ques'tri·an (i kwes'trē ən) adj. 1. of horse riders or horsemanship. —n. 2. Also, for a woman, **e·ques'tri·enne'.** horse rider.

e'qui·dis'tant (ē'kwi dis'tənt) adj. equally distant.

e'qui·lat'er·al, adj. having all sides equal.

e'qui·lib'ri·um (-lib'rē əm) n., pl. **-riums, -ria.** balance.

e'quine (ē'kwīn) adj. of horses.

e'qui·nox' (ē'kwə noks') n. time when night and day are of equal length.

e·quip' (i kwip') v., **equipped, equipping.** furnish. —**e·quip'ment,** n.

eq'ui·ta·ble (ek'wi tə bəl) adj. fair.

eq'ui·ty, n., pl. **-ties.** fairness. 2. share.

e·quiv'a·lent (i kwiv'ə lənt) adj., n. equal. —**e·quiv'a·lence,** n.

e·quiv'o·cal (i kwiv'ə kəl) adj. 1. ambiguous. 2. questionable.

e·quiv'o·cate' (-kāt') v., **-cated, -cating.** express oneself ambiguously or indecisively. —**e·quiv'o·ca'tion,** n.

ER, emergency room.

-er, suffix meaning: person occupied with or working at something, as roofer; resident, as southerner; person or thing associated with particular characteristic or circumstance, as teenager; one that performs or is used in performing action, as fertilizer.

e'ra (ēr'ə, er'ə) n. period of time.

ERA, 1. Also, **era.** earned run average. 2. Equal Rights Amendment.

e·rad'i·cate' (i rad'i kāt') v., **-cated, -cating.** remove completely.

e·rase' (i rās') v., **erased, erasing.** rub out. —**e·ras'a·ble,** adj. —**e·ra'sure,** n.

ere (âr) prep., conj. Archaic. before.

e·rect' (i rekt') adj. 1. upright. —v. 2. build.

e·rec'tion (-shən) n. 1. something erected. 2. erect state of an organ, as the penis.

erg (ûrg) n. unit of work or energy.

er'go (ûr'gō, er'gō) conj., adv. therefore.

er'go·nom'ics (ûr'gə nom'iks) n. applied science that coordinates workplace design and equipment with workers' needs.

er'mine (ûr'min) n. kind of weasel.

e·rode' (i rōd') v., **eroded, eroding.** wear away. —**e·ro'sion,** n.

e·rog'e·nous (i roj'ə nəs) adj. sensitive to sexual stimulation.

e·rot'ic (i rot'ik) adj. 1. of sexual love. 2. arousing sexual desire. —**e·rot'i·cism** (-ə siz'əm) n.

e·rot'i·ca (-i kə) n.pl. erotic literature and art.

err (ûr, er) v. 1. be mistaken. 2. sin.

er'rand (er'ənd) n. trip for special purpose.

er'rant (er'ənt) adj. roving.

er·rat'ic (i rat'ik) adj. uncontrolled or irregular.

er·ra'tum (i rä'təm, i rat'əm) n., pl. **-ta.** (usually pl.) error in printing.

er·ro'ne·ous (ə rō'nē əs, e rō'-) adj. incorrect.

er'ror (er'ər) n. 1. mistake. 2. sin.

er·satz' (er zäts') adj. artificial.

erst'while', adj. former.

ERT, estrogen replacement therapy.

er'u·dite' (er'yŏŏ dīt') adj. learned.

e·rupt' (i rupt') v. burst forth. —**e·rup'tion,** n.

-ery, suffix meaning: things or people collectively (machinery; peasantry); occupation, activity, or condition (archery); place for (winery); characteristic conduct (prudery).

es'ca·late' (es'kə lāt') v., **-lated, -lating.** increase in intensity or size.

es'ca·la'tor, n. moving stairway.

es·cal'lop (e skol'əp, e skal'-) v. 1. finish with scallops (def. 2) 2. bake in breadcrumb-topped sauce. —n. 3. scallop.

es'ca·pade' (es'kə pād') n. wild prank.

es·cape' (i skāp') v., **-caped, -caping,** n. —v. 1. get away. 2. avoid; elude. —n. 3. act or means of escaping. —**es·cap'ee,** n.

—**Usage.** ESCAPE, ELUDE, EVADE mean to keep away from something. To ESCAPE is to manage to keep away from danger, pursuit, observation, etc.: to escape punishment. To ELUDE is to slip through an apparently tight net, and implies using skill or cleverness: The fox eluded the hounds. To EVADE is to turn aside from or go out of reach of a person or thing, usually by moving or directing attention elsewhere: We evaded the traffic jam by taking an alternate route.

es·cape′ment (i skāp′mənt) *n.* part of clock that controls speed.

es·cap′ism, *n.* attempt to forget reality through fantasy. **—es·cap′ist,** *n., adj.*

es′ca·role′ (es′kə rōl′) *n.* broad-leaved endive.

es·carp′ment (i skärp′mənt) *n,* long clifflike ridge.

es·chew′ (es chōō′) *v.* avoid.

es′cort, *n.* (es′kôrt) **1.** accompanying person or persons. **—v.** (i-skôrt′) **2.** accompany as escort.

es·cutch′eon (i skuch′ən) *n.* coat of arms.

Es′ki·mo′ (es′kə mō′) *n.* Arctic North American people or language.

ESL, English as a second language.

e·soph′a·gus (i sof′ə gəs) *n., pl.* **-gi** (-jī′). tube connecting mouth and stomach.

es′o·ter′ic (es′ə ter′ik) *adj.* understood by a select few.

ESP, extrasensory perception.

esp., especially.

es′pa·drille′ (es′pə dril′) *n.* flat shoe with cloth upper and rope sole.

es·pe′cial (i spesh′əl) *adj.* special.

Es′pe·ran′to (es′pə rän′tō, -ran′-) *n.* artificial language based on major European languages.

es′pi·o·nage′ (es′pē ə näzh′, -nij) *n.* work or use of spies.

es′pla·nade′ (es′plə näd′, -nād′) *n.* open level space for public walks.

es·pouse′ (i spouz′, i spous′) *v.,* **-poused, -pousing. 1.** advocate. **2.** marry. **—es·pous′al,** *n.*

es·pres′so (i spres′ō) *n.* strong coffee made with steam.

es·prit′ de corps′ (ē sprē′ də kôr′) sense of common purpose.

es·py′ (i spī′) *v.,* **-pied, -pying.** catch sight of.

Es·quire′ (es′kwīr′) *n. Brit.* title of respect after man's name., in the U.S. chiefly applied to lawyers. *Abbr.:* Esq.

es′say, *n.* (es′ā) **1.** literary composition. **2.** attempt. **—v.** (e sā′) **3.** try.

es′say·ist, *n.* writer of essays.

es′sence (es′əns) *n.* **1.** intrinsic nature. **2.** concentrated form of substance or thought.

es·sen′tial (ə sen′shəl) *adj.* **1.** necessary. **2.** necessary thing.

es·sen′tial·ly, *adv.* basically; necessarily.

EST, Eastern Standard Time.

est., **1.** established. **2.** estimate. **3.** estimated.

es·tab′lish (i stab′lish) *v.* **1.** set up permanently. **2.** prove.

es·tab′lish·ment, *n.* **1.** act of establishing. **2.** institution or business.

3. (*often cap.*) group controlling government and social institutions.

es·tate′ (i stāt′) *n.* **1.** landed property. **2.** one's possessions.

es·teem′ (i stēm′) *v.* **1.** regard. **—n. 2.** opinion.

es′ter (es′tər) *n.* chemical compound produced by reaction between an acid and an alcohol.

es·thete, *n.* aesthete.

es′ti·ma·ble (es′tə mə bəl) *adj.* worthy of high esteem.

es′ti·mate′ (es′tə māt′) *v.,* **-mated, -mating, *n.* —v.** **1.** calculate roughly. **—n.** (-mit) **2.** rough calculation. **3.** opinion. **—es′ti·ma′tion,** *n.*

es·trange′ (i strānj′) *v.,* **-tranged, -tranging.** alienate.

es′tro·gen (es′trə jən) *n.* any of several female sex hormones.

es′tu·ar′y (es′chōō er′ē) *n., pl.* **-ar·ies.** part of river affected by sea tides.

ETA, estimated time of arrival.

et al. (et al′, äl′, ôl′) and so on. *Abbr.:* etc.

et cet′er·a (et set′ər ə, se′trə) and so on. *Abbr.:* etc.

etch (ech) *v.* cut design into (metal, etc.) with acid. **—etch′ing,** *n.*

e·ter′nal (i tûr′nl) *adj.* **1.** without beginning or end. **—n. 2.** (*cap.*) God. **—e·ter′ni·ty,** *n.*

eth′ane (eth′ān) *n.* flammable gas used chiefly as a fuel.

e′ther (ē′thər) *n.* **1.** colorless liquid used as an anesthetic. **2.** upper part of space.

e·the′re·al (i thēr′ē əl) *adj.* **1.** delicate. **2.** heavenly.

eth′ics (eth′iks) *n.pl.* principles of conduct. **—eth′i·cal,** *adj.*

eth′nic (eth′nik) *adj.* **1.** sharing a common culture. **—n. 2.** member of minority group.

eth·nic′i·ty (-nis′i tē) *n.* ethnic traits or association.

eth·nol′o·gy (eth nol′ə jē) *n.* branch of anthropology dealing with cultural comparisons.

e·thol′o·gy (ē thol′ə jē) *n.* scientific study of animal behavior.

e′thos (ē′thos, eth′ōs) *n.* distinguishing characteristics of person, group, or culture.

eth′yl (eth′əl) *n.* fluid containing lead, added to gasoline.

et′i·quette (et′i kit, -ket′) *n.* conventions of social behavior.

et seq., and the following.

é′tude (ā′tōōd, ā′tyōōd) *n.* musical composition played to improve technique but also for its artistic merit.

et′y·mol′o·gy (et′ə mol′ə jē) *n., pl.* **-gies.** history of word or words.

eu-

eu-, prefix meaning good, as *eugenics.*

eu/ca·lyp/tus (yōō'kə lip'təs) *n., pl.* **-ti.** Australian tree.

Eu/cha·rist (yōō'kə rist) *n.* Holy Communion.

eu·gen/ics (yōō jen'iks) *n.* science of improving human race.

eu/lo·gy (yōō'lə jē) *n., pl.* **-gies.** formal praise. —**eu/lo·gize/,** *v.*

eu/nuch (yōō'nək) *n.* castrated man.

eu/phe·mism (yōō'fə miz/əm) *n.* substitution of mild expression for blunt one. —**eu/phe·mis/tic,** *adj.*

eu/pho·ny (yōō'fə nē) *n., pl.* **-nies.** pleasant sound. —**eu·pho/ni·ous** (-fō'nē əs) *adj.*

eu·pho/ri·a (yōō fôr'ē ə) *n.* strong feeling of happiness or well-being. —**eu·phor/ic,** *adj.*

Eur·a/sian (yōō rā'zhən) *adj.* of or originating in both Europe and Asia, or in the two considered as one continent.

eu·re/ka (yōō rē'kə) *interj.* (exclamation of triumph at a discovery).

Eu/ro·pe/an (yōōr'ə pē'ən) *n.* native of Europe. —**Eu/ro·pe/an,** *adj.*

European plan, system of paying a fixed hotel rate that covers lodging only.

Eu·sta/chian tube (yōō stā'shən) *(often l.c.)* canal between middle ear and pharynx.

eu/tha·na/sia (yōō'thə nā'zhə) *n.* mercy killing.

e·vac/u·ate/ (i vak'yōō āt') *v.,* **-ated, -ating. 1.** vacate; empty. **2.** remove. —**e·vac/u·a/tion,** *n.*

e·vade/ (i vād') *v.,* **evaded, evading.** avoid or escape from by cleverness. —**e·va/sion,** *n.* —**e·va/sive,** *adj.* —**Usage.** see ESCAPE.

e·val/u·ate/ (i val'yōō āt') *v.,* **-ated, -ating.** appraise.

ev/a·nes/cent (ev'ə nes'ənt) *adj.* fading away.

e/van·gel/i·cal (ē'van jel'i kəl, ev'ən-) *adj.* **1.** of or in keeping with Gospel. **2.** of those Protestant churches that stress personal conversion through faith.

e·van/ge·list (i van'jə list) *n.* **1.** preacher. **2.** One of the writers of Gospel. —**e·van/ge·lism,** *n.* —**e·van/ge·lize/,** *v.*

e·vap/o·rate/ (i vap'ə rāt') *v.,* **-ated, -ating.** change into vapor.

eve (ēv) *n.* evening before.

e/ven (ē'vən) *adj.* **1.** smooth. **2.** uniform. **3.** equal. **4.** divisible by 2. **5.** calm. —*adv.* **6.** still; yet. **7.** indeed. —*v.* **8.** make even.

e/ven·hand/ed, *adj.* impartial; fair.

eve/ning (ēv'ning) *n.* early part of night; end of day.

evening star, bright planet, esp. Venus, visible around sunset.

e·vent/ (i vent') *n.* anything that happens. —**e·vent/ful,** *adj.*

e·ven/tu·al (i ven'chōō əl) *adj.* final. —**e·ven/tu·al·ly,** *adv.*

e·ven/tu·al/i·ty, *n., pl.* **-ties.** possible event.

ev/er (ev'ər) *adv.* at all times.

ev/er·glade/ *n.* tract of low, swampy ground.

ev/er·green/, *adj.* **1.** having its leaves always green. —*n.* **2.** evergreen plant.

ev/er·last/ing, *adj.* lasting forever or indefinitely.

eve/ry (ev'rē) *adj.* **1.** each. **2.** all possible. —**ev/er·y·bod/y** (-bod'ē, -bud'ē), **ev/er·y·one/,** *pron.* —**eve/ry·thing,** *pron.* —**ev/er·y·where/,** *adv.* —**eve/ry·day/,** *adj.*

e·vict/ (i vikt') *v.* legally remove from property. —**e·vic/tion,** *n.*

ev/i·dence (ev'i dəns) *n., v.,* **-denced, -dencing.** —*n.* **1.** grounds for belief. —*v.* **2.** prove.

ev/i·dent, *adj.* clearly so. —**ev/i·dent·ly** (ev'i dant lē, ev'i dent/lē) *adv.*

e/vil (ē'vəl) *adj.* **1.** wicked. **2.** unfortunate. —**e/vil·do/er,** *n.*

evil eye, look thought capable of doing harm.

e·vince/ (i vins') *v.,* **evinced, evincing.** show.

e·vis/cer·ate/ (i vis'ə rāt') *v.,* **-ated, -ating. 1.** remove entrails of. **2.** deprive of vital or essential parts.

e·voke/ (i vōk') *v.,* **evoked, evoking.** call forth. —**ev/o·ca/tion** (ev'ə kā'shən) *n.* —**e·voc/a·tive** (i vok'-) *adj.*

e·volve/ (i volv') *v.,* **evolved, evolving.** develop gradually. —**ev/o·lu/tion,** *n.*

ewe (yōō) *n.* female sheep.

ew/er (yōō'ər) *n.* wide-mouthed pitcher.

ex-, prefix meaning: **1.** out of or from, as *export.* **2.** utterly or thoroughly, as *exacerbate.* **3.** former, as *ex-governor.*

ex., 1. example. **2.** except. **3.** exception. **4.** exchange.

ex·ac/er·bate/ (ig zas'ər bāt', ek sas'-) *v.,* **-bated, -bating.** make more severe or violent.

ex·act/ (ig zakt') *adj.* **1.** precise; accurate. —*v.* **2.** demand; compel. —**ex·act/ing,** *adj.* severe.

ex·ag/ger·ate/ (ig zaj'ə rāt') *v.,* **-ated, ating.** magnify beyond truth.

ex·alt/ (ig zôlt') *v.* **1.** elevate. **2.** extol. —**ex/al·ta/tion,** *n.*

ex·am′ (ig zam′) n. *Informal.* examination.

ex·am′ine (-in) v., -ined, -ining. **1.** investigate. **2.** test. **3.** interrogate. —**ex·am′i·na′tion,** n. —**ex·am′in·er,** n.

ex·am′ple (ig zam′pəl) n. **1.** typical one. **2.** model. **3.** illustration.

ex·as′per·ate′ (ig zas′pə rāt′) v., -ated, -ating. make angry.

ex′ca·vate′ (eks′kə vāt′) v., -vated, -vating. **1.** dig out. **2.** unearth. —**ex′ca·va′tion,** n. —**ex′ca·va′tor,** n.

ex·ceed′ (ik sēd′) v. go beyond; surpass.

ex·ceed′ing·ly, adv. very.

ex·cel′ (ik sel′) v., -celled, -celling. do very well; be superior (to).

ex′cel·len·cy (ek′sə lən sē) n., pl. -cies. **1.** (cap.) title of honor. **2.** excellence.

ex′cel·lent, adj. remarkably good. —**ex′cel·lence,** n.

ex·cept′ (ik sept′) prep. **1.** Also, **ex·cept′ing.** other than; excluding. —v. **2.** leave out; exclude. **3.** object. —**Usage.** See ACCEPT.

ex·cep′tion·a·ble, adj. causing objections.

ex·cep′tion·al, adj. unusual.

ex′cerpt′ (n. ek′sûrpt) **1.** passage from longer writing. —v. (ik sûrpt′, ek′sûrpt) **2.** take (passage) from a book, film, etc.

ex·cess′ (ik ses′) **1.** amount over that required. —adj. (ek′ses) **2.** more than necessary, usual, or desirable.

ex·ces′sive, adj. more than desirable. —**ex·ces′sive·ly,** adv.

ex·change′ (iks chānj′) v., -changed, -changing. —v. **1.** change for something else. —n. **2.** act of exchanging. **3.** thing exchanged. **4.** trading place.

ex·cheq′uer (iks chek′ər) n. Brit. treasury.

ex′cise, n., v., -cised, -cising. —n. (ek′sīz) **1.** tax on certain goods. —v. (ik sīz′) **2.** cut out.

ex·cite′ (ik sīt′) v., -cited, -citing. **1.** stir up (emotions, etc.). **2.** cause. —**ex·cit′a·ble,** adj. —**ex·cite′ment,** n.

ex·claim′ (ik sklām′) v. cry out. —**ex′cla·ma′tion,** n.

ex·clude′ (ik sklōōd′) v., -cluded, -cluding. shut out. —**ex·clu′sion,** n.

ex·clu′sive (ik sklōō′siv) adj. **1.** belonging or pertaining to one. **2.** excluding others. **3.** stylish; chic.

ex′com·mu′ni·cate′ (eks′kə myōō′ni kāt′) v., -cated, -cating. cut off

from membership of church. —**ex′com·mu′ni·ca′tion,** n.

ex·co′ri·ate′ (ik skôr′ē āt′) v., -ated, -ating. denounce.

ex′cre·ment (ek′skrə mənt) n. bodily waste.

ex·cres′cence (ik skres′əns) n. abnormal growth. —**ex·cres′cent,** adj.

ex·crete′ (ik skrēt′) v., -creted, -creting. eliminate from body. —**ex·cre′tion,** n.

ex·cru′ci·at′ing (ik skrōō′shē ā′ting) adj. **1.** causing intense suffering. **2.** intense or extreme.

ex·cul′pate′ (ik skul′pāt′, ek skul′pāt) v., -pated, -pating. free of blame. —**ex′cul·pa′tion,** n.

ex·cur′sion (ik skûr′zhən) n. short trip.

ex·cuse′, v., -cused, -cusing, n. —v. (ik skyōōz′) **1.** pardon. **2.** justify. **3.** justify. **4.** seek or grant release. —n. (ik skyōōs′) **5.** reason for being excused.

ex′e·crate′ (ek′si krāt′) v., -crated, -crating. **1.** abominate. **2.** curse. —**ex′e·cra·ble,** adj.

ex′e·cute′ (ek′si kyōōt′) v., -cuted, -cuting. **1.** do. **2.** kill legally. —**ex′e·cu′tion,** n. —**ex′e·cu′tion·er,** n.

ex·ec′u·tive (ig zek′yə tiv) adj. **1.** responsible for directing affairs. —n. **2.** administrator.

ex·ec′u·tor (-tər) n. person named to carry out provisions of a will. —**ex·ec′u·trix′,** n.fem.

ex·em′plar (ig zem′plär, -plər) n. model or pattern.

ex·em′pla·ry (-plə rē) adj. worthy of imitation.

ex·em′pli·fy′ (-plə fī′) v., -fied, -fying. show or serve as example.

ex·empt′ (ig zempt′) v., adj. free from obligation. —**ex·emp′tion,** n.

ex′er·cise′ (ek′sər sīz′) n., v., -cised, -cising. —n. **1.** action to increase skill or strength. **2.** performance. **3.** (pl.) ceremony. —v. **4.** put through exercises. **5.** use.

ex·ert′ (ig zûrt′) v. put into action. —**ex·er′tion,** n.

ex·hale′ (eks hāl′) v., -haled, -haling. breathe out; emit breath.

ex·haust′ (ig zôst′) v. **1.** use up. **2.** fatigue greatly. —n. **3.** used gases from engine. —**ex·haus′tion,** n.

ex·haus′tive, adj. thorough.

ex·hib′it (ig zib′it) v., n. display. —**ex·hi·bi′tion** (ek′sə bish′ən) n. —**ex·hib′i·tor,** n.

ex′hi·bi′tion·ism (-bish′ə niz′əm) n. desire or tendency to display oneself. —**ex′hi·bi′tion·ist,** n.

ex·hil′a·rate′ (ig zil′ə rāt′) v., -rated, -rating. cheer; stimulate. —**ex·hil′a·ra′tion,** n.

exhort

ex·hort' (ig zôrt') v. advise earnestly. —**ex·hor·ta·tion** (eg'zôr tā'shən) n.

ex·hume' (ig zōōm', -zyōōm') v., -humed, -huming. dig up a dead body, etc.

ex·i·gen·cy (ek'si jan sē) n., pl. -cies. urgent requirement. —**ex·i·gent,** adj.

ex·ile (eg'zīl, ek'sīl) n., v., -iled, -iling. —n. 1. enforced absence from one's country or home. 2. one so absent. —v. 3. send into exile.

ex·ist' (ig zist') v. be; live. —**ex·ist'ence,** n. —**ex·ist'ent,** adj.

ex·is·ten·tial (eg'zi sten'shal, ek'si-) adj. of human life; based on experience.

ex·is·ten·tial·ism, n. philosophy that stresses personal liberty and responsibility. —**ex·is·ten'tial·ist,** n., adj.

ex·it (eg'zit, ek'sit) n. 1. way out. 2. departure. —v. 3. leave.

exo-, prefix meaning outside or outer, as *exosphere*.

ex·o·crine (ek'sə krin, -krīn') adj. secreting externally through a duct.

ex·o·dus (ek'sə dəs) n. departure.

ex' of·fi'ci·o' (eks' ə fish'ē ō') because of one's office.

ex·on·er·ate (ig zon'ə rāt') v., -ated, -ating. free of blame. —**ex·on'er·a'tion,** n.

ex·or·bi·tant (ig zôr'bi tant) adj. excessive, esp. in cost.

ex·or·cise (ek'sôr sīz', -sər-) v., -cised, -cising. expel (evil spirit). —**ex'or·cism,** n. —**ex'or·cist,** n.

ex·o·sphere (ek'sō sfēr') n. highest region of the atmosphere.

ex·ot'ic (ig zot'ik) adj. 1. foreign; alien. 2. strikingly unusual.

ex·pand' (ik spand') v. increase; spread out. —**ex·pan'sion,** n.

ex·panse (ik spans') n. wide extent.

ex·pan'sive (ik span'siv) adj. warm and benevolent.

ex·pa'ti·ate (ik spā'shē āt') v., -ated, -ating. talk or write at length.

ex·pa·tri·ate, v., -ated, -ating, n., adj. —v. (eks pā'trē āt') 1. expel. 2. remove (oneself) from homeland. —n. (-it) 3. expatriated person. —adj. (-it) 4. exiled; banished.

ex·pect' (ik spekt') v. look forward to. —**ex·pect'an·cy,** n. —**ex·pect'ant,** adj. —**ex·pec·ta'tion,** n.

ex·pec·to·rate (-rāt') v., -rated, -rating. spit. —**ex·pec·to·ra'tion,** n.

ex·pe·di·ent, adj. 1. desirable in given circumstances. 2. conducive to advantage. —n. 3. expedient means. —**ex·pe'di·en·cy,** n.

ex·pe·dite (ek'spi dīt') v., -dited, -diting. speed up.

ex·pe·di'tion (ek'spi dish'ən) n. 1. journey to explore or fight. 2. promptness.

ex·pe·di'tious, adj. prompt.

ex·pel' (ik spel') v., -pelled, -pelling. force out.

ex·pend' (ik spend') v. 1. use up. 2. spend. —**ex·pend'i·ture,** n.

ex·pend·a·ble, adj. 1. available for spending. 2. that can be sacrificed if necessary.

ex·pense (ik spens') n. 1. cost. 2. cause of spending.

ex·pen'sive, adj. costing much.

ex·pe'ri·ence (ik spēr'ē əns) n., v., -enced, -encing. —n. 1. something lived through. 2. knowledge from such things. —v. 3. have experience of.

ex·pe'ri·enced, adj. wise or skillful through experience.

ex·per'i·ment, n. (ik sper'ə mənt) 1. test to discover or check something. —v. (-ment') 2. perform experiment. —**ex·per'i·men·tal** (-men'tl) adj. —**ex·per'i·men·ta'tion,** n. —**ex·per'i·ment'er,** n.

ex'pert (eks'pûrt) n. 1. skilled person. —adj. (eks'pûrt; also iks·pûrt') 2. skilled. —**ex·pert'ly,** adv.

ex'per·tise' (ek'spər tēz') n. expert skill.

ex'pi·ate (ek'spē āt') v., -ated, -ating. atone for. —**ex'pi·a'tion,** n.

ex·pire' (ik spīr') v., -pired, -piring. 1. end. 2. die. 3. breathe out.

ex·plain' (ik splān') v. 1. make clear. 2. account for. —**ex·pla·na'tion,** n. —**ex·plan'a·to·ry** (ik-splan'-) adj.

ex'ple·tive (ik'spli tiv) n. exclamatory oath, usu. profane.

ex·pli·cate (-kāt') v., -cated, -cating. explain in detail.

ex·plic'it (ik splis'it) adj. 1. clearly stated. 2. outspoken. 3. having sexual acts or nudity clearly depicted.

ex·plode (ik splōd') v., -ploded, -ploding. 1. burst violently. 2. disprove; discredit. —**ex·plo'sion,** n. —**ex·plo'sive,** n., adj.

ex'ploit (eks'ploit) n. 1. notable act. —v. (ik sploit') 2. use, esp. selfishly. —**ex'ploi·ta'tion,** n. —**ex·ploit'a·tive,** adj.

ex·plore' (ik splôr') v., -plored, -ploring. examine from end to end. —**ex·plo·ra'tion** (ek'splə rā'shən) n. —**ex·plor'er,** n. —**ex·plor'a·to·ry,** adj.

ex·po'nent (ik spō'nənt or, esp. for 3, ek'spō nant) n. 1. person who explains. 2. symbol. 3. *Math.* symbol placed to the upper right of another to indicate the power to which the latter is to be raised.

ex·port′, v. (ik spôrt′) **1.** send to other countries. —n. (ek′spôrt) **2.** what is sent. —**ex′por·ta′tion,** n.

ex·pose′ (ik spōz′) v., **-posed, -posing. 1.** lay open to harm, etc. **2.** reveal. **3.** allow light to reach (film). —**ex·po′sure,** n.

ex′po·sé′ (ek′spō zā′) n. exposure of wrongdoing.

ex′po·si′tion (ek′spə zish′ən) n. **1.** public show. **2.** explanation.

ex·pos′i·to·ry (ik spozi tôr′ē) adj. serving to expound or explain.

ex post facto (eks′ pōst′ fak′tō) adj. made or done after the fact; retroactive.

ex·pos′tu·late (ik spos′chə lāt′) v., **-lated, -lating.** protest.

ex·pound′ (ik spound′) v. state in detail.

ex·press′ (ik spres′) v. **1.** convey in words, art, etc. **2.** press out. —adj. **3.** definite. —n. **4.** fast or direct train, etc. **5.** delivery system. —**ex·pres′sion,** n. —**ex·pres′sive,** adj.

ex·press′way′, n. road for high-speed traffic.

ex·pro′pri·ate′ (eks prō′prē āt′) v., **-ated, -ating.** take for public use.

ex·pul′sion (ik spul′shən) n. act of driving out.

ex·punge′ (ik spunj′) v., **-punged, -punging.** obliterate.

ex′pur·gate′ (ek′spər gāt′) v., **-gated, -gating.** remove objectionable parts from.

ex′qui·site (ik skwiz′it, ek′skwi zit) adj. delicately beautiful.

ex′tant (ik stant, ik stant′) adj. still existing.

ex·tem′po·ra′ne·ous (ik stem′pə rā′nē əs) adj. impromptu. —**ex·tem′po·re** (ik stem′pə rē) adj or adv.

ex·tend′ (ik stend′) v. **1.** stretch out. **2.** offer. **3.** reach. **4.** increase. —**ex·ten′sion,** n.

extended family, family comprising a married couple, their children, and close relatives.

ex·ten′sive (-siv) adj. far-reaching.

ex·tent′ (ik stent′) n. degree; breadth.

ex·ten′u·ate′ (ik sten′yōō āt′) v., **-ated, -ating.** lessen seriousness of (fault).

ex·te′ri·or (ik stēr′ē ər) adj. **1.** outer. —n. **2.** outside.

ex·ter′mi·nate′ (ik stûr′mə nāt′) v., **-nated, -nating.** get rid of by destroying. —**ex·ter′mi·na′tion,** n. —**ex·ter′mi·na′tor,** n.

ex·ter′nal (ik stûr′nl) adj. outer.

ex·tinct′ (ik stingkt′) adj. no longer existing. —**ex·tinc′tion,** n.

ex·tin′guish (ik sting′gwish) v. put out; end. —**ex·tin′guish·er,** n.

ex′tir·pate′ (ik′star pāt′) v., **-pated, -pating.** destroy totally.

ex·tol′ (ik stōl′) v., **-tolled, -tolling.** praise highly.

ex·tort′ (ik stôrt′) v. get by force, threat, etc. —**ex·tor′tion,** n.

ex·tor′tion·ate (ik stôr′shə nit) adj. excessive.

ex′tra (ek′strə) adj. additional.

extra-, prefix meaning outside or beyond, as extrasensory.

ex·tract′ (ik strakt′) v. **1.** draw out. —n. (ek′strakt) **2.** something extracted. —**ex·trac′tion,** n.

ex′tra·cur·ric′u·lar (ek′strə kə rik′yə lər) adj. outside the regular curriculum, as of a school.

ex′tra·dite′ (ek′strə dīt′) v., **-dited, -diting.** deliver (fugitive) to another state. —**ex′tra·di′tion** (-dish′ən) n.

ex′tra·le′gal, adj. beyond the authority of law.

ex′tra·mu′ral (-myōōr′əl) adj. involving members of more than one school.

ex·tra′ne·ous (ik strā′nē əs) adj. irrelevant. —**ex·tra′ne·ous·ly,** adv.

ex·traor′di·nar′y (ik strôr′dn er′ē, ek′strə ôr′-) adj. unusual or remarkable. —**ex·traor′di·nar′i·ly,** adv.

ex·trap′o·late′ (ik strap′ə lāt′) v., **-lated, -lating.** infer from known data. —**ex·trap′o·la′tion,** n.

ex′tra·sen′so·ry (ek′strə sen′sə rē) adj. beyond one's physical senses.

ex′tra·ter·res′tri·al, adj. **1.** being or from outside the earth's limits. —n. **2.** extraterrestrial being.

ex·trav′a·gant (ik strav′ə gənt) adj. **1.** spending imprudently. **2.** immoderate. —**ex·trav′a·gance,** n.

ex·trav′a·gan′za (-gan′zə) n. lavish production.

ex·treme′ (ik strēm′) adj. **1.** not moderate or ordinary. **2.** very great. **3.** outermost. —n. **4.** utmost degree.

ex·trem′ism, n. tendency to take extreme measures, esp. in politics.

ex·trem′i·ty (ik strem′i tē) n., pl. **-ties. 1.** farthest part. **2.** arm or leg. **3.** distress.

ex′tri·cate′ (ek′stri kāt′) v., **-cated, -cating.** disentangle.

ex·trin′sic (ik strin′sik, -zik) adj. **1.** not inherent or essential. **2.** being or coming from without; external.

ex′tro·vert′ (ek′strə vûrt′) n. outgoing person. —**ex′tro·ver′sion,** n. —**ex′tro·vert′ed,** adj.

ex·trude' (ik strōōd') v., **-truded,** **-truding.** force or press out.

ex·u·ber·ant (ig zōō'bər ənt) adj. 1. joyful; vigorous. 2. abundant. —**ex·u·ber·ance,** n.

ex·ude' (ig zōōd', ik sōōd') v., **-uded, -uding.** 1. ooze out. 2. radiate. —**ex'u·da'tion,** n.

ex·ult' (ig zult') v. rejoice. —**ex·ult'ant,** adj. —**ex'ul·ta'tion,** n.

eye (ī) n., v., **eyed, eying** or **eyeing.** —n. 1. organ of sight. 2. power of seeing. 3. close watch. —v. 4. watch closely. —**eye'ball',** n., v. —**eye'sight',** n.

eye'brow', n. ridge and line of short hairs over eye.

eye'ful, (ī'fōōl) n., pl. **-fuls.** 1. thorough view. 2. *Informal.* attractive person.

eye'glass'es, n.pl. pair of corrective lenses in a frame.

eye'lash', n. short hair at edge of eyelid.

eye'let (ī'lit) n. small hole.

eye'lid', n. movable skin covering the eye.

eye'o'pen·er, n. something that causes sudden enlightenment.

eye'sore', n. something unpleasant to look at.

eye'tooth', n. canine tooth in upper jaw.

eye'wash', n. 1. soothing solution for eyes. 2. nonsense.

eye'wit'ness, n. person who sees event.

ey'rie (âr'ē, ēr'ē) n., pl. **-ies.** aerie.

F

F, f (ef) n. sixth letter of English alphabet.

F, 1. Fahrenheit. **2.** female.

f., 1. feet. **2.** female. **3.** folio. **4.** foot. **5.** franc.

FAA, Federal Aviation Administration.

fa·ble (fā'bəl) n. 1. short tale with moral. 2. untrue story.

fab'ric (fab'rik) n. cloth.

fab'ri·cate' (-ri kāt') v., **-cated, -cating.** 1. construct. 2. invent (lie).

fab'u·lous (fab'yə ləs) adj. 1. marvelous. 2. suggesting fables.

fa·çade' (fa säd') n. 1. building front. 2. superficial appearance.

face (fās) n., v., **faced, facing.** —n. 1. front part of head. 2. surface. 3. appearance. 4. dignity. —v. 5. look toward. 6. confront. —**fa'cial** (fā'shəl) adj.

face'less, adj. lacking identity.

face'-lift', n. 1. surgery to eliminate facial sagging. 2. renovation to improve appearance of building.

face'-sav'ing, adj. saving one's prestige or dignity.

fac'et (fas'it) n. 1. surface of cut gem. 2. aspect.

fa·ce'tious (fa sē'shəs) adj. joking, esp. annoyingly so.

face value (fās' val'yōō for 1; fās' val'yōō for 2) 1. value printed on the face of a stock, bond, etc. 2. apparent value.

fac'ile (fas'il) adj. easy; effortless.

fa·cil'i·tate' (fə sil'i tāt') v., **-tated, -tating.** make easier. —**fa·cil'i·ta'tion,** n. —**fa·cil'i·ta'tor,** n.

fa·cil'i·ty (-i tē) n., pl. **-ties.** 1. something designed or installed for a purpose. 2. ease.

fac'ing (fā'sing) n. 1. decorative or protective outer material. 2. lining.

fac·sim'i·le (fak sim'ə lē) n. exact copy.

fact (fakt) n. truth. —**fac'tu·al,** adj.

fac'tion (fak'shən) n. competing internal group. —**fac'tion·al,** adj.

fac'tious, adj. causing strife.

fac'tor (fak'tər) n. 1. element. 2. one of two numbers multiplied.

fac'to·ry (fak'tə rē) n., pl. **-ries.** place where goods are made.

fac'ul·ty (fak'əl tē) n., pl. **-ties.** 1. special ability. 2. power. 3. body of teachers.

fad (fad) n. temporary fashion.

fade (fād) v., **faded, fading.** 1. lose freshness, color, or vitality. 2. disappear gradually.

fag (fag) v., **fagged, fagging.** —v. 1. exhaust. —n. 2. Also, **fag'got.** *Offensive.* homosexual.

fag'ot (fag'ət) n. bundle of firewood.

Fahr'en·heit' (far'ən hīt') adj. measuring temperature so that water freezes at 32° and boils at 212°.

fail (fāl) v. 1. be unsuccessful or lacking (in). 2. become weaker. 3. cease functioning.

fail'ing, n. 1. weak point of character. —prep. 2. in the absence of.

faille (fīl, fāl) n. ribbed fabric.

fail'-safe', adj. ensured against failure of a mechanical system, etc. or against consequences of its failure.

faint (fānt) adj. 1. lacking strength. 2. lose consciousness briefly.

faint'heart'ed, adj. lacking courage.

fair (fâr) adj. 1. behaving justly. 2. moderately good. 3. sunny. 4. light-hued. 5. attractive. —n. 6. ex-

far-off

hibition. —**fair′ly,** adv. —**fair′ness,** n.

fair shake, just and equal opportunity or treatment.

fair′y (fãr′ē) n., pl. **fairies.** 1. tiny supernatural being. 2. Offensive. homosexual. —**fair′y·land,** n.

fairy tale, 1. story, usu. for children, about magical creatures. 2. misleading account.

faith (fāth) n. 1. confidence. 2. religious belief. 3. loyalty.

faith′ful, adj. 1. loyal. 2. having religious belief. 3. copying accurately.

fake (fāk) v., **faked, faking,** n. Informal. —v. 1. counterfeit. —n. 2. thing faked. —adj. 3. deceptive.

fa·kir′ (fə kēr′) n. Muslim or Hindu monk.

fa·la′fel (fə lä′fəl), n. fried ball of ground chickpeas.

fal′con (fôl′kən, fal′-) n. bird of prey. —**fal′con·ry,** n.

fall (fôl) v., **fell** (fel), **fallen, falling,** n. —v. 1. drop. 2. happen. —n. 3. descent. 4. autumn.

fal′la·cy (fal′ə sē) n., pl. **-cies.** 1. false belief. 2. unsound argument. —**fal·la′cious** (fə lā′shəs) adj.

fall guy, Slang. 1. easy victim. 2. scapegoat.

fal′li·ble (fal′ə bəl) adj. liable to error. —**fal·li·bil′i·ty,** n.

fall′ing-out′, n., pl. **fallings-out, falling-out.** quarrel.

fal·lo′pian tube (fə lō′pē ən) either of pair of ducts in female abdomen that transport ova from ovary to uterus. Also, **Fallopian tube.**

fall′out′, n. 1. radioactive particles carried by air. 2. incidental outcome or product.

fal′low (fal′ō) adj. plowed and not seeded.

fallow deer, Eurasian deer with yellowish coat that is white-spotted in summer.

false (fôls) adj., **falser, falsest.** 1. not true. 2. faithless. 3. deceptive. —**false′hood,** n. —**false′ly,** adv. —**fal′si·fy,** v., **-fied, -fying.**

fal·set′to (fôl set′ō) n., pl. **-tos.** unnaturally high voice.

fal′ter (fôl′tər) v. hesitate; waver.

fame (fām) n. widespread reputation; renown. —**famed,** adj.

fa·mil′iar (fə mil′yər) adj. 1. commonly known. 2. intimate. —**fa·mil′i·ar·i·ty** (-ē ar′i tē, -yar′-) n. —**fa·mil′iar·ize,** v., **-ized, -izing.**

fam′i·ly (fam′ə lē, fam′lē) n., pl. **-lies.** 1. parents and their children. 2. relatives. —**fa·mil′ial** (fə mil′yəl) adj.

family tree, genealogical chart of a family.

fam′ine (fam′in) n. scarcity of food.

fam′ish (fam′ish) v. starve.

fa′mous (fā′məs) adj. widely known; renowned.

fa′mous·ly, adv. very well.

fan (fan) n., v., **fanned, fanning.** —n. 1. device for causing current of air. 2. Informal. devotee. —v. 3. blow upon with fan. 4. stir up.

fa·nat′ic (fə nat′ik) n. person excessively devoted to cause. —**fa·nat′i·cal,** adj. —**fa·nat′i·cism** (-ə siz′əm) n.

fan′ci·er (fan′sē ər) n. person interested in something, as dogs.

fan′cy (fan′sē) n., pl. **-cies,** adj., **-cier, -ciest,** v., **-cied, -cying.** —n. 1. imagination. 2. thing imagined. 3. whim. 4. taste. —adj. 5. ornamental. —v. 6. imagine. 7. crave.

fan′cy-free′, adj. free from emotional ties, esp. from love.

fan′cy·work′, n. ornamental needlework.

fan′fare′, n. 1. chorus of trumpets. 2. showy flourish.

fang (fang) n. long, sharp tooth.

fan′ny, n., pl. **-nies.** Informal. buttocks.

fan·ta′sia (fan tā′zhə) n. fanciful musical work.

fan′ta·size′ (-tə sīz′) v., **-sized, -sizing.** have fantasies.

fan·tas′tic (-tas′tik) adj. 1. wonderful and strange. 2. fanciful.

fan′ta·sy (-tə sē, -zē) n., pl. **-sies.** 1. imagination. 2. hallucination.

far (fär) adv., adj., **farther, farthest.** at or to great distance.

far′a·way′ (fär′ə wā′) adj. 1. distant. 2. preoccupied; dreamy.

farce (färs) n. light comedy. —**far′ci·cal,** adj.

fare (fãr) n., v., **fared, faring.** —n. 1. price of travel. 2. food. —v. 3. get along.

Far East, countries of east and southeast Asia.

fare′well′ (fãr′wel′) interj., n., adj. good-by.

far′-fetched′, adj. not reasonable or probable.

far′-flung′, adj. 1. extending over a great distance or wide area. 2. widely distributed.

fa·ri′na (fə rē′nə) n. flour or grain cooked as a cereal.

farm (färm) n. 1. tract of land for agriculture. —v. 2. cultivate land. —**farm′er,** n. —**farm′house′,** n. —**farm′ing,** n. —**farm′yard′,** n.

far′o (fãr′ō) n. gambling game in which players bet on cards.

far′-off′, adj. distant.

far′-out′, *adj. Slang.* extremely un-conventional.

far′-reach′ing, *adj.* of widespread influence.

far′row (far′ō) *n.* **1.** litter of pigs. —*v.* **2.** (of swine) bear.

far′-sight′ed (-sī′tid, -sī′-) *adj.* **1.** seeing distant objects best. **2.** planning for future.

far′ther (fär′t͟hər) *compar.* of **far.** *adv.* **1.** at or to a greater distance. —*adj.* **2.** more distant. **3.** additional. **——Usage.** FARTHER is used to indicate physical distance: *Is it much farther to the hotel?* FURTHER is used to refer to additional time, amount, or abstract ideas: *I would rather not talk about this further.* But both FARTHER and FURTHER are often used for distance of any kind: *Here is the solution; look no farther/further. His study of the novel reaches farther/ further than any earlier one.*

far′thest (-t͟hist) *superl.* of **far.** *adv.* **1.** at or to the greatest distance. —*adj.* **2.** most distant.

fas′ci·nate (fas′ə nāt′) *v.,* **-nated, -nating.** attract irresistibly. —**fas′ci·na′tion,** *n.*

fas′cism (fash′iz əm) *n.* principle of strong undemocratic government. —**fas′cist,** *n., adj.* —**fa·scis′tic,** *adj.*

fash′ion (fash′ən) *n.* **1.** prevailing style. **2.** manner. —*v.* **3.** make. —**fash′ion·a·bly,** *adv.*

fash′ion·a·ble, *adj.* of the latest style. —**fash′ion·a·bly,** *adv.*

fast (fast) *adj.* **1.** quick; swift. **2.** secure. —*adv.* **3.** tightly. **4.** swiftly. —*v.* **5.** abstain from food. —*n.* **6.** such abstinence.

fas′ten (fas′ən) *v.* fix or attach securely. —**fas′ten·er,** *n.*

fast′-food′, *adj.* specializing in food that is prepared and served quickly.

fas·tid′i·ous (fa stid′ē əs, fə-) *adj.* highly critical and demanding.

fast′ness, *n.* fortified place.

fat (fat) *n., adj.,* **fatter, fattest.** —*n.* **1.** greasy substance. —*adj.* **2.** fleshy. —**fat′ty,** *adj.*

fa′tal (fāt′l) *adj.* causing death or ruin. —**fa′tal·ly,** *adv.*

fa′tal·ism, *n.* belief in unchangeable destiny. —**fa′tal·ist,** *n.*

fa·tal′i·ty (fā tal′i tē, fə-) *n., pl.* **-ties. 1.** death by a disaster. **2.** fate.

fate (fāt) *n., v.,* **fated, fating.** —*n.* **1.** destiny. **2.** death or ruin. —*v.* **3.** destine.

fat′ed, *adj.* subject to fate; destined.

fate′ful, *adj.* involving important or disastrous events.

fa′ther (fä′t͟hər) *n.* **1.** male parent.

2. (*cap.*) God. **3.** priest. —**fa′ther·hood,** *n.* —**fa′ther·ly,** *adv.*

fa′ther-in-law′, *n., pl.* **fathers-in-law.** spouse's father.

fa′ther·land, *n.* **1.** one's native country. **2.** land of one's ancestors.

fath′om (fat͟h′əm) *n.* **1.** nautical measure equal to six feet. —*v.* **2.** understand.

fa·tigue′ (fə tēg′) *n., v.,* **-tigued, -tiguing.** —*n.* **1.** weariness. **2.** (*pl.*) military work clothes. —*v.* **3.** weary.

fat′ten, *v.* grow fat or wealthy.

fatty acid, organic acid found in animal and vegetable fats.

fat′u·ous (fach′ō͝o əs) *adj.* foolish or stupid.

fau′cet (fô′sit) *n.* valve for controlling flow of liquids.

fault (fôlt) *n.* defect. —**faul′ty,** *adj.*

faun (fôn) *n.* Roman deity, part man and part goat.

fau′na (fô′nə) *n., pl.* **-nas, -nae** (-nē). animals or animal life of particular region or period.

faux pas′ (fō pä′) social error.

fa′vor (fā′vər) *n.* **1.** kind act. **2.** high regard. —*v.* **3.** prefer. **4.** resemble. —**fa′vor·a·ble,** *adj.*

fa′vor·ite, *n.* **1.** one preferred. **2.** one most likely to win. —*adj.* **3.** preferred.

fa′vor·it·ism (fā′vər ə tiz′əm) *n.* preference shown toward certain persons.

fawn (fôn) *n.* **1.** young deer. —*v.* **2.** seek favor by servility.

fax (faks) *n.* **1.** method of sending documents by telephone. **2.** item sent in this way. —*v.* **3.** send by fax. **4.** communicate with by fax.

faze (fāz) *v.,* **fazed, fazing.** *Informal.* daunt.

FBI, Federal Bureau of Investigation.

FCC, Federal Communications Commission.

FDA, Food and Drug Administration.

FDIC, Federal Deposit Insurance Corporation.

fear (fēr) *n.* **1.** feeling of impending harm. **2.** awe. —*v.* **3.** be afraid of. **4.** hold in awe. —**fear′ful,** *adj.*

fea′si·ble (fē′zə bəl) *adj.* able to be done. —**fea/si·bil′i·ty,** *n.*

feast (fēst) *n.* **1.** sumptuous meal. **2.** religious celebration. —*v.* **3.** provide with or have feast.

feat (fēt) *n.* remarkable deed.

feath′er (fet͟h′ər) *n.* **1.** one of the growths forming bird's plumage.

fea′ture (fē′chər) *n., v.,* **-tured, -turing.** —*n.* **1.** part of face. **2.** prominent part, article, etc. —*v.* **3.** give prominence to.

Feb., February.

Feb·ru·ar·y (feb′rōō er′ē, feb′yōō-) *n., pl.* **-aries** second month of year. **—Pronunciation.** The second pronunciation for FEBRUARY shown above, with the first (r) is replaced by (y), occurs because neighboring sounds that are alike tend to become different. This word also conforms to the pattern (-yōō er′ē) by analogy with the pronunciation of the first month of the year, *January.* Although the pronunciation of FEBRUARY with (y) is often criticized, both pronunciations are used by educated speakers and are considered standard.

fe·ces (fē′sēz) *n.pl.* excrement.

feck·less (fek′lis) *adj.* **1.** incompetent. **2.** irresponsible and lazy.

fe·cund (fē′kund) *adj.* productive.

fed., 1. federal. **2.** federated. **3.** federation.

fed·er·al (fed′ər əl) *adj.* **1.** of states in permanent union. **2.** (*sometimes cap.*) of U.S. government.

fed·er·ate′ (fed′ə rāt′) *v.,* **-ated, -ating.** unite in league.

fe·do·ra (fi dōr′ə) *n.* soft felt hat.

fee (fē) *n.* payment for services, etc.

fee·ble (fē′bəl) *adj.,* **-bler, -blest.** weak. **—fee′bly,** *adv.*

feed (fēd) *v.,* fed (fed), **feeding.** *v.* **1.** give food to. **2.** eat. **—n. 3.** food for livestock. **—feed′er,** *n.*

feed′back′, *n.* **1.** return of part of output of a process to its input. **2.** informative response.

feel (fēl) *v.,* felt (felt), **feeling,** *n. —v.* **1.** perceive or examine by touch. **2.** be conscious of. **3.** have emotions. **—n. 4.** touch.

feel′er, *n.* **1.** proposal or remark designed to elicit opinion or reaction. **2.** organ of touch, as an antenna.

feign (fān) *v.* pretend.

feint (fānt) *n.* **1.** deceptive move. **—v. 2.** make feint.

feist·y (fī′stē) *adj.,* **-ier, -iest.** **1.** full of energy; spirited. **2.** ready to argue or fight; pugnacious.

fe·lic·i·tate′ (fə lis′i tāt′) *v.,* **-tated, -tating.** congratulate.

fe·lic·i·tous (-təs) *adj.* suitable.

fe·lic·i·ty, *n., pl.* **-ties.** happiness.

fe·line (fē′līn) *adj.* **1.** of or like cats. **—n. 2.** animal of the cat family.

fell (fel) *v.* cut or strike down.

fel·low (fel′ō) *n.* **1.** man. **2.** companion. **3.** peer. **4.** member of learned or professional group. **—fel′low·ship′,** *n.*

fel·on (fel′ən) *n.* criminal.

fel·o·ny (fə lō′nē as) *n., pl.* **-nies.** serious crime. **—fe·lo′ni·ous,** *adj.*

felt (felt) *n.* **1.** matted fabric. **—adj. 2.** of felt.

fem., 1. female. **2.** feminine.

fe·male (fē′māl) *adj.* **1.** belonging to sex that has babies. **—n. 2.** female person or animal.

fem·i·nine (fem′ə nin) *adj.* of women. **—fem′i·nin′i·ty,** *n.*

fem·i·nism (-i niz′əm) *n.* support of equal rights for women. **—fem′i·nist,** *adj., n.*

fe·mur (fē′mər) *n.* thigh bone.

fen (fen) *n.* swampy ground; marsh.

fence (fens) *n., v.,* **fenced, fencing. —n. 1.** wall-like enclosure around open area. **2.** person who receives and disposes of stolen goods. **—v. 3.** fight with sword for sport. **4.** sell to a fence.

fend (fend) *v.* ward off.

fend′er, *n.* metal part over automobile wheel.

fen′nel (fen′l) *n.* plant with seeds used for flavoring.

fe·ral (fēr′al, fer′-) *adj.* in a wild state; not tamed.

fer·ment *n.* (fûr′ment) **1.** substance causing fermentation. **2.** agitation. **—v.** (far ment′) **3.** cause or undergo fermentation.

fer·men·ta′tion, *n.* chemical change involving effervescence or decomposition.

fern (fûrn) *n.* nonflowering plant with feathery leaves.

fe·ro·cious (fə rō′shəs) *adj.* savagely fierce. **—fe·roc′i·ty** (fə ros′i·tē) *n.*

fer′ret (fer′it) *n.* **1.** kind of weasel. **—v. 2.** search intensively.

Fer′ris wheel (fer′is) amusement ride consisting of large upright wheel with suspended seats.

fer′rous (fer′əs) *adj.* of or containing iron. Also, **fer′ric** (ik).

fer′ry (fer′ē) *n., pl.* **-ries,** *v.,* **-ried, -rying. —n. 1.** Also, **fer′ry·boat′.** boat making short crossings. **2.** place where ferries operate. **—v. 3.** carry or pass in ferry.

fer′tile (fûr′tl) *adj.* **1.** producing abundantly. **2.** able to bear young.

fer′ti·lize′ *v.* **1.** make new life begin. **2.** make fertile. **—fer′ti·li·za′tion,** *n.* **—fer′ti·liz′er,** *n.*

fer′vent (fûr′vənt) *adj.* ardent; passionate. **—fer′ven·cy, fer′vor,** *n.*

fer′vid (-vid) *adj.* vehement.

fes′ter (fes′tər) *v.* **1.** generate pus. **2.** rankle.

fes′ti·val (fes′tə vəl) *n.* celebration. Also, **fes·tiv′i·ty** (-tiv′i·tē) *n.* **fes′tive,** *adj.* **—fes′tive·ly,** *adv.*

fes·toon′ (fe stōōn′) n. **1.** garland hung between two points. —v. **2.** adorn with festoons.

fet′a (fet′a) n. Greek cheese usu. from sheep's or goat's milk.

fetch (fech) v. go and bring.

fetch′ing, adj. attractive.

fete (fāt, fet) n., v., **feted, feting.** —n. **1.** festival. **2.** party. —v. **3.** honor with a fete.

fet′id (fet′id) adj. stinking.

fe′tish (fet′ish, fē′tish) n. object worshiped. —**fet′ish·ism,** n.

fet′lock (fet′lok′) n. **1.** part of horse's leg behind hoof. **2.** tuft of hair on this part.

fet′ter (fet′ər) n. **1.** shackle for feet. **2.** (pl.) anything that restrains. —v. **3.** put fetters on. **4.** restrain.

fet′tle (fet′l) n. condition.

fe′tus (fē′təs) n. unborn offspring. —**fe′tal,** adj.

feud (fyōōd) n. **1.** lasting hostility. —v. **2.** engage in feud.

feu′dal·ism (fyōōd′l iz′əm) n. system by which land is held in return for service. —**feu′dal,** adj.

fe′ver (fē′vər) n. **1.** high body temperature. **2.** intense nervous excitement. —**fe′ver·ish,** adj.

few (fyōō) adj., n. not many. —**Usage.** See LESS.

fey (fā) adj. **1.** strange; whimsical. **2.** supernatural; enchanted.

fez (fez) n., pl. **fezzes.** cone-shaped felt hat.

ff, folios. **2.** (and the following (pages, verses, etc.).

FG, field goal(s).

fi·an·cé′ (fē′än sā′, fē än′sā) n. betrothed man. —**fi·an·cée′,** n.fem.

fi·as′co (fē as′kō) n., pl. **-cos, -coes.** failure.

fi′at (fē′ät, fī′ät) n. decree.

fib (fib) n., v., **fibbed, fibbing.** —n. **1.** mild lie. —v. **2.** tell a fib.

fi′ber (fī′bər) n. **1.** threadlike piece, esp. one that can be worn. **2.** any of the threadlike structures that form plant or animal tissue. **3.** roughage. Also, **fi′bre.** —**fi′brous,** adj. —**fi′broid,** adj.

fi′ber·glass′, n. material composed of fine glass fibers.

fiber optics, technology of sending light and images through glass or plastic fibers. —**fi′ber·op′tic,** adj.

fib′ril·la′tion (fib′rə lā′shən), n. abnormally fast and irregular heartbeat. —**fib′ril·late,** v.

fib′u·la (fib′yə lə) n., pl. **-lae** (-lē), **-las.** outer thinner bone from knee to ankle.

FICA (fī′kə, fē′-) Federal Insurance Contributions Act.

fiche (fēsh) n. microfiche.

fick′le (fik′əl) adj. inconstant.

fic′tion (fik′shən) n. **1.** narrative of imaginary events. **2.** something made up. —**fic′tion·al,** adj.

fic·ti′tious (-tish′əs) adj. false.

fid′dle (fid′l) n., v., **-dled, -dling.** —n. **1.** violin. —v. **2.** play tunes on violin. **3.** move hands nervously.

fid′dle·sticks′, interj. (exclamation of impatience, disbelief, etc.).

fi·del′i·ty (fi del′i tē, fī-) n., pl. **-ties.** faithfulness.

fidg′et (fij′it) v. **1.** move restlessly. —n. **2.** (pl.) restlessness.

fi·du·ci·ar′y (-shē er′ē) adj., n., pl. **-ies.** —adj. **1.** being a trustee. **2.** held in trust. —n. **3.** trustee.

field (fēld) n. **1.** open ground. **2.** area of interest.

field day, 1. day for outdoor sports or contests. **2.** chance for unrestricted enjoyment.

fiend (fēnd) n. **1.** devil. **2.** cruel person. **3.** Informal. addict; fan. —**fiend′ish,** adj.

fierce (fērs) adj., **fiercer, fiercest.** **1.** wild; violent. —**fierce′ly,** adv.

fi′er·y (fī′ə rē, fī′rē) adj., **-ier, -iest. 1.** of or like fire. **2.** ardent.

fi·es′ta (fē es′tə) n. festival.

fife (fīf) n. high-pitched flute.

fif′teen′ (fif′tēn′) n., adj. ten plus five. —**fif·teenth′,** adj., n.

fifth (fifth) adj. **1.** next after fourth. —n. **2.** fifth part.

fifth column, traitorous group within a country.

fifth wheel, one that is unnecessary or unwanted.

fif′ty (fif′tē) n., adj. ten times five. —**fif′ti·eth,** adj., n.

fig (fig) n. fruit of semitropical tree.

fig. **1.** figurative. **2.** figuratively. **3.** figure.

fight (fīt) n., v., **fought, fighting.** battle or argue. —**fight′er,** n.

fig′ment (fig′mənt) n. something imagined.

fig′ur·a·tive (-yər ə tiv) adj. not literal. —**fig′ur·a·tive·ly,** adv.

fig′ure, n., v., **-ured, -uring.** —n. **1.** written symbol, esp. numerical. **2.** amount. **3.** shape. —v. **4.** calculate. **5.** be prominent.

fig′ure·head′, n. powerless leader.

figure of speech, use of words in nonliteral sense.

fig′ur·ine′ (-yə rēn′) n. miniature statue.

fil′a·ment (fil′ə mənt) n. fine fiber.

fil′bert (fil′bərt) n. kind of hazelnut.

filch (filch) v. steal.

file (fīl) n., v., **filed, filing.** —n. **1.** storage place for documents. **2.** line of persons, etc. **3.** metal rubbing tool. —v. **4.** arrange or keep in file. **5.** march in file. **6.** rub with file.

fil·i·al (fil′ē al) adj. befitting sons and daughters.

fil·i·bus·ter (fil′ə bus′tər) n. **1.** delay of legislation by long speeches. —v. **2.** use filibuster to impede legislation.

fil·i·gree′ (-i grē′) n. ornamental work of fine wires.

Fil·i·pi·no (fil′ə pēnō) n. native of the Philippines.

fill (fil) v. **1.** make full. **2.** pervade. **3.** supply. —n. **4.** full supply.

fil·let (fi lā′) n. narrow strip, esp. of meat or fish. Also, **fi′let.**

fil·lip (fil′əp) n. thing that excites.

fil·ly (fil′ē) n., pl. **-lies.** young female horse.

film (film) n. **1.** thin coating. **2.** roll or sheet with photographically sensitive coating. **3.** motion picture. —v. **4.** make motion picture of.

film′strip′, n. length of film containing still pictures for projecting on screen.

film′y, adj., **-ier, -iest. 1.** partly transparent. **2.** blurred.

fil·ter (fil′tər) n. **1.** device for straining substances. —v. **2.** remove by or pass through filter. —**fil·tra′tion,** n.

filth (filth) n. **1.** dirt. **2.** obscenity; offensive indecency. —**filth′y,** adj.

fin (fin) n. winglike organ on fishes.

fi·na·gle (fi nā′gal) v., **-gled, -gling.** practice or obtain by trickery.

fi·nal (fīn′l) adj. last. —**fi′nal·ist,** n. —**fi·nal′i·ty** (fi nal′i tē) n. —**fi′nal·ize′,** v., **-ized, -izing.**

fi·na·le (fi nä′lē) n. last part.

fi·nance (fi nans′, fī′nans) n., v., **-nanced, -nancing.** —n. **1.** money matters. **2.** (pl.) funds. —v. **3.** supply with money. —**fi·nan′cial,** adj.

fin·an·cier′ (fin′ən sēr′, fī′nən-) n. professional money handler.

finch (finch) n. small songbird.

find (fīnd) v., **found** (found), **finding,** n. —v. **1.** come upon. **2.** learn. —n. **3.** discovery.

fine (fīn) adj., **finer, finest,** n., v., **fined, fining.** —adj. **1.** excellent. **2.** delicate; thin. —n. **3.** money exacted as penalty. —v. **4.** subject to fine.

fine art, (usually pl.) painting, sculpture, etc., created primarily for beauty.

fin·er·y, n. showy dress.

fi·nesse′ (fi ness′) n. delicacy of performance or skill.

fin′ger (fing′gər) n. **1.** one of five parts on end of hand. **2.** touch with fingers. —**fin′ger·nail′,** n. —**fin′ger·tip,** n.

fin′ger·print′, n. **1.** impression of markings of surface of finger, used for identification. —v. **2.** take or record fingerprints of.

fin′ick·y (fin′i kē) adj., **-ier, -iest.** fussy. Also, **fin′ic·al.**

fi′nis (fin′is, fē nē′, fī′nis) n. end.

fin′ish (fin′ish) v. **1.** end. **2.** perfect. **3.** give desired surface to. —n. **4.** completion. **5.** surface coating or treatment.

fi′nite (fī′nīt) adj. having bounds or limits. —**fi′nite·ly,** adv.

Finn (fin) n. native of Finland.

Finn′ish (fin′ish) n. **1.** language of Finland. —adj. **2.** of Finland, the Finns, or Finnish.

fiord (fyôrd, fē ôrd′) n. narrow arm of sea. Also, **fjord.**

fir (fûr) n. cone-bearing evergreen tree.

fire (fīᵉr) n., v., **fired, firing.** —n. **1.** burning. **2.** ardor. **3.** discharge of firearms. —v. **4.** set on fire. **5.** discharge. **6.** Informal. gun.

fire′arm′, n. gun.

fire′bomb′, n. **1.** incendiary bomb. —v. **2.** attack with firebombs.

fire′crack′er, n. small firework that makes a noise.

fire′fight′er, n. person who fights destructive fires.

fire′fly′, n., pl. **-flies.** nocturnal beetle that produces light.

fire′man (fīr′mən) n., pl. **-men. 1.** firefighter. **2.** stoker.

fire′place′, n. semiopen place for fire.

fire′plug′, n. hydrant with water for fighting fires.

fire′proof′, adj. safe against fire.

fire′side′, n. area close to fireplace.

fire′trap′, n. dilapidated building.

fire′works′, n.pl. devices ignited for display of light.

firm (fûrm) adj. **1.** hard or stiff. **2.** fixed. **3.** resolute. —v. **4.** make or become firm. —n. **5.** business organization.

fir′ma·ment (fûr′mə mənt) n. sky.

first (fûrst) adj., adv. **1.** before all others. —n. **2.** first thing, etc.

first aid, emergency treatment.

first class, 1. highest class or grade. **2.** most expensive class in travel. **3.** class of mail sealed against inspection. —**first′-class′,** adj.

first′hand′, adj., adv. from the first or original source.

first′-rate′, adj. **1.** of the highest quality. —adv. **2.** very well.

fis′cal (fis′kəl) adj. financial.

fish (fish) n., pl. **fish, fishes,** —n. **1.** cold-blooded aquatic verte-

brate. —*v.* **2.** try to catch fish.
—**fish′er·man**, *n.* —**fish′er·y**, *n.*

fish′y, *adj.*, **-ier**, **-iest**. **1.** like a fish, esp. in taste or smell. **2.** questionable; dubious. —**fish′i·ness**, *n.*

fis′sion (fish′ən) *n.* division into parts. —**fis′sion·a·ble**, *adj.*

fis′sure (fish′ər) *n.* narrow opening caused by break; crack.

fist (fist) *n.* closed hand.

fist′ful (-fŏŏl) *n.*, *pl.* **fuls**. handful.

fist′i·cuffs′ (-i kufs′) *n.pl.* fight with the fists.

fit (fit) *adj.*, **fitter**, **fittest**, *v.*, **fitted**, **fitting**, *n.* —*adj.* **1.** suitable. **2.** healthy. —*v.* **3.** be or make suitable. **4.** equip. —*n.* **5.** manner of fitting. **6.** sudden attack of illness or emotion. —**fit′ness**, *n.*

fit′ful, *adj.* irregular.

fit′ting, *adj.* **1.** appropriate. —*n.* **2.** attached part. **3.** trial of new clothes, etc., for fit.

five (fīv) *n.*, *adj.* four plus one.

fix (fiks) *v.* **1.** make fast or steady. **2.** repair. **3.** prepare.

fix·a′tion (fik sā′shən) *n.* obsession.

fixed, *adj.* not changing.

fix′ings, *n.pl. Informal.* things accompanying main item.

fix′ture (-chər) *n.* thing fixed in place.

fizz (fiz) *v.*, *n.* hiss.

fiz′zle (fiz′əl) *v.*, **-zled**, **-zling**, *n.* —*v.* **1.** hiss weakly. **2.** *Informal.* fail. —*n.* **3.** act of fizzling.

fjord (fyôrd, fē ôrd′) *n.* fiord.

FL, Florida.

fl., **1.** (he or she) flourished. **2.** fluid.

Fla., Florida.

flab (flab) *n.* loose, excessive flesh.

flab′ber·gast′ (flab′ər gast′) *v. Informal.* astound.

flab′by (flab′ē) *adj.*, **-bier**, **-biest**. not firm. —**flab′bi·ness**, *n.*

flac′cid (flak′sid, flas′id) *adj.* flabby.

flag (flag) *n.*, *v.*, **flagged**, **flagging**. —*n.* **1.** cloth with symbolic colors or design. **2.** plant with long narrow leaves. **3.** Also, **flag′stone′**. paving stone. —*v.* **4.** signal with flags (def. 1). **5.** lose vigor, energy, etc.

flag′el·late′ (flaj′ə lāt′) *v.*, **-lated**, **-lating**. whip; flog.

flag′on (flag′ən) *n.* large bottle.

fla′grant (flā′grənt) *adj.* glaring.

flag′ship′, *n.* ship of commander.

flail (flāl) *n.* **1.** hand instrument for threshing grain. —*v.* **2.** strike or strike at as with flail.

flair (flâr) *n.* aptitude; talent.

flak (flak) *n.* **1.** antiaircraft fire. **2.** critical or hostile reaction.

flake (flāk) *n.*, *v.*, **flaked**, **flaking**. —*n.* **1.** small thin piece. —*v.* **2.** separate into flakes.

flak′y, *adj.*, **-ier**, **-iest**. **1.** of or like flakes. **2.** lying or coming off in flakes. **3.** *Slang.* eccentric; odd.

flam·bé (fläm bā′) *adj.* served in flaming liquor.

flam′boy·ant (flam boi′ənt) *adj.* showy; colorful.

flame (flām) *n.*, *v.*, **flamed**, **flaming**. blaze.

fla·men′co (flə meng′kō) *n.* Spanish gypsy dance and music style.

fla·min′go (flə ming′gō) *n.*, *pl.* **-gos**, **-goes**. tall, red, aquatic bird.

flam′ma·ble (flam′ə bəl) *adj.* easily set on fire. —**flam′ma·bil′i·ty**, *n.*

flange (flanj) *n.* projecting rim.

flank (flangk) *n.* **1.** side. —*v.* **2.** be at side of. **3.** pass around side of.

flan′nel (flan′l) *n.* soft wool fabric.

flap (flap) *v.*, **flapped**, **flapping**, *n.* —*v.* **1.** swing loosely and noisily. **2.** move up and down. —*n.* **3.** flapping movement. **4.** something flat hanging loosely. **5.** *Informal.* emotionally agitated state.

flare (flâr) *v.*, **flared**, **flaring**, *n.* —*v.* **1.** suddenly become brighter or excited. **2.** spread outward. —*n.* **3.** signal fire.

flare′up′, *n.* sudden outburst or outbreak.

flash (flash) *n.* **1.** brief light. **2.** instant. **3.** news dispatch. —*v.* **4.** gleam suddenly.

flash′back′, *n.* **1.** earlier event inserted out of order in a story. **2.** sudden recollection of a past event.

flash′bulb′, *n.* bulb giving burst of light for photography.

flash′light′, *n.* portable battery-powered light.

flash′y, *adj.*, **-ier**, **-iest**. showy.

flask (flask) *n.* kind of bottle.

flat (flat) *adj.*, **flatter**, **flattest**, *n.* —*adj.* **1.** level. **2.** horizontal. **3.** not thick. **4.** absolute. **5.** dull. **6.** below musical pitch. —*n.* **7.** something flat. **8.** apartment. —**flat′ten**, *v.*

flat′bed′, *n.* truck with trailer platform open on all sides.

flat′car′, *n.* railroad car without sides or top.

flat′fish′, *n.* fish with broad, flat body, as flounder.

flat′foot′, *n.*, *pl.* **-feet** for 1, **-foots** for 2. **1.** flattened condition of arch of foot. **2.** *Slang.* police officer.

flat′out′, *adj. Informal.* **1.** using full speed, resources, etc. **2.** downright.

flub

flat/ter (flat/ər) v. praise insincerely. —**flat/ter·y,** n.

flat/u·lent (flach/ə lənt) adj. **1.** having an accumulation of gas in the intestines. **2.** inflated and empty; pompous. —**flat/u·lence,** n.

flat/ware', n. table utensils.

flaunt (flônt) v. display boldly.

fla/vor (flā/vər) n. **1.** taste. —v. **2.** give flavor to. —**fla/vor·ing,** n.

flaw (flô) n. defect. —**flawed,** adj.

flax (flaks) n. linen plant. —**flax/-en,** adj.

flay (flā) v. strip skin from.

flea (flē) n. small, bloodsucking insect.

flea market, market, often outdoors, where used articles, antiques, etc., are sold.

fleck (flek) n. **1.** speck. —v. **2.** spot.

fledg/ling (flej/ling) n. young bird.

flee (flē) v., **fled** (fled), **fleeing.** run away from.

fleece (flēs) n., v., **fleeced, fleecing.** —n. **1.** wool of sheep. —v. **2.** swindle. —**fleec/y,** adj.

fleet (flēt) n. **1.** organized group of ships, aircraft, or road vehicles. —adj. **2.** swift.

fleet/ing, adj. temporary.

flesh (flesh) n. **1.** muscle and fat of animal body. **2.** body. **3.** soft part of fruit or vegetable. —**flesh/y,** adj.

flesh/pot', n. place of unrestrained pleasure.

flex (fleks) v. bend.

flex/i·ble, adj. **1.** capable of bending. **2.** adaptable.

flick (flik) n. **1.** light stroke. —v. **2.** strike lightly.

flick/er, v. **1.** glow unsteadily. —n. **2.** unsteady light.

fli/er (flī/ər) n. aviator.

flight (flīt) n. **1.** act or power of flying. **2.** trip through air. **3.** series of steps. **4.** hasty departure.

flight/less, adj. incapable of flying.

flight/y, adj., **-ier, -iest.** frivolous.

flim/sy (flim/zē) adj., **-sier, -siest.** weak or thin. —**flim/si·ness,** n.

flinch (flinch) v. shrink; wince.

fling (fling) v., **flung** (flung), **flinging.** n. —v. **1.** throw violently. —n. **2.** act of flinging.

flint (flint) n. hard stone that strikes sparks. —**flint/y,** adj.

flip (flip) v., **flipped, flipping,** n., adj., **flipper, flippest.** —v. **1.** move with sudden stroke. **2.** turn over with sudden stroke. —n. **3.** such movement. —adj. **4.** flippant.

flip/-flop', n. **1.** sudden reversal, as of opinion. **2.** backward somersault.

flip/pant (flip/ənt) adj. pert; disrespectful. —**flip/pan·cy,** n.

flip/per, n. broad flat limb for swimming.

flirt (flûrt) v. **1.** act amorously without serious intentions. —n. **2.** person who flirts. —**flir·ta/tion,** n. —**flir·ta/tious,** adj.

flit (flit) v., **flitted, flitting.** move swiftly and lightly.

float (flōt) v. **1.** rest or move on or in liquid, air, etc. —n. **2.** something that floats. **3.** decorated parade wagon. —**flo·ta/tion,** n.

flock (flok) n. **1.** group of animals. —v. **2.** gather in flock.

floe (flō) n. field of floating ice.

flog (flog) v., **flogged, flogging.** beat; whip.

flood (flud) n. **1.** overflowing of water. —v. **2.** overflow or cover with water, etc.

flood/light', n. artificial light for large area.

floor (flôr) n. **1.** bottom surface of room, etc. **2.** level in building. **3.** right to speak. —v. **4.** furnish with floor. **5.** knock down.

floor/ing, n. floor covering.

flop (flop) v., **flopped, flopping,** n. Informal. —v. **1.** fall heavily. **2.** fail. —n. **3.** flap. —n. **4.** act of flopping.

flop/py, adj. **-pier, -piest.** limp.

floppy disk, thin plastic disk for storing computer data.

flo/ra (flôr/ə) n., pl. **floras, florae** (flôr/ē). plants or plant life of a particular region or period.

flo/ral, adj. of flowers.

flor/id (flôr/id) adj. ruddy.

flo/rist, n. dealer in flowers.

floss (flôs) n. **1.** silky fiber from certain plants. **2.** thread used to clean between teeth. —v. **3.** use dental floss. —**floss/y,** adj.

flo·til/la (flō til/ə) n. small fleet.

flot/sam (flot/səm) n. floating wreckage.

flounce (flouns) v., **flounced, flouncing.** n. —v. **1.** go with exaggerated movements. —n. **2.** flouncing movement. **3.** ruffle.

floun/der (floun/dər) v. **1.** struggle clumsily. —n. **2.** flat edible fish.

flour (flou²r, flou²ər) n. finely ground grain.

flour/ish (flûr/ish) v. **1.** thrive. **2.** brandish. —n. **3.** act of brandishing. **4.** decoration.

flout (flout) v. mock; scorn.

flow (flō) v. **1.** move in stream. —n. **2.** act or rate of flowing.

flow chart, chart showing steps in procedure or system.

flow/er (flou/ər) n., v. blossom.

flu (flōō) n. influenza.

flub (flub) v., **flubbed, flubbing.** botch; bungle.

fluc/tu•ate/ (fluk/chŏŏ āt/) v., -ated, -ating. vary irregularly.

flue (flŏŏ) n. duct for smoke, etc.

flu/ent (flŏŏ/ənt) adj. writing and speaking with ease. —**flu/en•cy,** n.

fluff (fluf) n. downy particles.

flu/id (flŏŏ/id) n. 1. substance that flows. —adj. 2. liquid or gaseous.

fluke (flŏŏk) n. 1. lucky chance. 2. flounder (def. 2).

flume (flŏŏm) n. channel; trough.

flunk (flungk) v. Informal. fail, esp. in a course or examination.

flun/ky, n., pl. -kies. servant or follower.

fluo•res/cence (flŏŏ res/əns, flô) n. emission of light upon exposure to radiation, etc. —**fluo•res/cent,** adj.

fluorescent lamp, tubular lamp using phosphors to produce radiation of light.

fluor/i•da/tion (flŏŏr/i dā/shən, flôr/-) n. addition of fluorides to drinking water to reduce tooth decay.

fluor/ide/ (-īd) n. chemical compound containing fluorine.

fluor/ine (-ēn) n. yellowish toxic gaseous element.

flur/ry (flûr/ē) n., pl. -ries. 1. light snowfall. 2. agitated state.

flush (flush) n. 1. rosy glow. —v. 2. redden. 3. wash out with water. —adj. 4. even with surrounding surface. 5. well supplied.

flus/ter (flus/tər) v. confuse.

flute (flŏŏt) n., v., **fluted, fluting.** —n. 1. musical wind instrument. 2. groove. —v. 3. form grooves in.

flut/ist (flŏŏ/tist) n. flute player. Also, **flau/tist** (flô/tist, flou/-).

flut/ter (flut/ər) v. 1. wave in air. —n. 2. agitation. —**flut/tery,** adj.

flux (fluks) n. 1. a flowing. 2. continuous change. 3. substance that promotes fusion of metals.

fly (flī) v., **flew** (flŏŏ), **flown** (flōn), **flying,** n., pl. **flies.** —v. 1. move or direct through air. 2. move swiftly. —n. 3. winged insect. —**fly/er,** n.

fly/-blown/, adj. tainted; spoiled.

fly/-by-night/, adj. unreliable.

flying saucer, disk-shaped missile or plane, thought to come from outer space.

fly/leaf/, n., pl. -**leaves.** blank page in front or back of a book.

fly/wheel/, n. wheel for equalizing speed of machinery.

foal (fōl) n. young horse.

foam (fōm) n. 1. mass of tiny bubbles. —v. 2. form foam.

foam rubber, spongy rubber used esp. in cushions.

fob (fob) n. watch chain.

fo/cus (fō/kəs) n., pl. -**cuses, -ci** (-sī), v., -**cused, -cusing.** —n. 1. point at which refracted rays meet. 2. state of sharpness for image from optical device. 3. central point. —v. 4. bring into focus. —**fo/cal,** adj.

fod/der (fod/ər) n. livestock food.

foe (fō) n. enemy.

fog (fog) n., v., **fogged, fog•ging.** —n. 1. thick mist. 2. mental confusion. —v. 3. make or become enveloped with fog. —**fog/gy,** adj.

fo/gy (fō/gē) n., pl. -**gies.** old-fashioned person.

foi/ble (foi/bəl) n. weak point.

foil (foil) v. 1. frustrate. —n. 2. thin metallic sheet. 3. thing that sets off another by contrast. 4. thin sword.

foist (foist) v. impose unjustifiably.

fold (fōld) v. 1. bend over upon itself. 2. wrap. 3. collapse. —n. 4. folded part. 5. enclosure for sheep.

-fold, suffix meaning: 1. having so many parts, as a fourfold plan. 2. times as many, as to increase tenfold.

fold/er, n. 1. folded printed sheet. 2. outer cover.

fo/li•age (fō/lē ij) n. leaves.

folic acid (fō/lik, fol/ik) vitamin used in treating anemia.

fo/li•o/ (fō/lē ō/) n., pl. -**ios.** sheet of paper folded once.

folk (fōk) n., pl. **folk** or **folks.** 1. people. —adj. 2. of or from the common people.

folk/lore/, n. customs and beliefs of common people.

folk/lor/ist, n. expert on folklore.

folk song, song originating among the common people.

folk/sy, adj., -**sier, -siest.** Informal. suggesting simple simplicity.

fol/li•cle (fol/i kəl) n. 1. seed vessel. 2. small cavity, sac, or gland.

fol/low (fol/ō) v. 1. come or go after. 2. pursue. 3. conform to. 4. move along. 5. watch or understand. 6. result.

fol/low•er, n. 1. person who follows. 2. disciple.

fol/low•ing, n. group of admirers or disciples.

fol/low-through/, n. 1. last part of a motion, as after a ball has been struck. 2. act of continuing a plan, program, etc., to completion.

fol/ly (fol/ē) n., pl. -**lies.** foolishness.

fo•ment/ (fō ment/) v. foster.

fond (fond) adj. 1. having affection. 2. foolish. —**fond/ly,** adv.

fon/dant (fon/dənt) n. sugar paste used in candies.

fon•dle (fon′dl) v., -dled, -dling. caress.

fon•due′ (fon dōō′, -dyōō′) n. dip of melted cheese, liquor, and seasonings.

font (font) n. **1.** receptacle for baptismal water. **2.** printing type style.

food (fōōd) n. what is taken in for nourishment.

food processor, appliance for chopping, shredding or otherwise processing food.

fool (fōōl) n. **1.** person acting stupidly. —v. **2.** trick. **3.** act frivolously. —**fool′ish,** adj.

fool′har′dy, adj., -dier, -diest. rash.

fool′proof′, adj. proof against misuse or mistake.

foot (fōōt) n., pl. **feet** (fēt), v. —n. **1.** part of leg on which body stands. **2.** unit of length equal to 12 inches. **3.** lowest part. **4.** group of syllables. —v. **5.** pay. —**foot′print′,** n.

foot′ball′, n. game played with pointed leather ball.

foot′hill′, n. hill at foot of mountains.

foot′hold′, n. secure place for foot to rest.

foot′ing, n. **1.** secure position. **2.** basis for relationship.

foot′less, adj. having no basis.

foot′lights′, n.pl. **1.** lights at the front of a stage floor. **2.** acting.

foot′lock′er, n. small trunk.

foot′loose′, adj. free to go or travel about.

foot′man, n. male servant.

foot′note′, n. note at foot of page.

foot′-pound′, n. work done by force of one pound moving through distance of one foot.

foot′step′, n. sound of walking.

foot′stool′, n. low stool for resting the feet.

fop (fop) n. overdressed man.

for (fôr; unstressed fər) prep. **1.** with the purpose of. **2.** in the interest of. **3.** in place of. **4.** in favor of. **5.** during. —conj. **6.** because.

for′age (fôr′ij) n., v., -aged, -aging. —n. **1.** food for animals. —v. **2.** search for supplies.

for′ay (fôr′ā) n. **1.** raid. **2.** venture.

for•bear′ (fôr bâr′) v., -bore (-bôr′), -borne (-bôrn′), -bearing. **1.** refrain from. **2.** be patient.

for•bid′ (fər bid′) v., -bade (-bad′, -bād′) or -bad, -bidden or -bid, -bidding. give order against.

for•bid′ding, adj. intimidating or discouraging.

force (fôrs) n., v., forced, forcing. —n. **1.** strength. **2.** coercion. **3.**

armed group. **4.** influence. —v. **5.** compel. **6.** make yield.

for′ceps (fôr′səps, -seps) n. medical tool for seizing and holding.

for′ci•ble (fôr′sə bəl) adj. by means of force. —**for′ci•bly,** adv.

ford (fôrd) n. **1.** place for crossing water by wading. —v. **2.** cross at ford. —**ford′a•ble,** adj.

fore (fôr) adj., adv. **1.** at the front. **2.** earlier. —n. **3.** front.

fore-, prefix meaning: **1.** before, as forewarn. **2.** front, as forehead. **3.** preceding, as forefather. **4.** chief, as foreman.

fore′arm′, n. arm between elbow and wrist.

fore′bear′, n. ancestor.

fore•bode′, v., -boded, -boding. portend.

fore′cast′, v., -cast, -casting, n. —v. **1.** predict. —n. **2.** prediction.

fore′cas•tle (fōk′səl, fôr′kas′əl) n. forward part of vessel's upper deck.

fore•close′ (-klōz′) v., -closed, -closing. deprive of the right to redeem (mortgage, etc.).

fore′fa′ther, n. ancestor. —**fore′mother,** n.fem.

fore′fin′ger, n. finger next to thumb.

fore′front′, n. foremost place.

fore•go′ing, adj. previous.

fore′gone′ conclusion, inevitable result.

fore′ground′, n. nearest area.

fore′hand′, n. in sports, stroke made with palm of hand facing direction of movement. —**fore′hand′,** adj.

fore′head (fôr′id, fôr′hed′) n. part of face above eyes.

for′eign (fôr′in) adj. **1.** of or from another country. **2.** from outside.

fore′man -wom′an or **-per′son** n., pl. **-men** or **-women** or **-persons.** person in charge of work crew or jury.

fore′most′, adj., adv. first.

fore′noon′, n. daylight time before noon.

fo•ren′sic (fə ren′sik) adj. of or for public discussion or courtroom procedure.

fore′play′, n. sexual stimulation leading to intercourse.

fore′run′ner, n. predecessor.

fore•see′, v., -saw, -seen, -seeing. see beforehand. —**fore′sight′,** n.

fore•shad′ow, v. indicate beforehand.

fore′skin′, n. skin on end of penis.

for′est (fôr′ist) n. land covered with trees. —**for′est•ry,** n.

fore•stall′, v. thwart by earlier action.

for·est·a'tion (fôr'ə stā'shən) n. planting of forests.

forest ranger, officer who supervises care of forests.

fore·tell', v., **-told, -telling.** predict.

fore'thought' n. prudence.

fore·ev'er (fôr ev'ər, fər-) adv. always.

fore·warn', v. warn in good time.

fore'word' n. introduction.

for·feit (fôr'fit) n. **1.** penalty. —v. **2.** lose as forfeit. —adj. **3.** forfeited.

for·gath·er, v. assemble.

forge (fôrj) n., v., **forged, forging.** —n. **1.** place for heating and shaping metal. —v. **2.** form by heating and hammering. **3.** imitate fraudulently. **4.** press ahead. —**for'ger·y,** n.

for·get' (far get') v., **-got** (-got'), **-gotten, -getting.** fail to remember. —**for·get'ful,** adj.

for·get'-me-not', n. small plant with blue flowers.

for·give' (far giv') v., **-gave** (-gāv'), **-given, -giving.** grant pardon.

for·go' (fôr gō') v., **-went** (-went'), **-gone** (-gon'), **-going.** do without.

fork (fôrk) n. **1.** pronged instrument. **2.** point of division. —v. **3.** branch.

fork'lift', n. vehicle with two power-operated prongs for lifting heavy weights.

for·lorn' (fôr lôrn') adj. abandoned.

form (fôrm) n. **1.** shape. **2.** mold. **3.** custom; standard practice. **4.** document to be filled in. —v. **5.** shape.

for·mal (fôr'məl) adj. **1.** according to custom or standard practice. **2.** ceremonious. **3.** precisely stated. —**for'mal·ize',** v.

form·al'de·hyde (fôr mal'də hīd', far-) n. solution used as disinfectant and preservative.

for·mal'i·ty (-mal'i tē) n., pl. **-ties. 1.** accordance with custom. **2.** act done as matter of standard practice.

for·mat (fôr'mat) n., v., **-matted, -matting.** —n. **1.** general arrangement. —v. **2.** prepare (a computer disk) for writing and reading.

for·ma'tion (fôr mā'shən) n. **1.** act of forming. **2.** material that forms. **3.** pattern of ships, aircraft, etc., moving together.

form'a·tive (fôr'mə tiv) adj. **1.** giving or acquiring form. **2.** relating to formation and development.

for·mer (fôr'mər) adj. **1.** earlier. **2.** first-mentioned. —**for'mer·ly,** adv.

for·mi·da·ble (fôr'mi də bəl) adj. awesome. —**for'mi·da·bly,** adv.

form letter, standardized letter that can be sent to many people.

for'mu·la (fôr'myə lə) n., pl. **-las, -lae** (-lē'). **1.** scientific description in figures and symbols. **2.** set form of words. **3.** milk mixture for baby.

for'mu·late' (fôr'myə lāt') v., **-lated, -lating. 1.** state systematically. **2.** devise.

for·ni·cate' (fôr'ni kāt') v., **-cated, -cating.** have illicit sexual relations.

for·sake' (fôr sāk') v., **-sook** (-sŏŏk'), **-saken, -saking.** desert.

for·swear', v., **-swore, -sworn, -swearing. 1.** renounce. **2.** perjure.

for·syth'i·a (fôr sith'ē ə, far-) n. shrub bearing yellow flowers.

fort (fôrt) n. fortified place.

forte (fôrt) n. **1.** one's strong point. —adv. (fôr'tā). **2.** Music. loudly. —**Pronunciation.** In the noun sense (She draws pretty well, but sculpture is really her forte), the established, traditional pronunciation of FORTE is with one syllable: (fôrt). However, the two-syllable pronunciation (fôr'tā), which is correct for the adverb (a musical term borrowed from Italian), is increasingly heard for the noun as well, and is now also considered standard.

forth (fôrth) adv. onward.

forth'com'ing, adj. about to appear.

forth'right', adj. direct in manner or speech.

forth'with', adv. at once.

for'ti·fi·ca'tion (fôr'tə fi kā'shən) n. defensive military construction.

for'ti·fy' (fôr'tə fī') v., **-fied, -fying.** strengthen.

for·tis'si·mo' (fôr tis'ə mō') adj., adv. Music. very loud.

for'ti·tude' (fôr'ti tōōd', -tyōōd') n. patient courage.

fort'night', n. two weeks.

FORTRAN (fôr'tran) n. computer programming language used esp. for solving problems in science and engineering.

for'tress (fôr'tris) n. fortified place.

for·tu'i·tous (fôr tōō'i təs, -tyōō'-) adj. **1.** accidental. **2.** lucky.

for'tu·nate (fôr'chə nit) adj. lucky. —**for'tu·nate·ly,** adv.

for'tune, n. **1.** wealth. **2.** luck.

for'tune-tell'er, n. person who claims to read the future.

for'ty (fôr'tē) n., adj. ten times four. —**for'ti·eth,** adj., n.

fo'rum (fôr'əm) n. assembly for public discussion.

for'ward (fôr'wərd) adv. **1.** onward. —adj. **2.** advanced. **3.** bold. —v. **4.** send on. —**for'ward·er,** n.

fos'sil (fos'əl) n. petrified remains of animal or plant. —**fos'sil·i·za'tion,** n. —**fos'sil·ize',** v.

fos·ter (fôs′tər) v. **1.** promote growth. —adj. **2.** reared in a family but not related.

foul (foul) adj. **1.** filthy; dirty. **2.** abominable. **3.** unfair. —n. **4.** violation of rules in game. —v. **5.** make or become foul. **6.** entangle.

foul′-up′, n. mix-up caused esp. by bungling.

found (found) v. establish.

foun·da′tion, n. **1.** base for building, etc. **2.** organization endowed for public benefit. **3.** act of founding.

found′er (foun′dər) v. **1.** sink. —n. **2.** person who founds.

found′ling, n. abandoned child.

found′ry (foun′drē) n., pl. **-ries.** place where molten metal is cast

foun′tain (foun′tn) n. **1.** spring of water. **2.** source. Also, **fount.**

foun′tain·head′, n. source.

four (fôr) n., adj. three plus one. —**fourth,** n., adj.

four′-flush′, v. bluff.

four′score′, adj. eighty.

four′some (-səm) n. **1.** group of four. **2.** golf match between two pairs.

four′square′, adj. **1.** firm; forthright. —adv. **2.** firmly; frankly.

four·teen′, n., adj. ten plus four. —**four′teenth′,** adj., n.

fowl (foul) n. bird, esp. hen or rooster.

fox (foks) n. **1.** carnivorous animal of dog family. **2.** crafty person. —v. **3.** trick.

fox′glove′, n. tall plant with bell-shaped flowers.

fox′hole′, n. small pit used for cover in battle.

fox trot, dance for couples.

fox′y, adj., **-ier, -iest. 1.** cunning. **2.** Slang. attractive.

foy′er (foi′ər, foi′ā) n. lobby.

FPO, v. field post office. **2.** fleet post office.

Fr., **1.** Father. **2.** French. **3.** Friar. **4.** Friday.

fra′cas (frā′kəs, frak′əs) n. tumult.

frac′tion (frak′shən) n. part of whole. —**frac′tion·al,** adj.

frac′tious (frak′shəs) adj. unruly.

frac′ture (frak′chər) n., v., **-tured, -turing.** break or crack.

frag′ile (fraj′əl) adj. easily damaged. —**fra·gil′i·ty** (frə jil′i tē) n.

frag′ment, n. (frag′mənt) **1.** broken part. **2.** bit. —v. (fragment′, frag′ment′) **3.** break into fragments.

fra′grance (frā′grəns) n. pleasant smell. —**fra′grant,** adj.

frail (frāl) adj. weak; fragile.

frame (frām) n., v., **framed, framing.** —n. **1.** enclosing border. **2.**

skeleton. —v. **3.** devise. **4.** put in frame. —**frame′work′,** n.

frame′-up′, n. fraudulent incrimination.

franc (frangk) n. French coin.

fran′chise (fran′chīz) n. **1.** right to vote. **2.** right to do business.

frank (frangk) adj. **1.** candid. —v. **2.** mail without charge.

frank′furt·er (frangk′fər tər) n. cooked sausage.

frank′in·cense′ (frang′kin sens′) n. aromatic resin.

fran′tic (fran′tik) adj. wildly emotional. —**fran′ti·cal·ly,** adv.

fra·ter′nal (frə tûr′nl) adj. brotherly. —**fra·ter′nal·ly,** adv.

fra·ter′ni·ty, n., pl. **-ties.** male society.

frat′er·nize′ (frat′ər nīz′) v., **-nized, -nizing.** associate fraternally or intimately.

frat′ri·cide′ (fra′tri sīd′, frā′-) n. **1.** act of killing one's brother. **2.** person who kills his or her brother.

fraud (frôd) n. trickery. —**fraud′u·lent,** adj. —**fraud′u·lent·ly,** adv.

fraught (frôt) adj. full; charged.

fray (frā) n. **1.** brawl. —v. **2.** ravel.

fraz′zle (fraz′əl) v., **-zled, -zling,** n. Informal. —v. **1.** fray. **2.** fatigue. —n. **3.** state of fatigue.

freak (frēk) n. abnormal phenomenon, person, or animal.

freck′le (frek′əl) n. small brownish spot on skin. —**freck′led,** adj.

free (frē) adj., **freer, freest,** adv., v., **freed, freeing.** —adj. **1.** having personal rights or liberty. **2.** independent. **3.** open. **4.** without charge. —adv. **5.** without charge. —v. **6.** make free. —**free′dom,** n.

free′boot·er, n. pirate.

free′-for-all′, n. Informal. brawl; melee.

free′lance′ (-lans′) adj., n., v., **-lanced, -lancing.** adj. **1.** hiring out one's work job by job. —n. **2.** Also, **free′lanc′er.** work as freelance.

free′load′, v. Informal. take advantage of the generosity of others.

Free′ma′son, n. member of secret fraternal association for mutual assistance. —**Free′ma′son·ry,** n.

free radical, molecule capable of multiplying rapidly and harming the immune system.

free′think′er, n. person with original religious opinions.

free′way′, n. major highway.

freeze (frēz) v., **froze** (frōz), **frozen, freezing,** n. —v. **1.** harden into ice. **2.** fix (prices, etc.) at a specific level. **3.** make unnegotiable. —n. **4.** act of freezing.

freight (frāt) *n.* **1.** conveyance of goods. **2.** goods conveyed. **3.** price paid.

freight/er, *n.* ship carrying mainly freight.

French (french) *n.* language or people of France. —**French,** *adj.*

French dressing, **1.** salad dressing of oil and vinegar. **2.** creamy or orange salad dressing.

French fries, strips of potato that have been deep-fried.

French horn, coiled brass wind instrument.

fre·net/ic (fra net/ik) *adj.* frantic.

fren/zy (fren/zē) *n., pl.* **-zies.** wild excitement. —**fren/zied,** *adj.*

fre/quen·cy (frē/kwan sē) *n., pl.* **-cies. 1.** state of being frequent. **2.** rate of recurrence. **3.** *Physics.* number of cycles in a unit of time.

fre/quent *adj.* (frē/kwant) **1.** occurring often. —*v.* (fri kwent/) **2.** visit often.

fres/co (fres/kō) *n., pl.* **-coes, -cos.** painting on damp plaster.

fresh (fresh) *adj.* **1.** new. **2.** not salty, as water. **3.** not preserved. **4.** *Informal.* impudent. —**fresh/en,** *v.*

fresh/et (fresh/it) *n.* sudden flooding of a stream.

fresh/man, *n., pl.* **-men.** first-year student.

fresh/wa/ter, *adj.* of or living in water that is not salty.

fret (fret) *v.,* **fretted, fretting.** —*n.* **1.** vexation. **2.** interlaced design. **3.** metal or wood ridge across strings of an instrument, as a guitar. —*v.* **4.** ornament with fret. **5.** worry. —**fret/ful,** *adj.*

Freud/i·an (froi/dē an) *adj.* **1.** relating to psychoanalytical theories of Sigmund Freud. —*n.* **2.** person who follows Freud's theories.

Fri., Friday.

fri/a·ble (frī/a bal) *adj.* crumbly.

fri/ar (frī/ar) *n.* member of Roman Catholic order. —**fri/ar·y,** *n.*

fric/as·see/ (frik/a sē/) *n.* stewed meat or fowl.

fric/tion (frik/shan) *n.* **1.** act or effect of rubbing together. **2.** conflict.

Fri/day (frī/dā, -dē) *n.* sixth day of week.

friend (frend) *n.* **1.** person one likes. **2.** *cap.*) Quaker; member of **Society of Friends,** a Christian sect. —**friend/ly,** *adj.* —**friend/ship,** *n.*

frieze (frēz) *n.* decorative, often carved band, as around a room.

frig/ate (frig/it) *n.* **1.** fast sailing warship. **2.** destroyerlike warship.

fright (frīt) *n.* **1.** sudden fear. **2.** shocking thing. —**fright/en,** *v.*

fright/ful, *adj.* **1.** causing fright. **2.** *Informal.* ugly; tasteless. —**fright/ful·ly,** *adv.* *Informal.* very.

frig/id (frij/id) *adj.* **1.** very cold. **2.** coldly disapproving. **3.** lacking sexual appetite. —**fri·gid/i·ty,** *n.*

frill (fril) *n.* **1.** ruffle. **2.** unnecessary feature. —*v.* **3.** ruffle. —**frill/y,** *adj.*

fringe (frinj) *n.* border of lengths of thread, etc.

frip/per·y (frip/a rē) *n., pl.* **-peries.** cheap finery.

frisk (frisk) *v.* **1.** frolic. **2.** search (person) for concealed weapon, drugs, etc.

frisk/y, *adj.* playful.

frit/ter (frit/ar) *v.* **1.** squander little by little. —*n.* **2.** fried batter cake.

friv/o·lous (friv/a las) *adj.* not serious or appropriate. —**fri·vol/i·ty** (fri vol/i tē) *n.*

frizz (friz) *v., n.,* curl. —**friz/zy,** *adj.*

fro (frō) *adv.* from; back.

frock (frok) *n.* **1.** dress. **2.** loose robe.

frog (frog) *n.* **1.** small, tailless amphibian. **2.** hoarseness.

frol/ic (frol/ik) *n., v.,* **-icked, -icking.** —*n.* **1.** fun; gaiety. —*v.* **2.** play merrily. —**frol/ic·some,** *adj.*

from (frum, from; *unstressed* fram) *prep.* **1.** because of. **3.** starting at.

frond (frond) *n.* divided leaf.

front (frunt) *n.* **1.** foremost part. **2.** area of battle. **3.** appearance; pretense. **4.** false operation concealing illegal activity. —*adj.* **5.** of or at the front. —*v.* **6.** face. —**fron/tal,** *adj.*

front/age (frun/tij) *n.* front extent of property.

front burner, condition of top priority.

fron·tier/ (frun tēr/) *n.* **1.** border of a country. **2.** outer edge of civilization. —**fron·tiers/man,** *n.*

fron/tis·piece/ (frun/tis pēs/, fron/-) *n.* picture preceding title page.

front/-run/ner, *n.* person who leads in a competition.

frost (frôst) *n.* **1.** state of freezing. **2.** cover of ice particles. —*v.* **3.** cover with frost or frosting.

frost/bite/, *n.* gangrenous condition caused by extreme cold.

frost/ing, *n.* sweet preparation for covering cakes.

froth (frôth) *n., v.* foam.

fro/ward (frō/ward, frō/ard) *adj.* perverse.

frown (froun) *v.* **1.** show concentration or displeasure on face. —*n.* **2.** frowning look.

frowz'y (frou'zē) *adj.* **-ier, -iest.** slovenly.

fruc·ti·fy' (fruk'tə fī', frŏŏk'-) *v.*, **-fied, -fying. 1.** bear fruit. **2.** make productive. **—fruc'ti·fi·ca'tion,** *n.*

fruc'tose (-tōs) *n.* sweet sugar in honey and many fruits.

fru'gal (frōō'gəl) *adj.* thrifty.

fruit (frōōt) *n.* **1.** edible product of a plant. **2.** result.

fruit'ful, *adj.* productive; successful.

fru·i'tion (frōō ish'ən) *n.* attainment.

fruit'less, *adj.* unsuccessful.

frump (frump) *n.* dowdy, unattractive woman. **—frump'y,** *adj.*

frus'trate (frus'trāt) *v.*, **-trated, -trating.** thwart. **—frus·tra'tion,** *n.*

fry (frī) *v.*, **fried, frying,** *n.*, *pl.* **fries,** (for 4) **fry. —v. 1.** cook in fat over direct heat. **—n. 2.** something fried. **3.** feast of fried things. **4.** young fish.

ft., **1.** feet. **2.** foot. **3.** fort.

FTC, Federal Trade Commission.

fuch'sia (fyōō'shə) *n.* **1.** plant with drooping flowers. **2.** bright purplish red color.

fudge (fuj) *n.* kind of soft candy.

fuel (fyōō'əl) *n.*, *v.*, **fueled, fueling. —n. 1.** substance that maintains fire. **—v. 2.** supply with or take in fuel.

fu'gi·tive (fyōō'ji tiv) *n.* **1.** fleeing person. **—adj. 2.** fleeing. **3.** impermanent.

-ful, suffix meaning: **1.** full of or characterized by, as *beautiful*. **2.** tending to or able to, as *harmful*. **3.** as much as will fill, as *spoonful*.

ful'crum (fōōl'krəm, ful'-) *n.*, *pl.* **-crums, -cra.** support on which levers turns.

ful·fill' (fōōl fil') *v.* **1.** carry out. **2.** satisfy. **—ful·fill'ment,** *n.*

full (fōōl) *adj.* **1.** filled. **2.** complete. **3.** abundant. **4.** complete. **5.** very. **—full'y,** *adv.*

full'back', *n.* (in football) running back positioned behind the quarterback.

full'-bod'ied, *adj.* of full strength, flavor, or richness.

full'-fledged', *adj.* fully developed.

full'-scale', *adj.* **1.** of exact size as an original. **2.** all-out.

ful'mi·nate' (ful'mə nāt') *v.*, **-nated, -nating. 1.** explode loudly. **2.** issue denunciations.

ful'some (fōōl'səm, ful'-) *adj.* excessive.

fum'ble (fum'bəl) *v.*, **-bled, -bling,** *n.* **—v. 1.** grope clumsily. **2.** drop. **—n. 3.** act of fumbling.

fume (fyōōm) *n.*, *v.*, **fumed, fum-**

-ing. —n. 1. vapor. **—v. 2.** emit fumes. **3.** show anger.

fu'mi·gate' (fyōō'mi gāt') *v.*, **-gated, -gating.** disinfect with fumes. **—fu'mi·ga'tion,** *n.*

fun (fun) *n.* play; joking.

func'tion (fungk'shən) *n.* **1.** proper activity. **2.** formal social gathering. **—v. 3.** act; operate.

func'tion·ar'y (-shə ner'ē) *n.*, *pl.* **-aries.** official.

fund (fund) *n.* **1.** stock of money. **—v. 2.** pay for.

fun'da·men'tal (fun'də men'tl) *adj.* **1.** basic. **—n. 2.** basic principle.

fun'da·men'tal·ist, *n.* believer in literal interpretation of a religious text, as the Bible.

fu'ner·al (fyōō'nər əl) *n.* burial rite.

fu·ne're·al (-nēr'ē əl) *adj.* **1.** mournful. **2.** of funerals.

fun'gus (fung'gəs) *n.*, *pl.* **fungi** (fun'jī). plant of group including mushrooms and molds.

funk (fungk) *n. Informal.* depression.

funk'y (fung'kē) *adj.*, **-ier, -iest. 1.** earthy, as blues-based jazz. **2.** *Slang.* offbeat.

fun'nel (fun'l) *n.*, *v.*, **-neled, -nel-ing. —n. 1.** cone-shaped tube. **2.** smokestack of vessel. **—v. 3.** channel or focus.

fun'ny (fun'ē) *adj.*, **-nier, -niest. 1.** amusing. **2.** strange.

funny bone, part of elbow that tingles when the nerve is hit.

fur (fûr) *n.*, *v.*, **furred, furring. —n. 1.** thick hairy skin of animal. **2.** garment made of fur. **—v. 3.** trim with fur. **—fur'ry,** *adj.*

fur'bish (fûr'bish) *v.* polish; renew.

fu'ri·ous (fyōōr'ē əs) *adj.* very angry.

furl (fûrl) *v.* roll tightly.

fur'long (fûr'lông) *n.* ⅛ of mile; 220 yards.

fur'lough (fûr'lō) *n.* **1.** leave of absence. **—v. 2.** give a furlough to.

fur'nace (fûr'nis) *n.* structure in which to generate heat.

fur'nish (fûr'nish) *v.* **1.** provide. **2.** fit out with furniture.

fur'nish·ing, *n.* **1.** article of furniture, etc. **2.** clothing accessory.

fur'ni·ture (-ni chər) *n.* tables, chairs, beds, etc.

fu'ror (fyōōr'ôr, -ər) *n.* general excitement.

fur'ri·er (fûr'ē ər) *n.* dealer in furs.

fur'row (fûr'ō) *n.* **1.** trench made by plow. **2.** wrinkle. **3.** make furrows in.

fur'ther (fûr'thər) *adv.* **1.** to a greater distance or extent. **2.** moreover. —*adj.* **3.** more. —*v.* **4.** promote. —**fur′ther·ance,** *n.*

—**Usage.** See FARTHER.

fur′ther·more′, *adv.* in addition.

fur′ther·most′, *adj.* most distant.

fur′thest (-thist) *adj.* **1.** most distant or remote. —*adv.* **2.** to greatest distance.

fur′tive (-tiv) *adj.* stealthy.

fu′ry (fyŏŏr′ē) *n., pl.* **-ries. 1.** violent passion, esp. anger. **2.** violence.

fuse (fyŏŏz) *n., v.,* **fused, fusing.** —*n.* **1.** safety device that breaks an electrical connection under excessive current. Also, **fuze.** device for igniting explosive. —*v.* **3.** blend, esp. by melting together. —**fu′si·ble,** *adj.* —**fu′sion** (fyŏŏ′zhən) *n.*

fu′se·lage′ (fyŏŏ′sə läzh′, -lij) *n.* framework of an airplane.

fu′sil·lade′ (fyŏŏ′sə läd′, -läd′) *n.* simultaneous gunfire.

fuss (fus) *n.* **1.** needless concern or activity. —*v.* **2.** make a fuss.

fus′ty (fus′tē) *adj.,* **-tier, -tiest. 1.** moldy; musty. **2.** old fashioned; out-of-date.

fu′tile (fyŏŏt′l, fyŏŏ′tīl) *adj.* useless; unsuccessful. —**fu·til·i·ty** (-til′i·tē) *n.*

fu′ton (fŏŏ′ton) *n.* thin, quiltlike mattress.

fu′ture (fyŏŏ′chər) *n.* **1.** time to come. —*adj.* **2.** that is to come. —**fu′tur·is′tic,** *adj.*

fuzz (fuz) *n.* fluff.

fuzz′y, *adj.,* **-ier, -iest. 1.** covered with fuzz. **2.** blurred. —**fuzz′i·ly,** *adv.* —**fuzz′i·ness,** *n.*

FYI, for your information.

G

G, g (jē) *n.* seventh letter of English alphabet.

G, motion picture rating: general; suitable for all ages.

g, 1. good. **2.** gram. **3.** gravity.

GA, 1. Gamblers Anonymous. **2.** general of the army. **3.** Georgia.

Ga., Georgia.

gab (gab) *n., v.,* **gabbed, gabbing.** *Informal.* chatter. —**gab′by,** *adj.*

gab′ar·dine′ (gab′ər dēn′) *n.* twill fabric.

gab′ble (gab′əl) *n., v.,* **-bled, -bling.** —*n.* **1.** rapid, unintelligible talk. —*v.* **2.** talk gabble.

ga′ble (gā′bəl) *n.* triangular wall from eaves to roof ridge.

gad (gad) *v.,* **gadded, gadding.** wander restlessly.

gad′a·bout′, *n.* person who flits from one social activity to another.

gad′fly′, *n., pl.* **-flies.** annoyingly critical person.

gadg′et (gaj′it) *n.* any ingenious device. —**gad′get·ry,** *n.*

gaff (gaf) *n.* hook for landing fish.

gaffe (gaf) *n.* social blunder.

gaf′fer, *n.* **1.** chief electrician on a film or TV show. **2.** *Informal.* old man.

gag (gag) *v.,* **gagged, gagging.** —*v.* **1.** stop up mouth to keep (person) silent. **2.** suppress statements of. **3.** retch. —*n.* **4.** something that gags. **5.** *Informal.* joke.

gage (gāj) *n., v.,* **gaged, gaging.** —*n.* **1.** token of challenge. **2.** pledge. **3.** gauge. —*v.* **4.** gauge.

gag′gle (gag′əl) *n.* flock of geese.

gai·e·ty (gā′i tē) *n., pl.* **-ties.** merriment.

gai′ly (gā′lē) *adv.* merrily.

gain (gān) *v.* **1.** obtain. **2.** earn. **3.** improve. **4.** move faster than another. —*n.* **5.** profit.

gain′say′ (gān′sā′, gān sā′) *v.,* **-said, -saying.** contradict.

gait (gāt) *n.* manner of walking.

gal (gal) *n. Informal.* girl.

gal., gallon.

ga′la (gā′lə, gal′ə; *esp. Brit.* gä′lə) *adj.* festive. —*n.* **2.** festive occasion.

gal′ax·y (gal′ək sē) *n., pl.* **-axies. 1.** (*often cap.*) Milky Way. **2.** brilliant assemblage. —**ga·lac·tic** (gə-lak′tik) *adj.*

gale (gāl) *n.* **1.** strong wind. **2.** noisy outburst, as of laughter.

gall (gôl) *v.* **1.** chafe. **2.** irritate. —*n.* **3.** sore due to rubbing. **4.** bile. **5.** *Informal.* impudence. **6.** abnormal growth on plants.

gal′lant (gal′ənt; *for also* gə lant′, -länt′) *adj.* chivalrous.

gall bladder, sac on liver in which bile is stored.

gal′le·on (gal′ē ən, gal′yən) *n.* large sailing vessel.

gal′ler·y (gal′ə rē) *n.* **1.** corridor. **2.** balcony. **3.** place for art exhibits.

gal′ley (gal′ē) *n.* **1.** vessel propelled by many oars. **2.** kitchen of ship.

gal′li·vant′ (gal′ə vant′) *v.* travel about, seeking pleasure.

gal′lon (gal′ən) *n.* unit of capacity equal to 4 quarts.

gal′lop (gal′əp) *v.* **1.** run at full speed. —*n.* **2.** fast gait.

gal′lows (gal′ōz, -əz) *n.* wooden frame for execution by hanging.

gall′stone′, *n.* stone formed in bile passages.

ga·lore' (gə lôr') *adv.* in abundance.

ga·losh'·es (gə losh'əz) *n.pl.* overshoes.

gal·va·nize' (gal'və nīz') *v.,* -nized, -nizing. **1.** stimulate by or as by electric current. **2.** coat with zinc.

gam'bit (gam'bit) *n.* **1.** sacrificial move in chess. **2.** clever tactic.

gam'ble (gam'bəl) *v.,* -bled, -bling, *n.* —*v.* **1.** play for stakes at game of chance. **2.** wager; risk. —*n.* **3.** uncertain venture. —**gam'bler,** *n.*

gam'bol (gam'bəl) *v.,* -boled, -boling, *n.* frolic.

game (gām) *n.* **1.** pastime or contest. **2.** wild animals, hunted for sport. —*adj.* **3.** brave and willing. **4.** lame. —**game'ly,** *adv.*

game plan, carefully planned strategy or course of action.

gam·ete (gam'ēt) *n.* mature sexual reproductive cell that unites with another to form a new organism.

gam'ut (gam'ət) *n.* full range.

gam'y (gā'mē) *adj.,* -ier, -iest. having the strong flavor of game.

gan'der (gan'dər) *n.* male goose.

gang (gang) *n.* **1.** group; band. **2.** work crew. **3.** band of criminals.

gan'gling (gang'gling) *adj.* awkwardly tall and thin.

gan'gli·on (gang'glē ən) *n., pl.* -glia, -glions. nerve center.

gang'plank' (gang'plangk') *n.* temporary bridge to docked vessel.

gan'grene (gang'grēn) *n.* death of body tissue. —**gan'gre·nous,** *adj.*

gang'ster, *n.* member of a criminal gang.

gang'way' (*n.* gang'wā'; *interj.* gang'wā') *n.* **1.** entrance to ship. **2.** narrow passage. —*interj.* **3.** (make way!)

gan'try (gan'trē) *n., pl.* -tries. framework for traveling crane or rocket.

gaol (jāl) *n., v. Brit.* jail.

gap (gap) *n.* **1.** opening; vacant space. **2.** ravine.

gape (gāp, gap) *v.,* gaped, gaping. **1.** open mouth as in wonder. **2.** open wide.

ga·rage' (gə räzh', -räj') *n.* place where motor vehicles are kept or repaired.

garb (gärb) *n.* **1.** clothes. —*v.* **2.** clothe.

gar'bage (gär'bij) *n.* refuse; trash.

gar'ble (gär'bəl) *v.,* -bled, -bling. misquote or mix up.

gar'den (gär'dn) *n.* **1.** area for growing plants. —*v.* **2.** make or tend garden. —**gar'den·er,** *n.*

gar·de'nia (gär dēn'yə, -nē ə) *n.* flowering evergreen shrub.

gar'den-va·ri'ety, *adj.* common.

gar·gan'tu·an (gär gan'chōō ən) *adj.* gigantic; colossal.

gar'gle (gär'gəl) *v.,* -gled, -gling, *n.* **1.** rinse throat. —*n.* **2.** liquid for gargling.

gar'goyle (gär'goil) *n.* grotesquely carved figure.

gar'ish (gâr'ish, gar'-) *adj.* glaring; showy. —**gar'ish·ly,** *adv.*

gar'land (gär'lənd) *n.* **1.** wreath of flowers, etc. —*v.* **2.** deck with garland.

gar'lic (gär'lik) *n.* plant with edible, pungent bulb. —**gar'lick·y,** *adj.*

gar'ment (gär'mənt) *n.* article of clothing.

gar'ner (gär'nər) *v.* gather; acquire.

gar'net (gär'nit) *n.* deep-red gem.

gar'nish (gär'nish) *v.* **1.** adorn. **2.** decorate (food). —*n.* **3.** decoration for food.

gar·nish·ee' (gär'ni shē') *v.,* -nisheed, -nisheeing. attach (money or property of defendant).

gar'ret (gar'it) *n.* attic.

gar'ri·son (gar'ə sən) *n.* **1.** body of defending troops. **2.** military post. —*v.* **3.** provide with garrison.

gar·rote' (gə rot', -rōt') *n., v.,* -roted, -roting. —*n.* **1.** strangulation. —*v.* **2.** strangle.

gar·ru·lous (gar'ə ləs, gar'yə-) *adj.* talkative. —**gar·ru'li·ty,** *n.*

gar'ter (gär'tər) *n.* fastening to hold up stocking.

garter snake, common, harmless striped snake.

gas (gas) *n., pl.* **gases,** *v.,* **gassed,** gassing. —*n.* **1.** fluid substance, often burned for light or heat. **2.** gasoline. —*v.* **3.** overcome with gas.

gash (gash) *n.* **1.** long deep cut. —*v.* **2.** make gash in.

gas'ket (gas'kit) *n.* ring or strip used to make joint watertight.

gas'o·line' (gas'ə lēn', gas'ə lēn') *n.* inflammable liquid from petroleum, used esp. as motor fuel.

gasp (gasp) *n.* **1.** sudden short breath. —*v.* **2.** breathe in gasps.

gas'tric (gas'trik) *adj.* of stomach.

gas·tro·nom'i·cal (gas'trə nom'i kəl) *adj.* of good eating. —**gas·tron'o·my** (gə stron'ə mē) *n.*

gate (gāt) *n.* movable hinged barrier.

gate'way', *n.* passage or entrance.

gath'er (gath'ər) *v.* **1.** bring or come together. **2.** infer. **3.** harvest. —*n.* **4.** pucker. —**gath'er·ing,** *n.*

gauche (gōsh) *adj.* unsophisticated; socially clumsy.

gaud'y (gô'dē) *adj.,* -ier, -iest. vulgarly showy. —**gaud'i·ly,** *adv.*

gauge (gāj) v., gauged, gauging, n. —v. 1. estimate. 2. measure. —n. 3. standard of measure. 4. device for measuring. 5. distance between railroad rails.

gaunt (gônt) adj. haggard; bleak.

gaunt/let (gônt/lit, gänt/-) n. 1. large-cuffed glove. 2. Also, **gant/let** (gant/-). ordeal.

gauze (gôz) n. transparent fabric.

gav/el (gav/əl) n. chairperson's mallet.

gawk (gôk) v. stare stupidly.

gawk/y, adj., **-ier, -iest.** clumsy.

gay (gā) adj., gayer, gayest, n. —adj. 1. joyous. 2. bright. 3. Slang. homosexual. —n. 4. Slang. homosexual. —**gay/ly,** adv.

gaze (gāz) v., gazed, gazing, n. —v. 1. look steadily. —n. 2. steady look.

ga.ze/bo (gə zā/bō, -zē/-) n., pl. **-bos, -boes.** open structure on a site with a pleasant view in a garden.

ga.zelle/ (gə zel/) n. small antelope.

ga.zette/ (gə zet/) n. newspaper.

gaz/et.teer/ (gaz/i tēr/) n. geographical dictionary.

gaz.pa/cho (gäz pä/chō) n. Spanish chilled vegetable soup.

gear (gēr) n. 1. toothed wheel that engages with another. 2. equipment. —v. 3. connect by gears. 4. adjust.

gear/shift/, n. gear-changing lever in automotive transmission system.

geck/o (gek/ō) n., pl. **-os** or **-oes.** small tropical lizard.

GED, general equivalency diploma.

gee (jē) interj. (exclamation of surprise or disappointment.)

gee/zer (gē/zər) n. odd or eccentric man, esp. an older one.

Gei/ger counter (gī/gər) instrument for measuring radioactivity.

gei/sha (gā/shə, gē/-) n. Japanese woman trained to provide entertainment and companionship for men.

gel (jel) n., v., gelled, gelling. —n. 1. jellylike or gluelike substance. —v. 2. become gel.

gel/a.tin (jel/ə tn) n. substance from animal skins, etc., used in jellies, glue, etc. —**ge.lat/i.nous** (-latn əs) adj.

geld/ing (gel/ding) n. castrated male horse. —**geld,** v.

gel/id (jel/id) adj. icy.

gem (jem) n. precious stone.

Gen., General.

gen/darme (zhän/därm) n. French police officer.

gen/der (jen/dər) n. 1. Gram. set of classes including all nouns, distinguished as masculine, feminine, neuter. 2. character of being male or female; sex.

gene (jēn) n. biological unit that carries inherited traits.

ge/ne.al/o.gy (jē/nē ol/ə jē, -al/-, jen/ē-) n., pl. **-gies.** study or account of ancestry.

gen/er.al (jen/ər əl) adj. 1. of or including all. 2. usual. 3. undetailed. —n. 4. highest-ranking army officer. —**gen/er.al.ly,** adv.

gen/er.al/i.ty (-al/i tē) n., pl. **-ties.** general statement.

gen/er.al.ize/, v., **-ized, -izing.** make generalities.

general practitioner, doctor whose practice is not limited to any specific branch of medicine.

gen/er.ate/ (jen/ə rāt/) v., **-ated, -ating.** produce.

gen/er.a/tion, n. 1. all individuals born in one period. 2. such period (about 30 years). 3. production.

Generation X (eks) the generation born in the U.S. after 1965.

gen/er.a/tor, n. device for producing electricity, gas, etc.

ge.ner/ic (jə ner/ik) adj. 1. of entire categories. 2. (of merchandise) unbranded. —**ge.ner/i.cal.ly,** adv.

gen/er.ous (jen/ər əs) adj. 1. giving freely. 2. abundant. —**gen/er.os/i.ty** (-ə ros/i tē) n.

gen/e.sis (-ə sis) n. birth or origin.

ge.net/ics (jə net/iks) n. science of heredity. —**ge.net/ic,** adj.

gen., genl., general.

gen/ial (jēn/yəl, jē/nē əl) adj. openly friendly.

ge/nie (jē/nē) n. spirit, often appearing in human form.

gen/i.ta/li.a (jen/i tāl/ē ə, -tāl/yə) n.pl. genitals.

gen/i.tive (jen/i tiv) n. 1. grammatical case usu. indicating possession. —adj. 2. of or relating to this case.

gen/ius (jēn/yəs) n. 1. exceptional natural ability. 2. person having such ability.

gen/o.cide/ (jen/ə sīd/) n. planned extermination of national or racial group.

gen/re (zhän/rə) n. class or category of artistic work.

gen.teel/ (jen tēl/) adj. well-bred; refined. —**gen.til/i.ty** (-til/i tē) n.

gen/tian (jen/shən) n. plant with blue flowers.

gen/tile (jen/tīl) adj. (sometimes cap.) not Jewish or Mormon.

gen/tle (jen/tl) adj., **-tler, -tlest.** 1. mild; kindly. 2. respectable. 3. careful in handling things.

gen/tle·man, *n., pl.* **-men. 1.** man of good breeding and manners. **2.** (used as polite term) any man.

gen/tri·fi·ca/tion (jen/tra fi kā/shan) *n.* replacement of existing population by others with more wealth or status. —**gen/tri·fy,** *v.,* **-fied, -fying.**

gen/try, *n.* wellborn people.

gen/u·flect/ (-yōo flekt/) *v.* kneel partway in reverence.

gen/u·ine (-in or, sometimes, -īn/) *adj.* real. —**gen/u·ine·ly,** *adv.*

ge/nus (jē/nas) *n., pl.* **genera, genuses.** biological group including one or several species.

Gen X (jen/ eks/) Generation X. Also, **GenX.**

geo-, prefix meaning the earth or ground, as *geography.*

ge/ode (jē/ōd) *n.* hollow nodular stone often lined with crystals.

ge/o·des/ic dome (jē/a des/ik, -dē/sik) dome with framework of straight members that form grid.

ge·og/ra·phy (jē og/ra fē) *n.* study of earth's surface, climate, etc. —**ge·og/ra·pher,** *n.* —**ge/o·graph/i·cal** (a grafi kal) *adj.*

ge·ol/o·gy (jē ol/a jē) *n.* science of earth's structure. —**ge·ol/o·gist,** *n.*

ge/o·mag·net/ic (jē/ō mag net/ik) *adj.* of the earth's magnetism.

ge·om/e·try (jē om/i trē) *n.* branch of mathematics dealing with shapes. —**ge/o·met/ric** (-a me/trik) *adj.*

ge/o·phys/ics (jē/ō fiz/iks) *n.* science of the physics of the earth and its atmosphere.

ge/o·pol/i·tics, *n.* study of politics in relation to geography.

ge/o·sta/tion·ar/y, *adj.* of an orbiting satellite remaining in same spot over the earth.

ge/o·ther/mal, *adj.* of the earth's internal heat.

ge·ra/ni·um (ji rā/nē am) *n.* small plant with showy flowers.

ger/bil (jûr/bal) *n.* small burrowing rodent, popular as a pet.

ger/i·at/rics (jer/ē a/triks, jēr/-) *n.* branch of medicine dealing with aged persons. —**ger/i·at/ric,** *adj.*

germ (jûrm) *n.* **1.** microscopic disease-producing organism. **2.** seed or origin.

Ger/man (jûr/man) *n.* native or language of Germany. —**German,** *adj.*

ger·mane/ (jar mān/) *adj.* pertinent.

German measles, rubella.

German shepherd, large dog with thick, usually gray or black-and-tan coat.

ger/mi·cide/ (jûr/ma sīd/) *n.* agent that kills germs. —**ger/mi·cid/al,** *adj.*

ger/mi·nate/, *v.,* **-nated, -nating.** begin to grow. —**ger/mi·na/tion,** *n.*

ger/on·tol/o·gy (jer/an tol/a jē, jēr/-) *n.* study of aging and problems and care of old people.

ger/ry·man/der (jer/i man/dar) *v.* divide into voting districts so as to give one group or area an unequal advantage.

ger/und (jer/and) *n.* noun form of a verb.

ges·ta/tion (je stā/shan) *n.* period of being carried in womb.

ges·tic/u·late/ (je stik/ya lāt/) *v.,* **-lated, -lating.** make gestures.

ges/ture (jes/char) *n., v.,* **-tured, -turing.** —*n.* **1.** expressive movement of body, head, etc. **2.** act demonstrating attitude or emotion. —*v.* **3.** make expressive movements.

get (get) *v.,* **got** (got), **got** or **gotten, getting. 1.** obtain. **2.** cause to be or do. **3.** be obliged to. **4.** arrive. **5.** become.

get/a·way/, *n.* **1.** escape. **2.** start of race. **3.** place for relaxing, etc.

get/-up/, *n. Informal.* outfit.

gey/ser (gī/zar, -sar) *n.* hot spring that emits jets of water.

ghast/ly (gast/lē) *adj.,* **-lier, -liest. 1.** frightful. **2.** deathly pale.

gher/kin (gûr/kin) *n.* **1.** small cucumber. **2.** small pickle.

ghet/to (get/ō) *n., pl.* **-tos, -toes. 1.** (formerly) Jewish part of city. **2.** city area in which mostly poor minorities live. —**ghet/to·ize,** *v.,* **-ized, -izing.**

ghost (gōst) *n.* disembodied soul of dead person. —**ghost/ly,** *adj.*

ghost/writ/er, *n.* person who writes for another who is presumed to be the author. —**ghost/write/,** *v.*

ghoul (gōōl) *n.* **1.** spirit that preys on dead. **2.** person morbidly interested in misfortunes.

G.I. (jē/ī/) enlisted soldier.

gi/ant (jī/ant) *n.* **1.** being of superhuman size. **2.** person of great accomplishments. —**gi/ant·ess,** *n. fem.*

gib/ber (jib/ar) *v.* speak unintelligibly. —**gib/ber·ish,** *n.*

gib/bet (jib/it) *n.* gallows with projecting arm.

gib/bon (gib/an) *n.* small, long-armed ape.

gibe (jīb) *v.,* gibed, gibing, *n.* jeer.

gib/lets (jib/lits) *n.pl.* heart, liver, and gizzard of a fowl.

gid/dy (gid/ē) *adj.,* **-dier, -diest. 1.** frivolous. **2.** dizzy.

gift (gift) *n.* **1.** present. **2.** act of giving. **3.** talent.

gift'ed, *adj.* **1.** talented. **2.** highly intelligent.

gig (gig) *n.* **1.** carriage drawn by one horse. **2.** light boat. **3.** *Slang.* engagement, as of musician.

gi·gan'tic (ji gan'tik, ji-) *adj.* befitting a giant. —**gi·gan'ti·cal·ly,** *adv.*

gig'gle (gig'əl) *v.,* **-gled, -gling.** —*v.* **1.** laugh lightly in a silly way. —*n.* **2.** silly laugh.

GIGO (gi'gō) *n.* axiom that faulty data input to a computer will result in faulty output.

gig'o·lo (jig'ə lō') *n., pl.* **-los.** man supported by his female lover.

Gi'la monster (hē'lə) *n.* large, venomous lizard.

gild (gild) *v.,* **gilded** or **gilt, gilding.** coat with gold.

gill *n.* **1.** (gil) breathing organ on fish. **2.** (jil) unit of liquid measure, ¼ pint (4 fluid ounces).

gilt (gilt) *n.* gold used for gilding.

gilt'-edged', *adj.* of the highest quality. Also, **gilt'-edge'.**

gim'let (gim'lit) *n.* small tool for boring holes.

gim'mick (gim'ik) *n.* device or trick.

gimp'y (gim'pē) *adj.,* **gimpier, gimpiest.** *Slang.* limping or lame.

gin (jin) *n.,* *v.,* **ginned, ginning.** —*n.* **1.** flavored alcoholic drink. **2.** machine for separating cotton from its seeds. **3.** trap. **4.** card game. —*v.* **5.** put (cotton) through gin.

gin'ger (jin'jər) *n.* plant with spicy root used in cookery.

ginger ale, carbonated soft drink flavored with ginger.

gin'ger·bread' *n.* cake flavored with ginger and molasses.

gin'ger·ly, *adj.* **1.** wary. —*adv.* **2.** warily.

gin'ger·snap', *n.* crisp cookie flavored with ginger.

ging'ham (ging'əm) *n.* checked cotton fabric.

gin'gi·vi'tis (jin'jə vī'tis) *n.* inflammation of the gums.

gink'go (ging'kō, jing'-) *n., pl.* **-goes.** shade tree native to China, with fan-shaped leaves.

gin'seng (jin'seng) *n.* plant with a medicinal root.

gi·raffe' (ja raf') *n.* tall, long-necked animal of Africa.

gird (gûrd) *v.,* **girt** or **girded, girding.** **1.** encircle with or as with belt. **2.** prepare.

gird'er, *n.* horizontal structural beam.

gir'dle (gûr'dl) *n., v.,* **-dled, -dling.** —*n.* **1.** encircling band. **2.** light corset. —*v.* **3.** encircle.

girl (gûrl) *n.* female child. —**girl'hood',** *n.* —**girl'ish,** *adj.*

girl'friend', *n.* frequent or favorite female companion.

Girl Scout, member of organization for girls (**Girl Scouts**).

girth (gûrth) *n.* **1.** distance around. —*v.* **2.** gird.

gis'mo (giz'mō) *n.* gadget.

gist (jist) *n.* essential meaning.

give (giv) *v.,* **gave** (gāv), **given, giving,** *n.* —*v.* **1.** bestow. **2.** emit. **3.** present. **4.** yield. —*n.* **5.** elasticity.

give'a·way', *n.* **1.** revealing act, remark, etc. **2.** TV show in which contestants compete for prizes.

giv'en, *adj.* **1.** stated. **2.** inclined. —*n.* **3.** established fact or condition.

giz'zard (giz'ərd) *n.* muscular stomach of birds.

gla'cial (glā'shal) *adj.* **1.** of glaciers or ice sheets. **2.** bitterly cold.

gla'cier, *n.* mass of ice moving slowly down slope.

glad (glad) *adj.,* **gladder, gladdest. 1.** pleased; happy. **2.** causing joy. —**glad'den,** *v.* —**glad'ness,** *n.*

glade (glād) *n.* open space in forest.

glad'i·a'tor (glad'ē ā'tər) *n.* Roman swordsman fighting for public entertainment.

glad'i·o'lus (-ō'ləs) *n., pl.* **-lus, -li** (-lī), **-luses.** plant bearing tall spikes of flowers. Also, **glad'i·o'la.**

glad'ly, *adv.* **1.** with pleasure. **2.** willingly.

glam'or·ize' (glam'ə rī') *v.,* **-ized, -izing.** make glamorous.

glam'our (glam'ər) *n.* alluring charm. —**glam'or·ous,** *adj.*

glance (glans) *v.,* **glanced, glancing,** *n.* —*v.* **1.** look briefly. **2.** strike obliquely. —*n.* **3.** brief look.

gland (gland) *n.* body organ that secretes some substance.

glans (glanz) *n.* head of penis or clitoris.

glare (glâr) *n., v.,* **glared, glaring. 1.** strong light. **2.** fierce look. —*v.* **3.** shine with strong light. **4.** stare fiercely.

glar'ing, *adj.* very obvious.

glass (glas) *n.* **1.** hard, brittle, transparent substance. **2.** (*pl.*) eyeglasses. **3.** drinking vessel of glass. **4.** anything made of glass. —*adj.* **5.** of glass. —*v.* **6.** cover with glass. —**glass'ware',** *n.*

glass ceiling, not generally acknowledged upper limit to professional advancement, esp. for women or minorities.

glass'y, *adj.,* **-ier, -iest. 1.** like glass. **2.** without expression; dull.

glau·co'ma (glô kō'mə, glou-) *n.* condition of elevated fluid pressure within the eyeball, causing increasing loss of vision.

glaze (glāz) *v.,* **glazed, glazing,** *n.* —*v.* **1.** fit with glass. **2.** put glossy surface on. **3.** make (eyes) expressionless. —*n.* **4.** glossy coating.

gla'zier (glā'zhər) *n.* person who installs glass.

gleam (glēm) *n.* **1.** flash of light. —*v.* **2.** emit gleams.

glean (glēn) *v.* gather laboriously, as grain left by reapers.

glee (glē) *n.* mirth. —**glee'ful,** *adj.*

glen (glen) *n.* narrow valley.

glib (glib) *adj.* ungraciously fluent.

glide (glīd) *v.,* **glided, gliding,** *n.* —*v.* **1.** move smoothly and effortlessly. —*n.* **2.** gliding movement.

glid'er, *n.* motorless aircraft.

glim'mer (glim'ər) *n.* **1.** faint unsteady light. **2.** small amount. —*v.* **3.** shine faintly. —**glim'mer·ing,** *n.*

glimpse (glimps) *n.,* *v.,* **glimpsed, glimpsing,** —*n.* **1.** brief view. —*v.* **2.** catch glimpse of.

glint (glint) *n.,* *v.* gleam.

glis·ten (glis'ən) *v.,* *n.* sparkle.

glitch (glich) *n. Informal.* defect or error.

glit'ter (glit'ər) *v.* **1.** reflect light with a brilliant sparkle. **2.** make a brilliant show. —*n.* **3.** sparkling light or luster. **4.** showy brilliance. **5.** small glittering ornaments.

glitz'y (glit'sē) *adj.,* *-ier, -iest. Informal.* tastelessly showy; flashy and pretentious.

gloam'ing (glō'ming) *n.* dusk.

gloat (glōt) *v.* gaze or speak with unconcealed triumph.

glob (glob) *n.* rounded lump or mass.

global warming (glō'bal) increase in the average temperature of the earth's atmosphere, causing changes in climate.

globe (glōb) *n.* **1.** earth; world. **2.** sphere depicting the earth. **3.** any sphere. —**glob·al,** *adj.*

globe'trot·ter, *n.* one who travels regularly all over the world.

glob'ule (glob'yōōl) *n.* small sphere. —**glob·u·lar,** *adj.*

gloom (glōōm) *n.* **1.** low spirits. **2.** darkness.

gloom'y, *adj.,* *-ier, -iest.* **1.** dejected; low-spirited. **2.** depressing. **3.** dark; dismal. —**gloom'i·ly,** *adv.*

glop (glop) *n.* messy mixture.

glo'ri·fy (glôr'ə fī') *v.,* **-fied, -fying. 1.** extol. **2.** make glorious.

glo'ry, *n.,* *pl.* **-ries,** *v.,* **-ried, -rying.** —*n.* **1.** great praise or honor. **2.** magnificence. **3.** heavenly bliss. —*v.* **4.** exult. —**glor'i·ous,** *adj.*

gloss (glos) *n.* **1.** external show. **2.** shine. **3.** explanation of text. —*v.* **4.** put gloss on. **5.** annotate. **6.** explain away. —**glos'sy,** *adj.*

glos'sa·ry (glos'ə rē) *n.,* *pl.* **-ries.** list of key words with definitions.

glot'tis (glot'is) *n.* opening at upper part of larynx. —**glot'tal,** *adj.*

glove (gluv) *n.,* *v.,* **gloved, gloving.** —*n.* **1.** hand covering with piece for each finger. —*v.* **2.** cover with glove. —**gloved,** *adj.*

glow (glō) *n.* **1.** light emitted by substance. **2.** brightness or warmth. —*v.* **3.** shine.

glow'er (glou'ər) *v.* **1.** frown sullenly. —*n.* **2.** frown.

glow'worm' (glō'wûrm') *n.* kind of firefly.

glu'cose (glōō'kōs) *n.* sugar found in fruits and animal tissues.

glue (glōō) *n.,* *v.,* **glued, gluing.** —*n.* **1.** adhesive substance, esp. from gelatin. **2.** join with glue.

glum (glum) *adj.,* **glummer, glummest.** gloomily sullen.

glut (glut) *v.,* **glutted, glutting,** *n.* —*v.* **1.** feed or fill to excess. —*n.* **2.** full supply. **3.** surfeit.

glu'ten (glōōt'n) *n.* substance left in flour after starch is removed.

glu'ti·nous, *adj.* gluelike.

glut'ton (glut'n) *n.* greedy person. —**glut'ton·ous,** *adj.* —**glut'ton·y,** *n.*

glyc'er·in (glis'ər in) *n.* thick liquid used as a sweetener, lotion, etc. Also, **glyc'er·ine.**

gnarl (närl) *n.* knot on a tree.

gnarled (närld) *adj.* bent and distorted.

gnash (nash) *v.* grind (the teeth) together, as in rage.

gnat (nat) *n.* small fly.

gnaw (nô) *v.* **1.** wear away by biting. **2.** distress. —**gnaw'ing,** *adj.*

gnome (nōm) *n.* dwarf in fairy tales.

GNP, gross national product.

gnu (nōō, nyōō) *n.,* *pl.* **gnus, gnu.** African antelope.

go (gō) *v.,* *n.* **went** (went), **gone** (gôn), **going,** *pl.* **goes.** —*v.* **1.** move; depart. **2.** act. **3.** become. **4.** harmonize. —*n.* **5.** energy. **6.** attempt.

goad (gōd) *n.* **1.** stimulus. —*v.* **2.** tease; taunt.

goal (gōl) *n.* **1.** aim. **2.** terminal or

target in race or game. **3.** single score in various games.

goal/keep/er, *n.* in sports, player whose chief duty is to prevent opposition from scoring a goal. Also, **goal/tend/er;** *Informal.* **goal/ie.**

goat (gōt) *n.* horned mammal related to sheep.

goat•ee/ (gō tē/) *n.* pointed beard.

gob (gob) *n.* mass.

gob/ble (gob/al) *v.,* **-bled, -bling,** *n.* —*v.* **1.** eat greedily. **2.** make cry of male turkey. —*n.* **3.** this cry.

gob•ble•de•gook/ (-dē gŏŏk/) *n.* nonsense.

gob/bler, *n.* male turkey.

go/-be•tween/, *n.* intermediary.

gob/let (gob/lit) *n.* stemmed glass.

gob/lin (gob/lin) *n.* elf.

God (god) *n.* **1.** Supreme Being. **2.** (*l.c.*) deity. —**god/dess,** *n.fem.*

god/ly, *adj.,* **-lier, -liest.** of God or gods. **2.** conforming to religion.

god/par/ent, *n.* sponsor of child at baptism. —**god/child/,** *n.* —**god/daugh/ter,** *n.* —**god/fath/er,** *n.* —**god/moth/er,** *n.* —**god/son/,** *n.*

god/send/, *n.* anything unexpected but welcome.

goes (gōz) third pers. sing. pres. indic. of **go.**

go/fer (gō/fər) *n. Slang.* employee who mainly runs errands.

gog/gle (gog/al) *n., v.,* **-gled, -gling.** —*n.* **1.** (*pl.*) protective eyeglasses. —(*v.*) **2.** stare with wide-open eyes.

goi/ter (goi/tər) *n.* enlargement of thyroid gland.

gold (gōld) *n.* **1.** precious yellow metal. **2.** bright yellow. —**gold, gold/en,** *adj.*

gold/brick/, *Slang.* —*n.* **1.** Also, **gold/brick/er.** person who shirks work. —*v.* **2.** shirk work.

gold/en•rod/, *n.* plant bearing clusters of yellow flowers.

gold/finch/, *n.* yellow-feathered American finch.

gold/fish/, *n.* small, gold-colored fish.

golf (golf) *n.* game played on outdoor course with special clubs and small ball. —**golf/er,** *n.*

go/nad (gō/nad, gon/ad) *n.* ovary or testis. —**go•nad/al,** *adj.*

gon/do•la (gon/dl ə *or, esp. for 0,* gon dō/la) *n.* narrow canal boat used in Venice. —**gon/do•lier/** (-lēr/) *n.*

gon/er (gō/nər) *n. Informal.* person or thing that is dying or past help.

gong (gông) *n.* brass or bronze disk sounded with soft hammer.

gon•or•rhe/a (gon/ə rē/ə) *n.* contagious venereal disease.

goo (gōō) *n., pl.* **goos. 1.** thick or sticky substance. **2.** sentimentality.

good (gŏŏd) *adj.* **1.** morally excellent. **2.** of high or adequate quality. **3.** kind. **4.** skillful. —*n.* **5.** benefit. **6.** excellence. **7.** (*pl.*) possessions.

good/-bye/, *interj., n., pl.* **-byes.** farewell. Also, **good/-bye/.**

Good Friday, Friday before Easter.

good/ly, *adj.,* **-lier, -liest.** numerous; abundant.

good Sa•mar/i•tan (sə mar/i tn) person who helps those in need.

good/will/, *n.* friendly feelings or intentions.

good/y (gŏŏd/ē) *n., pl.* **-ies.** food pleasing to eat, as candy.

goof (gōōf) *Informal.* —*n.* **1.** fool. **2.** blunder. —*v.* **3.** blunder. —**goof/y,** *adj.*

goon (gōōn) *n. Slang.* **1.** hoodlum hired to threaten or commit violence. **2.** stupid, foolish, or awkward person.

goose (gōōs) *n., pl.* **geese.** web-footed water bird.

goose/ber/ry, *n., pl.* **-ries.** tart edible fruit.

goose flesh, bristling of hair on the skin, as from cold or fear. Also, **goose pimples, goose bumps.**

G.O.P., Grand Old Party (epithet of the Republican Party).

go/pher (gō/fər) *n.* burrowing rodent.

gore (gôr) *n., v.,* **gored, goring.** —*n.* **1.** clotted blood. **2.** triangular insert of cloth. —*v.* **3.** pierce with horn or tusk. —**gor/y,** *adj.*

gorge (gôrj) *n., v.,* **gorged, gorging.** —*n.* **1.** narrow rocky cleft. —*v.* **2.** stuff with food.

gor/geous (gôr/jəs) *adj.* **1.** splendid. **2.** very beautiful.

go•ril/la (gə ril/ə) *n.* large African ape.

gos/ling (goz/ling) *n.* young goose.

gos/pel (gos/pəl) *n.* **1.** teachings of Christ and apostles. **2.** absolute truth.

gos/sa•mer (gos/ə mər) *n.* **1.** filmy cobweb. —*adj.* **2.** like gossamer.

gos/sip (gos/əp) *n., v.,* **-siped, -siping.** —*n.* **1.** idle talk, esp. about others. **2.** person who spreads gossip. —*v.* **3.** talk idly about others.

Goth/ic (goth/ik) *adj.* **1.** noting a style of European architecture from the 12th to 16th centuries. **2.** (*often l.c.*) noting a style of literature marked by gloomy settings and sinister events.

Gou/da (gou/da, gōō/-) *n.* mild, yellowish Dutch cheese.

gouge (gouj) *n., v.,* **gouged, gouging.** —*n.* **1.** chisel with hollow blade. —v. **2.** dig out with gouge. **3.** extract by coercion.

gou/lash (gōō/läsh, -lash), n. seasoned stew.

gourd (gôrd, gōōrd), n. dried shell of squash.

gour•mand/ (gŏŏr mänd′, gŏŏr′-mand) n. enthusiastic eater.

gour•met/ (gŏŏr mā′, gŏŏr′mā) n. lover of fine food.

gout (gout) n. painful disease of joints. —**gout/y,** adj.

gov., Government.

gov/er•nor (guv/ər n) v. **1.** rule. **2.** influence. **3.** regulate.

gov•ern•ess, n. woman who teaches children in their home.

gov•ern•ment (-ərn mənt, -ər mənt) n. **1.** system of rule. **2.** political governing body.

gov/er•nor (-ər nər, -ə nər) n. **1.** person who governs, esp. head of a state in the U.S. **2.** device that controls speed.

govt., government.

gown (goun) n. **1.** woman's dress. **2.** loose robe.

G.P., General Practitioner.

grab (grab) v., **grabbed, grabbing,** n. —v. **1.** seize eagerly. —n. **2.** act of grabbing.

grace (grās) n., v., **graced, gracing.** —n. **1.** beauty of form, movement, etc. **2.** goodwill. **3.** God's love. **4.** prayer said at table. —v. **5.** lend grace to; favor. —**grace/ful,** adj.

gra/cious (grā/shəs) adj. kind.

grack/le (grak/əl) n. blackbird with iridescent black plumage.

gra•da/tion (grā dā/shən) n. step in series of stages.

grade (grād) n., v., **graded, grading.** —n. **1.** degree in a scale. **2.** scholastic division. **3.** Also, **gra/di•ent,** slope. —v. **4.** arrange in grades. **5.** level.

grade crossing, intersection of a railroad track and a road.

grade school, elementary school.

grad/u•al (graj/ōō əl) adj. changing, moving, etc., by degrees.

grad/u•ate, (-it) *n.* **1.** recipient of diploma. —adj. (-it) **2.** graduated. **3.** of or in academic study beyond the baccalaureate level. —v. (-āt′) **4.** receive or confer diploma or degree. **5.** mark in linear measuring degrees.

graf•fi/ti (grə fē/tē) n.pl., sing. **-to** (-tō). markings written on public walls, etc.

graft (graft) n. **1.** twig, etc., inserted in another plant to unite with it. **2.** profit through dishonest use of one's position. —v. **3.** make graft. **4.** make dishonest profits.

gra/ham (grā/əm) adj. made of unsifted whole-wheat flour.

Grail (grāl) n. in medieval legend, the cup or chalice used at the last supper of Christ with the apostles.

grain (grān) n. **1.** seed of cereal plant. **2.** particle. **3.** pattern of wood fibers. —**grain/y,** adj.

gram (gram) n. metric unit of weight.

-gram, suffix meaning something written or drawn, as *diagram.*

gram/mar (gram/ər) n. **1.** features of a language as a whole. **2.** knowledge or usage of the preferred forms in speaking or writing. —**gram•mar/i•an** (grə mâr/ē ən) n. —**gram•mat/i•cal** (-mat/i kəl) adj.

gran/a•ry (grā/nə rē, gran/ə-) n., pl. **-ries.** storehouse for grain.

grand (grand) adj. **1.** large; major. **2.** impressive. **3.** grand piano. **4.** *Informal.* a thousand dollars.

grand/child/ (gran/chīld′) n. child of one's son or daughter. —**grand/son/,** n. —**grand/daugh/ter,** n.fem.

gran•dee/ (gran dē′) n. nobleman.

gran/deur (gran/jər, -jŏŏr) n. imposing greatness.

gran•dil/o•quence (gran dil/ə-kwəns) n. lofty, often pompous speech. —**gran•dil/o•quent,** adj.

gran/di•ose/ (gran/dē ōs′) adj. grand or pompous.

grand jury, jury designated to determine if a law has been violated and whether the evidence warrants prosecution.

grand/par/ent, n. parent of parent. —**grand/fa/ther,** n. —**grand/mother,** n.fem.

grand piano, large piano with a horizontal case on three legs.

grand slam, home run with three runners on base.

grand/stand/ (gran/-, grand/-) n. **1.** sloped open-air space for spectators. —v. **2.** conduct oneself or perform to impress onlookers.

grange (grānj) n. farmers' organization.

gran/ite (gran/it) n. granular rock.

gra•no/la (grə nō/lə) n. cereal of dried fruit, grains, nuts, etc.

grant (grant) v. **1.** bestow. **2.** admit. —n. **3.** thing granted.

grants/man•ship/, n. skill in securing grants, as for research.

gran/u•late/ (gran/yə lāt′) v., **-lated, -lating.** form into granules.

gran/ule (-yōōl) n. small grain.

grape (grāp) n. smooth-skinned fruit that grows in clusters.

grape/fruit/, n. large yellow citrus fruit.

grape/vine/, n. **1.** vine on which

graph 134

grapes grow. **2.** person-to-person route by which gossip spreads.

graph (graf) *n.* diagram showing relations by lines, etc.

-graph, suffix meaning: something written or drawn, as *autograph*. **2.** instrument that writes or records, as *seismograph*.

graph'ic (-ik) *adj.* **1.** vivid. **2.** of writing, drawing, engraving, etc.

graph'ics, *n.pl.* **1.** the arts of drawing, engraving, etc. **2.** drawings, charts, etc.

graph'ite (-īt) *n.* soft, dark mineral.

graph-ol'o-gy (gra fol'ə jē) *n.* study of handwriting.

-graphy, suffix meaning: **1.** process or form of writing, printing, recording, or describing, as *biography*. **2.** art or science concerned with these, as *geography*.

grap'nel (grap'nl) *n.* hooked device for grasping.

grap'ple (grap'əl) *n., v.,* **-pled, -pling.** —*n.* **1.** hook for grasping. —*v.* **2.** try to grasp. **3.** try to cope.

grasp (grasp) *v.* **1.** seize and hold. **2.** understand. —*n.* **3.** act of gripping. **4.** mastery.

grasp'ing, *adj.* greedy.

grass (gras) *n.* ground-covering plant. —**grass'y,** *adj.*

grass'hop'per, *n.* leaping insect.

grass'land', *n.* open grass-covered land; prairie.

grass roots, ordinary citizens, as contrasted with leadership or elite. —**grass'-roots',** *adj.*

grass widow, woman who is separated or divorced.

grate (grāt) *v.,* **grated, grating,** —*v.* **1.** irritate. **2.** make harsh sound. **3.** rub into small bits. —*n.* **4.** Also, **grat'ing.** metal framework.

grate'ful, *adj.* **1.** thankful. **2.** welcome as news. —**grate'ful·ly,** *adv.*

grat'i·fy' (grat'ə fī') *v.,* **-fied, -fying.** please. —**grat'i·fi·ca'tion,** *n.*

gra'tis (grat'is, grā'tis) *adv., adj.* free of charge.

grat'i·tude' (grat'i tōōd', -tyōōd') *n.* thankfulness.

gra·tu'i·tous (gra tōō'i təs, -tyōō'-) *adj.* **1.** free of charge. **2.** without reasonable cause.

gra·tu'i·ty, *n., pl.* **-ties.** tip.

grave (grāv) *n., adj.* **graver, gravest.** —*n.* **1.** place of or excavation for burial. —*adj.* **2.** solemn. **3.** important. —**grave'yard',** *n.*

grav'el (grav'əl) *n.* small stones.

grav'el·ly, *adj.* **1.** made up of or like gravel. **2.** harsh-sounding.

graveyard shift, work shift usu. beginning about midnight.

grav'i·ta'tion (grav'i tā'shən) *n.*

force of attraction between bodies. —**grav'i·tate',** *v.,* **-tated, -tating.**

grav'i·ty, *n., pl.* **-ties. 1.** force attracting bodies to the earth's center. **2.** seriousness.

gra'vy (grā'vē) *n., pl.* **-vies.** juices from cooking meat.

gray (grā) *n.* **1.** color between black and white. —*adj.* **2.** of this color. **3.** ambiguous. **4.** vaguely depressing.

gray matter, *Informal.* brains.

graze (grāz) *v.,* **grazed, grazing. 1.** feed on grass. **2.** brush in passing.

grease (n. grēs; v. grēs, grēz) *n.* **1.** animal fat. **2.** fatty or oily matter. —*v.* **3.** put grease on or in. —**greas'y,** *adj.*

great (grāt) *adj.* **1.** very large. **2.** important. —**great'ly,** *adv.*

Great Dane, kind of very large dog.

grebe (grēb) *n.* diving bird.

greed (grēd) *n.* excessive desire. —**greed'i·ly,** *adv.* —**greed'y,** *adj.*

Greek (grēk) *n.* native or language of Greece. —**Greek,** *adj.*

green (grēn) *adj.* **1.** of color of vegetation. **2.** unripe. **3.** inexperienced. —*n.* **4.** green color. **5.** grassy land.

green'back', *n.* U.S. legal-tender note.

green'belt', *n.* area of open land surrounding a community.

green'er·y, *n., pl.* **-eries.** plants.

green'gro'cer, *n.* retailer of fresh fruit and vegetables.

green'horn', *n.* **1.** novice. **2.** naive or gullible person.

green'house', *n.* building where plants are grown.

greenhouse effect, heating of atmosphere resulting from absorption by certain gases of solar radiation.

green'room', *n.* lounge in theater for use by performers.

green thumb, exceptional skill for growing plants.

greet (grēt) *n.* **1.** address on meeting. **2.** react to. —**greet'ing,** *n.*

gre·gar'i·ous (gri gâr'ē əs) *adj.* fond of company.

grem'lin (grem'lin) *n.* mischievous elf.

gre·nade' (gri nād') *n.* hurled explosive.

gren'a·dier' (gren'ə dēr') *n. Brit.* member of special infantry regiment.

grey (grā) *n., adj.* gray.

grey'hound', *n.* slender swift dog.

grid (grid) *n.* **1.** covering of crossed bars. **2.** system of crossed lines.

grid'dle (grid'l) *n.* shallow frying pan.

grid'i'ron, *n.* **1.** grill. **2.** football field.

grid/lock/, n. **1.** complete stoppage of movement in all directions due to traffic. **2.** stoppage of a process, as legislation.

grief (grēf) n. keen sorrow.

griev/ance (grē/vəns) n. **1.** wrong. **2.** complaint against wrong.

grieve (grēv) v., **grieved, grieving.** feel sorrow; inflict sorrow on.

griev/ous, adj. causing grief.

grif/fin (grif/in) n. monster of fable with head and wings of eagle and body of lion. Also, **gryph/on.**

grill (gril) n. **1.** barred utensil for broiling. —v. **2.** broil on grill. **3.** question persistently.

grille (gril) n. ornamental metal barrier.

grim (grim) adj., **grimmer, grimmest. 1.** stern. **2.** harshly threatening. —**grim/ly,** adv.

grim/ace (grim/əs, grī mās/) n., v., **-maced, -macing.** —n. **1.** twisted expression. —v. **2.** twist the face.

grime (grīm) n. dirt. —**grim/y,** adj.

grin (grin) v., **grinned, grinning,** n. —v. **1.** smile openly and broadly. —n. **2.** broad smile.

grind (grīnd) v., **ground** (ground), **grinding,** n. —v. **1.** wear, crush, or sharpen by friction. **2.** operate by turning crank. —n. **3.** Informal. dreary routine. —**grind/stone,** n.

grip (grip) n., v., **gripped, gripping.** —n. **1.** grasp. **2.** small suitcase. **3.** handle. —v. **4.** grasp.

gripe (grīp) v., **griped, griping,** n. —v. **1.** produce pain in bowels. **2.** Informal. complain. —n. **3.** Informal. complaint. —**grip/er,** n.

grippe (grip) n. influenza.

gris/ly (griz/lē) adj., **-lier, -liest.** gruesome.

grist (grist) n. grain to be ground.

gris/tle (gris/əl) n. cartilage.

grit (grit) n., v., **gritted, gritting.** —n. **1.** fine particles. **2.** courage. —v. **3.** cause to grind together.

grits (grits) n.pl. ground grain.

griz/zly (griz/lē) adj., **-zlier, -zliest.** gray, as hair or fur. Also, **griz/zled.**

grizzly bear, large bear of western U.S. and Canada.

groan (grōn) n. **1.** moan of pain, derision, etc. —v. **2.** utter groans.

gro/cer (grō/sər) n. dealer in foods, etc.

gro/cer·y, n., pl. **-ies. 1.** store selling food. **2.** (usually pl.) food bought at a store.

grog (grog) n. **1.** mixture of rum and water. **2.** any alcoholic drink.

grog/gy, adj., **-gier, -giest.** dizzy.

groin (groin) n. hollow where thigh joins abdomen.

grom/met (grom/it, grum/-) n. eyelet.

groom (grōōm, grŏŏm) n. **1.** person who takes care of horses. **2.** bridegroom. —v. **3.** make neat.

grooms/man, n., pl. **-men.** attendant of bridegroom.

groove (grōōv) n., v., **grooved, grooving.** —n. **1.** furrow. —v. **2.** form groove in.

grope (grōp) v., **groped, groping.** feel blindly.

gros/beak/ (grōs/bēk/) n. finch with a thick, conical bill.

gross (grōs) adj. **1.** before deductions. **2.** disgusting. **3.** very fat. **4.** flagrant. —n. **5.** amount before deductions. **6.** twelve dozen.

gross national product, total monetary value of all goods produced in a country during one year.

gro·tesque/ (grō tesk/) adj. fantastically ugly or absurd.

grot/to (grot/ō) n., pl. **-tos, -toes.** cave.

grouch (grouch) v. **1.** sulk. —n. **2.** sulky person. **3.** sullen mood. —**grouch/y,** adj.

ground (ground) n. **1.** earth's solid surface. **2.** tract of land. **3.** motive. **4.** (pl.) dregs. **5.** rational basis. —adj. **6.** of or on ground. —v. **7.** teach the basics to. **8.** run aground.

ground ball, batted baseball that rolls or bounces along the ground.

ground/hog/, n. woodchuck.

ground/less, adj. without rational basis.

ground rules, basic rule of conduct in a situation.

ground/swell/, n. surge of feelings, esp. among the general public.

ground/work/, n. basic work.

group (grōōp) n. **1.** number of persons or things considered together. —v. **2.** place in or form group.

group/er (grōō/pər) n., pl. **-ers, -er.** large sea bass of warm waters.

group/ie, n., pl. **-ies.** young fan of rock group or celebrity.

grouse (grous) n. game bird of America and Britain.

grout (grout) n. thin, coarse mortar, used between tiles.

grove (grōv) n. small wood.

grov/el (grov/əl, gruv/-) v., **-eled, -eling.** humble oneself.

grow (grō) v., **grew** (grōō), **grown, growing. 1.** increase in size; develop. **2.** cultivate. —**grow/er,** n.

growl (groul) n. **1.** guttural, angry sound. —v. **2.** utter growls.

grown/up/, n. adult. —**grown/-up/,** adj.

growth (grōth) n. **1.** act of growing. **2.** something that has grown.

grub

grub (grub) *n.*, *v.*, **grubbed, grub-bing.** —*n.* **1.** larva. **2.** *Informal.* food. —*v.* **3.** dig.

grub'by, *adj.* **-bier, -biest.** dirty.

grudge (gruj) *n. v.*, **grudged, grudging.** —*n.* **1.** lasting malice. —*v.* **2.** begrudge.

gru'el (grōō'al) *n.* thin cereal.

gru'el·ing (grōō'a ling, grōō'ling) *adj.* exhausting; arduous.

grue'some (grōō'səm) *adj.* causing horror and repugnance.

gruff (gruf) *adj.* surly.

grum'ble (grum'bal) *v.*, **-bled, -bling.** murmur in discontent.

grump'y (grum'pē) *adj.*, **grumpier, grumpiest.** surly.

grun'gy (grun'jē) *adj.*, **-gier, -giest.** *Slang.* dirty or run down.

grunt (grunt) *n.* **1.** guttural sound. —*v.* **2.** utter grunts.

gryph'on (grif'an) *n.* griffin.

gua'no (gwä'nō) *n.* manure; excrement of sea birds.

guar., guarantee(d).

guar'an.tee' (gar'an tē') *n.*, *v.*, **-teed, -teeing.** —*n.* **1.** pledge given as security. —*v.* **2.** pledge. **3.** assure. Also, **guar·an'ty.** —**guar'an.tor'** (-tôr') *n.*

guard (gärd) *v.* **1.** watch over. —*n.* **2.** person who guards. **3.** body of guards. **4.** close watch.

guard'ed, *adj.* **1.** cautious; prudent. **2.** protected or restrained.

guard'i·an, *n.* **1.** person who guards. **2.** person entrusted with care of another.

gua'va (gwä'və) *n.* large yellow fruit of tropical tree.

gu'ber.na.to'ri·al (gōō'bər na tôr'ē-al, gyōō'-) *adj.* of governors.

guer·ril'la (gə ril'ə) *n.* member of band of soldiers that harasses the enemy.

guess (ges) *v.* **1.** form opinion on incomplete evidence. **2.** be right in such opinion. —*n.* **3.** act of guessing.

guess'work', *n.* **1.** act of guessing. **2.** conclusions from guesses.

guest (gest) *n.* **1.** visitor. **2.** customer at hotel, restaurant, etc.

guf.faw' (gu fô', gə-) *n.* **1.** loud laughter. —*v.* **2.** laugh loudly.

guid'ance (gīd'ns) *n.* **1.** act or instance of guiding. **2.** advice over period of time.

guide (gīd) *v.*, **guided, guiding.** —*v.* **1.** show the way. —*n.* **2.** one that guides.

guide'book', *n.* book of directions, advice, and information, as for tourists.

guided missile, radio-controlled aerial missile.

guide'line', *n.* guide or indication of future course of action.

guild (gild) *n.* commercial organization for common interest.

guile (gīl) *n.* cunning.

guil'lo.tine' (gil'ə tēn', gē'ə-) *n.* machine for beheading.

guilt (gilt) *n.* fact or feeling of having committed a wrong. —**guilt'i.ly,** *adv.* —**guilt'y**.

guin'ea (gin'ē) *n.*, *pl.* **-eas.** former British coin, worth 21 shillings.

guinea fowl, domesticated fowl. Also, **guinea hen.**

guinea pig, 1. South American rodent. **2.** subject of experiment.

guise (gīz) *n.* outward appearance.

gui.tar' (gi tär') *n.* stringed musical instrument. —**gui.tar'ist,** *n.*

gulch (gulch) *n.* ravine.

gulf (gulf) *n.* **1.** arm of sea. **2.** abyss.

gull (gul) *n.* **1.** web-footed sea bird. **2.** dupe. —*v.* **3.** cheat; trick.

gul'let (gul'it) *n.* throat.

gul'li.ble (gul'ə bəl) *adj.* easily deceived. —**gul'li.bil'i.ty,** *n.*

gul'ly (gul'ē) *n.*, *pl.* **-lies.** deep channel cut by running water.

gulp (gulp) *v.* **1.** swallow in large mouthfuls. —*n.* **2.** act of gulping.

gum (gum) *n.*, *v.*, **gummed, gumming.** —*n.* **1.** sticky substance. **2.** chewing gum. **3.** tissue around teeth. —*v.* **4.** smear with gum.

gum'bo (gum'bō) *n.*, *pl.* **-bos.** soup made with okra.

gum'drop', *n.* small chewy candy.

gump'tion (gump'shən) *n.* **1.** initiative; resourcefulness. **2.** courage.

gum'shoe', *n.*, *pl.* **-shoes.** *Slang.* detective. **2.** rubber overshoe.

gun (gun) *n.*, *v.*, **gunned, gunning.** —*n.* **1.** tubular weapon which shoots missiles with explosives. —*v.* **2.** hunt with gun. **3.** cause (an engine) to speed up quickly.

gun'fire', *n.* the firing of guns.

gung'-ho' (gung'hō') *adj. Informal.* thoroughly enthusiastic and loyal.

gunk (gungk) *n. Slang.* sticky or greasy matter.

gun'man, *n.*, *pl.* **-men.** armed criminal.

gun'ny, *n.*, *pl.* **-nies.** coarse material used for sacks.

gun'pow'der, *n.* explosive mixture.

gun'shot', *n.* shot fired from gun.

gun'smith', *n.* person who makes or repairs firearms.

gun'wale (gun'l) *n.* upper edge of vessel's side.

gup'py (gup'ē) *n.*, *pl.* **-pies.** tiny tropical fish.

gur'gle (gûr'gal) *v.*, **-gled, -gling,**

n. —*v.* **1.** flow noisily. —*n.* **2.** sound of gurgling.

gur'ney (gûr'nē) *n.* wheeled table or stretcher for transporting patients.

gu'ru (gŏŏr'ōŏ, gŏŏ rōŏ') *n.* **1.** Hindu spiritual teacher. **2.** any respected leader.

gush (gush) *v.* **1.** flow or emit suddenly. **2.** talk effusively. —*n.* **3.** sudden flow. —**gush'y,** *adj.*

gush'er, *n.* jet of petroleum from underground.

gus'set (gus'it) *n.* angular insertion, as in clothing.

gus'sy (gus'ē) *v.,* **-sied, -sying.** dress up or decorate showily.

gust (gust) *n.* **1.** blast of wind. **2.** outburst. —**gust'y,** *adj.*

gus'ta·to·ry (gus'tə tôr'ē) *adj.* of taste.

gus'to (gus'tō) *n., pl.* **-toes.** keen enjoyment.

gut (gut) *n., v.,* **gutted, gutting.** —*n.* **1.** intestine. **2.** (*pl.*) *Informal.* courage. —*v.* **3.** destroy interior of.

guts'y, *adj.,* **gutsier, gutsiest.** daring or courageous. —**guts'i·ness,** *n.*

gut'ter (gut'ər) *n.* channel for leading off rainwater.

gut'tur·al (gut'ər əl) *adj.* **1.** of or in throat. —*n.* **2.** guttural sound.

guy (gī) *n.* **1.** rope used to steady object. **2.** *Informal.* fellow.

guz'zle (guz'əl) *v.,* **-zled, -zling.** eat or drink greedily. —**guz'zler,** *n.*

gym·na'si·um (jim nā'zē əm) *n., pl.* **-siums, -sia.** place for physical exercise. *Informal.* **gym.**

gym'nast (jim'nast, -nast) *n.* performer of gymnastics.

gym·nas'tics (-nas'tiks) *n.pl.* physical exercises that demonstrate strength, balance, or agility.

gy'ne·col'o·gy (gī'ni kol'ə jē, jin'i-) *n.* branch of medicine dealing with care of women.

gyp (jip) *v.,* **gypped, gypping.** *Informal.* cheat.

gyp'sum (jip'səm) *n.* soft common mineral.

Gyp'sy (jip'sē) *n., pl.* **-sies.** member of wandering people.

gy'rate (jī'rāt, jī rāt') *v.,* **-rated, -rating.** whirl. —**gy·ra'tion,** *n.*

gy'ro·scope' (jī'rə skōp') *n.* rotating wheel mounted to maintain equilibrium and determine direction.

H

H, h (āch) *n.* eighth letter of English alphabet.

ha (hä) *interj.* (exclamation of surprise, suspicion, etc.)

ha'be·as cor'pus (hā'bē əs kôr'pəs) writ requiring that arrested person be brought before court to determine whether he or she is legally detained.

hab'er·dash'er·y (hab'ər dash'ə rē) *n., pl.* **-eries.** shop selling men's items. —**hab'er·dash'er,** *n.*

hab'it (hab'it) *n.* **1.** customary practice or act. **2.** monk's or nun's clothing. **3.** addiction. —**ha·bit'u·al** (hə bich'ŏŏ əl) *adj.*

hab'it·a·ble (hab'i tə bəl) *adj.* able to be inhabited.

hab'i·tat' (-tat') *n.* natural dwelling.

hab'i·ta'tion, *n.* abode.

ha·bit'u·ate' (hə bich'ŏŏ āt') *v.,* **-ated, -ating.** accustom.

ha·bit'u·é' (-ŏŏ ā') *n.* habitual visitor.

hack (hak) *v.* **1.** cut. **2.** cough sharply. —*n.* **3.** cut or notch. **4.** artistic drudge. **5.** vehicle for hire. —*adj.* **6.** routine.

hack'er, *n. Slang.* **1.** skilled computer enthusiast. **2.** computer user who tries to gain unauthorized access to systems.

hack'les (hak'əlz) *n.pl.* **1.** hair that can bristle on the back of an animal's neck. **2.** anger.

hack'ney (-nē) *n., pl.* **-neys.** horse or carriage for hire.

hack'neyed, *adj.* trite; common.

hack'saw', *n.* saw for cutting metal.

had'dock (had'ək) *n.* food fish of northern Atlantic.

Ha'des (hā'dēz) *n.* hell.

haft (haft) *n.* handle.

hag (hag) *n.* repulsive old woman.

hag'gard (hag'ərd) *adj.* gaunt with fatigue.

hag'gle (hag'əl) *v.,* **-gled, -gling.** argue over price.

hail (hāl) *n.* **1.** ice pellets (**hail'stones**) **2.** shower. **3.** call or greeting. —*v.* **4.** pour down hail. **5.** greet. **6.** call out to.

hair (hâr) *n.* **1.** filament on human head, animal body, etc. **2.** hairs collectively. —**hair'y,** *adj.* —**hair'dres'ser,** *n.* —**hair'pin',** *n.*

hair'breadth', *n.* narrow margin of safety. Also, **hairs'breadth'.**

hair'cut', *n.* **1.** act of cutting hair. **2.** hair style.

hair'do' (-dōo) *n., pl.* **-dos.** hair arrangement.

hair'piece', *n.* toupee or wig.

hair'-rais'ing, *adj.* terrifying.

hair/spray/, n. liquid spray for holding the hair in place.

hair/style/, n. way of cutting or arranging hair. —**hair/styl/ist**, n.

hair/-trig/ger, adj. easily set off.

hake (hāk) n. codlike marine food fish.

hal/cy·on (hal/sē ən) adj. peaceful; happy; carefree.

hale (hāl) v., **haled, haling**, adj. —v. **1.** compel to go. —adj. **2.** healthy.

half (haf) n., pl. **halves**, adj., adv. —n. **1.** one of two equal parts. —adj. **2.** being half. **3.** incomplete. —adv. **4.** partly.

half/back/, n. (in football) one of two backs who line up on each side of the fullback.

half/-baked/, adj. **1.** not sufficiently planned or prepared. **2.** foolish.

half/-breed/, n. Offensive. offspring of parents of two races.

half brother, brother related through one parent only.

half/-cocked/, adj. ill-prepared.

half/-heart/ed, adj. unenthusiastic.

half sister, sister related through one parent only.

half/-truth/, n. deceptive statement that is only partly true.

half/way/ (-wā/, -wā/) adv. **1.** to the midpoint. **2.** partially or almost. —adj. **3.** midway. **4.** partial or inadequate.

halfway house, residence for persons released from hospital, prison, etc., to ease their return to society.

half/-wit/, n. foolish person.

hal/i·but (hal/ə bət, hol/-) n. large edible fish.

hal/i·to/sis (hal/i tō/sis) n. bad breath.

hall (hôl) n. **1.** corridor. **2.** large public room.

hal/le·lu/jah (hal/ə lōō/yə) interj. Praise ye the Lord!

hall/mark/ (hôl/-) n. **1.** mark or indication of genuineness or quality. **2.** distinguishing characteristic.

hal/low (hal/ō) v. consecrate.

Hal/low·een/ (hal/ə wēn/, -ō ēn/, hol/-) n. the evening of October 31, observed by dressing in costumes. Also, **Hal/low·e'en/**.

hal·lu/ci·na/tion (hə lōō/sə nā/shən) n. perception of something that is not real. —**hal·lu/ci·nate/**, v.

hal·lu/ci·no·gen (-nə jən) n. substance that produces hallucinations.

hall/way/, n. corridor.

ha/lo (hā/lō) n., pl. **-los, -loes**. radiance surrounding a head.

halt (hôlt) v. **1.** falter; limp. **2.** stop. —adj. **3.** lame. **4.** stop.

hal/ter (hôl/tər) n. **1.** strap for

horse. **2.** noose. **3.** woman's top tied behind the neck and back.

halve (hav) v., **halved, halving**. divide in half.

ham (ham) n., v. **hammed, hamming**. —n. **1.** meat from rear thigh of hog. **2.** amateur radio operator. **3.** performer who overacts. —v. **4.** overact. —**ham/my**, adj.

ham/burg/er (ham/bûr/gər) n. sandwich of ground beef in bun.

ham/let (ham/lit) n. small village.

ham/mer (ham/ər) n. **1.** tool for pounding. **2.** pound with hammer.

ham/mock (ham/ək) n. hanging bed of canvas, etc.

ham/per (ham/pər) v. **1.** impede. —n. **2.** large basket.

ham/ster (ham/stər) n. small burrowing rodent kept as a pet.

ham/string/, n., v., **-strung, -stringing**. —n. **1.** tendon behind the knee. —v. **2.** disable by cutting hamstring. **3.** make powerless or ineffective.

hand (hand) n. **1.** terminal part of arm. **2.** worker. **3.** side or direction. **4.** style of handwriting. **5.** pledge of marriage. **6.** cards held by player. —v. **7.** pass by hand.

hand/bag/, n. woman's purse.

hand/ball/, n. ball game played against a wall.

hand/bill/, n. small printed notice usu. distributed by hand.

hand/book/, n. small manual.

hand/cuff/, n. **1.** metal ring for prisoner's wrist. —v. **2.** put handcuff on.

hand/ful (-fööl) n., pl. **-fuls. 1.** amount hand can hold. **2.** difficult person or thing.

hand/gun/, n. pistol.

hand/i·cap/ (han/dē kap/) n., v., **-capped, -capping**. —n. **1.** disadvantage. —v. **2.** subject to disadvantage.

hand/i·craft/, n. **1.** manual skill. **2.** work or products requiring such skill. Also, **hand/craft/**.

hand/i·work/, n. **1.** work done by hand. **2.** personal work or accomplishment.

hand/ker·chief (hang/kər chif, -chēf/) n. small cloth for wiping nose.

han/dle (han/dl) n., v., **-dled, -dling**. —n. **1.** part to be grasped. —v. **2.** feel or grasp. **3.** manage. **4.** Informal. endure. **5.** deal in.

hand/made/, adj. made individually by worker.

hand/out/, n. **1.** something given to a beggar. **2.** item of publicity.

hand'shake', *n.* clasping of hands in greeting or agreement.

hands'-off', *adj.* characterized by nonintervention.

hand'some (han'səm) *adj.* **1.** good-looking. **2.** generous.

hands'-on', *adj.* involving active personal participation.

hand'spring', *n.* complete flipping of body, landing first on hands, then on feet.

hand'-to-mouth', *adj.* providing bare existence; precarious.

hand'writ'ing, *n.* writing done by hand. —**hand'writ'ten** (-rit'n) *adj.*

hand'y (han'dē) *adj.*, **-ier, -iest. 1.** convenient. **2.** dexterous. **3.** useful.

han'dy·man', *n., pl.* **-men.** worker at miscellaneous physical chores.

hang (hang) *v.*, **hung** (hung), or **hanged, hanging**, *n.* —*v.* **1.** suspend. **2.** suspend by neck until dead. —*n.* **3.** manner of hanging. —**hang'man**, *n.*

hang'ar (hang'ər) *n.* shed, esp. for aircraft.

hang'dog', *adj.* shamefaced or cowed.

hang glider, kitelike glider for soaring through the air from hilltops, etc. (**hang gliding**).

hang'nail', *n.* small piece of loose skin around fingernail.

hang'o'ver, *n.* ill feeling from too much alcohol.

hang'up', *n. Informal.* obsessive problem.

hank (hangk) *n.* skein of yarn.

han'ker (hang'kər) *v.* yearn.

hank'y-pank'y (hang'kē pang'kē) *n. Informal.* **1.** mischief. **2.** illicit sexual relations.

han'som (han'səm) *n.* two-wheeled covered cab.

Ha'nuk·kah (кнä'nə kə, hä'-) *n.* annual Jewish festival.

hap'haz'ard (hap haz'ərd) *adj.* **1.** accidental. —*adv.* **2.** by chance.

hap'less, *adj.* unlucky.

hap'pen (hap'ən) *v.* occur. —**hap'pen·ing**, *n.*

hap'pen·stance' (-stans') *n.* chance happening or event.

hap'py (hap'ē) *adj.*, **-pier, -piest. 1.** pleased; glad. **2.** pleasurable. **3.** bringing good luck.

ha·rangue' (hə rang') *n., v.*, **-rangued, -ranguing.** —*n.* **1.** vehement speech. —*v.* **2.** address in harangue.

ha·rass' (hə ras', har'əs) *v.* annoy; disturb. —**har·ass'ment**, *n.*
—**Pronunciation.** HARASS has traditionally been pronounced (har'əs). A newer pronunciation, (hə ras'), which has developed in North

American but not British English, is sometimes criticized. However, it is now the more common pronunciation among younger educated U.S. speakers, some of whom are barely familiar with the older form.

har'bin·ger (här'bin jər) *n., v.* herald.

har'bor (här'bər) *n.* **1.** sheltered water for ships. **2.** shelter. —*v.* **3.** give shelter.

hard (härd) *adj.* **1.** firm; not soft. **2.** difficult. **3.** severe. **4.** indisputable. —**hard'en**, *v.* —**hard'ness**, *n.*

hard'-bit'ten, *adj.* tough; stubborn.

hard'-boiled', *adj.* **1.** boiled long enough for yolk and white to solidify. **2.** not sentimental; tough.

hard cider, fermented cider.

hard'core', *adj.* graphic; explicit.

hard'hat', *n.* **1.** worker's helmet. **2.** working-class conservative.

hard'head'ed, *adj.* **1.** practical; realistic; shrewd. **2.** obstinate; willful.

hard'heart'ed, *adj.* unfeeling.

hard'line', *adj.* uncompromising, as in politics. Also, **hard'line'**.

hard'ly, *adv.* barely.

hard'-nosed', *adj. Informal.* **1.** practical and shrewd. **2.** tough; stubborn. —**hard'nose'**, *n.*

hard'ship, *n.* suffering or need.

hard'tack', *n.* hard biscuit.

hard'ware', *n.* **1.** metalware. **2.** the machinery of a computer.

hard'wood', *n.* hard, compact wood of various trees.

har'dy (här'dē) *adj.*, **-dier, -diest.** able to endure hardship.

hare (hâr) *n.* mammal resembling rabbit.

hare'brained', *adj.* foolish.

hare'lip', *n.* split upper lip.

har'em (hâr'əm, har'-) *n.* **1.** women's section of Muslim palace. **2.** the women there.

hark (härk) *v.* listen. Also, **hark'en.**

har'le·quin (här'lə kwin, -kin) *n.* masked clown in theater.

har'lot (här'lət) *n.* prostitute.

harm (härm) *n.* **1.** injury. **2.** evil. —*v.* **3.** injure. —**harm'ful**, *adj.*

harm'less, *adj.* **1.** causing no harm. **2.** immune from legal action.

har·mon'i·ca (här mon'i kə) *n.* small wind instrument with metal reeds.

har'mo·ny (här'mə nē) *n., pl.* **-nies. 1.** agreement. **2.** combination of agreeable musical sounds. —**har'mo·nize'**, *v.*, **-nized, -nizing.** —**har·mon'i·ous** (-mō'nē əs) *adj.*

har'ness (här'nis) *n.* **1.** horse's working gear. —*v.* **2.** put harness on. **3.** make use of.

harp (härp) *n.* **1.** plucked musical

harpoon

string instrument. —v. **2.** repeat tediously. —**harp′ist, harp′er,** n.

har·poon′ (här poon′) n. **1.** spear used against whales. —v. **2.** strike with harpoon.

harp′si·chord′ (härp′si kôrd′) n. keyboard instrument with plucked strings. —**harp′si·chord′ist,** n.

har′ri·dan (har′i dn) n. scolding, vicious woman.

har′ri·er (har′ē ər) n. hunting dog.

har′row (har′ō) n. **1.** implement for leveling or breaking up plowed land. —v. **2.** draw a harrow over. **3.** distress. —**har′row·ing,** adj.

har′ry (har′ē) v., **-ried, -rying.** harass.

harsh (härsh) adj. **1.** rough. **2.** unpleasant. **3.** highly severe.

har′vest (här′vist) n. **1.** gathering of crops. **2.** season for this. **3.** crop. —v. **4.** reap. —**har′vest·er,** n.

has (haz; unstressed haz, əz) v. third pers. sing. pres. indic. of **have.**

has′-been′, n. one that is no longer effective, successful, etc.

hash (hash) n. **1.** chopped meat and potatoes. **2.** Slang. hashish. **3.** chop.

hash′ish (hash′ēsh, -ish) n. narcotic of Indian hemp.

hasn′t (haz′ənt) contraction of **has not.**

hasp (hasp) n. clasp for door or lid.

has′sle (has′əl) n., v., **-sled, -sling.** Informal. n. **1.** disorderly dispute. **2.** troublesome situation. —v. **3.** bother; harass.

has′sock (has′ək) n. cushion used as footstool, etc.

haste (hāst) n. **1.** swiftness of motion. **2.** rash action. —**hast′y,** adj. —**hast′i·ness,** n.

has′ten (hā′sən) v. hurry.

hat (hat) n. covering for head.

hatch (hach) v. **1.** bring forth young from egg. **2.** be hatched. —n. **3.** cover for opening. —**hatch′er·y,** n.

hatch′et (hach′it) n. small ax.

hatchet job, maliciously destructive critique.

hatch′way′, n. opening in ship's deck.

hate (hāt) v., **hated, hating,** n. **1.** feel enmity. —n. **2.** Also, **hat′red.** strong dislike.

hate′ful, adj. **1.** full of hate. **2.** arousing hate. —**hate′ful·ly,** adv.

haugh′ty (hô′tē) adj., **-tier, -tiest.** disdainfully proud.

haul (hôl) v. **1.** pull; drag. —n. **2.** pull. **3.** distance of carrying. **4.** thing hauled. **5.** amount collected.

haunch (hônch, hänch) n. hip.

haunt (hônt, hänt) v. **1.** visit or inhabit as ghost. **2.** visit often. —n. **3.** place of frequent visits. —**haunt′ed,** adj.

haunt′ing, adj. lingering in the mind.

haute cou·ture′ (ōt′ koo toor′) high fashion.

haute cui·sine′ (ōt′ kwi zēn′) gourmet cooking.

have (hav; unstressed həv, əv; for usually haf) v., **had, having.** **1.** possess; contain. **2.** get. **3.** be forced or obligated. **4.** be affected by. **5.** give birth to. —**Usage.** See **of.**

ha′ven (hā′vən) n. **1.** harbor. **2.** place of shelter.

have′-not′, n. (usually pl.) individual or group without wealth.

haven′t (hav′ənt) contraction of **have not.**

hav′er·sack′ (hav′ər sak′) n. bag for carrying supplies.

hav′oc (hav′ək) n. devastation.

Haw. (hô) Hawaii.

hawk (hôk) n. **1.** bird of prey. —v. **2.** hunt with hawks. **3.** peddle. —**hawk′er,** n.

hawk′er, n. peddler.

haw′thorn′ (hô′thôrn′) n. small tree with thorns and red berries.

hay (hā) n. grass cut and dried for fodder. —**hay′stack′,** n.

hay fever, disorder of eyes and respiratory tract, caused by pollen.

hay′wire′, adj. Informal. amiss.

haz′ard (haz′ərd) n., v. risk.

haze (hāz) n., v., **hazed, hazing,** —v. **1.** play abusive tricks on. —n. **2.** fine mist. —**ha′zy,** adj.

ha′zel (hā′zal) n. **1.** tree bearing edible nut (**ha′zel·nut′**). **2.** light reddish brown.

H′-bomb′, n. hydrogen bomb.

hdqrs., headquarters.

HDTV, high-definition television.

he (hē; unstressed ē) pron. **1.** male last mentioned. **2.** male.

head (hed) n. **1.** part of body joined to trunk by neck. **2.** leader. **3.** top or foremost part. —adj. **4.** at the head. **5.** leading or main. —v. **6.** lead. **7.** move in certain direction.

head′ache′, n. **1.** pain in upper part of head. **2.** worrying problem.

head′dress′, n. covering or decoration for the head.

head′first′, adv. headlong.

head′ing, n. caption.

head′light′, n. light with reflector at front of vehicle.

head′line′, n. title of news story.

head′long′, adj., adv. **1.** with the head foremost. **2.** in impulsive manner.

head'-on', *adj.*, *adv.* with the head or front foremost.

head'phone', *n.* (*usually pl.*) device worn over the ears for listening to an audiotape, etc.

head'quar'ters, *n.* center of command or operations.

head'stone', *n.* stone marker at head of grave.

head'strong', *adj.* willful.

head'way', *n.* progress.

head'y, *adj.*, **headier, headiest. 1.** impetuous. **2.** intoxicating.

heal (hēl) *v.* **1.** restore to health. **2.** get well.

health (helth) *n.* **1.** soundness of body or mind. **2.** physical condition. **—health'ful**, **—health'y**, *adj.*

heap (hēp) *n.*, *v.* pile (defs. 1, 2, 8, 9).

hear (hēr) *v.*, **heard** (hûrd), **hearing. 1.** perceive by ear. **2.** listen. **3.** receive report.

hear'say', *n.* gossip; indirect report.

hearse (hûrs) *n.* vehicle used to carry coffin.

heart (härt) *n.* **1.** muscular organ keeping blood in circulation. **2.** seat of life or emotion. **3.** compassion. **4.** vital part. **5.** (*pl.*) suit of playing cards. **—heart'less**, *adj.*

heart'ache', *n.* grief.

heart attack, sudden insufficiency of oxygen supply to heart that results in heart muscle damage.

heart'break', *n.* great sorrow or anguish. **—heart'bro'ken**, *adj.*

heart'burn', *n.* burning sensation in stomach and esophagus, sometimes caused by rising stomach acid.

heart'en, *v.* encourage.

heart'felt', *adj.* deeply felt.

hearth (härth) *n.* place for fires.

heart'-rend'ing, *adj.* causing intense grief.

heart'sick', *adj.* extremely sad.

heart'-to-heart', *adj.* sincere and intimate.

heart'y, *adj.*, **-ier, -iest. 1.** cordial. **2.** genuine. **3.** vigorous. **4.** substantial. **—heart'i·ly**, *adv.*

heat (hēt) *n.* **1.** warmth. **2.** form of energy raising temperature. **3.** intensity of emotion. **4.** sexual receptiveness in animals. **—v. 5.** make or become hot. **6.** excite. **—heat'er**, *n.*

heat'ed, *adj.* **1.** supplied with heat. **2.** emotionally charged.

heath (hēth) *n.* **1.** Also, **heath'er.** low evergreen shrub. **2.** uncultivated land overgrown with shrubs.

hea'then (hē'thən) *n.*, *adj.* pagan.

heat'stroke', *n.* headache, fever, etc., caused by too much heat.

heave (hēv) *v.*, **heaved, heaving**, *n.* **—v. 1.** raise with effort. **2.** lift and throw. **3.** *Slang.* vomit. **4.** rise and fall. **—n. 5.** act of heaving.

heav'en (hev'ən) *n.* **1.** abode of God, angels, and spirits of righteous dead. **2.** (*often pl.*) sky. **3.** bliss.

heav'y (hev'ē) *adj.*, **-ier, -iest. 1.** of great weight. **2.** substantial. **3.** clumsy; indelicate. **—heav'i·ly**, *adv.*

heav'y-du'ty, *adj.* made for hard use.

heav'y-hand'ed, *adj.* tactless; clumsy.

heav'y-heart'ed, *adj.* preoccupied with sorrow or worry.

heav'y-set', *adj.* large in body.

He'brew (hē'brōō) *n.* **1.** member of people of ancient Palestine. **2.** their language, now the national language of Israel. **—He'brew**, *adj.*

heck'le (hek'əl) *v.*, **-led, -ling.** harass with comments or questions.

hec'tare (hek'tãr) *n.* 10,000 square meters (2.47 acres).

hec'tic (-tik) *adj.* marked by excitement, passion, etc.

hec'tor (-tər) *v.* bully.

hedge (hej) *n.*, *v.*, **hedged, hedging. —n. 1.** fence of bushes or small trees. **—v. 2.** surround with hedge. **3.** offset (risk, bet, etc.).

hedge'hog', *n.* spiny mammal.

he'don·ist (hēd'n ist) *n.* person living for pleasure.

heed (hēd) *v.* **1.** notice. **2.** pay serious attention to. **—heed**, *n.* **—heed'ful**, **—heed'less**, *adj.*

heel (hēl) *n.* **1.** back of foot below ankle. **2.** part of shoe, etc., covering this. **—v. 3.** furnish with heels. **4.** lean to one side.

heft (heft) *n.* **1.** heaviness. **2.** significance. **—v. 3.** weigh by lifting.

hef'ty, *adj.*, **-tier, -tiest. 1.** heavy. **2.** sturdy. **3.** substantial.

he·gem'o·ny (hi jem'ə nē, hej'ə mō'-) *n.*, *pl.* **-nies.** domination or leadership.

heif'er (hef'ər) *n.* young cow that has not calved.

height (hīt) *n.* **1.** state of being high. **2.** altitude. **3.** apex. **—height'en**, *v.*

Heim'lich maneuver (hīm'lik) procedure to aid choking person by applying pressure to upper abdomen.

hei'nous (hā'nəs) *adj.* hateful.

heir (âr) *n.* inheritor. **—heir'ess**, *n. fem.*

heir'loom', *n.* possession long kept in family.

heist (hīst) *Slang.* **—n. 1.** robbery. **—v. 2.** rob.

hel/i·cop/ter (hel/i kop/tər, hē/li-) *n.* aircraft lifted by rotating blades.

he/li·um (hē/lē əm) *n.* light, gaseous element.

he/lix (hē/liks) *n.,* pl. **hel/i·ces** (hel/ə sēz/), **helixes.** spiral.

hell (hel) *n.* abode of condemned spirits. —**hell/ish,** *adj.*

Hel·len/ic (he len/ik, -lē/nik) *adj.* Greek.

hel·lo/ (he lō/, hə-, hel/ō) *interj.* (exclamation of greeting.)

helm (helm) *n.* 1. control of rudder. 2. steering apparatus.

hel/met (hel/mit) *n.* protective head covering.

help (help) *v.* 1. aid. 2. save. 3. relieve. 4. avoid. —*n.* 5. aid; relief. 6. helping person or thing. —**help/er,** *n.* —**help/ful,** *adj.*

help/ing, *n.* portion of food served.

help/less, *adj.* unable to act for oneself. —**help/less·ly,** *adv.*

help/mate/, *n.* companion and helper. Also, **help/meet/.**

hel/ter-skel/ter (hel/tər skel/tər) *adv.* in a disorderly way.

hem (hem) *v.,* **hemmed, hemming,** *n.* —*v.* 1. confine. 2. fold and sew down edge of cloth. 3. make throat-clearing sound. —*n.* 4. hemmed border.

hem/i·sphere/ (hem/i sfēr/) *n.* 1. half the earth or sky. 2. half sphere.

hem/lock (hem/lok/) *n.* 1. coniferous tree. 2. poisonous plant.

he/mo·glo/bin (hē/mə glō/bin, hem/ə-) *n.* oxygen-carrying compound in red blood cells.

he/mo·phil/i·a (hē/mə fil/ē ə) *n.* genetic disorder marked by excessive bleeding. —**he/mo·phil/i·ac/,** *n.*

hem/or·rhage (hem/ər ij) *n.* discharge of blood.

hem/or·rhoid/ (hem/ə roid/) *n.* (*usually pl.*) painful dilation of blood vessels in anus.

hemp (hemp) *n.* 1. herb fiber used for rope. 2. intoxicating drug made from hemp plant.

hen (hen) *n.* 1. female domestic fowl 2. female bird.

hence (hens) *adv.* 1. therefore. 2. from now on. 3. from this place.

hence/forth/ (hens/fôrth/, hens/-fôrth/) *adv.* from now on.

hench/man (hench/mən) *n., pl.* **-men.** 1. associate in wrongdoing. 2. trusted attendant.

hen/na (hen/ə) *n.* red dye.

hen/pecked/, *adj.* nagged or controlled by one's wife.

hep/a·ti/tis (hep/ə tī/tis) *n.* inflammation of the liver.

her (hûr; *unstressed* hər, ər) *pron.*

1. objective case of **she.** —*adj.* 2. of or belonging to female.

her/ald (her/əld) *n.* 1. messenger or forerunner. 2. proclaimer. —*v.* 3. proclaim. 4. give promise of.

her/ald·ry (her/əl drē) *n.* art of devising and describing coats of arms, tracing genealogies, etc. —**he·ral/dic** (he ral/dik, hə-) *adj.*

herb (ûrb; *esp. Brit.* hûrb) *n.* flowering plant with nonwoody stem. —**her·ba/ceous** (hûr bā/shəs, ûr-) *adj.* —**herb·al** (ûr/bəl, hûr/-) *adj.*

herb/i·cide/ (hûr/bə sīd/, ûr/-) *n.* substance for killing plants, esp. weeds. —**her/bi·cid/al,** *adj.*

her·biv/o·rous (hûr biv/ər əs, ûr-) *adj.* feeding on plants. —**her/bi·vore/** (hûr/bə vôr/, ûr/-) *n.*

her/cu·le/an (hûr/kyə lē/ən, hûr-kyōō/lē-) *adj.* requiring extraordinary strength or effort.

herd (hûrd) *n.* 1. animals feeding or moving together. —*v.* 2. go in herd. 3. tend herd.

here (hēr) *adv.* 1. in or to this place. 2. present.

here/a·bout/ *adv.* in this vicinity. Also, **here/a·bouts/.**

here·af/ter, *adv.* 1. in the future. —*n.* 2. future life.

here·by/, *adv.* by this.

he·red/i·tar/y (hə red/i ter/ē) *adj.* 1. passing from parents to offspring. 2. of heredity. 3. by inheritance.

he·red/i·ty, *n.* transmission of traits from parents to offspring.

here·in/, *adv.* in this place.

her/e·sy (her/ə sē) *n., pl.* **-sies.** unorthodox opinion or doctrine. —**her·et/ic** (her/i-) *n.*

here/to·fore/, *adv.* before now.

here/with/, *adv.* along with this.

her/it·a·ble (her/i tə bəl) *adj.* capable of being inherited.

her/it·age (her/i tij) *n.* 1. inheritance. 2. traditions and history.

her·maph/ro·dite/ (hûr maf/rə dīt/) *n.* animal or plant with reproductive organs of both sexes.

her·met/ic (hûr met/ik) *adj.* airtight. Also, **hermet/i·cal.**

her/mit (hûr/mit) *n.* recluse.

her/mit·age (-mi tij) *n.* hermit's abode.

her/ni·a (hûr/nē ə) *n.* rupture in abdominal wall, etc.

he/ro (hēr/ō) *n., pl.* **-roes.** 1. man admired for bravery. 2. main male character in story. —**he/ro·ine** (her/ō in) *n.fem.* —**he·ro/ic** (hi rō/ik) *adj.* —**her/o·ism** (her/ō iz/əm) *n.*

her/o·in (her/ō in) *n.* illegal morphinelike drug.

her/on (her/ən) *n.* long-legged wading bird.

hero sandwich, large sandwich of cold cuts, etc., in long roll.

her'pes (hûr'pēz) *n.* viral disease characterized by blisters on skin or mucous membranes.

her'ring (her'ing) *n.* north Atlantic food fish.

her'ring·bone', *n.* **1.** pattern of slanting lines in vertical rows. **2.** fabric of this.

hers (hûrz) *pron.* **1.** possessive form of **she,** used predicatively. **2.** her belongings or family.

her·self', *pron.* emphatic or reflexive form of **her.**

hertz (hûrts) *n.,* pl. **hertz.** radio frequency of one cycle per second.

hes'i·tate' (hez'i tāt') *v.,* -tated, -tating. **1.** hold back in doubt. **2.** pause. **3.** stammer. —**hes'i·tant** (-tənt) *adj.* —**hes'i·ta'tion, hes'i·tan·cy,** *n.*

het'er·o·dox' (het'ər ə doks') *adj.* unorthodox. —**het'er·o·dox'y,** *n.*

het'er·o·ge'ne·ous (-jē'nē əs) *adj.* **1.** unlike. **2.** varied.

het'er·o·sex'u·al, *adj.* sexually attracted to opposite sex.

hew (hyōō) *v.,* hewed, hewed or hewn, hewing. **1.** chop or cut. **2.** cut down. —**hew'er,** *n.*

hex (heks) *v.* **1.** cast spell on. **2.** bring bad luck to. —*n.* **3.** jinx.

hex'a·gon' (hek'sa gon', -gən) *n.* six-sided polygon. —**hex·ag'o·nal** (hek sag'ə nl) *adj.*

hey'day' (hā'dā') *n.* time of greatest success, popularity, etc.

hgt., height.

hgwy., highway.

HI, Hawaii.

hi·a'tus (hī ā'təs) *n.,* pl. **-tuses, -tus.** break or interruption in a series, action, etc.

hi·ba'chi (hi bä'chē) *n.* small charcoal brazier covered with a grill.

hi'ber·nate' (hī'bər nāt') *v.,* -nated, -nating. spend winter in dormant state. —**hi'ber·na'tion,** *n.*

hi·bis'cus (hī bis'kəs, hi-) *n.* plant with large flowers.

hic'cup (hik'up, -əp) *n.* **1.** sudden involuntary drawing in of breath. —*v.* **2.** have hiccups. Also, **hic'cough** (hik'up).

hick (hik) *n.* provincial, unsophisticated person.

hick'o·ry (hik'ə rē) *n.,* pl. **-ries.** tree bearing edible nut.

hide (hīd) *v.,* hid (hid), hidden or hid, hiding, *n.* —*v.* **1.** conceal or be concealed. —*n.* **2.** animal's skin.

hide'a·way', *n.* private retreat.

hide'bound', *adj.* narrow and rigid in opinion.

hid'e·ous (hid'ē əs) *adj.* **1.** very ugly. **2.** revolting.

hide'-out', *n.* safe place to hide, esp. from the law.

hi'er·ar'chy (hī'ə rär'kē) *n.,* pl. -chies. graded system of officials.

hi'er·o·glyph'ic (hī'ər ə glif'ik, hī'rə-) *adj.* **1.** of picture writing, as among ancient Egyptians. —*n.* **2.** hieroglyphic symbol.

hi-fi' (hī'fī') *adj.* of high fidelity. —**hi'-fi',** *n.*

high (hī) *adj.* **1.** tall. **2.** lofty. **3.** expensive. **4.** shrill. **5.** *Informal.* exuberant with drink or drugs. **6.** greater than normal. **7.** elevated in pitch. —*adv.* **8.** at or to high place, rank, etc.

high'ball', *n.* drink of whiskey mixed with club soda or ginger ale.

high'brow', *n.* **1.** cultured person. —*adj.* **2.** typical of a highbrow.

high fidelity, reproduction of sound without distortion.

high'-flown', *adj.* **1.** pretentious. **2.** bombastic.

high frequency, radio frequency between 3 and 30 megahertz.

high'-hand'ed, *adj.* overbearing.

high'lands (-ləndz) *n.* elevated part of country.

high'light', *v.* **1.** emphasize. —*n.* **2.** important event, scene, etc. **3.** area of strong reflected light.

high'ly, *adv.* very; extremely.

high'-mind'ed, *adj.* noble in feelings or principles.

high'ness (-nis) *n.* **1.** high state. **2.** (*cap.*) title of royalty.

high'-pres'sure, *adj., v.,* -sured, -suring. *adj.* **1.** stressful. —*v.* **2.** persuade aggressively.

high'rise', *n.* high building. —**high'rise',** *adj.*

high'road', *n.* highway.

high' school', *n.* school for grades 9 through 12.

high seas, ocean space, esp. beyond territorial waters.

high'-spir'it·ed, *adj.* lively.

high'-strung', *adj.* nervous.

high'-tech', *n.* **1.** technology using highly sophisticated and advanced equipment and techniques. —*adj.* **2.** using or suggesting high-tech.

high'-ten'sion, *adj.* of relatively high voltage.

high'way', *n.* main road.

high'way·man, *n., pl.* -men. highway robber.

hi'jack' (hī'jak') *v.* seize (plane, truck, etc.) by force.

hike (hīk) *v.,* hiked, hiking, *n.* —*v.* **1.** walk long distance. —*n.* **2.** long walk. —**hik'er,** *n.*

hi·lar'i·ous (hi lâr'ē əs, -lar'-) *adj.*

1. very funny. **2.** very cheerful.
—**hi•lar′i•ty**, *n.*

hill (hil) *n.* high piece of land.
—**hill′y**, *adj.*

hill′bil′ly (-bil′ē) *n., pl.* **-lies.** *Sometimes Offensive.* someone from a backwoods area.

hill′ock (-ək) *n.* little hill.

hilt (hilt) *n.* sword handle.

him (him) *pron.* objective case of **he.**

him•self′ (him self′; *medially often* im-) *pron.* reflexive or emphatic form of **him.**

hind (hīnd) *adj.* **1.** rear. —*n.* **2.** female red deer.

hin′der (hin′dər) *v.* **1.** retard. **2.** stop. —**hin′drance**, *n.*

hind′most′ (hīnd′mōst′) *adj.* last.

hind′sight′, *n.* keen awareness of how one should have avoided past mistakes.

Hin′du (hin′dōō) *n.* adherent of Hinduism. —**Hindu**, *adj.*

Hin′du•ism, *n.* major religion of India.

hinge (hinj) *n., v.*, **hinged, hinging.** —*n.* **1.** joint on which door, lid, etc., turns. —*v.* **2.** depend. **3.** furnish with hinges.

hint (hint) *n.* **1.** indirect suggestion. —*v.* **2.** give hint.

hin′ter•land′ (hin′tər land′) *n.* land remote from cities.

hip (hip) *n.* **1.** projecting part of each side of body below waist. —*adj. Slang.* **2.** familiar with the latest styles or ideas.

hip′-hop′, *n. Slang.* popular subculture as characterized by rap music.

hip′pie (hip′ē) *n.* person of 1960s who rejected conventional cultural and moral values.

hip′po (hip′ō) *n., pl.* **-pos.** hippopotamus.

hip′po•drome′ (hip′ə drōm′) *n.* arena, esp. for horse events.

hip′po•pot′a•mus (hip′ə pot′ə məs) *n., pl.* **-muses, -mi** (-mī′) large African water mammal.

hire (hīᵖr) *v.*, **hired, hiring.** —*v.* **1.** purchase services or use of. —*n.* **2.** payment for services or use.

hire′ling (-ling) *n.* person whose loyalty can be bought.

hir′sute (hûr′sōōt, hûr sōōt′) *adj.* hairy. —**hir′sute•ness**, *n.*

his (hiz; *unstressed* iz) *pron.* **1.** possessive form of **he. 2.** his belongings.

His•pan′ic (hi span′ik) *n.* person of Spanish or Latin-American descent. —**Hispanic,** *adj.*

hiss (his) *v.* **1.** make prolonged *s* sound. **2.** express disapproval in this way. —*n.* **3.** hissing sound.

his•tor′ic (hi stôr′ik) *adj.* **1.** Also, **his•tor′i•cal.** of history. **2.** important in or surviving from the past.

his′to•ry (his′tə rē, -trē) *n., pl.* **-ries. 1.** knowledge, study, or record of past events. **2.** pattern of events determining future. —**his•to′ri•an** (hi stôr′ē ən) *n.*

his′tri•on′ics (his′trē on′iks) *n.pl.* exaggerated, esp. melodramatic, behavior. —**his′tri•on′ic,** *adj.*

hit (hit) *v.*, **hit, hitting.** —*v.* **1.** strike. **2.** collide with. **3.** meet. **4.** guess. —*n.* **5.** collision. **6.** blow. **7.** success. **8.** *Slang.* murder.

hitch (hich) *v.* **1.** fasten. **2.** harness to cart, etc. **3.** raise or move jerkily. —*n.* **4.** fastening or knot. **5.** obstruction or problem.

hitch′hike′, *v.*, **-hiked, -hiking.** beg a ride from a stranger.

hith′er (hith′ər) *adv.* to this place.

hith′er•to′, *adv.* until now.

HIV, human immunodeficiency virus, the cause of AIDS.

hive (hīv) *n.* shelter for bees.

hives (hīvz) *n.pl.* eruptive skin condition.

HMO, *pl.* **HMOs, HMO's.** health maintenance organization: healthcare plan that provides comprehensive services to subscribers.

H.M.S., Her (or His) Majesty's Ship.

hoa′gie (hō′gē) *n.* hero sandwich. Also, **hoa′gy.**

hoard (hōrd) *n.* **1.** accumulation for future use. —*v.* **2.** accumulate as hoard. —**hoard′er,** *n.*

hoar′frost′ (hôr′frôst′) *n.* frost (def. 2).

hoarse (hôrs) *adj.* gruff in tone.

hoar′y (hôr′ē) *adj.* white with age.

hoax (hōks) *n.* **1.** mischievous deception. —*v.* **2.** deceive; trick.

hob′ble (hob′əl) *v.*, **-bled, -bling.** **1.** limp. **2.** fasten legs to prevent free movement.

hob′by (hob′ē) *n., pl.* **-bies.** favorite activity or pastime.

hob′by•horse′, *n.* **1.** rocking toy for riding. **2.** favorite subject for discussion.

hob′gob′lin, *n.* something causing superstitious fear.

hob′nob′ (-nob′) *v.*, **-nobbed, -nobbing.** associate socially.

ho′bo (hō′bō) *n., pl.* **-bos, -boes.** tramp; vagrant.

hock (hok) *n.* **1.** joint in hind leg of horse, etc. —*v.* **2.** pawn.

hock′ey (hok′ē) *n.* game played with bent clubs (**hockey sticks**) and ball or disk.

hock′shop′, *n.* pawnshop.

ho′cus-po′cus (hō′kəs pō′kəs) *n.* **1.** sleight of hand. **2.** trickery.

hod (hod) *n.* **1.** trough for carrying mortar, bricks, etc. **2.** coal scuttle.

hodge′podge′ (hoj′poj′) *n.* mixture; jumble.

hoe (hō) *n., v.,* **hoed, hoeing.** —*n.* **1.** tool for breaking ground, etc. —*v.* **2.** use hoe on.

hog (hôg) *n., v.,* **hogged, hogging.** —*n.* **1.** domesticated swine. **2.** greedy or filthy person. —*v.* **3.** take greedily. —**hog′gish,** *adj.*

hogs′head′, *n.* large cask.

hog′wash′, *n.* nonsense; bunk.

hog′-wild′, *adj.* wildly enthusiastic.

hoi′ pol·loi′ (hoi′ pə loi′) common people; the masses.

hoist (hoist) *v.* **1.** lift, esp. by machine. —*n.* **2.** hoisting apparatus. **3.** act of lifting.

hok′ey (hō′kē) *adj.,* **hokier, hokiest. 1.** mawkish **2.** obviously contrived. —**hok′i·ness,** *n.*

hold (hōld) *v.,* **held** (held)**, holding,** *n.* —*v.* **1.** have in hand. **2.** possess. **3.** sustain. **4.** adhere. **5.** celebrate. **6.** restrain or detain. **7.** believe. **8.** consider. —*n.* **9.** grasp. **10.** influence. **11.** cargo space below ship's deck. —**hold′er,** *n.*

hold′ing, *n.* **1.** leased land, esp. for farming. **2.** (*pl.*) legally owned property, esp. securities.

hold′out′, *n.* one who refuses to take part, give in, etc.

hold′up′, *n.* **1.** delay. **2.** robbery at gunpoint.

hole (hōl) *n., v.,* **holed, holing.** —*n.* **1.** opening. **2.** cavity. **3.** burrow. **4.** in golf, one of the cups into which the ball is driven. —*v.* **5.** drive into hole. **6.** make a hole in.

hol′i·day′ (hol′i dā′) *n.* **1.** day or period without work. —*adj.* **2.** festive.

ho′li·ness (hō′lē nis) *n.* holy state or character.

ho·lis′tic (hō lis′tik) *adj.* of or using therapies that consider the body and the mind as an integrated whole.

hol′low (hol′ō) *adj.* **1.** empty within. **2.** sunken. **3.** dull. **4.** unreal. —*n.* **5.** cavity. —*v.* **6.** make hollow.

hol′ly (hol′ē) *n., pl.* **-lies.** shrub with glossy leaves and bright red berries.

hol′ly·hock′ (-hok′, -hôk′) *n.* tall flowering plant.

hol′o·caust′ (hol′ə kôst′, hō′lə-) *n.* **1.** great destruction, esp. by fire. **2.** (*cap.*) Nazi killing of Jews during World War II.

hol′o·gram′ (hol′ə gram′, hō′lə-) *n.*

three-dimensional image made by a laser.

ho·log′ra·phy (hə log′rə fē) *n.* process of making holograms.

hol′ster (hōl′stər) *n.* case for pistol.

ho′ly (hō′lē) *adj.,* **-lier, -liest. 1.** sacred. **2.** dedicated to God.

Holy Ghost, third member of Trinity. Also, **Holy Spirit.**

hom′age (hom′ij, om′-) *n.* reverence or respect.

home (hōm) *n.* **1.** residence. **2.** native place or country. —*adv.* **3.** to or at home. —**home′land′,** *n.* —**home′ward,** *adv., adj.* —**home′less,** *adj.* —**home′made′,** *adj.*

home′ly, *adj.,* **-lier, -liest. 1.** plain; not beautiful. **2.** simple.

home′mak′er, *n.* person who manages a home.

ho′me·op′a·thy (hō′mē op′ə thē) *n.* method of treating homeopathy with small doses of drugs that in a healthy person would cause symptoms like those of the disease. —**ho′me·o·path′ic** (-ə path′ik) *adj.*

home′sick′, *adj.* longing for home.

home′spun′, *adj.* **1.** spun at home. **2.** unpretentious. —*n.* **3.** cloth made at home.

home′stead (-sted, -stid) *n.* dwelling with its land and buildings.

home′stretch′, *n.* last part of racetrack, endeavor, etc.

hom′ey (hō′mē) *adj.,* **-ier, -iest.** cozy.

hom′i·cide′ (hom′ə sīd′, hō′mə-) *n.* killing of one person by another. —**hom′i·cid′al,** *adj.*

hom′i·ly (hom′ə lē) *n., pl.* **-lies.** sermon. —**hom′i·let′ic** (-let′ik) *adj.*

hom′i·ny (hom′ə nē) *n.* **1.** hulled corn. **2.** coarse flour from corn.

homo-, prefix meaning same or identical, as *homosexuous.*

ho′mo·ge′ne·ous (hō′mə jēn′ē əs) *adj.* **1.** unvaried in content. **2.** alike. —**ho′mo·ge·ne′i·ty** (-ji nē′ə tē) *n.*

ho·mog′e·nize′ (hə moj′ə nīz′, hō-) *v.,* **-nized, -nizing.** form by mixing and emulsifying.

hom′o·graph′ (hom′ə graf′, hō′mə-) *n.* word spelled the same as another but having a different meaning.

hom′o·nym′ (hom′ə nim) *n.* word like another in sound, but not in meaning.

ho′mo·pho′bi·a (hō′mə fō′bē ə) *n.* unreasoning hatred of homosexuals.

Ho′mo sa′pi·ens (hō′mō sā′pē ənz) human being.

ho′mo·sex′u·al (hō′mə sek′shoō əl) *adj.* **1.** sexually attracted to same

sex. —*n.* **2.** homosexual person.
—**ho'mo•sex'u•al'i•ty** (-al'i tē) *n.*

Hon., **1.** Honorable. **2.** Honorary.

hon'cho (hon'chō) *n., pl.* **-chos.**
Slang. leader or important person.

hone (hōn) *n., v.,* **honed, honing.**
—*n.* **1.** fine whetstone. —*v.* **2.**
sharpen to fine edge.

hon'est (on'ist) *adj.* **1.** trustworthy.
2. sincere. **3.** virtuous. —**hon'est•ly,** *adv.* —**hon'es•ty,** *n.*

hon'ey (hun'ē) *n.* **1.** sweet fluid produced by bees (**hon'ey•bees'**)

hon'ey•comb', *n.* **1.** wax structure built by bees to store honey.

hon'ey•dew' melon, sweet muskmelon.

hon'ey•moon', *n.* vacation taken by newly married couple.

hon'ey•suck'le, *n.* shrub bearing tubular flowers.

honk (hongk) *n.* **1.** sound of automobile horn, goose, etc. —*v.* **2.** make such sound.

hon'or (on'ər) *n.* **1.** public or official esteem. **2.** something as token of this. **3.** good reputation. **4.** high ethical character. **5.** chastity. —*v.* **6.** revere. **7.** confer honor. **8.** show regard for. **9.** accept as valid.

hon'or•a•ble, *adj.* **1.** worthy of honor. **2.** of high principles.

hon'or•ar'y (-rer'ē) *adj.* conferred as honor.

hood (hŏŏd) *n.* **1.** covering for head and neck. **2.** automobile engine cover. **3.** hoodlum. —**hood'ed,** *adj.*

hood'lum (hŏŏd'ləm, hŏŏd'-) *n.* violent petty criminal.

hoof (hŏŏf, hŏŏf) *n., pl.* **hoofs,
hooves** (hŏŏvz, hŏŏvz). horny covering of animal foot. —**hoofed,** *adj.*

hook (hŏŏk) *n.* **1.** curved piece of metal for catching, etc. **2.** fishhook. **3.** sharp curve. —*v.* **4.** seize, etc., with hook.

hook'er, *n. Slang.* prostitute, esp. one who solicits on the street.

hook'up', *n.* connection of parts or apparatus in circuit, network, machine, or system.

hoo'li•gan (hōō'li gən) *n.* noisy, violent person.

hoop (hŏŏp, hŏŏp) *n.* circular band.

hoop'la (hōōp'lä) *n. Informal.* **1.** commotion. **2.** sensational publicity.

hoo•ray' (hŏŏ rā') *interj., n.* (hurrah.)

hoot (hōōt) *v.* **1.** shout in derision. **2.** (of owl) utter cry. —*n.* **3.** owl's cry. **4.** shout of derision.

hop (hop) *v.,* **hopped, hopping,** *n.* —*v.* **1.** leap, esp. on one foot. —*n.*

2. such a leap. **3.** plant bearing cones used in brewing. **4.** (*pl.*) the cones of this plant.

hope (hōp) *n., v.,* **hoped, hoping.** —*n.* **1.** feeling that something desired is possible. **2.** object of this. **3.** confidence. —*v.* **4.** look forward to with hope. —**hope'ful,** *adj.*

Ho'pi (hō'pē) *n., pl.* **-pi, -pis.** member of an American Indian people of the southwest.

hop'per (hop'ər) *n.* funnel-shaped trough for grain, etc.

horde (hôrd) *n.* **1.** multitude. **2.** nomadic group.

ho•ri'zon (hə rī'zən) *n.* apparent line between earth and sky.

hor'i•zon'tal (hôr'ə zon'tl) *adj.* **1.** at right angles to vertical. **2.** level. —*n.* **3.** horizontal line, etc.

hor'mone (hôr'mōn) *n.* endocrine gland secretion that activates specific organ, mechanism, etc.

horn (hôrn) *n.* **1.** hard growth on heads of cattle, goats, etc. **2.** hornlike part. **3.** brass wind instrument.

hor'net (hôr'nit) *n.* large wasp.

horn'pipe', *n.* lively dance.

hor'o•scope' (hôr'ə skōp') *n.* chart of heavens used in astrology.

hor•ren'dous (hə ren'dəs) *adj.* dreadful; horrible.

hor'ri•ble (hôr'ə bəl) *adj.* dreadful.

hor'rid (-id) *adj.* abominable.

hor'ror (hôr'ər) *n.* intense fear or repugnance. —**hor'ri•fy',** *v.,* **-fied, -fying.**

hors•d'oeuvre (ôr dûrv') *n., pl.* **-d'oeuvres** (-dûrv', -dûrvz'). tidbit served before meal.

horse (hôrs) *n.* **1.** large domesticated quadruped. **2.** cavalry. **3.** frame with legs for bearing work, etc. —**horse'back',** *n., adv.* —**horse'man,** *n.* —**horse'wo•man,** *n.fem.*

horse'play', *n.* boisterous play.

horse'pow'er, *n.* unit of power, equal to 550 foot-pounds per second.

horse'rad'ish, *n.* cultivated plant with pungent root.

horse sense, common sense.

horse'shoe', *n.* **1.** U-shaped iron plate nailed to horse's hoof. **2.** arrangement in this form. **3.** (*pl.*) game in which horseshoes are tossed.

hors'y, *adj.,* **-ier, -iest.** of or like a horse.

hor'ti•cul'ture (hôr'ti kul'chər) *n.* cultivation of gardens.

ho•san'na (hō zan'ə) *interj.* (praise the Lord!)

hose (hōz) *n.* **1.** stockings. **2.** flexible tube for water, etc.

ho′sier·y (hō′zhə rē) *n.* stockings.

hos′pice (hos′pis) *n.* **1.** shelter for pilgrims, strangers, etc. **2.** facility for supportive care of dying persons.

hos·pi·ta·ble (hos′pi tə bəl, hos-pit′ə-) *adj.* showing hospitality.

hos′pi·tal (hos′pi tl) *n.* institution for treatment of sick and injured. —**hos′pi·tal·i·za′tion,** *n.* —**hos′pi·tal·ize′, -ized, -izing.**

hos′pi·tal′i·ty (-tal′i tē) *n., pl.* **-ties.** warm reception of guests, etc.

host (hōst) *n.* **1.** entertainer of guests. **2.** great number. **3.** (*cap.*) bread consecrated in Eucharist. —**host′ess,** *n.fem.*

hos′tage (hos′tij) *n.* person given or held as security.

hos′tel (hos′tl) *n.* inexpensive transient lodging.

hos′tile (hos′tl; *esp. Brit.* -tīl) *adj.* **1.** opposed; unfriendly. **2.** of enemies. —**hos·til′i·ty** (ho stil′i tē) *n.*

hot (hot) *adj.,* **hotter, hottest. 1.** of high temperature. **2.** feeling great heat. **3.** sharp-tasting. **4.** ardent. **5.** fresh or new. **6.** *Informal.* currently popular. **7.** *Informal.* performing very well. **8.** *Slang.* recently stolen.

hot′bed′, *n.* **1.** covered and heated bed of earth for growing plants. **2.** place where something thrives and spreads.

hot′-blood′ed, *adj.* excitable.

hot cake, pancake.

hot dog, **1.** frankfurter. **2.** *Slang.* show-off.

ho·tel′ (hō tel′) *n.* building offering food, lodging, etc.

hot flash, sudden, brief feeling of heat experienced by some menopausal women.

hot′head′, *n.* impetuous or rash person. —**hot′head′ed,** *adj.*

hot′house′, *n.* greenhouse.

hot line, system for instantaneous communications of major importance.

hot plate, portable electrical appliance for cooking.

hot potato, *Informal.* unpleasant or risky situation or issue.

hot rod, *Slang.* car with speeded-up engine. —**hot rodder.**

hot′shot′, *n.* *Slang.* skillful and often vain person.

hot tub, large tub of hot water big enough for several persons.

hot water, *Informal.* trouble.

hound (hound) *n.* **1.** any of several breeds of hunting dog. —*v.* **2.** hunt or track.

hour (ou³r, ou′ər) *n.* period of 60 minutes. —**hour′ly,** *adj., adv.*

hour′glass′, *n.* timepiece operating by visible fall of sand.

house *n., v.,* **housed, housing.** —*n.* (hous) **1.** building, esp. for residence, rest, etc. **2.** family. **3.** legislative or deliberative body. **4.** commercial firm. —*v.* (houz) **5.** provide with a house.

house′break′er, *n.* person who breaks into another's house to steal.

house′bro′ken, *adj.* trained to excrete outdoors or to behave appropriately indoors.

house′fly′, *n., pl.* **-flies.** common insect.

house′hold′, *n.* **1.** people of house. —*adj.* **2.** domestic.

house′hold′er, *n.* **1.** person who owns house. **2.** head of household.

house′hus′band, *n.* married man who stays at home to manage the household.

house′keep′er, *n.* person who manages a house.

house′plant′, *n.* ornamental plant grown indoors.

house′warm′ing, *n.* party to celebrate a new home.

house′wife′, *n., pl.* **-wives.** woman in charge of home.

house′work′, *n.* work done in housekeeping.

hous′ing (hou′zing) *n.* **1.** dwellings collectively. **2.** container.

hov′el (huv′əl, hov′-) *n.* small mean dwelling.

hov′er (huv′ər, hov′-) *v.* **1.** stay suspended in air. **2.** linger about.

Hov′er·craft′, *n.* *Trademark.* vehicle that can skim over water on cushion of air.

how (hou) *adv.* **1.** in what way. **2.** to, at, or in what extent, price, or condition. **3.** why.

how·ev′er, *conj.* **1.** nevertheless. —*adv.* **2.** to whatever extent.

how′itz·er (hou′it sər) *n.* short-barreled cannon.

howl (houl) *v.* **1.** utter loud long cry. **2.** wail. —*n.* **3.** cry of wolf, etc. **4.** wail.

how′so·ev′er, *adv.* however.

hoy′den (hoid′n) *n.* tomboy.

HP, horsepower.

HQ, headquarters.

hr., hour.

H.R., House of Representatives.

H.S., High School.

ht., height.

hub (hub) *n.* central part of wheel.

hub′bub (hub′ub) *n.* confused noise.

hu′bris (hyōō′bris, hōō′-) *n.* excessive pride or self-confidence.

huck′le·ber′ry (huk′əl ber′ē) n., pl. **-ries.** edible berry of heath shrub.

huck′ster (huk′stər) n. peddler.

HUD (hud) Department of Housing and Urban Development.

hud·dle (hud′l) v., **-dled, -dling,** n. —v. **1.** crowd together. —n. **2.** confused heap or crowd.

hue (hyōō) n. **1.** color. **2.** outcry.

huff (huf) n. fit of anger.

hug (hug) v., **hugged, hugging,** n. —v. **1.** clasp in arms. **2.** stay close to. —n. **3.** tight clasp.

huge (hyōōj; often yōōj) adj., **huger, hugest.** very large in size or extent.

hu′la (hōō′lə) n. Hawaiian dance.

hulk (hulk) n. hull remaining from old ship.

hulk′ing, adj. bulky. Also, **hulk′y.**

hull (hul) n. **1.** outer covering of seed or fruit. **2.** body of ship. —v. **3.** remove hull of.

hul·la·ba·loo′ (hul′ə bə lōō′) n., pl. **-loos.** Informal. uproar.

hum (hum) v., **hummed, humming,** n. —v. **1.** make low droning sound. **2.** sing with closed lips. **3.** be busy or active. —n. **4.** indistinct murmur.

hu′man (hyōō′mən) adj. **1.** of or like people or their species. —n. **2.** Also, **human being.** a person.

hu·mane′ (-mān′) adj. tender; compassionate. —**hu·mane′ly,** adv.

hu′man·ism, n. system of thought focusing on human interests, values, and dignity. —**hu′man·ist,** n., adj.

hu·man′i·tar′i·an (-man′i târ′ē ən) adj. **1.** philanthropic. —n. **2.** philanthropist.

hu·man′i·ty, n., pl. **-ties. 1.** humankind. **2.** human state or quality. **3.** kindness. **4.** (pl.) literature, philosophy, etc., as distinguished from the sciences.

hu′man·ize′ (-mə nīz′) v., **-ized, -izing.** make or become human or humane. —**hu′man·i·za′tion,** n.

hu′man·kind′, n. people collectively.

hu′man·ly, adv. by human means.

hum′ble (hum′bəl, um′-) adj., **-bler, -blest,** v., **-bled, -bling.** —adj. **1.** low in rank, etc. **2.** meek. —v. **3.** abase. —**hum′bly,** adv.

hum′bug (hum′bug′) n. **1.** hoax. **2.** falseness.

hum′drum′ (hum′drum′) adj. dull.

hu′mid (hyōō′mid) adj. (of air) moist. —**hu·mid′i·fy,** v., **-fied, -fying.** —**hu·mid′i·fi·er,** n.

hu·mi·dor′ (-mi dôr′) n. humid box or chamber.

hu·mil′i·ate′ (hyōō mil′ē āt′) v., **-ated, -ating.** harm the pride or self-respect of. —**hu·mil′i·a′tion,** n.

hu·mil′i·ty, n. humbleness.

hum′ming·bird′, n. very small American bird.

hum′mock (hum′ək) n. hillock.

hu·mon′gous (hyōō mung′gəs, -mong′-) adj. Slang. extraordinarily large.

hu′mor (hyōō′mər) n. **1.** funniness. **2.** mental disposition. **3.** whim. —v. **4.** indulge mood or whim of. —**hu′mor·ist,** n. —**hu′mor·ous,** adj.

hump (hump) n. **1.** rounded protuberance. —v. **2.** raise in hump.

hump′back′, n. **1.** back with hump. **2.** person with such a back. Also, **hunch′back′.**

hu′mus (hyōō′məs) n. dark organic material in soils, produced by decomposing matter.

hunch (hunch) v. **1.** push out or up in a hump. —n. **2.** hump. **3.** guess.

hun′dred (hun′drid) n., adj. ten times ten. —**hun′dredth,** adj., n.

Hun·gar′i·an (hung gâr′ē ən) n. native or language of Hungary. —**Hun·gar′i·an,** adj.

hun′ger (hung′gər) n. **1.** feeling caused by need of food. **2.** strong desire. —v. **3.** be hungry.

hun′gry, adj., **-grier, -griest.** **1.** craving food. **2.** desirous.

hunk (hungk) n. **1.** large piece. **2.** Slang. handsome, muscular man

hun′ker (hung′kər) v. squat down.

hunt (hunt) v. **1.** chase to catch or kill. **2.** search for. —n. **3.** act of hunting. **4.** search. —**hunt′er,** n. —**hunt′ress,** n.fem.

hur′dle (hûr′dl) n., v., **-dled, -dling.** n. **1.** barrier in race track. —v. **2.** leap over.

hurl (hûrl) v. throw with great force. —**hurl′er,** n.

hur′ly-bur′ly (hûr′lē bûr′lē) n. noisy disorder and confusion.

hur·rah′ (hə rä′, -rô′) interj., n. (exclamation of joy, triumph, etc.)

hur′ri·cane′ (hûr′i kān′, hur′-) n. violent storm.

hur′ry (hûr′ē, hur′ē) v., **-ried, -rying,** n., pl. **-ries.** —v. **1.** move or act with haste. —n. **2.** need for haste. **3.** haste. —**hur′ried·ly,** adv.

hurt (hûrt) v., **hurt, hurting,** n. —v. **1.** cause pain. **2.** harm. **3.** offend. —n. **4.** injury or damage.

hur′tle (hûr′tl) v., **-tled, -tling.** strike or rush violently.

hus′band (huz′bənd) n. **1.** man of married pair. —v. **2.** manage prudently.

hus•band•ry, *n.* farming and raising of livestock.

hush (hush) *interj.* **1.** (command to be silent.) —*n.* **2.** silence.

husk (husk) *n.* **1.** dry covering of seeds. —*v.* **2.** remove husk.

husk′y, *adj., -ier, -iest, n., pl. -ies.* —*adj.* **1.** big and strong. **2.** hoarse. —*n.* **3.** (*sometimes cap.*) sturdy sled dog of arctic regions.

hus′sy (hus′ē, huz′ē) *n., pl. -sies.* **1.** ill-behaved girl. **2.** lewd woman.

hus′tle (hus′əl) *v., -tled, -tling, n.* —*v.* **1.** work energetically. —*n.* **2.** energetic activity.

hus′tler, *n. Slang.* **1.** person eager for success. **2.** swindler. **3.** prostitute.

hut (hut) *n.* small humble dwelling.

hutch (huch) *n.* **1.** pen for small animals. **2.** chestlike cabinet with open shelves above.

hwy., highway.

hy′a•cinth (hī′ə sinth) *n.* bulbous flowering plant.

hy′brid (hī′brid) *n.* offspring of organisms of different breeds, species, etc.

hy′brid•ize, *v., -ized, -izing,* produce or cause to produce hybrids.

hy•dran′gea (hī drān′jə) *n.* flowering shrub.

hy′drant (hī′drənt) *n.* water pipe with outlet.

hy•drau′lic (hī drô′lik) *adj.* **1.** of or operated by liquid. **2.** of hydraulics.

hy•drau′lics, *n.* science of moving liquids.

hydro-, prefix meaning: **1.** water. **2.** hydrogen.

hy′dro•car′bon (hī′drə kär′bən) *n.* compound containing only hydrogen and carbon.

hy′dro•e•lec′tric (hī′drō-) *adj.* of electricity generated from hydraulic energy. —**hy′dro•e•lec•tric′i•ty,** *n.*

hy′dro•foil′ (hī′drə foil′) *n.* powered vessel that can skim on water.

hy′dro•gen (-jən) *n.* inflammable gas, lightest of elements.

hy′dro•gen•ate′ (hī′drə jə nāt′, hī droj′ə-) *v., -ated, -ating.* combine with or treat with hydrogen.

hydrogen bomb, powerful bomb utilizing thermonuclear fusion.

hydrogen peroxide, liquid used as antiseptic and bleach.

hy′dro•pho′bi•a (hī′drə fō′bē ə) *n.* **1.** rabies. **2.** fear of water.

hy′dro•plane′, *n.* **1.** airplane that lands on water. **2.** light, high-speed motorboat.

hy′dro•ther′a•py, *n.* use of water externally to treat disease or injury.

hy•e′na (hī ē′nə) *n.* carnivorous African mammal.

hy′giene (hī′jēn) *n.* **1.** the application of scientific knowledge to the preservation of health. **2.** a condition or practice conducive to health, as cleanliness. —**hy•gi•en′ic** (-jē en′ik, -jen′-, -jē′nik) *adj.*

hy•grom′e•ter (hī grom′i tər) *n.* instrument for measuring humidity.

hy′men (hī′mən) *n.* fold of mucous membrane partly enclosing the vagina in a virgin.

hymn (him) *n.* song of praise.

hym′nal (him′nəl) *n.* book of hymns. Also, **hymn′book′.**

hype (hīp) *v., hyped, hyping, n. Informal.* —*v.* **1.** create interest in by flamboyant methods. —*n.* **2.** exaggerated promotion.

hyper-, prefix meaning over, above, or excessive, as *hyperactive.*

hy′per•ac′tive (hī′pər-) *adj.* abnormally active.

hy•per′bo•le (hī pûr′bə lē) *n.* exaggeration for rhetorical effect.

hy′per•crit′i•cal (hī′pər-) *adj.* excessively critical.

hy′per•gly•ce′mi•a (-glī sē′mē ə) *n.* abnormally high level of glucose in the blood.

hy′per•ten′sion, *n.* abnormally high blood pressure.

hy′per•ven′ti•la′tion, *n.* prolonged rapid or deep breathing. —**hy′per•ven′ti•late′,** *v.*

hy′phen (hī′fən) *n.* short line (-) connecting parts or syllables of a word. —**hy′phen•ate′,** *v.*

hyp•no′sis (hip nō′sis) *n., pl. -ses* (-sēz). artificially produced sleeplike state. —**hyp•not′ic** (-not′ik) *adj.* —**hyp′no•tism′** (-nə tiz′əm) *n.* —**hyp′no•tist,** *n.* —**hyp′no•tize′,** *v.*

hy′po (hī′pō) *n., pl. -pos.* hypodermic needle or injection.

hy′po•al′ler•gen′ic, *adj.* designed to minimize the chance of an allergic reaction.

hy′po•chon′dri•a (hī′pə kon′drē ə) *n.* morbid preoccupation with one's health. —**hy′po•chon′dri•ac′,** *n., adj.*

hy•poc′ri•sy (hī pok′rə sē) *n., pl. -sies.* pretense of virtue, piety, etc.

hyp′o•crite (hip′ə krit) *n.* person given to hypocrisy. —**hyp′o•crit′i•cal,** *adj.*

hy′po•der′mic (hī′pə dûr′mik) *adj.* **1.** introduced under the skin, as needle. —*n.* **2.** syringe and needle for hypodermic injections.

hy′po•gly•ce′mi•a (hī′pō glī sē′mē ə) *n.* abnormally low level of glucose in the blood.

hy•pot′e•nuse (hī pot′n ōōs′, -yōōs′) *n.* side of right triangle opposite right angle.

hy·po·ther′mi·a (hī′pə thûr′mē ə) n. body temperature below normal.

hy·poth′e·sis (hī poth′ə sis, hi-) n., pl. -ses (-sēz′). 1. proposed explanation. 2. guess. —**hy′po·thet′i·cal** (-pə thet′i kal) adj.

hys·ter·ec′to·my (his′tə rek′tə mē) n., pl. -mies. removal of uterus.

hys·te′ri·a (hi ster′ē ə, -stēr′-) n. 1. uncontrollable emotion. 2. psychological disorder. —**hys·ter′i·cal** (-ster′-) adj. —**hys·ter′i·cal·ly,** adv.

hys·ter′ics (-ster′iks) n.pl. fit of hysteria.

Hz, hertz.

I

I, i (ī) n. ninth letter of English alphabet.

I (ī) pron. subject form of first pers. sing. pronoun.

IA, Iowa. Also, **Ia.**

-iatrics, suffix meaning medical care or treatment, as *geriatrics.*

-iatry, suffix meaning healing or medical practice, as *psychiatry.*

i′bex (ī′beks) n., pl. **i′bex·es, ib′i·ces′** (ib′ə sēz′, ī′bə-), **i′bex.** wild goat with backward-curving horns.

ibid. (ib′id) in the same book, chapter, etc., previously cited.

-ible, variant of *-able.*

i′bis (ī′bis) n. wading bird.

i′bu·pro′fen (ī′byoo prō′fən) n. anti-inflammatory drug.

-ic, 1. adjective suffix meaning: of or pertaining to, as *prophetic;* like or characteristic of, as *idyllic;* containing or made of, as *alcoholic;* produced by or suggestive of, as *Homeric.* **2.** noun suffix meaning: person having, as *arthritic;* agent or drug, as *cosmetic;* follower, as *Socratic.*

ICC, Interstate Commerce Commission.

ice (īs) n., v., **iced, icing.** —n. **1.** water frozen solid. **2.** frozen dessert. —v. **3.** cover with ice or frosting. **4.** cool with ice. —**iced,** adj. —**i′ci·ly,** adv. —**i′ci·ness,** n. —**i′cy,** adj.

ice′berg′ (-bûrg) n. mass of ice floating at sea.

ice′box′, n. food chest cooled by ice.

ice cream, frozen dessert made with cream and flavorings.

ice skate, shoe with metal blade for skating on ice. —**ice-skate,** v.

ich′thy·ol′o·gy (ik′thē ol′ə jē) n. study of fishes.

i′ci·cle (ī′si kal) n. hanging tapering mass of ice.

ic′ing, n. cake covering.

i′con (ī′kon) n. sacred image.

i·con′o·clast′ (-ə klast′) n. attacker of cherished beliefs. —**i·con′o·clas′tic,** adj.

-ics, suffix meaning: **1.** art, science, or field, as *physics.* **2.** activities or practices of a certain kind, as *acrobatics.*

ICU, intensive care unit.

id (id) n. unconscious, instinctive part of the psyche.

ID (ī′dē′) pl. **IDs, ID's.** document, card, or other means of identification.

ID, Idaho. Also, **Id., Ida.**

i·de′a (ī dē′ə, ī dē′) n. conception in mind; thought.

i·de′al (ī dē′əl, ī dēl′) n. **1.** conception or standard of perfection. —*adj.* **2.** being an ideal. **3.** not real. —**i·de·al·ize,** v., -**ized, -izing.**

i·de′al·ism′, n. belief in or behavior according to ideals. —**i·de′al·ist,** n.

i·den′ti·cal (ī den′ti kal, i den′-) adj. same. —**i·den′ti·cal·ly,** adv.

i·den′ti·fy′, v., -**fied, -fying. 1.** recognize as particular person or thing. **2.** associate. —**i·den′ti·fi·ca′tion,** n.

i·den′ti·ty (-tē) n., pl. -**ties. 1.** fact of being same. **2.** self.

i′de·ol′o·gy (ī′dē ol′ə jē, id′ē-) n., pl. -**gies.** beliefs of group, esp. political. —**i′de·o·log′i·cal,** adj.

id′i·om (id′ē əm) n. **1.** expression peculiar to a language. **2.** dialect. —**id′i·o·syn′cra·sy** (-sing′krə sē, -sin′-) n., pl. -**sies.** unusual individual trait. —**id′i·o·syn·crat′ic,** adj.

id′i·ot (id′ē ət) n. foolish person. —**id′i·ot′ic** (-ot′ik) adj. —**id′i·ot′i·cal·ly,** adv. —**id′i·o·cy,** n.

i′dle (īd′l) adj., v., **idled, idling.** —*adj.* **1.** not working. **2.** worthless. **3.** lazy. —v. **4.** do nothing. —**i′dler,** n. —**i′dly,** adv.

i′dol (īd′l) n. object worshiped or adored. —**i′dol·ize′,** v.

i·dol′a·try (ī dol′ə trē) n., pl. -**tries.** worship of idols. —**i·dol′a·ter,** n.

i′dyll (īd′l) n. composition describing pastoral scene. Also, **i′dyl.** —**i·dyl′lic** (ī dil′ik) adj.

i.e., that is.

if (if) conj. **1.** in case that. **2.** whether. **3.** though.

if′fy, adj., -**fier, -fiest.** *Informal.* not resolved; indefinite.

ig′loo (ig′loō) n., pl. -**loos.** snow hut.

ig′ne·ous (ig′nē əs) adj. **1.** produced by great heat. **2.** of fire.

ig·nite' (ig nīt') v., -nited, -niting. set on or catch fire. —**ig·ni'tion** (-nish'ən) n.

ig·no'ble (ig nō'bəl) adj. 1. dishonorable. 2. humble.

ig'no·min'i·ous (ig'nə min'ē əs) adj. 1. humiliating. 2. contemptible.

ig'no·ra'mus (-rā'məs, -ram'əs) n. ignorant person.

ig'no·rant (ig'nər ənt) adj. 1. lacking knowledge. 2. unaware. —**ig'no·rance,** n.

ig·nore' (ig nôr') v., -nored, -noring. disregard.

i·gua'na (i gwä'nə) n. large tropical lizard.

IL, Illinois.

il-, prefix equivalent to *in-*, as *illogical.*

ilk (ilk) n. family or kind.

ill (il) adj. 1. sick. 2. evil. 3. unfavorable. —n. 4. harm. 5. ailment. —adv. 6. badly. 7. with difficulty.

Ill., Illinois.

ill'-bred', adj. rude.

il·le'gal (i lē'gəl) adj. unlawful.

il·leg'i·ble (i lej'ə bəl) adj. hard to read.

il'le·git'i·mate (il'i jit'ə mit) adj. 1. unlawful. 2. born to unmarried parents. —**il'le·git'i·ma·cy** (-mə sē) n.

ill'-fat'ed, adj. doomed.

il·lib'er·al, adj. 1. not generous. 2. narrow in attitudes or beliefs.

il·lic'it, adj. unlawful; not allowed.

il·lim'it·a·ble (i lim'i tə bəl) adj. boundless.

il·lit'er·ate (i lit'ər it) adj. 1. unable to read and write. —n. 2. illiterate person. —**il·lit'er·a·cy,** n.

ill'-man'nered, adj. having bad manners.

ill'ness, n. 1. state of being ill. 2. particular ailment; sickness.

il·log'i·cal (i loj'i kəl) adj. not logical. —**il·log'i·cal·ly,** adv.

ill'-starred', adj. unlucky; ill-fated.

ill'-treat', v. abuse. —**ill'-treat'ment,** n.

il·lu'mi·nate' (i lōō'mə nāt') v., -nated, -nating. supply with light. —**il·lu'mi·na'tion,** n.

illus., illustrated. 2. illustration.

ill'-use' (-ūs', -ūsed, -using, v. —v. (il'yōōz') v. 1. treat badly or unjustly. —n. (-yōōs') 2. bad or unjust treatment.

il·lu'sion (i lōō'zhən) n. false impression or appearance. —**il·lu'so·ry** (-sə rē, -zə-) adj.

il'lus·trate' (il'ə strāt', i lus'trāt) v., -trated, -trating. 1. explain with examples, etc. 2. furnish with pictures. —**il'lus·tra'tion,** n. —**il'lus·tra'tor,** n.

---

il·lus'tri·ous (i lus'trē əs) adj. 1. famous. 2. glorious.

ill will, hostile feeling.

im-, suffix equivalent to *in-*, as *immature.*

im'age (im'ij) n. 1. likeness. 2. picture in the mind. 3. conception of one's character. —v. 4. mirror.

im'age·ry, n., pl. -ries. 1. mental images collectively. 2. use of figures of speech.

im·ag'ine (i maj'in) v., -ined, -ining. 1. form mental images. 2. think; guess. —**im·ag'i·na'tion** (-nā'shən) n. —**im·ag'i·na·tive** (-na tiv) adj. —**im·ag'i·nar'y** (-ner'-ē) adj. —**im·ag'i·na·ble,** adj.

i·mam' (i mäm') n. Muslim religious leader.

im·bal'ance (im bal'əns) n. lack of balance.

im'be·cile (im'bə sil) n. a foolish person. —**im·be·cil'i·ty** (-sil'i tē) n.

im·bibe' (im bīb') v., -bibed, -bibing. drink. —**im·bib'er,** n.

im·bro'glio (im brōl'yō) n., pl. -glios. complicated affair.

im·bue' (im byōō') v., -bued, -buing. 1. inspire. 2. saturate.

im'i·tate' (im'i tāt') v., -tated, -tating. 1. copy. 2. counterfeit. —**im'i·ta'tive,** adj. —**im'i·ta'tion,** n.

im·mac'u·late (i mak'yə lit) adj. 1. spotlessly clean. 2. pure.

im'ma·nent (i'mə nənt) adj. being within. —**im'ma·nence,** n.

im'ma·te'ri·al (im'ə tēr'ē əl) adj. 1. unimportant. 2. spiritual.

im'ma·ture', adj. not mature.

im·meas'ur·a·ble, adj. limitless.

im·me'di·ate (i mē'dē it) adj. 1. without delay. 2. nearest. 3. present. —**im·me'di·a·cy** (-ə sē) n.

im'me·mo'ri·al, adj. beyond memory or record.

im·mense' (i mens') adj. vast. —**im·men'si·ty,** n.

im·merse' (i mûrs') v., -mersed, -mersing. 1. plunge into liquid. 2. absorb. —**im·mer'sion,** n.

im'mi·grant (im'i grənt) n. person who immigrates.

im'mi·grate' (-grāt') v., -grated, -grating. come to new country. —**im'mi·gra'tion,** n.

im'mi·nent (im'ə nənt) adj. about to happen. —**im'mi·nence,** n.

im·mo'bile (i mō'bəl, -bēl) adj. not moving. —**im'mo·bil'i·ty,** n. —**im·mo'bi·lize',** v.

im·mod'er·ate (-it) adj. excessive.

im·mod'est, adj. not modest.

im'mo·late' (im'ə lāt') v., -lated, -lating. 1. sacrifice. 2. destroy by fire. —**im'mo·la'tion,** n.

im·mor·al, *adj.* not moral. —**im·mo·ral·i·ty**, *n.*

im·mor·tal, *adj.* **1.** not subject to death or oblivion. —*n.* **2.** immortal being. —**im·mor·tal·i·ty**, *n.* —**im·mor·tal·ize**, *v.*

im·mov·a·ble (i mōō′va bəl) *adj.* **1.** fixed. **2.** unchanging.

im·mune (i myōōn′) *adj.* **1.** protected from disease. **2.** exempt. —**im·mu·ni·ty**, *n.* —**im·mu·ni·za·tion**, *n.* —**im·mu·nize**, *v.*

immune system, network of cells and tissues that protects the body from pathogens.

im·mu·nol·o·gy (-nol′ə jē) *n.* branch of science dealing with the immune system.

im·mure (i myōōr′) *v.*, **-mured, -muring.** confine within walls.

im·mu·ta·ble, *adj.* unchangeable.

imp (imp) *n.* **1.** little demon. **2.** mischievous child. —**imp′ish**, *adj.*

im′pact *n.* (im′pakt) **1.** collision. **2.** influence; effect. —*v.* (im pakt′) **3.** collide with. **4.** have effect.

im·pact′ed, *adj.* (of a tooth) wedged too tightly in its socket to erupt properly.

im·pair′ (im pâr′) *v.* damage; weaken. —**im·pair′ment**, *n.*

im·pale′ (im pāl′) *v.*, **-paled, -paling.** fix upon sharp stake, etc.

im·pal′pa·ble, *adj.* that cannot be felt or understood.

im·pan′el, *v.*, **-eled, -eling.** list for jury duty.

im·part′, *v.* **1.** tell. **2.** give.

im·par′tial, *adj.* unbiased. —**im·par·ti·al·i·ty** (-shē al′i tē) *n.*

im·pas′sa·ble, *adj.* not able to be passed through or along.

im′passe (im′pas, im pas′) *n.* deadlock.

im·pas′sioned, *adj.* full of passion.

im·pas′sive, *adj.* **1.** emotionless. **2.** calm. —**im·pas′sive·ly**, *adv.*

im·pa′tience, *n.* lack of patience. —**im·pa′tient**, *adj.*

im·peach′ (im pēch′) *v.* charge with misconduct in office. —**im·peach′ment**, *n.*

im·pec′ca·ble (im pek′ə bəl) *adj.* faultless. —**im·pec′ca·bly**, *adv.*

im′pe·cu′ni·ous (im′pi kyōō′nē əs) *adj.* having no money.

im·pede′ (im pēd′) *v.*, **-peded, -peding.** hinder.

im·ped′i·ment (im ped′ə mənt) *n.* **1.** hindrance. **2.** speech defect.

im·pel′ (im pel′) *v.*, **-pelled, -pelling.** urge forward.

im·pend′ (im pend′) *v.* be imminent.

im·pen′e·tra·ble, *adj.* that cannot be penetrated. —**im·pen′e·tra·bil·i·ty**, *n.* —**im·pen′e·tra·bly**, *adv.*

im·per′a·tive (im per′ə tiv) *adj.* **1.** necessary. **2.** *Gram.* denoting command.

im′per·cep′ti·ble, *adj.* **1.** very slight. **2.** not perceptible.

im·per′fect, *adj.* **1.** having defect. **2.** not complete. **3.** *Gram.* denoting action in progress. —**im·per′fec′tion**, *n.* —**im·per′fect·ly**, *adv.*

im·pe′ri·al (im pēr′ē əl) *adj.* of an empire or emperor.

im·pe′ri·al·ism, *n.* policy of extending rule over other peoples. —**im·pe′ri·al·ist**, *n.*, *adj.*

im·per′il, *v.*, **-iled, -iling.** endanger.

im·pe′ri·ous (im pēr′ē əs) *adj.* domineering.

im·per′ish·a·ble, *adj.* immortal; not subject to decay.

im·per′me·a·ble, *adj.* not permitting penetration. —**im·per′me·a·bil′i·ty**, *n.*

im·per′son·al, *adj.* without personal reference or bias.

im·per′son·ate′ (im pûr′sə nāt′) *v.*, **-ated, -ating.** act the part of. —**im·per′son·a′tion**, *n.* —**im·per′son·a′tor**, *n.*

im·per′ti·nence, *n.* **1.** rude presumption. **2.** irrelevance. —**im·per′ti·nent**, *adj.*

im′per·turb′a·ble, *adj.* calm.

im·per′vi·ous (im pûr′vē əs) *adj.* **1.** not allowing penetration. **2.** incapable of being affected.

im·pe·ti′go (im′pi tī′gō) *n.* contagious skin infection.

im·pet′u·ous (im pech′ōō əs) *adj.* rash or hasty. —**im·pet′u·os′i·ty** (-os′i tē) *n.*

im′pe·tus (im′pi təs) *n.* **1.** stimulus. **2.** force of motion.

im·pi′e·ty, *n.*, *pl.* **-ties. 1.** lack of piety. **2.** act showing this.

im·pinge′ (im pinj′) *v.*, **-pinged, -pinging. 1.** strike. **2.** encroach.

im′pi·ous (im′pē əs, im pī′-) *adj.* **1.** irreligious. **2.** disrespectful.

im·pla′ca·ble (im plak′ə bəl, -plā′ka-) *adj.* not to be placated.

im·plant′ *v.* (im plant′) **1.** instill. —*n.* (im′plant′) **2.** device or material used to repair or replace part of the body.

im·plau′si·ble, *adj.* not plausible. —**im·plau′si·bil′i·ty**, *n.*

im′ple·ment (im′plə mənt) *n.* **1.** instrument or tool. —*v.* (-ment′, -mənt) **2.** put into effect. —**im′ple·men·ta′tion**, *n.*

im′pli·cate′ (im′pli kāt′) *v.*, **-cated, -cating.** involve as guilty.

im′pli·ca′tion, *n.* **1.** act of imply-

inalienable

ing. **2.** thing implied. **3.** act of implicating.

im·plic'it (im plis'it) *adj.* **1.** unquestioning; complete. **2.** implied.

im·plode' (im plōd') *v.*, **-ploded, -ploding.** burst inward. —**im·plo'sion,** *n.*

im·plore' (im plôr') *v.*, **-plored, -ploring.** urge or beg.

im·ply' (im plī') *v.*, **-plied, -plying. 1.** indicate. **2.** suggest.

im·po·lite', *adj.* rude.

im·pol'i·tic, *adj.* not wise or prudent.

im·pon'der·a·ble, *adj.* that cannot be weighed, measured or evaluated.

im·port' *v.* (im pôrt') **1.** bring in from another country. **2.** matter; signify. —*n.* (im'pôrt) **3.** anything imported. **4.** significance. —**im'por·ta'tion,** *n.* —**im·port'er,** *n.*

im·por'tant, *adj.* **1.** of some consequence. **2.** prominent. —**im·por'tance,** *n.*

im·por·tune' (im'pôr tōōn', -tyōōn', im pôr'chan) *v.*, **-tuned, -tuning.** beg persistently. —**im·por'tu·nate,** *adj.*

im·pose' (im pōz') *v.*, **-posed, -posing. 1.** set as obligation. **2.** intrude (oneself). —**im'po·si'tion** (-pa-zish'shan) *n.*

im·pos'ing, *adj.* impressive.

im·pos'si·ble, *adj.* that cannot exist or be done. —**im·pos'si·bil'i·ty,** *n.*

im'post (im'pōst) *n.* tax or duty.

im·pos'tor (im pos'tar) *n.* person who deceives under false name. Also, **im·pos'ter.**

im'po·tence (im'pa tans) *n.* **1.** lack of power. **2.** lack of sexual powers. —**im'po·tent,** *adj.*

im·pound', *v.* seize by law.

im·pov'er·ish (im pov'ar ish, -pov'rish) *v.* make poor.

im·prac'ti·ca·ble (im prak'ti ka bal) *adj.* incapable of being put into practice or use.

im·prac'ti·cal, *adj.* not usable or useful.

im'pre·ca'tion (-pri kā'shan) *n.* curse. —**im'pre·cate,** *v.*

im'pre·cise', *adj.* not precise.

im·preg'na·ble (im preg'na bal) *adj.* resistant to attack.

im·preg'nate (-nāt) *v.*, **-nated, -nating. 1.** make pregnant. **2.** saturate; infuse. —**im'preg·na'tion,** *n.*

im'pre·sa'ri·o (im'pra sär'ē ō', -sär'-) *n.* person who organizes or manages entertainment events.

im·press' *v.* (im pres') **1.** affect with respect, etc. **2.** fix in mind. **3.** stamp. **4.** force into public service. —*n.* (im'pres) **5.** act of impressing. —**im·pres'sive,** *adj.*

im·pres'sion (im presh'an) *n.* **1.** effect on mind or feelings. **2.** notion. **3.** printed or stamped mark.

im·pres'sion·a·ble, *adj.* easily influenced, esp. emotionally.

im·pres'sion·ism, *n.* (often cap.) style of 19th-century painting characterized by short brush strokes to represent the effect of light on objects. —**im·pres'sion·ist,** *n., adj.* —**im·pres'sion·is'tic,** *adj.*

im'pri·ma'tur (im'pri mä'tar, -mä'-) *n.* sanction; approval.

im'print (im'print) *n.* mark made by pressure.

im·pris'on, *v.* put in prison. —**im·pris'on·ment,** *n.*

im·prob'a·ble, *adj.* unlikely. —**im·prob'a·bil'i·ty,** *n.*

im·promp'tu (im promp'tōō, -tyōō) *adj., adv.* without preparation.

im·prop'er, *adj.* not right, suitable, or proper. —**im'pro·pri'e·ty** (im'pra prī'i tē) *n.* —**im·prop'er·ly,** *adv.*

im·prove', *v.*, **-proved, -proving.** make or become better. —**im·prove'ment,** *n.*

im·prov'i·dent, *adj.* not providing for the future. —**im·prov'i·dence,** *n.* —**im·prov'i·dent·ly,** *adv.*

im'pro·vise' (im'pra vīz') *v.*, **-vised, -vising.** make, arrange, or perform at short notice. —**im·prov'i·sa'tion** (im prov'a zā'shan) *n.*

im·pru'dent, *adj.* not prudent; unwise.

im'pu·dent (im'pya dant) *adj.* insolent. —**im'pu·dence,** *n.*

im·pugn' (im pyōōn') *v.* cast doubt on.

im'pulse (im'puls) *n.* **1.** inciting influence. **2.** sudden inclination. —**im·pul'sive,** *adj.*

im·pu'ni·ty (im pyōō'ni tē) *n.* exemption from punishment.

im·pure', *adj.* not pure. —**im·pu'ri·ty,** *n.*

im·pute' (im pyōōt') *v.*, **-puted, -puting.** attribute.

in (in) *prep.* **1.** within. **2.** into. **3.** while; during. **4.** into some place. —*adv.* **5.** inside; within.

IN, Indiana.

in-, *prefix* meaning not or lacking, as *inexperience.*

in., inch.

in ab·sen'tia (in ab sen'sha, -shē ə) *adv. Latin.* in absence.

in·ac'ti·vate' (in ak'ta vāt') *v.*, **-vated, -vating.** make inactive.

in'ad·vert'ent (in'ad vûr'tnt) *adj.* **1.** heedless. **2.** unintentional. —**in'ad·vert'ent·ly,** *adv.*

in·al'ien·a·ble, *adj.* not to be taken away or transferred.

in·am·o·ra·ta (in am′ə rä′tə, in′-am-) n. female lover.

in·ane′ (i nān′) adj. silly; ridiculous. —**in·an′i·ty** (i nan′i tē) n.

in·ar·tic′u·late (-lit) adj. not clear in expression.

in′as·much′ as, seeing that.

in·au′gu·rate′ (in ô′gyə rāt′) v., -rated, -rating. 1. induct into office. 2. begin. —**in·au′gu·ral,** adj., n. —**in·au′gu·ra′tion,** n.

in′board′, adj., adv. inside a hull or aircraft.

in′born′, adj. present at birth.

in′bound′, adj. inward bound.

in′breed′, v. produce by breeding of related individuals. —**in′breed′ing,** n. —**in′bred′,** adj.

inc., 1. incomplete. 2. incorporated. 3. increase.

In′ca (ing′kə) n., pl. -cas. member of South American Indian people dominant in Peru before the Spanish conquest. —**In′can,** adj.

in·can·des′cence (in′kən des′əns) n. glow of intense heat. —**in·can·des′cent,** adj.

in·can·ta′tion (in′kan tā′shən) n. 1. magic ritual. 2. spell.

in·ca·pac′i·tate′ (in′kə pas′i tāt′) v., -tated, -tating. make unfit or unable. —**in·ca·pac′i·ty,** n.

in·car′cer·ate′ (in kär′sə rāt′) v., -ated, -ating. imprison.

in·car′nate (in kär′nit, -nāt) adj. 1. embodied in flesh. 2. typified.

in·cen′di·ar′y (in sen′dē er′ē) adj., n., pl. -aries. —adj. 1. of or for setting fires. 2. arousing strife. —n. 3. person who maliciously sets fires.

in·cense′ v., -censed, -censing. —v. (in sens′) 1. enrage. —n. (in′sens) 2. substance burned to give a sweet odor.

in·cen′tive (in sen′tiv) n. stimulus.

in·cep′tion (in sep′shən) n. beginning.

in·ces′sant (in ses′ənt) adj. unceasing. —**in·ces′sant·ly,** adv.

in′cest (in′sest) n. sexual relations between close relatives. —**in·ces′tu·ous** (-ses′chŏŏ əs) adj.

inch (inch) n. unit of length, $\frac{1}{12}$ foot.

in·cho′ate (in kō′it) adj. just begun; not fully developed.

inch′worm′, n. moth larva that moves in looping motion.

in′ci·dence (in′si dəns) n. range of occurrence or effect.

in′ci·dent, n. 1. occurrence. 2. side event. —adj. 3. dependent. —**in′ci·den′tal** (-den′tl) adj., n. —**in′ci·den′tal·ly,** adv.

in·cin′er·ate′ (in sin′ə rāt′) v., -ated, -ating. burn to ashes. —**in·cin′er·a′tor,** n.

in·cip′i·ent (in sip′ē ənt) adj. beginning. —**in·cip′i·ence,** n.

in·cise′ (in sīz′) v., -cised, -cising. cut into; engrave. —**in·ci′sion,** n.

in·ci′sive (-sī′siv) adj. sharp.

in·ci′sor (-sī′zər) n. cutting tooth.

in·cite′ (in sīt′) v., -cited, -citing. urge to action. —**in·cite′ment,** n.

incl., including.

in·cline′ v., -clined, -clining. n. —v. (in klīn′) 1. tend. 2. lean. 3. dispose. —n. (in′klīn) 4. slanted surface. —**in·cli·na′tion,** n.

in·clude′ (in klŏŏd′) v., -cluded, -cluding. 1. contain. 2. have among others. —**in·clu′sion** (-klŏŏ′zhən) n. —**in·clu′sive** (-siv) adj.

in·cog′ni·to′ (in′kog nē′tō, in kog′ni tō′) adj., adv. using assumed identity.

in′come (in′kum) n. money received.

in′com′ing, adj. coming in.

in′com·mu′ni·ca′do (in′kə myŏŏ′ni kä′dō) adv., adj. without means of communicating.

in·com′pa·ra·ble, adj. unequaled.

in′con·sid′er·ate, adj. thoughtless.

in·con'ti·nent, *adj.* **1.** unable to control bodily discharges. **2.** lacking sexual self-restraint. **—in·con'ti·nence,** *n.*

in·cor'po·rate' (-pə rāt') *v.,* **-rated, -rating. 1.** form a corporation. **2.** include as part.

in·cor·po're·al, *adj.* not corporeal or material.

in·cor'ri·gi·ble (in kôr'i jə bəl, -kor'-) *adj.* not to be reformed.

in·crease', (in krēs') *v.,* **-creased, -creasing,** *n.* **1.** make or become more or greater. **—n.** (in' krēs) **2.** instance of increasing. **3.** growth or addition. **—in·creas'ing·ly,** *adv.*

in·cred'i·ble, *adj.* unbelievable; amazing. **—in·cred'i·bly,** *adv.*

in·cred'u·lous, *adj.* not believing. **—in'cre·du'li·ty,** *n.*

in'cre·ment (in'krə mənt, ing'-) *n.* addition; increase. **—in'cre·men'tal** (-men'tl) *adj.*

in·crim'i·nate' (in krim'ə nāt') *v.,* **-nated, -nating.** charge with or involve in a crime. **—in·crim'i·na'tion,** *n.*

in'cu·bate' (in'kyə bāt', ing'-) *v.,* **-bated, -bating.** keep warm, as eggs for hatching. **—in'cu·ba'tion,** *n.*

in'cu·ba'tor, *n.* **1.** heated case for incubating. **2.** apparatus in which premature infants are cared for.

in·cul'cate (in kul'kāt, in'kul kāt') *v.,* **-cated, -cating.** teach; instill. **—in'cul·ca'tion,** *n.*

in·cum'bent (in kum'bənt) *adj.* **1.** obligatory. **—n. 2.** office holder.

in·cur' (in kûr') *v.,* **-curred, -curring.** bring upon oneself.

in·cur'sion (in kûr'zhən, -shən) *n.* raid.

Ind., Indiana.

in·debt'ed, *adj.* obligated by debt.

in·de·ci'pher·a·ble, *adj.* illegible.

in·de·ci'sion, *n.* inability to decide.

in·deed' (in dēd') *adv.* **1.** in fact. **—interj. 2.** (used to express surprise, contempt, etc.)

in·de·fat'i·ga·ble (in'di fat'i gə bəl) *adj.* tireless.

in·del'i·ble (in del'ə bəl) *adj.* unerasable.

in·dem'ni·fy' (in dem'nə fī') *v.,* **-fied, -fying.** compensate for or insure against loss, damage. **—in·dem'ni·ty,** *n.*

in·dent' (in dent') *v.* **1.** notch. **2.** set in from margin.

in·den'ture (in den'chər) *n., v.,* **-tured, -turing.** **—n. 1.** contract binding one to service. **—v. 2.** bind by indenture.

in·de·pend'ent, *adj.* **1.** free. **2.** not influenced by or dependent on others. **—in·de·pend'ence,** *n.*

in'-depth', *adj.* intensive; thorough.

in·de·struct'i·ble, *adj.* that cannot be destroyed.

in'dex (in'deks) *n., pl.* **-dexes, -dices** (-də sēz'), *v.* **—n. 1.** list with page references. **2.** indicator. **—v. 3.** provide with index.

In'di·an (-dē ən) *n.* **1.** native of India. **2.** Also, **Amer'ican In'dian.** member of the aboriginal peoples of N. and S. America. **—In'dian,** *adj.*

Indian summer, period of mild, dry weather in late fall.

in'di·cate' (in'di kāt') *v.,* **-cated, -cating.** **1.** be a sign of. **2.** point to. **—in'di·ca'tion,** *n.* **—in·dic'a·tive** (-dik'ə tiv) *adj.* **—in'di·ca'tor,** *n.*

in·dict' (in dīt') *v.* charge with crime. **—in·dict'ment,** *n.*

in·dif'fer·ent, *adj.* **1.** without interest or concern. **2.** moderate. **—in·dif'fer·ence,** *n.*

in·dig'e·nous (in dij'ə nəs) *adj.* native.

in'di·gent (in'di jənt) *adj.* needy; destitute. **—in'di·gence,** *n.*

in·di·ges'tion, *n.* difficulty in digesting food.

in·dig·na'tion (in'dig nā'shən) *n.* righteous anger. **—in·dig'nant,** *adj.*

in·dig′ni·ty, *n., pl.* **-ties. 1.** loss of dignity. **2.** cause of this.

in′di·go′ (in′di gō′) *n., pl.* **-gos, -goes.** blue dye.

in′dis·crim′i·nate (in′di skrim′ə nit) *adj.* done at random; haphazard

in′dis·posed′, *adj.* **1.** mildly ill. **2.** unwilling. **—in′dis·po·si′tion,** *n.*

in′dis·sol′u·ble (in′di sol′yə bəl) *adj.* that cannot be dissolved, decomposed, undone, or destroyed.

in′di·vid′u·al (in′də vij′ōō əl) *adj.* **1.** single; particular. **2.** of or for one only. —*n.* **3.** single person, animal, or thing. **—in′di·vid′u·al′i·ty** (-al′i-tē) *n.* **—in′di·vid′u·al·ly,** *adv.*

in′di·vid′u·al·ist, *n.* person dependent only on self.

in·doc′tri·nate′ (in dok′trə nāt′) *v.,* **-nated, -nating.** train to accept doctrine. **—in·doc′tri·na′tion,** *n.*

in′do·lent (in′dl ənt) *adj.* lazy. **—in′do·lence,** *n.*

in·dom′i·ta·ble (in dom′i tə bəl) *adj.* that cannot be dominated.

in′door′, *adj.* inside a building. **—in·doors′,** *adv.*

in′du·bi·ta·ble (in dōō′bi tə bəl, -dyōō′-) *adj.* undoubted.

in·duce′ (in dōōs′, -dyōōs′) *v.,* **-duced, -ducing. 1.** persuade; influence. **2.** cause; bring on. **—in·duce′ment,** *n.*

in·duct′ (in dukt′) *v.* bring into office, military service, etc. **—in·duc′tion,** *n.*

in·duc′tion, *n.* **1.** reasoning from particular facts. **2.** act of inducting.

in·dulge′ (in dulj′) *v.,* **-dulged, -dulging. 1.** accommodate whims, appetites, etc., of. **2.** yield to. **—in·dul′gence,** *n.* **—in·dul′gent,** *adj.*

in·dus′tri·al·ist (in dus′trē ə list) *n.* owner of industrial plant.

in·dus′tri·al·ize′, *v.,* **-ized, -izing.** convert to modern industrial methods.

in·dus′tri·ous, *adj.* hard-working.

in′dus·try (in′də strē) *n., pl.* **-tries. 1.** trade or manufacture, esp. with machinery. **2.** diligent work. **—in·dus′tri·al,** *adj.*

in·e′bri·ate′ *v.,* **-ated, -ating.** —*v.* (in ē′brē āt′) **1.** make drunk. —*n.* (-it) **2.** drunken person.

in·ef′fa·ble (in ef′ə bəl) *adj.* that cannot be described.

in·ef·fec′tu·al, *adj.* futile.

in·ept′ (in ept′, i nept′) *adj.* incompetent; foolish. **—in·ept′i·tude′,** *n.* **—in·ept′ly,** *adv.*

in·eq′ui·ty, *n., pl.* **-ties.** injustice.

in·ert′ (in ûrt′, i nûrt′) *adj.* without inherent power to move, resist, or act. **2.** slow-moving. **—in·er′tia,** *n.*

in·ev′i·ta·ble (in ev′i tə bəl) *adj.* not to be avoided. **—in·ev′i·ta·bil′i·ty,** *n.* **—in·ev′i·ta·bly,** *adv.*

in·ex′o·ra·ble (in ek′sər ə bəl) *adj.* unyielding. **—in·ex′o·ra·bly,** *adv.*

in·ex·pert′ (in eks′pûrt, in′ik spûrt′) *adj.* unskilled.

in·ex′pli·ca·ble (in ek′spli kə bəl, in′ik splik′ə-) *adj.* incapable of being explained.

in·ex′tri·ca·ble (in ek′stri kə bəl, in′ik strik′ə-) *adj.* that cannot be freed or disentangled.

in·fal′li·ble, *adj.* never failing or making mistakes.

in′fa·my (in′fə mē) *n., pl.* **-mies.** evil repute. **—in′fa·mous,** *adj.*

in′fant (in′fant) *n.* very young baby. **—in′fan·cy,** *n.* **—in′fan·tile** (-fan til′) *adj.*

in′fan·try (in′fən trē) *n., pl.* **-tries.** soldiers who fight on foot. **—in′fan·try·man,** *n.*

in·farct′ (in′ färkt′, in färkt′) *n.* area of dead or dying tissue, as in the heart. Also, **in·farc′tion.**

in·fat′u·ate′ (in fach′ōō āt′) *v.,* **-ated, -ating.** inspire with foolish love. **—in·fat·u·a′tion,** *n.*

in·fect′ (in fekt′) *v.* contaminate, esp. with disease germs. **—in·fec′tion,** *n.*

in·fec′tious, *adj.* spreading readily.

in·fer′ (in fûr′) *v.,* **-ferred, -ferring.**

in·flex′i·ble
in·for′mal
in·for·mal′i·ty
in·fre′quen·cy
in·fre′quent
in·glo′ri·ous
in·grat′i·tude′
in·har·mon′ic
in·har·mo′ni·ous
in·hos′pi·ta·ble
in·hu′mane′
in·ju·di′cious
in·jus′tice
in·of·fen′sive

in·op′er·a·tive
in·op′por·tune′
in·or·gan′ic
in·se·cure′
in·sen′si·tive
in·sep′a·ra·ble
in·sig·nif′i·cance
in·sig·nif′i·cant
in·sin·cere′
in·sin·cer′i·ty
in·sol′u·ble
in·sta·bil′i·ty
in·sub·or′di·nate
in·sub·or′di·na′tion

in·suf′fer·a·ble
in·suf·fi′cient
in·sup·press′i·ble
in·sur·mount′a·ble
in·sus·cep′ti·ble
in·tan′gi·ble
in·tem′per·ance
in·tem′per·ate
in·tol′er·a·ble
in·tol′er·ance
in·tol′er·ant
in·var′i·a·ble
in·vis′i·ble
in·vis′i·bly

conclude or deduce. —**in′fer·ence**, n.

in·fe′ri·or (in fēr′ē ər) adj. **1.** less good, important, etc. —n. **2.** person inferior to others. —**in·fe′ri·or′i·ty** (-ôr′i tē) n.

in·fer′nal (in fûr′nl) adj. **1.** of hell. **2.** Informal. outrageous.

in·fer′no (-nō) n., pl. **-nos.** hell.

in·fest′ (in fest′) v. overrun; trouble. —**in·fes·ta′tion**, n.

in′fi·del (in′fi dl, -del′) n. unbeliever.

in′field′, n. **1.** area of baseball field inside base lines. **2.** players in infield. —**in′field′er,** n.

in′fight′ing, n. conflict within group.

in·fil′trate (in fil′trāt, in′fil trāt′) v., **-trated, -trating.** pass in without being noticed. —**in′fil·tra′tion,** n.

in′fi·nite (in′fə nit) adj. **1.** vast; endless. —n. **2.** that which is infinite. —**in′fi·nite·ly** (in fin′i tē) n.

in·fin·i·tes′i·mal (in′fin i tes′ə mal) adj. immeasurably small.

in·fin′i·tive (in fin′i tiv) n. simple form of verb.

in·firm′ (-fûrm′) adj. feeble; weak. —**in·fir′mi·ty,** n.

in·fir′ma·ry (-fûr′mə rē) n., pl. **-ries.** hospital.

in·flame′, v., **-flamed, -flaming. 1.** excite. **2.** cause bodily reaction marked by redness, pain, etc. —**in·flam′ma·ble** (-flam′ə bal) adj. —**in·flam′ma·to′ry** (-tô′rē) adj. —**in·flam·ma′tion** (-flə mā′shən) n.

in·flate′ (in flāt′) v., **-flated, -flating. 1.** swell or expand with air or gas. **2.** increase unduly.

in·fla′tion (-shən) n. **1.** rise in prices when currency or credit expands faster than available goods or services. **2.** act of inflating.

in·flect′ (in flekt′) v. **1.** bend. **2.** modulate. **3.** display forms of a word. —**in·flec′tion,** n.

in·flict′ (in flikt′) v. impose harmfully. —**in·flic′tion,** n.

in′flu·ence (in′flōō əns) n., v., **-enced, -encing. 1.** power to affect another. **2.** something that does this. —v. **3.** affect or alter. —**in′flu·en′tial** (-en′shəl) adj.

in′flu·en′za (-en′zə) n. contagious disease caused by virus.

in′flux′, n. instance of flowing in.

in′fo·mer′cial (in′fō mûr′shəl) n. program-length television commercial designed to appear to be standard programming rather than an advertisement.

in·form′ (in fôrm′) v. supply with information. —**in·form′ant,** n.

—**in·form′er,** n. —**in·form′a·tive,** adj.

in′for·ma′tion (-fər mā′shən) n. factual knowledge. —**in·for·ma′tion·al,** adj.

information superhighway, large-scale communications network linking computers, television sets, etc.

in′fo·tain′ment (in′fō tān′mənt) n. broadcasting or publishing that treats factual matter in an entertaining way, as by dramatizing real events.

in·frac′tion (in frak′shən) n. violation.

in′fra·red′ (in′frə-) n. part of invisible spectrum.

in′fra·struc′ture, n. **1.** basic framework of system or organization. **2.** basic facilities, as transportation and communications systems.

in·fringe′ (in frinj′) v., **-fringed, -fringing.** violate; encroach.

in·fu′ri·ate (in fyŏŏr′ē āt′) v., **-ated, -ating.** enrage.

in·fuse′ (in fyŏŏz′) v., **-fused, -fusing. 1.** instill; fortify. **2.** steep. —**in·fu′sion,** n.

in·gen′ious (in jēn′yas) adj. inventive; clever. —**in·ge·nu′i·ty** (in′jə·nōō′i tē, -nyōō′-) n.

in′ge·nue′ (an′zhə nōō′) n. innocent young woman in a play.

in·gen′u·ous (in jen′yŏŏ əs) adj. innocent.

in·gest′ (in jest′) v. take into the body, as food or liquid.

in′got (ing′gət) n. cast block of metal.

in·grained′, adj. fixed firmly.

in′grate (in′grāt) n. ungrateful person.

in·gra′ti·ate′ (in grā′shē āt′) v., **-ated, -ating.** get (oneself) into someone's good graces.

in·gre′di·ent (in grēd′ē ənt) n. element or part of mixture.

in′gress (in′gres) n. entrance.

in·hab′it (in hab′it) v. live in. —**in·hab′it·ant,** n.

in·ha′la·tor (in′hə lā′tər) n. **1.** apparatus to help one inhale medicine, etc. **2.** respirator.

in·hale′ (in hāl′) v., **-haled, -haling.** breathe in. —**in′ha·la′tion,** n.

in·hal′er, n. inhalator.

in·here′ (in hēr′) v., **-hered, -hering.** be inseparable part or element. —**in·her′ent** (-hēr′ənt, -her′-) adj.

in·her′it (in her′it) v. become heir to. —**in·her′it·ance,** n.

in·hib′it (in hib′it) v. restrain or hinder. —**in′hi·bi′tion,** n.

in′house′ (adj. in′hous′; adv.

-hous/) *adj.*, *adv.* using an organization's own staff or resources.

in·hu/man, *adj.* **1.** brutal; heartless. **2.** not human. **—in/hu·man/i·ty,** *n.*

in·im/i·cal (i nim/i kəl) *adj.* **1.** adverse. **2.** hostile.

in·im/i·ta·ble (i nim/i tə bəl) *adj.* not to be imitated.

in·iq/ui·ty (i nik/wi tē) *n.*, *pl.* **-ties. 1.** wicked injustice. **2.** sin.

in·i/tial (i nish/əl) *adj.* **1.** of or at beginning. **—n. 2.** first letter of word. **—v. 3.** sign with initials of one's name. **—in·i/tial·ly,** *adv.*

in·i/ti·ate/ (i nish/ē āt/) *v.*, **-ated, -ating. 1.** begin. **2.** admit with ceremony. **—in·i/ti·a/tion,** *n.*

in·i/ti·a·tive (i nish/ē ə tiv) *n.* **1.** introductory step. **2.** readiness to proceed.

in·ject/ (in jekt/) *v.* force, as into tissue. **—in·jec/tion,** *n.*

in·junc/tion (in jungk/shən) *n.* order or admonition.

in/jure (in/jər) *v.*, **-jured, -juring. 1.** hurt. **2.** do wrong to. **—in·ju/ri·ous** (-jŏŏr/ē əs) *adj.* **—in/ju·ry,** *n.*

ink (ingk) *n.* **1.** writing fluid. **—v. 2.** mark with ink. **—ink/y,** *adj.*

ink/ling (ingk/ling) *n.* hint.

in/land (*adj.*, in/land; *adv.*, n. -land/, -lond) *adj.* **1.** of or in the interior of a region. **—adv. 2.** of or toward inland area. **—n. 3.** inland area.

in/law/ (in/lô/, -lō/) *n.* relative by marriage.

in·lay/, *v.*, **-laid, -laying,** *n.* **—v.** (in/lā/, in/lā/) **1.** ornament with design set in surface. **—n.** (in/lā/) **2.** inlaid work.

in/let (-let, -lit) *n.* narrow bay.

in-line skate, roller skate with four wheels in a straight line.

in/mate/ *n.* person confined in prison, hospital, etc.

in me·mo/ri·am (in mə môr/ē əm) in memory of.

in/most/, *adj.* farthest within. Also, **in/ner·most/.**

inn (in) *n.* **1.** hotel. **2.** tavern.

in·nards (in/ərdz) *n.pl.* internal parts.

in·nate/ (i nāt/, in/āt) *adj.* natural; born in one.

in/ner (in/ər) *adj.* **1.** being farther within. **2.** spiritual.

inner city, central part of city.

in/ner-di·rect/ed, *adj.* guided by one's own values.

in/ning (in/ing) *n.* Baseball. one round of play for both teams.

in/no·cence (in/ə səns) *n.* **1.** freedom from guilt. **2.** lack of worldly knowledge. **—in/no·cent,** *adj.*, *n.*

in·noc/u·ous (i nok/yŏŏ əs) *adj.* harmless.

in/no·vate/ (in/ə vāt/) *v.*, **-vated, -vating.** bring in something new. **—in/no·va/tion,** *n.* **—in/no·va/tor,** *n.* **—in/no·va/tive,** *adj.*

in/nu·en/do (in/yŏŏ en/dō) *n.*, *pl.* **-dos, -does.** indirect remark about sex or something bad.

in·nu/mer·a·ble, *adj.* **1.** very numerous. **2.** that cannot be counted.

in·oc/u·late/ (i nok/yə lāt/) *v.*, **-lated, -lating.** immunize. **—in·oc/u·la/tion,** *n.*

in·or/di·nate (in ôr/dn it) *adj.* excessive. **—in·or/di·nate·ly,** *adv.*

in/pa/tient, *n.* patient who stays in hospital while receiving care.

in/put/, *n.*, *v.*, **-putted** or **-put, -putting. —n. 1.** power, etc., supplied to machine. **2.** information given to computer. **—v. 3.** enter (data) into computer. **—in/put/ter,** *n.*

in/quest, *n.* legal inquiry.

in·quire/ (in kwīr/) *v.*, **-quired, -quiring. 1.** ask. **2.** make investigation. **—in·quir/y** (in kwīr/ē, in/kwə rē) *n.*

in/qui·si/tion (in/kwə zish/ən, ing/-) *n.* investigation. **—in·quis/i·tor,** *n.*

in·quis/i·tive (-kwiz/i tiv) *adj.* very curious.

in/road/, *n.* encroachment.

ins., **1.** inches. **2.** insurance.

in·sane/ (in sān/) *adj.* mentally deranged. **—in·san/i·ty** (-san/i tē) *n.*

in·sa/ti·a·ble (in sā/shə bəl, -shē ə-) *adj.* impossible to satisfy.

in·scribe/ (in skrīb/) *v.*, **-scribed, -scribing. 1.** write or engrave. **2.** dedicate. **—in·scrip/tion** (-skrip/shən) *n.*

in·scru/ta·ble (in skrŏŏ/tə bəl) *adj.* that cannot be understood. **—in·scru/ta·bil/i·ty,** *n.*

in/sect (in/sekt) *n.* small six-legged animal with body in three parts.

in·sec/ti·cide/ (-sek/tə sīd/) *n.* chemical for killing insects.

in·sem/i·nate/ (in sem/ə nāt/) *v.*, **-nated, -nating. 1.** sow seed in. **2.** impregnate. **—in·sem/i·na/tion,** *n.*

in·sen/si·ble, *adj.* **1.** incapable of feeling or perceiving. **2.** unaware; unconscious. **—in·sen/si·bil/i·ty,** *n.*

in·sert/, *v.* (in sûrt/) **1.** put or set in. **—n.** (in/sûrt) **2.** something inserted. **—in·ser/tion,** *n.*

in/shore/, *adj.*, *adv.* **1.** on or close to the shore. **—adv. 2.** toward the shore.

in/side/ (in/sīd/, in/sīd/) *prep.*, *adv.* **1.** within. **—n. 2.** inner part. **—adj. 3.** inner.

in/sid/er, *n.* person who has influence, esp. because privy to confidential information.

in·sid/i·ous (in sid/ē əs) *adj.* artfully treacherous.

in/sight/, *n.* discernment.

in·sig/ni·a (in sig/nē ə) *n., pl.* **-nia** or **-nias.** badge or other symbol of rank, honor, etc.

in·sin/u·ate/ (in sin/yōō āt/) *v.,* **-ated, -ating. 1.** hint slyly. **2.** put into mind. **3.** make one's way artfully. **—in·sin/u·a/tion,** *n.*

in·sip/id (in sip/id) *adj.* without distinctive qualities; vapid.

in·sist/ (in sist/) *v.* be firm or persistent. **—in·sist/ence,** *n.* **—in·sist/ent,** *adj.*

in/so·far/, *adv.* to such extent.

in/sole/, *n.* inner sole of shoe.

in/so·lent (in/sə lənt) *adj.* boldly rude. **—in/so·lence,** *n.*

in·sol/vent, without funds to pay one's debts. **—in·sol/ven·cy,** *n.*

in·som/ni·a (in som/nē ə) *n.* sleeplessness.

in/so·much/, *adv.* **1.** to such a degree (that). **2.** inasmuch (as).

in·sou/ci·ant (in sōō/sē ənt) *adj.* free from concern or anxiety.

in·spect/ (in spekt/) *v.* view critically or officially. **—in·spec/tion,** *n.*

in·spec/tor, *n.* **1.** person with duty to inspect. **2.** minor police official.

in·spire/ (in spīr/) *v.,* **-spired, -spiring. 1.** arouse (emotion, etc.). **2.** prompt to extraordinary actions. **3.** inhale. **—in/spi·ra/tion,** (in/spə rā/shən) *n.* **—in/spi·ra/tion·al,** *adj.*

Inst., **1.** Institute. **2.** Institution.

in·stall/ (in stôl/) *v.* **1.** put in position for use. **2.** establish. **—in/stal·la/tion,** *n.*

in·stall/ment, *n.* division, as of payment or story. Also, **in·stal/ment.**

installment plan, system for paying in installments.

in/stance (in/stəns) *n., v.,* **-stanced, -stancing. —n. 1.** case; example. **—v. 2.** cite.

in/stant, *n.* **1.** moment. **2.** point of time now present. **—adj. 3.** immediate. **—in/stant·ly,** *adv.*

in/stan·ta/ne·ous (-stan tā/nē əs) *adj.* occurring, etc., in an instant. **—in/stan·ta/ne·ous·ly,** *adv.*

in·stead/ (in sted/) *adv.* in place of.

in/step/, *n.* upper arch of foot.

in/sti·gate/ (in/sti gāt/) *v.,* **-gated, -gating.** incite to action. **—in/sti·ga/tion,** *n.* **—in/sti·ga/tor,** *n.*

in·still/ (in stil/) *v.* introduce slowly.

in/stinct (in/stingkt) *n.* natural impulse or talent. **—in·stinc/tive,** *adj.*

in/sti·tute/ (in/sti tōōt/, -tyōōt/) *v.,* **-tuted, -tuting. 1.** establish. **2.** put into effect. **—n. 3.** society or organization. **4.** established law, custom, etc.

in/sti·tu/tion, *n.* **1.** organization with public purpose. **2.** established tradition, etc. **3.** act of instituting. **—in/sti·tu/tion·al,** *adj.* **—in/sti·tu/tion·al·ize/,** *v.,* **-ized, -izing.**

in·struct/ (in strukt/) *v.* **1.** order. **2.** teach. **—in·struc/tion,** *n.* **—in·struc/tive,** *adj.* **—in·struc/tor,** *n.*

in/stru·ment (in/strə mənt) *n.* **1.** tool. **2.** device for producing music. **3.** means; agent. **4.** legal document. **—in/stru·men/tal** (-mən/tl) *adj.*

in/su·lar (in/sə lər, ins/yə-) *adj.* **1.** of islands. **2.** narrow in viewpoint.

in/su·late/ (-lāt/) *v.,* **-lated, -lating.** cover with material that prevents passage of heat, electricity, or sound. **—in/su·la/tion,** *n.* **—in/su·la/tor,** *n.*

in/su·lin (in/sə lin, ins/yə-) *n.* synthetic hormone used to treat diabetes.

in·sult/ *v.* (in sult/) **1.** treat with open contempt. **—n.** (in/sult) **2.** insulting remark or act.

in·su/per·a·ble (in sōō/pər ə bəl) *adj.* that cannot be overcome.

in·sure/, *v.,* **-sured, -suring. 1.** make certain. **2.** guarantee payment in case of harm to or loss of. **—in·sur/ance,** *n.* **—in·sur/er,** *n.*

in·sur/gent (in sûr/jənt) *n.* **1.** rebel. **—adj. 2.** rebellious.

in/sur·rec/tion (in/sə rek/shən) *n.* armed revolt.

int., **1.** interest. **2.** interior. **3.** interjection. **4.** international. **5.** intransitive.

in·tact/ (in takt/) *adj.* undamaged.

in/take/, *n.* **1.** point at which something is taken in. **2.** what is taken in.

in/te·ger (in/ti jər) *n.* whole number.

in/te·gral (in/ti grəl, in teg/rəl) *adj.* necessary to completeness.

in/te·grate/ (in/ti grāt/) *v.,* **-grated, -grating. 1.** unite. **2.** abolish segregation by race. **—in/te·gra/tion,** *n.*

in·teg/ri·ty (in teg/ri tē) *n.* **1.** soundness of character; honesty. **2.** perfect condition.

in·teg/u·ment (in teg/yə mənt) *n.* skin, rind, etc.

in/tel·lect/ (in/tl ekt/) *n.* **1.** reasoning. **2.** mental capacity.

in/tel·lec/tu·al, *adj.* **1.** of intellect. **2.** devising concepts in dealing with problems. **—n. 3.** person who pursues intellectual interests.

in·tel/li·gence (in tel/i jəns) *n.* **1.** ability to learn and understand. **2.** news. **3.** gathering of secret information.

in•tel′li•gent, adj. having a high mental capacity.

in•tel′li•gi•ble (-jə bəl) adj. understandable. —in•tel′li•gi•bil′i•ty, n.

in•tend′ (in tend′) v. plan; design.

in•tend′ed, n. Informal. person one plans to marry.

in•tense′ (in tens′) adj. 1. extremely powerful. 2. emotional. —in•ten′si•fy v., -fied, -fying. —in•ten′si•ty, n.

in•ten′sive, adj. thorough.

in•tent′ (in tent′) n. 1. purpose. —adj. 1. firmly concentrated. 2. firmly purposeful. —in•tent′ly, adv.

in•ten′tion, n. 1. purpose. 2. meaning. —in•ten′tion•al, adj.

in•ter′ (in tûr′) v. -terred, -terring. bury.

inter-, prefix meaning: 1. between or among, as interdepartmental. 2. reciprocally, as interdependent.

in′ter•act′ (in′tər akt′) v. act upon one another. —in′ter•ac′tion, n. —in′ter•ac′tive, adj.

in′ter•breed′, v., -bred, -breeding. crossbreed (plant or animal).

in′ter•cede′ (-sēd′) v., -ceded, -ceding. act or plead in behalf. —in′ter•ces′sion, n.

in′ter•cept′ (-sept′) v. stop or check progress.

in′ter•change′, v., -changed, -changing, n. —v. (in′tər chānj′) 1. exchange. 2. alternate. —n. (in′tər chānj′) 3. act or place of interchanging.

in′ter•con′ti•nen′tal, adj. between or among continents.

in′ter•course′, n. 1. dealings. 2. sexual relations.

in′ter•de•nom′i•na′tion•al, adj. between or involving different religious denominations.

in′ter•de•pen′dent, adj. mutually dependent. —in′ter•de•pen′dence, n.

in′ter•dict′ n. (in′tər dikt′) 1. decree that prohibits. —v. (in′tər dikt′) 2. prohibit. —in′ter•dic′tion, n.

in′ter•est (in′tər ist, -trist) n. 1. feeling of attention, curiosity, etc. 2. business or ownership. 3. benefit. 4. payment for use of money. —v. 5. excite or hold interest of.

interest group, group acting together because of a common interest, etc.

in′ter•est•ing (in′tər ə sting, -tra res′ting) adj. engaging the attention or curiosity.

in′ter•face′, n., v., -faced, -facing, v. —n. (in′tər fās′) 1. common boundary. 2. computer hardware or software that communicates information between entities, as between computer and user. —v. (in′tər fās′, in′tər fās′) 3. interact or coordinate smoothly.

in′ter•fere′ (-fēr′) v., -fered, -fering. 1. hamper. 2. intervene. 3. obstruct. —in′ter•fer′ence, n.

in′ter•im (in′tər əm) n. 1. meantime. —adj. 2. temporary.

in•te′ri•or (in tēr′ē ər) adj. 1. inside. 2. inland. —n. 3. interior part.

in′ter•ject′ (in′tər jekt′) v. add or include abruptly.

in′ter•jec′tion (-jek′shən) n. 1. act of interjecting. 2. something interjected. 3. interjected word that forms a complete utterance, as indeed!

in′ter•lace′, v., -laced, -lacing. weave together; intertwine.

in′ter•lock′, v., lock, join, or fit together closely.

in′ter•loc′u•tor (-lok′yə tər) n. participant in conversation.

in′ter•loc′u•to•ry (-tôr′ē) adj. 1. of or in conversation. 2. Law. not final.

in′ter•lop′er (-lō′pər) n. intruder.

in′ter•lude (-lōōd′) n. intervening episode, time, etc.

in′ter•mar′ry, v., -ried, -rying. 1. (of groups) become connected by marriage. 2. marry outside one's religion, ethnic group, etc. —in′ter•mar′riage, n.

in′ter•me′di•ar′y (-mē′dē er′ē) adj., n., pl. -aries. —adj. 1. intermediate. —n. 2. negotiator.

in′ter•me′di•ate (-it) adj. being or acting between two others.

in•ter′ment (in tûr′mənt) n. burial.

in′ter•mi•na•ble (in tûr′mə nə bəl) adj. seeming to be without end; endless. —in•ter′mi•na•bly, adv.

in′ter•mis′sion (in tûr mish′ən) n. interval between acts in drama, etc.

in′ter•mit′tent (-mit′nt) adj. alternately ceasing and starting again.

in•tern′ (in tûrn′) v. 1. confine, esp. prisoner of war. —n. (in′tûrn) 2. Also, in′terne. resident assistant physician on hospital staff. —in•tern′ment, n. —in′tern•ship′, n.

in•ter′nal (in tûr′nl) adj. 1. interior; inner. 2. not foreign; domestic.

internal medicine, branch of medicine dealing with diagnosis and nonsurgical treatment of diseases.

in′ter•na′tion•al, adj. 1. among nations. 2. of many nations.

in′ter•na′tion•al•ism, n. principle of international cooperation.

in′ter•na′tion•al•ize′, v., -ized, -izing. 1. make international. 2. bring under international control.

in·ter·ne·cine (-nē′sēn, -sīn, -nes′ēn, -īn) *adj.* **1.** of conflict within a group. **2.** mutually destructive.

In·ter·net′, *n.* large computer network linking smaller networks worldwide.

in·tern·ist (in′tûr nist, in tûr′nist) *n.* doctor specializing in internal medicine.

in·ter·per·son·al, *adj.* between persons.

in·ter·plan·e·tar·y, *adj.* between planets.

in·ter·play′, *n.* reciprocal action.

in·ter·po·late′ (in tûr′pə lāt′) *v.,* **-lated, -lating.** insert to alter or clarify meaning.

in·ter·pose′, *v.,* **-posed, -posing. 1.** place between things. **2.** intervene.

in·ter·pret (in tûr′prit) *v.* **1.** explain. **2.** construe. **3.** translate. —**in·ter′pre·ta′tion,** *n.* —**in·ter′pret·er,** *n.*

in·ter·ra′cial, *adj.* of, for, or between persons of different races.

in·ter·re·lat′ed, *adj.* closely associated.

in·ter·ro·gate′ (in ter′ə gāt′) *v.,* **-gated, -gating.** question. —**in·ter′ro·ga′tion,** *n.* —**in·ter·rog′a·tive** (in′tə rog′ə tiv) —**in·ter′ro·ga′tor,** *n.*

in·ter·rupt′ (in′tə rupt′) *v.* break in; stop. —**in·ter·rup′tion,** *n.*

in·ter·scho·las′tic, *adj.* existing or occurring between schools.

in·ter·sect′ (-sekt′) *v.* divide by crossing; cross.

in·ter·sec′tion, *n.* **1.** place where roads meet. **2.** act of intersecting.

in·ter·sperse′ (-spûrs′) *v.,* **-spersed, -spersing.** scatter at random.

in·ter·state′, *adj.* involving number of states.

in·ter·stel′lar, *adj.* situated or occurring between the stars.

in·ter·stice (in tûr′stis) *n.* space between.

in·ter·twine′, *v.,* **-twined, -twining.** unite by twining together.

in·ter·ur·ban, *adj.* between cities.

in·ter·val (in′tər val) *n.* **1.** intervening time or space. **2.** difference in musical pitch between two tones.

in·ter·vene′ (-vēn′) *v.,* **-vened, -vening. 1.** come or be between. **2.** mediate. —**in·ter·ven′tion** (-ven′shən) *n.* —**in′ter·ven′tion·ist,** *n.*

in·ter·view′, *n.* **1.** meeting to assess someone or get information. —*v.* **2.** have interview with.

in·tes·tate (in tes′tāt, -tit) *adj.* without having made a will.

in·tes·tine (in tes′tin) *n.* lower part

of alimentary canal. —**in·tes′ti·nal,** *adj.*

in·ti·mate, *adj., n., v.,* **-mated, -mating.** —*adj.* (in′tə mit) **1.** close; friendly. **2.** private. **3.** thorough. —*n.* (-mit) **4.** intimate friend. —*v.* (-māt′) **5.** imply. —**in′ti·ma·cy** (-mə sē) *n.* —**in′ti·ma′tion,** *n.*

in·tim′i·date′ (in tim′i dāt′) *v.,* **-dated, -dating.** frighten.

in′to (in′tōō; *unstressed* -tŏō, -tə) *prep.* to inside of.

in·tone′, *v.,* **-toned, -toning. 1.** use particular spoken tone. **2.** chant.

in·tox′i·cate′ (in tok′si kāt′) *v.,* **-cated, -cating.** make drunk.

in·trac′ta·ble, *adj.* stubborn.

in·tra·mu′ral (in′trə myŏōr′əl) *adj.* within one school.

in·tran′si·gent (in tran′si jənt) *adj.* uncompromising. —**in·tran′si·gence,** *n.*

in·tran′si·tive (-tiv) *adj.* (of verb) not having a direct object.

in·tra·ve′nous (in′trə vē′nəs) *adj.* within vein.

in·trep′id (in trep′id) *adj.* fearless. —**in′tre·pid′i·ty** (-tre pid′i tē) *n.*

in·tri·cate (in′tri kit) *adj.* complicated. —**in′tri·ca·cy** (-kə sē) *n.*

in·trigue′, *n., v.,* **-trigued, -triguing.** —*v.* (in trēg′) **1.** interest by puzzling. **2.** plot. —*n.* (in trēg′, in′trēg) **3.** crafty design or plot.

in·trin·sic (in trin′sik, -zik) *adj.* inherent. —**in·trin′si·cal·ly,** *adv.*

in·tro·duce′ (in′trə dōōs′, -dyōōs′) *v.,* **-duced, -ducing. 1.** bring to notice, use, etc. **2.** be preliminary to. **3.** make (person) known to another. —**in′tro·duc′tion** (-duk′shən) *n.* —**in′tro·duc′to·ry** (-duk′tə rē) *adj.*

in·tro·spec·tion (in′trə spek′shən) *n.* examination of one's own thoughts and motives. —**in′tro·spec′tive,** *adj.*

in·tro·vert′ (-vûrt′) *n.* person concerned chiefly with inner thoughts or feelings. —**in′tro·ver′sion** (-vûr′zhən) *n.* —**in′tro·vert′ed,** *adj.*

in·trude′ (in trōōd′) *v.,* **-truded, -truding.** come or bring in without welcome. —**in·tru′sion** (-trōō′zhən) *n.* —**in·tru′sive** (-siv) *adj.*

in·tu·i′tion (in′tōō ish′ən, -tyōō-) *n.* instinctive perception. —**in·tu′i·tive** (-i tiv) *adj.* —**in·tu′i·tive·ly,** *adv.*

in·un·date′ (in′ən dāt′, -un-) *v.,* **-dated, -dating.** flood. —**in′un·da′tion,** *n.*

in·ure′ (in yŏŏr′, i nŏŏr′) *v.,* **-ured, -uring.** accustom; harden.

in·vade′ (in vād′) *v.,* **-vaded, -vad-**

ing. 1. enter as an enemy. **—in·vad′er,** *n.* **—in·va′sion** (-vā′zhən) *n.*

in·va·lid, *n.* **1.** (in′və lid) sick person. **—adj. 2.** (in′və lid) sick. **3.** (in′və lid) for invalids. **4.** (in val′id) not valid.

in·val′i·date (in val′i dāt′) *v.* **-dated, -dating.** make invalid.

in·val′u·a·ble, *adj.* priceless.

in·vec′tive (in vek′tiv) *n.* abuse.

in·veigh′ (in vā′) *v.* attack violently in words.

in·vei′gle (in vā′gəl, -vē′-) *v.* **-gled, -gling.** lure into action.

in·vent′ (in vent′) *v.* devise (something new). **—in·ven′tion,** *n.* **—in·ven′tive,** *adj.* **—in·ven′tor,** *n.*
—Usage. See DISCOVER.

in′ven·to·ry (in′vən tôr′ē) *n., pl.* **-tories.** list or stock of goods.

in·verse′ (in vûrs′, in′vûrs) *adj.* **1.** reversed. **2.** opposite. **3.** inverted. **—in·verse′ly,** *adv.*

in·vert′ (-vûrt′) *v.* **1.** turn upside down. **2.** reverse. **3.** make contrary. **—in·ver′sion,** *n.*

in·ver′te·brate, *adj.* **1.** without backbone. **—n. 2.** invertebrate animal.

in·vest′ (in vest′) *v.* **1.** spend money in hope of profit. **2.** give or devote (time, etc.). **3.** give power or authority to. **—in·vest′ment,** *n.* **—in·ves′tor,** *n.*

in·ves′ti·gate (in ves′ti gāt′) *v.* **-gated, -gating.** examine in detail. **—in·ves′ti·ga′tion,** *n.* **—in·ves′ti·ga′tive, -ga′to·ry,** *adj.* **—in·ves′ti·ga′tor,** *n.*

in·vet′er·ate (in vet′ər it) *adj.* confirmed in habit.

in·vid′i·ous (in vid′ē əs) *adj.* **1.** likely to arouse envy. **2.** unjust.

in·vig′or·ate (in vig′ə rāt′) *v.* **-ated, -ating.** fill with energy.

in·vin′ci·ble (in vin′sə bəl) *adj.* unconquerable. **—in·vin′ci·bil′i·ty,** *n.*

in·vi′o·la·ble (in vī′ə lə bəl) *adj.* that must not or cannot be violated.

in·vi′o·late (-lit, -lāt′) *adj.* **1.** not hurt or desecrated. **2.** undisturbed.

in·vite′ (-vīt′) *v.* **-vited, -viting. 1.** ask politely. **2.** act so as to make likely. **3.** attract. **—in′vi·ta′tion** (in′vi täh′shən) *n.*

in·vit′ing, *adj.* attractive or tempting.

in vi′tro (in vē′trō) developed or maintained in a controlled nonliving environment, as a laboratory vessel.

in′vo·ca′tion (in′və kā′shən) *n.* prayer for aid, guidance, etc.

in′voice (in′vois) *n., v.* **-voiced, -voicing. —n. 1.** bill with prices of goods sent to buyer. **—v. 2.** list on invoice.

in·voke′ (in vōk′) *v.* **-voked, -vok-**

ing. 1. beg for. **2.** call on in prayer. **3.** cite as authoritative.

in·vol′un·tar′y, *adj.* not done intentionally.

in·volve′ (in volv′) *v.* **-volved, -volving. 1.** include as necessary. **2.** complicate. **3.** implicate. **4.** engross. **—in·volve′ment,** *n.*

in′ward (in′wərd) *adv.* **1.** Also, **in′wards.** toward the interior. **—adj. 2.** toward the interior. **3.** inner. **—n. 4.** inward part. **—in′ward·ly,** *adv.*

in′-your-face′, *adj. Informal.* involving confrontation; defiant; provocative.

Io., Iowa.

I/O, input/output.

i′o·dine′ (ī′ə dīn′, -din) *n.* in Chem. also -dēn′) *n.* nonmetallic element used in medicine.

i′on (ī′ən, ī′on) *n.* electrically charged particle.

-ion, suffix meaning: action or process (*inspection*); result of action (*creation*); state or condition (*depression*).

i′on·ize′ (ī′ə nīz′) *v.,* **-nized, -nizing. 1.** separate or change into ions. **2.** produce ions in. **3.** become ionized. **—i′on·i·za′tion,** *n.*

i·on′o·sphere (ī on′ə sfēr′) *n.* outermost region of earth's atmosphere, consisting of ionized layers.

i·o′ta (ī ō′tə) *n.* very small quantity.

IOU, written acknowledgment of debt.

ip·so fac′to (ip′sō fak′tō) by the fact itself.

IQ, intelligence quotient.

IRA (pronounced as initials or ī′rə) individual retirement account.

I·ra′ni·an (i rā′nē ən, i rā′-) *n.* native of Iran. **—I·ra′ni·an,** *adj.*

I·ra′qi (i rak′ē, i rä′ kē) *n., pl.* **-qis.** native of Iraq. **—I·ra′qi,** *adj.*

i·ras′ci·ble (i ras′ə bəl) *adj.* easily angered.

ire (īr) *n.* anger. **—i′rate** (ī rāt′, ī′rāt) *adj.*

ir′i·des′cence (ir′i des′əns) *n.* play of rainbowlike colors. **—ir′i·des′cent,** *adj.*

i′ris (ī′ris) *n.* **1.** colored part of the eye. **2.** perennial plant with showy flowers.

I′rish (ī′rish) *n.* language or people of Ireland. **—Irish,** *adj.*

irk (ûrk) *v.* annoy. **—irk′some,** *adj.*

i′ron (ī′ərn) *n.* **1.** metallic element. **2.** implement for pressing cloth. **3.** (*pl.*) shackles. **—adj. 4.** of or like iron. **—v. 5.** press with iron.

i′ron·clad′, *adj.* **1.** iron-plated, as a ship. **2.** very rigid or exacting.

itch

iron curtain, (formerly) barrier between Communist and non-Communist areas.

i·ro·ny (ī′rə nē, ī′ər-) *n., pl.* **-nies.** 1. figure of speech in which meaning is opposite to what is said. 2. outcome contrary to expectations. —i·ron′ic (ī ron′ik), *adj.*

Ir·o·quois′ (ir′ə kwoi′, -kwoiz′) *n., pl.* **-quois.** member of a group of North American Indians.

ir·ra·di·ate′ (i rā′dē āt′) *v.,* **-ated, -ating.** 1. illuminate. 2. expose to radiation. 3. shine.

ir·ra′tion·al (i rash′ə nl) *adj.* without reason or judgment.

ir·rec·on·cil′a·ble (i rek′ən sī′lə bəl) *adj.* 1. that cannot be brought into agreement. 2. bitterly opposed.

ir′re·deem′a·ble (ir′i dē′mə bəl) *adj.* that cannot be redeemed.

ir′re·duc′i·ble (ir′i dōō′sə bəl, -dyōō′-) *adj.* that cannot be reduced.

ir·ref′u·ta·ble (i ref′yə tə bəl) *adj.* impossible to refute.

ir·reg′u·lar (i reg′yə lər) *adj.* 1. not symmetrical. 2. not fixed. 3. not conforming to rule or normality.

ir·rel′e·vant (i rel′ə vənt) *adj.* not relevant. —ir·rel′e·vance, *n.*

ir′re·li′gious (ir′i lij′əs) *adj.* 1. not religious. 2. hostile to religion.

ir′re·par′a·ble (i rep′ər ə bəl) *adj.* that cannot be rectified.

ir′re·press′i·ble (ir′i pres′ə bəl) *adj.* that cannot be repressed.

ir′re·proach′a·ble (ir′i prō′chə bəl) *adj.* blameless.

ir′re·sist′i·ble (ir′i zis′tə bəl) *adj.* not to be withstood.

ir·res′o·lute′ (i rez′ə lōōt′) *adj.* undecided.

ir′re·spec′tive, *adj.* without regard to.

ir′re·spon′si·ble (ir′i spon′sə bəl) *adj.* not concerned with responsibilities. —ir′re·spon′si·bly, *adv.*

ir′re·triev′a·ble (ir′i trē′və bəl) *adj.* that cannot be recovered.

ir·rev′er·ent (i rev′ər ənt) *adj.* lacking respect.

ir·rev′o·ca·ble (i rev′ə kə bəl) *adj.* not to be revoked or annulled.

ir′ri·gate′ (ir′i gāt′) *v.,* **-gated, -gating.** supply with water. —ir′ri·ga′-tion, *n.*

ir′ri·ta·ble (ir′i tə bəl) *adj.* easily angered. —ir′ri·ta·bil′i·ty, *n.*

ir′ri·tate′ (-tāt′) *v.,* **-tated, -tating.** 1. anger. 2. make sore. —ir′ri·tant (-tnt) *n.* —ir′ri·ta′tion, *n.*

IRS, Internal Revenue Service.

is (iz) *v.* third pers. sing. pres. indic. of **be.**

-ish, suffix meaning: 1. of or be-

longing to, as *British.* 2. like or having characteristics of, as *baby-ish.* 3. inclined to, as *bookish.* 4. near or about, as *fiftyish.* 5. somewhat, as *reddish.*

Is·lam′ (is läm′, is′läm, iz′-) *n.* religious faith founded by Muhammad (A.D. 570-632). —Is·lam′ic, *adj.*

is′land (ī′lənd) *n.* body of land surrounded by water. —is′land·er, *n.*

isle (īl) *n.* small island.

is′let (ī′lit) *n.* tiny island.

ism (iz′əm) *n.* distinctive doctrine, theory, or system.

-ism, suffix meaning: action or practice (*baptism*); state or condition (*barbarism*); doctrine or principle (*Marxism*); distinctive feature or usage (*witticism*).

i′so·bar′ (ī′sə bär′) *n.* line on map connecting points at which barometric pressure is the same.

i′so·late′ (ī′sə lāt′) *v.,* **-lated, -lating.** place or keep alone. —i′so·la′tion, *n.*

i′so·la′tion·ist, *n.* person opposed to participation in world affairs.

i′so·met′rics, *n.pl.* exercises in which one body part is tensed against another. —i′so·met′ric, *adj.*

i·sos′ce·les′ (ī sos′ə lēz′) *adj.* (of triangle) having two sides equal.

i′so·tope′ (ī′sə tōp′) *n.* one of two or more forms of an element that vary in atomic weight.

Is·rae′li (iz rā′lē) *n., pl.* **-lis, -li.** native of Israel. —Is·rae′li, *adj.*

is′sue (ish′ōō) *v.,* **-sued, -suing,** *n.* —v. 1. send out. 2. publish. 3. distribute. 4. emit. 5. emerge. —n. 6. act of issuing. 7. thing issued. 8. point in question. 9. offspring. 10. result. —is′su·ance, *n.*

-ist, suffix meaning: 1. one who makes or professes, as *novelist.* 2. one who operates, as *machinist.* 3. advocate, as *socialist.*

isth′mus (is′məs) *n.* strip of land surrounded by water and connecting two larger bodies.

it (it) *pron.* third pers. sing. neuter pronoun.

ital., italic.

I·tal′ian (i tal′yən) *n.* native or language of Italy. —I·tal′ian, *adj.* —Pronunciation. The pronunciation of ITALIAN with the beginning sound (ī), (pronounced like *eye*) is heard primarily from uneducated speakers. This pronunciation is sometimes used as a joke and sometimes as an insult, but is considered pretentious in either case.

i·tal′ic (i tal′ik, ī tal′-) *n.* printing type that slopes to right.

itch (ich) *v.* 1. feel irritation of skin.

—*n.* **2.** itching sensation. **3.** restless desire. —*itch′y*, *adj.*

i′tem (ī′təm) *n.* separate article.

i′tem·ize′, *v.*, **-ized, -izing.** state by items; list. —*i′tem·i·za′tion, n.*

i·tin′er·ant (ī tin′ər ənt, i tin′-) *adj.* **1.** traveling. —*n.* **2.** person who goes from place to place.

i·tin′er·ar′y (-ə rer′ē) *n.*, *pl.* **-aries.** **1.** route. **2.** plan of travel.

-itis, suffix meaning inflammation of a body part, as *tonsillitis.*

its (its) *adj.* possessive form of **it.**

it's (its) contraction of **it is.**

it·self′, *pron.* reflexive form of **it.**

IV (ī′vē′) *n.*, *pl.* **IVs, IV's.** apparatus

for intravenous delivery of medicines, etc.

I've (īv) contraction of **I have.**

-ive, suffix meaning: tending to (de-*structive*); of the nature of (*festive*).

i′vo·ry (ī′və rē, ī′vrē) *n.*, *pl.* **-ries.** **1.** hard white substance in tusks. **2.** yellowish white.

ivory tower, remoteness or aloofness from wordly affairs.

i′vy (ī′vē) *n.*, *pl.* **vies.** climbing evergreen vine. —*i′vied, adj.*

-ize, suffix meaning: **1.** engage in, as *economize.* **2.** treat in a certain way, as *idolize.* **3.** become or form into, as *unionize.* **4.** make or cause to be, as *civilize.*

J

J, j (jā) *n.* tenth letter of English alphabet.

jab (jab) *v.*, **jabbed, jabbing,** *n.* poke; thrust.

jab′ber (jab′ər) *v.* **1.** talk rapidly or indistinctly. —*n.* **2.** such talk.

jack (jak) *n.* **1.** lifting device. **2.** knave in playing cards. **3.** electrical connecting device. **4.** flag; ensign. —*v.* **5.** raise with jack.

jack′al (jak′əl) *n.* wild dog.

jack′ass′, *n.* **1.** male donkey. **2.** fool.

jack′et (jak′it) *n.* short coat.

Jack Frost, frost personified.

jack′ham′mer, *n.* compressed-air portable drill for rock, etc.

jack′-in-the-box′, *n.*, *pl.* **-boxes.** toy consisting of box from which figure springs up when the lid is opened.

jack′knife′, *n.*, *pl.* **-knives,** **-knifed, -knifing.** —*n.* **1.** large folding pocketknife. —*v.* **2.** (of a trailer truck) have or cause to have the cab and trailer swivel into a V.

jack′pot′, *n.* cumulative prize in contest, lottery, etc.

jack rabbit, large rabbit of western America.

Ja·cuz′zi (jə kōō′zē) *n.*, *pl.* **-zis.** *Trademark.* brand name for type of whirlpool bath.

jade (jād) *n.* valuable green stone.

jad′ed, *adj.* weary.

jag (jag) *n.* *Slang.* drunken spree.

jag′ged, *adj.* sharply notched.

jag′uar (jag′wär) *n.* large South American wildcat.

jai′ a·lai′ (hī′ lī′, hī′ ə lī′) *n.* game played with basketlike rackets.

jail (jāl) *n.* **1.** prison. —*v.* **2.** put in prison. —*jail′er, n.*

ja·la·pe′ño (hä′lə pān′yō) *n.*, *pl.* **-ños.** Mexican hot pepper.

ja·lop′y (jə lop′ē) *n.*, *pl.* **-pies.** old, decrepit automobile.

jam (jam) *v.*, **jammed, jamming,** *n.* —*v.* **1.** push or squeeze. **2.** make or become unworkable. —*n.* **3.** people or objects jammed together. **4.** *Informal.* difficult situation. **5.** preserve of entire fruit.

jamb (jam) *n.* side post of door or window.

jam′bo·ree′ (jam′bə rē′) *n.* merry gathering.

Jan., January.

jan′gle (jang′gəl) *v.*, **-gled, -gling,** *n.* —*v.* **1.** sound harshly. —*n.* **2.** harsh sound.

jan′i·tor (jan′i tər) *n.* caretaker of building.

Jan′u·ar′y (jan′yōō er′ē) *n.* first month of year.

Jap′a·nese′ (jap′ə nēz′, -nēs′) *n.*, *pl.* **-nese.** native or language of Japan. —**Japanese,** *adj.*

jar (jär) *n.*, *v.*, **jarred, jarring.** —*n.* **1.** broad-mouthed bottle. **2.** sudden shock or shake. —*v.* **3.** shock or shake. **4.** conflict.

jar′gon (jär′gən, -gon) *n.* language meaningful only to a particular trade, etc.

jas′mine (jaz′min, jas′-) *n.* fragrant shrub.

jas′per (jas′pər) *n.* precious quartz.

jaun′dice (jôn′dis, jän′-) *n.* illness causing yellowed skin, etc.

jaun′diced, *adj.* **1.** skeptical. **2.** envious.

jaunt (jônt, jänt) *n.* short trip.

jaun′ty (jôn′tē, jän′-) *adj.*, **-tier, -tiest.** sprightly. —*jaun′ti·ly, adv.*

jave′lin (jav′lin, jav′ə-) *n.* spear.

jaw (jô) *n.* either of two bones forming mouth.

jaw′bone′, *n.*, *v.*, **-boned, -boning.**

—n. **1.** bone of the jaw. —v. **2.** influence by persuasion.

jay (jā) n. noisy colorful bird.

jay′walk′, v. cross street improperly. —**jay′walk′er,** n.

jazz (jaz) n. **1.** popular music of black American origin. **2.** Slang. insincere talk.

jazz′y, adj., **-ier, -iest. 1.** of or like jazz music. **2.** fancy.

J.D., 1. Doctor of Jurisprudence; Doctor of Laws. **2.** Doctor of Laws. **3.** Justice Department.

jeal′ous (jel′əs) adj. **1.** resentful of another's success, etc.; envious. **2.** vigilant in guarding something. —**jeal′ous•ly,** adv. —**jeal′ous•y,** n.

jeans (jēnz) n.pl. cotton trousers.

Jeep (jēp) n. Trademark. small rugged type of automobile.

jeer (jēr) v. **1.** deride. —n. **2.** deriding shout.

Je•ho′vah (ji hō′və) n. God.

je•june′ (ji jōōn′) adj. **1.** insipid. **2.** lacking maturity; childish.

jell (jel) v. **1.** become like jelly in consistency. **2.** become clear.

jel′ly (jel′ē) n., pl. **-lies,** v., **-lied, -lying.** —n. **1.** soft, semisolid food, as fruit juice boiled with sugar. —v. **2.** make into jelly.

jel′ly•bean′, n. small, bean-shaped, chewy candy.

jel′ly•fish′, n., pl. **-fish, -fishes.** marine animal with soft, jellylike body.

jelly roll, thin cake spread with jelly and rolled up.

jen′ny (jen′ē) n., pl. **-nies.** female donkey, wren, etc.

jeop′ard•ize′ (jep′ər dīz′) v., **-ized, -izing.** endanger. —**jeop′ard•y,** n.

jerk (jûrk) n. **1.** quick, sharp pull. **2.** Slang. stupid person. —v. **3.** pull with a jerk. —**jerk′y,** adj.

jer′kin (jûr′kin) n. close-fitting, usu. sleeveless jacket.

jerk′wa′ter, adj. insignificant and remote.

jer′ry-built′, adj. flimsily made.

jer′sey (jûr′zē) n. **1.** type of shirt. **2.** knitted fabric.

jest (jest) n., v. joke; banter. —**jest′er,** n.

Je′sus (jē′zəs, -zaz) n. founder of Christian religion. Also called **Jesus Christ.**

jet (jet) n., v., **jetted, jetting,** adj. —n. **1.** stream under pressure. Also, **jet plane.** plane operated by jet propulsion. **2.** black stone. —v. **4.** spout.

jet lag, fatigue after jet flight to different time zone.

jet′lin′er, n. jet plane carrying passengers.

jet propulsion, propulsion of plane, etc., by reactive thrust of jet. —**jet′-pro•pelled′,** adj.

jet′sam (jet′səm) n. goods thrown overboard to lighten distressed ship.

jet′ti•son (jet′ə sən, -zən) v. cast (jetsam) out.

jet′ty (jet′ē) n., pl. **-ties.** wharf; pier.

Jew (jōō) n. **1.** follower of Judaism. **2.** descendant of Biblical Hebrews. —**Jew′ish,** adj.

jew′el (jōō′əl) n. **1.** precious stone; gem. —v. **2.** adorn with jewels. —**jew′el•er,** n. —**jew′el•ry,** n.

jib (jib) n. triangular sail.

jibe (jīb) v., **jibed, jibing. 1.** gibe. **2.** Informal. be consistent.

jif′fy (jif′ē) n., pl. **-fies.** short time.

jig (jig) n., v., **jigged, jigging.** —n. **1.** lively folk dance. —v. **2.** dance a jig.

jig′ger (jig′ər) n. glass measure of liquor. $1\frac{1}{2}$ oz. (45 ml) for liquors.

jig′gle (jig′əl) v., **-gled, -gling,** n. —v. **1.** move back and forth, etc. —n. **2.** act of jiggling.

jig′saw′, n. saw with narrow vertical blade for cutting curves, patterns, etc.

jigsaw puzzle, set of irregularly cut flat pieces that form a picture when fitted together.

jilt (jilt) v. reject (a previously encouraged suitor).

Jim Crow (sometimes l.c.) policy of discrimination against blacks. —**Jim′-Crow′,** adj.

jim′my (jim′ē) n., pl. **-mies,** v., **-mied, -mying.** —n. **1.** short crowbar. —v. **2.** force open.

jim′son•weed′ (jim′sən wēd′) n. coarse weed with poisonous leaves.

jin′gle (jing′gəl) v., **-gled, -gling,** n. —v. **1.** make repeated clinking sound. —n. **2.** clink; tinkle. **3.** very simple verse.

jin′go•ism (jing′gō iz′əm) n. chauvinism marked by aggressive foreign policy. —**jin′go•is′tic,** adj.

jin•rik′i•sha (jin rik′shō, -shä) n. rickshaw. Also, **jin•rik′i•sha.**

jinx (jingks) n. **1.** cause of bad luck. —v. **2.** cause bad luck.

jit′ters, n.pl. Informal. nervousness. —**jit′ter•y,** adj.

jive (jīv) n., v., **jived, jiving.** —n. **1.** swing music or early jazz. **2.** deceptive or meaningless talk. —v. **3.** Slang. fool or kid.

job (job) n., v., **jobbed, jobbing.** —n. **1.** piece of work. **2.** employment. —v. **3.** sell wholesale.

job action, work slowdown by employees to win demands.

job′ber, n. **1.** wholesaler. **2.** dealer in odd lots of merchandise.

job lot, large assortment of goods sold as a single unit.

jock (jok) n. Informal. **1.** athlete. **2.** enthusiast.

jock′ey (jok′ē) n. **1.** rider of race horses. —v. **2.** maneuver.

jo·cose′ (jō kōs′, jə-) adj. merry. Also, **jo·cund** (jok′ənd, jō′kənd). —**jo·cose′ly,** adv.

joc′u·lar (jok′yə lər) adj. joking. —**joc′u·lar′i·ty** (-lar′i tē) n.

jodh′purs (jod′pərz) n.pl. riding breeches.

jog (jog) v., **jogged, jogging,** n. —v. **1.** nudge. **2.** run at steady pace. —n. **3.** nudge. **4.** steady pace. **5.** projection. —**jog′ger,** n.

joie de vi·vre (zhwad′ vē′vrə) French. delight in being alive.

join (join) v. **1.** put together. **2.** become member of.

join′er, n. assembler of woodwork. —**join′er·y,** n.

joint (joint) n. **1.** place or part in which things join. **2.** place where two bones join. **3.** cheap, sordid place. **4.** Slang. marijuana cigarette. —adj. **5.** common. **6.** join or divide at joint. —**joint′ly,** adv.

joist (joist) n. floor beam.

joke (jōk) n., v., **joked, joking.** —n. **1.** amusing remark, story, etc. —v. **2.** make or tell joke. **3.** speak only to amuse. —**jok′ing·ly,** adv.

jol′ly (jol′ē) adj., **-lier, -liest,** v., **-lied, -lying,** adv. —adj. **1.** merry. —v. **2.** try to keep (someone) in good humor. —adv. **3.** Brit. Informal. very. —**jol′li·ness,** n. —**jol′li·ty,** n.

jolt (jōlt) v., n. jar; shake.

jon′quil (jong′kwil, jon′-) n. fragrant yellow or white narcissus.

josh (josh) v. Informal. tease.

jos′tle (jos′əl) v., **-tled, -tling.** push or shove.

jot (jot) v., **jotted, jotting.** —n. **1.** bit. —v. **2.** write.

jounce (jouns) v., **jounced, jouncing,** n. —v. **1.** move joltingly. —n. **2.** jouncing movement.

jour′nal (jûr′nl) n. **1.** daily record. **2.** periodical.

jour·nal·ese′ (-ēz′, -ēs′) n. writing style typical of newspapers.

jour′nal·ism (-iz′əm) n. newspaper writing. —**jour′nal·ist,** n. —**jour′nal·is′tic,** adj.

jour′ney (jûr′nē) n. **1.** act or course of traveling. —v. **2.** travel.

jour′ney·man, n., pl. **-men.** hired skilled workman.

joust (joust) n. fight between mounted knights.

jo′vi·al (jō′vē əl) adj. hearty and good-humored. —**jo′vi·al′i·ty** (-al′i-tē) n.

jowl (joul) n. jaw or cheek.

joy (joi) n. gladness; delight. —**joy′ful, joy′ous,** adj.

joy′ride′, n. ride for pleasure, esp. in recklessly driven vehicle.

joy′stick′, n. **1.** Informal. control stick of airplane. **2.** lever for controlling action in computer game.

JP, Justice of the Peace.

Jr., junior. Also, **jr.**

ju′bi·lant (jōō′bə lənt) adj. rejoicing. —**ju′bi·la′tion** (-lā′shən) n.

ju′bi·lee′ (jōō′bə lē′) n. celebration, esp. of anniversary.

Ju′da·ism (jōō′dē iz′əm, -dā-) n. religion of the Jewish people.

judge (juj) n., v., **judged, judging.** —n. **1.** person who decides cases in court of law. **2.** person making authoritative decisions. **3.** discriminating person. —v. **4.** decide on.

judg′ment (-mənt) n. **1.** decision, as in court of law. **2.** good sense.

judg·men′tal (-men′tl) adj. making judgments, esp. on morality.

ju·di′cial (jōō dish′əl) adj. of justice, courts of law, or judges.

ju·di′ci·ar′y (-dish′ē er′ē, -dish′ə rē) n., pl. **-ies,** adj. —n. **1.** legal branch of government. —adj. **2.** of judges.

ju·di′cious, adj. wise; prudent.

ju′do (jōō′dō) n. martial art based on jujitsu.

jug (jug) n. **1.** container for liquids. **2.** Slang. prison.

jug′ger·naut′ (jug′ər nôt′) n. any overpowering, irresistible force.

jug′gle (jug′əl) v., **-gled, -gling.** perform tricks by tossing and catching objects. —**jug′gler,** n.

jug′u·lar (jug′yə lər) adj. **1.** of the neck. **2.** large vein in neck.

juice (jōōs) n. liquid part of plant, fruit, etc. —**juic′y,** adj.

juic′er, n. **1.** appliance for squeezing fruit and vegetable juice. **2.** Slang. heavy drinker.

ju·jit′su (jōō jit′sōō) n. Japanese method of wrestling and self-defense.

ju′jube (jōō′jōōb, jōō′jŏo bē′) n. chewy fruity lozenge.

juke box (jōōk′) coin-operated record player.

Jul., July.

ju·li·enne′ (jōō′lē en′) adj., v. (of vegetables) cut into thin strips.

Ju·ly′ (jōō lī′, jə-) n. seventh month of year.

jum′ble (jum′bal) n., v., **-bled, -bling.** —n. **1.** confused mixture. —v. **2.** make jumble of.

jum′bo (jum′bō) adj. very large.

jump (jump) v. **1.** spring up; leap. **2.** rise. —n. **3.** spring; leap. **4.** rise. **5.** Informal. advantage.

jump/er, n. **1.** one that jumps. **2.** sleeveless dress worn over blouse. **3.** electric cable for starting dead car battery.

jump/-start/, n. **1.** starting of car engine with jumpers (def. 3). —v. **2.** give a jump-start to. **3.** enliven or revive.

jump/suit/, n. one-piece suit.

jump/y, adj. **-ier, -iest.** nervous.

Jun., June.

junc/tion (jungk/shən) n. **1.** union. **2.** place of joining.

junc/ture (-chər) n. **1.** point of time. **2.** crisis. **3.** joint.

June (jōōn) n. sixth month of year.

jun/gle (jung/gəl) n. wildly overgrown tropical land.

jun/ior (jōōn/yər) adj. **1.** younger. **2.** lower. —n. **3.** third-year high school or college student.

junior college, two-year college.

junior high school, school usu. encompassing grades 7 through 9.

ju/ni-per (jōō/nə pər) n. coniferous evergreen shrub or tree.

junk (jungk) n. **1.** rubbish. **2.** type of Chinese ship. **3.** Slang. narcotics, esp. heroin. —v. **4.** discard.

junk/er, n. Informal. old vehicle ready to be scrapped.

junk/et (jung/kit) n. **1.** custard. **2.** trip by government official at public expense. —v. **3.** entertain.

junk food, high-calorie food of little nutritional value.

junk/ie, n. Informal. **1.** drug, esp. heroin, addict. **2.** person who craves or is enthusiastic for something.

junk mail, unsolicited commercial material mailed in bulk.

jun/ta (hōōn/tə, jun/-, hun/-) n. military group that seizes power.

—**Pronunciation.** When the word JUNTA was borrowed into English from Spanish in the early 17th century, its pronunciation was thoroughly Anglicized to (jun/tə). During the 20th century, esp. in North America, the pronunciation (hōōn/tə), which comes from Spanish (hōōn/tä) has come into frequent use, probably through people's renewed awareness of the word's Spanish origins. A hybrid form, combining English and Spanish influence, (hun/tə) is also heard. Any of these pronunciations is perfectly standard.

Ju/pi-ter (jōō/pi tər) n. largest of sun's planets.

ju/ris-dic/tion (jŏŏr/is dik/shən) n. authority, range of control, etc., of judge or the like.

ju/ris-pru/dence (-prōōd/ns) n. science of law.

ju/rist, n. expert in law.

ju/ror (jŏŏr/ər, -ôr) n. member of jury. Also, n. fem. **jur/y-wom/an.**

ju/ry (jŏŏr/ē) n., pl. **-ries.** group of persons selected to make decisions, esp. in law court.

just (just) adj. **1.** fair; right. **2.** legal. **3.** true. —adv. **4.** exactly. **5.** barely. **6.** only. **7.** very recently.

jus/tice (jus/tis) n. **1.** fairness; rightness. **2.** administration of law. **3.** high judge.

justice of the peace, local public officer who performs marriages, tries minor cases, etc.

jus/ti-fy/, v., **-fied, -fying. 1.** show to be true, right, etc. **2.** defend. —**jus/ti-fi-ca/tion,** n.

jut (jut) v., **jutted, jutting.** project.

jute (jōōt) n. East Indian plant whose fibers are used for fabrics.

ju/ve-nile (jōō/və nl, -nīl/) adj. **1.** young. —n. **2.** young person.

juvenile delinquency, illegal or antisocial behavior by a minor. —**juvenile delinquent.**

jux/ta-pose/ (juk/stə pōz/, juk/stə-pōz/) v. **-posed, -posing.** place close for comparison. —**jux/ta-po-si/tion** (-pə zish/ən) n.

K

K, k (kā) n. eleventh letter of English alphabet.

K, 1. karat. **2.** Kelvin. **3.** kilobyte. **4.** kilometer. **5.** thousand.

k, 1. karat. **2.** kilogram.

ka-bu/ki (kə bōō/kē, kä/bōō kē/) n. popular drama of Japan.

kai/ser (kī/zər) n. German emperor.

kale (kāl) n. type of cabbage.

ka-lei/do-scope/ (kə lī/də skōp/) n. optical device in which colored bits change patterns continually.

kan/ga-roo/ (kang/gə rōō/) n., pl. **-roos, -roo.** Australian marsupial with long hind legs used for leaping.

kangaroo court, self-appointed tribunal disregarding law or human rights.

Kans., Kansas.

kaolin

ka·o·lin (kā′ə lin) *n.* fine white clay.

ka′pok (kā′pok) *n.* silky down from seeds of certain trees.

ka·put′ (kä pŏŏt′, -pŏŏt′, ka-) *adj. Informal.* **1.** extinct. **2.** out of order.

ka′ra·o′ke (kar′ē ō′kē) *n.* act of singing along to music in which original vocals have been eliminated.

kar′at (kar′at) *n.* 1/24 part: unit for measuring purity of gold.

ka·ra′te (ka rä′tē) *n.* Japanese technique of unarmed combat.

kar′ma (kär′mə) *n.* fate as the result of one's actions in successive incarnations. —**kar′mic,** *adj.*

Kas., Kansas.

ka′ty·did (kā′tē did) *n.* large green grasshopper.

kay′ak (kī′ak) *n.* Eskimo canoe.

ka·zoo′ (kə zŏŏ′) *n.* tubular musical toy that vibrates and buzzes when one hums into it.

KB, kilobyte.

kc, kilocycle.

ke·bab′ (kə bob′) *n.* cubes of marinated meat broiled on a skewer.

keel (kēl) *n.* **1.** central framing member of ship's bottom. —*v.* **2.** fall sideways.

keen (kēn) *adj.* **1.** sharp. **2.** excellent. **3.** intense. **4.** eager. —*v.* **5.** wail; lament. —**keen′ly,** *adv.*

keep (kēp) *v.,* **kept** (kept), **keeping,** *n.* —*v.* **1.** continue. **2.** detain. **3.** support. **4.** maintain. **5.** withhold. **6.** observe. **7.** last. —*n.* **8.** board and lodging. —**keep′er,** *n.*

keep′ing, *n.* **1.** conformity. **2.** care.

keep′sake′, *n.* souvenir.

keg (keg) *n.* small barrel.

kelp (kelp) *n.* large brown seaweed.

Kel′vin (kel′vin) *adj.* of or noting an absolute scale of temperature in which 0° equals −273.16° Celsius.

ken (ken) *n.* knowledge.

Ken., Kentucky.

ken′nel (ken′l) *n.* **1.** doghouse. **2.** establishment where dogs are boarded and cared for.

ker′chief (kûr′chif, -chēf) *n.* cloth head covering.

ker′nel (kûr′nl) *n.* center part of nut.

ker′o·sene′ (ker′ə sēn′) *n.* type of oil.

kes′trel (kes′trəl) *n.* small falcon.

ketch′up (kech′əp, kach′-) *n.* type of thick tomato sauce with spices.

ket′tle (ket′l) *n.* pot for boiling liquids.

ket′tle·drum′, *n.* large drum with round copper bottom.

key (kē) *n.* **1.** metal piece for operating lock. **2.** explanation. **3.** operating lever. **4.** musical tonality. **5.** reef. —*adj.* **6.** chief. —*v.* **7.** excite.

key′board′, *n.* **1.** row of keys on piano, computer, etc. —*v.* **2.** insert (data) into computer. —**key′board′er,** *n.*

key′note′, *n.* **1.** tonic. **2.** theme of meeting, etc.

key′stone′, *n.* stone forming summit of arch.

kg, kilogram.

khak′i (kak′ē, kä′kē) *adj., n.* **1.** yellowish brown.

khan (kän, kan) *n.* Asian ruler.

kHz, kilohertz.

KIA, killed in action.

kib·butz′ (ki bŏŏts′, -bŏŏts′) *n., pl.* **-but·zim.** Israeli collective farm.

kib′itz·er (kib′it sər) *n. Informal.* person offering unwanted advice.

kick (kik) *v.* **1.** strike with foot. **2.** recoil. **3.** *Informal.* complain. —*n.* **4.** act of kicking. **5.** *Informal.* thrill.

kick′back′, *n.* portion of an income given, often secretly, to someone who made the income possible.

kick′off′, *n.* **1.** kick that begins play in football or soccer. **2.** beginning of anything.

kick′stand′, *n.* bar for holding cycle upright when not in use.

kid (kid) *n., v.,* **kidded, kidding.** —*n.* **1.** young goat. **2.** leather from its skin. **3.** *Informal.* child. —*v.* **4.** *Informal.* fool; tease. —**kid′der,** *n.*

kid′nap (kid′nap) *v.,* **-napped** or **-naped, -napping** or **-naping.** carry off by force, esp. for ransom; abduct. —**kid′nap·per, kid′nap·er,** *n.*

kid′ney (kid′nē) *n.* **1.** gland that secretes urine. **2.** kind.

kidney bean, plant cultivated for its edible seeds.

kidney stone, abnormal stony mass formed in kidney.

kill (kil) *v.* **1.** murder. **2.** destroy. —*n.* **3.** animal slain.

killer whale, large, predatory, black-and-white dolphin.

kill′ing, *n.* **1.** act of one that kills. **2.** quick, large profit. —*adj.* **3.** fatal. **4.** exhausting.

kill′joy′, *n.* person who spoils pleasure of others.

kiln (kil, kiln) *n.* large furnace for making bricks, firing pottery, etc.

ki′lo (kē′lō, kil′ō) *n., pl.* **-los.** **1.** kilogram. **2.** kilometer.

kilo-, prefix meaning thousand, as *kilowatt.*

kil′o·byte′, *n.* **1.** 1024 bytes. **2.** (loosely) 1000 bytes.

kil′o·gram′, *n.* 1000 grams. Also, **kilo.**

kil/o·hertz/, n., pl. **-hertz.** radio frequency of 1000 cycles per second.

kil/o·li/ter (-lē´-) n. 1000 liters.

ki·lom/e·ter (ki lom/ə tər, kil/ə mē´-) n. 1000 meters.

—Pronunciation. The first pronunciation of KILOMETER is something of a mystery. The usual pronunciation both for *units of measurement* starting with *kilo-* (*kilobyte*) and for *units of length* ending in *-meter* (*centimeter*) gives primary stress to the first syllable and secondary to the third *-me-*. Logically, KILOMETER should follow this pattern, and in fact has been pronounced (kil/ə-mē´tər) since the early 1800s. However, another pronunciation of KILO-METER, with stress on the *-om-*, or second syllable, has been around for nearly as long. It is reinforced by words for *instruments of measurement* (rather than *units of measurement*) that also end in *-meter* (*thermometer*, *barometer*). Although criticized because it does not fit the expected pattern, the pronunciation (ki lom/i tər) is very common in American English and has gained popularity in Britain. Both pronunciations are used by educated speakers, including scientists.

kil/o·watt/, n. 1000 watts.

kilt (kilt) n. man's skirt, worn in Scotland.

ki·mo/no (kə mō/nə, -nō) n., pl. **-nos.** loose dressing gown.

kin (kin) n. relatives. Also, **kins/folk/. —kins/man,** n. **—kins/wom/an,** n.fem.

kind (kīnd) adj. 1. compassionate; friendly. —n. 2. type; group.

kin/der·gar/ten (kin/dər gär/tn, -dn) n. school for very young children.

kind/heart/ed (kīnd/-) adj. having or showing kindness.

kin/dle (kin/dl) v., **-dled, -dling.** 1. set afire. 2. rouse.

kin/dling, n. material for starting fire.

kind/ly (kīnd/lē) adj., **-lier, -liest,** adv. —adj. 1. kind. —adv. 2. in kind manner. 3. favorably.

kin/dred (kin/drid) n. 1. related; similar. n. 2. relatives.

ki·net/ic (ki net/ik, kī-) adj. of motion.

king (king) n. sovereign male ruler. —king/ly, adj.

king/dom (-dəm) n. government ruled by king or queen.

king/fish/er (king/fish/ər) n. colorful, fish-eating bird.

king/-size/, adj. extra large.

kink (kingk) n., v. twist; curl. —kink/y, adj., **-ier, -iest.**

kin/ship, n. 1. family relationship. 2. affinity; likeness.

ki·osk (kē/osk, kē osk/) n. small open structure where newspapers, refreshments, etc., are sold.

kip/per (kip/ər) n. salted, dried fish.

kis/met (kiz/mit, -met, kis/-) n. fate.

kiss (kis) v. 1. touch with lips in affection, etc. —n. 2. act of kissing.

kit (kit) n. set of supplies, tools, etc.

kitch/en (kich/ən) n. room for cooking. —kitch/en·ware/,** n.

kite (kīt) n. 1. light, paper-covered frame flown in wind on long string. 2. type of falcon.

kith and kin (kith) friends and relations.

kitsch (kich) n. something tawdry designed to appeal to undiscriminating persons.

kit/ten (kit/n) n. young cat.

kit/ten·ish, adj. playfully coy or cute.

kit/ty-cor/nered, adj. cater-cornered. Also, **kit/ty-cor/ner.**

ki/wi (kē/wē) n. 1. flightless bird of New Zealand. 2. egg-sized brown fruit with edible green pulp.

KKK, Ku Klux Klan.

Klee/nex (klē/neks) Trademark. soft paper tissue.

klep/to·ma/ni·a (klep/tə mā/nē ə) n. irresistible desire to steal. —klep/to·ma/ni·ac/,** n.

klutz (kluts) n. Slang. clumsy person. —klutz/y, adj.

km, kilometer.

knack (nak) n. special skill.

knack/wurst (näk/wûrst, -wŏŏrst) n. spicy sausage.

knap/sack/ (nap/sak/) n. supply bag carried on back.

knave (nāv) n. dishonest rascal.

knead (nēd) v. work (dough) with the hands.

knee (nē) n. middle joint of leg.

knee/cap/, n. flat bone at front of knee.

knee/-jerk/, adj. Informal. reacting in an automatic, habitual way.

kneel (nēl) v., **knelt** (nelt) or **kneeled, kneeling.** to be on one's knees.

knell (nel) n. slow, deep sound of bell.

knick/ers (nik/ərz) n.pl. type of short breeches.

knick/knack/ (nik/nak/) n. trinket.

knife (nīf) n., pl. **knives** (nīvz). cutting blade in handle.

knight (nīt) n. 1. chivalrous medie-

knit

val soldier of noble birth. **2.** holder of honorary rank. **3.** piece in chess. —**knight**/**hood,** n. —**knight**/**ly,** adj.

knit (nit) v., **knitted** or **knit, knitting.** form netlike fabric.

knob (nob) n. rounded handle.

knock (nok) v. **1.** strike hard. **2.** Informal. criticize. —n. **3.** hard blow, etc. **4.** Informal. criticism.

knock/knee/, n. inward curvature of the legs at the knees.

knock/out/, n. **1.** boxing blow that knocks opponent to the canvas. **2.** Informal. one that is extremely attractive.

knoll (nōl) n. small hill.

knot (not) n., v., **knotted, knotting.** —n. **1.** intertwining of cords to bind. **2.** cluster. **3.** lump. **4.** hard mass where branch joins tree trunk. **5.** one nautical mile per hour. —v. **6.** tie or tangle. —**knot/ty,** adj.

know (nō) v., **knew** (noō, nyoō), **known, knowing,** n. —v. **1.** understand, remember, or experience. —n. **2.** Informal. state of knowledge, esp. of secrets. —**know/a•ble,** adj.

know/-how/, n. Informal. skill.

know/ing, adj. **1.** having knowledge. **2.** shrewd. **3.** deliberate.

knowl/edge (nol/ij) n. facts, etc., known.

knowl/edge•a•ble (-i ja bal) adj. well-informed.

knuck/le (nuk/al) n. **1.** joint of a finger. —v. **2. knuckle down,** apply

oneself earnestly. **3. knuckle under,** submit; yield.

knuck/le•head/, n. Informal. stupid, inept person.

KO (kā/ō/, kā/ō/) knockout.

ko•a/la (kō ä/la) n. gray, tree-dwelling Australian marsupial.

kohl•ra/bi (kōl rä/bē, -rab/ē) n., pl. **-bies.** variety of cabbage.

koi (koi) n., pl. **kois, koi.** colorful carp.

ko/la (kō/la) n. tropical African tree grown for its nuts, used to flavor soft drinks.

kook (kook) n. Slang. eccentric. —**kook/y,** adj.

Ko•ran/ (kə rän/, -ran/, kô-) n. sacred scripture of Islam.

Ko•re/an (ka rē/an) n. native or language of Korea. —**Ko•re/an,** adj.

ko/sher (kō/shar) adj. permissible to eat according to Jewish law.

kow/tow/ (kou/tou/, -tou/, kō/-) v. to act obsequiously.

kryp/ton (krip/ton) n. inert gas.

KS, Kansas.

ku/dos (koō/dōz, -dōs, -dos, kyoō/-) n. admiration and respect.

kum/quat (kum/kwot) n. small citrus fruit.

kung/ fu/ (kung/ foō/, koōng/) Chinese technique of unarmed combat.

kvetch (kvech) Slang. v. **1.** complain chronically. —n. **2.** person who kvetches.

KW, kilowatt. Also, **kw.**

KY, Kentucky. Also, **ky.**

L

L, l (el) n. twelfth letter of English alphabet.

L., 1. lake. **2.** large. **3.** Latin. **4.** left. **5.** length. **6.** Brit. pound. **7.** long.

l., 1. left. **2.** length. **3.** pl. **ll.** line. **4.** liter.

LA, Louisiana. Also, **La.**

lab (lab) n. laboratory.

la/bel (lā/bal) n., v., **-beled, -beling.** —n. **1.** tag bearing information. —v. **2.** put label on.

la/bi•um (lā/bē əm) n., pl. **-bia** (-bē ə). fold of skin bordering the vulva. —**la/bi•al,** adj.

la/bor (lā/bər) n. **1.** bodily toil; work. **2.** childbirth. **3.** workers as a group. —v. **4.** work. Also, Brit., **la/bour.** —**la/bor•er,** n.

lab/o•ra•to/ry (lab/rə tôr/ē, lab/ər-ə-) n., pl. **-ries.** place for scientific work.

la/bored, adj. done with difficulty.

la•bo/ri•ous (la bōr/ē əs) adj. involving much effort.

labor union, organization of workers for mutual aid, esp. by collective bargaining.

la•bur/num (lə bûr/nəm) n. poisonous tree with drooping yellow flowers.

lab/y•rinth (lab/ə rinth) n. maze.

lace (lās) n., v., **laced, lacing.** —n. **1.** fancy network of threads. **2.** cord for tying. —v. **3.** fasten with lace. —**lac/y,** adj.

lac/er•ate/ (las/ə rāt/) v., **-ated, -ating.** tear; mangle.

lach/ry•mal (lak/rə mal) adj. of or producing tears.

lach/ry•mose/ (-mōs/) adj. tearful.

lack (lak) n. **1.** deficiency. —v. **2.** be wanting.

lack/a•dai/si•cal (lak/ə dā/zi kal) adj. listless.

lack/ey (lak/ē) n. servile follower.

lack/lus/ter, adj. uninteresting.

la•con/ic (lə kon/ik) adj. using few words. —**la•con/i•cal•ly,** adv.

lac•quer (lak′ər) *n.* **1.** kind of varnish. —*v.* **2.** coat with lacquer.

la•crosse′ (lə krôs′) *n.* game of ball played with long rackets.

lac•tate (lak′tāt) *v.*, **-tated, -tating.** secrete milk. —**lac•ta′tion,** *n.*

lac•tose (-tōs) *n.* sweet crystalline substance in milk.

la•cu′na (lə kyoo′nə) *n., pl.* **-nae** (-nē), **-nas.** **1.** cavity. **2.** gap.

lad (lad) *n.* boy.

lad′der (lad′ər) *n.* structure of two sidepieces with steps between.

lad′en (lād′n) *adj.* loaded heavily.

lad′ing (lā′ding) *n.* cargo; freight.

la′dle (lād′l) *n., v.,* **-dled, -dling.** —*n.* **1.** large deep-bowled spoon. —*v.* **2.** serve with ladle.

la′dy (lā′dē) *n., pl.* **-dies.** **1.** refined woman. **2.** title of noblewoman.

la′dy•bug′, *n.* small spotted beetle. Also, **la′dy•bird′.**

la′dy•fin′ger, *n.* small oblong cake.

la′dy's-slip′per, *n.* orchid with slipper-shaped flower lips.

lag (lag) *v.,* **lagged, lagging,** *n.* —*v.* **1.** move slowly or belatedly. —*n.* **2.** instance of lagging. **3.** interval.

la′ger (lä′gər, lô′-) *n.* kind of beer.

lag′gard (lag′ərd) *adj.* **1.** lagging. —*n.* **2.** person who lags.

la•gniappe′ (lan yap′, lan′yap) *n.* **1.** small gift given with a purchase. **2.** gratuity. Also, **la•gnappe′.**

la•goon′ (lə goon′) *n.* shallow pond connected with a body of water.

laid′-back′ (lād′-) *adj. Informal.* relaxed; easygoing.

lair (lâr) *n.* den of beast.

lais•sez-faire′ (les′ā fâr′) *adj.* without interfering in trade, etc.

la′i•ty (lā′i tē) *n.* laypersons.

lake (lāk) *n.* large body of water enclosed by land.

La•ko′ta (lə kō′tə) *n., pl.* **-tas** or **-ta.** member of a Plains Indian people.

lam (lam) *n., v.,* **lammed, lamming.** *Slang.* —*n.* **1.** hasty escape. —*v.* **2.** escape; flee. **3.** on the lam, hiding or fleeing from the police.

la′ma (lä′mə) *n.* Tibetan or Mongolian Buddhist priest.

La•maze′ method (lə mäz′) method by which expectant mother is prepared for birth by classes, exercises, etc.

lamb (lam) *n.* young sheep.

lam•baste′ (lam bāst′, -bast′) *v.,* **-basted, -basting.** *Informal.* **1.** beat severely. **2.** reprimand harshly.

lam′bent (lam′bənt) *adj.* flickering or glowing lightly. —**lam′ben•cy,** *n.*

lame (lām) *adj., v.,*

lamed, laming. —*adj.* **1.** crippled. **2.** stiff. —*v.* **3.** make lame.

la•mé′ (la mā′, lä-) *n.* ornamental fabric with metallic threads.

lame duck (lām) elected official completing term after election of successor.

la•ment′ (lə ment′) *v.* **1.** mourn; regret. —*n.* **2.** Also, **lam′en•ta′tion** (lam′ən tā′shən) expression of grief.

lam′i•nate (lam′ə nāt′) *v.,* **-nated, -nating,** *adj.* —*v.* (lam′ə nāt′) **1.** split into thin layers. **2.** cover or form with layers. —*adj.* (-nāt′, -nit) **3.** Also, **lam′i•nat•ed.** made of layers.

lamp (lamp) *n.* light source.

—**lamp′shade′,** *n.* —**lamp′post′,** *n.*

lam•poon′ (lam poon′) *n.* **1.** vicious satire. —*v.* **2.** satirize.

lam′prey (lam′prē) *n.* eellike fish.

lance (lans) *n., v.,* **lanced, lancing.** —*n.* **1.** long spear. —*v.* **2.** open with lancet.

lan′cet (lan′sit) *n.* sharp-pointed surgical tool.

land (land) *n.* **1.** part of the earth's surface above water. **2.** country. —*v.* **3.** bring or come to land. **4.** fall to earth or floor.

lan′dau (lan′dô, -dou) *n.* carriage with folding top.

land′ed, *adj.* **1.** owning land. **2.** consisting of land.

land′fall′, *n.* **1.** sighting of land. **2.** land sighted.

land′fill′, *n.* **1.** area of land built up from refuse material. **2.** material deposited on landfill.

land′ing, *n.* **1.** act of one that lands. **2.** place for landing persons or goods. **3.** level part between stairs.

land′locked′, *adj.* **1.** shut in completely or almost completely by land. **2.** having no access to sea.

land′lord′, *n.* person who owns and leases property. —**land′la′dy,** *n.fem.*

land′lub′ber (-lub′ər) *n.* person unused to sea.

land′mark′, *n.* **1.** prominent object serving as a guide. **2.** anything prominent of its kind.

land′mass′, *n.* large area of land.

land′scape′ (-skāp′) *n., v.,* **-scaped, -scaping.** —*n.* **1.** broad view of rural area. —*v.* **2.** arrange trees, shrubs, etc., for effects. —**land′scap′er,** *n.*

land′slide′, *n.* fall of earth or rock.

lane (lān) *n.* narrow road.

lan′guage (lang′gwij) *n.* **1.** speech. **2.** any means of communication.

lan′guid (lang′gwid) *adj.* moving slowly and weakly.

lan′guish (-gwish) *v.* **1.** be or become

come weak. **2.** pine. —**lan′guor** (-gər) *n.* —**lan′guor•ous,** *adj.*

lank (langk) *adj.* **1.** thin. Also, **lank′y. 2.** straight and thin.

lan•o•lin (lan′l in) *n.* fat from wool.

lan′tern (lan′tərn) *n.* case for enclosing light.

lantern jaw, long, thin jaw. —**lan′tern-jawed′,** *adj.*

lan′yard (lan′yərd) *n.* short rope.

lap (lap) *v.,* **lapped, lapping,** *n.* —*v.* **1.** lay or lie partly over. **2.** wash against. **3.** take up with tongue. —*n.* **4.** overlapping part. **5.** one circuit of racecourse. **6.** thighs of sitting person.

la•pel′ (lə pel′) *n.* folded-back part on front of a garment.

lap′i•dar′y (lap′i der′ē) *n., pl.* **-ries.** worker in gems.

lap′in (lap′in) *n.* rabbit.

lap•is laz′u•li (lap′is laz′ŏŏ lē, -lī′, laz′yŏŏ-) **1.** deep blue semiprecious gem. **2.** sky-blue color; azure.

lapse (laps) *n., v.,* **lapsed, lapsing.** —*n.* **1.** slight error; negligence. **2.** interval of time. —*v.* **3.** pass slowly. **4.** make error. **5.** slip downward. **6.** become void.

lap′top′, *n.* portable microcomputer that fits on the lap.

lar•ce•ny (lär′sə nē) *n., pl.* **-nies.** theft. —**lar′ce•nist,** *n.*

larch (lärch) *n.* tree of pine family.

lard (lärd) *n.* rendered fat of hogs.

lard′er (lär′dər) *n.* pantry.

large (lärj) *adj.,* **larger, largest. 1.** great in size or number. **2. at large, a.** at liberty. **b.** in general.

large′ly, *adv.* mostly.

large′-scale′, *adj.* extensive.

lar•gess′ (lär jes′, lär′jis) *n.* generosity. Also, **lar•gesse′.**

lar′go (lär′gō) *adj., adv.* Music. slowly.

lar′i•at (lar′ē ət) *n.* long, noosed rope.

lark (lärk) *n.* **1.** songbird. **2.** frolic.

lark′spur′ (-spûr′) *n.* plant with flowers on tall stalks.

lar′va (lär′və) *n., pl.* **-vae** (-vē) young of insect between egg and pupal stages. —**lar′val,** *adj.*

lar′yn•gi′tis (lar′ən jī′tis) *n.* inflammation of larynx.

lar′ynx (lar′ingks) *n., pl.* **laryn•ges** (lə rin′jēz), **larynx•es.** cavity at upper end of windpipe. —**la•ryn′ge•al** (lə rinj′ē əl, lar′ən jēəl′) *adj.*

la•sa′gna (lə zän′yə, lä-) *n.* baked dish of wide strips of pasta layered with cheese, tomato sauce, and usu. meat. Also, **la•sa′gne.**

la•sciv′i•ous (lə siv′ē əs) *adj.* lewd.

la′ser (lā′zər) *n.* device for amplifying radiation of frequencies of visible light.

lash (lash) *n.* **1.** blow with whip. **2.** eyelash. —*v.* **3.** strike with or as with lash. **4.** bind.

lass (las) *n.* girl.

las′si•tude′ (las′i tŏŏd′, -tyŏŏd′) *n.* weariness.

las′so (las′ō, la sŏŏ′) *n., pl.* **-sos, soes,** *v.,* **-soed, -soing.** —*n.* **1.** lariat. —*v.* **2.** catch with lasso.

last (last) *adj.* **1.** latest. **2.** final. —*adv.* **3.** most recently. **4.** finally. —*n.* **5.** that which is last. **6.** footshaped form on which shoes are made. —*v.* **7.** endure.

last′ing, *adj.* going on or enduring a long time. —**last′ing•ly,** *adv.*

lat., latitude.

latch (lach) *n.* **1.** device for fastening door or gate. —*v.* **2.** fasten with latch.

late (lāt) *adj., adv.,* **later, latest. 1.** after proper time. **2.** being or lasting well along in time. **3.** recent. **4.** deceased.

late′ly, *adv.* recently.

la′tent (lāt′nt) *adj.* hidden.

lat•er•al (lat′ər əl) *adj.* on or from the side. —**lat′er•al•ly,** *adv.*

la′tex (lā′teks) *n.* milky plant juice used esp. in making rubber.

lath (lath) *n.* **1.** narrow wood strip. **2.** material for holding plaster. —*v.* **3.** cover with laths.

lathe (lāth) *n.* machine for turning wood, etc., against a shaping tool.

lath′er (lath′ər) *n.* **1.** froth made with soap and water. **2.** froth from sweating. —*v.* **3.** form or cover with lather.

Lat′in (lat′n) *n.* **1.** language of ancient Rome. **2.** member of any people speaking Latin-based language. —**Latin,** *adj.*

Latin America, countries in South and Central America where Spanish or Portuguese is spoken. —**Lat′in-A•mer′i•can,** *adj.*

La•ti′no (lə tē′nō, la-) *n.* Hispanic.

lat′i•tude′ (lat′i tŏŏd′, -tyŏŏd′) *n.* **1.** distance from equator. **2.** freedom.

la•trine′ (lə trēn′) *n.* toilet, esp. in military installation.

lat′ter (lat′ər) *adj.* **1.** being second of two. **2.** later.

lat′tice (lat′is) *n.* structure of crossed strips. —**lat′tice•work′,** *n.*

laud (lôd) *v.* praise. —**laud′a•to•ry,** *adj.*

laugh (laf) *v.* **1.** express mirth audibly. —*n.* **2.** act or sound of laughing.

laugh′a•ble, *adj.* ridiculous.

laugh′ing•stock′, *n.* object of ridicule.

launch (lônch, länch) v. **1.** set afloat or send off. **2.** start. **3.** throw. —n. **4.** large open motorboat. —**launch'er,** n.

launch pad, platform for launching rockets. Also, **launch'ing pad.**

laun·der (lôn'dər, län'-) v. wash and iron.

Laun·dro·mat' {-drə mat'} n. *Trademark.* self-service laundry with coin-operated machines.

laun·dry, n., pl. **-dries. 1.** clothes to be washed. **2.** place where clothes are laundered.

lau·re·ate (lôr'ē it) n. person who has been honored.

lau·rel (lôr'əl) n. **1.** small glossy evergreen tree. **2.** (pl.) honors.

la·va (lä'və, lav'ə) n. molten rock from volcano.

lav·a·to·ry (lav'ə tôr'ē) n., pl. **-ries. 1.** bathroom. **2.** washbowl.

lave (lāv) v., **laved, laving.** bathe.

lav·en·der (lav'ən dər) n. **1.** pale purple. **2.** fragrant shrub yielding **oil of lavender.**

lav·ish (lav'ish) adj. **1.** extravagant. —v. **2.** expend or give abundantly.

law (lô) n. **1.** rules established by government under which people live. **2.** rule. **3.** legal action. —**law'-a·bid'ing,** adj. —**law'break'er,** n. —**law'break'ing,** n., adj. —**law'less,** adj.

law'ful, adj. permitted by law.

lawn (lôn) n. **1.** grass-covered land kept mowed. **2.** thin cotton or linen fabric.

law'suit', n. prosecution of claim in court.

law'yer (lô'yər, loi'ər) n. person trained in law.

lax (laks) adj. **1.** careless. **2.** slack.

lax'a·tive (lak'sə tiv) adj. **1.** purgative. —n. **2.** laxative agent.

lay (lā) v., **laid, laying,** n., adj. —v. **1.** place or put down, esp. in flat position. **2.** produce eggs. **3.** ascribe. **4.** devise. **5.** put of. **lie.** —n. **6.** position. **7.** song. —adj. **8.** not clerical or professional. —**lay'man,** **lay'per·son,** n. —**lay'wom·an,** fem. —**Usage.** For many speakers, the verbs LAY and LIE are confused because both have the meaning of "in a flat position." LAY means "to put down" or "to place, especially in a flat position." A general rule to remember is that if the word "put" or "place" can be substituted in a sentence, then LAY is the verb to use: *Lay* (= *put, place) the books on the table. She laid* (= *put, placed) the baby in the cradle.* But the verb LIE means "to be in a flat position" or "to be situated."

Lie down and rest a moment. The baby is lying down. For many speakers, the problem comes in the past tense for these two verbs, because the past tense of LIE is *lay,* which looks like, but is not, the present tense of LIE: *The dog will want to lie in the shade; yesterday it* LAY *in the grass.* Note that we can LAY an infant down in a crib; he or she will LIE there until picked up.

lay'a·way plan, method of purchasing in which store reserves item until customer has completed payment.

lay'er, n. one thickness.

lay·ette' (-et') n. outfit for newborn child.

lay'off', n. temporary dismissal of employees.

lay'out', n. arrangement.

laze (lāz) v., **lazed, lazing.** pass (time) lazily.

la'zy (lā'zē) adj., **-zier, -ziest. 1.** unwilling to work. **2.** slow-moving.

lb., pl. **lbs., lb.** pound.

l.c., lowercase.

lea (lē, lā) n. meadow.

leach (lēch) v. **1.** soak through or in. **2.** dissolve by soaking.

lead (lēd *for 1–6; lēd for 5–7*), v., **led** (led), **leading,** n. —v. **1.** guide by going before or with. **2.** influence. **3.** go to. —n. **4.** position at front. **5.** heavy malleable metal. **6.** graphite used in pencils. —**lead'en,** adj. —**lead'er,** n. —**lead'er·ship,** n.

leading question (lē'ding) question worded to suggest the desired answer.

lead time (lēd) time between beginning of a process and appearance of results.

leaf (lēf) n., pl. **leaves** (lēvz), v. —n. **1.** flat green part on stem of plant. **2.** thin sheet. —v. **3.** thumb through. —**leaf'y,** adj.

leaf'let (-lit) n. **1.** pamphlet. **2.** small leaf.

league (lēg) n., v., **leagued, leaguing.** —n. **1.** alliance; pact. **2.** unit of distance, about three miles. —v. **3.** unite in league.

leak (lēk) n. **1.** unintended hole. —v. **2.** pass or let pass through leak. **3.** allow to be known unofficially. —**leak'age,** n. —**leak'y,** adj.

lean (lēn) v., **leaned** or **leant,** **leaning,** adj. —v. **1.** bend. **2.** depend. **3.** incline. —n. **4.** inclination. **5.** lean flesh. —adj. **6.** not fat.

lean'-to', n., pl. **-tos.** structure with single-sloped roof abutting a wall.

leap (lēp) v., **leaped** or **leapt** (lept,

lēpt), leaping, n. —v. **1.** spring through air; jump. —n. **2.** jump.

leap'frog', n., v., **-frogged, -frogging.** —n. **1.** game in which players leap over each other's backs. —v. **2.** jump over as in leapfrog.

leap year, year of 366 days.

learn (lûrn) v. acquire knowledge or skill. —**learn'er,** n. —**learn'ing,** n.

learn'ed (lûr'nid) adj. scholarly.

learning disability, difficulty in reading, writing, etc., associated with impairment of central nervous system.

lease (lēs) n., v., **leased, leasing.** —n. **1.** contract renting property to another for certain time. —v. **2.** get by means of lease.

leash (lēsh) n. strap for holding dog.

least (lēst) adj. **1.** smallest. —n. **2.** least amount, etc. —adv. **3.** to least extent, etc.

leath'er (leth'ər) n. prepared skin of animals. —**leath'er·y,** adj.

leath'er·neck', n. Informal. U.S. marine.

leave (lēv) v., **left** (left), **leaving,** n. —v. **1.** depart from. **2.** let remain or be. **3.** have remaining. **4.** bequeath. —n. **5.** permission. **6.** farewell. **7.** furlough.

leav'en (lev'ən) n. Also, **leav'en·ing.** fermenting agency to raise dough. —v. **2.** produce fermentation.

lech'er·ous (lech'ər əs) adj. lustful. —**lech'er·y,** n. —**lech'er,** n.

lec'tern (lek'tərn) n. stand for speaker's papers.

lec'ture (lek'chər) n., v., **-tured, -turing.** —n. **1.** instructive speech. —v. **2.** give lecture; moralize. —**lec'tur·er,** n.

ledge (lej) n. narrow shelf.

ledg'er (lej'ər) n. account book.

lee (lē) n. **1.** shelter. **2.** side away from the wind. **3.** (pl.) dregs. —**lee,** adj. —**lee'ward,** adj., adv., n.

leech (lēch) n. bloodsucking worm.

leek (lēk) n. plant related to onion.

leer (lēr) n. **1.** sly or insinuating glance. —v. **2.** look with leer.

leer'y (lēr'ē) adj., **-ier, -iest.** wary.

lee'way', n. **1.** Naut. drift due to wind. **2.** extra time, space, etc.

left (left) adj. **1.** on side toward west when facing north. —n. **3.** left side. **4.** political side favoring liberal or radical reform. —**left'-hand',** adj. —**left'-hand'ed,** adj. —**left'ist,** n., adj.

leg (leg) n. **1.** one of limbs supporting a body. **2.** any leglike part.

leg'a·cy (leg'ə sē) n., pl. **-cies.** anything bequeathed.

le'gal (lē'gəl) adj. of or according to law. —**le·gal'i·ty** (-gal'i tē) n. —**le'gal·ize,** v.

le'gal·ese' (lē'gə lēz', -lēs') n. excessive legal jargon.

le·ga'tion (li gā'shən) n. **1.** diplomatic minister and staff. **2.** official residence of minister.

le·ga'to (lə gä'tō) adj., adv. Music. smooth and connected.

leg'end (lej'ənd) n. **1.** story handed down by tradition. **2.** key; inscription. —**leg'end·ar'y,** adj.

leg'er·de·main' (lej'ər də mān') n. sleight of hand.

leg'ging, n. covering for leg.

leg'i·ble (lej'ə bəl) adj. easily read. —**leg'i·bly,** adv.

le'gion (lē'jən) n. **1.** military unit. **2.** multitude. —adj. **3.** very great in number. —**le'gion·naire',** n.

leg'is·late' (lej'is lāt') v., **-lated, -lating. 1.** make laws. **2.** control by law. —**leg'is·la'tion,** n. —**leg'is·la'tive,** adj. —**leg'is·la'tor,** n.

leg'is·la·ture (-chər) n. law-making body.

le·git'i·mate (li jit'ə mit) adj. **1.** lawful. **2.** after righter or established principles. **3.** born to a married couple. —**le·git'i·ma·cy** (-mə sē) n. —**le·git'i·mize',** v., **-mized, -mizing.** show to be or regard as legitimate.

leg'ume (leg'yōōm, li gyōōm') n. plant of group including peas and beans. —**le·gu'mi·nous,** adj.

lei (lā) n. flower wreath for neck.

lei'sure (lē'zhər, lezh'ər) n. **1.** free time. —adj. **2.** unoccupied; at rest. —**lei'sure·ly,** adj. unhurried.

leit'mo·tif' (līt'mō tēf') n. **1.** recurring musical phrase in an opera. **2.** dominant theme.

lem'ming (lem'ing) n. small rodent noted for periodic mass migrations.

lem'on (lem'ən) n. **1.** yellowish fruit of citrus tree. **2.** Informal. person or thing that is defective.

lem'on·ade' (-ə nād') n. beverage of lemon juice and water.

le'mur (lē'mər) n. small monkeylike animal.

lend (lend) v. **1.** give temporary use of. **2.** give. —**Usage.** See BORROW.

length (lengkth, length, lenth) n. size or extent from end to end. —**length'en,** v. —**length'wise',** adv. —**length'y,** adj.

le'ni·ent (lē'nē ənt, lēn'yənt) adj. tolerant; not severe. —**le'ni·en·cy,** n.

lens (lenz) n., pl. **lenses.** glass for changing convergence of light rays.

Lent (lent) *n.* season of fasting before Easter. —**Lent′en,** *adj.*

len′til (len′til, -tl) *n.* pealike plant.

le′o·nine′ (lē′ə nīn′) *adj.* of or like the lion.

leop′ard (lep′ərd) *n.* large fierce spotted feline.

le′o·tard′ (lē′ə tärd′) *n.* tight, flexible, one-piece garment worn by acrobats, dancers, etc.

lep′er (lep′ər) *n.* person afflicted with leprosy.

lep′re·chaun′ (lep′rə kôn′) *n.* Irish elf.

lep′ro·sy (lep′rə sē) *n.* disease marked by skin ulcerations.

les′bi·an (lez′bē ən) *n.* **1.** female homosexual. —*adj.* **2.** pertaining to female homosexuals.

lese majesty (lēz′) offense against the dignity of a ruler.

le′sion (lē′zhən) *n.* **1.** injury. **2.** morbid change in bodily part.

less (les) *adv.* **1.** to smaller extent. —*adj.* Also, **les′ser. 2.** smaller. **3.** lower in importance. —*n.* **4.** Also, **lesser,** smaller amount, etc. —*prep.* **5.** minus.
—**Usage. FEWER** is the comparative form of **FEW.** It is properly used before plural nouns that refer to individuals or things that can be counted (*fewer words; no fewer than 31 states*). **LESS** is the comparative form of **LITTLE.** It should modify only singular mass nouns that refer to things that are abstract or cannot be counted (*less sugar; less doubt*). **LESS** may be used before plural nouns only when they suggest combination into a unit or group (*less than $50; less than three miles*).

les·see′ (le sē′) *n.* one granted a lease.

les′ser, *adj.* compar. of **little.**

les′son (les′ən) *n.* **1.** something to be studied. **2.** reproof. **3.** useful experience.

les′sor (les′ôr, le sôr′) *n.* granter of lease.

lest (lest) *conj.* for fear that.

let (let) *v.,* **let, letting,** *n.* —*v.* **1.** permit. **2.** rent out. **3.** cause to. —*n.* **4.** hindrance.

-let, suffix indicating: **1.** small, as *booklet.* **2.** article worn on, as *anklet.*

let′down′, *n.* disappointment.

le′thal (lē′thəl) *adj.* deadly.

leth·ar′gy (leth′ər jē) *n.,* pl. **-gies.** drowsy dullness. —**le·thar′gic** (lə-thär′jik) *adj.*

let′ter (let′ər) *n.* **1.** written communication. **2.** written component of word. **3.** actual wording. **4.** (*pl.*) literature. —*v.* **5.** write with letters.

let′tered, *adj.* literate; learned.

let′ter·head′, *n.* **1.** printed information on stationery. **2.** paper with a letterhead.

let′ter·per′fect, *adj.* precise in every detail.

let′tuce (let′is) *n.* plant with large leaves used in salad.

let′up′, *n.* cessation; pause; relief.

leu·ke′mi·a (lōō kē′mē ə) *n.* cancerous disease of blood cells.

leu′ko·cyte (lōō′kə sīt′) *n.* white blood cell.

lev′ee (lev′ē) *n.* embankment.

lev′el (lev′əl) *adj., n., v.,* **-eled, -eling.** —*adj.* **1.** even. **2.** horizontal. **3.** well-balanced. —*n.* **4.** height. **5.** level position. **6.** device for determining horizontal plane. —*v.* **7.** make or become level. **8.** aim.

lev′el·head′ed, *adj.* sensible and judicious.

lev′er (lev′ər, lē′vər) *n.* bar moving on fixed support to exert force.

lev′er·age (-ij) *n.* power or action of lever.

le·vi′a·than (lə vī′ə thən) *n.* something of immense size or power.

lev′i·tate′ (lev′i tāt′) *v.,* **-tated, -tating.** rise or cause to rise into the air, esp. in apparent defiance of gravity. —**lev′i·ta′tion,** *n.*

lev′i·ty (lev′i tē) *n.* lack of seriousness.

lev′y (lev′ē) *v.,* **levied, levying,** *n.,* pl. **levies.** —*v.* **1.** raise or collect by authority. **2.** make (war). —*n.* **3.** act of levying. **4.** something levied.

lewd (lōōd) *adj.* obscene.

lex·i·cog′ra·phy (lek′si kog′rə fē) *n.* writing of dictionaries.

lex′i·con′ (-kon′, -kən) *n.* dictionary.

lg., **1.** large. **2.** long.

li′a·bil′i·ty (lī′ə bil′i tē) *n.,* pl. **-ties.** **1.** debt. **2.** disadvantage. **3.** state of being liable.

li′a·ble, *adj.* **1.** likely. **2.** subject to obligation or penalty.

li·ai·son (lē ā′zən, lē′ā zōn′) *n.* **1.** contact to ensure cooperation. **2.** intimacy; affair.

li′ar (lī′ər) *n.* person who tells lies.

li′bel (lī′bəl) *n., v.,* **-beled, -beling.** —*n.* **1.** defamation in writing or print. —*v.* **2.** publish libel against. —**li′bel·ous,** *adj.*

lib′er·al (lib′ər əl, lib′rəl) *adj.* **1.** favoring extensive individual liberty. **2.** tolerant. **3.** generous. —*n.* **4.** liberal person. —**lib′er·al·ism,** *n.* —**lib′er·al′i·ty** (-ə ral′i tē) *n.* —**lib′er·al·ize′,** *v.*

liberal arts, college courses comprising the arts, humanities, and natural and social sciences.

lib·er·ate' (-ǝ rāt') v., **-ated, -ating.** set free. —**lib'er·a'tion,** n. —**lib'er·a'tor,** n.

lib·er·tar·i·an (lib'ǝr târ'ē ǝn) n. person who advocates liberty in thought or conduct.

lib·er·tine' (-tēn', -tin) n. dissolute person.

lib·er·ty, n., pl. **-ties.** 1. freedom; independence. 2. right to use place. 3. impertinent freedom.

li·bi·do (li bē'dō) n., pl. **-dos.** 1. sexual desire. 2. instinctual energies and drives derived from all.

li·brar·y (lī'brer'ē, -brǝ rē, -brē) n., pl. **-ries.** 1. place for collection of books, etc. 2. collection of books, etc. —**li·brar'i·an,** n.
—**Pronunciation.** LIBRARY, with two barely separated r-sounds, is particularly vulnerable to the tendency for neighboring sounds that are alike to become different, or for one of them to disappear altogether. This can lead to forms like the pronunciation (lī'brer ē), which is likely to be heard from less educated or very young speakers and is often criticized. However, (lī'brē), the third pronunciation shown above, is considered perfectly standard, even though one of the r-sounds has been dropped.

li·bret·to (li bret'ō) n., pl. **-brettos, -bretti** (-bret'ē). words of musical drama. —**li·bret'tist,** n.

li·cense (lī'sǝns) n., v., **-censed, -censing.** —n. 1. formal permission. 2. undue freedom. —v. 3. grant license to. Also, **li'cence.**

li·cen·see' (-sǝ sē') n. person to whom a license is granted.

li·cen·tious (lī sen'shǝs) adj. lewd.

li·chen (lī'kǝn) n. crustlike plant on rocks, trees, etc.

lic·it (lis'it) adj. lawful.

lick (lik) v. 1. pass tongue over. 2. Informal. beat or defeat. —n. 2. act of licking.

lick'e·ty-split' (lik'i tē-) adv. Informal. at great speed.

lick'ing, n. Informal. 1. beating or thrashing. 2. defeat or setback.

lic·o·rice (lik'ǝr ish, -ǝ ris) n. plant root used in candy, etc.

lid (lid) n. 1. movable cover. 2. eyelid. —**lid'ded,** adj.

lie (lī) n., v., **lied, lying.** —n. 1. deliberately false statement. —v. 2. tell a lie.

lie (lī) v., **lay** (lā), **lain** (lān), **lying,** n. —v. 1. assume or have reclining position. 2. be or remain. —n. 3.

manner of lying. —**Usage.** See LAY.

lie detector, polygraph.

lien (lēn, lē'ǝn) n. right in another's property as payment on claim.

lieu (lōō) n. stead.

lieu·ten·ant (lōō ten'ǝnt; in Brit. use, except in the navy, lef ten'ǝnt) n. 1. commissioned officer in army or navy. 2. aide.

life (līf) n., pl. **lives** (līvz). 1. quality that distinguishes animals and plants from inanimate things. 2. period of being alive. 3. living things. 4. mode of existence. 5. animation. —**life'long',** adj. —**life'time',** n. —**life'like',** adj.

life'blood', n. 1. blood. 2. vital element.

life'boat', n. boat designed to rescue passengers from sinking ship.

life'guard', n. person employed to protect swimmers, as at a beach.

life preserver, buoyant device to keep a person afloat.

lif'er, n. person serving a term of imprisonment for life.

life'sav'er, n. person or thing that saves from death or a difficult situation. —**life'sav'ing,** adj., n.

life'-size', adj. of the actual size of a person, etc.

life'style', person's general pattern of living. Also, **life'-style'.**

life'-sup·port', adj. of equipment or techniques that sustain or substitute for essential body functions.

life'work', n. complete or principal work of a lifetime.

lift (lift) v. 1. move or hold upward. 2. raise or rise. —n. 3. act of lifting. 4. ride. 5. Brit. elevator.

lift'-off', n. departure from ground by rocket, etc., under own power.

lig·a·ment (lig'ǝ mǝnt) n. band of tissue holding bones together.

lig·a·ture (lig'ǝ chǝr, -chŏŏr') n. 1. surgical thread or wire for tying blood vessels.

light (līt) n., adj., v., **lighted** or **lit** (līt), **lighting.** —n. 1. something that makes things visible or gives illumination. 2. daylight. 3. aspect. 4. enlightenment. —adj. 5. not dark. 6. not heavy. 7. not serious. 8. ignite. 9. illuminate. 10. alight; land. 11. happen (upon).

light'en, v. 1. become or make less dark. 2. lessen in weight. 3. mitigate. 4. cheer.

light'er, n. 1. something that lights. 2. barge.

light'-fin·gered, adj. given to pilfering.

light'-head·ed, adj. as if about to faint.

light'-heart'ed, *adj.* cheerful; without worry.

light'house', *n.* tower displaying light to guide mariners.

light'ning (-ning) *n.* flash of light in sky caused by electrical discharge.

lightning bug, firefly.

lightning rod, metal rod to divert lightning from a structure into the ground.

light'-year', *n.* distance that light travels in one year.

lig'ne·ous (lig'nē əs) *adj.* of the nature of or resembling wood.

lig'nite (lig'nīt) *n.* kind of coal.

like (līk) *v.,* **liked, liking,** *adj., prep., conj., —v.* **1.** find agreeable. **2.** wish. —*adj.* **3.** resembling; similar to. —*prep.* **4.** in like manner with. —*conj.* **5.** *Informal.* as; as if. —*n.* **6.** like person or thing; match. **7.** preference. —**lik'a·ble, like'a·ble,** *adj.*

-like, suffix indicating: like or characteristic of, as *childlike.*

like'ly, *adj., -lier, -liest, adv. —adj.* **1.** probable. **2.** suitable. —*adv.* **3.** probably. —**like'li·hood',** *n.*

lik'en, *v.* compare.

like'ness, *n.* **1.** image; picture. **2.** fact of being like.

like'wise', *adv.* **1.** also. **2.** in like manner.

li'lac (lī'lak, -lăk, -lak) *n.* fragrant flowering shrub.

Lil'li·pu'tian (lĭl'ĭ pyoo'shən) *adj.* **1.** very small. **2.** trivial.

lilt (lĭlt) *n.* rhythmic cadence.

lil'y (lĭl'ē) *n., pl. -ies.* plant with erect stems and showy flowers.

lil'y-liv'ered (-lĭv'ərd) *adj.* cowardly.

lily of the valley, *n., pl.* **lilies of the valley.** plant with spike of bell-shaped flowers.

li'ma bean (lī'mə) flat, edible bean.

limb (lĭm) *n.* **1.** jointed part of an animal body. **2.** branch.

lim'ber (lĭm'bər) *adj.* **1.** flexible; supple. —*v.* **2.** make or become limber.

lim'bo (lĭm'bō) *n., pl. -bos.* **1.** region on border of hell or heaven. **2.** midway state or place. **3.** dance involving bending backward to pass under horizontal bar.

lime (līm) *n., v.,* **limed, liming.** —*n.* **1.** oxide of calcium, used in mortar. **2.** small, greenish, acid fruit of tropical tree. —*v.* **3.** treat with lime.

lime'light', *n.* public notice; fame.

lim'er·ick (lĭm'ər ĭk) *n.* humorous five-line verse.

lime'stone', *n.* rock consisting chiefly of powdered calcium.

lim'it (lĭm'ĭt) *n.* **1.** farthest extent; boundary. —*v.* **2.** fix or keep within limits. —**lim'i·ta'tion,** *n.*

lim'it·ed, *adj.* **1.** restricted **2.** (of trains, etc.) making few stops. —*n.* **3.** limited train.

lim'o (lĭm'ō) *n., pl. -os. Informal.* limousine.

lim'ou·sine' (lĭm'ə zēn', lĭm'ə zēn') *n.* luxurious automobile for several passengers.

limp (lĭmp) *v.* **1.** walk unevenly. —*n.* **2.** lame movement. —*adj.* **3.** not stiff or firm. —**limp'ly,** *adv.*

lim'pet (lĭm'pĭt) *n.* small cone-shelled marine animal.

lim'pid (-pĭd) *adj.* clear. —**lim·pid'i·ty, lim'pid·ness,** *n.*

linch'pin' (lĭnch'-) *n.* **1.** pin inserted through end of axle to keep wheel on. **2.** something that holds various parts of a structure together.

lin'den (lĭn'dən) *n.* tree with heart-shaped leaves.

line (līn) *n., v.,* **lined, lining.** —*n.* **1.** long thin mark. **2.** row; series. **3.** course of action, etc. **4.** boundary. **5.** string, cord, etc. **6.** occupation. —*v.* **7.** form line. **8.** mark with line. **9.** cover inner side of.

lin'e·age (lĭn'ē ĭj) *n.* ancestry.

lin'e·al (-al) *adj.* **1.** of direct descent. **2.** Also, **lin'e·ar** (-ar). of or a line.

lin'e·a·ment (-ə mənt) *n.* feature, as of face.

line drive, batted baseball that travels low, fast, and straight.

line'man, *n., pl. -men.* worker who repairs telephone, telegraph, etc., wires.

lin'en (lĭn'ən) *n.* **1.** fabric made from flax. **2.** articles of linen or cotton.

lin'er (lī'nər) *n.* **1.** ship or airplane on regular route. **2.** lining.

line'-up', *n.* order.

-ling, suffix meaning: **1.** person connected with, as *hireling.* **2.** little, as *duckling.*

lin'ger (ling'gər) *v.* **1.** stay on. **2.** persist. **3.** delay.

lin'ge·rie' (län'zhə rā', -jə-, län'-zhə rē') *n.* women's undergarments.

lin'go (ling'gō) *n., pl. -goes. Informal.* language.

lin·gui'ni (-gwē'nē) *n. pl.* pasta in slender flat form.

lin'guist (-gwist) *n.* person skilled in languages.

lin·guis'tics, *n.* science of language. —**lin·guis'tic,** *adj.*

lin′i•ment (lin′ə mənt) *n.* liquid applied to bruises, etc.

lin′ing (lī′ning) *n.* inner covering.

link (lingk) *n.* 1. section of chain. 2. bond. —*v.* 3. unite. —**link′age,** *n.*

links, *n.pl.* golf course.

link′up′ *n.* contact set up between military units.

lin′net (lin′it) *n.* small songbird.

li•no•le•um (li nō′lē əm) *n.* hard, washable floor covering.

lin′seed′ (lin′sēd′) *n.* seed of flax.

lin′sey-wool′sey (lin′zē wōōl′zē) *n.* fabric of linen and wool.

lint (lint) *n.* bits of thread.

lin′tel (lin′tl) *n.* beam above door or window.

li•on (lī′ən) *n.* large cat of Africa and Asia. —**li′on•ess,** *n.fem.*

li•on•heart′ed, *adj.* courageous.

li•on•ize′ *v.,* **-ized, -izing.** treat as a celebrity.

lip (lip) *n.* 1. fleshy margin of the mouth. 2. projecting edge. 3. *Slang.* impudent talk.

lip•o•suc′tion (lip′ə suk′shən, lī′pə-) *n.* surgical withdrawal of excess fat from under skin.

lip′read′ing, method of understanding spoken words by interpreting speaker's lip movements. —**lip′read′er,** *v.* —**lip′read′,** *v.*

lip service, insincere profession of friendship, admiration, support, etc.

lip′stick′, *n.* coloring for lips.

liq′ue•fy′ (lik′wə fī′) *v.,* **-fied, -fy-ing.** become liquid. —**liq′ue•fac′tion** (-fak′shən) *n.*

li•queur′ (li kûr′, -kyŏŏr′) *n.* strong sweet alcoholic drink.

liq′uid (lik′wid) *n.* 1. fluid of molecules remaining together. —*adj.* 2. of or being a liquid. 3. in or convertible to cash.

liq′ui•date′ (-wi dāt′) *v.,* **-dated, -dating.** 1. settle, as debts. 2. convert into cash. 3. eliminate. —**liq′ui•da′tion,** *n.* —**liq′ui•da′tor,** *n.*

liq′uor (lik′ər) *n.* 1. alcoholic beverage. 2. liquid.

lisle (līl) *n.* strong linen or cotton thread.

lisp (lisp) *n.* 1. pronunciation of *s* and *z* like *th.* —*v.* 2. speak with lisp. —**lisp′er,** *n.*

lis′some (lis′əm) *adj.* 1. lithe; lithesome. 2. nimble. Also, **lis′som.**

list (list) *n.* 1. series of words, names, etc. 2. inclination to side. —*v.* 3. make list. 4. incline.

lis′ten (lis′ən) *v.* pay attention in order to hear. —**lis′ten•er,** *n.*

list′less (list′lis) *adj.* having no interest in anything.

list price, retail price.

lit., 1. literally. 2. literature.

lit′a•ny (lit′n ē) *n., pl.* **-nies.** 1. form of prayer. 2. tedious account.

li′ter (lē′tər) *n.* metric unit of capacity, = 1.0567 U.S. quarts. Also, *Brit.,* **li′tre.**

lit′er•al (lit′ər əl) *adj.* 1. in accordance with strict meaning of words. 2. exactly as written or stated.

lit′er•al-mind′ed, *adj.* interpreting without imagination.

lit′er•ar′y (-ə rer′ē) *adj.* of books and writings.

lit′er•ate (-ər it) *adj.* 1. able to read and write. 2. skilled. 3. educated. —*n.* 4. literate person. —**lit′er•a•cy** (-ər ə sē) *n.*

lit•e•ra′ti (-ə rä′tē, -rä′-) *n.pl.* persons of scholarly or literary attainments.

lit′er•a•ture (lit′ər ə chər, -choŏr′, li′trə-) *n.* writings, esp. those of notable expression and thought.

lithe (līth) *adj.* limber; supple.

lith′i•um (lith′ē əm) *n.* soft silvery white metallic element.

lith′o•graph′ (-ə graf′) *n.* print made from prepared stone or plate. —**li•thog′ra•phy,** *n.*

lit′i•gant (lit′i gənt) *n.* person engaged in lawsuit.

lit′i•gate′ (-gāt′) *v.,* **-gated, -gating.** carry on lawsuit. —**lit′i•ga′tion,** *n.*

lit′mus (lit′məs) *n.* blue coloring matter turning red in acid solution.

litmus paper, paper treated with litmus for use as a chemical indicator.

litmus test, use of single issue or factor as basis for judgment.

Litt. D., Doctor of Letters; Doctor of Literature.

lit′ter (lit′ər) *n.* 1. disordered array. 2. young from one birth. 3. stretcher. 4. bedding for animals. 5. scattered rubbish, etc. —*v.* 6. strew in disorder.

lit′ter•bug′, *n.* person who litters public places with trash.

lit′tle (lit′l) *adj.,* **-tler, -tlest.** 1. small. 2. mean. —*adv.* 3. not much. —*n.* 4. small amount.

lit′tor•al (lit′ər əl) *adj.* of the shore of a lake, sea, or ocean.

lit′ur•gy (lit′ər jē) *n., pl.* **-gies.** form of worship. —**li•tur′gi•cal** (li-tûr′ji kəl) *adj.*

liv′a•ble (liv′ə bəl) *adj.* habitable.

live (liv for 1–5; līv for 6–8), *v.,* **lived, living.** 1. be alive. 2. endure in reputation. 3. rely for food, etc. 4. dwell. 5. pass (life). —*adj.* 6. alive. 7. connected to electric power. 8. not exploded.

live′li•hood′ (līv′lē hoŏd′) *n.* means of supporting oneself.

live′long′ (liv′-) *adj.* entire; whole.

live/ly (līv′lē) *adj.*, **-lier**, **-liest.** active; spirited.

liv/er (liv′ər) *n.* abdominal organ that secretes bile.

liv/er·wurst′ (-wûrst′) *n.* liver sausage.

liv/er·y (liv′ə rē, liv′rē) *n., pl.* **-eries. 1.** uniform of male servants. **2.** keeping of horses for hire.

live/stock′ (līv′stok′) *n.* domestic farm animals.

live wire (līv) *Informal.* energetic, vivacious person.

liv/id (liv′id) *adj.* **1.** dull blue. **2.** furious.

liv/ing (liv′ing) *adj.* **1.** live. **2.** sufficient for living. —*n.* **3.** condition of life. **4.** livelihood.

living room, room in home used for leisure activities, entertaining, etc.

living will, document stipulating that no extraordinary measures be taken to prolong signer's life during terminal illness.

liz/ard (liz′ərd) *n.* four-legged reptile.

lla/ma (lä′mə, yä′-) *n.* South American animal.

LL.B., Bachelor of Laws.

LL.D., Doctor of Laws.

load (lōd) *n.* **1.** cargo; anything carried. **2.** charge of firearm. —*v.* **3.** put load on. **4.** oppress. **5.** charge (firearm). —**load′er,** *n.*

loaf (lōf) *n., pl.* **loaves** (lōvz), *v.* —*n.* **1.** shaped mass of bread, etc. —*v.* **2.** idle. —**loaf/er,** *n.*

loam (lōm) *n.* loose fertile soil.

loan (lōn) *n.* **1.** act of lending. **2.** something lent. —*v.* **3.** lend.

loan shark, *Informal.* usurer. —**loan′shark′ing,** *n.*

loan/word′, *n.* word borrowed from another language.

loath (lōth, lōth) *adj.* reluctant.

loathe (lōth) *v.*, **loathed, loathing.** feel disgust at; despise. —**loath′some** (lōth′səm, lōth′-) *adj.*

lob (lob) *v.*, **lobbed, lobbing,** *n.* —*v.* **1.** strike or hurl in a high curve. —*n.* **2.** tennis ball so struck.

lob/by, *n., pl.* **-bies,** *v.*, **-bied, -bying. 1.** vestibule or entrance hall. **2.** group that tries to influence legislators. —*v.* **3.** try to influence legislators. —**lob/by·ist,** *n.*

lobe (lōb) *n.* roundish projection.

lo·bot/o·my (lə bot′ə mē, lō-) *n., pl.* **-mies.** surgical incision of brain lobe to treat mental disorder. —**lo·bot/o·mize′,** *v.*, **-mized, -mizing.**

lob/ster (lob′stər) *n.* edible marine shellfish.

lo/cal (lō′kəl) *adj.* **1.** of or in particular area. —*n.* **2.** local branch of

trade union. **3.** train that makes all stops. —**lo/cal·ly,** *adv.*

lo·cale′ (lō kal′, -kāl′) *n.* setting.

lo·cal/i·ty (-kal′i tē) *n., pl.* **-ties.** place; place.

lo/cal·ize′ (-kə līz′) *v.*, **-ized, -izing.** confine to particular place.

lo/cate (lō′kāt, lō kāt′) *v.*, **-cated, -cating.** find or establish place of.

lo·ca/tion, *n.* **1.** act or instance of locating. **2.** place where something is.

loc. cit. (lok′ sit′) in the place cited.

lock (lok) *n.* **1.** device for fastening door, lid, etc. **2.** place in canal, etc., for moving vessels from one water level to another. **3.** part of firearm. **4.** tress of hair. —*v.* **5.** secure with lock. **6.** shut in or out. **7.** join firmly.

lock/er, *n.* closet with lock.

lock/et (-it) *n.* small case worn on necklace.

lock/jaw′, *n.* disease in which jaws become tightly locked; tetanus.

lock/out′, *n.* business closure to force acceptance of employer's terms of work.

lock/smith′, *n.* person who makes or repairs locks.

lock/step′, *n.* way of marching in close file.

lock/up′, *n.* jail.

lo/co (lō′kō) *adj. Slang.* crazy.

lo·co·mo/tion (lō′kə mō′shən) *n.* act of moving about.

lo·co·mo/tive, *n.* engine that pulls railroad cars.

lo/co·weed′ (lō′kō-) *n.* plant causing a disease in livestock.

lo/cust (lō′kəst) *n.* **1.** kind of grasshopper. **2.** flowering American tree.

lo·cu/tion (lō kyōō′shən) *n.* phrase.

lode (lōd) *n.* mineral deposit.

lode/star′, *n.* guiding star.

lode/stone′, *n.* magnetic stone.

lodge (loj) *n.*, **lodged, lodging.** —*n.* **1.** hut or house. **2.** members or meeting place of fraternal organization. —*v.* **3.** live or house temporarily. **4.** fix or put; become fixed. —**lodg/er,** *n.*

lodg/ing, *n.* **1.** temporary housing. **2.** (*pl.*) rooms.

loft (lôft) *n.* attic or gallery.

loft/y, *adj.*, **-ier, -iest. 1.** tall. **2.** exalted or elevated. —**loft/i·ly,** *adv.*

log (lôg) *n.*, **logged, logging.** —*n.* **1.** section of trunk or limb of felled tree. **2.** Also, **log/book′.** record of events. —*v.* **3.** fell and cut up trees. **4.** record in log. **5.** log in or on, gain access to secured computer system. —**log/ger,** *n.*

lo/gan·ber/ry (lō′gən ber′ē) *n., pl.* **-ries.** dark red acid fruit.

log/a·rithm (lô′gə rith′əm) n. Math. symbol of number of times a number must be multiplied by itself to equal a given number.

loge (lōzh) n. box in theater.

log/ger·head/ (lô′gər hed′, log′ər-) n. at loggerheads, disputing.

log/ic (loj′ik) n. science of reasoning. —**lo·gi/cian** (lō jish′shən) n.

lo·gis/tics (lō jis′tiks, lə-) n. management of details of an operation.

log/jam/ (lôg′-) n. blockage or impasse.

lo/go (lō′gō) n. representation or symbol of company name, trademark, etc. Also, **lo/go·type/.**

log/roll/ing, n. exchange of support or favors, esp. in politics.

lo/gy (lō′gē) adj., -gier, -giest. heavy; dull.

-logy, suffix meaning science or study of, as theology.

loin (loin) n. part of body between ribs and hipbone.

loin/cloth/, n. cloth worn around the loins or hips.

loi/ter (loi′tər) v. linger.

loll (lol) v. 1. recline indolently. 2. hang loosely.

lol/li·pop/ (lol′ē pop′) n. hard candy on stick.

lone (lōn) adj. alone.

lone/ly (lōn′lē) adj., -lier, -liest. 1. alone. 2. wishing for company. 3. isolated. —**lone/li·ness,** n.

lon/er, n. person who spends much time alone.

lone/some (-səm) adj. 1. depressed by solitude. 2. lone.

long (lông) adj. 1. of great or specified length. —adv. 2. for long time. —v. 3. yearn.

lon·gev/i·ty (lon jev′i tē) n. long life.

long/hand/ (lông′-) n. ordinary handwriting.

lon/gi·tude/ (lon′ji tōōd′, -tyōōd′) n. distance east and west on earth's surface.

lon/gi·tu/di·nal (-tōōd′n l, -tyōōd′-) adj. 1. of longitude. 2. lengthwise.

long jump, jump for distance.

long/-lived/ (-līvd′, -livd′) adj. having a long life or duration.

long/-range/, adj. spanning a long distance or time.

long/shore/man, n. person who loads and unloads ships.

long shot, 1. racehorse, team, etc., with little chance for winning. 2. undertaking with little chance for success.

long/-term/, adj. involving a long time.

long/-wind/ed (-win′did) adj. continuing to speak for too long.

look (lŏŏk) v., 1. direct the eyes. 2. seem. 3. face. 4. seek. 5. care for. —n. 6. act of looking. 7. appearance.

looking glass, mirror.

look/out/, n. 1. watch. 2. person for keeping watch. 3. place for keeping watch.

loom (lōōm) n. 1. device for weaving fabric. —v. 2. appear as large and indistinct.

loon (lōōn) n. diving bird.

loon/y, adj., -ier, -iest. Informal. 1. lunatic; insane. 2. extremely foolish.

loop (lōōp) n. 1. circular form from length of material or line. —v. 2. form a loop.

loop/hole/, n. 1. small opening in wall, etc. 2. means of evasion.

loose (lōōs) adj., looser, loosest, v., loosed, loosing. —adj. 1. free; unconfined. 2. not firm or tight. 3. not exact. 4. dissolute. —v. 5. free. 6. shoot (missiles). —loos/en, v.

loot (lōōt) n. 1. spoils. —v. 2. plunder. —loot/er, n.

lop (lop) v., lopped, lopping. cut off.

lope (lōp) v., loped, loping, n. —v. 1. move or run with long, easy stride. —n. 2. long, easy stride.

lop/sid/ed, adj. uneven.

lo·qua/cious (lō kwā′shəs) adj. talkative. —**lo·quac/i·ty** (-kwas′ə-tē) n.

lord (lôrd) n. 1. master. 2. British nobleman. 3. (cap.) God. 4. (cap.) Jesus Christ. —v. 5. domineer. —**lord/ly,** adj. —**lord/ship,** n.

lore (lôr) n. learning.

lor/ry (lôr′ē) n., pl. -ries. Brit. truck.

lose (lōōz) v., lost (lôst), losing. 1. fail to keep. 2. misplace 3. be deprived of. 4. fail to win.

loss (lôs) n. 1. disadvantage from losing. 2. thing lost. 3. waste.

lot (lot) n. 1. object drawn to decide question by chance. 2. allotted share. 3. piece of land. 4. (often pl.) Informal. a great number or amount. —Usage. See ALOT.

Lo·thar/i·o (lō thâr′ē ō′) n., pl. -os. (often l.c.) man who obsessively seduces women.

lo/tion (lō′shən) n. liquid to rub on skin.

lot/ter·y (lot′ə rē) n., pl. -ies. sale of tickets on prizes to be awarded by lots.

lot/to (lot′ō) n. 1. game of chance similar to bingo. 2. lottery in which players choose numbers that are matched against those of the official drawing.

lo′tus (lō′təs) *n.* water lily of Egypt and Asia.

loud (loud) *adj.* **1.** strongly audible. **2.** blatant.

loud′-mouth′ (-mouth′) *n.* a braggart; gossip.

loud′speak′er, *n.* device for increasing volume of sound.

lounge (lounj) *v.,* **lounged, lounging,** *n.* —*v.* **1.** pass time idly. **2.** loll. —*n.* **3.** kind of sofa. **4.** public room.

louse (lous) *n., pl.* **lice** (līs). bloodsucking insect.

lous′y (lou′zē) *adj.,* **-ier, -iest.** *Informal.* bad; poor. **2.** troubled with lice. —**lous′i·ness,** *n.*

lout (lout) *n.* boor. —**lout′ish,** *adj.*

lou′ver (lōō′vər) *n.* arrangement of slits for ventilation.

lov′a·ble (luv′ə bəl) *adj.* attracting love. Also, **love·a·ble.**

love (luv) *n., v.,* **loved, loving.** —*n.* **1.** strong affection. **2.** sweetheart. **3.** have love for. —**lov′er,** *n.* —**lov′ing,** *adj.*

love′lorn′ (-lôrn′) *adj.* deprived of love or a lover.

love′ly (luv′lē) *adj.,* **-lier, -liest.** charming. —**love′li·ness,** *n.*

love′sick′, *adj.* sick from intensity of love.

loving cup, large two-handled drinking cup.

low (lō) *adj.* **1.** not high or tall. **2.** below normal level. **3.** sad. **4.** humble or inferior. **5.** not loud. **6.** base or unfavorable. —*adv.* **7.** in low position. **8.** in quiet tone. —*n.* **9.** thing that is low. **10.** moo. —*v.* **11.** moo.

low′brow′, *n.* uncultured person. —*adj.* **2.** typical of a lowbrow.

low′-cal′ (lō′kal′, -kal′) *adj.* with fewer calories than usual.

low′down′ *n.* (lō′doun′) **1.** real and unadorned facts. —*adj.* (-doun′) **2.** contemptible; mean.

low′er (lō′ər for *1, 2;* lou′ər for *3–5*) *v.* **1.** reduce or diminish. **2.** make or become lower. **3.** be threatening. **4.** frown. —*n.* **5.** lowering appearance.

low′er·case′ *n.* **1.** (of a letter) of a form often different from and smaller than its corresponding capital letter. —*n.* **2.** lowercase letter.

low frequency, radio frequency between 30 and 300 kilohertz.

low′-key′, *adj.* understated.

low′life′, *n., pl.* **-lifes.** disreputable or degenerate person.

low′ly, *adj.,* **-lier, -liest.** meek.

low′-mind′ed, *adj.* coarse; vulgar.

low profile, deliberately inconspicuous manner.

lox (loks) *n.* salmon cured in brine.

loy′al (loi′əl) *adj.* faithful; steadfast. —**loy′al·ly,** *adv.* —**loy′al·ty,** *n.*

loz′enge (loz′inj) *n.* **1.** flavored candy, often medicated. **2.** diamond shape.

LPN, licensed practical nurse.

LSD, lysergic acid diethylamide, a powerful psychedelic drug.

Lt., lieutenant.

Ltd., limited.

lub′ber (lub′ər) *n.* clumsy person.

lu′bri·cant (lōō′bri kənt) *n.* lubricating substance.

lu′bri·cate′ (-kāt′) *v.,* **-cated, -cating.** oil or grease, esp. to diminish friction. —**lu′bri·ca′tor,** *n.*

lu′cid (lōō′sid) *adj.* **1.** bright. **2.** clear in thought or expression. **3.** rational. —**lu·cid′i·ty,** *n.*

Lu′cite (lōō′sīt) *n. Trademark.* transparent plastic.

luck (luk) *n.* **1.** chance. **2.** good fortune. —**luck′less,** *adj.*

luck′y, *adj.,* **-ier, -iest.** having or due to good luck. —**luck′i·ly,** *adv.*

lu′cra·tive (lōō′krə tiv) *adj.* profitable.

lu′cre (lōō′kər) *n.* gain or money.

lu′di·crous (lōō′di krəs) *adj.* ridiculous. —**lu′di·crous·ly,** *adv.*

lug (lug) *v.,* **lugged, lugging,** *n.* —*v.* **1.** pull or carry with effort. **2.** haul. —*n.* **3.** projecting handle. **4.** *Slang.* awkward, clumsy fellow.

luge (lōōzh) *n., v.,* **luged, luging.** —*n.* **1.** small racing sled for one or two persons. —*v.* **2.** race on a luge.

lug′gage (lug′ij) *n.* baggage.

lug nut, large nut, esp. for attaching a wheel to a vehicle.

lu·gu′bri·ous (lōō gōō′brē əs, -gyōō′-) *adj.* excessively mournful.

luke′warm′ (lōōk′-) *adj.* slightly warm.

lull (lul) *v.* **1.** soothe, esp. to sleep. **2.** quiet.

lull′a·by (-ə bī′) *n., pl.* **-bies.** song to lull baby.

lum·ba′go (lum bā′gō) *n.* muscular pain in back.

lum′bar (lum′bər, -bär) *adj.* of or close to the loins.

lum′ber (lum′bər) *n.* **1.** timber made into boards, etc. —*v.* **2.** cut and prepare timber. **3.** encumber. **4.** move heavily.

lum′ber·jack′, *n.* person who fells trees.

lum′ber·yard′, *n.* yard where lumber is stored for sale.

lu′mi·nar′y (lōō′mə ner′ē) *n., pl.* **-ies.** **1.** celestial body. **2.** person who inspires many.

lu·min·es·cent (loo′mə nes′ənt) *adj.* luminous at relatively low temperatures. —**lu·min·es·cence**, *n.*

lu·mi·nous (-nəs) *adj.* giving or reflecting light. —**lu′mi·nos·i·ty** (-nos′i tē) *n.*

lum′mox (lum′əks) *n. Informal.* clumsy, stupid person.

lump (lump) *n.* 1. irregular mass. 2. swelling. —*adj.* 3. including many. —*v.* 4. put together. 5. endure.

lu·na·cy (loo′nə sē) *n., pl.* -**cies.** insanity.

lu·nar (-nər) *adj.* 1. of or according to moon. 2. crescent-shaped.

lu·na·tic (-tik) *n.* 1. insane person. —*adj.* 2. for the insane. 3. crazy.

lunch (lunch) *n.* 1. Also, **lunch′eon** (lun′chən). midday meal. —*v.* 2. eat lunch.

lunch′eon·ette′ (lun′chə net′) *n.* restaurant for quick, simple lunches.

lung (lung) *n.* respiratory organ.

lunge (lunj) *n., v.,* **lunged, lunging.** —*n.* 1. sudden forward movement. —*v.* 2. make lunge.

lu·pine (loo′pin) *n.* 1. plant with tall, dense clusters of flowers. —*adj.* 2. of or resembling the wolf.

lu·pus (loo′pəs) *n.* any of several diseases characterized by skin eruptions.

lurch (lûrch) *n.* 1. sudden lean to one side. 2. helpless plight. —*v.* 3. make lurch.

lure (loor) *n., v.,* **lured, luring.** —*n.* 1. bait. —*v.* 2. decoy; entice.

lu·rid (loor′id) *adj.* 1. glaringly lighted. 2. sensational.

lurk (lûrk) *v.* 1. loiter furtively. 2. exist unperceived.

lus·cious (lush′əs) *adj.* delicious.

lush (lush) *adj.* 1. tender and juicy. 2. abundant.

lust (lust) *n.* 1. strong desire. —*v.*

2. have strong desire. —**lust′ful,** *adj.*

lus·ter (lus′tər) *n.* gloss; radiance. Also, **lus′tre.** —**lus′trous,** *adj.*

lust′y, *adj.,* -**ier,** -**iest.** vigorous.

lute (loot) *n.* stringed musical instrument. —**lut′en·ist,** *n.*

Lu′ther·an (loo′thər ən) *adj.* of Protestant sect named for Martin Luther. —**Lu′ther·an·ism,** *n.*

lux·u·ri·ant (lug zhoor′ē ənt, luk-shoor′-) *adj.* profuse; abundant. —**lux·u′ri·ance,** *n.*

lux·u·ri·ate (-āt′) *v.,* -**ated, -ating.** revel; delight.

lux′u·ry (luk′shə rē, lug′zhə-) *n., pl.* -**ries.** something enjoyable but not necessary. —**lux·u′ri·ous** (lug-zhoor′ē əs, luk shoor′-) *adj.*

-ly, suffix meaning: in a specified manner, as *loudly*; according to, as *theoretically*; to or from a specified direction, as *inwardly*; like or characteristic of, as *saintly*; every, as *hourly.*

ly·ce′um (lī sē′əm) *n.* hall for lectures, etc.

lye (lī) *n.* alkali solution.

ly′ing-in′, *adj.* 1. of or for childbirth. —*n.* 2. childbirth.

lymph (limf) *n.* yellowish matter from body tissues. —**lym·phat′ic** (lim fat′ik) *adj.*

lym′pho·cyte′ (lim′fə sīt′) *n.* white blood cell producing antibodies.

lynch (linch) *v.* put to death without legal authority.

lynx (lingks) *n., pl.* **lynxes, lynx.** kind of wild cat.

lyre (lī�′r) *n.* ancient harplike instrument.

lyr′ic (lir′ik) *adj.* Also, **lyr′i·cal.** 1. (of poetry) musical. 2. of or writing such poetry. —*n.* 3. lyric poem. 4. (*pl.*) words for song. —**lyr′i·cism** (-ə siz′m) *n.* —**lyr′i·cist,** *n.*

M

M, m (em) *n.* thirteenth letter of English alphabet.

ma (mä) *n. Informal.* mother.

MA, Massachusetts.

M.A., Master of Arts.

ma′am (mam, mäm; *unstressed* məm) *n. Informal.* madam.

ma·ca′bre (mə kä′brə, -käb′) *adj.* gruesome.

mac·ad′am (mə kad′əm) *n.* road-making material containing broken stones. —**mac·ad′am·ize′,** *v.,* -**ized, -izing.**

mac′a·ro′ni (mak′ə rō′nē) *n.* tube-shaped food made of wheat.

mac′a·roon′ (mak′ə roon′) *n.* almond or coconut cookie.

ma·caw′ (mə kô′) *n.* parrot.

mace (mās) *n.* 1. spiked war club. 2. staff of office. 3. spice from part of nutmeg seed. 4. (*cap.*) *Trademark.* chemical spray for subduing rioters, attackers etc.

mac′er·ate′ (mas′ə rāt′) *v.,* -**ated, -ating.** soften by steeping in liquid.

ma·che′te (mə shet′ē, -chet′ē) *n.* heavy knife.

Mach′i·a·vel′li·an (mak′ē ə vel′ē-ən) *adj.* unscrupulously wily.

mach′i·na′tion (mak′ə nā′shən) n. cunning plan.

ma·chine′ (mə shēn′) n. **1.** apparatus or mechanical device. **2.** group controlling political organization.

machine gun, firearm capable of firing continuous stream of bullets.

ma·chin′er·y, n., pl. -**er·ies.** machines or mechanisms.

ma·chin′ist, n. operator of powered tool, ship's engines, etc.

ma·chis′mo (mä chēz′mō) n. exaggerated masculinity as basis for code of behavior.

Mach′ num′ber (mäk) ratio of speed of object to speed of sound.

ma′cho (mä′chō) adj. aggressively virile.

mack′er·el (mak′ər al) n. common food fish.

mack′i·naw′ (mak′ə nô′) n. short, heavy, woolen coat.

mack′in·tosh′ (mak′in tosh′) n. raincoat.

mac′ra·mé′ (mak′rə mā′) n. decorative work of knotted cords.

macro-, prefix meaning large, as macrocosm.

mac′ro·bi·ot′ic (mak′rō bī ot′ik) adj. of or giving long life.

mac′ro·cosm (mak′rə koz′əm) n. universe.

ma′cron (mā′kron, mak′ron) n. horizontal line over vowel to show it is long.

mad (mad) adj., **madder, maddest. 1.** insane. **2.** Informal. angry. **3.** violent. —**mad′den,** v.

mad′am (mad′əm) n. **1.** female term of address. **2.** woman in charge of brothel.

made, pt. of **make.**

mad′e·moi·selle′ (mad′ə mə zel′, mad′mwə-, mam zel′) n., pl. **mademoiselles, mesdemoiselles** (mā′də mə zel′, -zelz′, mād′mwə-) French term of address for unmarried woman.

mad′man′, n. man who is or seems mentally ill. —**mad′wo′man,** n.fem.

Ma·don′na (mə don′ə) n. Virgin Mary.

mad′ras (mad′rəs, mə dras′, -dräs′) n. light cotton fabric.

mad′ri·gal (mad′ri gal) n. song for several voices unaccompanied.

mael′strom (māl′strəm) n. **1.** whirlpool. **2.** confusion.

maes·tro (mī′strō) n., pl. -**tros.** master, esp. of music.

Ma′fi·a (mä′fē ə, maf′ē ə) n. criminal society.

ma′fi·o′so (mä′fē ō′sō), n., pl. -**si** (-sē), -**sos.** member of Mafia.

mag′a·zine′ (mag′ə zēn′) n. **1.** periodical publication. **2.** storehouse for ammunition, etc. **3.** cartridge container in repeating weapon.

ma·gen′ta (mə jen′tə) n. reddish purple.

mag′got (mag′ət) n. larva of fly.

Ma′gi (mā′jī) n.pl. Bible. the three wise men.

mag′ic (maj′ik) n. **1.** supernatural power. —adj. Also, **mag′i·cal. 2.** sleight of hand. **3.** of magic. **4.** enchanting. —**ma·gi′cian** (mə jish′ən) n.

mag·is·te′ri·al (maj′ə stēr′ē əl) adj. masterlike; authoritative.

mag′is·trate′ (-strāt′, -strit) n. civil public official.

mag′ma (mag′mə) n. molten rock.

mag·nan′i·mous (mag nan′ə məs) adj. generous; high-minded. —**mag·na·nim′i·ty** (-nə nim′i tē) n.

mag′nate (-nāt, -nit) n. business leader.

mag·ne′sia (mag nē′zhə) n. magnesium oxide, used as laxative.

mag·ne′si·um (-zē əm, -zhəm) n. light, silvery, metallic element.

mag′net (mag′nit) n. metal body that attracts iron or steel.

mag·net′ic (-net′ik) adj. **1.** of a magnet or magnetism. **2.** attractive.

magnetic field, space near magnet, electric current, moving charged particle in which magnetic force acts.

mag′net·ism (mag′ni tiz′əm) n. **1.** characteristic property of magnets. **2.** science of magnets. **3.** great personal charm. —**mag′net·ize′,** v., -**ized, -izing.**

mag′net·ite′ (mag′ni tīt′) n. common black mineral.

mag·ne′to (mag nē′tō) n., pl. -**tos.** small electric generator.

mag·nif′i·cent (mag nif′ə sənt) adj. **1.** splendid. **2.** noble.

mag′ni·fy′ (mag′nə fī′) v., -**fied, -fying. 1.** increase apparent size. **2.** enlarge. **e** —**mag′ni·fi′er,** n.

mag′ni·tude′ (-ni tōōd′, -tyōōd′) n. size or extent.

mag·no′li·a (mag nōl′yə, -nō′lē ə) n. tree with large fragrant flowers.

magnum opus (mag′nəm ō′pəs) chief work.

mag′pie′ (mag′pī′) n. black and white bird that steals.

ma·ha·ra′jah (mä′hə rä′jə, -zhə) n. (formerly) ruling prince in India. —**ma·ha·ra′nee** (-nē) n.fem.

ma·hat′ma (mə hät′mə, -hat′-) n. person, esp. in India, held in highest esteem for wisdom and saintliness.

mah/-jongg/ (mä/jông/, -zhông/) *n.* Chinese game.

ma.hog.a.ny (ma hog/a nē) *n., pl.* **-nies.** tropical American tree or its red-brown wood.

Ma.hom/et (ma hom/it) *n.* Muhammad.

maid (mād) *n.* **1.** unmarried woman. **2.** female servant.

maid/en (-n) *n.* **1.** unmarried woman. —*adj.* **2.** of maidens. **3.** unmarried. **4.** initial. —**maid/en.ly,** *adj.*

maid/en.hair/, *n.* fern with finely divided fronds.

mail (māl) *n.* **1.** material delivered by postal system. **2.** postal system. **3.** armor, usually flexible. —*adj.* **4.** of mail. —*v.* **5.** send by mail. —**mail/box/,** *n.* —**mail carrier,** *n.* —**mail/man/,** *n.*

maim (mām) *v.* cripple; impair.

main (mān) *adj.* **1.** chief; principal. —*n.* **2.** chief pipe or duct. **3.** strength. **4.** ocean. —**main/ly,** *adv.*

main/frame/, *n.* large computer, often the hub of a system serving many users.

main/land/ (-land/, -land) *n.* continental land rather than island.

main/stay/, *n.* chief support.

main/stream/, *n.* customary trend of behavior, opinion, etc.

main.tain/ (mān tān/) *v.* **1.** support. **2.** assert. **3.** keep in order or condition. —**main/te.nance** (-tanans) *n.*

mai/tre d'hô/tel/ (mā/tra dō tel/) headwaiter. Also, **mai/tre d'** (mā/tar dē/).

maize (māz) *n.* corn.

maj/es.ty (maj/ə stē) *n., pl.* **-ties. 1.** regal grandeur. **2.** sovereign. —**ma.jes/tic** (ma jes/tik) *adj.*

ma.jol/i.ca (ma jol/i ka, ma yol/-) *n.* kind of pottery.

ma/jor (mā/jər) *n.* **1.** army officer above captain. **2.** person of legal age. —*adj.* **3.** larger or more important.

ma/jor-do/mo (-dō/mō) *n.* steward.

ma/jor.ette/ (-ja ret/) *n.* female leader of marchers.

major general, army officer above brigadier general.

ma.jor/i.ty (ma jôr/i tē) *n., pl.* **-ties. 1.** greater number. **2.** full legal age.

make (māk) *v.,* **made** (mād), **making,** *n.* —*v.* **1.** bring into existence. **2.** force. **3.** earn. **4.** accomplish. —*n.* **5.** style. **6.** manufacture.

make/-be.lieve/, *n.* **1.** pretending that fanciful thing is true. —*adj.* **2.** imaginary.

make/shift/, *n., adj.* substitute.

make/up/, *n.* **1.** cosmetics. **2.** organization; composition.

mal-, prefix meaning bad or ill, as *maladjustment.*

mal/a.chite/ (mal/ə kīt/) *n.* green mineral, an ore of copper.

mal/ad.just/ed, *adj.* badly adjusted, esp. to social conditions.

mal/a.droit/ (mal/ə droit/) *adj.* awkward.

mal/a.dy (mal/ə dē) *n., pl.* **-dies.** illness.

ma.laise/ (ma lāz/, -lez/, ma-) *n.* **1.** weakness. **2.** vague uneasiness.

mal/a.mute/ (mal/ə myōōt/) *n.* Alaskan breed of large dogs.

mal/a.prop.ism (mal/ə prop iz/əm) *n.* ludicrous misuse of similar words.

ma.lar/i.a (ma lâr/ē ə) *n.* mosquito-borne disease. —**ma.lar/i.al,** *adj.*

ma.lar/key (ma lär/kē) *n. Informal.* nonsense.

mal/con.tent/ (mal/kən tent/) *n.* dissatisfied person.

mal de mer (mʌl də meʀ/) seasickness.

male (māl) *adj.* **1.** of sex that produces sperm, etc. —*n.* **2.** male person, etc.

mal/e.dic/tion (mal/i dik/shən) *n.* curse.

mal/e.fac/tor (mal/ə fak/tər) *n.* person who does wrong.

ma.lev/o.lent (ma lev/ə lənt) *adj.* wishing evil. —**ma.lev/o.lence,** *n.*

mal.fea/sance (mal fē/zəns) *n.* misconduct in office.

mal.formed/, *adj.* badly formed. —**mal/for.ma/tion,** *n.*

mal/ice (mal/is) *n.* evil intent. —**ma.li/cious** (ma lish/shəs) *adj.*

ma.lign/ (ma līn/) *v.* **1.** speak ill of. —*adj.* **2.** evil.

ma.lig/nan.cy (ma lig/nən sē) *n., pl.* **-cies. 1.** malignant state. **2.** cancerous growth.

ma.lig/nant (-nənt) *adj.* **1.** causing harm or suffering. **2.** deadly.

ma.lig/ni.ty (-ni tē) *n., pl.* **-ties. 1.** state of being malignant. **2.** instance of malignant feeling or behavior.

ma.lin/ger (ma ling/gər) *v.* feign sickness. —**ma.lin/ger.er,** *n.*

mall (môl) *n.* **1.** shaded walk. **2.** covered shopping center.

mal/lard (mal/ərd) *n.* wild duck.

mal/le.a.ble (mal/ē ə bəl) *adj.* **1.** that may be hammered or rolled into shape. **2.** readily influenced.

mal/let (mal/it) *n.* wooden-headed hammer.

mal/nu.tri/tion, *n.* improper nutrition.

mal·o·dor·ous, *adj.* smelling bad.

mal·prac'tice, *n.* improper professional behavior.

malt (môlt) *n.* germinated grain used in liquor-making.

mal·treat' (mal trēt') *v.* abuse.

ma'ma (mä'mə, mə mä') *n. Informal.* mother.

mam'mal (mam'əl) *n.* vertebrate animal whose young are suckled.

mam'ma·ry (mam'ə rē) *adj.* of breasts.

mam'mo·gram' (mam'ə gram') *n.* x-ray photograph of a breast, for detection of tumors.

mam'mon (mam'ən) *n.* material wealth, esp. as influence for evil.

mam'moth (mam'əth) *n.* **1.** large extinct kind of elephant. —*adj.* **2.** huge.

mam'my (mam'ē) *n., pl.* -mies. *Informal.* mother.

man (man) *n., pl.* **men** (men), *v.,* **manned, manning.** —*n.* **1.** male person. **2.** person. **3.** human race. —*v.* **4.** supply with crew. **5.** operate.

man'a·cle (man'ə kəl) *n., v.,* -cled, -cling. handcuff.

man'age (man'ij) *v.,* -aged, -aging. **1.** take care of. **2.** direct. **3.** cope. —**man'ag·er,** *n.* —**man'a·ge'ri·al** (-i jēr'ē əl) *adj.*

man'age·ment *n.* **1.** direction. **2.** persons in charge.

ma·ña'na (mä nyä'nä) *n. Spanish.* tomorrow.

man'a·tee' (man'ə tē') *n.* plant-eating aquatic mammal.

man'da·rin (man'də rin) *n.* **1.** public official in Chinese Empire. **2.** (*cap.*) dialect of Chinese.

man'date (man'dāt) *n.* **1.** authority over territory granted to nation by other nations. **2.** territory under such authority. **3.** command, as to take office. —**man'date,** *v.*

man'da·to·ry (man'də tôr'ē) *adj.* officially required.

man'di·ble (man'də bəl) *n.* bone comprising the lower jaw.

man'do·lin (man'dl in, man'dl in') *n.* stringed musical instrument.

man'drake (man'drāk, -drik) *n.* narcotic herb.

mane (mān) *n.* long hair at neck of some animals.

ma·neu'ver (mə noō'vər) *n.* **1.** planned movement, esp. in war. —*v.* **2.** change position by maneuver. **3.** put in certain situation by intrigue. —**ma·neu'ver·a·ble,** *adj.*

man Friday, *pl.* **men Friday.** reliable male assistant.

man'ful, *adj.* resolute.

man'ga·nese' (mang'gə nēs', -nēz') *n.* hard metallic element.

mange (mānj) *n.* skin disease of animals. —**man'gy,** *adj.*

man'ger (mān'jər) *n.* trough for feeding livestock.

man'gle (mang'gəl) *v.,* -gled, -gling, *n.* —*v.* **1.** disfigure, esp. by crushing. **2.** put through mangle. —*n.* **3.** device with rollers for removing water in washing clothes.

man'go (mang'gō) *n., pl.* -goes. fruit of tropical tree.

man'grove (mang'grōv, man'-) *n.* kind of tropical tree.

man'han·dle (man'han'dl) *v.,* -dled, -dling. handle roughly.

man·hat'tan (man hat'n, man-) *n.* cocktail of whiskey and vermouth.

man'hole' *n.* access hole to sewer.

man'hood, *n.* **1.** manly qualities. **2.** state of being a man.

man'-hour', *n.* ideal amount of work done by a person in an hour.

man'hunt', *n.* intensive search for fugitive.

ma'ni·a (mā'nē ə) *n.* **1.** great excitement. **2.** violent insanity.

ma'ni·ac', *n.* lunatic. —**ma·ni'a·cal** (mə nī'ə kəl) *adj.*

man'ic (man'ik) *adj.* irrationally excited or lively.

man'ic-depres'sive, *adj.* suffering from mental disorder in which mania alternates with depression.

man'i·cure' (man'i kyōōr') *n.* skilled care of fingernails and hands. —**man'i·cure',** *v.*

man'i·fest' (man'ə fest') *adj.* **1.** evident. —*v.* **2.** show plainly. —*n.* **3.** list of cargo and passengers. —**man'i·fes·ta'tion,** *n.*

man'i·fes'to (-fes'tō) *n., pl.* -toes. public declaration of intentions.

man'i·fold' (man'ə fōld') *adj.* **1.** of many kinds or parts. —*v.* **2.** copy. —*n.* **3.** pipe with many outlets.

man'i·kin (man'i kin) *n.* model of human body.

Ma·nil'a paper (mə nil'ə) strong, light brown or buff paper.

man in the street, ordinary person.

ma·nip'u·late' (mə nip'yə lāt') *v.,* -lated, -lating. handle with skill or cunning. —**ma·nip'u·la'tor,** *n.*

man'kind' (man'kīnd') *n.* human race.

man'ly, *adj.,* -lier, -liest. virile.

man'na (man'ə) *n.* divine food given to Israelites.

man'ne·quin (man'i kin) *n.* model for displaying clothes.

man'ner (man'ər) *n.* **1.** way of doing, acting, etc. **2.** (*pl.*) way of acting in society. **3.** sort.

man'ner·ism, n. peculiarity of manner.

man'ner·ly, adj. polite.

man'nish, adj. like a man.

man'-of-war', n., pl. men-of-war. warship.

man'or (man'ər) n. large estate.

man'pow'er, n. available labor force.

man·qué' (mäng kā') adj. unfulfilled.

man'sard (man'särd) n. roof with two slopes of different pitch on all sides.

manse (mans) n. house and land of parson.

man'serv'ant, n. male servant, as valet.

man'sion (man'shən) n. stately house.

man'slaugh'ter, n. unlawful killing of person without malice.

man'tel (man'tl) n. ornamental structure around fireplace.

man·til'la (man til'ə, -tē'ə) n. lace head scarf of Spanish women.

man'tis (man'tis) n. kind of carnivorous insect.

man'tle (man'tl) n., v., -tled, -tling. —n. 1. loose cloak. —v. 2. envelop.

man'tra (man'trə, män'-) n. Hindu or Buddhist chant for recitation.

man'u·al (man'yōō əl) adj. 1. of or done with hands. 2. small informational book. 3. hand powered typewriter. —**man'u·al·ly,** adv.

man'u·fac'ture (man'yə fak'chər) n., v., -tured, -turing. —n. 1. making of things, esp. in great quantity. 2. thing made. —v. 3. make.

man'u·mit' (man'yə mit') v., -mitted, -mitting. release from slavery. —**man'u·mis'sion,** n.

ma·nure' (mə nŏŏr', -nyŏŏr') n. animal dung used as fertilizer.

man'u·script' (man'yə skript') n. handwritten or typed document.

man'y (men'ē) adj. 1. comprising a large number; numerous. —n. 2. large number.

Mao'ism (mou'izm) n. policies of Chinese Communist leader Mao Zedong. —**Mao'ist,** n., adj.

map (map) n., v., mapped, mapping. —n. 1. flat representation of earth, etc. —v. 2. show by map. 3. plan.

ma'ple (mā'pəl) n. northern tree.

mar (mär) v., marred, marring. damage.

Mar., March.

ma·ra'ca (mə rä'kə, -rak'ə) n. gourd-shaped rattle filled with seeds or pebbles, used as rhythm instrument.

maraschino cherry, (mar'ə skē'nō) cherry preserved in cherry cordial.

mar'a·thon' (mar'ə thon', -thən) n. long contest, esp. a foot race of 26 miles, 385 yards.

ma·raud' (mə rôd') v. plunder.

mar'ble (mär'bəl) n. 1. crystalline limestone used in sculpture and building. 2. small glass ball used in children's game. —adj. 3. of marble.

mar'bling, n. intermixture of fat with lean in meat.

march (märch) v. 1. walk with measured tread. 2. advance. —n. 3. act of marching. 4. distance covered in march. 5. music for marching.

March (märch) n. third month of year.

mar'chion·ess (mär'shə nis, -nes') n. 1. wife or widow of marquess. 2. woman of rank equal to marquess.

Mar'di Gras (mär'dē grä', grä') the Tuesday before Lent, often celebrated as a carnival.

mare (mâr) n. female horse.

mare's'-nest', n. complicated situation.

mar'ga·rine (mär'jər in) n. butterlike product made from vegetable oils and water or milk.

mar'gin (mär'jin) n. 1. edge. 2. amount beyond what is necessary.

mar'gin·al, adj. 1. of or at margin. 2. barely acceptable.

mar'gue·rite' (mär'gə rēt') n. daisylike chrysanthemum.

mar'i·gold' (mar'i gōld') n. common, yellow-flowered plant.

ma'ri·jua'na (mar'ə wä'nə) n. narcotic plant.

ma·rim'ba (mə rim'bə) n. xylophone with chambers for resonance.

ma·ri'na (mə rē'nə) n. docking area for small boats.

mar'i·nade' (mar'ə nād') n. pungent liquid mixture for steeping food.

mar'i·nate', v. -nated, -nating. season by steeping.

ma·rine' (mə rēn') adj. 1. of the sea. —n. 2. member of U.S. Marine Corps. 3. fleet of ships.

Marine Corps, military branch of U.S. Navy.

mar'i·ner (mar'ə nər) n. sailor.

mar'i·o·nette' (mar'ē ə net') n. puppet on strings.

mar'i·tal (mar'i tl) adj. of marriage.

mar'i·time' (mar'i tīm') adj. of sea or shipping.

mar'jo·ram (mär'jər əm) n. herb used as seasoning.

mark (märk) *n.* **1.** any visible sign. **2.** object aimed at. **3.** rating; grade. **4.** lasting effect. **5.** German monetary unit. —*v.* **6.** be feature of. **7.** put mark on, as grade or price. **8.** pay attention to. —**mark′er,** *n.*

mark′down′, *n.* price reduction.

marked, *adj.* **1.** conspicuous. **2.** ostentatious. **3.** singled out for revenge. —**mark′ed·ly,** *adv.*

mar′ket (mär′kit) *n.* **1.** place for selling and buying. —*v.* **2.** sell or buy. —**mar′ket·a·ble,** *adj.*

mar′ket·place′, *n.* **1.** open area where market is held. **2.** the world of business, trade, and economics.

marks′man, *n., pl.* **-men.** person who shoots well. —**marks′man·ship′,** *n.* —**marks′wom′an,** *n.fem.*

mark′up′, *n.* price increase by retailer.

mar′lin (mär′lin) *n.* large game fish.

mar′ma·lade (mär′mə lād′) *n.* fruit preserve.

mar′mo·set′ (mär′mə zet′, -set′) *n.* small, tropical American monkey.

mar′mot (mär′mət) *n.* bushy-tailed rodent.

ma·roon′ (mə rōōn′) *n., adj.* **1.** dark brownish-red. —*v.* **2.** abandon ashore. **3.** isolate without aid.

mar·quee′ (mär kē′) *n.* **1.** projecting shelter over outer door. **2.** large tent.

mar′que·try (mär′ki trē) *n.* inlaid work forming pattern.

mar′quis (mär′kwis, mär kē′) *n.* rank of nobility below duke. Also, *Brit.* **mar′quess** (-kwis). —**mar′quise′** (-kēz′) *n.fem.*

mar′riage (mar′ij) *n.* **1.** legal union of man and woman. **2.** wedding. —**mar′riage·a·ble,** *adj.*

mar′row (mar′ō) *n.* soft inner tissue of bone.

mar′ry (mar′ē) *v.,* **-ried, -rying.** take, give, or unite in marriage.

Mars (märz) *n.* one of the planets.

marsh (märsh) *n.* low, wet land. —**marsh′y,** *adj.*

mar′shal (mär′shəl) *n., v.,* **-shaled, -shaling.** —*n.* **1.** federal officer. —*v.* **2.** lead; organize.

marsh gas, decomposition product of organic matter.

marsh′mal·low (-mel′ō, -mal′ō) *n.* soft confection made from gelatin.

marsh marigold, yellow-flowered plant of buttercup family.

mar·su′pi·al (mär sōō′pē əl) *n.* animal carrying its young in pouch, as the kangaroo. —**mar·su′pi·al,** *adj.*

mart (märt) *n.* market.

mar′ten (mär′tn) *n.* small, American, fur-bearing animal.

mar′tial (mär′shəl) *adj.* warlike; military. —**mar′tial·ly,** *adv.*

martial art, of various forms of East Asian self-defense or combat.

martial law, law imposed by military forces.

mar′tin (mär′tn) *n.* bird of swallow family.

mar·ti·net′ (mär′tn et′) *n.* disciplinarian.

mar·ti′ni (mär tē′nē) *n.* cocktail of gin and vermouth.

mar′tyr (mär′tər) *n.* **1.** person who willingly dies for a belief. —*v.* **2.** make martyr of. —**mar′tyr·dom,** *n.*

mar′vel (mär′vəl) *n., v.,* **-veled, -veling.** —*v.* **1.** wonderful thing. —*v.* **2.** wonder (at). —**mar′vel·ous,** *adj.*

Marx′ism (märk′siz əm) *n.* doctrine of classless society; communism. —**Marx′ist,** *n., adj.*

mar′zi·pan′ (mär′zə pan′) *n.* confection of almond paste and sugar.

mas·car′a (ma skar′ə) *n.* cosmetic for eyelashes.

mas′cot (mas′kot, -kət) *n.* person or thing that brings good luck.

mas′cu·line (mas′kyə lin) *adj.* of or like men. —**mas′cu·lin′i·ty,** *n.*

ma′ser (mā′zər) *n.* device for producing electromagnetic waves.

mash (mash) *n.* **1.** soft pulpy mass. —*v.* **2.** crush. —**mash′er,** *n.*

mask (mask) *n.* **1.** disguise or protection for face. —*v.* **2.** disguise or cover.

mas′och·ism (mas′ə kiz′əm, maz′-) *n.* pleasure in suffering.

ma′son (mā′sən) *n.* builder with stone, brick, etc. —**ma′son·ry,** *n.*

mas′quer·ade′ (mas′kə rād′) *n., v.,* **-aded, -ading.** —*n.* **1.** disguise. **2.** party at which guests wear disguise. —*v.* **3.** wear disguise.

mass (mas) *n.* **1.** body of coherent matter. **2.** quantity or size. **3.** weight. **4.** (*cap.*) celebration of the Eucharist. **5. the masses,** common people as a whole. —*v.* **6.** form into a mass. —*adj.* **7.** of or affecting the masses. **8.** done on a large scale.

Mass., Massachusetts.

mas′sa·cre (mas′ə kər) *n., v.,* **-cred, -cring.** —*n.* **1.** killing of many. —*v.* **2.** slaughter.

mas·sage (mə säzh′, -säj′) *v.,* **-saged, -saging.** —*n.* **1.** treat body by rubbing or kneading. —*n.* **2.** such treatment. —**mas·seur′** (mə sûr′), *n.* —**mas·seuse′** (mə-sōōs′ -sōōz′) *n.fem.*

mas′sive (mas′iv) *adj.* large; heavy.

mass media, means of communication that reaches large numbers of people.

mass noun, noun referring to indefinitely divisible substance or abstract noun.

mass'-produce', v., **-duced, -ducing.** produce in large quantities. —**mass production.**

mast (mast) n. upright pole.

mas·tec'to·my (ma stek'tə mē) n., pl. **-mies.** surgical removal of a breast.

mas'ter (mas'tər) n. **1.** person in control. **2.** male teacher. **3.** skilled person. —adj. **4.** chief. —v. **5.** conquer. **6.** become expert in.

mas'ter·ful, adj. asserting power.

mas'ter·ly, adj. highly skilled.

mas'ter·mind', n. **1.** supreme planner. —v. **2.** plan as mastermind.

master of ceremonies, person who conducts events.

mas'ter·piece', n. work of highest skill.

master's degree, academic degree awarded to student who has completed at least one year of graduate study.

master sergeant, noncommissioned officer of highest rank.

mas'ter·stroke', n. extremely skillful action.

mas'ter·y, n., pl. **-teries.** control.

mas'ti·cate' (mas'ti kāt') v., **-cated, -cating.** chew. —**mas'ti·ca'tion,** n.

mas'tiff (mas'tif) n. powerful dog.

mas'to·don' (mas'tə don') n. large extinct elephantlike mammal.

mas'toid (mas'toid) n. protuberance of bone behind ear.

mas'tur·bate' (mas'tər bāt') v., **-bated, -bating.** practice sexual self-gratification. —**mas'tur·ba'tion,** n.

mat (mat) n., v., **matted, matting,** adj. —n. **1.** covering for floor or other surface. **2.** border for picture. **3.** padding. **4.** thick mass. **5.** matte. —v. **6.** cover with mat. **7.** form into mat. —adj. **8.** matte.

mat'a·dor' (mat'ə dôr') n. bullfighter.

match (mach) n. **1.** stick chemically tipped to strike fire. **2.** person or thing resembling or equaling another. **3.** game. **4.** marriage. —v. **5.** equal. **6.** fit together. **7.** arrange marriage for.

match'less, adj. unequaled.

match'mak'er, n. arranger of marriages.

mate (māt) n., v., **mated, mating.** —n. **1.** one of pair. **2.** officer of merchant ship. —v. **3.** join; pair. **4.** copulate.

ma·te'ri·al (mə tēr'ē əl) n. **1.** sub-

stance of which thing is made. **2.** fabric. —adj. **3.** physical. **4.** pertinent. —**ma·te'ri·al·ly,** adv.

ma·te'ri·al·ism, n. **1.** devotion to material objects or wealth. **2.** belief that all reality is material.

ma·te'ri·al·ize', v., **-ized, -izing.** give or assume material form.

ma·te'ri·el' (mə tēr'ē el') n. supplies, esp. military.

ma·ter'ni·ty (mə tûr'ni tē) n. motherhood. —**ma·ter'nal,** adj.

math'e·mat'ics (math'ə mat'iks) n. science of numbers. —**math'e·mat'i·cal,** adj. —**math'e·ma·ti'cian** (-mə tish'ən) n.

mat'i·née' (mat'n ā') n. afternoon performance.

mat'ins (mat'nz) n. morning prayer.

ma'tri·arch' (mā'trē ärk') n. female ruler. —**ma'tri·ar'chy,** n.

mat'ri·cide' (ma'tri sīd', mā'-) n. killing one's mother.

ma·tric'u·late' (mə trik'yə lāt') v., **-lated, -lating.** enroll in school.

mat'ri·mo'ny (ma'trə mō'nē) n., pl. **-nies.** marriage. —**mat'ri·mo'ni·al,** adj.

ma'trix (mā'triks, ma'-) n., pl. **-trices** (-tri sēz'), **-trixes.** **1.** place or point where something originates. **2.** mold; model.

ma'tron (mā'trən) n. **1.** dignified married woman. **2.** female institutional officer. —**ma'tron·ly,** adj.

matte (mat) adj. **1.** having a dull surface, without luster. —n. **2.** dull surface or finish. Also, **mat.**

mat'ter (mat'ər) n. **1.** material. **2.** affair or trouble. **3.** pus. **4.** importance. —v. **5.** be of importance.

mat'ter-of-fact', adj. adhering to fact; straightforward.

mat'ting (mat'ing) n. mat of rushes.

mat'tock (mat'ək) n. digging tool.

mat'tress (ma'tris) n. thick filled case for sleeping on.

ma·ture' (mə tŏŏr', -tyŏŏr', -chŏŏr') adj., **-turer, -turest,** v., **-tured, -turing.** —adj. **1.** grown or developed. **2.** adult in manner or thought. **3.** payable. —v. **4.** become or make mature. —**ma·tu'ri·ty,** n.

mat'zo (mät'sə) n., pl. **-zos.** unleavened bread.

maud'lin (môd'lin) adj. weakly sentimental.

maul (môl) v. handle roughly.

maun'der (môn'dər) v. **1.** talk meanderingly. **2.** wander.

mau·so·le'um (mô'sə lē'əm, -zə-) n., pl. **-leums, -lea** (-lē'ə) n. tomb in form of building.

mauve (mōv, môv) n. pale purple.

ma'ven (mā'vən) n. expert.

mav'er.ick (mav'ər ik) n. **1.** unbranded calf. **2.** nonconformist.

maw (mô) n. mouth.

mawk'ish (mô'kish) adj. sickly sentimental. —**mawk'ish.ly,** adv.

max'i (mak'sē) n., pl. **-is.** anklelength coat or skirt.

max'im (mak'sim) n. general truth.

max'i.mum (mak'sə məm) n. **1.** greatest degree or quantity. —adj. **2.** greatest possible.

may (mā) v., pt. **might** (mīt). (auxiliary verb of possibility or permission.)

May (mā) n. fifth month of year.

may'be, adv. perhaps.

May'day', n. international radio distress call.

may'flow'er, n. plant that blossoms in May.

may'fly', n., pl. **-flies.** insect with large transparent forewings.

may'hem (mā'hem, -əm) n. random violence.

may'on.naise' (mā'ə nāz') n. salad dressing made chiefly of egg yolks, oil, and vinegar. Also, Informal. **may.o.**

may'or (mā'ər) n. chief officer of city. —**may'or.al,** adj. —**may'or.al.ty,** n.

maze (māz) n. confusing arrangement of paths.

MD, Maryland. Also, **Md.**

M.D., Doctor of Medicine.

me (mē) pers. pronoun. objective case of **I.**

ME, Maine.

mead (mēd) n. liquor of fermented honey.

mead'ow (med'ō) n. level grassland.

mead'ow.lark', n. common American songbird.

mea'ger (mē'gər) adj. poor; scanty. Also, **mea'gre.**

meal (mēl) n. **1.** food served or eaten. **2.** coarse grain.

meal'y-mouthed', adj. avoiding candid speech.

mean (mēn) v., meant (ment), meaning, adj. —v. **1.** intend (to do or signify). **2.** signify. —adj. **3.** poor; shabby. **4.** hostile; malicious. **5.** middle. —n. **6.** (pl.) method of achieving purpose. **7.** (pl.) money or property. **8.** intermediate quantity. —**mean'ly,** adv.

me.an'der (mē an'dər) v. wander aimlessly.

mean'ing, n. **1.** significance. **2.** significant. —**mean'ing.ful,** adj.

mean'time', n. **1.** time between. —adv. Also, **mean'while'.** **2.** in time between.

mea'sles (mē'zalz) n. infectious disease marked by small red spots.

mea'sly (mē'zlē) adj., **-slier, -sliest.** Informal. miserably small.

meas'ure (mezh'ər) v., **-ured, -uring.** —v. **1.** ascertain size or extent. —n. **2.** process of measuring. **3.** dimensions. **4.** instrument or system of measuring. **5.** action. —**meas'ure.ment,** n.

meas'ured, adj. careful, deliberate.

meat (mēt) n. **1.** flesh of animals used as food. **2.** edible part of fruit, nut, etc. **3.** essential part; gist. **meat'y,** adj., **-ier, -iest. 1.** with much meat. **2.** rewarding attention.

Mec'ca (mek'ə) n. **1.** city in Saudi Arabia, spiritual center of Islam. **2.** (often l.c.) place that attracts many.

me.chan'ic (mə kan'ik) n. skilled worker with machinery.

me.chan'i.cal, adj. of or operated by machinery.

me.chan'ics, n. science of motion and of action of forces on bodies.

mech'an.ism (mek'ə niz'əm) n. **1.** structure of machine. **2.** piece of machinery. —**mech'a.nist,** n.

mech'a.nize', v., **-nized, -nizing.** adapt to machinery.

med'al (med'l) n. badgelike metal object given for merit.

med'al.ist, n. medal winner.

me.dal'lion (mə dal'yən) n. large medal or medallike ornament.

med'dle (med'l) v., **-dled, -dling.** interfere; tamper. —**med'dler,** n. —**med'dle.some,** adj.

me'di.a (mē'dē ə) n.pl. the means of mass communication.

me'di.an (mē'dē ən) adj., n. middle.

me'di.ate' (mē'dē āt') v., **-ated, -ating.** settle (dispute) between parties. —**me'di.a'tor,** n.

med'ic (med'ik) n. Informal. doctor or medical aide.

Med'i.caid' (med'i kād') n. state- and federal-supported medical care for low-income persons.

med'i.cal, adj. **1.** of medicine. **2.** curative. —**med'i.cal.ly,** adv.

me.dic'a.ment (mə dik'ə mənt, med'i kə-) n. healing substance.

Med'i.care' (med'i kār') n. government-supported medical insurance for those 65 years old or more.

med'i.cate', v., **-cated, -cating.** treat with medicine. —**med'i.ca'tion,** n.

me.dic'i.nal (mə dis'ə nl) adj. curative. —**me.dic'i.nal.ly,** adv.

med'i.cine (med'ə sin) n. **1.** substance used in treating disease. **2.** art of restoring physical health.

medicine man, among American Indians, person believed to have magical powers.

me·di·e·val (mē'dē ēr'vəl, mid ē'-) *adj.* of the Middle Ages. Also, **me'di·ae·val.**

me·di·e·val·ism, *n.* a characteristic of the Middle Ages.

me·di·e·val·ist, *n.* expert in medieval history, etc.

me·di·o·cre (mē'dē ō'kər) *adj.* undistinguished. —**me'di·oc'ri·ty** (-ok'ri tē) *n.*

med·i·tate (med'i tāt') *v.,* -tated, -tating. think intensely. —**med'i·ta'tion,** *n.* —**med'i·ta'tive,** *adj.*

me·di·um (mē'dē əm) *n., pl.* **-di·ums** for 1–5, **-dia** (-dē ə) for 1–3, 5, *adj.* —*n.* **1.** something intermediate or moderate. **2.** means of doing. **3.** environment. **4.** person believed able to communicate with dead. **5.** means of mass communication. —*adj.* **6.** intermediate.

med·ley (med'lē) *n.* mixture, as of tunes.

meek (mēk) *adj.* submissive.

meer·schaum (mēr'shəm, -shôm) *n.* claylike mineral, used for tobacco pipes.

meet (mēt) *v.,* **met** (met), **meeting,** *n., adj.* —*v.* **1.** come into contact with. **2.** make acquaintance of. **3.** satisfy. —*n.* **4.** equal. **5.** meeting, esp. for sport. —*adj.* **6.** proper.

meet·ing, *n.* **1.** a coming together. **2.** persons gathered.

mega-, *prefix.* **1.** one million. **2.** large.

meg·a·hertz (meg'ə hûrts') *n., pl.* **-hertz.** *Elect.* one million cycles per second.

meg·a·lo·ma·ni·a (meg'ə lō mā'nē ə) *n.* delusion of greatness, riches, etc.

meg·a·phone (meg'ə fōn') *n.* cone-shaped device for magnifying sound.

meg·a·ton' *n.* one million tons, esp. of TNT, as equivalent in explosive force.

mel·a·mine (mel'ə mēn') *n.* crystalline solid used in manufacturing resins.

mel·an·cho·li·a (mel'ən kō'lē ə) *n.* mental state of severe depression.

mel·an·chol·y (mel'ən kol'ē) *n., pl.* **-cholies.** **1.** low spirits; depression. —*adj.* **2.** sad.

mé·lange (mā länzh', -länj') *n.* mixture.

mel·a·nin (mel'ə nin) *n.* pigment accounting for dark color of skin, hair, etc.

mel·a·no·ma (-nō'mə) *n.* darkly pigmented skin tumor.

meld (meld) *v.* display combination of cards for a score.

me·lee (mā'lā) *n.* confused, general fight.

mel·io·rate (mēl'yə rāt') *v.,* -rated, -rating. improve.

mel·lif·lu·ous (mə lif'lŏo əs) *adj.* soft and sweet in speech.

mel·low (mel'ō) *adj.* **1.** soft and rich. **2.** genial. —*v.* **3.** make or become mellow.

me·lo·de·on (mə lō'dē ən) *n.* reed organ.

me·lo·di·ous, *adj.* tuneful.

mel·o·dra·ma (mel'ə drä'mə, -dram'ə) *n.* play emphasizing theatrical effects and strong emotions.

mel·o·dra·mat·ic, *adj.* **1.** of melodrama. **2.** overly emotional.

mel·o·dy (mel'ə dē) *n., pl.* **-dies.** arrangement of musical sounds. —**me·lod·ic** (mə lod'ik) *adj.*

mel·on (mel'ən) *n.* edible fruit of certain annual vines.

melt (melt) *v.,* **melted, melted** or **molten, melting.** **1.** make or become liquid, esp. by heat. **2.** soften.

melt/down', *n.* melting of nuclear reactor core, causing escape of radiation.

melting pot, place where blending of peoples, races, or cultures takes place.

mem·ber (mem'bər) *n.* **1.** part of structure. **2.** one belonging to organization. —**mem'ber·ship',** *n.*

mem·brane (mem'brān) *n.* thin film of tissue in animals and plants.

me·men·to (mə men'tō) *n., pl.* **-tos, -toes.** reminder.

mem·oir (mem'wär, -wôr) *n.* **1.** autobiography. —*pl.* **2.** personal recollection.

mem·o·ra·bil·i·a (-ə bil'ē ə, -bil'yə) *n.pl.* souvenirs.

mem·o·ra·ble, *adj.* worth remembering. —**mem'o·ra·bly,** *adv.*

mem·o·ran·dum (mem'ə ran'dəm) *n., pl.* **-dums, -da** (-də). written statement or reminder. Also, **mem'o** (mem'ō).

me·mo·ri·al (mə môr'ē əl) *n.* **1.** something honoring memory of a person or event. —*adj.* **2.** serving as memorial.

mem·o·rize (mem'ə rīz') *v.,* -rized, -rizing. commit to memory.

mem·o·ry (mem'ə rē) *n., pl.* **-ries.** **1.** faculty of remembering. **2.** something that is remembered. **3.** length of time of recollection. **4.** capacity of computer to store data.

men·ace (men'is) *v.,* -aced, -acing, *n.* —*v.* **1.** threaten evil to. —*n.* **2.** something that threatens.

metabolism

me·nag′er·ie (mə naj′ə rē, -nazh′-) *n.* collection of animals.

mend (mend) *v.* repair; improve.

men·da′cious (men dā′shəs) *adj.* untruthful. —**men·dac′i·ty** (-das′i-tē) *n.*

men′di·cant (men′di kənt) *n.* beggar.

me′ni·al (mē′nē əl) *adj.* 1. humble; servile. —*n.* 2. servant.

me·nin′ges (mi nin′jēz) *n.pl., sing.* **me′ninx** (mē′ningks). three membranes covering brain and spinal cord.

men′in·gi′tis (men′in jī′tis) *n.* inflammation of meninges.

men′o·pause′ (men′ə pôz′) *n.* cessation of menses, usually between ages of 45 and 50.

me·nor′ah (mə nôr′ə) *n.* symbolic candelabrum used by Jews during Hanukkah.

men′stru·a′tion (men′strŏŏ ā′shən) *n.* monthly discharge of blood from uterus. —**men′stru·al,** *adj.* —**men′stru·ate′,** *v.,* -ated, -ating.

men′sur·a·ble (-shər ə bəl, -sər ə-bəl) *adj.* measurable.

mens′wear′, *n.* clothing for men.

-ment, suffix meaning: action or resulting state, as *abridgment;* product, as *fragment;* means, as *ornament.*

men′tal (men′tl) *adj.* of or in the mind. —**men′tal·ly,** *adv.*

men·tal′i·ty (-tal′i tē) *n., pl.* -ties. 1. mental ability. 2. characteristic mental attitude.

men′thol (men′thôl, -thol) *n.* colorless alcohol from peppermint oil. —**men′thol·at′ed** (-thə lā′tid) *adj.*

men′tion (men′shən) *v.* speak or write. —*n.* 2. reference.

men′tor (men′tôr, -tər) *n.* adviser.

men′u (men′yŏŏ, mā′nyŏŏ) *n.* list of dishes that can be served.

me·ow′ (mē ou′, myou) *n.* 1. sound cat makes. —*v.* 2. make such sound.

mer′can·tile′ (mûr′kən tēl′, -tīl′, -til) *adj.* of or engaged in trade.

mer′ce·nar′y (mûr′sə ner′ē) *adj., n., pl.* -naries. —*adj.* 1. acting only for profit. —*n.* 2. hired soldier.

mer′chan·dise′, *n., v., -dised, -dis-ing.* —*n.* (mûr′chən dīz′, -dīs′) 1. goods; wares. —*v.* (-dīz′) 2. buy and sell.

mer′chant (mûr′chənt) *n.* person who buys and sells goods for profit.

merchant marine, commercial vessels of nation.

mer·cu′ri·al (mər kyŏŏr′ē əl) *adj.* 1. of mercury. 2. unpredictable.

mer′cu·ry (mûr′kyə rē) *n.* 1. heavy

metallic element. 2. (*cap.*) one of the planets.

mer′cy (mûr′sē) *n., pl.* -cies. 1. pity; compassion. 2. act of compassion. —**mer′ci·ful,** *adj.*

mere (mēr) *adj.* only. —**mere′ly,** *adv.*

merge (mûrj) *v.,* merged, merging. combine. —**merg′er,** *n.*

me·rid′i·an (mə rid′ē ən) *n.* circle on earth's surface passing through the poles.

me·ringue′ (mə rang′) *n.* egg whites and sugar beaten together.

me·ri′no (mə rē′nō) *n., pl.* -nos. 1. kind of sheep. 2. soft woolen yarn.

mer′it (mer′it) *n.* 1. excellence or good quality. —*v.* 2. deserve. —**mer′i·to′ri·ous** (-i tôr′ē əs) *adj.*

mer′maid′ (mûr′mād′) *n.* imaginary sea creature, half woman and half fish. —**mer′man′,** *n.masc.*

mer′ry (mer′ē) *adj.,* -rier, -riest. gay; joyous. —**mer′ri·ly,** *adv.*

mer′ry-go-round′, *n.* revolving amusement ride.

mer′ry·mak′ing, *n.* festivities; hilarity. —**mer′ry·mak′er,** *n.*

me′sa (mā′sə) *n.* high, steep-walled plateau.

mesh (mesh) *n.* 1. open space of net. 2. net itself. 3. engagement of gears. —*v.* 4. catch in mesh. 5. engage. 6. match or interlock.

mes′mer·ize′ (mez′mə rīz′) *v.,* -ized, -izing. hypnotize; spellbind. —**mes′mer·ism** (-mə riz′əm) *n.*

Mes·o·zo′ic (mez′ə zō′ik) *adj.* pertaining to geologic era occurring between 230 and 65 million years ago.

mes·quite′ (me skēt′, mes′kēt) *n.* tree of southwest U.S.

mess (mes) *n.* 1. dirty or disorderly condition. 2. group taking meals together regularly. 3. Meals so taken. —*v.* 4. make dirty or untidy. 5. eat in company. —**mess′y,** *adj.*

mes′sage (mes′ij) *n.* communication.

mes′sen·ger (mes′ən jər) *n.* bearer of message.

Mes·si′ah (mi sī′ə) *n.* 1. expected deliverer. 2. (in Christian theology) Jesus Christ.

mes·ti′zo (me stē′zō) *n., pl.* -zos, -zoes. person part-Spanish, part-Indian. Also, **mes·ti′za** (-zə) *fem.*

meta-, prefix meaning: 1. after or beyond, as *metaphysics.* 2. behind, as *metacarpus.* 3. change, as *metamorphosis.*

me·tab′o·lism (mə tab′ə liz′əm) *n.* biological processes of converting food into matter and matter into energy. —**met′a·bol′ic** (met′ə bol′ik) *adj.*

met′al (met′l) *n.* 1. elementary substance such as gold or copper. 2. **mettle** —**me·tal′lic** (mə tal′ik) *adj.* —**met′al·ware′,** *n.*

met′al·lur′gy (met′l ûr′jē) *n.* science of working with metals.

met′a·mor′phose (met′ə môr′fōz, -fōs) *v.,* -**phosed,** -**phosing.** transform.

met′a·mor·pho·sis (-fə sis) *n., pl.* -**ses** (-sēz′). change.

met′a·phor (met′ə fôr′, -fər) *n.* figure of speech using analogy. —**met′a·phor′i·cal,** *adj.*

met′a·phys′ics, *n.* branch of philosophy concerned with ultimate nature of reality. —**met′a·phys′i·cal,** *adj.* —**met′a·phy·si′cian,** *n.*

me·tas′ta·size′ (mə tas′tə sīz′) *v.,* -**sized,** -**sizing.** spread from one to another part of the body. —**me·tas′ta·sis** (-sis) *n.*

mete (mēt) *v.,* **meted, meting.** allot.

me′te·or (mē′tē ər, -ôr′) *n.* celestial body passing through earth's atmosphere.

me′te·or′ic (-ôr′ik) *adj.* 1. of meteors. 2. sudden and spectacular.

me′te·or·ite′ (-ə rīt′) *n.* meteor reaching earth.

me′te·or·ol′o·gy (-ə rol′ə jē) *n.* science of atmospheric phenomena, esp. weather. —**me′te·or·o·log′i·cal** (-ər ə loj′i kəl) *adj.* —**me′te·or·ol′o·gist,** *n.*

me′ter (mē′tər) *n.* 1. unit of length in metric system, equal to 39.37 inches. 2. rhythmic arrangement of words. 3. device for measuring flow. —*v.* 4. measure. Also, *Brit.,* **me′tre.** —**met′ric** (me′trik), **met′ri·cal,** *adj.*

meth′a·done′ (meth′ə dōn′) *n.* synthetic narcotic used in treating heroin addiction.

meth′ane (meth′ān) *n.* colorless, odorless, flammable gas.

meth′a·nol′ (meth′ə nôl′) *n.* colorless liquid used as solvent, fuel, or antifreeze. Also, **methyl alcohol.**

meth′od (meth′əd) *n.* system of doing. —**me·thod′i·cal** (mə thod′i kəl), *adj.* —**me·thod′i·cal·ly,** *adv.*

meth′od·ol′o·gy (-ə dol′ə jē) *n., pl.* -**gies.** system of methods and principles.

me·tic′u·lous (mə tik′yə ləs) *adj.* minutely careful.

mé′ti·er (mā′tyā) *n.* field of activity in which one has special ability. Also, **me′tier.**

met′ric (me′trik) *adj.* of decimal system of weights and measures, based on meter and gram.

met′ro·nome′ (me′trə nōm′) *n.* device for marking tempo.

me·trop′o·lis (mi trop′ə lis) *n.* great city.

met′ro·pol′i·tan (me′trə pol′i tn) *adj.* 1. of or in a city. 2. of cities and urban areas.

met′tle (met′l) *n.* 1. spirit. 2. disposition.

met′tle·some (-səm) *adj.* spirited; courageous.

mew (myōō) *n.* 1. cry of a cat. —*v.* 2. emit a mew.

mews, *n.* street with dwellings converted from stables.

Mex′i·can, (mek′si kan) *n.* native of Mexico. —**Mexican,** *adj.*

mez′za·nine′ (mez′ə nēn′, mez/ə nēn′) *n.* low story between two main floors; balcony.

mez′zo-so·pra′no (met′sō-, med′zō-) *n.* voice, musical part, or singer intermediate in range between soprano and contralto.

M.F.A., Master of Fine Arts.

MI, Michigan.

mi·as′ma (mī az′mə, mē-) *n., pl.* -**mata** (-mə tə), -**mas.** vapors from decaying organic matter.

mi′ca (mī′kə) *n.* shiny mineral occurring in thin layers.

Mich., Michigan.

micro-, prefix meaning: 1. extremely small. 2. one millionth.

mi′crobe (mī′krōb) *n.* microorganism, esp. one causing disease.

mi′cro·brew′er·y, *n.* small brewery usu. producing exotic or high quality beer.

mi′cro·chip′, *n.* chip (def. 3).

mi′cro·com·put′er, *n.* compact computer with less capability than minicomputer.

mi′cro·cosm (mī′krə koz′əm) *n.* world in miniature.

mi′cro·fiche′ (-fēsh′) *n.* small sheet of microfilm.

mi′cro·film′, *n.* 1. very small photograph of book page, etc. —*v.* 2. make microfilm of.

mi·crom′e·ter (mī krom′i tər) *n.* device for measuring minute distances.

mi′cron (mī′kron) *n.* millionth part of a meter.

mi′cro·or′gan·ism′ (mī′krō-) *n.* microscopic organism.

mi′cro·phone′ (mī′krə fōn′) *n.* instrument for changing sound waves into changes in electric current.

mi′cro·pro·ces′sor (mī′krō pros′es-ər, -ə sər; *esp. Brit.* -prō′ses ər, -sə sər) *n.* computer circuit that performs all functions of CPU.

mi′cro·scope′ (mī′krə skōp′) *n.* instrument for inspecting minute objects.

mi′cro·scop′ic (-skop′ik) *adj.* **1.** of microscopes. **2.** extremely small.

mi′cro·sur′ger·y (mī′krō sûr′jə rē) *n.* surgery performed under magnification.

mi′cro·wave′, *n.* **1.** short radio wave used in radar, cooking, etc. **2.** oven that uses microwaves to cook food. —*v.* **3.** cook in microwave oven.

mid (mid) *adj.* middle. —*prep.* **2.** amid.

mid′day′ (-dā′, -dā′) *n.* noon.

mid′dle (mid′l) *adj.* **1.** equally distant from given limits. **2.** medium. —*n.* **3.** middle part.

Middle Ages, period of European history, about A.D. 476 to 1500.

middle class, class of people intermediate between the poor and the wealthy.

Middle East, area including Israel and Arab countries of NE Africa and SW Asia.

Middle English, English language of period c1150–1475.

mid′dle·man′, *n.* merchant who buys direct from producer.

middle-of-the-road, *adj.* moderate.

middle school, school encompassing grades 5 or 6 through 8.

mid′dling, *adj.* **1.** medium. **2.** mediocre.

midge (mij) *n.* minute fly.

midg′et (mij′it) *n.* very small person or thing.

mid′land (-lənd) *n.* interior of country.

mid′night′, *n.* 12 o'clock at night.

mid′point′, *n.* point at or near the middle.

mid′riff (-rif) *n.* part of body between the chest and abdomen.

mid′ship′man, *n.,* *pl.* **-men.** rank of student at U.S. Naval or Coast Guard academy.

midst (midst) *n.* middle.

mid′sum′mer (-sum′ər, sum′-) *n.* middle of the summer.

mid′term′, *n.* **1.** halfway point of school term. **2.** examination given at midterm.

mid′way′ *adj., adv.* (mid′wā′) **1.** in or to middle. —*n.* (-wā′) **2.** area of games and shows at carnival.

mid′wife′, *n., pl.* **-wives.** woman who assists at childbirth.

mid′win′ter (-win′tər, -win′-) *n.* middle of winter.

mien (mēn) *n.* air; bearing.

miff (mif) *n.* petty quarrel.

miffed (mift) *adj.* irritated; offended.

might (mīt) *v.* **1.** pt. of **may.** —*n.* **2.** strength; power.

might′y, *adj.,* **-ier, -iest,** *adv.* —*adj.* **1.** powerful; huge. —*adv.* **2.** *Informal.* very. —**might′i·ness,** *n.*

mi′graine (mī′grān) *n.* painful headache.

mi′grate (-grāt) *v.,* **-grated, -grating.** go from one region to another. —**mi·gra′tion,** *n.* —**mi′gra·to′ry** (-grə tôr′ē) *adj.* —**mi′grant,** *adj., n.*

mi·ka′do (mi kä′dō) *n., pl.* **-dos.** a title of emperor of Japan.

mike (mīk) *n. Informal.* microphone.

mil (mil) *n.* one thousandth of inch.

mild (mīld) *adj.* gentle; temperate.

mil′dew′ (mil′dōō′, -dyōō′) *n.* discoloration caused by fungus. —*v.* **2.** affect with mildew.

mile (mīl) *n.* unit of distance, equal on land to 5280 ft.

mile′age (mī′lij) *n.* **1.** miles traveled. **2.** travel allowance.

mile′stone′, *n.* **1.** marker showing road distance. **2.** important event.

mi·lieu′ (mil yōō′, mēl-; *Fr.* mēlyœ′) *n., pl.* **-lieus, -lieux.** environment.

mil′i·tant (mil′i tənt) *adj.* warlike; aggressive.

mil′i·ta·rism (-tə riz′əm) *n.* **1.** military spirit. **2.** domination by military. —**mil′i·ta·rist,** *n.*

mil′i·ta·rize′, *v.,* **-ized, -izing.** equip with military weapons.

mil′i·tar·y (-ter′ē) *adj., n., pl.* **-ta·ries.** —*adj.* **1.** of armed forces, esp. on land. —*n.* **2.** armed forces or soldiers collectively.

military police, soldiers who perform police duties within army.

mi·li′tia (mi lish′ə) *n.* organization for emergency military service. —**mi·li′tia·man,** *n.*

milk (milk) *n.* **1.** liquid secreted by female mammals to feed their young. —*v.* **2.** draw milk from. —**milk′y,** *adj.* —**milk′maid′,** *n.*

milk′man′, *n., pl.* **-men.** man who sells or delivers milk.

milk′weed′, *n.* plant with milky juice.

Milk′y Way′, *Astron.* galaxy containing sun and earth.

mill (mil) *n.* **1.** place where manufacturing is done. **2.** device for grinding. **3.** place where grain is ground. **4.** one tenth of a cent. —*v.* **5.** grind or treat with mill. **6.** groove edges of (coin). **7.** move about in confusion. —**mill′er,** *n.*

mil·len′ni·um (mi len′ē əm) *n., pl.*

-niums, -nia (-nē ə). period of a thousand years.

mil′let (-it) n. cereal grass.

milli-, prefix meaning thousand or thousandth.

mil′liard (mil′yard, -yärd) n. Brit. one billion.

mil′li•gram′ (mil′i gram′) n. one thousandth of gram.

mil′li•li′ter, n. one thousandth of liter.

mil′li•me′ter, n. one thousandth of meter.

mil′li•ner (mil′ə nər) n. person who makes or sells women's hats.

mil′li•ner′y (-ner′ē, -nə rē) n. 1. women's hats. 2. business or trade of a milliner.

mil′lion (mil′yən) n., adj. 1000 times 1000. —**mil′lionth,** adj., n.

mil′lion•aire′ (mil′yə nâr′) n. person having a million dollars or more.

mill′race′, n. channel for current of water driving mill wheel.

mill′stone′, n. 1. stone for grinding grain. 2. heavy mental or emotional burden.

mill′stream′, n. stream in millrace.

mime (mīm, mēm) n. pantomimist; clown.

mim•e•o•graph′ (mim′ē ə graf′) n. 1. stencil device for duplicating. —v. copy with mimeograph.

mim′ic (mim′ik) v., -icked, -icking, n. —v. 1. imitate speech or actions of. —n. 2. person who mimics. —**mim′ic•ry,** n.

mi•mo′sa (mi mō′sa, -za) n. semitropical tree or shrub.

min′a•ret′ (min′ə ret′) n. tower for calling Muslims to prayer.

mince (mins) v., minced, mincing. 1. chop fine. 2. speak, move, or behave with affected elegance.

mince′meat′, n. cooked mixture of finely chopped meat, raisins, spices, etc., used in pies.

mind (mīnd) n. 1. thinking part of human or animal. 2. intellect. 3. inclination. —v. 4. heed; obey.

mind′-blow′ing, adj. 1. astounding. 2. producing hallucinogenic effect.

mind′ful, adj. careful.

mind′less, adj. 1. heedless. 2. requiring no intelligence.

mine (mīn) pron., n., v., mined, mining. —pron. 1. possessive form of I. —n. 2. excavation in earth for resources. 3. stationary explosive device used in war. 4. abundant source. —v. 5. lay explosive mines. 6. work in mine. —**min′er,** n.

min′er•al (min′ər əl) n. 1. inorganic substance. 2. substance obtained by mining. —adj. 3. of minerals.

min•er•al•o•gy (-ə rol′ə jē, -ral′ə-) n. science of minerals.

mineral water, water containing dissolved mineral salts or gases.

min•e•stro′ne (min′ə strō′nē) n. thick vegetable soup.

mine′sweep′er, n. ship used to remove explosive mines.

min′gle (ming′gəl) v., -gled, -gling. associate; mix.

min′i (min′ē) n. small version.

mini-, prefix meaning. 1. smaller than others of its kind. 2. very short.

min′i•a•ture (min′ē ə chər, min′ə-) n. 1. greatly reduced form. 2. tiny painting. —adj. 3. on small scale.

min′i•a•tur•ize′ (-ə rīz′) v., -ized, -izing. make in or reduce to very small size. —**min′i•a•tur•i•za′tion,** n.

min′i•bus′, n. small bus.

min′i•com•put′er, n. computer with capabilities between those of microcomputer and mainframe.

min′im (min′əm) n. smallest unit of liquid measure.

min′i•mal•ism (-mə liz′əm) n. style, as in art or music, that is spare and simple.

min′i•mize′ (-mīz′) v., -mized, -mizing. make minimum.

min′i•mum (-məm) n. 1. least possible quantity, degree, etc. —adj. 2. Also, min′i•mal (-məl) lowest.

min′ion (min′yən) n. servile follower.

min′is•ter (min′ə stər) n. 1. person authorized to conduct worship. 2. government representative abroad. 3. head of governmental department. —v. 4. give care. —**min′is•te′ri•al** (-stēr′ē əl) adj. —**min′is•tra′tion,** n.

min′is•try (-ə strē) n., pl. -tries. 1. religious calling. 2. clergy. 3. duty or office of a department of government. 4. body of executive officials. 5. act of ministering.

min′i•van′, n. small passenger van.

mink (mingk) n. 1. semiaquatic mammal or its soft brown fur.

Minn., Minnesota.

min′now (min′ō) n. tiny fish.

mi′nor (mī′nər) n. 1. lesser in size or importance. 2. person under legal age. —n. 3. person under legal age.

mi•nor′i•ty (mi nôr′i tē, mī-) n., pl. -ties. 1. smaller number or part. 2. relatively small population group. 3. state or time of being under legal age.

min′strel (min′strəl) n. 1. musician or singer, esp. in Middle Ages. 2.

white performer with face blacked singing black Americn songs.

mint (mint) *n.* **1.** aromatic herb. **2.** place where money is coined. **3.** huge sum. —*v.* **4.** make coins.

min′u·et′ (min′yŏŏ et′) *n.* stately dance.

mi′nus (mī′nəs) *prep.* **1.** less. —*adj.* **2.** less than.

mi′nus·cule′ (min′ə skyŏŏl′, minus′kyŏŏl) *adj.* tiny.

min′ute (min′it) **1.** sixty seconds. **2.** (*pl.*) record of proceedings. —*adj.* (mī nŏŏt′, -nyŏŏt′) **3.** extremely small. **4.** attentive to detail. —**mi·nute′ly,** *adv.*

mi·nu′ti·ae′ (mi nŏŏ′shē ē′) *n.pl.* trifling matters.

minx (mingks) *n.* saucy girl.

mir′a·cle (mir′ə kəl) *n.* supernatural act or effect. —**mi·rac′u·lous** (mi rak′yə ləs) *adj.*

mi·rage′ (mi räzh′) *n.* atmospheric illusion in which images of far-distant objects are seen.

mire (mī°r) *n., v.,* **mired, miring.** —*n.* **1.** swamp. **2.** deep mud. —*v.* **3.** stick fast in mire. **4.** soil.

mir′ror (mir′ər) *n.* **1.** reflecting surface. —*v.* **2.** reflect.

mirth (mûrth) *n.* gaiety and laughter. —**mirth′less,** *adj.*

mis-, prefix meaning: **1.** wrong, as *misconduct.* **2.** lack of, as *mistrust.*

mis′ad·ven′ture (mis′ad ven′chər) *n.* bad luck.

mis·al·li′ance, *n.* incompatible association.

mis′an·thrope′ (mis′ən thrōp′, miz′-) *n.* hater of humanity. —**mis′an·throp′ic** (-throp′ik) *adj.*

mis′ap·ply′, *v.,* **-plied, -plying.** use wrongly. —**mis′ap·pli·ca′tion,** *n.*

mis′ap·pre·hend′, *v.* misunderstand. —**mis′ap·pre·hen′sion** (-hen′shən) *n.*

mis′ap·pro′pri·ate′ (-āt′) *v.,* **-ated, -ating.** use wrongly as one's own.

mis′be·got′ten, *adj.* ill-conceived.

mis′be·have′, *v.,* **-haved, -having.** behave badly. —**mis′be·hav′ior,** *n.*

misc., miscellaneous.

mis·cal′cu·late′, *v.,* **-lated, -lating.** judge badly.

mis·call′, *v.* call by a wrong name.

mis·car′riage, *n.* **1.** premature birth resulting in death of fetus. **2.** failure.

mis·car′ry (mis kar′ē; *for 1 also* mis′kar′ē) *v.,* **-ried, -rying. 1.** have miscarriage. **2.** go wrong.

mis·cast′, *v.* cast in unsuitable role.

mis′cel·la′ne·ous (-lā′nē əs) *adj.* unclassified; various. —**mis′cel·la′ny** (-lā′nē) *n.*

mis·chance′, *n.* bad luck.

mis′chief (mis′chif) *n.* **1.** trouble, caused willfully. **2.** tendency to tease. —**mis′chie·vous** (mis′chə vəs), *adj.* —**Pronunciation.** The word MISCHIEVOUS is pronounced with three syllables. The pronunciation (mis chē′vē əs), with four syllables, is usually considered nonstandard. Note that although a spelling *mischievious,* which reflects this nonstandard pronunciation by including an extra *i* after the *v,* was occasionally seen between the 16th and 19th centuries, it is not considered a correct spelling today.

mis′con·ceive′, *v.,* **-ceived, -ceiving.** misunderstand. —**mis′con·cep′tion,** *n.*

mis′con·duct (-kon′dukt) *n.* improper or illegal conduct.

mis′con·strue′ (mis′kən strōō′) *v.,* **-strued, -struing.** misinterpret.

mis′cre·ant (mis′krē ənt) *n.* villain.

mis·deed′, *n.* immoral deed.

mis′de·mean′or, *n.* minor offense.

mise-en-scène′ (mē zän sen′) *n., pl.* **-scènes** (-sens′). **1.** placement of actors, scenery, and properties on stage. **2.** surroundings.

mi′ser (mī′zər) *n.* hoarder of wealth. —**mi′ser·ly,** *adj.*

mis′er·a·ble (miz′ər ə bəl) *adj.* **1.** wretched. **2.** deplorable. **3.** contemptible; despicable.

mis′er·y, *n., pl.* **-eries.** wretched condition.

mis·fea′sance (mis fē′zəns) *n.* wrongful exercise of lawful authority.

mis·fire′ (mis fī°r′) *v.,* **-fired, -firing.** fail to fire.

mis·fit′ (mis fit′, mis′fit′) **1.** (mis′fit′) poor fit. **2.** (mis′fit′) maladjusted person.

mis·for′tune, *n.* bad luck.

mis·giv′ing, *n.* doubt.

mis·guid′ed, *adj.* mistaken; ill-informed.

mis·han′dle, *v.,* **-dled, -dling. 1.** handle roughly. **2.** manage badly.

mis′hap (mis′hap, mis hap′) *n.* unlucky accident.

mish′mash′ (mish′mäsh′, -mash′) *n.* jumble; hodgepodge.

mis′in·form′, *v.* give false information to. —**mis′in·for·ma′tion,** *n.*

mis′in·ter′pret, *v.* interpret wrongly.

mis·judge′, *v.,* **-judged, -judging.** judge wrongly.

mis·lay′, *v.,* **-laid, -laying. 1.** put in place later forgotten. **2.** misplace.

mis·lead′ (-lēd′) *v.,* **-led, -leading. 1.** lead in wrong direction. **2.** lead into error, as in conduct.

mis·man′age, *v.,* **-aged, -aging.** manage badly.

mis·match′ v. 1. (mis mach′) match unsuitably. —n. (mis mach′, mis′mach′) 2. unsuitable match.

mis·no′mer (mis nō′mər) n. misapplied name.

mi·sog′a·my (mi sog′ə mē, mī-) n. hatred of marriage.

mi·sog′y·ny (mi soj′ə nē, mī-) n. hatred of women. —**mi·sog′y·nist,** n.

mis·place′, v., **-placed, -placing.** 1. forget location of. 2. place unwisely.

mis·print′ (mis′print′, mis print′) n. error in printing.

mis·pro·nounce′, v., **-nounced, -nouncing.** pronounce wrongly.

mis·quote′, v., **-quoted, -quoting.** quote incorrectly.

mis·read′ (-rēd′) v., **-read** (red′), **-reading.** 1. read wrongly. 2. misinterpret.

mis·rep·re·sent′, v. give wrong idea of.

mis·rule′, n. bad or unwise rule. —**mis·rule′,** v.

miss (mis) v. 1. fail to hit, catch, meet, do, etc. 2. feel absence of. —n. 3. (cap.) title of respect for unmarried woman. 4. girl. 5. failure to hit successfully.

Miss., Mississippi.

mis′sal (mis′əl) n. book of prayers, etc., for celebrating Mass.

mis·shap′en, adj. deformed.

mis′sile (mis′əl; esp. Brit. -īl) n. object thrown or shot, as lance or bullet.

mis′sion (mish′ən) n. 1. group sent abroad for specific work. 2. duty. 3. air operation against enemy. 4. missionary post.

mis′sion·ar′y (-ə ner′ē) n., pl. **-aries,** adj. —n. 1. person sent to propagate religious faith. —adj. 2. of religious missions.

mis′sive (mis′iv) n. letter.

mis·spell′, v. spell wrongly.

mis·spend′, v., **-spent, -spending.** squander.

mis·state′, v., **-stated, -stating.** state wrongly.

mis·step′, n. error.

mist (mist) n. light, thin fog. —**mist′y,** adj.

mis·take′ (mi stāk′) n., v., **-took, -taken, -taking.** —n. 1. error in judgment, action, or belief. —v. 2. take or regard wrongly. 3. misunderstand. 4. be in error.

Mis′ter (mis′tər) n. title of address for man. Abbr.: **Mr.**

mis′tle·toe′ (mis′əl tō′) n. parasitic plant with waxy white berries.

mis·treat′, v. treat badly. —**mis·treat′ment,** n.

mis′tress (mis′tris) n. 1. female in control. 2. female lover of married man.

mis·tri′al, n. trial ended without verdict because of legal error or inability of jury to agree on verdict.

mis·trust′, n. lack of trust. —**mis·trust′,** v.

mis·un·der·stand′, v., **-stood, -standing.** understand wrongly. —**mis·un·der·stand′ing,** n.

mis·use′ n., v., **-used, -using.** —n. (-yōōs′) 1. improper use. —v. (-yōōz′) 2. use badly or wrongly. 3. abuse.

mite (mīt) n. 1. tiny parasitic insect. 2. small thing or bit.

mi′ter (mī′tər) n. 1. join two pieces on diagonal. —n. 2. such joint. 3. tall cap worn by bishops. Also, Brit., **mi′tre.**

mit′i·gate′ (mit′i gāt′) v., **-gated, -gating.** make less severe.

mi·to′sis (mī tō′sis) n. method of cell division.

mitt (mit) n. thick glove.

mit′ten (mit′n) n. fingerless glove.

mix (miks) v., n. —v. 1. put together; combine. 2. associate. 3. confuse. n. 4. mixture. 5. mess.

mixed number, number consisting of whole number and fraction or decimal.

mix′ture (-chər) n. act or product of mixing.

mix′-up′, n. state of confusion.

mm, millimeter.

MN, Minnesota.

mne·mon′ic (ni mon′ik) adj. aiding memory.

MO, 1. Also, **Mo.** Missouri. 2. modus operandi.

moan (mōn) n. 1. low groan. —v. 2. utter moans.

moat (mōt) n. deep, water-filled ditch around castle.

mob (mob) n., v., **mobbed, mobbing.** —n. 1. crowd, esp. disorderly one. —v. 2. attack as a mob.

mo′bile (mō′bəl, -bēl) adj. 1. capable of moving or being moved. —n. (-bēl) 2. suspended artwork with parts that move in the breeze. —**mo·bil′i·ty,** n.

mo′bi·lize′ (mō′bə līz′) v., **-lized, -lizing.** make ready for war.

mob′ster (mob′stər) n. member of criminal mob.

moc′ca·sin (mok′ə sin, -zən) n. 1. soft shoe. 2. poisonous snake.

mo′cha (mō′kə) n. 1. kind of coffee. 2. flavoring made from coffee and chocolate.

mock (mok) v. 1. mimic or ridicule. —adj. 2. imitation.

mock′er·y, *n., pl.* **-ies. 1.** derision. **2.** dishonest imitation; travesty.

mock′ing·bird′, *n.* songbird with imitative voice.

mock′-up′, *n.* scale model.

mode (mōd) *n.* prevailing style.

mod′el (mod′l) *n., adj., v.,* **-eled, -eling. —n. 1.** standard for imitation. **2.** person who poses, as for artist or photographer. **—adj. 3.** serving as model. **—v. 4.** pattern after model. **5.** wear as model. **6.** form.

mo′dem (mō′dam, -dem) *n.* device enabling transmission of data between computers via telephone lines.

mod′er·ate *adj., n., v.,* **-ated, -at-ing. —adj.** (mod′ar it) **1.** not extreme. **—n.** (-ar it) **2.** person having moderate views. **—v.** (-a rāt′) **3.** make or become less violent or intense. **4.** preside over.

mod′er·a′tor, *n.* director of group discussion.

mod′ern (mod′arn) *adj.* of recent time. **—mo·der′ni·ty** (-dûr′ni tē) *n.* **—mod′ern·ize′,** *v.*

Modern English, English language since c1475.

mod′ern·ism, *n.* **1.** modern character or tendencies. **2.** modern usage.

mod′est (mod′ist) *adj.* **1.** humble in estimating oneself. **2.** simple; moderate. **3.** decent, moral. **—mod′est·ly,** *adv.* **—mod′es·ty,** *n.*

mod′i·cum (mod′a kam) *n.* small amount.

mod′i·fy (mod′a fī′) *v.,* **-fied, -fy-ing.** alter or moderate. **—mod′i·fi-ca′tion,** *n.* **—mod′i·fi′er,** *n.*

mod′ish (mō′dish) *adj.* fashionable.

mo·diste′ (mō dēst′) *n.fem.* maker of women's attire.

mod′u·late′ (moj′a lāt′) *v.,* **-lated, -lating. 1.** soften. **2.** *Radio.* alter (electric current) in accordance with sound waves. **3.** alter the pitch or key of. **—mod′u·la′tion,** *n.*

mod′ule (moj′ōol) *n.* **1.** building unit. **2.** self-contained element of spacecraft. **—mod′u·lar,** *adj.*

mo′dus op·e·ran′di (mō′das op′a-ran′dē, -dī) *n.,* **modi op·e·ran′-di** (mō′dē, -dī). method of operating.

mo′gul (mō′gal) *n.* powerful or influential person.

mo′hair′ (mō′hâr′) *n.* fabric from fleece of the Angora goat.

Mo·ham′med·an·ism (mōō ham′i-dn iz′am, mō-) *n.* Islam. **—Mo·ham′med·an,** *n., adj.*

moi·ré′ (mwä rā′, mō-) *n., pl.* **-rés.** fabric with watery appearance.

moist (moist) *adj.* damp. **—mois′-ten** (moi′san) *v.* dampness.

mois′ture (-char) *n.* dampness.

mois′tur·ize′ *v.,* **-ized, -izing.** add moisture to. **—mois′tur·iz′er,** *n.*

mo′lar (mō′lar) *n.* broad back tooth.

mo·las′ses (ma las′iz) *n.* thick, dark syrup produced in refining sugar.

mold (mōld) *n.* **1.** form for shaping molten or plastic material. **2.** thing so formed. **3.** fungus growth on animal or vegetable matter. **4.** loose rich earth. **—v. 5.** shape or form. **6.** become or make covered with mold (def. 3). **—mold′y,** *adj.*

mold′er, *v.* **1.** decay. **—n. 2.** person who molds.

mold′ing, *n.* decorative strip with special cross section.

mole (mōl) *n.* **1.** small dark spot on skin. **2.** small, furred, underground mammal. **3.** spy who works against government agency he or she is employed by.

mol′e·cule′ (mol′a kyōol′) *n.* smallest physical unit of a chemical element or compound. **—mo·lec′u·lar** (ma lek′ya lar) *adj.*

mole′hill′, *n.* **1.** small mound of earth raised by moles. **2.** something small and insignificant.

mole′skin′, *n.* **1.** fur of mole. **2.** heavy cotton fabric.

mo·lest′ (ma lest′) *v.* **1.** annoy or bother. **2.** make indecent sexual advances to. **—mo·lest′er** *n.*

moll (mol) *n. Slang.* female companion of gangster.

mol′li·fy′ (mol′a fī′) *v.,* **-fied, -fy-ing.** appease in temper.

mol′lusk (mol′ask) *n.* hard-shelled invertebrate animal. Also, **mol′lusc.**

mol′ly·cod′dle (mol′ē kod′l) *v.,* **-dled, -dling.** pamper.

molt (mōlt) *v.* shed skin or feathers.

mol′ten (mōl′tan) *adj.* melted.

mom (mom) *n. Informal.* mother.

mo′ment (mō′mant) *n.* **1.** short space of time. **2.** importance.

mo′men·tar′y (-man ter′ē) *adj.* very brief. **—mo′men·tar′i·ly,** *adv.*

mo·men·tous (-men′tas) *adj.* important.

mo·men·tum (-tam) *n., pl.* **-ta** (-ta), **-tums.** force of moving body.

mom′my (mom′ē) *n., pl.* **-mies.** *Informal.* mother.

Mon., Monday.

mon′arch (mon′ark, -ärk) *n.* hereditary sovereign.

mon′ar·chy, *n., pl.* **-chies. 1.** government by monarch. **2.** country governed by monarch. **—mon′ar•chism,** n. **—mon′ar•chist,** n., adj.

mon•as•ter•y (mon′ə ster′ē) n., pl. **-teries.** residence of monks. **—mo•nas′tic** (mə nas′tik) adj. **—mo•nas′ti•cism** (-siz′əm) n.

Mon′day (mun′dā, -dē) n. second day of week.

mon′e•tar′y (mon′i ter′ē, mun′-) adj. of money.

mon′ey (mun′ē) n., pl. **moneys, monies. 1.** pieces of metal or certificates used to buy and sell. **2.** wealth.

mon′eyed (-ēd) adj. wealthy.

mon′ger (mung′gər, mong′-) n. Brit. dealer.

mon′gol•ism (mong′gə liz′əm, mon′-) n. Offensive. (earlier term for) Down syndrome.

Mon′gol•oid′ (-loid′) adj. designating division of human race including most peoples of eastern Asia.

mon′goose (mong′gōōs′, mon′-) n., pl. **-gooses.** carnivorous animal of Asia.

mon′grel (mung′grəl, mong′-) n. **1.** animal or plant resulting from crossing of different breeds. **—adj. 2.** of mixed breeds.

mon′i•ker (mon′i kər) n. Slang. name. Also, **mon′ick•er.**

mon′i•tor (mon′i tər) n. **1.** pupil who assists teacher. **2.** television or computer screen. **—v. 3.** check continuously.

monk (mungk) n. man who is a member of a religious order.

mon′key (mung′kē) n. **1.** mammal strongly resembling a human being. **—v. 2.** fool. **3.** tamper.

monkey business, mischievous behavior.

monkey wrench, wrench with adjustable jaws.

mono-, prefix meaning one, single, or lone.

mon′o•chrome (mon′ə krōm′) adj. of one color.

mon′o•cle (mon′ə kəl) n. eyeglass for one eye.

mon′o•cot′y•le′don (mon′ə kot′l-ēd′n) n. plant having embryo containing single seed leaf.

mo•noc′u•lar (mə nok′yə lər) adj. **1.** having one eye. **2.** for use of only one eye.

mo•nog′a•my (mə nog′ə mē) n. marriage of one woman with one man. **—mo•nog′a•mous,** adj. **—mo•nog′a•mist,** n.

mon′o•gram′ (mon′ə gram′) n. design made of one's initials. **—mon′o•grammed,** adj.

mon′o•graph (mon′ə graf′) n. treatise on one subject.

mon′o•lith (-lith) n. structure of single block of stone. **—mon′o•lith′ic,** adj.

mon′o•logue′ (-lôg′) n. talk by single speaker. Also, **mon′o•log′.**

mon′o•ma′ni•a, n. obsessive zeal for or interest in single thing. **—mon′o•ma′ni•ac,** n.

mon′o•nu•cle•o′sis (-nōō′klē ō′sis, -nyōō′-) n. infectious disease characterized by fever, swelling of lymph nodes, etc.

mon′o•plane′, n. airplane with one wing on each side.

mo•nop′o•ly (mə nop′ə lē) n., pl. **-lies. 1.** exclusive control. **2.** thing so controlled. **3.** company having such control. **—mo•nop′o•lize′,** v.

mon′o•rail′ (mon′ə rāl′) n. **1.** single rail serving as track for wheeled vehicles. **2.** car or train moving on such a rail.

mon′o•so′di•um glu′ta•mate′ (mon′ə sō′dē əm glōō′tə māt′) white crystalline powder used to intensify flavor of foods.

mon′o•syl′la•ble, n. word of one syllable. **—mon′o•syl•lab′ic,** adj.

mon′o•the•ism, n. doctrine or belief that there is only one God.

mon′o•tone′, n. single tone of unvarying pitch.

mo•not′o•ny (mə not′n ē) n. wearisome uniformity. **—mo•not′o•nous,** adj.

mon•sieur (mə syœ′) n., pl. **mes•sieurs′** (me syœ′) French term of address for man.

mon•si•gnor (mon sē′nyər, mon′sē•nyôr′, mōn′-) n., pl. **-gnors, -gno′ri** (mōn′sē nyôr′ē) title of certain Roman Catholic priests.

mon•soon′ (mon sōōn′) n. seasonal wind of Indian Ocean.

mon′ster (mon′stər) n. **1.** animal or plant of abnormal form. **2.** wicked creature. **3.** anything huge.

mon•stros•i•ty (mon stros′i tē) n., pl. **-ties.** grotesquely abnormal thing.

mon′strous (-strəs) adj. **1.** huge. **2.** frightful.

Mont., Montana.

mon•tage′ (mon tazh′; Fr. môn tazh′) n. blending of elements from several pictures into one.

month (munth) n. any of twelve parts of calendar year.

month′ly, n., pl. **-lies,** adv. **—adj. 1.** occurring, appearing, etc., once a month. **2.** lasting for a month. **—n. 3.** periodical published once a month. **—adv. 4.** once a month. **5.** by the month.

mon′u•ment (mon′yə mənt) n. memorial structure.

mon'u•men'tal (-men'tl) adj. **1.** imposing. **2.** serving as monument.

moo (mōō) n. **1.** sound cow makes. —v. **2.** utter such sound.

mooch (mōōch) Slang. —v. **1.** try to get without paying. —n. **2.** Also, **mooch'er.** person who mooches.

mood (mōōd) n. **1.** frame of mind.

mood'y, adj., **-ier, -iest.** given to bad moods. —**mood'i•ly,** adv.

moon (mōōn) n. **1.** body which revolves around earth monthly. **2.** month. —v. **3.** gaze dreamily.

moon'light', n. **1.** light from moon. —v. **2.** work at second job after principal one.

moon'shine', n. illegally made liquor. —**moon'shin'er,** n.

moon'stone', n. pearly gem.

moor (mōōr) v. **1.** secure (ship), as at a dock. —n. **2.** Brit. open peaty wasteland.

moor'ing, n. **1.** (pl.) cables, etc., by which ship is moored. **2.** place where ship is moored.

moose (mōōs) n., pl. **moose.** large animal of deer family.

moot (mōōt) adj. debatable.

mop (mop) n., v., **mopped, mopping.** —n. **1.** piece of cloth, etc., fastened to stick, for washing or dusting. —v. **2.** clean with mop. **3.** Mil. **mop up,** destroy final resisting elements.

mope (mōp) v., **moped, moping.** be in low spirits.

mo'ped' (mō'ped') n. motorized bicycle.

mop'pet (mop'it) n. child.

mor'al (môr'əl) adj. **1.** of or concerned with right conduct. **2.** virtuous. —n. **3.** (pl.) principles of conduct. **4.** Moral lesson. —**mor'al•ist,** n. —**mor'al•is'tic, adj.**

mo•rale' (mə ral') n. spirits; mood.

mo•ral'i•ty (mə ral'i tē, mô-) n. **1.** conformity to rules of right conduct. **2.** moral quality.

mor'al•ize' (môr'ə līz') v., **-ized, -izing.** think or pronounce on moral questions.

mor'al•ly, adv. **1.** according to morals. **2.** in one's honest belief.

mo•rass' (mə ras') n. swamp.

mor'a•to'ri•um (môr'ə tôr'ē əm) n., pl. **-to•ri•a** (tôr'ē ə), **-to•ri•ums. 1.** legal permission to delay payment of debts. **2.** any temporary cessation.

mo'ray (môr'ā, mô rā') n. tropical eel.

mor'bid (môr'bid) adj. **1.** unwholesome. **2.** of disease. —**mor'bid'i•ty,** n. —**mor'bid•ly,** adv.

mor'dant (môr'dnt) adj. **1.** sarcastic; biting. **2.** burning; corrosive.

more (môr) adj. **1.** in greater amount or degree. **2.** additional. —n. **3.** additional or greater quantity or degree. —adv. **4.** in addition.

mo•rel' (mə rel') n. edible mushroom.

more•o•ver, adv. besides.

mo'res (môr'āz, -ēz) n.pl. social and moral customs of group.

morgue (môrg) n. place where corpses are taken for identification.

mor'i•bund' (môr'ə bund') adj. dying.

Mor'mon•ism (môr'mən iz'əm) n. religion founded in U.S. in 1830. —**Mor'mon,** n., adj.

morn (môrn) n. morning.

morn'ing, n. **1.** first part of day. —adj. **2.** done, or occurring, in the morning.

morn'ing-glo'ry, n., pl. **-ries.** vine with funnel-shaped flowers.

morning sickness, nausea occurring early in the day during the first months of pregnancy.

mo•roc'co (mə rok'ō) n. fine leather.

mo'ron (môr'on) n. stupid person. —**mo•ron'ic** (mə ron'ik) adj.

mo•rose' (mə rōs') adj. gloomily ill-humored. —**mo•rose'ly,** adv.

mor'pheme (môr'fēm) n. minimal grammatical unit.

mor'phine (môr'fēn) n. narcotic found in opium.

mor•phol'o•gy (môr fol'ə jē) n. **1.** branch of biology dealing with form and structure of organisms. **2.** study of word formation.

Morse code (môrs) n. telegraphic code of long and short signals.

mor'sel (môr'səl) n. small amount.

mor'tal (môr'tl) adj. **1.** liable to death. **2.** causing death. **3.** extreme. —n. **4.** human being.

mor•tal'i•ty (môr tal'i tē) n., pl. **-ties. 1.** mortal nature. **2.** relative death rate.

mor'tar (môr'tər) n. **1.** bowl in which drugs, etc., are pulverized. **2.** short cannon. **3.** material used to bind masonry.

mor'tar•board', n. academic cap with square, flat top and tassel.

mort'gage (môr'gij) n., v., **-gaged, -gaging.** —n. **1.** conditional transfer of property as security for debt. —v. **2.** put mortgage on.

mor•ti'cian (môr tish'ən) n. undertaker.

mor'ti•fy' (môr'tə fī') v., **-fied, -fying. 1.** humiliate or shame. **2.** subdue (body) by abstinence or pain.

mor'tise (môr'tis) n., v., **-tised, -tis-**

ing. —n. **1.** slot in wood for tenon. —v. **2.** fasten by mortise.

mor'tu·ar'y (môr'chōo er'ē) n., pl. **-aries.** place where bodies are prepared for burial.

mo·sa'ic (mō zā'ik) n. **1.** design made of small colored pieces of stone.

mo'sey (mō'zē) v. Informal. stroll.

Mos'lem (moz'ləm, mos'-) n., adj. Muslim.

mosque (mosk) n. Muslim place of prayer.

mos·qui'to (mə skē'tō) n., pl. **-toes, -tos.** common biting insect.

moss (môs) n. **1.** small, leafy-stemmed plant growing on rocks, etc. —v. **2.** cover with moss.

moss'back' n. Informal. person having antiquated ideas.

most (mōst) adj. **1.** in greatest amount. **2.** majority of. —n. **3.** greatest quantity. —adv. **4.** to greatest extent.

most'ly, adv. **1.** in most cases. **2.** in greater part.

mote (mōt) n. small particle.

mo·tel' (mō tel') n. roadside hotel for automobile travelers.

moth (môth) n. insect, some of whose larvae eat cloth.

moth'ball' n. ball of camphor, etc., for repelling moths.

moth'er (muⁿ'ər) n. **1.** female parent. **2.** head of group of nuns. **3.** source. —adj. **4.** of, like, or being mother. **5.** native. —v. **6.** act as or like mother to. —**moth'er·hood'**, n. —**moth'er·ly,** adj.

moth'er-in-law', n., pl. **mothers-in-law.** mother of one's spouse.

moth'er·land', n. **1.** one's native land. **2.** land of one's ancestors.

moth'er-of-pearl', n. inner layer of certain shells.

mo·tif' (mō tēf') n. recurring subject or theme.

mo'tile (mōt'l, mō'til) adj. Biology. capable of moving spontaneously.

mo'tion (mō'shən) n. **1.** process of changing position. **2.** action or power of movement. **3.** formal proposal made in meeting. —v. **4.** indicate by gesture.

motion picture, series of photographs projected so rapidly that objects seem to be moving.

mo'ti·vate' (mō'tə vāt') v., **-vated, -vating.** give motive to. —**mo'ti·va'tion,** n.

mo'tive (-tiv) n. **1.** purpose; goal. —adj. **2.** of or causing motion.

mot'ley (mot'lē) adj. widely, often grotesquely, varied.

mo'to·cross' (mō'tə krôs') n. motorcycle race over rough terrain.

mo'tor (mō'tər) n. **1.** small, power-

ful engine. —adj. **2.** of or causing motion. **3.** of or operated by motor. —v. **4.** travel by automobile.

mo'tor·bike' n. small motorcycle.

mo'tor·boat' n. boat run by motor.

mo'tor·cade' (-kād') n. procession of automobiles.

mo'tor·car' n. automobile.

mo'tor·cy'cle, n. heavy motor-driven bicycle. —**mo'tor·cy'clist,** n.

mo'tor·ist, n. automobile driver.

mo'tor·ize', v., **-ized, -izing.** furnish with motors or motor-driven vehicles.

mot'tle (mot'l) v., **-tled, -tling.** mark with spots or blotches.

mot'to (mot'ō) n., pl. **-toes, -tos.** phrase expressing one's guiding principle.

moue (mōō) n., pl. **moues** (mōō) pouting grimace.

mould n. mold.

mould'er, v. molder.

moult (mōlt) v., n. molt.

mound (mound) n. heap of earth; hill.

mount (mount) v. **1.** go up; get on; rise. **2.** prepare for use or display. **3.** fix in setting. —n. **4.** act or manner of mounting. **5.** horse for riding. **6.** Also, **mounting.** support, setting, etc. **7.** hill.

moun'tain (moun'tn) n. lofty natural elevation on earth's surface. —**moun'tain·ous,** adj.

mountain bike, bicycle designed for off-road use, usu. having smaller frame and wider tires.

moun'tain·eer' n. **1.** mountain climber. —**moun'tain·eer'ing,** n.

mountain lion, cougar.

moun'te·bank' (moun'tə bangk') n. charlatan.

mourn (môrn) v. grieve; feel or express sorrow (for). —**mourn'er,** n. —**mourn'ful,** —**mourn'ing,** n.

mouse (n. mous; v. also mouz) n., pl. **mice** (mīs), v., **moused, mousing.** —n. **1.** small rodent. **2.** palm-sized device used to select items on computer screen. —v. (mouz) **3.** hunt for mice.

mousse (mōōs) n. **1.** frothy dessert. **2.** foamy preparation used to style hair.

mous·tache' (mus'tash, mə stash') n. mustache.

mous'y (mou'sē, -zē) adj., **-ier, -iest.** drably quiet.

mouth n., adj. **mouths,** v. —n. (mouth) **1.** opening through which animal eats. **2.** any opening. —v. (mouth) **3.** utter pompously or dishonestly. —**mouth'ful',** n.

mouth organ, harmonica.

mouth′piece′, n. **1.** piece held in or to mouth. **2.** spokesperson.

mouth′wash′, n. solution for cleaning the mouth.

mouth′-wa′ter·ing, adj. appetizing, as in appearance or aroma.

mou′ton (mōō′ton) n. processed sheepskin.

move (mōōv) v., moved, moving, n. —v. **1.** change place or position. **2.** change one's abode. **3.** advance. **4.** make formal proposal in meeting. **5.** affect emotionally. —n. **6.** act of moving. **7.** purposeful action.

move′ment, n. **1.** act or process of moving. **2.** trend in thought. **3.** works of mechanism. **4.** principal division of piece of music.

moving picture, motion picture. Also, **mov′ie.**

mow, v., mowed, mowed or mown, mowing, n. —v. (mō) **1.** cut (grass, etc.). **2.** kill indiscriminately. —n. (mou) **3.** place in barn where hay, etc., are stored. **—mow′er,** n.

moz′za·rel′la (mot′sə rel′lə, mōt′-) n. mild, white, semisoft cheese.

MP, 1. a member of Parliament. **2.** Military Police.

mph, miles per hour.

Mr. (mis′tər) pl. **Messrs.** (mes′ərz) Mister; title of address for man.

MRI, magnetic resonance imaging: process of producing images of the body using strong magnetic field and low-energy radio waves.

Mrs. (mis′iz, miz′iz) pl. **Mmes.** (mā dām′, -dam′) title of address for married woman.

MS, 1. Also, **ms, ms** manuscript. **2.** Mississippi. **3.** multiple sclerosis.

Ms. (miz) title of address for woman not to be distinguished as married or unmarried.

M.S., Master of Science.

MSG, monosodium glutamate.

MT, Montana.

much (much) adj. **1.** in great quantity or degree. —n. **2.** great quantity. **3.** notable thing. —adv. **4.** greatly. **5.** generally.

mu′ci·lage (myōō′sə lij) n. gummy adhesive.

muck (muk) n. **1.** filth. **2.** moist barn refuse. **—muck′y,** adj.

muck′rake′, v., -raked, -raking. expose scandal. **—muck′rak′er,** n.

mu′cous (myōō′kəs) adj. **1.** secreting mucus. **2.** of or like mucus.

mucous membrane, membrane lining internal surface of organ.

mu′cus (-kəs) n. sticky secretion of mucous membrane.

mud (mud) n. **1.** wet soft earth. **2.**

malicious statements. **—mud′dy,** adj., v.

mud′dle (mud′l) v., -dled, -dling. —v. **1.** mix up; confuse. —n. **2.** confusion.

mud′dle·head′ed, adj. confused in one's thinking.

mud′sling′ing, n. efforts to discredit opponent by malicious remarks.

mu·ez′zin (myōō ez′in, mōō-) n. crier who summons Muslims to prayer.

muff (muf) n. **1.** tubular covering for hands. —v. **2.** bungle. **3.** drop (ball) after catching.

muf′fin (muf′in) n. small round bread.

muf′fle (muf′əl) v., -fled, -fling. **1.** wrap in scarf, cloak, etc. **2.** deaden (sound).

muf′fler (muf′-) n. **1.** heavy neck scarf. **2.** device for deadening sound.

muf′ti (muf′tē) n. civilian dress.

mug (mug) n., v., mugged, mugging. —n. **1.** drinking cup. **2.** Slang. face. —v. **3.** assault, usually with intent to rob. **—mug′ger,** n.

mug′gy, adj., -gier, -giest. hot and humid.

mug shot, photograph of the face of a criminal suspect.

Mu·ham′mad (mōō ham′əd, -hä′mad) n. founder of Islam, A.D. 570–632.

mu·lat′to (mə lat′ō, -lä′tō) n., pl. -toes. person with mixed black and white ancestry.

mul′ber′ry (mul′ber′ē, -bə rē) n., pl. -ries. tree, the leaves of some of whose species are used as food by silkworms.

mulch (mulch) n. **1.** loose covering of leaves, straw, etc., on plants. —v. **2.** surround with mulch.

mulct (mulkt) v. **1.** deprive of by trickery. **2.** fine.

mule (myōōl) n. **1.** offspring of donkey and mare. **2.** woman's house slipper.

mul′ish (myōō′lish) adj. obstinate.

mull (mul) v. **1.** study or ruminate (over). **2.** heat and spice.

mul′let (mul′it) n. common food fish.

mul′li·gan (mul′i gən) n. stew of meat and vegetables.

mul′li·ga·taw′ny (-gə tô′nē) n. curry-flavored soup.

mul′lion (mul′yən) n. vertical member separating lights of window.

multi-, prefix meaning many.

mul′ti·cul′tur·al·ism (mul′tē kul′-char ə liz′əm, mul′tī-) n. recognition of different cultural identities within unified society.

mul′ti·far′i·ous (mul′tə fâr′ē əs) *adj.* many and varied.

mul′ti·me′di·a (mul′tē-, mul′tī-) *n.* (*used with sing. v.*) combined use of several media or mass media.

mul′ti·na′tion·al, *n.* **1.** corporation with operations in many countries. —*adj.* **2.** pertaining to several nations or multinationals.

multiple sclerosis, disease marked by destruction of areas of brain and spinal cord.

mul′ti·plic′i·ty (-plis′i tē) *n.,* *pl.* **-ties.** great number or variety.

mul′ti·ply′ (mul′tə plī′) *v.,* **-plied, -plying. 1.** increase the number of. **2.** add (number) to itself a stated number of times. —**mul′ti·pli′er,** *n.* —**mul′ti·pli·ca′tion,** *n.*

mul′ti·tude′ (mul′ti tōōd′, -tyōōd′) *n.* great number.

mul′ti·tu′di·nous, *adj.* **1.** numerous. **2.** having many parts.

mum (mum) *adj.* silent.

mum′ble (mum′bəl) *v.,* **-bled, -bling,** *n.* —*v.* **1.** speak quietly and unintelligibly. —*n.* **2.** mumbling sound.

mum′ble·ty·peg′ (mum′bəl tē peg′) *n.* game in which pocketknife is flipped so it sticks in ground. Also, **mum′ble-the-peg′** (-thə-).

mum′bo jum′bo (mum′bō jum′bō) senseless language.

mum′mer (mum′ər) *n.* **1.** person in festive disguise. **2.** actor.

mum′my (mum′ē) *n.,* *pl.* **-mies.** dead body treated to prevent decay.

mumps (mumps) *n.pl.* disease marked by swelling of salivary glands.

munch (munch) *v.* chew.

mun·dane′ (mun dān′, mun′dān) *adj.* commonplace.

mu·nic′i·pal (myōō nis′ə pəl) *adj.* of a city.

mu·nic′i·pal′i·ty (-pal′i tē) *n.,* *pl.* **-ties.** self-governing city.

mu·nif′i·cent (myōō nif′ə sənt) *adj.* extremely generous. —**mu·nif′i·cence,** *n.* —**mu·nif′i·cent·ly,** *adv.*

mu·ni′tions (myōō nish′ənz) *n.pl.* weapons and ammunition.

mu′ral (myōōr′əl) *n.* **1.** picture painted on wall. —*adj.* **2.** of walls.

mur′der (mûr′dər) *n.* **1.** unlawful willful killing. —*v.* **2.** commit murder. —**mur′der·er,** *n.* —**mur′der·ess,** *n.fem.* —**mur′der·ous,** *adj.*

murk (mûrk) *n.* darkness.

murk′y, *adj.,* **-ier, -iest.** dark and gloomy. —**murk′i·ness,** *n.*

mur′mur (mûr′mər) *n.* **1.** low, continuous, indistinct sound. **2.** complaint. —*v.* **3.** speak softly or indistinctly. **4.** complain.

mus′ca·dine (mus′kə din, -dīn′) *n.* American grape.

mus′cat (mus′kat, -kət) *n.* sweet grape.

mus·ca·tel′ (mus′kə tel′) *n.* wine made from muscat grapes.

mus′cle (mus′əl) *n.,* *v.,* **-cled, -cling.** —*n.* **1.** bundle of fibers in animal body that contract to produce motion. **2.** brawn. —*v.* **3.** *Informal.* force one's way. —**mus′cu·lar** (-kyə lər) *adj.*

mus′cle·bound′, *adj.* having enlarged and inelastic muscles.

muscular dys′tro·phy (dis′trə fē) hereditary disease characterized by gradual wasting of muscles.

muse (myōōz) *v.,* **mused, musing.** reflect quietly.

Muse (myōōz) *n.* one of nine goddesses of the arts.

mu·se′um (myōō zē′əm) *n.* place for permanent public exhibits.

mush (mush *or,* *esp.* for 2, 3, mōōsh) *n.* **1.** meal boiled in water until thick, used as food. **2.** anything soft. **3.** *Informal.* maudlin sentiment. —*v.* **4.** travel on foot, esp. with dog team. —**mush′y,** *adj.*

mush′room (mush′rōōm, -rōōm) *n.* **1.** fleshy fungus, usu. umbrella-shaped, sometimes edible. —*v.* **2.** grow quickly.

mu′sic (myōō′zik) *n.* **1.** art of arranging sounds for effect by rhythm, melody, etc. **2.** score of musical composition. —**mu·si′cian** (-zish′ən) *n.*

mus′i·cal, *adj.* **1.** of music. **2.** pleasant-sounding. **3.** sensitive to or skilled in music. —*n.* **4.** Also, **mus′ical com′edy.** a play with music.

mu′si·col′o·gy (-zi kol′ə jē) *n.* scholarly or scientific study of music. —**mu′si·col′o·gist,** *n.*

music video, videotape featuring rendition of pop song.

musk (musk) *n.* fragrant animal secretion, used in perfume. —**musk′y,** *adj.*

mus′ket (mus′kit) *n.* early rifle.

mus·ket·eer′, *n.* soldier armed with musket.

musk′mel′on, *n.* sweet edible melon.

musk′ox′, *n.,* *pl.* **-oxen.** large mammal of arctic regions.

musk′rat′, *n.* large aquatic American rodent.

Mus•lim (muz′lim, mŏŏz′-, mŏŏs′-) *n.* **1.** follower of Islam. —*adj.* **2.** of or pertaining to Islam.

mus•lin (muz′lin) *n.* plain-weave cotton fabric.

muss (mus) *Informal.* —*n.* **1.** disorder. —*v.* **2.** rumple. —**muss′y,** *adj.*

mus•sel (mus′əl) *n.* bivalve mollusk, sometimes edible.

must (must) *aux. v.* **1.** be obliged to. **2.** may be assumed to. —*adj.* **3.** necessary. —*n.* **4.** anything necessary. **5.** new wine not yet fermented.

mus•tache (mus′tash, mə stash′) *n.* hair growing on upper lip.

mus•tang (mus′tang) *n.* small wild horse of western U.S.

mus•tard (mus′tərd) *n.* pungent yellow powder made from seeds of mustard plant.

mustard gas, oily liquid with poisonous properties, used in warfare.

mus•ter (mus′tər) *v.* **1.** assemble, as troops; gather. —*n.* **2.** assembly.

mus•ty (mus′tē) *adj.,* **-tier, -tiest. 1.** stale-smelling. **2.** out-dated.

mu•ta•ble (myōō′tə bəl) *adj.* subject to change. —**mu′ta•bil′i•ty,** *n.*

mu•tant (myōōt′nt) *n.* organism resulting from mutation. —*adj.* **2.** resulting from mutation.

mu•tate (myōō′tāt) *v.,* **-tated, -tating.** change or cause to change.

mu•ta′tion, *n.* **1.** sudden change in genetic characteristic. **2.** individual or species characterized by such change. **3.** change.

mute (myōōt) *adj.,* **muter, mutest,** *n., v.,* **muted, muting.** —*adj.* **1.** silent. **2.** incapable of speech. —*n.* **3.** person unable to utter words. **4.** device for muffling musical instrument. —*v.* **5.** deaden sound of.

mu•ti•late (myōōt′l āt′) *v.,* **-lated, -lating.** injure by depriving of or damaging part. —**mu′ti•la′tion,** *n.*

mu•ti•ny (myōōt′n ē) *n., pl.* **-nies,** *v.,* **-nied, -nying.** revolt against lawful authority. —**mu′ti•neer′,** *n.* —**mu′ti•nous,** *adj.*

mutt (mut) *n. Slang.* mongrel dog.

mut•ter (mut′ər) *v.* **1.** speak low and indistinctly; grumble. —*n.* **2.** act or sound of muttering.

mut•ton (mut′n) *n.* flesh of sheep, used as food.

mut•ton-chops′, *n.pl.* side whiskers that are narrow at temples and broad and short at jawline.

mu•tu•al (myōō′chŏŏ əl) *adj.* **1.** done, etc., by two or more in relation to each other. **2.** common.

mutual fund, investment company that invests money of its shareholders.

muz•zle (muz′əl) *n., v.,* **-zled, -zling.** —*n.* **1.** mouth of firearm. **2.** animal's jaws. **3.** cage for this. —*v.* **4.** put muzzle on. **5.** silence.

my (mī) *pron.* possessive form of **I** used before noun.

my•col•o•gy (mī kol′ə jē) *n.* study of fungi. —**my•col′o•gist,** *n.*

my′na (mī′nə) *n.* Asiatic bird sometimes taught to talk.

my•o•pi•a (mī ō′pē ə) *n.* nearsightedness. —**my•op′ic** (-op′ik, -ō′pik) *adj.*

myr′i•ad (mir′ē əd) *n., adj.* very great number.

myrrh (mûr) *n.* aromatic substance from certain plants.

myr′tle (mûr′tl) *n.* **1.** evergreen shrub. **2.** periwinkle (def. 2).

my•self′, *pron.,* pl. **ourselves. 1.** intensive form of **I** or **me. 2.** reflexive form of **me.**

mys•ter•y (mis′tə rē) *n., pl.* **-teries. 1.** anything secret, unknown, or unexplained. **2.** obscurity. **3.** secret rite. —**mys•te′ri•ous** (mi stēr′ē əs) *adj.* —**mys•te′ri•ous•ly,** *adv.*

mys•tic (mis′tik) *adj.* Also, **mys′ti•cal. 1.** mysterious or occult. **2.** spiritual. —*n.* **3.** believer in mysticism.

mys•ti•cism (-tə siz′əm) *n.* doctrine of direct spiritual intuition of God, truth, etc.

mys•ti•fy′, *v.,* **-fied, -fying.** bewilder purposely.

mys•tique′ (mi stēk′) *n.* aura of mystery or power.

myth (mith) *n.* **1.** legendary story, person, etc. **2.** false popular belief. —**myth′i•cal,** *adj.*

my•thol•o•gy (mi thol′ə jē) *n., pl.* **-gies.** body of myths. —**myth′o•log′i•cal** (mith′ə loj′i kəl) *adj.*

N

N, n (en) *n.* fourteenth letter of English alphabet.

N, north, northern.

nab (nab) *v.,* **nabbed, nabbing.** *Informal.* seize; arrest.

na′bob (nā′bob) *n.* wealthy, influential, or powerful person.

na′cre (nā′kər) *n.* mother-of-pearl.

na′dir (nā′dər, -dēr) *n.* **1.** lowest point. **2.** point of celestial sphere directly below given point.

nag (nag) *v.,* **nagged, nagging.** —*v.* **1.** scold constantly. —*n.* **2.** person who nags. **3.** old horse.

nai′ad (nā′ad, -əd, nī′-) *n.* water nymph.

nail (nāl) *n.* **1.** slender piece of metal for holding pieces of wood together. **2.** horny plate at end of finger or toe. —*v.* **3.** fasten with nails. **4.** *Informal.* secure or seize.

na·ive′ (nä ēv′) *adj.* simple; unsophisticated. Also, **na·ïve·té′.**

na·ive·té′ (nä ēv tā′) *n.* artless simplicity. Also, **na·ïve·té′.**

na′ked (nā′kid) *adj.* **1.** without clothing or covering. **2.** (of eye) unassisted in seeing. **3.** plain.

name (nām) *n., v.,* **named, naming.** —*n.* **1.** word or words by which a person, place, or thing is designated. **2.** reputation. **3.** behalf or authority. —*v.* **4.** give name to. **5.** specify. **6.** appoint.

name′less, *adj.* **1.** having no name. **2.** not referred to by name.

name′ly, *adv.* that is to say.

name′sake′, *n.* one having same name as another.

nan′ny (nan′ē) *n., pl.* **-nies.** child's nursemaid.

nanny goat, female goat.

nan′o·sec′ond (nan′ə sek′ənd, na-) *n.* one billionth of a second.

nap (nap) *n., v.,* **napped, napping.** —*n.* **1.** short sleep. **2.** short, fuzzy fibers on the surface of cloth. —*v.* **3.** raise fuzz on. **4.** have short sleep.

na′palm (nā′päm) *n.* **1.** highly incendiary jellylike substance used in bombs, etc. —*v.* **2.** bomb or attack with napalm.

nape (nāp, nap) *n.* back of neck.

naph′tha (naf′thə, nap′-) *n.* petroleum derivative.

nap′kin (nap′kin) *n.* piece of cloth or paper used at table to wipe lips or fingers.

na·po·le·on (nə pō′lē ən, -pōl′yən) *n.* flaky pastry with cream filling.

nar·cis·sis′tic (-sis′tik) *adj.* excessive admiration of oneself. —**nar′cis·sis′tic** (-sis′tik) *adj.*

nar·cis′sus (när sis′əs) *n.* spring-blooming plant, as daffodil or jonquil.

nar·co′sis (när kō′sis) *n.* stupor.

nar·cot′ic (-kot′ik) *adj.* **1.** sleep-inducing. —*n.* **2.** substance that dulls pain, induces sleep, etc. **3.** addictive drug, esp. an illegal one.

nar′rate (nar′āt, na rāt′) *v.,* **-rated, -rating.** tell. —**nar·ra′tion,** *n.* —**nar′ra·tor,** *n.*

nar′ra·tive (-ə tiv) *n.* **1.** story of events. —*adj.* **2.** that narrates. **3.** of narration.

nar′row (nar′ō) *adj.* **1.** not broad or wide. **2.** literal or strict in interpreting rules, etc. **3.** minute. —*v.* **4.** make or become narrow. —*n.* **5.** narrow place, thing, etc.

nar′row-mind′ed, *adj.* unwilling to accept new ideas.

nar′whal (när′wəl) *n.* Arctic whale.

NASA (nas′ə) *n.* National Aeronautics and Space Administration.

na′sal (nā′zəl) *adj.* **1.** of noses. **2.** spoken through nose. —*n.* **3.** nasal sound. —**na′sal·ly,** *adv.*

nas′cent (nas′ənt, nā′sənt) *adj.* beginning to exist or develop.

na·stur′tium (nə stûr′shəm, na-) *n.* garden plant with yellow, orange, or red flowers.

nas′ty (nas′tē) *adj.,* **-tier, -tiest. 1.** disgustingly unclean. **2.** objectionable. —**nas′ti·ly,** *adv.*

na′tal (nāt′l) *adj.* of one's birth.

na′tion (nā′shən) *n.* **1.** people living in one territory under same government. **2.** people related by tradition or ancestry. —**na′tion·al** (nash′ə nl) *adj., n.*

na′tion·al·ism (nash′ə nl iz′əm) *n.* devotion to one's nation. —**na′tion·al·ist,** *n., adj.*

na′tion·al′i·ty (nash′ə nal′i tē) *n., pl.* **-ties. 1.** condition of being member of a nation. **2.** nation.

na′tion·al·ize′, *v.,* **-ized, -izing.** bring under national control.

na′tion·wide′ (nā′shən-) *adj., adv.* across entire nation.

na′tive (nā′tiv) *adj.* **1.** belonging to by birth, nationality, or nature. **2.** of natives. **3.** being the place of origin of a person or thing. —*n.* **4.** person, animal, or plant native to region.

Native American, American Indian.

na·tiv′i·ty (nə tiv′i tē) *n., pl.* **-ties.** birth.

NATO (nā′tō) *n.* North Atlantic Treaty Organization.

nat′ty (nat′ē) *adj.,* **-tier, -tiest.** neat; trim.

nat′u·ral (nach′ər əl) *adj.* **1.** of, existing in, or formed by nature. **2.** to be expected in circumstances. **3.** without affectation. **4.** *Music.* neither sharp nor flat. —**nat′u·ral·ly,** *adv.* —**nat′u·ral·ness,** *n.*

natural childbirth, childbirth without use of drugs.

natural gas, mixture of gaseous hydrocarbons that accumulates in porous sedimentary rocks.

natural history, study of natural objects.

nat′u·ral·ism (-ər ə liz′əm) *n.* artistic or literary style that represents objects or events as they occur in nature or real life. —**nat′u·ral·is′tic,** *adj.*

nat′u·ral·ist, *n.* **1.** student of nature. **2.** adherent of naturalism.

nat′u·ral·ize′, *v.,* **-ized, -izing. 1.** confer citizenship upon. **2.** introduce to region.

natural resource, source of wealth occurring in nature.

natural selection, process by which life forms having traits that enable them to adapt to the environment will survive in greater numbers.

na′ture (nā′chər) *n.* **1.** natural world. **2.** universe. **3.** one's character. **4.** kind or sort.

naught (nôt) *n.* zero.

naugh′ty (nô′tē) *adj.,* **-tier, -tiest. 1.** disobedient; bad. **2.** improper.

nau′sea (nô′zē ə, -zhə, -sē ə, -shə) *n.* **1.** feeling of impending vomiting. **2.** disgust. —**nau′se·ate** (-zē āt′, -zhē-, -sē-, -shē-) *v.* —**nau′seous** (-shəs, -zē əs) *adj.*

nau′ti·cal (nô′ti kəl) *adj.* of ships, sailors, or navigation.

nautical mile, unit of distance equal to 1.852 kilometers.

nau′ti·lus (nôt′l əs) *n.* mollusk having pearly shell.

Nav′a·jo′ (nav′ə hō′, nä′və-) *n., pl.* **-jo, -jos, -joes.** member of an American Indian people of the Southwest.

na′val (nā′vəl) *adj.* of ships or navy.

nave (nāv) *n.* main lengthwise part of church.

na′vel (nā′vəl) *n.* pit in center surface of belly.

nav′i·gate′ (nav′i gāt′) *v.,* **-gated, -gating. 1.** traverse (water or air). **2.** direct on a course. —**nav′i·ga·tor,** *n.* —**nav′i·ga·ble,** *adj.*

na′vy (nā′vē) *n., pl.* **-vies.** a nation's warships and crews.

navy blue, dark blue.

nay (nā) *adv., n.* no.

Na′zi (nät′sē, nat′-) *n.* member of the National Socialist party in Germany, headed by Adolf Hitler. —**Na′zism,** *n.*

NB, nota bene.

NC, North Carolina. Also, **N.C.**

NC-17 (en′sē′sev′ən tēn′) *Trademark.* motion-picture rating advising that persons under 17 will not be admitted.

ND, North Dakota. Also, **N.D.**

N.Dak., North Dakota.

NE, 1. Nebraska. **2.** northeast.

neap tide (nēp) tide having lowest high point.

near (nēr) *adv.* **1.** close by. —*adj.* **2.** close. **3.** intimate. —*v.* **4.** approach. —**near′ness,** *n.*

near′by′, *adj.* close by.

near′ly, *adv.* almost.

near′sight′ed (-sī′tid, -sī′-) *adj.* seeing distinctly only at short distance. —**near′sight′ed·ness,** *n.*

neat (nēt) *adj.* **1.** orderly. **2.** skillful. **3.** undiluted. —**neat′ly,** *adv.*

neb (neb) *n.* bill or beak.

Nebr., Nebraska.

neb′u·la (neb′yə lə) *n., pl.* **-lae** (-lē′), **-las.** luminous mass of gas or stars. —**neb′u·lar,** *adj.*

neb′u·lous (neb′yə ləs) *adj.* **1.** hazy; vague. **2.** cloudlike.

nec′es·sar′y (nes′ə ser′ē) *adj., n., pl.* **-saries. 1.** that cannot be dispensed with. **2.** required by reason or reason; unavoidable. —*n.* **3.** something necessary.

ne·ces′si·tate′ (nə ses′i tāt′) *v.,* **-tated, -tating.** make necessary.

ne·ces′si·ty, *n., pl.* **-ties. 1.** something necessary. **2.** fact of being necessary. **3.** poverty.

neck (nek) *n.* **1.** part connecting head and trunk. —*v.* **2.** *Slang.* kiss and embrace amorously.

neck′er·chief (nek′ər chif, -chēf′) *n.* cloth worn around neck.

neck′lace (-lis) *n.* ornament of gems, etc., worn around neck.

neck′tie′, *n.* cloth strip worn under collar and tied in front.

nec′ro·man′cy (nek′rə man′sē) *n.* magic. —**nec′ro·man′cer,** *n.*

ne·cro′sis (nə krō′sis) *n.* death of tissue or of organ.

nec′tar (nek′tər) *n.* **1.** sweet secretion of flower. **2.** drink of gods.

nec′tar·ine′ (nek′tə rēn′) *n.* downless peach.

nee (nā) *adj.* (of woman) born; having as maiden name. Also, **née.**

need (nēd) *n.* **1.** requirement. **2.** condition marked by necessity. —*v.* **3.** depend absolutely or strongly. **4.** be obliged. —**need′less,** *adj.*

nee′dle (nēd′l) *n., v.,* **-dled, -dling.** —*n.* **1.** slender pointed implement for sewing, knitting, etc. **2.** anything similar, as indicator or gauge. **3.** hypodermic syringe. —*v.* **4.** prod.

nee′dle·point′, *n.* embroidery on canvas.

nee′dle·work′, *n.* art or product of working with a needle.

needs (nēdz) *adv.* necessarily.

need′y, *adj.,* **-ier, -iest.** very poor.

ne′er′-do·well′ (nâr′-) *n.* person who habitually fails.

ne·far′i·ous (ni fâr′ē əs) *adj.* wicked.

ne·gate′ (ni gāt′, neg′āt) *v.,* **-gated, -gating.** deny; nullify.

neg′a·tive (neg′ə tiv) *adj.* **1.** expressing denial or refusal. **2.** lacking positive attributes. **3.** *Math.* minus. *4. Photog.* having light and shade reversed. —*n. 5.* negative statement, etc. *6. Photog.* negative image.

ne·glect' (ni glekt') *v.* **1.** disregard; fail to do. **2.** disregard; negligence. —**ne·glect'ful,** *adj.*

neg'li·gee' (neg'li zhā', neg'li zhā') *n.* woman's house robe.

neg'li·gent (neg'li jant) *adj.* neglectful. —**neg'li·gence,** *n.*

neg'li·gi·ble (-jə bəl) *adj.* very small; unimportant.

ne·go'ti·a·ble (ni gō'shē ə bəl, -shə bəl) *adj.* transferable, as securities. —**ne·go'ti·a·bil'i·ty,** *n.*

ne·go'ti·ate' (-shē āt') *v.,* **-ated, -ating. 1.** deal with; bargain. **2.** dispose of. —**ne·go'ti·a'tion,** *n.* —**ne·go'ti·a'tor,** *n.*

Ne'gro (nē'grō) *n., pl.* **-groes.** *Sometimes Offensive.* member of racial group having brown to black skin. —**Ne'gro,** *adj.* —**Ne'groid** (-groid) *adj.*

neigh (nā) *n.* **1.** cry of horse; whinny. —*v.* **2.** make cry of horse.

neigh'bor (nā'bər) *n.* **1.** person or thing near another. —*v.* **2.** be near.

neigh'bor·hood, *n.* **1.** surrounding area. **2.** district having separate identity.

nei'ther (nē'thər, nī'-) *conj., adj.* not either. —**Pronunciation.** See EITHER.

nem'e·sis (nem'ə sis) *n., pl.* **-ses.** cause of one's downfall.

neo-, prefix meaning new, recent, or revived.

Ne'o·lith'ic (nē'ə lith'ik) *adj.* of the later Stone Age.

ne·ol'o·gism (nē ol'ə jiz'əm) *n.* new word or phrase.

ne'on (nē'on) *n.* gas used in electrical signs.

ne'o·nate' (nē'ə nāt') *n.* newborn child. —**ne'o·na'tal,** *adj.*

ne'o·phyte' (-fīt') *n.* beginner.

ne'o·plasm (nē'ə pla'zəm) *n.* tumor.

neph'ew (nef'yoo) *n.* son of one's brother or sister.

ne·phri'tis (nə frī'tis) *n.* inflammation of the kidneys.

ne'plus'ul'tra (nē' plus' ul'trə, nā') highest point.

nep'o·tism (nep'ə tiz'əm) *n.* favoritism based on family relationship.

Nep'tune (nep'tōōn, -tyōōn) *n.* planet eighth from the sun.

nerd (nûrd) *n. Slang.* **1.** dull, ineffectual, or unattractive person. **2.** person devoted to nonsocial pursuit.

nerve (nûrv) *n., v.,* **nerved, nerving.** —*n.* **1.** bundle of fiber that conveys impulses between brain and other parts of body. **2.** courage. **3.** *Informal.* presumption. **4.** (*pl.*) anxiety; unease. —*v.* **5.** give courage to.

nerve gas, poison gas that interferes with nerve functions.

nerv'ous, *adj.* **1.** of nerves. **2.** having or caused by disordered nerves. **3.** anxious. —**nerv'ous·ly,** *adv.*

nerv'y, *adj.,* **-ier, -iest.** *Informal.* presumptuous.

-ness, suffix meaning: quality or state, as *goodness.*

nest (nest) *n.* **1.** place used by animal for rearing its young. **2.** group of things fitting tightly together. —*v.* **3.** settle in nest. **4.** fit one within another.

nest egg, money saved for emergencies, retirement, etc.

nes'tle (nes'əl) *v.,* **-tled, -tling.** lie close and snug.

net (net) *adj., n., v.,* **netted, netting.** —*adj.* **1.** exclusive of loss, expense, etc. —*n.* **2.** net profit. **3.** Also, **net'ting.** lacelike fabric of uniform mesh. **4.** bag of such fabric. —*v.* **5.** gain as clear profit. **6.** cover with net. **7.** ensnare.

neth'er (neth'ər) *adj.* lower.

net'tle (net'əl) *n., v.,* **-tled, -tling.** —*n.* **1.** plant with stinging hairs. —*v.* **2.** irritate; sting.

net'tle·some (-səm) *adj.* **1.** causing irritation. **2.** easily provoked.

net'work', *n.* **1.** netlike combination. **2.** group of associated radio or television stations, etc. **3.** any system of interconnected elements. —*v.* **4.** share information informally with others who have common interests.

neu'ral (nŏŏr'əl, nyŏŏr'-) *adj.* of nerves or nervous system.

neu·ral'gia (nŏŏ ral'jə, nyŏŏ-) *n.* sharp pain along nerve.

neu·ri'tis (nŏŏ rī'tis, nyŏŏ-) *n.* inflammation of nerve.

neu·rol'o·gy (-rol'ə jē) *n.* study of nerves. —**neu·rol'o·gist,** *n.* —**neu'ro·log'i·cal** (nŏŏr'ə loj'i kəl) *adj.*

neu'ron (nŏŏr'on, nyŏŏr'-) *n.* cell that is basic to nervous system.

neu·ro'sis (nŏŏ rō'sis, nyŏŏ-) *n., pl.* **-ses.** psychoneurosis. —**neu·rot'ic** (-rot'ik) *adj., n.*

neu'ro·sur'ger·y (nŏŏr'ō sûr'jə rē, nyŏŏr'-) *n.* surgery of the brain or other nerve tissue.

neu'ro·trans·mit'ter, *n.* chemical substance that transmits nerve impulses across synapse.

neu'ter (nŏŏ'tər, nyŏŏ'-) *adj.* **1.** neither male nor female. —*v.* **2.** spay or castrate. —**neu'ter,** *n.*

neu′tral (nōō′trəl, nyōō′-) adj. **1.** taking no side in controversy. **2.** not emphatic or positive. —n. **3.** neutral person or state. —**neu′tral·i·ty** (-tral′i tē) n. —**neu′tral·ize′**, v., **-ized, -izing.** —**neu′tral·ly,** adv.

neu′tron (nōō′tron, nyōō′-) n. particle in nucleus of atom.

Nev., Nevada.

nev′er (nev′ər) adv. not ever.

nev·er·the·less′, adv. in spite of what has been said.

new (nōō, nyōō) adj. **1.** of recent origin or existence. **2.** unfamiliar. —adv. **3.** recently; freshly.

new′el (nōō′əl, nyōō′-) n. post at the head and foot of stair.

New England, group of states in northeast U.S.

new′fan′gled (-fang′gəld) adj. of a new kind or fashion.

new′ly, adv. **1.** recently. **2.** anew.

new′ly·wed′, n. newly married person.

news (nōōz, nyōōz) n. report of recent event.

news′cast′, n. broadcast of news. —**news′cast′er,** n.

news′let′ter, n. small informative periodical for specialized group.

news′man′, n. journalist. Also, **news′wom′an,** n.fem.

news′pa′per (nōōz′-, nyōōz′-) n. periodical containing news, etc.

news′print′, n. paper on which newspapers are printed.

news′reel′, n. motion picture of news events.

news′stand′, n. sales booth for periodicals.

news′wor′thy, adj. interesting enough to warrant press coverage.

newt (nōōt, nyōōt) n. salamander.

New Testament, portion of Christian Bible recording life and teachings of Christ and His disciples.

new′ton (nōōt′ən, nyōōt′n) n. unit of force.

new wave, movement that breaks with traditional values, etc.

new year, 1. (cap.) first day of year. **2.** year approaching.

next (nekst) adj. **1.** nearest after. —adv. **2.** in nearest place after. **3.** at first subsequent time.

next′-door′, adj. in the next house, apartment, etc.

nex′us (nek′səs) n., pl. **nexus.** link or connection.

NH, New Hampshire. Also, **N.H.**

ni′a·cin (nī′ə sin) n. nicotinic acid.

nib (nib) n. pen point.

nib′ble, v., **-bled, -bling.** —v. **1.** bite off in small bits. —n. **2.** small morsel.

nice (nīs) adj., **nicer, nicest. 1.** agreeable. **2.** precise. **3.** fastidious.

ni′ce·ty (nī′si tē) n., pl. **-ties. 1.** subtle point. **2.** refinement.

niche (nich) n. **1.** recess in wall. **2.** proper niche or vocation.

nick (nik) n. **1.** notch or hollow place in surface. **2.** precise or opportune moment. —v. **3.** make nick in.

nick′el (nik′əl) n. **1.** hard silver-white metal. **2.** five-cent coin.

nick′name′, n., v., **-named, -naming.** —n. **1.** name used informally. —v. **2.** give nickname to.

nic′o·tine (nik′ə tēn′) n. alkaloid found in tobacco.

niece (nēs) n. daughter of one's brother, sister, brother-in-law, or sister-in-law.

nif′ty (nif′tē) adj., **-tier, -tiest.** Informal. smart; fine.

nig′gard·ly (nig′ərd lē) adj. stingy.

nig′gling (nig′ling) adj. trivial.

nigh (nī) adv., adj. near.

night (nīt) n. period between sunset and sunrise.

night′cap′, n. **1.** alcoholic drink taken before bed. **2.** cap worn while sleeping.

night′club′, n. establishment open at night, offering food, drink, and entertainment.

night crawler, earthworm.

night′fall′, n. coming of night.

night′gown′, n. gown for sleeping.

night′hawk′, n. nocturnal American bird.

night′in·gale′, n. small European song bird.

night′ly, adj., adv. every night.

night′mare′ (-mâr′) n. **1.** bad dream. **2.** harrowing event.

night owl, person who often stays up late at night.

night′shade′, n. plant sometimes used in medicine.

night′shirt′, n. loose shirtlike garment worn in bed.

night stick, club carried by police officers.

ni′hil·ism (nī′ə liz′əm, nē′-) n. total disbelief in principles. —**ni′hil·ist,** n. —**ni′hil·is′tic,** adj.

nil (nil) n. nothing.

nim′ble (nim′bəl) adj., **-bler, -blest.** agile; quick. —**nim′bly,** adv.

nim′bus (nim′bəs) n., pl. **-bi** (-bī), **-buses. 1.** halo. **2.** rain cloud.

nim′rod (nim′rod) n. hunter.

nin′com·poop′ (nin′kəm pōōp′, ning′-) n. fool.

nine (nīn) n., adj. eight plus one. —**ninth,** n., adj.

nine′pins′, n.pl. bowling game played with nine wooden pins.

nine·teen', n., adj. ten plus nine.
—**nine·teenth'**, n., adj.

nine·ty, n., adj. ten times nine.
—**nine·ti·eth**, adj., n.

nin'ny, n., pl. -nies. fool.

nip (nip) v., nipped, nipping, n.
—v. 1. pinch or bite. 2. check
growth of. 3. affect sharply. 4. sip.
—n. 5. pinch. 6. biting quality. 7.
sip.

nip'ple, n. 1. milk-discharging protuberance on breast. 2. nipple-
shaped object.

nip'py, adj., -pier, -piest. 1. chilly.
2. pungent.

nir·va'na (nir vä'nə, -van'ə, nər-')
n. 1. (in Buddhism) freedom from
all passion. 2. state of bliss.

nit (nit) n. egg of louse.

ni'ter (nī'tər) n. white salt used in
gunpowder, etc. Also, **ni'tre**.

nit'-pick', v. Informal. argue or find
fault pettily.

ni'trate (nī'trāt, -trit) n. salt of ni-
tric acid.

ni'tric acid (nī'trik) caustic liquid
used in manufacture of explosives,
fertilizers, etc.

ni'tro·gen (nī'trə jən) n. colorless,
odorless, tasteless gas.

ni'tro·glyc·er·in (nī'trə glis'ər in) n.
colorless, highly explosive oil.

ni'trous (nī'trəs) adj. 1. of niter. 2.
Also, **ni'tric**. containing nitrogen.

nit'ty-grit'ty (nit'ē grit'ē) n. Slang.
essentials of situation.

nit'wit', n. stupid person.

nix (niks) adv. Informal. no.

NJ, New Jersey. Also, **N.J.**

NM, New Mexico.

N. Mex., New Mexico.

no (nō) adv., n., adj. **noes**, adj.
—adv. 1. word used to express dis-
sent, denial or refusal. —n. 2. negative vote. —adj. 3. not any.

no., 1. north. 2. number.

no·bil'i·ty (nō bil'i tē) n., pl. -ties.
1. noble class. 2. noble quality.

no'ble (nō'bəl) adj., -bler, -blest, n.
—adj. 1. of high rank by birth. 2.
admirable or magnificent. —n. 3.
person of noble rank. —**no'ble·**
man, n. —**no'ble·wom'an**, n.fem.

no·blesse' o·blige' (nō bles' ō-
blēzh') moral obligation of the rich
to display noble conduct.

no'bod'y, n., pl. -bodies. 1. no one. 2. no
one of importance.

no'-brain'er, n. Informal. something requiring little thought.

noc·tur'nal (nok tûr'nl) adj. 1. of
night. 2. occurring or active by
night.

noc'turne (-tûrn) n. dreamy or
pensive musical composition.

nod (nod) v., nodded, nodding, n.
—v. 1. incline head briefly. 2. become sleepy. 3. sway gently. —n.
4. brief inclination of head, as in
assent.

node (nōd) n. 1. protuberance. 2.
joint in plant stem.

nod'ule (noj'ōōl) n. small knob or
lump. —**nod'u·lar**, adj.

No·el' (nō el') n. Christmas.

no'-fault', adj. (of auto accident insurance, divorces, etc.) effective
without establishing fault.

nog'gin (nog'ən) n. small mug.

noise (noiz) n., v., noised, nois·ing.
—n. 1. sound, esp. loud or harsh.
—v. 2. spread rumors. —**nois'y**,
adj. —**nois'i·ly**, adv.

noi'some (noi'səm) adj. offensive.

no'mad (nō'mad) n. wanderer.
—**no·mad'ic**, adj.

no man's land, area between warring armies.

nom de plume (nom' də plōōm')
name assumed by writer.

no'men·cla'ture (nō'mən klā'chər)
n. set or system of names.

nom'i·nal (nom'ə nl) adj. 1. in
name only; so-called. 2. trifling.

nom'i·nate' (-nāt') v., -nated, -nat-
ing. 1. propose as candidate. 2. appoint. —**nom'i·na'tion**, n.

nom'i·na·tive (nom'ə nə tiv) adj.
1. denoting noun or pronoun used
as the subject of a sentence. —n.
2. nominative case.

nom'i·nee', n. one nominated.

non-, prefix meaning not.

non'age (non'ij, nō'nij) n. period
of legal minority.

non'a·ge·nar'i·an (non'ə jə när'ē-
ən, nō'nə-) n. person 90 to 99
years old.

non'cha·lant' (non'shə länt') adj.
coolly unconcerned. —**non'cha·**
lance', n. —**non'cha·lant'ly**, adv.

non'com·bat'ant (non'kəm bat'nt,
non kom'bə tnt) n. 1. member of
military force who is not a fighter.
2. civilian in wartime.

non'com·mis'sioned, adj. Mil. not
commissioned.

non'com·mit'tal, adj. not committing oneself.

non' com'pos men'tis (non' kom'-
pəs men'tis) Law. not of sound
mind.

non·con·duc'tor, n. substance that
does not readily conduct heat, electricity, etc.

non'con·form'ist, n. person who
refuses to conform.

non'de·script' (non'di skript') adj.
of no particular kind.

none (nun) pron. sing. and pl. 1.

not one; not any. —*adv.* **2.** in no way.

non·en·ti·ty, *n., pl.* **-ties.** unimportant person or thing.

none·the·less, *adv.* nevertheless.

no'-no', *n. Informal.* forbidden thing.

non·pa·reil' (non'pə rel') *adj.* **1.** having no equal. —*n.* **2.** person or thing without equal.

non·par·ti·san, *adj.* **1.** not taking sides. **2.** belonging to no party.

non·plus' (non plus', non'plus) *v.* confuse.

non·prof'it, *adj.* not profit motivated.

non·rep·re·sen·ta'tion·al, *adj.* not resembling any object in nature.

non·sec·tar'i·an, *adj.* of no one sect. —**nonsectarian,** *n.*

non'sense (non'sens, -səns) *n.* senseless or absurd words or action. —**non·sen'si·cal,** *adj.*

non se'qui·tur (non sek'wi tər, -toŏr') statement unrelated to preceding one.

non'stand'ard, *adj.* not conforming to usage considered acceptable by educated native speakers.

non'stop', *adj., adv.* without intermediate stops. Also, **non-stop.**

non'sup·port', *n.* failure to provide financial support.

non·un'ion, *adj.* **1.** not belonging to labor union. **2.** not produced by union workers.

non·vi'o·lence, *n.* policy of refraining from using violence. —**non·vi'o·lent,** *adj.*

noo'dle (nood'l) *n.* thin strip of dough, cooked in soup, etc.

nook (noŏk) *n.* corner of room.

noon (noon) *n.* 12 o'clock in daytime. —**noon'time', noon'tide',** *n.*

no one, not anyone.

noose (noos) *n., v.,* **noosed, noosing.** —*n.* **1.** loop with running knot that pulls tight. —*v.* **2.** catch by noose.

nor (nôr; *unstressed* nər) *conj.* or not: used with **neither.**

Nor'dic (nôr'dik) *n.* person marked by tall stature, blond hair, and blue eyes. —**Nor'dic,** *adj.*

norm (nôrm) *n.* standard.

nor'mal (nôr'məl) *adj.* **1.** of standard type; usual. —*n.* **2.** standard; average. —**nor'mal·cy, nor·mal'i·ty** (-mal'i tē) *n.* —**nor'mal·ize',** *v.,* **-ized, -izing.**

normal school, school for training teachers.

nor'ma·tive (nôr'mə tiv) *adj.* establishing a norm.

Norse (nôrs) *n.* inhabitants or speech of medieval Scandinavia.

north (nôrth) *n.* **1.** cardinal point of compass, on one's right facing the setting sun. **2.** territory or area to north. —*adj., adv.* **3.** toward, in, or from north. —**north'er·ly,** *adj., adv.* —**north'ern,** *adj.* —**north'ern·er,** *n.* —**north'ward,** *adj., adv.*

north'east', *n.* point or direction midway between north and east. —**north'east',** *adj., adv.* —**north'east'ern,** *adj.*

North Star, Polaris.

north'west', *n.* point or direction midway between north and west. —**north'west',** *adj., adv.* —**north'west'ern,** *adj.*

nose (nōz) *n., v.,* **nosed, nosing.** —*n.* **1.** part of head containing nostrils. **2.** sense of smell. **3.** projecting part. —*v.* **4.** smell. **5.** pry. **6.** head cautiously.

nose'cone', *n.* forward section of rocket.

nose'dive', *n.* **1.** downward plunge. —*v.* **2.** go into a nosedive.

nose'gay', *n.* small bouquet.

nosh (nosh) *Informal.* —*v.* **1.** snack (on). —*n.* **2.** snack.

no'-show', *n.* person who neither uses nor cancels reservation.

nos·tal'gia (no stal'jə) *n.* yearning for the past.

nos'tril (nos'trəl) *n.* external opening of nose for breathing.

nos'trum (nos'trəm) *n.* favorite or quack remedy.

nos'y (nō'zē) *adj.,* **-ier, -iest.** *Informal.* unduly inquisitive.

not (not) *adv.* word expressing negation, denial, or refusal.

no'ta be'ne (nō'tä ben'ē) *Latin.* note well.

no'ta·ble (nō'tə bəl) *adj.* **1.** worthy of note; important. —*n.* **2.** prominent person. —**no'ta·bly,** *adv.*

no'ta·rize' (nō'tə rīz') *v.,* **-rized, -rizing.** authenticate by notary.

no'ta·ry (nō'tə rē) *n., pl.* **-ries.** official authorized to verify documents. Also, **notary public.**

no·ta'tion (nō tā'shən) *n.* note. —**no·ta'tion·al,** *adj.*

notch (noch) *n.* **1.** angular cut. —*v.* **2.** make notch in.

note (nōt) *n., v.,* **noted, noting.** —*n.* **1.** brief record, comment, etc. **2.** short letter. **3.** importance. **4.** notice. **5.** paper promising payment. **6.** musical sound or written symbols. —*v.* **7.** write down. **8.** notice.

note'book', *n.* **1.** book with blank pages for writing notes. **2.** laptop computer.

not'ed, *adj.* famous.

note'wor'thy, *adj.* notable.

noth′ing (nuth′ing) *n.* **1.** not anything. **2.** trivial action, thing, etc. —*adv.* **3.** not at all.

noth′ing·ness, *n.* **1.** lack of being. **2.** unconsciousness.

no′tice (nō′tis) *n., v.,* **-ticed, -ticing.** —*n.* **1.** information; warning. **2.** note, etc., that informs or warns. **3.** attention; heed. —*v.* **4.** pay attention to; perceive. **5.** mention.

no′ti·fy, *v.,* **-fied, -fying.** give notice to. —**no′ti·fi·ca′tion,** *n.*

no′tion (nō′shan) *n.* **1.** idea; conception. **2.** opinion. **3.** whim. **4.** (*pl.*) small items, as pins or trim.

no·to′ri·ous (nō tôr′ē as, na-) *adj.* widely known, esp. unfavorably. —**no′to·ri′e·ty** (-ta rī′i tē) *n.*

not′with·stand′ing, *prep.* **1.** in spite of. —*adv.* **2.** nevertheless. —*conj.* **3.** although.

nou′gat (nōō′gat) *n.* pastelike candy with nuts.

nought (nôt) *n.* naught.

noun (noun) *n.* word denoting person, place, or thing.

nour′ish (nûr′ish, nur′-) *v.* sustain with food. —**nour′ish·ment,** *n.*

nou′veau riche′ (nōō′vō rēsh′) *pl.* **nou′veaux riches** (nōō′vō rēsh′). newly rich person.

nou·velle′ cuisine (nōō vel′) cooking that emphasizes fresh fruits and vegetables and light sauces.

Nov., November.

no′va (nō′va) *n., pl.* **-vas, -vae** (-vē). star that suddenly becomes much brighter, then gradually fades.

nov′el (nov′al) *n.* **1.** long fictitious narrative. —*adj.* **2.** new or strange. —**nov′el·ist,** *n.*

nov′el·ty, *n., pl.* **-ties. 1.** unfamiliarity. **2.** new or amusing thing.

No·vem·ber (nō vem′bar) *n.* eleventh month of year.

no·ve·na (nō vē′na, na-) *n., pl.* **-nae** (-nē), **-nas.** Roman Catholic devotion occurring on nine consecutive days.

nov′ice (nov′is) *n.* **1.** beginner. **2.** person just received into a religious order.

no·vi′ti·ate (nō vish′ē it, -āt′) *n.* period of being novice.

No′vo·caine′ (nō′va kān′) *Trademark.* local anesthetic.

now (nou) *adv.* **1.** at present time. **2.** immediately. —*conj.* **3.** since. —*n.* **4.** the present.

now′a·days′ (-a dāz′) *adv.* in these times.

no′where′, *adv.* not anywhere.

nox′ious (nok′shas) *adj.* harmful.

noz′zle (noz′al) *n.* projecting spout.

nth (enth) *adj.* utmost.

nu′ance (nōō′äns, nyōō′-) *n.* shade of expression, tone.

nub (nub) *n.* gist.

nu′bile (nōō′bil, -bīl, nyōō′-) *adj.* (of a young woman) **1.** marriageable. **2.** sexually attractive.

nu′cle·ar (nōō′klē ar, nyōō′-) *adj.* **1.** of or involving atomic weapons. **2.** of or forming a nucleus.

nuclear energy, energy released by reactions within atomic nuclei, as in nuclear fission or fusion.

nuclear family, social unit composed of father, mother, and children.

nuclear physics, branch of physics dealing with atoms.

nuclear winter, devastation, darkness, and cold that could result from nuclear war.

nu′cle·on (nōō′klē on′, nyōō′-) *n.* proton or neutron.

nu′cle·us (-klē as) *n., pl.* **-cle·i** (-klē ī′), **-cleuses. 1.** central part. **2.** central body of living cell. **3.** core of atom.

nude (nōōd, nyōōd) *adj.* **1.** naked. —*n.* **2.** naked human figure.

nudge (nuj) *v.,* **nudged, nudging,** *n.* —*v.* **1.** push slightly. —*n.* **2.** slight push.

nud′ism (nōō′diz əm, nyōō′-) *n.* practice of going naked. —**nud′ist,** *n.*

nug′get (nug′it) *n.* lump.

nui′sance (nōō′səns, nyōō′-) *n.* annoying thing or person.

nuke (nōōk, nyōōk) *n., v.,* **nuked, nuking.** *Slang.* —*n.* **1.** nuclear weapon or power plant. —*v.* **2.** attack with nuclear weapons.

null (nul) *adj.* of no effect.

null/i·fy, *v.,* **-fied, -fying. 1.** make null. **2.** make legally void.

numb (num) *adj.* **1.** deprived of feeling. —*v.* **2.** make numb.

num′ber (num′bar) *n.* **1.** sum of group of units. **2.** numeral. **3.** one of series or group. **4.** large quantity. —*v.* **5.** mark with number. **6.** count. **7.** amount to in numbers. —**Usage.** See AMOUNT.

num′ber·less, *adj.* too numerous to count.

nu′mer·al (nōō′mar al, nyōō′-) *n.* **1.** word or sign expressing number. —*adj.* **2.** of numbers.

nu′mer·ate′ (-ma rāt′) *v.,* **-ated, -ating.** number; count.

nu′mer·a′tor, *n.* part of fraction written above the line, showing number to be divided.

nu·mer′i·cal (nōō mer′i kəl, nyōō-) *adj.* of, denoting number.

nu′mer·ol′o·gy (nōō′ma rol′a jē,

nyōō'-) *n.* study of numbers to determine supernatural meaning.

nu•mer•ous (-mər əs) *adj.* very many.

nu•mis•mat•ics (nōō'miz mat'iks, -mis-, nyōō'-) *n.* science of coins and medals.

num/skull' (num'skul') *n. Informal.* dunce. Also, **numb/skull'.**

nun (nun) *n.* woman living with religious group under vows.

nun/ner•y (nun/ə rē) *n., pl.* -neries. convent.

nup/tial (nup'shəl, -chəl) *adj.* 1. of marriage. —*n.* 2. (*pl.*) marriage ceremony.

nurse (nûrs) *n., v.,* **nursed, nursing.** —*n.* 1. person who cares for sick or children. —*v.* 2. tend in sickness. 3. look after carefully. 4. suckle.

nurs/er•y *n., pl.* -eries. 1. room set apart for young children. 2. place where young plants are grown.

nursery school, school level below kindergarten age.

nur/ture (nûr/chər) *v.,* -tured, -turing, *n.* —*v.* 1. feed and care for during growth. —*n.* 2. upbringing. 3. nourishment.

nut (nut) *n.* 1. dry fruit consisting of edible kernel in shell. 2. the kernel. 3. perforated, threaded metal block used to screw on end of bolt. —**nut/crack/er,** *n.* —**nut/shell/,** *n.*

nut/hatch', *n.* small songbird that seeks food along tree trunks.

nut/meg (-meg) *n.* aromatic seed of East Indian tree.

nu/tri•ent (nōō'trē ənt, nyōō'-) *adj.* 1. nourishing. —*n.* 2. nutrient substance.

nu/tri•ment (-trə mənt) *n.* nourishment.

nu•tri/tion (-trish'ən) *n.* 1. process of nourishing or being nourished. 2. study of dietary requirements. —**nu•tri/tious, nu/tri•tive,** *adj.* —**nu•tri/tion•ist,** *n.*

nuts (nuts) *adj. Informal.* crazy.

nut/ty, *adj.,* -tier, -tiest. 1. tasting of or like nuts. 2. *Informal.* insane; senseless. —**nut/ti•ness,** *n.*

nuz/zle (nuz/əl) *v.,* -zled, -zling. 1. rub noses against. 2. cuddle.

NV, Nevada.

NW, northwest. Also, **N.W.**

NY, New York. Also, **N.Y.**

ny/lon (nī/lon) *n.* 1. tough, elastic synthetic substance used for yarn, bristles, etc. 2. (*pl.*) stockings of nylon.

nymph (nimf) *n.* 1. beautiful goddess. 2. beautiful girl.

nym/pho•ma/ni•a (nim'fə mā'nē ə) *n.* uncontrollable sexual desire in women. —**nym/pho•ma/ni•ac',** *n.*

O

O, o (ō) *n.* fifteenth letter of English alphabet.

O (ō) *interj.* (expression of surprise, gladness, pain, etc.)

o' (ə, ō) *prep.* shortened form of **of.**

oaf (ōf) *n.* clumsy, rude person. —**oaf/ish,** *adj.*

oak (ōk) *n.* tree having hard wood.

oar (ōr) *n.* 1. flat-bladed shaft for rowing boat. —*v.* 2. row. —**oars/man,** *n.*

oar/lock', *n.* support on gunwale for oar.

o•a/sis (ō ā'sis) *n., pl.* -ses. fertile place in desert.

oat (ōt) *n.* cereal grass having edible seed.

oath (ōth) *n.* 1. solemn affirmation; vow. 2. curse.

oat/meal/, *n.* 1. meal made from oats. 2. cooked breakfast food.

ob/du•rate (ob'dōō rit, -dyōō-) *adj.* stubborn; not sorry or penitent.

o•bei/sance (ō bā'səns, ō bē'-) *n.* 1. bow or curtsy. 2. homage.

ob/e•lisk (ob'ə lisk) *n.* tapering, four-sided monumental pillar.

o•bese/ (ō bēs') *adj.* very fat. —**o•bes/i•ty,** *n.*

o•bey/ (ō bā') *v.* 1. do as ordered by. 2. respond to, as controls. —**o•be/di•ence** (ō bē'dē əns) *n.* —**o•be/di•ent,** *adj.*

ob/fus•cate (ob'fə skāt', ob fus'kāt) *v.,* -cated, -cating. confuse; make unclear. —**ob/fus•ca'tion,** *n.*

ob/i•ter dic/tum (ob'i tər dik'təm) *pl.* **obiter dicta** (-tə) incidental remark.

o•bit/u•ar/y (ō bich'ōō er'ē) *n., pl.* -aries. notice of death.

obj., 1. object. 2. objective.

ob•ject/ *n.* (ob'jikt, -jekt) 1. something solid. 2. thing or person to which attention is directed. 3. end; motive. 4. noun or pronoun that represents goal of action. —*v.* (əb jekt') 5. make protest. —**ob•jec/tor,** *n.*

ob•jec/tion (əb jek'shən) *n.* 1. argument against. 2. act of objecting.

ob•jec/tion•a•ble (əb jek'shə nə bəl) *adj.* causing disapproval; offensive.

ob•jec/tive, *n.* 1. something aimed at. 2. objective case. —*adj.* 3. real or factual. **4.** unbiased. **5.** denoting word used as object of sentence. —**ob·jec·tiv′i·ty** (ob′jik tiv′i tē) *n.*

object lesson, practical illustration of principle.

ob·jet d'art (ob′zhā där′) *pl.* **objets d'art** (ob′zhā där′). object of artistic worth.

ob·late (ob′lāt, ō blāt′) *adj.* (of spheroid) flattened at poles.

ob·la′tion (o blā′shən) *n.* offering; sacrifice.

ob′li·gate (ob′li gāt′) *v.*, **-gated, -gating.** bind morally or legally. —**ob′li·ga′tion,** *n.*

ob·lig·a·to·ry (ə blig′ə tôr′ē) *adj.* compulsory.

o·blige′ (ə blīj′) *v.*, **obliged, obliging. 1.** require. **2.** do a favor for.

o·blig′ing, *adj.* willing to help.

ob·lique′ (ə blēk′, ō blēk′) *adj.* **1.** slanting. **2.** indirect. —**ob·lique′ly,** *adv.* —**ob·lique′ness,** *n.*

ob·lit′er·ate′ (ə blit′ə rāt′) *v.*, **-ated, -ating.** remove all traces of.

ob·liv·i·on (ə bliv′ē ən) *n.* state of being forgotten. **2.** forgetfulness. —**ob·liv′i·ous,** *adj.*

ob′long (ob′lông) *adj.* **1.** longer than broad. —*n.* **2.** oblong figure.

ob′lo·quy (ob′lə kwē) *n., pl.* **-quies.** public disgrace.

ob·nox′ious (əb nok′shəs) *adj.* offensive. —**ob·nox′ious·ly,** *adv.* —**ob·nox′ious·ness,** *n.*

o′boe (ō′bō) *n.* wind instrument. —**o′bo·ist,** *n.*

obs., obsolete.

ob·scene′ (əb sēn′) *adj.* offensive to decency. —**ob·scene′ly,** *adv.* —**ob·scen·i·ty** (-sen′i tē, -sē′ni-) *n.*

ob·scu′rant·ism (əb skyōōr′ən tiz′əm, əb·skyōō ran′tiz əm) *n.* willful obscuring of something presented to public. —**ob·scu′rant·ist,** *n.,*

ob·scure′ (əb skyōōr′) *adj., v.,* **-scured, -scuring.** —*adj.* **1.** not clear. **2.** not prominent. **3.** dark. —*v.* **4.** make obscure. —**ob·scu′ri·ty,** *n.* —**ob·scure′ly,** *adv.*

ob·se′qui·ous (əb sē′kwē əs) *adj.* servilely deferential.

ob′se·quy (ob′si kwē) *n., pl.* **-quies.** funeral rite.

ob·serv′ance (əb zûr′vəns) *n.* **1.** act of observing or conforming. **2.** due celebration of holiday or ritual.

ob·serv′ant, *adj.* quick to notice.

ob·serv·a·to·ry (əb zûr′və tôr′ē) *n., pl.* **-ries.** place equipped for observing stars.

ob·serve′ *v.,* **-served, -serving. 1.** see; notice; watch. **2.** remark. **3.** celebrate by ritual. —**ob′ser·va′tion** (ob′zər vā′shən) *n.*

ob·sess′ (əb ses′) *v.* be constantly

in the thoughts of. —**ob·ses′sion** (-sesh′ən) *n.* —**ob·ses′sive,** *adj.*

ob′so·les′cent (ob′sə les′ənt) *adj.* becoming obsolete. —**ob′so·les′cence,** *n.*

ob′so·lete′ (-lēt′) *adj.* no longer in use.

ob′sta·cle (ob′stə kəl) *n.* something in the way.

ob·stet′rics (əb ste′triks) *n.* branch of medicine concerned with childbirth. —**ob′ste·tri′cian** (ob′sti-trish′ən) *n.* —**ob·stet′ric,** *adj.*

ob′sti·nate (ob′stə nit) *adj.* **1.** firm; stubborn. **2.** not yielding to treatment. —**ob′sti·na·cy** (-nə sē) *n.* —**ob′sti·nate·ly,** *adv.*

ob·strep′er·ous (əb strep′ər əs) *adj.* unruly.

ob·struct′ (əb strukt′) *v.* block; hinder. —**ob·struc′tion,** *n.* —**ob·struc′tive,** *adj.*

ob·struc′tion·ism (-shə niz′əm) *n.* perverse desire to be obstructive.

ob·tain′ (əb tān′) *v.* **1.** get or acquire. **2.** prevail.

ob·trude′ (əb trōōd′) *v.,* **-truded, -truding.** thrust forward; intrude. —**ob·tru′sive** (-trō′siv) *adj.*

ob·tuse′ (əb tōōs′, -tyōōs′) *adj.* **1.** blunt. **2.** not perceptive. **3.** (of angle) between 90° and 180°.

ob′verse (n. ob′vûrs) *n.* **1.** front. **2.** side of coin having principal design. **3.** counterpart. —*adj.* (obvûrs′, ob′vûrs) **1.** facing. **2.** corresponding.

ob′vi·ate′ (ob′vē āt′) *v.,* **-ated, -ating.** make unnecessary.

ob′vi·ous (ob′vē əs) *adj.* **1.** readily perceptible. **2.** not subtle. —**ob′vi·ous·ly,** *adv.* —**ob′vi·ous·ness,** *n.*

oc′a·ri′na (ok′ə rē′nə) *n.* eggshaped wind instrument.

oc·ca′sion (ə kā′zhən) *n.* **1.** particular time. **2.** important time. **3.** opportunity. **4.** reason. —*v.* **5.** give cause for. —**oc·ca′sion·al,** *adj.* —**oc·ca′sion·al·ly,** *adv.*

Oc′ci·dent (ok′si dənt) *n.* West, esp. Europe and Americas. —**Oc′ci·den′tal** (-den′tl) *adj.*

oc·cult′ (ə kult′, ok′ult) *adj.* **1.** outside ordinary knowledge. —*n.* **2.** occult studies.

oc′cu·pa′tion (ok′yə pā′shən) *n.* **1.** trade. **2.** possession. **3.** military seizure. —**oc′cu·pa′tion·al,** *adj.*

occupational therapy, therapy utilizing activities for psychological or physical rehabilitation.

oc′cu·py, *v.,* **-pied, -pying. 1.** inhabit or be in. **2.** require as space. **3.** take possession of. **4.** hold attention of. —**oc′cu·pan·cy,** *n.* —**oc′cu·pant,** *n.*

oc·cur′ (ə kûr′) v., -curred, -curr- ing. **1.** take place. **2.** appear. **3.** come to mind. —**oc·cur′rence,** n.

o′cean (ō′shən) n. **1.** large body of salt water covering much of earth. **2.** any of its five main parts. —**o′- ce·an′ic** (ō′shē an′ik) adj.

o′cea·nog′ra·phy (ō′shə nog′rə fē, ō′shē ə-) n. study of oceans.

o′ce·lot′ (os′ə lot′, ō′sə-) n. small American wildcat.

o′cher (ō′kər) n. yellow-to-red earth used as pigment. Also, **o′- chre.**

o′clock′ (ə klok′) adv. by the clock.

Oct., October.

oc·ta·gon′ (ok′tə gon′, -gən) n. plane figure with eight sides.

oc′tane (ok′tān) n. colorless liquid hydrocarbon found in petroleum.

octane number, designation of quality of gasoline.

oc′tave (ok′tiv, -tāv) n. Music. **1.** eighth tone from given tone. **2.** in- terval between such tones.

oc·tet′ (ok tet′) n. group of eight, esp. musicians. Also, **oc·tette′.**

Oc·to′ber (ok tō′bər) n. tenth month of year.

oc′to·ge·nar′i·an (ok′tə jə nâr′ē- ən) n. person 80 to 89 years old.

oc′to·pus (ok′tə pəs) n., pl. -puses, -pi (-pī). eight-armed sea mollusk.

oc′u·lar (ok′yə lər) adj. of eyes.

oc′u·list (-list) n. doctor skilled in treatment of eyes.

OD (ō′dē′) n., pl. **ODs** or **OD's,** v., **OD'd** or **ODed, OD'ing.** Slang. —n. **1.** overdose of a drug, esp. a fatal one. —v. **2.** take a drug overdose.

odd (od) adj. **1.** eccentric; bizarre. **2.** additional; not part of set. **3.** not evenly divisible by two.

odd′ball′, n. Informal. peculiar per- son or thing.

odd′i·ty, n., pl. -ties. **1.** queerness. **2.** odd thing.

odds (odz) n. **1.** chances; probabil- ity for or against. **2.** state of disa- greement. **3.** odd things.

odds and ends, **1.** miscellany. **2.** remnants.

odds′-on′, adj. most likely.

ode (ōd) n. poem of praise.

o′di·ous (ō′dē əs) adj. hateful.

o′di·um (-am) n. **1.** discredit; re- proach. **2.** hatred.

o′dor (ō′dər) n. quality that affects sense of smell. —**o′dor·ous,** adj.

o′dor·if′er·ous (ō′də rif′ər əs) adj. having odor, esp. unpleasant.

od′ys·sey (od′ə sē) n. long, adven- turous journey.

oed′i·pal (ed′ə pəl, ē′də-) adj. (of- ten cap.) resulting from the Oedipus complex.

Oedipus complex, libidinous feelings of son toward mother.

o′er (ōr) prep., adv. Poetic. over.

oeu′vre (Fr. œ′vrə′) n., pl. **oeu·vres** (Fr. œ′vrə′). all the works of a writer, painter, etc.

of (uv, ov; unstressed əv or, esp. be- fore consonants, ə) prep. particle in- dicating: **1.** belonging to. **2.** belong- ing to. —aux. v. **3.** Nonstandard. have. —**Usage.** Because the preposition OF, when unstressed (a piece of cake), and the unstressed or contracted auxiliary verb HAVE (could have gone; could've gone) are both pronounced (əv) or (ə) in con- nected speech, inexperienced writ- ers commonly confuse the two words, spelling HAVE as OF (I would of handed in my book report, but the dog ate it). Professional writers use this spelling deliberately, espe- cially in fiction, to represent the speech of the uneducated: If he could of went home, he would of.

off (ôf) adv. **1.** up or away. **2.** devi- ating. **3.** out of operation or effect. —prep. **4.** up or away from. —adj. **5.** not operating or in effect. **6.** in error. **7.** starting on one's way.

off′al (ô′fəl) n. waste parts of butchered animal.

off′beat′ adj. Informal. unconven- tional.

off′-col′or, adj. **1.** not having the usual color. **2.** of questionable taste.

of·fend′ (ə fend′) v. **1.** err. **2.** an- noy greatly.

of·fend′er, n. **1.** person who of- fends. **2.** criminal.

of·fense′ (ə fens′) n. **1.** (ə fens′) wrong; sin. **2.** (ə fens′) displeasure. **3.** (ə fens′) attack. **4.** (ôf′ens) attacking side. Also, **of·fence′.**

of·fen′sive, adj. **1.** causing offense. —n. **2.** attack.

of′fer (ô′fər) v. **1.** present. **2.** pro- pose; suggest. —n. **3.** proposal; bid. —**of′fer·ing,** n.

of′fer·to·ry (-tôr′ē) n., pl. -ries. **1.** Rom. Cath. Ch. offering to God of bread and wine during Mass. **2.** collection at religious service.

off′hand′ adj. **1.** Also, **off′hand′- ed.** done without previous thought. **2.** curt. —**off′hand′ed·ly,** adv.

of′fice (ô′fis) n. **1.** place of busi- ness. **2.** position of authority. **3.** duty; task. **4.** religious service.

of′fice·hold′er, n. public official.

of′fi·cer, n. person of rank or au- thority.

of·fi′cial (ə fish′əl) n. **1.** person

who holds office. —*adj.* **2.** authorized. **3.** pertaining to public office.

of·fi·ci·ant (ə fish′ē ənt) *n.* cleric at religious service.

of·fi·ci·ate′ (-āt′) *v.,* **-ated, -ating.** perform official duties.

of·fi·cious, *adj.* too forward in offering unwanted help.

off′ing′ *n.* future.

off′-key′, *adj.* **1.** not in tune. **2.** somewhat incongruous or abnormal.

off′-lim′its, *adj.* forbidden to be patronized, used, etc.

off′-put′ting, *adj.* provoking uneasiness, annoyance, etc.

off·set′, *v.,* **-set, -setting.** compensate for.

off′shoot′, *n.* branch.

off′shore′, *adj., adv.* in water and away from shore.

off′spring′, *n.* children or descendants.

off′stage′, *adv., adj.* out of sight of audience.

off′-the-cuff′, *adj.* impromptu.

off′-the-rec′ord, *adj.* not to be quoted.

off′-the-wall′, *adj. Informal.* bizarre.

off year, 1. year without major election. **2.** year marked by reduced production.

oft (ôft) *adv. Poetic.* often.

of·ten (ôf′ən, ôf′tən) *adv.* **1.** frequently. **2.** in many cases.

o′gle (ō′gəl) *v.,* **ogled, ogling,** *n.* —*v.* **1.** eye with impertinent familiarity. —*n.* **2.** ogling glance.

o′gre (ō′gər) *n.* **1.** hideous giant who eats human flesh. **2.** cruel person. —**o′gress,** *n. fem.*

oh (ō) *interj.* (exclamation of surprise, etc.)

OH, Ohio.

ohm (ōm) *n.* unit of electrical resistance.

-oid, suffix meaning resembling or like.

oil (oil) *n.* **1.** greasy combustible liquid used for lubricating, heating, etc. —*v.* **2.** supply with oil. —*adj.* **3.** of oil. —**oil′y,** *adj.*

oil′cloth′, *n.* fabric made waterproof with oil.

oil′skin′, *n.* **1.** fabric made waterproof with oil. **2.** (*often pl.*) garment made of this.

oint′ment (oint′mənt) *n.* salve.

OK, Oklahoma.

OK (ō′kā′) *adj., adv., v.,* **OK′d, OK′ing,** *n., pl.* **OK′s.** —*adj., adv.* **1.** all right. —*v.* **2.** approve. —*n.* **3.** approval. Also, **O.K., o′kay′.**

Okla., Oklahoma.

o′kra (ō′krə) *n.* leafy vegetable with edible pods.

old (ōld) *adj.* **1.** far advanced in years or time. **2.** of age. **3.** Also, **old′en.** former; ancient. **4.** longstanding. —*n.* **5.** former time.

Old English, English language before c1150.

old′-fash′ioned, *adj.* having style, ideas, etc. of an earlier time.

Old Guard, (*sometimes l.c.*) conservative members of any group.

old hand, person with long experience.

old hat, old-fashioned; dated.

old school, supporters of established custom.

old′ster, *n. Informal.* elderly person.

Old Testament, complete Bible of the Jews, being first division of Christian Bible.

old′-tim′er, *n. Informal.* elderly person.

Old World, Europe, Asia, and Africa. —**old′-world′,** *adj.*

o′le·ag′i·nous (ō′lē aj′ə nəs) *adj.* **1.** oily. **2.** unctuous; fawning.

o′le·an′der (ō′lē an′dər) *n.* poisonous evergreen flowering shrub.

o′le·o·mar′ga·rine (ō′lē ō-) *n.* margarine. Also, **o′le·o′.**

ol·fac′to·ry (ol fak′tə rē, ōl-) *adj.* pertaining to sense of smell.

ol′i·gar′chy (-gär′kē) *n., pl.* **-chies.** government by small group.

ol′ive (ol′iv) *n.* **1.** evergreen tree valued for its small, oily fruit. **2.** fruit of this tree. **3.** yellowish green.

om·buds′man′ (om′badz mən, ombŏŏdz′-) *n., pl.* **-men.** official who investigates private individuals' complaints against government. Also, *fem.* **om·buds·wom′an.**

o·me′ga (ō mē′gə, ō meg′ə) *n.* last letter of Greek alphabet.

om′e·let (om′lit, om′ə-) *n.* eggs beaten and fried. Also, **om′e·lette.**

o′men (ō′mən) *n.* sign indicative of future.

om′i·nous (om′ə nəs) *adj.* threatening evil. —**om′i·nous·ly,** *adv.*

o·mit′ (ō mit′) *v.,* **omitted, omitting.** **1.** leave out. **2.** fail to do, etc. —**o·mis′sion** (ō mish′ən) *n.*

omni-, prefix meaning all.

om′ni·bus′ (om′nə bus′, -bəs) *n., pl.* **-buses. 1.** bus. **2.** anthology.

om·nip′o·tent (om nip′ə tənt) *adj.* almighty.

om′ni·pres′ent (om′nə prez′ənt) *adj.* everywhere at once.

om·nis′cient (om nish′ənt) *adj.* knowing all things.

om·niv·o·rous (om niv′ə əs) *adj.* eating all kinds of foods.

on (ôn) *prep.* particle expressing: **1.** position in contact with supporting surface. **2.** support; reliance. **3.** situation or direction. **4.** basis. *—adv.* **5.** onto a thing, place, or person. **6.** forward. **7.** into operation. *—adj.* **8.** in use. *—Usage.* See ABOUT.

once (wuns) *adv.* **1.** formerly. **2.** single time. **3.** at any time. *—conj.* **4.** if ever; whenever.

once′-o′ver, *n.* Informal. quick survey.

on·col·o·gy (-kol′ə jē) *n.* branch of medical science dealing with tumors and cancer. *—on·col′o·gist, n.*

on′com′ing, *adj.* approaching.

one (wun) *adj.* **1.** single. **2.** in particular. **3.** common to all. *—n.* **4.** first and lowest whole number. **5.** single person or thing. *—pron.* **6.** person or thing.

one′ness, *n.* unity.

on′er·ous (on′ər əs, ōn′ar-) *adj.* burdensome.

one·self′ (wun self′, wunz-) *pron.* person's self. Also, **one′s self.**

one′-sid′ed, *adj.* **1.** with all advantage on one side. **2.** biased.

one′-time′, *adj.* former.

one′-track′, *adj.* Informal. obsessed with one subject.

one′-way′, *adj.* moving or allowing movement in one direction only.

on′go′ing, *adj.* in progress.

on′ion (un′yən) *n.* common plant having edible bulb.

on′-line′, *adj.* operating under the direct control of, or connected to, a main computer.

on′look′er, *n.* spectator; witness.

on′ly (ōn′lē) *adv.* **1.** alone; solely. **2.** merely. *—adj.* **3.** sole. *—conj.* **4.** but.

on′o·mat′o·poe′ia (on′ə mat′ə pē′ə, -mä′tə-) *n.* formation of word by imitation of a sound.

on′rush′, *n.* rapid advance.

on′set′, *n.* **1.** beginning. **2.** attack.

on′slaught′ (on′slôt′) *n.* attack.

on′to, *prep.* upon; on to.

on·tol′o·gy (on tol′ə jē) *n.* branch of metaphysics studying existence or being.

o′nus (ō′nəs) *n.* burden.

on′ward (ōn′wərd) *adv.* **1.** forward. *—adj.* **2.** moving forward.

on′yx (on′iks, ō′niks) *n.* varicolored quartz.

oo′dles (ōōd′lz) *n.pl.* Informal. large quantity.

ooze (ōōz) *v.* **1.** oozed, oozing. *—v.* **1.** leak out slowly. *—n.* **2.** something that oozes. **3.** soft mud.

o·pac′i·ty (ō pas′i tē) *n., pl.* -ties. state of being opaque.

o′pal (ō′pəl) *n.* precious stone, often iridescent.

o′pa·les′cent (ō′pə les′ənt) *adj.* with opallike play of color.

o·paque′ (ō pāk′) *adj.* **1.** not transmitting light. **2.** not shining. **3.** not clear.

op. cit. (op′ sit′) in the work cited.

OPEC (ō′pek) *n.* Organization of Petroleum Exporting Countries.

Op′-Ed′ (op′ed′) *n.* newspaper section devoted to signed articles and letters.

o′pen (ō′pən) *adj.* **1.** not shut. **2.** not enclosed or covered. **3.** available; accessible. **4.** candid. *—v.* **5.** make or become open. **6.** begin. **7.** come apart. *—n.* **8.** any open space.

o′pen-and-shut′, *adj.* easily solved or decided; obvious.

o′pen-end′ed, *adj.* **1.** unrestricted. **2.** having no fixed answer.

o′pen-hand′ed, *adj.* generous.

o′pen·ing, *n.* **1.** unobstructed or unoccupied space. **2.** gap or hole. **3.** beginning. **4.** opportunity.

o′pen-mind′ed, *adj.* without prejudice. *—o′pen-mind′ed·ness, n.*

op′er·a (op′ər ə, op′rə) *n.* sung drama. *—op′er·at′ic* (-ə rat′ik) *adj.*

op′er·a·ble (op′ər ə bəl) *adj.* **1.** able to be operated. **2.** curable by surgery.

opera glasses, small, low-power binoculars.

op′er·ate′ (-ə rāt′) *v.,* -ated, -ating. **1.** work or run. **2.** exert force or influence. **3.** perform surgery. *—op′er·a′tion, n.* *—op′er·a′tor, n.*

operating system, software that directs computer's operations.

op′er·a′tion·al, *adj.* concerning operations. **2.** in operation.

op′er·a·tive (-ə tiv, -ə rā′tiv) *n.* **1.** worker. **2.** spy. *—adj.* **3.** in operation.

op′er·et′ta (op′ə ret′ə) *n.* light opera.

oph·thal·mol·o·gy (of′thal mol′ə jē, -thə-, -thal-, op′-) *n.* branch of medicine dealing with eye. *—oph′thal·mol′o·gist, n.*

o′pi·ate (ō′pē it, -āt′) *n.* medicine containing opium.

o·pine′ (ō pīn′) *v.,* -pined, -pining. express an opinion.

o·pin′ion (ə pin′yən) *n.* belief or judgment.

o·pin′ion·at′ed (-yə nā′tid) *adj.* stubborn in opinions.

o′pi·um (ō′pē əm) *n.* narcotic juice of poppy.

o·pos·sum (ə pos'əm, pos'əm) n. pouched mammal of southern U.S.

op·po·nent (ə pō'nənt) n. 1. person on opposite side, as in contest. 2. person opposed to something.

op·por·tune' (op'ər tōōn', -tyōōn') adj. appropriate; timely.

op·por·tun·ism' n. unprincipled use of opportunities. —**op'por·tun'ist**, n. —**op'por·tun·is'tic**, adj.

op·por·tu'ni·ty, n., pl. -ties. temporary possible advantage.

op·pose' (ə pōz') v., -posed, -posing. 1. resist or compete with. 2. hinder. —**op'po·si'tion**, n.

op'po·site (op'ə zit, -sit) adj. 1. in corresponding position on other side. 2. completely different. —n. 3. one that is opposite.

op·press' (ə pres') v. 1. weigh down. 2. treat harshly as a matter of policy. —**op·pres'sion** (ə presh'ən), n. —**op·pres'sive**, adj. —**op·pres'sor**, n.

op·pro'bri·um (ə prō'brē əm) n. disgrace and reproach.

opt (opt) v. make a choice.

op'tic (op'tik) adj. of eyes.

op'ti·cal, adj. 1. made to assist sight. 2. visual. 3. of optics.

optical disc, disk on which digital data is stored and read by laser.

optical scanner, device for scanning and digitizing printed material.

op·ti'cian (ə tish'ən) n. eyeglass maker.

op'tics, n. branch of science dealing with light and vision.

op'ti·mal, adj. optimum.

op'ti·mism (op'tə miz'əm) n. 1. disposition to hope for best. 2. belief that good will prevail. —**op'ti·mist**, n. —**op'ti·mis'tic**, adj.

op'ti·mum (-məm) adj., n. best.

op'tion (op'shən) n. 1. ability to choose. 2. choice. —**op'tion·al**, adj.

op·tom'e·try (op tom'i trē) n. art of testing eyes for eyeglasses. —**op·tom'e·trist**, n.

op'u·lent (op'yə lənt) adj. wealthy. —**op'u·lence**, n.

o'pus (ō'pəs) n., pl. **op·er·a** (op'ər ə, op'rə). work, esp. musical, usually numbered.

or (ôr; unstressed ər) conj. (used to connect alternatives).

OR, 1. operating room. 2. Oregon.

-or, suffix meaning: condition or quality, as pallor; person or thing that does something, as orator.

or'a·cle (ôr'ə kəl) n. 1. one who gave answers from the gods to questions. 2. wise person.

o'ral (ôr'əl) adj. 1. spoken. 2. of mouths. —**o'ral·ly**, adv.

or'ange (ôr'inj) n. 1. round, reddish-yellow citrus fruit. 2. reddish yellow.

or'ange·ade' (-ād') n. drink with base of orange juice.

o·rang'u·tan' (ō rang'ŏŏ tan', ə rang'-) n. large, long-armed ape.

o·ra'tion, n. formal speech.

or'a·tor (ôr'ə tər), n. eloquent public speaker.

or'a·to'ri·o' (-tôr'ē ō', n., pl. -rios. religious work for voices and orchestra in dramatic form.

or'a·to'ry, n., pl. -ries. 1. eloquent speaking. 2. small room for prayer.

orb (ôrb) n. 1. sphere. 2. any of heavenly bodies.

or'bit (ôr'bit) n. 1. path of planet, etc., around another body. —v. 2. travel in orbit. —**or'bit·al**, adj.

or'chard (ôr'chərd) n. plot of fruit trees.

or'ches·tra (ôr'kə strə, -kes trə) n. 1. Music. large company of instrumental performers. 2. main floor of theater. —**or·ches'tral**, adj.

or'ches·trate' (ôr'kə strāt') v., -trated, -trating. 1. arrange music for orchestra. 2. arrange elements of. —**or'ches·tra'tion**, n.

or'chid (ôr'kid) n. tropical plant with oddly shaped blooms.

or·dain' (ôr dān') v. 1. invest as a member of the clergy. 2. direct.

or·deal' (ôr dēl', ôr'dēl) n. severe test.

or'der (ôr'dər) n. 1. authoritative command. 2. harmonious arrangement. 3. group bound by common religious rules. 4. list of items desired. —v. 5. give an order. 6. arrange.

or'der·ly, adj., adv., n., pl. -lies. —adj. 1. methodical. 2. well-behaved. —adv. 3. according to rule. —n. 4. hospital attendant.

or'di·nal (ôr'dn əl) adj. 1. showing position in series, as first, second, etc. —n. 2. ordinal number.

or'di·nance (ôr'dn əns) n. law.

or'di·nar'y (-dn er'ē) adj., n., pl. -ies. —adj. 1. normal. —n. 2. ordinary condition, etc. —**or'di·nar'i·ly**, adv.

or'di·na'tion (ôr'dn ā'shən) n. act or ceremony of ordaining.

ord'nance (ôrd'nəns) n. military weapons of all kinds.

or'dure (ôr'jər, -dyŏŏr) n. dung.

ore (ôr) n. metal-bearing rock.

Ore., Oregon.

o·reg'a·no (ə reg'ə nō') n. plant with leaves used as seasoning.

or'gan (ôr'gən) n. 1. large musical keyboard instrument sounded by air forced through pipes, etc. 2. part of animal or plant with specific function. **3.** periodical. **—or·gan·ist,** n.

or·gan·dy (ôr′gən dē) n., pl. **-dies.** thin stiff cotton fabric.

or·gan·ic (ôr gan′ik) adj. **1.** of carbon compounds. **2.** of living organisms. **3.** raised or grown without synthetic fertilizers, pesticides, etc.

or·gan·ism (-gə niz′əm) n. anything living or formerly alive.

or·gan·ize′ (-gə nīz′) v., **-ized, -izing.** form into coordinated whole; systematize. **—or·gan′i·za′tion,** n. **—or·gan·i·za·tion·al,** adj.

or·gan·za (ôr gan′zə) n. sheer fabric of rayon, nylon, or silk.

or·gasm (ôr′gaz əm) n. sexual climax.

or·gy (ôr′jē) n., pl. **-gies.** unrestrained indulgence, esp in sexual activities.

o·ri·el (ôrē al) n. bay window.

o·ri·ent (ôrē ənt, -ē ent′) **1.** (cap.) countries of Asia. **—v.** (ôrē ent′) **2.** set facing certain way. **3.** inform about one's situation. **—O·ri·en′tal,** adj. **—o′ri·en·ta′tion,** n.

o′ri·en·teer·ing (-tēr′ing) n. sport of navigating unknown terrain.

or·i·fice (ôr′ə fis) n. opening.

o·ri·ga·mi (ôr′i gä′mē) n. Japanese art of folding paper.

or·i·gin (ôr′i jin) n. **1.** source. **2.** beginning. **3.** birth or ancestry.

o·rig·i·nal (ə rij′ə nl) adj. **1.** first. **2.** novel. **3.** being new work. **4.** capable of creating something original. **—n. 5.** primary form. **6.** thing copied. **—o·rig′i·nal′i·ty** (-nal′i tē) n. **—o·rig′i·nal·ly,** adv. **1.** at first. **2.** in original manner.

o·rig·i·nate′, v., **-nated, -nating. 1.** come to be. **2.** give origin to.

o·ri·ole (ôrē ōl′) n. bright-colored bird of Europe and America.

o·ri·son (ôr′i zən) n. prayer.

Or·lon (ôr′lon) n. Trademark. synthetic fabric resembling nylon.

or·mo·lu (ôr′mə lōō′) n., pl. **-lus.** copper-zinc alloy.

or·na·ment (ôr′nə mənt) n. **1.** something to beautify. **—v.** (-mənt′, -mənt) **2.** adorn; decorate. **—or′na·men′tal,** adj.

or·nate′ (ôr nāt′) adj. lavish. **—or·nate′ly,** adv.

or·ner·y (ôr′nə rē) adj. Informal. ill-tempered.

or·ni·thol·o·gy (ôr′nə thol′ə jē) n. study of birds.

o·ro·tund′ (ôr′ə tund′) adj. **1.** rich and clear in voice. **2.** pompous.

or·phan (ôr′fən) n. **1.** child whose parents are both dead. **—adj. 2.** of or for orphans. **—v. 3.** bereave of parents.

or·phan·age (-fə nij) n. home for orphans.

or·tho·don·tics (ôr′thə don′tiks) n. branch of dentistry dealing with irregular teeth. **—or·tho·don′tic,** adj. **—or·tho·don′tist,** n.

or·tho·dox′ (ôr′thə doks′) adj. **1.** sound and correct in doctrine. **2.** conventional. **3.** (cap.) of Christian churches of eastern Europe.

or·thog·ra·phy (ôr thog′rə fē) n., pl. **-phies.** spelling. **—or′tho·graph′ic** (ôr′thə graf′ik), adj.

or·tho·pe′dics (ôr′thə pē′diks) n. branch of medicine dealing with the skeletal system.

-ory, suffix meaning: **1.** of, characterized by, or serving to, as excretory. **2.** place or instrument for, as crematory.

os′cil·late′ (os′ə lāt′) v., **-lated, -lating.** swing to and fro. **—os′cil·la′tion,** n. **—os′cil·la′tor,** n.

os·cil′lo·scope′ (ə sil′ə skōp′) n. device that uses cathode-ray tube to display changes in electric quantity.

os′cu·late′ (os′kyə lāt′) v., **-lated, -lating.** kiss. **—os′cu·la′tion,** n.

o′sier (ō′zhər) n. tough flexible twig used in wickerwork.

-osis, suffix meaning: **1.** action or condition, as osmosis. **2.** abnormal state, as tuberculosis.

os·mo′sis (oz mō′sis, os-) n. diffusion of liquid through membrane.

os′prey (os′prē, -prā) n. large hawk.

os′se·ous (os′ē əs) adj. of, like, or containing bone.

os′si·fy′ (os′ə fī′) v., **-fied, -fying.** make or become bone.

os·ten′si·ble (o sten′sə bəl) adj. merely apparent or pretended. **—os·ten′si·bly,** adv.

os′ten·ta′tion (os′ten tā′shən, -tan-) n. pretentious display. **—os′ten·ta′tious,** adj.

os′te·o·ar·thri′tis (os′tē ō är thrī′tis) n. arthritis marked by decay of cartilage in joints.

os′te·op′a·thy (os′tē op′ə thē) n. treatment of disease by manipulating affected part. **—os′te·o·path′** (-ə path′) n. **—os′te·o·path′ic,** adj.

os′te·o·po·ro′sis (os′tē ō pə rō′sis) n. disorder in which bones become increasingly brittle, porous, and prone to fracture.

os′tra·cize′ (os′trə sīz′) v., **-cized, -cizing.** exclude from society; banish. **—os′tra·cism** (-siz′əm) n.

os′trich (ô′strich) n. large, swiftfooted, flightless bird.

oth′er (uth′ər) adj. **1.** additional. **2.** different. **3.** remaining. **4.** former. **—pron. 5.** other person or thing.

oth′er·wise′, *adv.* **1.** in other ways or circumstances. —*adj.* **2.** of other sort.

oth′er·world′ly, *adj.* concerned with spiritual or imaginary world.

ot′ter (ot′ər) *n.* aquatic mammal.

ot′to·man (ot′ə mən) *n.* low, cushioned seat.

ought (ôt) *aux. v.* used to express obligation or advisability. —*n.*

ounce (ouns) *n.* unit of weight equal to $\frac{1}{16}$ lb. avoirdupois or $\frac{1}{12}$ lb. troy.

our (ou⁰r, ou′ər; *unstressed* ər) *pron.* possessive form of **we,** used before noun.

ours, *pron.* possessive form of **we,** used predicatively.

our·selves′, *pron.* **1.** reflexive substitute for **us. 2.** intensive with or substitute for **we** or **us.**

-ous, suffix meaning full of or characterized by.

oust (oust) *v.* eject; force out.

oust′er, *n.* ejection.

out (out) *adv.* **1.** away from some place. **2.** so as to emerge or project. **3.** until conclusion. **4.** to depletion. **5.** so as to be extinguished, etc. —*adj.* **6.** away from some place. **7.** extinguished, etc. —*prep.* **8.** out from. **9.** away along. —*n.* **10.** means of evasion.

out-, prefix meaning: **1.** outward, as *outburst.* **2.** outside, as *outbuilding.* **3.** surpass, as *outlast.*

out′age (ou′tij) *n.* interruption or failure in supply of power.

out′-and-out′, *adj.* utter; thorough.

out′back′, *n.* remote area.

out′board′, *adj., adv.* on exterior of ship or boat.

out′break′, *n.* sudden occurrence. **2.** riot.

out′build′ing, *n.* detached building subordinate to main building.

out′burst′, *n.* violent outpouring.

out′cast′, *n.* exiled person.

out′class′, *v.* outdo in style or excellence.

out′come′, *n.* consequence.

out′crop′, *n.* emerging stratum at earth's surface.

out′cry′, *n., pl.* **-cries.** expression of distress or protest.

out·dat′ed, *adj.* obsolete.

out·dis′tance, *v.,* **-tanced, -tancing.** leave behind, as in racing.

out·do′, *v.,* **-did, -done, -doing.** surpass.

out′door′, *adj.* done or occurring in open air. —**out′doors′,** *adv.*

out′er, *adj.* **1.** farther out. **2.** on outside.

out′er·most′, *adj.* farthest out.

outer space, space beyond the earth's atmosphere.

out′field′, *n.* part of baseball field beyond diamond. —**out′field′er,** *n.*

out′fit′, *n., v.,* **-fitted, -fitting.** —*n.* **1.** set of articles for any purpose. **2.** set of clothes. **3.** organized group of persons. —*v.* **4.** equip.

out′go′, *n., pl.* **-goes.** expenditure.

out′go·ing *adj.* **1.** (-gō′ing) departing. **2.** (-gō′ing) retiring from a position or office. **3.** -gō′ing, -gō′-) friendly; sociable.

out′grow′, *v.,* **-grew, -grown, -growing.** grow too large or mature for.

out′growth′, *n.* **1.** natural result. **2.** offshoot.

out′house′, *n.* separate building serving as toilet.

out′ing, *n.* pleasure trip.

out·land′ish (-lan′dish) *adj.* strange.

out·last′, *v.* endure after.

out′law′, *n.* **1.** habitual criminal. **2.** person excluded from protection of law. —*v.* **3.** prohibit by law. **4.** deny protection of law to.

out′lay′, *n.* expenditure.

out′let (-let, -lit) *n.* **1.** opening or passage out. **2.** market for goods.

out′line′, *n., v.,* **-lined, -lining.** —*n.* **1.** line by which object is bounded. **2.** drawing showing only outer contour. **3.** general description. —*v.* **4.** draw or represent in outline.

out·live′ (-liv′) *v.,* **-lived, -living.** live longer than.

out′look′, *n.* **1.** view from place. **2.** mental view. **3.** prospect.

out′ly·ing, *adj.* remote.

out·mod′ed (-mō′did) *adj.* obsolete.

out·num′ber, *v.* be more numerous than.

out′-of-bod′y, *adj.* characterized by sensation that the mind has left the body.

out′-of-date′, *adj.* obsolete.

out′-of-doors′, *n.* outdoors.

out′-of-the-way′, *adj.* isolated.

out′pa′tient, *n.* patient visiting hospital to receive treatment.

out′place′ment, *n.* assistance in finding new job, provided by company for employee being let go.

out′post′, *n.* **1.** sentinel station away from main army. **2.** place away from main area.

out′put′, *n.* **1.** production. **2.** quantity produced.

out′rage′, *n., v.,* **-raged, -raging.** —*n.* **1.** gross violation. **2.** anger. —*v.* **3.** subject to outrage.

out·ra′geous (-rā′jəs) *adj.* very offensive.

ou·tré′ (ōō trā′) *adj.* unconventional; bizarre.

out′reach′ *adj.* concerned with extending services.

out′right′ *adj.* (-rīt′) **1.** utter; thorough. —*adv.* (-rīt′, -rīt′) **2.** at once; completely.

out·run′, *v.*, **-ran**, **-run**, **-running. 1.** run faster or farther than. **2.** exceed.

out·sell′, *v.*, **-sold**, **-selling.** exceed in number of sales.

out′set′, *n.* beginning.

out·shine′, *v.*, **-shone** or **-shined**, **-shining. 1.** shine more brightly than. **2.** surpass in excellence.

out′side′ *n.* (out′sīd′, -sīd′) **1.** outer side, aspect, etc. **2.** space beyond enclosure. —*adj.* (out′sīd′, out′-) **3.** being, done, etc., on the outside. **4.** remote. —*adv.* (out′sīd′) **5.** on or to the outside. —*prep.* (out′sīd′, out′sīd′) **6.** at the outside of.

out·sid′er, *n.* person not belonging.

out′skirts′, *n.pl.* outlying districts.

out·smart′, *v.* outwit.

out′spo′ken, *adj.* candid.

out′spread′, *adj.* extended.

out·stand′ing, *adj.* **1.** prominent. **2.** not yet paid.

out·strip′, *v.*, **-stripped**, **-stripping. 1.** excel. **2.** outdistance.

out′take′, *n.* segment of film edited from published version.

out′ward (-ward) *adj.* **1.** external. —*adv.* **2.** Also, **out′wards.** toward the outside. —**out′ward·ly**, *adv.*

out·weigh′, *v.*, exceed in importance.

out·wit′, *v.*, **-witted**, **-witting.** get the better of by superior cleverness.

o′va (ō′və) *n.* pl. of **ovum.**

o′val (ō′vəl) *adj.* egg-shaped.

o·va·ry (ō′və rē) *n.*, *pl.* **-ries.** female reproductive gland. —**o·var′i·an** (ō vâr′ē ən) *adj.*

o′vate (ō′vāt) *adj.* egg-shaped.

o·va′tion (ō vā′shən) *n.* enthusiastic applause.

ov′en (uv′ən) *n.* chamber for baking or drying.

o′ver (ō′vər) *prep.* **1.** above in place, authority, etc. **2.** on. **3.** across; through. **4.** in excess of. **5.** concerning. **6.** during. —*adv.* **7.** so as to affect whole surface. **8.** above. **9.** again. —*adj.* **10.** finished. **11.** remaining. **12.** upper.

o′ver·a·chieve′, *v.*, **-chieved**, **-chieving.** perform better than expected, esp. in school.

o′ver·act′, *v.* perform in an exaggerated manner.

o′ver·age (ō′vər ij) *n.* surplus.

—*adj.* (ō′vər āj′) **2.** beyond desirable age.

o′ver·all′ (ō′vər ôl′) *adj.* **1.** including everything. —*n.* **2.** (*pl.*) loose, stout trousers.

o′ver·awe′, *v.*, **-awed**, **-awing.** dominate with impressiveness.

o′ver·bear′ing, *adj.* arrogant.

o′ver·bite′, *n.* occlusion in which upper incisor teeth overlap lower ones.

o′ver·blown′, *adj.* pretentious.

o′ver·board′, *adv.* over side of ship into water.

o′ver·cast′ (-kast′, -kast′) *adj.* **1.** cloudy. **2.** gloomy.

o′ver·charge′, *v.*, **-charged**, **-charging. 1.** charge too high a price. **2.** overload. —*n.* (ō′vər chärj′) **3.** charge exceeding fair price. **4.** excessive load.

o′ver·coat′, *n.* coat worn over ordinary clothing.

o′ver·come′, *v.*, **-came**, **-come**, **-coming.** defeat; overpower.

o′ver·do′, *v.*, **-did**, **-done**, **-doing. 1.** do to excess. **2.** exaggerate.

o′ver·dose′, *n.*, *v.*, **-dosed**, **-dosing.** —*n.* **1.** excessive dose. —*v.* **2.** take such a dose.

o′ver·draft′, *n.* **1.** act of overdrawing. **2.** amount overdrawn.

o′ver·draw′, *v.*, **-drew**, **-drawn**, **-drawing.** draw upon in excess of.

o′ver·drive′, *n.* mechanism that reduces power required to maintain speed by lowering gear ratio.

o′ver·due′, *adj.* due some time before.

o′ver·flow′ *v.*, **-flowed**, **-flown**, **-flowing**, *n.* —*v.* (ō′vər flō′) **1.** flow or run over; flood. —*n.* (ō′vər flō′) **2.** instance of flooding. **3.** something that runs over.

o′ver·grow′, *v.*, **-grew**, **-grown**, **-growing.** cover with growth.

o′ver·hand′, *adv.* with hand above shoulder.

o′ver·hang′ *v.*, **-hung**, **-hanging**, *n.* —*v.* (ō′vər hang′) **1.** project over. —*n.* (ō′vər hang′) **2.** projection.

o′ver·haul′ *v.* (ō′vər hôl′, ō′vər hôl′) **1.** investigate thoroughly, as for repair. **2.** overtake. —*n.* (ō′vər hôl′) **3.** complete examination.

o′ver·head′ *adv.* (ō′vər hed′) **1.** aloft. —*n.* (ō′vər hed′) **2.** general business expense.

o′ver·hear′, *v.*, **-heard**, **-hearing.** hear without speaker's intent.

o′ver·joyed′ (-joid′) *adj.* very happy.

o′ver·kill′, *n.* any greatly excessive amount.

o′ver·land′ (-land′, -land) *adv.*, *adj.* across open country.

o'ver·lap' v., -lapped, -lapping, n. —v. (ō'vər lap') **1.** extend over and beyond. —n. (ō'vər lap') **2.** overlapping part.

o'ver·lay' v., -laid, -laying, —n. **1.** spread over. —n. **2.** something used in overlaying.

o'ver·lie' v. -lay, -lain, -lying. lie over or on.

o'ver·look' v. **1.** fail to notice. **2.** afford view over.

o'ver·ly adv. Informal. excessively.

o'ver·night' adv. (-nīt') **1.** during the night. **2.** suddenly. —adj. (-nīt') **3.** done, made, etc., during the night. **4.** staying for one night.

o'ver·pass' n. bridge crossing other traffic.

o'ver·play' v. exaggerate.

o'ver·pow'er v. **1.** overwhelm in feeling. **2.** subdue.

o'ver·rate' v., -rated, -rating. esteem too highly.

o'ver·reach' v. **1.** extend beyond. **2.** try too hard.

o'ver·re·act' v. react too emotionally. —**o'ver·re·ac'tion,** n.

o'ver·ride' v., -rode, -ridden, -riding. prevail over; supersede.

o'ver·rule' v., -ruled, -ruling. rule against.

o'ver·run' v., -ran, -run, -running. **1.** swarm over. **2.** overgrow.

o'ver·seas' adv. over or across the sea.

o'ver·see' v., -saw, -seen, -seeing. supervise. —**o'ver·se'er,** n.

o'ver·shad'ow v. be more important than.

o'ver·shoe' n. protective shoe worn over another shoe.

o'ver·shoot' v., -shot, -shooting. shoot or go beyond.

o'ver·sight' n. error of neglect.

o'ver·sleep' v., -slept, -sleeping. sleep beyond desired time.

o'ver·state' v., -stated, -stating. exaggerate in describing. —**o'ver·state'ment,** n.

o'ver·stay' v., -stayed, -staying. stay too long.

o'ver·step' v., -stepped, -stepping. exceed.

o·vert' (ō vûrt', ō'vûrt) adj. not concealed.

o'ver·take' v., -took, -taken, -taking. catch up with or pass.

o'ver-the-count'er, adj. **1.** not listed or traded through an organized securities exchange. **2.** sold legally without a prescription.

o'ver·throw' v., -threw, -thrown, -throwing. —n. (ō'vər thrō') **1.** defeat; put down. —n. (ō'vər thrō') **2.** act of overthrowing.

o'ver·time', n. time worked in addition to regular hours. —**o'ver·time',** adv., adj.

o'ver·tone', n. **1.** additional meaning. **2.** musical tone added to basic tone.

o'ver·ture (ō'vər chər, -chŏŏr') n. **1.** offer. **2.** musical prelude.

o'ver·turn', v. **1.** tip off base. **2.** defeat.

o'ver·view', n. overall perception or description.

o'ver·ween'ing (-wē'ning) adj. **1.** conceited. **2.** excessive.

o'ver·weight', n. **1.** excess of weight. —adj. (ō'vər wāt') **2.** weighing more than is normal.

o'ver·whelm' (-hwelm', -welm') v. completely overcome.

o'ver·work', v., -worked or -wrought, -working. —n. (ō'vər wûrk') **1.** work too hard. —n. (ō'vər wûrk') **2.** work beyond one's strength.

o'ver·wrought' (ō'vər rôt', ō'vər-) adj. highly excited.

o'vi·duct' (ō'vi dukt') n. tube through which ova are passed.

o·void' (ō'void) adj. egg-shaped.

ov'u·late (ov'yə lāt', ō'vyə-) v., -lated, -lating. produce and discharge eggs (ova) from ovary.

ov'ule (ov'yŏŏl, ō'vyŏŏl) n. **1.** structure that develops into seed. **2.** small egg.

o'vum (ō'vəm) n., pl. ova (ō'və). female reproductive cell.

owe (ō) v., owed, owing. be obligated to pay or give to another.

owl (oul) n. nocturnal bird of prey.

own (ōn) adj. **1.** of or belonging to. —v. **2.** possess. **3.** acknowledge. —**own'er,** n. —**own'er·ship,** n.

ox (oks) n., pl. oxen. adult castrated male bovine.

ox'blood', n. deep, dull red color.

ox'ford (oks'fərd) n. low shoe laced over instep.

ox'i·dant (ok'si dant) n. chemical agent that oxidizes.

ox'ide (ok'sīd, -sid) n. compound of oxygen and another element.

ox'i·dize' (ok'si dīz') v., -dized, -dizing. add oxygen to. —**ox'i·di·za'tion, ox·i·da'tion,** n.

ox'y·a·cet'y·lene' (ok'sē ə set'l-ēn', -in) adj. denoting a mixture of oxygen and acetylene used for cutting and welding steel.

ox'y·gen (ok'si jən) n. colorless, odorless gas necessary to life and fire.

ox'y·gen·ate' (-jə nāt') v., -ated, -ating. enrich with oxygen.

ox'y·mo'ron (ok'si môr'on) n., pl. -mora. figure of speech that uses seeming contradictions.

oys/ter (oi/stər) *n.* edible, irregularly shaped mollusk.

oz., ounce.

o/zone (ō/zōn, ō zōn/) *n.* form of oxygen in upper atmosphere.

ozone hole, part of ozone layer depleted by atmospheric pollution.

ozone layer, layer of upper atmosphere where most ozone is concentrated.

P

P, p (pē) *n.* sixteenth letter of English alphabet.

PA, 1. Also, **Pa.** Pennsylvania. **2.** public-address system.

PAC (pak) *n., pl.* **PACs, PAC's.** political action committee.

pace (pās) *n., v.,* **paced, pacing.**
—*n.* **1.** rate of movement or progress. **2.** linear measure. **3.** step or gait. —*v.* **4.** set pace for. **5.** step regularly. —**pac/er,** *n.*

pace/mak/er, *n.* **1.** one that sets pace. **2.** electrical device for controlling heartbeat.

pace/set/ter, *n.* leader.

pach/y.derm/ (pak/i dûrm/) *n.* thick-skinned mammal, as the elephant.

pa.cif/ic (pə sif/ik) *adj.* peaceful.

pac/i.fism (pas/ə fiz/əm) *n.* principle of abstention from violence. —**pac/i.fist,** *n.* —**pac/i.fis/tic,** *adj.*

pac/i.fy/ (-fī/) *v.,* **-fied, -fying. 1.** calm. **2.** appease. —**pac/i.fi/er,** *n.*

pack (pak) *n.* **1.** bundle. **2.** group or complete set. —*v.* **3.** make into compact mass. **4.** fill with objects. **5.** cram. —**pack/er,** *n.*

pack/age (-ij) *n., v.,* **-aged, -aging.**
—*n.* **1.** bundle; parcel. **2.** container. —*v.* **3.** put into package.

pack/et, *n.* **1.** small package. **2.** passenger boat, esp. with fixed route.

pack rat, 1. rat that carries off shiny articles to its nest. **2.** *Informal.* person who saves useless items.

pact (pakt) *n.* agreement.

pad (pad) *n., v.,* **padded, padding.**
—*n.* **1.** soft, cushionlike mass. **2.** bound package of writing paper. **3.** dull sound of walking. —*v.* **4.** furnish with padding. **5.** expand with false or useless matter. **6.** walk with dull sound.

pad/ding, *n.* material with which to pad.

pad/dle (pad/l) *n., v.,* **-dled, -dling.**
—*n.* **1.** short oar for two hands. —*v.* **2.** propel with paddle. **3.** play in water.

pad/dock (pad/ək) *n.* field for horses.

pad/dy (pad/ē) *n., pl.* **-dies.** rice field.

paddy wagon, van for transporting prisoners.

pad/lock/ *n.* **1.** portable lock. —*v.* **2.** lock with padlock.

pa/dre (pä/drā) *n., pl.* **-dres.** clergyman.

pae/an (pē/ən) *n.* song of praise.

pa/gan (pā/gən) *n.* **1.** worshiper of idols. —*adj.* **2.** idolatrous; heathen. —**pa/gan.ism,** *n.*

page (pāj) *n., v.,* **paged, paging.**
—*n.* **1.** written or printed surface. **2.** boy servant. —*v.* **3.** summon by calling name.

pag/eant (paj/ənt) *n.* elaborate spectacle. —**pag/eant.ry,** *n.*

pag/i.nate/ (-ə nāt/) *v.,* **-nated, -nating.** number the pages of (a book, etc.). —**pag/i.na/tion,** *n.*

pa.go/da (pə gō/də) *n.* Far Eastern temple tower, esp. Buddhist.

pail (pāl) *n.* bucket.

pain (pān) *n.* **1.** bodily or mental suffering. **2.** (*pl.*) effort. **3.** penalty. —*v.* **4.** hurt. —**pain/ful,** *adj.*

pain/kil/ler, *n.* something that relieves pain.

pains/tak/ing, *adj.* careful.

paint (pānt) *n.* **1.** liquid coloring matter used as coating. —*v.* **2.** represent in paint. **3.** apply paint to. —**paint/er,** *n.* —**paint/ing,** *n.*

pair (pâr) *n., pl.* **pairs, pair,** *v.* —*n.* **1.** combination of two. —*v.* **2.** arrange in pairs. —**Usage.** See COUPLE.

pais/ley (pāz/lē) *adj.* having a colorful, detailed pattern.

pa.jam/as (pə jä/məz, -jam/əz) *n.pl.* nightclothes.

pal (pal) *n. Informal.* close friend.

pal/ace (pal/is) *n.* official residence of sovereign.

pal/at.a.ble (pal/ə tə bəl) *adj.* agreeable to taste.

pal/ate (-it) *n.* **1.** roof of mouth. **2.** sense of taste. —**pal/a.tal,** *adj.*

pa.la/tial (pə lā/shəl) *adj.* splendidly built or furnished.

pal/a.tine (pal/ə tīn/, -tin) *n.* vassal exercising royal privileges in province. —**pa.lat/i.nate/** (pə lat/n āt/, -it) *n.*

pa.lav/er (pə lav/ər, -lä/vər) *n.* idle talk.

pale (pāl) *adj.,* **paler, palest,** *v.,* **paled, paling,** *n.* —*adj.* **1.** without much color; near-white. **2.** dim. —*v.* **3.** become or make pale. —*n.*

4. stake. 5. bounds. 6. enclosed area.

Pa/le·o·lith/ic (pā/lē ə lith/ik) *adj.* denoting early Stone Age.

pa/le·on·tol/o·gy (-ən tol/ə jē) *n.* science of early life forms, as represented by fossils.

Pa/le·o·zo/ic (-ə zō/ik) *adj.* pertaining to geologic era 570 to 230 million years ago.

pal/ette (pal/it) *n.* board on which painter lays and mixes colors.

pal/i·mo/ny (pal/ə mō/nē) *n.* alimony awarded to member of unmarried couple.

pal/imp·sest/ (pal/imp sest/) *n.* manuscript with text erased to make room for other text.

pal/in·drome/ (pal/in drōm/) *n.* word or verse reading the same backward as forward.

pal/ing (pā/ling) *n.* fence of pales.

pal/i·sade/ (pal/ə sād/) *n.* **1.** fence of pales. **2.** line of tall cliffs.

pall (pôl) *n.* **1.** cloth spread on coffin. **2.** something gloomy. —*v.* **3.** become wearisome or distasteful.

pall/bear/er, *n.* person who carries coffin at funeral.

pal/let (pal/it) *n.* **1.** straw mattress. **2.** portable platform for cargo.

pal/li·ate/ (pal/ē āt/) *v.,* **-ated, -ating.** mitigate; excuse.

pal/li·a/tive (-ā/tiv, -ə tiv) *n.* drug that relieves symptoms but does not cure disease.

pal/lid (pal/id) *adj.* pale.

pal/lor (pal/ər) *n.* paleness.

palm (päm) *n.* **1.** inner surface of hand. **2.** tall, unbranched tropical tree. —*v.* **3.** conceal in hand.

pal·met/to (pal met/ō, päl-, päl-) *n., pl.* **-tos, -toes.** species of palm.

palm/is·try (pä/mə strē) *n.* art of telling fortunes from pattern of lines on palms of hands. **palm/ist,** *n.*

palm/y, *adj.,* **palmier, palmiest.** thriving.

pal/o·mi/no (pal/ə mē/nō) *n., pl.* **-nos.** light-tan horse.

pal/pa·ble (pal/pə bəl) *adj.* obvious; tangible. **pal/pa·bly,** *adv.*

pal/pate (pal/pāt) *v.,* **-pated, -pating.** examine by touch. **—pal·pa/tion,** *n.*

pal/pi·tate/ (pal/pi tāt/) *v.,* **-tated, -tating.** pulsate with unnatural rapidity. —**pal/pi·ta/tion,** *n.*

pal/sy (pôl/zē) *n., pl.* **-sies. 1.** paralysis. **2.** condition with tremors.

pal/try (pôl/trē) *adj.,* **-trier, -triest.** trifling. —**pal/tri·ness,** *n.*

pam/pas (pam/pəz; *attributively* -pas) *n.* vast South American plains.

pam/per (pam/pər) *v.* indulge; spoil.

pam/phlet (pam/flit) *n.* **1.** thin booklet. **2.** argumentative treatise.

pam/phlet·eer/, *n.* writer of pamphlets.

pan (pan) *n., v.,* **panned, panning.** —*n.* **1.** dish for cooking. —*v.* **2.** wash (gravel, etc.) to search for gold. **3.** *Informal.* criticize harshly. **4.** film panoramically.

Pan, *n.* Greek god of shepherds.

pan-, *prefix* meaning all.

pan/a·ce/a (pan/ə sē/ə) *n.* cure-all.

pa·nache/ (pə nash/, -näsh/) *n.* grand or flamboyant manner; flair.

pan/cake/, *n.* flat fried batter cake.

pan/cre·as (pan/krē əs, pang/-) *n.* gland near stomach secreting a digestive fluid. —**pan/cre·at/ic,** *adj.*

pan/da (pan/də) *n.* black and white bearlike animal native to Asia.

pan·dem/ic (pan dem/ik) *adj.* epidemic over large area.

pan/de·mo/ni·um (pan/də mō/nē əm) *n.* uproar.

pan/der (pan/dər) *n.* **1.** person who caters to base passions of others. —*v.* **2.** act as pander. —**pan/der·er,** *n.*

pane (pān) *n.* glass section of window.

pan/e·gyr/ic (pan/i jir/ik, -jī/rik) *n.* eulogy.

pan/el (pan/l) *n., v.,* **-eled, -eling.** —*n.* **1.** bordered section of wall, door, etc. **2.** list of persons called for jury duty. **3.** public discussion group. —*v.* **4.** arrange in or ornament with panels. —**pan/el·ing,** *n.*

pan/el·ist, *n.* member of panel.

pang (pang) *n.* sudden feeling of distress.

pan/han/dle, *v.,* **-dled, -dling.** *Informal.* beg from passerby.

pan/ic (pan/ik) *n.* demoralizing terror. —**pan/ick·y,** *adj.* —**pan/ic·strick/en,** *adj.*

pan/nier (pan/yər, -ē ər) *n.* large basket for carrying goods.

pan/o·ply (pan/ə plē) *n., pl.* **-plies. 1.** impressive display. **2.** suit of armor.

pan/o·ram/a (pan/ə ram/ə, -rä/mə) *n.* **1.** view over wide area. **2.** passing scene. —**pan/o·ram/ic,** *adj.*

pan/sy (pan/zē) *n., pl.* **-sies. 1.** species of violet. **2.** *Brit.* (*Offensive*) homosexual.

pant (pant) *v.* **1.** breathe hard and quickly. **2.** long eagerly.

pan·ta·loons/ (pan/tl oonz/) *n.pl. Archaic.* trousers.

pan/the·ism (pan/thē iz/əm) *n.* religious belief or philosophical doctrine that identifies God with the universe. —**pan/the·is/tic,** *adj.*

pan·the·on (pan′thē on′) n. **1.** building with tombs or memorials of a nation's illustrious dead. **2.** heroes of a nation, etc., as a group.

pan·ther (pan′thər) n. cougar or leopard.

pan·ties (pan′tēz) n.pl. women's underpants. Also, **pan·ty.**

pan·to·mime′ (pan′tə mīm′) n., v., **-mimed, -miming.** —n. **1.** expression by mute gestures. **2.** play in this form. —v. **3.** express in pantomime. —**pan′to·mim′ist,** n.

pan·try (pan′trē) n., pl. **-tries.** room for kitchen supplies.

pants (pants) n.pl. Informal. trousers.

pant′y·hose′, n. one-piece stockings plus panties for women.

pant′y·waist′, n. sissy.

pan·zer (pan′zər) adj. **1.** armored. —n. **2.** tank or armored vehicle.

pap (pap) n. soft food.

pa·pa (pä′pə, pə pä′) n. Informal. father.

pa·pa·cy (pā′pə sē) n., pl. **-cies.** office or reign of the pope.

pa·pal (pā′pəl) adj. of the pope.

pa·pa·ya (pə pä′yə) n. melonlike tropical American fruit.

pa·per (pā′pər) n. **1.** thin fibrous sheet for writing, etc. **2.** document. **3.** treatise. **4.** newspaper. —v. **5.** decorate with wallpaper. —adj. **6.** of paper. —**pa′per·y,** adj.

pa′per·back′, n. book cheaply bound in paper.

paper tiger, person or nation that seems strong but is actually weak.

pa′per·weight′, n. small, heavy object placed on papers to keep them from scattering.

pa·pier-mâ·ché′ (pā′pər mə shā′) n. molded paper pulp.

pa·pist (pā′pist) n., adj. Disparaging. Roman Catholic. —**pa′pism** (-piz′əm) n.

pa·poose′ (pa pōōs′) n. North American Indian baby.

pap·ri·ka (pa prē′kə) n. spice from pepper plant.

Pap test (pap) test for cancer of the cervix.

pa·py·rus (pə pī′rəs) n., pl. **-ri.** tall aquatic plant made into paper by ancient Egyptians.

par (pär) n. **1.** equality in value or standing. **2.** average amount, etc. **3.** in golf, standard number of strokes.

para- prefix meaning: **1.** beside, as paradigm. **2.** beyond, as parapsychology. **3.** auxiliary, as paramedical.

par·a·ble (par′ə bəl) n. moral allegory.

pa·rab′o·la (pə rab′ə lə) n. a U-shaped curve, surface, object, etc.

par·a·chute′ (par′ə shōōt′) n., v., **-chuted, -chuting.** —n. **1.** umbrella-like apparatus used to fall safely through air. —v. **2.** drop or fall by parachute. —**par′a·chut′ist,** n.

pa·rade′ (pə rād′) n., v., **-raded, -rading.** —n. **1.** public procession or assembly for display. —v. **2.** march in procession. **3.** display ostentatiously. —**pa·rad′er,** n.

par·a·digm′ (par′ə dīm′, -dim) n. example or model.

par·a·dise′ (-dīs′, -dīz′) n. **1.** heaven. **2.** garden of Eden. **3.** ideal. —**par′a·dis′i·cal,** adj.

par·a·dox′ (-doks′) n. statement that seems self-contradictory. —**par′a·dox′i·cal,** adj.

par·af·fin (-fin) n. waxy substance from petroleum, used in candles.

par·a·gon′ (-gon′, -gən) n. ideal model.

par·a·graph′ (-graf′) n. **1.** unit of written or printed matter, begun on new line. —v. **2.** divide into paragraphs.

par′a·keet′ (-kēt′) n. small parrot.

par′a·le′gal, n. attorney's assistant.

par′al·lax′ (-ə laks′) n. apparent displacement of object viewed due to changed position of observer.

par′al·lel′ (-ə lel′, -ləl) adj., n., v., **-leled, -leling.** —adj. **1.** having same direction and being same distance apart. **2.** having same characteristics. —n. **3.** parallel line or plane. **4.** anything parallel. —v. **5.** be parallel to. —**par′al·lel·ism,** n.

par′al·lel′o·gram (-lel′ə gram′) n. a four-sided figure whose opposite sides are parallel.

pa·ral′y·sis (pə ral′ə sis) n., pl. **-ses.** loss of voluntary muscular control. —**par′a·lyt′ic** (par′ə lit′ik) n., adj. —**par′a·lyze′, -lyzed, -lyzing.**

par′a·med′ic, n. person with paramedical duties.

par′a·med′i·cal, adj. of supplementary medicine.

pa·ram′e·ter (pə ram′i tər) n. determining factor.

par′a·mil′i·tar′y (par′ə mil′i ter′ē) adj. of organizations operating in place of or in addition to a regular military force.

par′a·mount′ (par′ə mount′) adj. greatest; utmost.

par′a·mour′ (par′ə mŏŏr′) n. lover of married person.

par′a·noi′a (par′ə noi′ə) n. mental disorder marked by systematized delusions ascribing hostile intentions to other persons.

par·a·pet (par'ə pit, -pet') n. wall at edge of roof or terrace.

par·a·pher·nal·ia (-fər nāl'yə, -fə-) n.pl. 1. equipment. 2. belongings.

par·a·phrase/, v., -phrased, -phrasing, n. —v. 1. rephrase. —n. 2. such restatement.

par·a·ple·gi·a (-plē'jē ə, -jə) n. paralysis of lower part of body. —**par·a·ple'gic** n., adj.

par·a·pro·fes'sion·al, adj. engaged in profession in partial or secondary capacity.

par·a·psy·chol'o·gy, n. branch of psychology that studies psychic phenomena.

par·a·site' (par'ə sīt') n. animal or plant that lives on another organism. —**par·a·sit'ic** (-sit'ik) adj.

par·a·sol' (par'ə sôl') n. sun umbrella.

par·a·thy'roid gland, small gland that regulates blood levels of calcium and phosphate.

par·a·troops', n. force of soldiers who reach battle by parachuting from planes.

par·boil' (pär'boil') v. precook.

par·cel (pär'səl) n., v., -celed, -celing. —n. 1. goods wrapped together; bundle. 2. part. —v. 3. divide.

parch (pärch) v. dry by heat.

par·chee'si (pär chē'zē) n. game resembling backgammon.

parch·ment (pärch'mənt) n. skin of sheep, etc., prepared for writing on.

par·don (pär'dn) n. 1. legal release. 2. forgiveness. —v. 3. excuse; forgive. —**par'don·a·ble**, adj.

pare (pâr) v., pared, paring. cut off outer part of.

par·ent (pâr'ənt, par'-) n. father or mother. —**pa·ren'tal** (pə ren'tl) adj. —**par'ent·hood'**, n.

par·ent·age (-ən tij) n. descent.

pa·ren'the·sis (pə ren'thə sis) n., pl. -ses (-sēz). 1. upright curves ( ) used to mark off inserted word or phrase. 2. material so inserted.

par excellence (pär ek'sə läns') superior.

par·fait' (pär fā') n. frothy frozen dessert.

pa·ri'ah (pə rī'ə) n. outcast.

par·i-mu'tu·el (par'i myōō'chōō əl) n. form of betting on races.

par·ish (par'ish) n. ecclesiastical district. —**pa·rish'ion·er,** n.

par'i·ty (par'i tē) n. 1. equality. 2. similarity. 3. guaranteed level of farm prices.

park (pärk) n. 1. tract of land set apart for public. —v. 2. put vehicle in a place.

par·ka (pär'kə) n. hooded garment.

Par'kin·son's disease (pär'kin səns) neurological disease characterized by tremors and shuffling.

park'way', n. broad thoroughfare with dividing strip or side strips planted with trees, etc.

par'lance (pär'ləns) n. way of speaking.

par·lay' (pär'lā, -lē) v. reinvest original amount and its earnings.

par·ley (pär'lē) n. 1. conference between combatants. 2. hold parley.

par·lia·ment (pär'lə mənt) n. legislative body, esp. (cap.) that of the United Kingdom.

par·lia·men·tar'ian (-men târ'ē ən, -mən-) n. expert in parliamentary rules.

par·lia·men'ta·ry (-men'tə rē) adj. 1. of, by, or having a parliament. 2. in accordance with rules of debate.

par'lor (pär'lər) n. room for receiving guests.

Par'me·san' (pär'mə zän', -zən) n. hard, dry Italian cheese.

par·mi·gia'na (pär'mə zhä'nə, -zhän') adj. cooked with Parmesan cheese.

pa·ro'chi·al (pə rō'kē əl) adj. 1. of a parish. 2. narrow; provincial.

parochial school, school run by religious organization.

par'o·dy (par'ə dē) n., pl. -dies, v., -died, -dying. —n. 1. humorous imitation. —v. 2. satirize.

pa·role' (pə rōl') n., v., -roled, -roling. —n. 1. conditional release from prison. —v. 2. put on parole. —**pa·rol·ee'** (-rō lē') n.

par'ox·ysm (par'ək siz'əm) n. 1. outburst. —**par·ox·ys'mal,** adj.

par·quet' (pär kā') n. floor of inlaid design.

par'ri·cide' (par'ə sīd') n. crime of killing one's close relative.

par'rot (par'ət) n. 1. hook-billed, bright-colored bird capable of being taught to talk. —v. 2. repeat senselessly.

par'ry (par'ē) v., -ried, -rying, n., pl. -ries. —v. 1. ward off; evade. —n. 2. act of parrying.

parse (pärs) v., parsed, parsing. analyze (word or sentence) grammatically.

par'si·mo'ny (pär'sə mō'nē) n. excessive frugality. —**par·si·mo'ni·ous,** adj.

pars'ley (pärs'lē) n. garden herb used in seasoning.

pars'nip (pärs'nip) n. plant with white edible root.

par'son (pär'sən) n. member of clergy.

par·son·age (-sə nij) *n.* house provided for parson.

part (pärt) *n.* **1.** portion of a whole. **2.** share. **3.** role. —*v.* **4.** separate.

par·take′ (pär tāk′) *v.*, **-took, -taken, -taking.** have or take a share.

par·terre′ (pär târ′) *n.* rear section of theater seats under balcony.

par·the·no·gen·e·sis (pär′thə nō-jen′ə sis) *n.* development of egg without fertilization.

par·tial (pär′shəl) *adj.* **1.** being part; incomplete. **2.** biased. **3.** especially fond. —**par·tial′i·ty,** *n.*

par·tic·i·pate (pär tis′ə pāt′) *v.*, **-pated, -pating.** take part; share (in). —**par·tic·i·pant,** *n.* —**par·tic·i·pa′tion,** *n.*

par·ti·ci·ple (pär′tə sip′əl) *n.* adjective derived from verb.

par·ti·cle (pär′ti kəl) *n.* **1.** tiny piece. **2.** functional word.

par·tic·u·lar (pər tik′yə lər, pə-) *adj.* **1.** pertaining to a specific. **2.** noteworthy. **3.** attentive to details. —*n.* **4.** detail. —**par·tic·u·lar·ize′,** *v.,* **-ized, -izing.** give details.

par·tic·u·lar·ly, *adv.* **1.** especially. **2.** specifically.

par·tic·u·late (-lit, -lāt′, pär-) *adj.* composed of particles.

part′ing, *n.* departure or separation.

par·ti·san (pär′tə zən, -sən) *n.* **1.** adherent. **2.** guerrilla.

par·ti·tion (pär tish′ən) *n.* **1.** division into portions. **2.** interior wall. —*v.* **3.** divide into parts.

part′ly, *adv.* not wholly.

part′ner (pärt′nər) *n.* **1.** sharer; associate. **2.** joint owner. **3.** spouse or lover. —**part′ner·ship,** *n.*

par·tridge (pär′trij) *n.* game bird.

part′-song, *n.* song with parts for several voices.

part′-time, (-tīm′) **1.** involving or working less than the usual or full time. —*adv.* (-tīm′) **2.** on a part-time basis.

par·tu·ri·tion (pär′tŏŏ rish′ən, -tyŏŏ-) *n.* childbirth.

par′ty (pär′tē) *n., pl.* **-ties. 1.** group with common purpose. **2.** social gathering. **3.** persons concerned.

party line, 1. guiding policy of political party. **2.** telephone line connecting telephones of several subscribers.

par·ve·nu′ (pär′və nōō′, -nyōō′) *n., pl.* **-nus.** person with new wealth but not social acceptance.

pass (pas) *v.,* **passed, passed** or **past, passing,** —*v.* **1.** go up, by, or through. **2.** succeed. **3.**
transfer. **4.** approve. **5.** proceed. **6.** go by; elapse. **7.** die. **8.** be accepted. **9.** go unchallenged. —*n.* **10.** narrow route through barrier. **11.** permission or license. **12.** free ticket. **13.** state of affairs. —**pass′er,** *n.*

pass′a·ble, *adj.* adequate.

pas·sage (pas′ij) *n.* **1.** section of writing, etc. **2.** freedom to pass. **3.** movement; transportation. **4.** corridor. **5.** lapse. **6.** act of passing. —**pas′sage·way,** *n.*

pass′book, *n.* record of depositor's bank balance.

pas·sé′ (pa sā′) *adj.* out-of-date.

pas′sen·ger (pas′ən jər) *n.* traveler on vehicle or craft.

pass′er·by′, *n., pl.* **passers·by.** person who passes by.

pass′ing, *adj.* brief; transitory.

pas·sion (pash′ən) *n.* **1.** very strong emotion. **2.** sexual love. **3.** (*cap.*) sufferings of Christ. —**pas′sion·ate,** *adj.* —**pas′sion·ate·ly,** *adv.*

pas·sive (pas′iv) *adj.* **1.** not in action. **2.** acted upon. **3.** submitting without resistance. **4.** designating voice of verbs indicating subject acted upon. —**pas′sive·ly,** *adv.* —**pas′sive·ness, pas·siv′i·ty,** *n.*

passive resistance, nonviolent opposition.

passive smoking, inhaling of others' cigarette, cigar, or pipe smoke.

pass′key′, *n.* master key.

Pass′o·ver (pas′ō′vər) *n.* annual Jewish festival.

pass′port, *n.* official document giving permission to travel abroad.

pass′word′, *n.* secret word used to gain access.

past (past) *adj.* **1.** gone by, as in time. **2.** of an earlier time. **3.** designating a tense or verb formation showing time gone by. —*n.* **4.** time or events gone by. **5.** past tense. —*adv.* **6.** so as to pass by. —*prep.* **7.** after. **8.** beyond.

pas′ta (pä′stə) *n.* Italian flour-and-egg mixture, as spaghetti.

paste (pāst) *n., v.,* **pasted, pasting. 1.** soft, sticky mixture. **2.** glass for gems. —*v.* **3.** fasten with paste.

paste′board′, *n.* firm board made of layers of paper.

pas·tel′ (pa stel′) *n.* soft color.

pas·teur·ize′ (pas′chə rīz′) *v.,* **-ized, -izing.** heat (milk, etc.) to destroy certain bacteria.

pas·tiche′ (pa stēsh′) *n.* artistic work made up of borrowed details.

pas·tille′ (pa stēl′) *n.* lozenge.

pas′time′ (pas′tīm′) *n.* diversion.

past master, expert.

pas·tor (pas'tər) *n.* minister.

pas·to·ral, *adj.* **1.** having rural charm. **2.** of shepherds. **3.** of pastors or spiritual guidance.

pas·to·rale' (-räl') *n.* dreamy musical composition.

pas·tra·mi (pə strä'mē) *n.* seasoned smoked or pickled beef.

pas·try (pā'strē) *n., pl.* **-tries.** food made of rich paste, as pies.

pas·ture (pas'chər) *n., v.,* **-tured, -turing.**
—*n.* **1.** grassy ground for grazing.
—*v.* **2.** graze on pasture.

past·y (pā'stē) *adj.* like paste in texture or color.

pat (pat) *v.,* patted, patting, *n., adj., adv.* —*v.* **1.** strike gently. —*n.* **2.** light stroke. **3.** small mass. —*adj.* **4.** apt; to the point. —*adv.* **5.** perfectly. **6.** unwaveringly.

patch (pach) *n.* **1.** piece of material used to mend or protect. **2.** any small piece. —*v.* **3.** mend, esp. with patches. —**patch'work**, *n.*

patch test, allergy test where patch of material containing allergen is applied to skin.

patch·y, *adj.,* **-ier, -iest.** irregular in surface or quality.

pate (pāt) *n.* crown of head.

pâ·té (pä tā', pä-) *n.* paste of puréed or chopped meat, liver, etc.

pa·tel·la (pə tel'ə) *n., pl.* **-tellae** (tel'ē) *.* kneecap.

pat'ent (pat'nt) *n.* **1.** exclusive right to invention. —*adj.* **2.** protected by patent. **3.** evident. —*v.* **4.** secure patent on.

patent leather, hard, glossy, smooth leather.

patent medicine, drug protected by trademark.

pa·ter·nal (pə tûr'nl) *adj.* **1.** fatherly. **2.** related through father. —**pa·ter'nal·ly**, *adv.*

pa·ter·nal·ism, benevolent control. —**pa·ter'nal·is'tic**, *adj.*

pa·ter·ni·ty (-ni tē) *n.* fatherhood.

pa·ter·nos·ter (pā'tər nos'tər) *n.* Lord's Prayer.

path (path) *n.* **1.** Also, **path'way,** narrow way. **2.** route. **3.** course of action.

pa·thet·ic (pə thet'ik) *adj.* arousing pity. —**pa·thet'i·cal·ly**, *adv.*

path·o·gen (path'ə jən, -jen') *n.* disease-producing agent.

path·o·log·i·cal (-loj'i kəl) *adj.* sick; morbid.

pa·thol·o·gy (pə thol'ə jē) *n.* study of disease. —**pa·thol'o·gist**, *n.*

pa·thos (pā'thos, -thōs) *n.* quality or power of arousing pity.

-pathy, suffix meaning: **1.** feeling, as *antipathy.* **2.** method of treatment, as *osteopathy.*

pa·tient (pā'shənt) *n.* **1.** person under care of a doctor. —*adj.* **2.** enduring calmly. —**pa'tience**, *n.*

pa·ti·na (pat'n ə, pə tē'nə) *n.* film on old bronze, etc.

pa·ti·o (pat'ē ō') *n., pl.* **-tios.** inner open court.

pa·tri·arch (pā'trē ärk') *n.* **1.** venerable old man. **2.** male head of family. —**pa'tri·ar'chal**, *adj.*

pa·tri·ar·chy (-är'kē) *n., pl.* **-chies.** family group ruled by a father.

pa·tri·cian (pə trish'ən) *n.* aristocrat. —*adj.* **2.** aristocratic.

pat·ri·cide (pa'trə sīd') *n.* killing one's father. —**pat'ri·cid'al**, *adj.*

pat·ri·mo·ny (-mō'nē) *n., pl.* **-nies.** inherited estate.

pa·tri·ot (pā'trē ət, -ot') *n.* person who supports country. —**pa·tri·ot·ic**, *adj.* —**pa'tri·ot·ism** (-ə tiz'əm) *n.* —**pa'tri·ot·i·cal·ly**, *adv.*

pa·trol (pə trōl') *v.,* **-trolled, -trolling,** *n.* —*v.* **1.** pass through or around in guarding. —*n.* **2.** person or group assigned to patrol.

pa·trol·man, *n., pl.* **-men.** police officer who patrols.

pa·tron (pā'trən) *n.* **1.** supporter. **2.** regular customer.

pa·tron·age (pā'trə nij, pa'-) *n.* **1.** support by patron. **2.** political control of appointments to office.

pa·tron·ize' (-īz, pa'-) *v.,* **-ized, -izing.** **1.** buy from, esp. regularly. **2.** treat condescendingly.

patron saint, saint regarded as special guardian.

pat·sy (pat'sē) *n., pl.* **-sies.** *Slang.* person easily manipulated.

pat·ter (pat'ər) *v.* **1.** tap lightly and quickly. **2.** speak glibly. —*n.* **3.** pattering sound. **4.** rapid, glib talk.

pat·tern (pat'ərn) *n.* **1.** surface design. **2.** characteristic mode of development, etc. **3.** model for copying. —*v.* **4.** make after pattern.

pat·ty (pat'ē) *n., pl.* **-ties.** flat cake of ground or minced food.

pau·ci·ty (pô'si tē) *n.* scarceness.

paunch (pônch) *n.* belly, esp. when large. —**paunch'y**, *adj.*

pau·per (pô'pər) *n.* poor person.

pause (pôz) *n., v.,* **paused, pausing.** —*n.* **1.** temporary stop. —*v.* **2.** make pause.

pave (pāv) *v.,* **paved, paving.** **1.** cover with solid road surface. **2.** prepare. —**pave'ment,** *n.*

pa·vil·ion (pə vil'yən) *n.* **1.** light open shelter. **2.** tent.

paw (pô) *n.* **1.** foot of animal. —*v.* **2.** scrape with paw. **3.** touch clumsily.

pawn (pôn) *v.* **1.** deposit as security for loan. —*n.* **2.** state of being pawned. **3.** piece used in chess. —**pawn′shop′,** n.

pawn′bro′ker, n. person who lends money on pledged articles.

paw′paw′ (pô′pô′) n. small tree bearing purple flowers.

pay (pā) v., **paid, paying.** —v. **1.** give money required to. **2.** give as compensation. **3.** yield profit. **4.** let out (rope). —n. **5.** wages. **6.** paid employ. —**pay′a·ble,** adj. —**pay′ment,** n.

pay dirt. 1. profitable soil to mine. **2.** Informal. any source of wealth.

pay′load′, n. **1.** revenue-producing freight, etc. **2.** explosives, passengers, or cargo carried by an aircraft.

pay′mas′ter, n. person in charge of paying out wages.

pay′off′, n. **1.** Informal. final consequence. **2.** awaited payment.

pay·o′la (pā ō′lə) n. bribe.

pay′roll, n. **1.** list of employees to be paid. **2.** total of these amounts.

PC, 1. pl. **PCs** or **PC's.** personal computer. **2.** politically correct.

PE, physical education.

pea (pē) n. round edible seed of legume.

peace (pēs) n. **1.** freedom from war, trouble, or disturbance. —**peace′mak′er,** n. —**peace′time′,** n.

peace′ful, adj. **1.** at peace. **2.** desiring peace. Also, **peace′a·ble.**

peach (pēch) n. sweet juicy pinkish fruit.

pea′cock′ (pē′kok′) n. male peafowl, having iridescent tail feathers.

pea′fowl′, n. bird of pheasant family.

pea′hen′, n. female peafowl.

pea jacket, short heavy coat.

peak (pēk) n. **1.** pointed top. **2.** highest point.

peaked, adj. **1.** (pēkt) having peak. **2.** (pē′kid) sickly, haggard.

peal (pēl) n. **1.** prolonged sound, as of bells or thunder. **2.** set of bells. —v. **3.** sound in a peal.

pea′nut′, n. pod or edible seed of leguminous plant that ripens underground.

pear (pâr) n. elongated edible fruit.

pearl (pûrl) n. **1.** hard, smooth, near-white gem formed within an oyster. —**pearl′y,** adj.

peas′ant (pez′ənt) n. farm worker.

peat (pēt) n. organic soil dried for fuel. —**peat′y,** adj.

peb′ble (peb′əl) n. small, rounded stone. —**peb′bly,** adj.

pe·can′ (pi kän′, -kan′) n. smooth-shelled nut.

pec′ca·dil′lo (pek′ə dil′ō) n., pl. **-loes, -los.** trifling sin.

pec′ca·ry (pek′ə rē) n., pl. **-ries.** wild American pig.

peck (pek) v. **1.** strike with beak. —n. **2.** pecking stroke. **3.** dry measure of eight quarts.

pecking order, hierarchy within group.

pec′tin (pek′tin) n. substance in ripe fruit that forms jelly.

pec′to·ral (pek′tər əl) adj. **1.** of the chest. —n. **2.** pectoral muscle.

pe·cul′iar (pi kyōōl′yər) adj. **1.** strange; odd. **2.** uncommon. **3.** exclusive. —**pe·cu′li·ar′i·ty** (-lē ar′i-tē) n. —**pe·cul′iar·ly,** adv.

pe·cu′ni·ar′y (pi kyōō′nē er′ē) adj. of money.

ped·a·gogue (ped′ə gog′) n. teacher. —**ped′a·go·gy** (-gō′jē, -goj′ē) n. —**ped·a·gog′ic, ped·a·gog′i·cal,** adj.

ped′al (ped′l) n., v., **-aled, -aling,** adj. —n. **1.** lever worked by foot. —v. **2.** work pedals of. —adj. **3.** (pēd′al) of feet.

ped′ant (ped′nt) n. person excessively concerned with details. —**pe·dan′tic,** adj. —**ped′ant·ry,** n.

ped′dle (ped′l) v., **-dled, -dling.** carry about for sale. —**ped′dler,** n.

ped·er·as·ty (ped′ə ras′tē, pē′də-) n. sexual relations between a man and a boy. —**ped′er·ast′,** n.

ped′es·tal (ped′ə stl) n. base for object.

pe·des′tri·an (pə des′trē ən) n. **1.** walker. —adj. **2.** walking. **3.** prosaic.

pe′di·at′rics (pē′dē a′triks) n. study of care and diseases of children. —**pe′di·a·tri′cian** (pē′dē ə trish′ən) n. —**pe′di·at′ric,** adj.

ped′i·cure′ (ped′i kyōōr′) n. professional care of the feet.

ped′i·gree′ (ped′i grē′) n. **1.** certificate of ancestry. **2.** ancestry.

ped′i·ment (ped′ə mənt) n. triangular gablelike architectural feature.

pe·dom′e·ter (pə dom′i tər) n. device that measures distance walked.

peek (pēk) v., n. peep (defs. 1-3; 5).

peel (pēl) v. **1.** remove or lose skin, bark, etc. —n. **2.** skin of fruit, etc.

peep (pēp) v. **1.** look through small opening. **2.** look furtively. **3.** show slightly. **4.** utter shrill little cry. —n. **5.** quick look. **6.** weak sound.

peer (pēr) n. **1.** equal. **2.** noble. —v. **3.** look closely.

peer′age (-ij) n. rank of peer.

peer′less, adj. without equal.

peeve (pēv) n., v., **peeved, peeving.** —n. **1.** complaint. —v. **2.** vex.

peev′ish (pē′vish) adj. cross.

pee·wee (pē′wē′) n. Informal. person or thing that is unusually small.

peg (peg) *n., v.,* **pegged, pegging.** —*n.* **1.** pin of wood, metal, etc. —*v.* **2.** fasten with peg.

peg leg, wooden leg.

peign·oir′ (pān wär′, pen-) *n.* woman's loose dressing gown.

pe·jo·ra·tive (pi jôr′ə tiv) *adj.* disparaging; negative.

Pe′king·ese′ (pē′kə nēz′, -nēs′) *n., pl.* **-ese.** long-haired Chinese dog with flat muzzle.

pel′i·can (pel′i kən) *n.* large-billed bird.

pel·la′gra (pə lag′rə, -lā′grə, -lä′-) *n.* chronic disease from inadequate diet.

pel′let (pel′it) *n.* little ball.

pell′-mell′ (pel′mel′) *adv.* in disorderly haste.

pel·lu′cid (pə lōō′sid) *adj.* **1.** translucent. **2.** clear.

pelt (pelt) *v.* **1.** throw. **2.** assail. —*n.* **3.** a blow. **4.** skin of beast.

pel′vis (pel′vis) *n.* **1.** cavity in lower body trunk. **2.** bones forming this cavity. —**pel′vic,** *adj.*

pen (pen) *n., v.,* **penned** or (for 4) **pent, penning.** —*n.* **1.** device for writing with ink. **2.** small enclosure. —*v.* **3.** write with pen. **4.** confine in pen.

pe′nal (pēn′l) *adj.* of punishment. —**pe′nal·ize′,** *v.*

pen′al·ty (pen′l tē) *n., pl.* **-ties. 1.** punishment. **2.** disadvantage.

pen′ance (-əns) *n.* punishment as penitence for sin.

pence (pens) *n.* Brit. pl. of **penny.**

pen′chant (pen′chənt) *n.* liking.

pen′cil (pen′səl) *n.* enclosed stick of graphite, etc., for marking.

pend (pend) *v.* remain undecided.

pend′ant (pen′dənt) *n.* hanging ornament.

pend′ent (pen′dənt) *adj.* hanging.

pend′ing, *prep.* **1.** until. —*adj.* **2.** undecided.

pen′du·lous (pen′jə ləs, pen′dyə-) *adj.* hanging loosely.

pen′du·lum (-ləm) *n.* hung weight.

pen′e·trate′ (pen′i trāt′) *v.,* **-trated, -trating. 1.** pierce; permeate. **2.** enter. **3.** understand; have insight. —**pen′e·tra′tion,** *n.*

pen′guin (peng′gwin, pen′-) *n.* flightless aquatic bird.

pen′i·cil′lin (pen′ə sil′in) *n.* antibacterial substance produced in certain molds.

pen·in′su·la (pə nin′sə lə) *n.* piece of land nearly surrounded by water. —**pen·in′su·lar,** *adj.*

pe′nis (pē′nis) *n.* male sex organ. —**pe′nile** (pēn′l) *adj.*

pen′i·tent (pen′i tənt) *adj.* **1.** sorry for sin or fault. —*n.* **2.** penitent person. —**pen′i·tence,** *n.*

pen′i·ten′tia·ry (-ten′shə rē) *n., pl.* **-ries.** prison.

pen′knife′, *n.* small pocket knife.

pen′light′, *n.* flashlight shaped like fountain pen.

pen′man, *n., pl.* **-men.** one who writes. —**pen′man·ship′,** *n.*

Penn., Pennsylvania. Also, **Penna.**

pen name, pseudonym.

pen′nant (pen′ənt) *n.* flag, usually tapered. Also, **pen′non.**

pen′ny (pen′ē) *n., pl.* **-nies,** Brit. **pence.** small coin, equal to one cent in the U.S. and Canada, and to 1/100 pound in United Kingdom. —**pen′ni·less,** *adj.*

penny pincher, stingy person. —**pen′ny-pinch′ing,** *adj.*

pen′ny·weight′, *n.* (in troy weight) 24 grains, or 1/20 of an ounce.

pen pal, person with whom one exchanges letters.

pen·sion (pen′shən) *n.* **1.** fixed periodic payment for past service, etc. **2.** (pän sē ôn′) (in France) boarding house or school. —*v.* **3.** give pension to.

pen·sion·er, *n.* person receiving pension.

pen′sive (pen′siv) *adj.* gravely thoughtful. —**pen′sive·ly,** *adv.*

pent (pent) *adj.* confined.

penta-, prefix meaning five.

pen′ta·gon′ (pen′tə gon′) *n.* plane figure having five sides.

pen′ta·gram′ (-gram′) *n.* five-pointed, star-shaped symbol.

pen·tam′e·ter (pen tam′i tər) *n.* verse or line of five feet.

Pen′ta·teuch′ (pen′tə tōōk′, -tyōōk′) *n.* Bible. first five books of the Old Testament.

pen·tath′lon (pen tath′lən, -lon) *n.* athletic contest of five events.

Pen′te·cost′ (pen′ti kôst′) *n.* Christian festival; Whitsunday.

Pen′te·cos′tal, *adj.* of Christian groups that emphasize the Holy Spirit.

pent′house′ (pent′hous′) *n.* rooftop apartment or dwelling.

pent′-up′, *adj.* restrained; confined.

pe·nul′ti·mate (pi nul′tə mit) *adj.* being or occurring next to last.

pe·num′bra (pə num′brə) *n., pl.* **-brae** (-brē), **-bras.** partial shadow outside complete shadow of celestial body in eclipse. —**pe·num′bral,** *adj.*

pe·nu′ri·ous (pə nŏŏr′ē əs, -nyŏŏr′-) *adj.* **1.** stingy. **2.** very poor.

pen′u·ry (pen′yə rē) *n.* poverty.

pe·on (pē′an, -on) *n.* **1.** unskilled worker. **2.** indentured worker.

pe·on·age (-a nij) *n.* work of peon.

pe·o·ny (pē′a nē) *n., pl.* **-nies.** perennial plant with large flowers.

peo·ple (pē′pal) *n., v.* **-pled, -pling.** —*n.* **1.** body of persons constituting nation or ethnic group. **2.** persons in general. **3.** person's relatives. —*v.* **4.** populate.

pep (pep) *Informal.* —*n.* **1.** vigor. —*v.* **2.** give vigor to. —**pep′py**, *adj.*

pep·per (pep′ar) *n.* **1.** condiment from dried berries. **2.** edible fruit of certain plants. —*v.* **3.** season with pepper. **4.** pelt with shot. —**pep′per·y,** *adj.*

pep′per·corn′, *n.* dried berry of pepper plant.

pepper mill, device for grinding peppercorns.

pep·per·mint′ (-mint′) *n.* aromatic oil of herb, used as flavoring.

pep·per·o·ni (pep′a rō′nē) *n., pl.* **-nis.** highly seasoned sausage.

pep·sin (pep′sin) *n.* juice secreted in stomach that digests proteins.

pep·tic (pep′tik) *adj.* digestive.

per (pûr; *unstressed* par) *prep.* for; by means of.

per·am·bu·late′, *v.,* **-lated, -lating.** walk about or through.

per·am·bu·la′tor, *n.* baby carriage.

per an′num (par an′am) yearly.

per·cale′ (par kāl′) *n.* smooth, closely woven cotton fabric.

per cap′i·ta (par kap′i ta) by or for each person.

per·ceive′ (par sēv′) *v.,* **-ceived, -ceiving.** **1.** gain knowledge of by seeing, hearing, etc. **2.** understand. —**per·ceiv′a·ble,** *adj.*

per·cent′ (par sent′) *n.* number of parts in each hundred.

per·cent′age (-sen′tij) *n.* proportion or rate per hundred.

per·cen·tile (-tīl, -til) *n.* value of statistical variable that divides distribution of variable into 100 equal parts.

per·cep·ti·ble (-sep′ta bal) *adj.* capable of being perceived.

per·cep′tion, *n.* **1.** act or faculty of perceiving. **2.** intuition; insight. **3.** result or product of perceiving.

per·cep′tive, *adj.* **1.** keen. **2.** showing perception.

per·cep′tu·al (-chōō al) *adj.* involving perception.

perch (pûrch) *n.* **1.** place for roosting. **2.** linear measure of 5½ yards. **3.** square rod (30½ sq. yards). **4.** common food fish. **5.** set or rest on perch.

per·chance′ (par chans′) *adv. Poetic.* maybe; by chance.

per′co·late′ (pûr′ka lāt′) *v.,* **-lated, -lating.** filter through.

per′co·la′tor, *n.* coffee pot.

per·cus′sion (par kush′an) *n.* **1.** violent impact. —*adj.* **2.** musical instruments sounded by striking.

per di′em (par dē′am) *adv.* **1.** by the day. —*n.* **2.** daily pay or allowance for expenses.

per·di′tion (par dish′an) *n.* ruin; hell.

per′e·gri·nate′ (per′i gra nāt′) *v.,* **-nated, -nating.** travel, esp. on foot. —**per′e·gri·na′tion,** *n.*

peregrine falcon (per′i grin, -grēn′) bird of prey.

per·emp′to·ry (pa remp′ta rē) *adj.* permitting no denial or refusal. —**per·emp′to·ri·ly,** *adv.*

per·en′ni·al (pa ren′ē al) *adj.* **1.** lasting indefinitely. **2.** living more than two years. —*n.* **3.** perennial plant. —**per·en′ni·al·ly,** *adv.*

per′fect (pûr′fikt) *adj.* **1.** faultless. **2.** designating verb tense indicating action already completed. —*n.* **3.** *Gram.* perfect tense. —*v.* (par fekt′) **4.** make faultless. —**per·fec′tion** (par fek′shan) *n.*

per·fec′tion·ism, *n.* insistence on perfection. —**per·fec′tion·ist,** *n.*

per′fi·dy (pûr′fi dē) *n., pl.* **-dies.** treachery. —**per·fid′i·ous,** *adj.*

per′fo·rate′ (pûr′fa rāt′) *v.,* **-rated, -rating.** make holes through. —**per′fo·ra′tion,** *n.*

per·force′ (par fôrs′) *adv.* of necessity.

per·form′ (-fôrm′) *v.* **1.** carry out; do. **2.** act, as on stage. —**per·for′mance,** *n.* —**per·form′er,** *n.*

performing arts, arts requiring public performance.

per·fume, *n., v.,* **-fumed, -fuming.** —*n.* (pûr′fyōōm, par fyōōm′) **1.** sweet-smelling liquid. **2.** sweet smell. —*v.* (par fyōōm′, pûr′fyōōm) **3.** impart fragrance to. —**per·fum′er·y,** *n.*

per·func′to·ry (par fungk′ta rē) *adj.* done without care or attention. —**per·func′to·ri·ly,** *adv.*

per·haps′ (par haps′) *adv.* maybe.

peri-, prefix meaning around, surrounding, or near.

per′i·car′di·um (per′i kär′dē am) *n.* membranous sac enclosing the heart.

per·il (per′al) *n.* **1.** danger. —*v.* **2.** endanger. —**per′il·ous,** *adj.*

per·im′e·ter (pa rim′i tar) *n.* outer boundary of plane figure.

per′i·ne′um (per′a nē′am) *n., v.,*

-nea. area between genitals and anus.

pe·ri·od (pēr'ē əd) *n.* **1.** portion of time. **2.** mark (.) ending sentence.

pe·ri·od·ic (-od'ik) *adj.* recurring regularly or intermittently. —**pe'ri·od'i·cal·ly,** *adv.*

pe·ri·od·i·cal *n.* **1.** publication issued at regular intervals. —*adj.* **2.** periodic.

periodic table, table showing chemical elements in related groups.

per·i·pa·tet·ic (per'ə pə tet'ik) *adj.* walking or traveling about; itinerant.

pe·riph·er·al (pə rif'ər əl) *adj.* **1.** located on periphery. **2.** only partly relevant.

pe·riph·er·y, *n., pl.* **-eries. 1.** external boundary. **2.** external surface.

pe·riph·ra·sis (pə rif'rə sis) *n., pl.* **-ses** (-sēz'). use of roundabout form of expression.

per·i·scope (per'ə skōp') *n.* optical instrument consisting of a tube in which mirrors or prisms reflect to give a view from below or behind an obstacle.

per·ish (per'ish) *v.* **1.** die. **2.** decay. —**per'ish·a·ble,** *adj.,*

per·i·stal·sis (per'ə stöl'sis, -stal'-) *n., pl.* **-ses** (-sēz). muscle contractions and relaxations that move food along alimentary canal.

per·i·to·ne·um (per'i tn ē'əm, -tō'-) *n.* lining of abdominal cavity.

per·i·to·ni·tis (-tn i'tis) *n.* swelling of peritoneum.

per·i·win·kle (per'ə wing'kəl) *n.* **1.** edible marine snail. **2.** trailing evergreen plant.

per·jure (pûr'jər) *v.,* **-jured, -juring.** lie under oath. —**per'jur·er,** *n.*

per·ju·ry (pûr'jə rē) *n., pl.* **-ries.** false statement made under oath.

perk (pûrk) *v.* **1.** move up jauntily. **2.** become lively. —*n.* **3.** perquisite.

perk'y *adj.* cheerful.

per·ma·frost (pûr'mə frôst') *n.* permanently frozen subsoil.

per·ma·nent (-nənt) *adj.* **1.** lasting indefinitely. —*n.* **2.** curl chemically set in hair. —**per'ma·nence,** *n.* —**per'ma·nent·ly,** *adv.*

per·me·a·ble (pûr'mē ə bəl) *adj.* letting fluids through.

per·me·ate' (-āt') *v.,* **-ated, -ating.** penetrate; pervade.

per·mis·sion (-mish'ən) *n.* authorization. —**per·mis'si·ble,** *adj.*

per·mis·sive (-mis'iv) *adj.* **1.** giving permission. **2.** loose or lax in discipline.

per·mit' *v.,* **-mitted, -mitting,** *n.* —*v.* (pər mit') **1.** allow; agree to. **2.** afford opportunity. —*n.* (pûr'-

mit, pər mit') **3.** written order giving permission.

per·mu·ta·tion (pûr'myōō tā'shən) *n.* alteration; change in order.

per·ni·cious (pər nish'əs) *adj.* **1.** highly hurtful. **2.** deadly.

per·ox·ide (pə rok'sīd) *n.* **1.** oxide containing large amount of oxygen. **2.** hydrogen peroxide.

per·pen·dic·u·lar (pûr'pən dik'yə lər) *adj.* **1.** vertical. **2.** meeting given line at right angles. —*n.* **3.** perpendicular line or plane.

per·pe·trate' (pûr'pi trāt') *v.,* **-trated, -trating.** commit (crime, etc.). —**per'pe·tra'tion,** *n.* —**per'·pe·tra'tor,** *n.*

per·pet·u·al (par pech'ōō əl) *adj.* **1.** lasting forever. **2.** unceasing. —**per·pet'u·ate',** *v.*

per·pe·tu·i·ty (pûr'pi tōō'i tē, -tyōō'-) *n.* forever.

per·plex' (pər pleks') *v.* confuse mentally. —**per·plex'i·ty,** *n.*

per'qui·site (pûr'kwə zit) *n.* incidental profit.

per se (pûr sā', sē', pər) by, of, for, or in itself; intrinsically.

per·se·cute' (pûr'si kyōōt') *v.,* **-cuted, -cuting.** oppress persistently, esp. for one's beliefs. —**per'se·cu'tion,** *n.* —**per'se·cu'tor,** *n.*

per·se·vere' (pûr'sə vēr') *v.,* **-vered, -vering.** continue steadfastly. —**per'se·ver'ance,** *n.*

per·sim·mon (pər sim'ən) *n.* soft fruit.

per·sist' (pər sist', -zist') *v.* **1.** continue firmly in spite of opposition. **2.** endure. —**per·sist'ence,** *n.* —**per·sist'ent,** *adj.*

per·snick·et·y (pər snik'i tē) *adj.* *Informal.* fussy.

per'son (pûr'sən) *n.* **1.** human being. **2.** individual personality. **3.** body.

per'son·a·ble, *adj.* attractive in appearance and manner.

per'son·age (-sə nij) *n.* distinguished person.

per'son·al (-sə nl) *adj.* **1.** of, by, or relating to a certain person. **2.** *Gram.* denoting class of pronouns that refer to speaker, person addressed, or person spoken of. **3.** *Law.* of property that is movable. —**per'son·al·ly,** *adv.*

personal computer, microcomputer designed for individual use.

personal effects, belongings.

per'son·al'i·ty (-sə nal'ə tē) *n., pl.* **-ties. 1.** distinctive personal character. **2.** famous person.

per'son·al·ize', *v.,* **-ized, -izing. 1.** make personal. **2.** treat as if human.

per·so/na non gra/ta (pər sō/nə non grä/tə) unwelcome.

per·son/i·fy/ (pər son/ə fī/) v., **-fied, -fying. 1.** attribute personal character to. **2.** embody; typify. —**per·son/i·fi·ca/tion,** n.

per·son·nel/ (pûr/sə nel/) n. employees.

per·spec/tive (pər spek/tiv) n. **1.** depiction as to show space relationships. **2.** mental view.

per·spi·ca/cious (pûr/spi kā/shəs) adj. mentally keen. —**per·spi·cac/i·ty** (-kas/i tē) n.

per·spire/ (pər spī°r/) v., **-spired, -spiring.** sweat. —**per·spi·ra/tion** (pûr/spə rā/shən) n.

per·suade/ (pər swād/) v., **-suaded, -suading. 1.** prevail on to act as suggested. **2.** convince. —**per·sua/sive,** adj. —**per·sua/sive·ly,** adv.

per·sua/sion (-swā/zhən) n. **1.** act or power of persuading. **2.** conviction or belief. **3.** religious system.

pert (pûrt) adj. bold; saucy.

per·tain/ (pər tān/) v. belong; have reference.

per/ti·nent (-tn ənt) adj. relevant. —**per/ti·nence,** n. —**per/ti·nent·ly,** adv.

per·turb/ (pər tûrb/) v. disturb greatly. —**per/tur·ba/tion,** n.

pe·ruke/ (pə rōōk/) n. man's wig.

pe·ruse/ (pə rōōz/) v., **-rused, -rusing.** read, esp. with care. —**pe·ru/sal,** n.

per·vade/ (pər vād/) v., **-vaded, -vading.** be present throughout. —**per·va/sive,** adj.

per·verse/ (pər vûrs/) adj. stubbornly contrary. —**per·ver/si·ty,** n.

per·vert/ v. (pər vûrt/) **1.** turn from right or moral sense or use. —n. (pûr/vûrt) **2.** perverted person. —**per·ver/sion,** n.

pe·se/ta (pə sā/tə) n., pl. **-tas.** monetary unit of Spain.

pes/ky (pes/kē) adj., **-kier, -kiest.** annoying; troublesome.

pe/so (pā/sō) n. monetary unit and coin in Latin America.

pes/si·mism (pes/ə miz/əm) n. **1.** disposition to expect worst. **2.** belief that all things tend to evil. —**pes/si·mist,** n. —**pes/si·mis/tic,** adj. —**pes/si·mis/ti·cal·ly,** adv.

pest (pest) n. troublesome person, animal, or thing.

pes/ter (pes/tər) v. annoy; harass.

pes/ti·cide/ (pes/tə sīd/) n. poison used to kill harmful insects or weeds.

pes·tif/er·ous (pe stif/ər əs) adj. **1.** bearing disease. **2.** troublesome.

pes/ti·lence (pes/tl əns) n. epidemic disease. —**pes/ti·lent,** adj.

pes/tle (pes/əl, pes/tl) n. instrument for pounding or crushing.

pes/to (pes/tō) n. sauce of basil, nuts, garlic, olive oil, and cheese.

pet (pet) n., adj., v., **petted, petting.** —n. **1.** tame animal that is cared for affectionately. **2.** favorite. **3.** tantrum. —adj. **4.** treated as pet. —v. **5.** caress.

pet/al (pet/l) n. leaf of blossom.

pe·tard/ (pi tärd/) n. explosive device.

pe/ter (pē/tər) v. Informal. diminish gradually.

pe·tite/ (pə tēt/) adj. small.

pe·ti/tion (pə tish/ən) n. **1.** request, esp. formal one. —v. **2.** present petition. —**pe·ti/tion·er,** n.

pet/rel (pe/trəl) n. small oceanic bird.

pet·ri·fy (pe/trə fī/) v., **-fied, -fying. 1.** turn into stone. **2.** paralyze with fear.

pe/tro·chem/i·cal (pe/trō kem/i kəl) n. chemical from petroleum.

pe·tro/le·um (pə trō/lē əm) n. oily liquid occurring underground; source of gasoline, kerosene, paraffin, etc.

pe·trol/o·gy (pi trol/ə jē) n. study of rocks.

pet/ti·coat/ (pe/tē kōt/) n. underskirt.

pet/ti·fog/ (pe/tē fog/) v., **-fogged, -fogging.** quibble over trifles.

pet/tish (pet/ish) adj. petulant.

pet/ty (pet/ē) adj., **-tier, -tiest.** small or trivial. **2.** small-minded. —**pet/ti·ness,** n.

petty cash, fund for paying minor expenses.

petty jury, jury in civil or criminal trial.

petty officer, noncommissioned officer in navy or coast guard.

pet/u·lant (pech/ə lənt) adj. showing impatient irritation. —**pet/u·lance,** n.

pe·tu/ni·a (pi tōō/nyə, -tyōō/-) n. plant with funnel-shaped flowers.

pew (pyōō) n. enclosed bench or seats in church.

pe/wee (pē/wē) n. any of certain small birds.

pew/ter (pyōō/tər) n. alloy rich in lead.

pf., (of stock) preferred.

PG, motion-picture rating: parental guidance recommended.

PG-13, motion-picture rating: material may be unsuitable for children under 13.

pg., page.

pH, symbol describing acidity or alkalinity of chemical solution.

pha·e·ton (fā′i tn, fā′ə tən) n. open carriage or automobile.

pha/lanx (fā′langks, fal′angks) n., pl. **phalanxes, phalanges** (fə lan′jēz). **1.** compact body, as of troops, etc. **2.** any bone of fingers or toes.

phal/lus (fal′əs) n., pl. **phal·li** (fal′ī). **1.** penis. **2.** image of penis as symbol of fertility. —**phal/lic,** adj.

phan/tasm (fan′taz əm) n. apparition.

phan·tas/ma·go/ri·a (-ma gôr′ē ə) n. shifting series of illusions.

phan/tom (-təm) n. **1.** ghostlike image. —adj. **2.** unreal.

Phar·aoh (fâr′ō) n. title of ancient Egyptian kings.

Phar/i·see (far′ə sē′) n. **1.** member of ancient Jewish sect. **2.** (l.c.) self-righteous person.

phar·ma·ceu/ti·cal (fär′mə sōō′ti-kəl) adj. pertaining to pharmacy.

phar·ma·col/o·gy (-kol′ə jē) n. study of drugs.

phar·ma·co·poe/ia (-kə pē′ə) n. book on medicines.

phar/ma·cy (-sē) n., pl. **-cies. 1.** art or practice of preparing medicines. **2.** place for dispensing medicines. —**phar/ma·cist,** n.

phar/ynx (far′ingks) n., pl. **pharyn·ges** (fə rin′jēz), **pharynxes.** tube connecting mouth and nasal passages with esophagus. —**pha·ryn/ge·al,** or —**phar/yn·gi/tis** (far′ən jī′tis) n.

phase (fāz) n. **1.** stage of change. **2.** aspect of changing thing.

phase/out/, n. **1.** gradual dismissal or termination.

Ph.D., Doctor of Philosophy.

pheas/ant (fez′ənt) n. large, long-tailed, brightly colored bird.

phe/no·bar/bi·tal/ (fē′nō bär′bi-tôl′, -tal′) n. white powder used as sedative.

phe/nol (fē′nôl) n. carbolic acid.

phe·nom/e·non/ (fi nom′ə non′, -nən) n., pl. **-e·na** (-ə nə). **1.** something observable. **2.** extraordinary thing or person. —**phe·nom/e·nal,** adj. —**phe·nom/e·nal·ly,** adv.

pher/o·mone/ (fer′ə mōn′) n. chemical substance released by animal that influences behavior of other members of species.

phi/al (fī′əl) n. vial.

phil-, prefix meaning loving, having affinity for.

phi·lan/der·er (fi lan′dər ər) n. a man who has many love affairs. —**phi·lan/der,** v.

phi·lan/thro·py (fi lan′thrə pē) n., pl. **-pies.** love of humanity. **2.** benevolent act, work, or institution.

—**phil/an·throp/ic** (fil′ən throp′ik), adj. —**phi·lan/thro·pist,** n.

phi·lat/e·ly (fi lat′l ē) n. collection and study of postage stamps, etc. —**phi·lat/e·list,** n.

-phile, suffix meaning one that loves or has strong enthusiasm for.

phil/har·mon/ic (fil′här mon′ik) adj. **1.** music-loving. —n. **2.** large orchestra.

phil/is·tine/ (fil′ə stēn′, -stīn′) n. person indifferent to culture.

phi/lo·den/dron (fil′ə den′drən) n., pl. **-drons, -dra.** tropical climbing plant.

phi·lol/o·gy (fi lol′ə jē) n. linguistics. —**phi·lol/o·gist,** n.

phi·los/o·pher (fi los′ə fər) n. **1.** person versed in philosophy. **2.** person guided by reason.

phi·los/o·phy (-fē) n., pl. **-phies. 1.** study of truths underlying being and knowledge. **2.** system of philosophical belief. **3.** principles of particular field of knowledge or action. **4.** calmness. —**phil/o·soph/ic** (fil′ə sof′ik), **phil/o·soph/i·cal,** adj. —**phi·los/o·phize/,** v.

phle·bi/tis (flə bī′tis) n. inflammation of a vein.

phle·bot/o·my (flə bot′ə mē) n., pl. **-mies.** practice of opening a vein to let blood. —**phle·bot/o·mize/,** v., **-mized, -mizing.**

phlegm (flem) n. **1.** thick mucus in the respiratory passages. **2.** apathy.

phleg·mat/ic (fleg mat′ik) adj. unemotional or unenthusiastic.

phlo/em (flō′em) n. tissue in plant through which food passes.

phlox (floks) n. garden plant with showy flowers.

-phobe, suffix meaning one who hates or fears.

pho/bi·a (fō′bē ə) n. morbid fear.

-phobia, suffix meaning fear or dread.

phoe/be (fē′bē) n. small American bird.

phoe/nix (fē′niks) n. mythical bird that burns, then rises from its ashes.

phone (fōn) n., v., **phoned, phoning.** Informal. telephone.

pho/neme (fō′nēm) n. minimal unit of speech sound that distinguishes one word from another.

pho·net/ics (fə net′iks) n. study of speech sounds. —**pho·net/ic,** adj.

phon/ics (fon′iks) n. method of teaching reading and spelling based on phonetics.

phono-, prefix meaning sound.

pho/no·graph/ (fō′nə graf′) n. sound-producing machine using records. —**pho/no·graph/ic,** adj.

pho·nol·o·gy (fə nol′ə jē) n., pl. **-gies.** study of sound changes in language.

pho′ny (fō′nē) adj., **-nier, -niest,** n., pl. **-nies.** Informal. —adj. **1.** false; fraudulent. —n. **2.** something phony. —**pho′ni·ness,** n.

phos′gene (fos′jēn) n. poisonous gas.

phos′phate (fos′fāt) n. **1.** salt of phosphoric acid. **2.** fertilizer containing phosphorus.

phos′phor (fos′fər) n. substance showing luminescence.

phos·pho·res·cent (-fə res′ənt) adj. luminous. —**phos·pho·res′cence,** n.

phos·pho·rus (fos′fər əs) n. solid nonmetallic element present in all forms of life. —**phos·phor′ic** (-fôr′ik), **phos′pho·rous,** adj.

pho′to (fō′tō) n., pl. **-tos.** Informal. photograph.

photo-, prefix meaning light.

pho′to·cop′y, n., pl. **-copies.** photographic copy. —**pho′to·cop′y,** v.

pho·to·e·lec′tric, adj. of or using electrical effects produced by light.

pho′to·en·grav′ing, n. photographic process of preparing printing plates for printing.

photo finish, finish of race so close as to require scrutiny of photograph to determine winner.

pho·to·gen′ic (fō′tə jen′ik) adj. looking attractive in photos.

pho′to·graph (-graf′) n. **1.** picture produced by photography. —v. **2.** take photograph. —**pho·tog′ra·pher** (fə tog′rə fər) n.

pho·tog·ra·phy (fə tog′rə fē) n. process of obtaining images on sensitized surface by action of light. —**pho·to·graph·ic** (fō′tə graf′ik) adj.

pho′ton (fō′ton) n. quantum of electromagnetic radiation.

pho·to·sen′si·tive, adj. sensitive to light.

Pho′to·stat′ (fō′tə stat′) n. **1.** Trademark. camera for photographing documents, etc. **2.** (l.c.) the photograph. —v. **3.** (l.c.) make photostatic copy. —**pho·to·stat′ic,** adj.

pho·to·syn′the·sis, n. conversion by plants of carbon dioxide and water into carbohydrates, aided by light and chlorophyll.

phrase (frāz) n., v., **phrased, phrasing.** —n. **1.** sequence of words used as unit. **2.** minor division of musical composition. —v. **3.** express in particular way.

phra·se·ol·o·gy (frā′zē ol′ə jē) n. manner of verbal expression.

phre·nol·o·gy (frə nol′ə jē) n. theory that mental powers are shown by shape of skull.

phy·log·e·ny (fī loj′ə nē) n. development of particular group of organisms.

phy′lum (fī′ləm) n., pl. **-la.** primary classification of plants or animals.

phys′ic (fiz′ik) n. medicine, esp. one that purges.

phys′i·cal, adj. **1.** of the body. **2.** of matter. **3.** of physics. —n. **4.** full examination of body.

physical anthropology, study of evolutionary changes in human body structure.

physical science, science that deals with inanimate matter or energy.

physical therapy, treatment of physical disability or pain by techniques such as exercise.

phy·si′cian (fi zish′ən) n. medical doctor.

phys′ics (fiz′iks) n. science of matter, motion, energy, and force. —**phys′i·cist,** n.

phys·i·og·no·my (fiz′ē og′nə mē, -on′ə-) n., pl. **-mies.** face.

phys·i·og·ra·phy (-og′rə fē) n. study of earth's surface.

phys·i·ol·o·gy (-ol′ə jē) n. science dealing with functions of living organisms. —**phys·i·o·log′i·cal** (-ə loj′i kal) adj. —**phys·i·ol′o·gist,** n.

phys·i·o·ther′a·py (fiz′ē ō-) n. treatment of disease by massage, exercise, etc.

phy·sique′ (fi zēk′) n. physical structure.

pi (pī) n. the Greek letter, used as symbol for ratio of circumference to diameter.

pi·a·nis·si·mo (pē′ə nis′ə mō′, pyä-) adv. Music. very softly.

pi·an·o (pē an′ō) n., pl. **-anos,** adv. —n. **1.** Also, **pi·an·o·for·te** (-fôr′tā). musical keyboard instrument in which hammers strike upon metal strings. —adv. (pē ä′nō) **2.** Music. softly. —**pi·an′ist** (pē an′ist, pē′ə-nist) n.

pi·az′za (pē az′ə or, for 0, -ät′sə) n. open public square, esp. in Italy.

pi′ca (pī′kə) n. **1.** size of printing type. **2.** unit of measure in printing.

pic·a·resque′ (pik′ə resk′) adj. of a form of fiction that describes adventures of roguish hero.

pic′a·yune′ (pik′ē yōōn′, pik′ə-) adj. insignificant; petty.

pic·ca·lil′li (pik′ə lil′ē) n. spiced vegetable relish.

pic′co·lo′ (pik′ə lō′) n., pl. **-los.** small shrill flute.

pick (pik) v. **1.** choose. **2.** pluck. **3.** dig or break into, esp. with pointed

instrument. **4.** nibble listlessly.
—*n.* **5.** choice. **6.** right to choose.
7. Also, **pick′ax′, pick′axe′.** sharp-pointed tool for breaking rock, etc.

pick′er•el (pik′ər əl) *n.* small pike.

pick′et (pik′it) *n.* **1.** pointed stake.
2. demonstration by labor union in front of workplace. **3.** troops posted to warn of enemy attack. —*v.* **4.** enclose with pickets. **5.** put pickets in front of.

picket line, line of strikers or other pickets.

pick′le (pik′əl) *n., v.,* **-led, -ling.**
—*n.* **1.** cucumber, etc. preserved in spiced vinegar. **2.** predicament.
—*v.* **3.** preserve in vinegar or brine.

pick′pock′et, *n.* person who steals from others' pockets.

pick′up′, *n.* **1.** ability to accelerate rapidly. **2.** open-body truck.

pick′y, *adj.,* **-ier, -iest.** extremely fussy or finicky.

pic′nic (pik′nik) *n., v.,* **-nicked, -nicking.** —*n.* **1.** outing and meal in the open. —*v.* **2.** have picnic.
—**pic′nick•er,** *n.*

pi′cot (pē′kō) *n.* decorative loop along edge of lace, ribbon, etc.

pic′ture (pik′chər) *n., v.,* **-tured, -turing.** —*n.* **1.** painting or photograph. **2.** motion picture. **3.** represent in picture. **4.** imagine.
—**pic•to′ri•al,** *adj.*

pic′tur•esque′ (-chə resk′) *adj.* visually charming or quaint.

pid′dling, *adj.* trivial; negligible.

pidg′in (pij′ən) *n.* language developed to allow speakers of two different languages to communicate.

pidgin English, English trade jargon used in other countries.

pie (pī) *n.* baked dish of fruit, meat, etc., in pastry crust.

pie′bald′ (pī′bôld′) *adj.* having patches of different colors.

piece (pēs) *n., v.,* **pieced, piecing.** —*n.* **1.** limited or single portion. **2.** one part of a whole. **3.** artistic work. **4.** rifle or cannon. —*v.* **5.** make or enlarge by joining pieces.

pièce de ré•sis•tance′ (pyes da RĀ-zē stäns′) *n., pl.* **pièces de résistance** (pyes-). **1.** principal dish of meal. **2.** principal item of series.

piece goods, goods sold at retail by linear measure.

piece′meal′, *adv.* gradually.

piece′work′, *n.* work done and paid for by the piece.

pie chart, graph in which sectors of circle represent quantities.

pied (pīd) *adj.* many-colored.

pied′-à-terre′ (pyä′dä târ′) *n., pl.* **pieds′-à-terre′** (pyä′-). apartment for part-time use.

pie′-eyed′, *adj. Slang.* drunk.

pier (pēr) *n.* **1.** structure at which vessels are moored. **2.** masonry support.

pierce (pērs) *v.,* **pierced, piercing. 1.** make hole or way through. **2.** make (hole) in.

pi′e•ty (pī′i tē) *n.* piousness.

pif′fle (pif′əl) *n. Informal.* nonsense. —**pif′fling,** *adj.*

pig (pig) *n.* **1.** swine. **2.** bar of metal. —**pig′gish,** *adj.*

pi′geon (pij′ən) *n.* short-legged bird with compact body.

pi′geon•hole′, *n., v.,* **-holed, -holing.** —*n.* **1.** small compartment, as in desk, etc. —*v.* **2.** classify. **3.** set aside and ignore.

pi′geon-toed′, *adj.* having toes or feet turned inward.

pig′gy•back′, *adv.* **1.** on the back or shoulders. —*adj.* **2.** astride the back. **3.** attached to something else.

pig′head•ed, *adj.* perversely stubborn.

pig iron, crude iron from furnace.

pig′let, *n.* baby pig.

pig′ment (-mənt) *n.* coloring matter. —**pig′men•tar′y,** *adj.*

pig′men•ta′tion, *n.* coloration.

pig′my (-mē) *n., pl.* **-mies.** pygmy.

pig′pen′, *n.* **1.** stall for pigs. **2.** filthy or untidy place. Also, **pig′ sty′.**

pig′tail′, *n.* braid of hair.

pike (pīk) *n.* **1.** large fresh-water fish. **2.** metal-headed weapon.

pik′er, *n. Slang.* person who does things cheaply or meanly.

pi′laf′ (pē′läf, pi läf′) *n.* Middle Eastern rice dish.

pi•las′ter (pi las′tər) *n.* shallow decorative feature similar to column.

pil′chard (pil′chərd) *n.* marine fish.

pile (pīl) *n., v.,* **piled, piling.** —*n.* **1.** group of things lying one on another. **2.** large amount of anything. **3.** device for producing energy by nuclear reaction. **4.** Also, **pil′ing.** upright driven into ground as foundation member or to retain earth. **5.** hair; down; wool; fur. **6.** *n.* (def. 2). **7.** *pl.* hemorrhoids. —*v.* **8.** lay in pile. **9.** accumulate.

pil′fer (pil′fər) *v.* steal, esp. small amounts. —**pil′fer•age,** *n.*

pil′grim (pil′grim, -grəm) *n.* **1.** traveler, esp. to sacred place. **2.** (*cap.*) early Puritan settler in America.
—**pil′grim•age,** *n.*

pill (pil) *n.* small mass of medicine to be swallowed.

pil′lage (pil′ij) *v.,* **-laged, -laging,** *n.* plunder.

pil/lar (pil'ər) n. upright shaft of masonry.

pill/box', n. **1.** small fort. **2.** box for pills.

pil/lo-ry (pil'ə rē) n., pl. -ries, v., -ried, -rying. —n. **1.** wooden framework used to confine and expose offenders. —v. **2.** put in pillory. **3.** expose to public contempt. —pil/low-case', n.

pil/low (pil'ō) n. bag of feathers, etc., used as support for head. —pil/low-case', n.

pi/lot (pī'lət) n. **1.** operator of aircraft. **2.** expert navigator. —v. **3.** steer. —adj. **4.** experimental.

pilot light, small flame used to relight main burners.

pi-men/to (pi men'tō) n., pl. -tos. red fruit of sweet pepper.

pi-mien/to (-myen'tō, -men'-) n., pl. -tos. pimento.

pimp (pimp) n., v. —n. **1.** manager of prostitutes. —v. **2.** act as pimp.

pim/ple (pim'pal) n. small swelling of skin. —pim/ply, adj.

pin (pin) n., v., pinned, pinning. —n. **1.** slender pointed piece of metal, wood, etc., for fastening. —v. **2.** fasten with pin. **3.** hold fast.

PIN (pin) personal identification number.

pin/a-fore' (pin'ə fôr') n. **1.** child's apron. **2.** sleeveless dress.

pin/ball', n. game in which spring-driven ball rolls against pins on sloping board.

pince/-nez' (pans'nā', pins'-) n., pl. **pince-nez.** eyeglasses supported by pinching the nose.

pin/cers (pin'sərz) n.pl. gripping tool with two pivoted limbs.

pinch (pinch) v. **1.** squeeze, as between finger and thumb. **2.** cramp or affect sharply. **3.** economize. —n. **4.** act of pinching. **5.** tiny amount. **6.** distress; emergency.

pinch/-hit', v., -hit, -hitting. substitute.

pine (pīn) v., pined, pining, n. —v. **1.** long painfully. **2.** fail in health from grief, etc. —n. **3.** evergreen tree with needle-shaped leaves.

pine/ap/ple, (pīn'ap'əl) n. tropical fruit.

pin/feath/er, n. undeveloped feather.

ping (ping) v. **1.** produce sharp sound like bullet striking metal. —n. **2.** pinging sound.

Ping/-Pong' (ping'pong') n. Trademark. table tennis.

pin/head', n. **1.** head of pin. **2.** stupid person.

pin/ion (pin'yən) n. **1.** feather or wing. **2.** small cogwheel. —v. **3.** bind (the arms).

pink (pingk) n. **1.** pale red. **2.** fragrant garden flower. **3.** highest degree. —pink, adj.

pink/eye', n. contagious inflammation of membrane covering eye.

pinking shears, shears with notched blades.

pin money, small sum set aside.

pin/na-cle (pin'ə kəl) n. lofty peak or position.

pin/nate (pin'āt, -it) adj. having leaflets on each side of common stalk.

pi/noch/le (pē'nuk əl, -nok-) n. game using 48 cards.

pin/point', v. identify.

pin/stripe', n. very thin stripe in fabric. —pin'striped', adj.

pint (pīnt) n. liquid and dry measure equal to one-half quart.

pin/to (pin'tō, pēn'-) adj., n., pl. -tos. —adj. **1.** piebald. —n. **2.** piebald horse.

pinto bean, bean with pinkish mottled seeds.

pin/up', n. large photograph of sexually attractive person.

pin/wheel', n. windmill-like toy that spins on stick.

pin/yin' (pin'yin') n. system for writing Chinese in Latin alphabet.

pi/o-neer' (pī'ə nēr') n. **1.** early arrival in new territory. **2.** first one in any effort. —v. **3.** act as pioneer.

pi/ous (pī'əs) adj. **1.** reverential; devout. **2.** sacred. —pi'ous-ly, adv.

pip (pip) n. **1.** small fruit seed. **2.** spot on playing card, domino, etc. **3.** disease of fowls.

pipe (pīp) n., v., piped, piping. —n. **1.** tube for conveying fluid. **2.** tube for smoking tobacco. **3.** tube used as musical instrument. —v. **4.** play on pipe. **5.** convey by pipe.

pipe dream, unrealistic hope.

pipe/line', n. **1.** linked pipes for transporting oil, water, etc. **2.** route for supplies. **3.** channel of information.

pip/ing, n. **1.** pipes. **2.** sound of pipes. **3.** kind of trimming.

pip/pin (pip'in) n. kind of apple.

pip/squeak' (pip'skwēk') n. Informal. small or unimportant person.

pi/quant (pē'kənt, -känt) adj. agreeably sharp. —pi/quan-cy, n.

pique (pēk) v., piqued, piquing, n. —v. **1.** arouse resentment in. **2.** excite (curiosity, etc.). —n. **3.** irritated feeling.

pi-qué/ (pi kā') n. corded cotton fabric.

pi/ra-cy (pī'rə sē) n., pl. -cies. **1.** robbery at sea. **2.** illegal use of material. —pi/rate, n., v.

pi-ra/nha (pi rän'yə, -ran'-, -rä'nə)

-ran′ə) n., pl. **-nhas, -nha.** small, fiercely predatory fish.

pir′ou·ette′ (pir′ōō et′) v., **-etted, -etting.** —v. **1.** whirl about on the toes. —n. **2.** such whirling.

pis·ta·chi·o′ (pi stash′ē ō′) n., pl. **-chios.** edible nut.

pis·til (pis′tl) n. seed-bearing organ of flower. —**pis′til·late** (-tl it, -āt′) adj.

pis·tol (pis′tl) n. short hand-held gun.

pis′tol-whip′, v., **-whipped, -whipping.** beat with pistol.

pis·ton (pis′tən) n. part moving back and forth in cylinder.

pit (pit) n., v., **pitted, pitting.** —n. **1.** hole in ground or other surface. **2.** hollow in body. **3.** part of main floor of theater. **4.** stone of fruit. —v. **5.** mark with pits. **6.** set in enmity or opposition. **7.** remove pit.

pi·ta (pē′tə) n. round, flat bread with pocket.

pitch (pich) v. **1.** throw. **2.** set at certain point. **3.** fall forward. **4.** drop and rise, as ship. —n. **5.** relative point or degree. **6.** musical tone. **7.** slope. **8.** sticky dark substance from coal tar. **9.** sales talk.

pitch′-black′, adj. extremely black.

pitch′-dark′, adj. very dark.

pitched, adj. fought with all available troops.

pitch·er (pich′ər) n. **1.** container with spout for liquids. **2.** person who pitches.

pitch·fork′, n. sharp-tined fork for handling hay.

pitch pipe, small pipe producing pitches.

pit·e·ous (pit′ē əs) adj. pathetic.

pit′fall′, n. trap; hazard.

pith (pith) n. **1.** spongy plant tissue. **2.** essence. —**pith′y**, adj.

pit·i·a·ble (pit′ē ə bəl) adj. deserving pity. **2.** contemptible. —**pit′i·a·bly**, adv.

pit·i·ful (-i fəl) adj. **1.** deserving pity. **2.** exciting contempt. **3.** full of pity. —**pit′i·ful·ly**, adv.

pit′tance (pit′ns) n. meager income.

pi·tu·i·tar·y (pi tōō′ə terē′, -tyōō-) adj. denoting gland at base of brain.

pit·y (pit′ē) n., pl. **-ies,** v., **-ied, pitying.** —n. **1.** sympathetic sorrow. **2.** cause for regret. —v. **3.** feel pity for. —**pit′i·less,** adj. —**pit′i·less·ly,** adv.

piv·ot (piv′ət) n. **1.** shaft on which something turns. —v. **2.** turn on pivot. —**piv′ot·al,** adj.

pix′el (pik′səl, -sel) n. smallest element of image in video display system.

pix·y (pik′sē) n., pl. **pixies.** fairy. Also, **pix·ie.**

pi·zazz′ (pə zaz′) n. Informal. **1.** energy. **2.** dash. Also, **piz·zazz′.**

piz′za (pēt′sə) n. dish of cheese, tomato sauce, etc., on baked crust.

piz·zer·i′a (pēt′sə rē′ə) n. restaurant serving mainly pizza.

piz′zi·ca·to (pit′si kä′tō) adj. Music. played by plucking strings with fingers.

pkg., package.

pkwy., parkway.

pl., **1.** place. **2.** plural.

plac·a·ble (plak′ə bəl, plā′kə-) adj. forgiving.

plac·ard (plak′ärt, -ərd) n. public notice.

pla·cate (plā′kāt, plak′āt) v., **-cated, -cating.** appease. —**pla·ca′tion,** n.

place (plās) n., v., **placed, placing.** —n. **1.** particular portion of space. **2.** function. **3.** social standing. **4.** stead. —v. **5.** put in place. **6.** identify from memory. —**place′ment,** n.

pla·ce·bo (plə sē′bō) n., pl. **-bos, -boes.** pill, etc., containing no medication, given to reassure patient or as control in testing drug.

pla·cen·ta (plə sen′tə) n. organ in uterus which attaches to and nourishes fetus.

plac·id (plas′id) adj. serene. —**pla·cid′i·ty,** n. —**plac′id·ly,** adv.

plack·et (plak′it) n. slit at neck, waist, or wrist of garment.

pla·gia·rize (plā′jə rīz′) v., **-rized, -rizing.** copy and present as one's own work. —**pla′gia·rism,** n.

plague (plāg) n., v., **plagued, plaguing.** —n. **1.** often fatal epidemic disease. **2.** affliction or vexation. —v. **3.** trouble; annoy.

plaid (plad) n. **1.** fabric woven in many-colored cross bars. —adj. **2.** having such pattern.

plain (plān) adj. **1.** distinct. **2.** evident. **3.** candid. **4.** ordinary; unpretentious. **5.** bare. **6.** flat. —adv. **7.** clearly. **8.** candidly. —n. **9.** level area. —**plain′ly,** adv.

plain·clothes′man, n., pl. **-men.** police officer who wears civilian clothes on duty.

plain′song′, n. ancient harmonic music of early Christian Church.

plaint (plānt) n. complaint.

plain′tiff (plān′tif) n. one who brings suit in court.

plain′tive (plān′tiv) adj. melancholy. —**plain′tive·ly,** adv.

plait (plāt, plat) n., v. **1.** braid. **2.** pleat.

plan (plan) n., v., **planned, plan-**

ning. —*n.* **1.** scheme of action or arrangement. **2.** drawing of projected structure. —*v.* **3.** make plan. —**plan/ner,** *n.*

plane (plān) *n., adj., v.,* **planed, planing.** —*n.* **1.** flat surface. **2.** level. **3.** airplane. **4.** tool for smoothing. —*adj.* **5.** flat. —*v.* **6.** glide. **7.** smooth with plane.

plan/et (plan/it) *n.* solid heavenly body revolving about sun. —**plan/e·tar/y,** *adj.*

plan/e·tar/i·um (-i târ/ē əm) *n., pl.* **-iums, -ia. 1.** optical device that projects a representation of heavens on a dome. **2.** museum with such device.

plane tree, large, spreading shade tree.

plank (plangk) *n.* **1.** long flat piece of timber. **2.** point in political platform. —**plank/ing,** *n.*

plank/ton (plangk/tən) *n.* microscopic organisms floating in water.

plant (plant) *n.* **1.** any member of vegetable group. **2.** equipment for business or process; factory. —*v.* **3.** set in ground for growth. **4.** furnish with plants. —**plant/er,** *n.*

plan/tain (plan/tin) *n.* **1.** tropical bananalike plant. **2.** common flat-leaved weed.

plan·ta/tion (plan tā/shən) *n.* large farm, esp. with one crop.

plaque (plak) *n.* **1.** monumental tablet. **2.** sticky, whitish film formed on tooth surfaces.

plas/ma (plaz/mə) *n.* clear liquid part of blood or lymph.

plas/ter (plas/tər) *n.* **1.** pasty mixture for covering walls, etc. **2.** medicinal preparation spread on cloth and applied to body. —*v.* **3.** cover or treat with plaster.

plas/ter·board/, *n.* material for insulating or covering walls.

plaster of Par/is (par/is) form of gypsum in powdery form, used in making plasters and casts.

plas/tic (plas/tik) *adj.* **1.** of or produced by molding. **2.** moldable. **3.** three-dimensional. **4.** organic material that is hardened after shaping. —**plas·tic/i·ty** (-tis/ə tē) *n.*

plastic surgery, branch of surgery dealing with repair, replacement, or reshaping of parts of body.

plate (plāt) *n., v.,* **plated, plating.** —*n.* **1.** shallow round dish for food. **2.** gold or silver ware. **3.** sheet of metal used in printing. **4.** shaped holder for false teeth. —*v.* **5.** coat with metal.

pla·teau/ (pla tō/) *n., pl.* **-teaus, -teaux** (-tōz/, -tōz). raised plain.

plate glass, smooth glass.

plat/en (plat/n) *n.* plate in printing press that presses paper against inked surface.

plat/form (plat/fôrm) *n.* **1.** raised flooring or structure. **2.** set of announced political principles.

plat/i·num (plat/n əm) *n.* precious, malleable metallic element.

plat/i·tude (plat/i tōōd´, -tyōōd´) *n.* trite remark.

pla·ton/ic (plə ton/ik) *adj.* without sexual involvement.

pla·toon/ (plə tōōn´) *n.* small military or police unit.

plat/ter (plat/ər) *n.* large serving dish.

plat/y·pus (plat/i pəs) *n., pl.* **-puses, -pi** (-pī´). duckbill.

plau/dit (plô/dit) *n.* (*us. pl.*) applause.

plau/si·ble (plô/zə bəl) *adj.* apparently true, reasonable, or trustworthy. —**plau/si·bil/i·ty,** *n.*

play (plā) *n.* **1.** dramatic work. **2.** recreation. **3.** fun. **4.** movement. —*v.* **5.** act in a play. **6.** engage in game. **7.** perform on musical instrument. **8.** amuse oneself. **9.** move about lightly. —**play/er,** *n.* —**play/ful,** *adj.* —**play/ful·ly,** *adv.* —**play/go/er,** *n.*

play/back/, *n.* **1.** reproduction of a recording. **2.** apparatus used in producing playbacks.

play/bill/, *n.* program or announcement of play.

play/boy/, *n.* man who pursues life of pleasure without responsibilities or attachments.

play/ground/, *n.* area used, esp. by children, for outdoor recreation.

play/house/, *n.* **1.** theater. **2.** small house for children to play in.

play/mate/, *n.* companion in play.

play/-off/, *n.* extra game played to break a tie.

play on words, pun.

play/pen/, *n.* small enclosure in which baby can play.

play/thing/, *n.* toy.

play/wright/ (-rīt´) *n.* writer of plays.

pla/za (plä/zə, plaz/ə) *n.* **1.** public square, esp. in Spanish-speaking countries. **2.** shopping center.

plea (plē) *n.* **1.** defense; justification. **2.** entreaty.

plea bargain, agreement in which criminal defendant pleads guilty to lesser charge.

plead (plēd) *v.,* **pleaded** or **pled** (pled), **pleading. 1.** make earnest entreaty. **2.** allege formally in court.

3. argue (case at law). **4.** allege in justification. —**plead′er,** *n.*

pleas′ant (plez′ənt) *adj.* agreeable; pleasing. —**pleas′ant·ly,** *adv.*

pleas′ant·ry, *n., pl.* **-ries.** good-humored remark.

please (plēz) *v.,* **pleased, pleasing.** give pleasure or satisfaction to.

pleas′ur·a·ble (plezh′ər ə bəl) *adj.* enjoyable.

pleas′ure, *n.* **1.** enjoyment. **2.** person's will or desire.

pleat (plēt) *n.* **1.** double fold of cloth. —*v.* **2.** fold in pleats.

ple·be′ian (pli bē′ən) *adj.* of common people.

pleb′i·scite (pleb′ə sīt′) *n.* direct vote by citizens on public question.

plec′trum (plek′trəm) *n., pl.* **-tra** (-trə), **-trums.** object for picking strings of musical instrument.

pledge (plej) *n., v.,* **pledged, pledging.** —*n.* **1.** solemn promise. **2.** property delivered as security on a loan. —*v.* **3.** bind by pledge. **4.** promise. **5.** deliver as pledge.

Pleis′to·cene′ (plīs′tə sēn′) *adj.* pertaining to geologic epoch forming earlier half of Quaternary Period.

ple′na·ry (plē′nə rē, plen′ə-) *adj.* full; complete.

plen′i·po·ten′ti·ar′y (plen′ə pə ten′shē er′ē, -sha rē) *n., pl.* **-aries,** *adj.* —*n.* **1.** diplomat with full authority. —*adj.* **2.** having full authority.

plen′i·tude (plen′i tōōd′, -tyōōd′) *n.* abundance.

plen′ty (plen′tē) *n.* **1.** abundant supply. —*adv. Informal.* **2.** very much.

pleth′o·ra (pleth′ər ə) *n.* superabundance.

pleu′ri·sy (plŏŏr′ə sē) *n.* inflammation of chest membrane.

Plex′i·glas′ (plek′si glas′) *Trademark.* light, durable transparent plastic.

pli′a·ble (plī′ə bəl) *adj.* easily bent or influenced. —**pli′a·bil′i·ty,** *n.*

pli′ant (-ənt) *adj.* pliable.

pli′ers (plī′ərz) *n.pl.* small pincers.

plight (plīt) *n.* **1.** distressing condition. —*v.* **2.** promise.

PLO, Palestine Liberation Organization.

plod (plod) *v.,* **plodded, plodding. 1.** walk heavily. **2.** work laboriously. —**plod′der,** *n.*

plop (plop) *v.,* **plopped, plopping.** —*n.* **1.** drop with sound like that of object hitting water. **2.** drop with direct impact. —*n.* **3.** plopping sound or fall.

plot (plot) *n., v.,* **plotted, plotting.** —*n.* **1.** secret scheme. **2.** main

story of fictional work. **3.** small area of ground. —*v.* **4.** plan secretly. **5.** mark (chart course) on. **6.** divide into plots. —**plot′ter,** *n.*

plov′er (pluv′ər, plō′vər) *n.* shore bird.

plow (plou) *n.* **1.** implement for cutting and turning soil. **2.** similar implement for removing snow. —*v.* **3.** cut or turn with plow. **4.** force way, as through water. Also, **plough.** —**plow′man,** *n.*

plow′share′, *n.* blade of plow.

ploy (ploi) *n.* maneuver; ruse.

pluck (pluk) *v.* **1.** pull out from fixed position. **2.** sound (strings of musical instrument). —*n.* **3.** pull or tug. **4.** courage.

pluck′y, *adj.,* **-ier, -iest.** courageous. —**pluck′i·ly,** *adv.*

plug (plug) *n., v.,* **plugged, plugging.** —*n.* **1.** object for stopping hole. **2.** device on electrical cord that establishes contact in socket. **3.** *Slang.* advertisement; favorable mention. —*v.* **4.** stop with or insert plug. **5.** *Slang.* mention favorably. **6.** work steadily.

plum (plum) *n.* **1.** oval juicy fruit. **2.** deep purple. **3.** *Informal.* favor widely desired.

plum′age (plōō′mij) *n.* feathers of bird.

plumb (plum) *n.* **1.** plummet. —*adj.* **2.** perpendicular. —*adv.* **3.** vertically. **4.** exactly. **5.** *Informal.* completely. —*v.* **6.** make vertical. **7.** measure depth of.

plumb′ing, *n.* system of water pipes, etc. —**plumb′er,** *n.*

plume (plōōm) *n., v.,* **plumed, pluming.** —*n.* **1.** feather, esp. large one. **2.** ornamental tuft. —*v.* **3.** preen. **4.** adorn with plumes.

plum′met (plum′it) *n.* **1.** weight on line for sounding or establishing verticals. —*v.* **2.** plunge.

plump (plump) *adj.* **1.** somewhat fat or thick. —*v.* **2.** make or become plump. **3.** drop heavily. —*n.* **4.** heavy fall. —*adv.* **5.** directly. **6.** heavily. —**plump′ness,** *n.*

plun′der (plun′dər) *v.* **1.** rob. —*n.* **2.** act of plundering. **3.** loot.

plunge (plunj) *v.,* **plunged, plunging,** *n.* —*v.* **1.** fall abruptly. **2.** rush. **3.** pitch forward. —*n.* **4.** dive.

plung′er, *n.* pistonlike part moving within the cylinder of certain machines. **2.** device with handle and suction cup, used to unclog drains.

plu′ral (plŏŏr′əl) *adj.* **1.** of, being, or containing more than one. —*n.* **2.** plural form. —**plu′ral·ize′,** *v.,* **-ized, -izing.**

plu·ral·ism, n. condition in which minority groups participate in society, yet maintain their distinctions. —**plu·ral·ist**, n.

plu·ral·i·ty (ploo ral′i tē) n., pl. **-ties.** 1. in election with three or more candidates, the excess of votes given leading candidate over next candidate. 2. majority.

plus (plus) prep. 1. increased by. —adj. 2. involving addition. 3. positive. —n. 4. something additional.

plush (plush) n. long-piled fabric.

Plu·to (ploo′tō) n. planet ninth in order from the sun.

plu·to·crat (ploo′tə krat′) n. 1. wealthy person. 2. member of wealthy governing class. —**plu·toc′ra·cy** (-tok′rə sē) n.

plu·to·ni·um (ploo tō′nē əm) n. radioactive element.

plu·vi·al (ploo′vē əl) adj. of rain.

ply (plī) v., **plied, ply·ing,** n., pl. **plies.** —v. 1. work with hand. 2. carry on, as trade. 3. supply or offer something repeatedly. 4. travel regularly. —n. 5. fold; thickness.

ply·wood′, n. sheets of wood.

p.m., after noon. Also, **P.M.**

PMS, premenstrual syndrome.

P.O., post office.

poach (pōch) v. 1. hunt illegally. 2. cook (eggs, fruit, etc.) in hot water. —**poach′er,** n.

pock·et (pok′it) n. 1. small bag sewed into garment. 2. pouch; cavity. —adj. 3. small. —v. 4. put into one's pocket. 5. take as profit.

pock′et·book′, n. purse.

pock′et·knife′, n. small folding knife.

pock′mark′, n. acne scar.

pod (pod) n., v. seed covering.

po·di·a·try (pə dī′ə trē) n. diagnosis and treatment of foot disorders.

po·di·um (pō′dē əm) n., pl. **-diums, -dia** (-dē ə). small raised platform.

po·em (pō′əm) n. composition in verse.

po·e·sy (-ə sē) n., pl. **-sies.** poetry.

po·et (pō′it) n. writer of poetry.

po·et·ry (-i trē) n. rhythmical composition of words. —**po·et′ic** (pō-et′ik), **po·et′i·cal,** adj.

po·grom′ (pə grum′, -grom′) n. organized massacre, esp. of Jews.

poign·ant (poin′yənt) adj. keenly distressing. —**poign′an·cy,** n.

poin·set·ti·a (poin set′ē ə, -set′ə) n. tropical plant with scarlet flowers.

point (point) n. 1. sharp end. 2. projecting part. 3. dot. 4. definite position or time. 5. compass direction. 6. basic reason, purpose, etc. 7. detail. 8. unit in accounting, scoring, etc. —v. 9. indicate. 10. direct.

point′-blank′, adj. 1. direct; plain. —adv. 2. directly.

point′ed, adj. 1. having a point. 2. sharp. 3. aimed at a particular person. 4. emphasized.

point′er, n. 1. one that points. 2. long stick for pointing. 3. breed of hunting dog.

poin·til·lism (pwan′tl iz′əm) n. technique in painting of using dots of pure color that are optically mixed into resulting hue by viewer.

point′less, adj. futile.

poise (poiz) n., v., **poised, pois·ing.** —n. 1. balance. 2. composure. —v. 3. balance. 4. be in position for action.

poi·son (poi′zən) n. 1. substance that kills or harms seriously. —v. 2. harm with poison. —**poi′son·er,** n. —**poi′son·ous,** adj.

poison ivy, n. vine or shrub having shiny leaves with three leaflets. 2. rash caused by touching poison ivy.

poke (pōk) v., **poked, pok·ing,** n. thrust.

pok′er (pō′kər) n. 1. rod for poking fires. 2. card game.

pok′er-faced′, adj. showing no emotion or intention.

pok′y (pō′kē) adj., **-ier, -iest.** Informal. slow; dull. Also, **poke′y.**

po·lar (pō′lər) adj. 1. arctic or antarctic. 2. of magnetic poles. —**po·lar′i·ty,** n.

polar bear, large white arctic bear.

Po·lar′is (pō lâr′is, -lar′-, pə-) n. bright star close to North Pole.

po·lar·i·za·tion (pō′lər ə zā′shən) n. 1. division of group into opposing factions. 2. state in which rays of light exhibit different properties in different directions. —**po′lar·ize′,** v., **-ized, -iz·ing.**

pole (pōl) n., v., **poled, pol·ing.** —n. 1. long slender rod. 2. unit of length equal to 16½ ft.; rod. 3. square rod, 30¼ sq. yards. 4. each end of axis. 5. each end showing strongest opposite force. 6. (cap.) native or citizen of Poland. —v. 7. propel with a pole.

pole′cat′, n. small bad-smelling mammal.

po·lem'ics (pə lem'iks) *n.* art or practice of argument. —**po·lem'ic**, *n., adj.* —**po·lem'i·cist,** *n.*

pole vault, athletic event in which vault over horizontal bar is performed with aid of long pole.

po·lice' (pə lēs') *n., v.,* **-liced, -lic·ing.** —*n.* 1. organized civil force for enforcing law. —*v.* 2. keep in order. —**po·lice'man,** *n.* —**po·lice'wom'an,** *n.*

pol'i·cy (pol'ə sē) *n., pl.* **-cies.** 1. definite course of action. 2. insurance contract.

pol'i·o·my'e·li'tis (pō'lē ō mī'ə lī'tis) *n.* infantile paralysis. Also, **po'li·o'.**

pol'ish (pol'ish) *v.* 1. make glossy. —*n.* 2. polishing substance. 3. gloss. 4. refinement.

Pol'ish (pō'lish) *n.* 1. language or people of Poland. —*adj.* 2. of Poland.

po·lite' (pə līt') *adj.* showing good manners; refined. —**po·lite'ly,** *adv.*

pol'i·tic (pol'i tik) *adj.* 1. prudent; expedient. 2. political.

politically correct, marked by progressive attitude on issues of race, gender, etc. —**political correctness,** *n.*

political science, social science dealing with political institutions and government.

po·lit'i·cize' (pə lit'ə sīz') *v.,* **-cized, -ciz·ing.** give a political bias to.

pol'i·tick'ing (pol'i tik'ing) *n.* political campaigning.

pol'i·tics (pol'i tiks) *n.* 1. science or conduct of government. 2. political affairs, methods, or principles. —**po·lit'i·cal** (pə lit'i kəl) *adj.* —**pol'i·ti'cian,** *n.*

pol'ka (pōl'kə, pō'kə) *n.* lively dance.

polka dot, pattern of dots.

poll (pōl) *n.* 1. voting or votes at election. 2. list of individuals, as for voting. 3. (*pl.*) place of voting. 4. analysis of public opinion. —*v.* 5. receive votes. 6. vote. 7. ask opinions of.

pol'len (pol'ən) *n.* powdery fertilizing element of flowers. —**pol'li·nate',** *v.* —**pol'li·na'tion,** *n.*

pol'li·wog' (pol'ē wog') *n.* tadpole.

poll'ster (pōl'stər) *n.* person who takes public-opinion polls.

pol·lute' (pə lōōt') *v.,* **-luted, -lut·ing.** contaminate or make foul. —**pol·lu'tion,** *n.* —**pol·lut'ant,** *n.*

po'lo (pō'lō) *n.* **-los.** game played on horseback.

pol'ter·geist' (pōl'tər gīst') *n.* boisterous, often destructive ghost.

pol·troon' (pol trōōn') *n.* coward.

poly-, prefix meaning many.

pol'y·an'dry (pol'ē an'drē) *n.* practice of having more than one husband at a time.

pol'y·es'ter (pol'ē es'tər) *n.* artificial material for synthetics.

pol'y·eth'yl·ene' (-eth'ə lēn') *n.* plastic polymer used esp. for containers and packaging.

po·lyg'a·my (pə lig'ə mē) *n.* practice of having many spouses, esp. wives, at one time. —**po·lyg'a·mist,** *n.* —**po·lyg'a·mous,** *adj.*

pol'y·glot' (pol'ē glot') *adj.* able to speak, read, or write several languages.

pol'y·gon' (pol'ē gon') *n.* figure having three or more straight sides.

pol'y·graph' (pol'i graf') *n.* instrument recording variations in certain body activities, sometimes used to detect lying.

pol'y·he'dron (pol'ē hē'drən) *n., pl.* **-drons, -dra** (-drə). solid figure having four or more sides.

pol'y·math' (pol'ē math') *n.* person of great learning in several fields.

pol'y·mer (pol'ə mər) *n.* compound formed by the combination of various molecules with water or alcohol removed. —**pol'y·mer·i·za'tion,** *n.*

pol'yp (pol'ip) *n.* projecting growth from mucous surface.

po·lyph'o·ny (pə lif'ə nē) *n.* music with two or more melodic lines in equitable juxtaposition. —**pol'y·phon'ic** (pol'ē fon'ik) *adj.*

pol'y·sty'rene (pol'ē stī'rēn, -stēr'ēn) *n.* polymer used in molded objects and as insulator.

pol'y·tech'nic (-tek'nik) *adj.* offering instruction in variety of technical subjects.

pol'y·the'ism, *n.* belief in more than one god.

pol'y·un·sat'u·rat'ed, *adj.* of a class of animal or vegetable fats associated with low cholesterol content.

po·made' (po mād', -mäd') *n.* hair ointment.

pome'gran'ate (pom'gran'it, pom'i-) *n.* red, many-seeded fruit of Asiatic tree.

pom'mel (pum'əl, pom'-) *n., v.,* **-meled, -meling.** —*n.* 1. knob on sword or saddle. —*v.* 2. strike; beat.

pomp (pomp) *n.* stately display.

pom'pa·dour' (pom'pə dôr', -dōōr')

n. arrangement of hair brushed up high from forehead.

pom'pom (pom'pŏm') *n.* ornamental tuft.

pomp'ous (pom'pəs) *adj.* affectedly dignified or serious. —**pom·pos'i·ty** (-pos'i tē) *n.* —**pomp'ous·ly,** *adv.*

pon'cho (pon'chō) *n., pl.* **-chos.** blanketlike cloak.

pond (pond) *n.* small lake.

pon'der (pon'dər) *v.* meditate.

pon'der·ous, *adj.* heavy; not graceful.

pon'iard (pon'yərd) *n.* dagger.

pon'tiff (pon'tif) *n.* **1.** pope. **2.** chief priest; bishop. —**pon·tif'i·cal,** *adj.*

pon·tif'i·cate' (pon tif'i kāt') *v.,* **-cated, -cating.** speak with affected air of authority.

pon·toon' (pon tōōn') *n.* floating support.

po'ny (pō'nē) *n., pl.* **-nies.** small horse.

po'ny·tail', *n.* hair gathered and fastened at the back of the head so as to hang freely.

poo'dle (pōōd'l) *n.* kind of dog with thick, curly hair.

pool (pōōl) *n.* **1.** body of still water. **2.** group of persons or things available for use. **3.** game resembling billiards. —*v.* **4.** put into common fund.

poop (pōōp) *n.* upper deck on stern of a ship.

poor (pŏŏr) *adj.* **1.** having little wealth. **2.** wanting. **3.** inferior. **4.** unfortunate. —*n.* **5.** poor persons.

poor'-mouth', *v. Informal.* complain about poverty, usu. as an excuse.

pop (pop) *v.,* **popped, popping,** *n., adv.* —*v.* **1.** make or burst with a short, quick sound. **2.** shoot. —*n.* **3.** short, quick sound. **4.** effervescent soft drink.

pop'corn', *n.* kind of corn whose kernels burst in dry heat.

pope (pōp) *n. (often cap.)* head of Roman Catholic Church.

pop'in·jay' (pop'in jā') *n.* vain, shallow person.

pop'lar (pop'lər) *n.* any of certain fast-growing trees.

pop'lin (pop'lin) *n.* corded fabric.

pop'o'ver, *n.* very light muffin.

pop'py (pop'ē) *n., pl.* **-pies.** showy-flowered herbs, one species of which yields opium.

pop'py·cock', *n.* nonsense.

pop'u·lace (pop'yə ləs) *n.* population.

pop'u·lar (-lər) *adj.* **1.** generally liked and approved. **2.** of the peo-

ple. **3.** prevalent. —**pop'u·lar'i·ty** (-lar'i tē) *n.* —**pop'u·lar·ize',** *v.,* **-ized, -izing.** —**pop'u·lar·ly,** *adv.*

pop'u·late' (-lāt') *v.,* **-lated, -lating.** inhabit.

pop'u·la'tion, *n.* **1.** total number of persons inhabiting given area. **2.** body of inhabitants.

pop'u·lism, *n.* political philosophy or movement promoting the interests of the common people. —**pop'u·list,** *n., adj.*

pop'u·lous, *adj.* with many inhabitants.

por'ce·lain (pôr'sə lin, pôrs'lin) *n.* glassy ceramic ware; china.

porch (pôrch) *n.* exterior shelter on building.

por'cu·pine' (pôr'kyə pīn') *n.* rodent with stout quills.

pore (pôr) *v.,* **pored, poring,** *n.* —*v.* **1.** ponder or read intently. —*n.* **2.** minute opening in skin.

pork (pôrk) *n.* flesh of hogs as food.

pork barrel, government funds available for popular local improvements.

por·nog'ra·phy (pôr nog'rə fē) *n.* obscene literature or art. —**por'no·graph'ic** (-nə graf'ik) *adj.* —**por·nog'ra·pher,** *n.*

po'rous (pôr'əs) *adj.* permeable by water, air, etc. —**po'rous·ness,** *n.*

por'poise (pôr'pəs) *n.* gregarious aquatic mammal.

por'ridge (pôr'ij, por'-) *n.* boiled cereal.

por'rin·ger (pôr'in jər, por'-) *n.* round dish for soup, etc.

port (pôrt) *n.* **1.** place where ships load and unload. **2.** harbor. **3.** left side of vessel, facing forward. **4.** sweet red wine. —**port,** *adj.*

port'a·ble, *adj.* easily carried.

por'tage (pôr'tij, pôr tázh') *n.* **1.** overland route between navigable streams. **2.** act of carrying.

por'tal (pôr'təl) *n.* door or gate, esp. a large one.

port·cul'lis (pôrt kul'is) *n.* heavy iron grating at gateway of castle.

por·tend' (pôr tend') *v.* indicate beforehand.

por'tent (-tent) *n.* **1.** omen. **2.** ominous significance. —**por·ten'tous,** *adj.*

por'ter (pôr'tər) *n.* **1.** railroad attendant. **2.** baggage carrier. **3.** person who cleans or maintains building, store, etc.

por'ter·house', *n.* choice cut of beefsteak.

port·fo'li·o (pôrt fō'lē ō') *n., pl.* **-lios. 1.** portable case for papers, etc. **2.** cabinet post.

port·hole, n. opening in ship's side.

por·ti·co (pôr'ti kō') n., pl. **-coes, -cos.** roof supported by columns.

por·tion (pôr'shən) n. **1.** part of a whole. **2.** share. —v. **3.** divide into shares.

port·ly (pôrt'lē) adj., **-lier, -liest. 1.** fat. **2.** stately. —**port·li·ness,** n.

port·man·teau (pôrt man'tō) n., pl. **-teaus, -teaux** (-tōz, tō). leather trunk.

por·trait (pôr'trit, -trāt) n. picture, sculpture, etc., showing specific person. —**por·trai·ture** (-tri chər) n.

por·trait·ist, n. person who makes portraits.

por·tray' (pôr trā') v. represent faithfully, as in picture. —**por·tray·al,** n.

Por·tu·guese' (-chə gēz', -gēs') n., pl. **-guese.** native or language of Portugal. —**Portuguese,** adj.

Portuguese man-of-war, poisonous marine animal.

pose (pōz) v., **posed, posing,** n. —v. **1.** assume or feign physical position, attitude, or character. **2.** take or give specific position. **3.** ask (question). —n. **4.** position or character assumed.

po'ser, n. person who poses, as for artist. **2.** difficult question.

po·seur' (pō zûr') n. affected person.

posh (posh) adj. elegant; luxurious.

pos'it (poz'it) v. lay down or assume as a fact or principle.

po·si'tion (pə zish'ən) n. **1.** place or attitude. **2.** belief or argument on question. **3.** social or organizational standing. **4.** job. —v. **5.** place.

pos'i·tive (poz'i tiv) adj. **1.** not denying or questioning. **2.** emphatic. **3.** confident. **4.** showing lights and shades of original. **5.** Gram. denoting first degree of comparison. **6.** denoting more than zero. **7.** deficient in electrons. **8.** revealing presence of thing tested for. —n. **9.** something positive. **10.** photographic image. —**pos'i·tive·ly,** adv.

pos'i·tron (poz'i tron') n. particle with same mass as electron but with positive charge.

pos'se (pos'ē) n. body of persons assisting sheriff.

pos·sess' (pə zes') v. **1.** have under ownership or domination. **2.** have as quality. **3.** obsess. —**pos·ses'sor,** —**pos·ses'sion** (-zesh'ən) n.

pos·sessed', adj. controlled by strong feeling or supernatural.

pos·ses'sive, adj. **1.** denoting pos-

session. **2.** obsessed with dominating another.

pos'si·ble (pos'ə bəl) adj. that may be, happen, etc. —**pos'si·bil'i·ty,** n. —**pos'si·bly,** adv.

pos'sum (pos'əm) n. opossum.

post (pōst) n. **1.** upright support. **2.** position of duty or trust. **3.** station for soldiers or traders. **4.** Chiefly Brit. mail. —v. **5.** put up. **6.** station at post. **7.** Chiefly Brit. mail. **8.** enter in ledger. **9.** hasten. **10.** inform.

post-, prefix meaning after or behind.

post'age (pō'stij) n. charge for mailing.

post'al (pōs'tl) adj. concerning mail.

post·bel'lum (-bel'əm) adj. after war, esp. U.S. Civil War.

post'card', n. small notecard usu. having picture on one side and space for stamp, address, and message on the other.

post·date' (pōst dāt', pōst'-) v., **-dated, -dating. 1.** mark with date later than actual date. **2.** follow in time.

post'er (pō'stər) n. large public notice.

pos·te'ri·or (po stēr'ē ər, pō-) adj. **1.** situated behind. **2.** later. —n. **3.** buttocks.

pos·ter'i·ty (po ster'i tē) n. descendants.

post·grad'u·ate (pōst graj'ōō it, -āt') n. **1.** of postgraduates. —n. **2.** student taking advanced work after graduation.

post'haste', adv. speedily.

post'hu·mous (pos'chə məs, -chōō-) adj. **1.** occurring after one's death. **2.** born after father's death.

post'man, n. mail carrier.

post'mark', n. official mark on mail showing place and time of mailing. —**post'mark',** v.

post'mas'ter, n. official in charge of post office.

post me·rid'i·em' (mə rid'ē əm, -em') afternoon.

post'mis'tress, n. woman in charge of post office.

post·mod'ern, adj. pertaining to late 20th century artistic movement that developed in reaction to modernism.

post·mor'tem (-môr'təm) —n. examination of dead body.

post·na'tal (-nāt'l) adj. after childbirth.

post office, government office responsible for postal service.

post'paid', adv., adj. with postage paid in advance.

post·par'tum (-pär'təm) *adj.* following childbirth.

post·pone' (pōst pōn', pōs-) *v.*, **-poned, -poning.** delay till later. **—post·pone'ment,** *n.*

post·script' *n.* note added to letter after signature.

pos·tu·late', *v.*, **-lated, -lating**, *n.* **—v.** (pos/cha lāt') **1.** require. **2.** assume. **—n.** (-lit) **3.** something postulated.

pos'ture (pos'chər) *n.*, *v.*, **-tured, -turing.** **—n. 1.** position of the body. **—v. 2.** place in particular position. **3.** behave affectedly; pose.

post'war', *adj.* after a war.

po'sy (pō'zē) *n.*, *pl.* **-sies.** flower or bouquet.

pot (pot) *n.*, *v.*, **potted, potting.** **—n. 1.** round deep container for cooking, etc. **2.** total stakes at cards. **3.** *Slang.* marijuana. **—v. 4.** put into pot.

po'ta·ble (pō'tə bəl) *adj.* drinkable.

pot'ash' (pot'ash') *n.* potassium carbonate, esp. from wood ashes.

po·tas'si·um (pa tas'ē əm) *n.* light metallic element.

po·ta'to (pa tā'tō, -tə) *n.*, *pl.* **-toes.** edible tuber.

pot'bel'ly, *n.*, *pl.* **-lies.** belly that sticks out. **—pot'bel'lied,** *adj.*

pot'boil'er, *n.* mediocre work of literature or art produced merely for financial gain.

po'tent (pōt'nt) *adj.* **1.** powerful. **2.** (of a male) capable of sexual intercourse. **—po'ten·cy,** *n.*

po'ten·tate' (-tāt') *n.* powerful person, as a sovereign.

po·ten'tial (pa ten'shal) *adj.* **1.** possible. **2.** latent. **3.** possibility. **—n.** **—po·ten'tial·ly,** *adv.*

poth'er (poth'ər) *n.*, *v.* fuss.

pot'hole', *n.* hole formed in pavement.

po'tion (pō'shən) *n.* medicinal or magical drink.

pot'luck', *n.* **1.** meal to which participants bring food to be shared. **2.** whatever happens to be available.

pot'pour·ri' (pō'poŏ rē') *n.* **1.** fragrant mixture of dried flowers and spices. **2.** miscellany.

pot'shot', *n.* **1.** casual or aimless shot. **2.** random or incidental criticism.

pot'ted, *adj.* **1.** grown in a pot. **2.** *Slang.* drunk.

pot'ter (pot'ər) *n.* **1.** person who makes earthen pots. **—v. 2.** putter (def. 1).

pot'ter·y, *n.*, *pl.* **-teries.** objects made of clay and baked.

pouch (pouch) *n.* **1.** bag or sack. **2.** baglike sac.

poul'tice (pōl'tis) *n.* soft moist mass applied as medicine.

poul'try (pōl'trē) *n.* domestic fowls.

pounce (pouns) *v.*, **pounced, pouncing**, *n.* **—v. 1.** swoop down or spring suddenly. **2.** seize eagerly. **—n. 3.** sudden swoop.

pound (pound) *n.*, *pl.* **pounds, pound**, *v.* **—n. 1.** unit of weight: in U.S., **pound avoirdupois** (16 ounces) and **pound troy** (12 ounces). **2.** British monetary unit. **3.** enclosure for stray animals. **—v. 4.** strike repeatedly and heavily. **5.** crush by pounding.

pound cake, rich, sweet cake.

pour (pôr) *v.* cause to flow; flow.

pout (pout) *v.* **1.** look sullen. **—n. 2.** sullen look or mood.

pov'er·ty (pov'ər tē) *n.* **1.** poorness. **2.** lack.

POW, *pl.* **POWs, POW's.** prisoner of war.

pow'der (pou'dər) *n.* **1.** solid substance crushed to fine loose particles. **—v. 2.** reduce to powder. **3.** apply powder to. **—pow'der·y**, *adj.*

powder keg, **1.** container for gunpowder. **2.** explosive situation.

pow'er (pou'ər) *n.* **1.** ability to act; strength. **2.** faculty. **3.** authority; control. **4.** person, nation, etc., having great influence. **5.** mechanical energy. **6.** product of repeated multiplications of number by itself. **7.** magnifying capacity of an optical instrument. **—pow'er·ful,** *adj.*

pow'er·house', *n.* **1.** building where electricity is generated. **2.** dynamic person.

power of attorney, written legal authorization for another person to act in one's place.

pow'wow' (pou'wou') *n. Informal.* conference.

pox (poks) *n.* disease marked by skin eruptions.

pp., **1.** pages. **2.** past participle.

ppd., **1.** postpaid. **2.** prepaid.

P.P.S., additional postscript. Also, **p.s.**

PR, public relations.

prac'ti·ca·ble (prak'ti kə bəl) *adj.* able to be put into practice; feasible.

prac'ti·cal, *adj.* **1.** of or from practice. **2.** useful. **3.** level-headed. **4.** concerned with everyday affairs. **5.** virtual. **—prac'ti·cal'i·ty,** *n.*

prac'ti·cal·ly, *adv.* **1.** almost. **2.** in a practical way.

prac'tice (-tis) *n.*, *v.*, **-ticed, -ticing.** **—n. 1.** habit; custom. **2.** action carried out. **3.** repeated performance in learning. **4.** professional activity.

—v. Also, *Brit.*, **prac'tise. 5.** do habitually or as profession. **6.** repeat to acquire skill.

prac·ti'tion·er (-tish'ə nər) *n.* person engaged in a profession.

prag·mat'ic (prag mat'ik) *adj.* concerned with practical values and results. —**prag'ma·tism,** *n.* —**prag'ma·tist,** *n.*

prai'rie (prâr'ē) *n.* broad, flat, treeless grassland.

prairie dog, burrowing squirrel of western North America.

praise (prāz) *n., v.*, **praised, praising.** —*n.* **1.** words of admiration or strong approval. **2.** grateful homage. —*v.* **3.** give praise to. **4.** worship. —**praise'wor'thy,** *adj.*

pra'line (prā'lēn, prä'-) *n.* confection of caramelized nuts and sugar.

pram (pram) *n. Brit. Informal.* baby carriage.

prance (prans) *v.*, **pranced, prancing,** —*v.* **1.** step about gaily or proudly. —*n.* **2.** act of prancing.

prank (prangk) *n.* playful trick. —**prank'ster,** *n.*

prate (prāt) *v.*, **prated, prating.** talk foolishly.

prat'fall' (prat'fôl') *n.* fall on the buttocks.

prat'tle (prat'l) *v.*, **-tled, -tling,** *n.* —*v.* **1.** chatter foolishly or childishly. —*n.* **2.** chatter.

prawn (prôn) *n.* large shrimplike shellfish.

pray (prā) *v.* make prayer.

prayer (prâr) *n.* **1.** devout petition to or spiritual communication with God. **2.** petition.

preach (prēch) *v.* **1.** advocate. **2.** deliver (sermon). —**preach'er,** *n.* —**preach'y,** *adj.*

pre·am'ble (prē'am'bəl, prē am'-) *n.* introductory declaration.

pre·can'cer·ous, *adj.* showing pathological changes that may be preliminary to malignancy.

pre·car'i·ous (pri kâr'ē as) *adj.* uncertain; dangerous.

pre·cau'tion (pri kô'shən) *n.* prudent advance measure. —**pre·cau'tion·ar'y,** *adj.*

pre·cede' (pri sēd') *v.*, **-ceded, -ceding.** go before.

prec'e·dence (pres'i dəns) *n.* **1.** priority. **2.** something that has gone before.

prec'e·dent (pres'i dənt) *n.* past case used as example or guide.

pre'cept (prē'sept) *n.* rule of conduct.

pre·cep'tor (pri sep'tər, prē'sep-) *n.* teacher.

pre'cinct (prē'singkt) *n.* bounded or defined area.

pre·ci·os'i·ty (presh'ē os'i tē) *n., pl.* **-ties.** fastidious refinement.

pre'cious (presh'əs) *adj.* **1.** valuable. **2.** beloved. **3.** affectedly refined. —**pre'cious·ly,** *adv.*

prec'i·pice (pres'ə pis) *n.* sharp cliff.

pre·cip'i·tate' *v.*, **-tated, -tating,** *adj.*, *n.* —*v.* (pri sip'i tāt') **1.** hasten occurrence of. **2.** separate (solid from solution). **3.** condense (as vapor into rain). **4.** fling down. —*adj.* (-tit) **5.** rash or impetuous; hasty. —*n.* (-tit) **6.** substance precipitated. **7.** condensed moisture. —**pre·cip'i·tate·ly,** *adv.* —**pre·cip'i·ta'tion,** *n.*

pre·cip'i·tous, *adj.* **1.** like a precipice. **2.** precipitate.

pre·cis' (prā sē', prā'sē) *n.* summary.

pre·cise' (pri sīs') *adj.* **1.** definite; exact. **2.** distinct. **3.** strict. —**pre·ci'sion** (-sizh'ən), **pre·cise'ness,** *n.*

pre·clude' (pri klōōd') *v.*, **-cluded, -cluding.** prevent. —**pre·clu'sion** (-klōō'zhən) *n.* —**pre·clu'sive,** *adj.*

pre·co'cious (pri kō'shəs) *adj.* forward in development. —**pre·coc'i·ty** (-kos'ə tē) *n.*

pre·cog·ni'tion (prē'kog nish'ən) *n.* knowledge of future event through extrasensory means.

pre'-Co·lum'bi·an, *adj.* of the period before the arrival of Columbus in the Americas.

pre·con·ceive' *v.*, **-ceived, -ceiving.** form an opinion beforehand. —**pre·con·cep'tion,** *n.*

pre·con·di'tion, *n.* something necessary for subsequent success.

pre·cur'sor (pri kûr'sər, prē'kûr-) *n.* **1.** predecessor. **2.** harbinger.

pred'a·tor (pred'ə tər) *n.* preying animal.

pred'a·to'ry, *adj.* **1.** plundering. **2.** feeding on other animals.

pred'e·ces'sor (-ses'ər) *n.* one who precedes another.

pre·des'ti·na'tion (pri des'tə nā'shən) *n.* **1.** determination beforehand. **2.** destiny. —**pre·des'tine,** *v.*

pre·de·ter'mine (prē'di tûr'min) *v.*, **-mined, -mining. 1.** decide in advance. **2.** predestine. —**pre'de·ter'mi·na'tion,** *n.*

pre·dic'a·ment (pri dik'ə mənt) *n.* trying or dangerous situation.

pred'i·cate, *v.*, **-cated, -cating,** *adj.*, *n.* —*v.* (pred'i kāt') **1.** declare. **2.** find basis for. —*adj.* (-kit) **3.** *Gram.* belonging to predicate. —*n.* (-kit) **4.** *Gram.* part of sentence that expresses what is said of subject.

pre·dict' (pri dikt') v. tell beforehand. —**pre·dic'tion,** n. —**pre·dict'a·ble,** adj. —**pre·dic'tor,** n.

pre'di·lec'tion (pred'l ek'shan, prēd'-) n. preference.

pre'dis·pose' v., **-posed, -posing.** 1. make susceptible. 2. incline. —**pre'dis·po·si'tion,** n.

pre·dom'i·nate' (pri dom'ə nāt') v., **-nated, -nating.** 1. be more powerful or common. 2. control. —**pre·dom'i·nance,** n. —**pre·dom'i·nant,** adj.

pre·em'i·nent (prē em'ə nənt) adj. superior; outstanding. —**pre·em'i·nence,** n. —**pre·em'i·nent·ly,** adv.

pre·empt' (prē empt') v. 1. acquire or reserve before others. 2. occupy to establish prior right to buy. Also, **pre-empt'.** —**pre·emp'tion,** n. —**pre·emp'tive,** adj.

preen (prēn) v. 1. trim or clean (feathers or fur). 2. dress (oneself) carefully.

pre·fab'ri·cate' v., **-cated, -cating.** build in parts for quick assembly. —**pre·fab'ri·ca'tion,** n. —**pre'fab,** n. Informal.

pref·ace (pref'is) n., v., **-aced, -acing.** —n. 1. preliminary statement. —v. 2. provide with or serve as preface. —**pref'a·to'ry** (-ə tôr'ē) adj.

pre'fect (prē'fekt) n. magistrate. —**pre'fec·ture** (-fek shər) n.

pre·fer' (pri fûr') v., **-ferred, -ferring.** 1. like better. 2. put forward; present (criminal charge, etc.).

pref'er·a·ble (pref'ər ə bəl) adj. more desirable.

pref'er·ence (-əns) n. 1. liking of one above others. 2. person or thing preferred. 3. granting of advantage to one. —**pref'er·en'tial** (-ə ren'shəl) adj.

pre·fer'ment (pri fûr'mənt) n. promotion.

pre·fig'ure (prē fig'yər) v., **-ured, -uring.** foreshadow.

pre'fix (prē'fiks) 1. syllable or syllables put before word to qualify its meaning. —v. (also prē fiks') 2. put before.

preg'nant (preg'nənt) adj. 1. being with child. 2. meaningful. —**preg'nan·cy,** n.

pre·hen'sile (pri hen'sil, -sīl) adj. adapted for grasping.

pre'his·tor'ic, adj. of time before recorded history.

pre·judge' v., **-judged, -judging.** judge prematurely.

prej'u·dice (prej'ə dis) n., v., **-diced, -dicing.** —n. 1. opinion formed without evidence. 2. disadvantage. —v. 3. affect with prejudice. —**prej'u·di'cial** (-dish'əl) adj.

prel'ate (prel'it) n. high church official.

pre·lim'i·nar'y (pri lim'ə ner'ē) adj., n., pl. **-naries.** —adj. 1. introductory. —n. 2. preliminary stage or action.

prel'ude (prel'yōōd, prā'lōōd) n. 1. Music. **a.** preliminary to a more important work. **b.** brief composition, esp. for piano. 2. preliminary to major action or event.

pre·mar'i·tal (prē mar'i tl) adj. before marriage.

pre·ma·ture', adj. 1. born, maturing, or occurring too soon. 2. overhasty. —**pre'ma·ture'ly,** adv.

pre·med'i·tate', v., **-tated, -tating.** plan in advance.

pre·mier' (pri mēr', -myēr') n. 1. prime minister. —adj. 2. chief.

pre·miere' (pri mēr', -myēr') n. first public performance.

prem'ise (prem'is) n. 1. (pl.) building with its grounds. 2. statement from which a conclusion is drawn.

pre'mi·um (prē'mē əm) n. 1. great value. 2. bonus. 3. periodic insurance payment.

pre'mo·ni'tion (prem'ə nish'ən, prē'mə-) n. foreboding.

pre·na'tal (prē nāt'l) adj. before birth or before giving birth.

pre·oc'cu·py' v., **-pied, -pying.** engross completely.

pre'or·dain', v. decree in advance.

prep (prep) v., **prepped, prepping.** get ready; prepare.

prep'ar·a·to'ry school (prep'ər ə tôr'ē) private secondary school preparing students for college. Also, **prep school.**

pre·pare' (pri pâr') v., **-pared, -paring.** 1. make or get ready. 2. manufacture. —**prep'a·ra'tion** (prep'ə-rā'shən), n. —**pre·par'a·to'ry,** adj. —**pre·par'ed·ness,** n.

pre·pay' (prē pā') v., **-paid, -paying.** pay beforehand.

pre·pon'der·ant (pri pon'dər ənt) adj. superior in force or numbers. —**pre·pon'der·ance,** n.

prep'o·si'tion (prep'ə zish'ən) n. word placed before noun or adjective to indicate relationship of space, time, means, etc.

pre'pos·sess'ing (prē'-) adj. impressing favorably.

pre·pos'ter·ous (pri pos'tər əs) adj. absurd.

prep'py (prep'ē) n., pl. **-pies,** adj., **-pier, -piest.** —n. 1. student or graduate of a preparatory school. 2. person who acts or dresses like a preppy. —adj. 3. characteristic of a preppy.

pre′puce (prē′pyōōs) *n.* skin covering head of penis.

pre′quel (prē′kwal) *n.* sequel to film, play, etc., that prefigures the original.

pre·req′ui·site (pri rek′wə zit, prē-) *adj.* 1. required in advance. —*n.* 2. something prerequisite.

pre·rog′a·tive (pri rog′ə tiv, pə rog′-) *n.* special right or privilege.

pres., 1. present. 2. president.

pres′age (pres′ij) *v.,* -**aged,** -**aging.** 1. portend. 2. predict.

pres′by·o′pi·a (prez′bē ō′pē ə, pres′-) *n.* farsightedness.

pres′by·ter (prez′bi tər, pres′-) *n.* 1. priest. 2. elder.

pres′by·te′ri·an (-bi tēr′ē ən) *adj.* 1. (of religious group) governed by presbytery. 2. (*cap.*) designating Protestant church so governed. —*n.* 3. (*cap.*) member of Presbyterian Church.

pres′by·ter′y, *n., pl.* -**ies.** body of church elders and (in Presbyterian churches) ministers.

pre′school′, *adj.* (prē′skōōl′) 1. of or for children between infancy and kindergarten age. —*n.* (-skōōl′) 2. nursery for preschool children.

pre′sci·ence (prē′shəns, -ē əns) *n.* foresight. —**pre′sci·ent,** *adj.*

pre·scribe′ (pri skrīb′) *v.,* -**scribed,** -**scribing.** 1. order for use, as medicine. 2. order. —**pre·scrip′tion** (-skrip′shən) *n.* —**pre·scrip′tive** (-skrip′tiv) *adj.*

pres′ence (prez′əns) *n.* 1. fact of being present. 2. vicinity. 3. impressive personal quality.

presence of mind, ability to think clearly and act appropriately, as during a crisis.

pres′ent, *adj.* (prez′ənt) 1. being or occurring now. 2. being at particular place. 3. *Gram.* denoting action or state now in progress. —*n.* (prez′ənt) 4. present time. 5. *Gram.* present tense. 6. thing bestowed as gift. —*v.* (pri zent′) 7. give, bring, or offer. 8. exhibit. —**pres·en·ta′tion,** *n.*

pres·ent′a·ble (pri zen′tə bal) *adj.* suitable in looks, dress, etc.

pre·sen′ti·ment (-mant) *n.* feeling of something impending, esp. evil.

pres′ent·ly (prez′ənt lē) *adv.* 1. at present. 2. soon.

pres·er·va′tion·ist (prez′ər vā′shə nist) *n.* one who advocates preservation of wildlife, etc.

pre·serve′ (pri zûrv′) *v.,* -**served,** -**serving,** *n.* —*v.* 1. keep alive. 2. keep safe. 3. maintain. 4. prepare (food) for long keeping. —*n.* 5. (*pl.*) preserved fruit. 6. place where

game is protected. —**pres′er·va′tion** (prez′ər vā′shən) *n.* —**pre·serv′a·tive,** *n., adj.*

pre·side′ (pri zīd′) *v.,* -**sided,** -**siding.** act as chairman.

pres′i·dent (prez′i dənt) *n.* 1. highest executive of republic. 2. chief officer. —**pres′i·den·cy,** *n.*

press (pres) *v.* 1. act upon with weight or force. 2. oppress; harass. 3. insist upon. 4. urge to hurry or comply. 5. smooth with iron. —*n.* 6. newspapers, etc., collectively. 7. device for pressing or printing. 8. crowd. 9. urgency. —**press′er,** *n.*

press agent, person employed to obtain favorable publicity.

press conference, interview with reporters.

press′ing, *adj.* urgent.

press release, statement distributed to the press.

pres′sure (presh′ər) *n.* 1. exertion of force by one body upon another. 2. stress. 3. urgency.

pressure cooker, pot for cooking quickly by steam under pressure.

pressure group, group that tries to influence legislation.

pres·sur·ize′, *v.,* -**ized,** -**izing.** produce normal air pressure at high altitudes. —**pres′sur·i·za′tion,** *n.*

pres′ti·dig′i·ta′tion (pres′ti dij′i tā′shən) *n.* sleight of hand.

pres·tige′ (pre stēzh′, -stēj′) *n.* distinguished reputation. —**pres·tig′ious** (-stij′əs) *adj.*

pres′to (pres′tō) *adv. Music.* quickly.

pre·sume′ (pri zōōm′) *v.,* -**sumed,** -**suming.** 1. take for granted. 2. act with unjustified boldness. —**pre·sum′a·bly,** *adv.* —**pre·sump′tu·ous** (-zump′chōō əs) *adj.*

pre·sump′tion (-zump′shən) *n.* 1. presumptuous attitude. 2. assumption.

pre·sup·pose′ (prē′sə pōz′) *v.,* -**posed,** -**posing.** assume.

pre·teen′ *n.* 1. child between 10 and 13 years old. —*adj.* 2. of or for preteens.

pre·tend′ (pri tend′) *v.* 1. make false appearance or claim. 2. make believe. 3. claim, as sovereignty. —**pre·tend′er,** *n.* —**pre·tense′,** *n.*

pre·ten′sion (pri ten′shən) *n.* 1. ostentation. 2. act of pretending.

pre·ten′tious *adj.* overly self-important. —**pre·ten′tious·ly,** *adv.*

pret′er·it (pret′ər it) *Gram.* —*adj.* 1. denoting action in past. —*n.* 2. preterit tense.

pre′ter·nat′u·ral (prē′tər nach′ər əl) *adj.* supernatural.

pre′text (prē′tekst) *n.* ostensible reason; excuse.

pret′ty (prit′ē) *adj.,* **-tier, -tiest,** *adv.* —*adj.* **1.** pleasingly attractive. —*adv.* **2.** moderately. **3.** very. —**pret′ti·fy′** *v.* —**pret′ti·ly,** *adv.*

pret′zel (pret′səl) *n.* crisp elongated or knotted biscuit.

pre·vail′ (pri vāl′) *v.* **1.** be widespread. **2.** exercise persuasion. **3.** gain victory.

pre·vail′ing, *adj.* **1.** most common. **2.** having superior influence.

prev′a·lent (prev′ə lənt) *adj.* widespread; general. —**prev′a·lence,** *n.*

pre·var′i·cate′ (pri var′i kāt′) *v.,* **-cated, -cating.** speak evasively; lie. —**pre·var′i·ca′tion,** *n.*

pre·vent′ (pri vent′) *v.* hinder; stop. —**pre·vent′a·ble,** *adj.* —**pre·ven′tion,** *n.* —**pre·ven′ta·tive,** *adj.,* *n.*

pre·view′ (prē′vyōō′) *n.,* *v.* view or show in advance.

pre′vi·ous (prē′vē əs) *adj.* occurring earlier. —**pre′vi·ous·ly,** *adv.*

prey (prā) *n.* **1.** animal hunted as food by another animal. **2.** victim. —*v.* **3.** seize prey. **4.** victimize another. **5.** be obsessive.

price (prīs) *n.,* *v.,* **priced, pricing.** —*n.* **1.** amount for which thing is sold. **2.** value. —*v.* **3.** set price on. **4.** *Informal.* ask the price of.

price′less, *adj.* too valuable to set price on.

pric′ey, *adj.,* **-ier, -iest.** *Informal.* expensive.

prick (prik) *n.* **1.** puncture by pointed object. —*v.* **2.** pierce. **3.** point.

prick′le, *n.* sharp point. —**prick′ly,** *adj.*

prickly heat, rash caused by inflammation of sweat glands.

pride (prīd) *n.,* *v.,* **prided, priding.** —*n.* **1.** high opinion of worth of oneself or that associated with oneself. **2.** self-respect. **3.** that which one is proud of. **4.** group of lions. —*v.* **5.** feel pride. —**pride′ful,** *adj.*

priest (prēst) *n.* person authorized to perform religious rites; member of clergy. —**priest′ess,** *n.fem.* —**priest′hood,** *n.*

prig (prig) *n.* self-righteous person. —**prig′gish,** *adj.*

prim (prim) *adj.* stiffly proper.

pri·ma·cy (prī′mə sē) *n.,* *pl.* **-cies.** supremacy.

pri·ma don·na (prē′mə don′ə, prim′ə) *n.* **1.** principal female opera singer. **2.** temperamental person.

pri·ma fa′ci·e (prī′mə fā′shē ē′, fā′shē) *adj. Law.* sufficient to establish a fact unless rebutted.

pri′mal (prī′məl) *adj.* **1.** first; original. **2.** most important.

pri·ma·ri·ly (prī mâr′ə lē, -mer′-) *adv.* **1.** chiefly. **2.** originally.

pri′ma·ry (prī′mer ē, -mə rē) *adj.,* *n.,* *pl.* **-ries.** —*adj.* **1.** first in importance or in order. **2.** earliest. —*n.* **3.** preliminary election for choosing party candidates.

pri′mate (prī′māt *or, esp. for 1,* -mit) *n.* **1.** high church official. **2.** mammal of order including humans, apes, and monkeys.

prime (prīm) *adj.,* *n.,* *v.,* primed, priming. —*adj.* **1.** first in importance or quality. **2.** original. —*n.* **3.** best stage or part. —*v.* **4.** prepare for special purpose or function.

prime meridian, meridian running through Greenwich, England, from which longitude east and west is reckoned.

prime minister, chief minister in some governments.

prim′er (prim′ər; *esp. Brit.* prī′mər) *n.* elementary book, esp. for reading.

prime rate, minimum interest rate charged by banks to best-rated customers.

prime time, hours considered to have largest television audience.

pri·me·val (prī mē′vəl) *adj.* of earliest time.

prim′i·tive (prim′i tiv) *adj.* **1.** earliest. **2.** simple; unrefined.

pri·mo·gen·i·ture (prī′mō jen′i char) *n.* state of being firstborn.

pri·mor′di·al (prī môr′dē əl) *adj.* primeval.

primp (primp) *v.* dress fussily.

prim′rose′ (prim′rōz′) *n.* early-flowering garden perennial.

prince (prins) *n.* **1.** high-ranking male member of royalty. —**prin′cess,** *n. fem.*

prince′ly, *adj.* lavish.

prin′ci·pal (prin′sə pəl) *adj.* **1.** chief. —*n.* **2.** chief; leader. **3.** head of school. **4.** person authorizing another to act for him. **5.** capital sum, distinguished from interest.

prin′ci·pal′i·ty (-pal′i tē) *n.,* *pl.* **-ties.** state ruled by prince.

prin′ci·ple (prin′sə pəl) *n.* **1.** rule of conduct or action. **2.** fundamental truth or cause.

print (print) *v.* **1.** reproduce from inked types, plates, etc. **2.** write in letters like those of print. **3.** produce (photograph) from negative. —*n.* **4.** printed state. **5.** (of book) present availability for sale. **6.** print lettering. **7.** anything printed.

print′out′, *n.* printed output of computer.

pri/or (prī/ər) *adj.* **1.** earlier. —*adv.* **2.** previously. —*n.* **3.** officer in religious house. —**pri/or·ess,** *n.fem.* —**pri/o·ry,** *n.*

pri·or/i·tize (prī ôr/i tīz/) *v.,* **-tized, -tizing.** arrange in order of priority.

pri·or/i·ty, *n., pl.* **-ties. 1.** state of being earlier. **2.** precedence.

prism (priz/əm) *n.* transparent body for dividing light into its spectrum.

pris/on (priz/ən) *n.* building for confinement of criminals. —**pris/on·er,** *n.*

pris/sy (pris/ē) *adj.,* **-sier, -siest.** excessively or affectedly improper.

pris/tine (pris/tēn, pri stēn/) *adj.* original; pure.

pri/vate (prī/vit) *adj.* **1.** belonging to particular person or group. **2.** personal. —*n.* **3.** soldier of lowest rank. —**pri/va·cy,** *n.* —**pri/vate·ly,** *adv.*

pri/va·teer/ (prī/və tēr/) *n.* privately owned vessel commissioned to fight. —**pri/va·teer/ing,** *n.*

private eye, *Informal.* private detective.

pri·va/tion (prī vā/shən) *n.* lack.

priv/et (priv/it) *n.* evergreen shrub.

priv/i·lege (priv/ə lij, priv/lij) *n., v.,* **-leged, -leging.** —*n.* **1.** special advantage. —*v.* **2.** grant privilege to.

priv/y (priv/ē) *adj., n., pl.* **privies.** —*adj.* **1.** sharing secret. **2.** private. —*n.* **3.** outdoor toilet.

privy council, board of personal advisors.

prize (prīz) *n., v.,* **prized, prizing.** —*n.* **1.** reward for victory, superiority, etc. **2.** thing worth striving for. —*v.* **3.** esteem highly.

pro (prō) *n., pl.* **pros,** *adv.* —*n.* **1.** argument in favor of something. **2.** *Informal.* professional. —*adv.* **3.** in favor of a plan, etc.

pro-, prefix meaning: **1.** favoring or supporting, as *prowar.* **2.** before or in front of, as *prognosis.*

prob/a·ble (prob/ə bəl) *adj.* **1.** likely to occur, etc. **2.** affording ground for belief. —**prob/a·bil/i·ty,** *n.* —**prob/a·bly,** *adv.*

pro/bate (prō/bāt) *n., adj., v.,* **-bated, -bating.** —*n.* **1.** authentication of will. —*adj.* **2.** of probate. —*v.* **3.** establish will's validity.

pro·ba/tion, *n.* **1.** act of testing. **2.** period of such testing. **3.** conditional release, as from prison.

probe (prōb) *v., n.,* **probed, probing.** —*v.* **1.** examine thoroughly. —*n.* **2.** device for exploring wounds, etc. **3.** investigation.

pro/bi·ty (prō/bi tē, prob/i-) *n.* honesty.

prob/lem (prob/ləm) *n.* matter involving uncertainty or difficulty. —**prob/lem·at/ic,** *adj.*

pro·bos/cis (prō bos/is, -kis) *n., pl.* **-cises.** flexible snout.

pro·ce/dure (prə sē/jər) *n.* course of action. —**pro·ce/dur·al,** *adj.*

pro·ceed/ (prə sēd/) *v.* **1.** go forward. **2.** carry on action. **3.** issue forth. —*n.* (prō/sēd) **4.** (*pl.*). sum derived from sale, etc.

pro·ceed/ing, *n.* **1.** action or conduct. **2.** (*pl.*) **a.** records of society. **b.** legal action.

proc/ess (pros/es; *esp. Brit.* prō/ses) *n.* **1.** series of actions toward given end. **2.** continuous action. **3.** legal summons. **4.** projecting growth. —*v.* **5.** treat by particular process.

pro·ces/sion (prə sesh/ən) *n.* ceremonial movement; parade.

pro·ces/sion·al, *n.* **1.** hymn sung during procession. **2.** hymnal.

pro·choice/ (prō chois/) *adj.* supporting the right to legalized abortion.

pro·claim/ (prō klām/, prə-) *v.* announce publicly. —**proc/la·ma/tion** (prok/lə mā/shən) *n.*

pro·cliv/i·ty (prō kliv/i tē) *n., pl.* **-ties.** natural tendency.

pro·cras/ti·nate/ (prō kras/tə nāt/, prə-) *v.,* **-nated, -nating.** delay. —**pro·cras/ti·na/tion,** *n.*

pro/cre·ate/ (prō/krē āt/) *v.* **-ated, -ating.** produce or have offspring. —**pro/cre·a/tion,** *n.*

proc/tor (prok/tər) *n.* **1.** person who watches over students at examinations. —*v.* **2.** supervise or monitor.

pro·cure/ (prō kyŏŏr/, prə-) *v.* **-cured, -curing. 1.** get; obtain. **2.** cause. **3.** hire prostitutes. —**pro·cur/a·ble,** *adj.* —**pro·cure/ment,** *n.* —**pro·cur/er,** *n.* **1.** one that procures. **2.** Also, **pro·cur/ess,** *fem.* person who arranges for prostitution.

prod (prod) *v.,* **prodded, prodding,** *n.* —*v.* **1.** poke. **2.** incite; goad. —*n.* **3.** poke. **4.** goading instrument.

prod/i·gal (prod/i gəl) *adj.* **1.** wastefully extravagant. **2.** lavish. —*n.* **3.** spendthrift.

prod/i·gal/i·ty (-gal/ə tē) *n., pl.* **-ties.** extravagance; lavishness.

pro·di/gious (prə dij/əs) *adj.* huge; wonderful. —**pro·di/gious·ly,** *adv.*

prod/i·gy (prod/i jē) *n., pl.* **-gies.** very gifted person.

pro·duce/ (*v.* prə dōōs/, -dyōōs/; *n.* prō/dōōs) *v.* **-duced, -ducing.** —*v.* (prə dōōs/, -dyōōs) **1.** bring into existence; create. **2.** bear, as young, fruit. **3.** exhibit. —*n.* (prod/ōōs, -yōōs, prō/dōōs, -dyōōs) **4.** product. **5.** agricultural products.

—pro·duc'tion *n.* —pro·duc'tive, *adj.*

prod'uct (prod'əkt) *n.* **1.** thing produced; result. **2.** result obtained by multiplying.

pro·duc·tiv·i·ty (prod'duk tiv'i tē, prod'ək), *n.* **1.** capability of being productive. **2.** rate at which things are produced.

pro·fane' (prə fān', prō-) *adj., v.,* **-faned, -faning.** —*adj.* **1.** secular. **2.** irreverent toward sacred things. —*v.* **3.** defile. **4.** treat (sacred thing) with contempt. —prof'a·na'tion (prof'ə nā'shən) *n.*

pro·fan'i·ty (-fan'i tē) *n., pl.* **-ties.** **1.** profane quality. **2.** blasphemous or vulgar language.

pro·fess' (prə fes') *v.* **1.** declare. **2.** affirm faith in. **3.** claim.

pro·fes'sion, *n.* **1.** learned vocation. **2.** declaration; assertion.

pro·fes·sion·al, *adj.* **1.** following occupation for gain. **2.** of or engaged in profession. —*n.* **3.** professional person.

pro·fes'sor (prə fes'ər) *n.* college teacher of highest rank.

prof'fer (prof'ər) *v.* **1.** offer. —*n.* **2.** offer.

pro·fi'cient (prə fish'ənt) *adj.* expert. —pro·fi'cien·cy, *n.*

pro'file (prō'fīl) *n.* **1.** side view. **2.** informal biographical sketch.

prof'it (prof'it) *n.* **1.** pecuniary gain from business transaction. **2.** net gain after costs. **3.** benefit. —*v.* **4.** gain advantage. **5.** make profit. —prof'it·a·ble, *adj.*

prof'it·eer', *n.* **1.** person who makes unfair profit. —*v.* **2.** act as profiteer.

prof'li·gate (prof'li git, -gāt') *adj.* **1.** immoral. **2.** extravagant. —prof'li·gate, *n.* —prof'li·ga·cy, *n.*

pro for'ma (prō fôr'mə) done as a matter of form or for the sake of form.

pro·found' (prə found') *adj.* **1.** thinking deeply. **2.** intense. **3.** deep. —pro·fun'di·ty (-fun'di tē) *n.*

pro·fuse' (-fyoos') *adj.* extravagant; abundant. —pro·fuse'ly, *adv.*

pro·gen'i·tor (prō jen'i tər) *n.* ancestor.

prog'e·ny (proj'ə nē) *n.pl.* children.

pro·ges'ter·one (prō jes'tə rōn') *n.* female hormone that prepares uterus for fertilized ovum.

prog·no'sis (prog nō'sis) *n., pl.* **-noses** (-nō'sēz). medical forecast.

prog·nos'ti·cate (-nos'ti kāt') *v.,* **-cated, -cating.** predict.

pro'gram (prō'gram, -grəm) *n., v.,* **-grammed, -gramming.** —*n.* **1.** plan of things to do. **2.** schedule of entertainments. **3.** television or radio show. **4.** plan for computerized problem solving. —*v.* **5.** make program for or including. —pro·gram'ma·ble, *adj.* —pro'gram·mer, *n.*

prog'ress, *n.* (prog'res, -rəs; *esp. Brit.* prō'gres) **1.** advancement. **2.** permanent improvement. **3.** growth. —*v.* (prə gres') **4.** make progress.

pro·gres'sion, *n.* **1.** advance. **2.** series.

pro·gres'sive, *adj.* **1.** advancing step by step. **2.** advocating reform.

pro·hib'it (prō hib'it) *v.* forbid; prevent.

pro'hi·bi'tion (prō'ə bish'ən) *n.* **1.** act of prohibiting. **2.** (*cap.*) period, 1920–33, when manufacture and sale of alcoholic drinks was forbidden in U.S. —pro'hi·bi'tion·ist, *n.*

pro·hib'i·tive (-hib'ə tiv) *adj.* **1.** serving to prohibit. **2.** too expensive.

proj'ect, *n.* (proj'ekt, -ikt; *esp. Brit.* prō'jekt) **1.** something planned. —*v.* (prə jekt') **2.** plan. **3.** impel forward. **4.** display upon surface, as motion picture or map. **5.** protrude. —pro·jec'tion, *n.* —pro·jec'tor, *n.*

pro·jec'tile (prə jek'til, -tīl) *n.* object fired with explosive force.

pro·jec'tion·ist (-shə nist) *n.* operator of motion-picture projector.

pro·le·tar'i·at (prō'li târ'ē ət) *n.* working or impoverished class. —pro'le·tar'i·an, *adj., n.*

pro-life', *adj.* opposed to legalized abortion.

pro·lif'er·ate (prə lif'ə rāt') *v.,* **-ated, -ating.** spread rapidly.

pro·lif'ic (-ik) *adj.* fruitful.

pro·lix' (prō liks', prō'liks) *adj.* tediously long and wordy.

pro'logue (prō'lôg) *n.* introductory part of novel, play, etc.

pro·long' (prə lông') *v.* lengthen. —pro'lon·ga'tion (prō'-) *n.*

prom (prom) *n.* formal dance at high school or college.

prom'e·nade' (prom'ə nād', -näd') *n., v.,* **-naded, -nading.** —*n.* **1.** leisurely walk. **2.** space for such walk. —*v.* **3.** stroll.

prom'i·nent (prom'ə nənt) *adj.* **1.** conspicuous. **2.** projecting. **3.** well-known. —prom'i·nence, *n.*

pro·mis'cu·ous (prə mis'kyōō əs) *adj.* having numerous sexual partners on a casual basis. —prom'is·cu'i·ty, (prom'i skyōō'i tē) *n.* —pro·mis'cu·ous·ly, *adv.*

prom'ise (prom'is) *n., v.,* **-ised, -ising.** —*n.* **1.** assurance that one will act as specified. **2.** indication of future excellence. —v. **3.** assure by promise. **4.** afford ground for expectation. —**prom'is·ing,** adj.

prom·is·so·ry (prom'ə sôr'ē) adj. containing promise of payment.

prom·on·to·ry (prom'ən tôr'ē) n., pl. **-ries.** high peak projecting into sea or overlooking low land.

pro·mote' (prə mōt') v., **-moted, -moting. 1.** further progress of. **2.** advance. **3.** organize. —**pro·mot'er,** n. —**pro·mo'tion,** n.

prompt (prompt) adj. **1.** ready to act. **2.** done at once. —v. **3.** incite to action. **4.** suggest (action, etc.). —**prompt'ness,** n.

prom·ul·gate (prom'əl gāt', prō-mul'gāt) v., **-gated, -gating.** proclaim formally.

prone (prōn) adj. **1.** likely; inclined. **2.** lying flat, esp. face downward.

prong (prông) n. point.

pro·noun' (prō'noun') n. word used as substitute for noun.

pro·nounce' (prə nouns') v., **-nounced, -nouncing. 1.** utter, esp. precisely. **2.** declare to be. **3.** announce. —**pro·nounce'ment,** n.

pro·nounced' adj. **1.** strongly marked. **2.** decided.

pron'to (pron'tō) adv. quickly.

pro·nun'ci·a'tion (prə nun'sē ā'shən) n. production of sounds of speech.

proof (prōōf) n. **1.** evidence establishing fact. **2.** standard strength, as of liquors. **3.** trial printing. —adj. **4.** resisting perfectly.

-proof, suffix meaning resistant.

proof'read' (-rēd') v., **-read** (red'), **-reading.** read (printers' proofs, etc.) to mark errors. —**proof'read'er,** n.

prop (prop) n., v., **propped, propping.** —n. **1.** rigid support. **2.** propeller. —v. **3.** support with prop.

prop'a·gan'da (prop'ə gan'də) n. doctrines disseminated by organization. —**prop'a·gan'dist,** n. —**prop'a·gan'dize,** v., **-dized, -dizing.**

prop'a·gate (prop'ə gāt') v., **-gated, -gating. 1.** reproduce. **2.** cause to increase. **3.** transmit (doctrine, etc.).

pro'pane (prō'pān) n. colorless flammable gas, used esp. as fuel.

pro·pel' (prə pel') v., **-pelled, -pelling.** drive forward. —**pro·pel'lant, pro·pel'lent,** n.

pro·pel'ler, n. screwlike propelling device.

pro·pen'si·ty (prə pen'si tē) n., pl. **-ties.** inclination.

prop'er (prop'ər) adj. **1.** suitable;

fitting. **2.** correct. **3.** designating particular person, place, or thing.

prop'er·ty, n., pl. **-ties. 1.** that which one owns. **2.** attribute.

proph'e·cy (prof'ə sī') n., **-sied, -sying.** predict. —**proph'e·cy** (-sē) n.

proph'et (-it) n. **1.** person who speaks for God. **2.** inspired leader. **3.** person who predicts. —**pro·phet'ic** (prə fet'ik) adj.

pro'phy·lax'is (prō'fə lak'sis) n. protection from or prevention of disease. —**pro'phy·lac'tic,** adj., n.

pro·pin'qui·ty (prō ping'kwi tē) n. nearness.

pro·pi'ti·ate' (prə pish'ē āt') v., **-ated, -ating.** appease.

pro·pi'tious (-pish'əs) adj. favorable. —**pro·pi'tious·ly,** adv.

pro·po'nent (prə pō'nənt) n. advocate; supporter.

pro·por'tion (prə pôr'shən) n. **1.** comparative or proper relation of dimensions or quantities. **2.** symmetry. **3.** (pl.) dimensions. —v. **4.** adjust in proper relation.

pro·por'tion·ate (-shə nit) adj. being in due proportion.

pro·pos'al (prə pō'zəl) n. **1.** proposition. **2.** offer of marriage.

pro·pose' (prə pōz') v., **-posed, -posing. 1.** suggest. **2.** intend. **3.** offer marriage.

prop'o·si'tion (prop'ə zish'ən) n. **1.** proposed plan. **2.** statement that affirms or denies. **3.** proposal of sex. —v. **4.** make proposition to.

pro·pound' (prə pound') v. offer for consideration.

pro·pri'e·tor (prə prī'ə tər) n. owner or manager. —**pro·pri'e·tar'y,** adj.

pro·pri'e·ty, n., pl. **-ties. 1.** appropriateness. **2.** (pl.) morality.

pro·pul'sion (prə pul'shən) n. propelling force.

pro·rate' (prō rāt', prō'rāt') v., **-rated, -rating.** divide proportionately.

pro·sa'ic (prō zā'ik) adj. commonplace. —**pro·sa'i·cal·ly,** adv.

pro·sce'ni·um (prō sē'nē əm, prə-) n., pl. **-niums, -nia** (-nē ə) arch separating stage from auditorium. Also, **proscenium arch.**

pro·scribe' (prō skrīb') v., **-scribed, -scribing.** prohibit.

prose (prōz) n. not verse; ordinary language.

pros'e·cute' (pros'i kyōōt') v., **-cuted, -cuting. 1.** begin legal proceedings against. **2.** go on with (task, etc.) to the end. —**pros'e·cu'tion,** n. —**pros'e·cu'tor,** n.

pros'e·lyte' (pros'ə līt') n., v.,

-lyted, -lyting. convert. **—pros′e·lyt·ize′** (-lə tīz′) v., **-ized, -izing.**

pros′pect (pros′pekt) n. **1.** likelihood of success. **2.** outlook; view. **3.** potential customer. —v. **4.** search. **—pro·spec′tive** (prə spek′tiv) adj. **—pros′pec·tor,** n.

pro·spec′tus (prə spek′təs) n. description of new investment or purchase.

pros′per (pros′pər) v. be successful. **—pros·per′i·ty** (-per′ə tē) n. **—pros′per·ous,** adj.

pros′tate (pros′tāt) n. gland in males at base of bladder.

pros·the′sis (pros thē′sis) n., pl. **-ses** (-sēz). device that substitutes for or supplements missing or defective body part. **—pros·thet′ic** (-thet′ik) adj.

pros′ti·tute′ (pros′ti tōōt′, -tyōōt′) n., v., **-tuted, -tuting.** —n. **1.** person who engages in sexual intercourse for money. —v. **2.** put to base use. **—pros′ti·tu′tion,** n.

pros′trate (pros′trāt) adj., v., **-trated, -trating.** —v. **1.** lay (oneself) face downward, esp. in humility. **2.** exhaust. —adj. **3.** lying flat. **4.** helpless. **5.** weak or exhausted.

pro·tag′o·nist (prō tag′ə nist) n. main character.

pro′te·an (prō′tē ən, prō tē′-) adj. assuming different forms.

pro·tect′ (prə tekt′) v. shield; defend, as from attack. **—pro·tec′tion,** n. **—pro·tec′tive,** adj. **—pro·tec′tor,** n.

pro·tec′tion·ism (-sha niz′əm) n. practice of protecting domestic industries from foreign competition by imposing import duties.

pro·tec′tor·ate (-tar it) n. **1.** relation by which strong state partly controls weaker state. **2.** such weaker state.

pro′té·gé′ (prō′tə zhā′) n. one under friendly patronage of another. **—pro′té·gée′,** n. fem.

pro′tein (prō′tēn, -tē in) n. nitrogenous compound.

pro tem·por·e (prō′ tem′pə rē′, -rā′) temporarily.

pro′test, n. (prō′test) **1.** objection. —v. (prə test′, prō′test) **2.** express objection. **3.** declare. **—prot′es·ta′tion,** n. **—pro·test′er,** n.

Prot′es·tant (prot′ə stənt) n. Christian who belongs to a church that began by breaking away from the Roman Catholic Church in the 16th century. **—Prot′es·tant·ism′,** n.

proto-, prefix meaning earliest or foremost.

pro′to·col′ (prō′tə kôl′) n. diplomatic etiquette.

pro′ton (prō′ton) n. part of atom bearing positive charge.

pro′to·plasm′ (prō′tə plaz′əm) n. basis of living matter.

pro′to·type′, n. model; first or typical version. **—pro′to·typ′i·cal,** adj.

pro′to·zo′an (-zō′ən) n., pl. **-zo·ans, -zoa** (-zō′ə). one-celled organism that obtains nourishment by ingesting food.

pro·tract′ (prō trakt′, prə-) v. lengthen. **—pro·trac′tion,** n.

pro·trac′tor, n. instrument for measuring angles.

pro·trude′ (prō trōōd′, prə-) v., **-truded, -truding.** project; extend. **—pro·tru′sion** (-trōō′zhən) n. **—pro·tru′sive** (-trōō′siv) adj.

pro·tu′ber·ant (prō tōō′bər ənt, -tyōō′-) adj. bulging out. **—pro·tu′ber·ance,** n.

proud (proud) adj. **1.** having pride. **2.** arrogant. **3.** magnificent. **—proud′ly,** adv.

prove (prōōv) v., **proved, proving. 1.** establish as fact. **2.** test. **3.** be or become ultimately.

prov′e·nance (prov′ə nəns, -näns′) n. place or source of origin.

prov′en·der (prov′ən dər) n. fodder.

prov′erb (prov′ərb) n. wise popular saying. **—pro·ver′bi·al** (prə vûr′bē əl) adj.

pro·vide′ (prə vīd′) v., **-vided, -viding. 1.** supply. **2.** yield. **3.** prepare beforehand. **—pro·vid′er,** n.

pro·vid′ed, conj. if.

prov′i·dence (prov′i dəns) n. **1.** God's care. **2.** economy.

prov′i·dent (-dənt) adj. showing foresight; prudent.

prov′i·den′tial (-den′shəl) adj. coming as godsend.

prov′ince (prov′ins) n. **1.** administrative unit of country. **2.** sphere.

pro·vin′cial (prə vin′shəl) adj. **1.** of province. **2.** narrow-minded; unsophisticated.

pro·vi′sion (prə vizh′ən) n. **1.** something stated as necessary or binding. **2.** act of providing. **3.** what is provided. **4.** arrangement beforehand. **5.** (pl.) food supply. —v. **6.** supply with provisions.

pro·vi′sion·al, adj. temporary.

pro·vi′so (prə vī′zō) n., pl. **-sos, -soes.** something required in an agreement; stipulation.

pro·voc′a·tive (prə vok′ə tiv) adj. stimulating; exciting.

pro·voke′ (-vōk′) v., **-voked, -voking. 1.** exasperate. **2.** arouse. **—prov′o·ca′tion** (prov′ə kā′shən) n.

pro′vost (prō′vōst) n. **1.** superintendent. **2.** high-ranking university administrator.

prow (prou) *n.* front part of ship or aircraft.

prow·ess (prou'is) *n.* **1.** exceptional ability. **2.** bravery.

prowl (proul) *v.* roam or search stealthily. —**prowl'er,** *n.*

prox·im·i·ty (prok sim'i tē) *n.* nearness.

prox·y (prok'sē) *n., pl.* **proxies.** agent.

prude (prōōd) *n.* person overly concerned with proprieties. —**prud'er·y,** *n.* —**prud'ish,** *adj.*

pru·dence (prōōd'ns) *n.* practical wisdom; caution. —**pru'dent,** *adj.* —**pru'dent·ly,** *adv.*

prune (prōōn) *n.* pruned, pruning, *n.* —*v.* **1.** cut off (branches, etc.). —*n.* **2.** dried plum.

pru·ri·ent (prōōr'ē ənt) *adj.* having lewd thoughts. —**pru'ri·ence,** *n.*

pry (prī) *v.,* **pried, prying,** *n.* —*v.* **1.** look or inquire too curiously. **2.** move with lever. —*n.* **3.** act of prying. **4.** prying person. **5.** lever.

P.S., **1.** Also, **p.s.** postscript. **2.** Public School.

psalm (säm) *n.* sacred song.

pseu·do (sōō'dō) *adj.* false.

pseu·do·nym (sōōd'n im) *n.* false name used by writer.

pso·ri·a·sis (sə rī'ə sis) *n.* chronic, inflammatory skin disease.

psych (sīk) *v.* *Informal.* **1.** intimidate. **2.** prepare psychologically.

psy·che (sī'kē) *n.* human soul or mind.

psy·che·del·ic (sī'ki del'ik) *adj.* noting a mental state of distorted sense perceptions and hallucinations.

psy·chi·a·try (si kī'ə trē, sī-) *n.* science of mental diseases. —**psy·chi·at·ric** (sī'kē a'trik) *adj.* —**psy·chi'a·trist,** *n.*

psy·chic (sī'kik) *adj.* **1.** of the psyche. **2.** pertaining to an apparently nonphysical force or agency. —*n.* **3.** person sensitive to psychic influences.

psy·cho·ac·tive (sī'kō-) *adj.* affecting mental state.

psy·cho·a·nal·y·sis (sī'kō ə nal'ə sis) *n.* **1.** study of conscious and unconscious psychological processes. **2.** treatment according to such study. —**psy'cho·an'a·lyst,** *n.* —**psy'cho·an'a·lyze,** *v.*

psy·cho·gen·ic (sī'kə jen'ik) *adj.* originating in mental process.

psy·chol·o·gy (sī kol'ə jē) *n.* science of mental states and behavior. —**psy'cho·log'i·cal** (-kə loj'i kəl) *adj.* —**psy·chol'o·gist,** *n.*

psy·cho·neu·ro·sis (sī'kō nōō rō'sis, -nyōō-) *n., pl.* **-ses.** emotional disorder.

psy·chop·a·thy (-kop'ə thē) *n., pl.* **-thies.** mental disease. —**psy'cho·path'** (sī'kə path') *n.* —**psy'cho·path'ic,** *adj.*

psy·cho·sis (-kō'sis) *n., pl.* **-ses** (-sēz). severe mental disease. —**psy·chot'ic** (-kot'ik) *adj.*

psy·cho·so·mat·ic (-sə mat'ik) *adj.* (of physical disorder) caused by one's emotional state.

psy·cho·ther·a·py, *n., pl.* **-pies.** treatment of mental disorders. —**psy'cho·ther'a·pist,** *n.*

psy·cho·tro·pic (-trō'pik) *adj.* affecting mental activity.

pt., **1.** part. **2.** pint. **3.** point.

ptar·mi·gan (tär'mi gən) *n.* species of mountain grouse.

pter·o·dac·tyl (ter'ə dak'til) *n.* extinct flying reptile.

pto·maine (tō'mān) *n.* substance produced during decay of plant and animal matter.

pub *n. Brit. Informal.* tavern.

pu·ber·ty (pyōō'bər tē) *n.* sexual maturity. —**pu'ber·tal,** *adj.*

pu·bes·cent (-bes'ənt) *adj.* arriving at puberty. —**pu·bes'cence,** *n.*

pu·bic (pyōō'bik) *adj.* of or near the genitals.

pub·lic (pub'lik) *adj.* **1.** of or for people generally. **2.** open to view or knowledge of all. —*n.* **3.** people.

pub·li·ca·tion, *n.* **1.** publishing of book, etc. **2.** item published.

public defender, lawyer who represents indigent clients at public expense.

public domain, legal status of material not protected by copyright or patent.

pub·lic·i·ty (pu blis'i tē) *n.* **1.** public attention. **2.** material promoting this.

pub·li·cize, *v.,* **-cized, -cizing.** bring to public notice.

public relations, actions of organization in promoting goodwill with the public.

pub·lish (pub'lish) *v.* **1.** issue (book, paper, etc.) for general distribution. **2.** announce publicly. —**pub'lish·er,** *n.*

puck (puk) *n.* black rubber disk hit into goal in hockey.

puck·er (puk'ər) *v., n.* wrinkle.

puck·ish (puk'ish) *adj.* mischievous.

pud·ding (pōōd'ing) *n.* soft, creamy dish, usually dessert.

pud·dle (pud'l) *n.* small pool of water.

pupil

pudg·y (puj′ē) adj., -ier, -iest. short and fat. —**pudg′i·ness**, n.

pu·er·ile (pyōō′ər il, -ə rīl′) adj. childish. —**pu′er·il′i·ty**, n.

puff (puf) n. **1.** short blast of wind. **2.** inflated part. **3.** anything soft and light. —v. **4.** blow with puffs. **5.** breathe hard and fast. **6.** inflate. —**puff′i·ness**, n. —**puff′y**, adj.

puf′fin (puf′in) n. sea bird.

pug (pug) n. kind of dog.

pu·gil·ism (pyōō′jə liz′əm) n. boxing. —**pu′gil·ist**, n.

pug·na·cious (pug nā′shəs) adj. always eager to fight. —**pug·nac′i·ty** (-nas′ə tē) n.

pug nose, short, broad, somewhat turned-up nose.

puke (pyōōk) v., puked, puking, n. Slang. vomit.

pul′chri·tude′ (pul′kri tōōd′, -tyōōd′) n. beauty.

pule (pyōōl) v., puled, puling, whine.

pull (pŏŏl) v. **1.** draw; haul. **2.** tear. **3.** move with force. —n. **4.** act of pulling. **5.** force. **6.** handle. **7.** Informal. influence in politics, etc. —**pull′er**, n.

pul′let (pŏŏl′it) n. young hen.

pul′ley (pŏŏl′ē) n. wheel for guiding rope.

Pull′man (pŏŏl′mən) n. sleeping car on railroad.

pull′out′, n. **1.** withdrawal. **2.** section of publication that can be pulled out.

pull′o′ver, adj. **1.** put on by being drawn over the head. —n. **2.** pullover garment.

pul′mo·nar′y (pul′mə ner′ē, pŏŏl-) adj. of lungs.

pulp (pulp) n. **1.** soft fleshy part, as of fruit or tooth. **2.** any soft mass. —v. **3.** make or become pulp.

pul′pit (pŏŏl′pit, pul′-) n. platform in church from which service is conducted or sermon is preached.

pul′sar (pul′sär) n. source of pulsating radio energy among stars.

pul·sate (pul′sāt) v., -sated, -sating. throb. —**pul·sa′tion**, n.

pulse (puls) n., v., pulsed, pulsing. —n. **1.** heartbeat. —v. **2.** pulsate.

pul′ver·ize′ (pul′və rīz′) v., -ized, -izing. reduce to powder.

pu′ma (pyōō′mə, pōō′-) n. cougar.

pum′ice (pum′is) n. porous volcanic glass used as abrasive.

pum′mel (pum′əl) v., -meled, -meling. strike; beat.

pump (pump) n. **1.** apparatus for raising or driving fluids. **2.** women's shoe. —v. **3.** raise or drive with pump. **4.** Informal. try to get information from.

pum′per·nick′el (pum′pər nik′əl) n. hard, sour rye bread.

pump′kin (pump′kin or, commonly, pung′kin) n. large orange squash of garden vine.

pun (pun) n., v., punned, punning. —n. **1.** play with words alike in sound but different in meaning. —v. **2.** make pun. —**pun′ster**, n.

punch (punch) n. **1.** thrusting blow. **2.** tool for piercing material. **3.** sweetened beverage. —v. **4.** hit with thrusting blow. **5.** drive (cattle). **6.** cut or indent with punch.

punch′-drunk′, adj. **1.** showing symptoms of cerebral injury. **2.** dazed.

punch line, climactic phrase in a joke.

punch′y, adj., -ier, -iest. **1.** befuddled. **2.** forceful.

punc·til′i·ous (pungk til′ē əs) adj. exact in observance of formalities.

punc′tu·al (pungk′chōō əl) adj. on time. —**punc′tu·al′i·ty**, n.

punc′tu·ate′ (-āt′) v., -ated, -ating. **1.** mark with punctuation. **2.** interrupt periodically.

punc′tu·a′tion, n. use of commas, semicolons, etc.

punc′ture (pungk′chər) n., v., -tured, -turing. —n. **1.** perforation. —v. **2.** perforate with pointed object.

pun′dit (pun′dit) n. learned person.

pun′gent (pun′jənt) adj. **1.** sharp in taste. **2.** biting. —**pun′gen·cy**, n.

pun′ish (pun′ish) v. subject to pain, confinement, loss, etc., for offense. —**pun′ish·ment**, n.

pu′ni·tive (pyōō′ni tiv) adj. punishing.

punk (pungk) n. **1.** substance that will smolder, used esp. to light fires. **2.** Slang. something or someone worthless or unimportant. **3.** Slang. young hoodlum. **4.** Also, **punk rock.** rock music marked by loudness and aggressive style. **5.** style of clothing, etc., suggesting defiance of social norms. **6.** Informal. poor in quality. **7.** of punk rock or punk style.

punt (punt) n. **1.** kick in football. **2.** shallow flat-bottomed boat. —v. **3.** kick (dropped ball) before it touches ground. **4.** propel (boat) with pole.

pu′ny (pyōō′nē) adj., -nier, -niest. small and weak.

pup (pup) n. young dog.

pu·pa (pyōō′pə) n., pl. -pae (-pē), -pas. insect in stage between larva and winged adult. —**pu′pal**, adj.

pu′pil (pyōō′pəl) n. **1.** person being taught. **2.** opening in iris of eye.

pup·pet (pup′it) *n.* **1.** doll or figure manipulated by hand or strings. **2.** person, government, etc., whose actions are controlled by another. —**pup′pet·ry,** *n.*

pup·pet·eer, *n.* person who manipulates puppets.

pup·py (pup′ē) *n., pl.* -**pies.** young dog.

pur·chase (pûr′chəs) *v.,* -chased, -chasing, *n.* —*v.* **1.** buy. —*n.* **2.** acquisition by payment. **3.** what is bought. **4.** leverage.

pure (pyŏŏr) *adj.,* purer, purest. **1.** free of pollutants. **2.** abstract. **3.** absolute. **4.** chaste. —**pure′ly,** *adv.*

pure′bred (pyŏŏr′bred′) **1.** having ancestors over many generations from a recognized breed. —*n.* (pyŏŏr′bred′) purebred animal.

pu·rée (pyŏŏ rā′, -rē′) *n., v.,* -réed, -réeing. —*n.* **1.** cooked food that has been sieved or blended. —*v.* **2.** make purée of.

pur·ga·to·ry (pûr′gə tôr′ē) *n., pl.* -ries. **1.** *Rom. Cath. Theol.* condition or place of purification, after death, from venial sins. **2.** any condition or place of temporary punishment.

purge (pûrj) *v.,* purged, purging, *n.* —*v.* **1.** cleanse; purify. **2.** rid. **3.** clear by causing evacuation. —*n.* **4.** act or means of purging. —**pur′ga·tive** (gə tiv) *adj., n.*

pu·ri·fy (pyŏŏr′ə fī′) *v.,* -fied, -fying. make or become pure.

Pu·rim (pŏŏr′im) *n.* Jewish commemorative festival.

pur·ism (pyŏŏr′iz əm) *n.* insistence on purity in language, style, etc.

Pu·ri·tan (pyŏŏr′i tn) *n.* **1.** member of strict Protestant group originating in 16th-century England. **2.** (*l.c.*) person of strict moral views. —**pu′ri·tan′i·cal,** *adj.*

pu·ri·ty (pyŏŏr′i tē) *n.* condition of being pure.

purl (pûrl) *v.* knit with inverted stitch.

pur′lieu (pûr′lōō, pûr′lyōō) *n., pl.* -lieus. (*pl.*) neighborhood.

pur·loin (pər loin′, pûr′loin) *v.* steal.

pur′ple (pûr′pəl) *n.* color blended of red and blue. —**purple.** *adj.*

pur·port (*v.* pər pôrt′) *v.* **1.** claim. **2.** imply. —*n.* (pûr′pôrt) **3.** meaning.

pur·pose (pûr′pəs) *n., v.,* -posed, -posing. —*n.* **1.** object; aim; intention. —*v.* **2.** intend. —**pur′pose·ful,** *adj.* —**pur′pose·less,** *adj.*

purr (pûr) *n.* **1.** low continuous sound made by cat. —*v.* **2.** make this sound.

purse (pûrs) *n., v.,* pursed, pursing. —*n.* **1.** bag for money and small things. **2.** sum of money offered as prize. —*v.* **3.** pucker.

purs′er, *n.* financial officer.

pur·su·ant (pər sōō′ənt) *adv.* according.

pur·sue, *v.,* -sued, -suing. **1.** follow. **2.** carry on (studies, etc.). —**pur·su′er,** *n.*

pur·suit′ (-sōōt′) *n.* **1.** act of pursuing. **2.** quest. **3.** occupation.

pur·vey′ (pər vā′) *v.* provide; supply. —**pur·vey′or,** *n.*

pus (pus) *n.* liquid matter found in sores, etc.

push (pŏŏsh) *v.* **1.** exert force on to send away. **2.** urge. **3.** peddle. —*n.* **4.** act of pushing. **5.** *Informal.* effort.

push′o·ver, *n. Informal.* one easily victimized or overcome.

push′y, *adj.,* -ier, -iest. obnoxiously self-assertive. —**push′i·ness,** *n.*

pu·sil·lan·i·mous (pyŏŏ′sə lan′ə məs) *adj.* cowardly.

puss·y (pŏŏs′ē) *n., pl.* pussies. cat. Also, **puss.**

puss′y·foot′, *v.* **1.** go stealthily. **2.** act timidly or irresolutely.

pussy willow, small American willow.

pus′tule (pus′chōōl) *n.* pimple containing pus.

put (pŏŏt) *v.,* put, putting, *n.* —*v.* **1.** move or place. **2.** set, as to task. **3.** express. **4.** apply. **5.** impose. **6.** throw.

pu·ta·tive (pyŏŏ′tə tiv) *adj.* reputed.

put′-down′, *n. Informal.* snubbing remark.

pu·tre·fy′ (pyŏŏ′trə fī′) *v.,* -fied, -fying. rot. —**pu·tre·fac′tion** (-fak′shən) *n.*

pu·tres·cent (-tres′ənt) *adj.* becoming putrid. —**pu·tres′cence,** *n.*

pu·trid (-trid) *adj.* rotten.

putsch (pŏŏch) *n.* sudden political revolt or uprising.

putt (put) *v.* **1.** strike (golf ball) gently. —*n.* **2.** such strike.

put′ter, (put′ər) *v.* **1.** busy oneself ineffectively. —*n.* **2.** club for putting.

put′ty (put′ē) *n., v.,* -tied, -tying. —*n.* **1.** cement of whiting and oil used in windows. —*v.* **2.** secure with putty.

puz·zle (puz′əl) *n., v.,* -zled, -zling. —*n.* **1.** device or question offering difficulties. —*v.* **2.** perplex.

Pvt., Private.

PX, post exchange.

pyg·my (pig′mē) *n., pl.* -mies. dwarf.

py•lon (pī′lon) *n.* tall thin structure.

pyr•a•mid (pir′ə mid) *n.* solid with triangular sides meeting in point. —*v.* 2. increase gradually. —**pyr•am•i•dal** (pə ram′ə dl) *adj.*

pyre (pīr) *n.* heap of wood, esp. for burning corpse.

py•rite (pī′rīt) *n.* common yellow mineral of low value.

py•ro•ma•ni•a (pī′rə mā′nē ə) *n.* mania for setting fires. —**py•ro•ma′ni•ac′**, *n.*

py•ro•tech•nics (-tek′niks) *n.* fireworks. —**py′ro•tech′nic**, *adj.*

py•thon (pī′thon) *n.* large snake that kills by constriction.

Q

Q, q (kyōō) *n.* seventeenth letter of English alphabet.

Q.E.D., which was to be shown or demonstrated.

qt., *pl.* **qt., qts.** quart.

qty., quantity.

quack (kwak) *n.* 1. pretender to medical skill. 2. sound that duck makes. —**quack′er•y,** *n.*

quad (kwod) *n.* 1. quadrangle. 2. quadruplet.

quad•ran•gle (-rang′gəl) *n.* 1. plane figure with four angles and four sides. 2. four-sided area surrounded by buildings. —**quad•ran•gu•lar** (kwo drang′gyə lar) *adj.*

quad•rant (-rənt) *n.* 1. arc of 90°. 2. instrument for measuring altitudes.

quad•ra•phon•ic (-rə fon′ik) *adj.* of sound reproduced through four recording tracks.

quad•ri•lat•er•al (-lat′ər əl) *adj.* 1. four-sided. —*n.* 2. four-sided plane figure.

qua•drille′ (kwo dril′, kwə-) *n.* square dance for four couples.

quad•ri•ple•gi•a (kwod′rə plē′jē ə, -jə) *n.* paralysis of the entire body below the neck. —**quad′ri•ple′gic,** *n., adj.*

quad•ru•ped′ (-rŏŏ ped′) *n.* four-footed animal.

quad•ru•ple (kwo drōō′pəl, -drup′əl) *adj., n., v.,* **-pled, -pling.** —*adj.* 1. of four parts. 2. four times as great. —*n.* 3. number, etc., four times as great as another. —*v.* 4. increase fourfold.

quad•ru•plet (-drup′lit, -drōō′plit) *n.* one of four children born at one birth.

quad•ru•pli•cate (-drōō′pli kit) *n.* group of four copies.

quaff (kwof, kwaf) *v.* drink heartily.

quag•mire′ (kwag′mīr′r′, kwog′-) *n.* boggy ground.

qua′hog (kwô′hog, kō′-) *n.* edible American clam.

quail (kwāl) *n., pl.* **quails, quail,** *v.* —*n.* 1. game bird resembling domestic fowls. —*v.* 2. lose courage; show fear.

quaint (kwānt) *adj.* pleasingly old-fashioned or odd. —**quaint′ly,** *adv.*

quake (kwāk) *v.,* **quaked, quaking,** *n.* —*v.* 1. tremble. —*n.* 2. earthquake.

Quak′er (kwā′kər) *n.* member of Society of Friends.

qual′i•fy′ (kwol′ə fī′) *v.,* **-fied, -fying.** 1. make proper or fit. 2. modify. 3. mitigate. 4. show oneself fit. —**qual′i•fi•ca′tion,** *n.*

qual′i•ty, (-i tē) *n., pl.* **-ties.** 1. characteristic. 2. relative merit. 3. excellence.

quality time, time devoted exclusively to nurturing cherished person or activity.

qualm (kwäm), *n.* 1. misgiving; scruple. 2. feeling of illness.

quan′da•ry (kwon′də rē, -drē) *n., pl.* **-ries.** dilemma.

quan′ti•fy′ (kwon′tə fī′) *v.,* **-fied, -fying.** measure.

quan′ti•ty (-ti tē) *n., pl.* **-ties.** 1. amount; measure. 2. *Math.* something having magnitude.

quan′tum (-təm) *n., pl.* **-ta,** *adj.* —*n.* 1. quantity or amount. 2. *Physics.* very small, indivisible quantity of energy. —*adj.* 3. sudden and significant.

quar′an•tine (kwôr′ən tēn′) *n., v.,* **-tined, -tining.** —*n.* 1. strict isolation to prevent spread of disease. 2. put in quarantine.

quark (kwôrk, kwärk) *n.* subatomic particle having fractional electric charge and thought to form basis of all matter.

quar′rel (kwôr′əl) *n., v.,* **-reled, -reling.** —*n.* 1. angry dispute. —*v.* 2. disagree angrily. —**quar′rel•some,** *adj.*

quar′ry (kwôr′ē) *n., pl.* **-ries,** *v.,* **-ried, -rying.** —*n.* 1. pit from which stone is taken. 2. object of pursuit. —*v.* 3. get from quarry.

quart (kwôrt) *n.* measure of capacity: in liquid measure, ¼ gallon; in dry measure, ⅛ peck.

quar′ter, *n.* 1. one of four equal parts. 2. coin worth 25 cents. 3. (*pl.*) place of residence. 4. mercy.

—v. **5.** divide into quarters. **6.** lodge.

quar·ter·back', n. position in football.

quar·ter·ly, adj., n., pl. **-lies**, adv. —adj. **1.** occurring, etc., each quarter year. **2.** quarterly publication. —adv. **3.** once each quarter year.

quar·ter·mas·ter, n. **1.** military officer in charge of supplies, etc. **2.** naval officer in charge of signals.

quar·tet' (kwôr tet') n. group of four. Also, **quar·tette'**.

quar'to (kwôr'tō) n., pl. **-tos.** book page of sheets folded twice.

quartz (kwôrts) n. crystalline mineral.

qua'sar (kwā'zär, -zär) n. astronomical source of powerful radio energy.

quash (kwosh) v. subdue; suppress.

qua'si (kwā'zī, -sī, kwä'sē, -zē) adj. resembling; to be regarded as if.

quasi-, prefix meaning somewhat.

Quat·er'nar·y (kwot'ər ner'ē, kwa-tûr'nə rē) adj. pertaining to present geologic period forming latter part of Cenozoic Era.

quat'rain (kwo'trān) n. four-line stanza.

qua'ver (kwā'vər) v. **1.** quiver. **2.** speak tremulously. —n. **3.** quavering tone.

quay (kē) n. landing beside water.

quea'sy (kwē'zē) adj., **-sier, -siest.** **1.** nauseated. **2.** uneasy.

queen (kwēn) n. **1.** wife of king. **2.** female sovereign. **3.** fertile female of bees, ants, etc. —v. **4.** reign as queen.

queer (kwēr) adj. **1.** strange; odd. —v. **2.** Offensive. homosexual. —v. **3.** Slang. ruin; impair.

quell (kwel) v. suppress.

quench (kwench) v. slake or extinguish.

quer'u·lous (kwer'ə ləs, kwer'yə-) adj. peevish.

que'ry (kwēr'ē) n., pl. **-ries,** v., **-ried, -rying.** question.

quest (kwest) n., v. search.

ques'tion (kwes'chən) n. **1.** sentence put in a form to elicit information. **2.** problem for discussion or dispute. —v. **3.** ask a question. **4.** doubt. —**ques'tion·a·ble,** adj. —**ques'tion·er,** n.

ques'tion·naire' (-chə nâr') n. list of questions.

queue (kyōō) n., v., **queued, queuing.** —n. **1.** line of persons. **2.** braid of hair hanging down the back. —v. **3.** form in a line.

quib'ble (kwib'əl) n., v., **-bled, -bling,** n. —v. **1.** speak ambiguously in evasion. **2.** make petty objections. —n. **3.** act of quibbling.

quiche (kēsh) n. pielike dish of cheese, onion, etc.

quick (kwik) adj. **1.** prompt; done promptly. **2.** swift. **3.** alert. —n. **4.** living persons. **5.** sensitive flesh. —adv. **6.** quickly. —**quick'ly,** adv.

quick'en, v. **1.** hasten. **2.** rouse. **3.** become alive.

quick'ie, n. something done or enjoyed in only a short time.

quick'lime', n. untreated lime.

quick'sand', n. soft sand yielding easily to weight.

quick'sil'ver, n. mercury.

quid (kwid) n. **1.** portion for chewing. **2.** Brit. Informal. one pound sterling.

quid pro quo (kwid' prō kwō') pl. **quid pro quos, quids pro quo.** something given or taken for something else.

qui·es'cent (kwē es'ənt, kwī-) adj. inactive. —**qui·es'cence,** n.

qui'et (kwī'it) adj. **1.** being at rest. **2.** peaceful. **3.** silent. **4.** restrained. —v. **5.** make or become quiet. **6.** tranquility. —**qui'et·ly,** adv.

quill (kwil) n. large feather.

quilt (kwilt) n. padded and lined bed covering. —**quilt'ed,** adj.

quince (kwins) n. yellowish acid fruit.

qui'nine (kwī'nīn) n. bitter substance used esp. in treating malaria.

quint (kwint) n. quintuplet.

quin·tes'sence (kwin tes'əns) n. essential substance. —**quin·tes·sen'tial** (-tə sen'shəl) adj.

quin·tet' (kwin tet') n. group of five. Also, **quin·tette'**.

quin·tu'plet (-tup'lit, -tōō'plit, -tyōō'-) n. one of five children born at one birth.

quip (kwip) n., v., **quipped, quipping.** —n. **1.** witty or sarcastic remark. —v. **2.** make quip.

quire (kwīr) n. set of 24 uniform sheets of paper.

quirk (kwûrk) n. peculiarity. —**quirk'y,** adj., **-i·er, -i·est.**

quis'ling (kwiz'ling) n. traitor.

quit (kwit) v., **quitted, quitting. 1.** stop. **2.** leave. **3.** relinquish.

quit'claim', n. **1.** transfer of one's interest. —v. **2.** give up claim to.

quite (kwīt) adv. **1.** completely. **2.** really.

quits (kwits) adj. with no further payment or revenge due.

quit'tance (kwit'ns) n. **1.** requital. **2.** discharge from debt.

quiv'er (kwiv'ər) v. **1.** tremble. —n. **2.** trembling. **3.** case for arrows.

quix·ot/ic (kwik sot/ik) *adj.* extravagantly idealistic; impractical.

quiz (kwiz) *v.,* **quizzed, quizzing,** *n., pl.* **quizzes.** —*v.* **1.** question. —*n.* **2.** informal questioning.

quiz/zi·cal, *adj.* **1.** comical. **2.** puzzled. —**quiz/zi·cal·ly,** *adv.*

quoin (koin, kwoin) *n.* **1.** external solid angle. **2.** cornerstone.

quoit (kwoit, koit) *n.* flat ring thrown to encircle peg in game of **quoits.**

quon/dam (kwon/dəm, -dam) *adj.* former.

quo/rum (kwôr/əm) *n.* number of members needed to transact business legally.

quo/ta (kwō/tə) *n.* proportional share due.

quote (kwōt) *v.,* **quoted, quoting,** *n.* —*v.* **1.** repeat verbatim. **2.** cite. **3.** state (price of). —*n.* **4.** *Informal.* quotation. —**quo·ta/tion,** *n.*

quo·tid/i·an (kwō tid/ē ən) *adj.* **1.** daily; everyday. **2.** ordinary.

quo/tient (kwō/shənt) *n. Math.* number of times one quantity is contained in another.

R

R, r (är) *n.* eighteenth letter of English alphabet.

R, motion-picture rating: those less than 17 years old must be accompanied by adult.

rab/bi (rab/ī) *n.* Jewish religious leader. —**rab·bin/ic** (rə bin/ik), **rab·bin/i·cal,** *adj.*

rab/bin·ate (rab/ə nit, -nāt/) *n.* **1.** office of a rabbi. **2.** rabbis collectively.

rab/bit (rab/it) *n.* small, long-eared mammal.

rab/ble (rab/əl) *n.* mob.

rab/ble-rous/er (-rou/zər) *n.* demagogue.

rab/id (rab/id) *adj.* **1.** irrationally intense. **2.** violent. **3.** having rabies.

ra/bies (rā/bēz) *n.* fatal disease transmitted by bite of infected animal.

rac·coon/ (ra koon/) *n.* small nocturnal carnivorous mammal.

race (rās) *n., v.,* **raced, racing.** —*n.* **1.** contest of speed. **2.** onward course or flow. **3.** group of persons of common origin. **4.** any class or kind. —*v.* **5.** engage in race. **6.** move swiftly. —**rac/er,** *n.* —**ra/cial** (rā/shəl) *adj.*

rac/ism (rā/siz əm) *n.* hatred of or prejudice against another race.

rack (rak) *n.* **1.** structure for storage. **2.** toothed bar engaging with teeth of pinion. **3.** torture device. **4.** destruction. —*v.* **5.** torture. **6.** strain.

rack/et (rak/it) *n.* **1.** noise. **2.** illegal or dishonest business. **3.** Also, **rac/quet.** netted bat used in tennis, etc.

rack/e·teer/, *n.* criminal engaged in racket.

rac/on·teur/ (rak/on tûr/, -tŏŏr/, -ən-) *n.* skilled storyteller.

ra·coon/ (ra kōōn/) *n.* raccoon.

rac/quet·ball (rak/it-) *n.* game similar to handball, played with rackets on four-walled court.

rac/y (rā/sē) *adj.,* **-ier, -iest. 1.** lively. **2.** risqué. —**rac/i·ly,** *adv.*

ra/dar (rā/där) *n.* electronic device capable of locating unseen objects by radio wave.

ra/di·al (-dē əl) *adj.* of rays or radii.

ra/di·ant (-ənt) *adj.* **1.** emitting rays of light. **2.** bright; exultant. **3.** emitted in rays, as heat. —**ra/di·ance,** *n.* —**ra/di·ant·ly,** *adv.*

ra/di·ate (-āt/) *v.,* -**ated, -ating. 1.** spread like rays from center. **2.** emit or issue in rays. —**ra/di·a/tion,** *n.*

ra/di·a/tor, *n.* heating device.

rad/i·cal (rad/i kal) *adj.* **1.** fundamental. **2.** favoring drastic reforms. —*n.* **3.** person with radical ideas. **4.** atom or group of atoms behaving as unit in chemical reaction. —**rad/i·cal·ism,** *n.* —**rad/i·cal·ly,** *adv.*

ra/di·o (rā/dē ō/) *n., pl.* -**dios. 1.** way of transmitting sound by electromagnetic waves, without wires. **2.** apparatus for sending or receiving such waves.

ra/di·o·ac/tive, *adj.* emitting radiation from the atomic nucleus. —**ra/di·o·ac·tiv/i·ty,** *n.*

ra/di·ol/o·gy (-ol/ə jē) *n.* use of radiation, as x-rays, for medical diagnosis and treatment.

rad/ish (rad/ish) *n.* crisp root of garden plant, eaten raw.

ra/di·um (rā/dē əm) *n.* radioactive metallic element.

ra/di·us (-əs) *n., pl.* -**dii** (-dē ī), -**di·uses. 1.** straight line from center of a circle to circumference. **2.** one of the bones of the forearm.

ra/don (rā/don) *n.* inert gaseous element produced by decay of radium.

RAF, Royal Air Force.

raf·fi·a (raf/ē ə) n. fiber made from leafstalks of palm tree.

raff·ish (raf/ish) adj. **1.** jaunty; rakish. **2.** gaudily vulgar or cheap.

raf·fle (raf/əl) n., v., **-fled, -fling.** —n. **1.** lottery in which chances are sold. —v. **2.** dispose of by raffle.

raft (raft) n. floating platform of logs.

raft·er (raf/tər) n. framing timber of roof.

rag (rag) n. worthless bit of cloth. —**rag·ged** (rag/id) adj.

ra·ga (rä/gə) n., pl. **-gas.** traditional melodic formula of Hindu music.

rag·a·muf·fin (rag/ə muf/in) n. ragged child.

rage (rāj) n., v., **raged, raging.** —n. **1.** violent anger. **2.** object of popular enthusiasm. —v. **3.** be violently angry. **4.** prevail violently.

ra·gout (ra gōō/) n. stew.

rag/time/, n. style of jazz.

rag/weed/, n. plant whose pollen causes hay fever.

raid (rād) n. **1.** sudden assault or attack. —v. **2.** attack suddenly.

rail (rāl) n. **1.** horizontal bar used as barrier, support, etc. **2.** one of pair of railroad tracks. **3.** railroad as means of transport. **4.** wading bird. —v. **5.** complain bitterly.

rail/ing, n. barrier of rails and posts.

rail·ler·y (rā/lə rē) n. banter.

rail/road/, n. **1.** road with fixed rails on which trains run. —v. **2.** transport by means of a railroad. **3.** coerce into hasty action or decision.

rail/way/, n. Chiefly Brit. railroad.

rai·ment (rā/mənt) n. clothing.

rain (rān) n. **1.** water falling from sky in drops. **2.** rainfall. —v. **3.** fall or send down as rain. —**rain/y,** adj.

rain/bow/ (-bō/) n. arc of colors sometimes seen in sky opposite sun during rain.

rain check, **1.** postponement of invitation. **2.** ticket for future admission to event postponed by rain.

rain/coat/, n. waterproof coat.

rain/fall/, n. amount of rain.

rain forest, tropical forest in area of high annual rainfall.

rain/mak/er, n. one who induces rain by artificial means.

raise (rāz) v., **raised, raising,** n. —v. **1.** lift up. **2.** set upright. **3.** cause to appear. **4.** grow. **5.** collect. **6.** rear. **7.** cause (dough) to expand. **8.** end (siege). —n. **9.** increase, esp. in pay.

rai·sin (rā/zin) n. dried sweet grape.

rai·son d'ê·tre (rā/zōn de/tra), n.,

pl. **rai·sons d'ê·tre.** reason for existence.

ra·jah (rä/jə) n. (formerly) Indian king or prince.

rake (rāk) n., v., **raked, raking.** —n. **1.** long-handled tool with teeth for gathering or smoothing ground. **2.** dissolute person. **3.** slope. —v. **4.** gather or smooth with rake. **5.** fire guns the length of (target).

rake/-off/, n. amount received, esp. illicitly.

rak/ish (rā/kish) adj. jaunty.

ral/ly (ral/ē) v., **-lied, -lying,** n., pl. **-lies.** —v. **1.** bring into order again. **2.** call or come together. **3.** revive. **4.** come to aid. —n. **5.** sharp rise. **6.** renewal of strength. **7.** mass meeting.

ram (ram) n., v., **rammed, ramming.** —n. **1.** male sheep. **2.** device for battering, forcing, etc. —v. **3.** strike forcibly.

RAM (ram) n. random-access memory: computer memory available for creating, loading, and running programs and temporarily storing data.

ram·ble v., **-bled, -bling,** n. —v. **1.** stroll idly. **2.** talk vaguely. —n. **3.** leisurely stroll. —**ram/bler,** n.

ram·bunc/tious (-bungk/shəs) adj. difficult to control or handle.

ram·i·fi·ca/tion (ram/ə fi kā/shən), n. consequence.

ram/i·fy/ (-ə fī/) v., **-fied, -fying.** divide into branches.

ramp (ramp) n. sloping surface between two levels.

ram/page, n., v., **-paged, -paging.** —n. **1.** violent behavior. —v. (ram pāj/) **2.** move furiously about.

ram/pant (ram/pant) adj. vigorous; unrestrained.

ram/part (-pärt, -pərt) n. mound of earth raised for defense.

ram/rod/, n. rod for cleaning or loading gun.

ram/shack/le, adj. rickety.

ranch (ranch) n. large farm, esp. for raising stock. —**ranch/er,** n.

ran/cid (ran/sid) adj. stale.

ran/cor (rang/kər) n. lasting resentment. —**ran/cor·ous,** adj.

rand (rand) n., pl. **rand.** monetary unit of South Africa.

ran/dom (ran/dəm) adj. occurring or done without aim or pattern.

rand/y (ran/dē) adj., **-ier, -iest.** sexually aroused; lustful.

range (rānj) n., v., **ranged, ranging.** —n. **1.** limits; extent. **2.** place for target shooting. **3.** distance between gun and target. **4.** row. **5.** mountain chain. **6.** grazing area. **7.**

cooking stove. —v. **8.** arrange. **9.** pass over (area). **10.** vary.

rang/er (rān/jer) n. **1.** warden of forest land. **2.** civil officer who patrols large area.

rang/y (rān/jē) adj., **-ier, -iest.** slender and long-limbed.

rank (rangk) n. **1.** class, group, or standing. **2.** high position. **3.** row. **4.** (pl.) enlisted personnel. —v. **5.** arrange. **6.** be in particular rank. —adj. **7.** growing excessively. **8.** offensively strong in smell. **9.** utter. **10.** grossly vulgar.

rank and file, 1. members apart from leaders. **2.** enlisted soldiers.

rank/ing, adj. **1.** senior. **2.** renowned.

ran/kle (rang/kal) v., **-kled, -kling.** irk.

ran/sack (ran/sak) v. search thoroughly.

ran/som (ran/sam) n. **1.** sum demanded for prisoner. —v. **2.** pay ransom for.

rant (rant) v. **1.** speak wildly. —n. **2.** violent speech. —**rant/er,** n.

rap (rap) v., **rapped, rapping.** —v. **1.** strike quickly and sharply. —n. **2.** sharp blow. **3.** popular music marked by rhythmical intoning of rhymed verses over repetitive beat. —**rap/per,** n.

ra•pa/cious (rə pā/shəs) adj. predatory; greedy.

rape (rāp) n., v., **raped, raping.** —n. **1.** forcing of sexual intercourse on someone. **2.** abduction or seizure. **3.** plant grown as forage and for its oil. —v. **4.** commit rape on. **5.** abduct or seize. —**rap/ist,** n.

rap/id (rap/id) adj. **1.** swift. —n. **2.** (pl.) swift-moving part of river. —**ra•pid/i•ty,** n. —**rap/id•ly,** adv.

ra/pier (rā/pē ər) n. slender sword.

rap/ine (rap/in) n. plunder.

rap•port/ (ra pôr/) n. sympathetic relationship.

rap•proche•ment/ (rap/rōsh mäw/) n. establishment of harmonious relations.

rap sheet, Slang. record of person's arrests and convictions.

rapt (rapt) adj. engrossed.

rap/ture (rap/chər) n. ecstatic joy. —**rap/tur•ous,** adj.

rare (râr) adj., **rarer, rarest. 1.** unusual. **2.** thin. **3.** (of meat) not thoroughly cooked. —**rar/i•ty,** n.

rare/bit (râr/bit) n. dish of melted cheese.

rar•e•fy (râr/ə fī/) v., **-fied, -fying.** make or become thin, as air.

rar/ing, adj. very eager or anxious.

ras/cal (ras/kəl) n. dishonest person.

rash (rash) adj. **1.** thoughtlessly hasty. —n. **2.** skin eruption.

rash/er, n. thin slice of bacon.

rasp (rasp) v. **1.** scrape, as with file. **2.** irritate. **3.** speak gratingly. —n. **4.** coarse file. **5.** rasping sound. —**rasp/y,** adj.

rasp/ber/ry (raz/ber/ē, -bə rē) n., pl. **-ries.** small juicy red or black fruit.

rat (rat) n. rodent larger than a mouse.

ratch/et (rach/it) n. wheel or bar with teeth.

rate (rāt) n., v., **rated, rating.** —n. **1.** charge in proportion to something that varies. **2.** degree of speed, etc. —v. **3.** estimate or fix rate. **4.** consider; judge.

rath/er (rath/ər) adv. **1.** somewhat. **2.** in preference. **3.** on the contrary.

raths/kel•ler (rät/skel/ər, rat/-) n. restaurant or bar below street level.

rat/i•fy (rat/ə fī/) v., **-fied, -fying.** confirm formally.

ra/tio (rā/shō, -shē ō/) n., pl. **-tios.** relative number or extent; proportion.

ra/ti•oc/i•na/tion (rash/ē os/ə nā/shən) n. reasoning.

ra/tion (rash/ən, rā/shən) n. **1.** fixed allowance. —v. **2.** apportion. **3.** put on ration.

ra/tion•al (rash/ə nl) adj. **1.** sensible. **2.** sane. —**ra/tion•al/i•ty,** n. —**ra/tion•al•ly,** adv.

ra/tion•ale/ (-nal/) n. reasonable basis for action.

ra/tion•al•ize/, v., **-ized, -izing. 1.** find reason for one's behavior or attitude. **2.** make rational.

rat race, exhausting, competitive routine activity.

rat•tan/ (ra tan/, rə-) n. hollow stem of climbing palm used for wickerwork.

rat/tle (rat/l) v., **-tled, -tling.** —v. **1.** make series of short sharp sounds. **2.** chatter. **3.** Informal. disconcert. —n. **4.** sound of rattling. **5.** child's toy that rattles.

rat/tle•snake/, n. venomous American snake.

rau/cous (rô/kəs) adj. **1.** hoarse; harsh. **2.** rowdy; disorderly.

raun/chy (rôn/chē, rän/-) adj. **-chier, -chiest. 1.** vulgar; smutty. **2.** lecherous. **3.** dirty; slovenly.

rav/age (rav/ij) n., v., **-aged, -aging. 1.** ruin. —**rav/ag•er,** n.

rave (rāv) v., **raved, raving.** talk wildly.

rav/el (rav/əl) v. **1.** disengage

threads. **2.** tangle. **3.** make clear. —*n.* **4.** tangle. **5.** disengaged thread.

ra'ven (rā'vən) *n.* large shiny black bird.

rav·en·ing (rav'ə ning) *adj.* greedy for prey.

rav·en·ous, *adj.* very hungry; greedy. —**rav'en·ous·ly,** *adv.*

ra·vine' (rə vēn') *n.* deep, narrow valley.

ra·vi·o·li (rav'ē ō'lē) *n.* small pockets of pasta filled esp. with cheese or meat.

rav·ish (rav'ish) *v.* **1.** fill with joy. **2.** rape.

rav·ish·ing, *adj.* extremely beautiful.

raw (rô) *adj.* **1.** in the natural state. **2.** uncooked. **3.** open. **4.** untrained. —*n.* **5.** raw condition or substance.

raw'boned', *adj.* lean and bony.

raw'hide', *n.* untanned hide, as of cattle.

ray (rā) *n.* **1.** narrow beam of light. **2.** trace. *n.* **3.** line outward from center. **4.** flat-bodied deep-sea fish.

ray'on (rā'on) *n.* silklike synthetic fabric.

raze (rāz) *v.,* **razed, razing.** demolish.

ra'zor (rā'zər) *n.* sharp-edged instrument for shaving.

R.C., Roman Catholic.

rd., road.

re, (rā) **1.** *Music.* second tone of scale. —*prep.* (rē) **2.** with reference to.

re-, prefix indicating; **1.** repetition, as *reprint, rearm.* **2.** withdrawal.

reach (rēch) *v.* **1.** come to. **2.** be able to touch. **3.** extend. —*n.* **4.** act of reaching. **5.** extent.

re·act' (rē akt') *v.* **1.** act upon each other. **2.** respond.

re·ac'tant (-ak'tənt) *n.* substance that undergoes change in chemical reaction.

re·ac'tion, *n.* **1.** extreme political conservatism. **2.** responsive action. **3.** chemical change. —**re·ac'tion·ar'y,** *n., adj.*

re·ac'tor, *n.* **1.** one that reacts. **2.** apparatus for producing useful nuclear energy.

read (rēd) *v.,* **read** (red), **reading. 1.** observe and understand (printed matter, etc.). **2.** register. **3.** utter aloud (something written or printed). **4.** obtain and store, as in computer memory. —**read'er,** *n.* —**read'er·ship,** *n.*

read·ing (rē'ding) *n.* **1.** something read. **2.** interpretation of written or musical work. **3.** data indicated on instrument.

read'-on·ly (rēd) *adj.* noting computer files or memory that can be read but not changed.

read'y (red'ē) *adj.,* **readier, readiest,** *v.,* **readied, readying,** *n.* —*adj.* **1.** fully prepared. **2.** willing. **3.** apt. —*v.* **4.** make ready. —*n.* **5.** state of being ready. —**read'i·ly,** *adv.* —**read'i·ness,** *n.*

read'y-made', *adj.* ready for use when bought.

re·a'gent (rē ā'jənt) *n.* chemical used in analysis and synthesis.

re'al (rē'əl, rēl) *adj.* **1.** actual. **2.** genuine. **3.** denoting immovable property. —**re·al'i·ty** (-al'i tē), **re'al·ness,** *n.* —**re'al·ly,** *adv.*

real estate, land with buildings, etc., on it. Also, **re'al·ty.**

re'al·ism, *n.* **1.** tendency to see things as they really are. **2.** representation of things as they really are. —**re'al·ist,** *n.* —**re'al·is'tic,** *adj.* —**re'al·is'ti·cal·ly,** *adv.*

re'al·ize', *v.,* **-ized, -izing. 1.** understand clearly. **2.** make real. **3.** get as profit. —**re'al·i·za'tion,** *n.*

realm (relm) *n.* **1.** kingdom. **2.** special field.

ream (rēm) *n.* twenty quires of paper.

reap (rēp) *v.* harvest. —**reap'er,** *n.*

rear (rēr) *n.* **1.** back part. —*adj.* **2.** of or at rear. —*v.* **3.** care for to maturity. **4.** raise; erect. **5.** rise on hind legs.

rear admiral, naval officer above captain.

re·arm' (rē ärm') *v.* arm again. —**re·arm'a·ment,** *n.*

rear'most' (-word) *adj.* farthest back.

rear'ward (-word) *adv.* **1.** Also, **rear'wards.** toward the rear. —*adj.* **2.** located in the rear.

rea'son (rē'zən) *n.* **1.** cause for belief, act, etc. **2.** sound judgment. **3.** sanity. —*v.* **4.** think or argue logically. **5.** infer. —**rea'son·ing,** *n.*

rea'son·a·ble (rē'zə nə bəl, rēz'nə-) *adj.* showing sound judgment.

re·as·sure' (rē'ə shoor', -shûr') *v.,* **-sured, -suring.** restore confidence of. —**re·as·sur'ance,** *n.*

re·bate' (rē'bāt, also ri bāt') *v.* **1.** return (part of amount paid). —*n.* (rē'bāt) **2.** amount rebated.

reb'el, *n.,* **rebelled, belling,** *v.* —*v.* (ri bel') **1.** rise in arms against one's government. **2.** resist any authority. —*n.* (reb'əl) **3.** one who rebels. —**re·bel'lion,** *n.* —**re·bel'lious,** *adj.* —**re·bel'lious·ly,** *adv.*

re·bound', *v.* (ri bound') **1.** bound back after impact. —*n.* (rē'bound) **2.** act of rebounding.

re·buff′ (ri buf′) n. **1.** blunt check or refusal. —v. **2.** check; repel.

re·buke′ (ri byŌŌk′) v., **-buked, -buking.** reprimand.

re·bus (rē′bəs) n. puzzle in which pictures and symbols combine to represent a word.

re·but′ (ri but′) v., **-butted, -butting.** refute. **—re·but′tal,** n.

re·cal′ci·trant (ri kal′si trənt) adj. resisting control.

re·call′, v. (ri kôl′) **1.** remember. **2.** call back. **3.** withdraw. —n. (rē′kôl) **4.** act of recalling.

re·cant′ (ri kant′) v. retract.

re′cap′ (rē′kap′) n., v., **-capped, -capping.** —n. **1.** recapitulation. **2.** tire reconditioned by adding strip of new rubber. —v. **3.** recapitulate. **4.** recondition a tire.

re′ca·pit′u·late (rē′kə pich′ə lāt′) v., **-lated, -lating.** review; sum up.

re·cap′ture, v., **-tured, -turing.** —v. **1.** capture again. **2.** experience again. —n. **3.** recovery by capture.

recd. or **rec′d.,** received.

re·cede′ (ri sēd′) v., **-ceded, -ceding.** move or appear to move back.

re·ceipt′ (ri sēt′) n. **1.** written acknowledgment of receiving. **2.** (pl.) amount received. **3.** act of receiving.

re·ceive′, v., **-ceived, -ceiving. 1.** take (something offered or delivered). **2.** experience. **3.** welcome (guests). **4.** accept.

re·ceiv′er, n. **1.** one that receives. **2.** device that receives electrical signals and converts them. **3.** person put in charge of property in litigation. **—re·ceiv′er·ship′,** n.

re′cent (rē′sənt) adj. happening, etc., lately. **—re′cent·ly,** adv.

re·cep′ta·cle (ri sep′tə kəl) n. container.

re·cep′tion (ri sep′shən) n. **1.** act of receiving. **2.** fact or manner of being received. **3.** social function.

re·cep′tion·ist, n. person who receives callers in an office.

re·cep′tive (-tiv) adj. quick to understand and consider ideas.

re·cep′tor (-tar) n. nerve ending that is sensitive to stimuli.

re·cess′ (ri ses′, rē′ses) n. **1.** temporary cessation of work. **2.** alcove. **3.** (pl.) inner part. —v. **4.** take or make recess.

re·ces′sion (-sesh′ən) n. **1.** withdrawal. **2.** economic decline.

re·ces′sive (-ses′iv) adj. receding.

re·cher·ché (rə shâr′shā, rə shâr′shā′) adj. **1.** very rare or choice. **2.** affectedly refined.

re·cid′i·vism (ri sid′ə viz′əm) re-

peated or habitual relapse, as into crime. **—re·cid′i·vist,** n., adj.

rec′i·pe (res′ə pē) n. formula, esp. in cookery.

re·cip′i·ent (ri sip′ē ənt) n. **1.** receiver. **—adj. 2.** receiving.

re·cip′ro·cal (ri sip′rə kəl) adj. **1.** mutual. **2.** thing in reciprocal position. **—re·cip′ro·cal·ly,** adv.

re·cip′ro·cate′ (-kāt′) v., **-cated, -cating. 1.** give, feel, etc., in return. **2.** move alternately backward and forward. **—re·cip′ro·ca′tion,** n.

rec′i·proc′i·ty (res′ə pros′i tē) n. interchange.

re·cit′al (ri sīt′l) n. musical entertainment.

rec′i·ta·tive′ (res′i tə tēv′) n. style of vocal music intermediate between speaking and singing.

re·cite′ (ri sīt′) v., **-cited, -citing. 1.** repeat from memory. **2.** narrate. **—rec·i·ta′tion** (res′i tā′shən) n.

reck′less (rek′lis) adj. careless.

reck′on (rek′ən) v. **1.** calculate. **2.** regard as; esteem. **3.** Informal. suppose. **4.** deal (with).

reck′on·ing, n. **1.** settling of accounts. **2.** navigational calculation.

re·claim′ (rē klām′) v. make usable, as land. **—rec′la·ma′tion** (rek′lə mā′shən) n.

re·cline′ (ri klīn′) v., **-clined, -clining.** lean back.

re·clin′er, n. chair with adjustable back and footrest.

re·cluse (rek′lōōs, ri klōōs′) n. person living in seclusion.

rec′og·ni′zance (ri kog′nə zəns, -kon′ə-) n. bond pledging one to do a particular act.

rec′og·nize (rek′əg nīz′) v., **-nized, -nizing. 1.** identify or perceive from previous knowledge. **2.** acknowledge formally. **3.** greet. **—rec′og·ni′tion** (-nish′ən) n.

re·coil′ (rē koil′) v. **1.** shrink back. **2.** spring back. **—n. 3.** act of recoiling.

rec′ol·lect′ (rek′ə lekt′) v. remember. **—rec′ol·lec′tion,** n.

rec′om·mend′ (rek′ə mend′) v. **1.** present as worthy. **2.** advise. **—rec′om·men·da′tion,** n.

rec′om·pense′ (rek′əm pens′) v., **-pensed, -pensing,** n. —v. **1.** repay or reward for services, injury, etc. —n. **2.** such compensation.

rec′on·cile′ (rek′ən sīl′) v., **-ciled, -ciling. 1.** bring into agreement. **2.** restore to friendliness. **—rec′on·cil′i·a′tion** (-sil′ē ā′shən) n.

rec′on·dite (rek′ən dīt′) adj. **1.** very profound, difficult, or abstruse. **2.** known by a few; esoteric.

re·con′nais·sance (ri kon′ə səns,

-zəns), *n.* survey of enemy territory.

re·con·noi·ter (rē'kə noi'tər, rek'ə-) *v.* search area, esp. for military information.

re·cord *v.* (ri kôrd') **1.** set down in writing. **2.** register for mechanical reproduction. —*n.* (rek'ərd) **3.** what is recorded. **4.** object from which sound is reproduced. **5.** best rate, etc., yet attained. —*adj.* (rek'ərd) **6.** making or being a record. —**re·cord'ing,** *n.*

re·cord'er, *n.* **1.** person who records. **2.** recording device. **3.** flute with eight finger holes.

re·count' *v.* (rē kount') **1.** narrate. **2.** count again. —*n.* (rē'kount') **3.** a second count.

re·coup' (ri kōōp') *v.* recover; make up.

re·course (rē'kôrs, ri kôrs') *n.* resort for help.

re·cov·er (ri kuv'ər) *v.* **1.** get back. **2.** reclaim. **3.** regain health. —**re·cov'er·a·ble,** *adj.* —**re·cov'er·y,** *n.*

re'-cre·ate' (rē'krē āt') *v.,* **-ated, -ating.** create anew.

rec're·a'tion, *n.* refreshing enjoyment. —**rec're·a'tion·al,** *adj.*

re·crim·i·nate (ri krim'ə nāt') *v.,* **-nated, -nating.** accuse in return. —**re·crim'i·na'tion,** *n.*

re·cruit' (ri krōōt') *n.* **1.** new member of military or other group. —*v.* **2.** enlist. —**re·cruit'ment,** *n.*

rec·tan·gle (rek'tang'gəl) *n.* parallelogram with four right angles. —**rec·tan'gu·lar** (-tang'gyə lər) *adj.*

rec·ti·fy (rek'tə fī') *v.,* **-fied, -fying.** correct. —**rec'ti·fi'a·ble,** *adj.* —**rec'ti·fi·ca'tion,** *n.*

rec'ti·lin'e·ar (rek'tl in'ē ər) *adj.* **1.** forming straight line. **2.** formed by straight lines.

rec'ti·tude' (rek'ti tōōd', -tyōōd') *n.* moral rightness.

rec'tor (rek'tər) *n.* **1.** member of clergy in charge of parish, etc. **2.** head of university, etc. —**rec'to·ry** (-tə rē) *n., pl.* **-ries.** parsonage.

rec'tum (rek'təm) *n.* lowest part of intestine. —**rec'tal,** *adj.*

re·cum·bent (ri kum'bənt) *adj.* lying down. —**re·cum'ben·cy,** *n.*

re·cu·per·ate' (ri kōō'pə rāt') *v.,* **-ated, -ating.** regain health. —**re·cu'per·a'tion,** *n.*

re·cur' (ri kûr') *v.,* **-curred, -curring. 1.** occur again. **2.** return in thought, etc. —**re·cur'rence,** *n.* —**re·cur'rent,** *adj.*

re·cy·cle (rē sī'kəl) *v.* **-cled, -cling.** treat (refuse) to extract reusable material.

red (red) *n., adj.,* **redder, reddest.**

—*n.* **1.** color of blood. **2.** leftist radical in politics. —*adj.* **3.** of or like red. **4.** radically to left in politics. —**red'den,** *v.* —**red'dish,** *adj.*

red blood cell, blood cell that contains hemoglobin and carries oxygen to cells and tissues.

red'cap', *n.* baggage porter.

re·deem' (ri dēm') *v.* **1.** pay off. **2.** recover. **3.** fulfill. **4.** deliver from sin by sacrifice. —**re·deem'er,** *n.* —**re·demp'tion** (-demp'shən) *n.*

red'-hand'ed, *adj., adv.* in the act of wrongdoing.

red'head', *n.* person with red hair. —**red'head'ed,** *adj.*

red herring, something intended to distract attention from the real problem or issue.

red'-hot', *adj.* **1.** red with heat. **2.** violent; furious. **3.** very fresh or new.

red'-let'ter, *adj.* memorable.

red'lin'ing, *n.* refusal by banks to grant mortgages in specified urban areas.

red·o·lent (red'l ənt) *adj.* **1.** odorous. **2.** suggestive.

re·doubt (ri dout') *n.* small isolated fort.

re·doubt'a·ble, *adj.* evoking fear or respect.

re·dound' (ri dound') *v.* occur as result.

re·dress' (ri dress') **1.** set right (a wrong). —*n.* (rē'dres) **2.** act of redressing.

red tape, excessive attention to prescribed procedure.

re·duce' (ri dōōs', -dyōōs') *v.,* **-duced, -ducing. 1.** make less in size, rank, etc. **2.** put into simpler form or state. **3.** remove weight. —**re·duc'er,** *n.* —**re·duc'i·ble,** *adj.* —**re·duc'tion** (-duk'shən) *n.*

re·dun'dant (ri dun'dənt) *adj.* **1.** excessive. **2.** wordy. —**re·dun'dance, re·dun'dan·cy,** *n.*

red'wood' (red'wŏŏd') *n.* huge evergreen tree of California.

reed (rēd) *n.* **1.** tall marsh grass. **2.** small piece of cane or metal at mouth of wind instrument. —**reed'y,** *adj.*

reef (rēf) *n.* **1.** narrow ridge near the surface of water.

reef'er, *n.* **1.** short heavy coat. **2.** *Slang.* marijuana cigarette.

reek (rēk) *v.* **1.** smell strongly and unpleasantly. —*n.* **2.** such smell.

reel (rēl) *n.* **1.** turning object for wound cord, film, etc. **2.** lively dance. —*v.* **3.** wind on reel. **4.** tell easily and at length. **5.** sway or stagger. **6.** whirl.

re·en'try (rē en'trē) *n., pl.* **-tries. 1.**

second entry. **2.** return into earth's atmosphere.

ref (ref) n., v. referee.

re·fec·to·ry (ri fek'tə rē) n., pl. **-ries.** dining hall.

re·fer' (ri fūr') v., **-ferred, -ferring. 1.** direct attention. **2.** direct or go for information. **3.** apply. **—re·fer'ral,** n.

ref·er·ee' (ref'ə rē') n. **1.** judge. **—v. 2.** act as referee.

ref'er·ence (ref'ər əns) n. **1.** act or fact of referring. **2.** something referred to. **3.** person from whom one seeks recommendation. **4.** testimonial.

ref·er·en·dum (ref'ə ren'dəm) n., pl. **-dums, -da.** submission to popular vote of law passed by legislature.

re·fill' v. (rē fil') **1.** fill again. —n. (rē'fil') **2.** second filling.

re·fine' (ri fīn') v., **-fined, -fining. 1.** free from impurities or error. **2.** teach good manners, taste, etc. **—re·fin'er,** n. **—re·fine'ment,** n.

re·fin'er·y, n., pl. **-eries.** establishment for refining, esp. petroleum.

re·flect' (ri flekt') v. **1.** cast back. **2.** show; mirror. **3.** bring (credit or discredit) on one. **4.** think. **—re·flec'tion,** n. **—re·flec'tive,** adj. **—re·flec'tor,** n.

re·flex (rē'fleks) adj. **1.** denoting involuntary action. **2.** bent. —n. **3.** involuntary movement.

re·flex'ive, adj. **1.** (of verb) having same subject and object. **2.** (of pronoun) showing identity with subject.

re·for·est (rē fôr'ist) v. replant with forest trees. **—re·for·est·a'tion,** n.

re·form' (rē fôrm') n. **1.** correction of what is wrong. —v. **2.** change for better. **—re·form'er,** n. **—ref'or·ma'tion** (ref'ər mā'shən) n.

re·form'a·to·ry (ri fôr'mə tôr'ē) n., pl. **-ries.** prison for young offenders.

re·frac'tion (ri frak'shən) n. change of direction of light or heat rays in passing to another medium. **—re·fract',** v. **—re·frac'tive,** adj. **—re·frac·to·ry,** adj. stubborn.

re·frain' (ri frān') v. **1.** keep oneself (from). —n. **2.** recurring passage in song, etc.

re·fresh' (ri fresh') v. **1.** reinvigorate. **2.** stimulate. **—re·fresh'ment,** n. **—re·fresh'ing,** adj.

re·frig·er·ate (ri frij'ə rāt') v., **-ated, -ating.** make or keep cold. **—re·frig'er·ant** (-ə rənt) n. **—re·frig'er·a'tion,** n.

re·frig'er·a'tor, n. cabinet for keeping food cold.

ref·uge (ref'yōōj) n. shelter from danger.

ref'u·gee' (ref'yŏō jē') n. person who flees from safety.

re·ful'gent (ri ful'jənt) adj. shining brightly; radiant. **—re·ful'gence,** n.

re·fund' v. (ri fund') **1.** give back (money). —n. (rē'fund) **2.** repayment. **—re·fund'a·ble,** adj.

re·fur·bish (rē fûr'bish) v. renovate.

re·fuse', v., **-fused, -fusing.** —v. (ri fyōōz') **1.** decline to accept. **2.** deny (request). —n. (ref'yōōs) **3.** rubbish. **—re·fus'al,** n.

re·fute' (ri fyōōt') v., **-futed, -futing.** prove wrong. **—ref'u·ta'tion,** n.

re·gain' (rē gān') v. get again.

re'gal (rē'gəl) adj. royal.

re·gale' (ri gāl') v., **-galed, -galing. 1.** entertain grandly. **2.** feast.

re·ga·lia (ri gāl'yə) n.pl. emblems of royalty, office, etc.

re·gard' (-gärd') v. **1.** look upon with particular feeling. **2.** respect. **3.** look at. **4.** concern. —n. **5.** reference. **6.** attention. **7.** respect and liking.

re·gard'ing, prep. concerning.

re·gard'less, adv. **1.** without regard; in spite of. —adj. **2.** heedless.

re·gat'ta (ri gat'ə, -gä'tə) n. organized series of boat races.

re·gen·er·ate v. (ri jen'ə rāt'), adj. (-ər it) —v. **1.** make over for the better. **2.** form anew. —adj. (-ər it) **3.** regenerated. **—re·gen'er·a'tion,** n. **—re·gen'er·a'tive,** adj.

re'gent (rē'jənt) n. **1.** person ruling in place of sovereign. **2.** university governor. **—re'gen·cy,** n.

reg·gae (reg'ā) n. Jamaican music blending blues, calypso, and rock.

reg'i·cide' (rej'ə sīd') n. killing of king.

re·gime' (rə zhēm', rā-) n. system of rule.

reg'i·men (rej'ə mən) n. **1.** course of diet, etc., for health. **2.** rule.

reg'i·ment (rej'ə mənt) n. **1.** infantry unit. —v. (rej'ə ment') **2.** subject to strict, uniform discipline. **—reg'i·men'tal,** adj.

re'gion (rē'jən) n. area; district. **—re'gion·al,** adj.

re'gion·al·ism, n. feature peculiar to geographical region.

reg'is·ter (rej'ə stər) n. **1.** written list; record. **2.** range of voice or instrument. **3.** device for controlling passage of warm air. —v. **4.** enter in register. **5.** show. **6.** enter oneself on list of voters. —**reg/is·tra/tion** (-strā/shan) *n.*

reg·is·trar/ (-strär/) *n.* official recorder.

reg·is·try, *n., pl.* **-tries. 1.** registration. **2.** place where register is kept. **3.** enrollment.

re·gress/ (ri gres/) *v.* return to previous, inferior state. —**re·gres/sion,** *n.* —**re·gres/sive,** *adj.*

re·gret/ (ri gret/) *v.,* **-gretted, -gretting,** *n.* —*v.* **1.** feel sorry about. —*n.* **2.** feeling of loss or sorrow. —**re·gret/ta·ble,** *adj.* —**re·gret/ful,** *adj.*

re·group/ (rē grōōp/) *v.* form into new group.

reg·u·lar (reg/ya lar) *adj.* **1.** usual. **2.** symmetrical. **3.** recurring at fixed times. **4.** orderly. **5.** denoting permanent army. —*n.* **6.** regular soldier. —**reg/u·lar/i·ty,** *n.* —**reg/u·lar·ize/,** *-ized, -izing.*

reg·u·late/ (-lāt/) *v.,* **-lated, -lating. 1.** control by rule, method, etc. **2.** adjust. —**reg/u·la/tion,** *n.* —**reg/u·la·to/ry** (-la tôr/ē) *adj.*

reg/u·la/tion, *n.* **1.** act of regulating. **2.** rule.

re·gur/gi·tate/ (ri gûr/ji tāt/) *v.,* **-tated, -tating.** bring back from stomach. —**re·gur/gi·ta/tion,** *n.*

re·ha·bil/i·tate/ (rē/ha bil/i tāt/, rē/a-) *v.,* **-tated, -tating.** restore to good condition. —**re/ha·bil/i·ta/tion,** *n.*

re·hash/ *v.* (rē hash/) rework or reuse in new form without significant change. —*n.* (rē/hash/) **2.** act of rehashing. **3.** something rehashed.

re·hearse/ (ri hûrs/) *v.,* **-hearsed, -hearsing. 1.** act or direct in practice for performance. **2.** recount in detail. —**re·hears/al,** *n.*

reign (rān) *n.* **1.** royal rule. —*v.* **2.** have sovereign power or title.

re/im·burse/ (rē/im bûrs/) *v.,* **-bursed, -bursing.** repay, as for expenses. —**re/im·burse/ment,** *n.*

rein (rān) *n.* narrow strap fastened to bridle for controlling animal.

re/in·car·na/tion (rē/in kär nā/shan) *n.* continuation of soul after death in new body.

rein/deer/ (rān/dēr/) *n.* large arctic deer.

re/in·force/ (rē/in fôrs/) *v.,* **-forced, -forcing.** strengthen with support, troops, etc. —**re/in·force/ment,** *n.*

re/in·state/ (rē/in stāt/) *v.,* **-stated, -stating.** put back into former position or state. —**re/in·state/ment,** *n.*

re·it/er·ate/ (rē it/a rāt/) *v.,* **-ated, -ating.** repeat. —**re·it/er·a/tion,** *n.*

re·ject/, (ri jekt/) *v.* refuse or dis-

card. —*n.* (rē/jekt) **2.** something rejected. —**re·jec/tion,** *n.*

re·joice/ (ri jois/) *v.,* **-joiced, -joicing.** be or make glad.

re·join/ (-join/) *v.* **1.** answer. **2.** join again.

re·join/der (-dar) *n.* response.

re·ju/ve·nate/ (ri jōō/va nāt/) *v.,* **-nated, -nating.** make young again.

re·lapse/ *v.,* **-lapsed, -lapsing.** —*v.* (ri laps/) **1.** fall back into former state or practice. —*n.* (ri laps/, rē/laps) **2.** act or instance of relapsing.

re·late/ (ri lāt/) *v.,* **-lated, -lating. 1.** tell. **2.** establish or have relation.

re·lat/ed, *adj.* **1.** associated. **2.** connected by blood or marriage.

re·la/tion, *n.* **1.** connection. **2.** relative. **3.** narrative. —**re·la/tion·ship/,** *n.*

rel/a·tive (rel/a tiv) *n.* **1.** person connected with another by blood or marriage. —*adj.* **2.** comparative. **3.** designating word that introduces subordinate clause.

relative humidity, ratio of water vapor in the air at a given temperature to the amount the air could hold.

rel/a·tiv/i·ty, *n.* principle that time, mass, etc. are relative, not absolute concepts.

re·lax/ (ri laks/) *v.* **1.** make or become less tense, firm, etc. **2.** slacken. —**re/lax·a/tion** (rē/lak sā/shan) *n.*

re/lay (rē/lā) *n.* **1.** fresh supply of persons, etc., to relieve others. —*v.* **2.** carry forward by relays.

re·lease/ (ri lēs/) *v.,* **-leased, -leasing,** *n.* —*v.* **1.** let go; discharge. —*n.* **2.** act or instance of releasing.

rel/e·gate/ (rel/i gāt/) *v.,* **-gated, -gating.** consign to inferior position. **2.** turn over.

re·lent/ (ri lent/) *v.* become more mild or forgiving. —**re·lent/less,** *adj.*

rel/e·vant (rel/a vant) *adj.* having to do with matter in question. —**rel/e·vance,** *n.*

re·li/a·ble (ri lī/a bal) *adj.* trustworthy. —**re·li/a·bil/i·ty,** *n.*

re·li/ance (-ans) *n.* **1.** trust. **2.** confidence. —**re·li/ant,** *adj.*

rel/ic (rel/ik) *n.* **1.** object surviving from past. **2.** personal memorial of sacred person.

re·lief/ (ri lēf/) *n.* **1.** alleviation of pain, distress, etc. **2.** help. **3.** pleasant change. **4.** projection.

re·lieve/ (ri lēv/) *v.,* **-lieved, -lieving. 1.** ease. **2.** break sameness of. **3.** discharge from duty.

re·li/gion (ri lij/an) *n.* **1.** spiritual recognition and worship. **2.** particular system of religious belief. —**re·li·gious,** adj. —**re·li·gious·ly,** adv.

re·lin·quish (ri ling'kwish) v. give up; surrender.

rel·i·quar·y (rel'i kwer'ē) n., pl. **-ies.** receptacle for religious relics.

rel·ish (rel'ish) n. **1.** enjoyment. **2.** chopped pickles, etc. —v. **1.** take enjoyment in.

re·live (rē liv') v., **-lived, -living.** experience again.

re·lo·cate (ri lō'kāt) v., **-cated, cating.** move. —**re·lo·ca'tion,** n.

re·luc·tant (ri luk'tənt) adj. unwilling. —**re·luc'tance,** n.

re·ly' (ri lī') v., **-lied, -lying.** put trust in.

REM (rem) n. quick, darting movement of eyes during sleep.

re·main (ri mān') v. **1.** continue to be. **2.** stay; be left. —n. pl. **3.** that which remains. **4.** corpse.

re·main·der (-dər) n. that which is left over.

re·mand (ri mand') v. send back, as to jail or lower court of law.

re·mark (ri märk') v. **1.** say casually. **2.** perceive; observe. —n. **3.** casual comment. **4.** notice.

re·mark·a·ble, adj. extraordinary.

rem·e·dy (rem'i dē) v., **-died, -dying,** n., pl. **-dies.** —v. **1.** cure or alleviate. **2.** correct. —n. **3.** something that remedies. —**re·me'di·al,** adj.

re·mem·ber (ri mem'bər) v. **1.** recall to or retain in memory. **2.** mention as sending greetings. —**re·mem'brance** (-brəns) n.

re·mind (ri mīnd') v. cause to remember. —**re·mind'er,** n.

rem·i·nisce (rem'ə nis') v., **-nisced, -niscing.** recall past experiences. —**rem'i·nis'cence,** n. —**rem'i·nis'cent,** adj.

re·miss (ri mis') adj. negligent.

re·mis·sion (ri mish'ən) n. **1.** act of forgiving. **2.** period when symptoms of disease subside.

re·mit (-mit') v., **-mitted, -mitting. 1.** send money. **2.** pardon. **3.** abate.

re·mit·tance (ri mit'əns) n. money, etc., sent.

rem·nant (rem'nənt) n. **1.** small remaining part. **2.** trace.

re·mod·el (rē mod'l) v., **-eled, -eling.** alter structure or form.

re·mon·strate (ri mon'strāt) v., **-strated, -strating.** protest; plead in protest.

re·morse (ri môrs') n. regret for wrongdoing. —**re·morse'ful,** adj. —**re·morse'less,** adj.

re·mote (ri mōt') adj. **1.** far distant. **2.** faint. —n. **3.** remote control (def. 2). —**re·mote'ly,** adv.

remote control, 1. control of an ap-paratus from a distance, as by radio signals. **2.** Also, **remote.** device used for such control.

re·move (ri mōōv') v., **-moved, -moving.** —v. **1.** take away or off. **2.** move to another place. —n. **3.** distance of separation. —**re·mov'al,** n. —**re·mov'a·ble,** adj.

re·mu'ner·ate (ri myōō'nə rāt') v., **-ated, -ating.** pay for work, etc. —**re·mu'ner·a'tion,** n.

ren·ais·sance (ren'ə säns') n. **1.** revival. **2.** (cap.) cultural period of the 14th-17th century marked by interest in culture of antiquity.

re·nal (rēn'l) adj. of the kidneys.

rend (rend) v. **1.** tear apart. **2.** disturb with noise. **3.** distress.

ren·der, v. **1.** cause to be. **2.** do, show, or furnish. **3.** perform. **4.** give back. **5.** melt (fat). —**ren·di'tion** (-dish'ən) n.

ren·dez·vous (rän'də vōō', -dā-) n., pl. **-vous.** appointment or place to meet.

ren·e·gade (ren'i gād') n. deserter.

re·nege (ri nig', -neg') v., **-neged, -neging.** Informal. break promise.

re·new' (ri nōō', -nyōō') v. **1.** begin or do again. **2.** make like new; replenish. —**re·new·al,** n.

ren·net (ren'it) n. **1.** membrane lining stomach of calf or other animal. **2.** preparation of this used in making cheese.

re·nounce (ri nouns') v., **-nounced, -nouncing.** give up voluntarily. —**re·nounce'ment,** n.

ren·o·vate (ren'ə vāt') v., **-vated, -vating.** repair; refurbish.

re·nown' (ri noun') n. fame. —**re·nowned',** adj.

rent (rent) n. **1.** Also, **rent'al.** payment for use of property. **2.** tear. —v. **3.** grant or use in return for rent.

rent·al, n. **1.** amount given or received as rent. **2.** act of renting. **3.** property rented.

re·nun·ci·a·tion (ri nun'sē ā'shən, -shē-) n. act of renouncing.

Rep., **1.** Representative. **2.** Republic. **3.** Republican.

re·pair' (ri pâr') v. **1.** restore to good condition. **2.** go. —n. **3.** work of repairing. **4.** good condition.

rep·a·ra·tion (rep'ə rā'shən) n. amends for injury.

rep·ar·tee' (rep'ər tē', -tā', -är-) n. exchange of wit; banter.

re·past' (ri past') n. meal.

re·pa·tri·ate (rē pā'trē āt') v., **-ated, -ating.** send back to one's native country.

re·pay (ri pā′) v., **-paid**, **-paying.** pay back. —**re·pay′ment,** n.

re·peal (ri pēl′) v. 1. revoke officially. —n. 2. revocation.

re·peat (ri pēt′) v. 1. say, tell, or do again. —n. 2. act of repeating. 3. musical passage to be repeated. —**re·peat′ed·ly,** adv.

re·peat·ed, adj. said or done again and again. —**re·peat′ed·ly,** adv.

re·pel′ (ri pel′) v., **-pelled, -pelling.** 1. drive back; thrust away. 2. excite disgust or suspicion. —**re·pel′lent,** adj., n.

re·pent′ (ri pent′) v. feel contrition. —**re·pent′ance,** n. —**re·pent′ant,** adj. —**re·pent′ant·ly,** adv.

re·per·cus·sion (rē′pər kush′ən) n. 1. indirect result. 2. echo.

rep·er·toire (rep′ər twär′, -twôr′, rep′ə-) n. group of works that performer or company can perform. Also, **rep′er·to·ry.**

rep·e·ti·tion (rep′ə tish′ən) n. repeated action, utterance, etc. —**rep·e·ti′tious,** adj. —**re·pet′i·tive** (ri pet′ə tiv) adj.

re·pine (ri pīn′) v., **-pined, -pining.** 1. complain. 2. yearn.

re·place (ri plās′) v., **-placed, -placing.** 1. take place of. 2. provide substitute for. 3. put back.

re·play, v., **-played, -playing.** —n. (rē plā′) v. 1. play again. —n. (rē′ plā) 2. act of replaying. 3. something replayed.

re·plen·ish (ri plen′ish) v. make full again. —**re·plen′ish·ment,** n.

re·plete (ri plēt′) adj. abundantly filled. —**re·ple′tion,** n.

rep·li·ca (rep′li kə) n. copy.

rep·li·cate (-kāt′) v., **-cated, -cating.** duplicate or reproduce.

re·ply′ (ri plī′) v., **-plied, -plying,** n., pl. **-plies.** answer.

re·port′ (ri pôrt′) n. 1. statement of events or findings. 2. rumor. 3. loud noise. —v. 4. tell of. 5. present oneself. 6. inform against. 7. write about for newspaper. —**re·port′er,** n.

re·pose (ri pōz′) n., v., **-posed, -posing.** —n. 1. rest or sleep. 2. tranquility. —v. 3. rest or sleep. 4. put, as trust. —**re·pose′ful,** adj.

re·pos·i·to·ry (ri poz′i tôr′ē) n., pl. **-tories.** place where things are stored.

re·pos·sess′ (rē′pə zes′) v. take back.

re·pre·hen·si·ble (rep′rə hen′sə bəl) adj. blameworthy.

rep·re·sent′ (rep′ri zent′) v. 1. express; signify. 2. act or speak for. 3. portray. —**rep·re·sen·ta′tion,** n.

rep·re·sent′a·tive (-zen′tə tiv) n. 1. one that represents another or others. 2. member of legislative body. —adj. 3. representing. 4. typical.

re·press (ri pres′) v. 1. inhibit. 2. suppress. —**re·pres′sive,** adj. —**re·pres′sion,** n.

re·prieve (ri prēv′) v., **-prieved, -prieving.** 1. respite.

rep·ri·mand (rep′rə mand′) n. 1. severe reproof. —v. 2. reprove severely.

re·pris·al (ri prī′zəl) n. infliction of injuries in retaliation.

re·proach (ri prōch′) v. 1. blame; upbraid. —n. 2. blame; discredit. —**re·proach′ful,** adj.

rep·ro·bate (rep′rə bāt′) n. 1. hopelessly bad person. —adj. 2. depraved. —**rep·ro·ba′tion,** n.

re·pro·duce (rē′prə dōōs′, -dyōōs′) v., **-duced, -ducing.** 1. copy or duplicate. 2. produce by propagation. —**re·pro·duc′tion** (-duk′shən) n. —**re·pro·duc′tive,** adj.

re·proof′ (-prōōf′) n. censure.

re·prove′ (-prōōv′) v., **-proved, -proving.** blame.

rep·tile (rep′til, -tīl) n. creeping animal, as lizard or snake.

re·pub·lic (ri pub′lik) n. state governed by representatives elected by citizens.

re·pub·li·can (ri pub′li kən) adj. 1. of or favoring republic. 2. (cap.) of **Republican Party,** one of two major political parties of U.S. —n. 3. (cap.) member of Republican Party.

re·pu·di·ate (ri pyōō′dē āt′) v., **-ated, -ating.** reject as worthless, not binding, or false.

re·pug·nant (ri pug′nənt) adj. distasteful. —**re·pug′nance,** n.

re·pulse (ri puls′) v., **-pulsed, -pulsing.** —v. 1. drive back with force. —n. 2. act of repulsing. 3. rejection. —**re·pul′sion,** n.

re·pul′sive, adj. disgusting.

rep·u·ta·ble (rep′yə tə bəl) adj. of good reputation.

rep·u·ta′tion (-tā′shən) n. 1. public estimation of character. 2. good name.

re·pute (ri pyōōt′) n., v., **-puted, -puting.** —n. 1. reputation. —v. 2. give reputation to.

re·quest′ (ri kwest′) v. 1. ask for. —n. 2. act of requesting. 3. what is requested.

Req·ui·em (rek′wē əm) n. Rom. Cath. Ch. mass for dead.

re·quire (ri kwīr′) v., **-quired, -quiring.** 1. need. 2. demand. —**re·quire′ment,** n.

req·ui·site (rek′wə zit) adj. 1. necessary. —n. 2. necessary thing.

req′ui·si′tion (-zish′ən) n. 1. formal order or demand. —v. 2. take for official use.

re.quite' (ri kwīt') v., -quited, -quiting. give or do in return. —re.quit'al (-kwīt'al) n.

re'run' (rē'run') n. 1. showing of motion picture or television program after its initial run. 2. the program shown.

re.scind' (ri sind') v. annul; revoke.

res'cue (res'kyoō) v., -cued, -cuing, n. —v. 1. free from danger, capture, etc. —n. 2. act of rescuing.

re.search' (ri sûrch', rē'sûrch) n. 1. diligent investigation. —v. 2. investigate carefully. —re.search'er, n.

re.sem'ble (ri zem'bal) v., -bled, -bling. be similar to. —re.sem'blance, n.

re.sent' (ri zent') v. feel indignant or injured at. —re.sent'ful, adj. —re.sent'ment, n.

res'er.va'tion (rez'ar vā'shan) n. 1. act of withholding or setting apart. 2. particular doubt or misgiving. 3. advance assurance of accommodations. 4. land for use of an Indian tribe.

re.serve' (ri zûrv') v., -served, -serving, n., adj. —v. 1. keep back. —n. 2. something reserved. 3. part of military force held in readiness to support active forces. 4. reticence. —adj. 5. kept in reserve.

re.served' adj. 1. held for future use. 2. self-restrained.

re.serv'ist, n. member of military reserves.

res'er.voir' (rez'ar vwär', -vwôr', rez'ə-) n. 1. place where water is stored for use. 2. supply.

re.side' (ri zīd') v., -sided, -siding. 1. dwell. 2. be vested, as powers.

res'i.dence (rez'i dans) n. 1. dwelling place. 2. fact or act of residing. —res'i.dent, n. —res'i.den'tial (-den'shal) adj.

res'i.den.cy, n., pl. -cies. 1. residence (def. 2). 2. period of advanced medical training.

res'i.due' (-dōo', -dyōo') n. remainder. —re.sid'u.al (ri zij'ōō əl) adj.

re.sign' (ri zīn') v. 1. give up (job, office, etc.), esp. formally. 2. submit, as to fate or force.

re.signed', adj. acquiescent.

re.sil'i.ent (ri zil'yant) adj. 1. springing back. 2. recovering readily from adversity. —re.sil'i.ence, n.

res'in (rez'in) n. exudation from some plants, used in medicines, art.

re.sist' (ri zist') v. withstand; offer opposition to. —re.sist'ant, adj.

re.sist'ance, n. 1. act of resisting.

2. ability to resist disease. 3. opposition to electric current.

re.sis'tor, n. device that introduces resistance into electrical circuit.

res'o.lute' (rez'ə lōōt') adj. determined on action or result.

res'o.lu'tion, n. 1. formal expression of group opinion. 2. determination. 3. solution of problem.

re.solve' (ri zolv') v., -solved, -solving, n. —v. 1. decide firmly. 2. state formally. 3. dispel. 4. solve. —n. 5. resolution.

res'o.nant (rez'ə nant) adj. 1. resounding. 2. rich in sound.

res'o.nate (-nāt') v., -nated, -nating. resound.

re.sort' (ri zôrt') v. 1. apply or turn (to) for use, help, etc. 2. go often. —n. 3. place much frequented, esp. for recreation. 4. recourse.

re.sound' (ri zound') v. echo.

re.sound'ing, adj. impressively complete. —re.sound'ing.ly, adv.

re.source' (rē'sôrs, ri sôrs') n. 1. source of aid or supply. 2. (pl.) wealth.

re.source'ful, adj. clever.

re.spect' (ri spekt') n. 1. detail; point. 2. reference. 3. esteem. —v. 4. hold in esteem. —re.spect'er, n.

re.spect'a.ble, adj. 1. worthy of respect. 2. decent.

re.spect'ful, adj. showing respect. —re.spect'ful.ly, adv.

re.spect'ing, prep. concerning.

re.spec'tive, adj. in order previously named.

res'pi.ra'tor (res'pə rā'tər) n. apparatus to produce artificial breathing.

re.spire' (ri spīr') v., -spired, -spiring. breathe. —res'pi.ra'tion (res'pə rā'shan) n. —res'pi.ra.to'ry, adj.

res'pite (res'pit) n., v., -pited, -piting. —n. 1. temporary relief or delay. —v. 2. relieve or cease temporarily.

re.splend'ent (ri splen'dant) adj. gleaming. —re.splend'ence, n.

re.spond' (ri spond') v. answer.

re.spond'ent, n. Law. defendant.

re.sponse' (ri spons') n. reply.

re.spon'si.bil'i.ty, n., pl. -ties. 1. state of being responsible. 2. obligation. 3. initiative.

re.spon'si.ble, adj. 1. causing or allowing things to happen. 2. capable of rational thought. 3. reliable.

re.spon'sive, adj. responding readily. —re.spon'sive.ly, adv.

rest (rest) n. 1. quiet or sleep. 2. cessation from motion, work, etc. 3. support. 4. Music. interval of silence. 5. remainder; others. —v. 6.

be quiet or at ease. **7.** cease from motion. **8.** lie or lay. **9.** be based. **10.** rely. **11.** continue to be. —**rest′ful,** *adj.* —**rest′ful•ly,** *adv.*

res′tau•rant (res′tər ənt, -tə ränt′) *n.* public eating place.

res′tau•ra•teur′ (-tər ə tûr′) *n.* restaurant owner.

res′ti•tu′tion (res′ti tōō′shən, -tyōō′-) *n.* **1.** reparation. **2.** return of rights, etc.

res′tive (res′tiv) *adj.* restless.

rest′less, *adj.* **1.** lacking rest. **2.** uneasy. **3.** always moving. —**rest′less•ly,** *adv.* —**rest′less•ness,** *n.*

re•store′ (ri stôr′) *v.,* **-stored, -stor•ing. 1.** bring back, as to use or good condition. **2.** give back. —**res′to•ra′tion,** *n.* —**re•stor′a•tive,** *adj.*

re•strain′ (ri strān′) *v.* **1.** hold back. **2.** confine.

re•straint′ (-strānt′) *n.* **1.** restraining influence. **2.** confinement. **3.** constraint.

re•strict′ (ri strikt′) *v.* confine; limit. —**re•stric′tion,** *n.* —**re•stric′tive,** *adj.*

rest room, room in public building with washbowls and toilets.

re•sult′ (ri zult′) *n.* **1.** outcome; consequence. —*v.* **2.** occur as result. **3.** end. —**re•sult′ant,** *adj., n.*

re•sume′ (ri zōōm′) *v.,* **-sumed, -suming.** go on again. —**re•sump′tion** (-zump′shən) *n.*

ré′su•mé′ (rez′ŏō mā′) *n.* summary, esp. of education and work.

re•sur•face (rē sûr′fis) *v.,* **-faced, -fac•ing. 1.** give new surface to. **2.** come to the surface again.

re•sur′gent (ri sûr′jənt) *adj.* rising again. —**re•sur′gence,** *n.*

res′ur•rect′ (rez′ə rekt′) *v.* bring to life again. —**res′ur•rec′tion,** *n.*

re•sus′ci•tate′ (ri sus′i tāt′) *v.* revive. —**re•sus′ci•ta′tion,** *n.*

re′tail (rē′tāl) *n.* **1.** sale of goods to consumer. —*v.* **2.** sell at retail.

re•tain′ (ri tān′) *v.* **1.** keep or hold. **2.** engage. —**re•tain′a•ble,** *adj.*

re•tain′er, *n.* **1.** fee paid to secure services. **2.** old servant.

re•take *v.,* **-took, -taken, -taking.** (rē tāk′) **1.** take again. **2.** photograph again. —*n.* (rē′ tāk) **3.** picture photographed again.

re•tal′i•ate′ (ri tal′ē āt′) *v.,* **-ated, -ating.** return like for like, esp. evil. —**re•tal′i•a′tion,** *n.* —**re•tal′i•a•to•ry** (-ə tôr′ē) *adj.*

re•tard′ (ri tärd′) *v.* **1.** delay; hinder.

re•tard′ed, *adj.* slow or weak in mental development.

retch (rech) *v.* try to vomit.

re•ten′tion (ri ten′shən) *n.* **1.** re-

taining. **2.** power of retaining. **3.** memory. —**re•ten′tive,** *adj.*

ret′i•cent (ret′ə sənt) *adj.* saying little. —**ret′i•cence,** *n.*

ret′i•na (ret′n ə) *n.* coating on back part of eyeball that receives images.

ret′i•nue (ret′n ōō′, -yōō′) *n.* train of attendants.

re•tire′ (ri tīr′) *v.,* **-tired, -tiring. 1.** withdraw. **2.** go to bed. **3.** end working life. **4.** put out (a batter, etc.) —**re•tire′ment,** *n.*

re•tired′, *adj.* **1.** withdrawn from office, occupation, etc. **2.** secluded.

re•tir′ee′, *n.* person who has retired.

re•tir′ing, *adj.* shy.

re•tort′ (ri tôrt′) *v.* **1.** reply smartly. —*n.* **2.** sharp or witty reply. **3.** long-necked vessel used in distilling.

re•touch′ (rē tuch′) *v.* touch up.

re•trace′ (rē trās′) *v.,* **-traced, -tracing.** go back over.

re•tract′ (ri trakt′) *v.* withdraw. —**re•trac′tion,** *n.* —**re•tract′a•ble,** *adj.*

re′tread′ (rē tred′) *n.* **1.** tire that has had new tread added. **2.** *Informal.* person returned to former position or occupation.

re•treat′ (ri trēt′) *n.* **1.** forced withdrawal. **2.** private place. —*v.* **3.** make a retreat. withdraw.

re•trench′ (ri trench′) *v.* reduce expenses. —**re•trench′ment,** *n.*

ret′ri•bu′tion (re′trə byōō′shən) *n.* requital according to merits, esp. for evil.

re•trieve′ (ri trēv′) *v.,* **-trieved, -trieving,** *n.* —*v.* **1.** regain or make restore. **2.** locate or access in a computer. **3.** recover (killed game). **4.** recovery. —**re•triev′er,** *n.*

ret′ro•ac′tive (re′trō ak′tiv) *adj.* applying also to past.

ret′ro•fit′, *v.,* **-fitted, -fitting.** refit with newly developed equipment.

ret′ro•grade′ (re′trə-) *adj., v.,* **-graded, -grading.** —*adj.* **1.** moving backward. —*v.* **2.** move backward. **3.** degenerate.

ret′ro•gress′ (re′trə gres′) *v.* return to earlier or more primitive condition. —**ret′ro•gres′sion,** *n.* —**ret′-ro•gres′sive,** *adj.*

ret′ro•spect′ (re′trə spekt′) *n.* occasion of looking back. —**ret′ro•spec′tive,** *adj.*

re•turn′ (ri tûrn′) *v.* **1.** go or come back to former place or condition. **2.** put or bring back. **3.** reply. —*n.* **4.** act or fact of returning. **5.** recurrence. **6.** requital. **7.** reply. **8.** (*often pl.*) profit. **9.** report of results.

re·turn·ee (ri tûr′nē, -tûr′nē) n., pl. **-ees.** person who has returned.

re·u·nite′ (rē′yə nīt′) v., **-nited, -niting.** unite after separation. —**re·un′ion,** n.

rev (rev) n., v., **revved, revving.** Informal. —n. **1.** revolution (as in machinery). —v. **2.** increase speed of (motor).

Rev., Reverend.

re·vamp′ (rē vamp′) v. renovate.

re·veal′ (ri vēl′) v. disclose.

rev·eil·le (rev′ə lē) n. Mil. signal for awakening.

rev·el (rev′əl) v., **-eled, -eling. 1.** enjoy greatly. **2.** make merry. —n. **3.** merry-making. —**rev′el·ry,** n.

rev·e·la·tion (rev′ə lā′shən) n. disclosure.

re·venge (ri venj′) n., v., **-venged, -venging. 1.** harm in return for harm; retaliation. **2.** vindictiveness. —v. **3.** take revenge. —**re·venge′ful,** adj. —**re·veng′er,** n.

rev·e·nue (rev′ən yōō′, -ə nōō′) n. income, esp. of government or business.

re·ver·ber·ate (ri vûr′bə rāt′) v., **-ated, -ating. 1.** echo back. **2.** reflect. —**re·ver·ber·a′tion,** n.

re·vere (ri vēr′) v., **-vered, -vering.** hold in deep respect.

rev·er·ence (rev′ər əns) n., v., **-enced, -encing.** —n. **1.** deep respect and awe. —v. **2.** regard with reverence. —**rev′er·ent, rev′er·en′tial** (-ə ren′shəl) adj.

Rev·er·end, adj. title used with name of member of the clergy.

rev·er·ie (rev′ə rē) n. daydream.

re·verse′ (ri vûrs′) adj., n., v., **-versed, -versing.** —adj. **1.** opposite in position, action, etc. **2.** of or for backward motion. —n. **3.** reverse part, position, etc. **4.** misfortune. —v. **5.** turn in the opposite direction. —**re·ver′sal,** n. —**re·vers′i·ble,** adj.

re·vert′ (-vûrt′) v. go back to earlier state, topic, etc.

re·view′ (ri vyōō′) n. **1.** critical article. **2.** repeated viewing. **3.** inspection. —v. **4.** view again. **5.** survey. **6.** inspect. **7.** write a review of. —**re·view′er,** n.

re·vile′ (ri vīl′) v., **-viled, -viling.** speak abusively to or about.

re·vise′ (ri vīz′) v., **-vised, -vising.** change or amend content of. —**re·vi′sion,** n. —**re·vis′er,** n.

re·vi′sion·ism (ri vizh′ə niz′əm) n. departure from accepted doctrine. —**re·vi′sion·ist,** n., adj.

re·vi·tal·ize (rē vīt′l īz′) v., **-ized, -izing.** bring new vitality to.

re·viv·al (ri vī′vəl) n. **1.** restoration to life, use, etc. **2.** religious awakening. —**re·viv′al·ist,** n.

re·vive′ v., **-vived, -viving.** bring back to life.

re·viv·i·fy (ri viv′ə fī′) v., **-fied, -fying.** bring back to life.

re·voke′ (ri vōk′) v., **-voked, -voking.** annul or repeal. —**rev′o·ca·ble** (rev′ə kə bəl) adj.

re·volt′ (ri vōlt′) v. **1.** rebel. **2.** turn away in disgust. **3.** fill with disgust. —n. **4.** rebellion. —**re·volt′ing,** adj.

rev·o·lu·tion (rev′ə lōō′shən) n. **1.** overthrow of government. **2.** fundamental change. **3.** rotation. —**rev′o·lu′tion·ar′y,** adj., n. —**rev′o·lu′tion·ize′,** v., **-ized, -izing.** cause fundamental change in.

re·volve′ (ri volv′) v., **-volved, -volving. 1.** turn round, as on axis. **2.** consider.

re·volv′er, n. pistol with revolving cylinder holding cartridges.

re·vue′ (ri vyōō′) n. theatrical show.

re·vul·sion (ri vul′shən) n. strong feeling of disgust.

re·ward′ (ri wôrd′) n. **1.** recompense for merit, service, etc. —v. **2.** give reward.

re·ward′ing, adj. giving satisfaction.

re·word′ (rē wûrd′) v. put into other words.

re·write′ v., **-wrote, -written, -writing. 1.** revise. **2.** write again.

RFD, rural free delivery.

rhap·so·dize′ (rap′sə dīz′) v., **-dized, -dizing.** talk with extravagant enthusiasm.

rhap·so·dy (-sə dē) n., pl. **-dies. 1.** exaggerated expression of enthusiasm. **2.** irregular musical composition.

rhe·o·stat′ (rē′ə stat′) n. device for regulating electric current.

rhet·o·ric (ret′ər ik) n. **1.** skillful use of language. **2.** exaggerated speech.

rhetorical question, question asked for effect, not answer.

rheu·ma·tism (rōō′mə tiz′əm) n. disease affecting joints or muscles. —**rheu·mat′ic** (rōō mat′ik) adj., n.

Rh factor, antigen in blood that may cause reverse reaction in individual lacking the substance.

rhine·stone (rīn′stōn′) n. artificial diamondlike gem.

rhi·noc·er·os (rī nos′ər əs) n. large thick-skinned mammal with horned snout.

rho·do·den·dron (rō′də den′drən) n. flowering evergreen shrub.

rhom·boid (rom′boid) n. oblique-angled parallelogram with only the opposite sides equal.

rhom′bus (-bəs) n., pl. **-buses, -bi** (-bī). oblique-angled parallelogram with all sides equal.

rhu′barb (rōō′bärb) n. garden plant with edible leaf stalks.

rhyme (rīm) n., v., **rhymed, rhyming.** —n. **1.** agreement in sounds of lines or words. **2.** verse with such correspondence. —v. **3.** make or form rhyme.

rhythm (rith′əm) n. movement with uniformly recurring beat. —**rhyth′mic, rhyth′mi·cal,** adj.

RI, Rhode Island. Also, **R.I.**

rib (rib) n., v., **ribbed, ribbing.** —n. **1.** one of the slender curved bones enclosing chest. **2.** riblike part. —v. **3.** furnish with ribs. **4.** Informal. tease.

rib′ald (rib′əld; spelling pron. rī′bald) adj. bawdy in speech. —**rib′ald·ry,** n.

rib′bon (rib′ən) n. strip of silk, rayon, etc.

ri′bo·fla′vin (rī′bō flā′vin, -bə-) n. important vitamin in milk, fresh meat, eggs, etc.

rice (rīs) n. edible starchy grain.

rich (rich) adj. **1.** having great possessions. **2.** abounding. **3.** costly. **4.** containing butter, eggs, cream, etc. **5.** strong; vivid. **6.** mellow. —n. **7.** rich people.

rich′es, n.pl. wealth.

Rich′ter scale (rik′tər) scale for indicating intensity of earthquake.

rick (rik) n. stack of hay, etc.

rick′ets (rik′its) n. childhood bone disease caused by lack of vitamin D.

rick′et·y (rik′i tē) adj., **-ier, -iest.** shaky.

rick′shaw (rik′shô, -shä) n. two-wheeled passenger vehicle pulled by person.

ric′o·chet′ (rik′ə shā′) n., v., **-cheted** (-shād′), **-cheting** (-shā′ing), n. —v. **1.** rebound from a flat surface. —n. **2.** such a movement.

ri·cot′ta (ri kot′ə, -kô′tə) n. soft Italian cheese.

rid (rid) v., **rid** or **ridded, ridding.** clear or free of. —**rid′dance,** n.

rid′dle (rid′l) n., v., **-dled, -dling.** —n. **1.** puzzling question or matter. **2.** coarse sieve. —v. **3.** speak perplexingly. **4.** pierce with many holes. **5.** put through sieve.

ride (rīd) v., **rode** (rōd), **ridden, riding,** n. —v. **1.** be carried in traveling. **2.** sit on and manage (horse, etc.). **3.** rest on something. —n. **4.** journey on a horse, etc. **5.** vehicle or device in which people ride for amusement.

rid′er, n. **1.** person that rides. **2.**

clause attached to legislative bill before passage.

ridge (rij) n., v., **ridged, ridging.** —n. **1.** long narrow elevation. —v. **2.** form with ridge.

rid′i·cule′ (rid′i kyōōl′) n., v., **-culed, -culing.** —n. **1.** derision. —v. **2.** deride.

ri·dic′u·lous (ri dik′yə ləs) adj. absurd. —**ri·dic′u·lous·ly,** adv.

rife (rīf) adj. **1.** widespread. **2.** abounding.

riff (rif) n. repeated phrase in jazz or rock music.

riff′raff′ (rif′raf′) n. rabble.

ri′fle (rī′fəl) n., v., **-fled, -fling.** —n. **1.** shoulder firearm with spirally grooved barrel. —v. **2.** cut spiral grooves in (gun barrel). **3.** search through to rob.

rift (rift) n. split.

rig (rig) v., **rigged, rigging,** n. —v. **1.** fit with tackle and other parts. **2.** put together as makeshift. **3.** manipulate fraudulently or artificially. —n. **4.** arrangement of masts, booms, tackle, etc. **5.** equipment.

rig′ging, n. ropes and chains that support and work masts, sails, etc.

right (rīt) adj. **1.** just or good. **2.** correct. **3.** in good condition. **4.** on side that is toward the east when one faces north. **5.** straight. —n. **6.** that which is right. **7.** right side. **8.** that justly due one. **9.** conservative side in politics. —adv. **10.** directly; completely. **11.** set correctly. **12.** in right position. **13.** correct. —**right′ly,** adv. —**right′ist,** adj., n.

right angle, 90-degree angle.

right′eous (rī′chəs) adj. virtuous.

right′ful, adj. belonging to or having just claim. —**right′ful·ly,** adv.

right′-hand′ed, adj. **1.** using the right hand more easily. **2.** for the right hand.

right of way, 1. right of one vehicle to proceed before another. **2.** path that may lawfully be used.

right′-to-life′, adj. advocating laws making abortion illegal. —**right′-to-lif′er,** n.

right wing, conservative element in organization. —**right′-wing′,** adj. —**right′-wing′er,** n.

rig′id (rij′id) adj. **1.** stiff; inflexible. **2.** rigorous. —**ri·gid′i·ty,** n.

rig′ma·role′ (rig′mə rōl′) n. **1.** confused talk. **2.** complicated procedure.

rig′or (rig′ər) n. **1.** strictness. **2.** hardship. —**rig′or·ous,** adj.

ri′gor mor′tis (rig′ər môr′tis) stiffening of body after death.

rile (rīl) v., **riled, riling.** Informal. vex.

rill (ril) *n.* small brook.

rim (rim) *n., v.,* **rimmed, rimming.** —*n.* **1.** outer edge. —*v.* **2.** furnish with rim.

rime (rīm) *n., v.,* **rimed, riming.** —*n.* **1.** rhyme. **2.** rough white frost. —*v.* **3.** cover with rime.

rind (rīnd) *n.* firm covering, as of fruit or cheese.

ring (ring) *n., v.,* **rang** (rang), **rung** (rung) (for 11), **ringed, ringing.** —*n.* **1.** round band for a finger. **2.** any circular band. **3.** enclosed area. **4.** group cooperating for selfish purpose. **5.** ringing sound. **6.** telephone call. —*v.* **7.** sound clearly and resonantly. **8.** seem; appear. **9.** be filled with sound. **10.** signal by bell. **11.** form ring around.

ring'er, *n.* person or thing that closely resembles another. **2.** athlete entered in competition in violation of eligibility rules.

ring'lead'er, *n.* leader in mischief.

ring'let (-lit) *n.* long curl of hair.

ring'mas'ter, *n.* person in charge of performances in circus ring.

ring'worm', *n.* contagious skin disease.

rink (ringk) *n.* floor or sheet of ice for skating on.

rinse (rins) *v.,* **rinsed, rinsing,** —*v.* **1.** wash lightly. —*n.* **2.** rinsing act. **3.** liquid for rinsing.

ri'ot (rī'ət) *n.* **1.** disturbance by mob. **2.** wild disorder. —*v.* **3.** take part in riot. —**ri'ot·ous,** *adj.*

rip (rip) *v.,* **ripped, ripping,** *n.* **1.** tear.

R.I.P., may he, she, or they rest in peace.

rip cord, cord that opens parachute.

ripe (rīp) *adj.,* **riper, ripest. 1.** fully developed; mature. **2.** ready. —**rip'en,** *v.* —**ripe'ness,** *n.*

rip'off', *n. Slang.* theft or exploitation.

ri·poste' (ri pōst') *n.* quick, sharp reply or reaction.

rip'ple (rip'əl) *v.,* **-pled, -pling,** *n.* —*v.* **1.** form small waves. —*n.* **2.** pattern of small waves.

rip'-roar'ing, *adj.* boisterously exciting.

rip'saw', *n.* saw for cutting wood with the grain.

rip'tide', *n.* tide that opposes other tides.

rise (rīz) *v.,* **rose** (rōz), **ris·en** (riz'ən), **rising,** *n.* —*v.* **1.** get up. **2.** revolt. **3.** appear. **4.** originate. **5.** move upward. **6.** increase. **7.** (of dough) expand. —*n.* **8.** upward movement. **9.** origin. **10.** upward slope. —**ris'er,** *n.*

risk (risk) *n.* **1.** dangerous chance.

—*v.* **2.** expose to risk. **3.** take risk of. —**risk'y,** *adj.*

ris·qué' (ri skā') *adj.* bawdy.

rite (rīt) *n.* ceremonial act.

rite of passage, event marking passage from one stage of life to another.

rit'u·al (rich'ōō əl) *n.* system of religious or other rites.

ri'val (rī'vəl) *n., adj., v.,* **-valed, -valing.** —*n.* **1.** competitor. **2.** equal. —*adj.* **3.** being a rival. —*v.* **4.** compete with. **5.** match. —**ri'val·ry,** *n.*

riv'er (riv'ər) *n.* large natural stream.

riv'et (riv'it) *n.* **1.** metal bolt hammered after insertion. —*v.* **2.** fasten with rivets.

riv'u·let (riv'yə lit) *n.* small stream.

RN, registered nurse.

roach (rōch) *n.* cockroach.

road (rōd) *n.* open way for travel.

road'block', *n.* obstruction placed across road to halt traffic.

road'run'ner, *n.* terrestrial cuckoo of western U.S.

roam (rōm) *v.* wander; rove.

roan (rōn) *adj.* **1.** horse with gray or white spots. —*n.* **2.** roan horse.

roar (rôr) *v.* **1.** make loud, deep sound. —*n.* **2.** loud, deep sound.

roast (rōst) *v.* **1.** cook by dry heat. —*n.* **2.** roasted meat. —**roast'er,** *n.*

rob (rob) *v.,* **robbed, robbing.** deprive of unlawfully. —**rob'ber,** *n.* —**rob'ber·y,** *n.*

robe (rōb) *n., v.,* **robed, robing.** —*n.* **1.** long loose garment. **2.** wrap or covering. —*v.* **3.** clothe.

rob'in (rob'in) *n.* red-breasted bird.

ro'bot (rō'bət, -bot) *n.* **1.** human-like machine that performs tasks. **2.** person who acts mechanically.

ro·bot'ics, *n.* technology of computer-controlled robots.

ro·bust' (rō bust', rō'bust) *adj.* healthy.

rock (rok) *n.* **1.** mass of stone. **2.** Also, **rock-'n'-roll.** popular music with steady, insistent rhythm. —*v.* **3.** move back and forth. —**rock'y,** *adj.*

rock bottom, lowest level.

rock'er, *n.* curved support of cradle or rocking chair.

rock'et (rok'it) *n.* tube propelled by discharge of gases from it.

rock'et·ry, *n.* science of rocket design.

rock salt, salt occurring in rocklike masses.

ro·co'co (rə kō'kō, rō'kə kō') *n.* elaborate decorative style of many curves. —**ro·co'co,** *adj.*

rod (rod) *n.* **1.** slender shaft. **2.** linear measure of 5½ yards.

ro'dent (rōd'nt) *n.* small gnawing or nibbling mammal.

ro'de·o' (rō'dē ō', rō dā'ō) *n., pl.* **-deos.** exhibition of cowboy skills.

roe (rō) *n., pl.* **roes, roe. 1.** small deer. **2.** fish eggs or spawn.

rog'er (roj'ər) *interj.* (message) received.

rogue (rōg) *n.* rascal. **—ro'guish,** *adj.* **—ro'guer·y,** *n.*

roil (roil) *v.* **1.** make muddy. **2.** vex.

role (rōl) *n.* part of function, as of character in play. Also, **rôle.**

role model, person imitated by others.

roll (rōl) *v.* **1.** move by turning. **2.** rock. **3.** have deep, loud sound. **4.** flatten with roller. **5.** form into roll or ball. **—n. 6.** list; register. **7.** anything cylindrical. **8.** small cake of bread. **9.** deep long sound.

roll'back', *n.* return to lower level.

roll call, calling of names for checking attendance.

Roll'er·blade', *n., v.,* **-blad·ed, -blad·ing. —n. 1. Trademark.** brand of in-line skates. **—v. 2.** (*often l.c.*) skate on in-line skates.

roller coaster, small railroad that moves along winding route with steep inclines.

roller skate, skate with four wheels. **—roller-skate,** *v.*

rol'lick·ing (rol'i king) *adj.* jolly.

roll'o'ver, *n.* reinvestment of funds.

roll'-top desk, desk with flexible sliding cover.

ro'ly-po'ly (rō'lē pō'lē, -pō'lē) *adj.* short and round.

ROM (rom) *n.* read only memory: non-modifiable part of computer memory containing instructions to system.

ro·maine' (rō mān', rə-) *n.* kind of lettuce.

Ro'man (rō'man) **1.** native or citizen of Rome or Roman Empire. **2.** (*l.c.*) upright style of printing type. **—Ro'man,** *adj.*

Roman candle, kind of firework.

Roman Catholic Church, Christian Church of which pope (Bishop of Rome) is head. **—Roman Catholic.**

ro·mance' (rō mans') *n., v.,* **-manced, -mancing. —n. 1.** colorful, imaginative tale. **2.** love affair. **—v. 4.** act romantically. **5.** tell fanciful, false story.

Roman numerals, system of numbers using letters as symbols: I = 1, V = 5, X = 10, L = 50, C = 100, D = 500, M = 1,000.

ro·man'tic (rō man'tik) *adj.* **1.** of romance. **2.** impractical or unrealistic. **3.** imbued with idealism. **4.** preoccupied with love. **5.** passionate; fervent. **6.** of a style of art stressing imagination and emotion. **—n. 7.** romantic person.

ro·man'ti·cism (-tə siz'əm) *n.* (*often cap.*) romantic spirit or cultural style or movement.

ro·man'ti·cize', *v.,* **-cized, -cizing.** invest with romantic character.

romp (romp) *v., n.* frolic.

romp'ers, *n.pl.* child's loose outer garment.

rood (rood) *n.* **1.** crucifix. **2.** one-quarter of an acre.

roof (roof, roof) *n., pl.* **roofs. 1.** upper covering of building. **—v. 2.** provide with roof. **—roof'er,** *n.*

rook (rook) *n.* **1.** European crow. **2.** chess piece; castle. **—v. 3.** cheat.

rook'ie, *n. Slang.* beginner.

room (room, room) *n.* **1.** separate space within building. **2.** space. **—v. 3.** lodge. **—room'er,** *n.* **—room'mate',** *n.* **—room'y,** *adj.*

roost (roost) *n.* **1.** perch where fowls rest. **—v. 2.** sit on roost.

roost'er, *n.* male chicken.

root (root, root) *n.* **1.** part of plant growing underground. **2.** embedded part. **3.** origin. **4.** quantity that, when multiplied by itself so many times, produces given quantity. **—v. 5.** establish roots. **6.** implant. **7.** root out, exterminate. **8.** dig with snout. **9.** *Informal.* cheer encouragingly. **—root'er,** *n.*

root beer, soft drink flavored with extracts of roots, barks, and herbs.

root canal, root portion of the pulp cavity of a tooth.

rope (rōp) *n., v.,* **roped, roping. —n. 1.** strong twisted cord. **—v. 2.** fasten or catch with rope.

Roque'fort (rōk'fərt) *n. Trademark.* strong cheese veined with mold, made from sheep's milk.

ro'sa·ry (rō'zə rē) *n., pl.* **-ries.** *Rom. Cath. Ch.* **1.** series of prayers. **2.** string of beads counted in saying rosary.

rose (rōz) *n.* **1.** thorny plant having showy, fragrant flowers.

ro·sé' (rō zā') *n.* pink wine.

rose'mar'y (rōz'mâr'ē, -ma rē) *n.* aromatic shrub used for seasoning.

ro·sette' (rō zet') *n.* rose-shaped ornament.

ros'ter (ros'tər) *n.* list of persons, groups, events, etc.

ros'trum (ros'trəm) *n., pl.* **-trums, -tra** (-trə). speakers' platform.

ros'y (rō'zē) *adj.,* **-ier, -iest. 1.** pink

rudder

or pinkish-red. **2.** cheerful; optimistic. **3.** bright. —**ros′i·ly,** adv.

rot (rot) v., **rotted, rotting.** —n. **1.** decay. **2.** decay. **3.** decay of tissue.

ro·tate (rō′tāt) v., **-tated, -tating.** turn on or as on axis. —**ro′ta·ry** (-tə rē) adj. —**ro·ta′tion,** n.

ROTC (är′ō tē sē′, är′tē sē) Reserve Officers Training Corps.

rote (rōt) n. **1.** routine way. **2.** by **rote,** from memory in mechanical way.

ro·tis·ser·ie (rō tis′ə rē) n. rotating machine for roasting.

ro′tor (rō′tər) n. rotating part.

ro·to·till·er (rō′tə til′ər) n. motorized device with rotating blades for tilling soil.

rot′ten (rot′n) adj. **1.** decaying. **2.** corrupt. —**rot′ten·ness,** n.

ro·tund (rō tund′) adj. round.

ro·tun·da (rō tun′də) n. round room.

rou·é (rōō ā′) n. dissolute man; rake.

rouge (rōōzh) n., v., **rouged, rouging.** —n. **1.** red cosmetic for cheeks and lips. —v. **2.** color with rouge.

rough (ruf) adj. **1.** not smooth. **2.** violent in action or motion. **3.** harsh. **4.** crude. —n. **5.** rough thing or part. —v. **6.** make rough. —**rough′age** (-ij) n. coarse or fibrous material in food.

rough′en, v. make or become rough.

rou·lette (rōō let′) n. gambling game based on spinning disk.

round (round) adj. **1.** circular, curved, or spherical. **2.** complete. **3.** expressed as approximate number. **4.** sonorous. —n. **5.** something round. **6.** complete course, series, etc. **7.** cut of beef between rump and leg. **8.** song in which voices enter at intervals. **9.** stage of competition, as in tournament. —adv. **10.** in or as in a circle. **11.** in circumference. —prep. **12.** around. —v. **13.** make round. **14.** travel around. **15.** bring together. —**round′ness,** n.

round′a·bout′, adj. indirect.

round′house′, n. building for servicing locomotives.

round′ly, adv. unsparingly.

round trip, trip to and back.

round′up′, n. **1.** bringing together. **2.** summary.

rouse (rouz) v., **roused, rousing.** stir up; arouse.

roust′a·bout′ (roust′ə bout′) n. laborer.

rout (rout) n. **1.** defeat ending in disorderly flight. —v. **2.** force to flee in disorder.

route (rōōt, rout) n., v., **routed, routing.** —n. **1.** course of travel. —v. **2.** send by route.

rou·tine′ (rōō tēn′) n. **1.** regular order of action. —adj. **2.** like or by routine. **3.** ordinary.

rove (rōv) v., **roved, roving.** wander aimlessly. —**rov′er,** n.

row (rō) v. **1.** propel by oars. **2.** (rou) dispute noisily. —n. **3.** trip in rowboat. **4.** persons or things in line. **5.** (rou) noisy dispute. —**row′boat′,** n.

row′dy (rou′dē) adj., **-dier, -diest,** n., pl. **-dies.** —adj. **1.** rough and disorderly. —n. **2.** rowdy person.

roy′al (roi′əl) adj. of kings or queens. —**roy′al·ly,** adv.

roy′al·ist, n. person favoring royal government. —**royalist,** adj.

roy′al·ty, n., pl. **-ties. 1.** royal persons. **2.** royal power. **3.** share of proceeds, paid to an author, inventor, etc.

rpm, revolutions per minute.

RR, 1. railroad. **2.** rural route.

RSVP, please reply.

rub (rub) v., **rubbed, rubbing.** —v. **1.** apply pressure to in cleaning, smoothing, etc. **2.** press against with friction. —n. **3.** act of rubbing. **4.** difficulty.

rub′ber (rub′ər) n. **1.** elastic material from a tropical tree. **2.** pl. overshoes. —**rub′ber·y,** adj.

rubber band, band of rubber used for holding things together.

rubber cement, adhesive.

rub′ber·neck′, Informal. —v. **1.** stare curiously. —n. **2.** curious onlooker. **3.** sightseer.

rubber stamp, stamp with rubber printing surface.

rub′bish (rub′ish) n. **1.** waste. **2.** nonsense.

rub′ble (rub′əl) n. broken stone.

rub′down′, n. massage.

ru·bel′la (rōō bel′ə) n. usu. mild viral infection. Also, **German measles.**

ru′ble (rōō′bəl) n. monetary unit of Russia and of some former Soviet states.

ru′bric (rōō′brik) n. **1.** title or heading. **2.** class or category.

ru′by (rōō′bē) n., pl. **-bies.** red gem.

ruck′sack′ (ruk′sak′, rōōk′-) n. knapsack.

ruck′us (ruk′əs) n. noisy commotion.

rud′der (rud′ər) n. turning flat piece for steering vessel or aircraft.

rud'dy (rud'ē) *adj.* **-dier, -diest.** having healthy red color.

rude (rood) *adj.* **ruder, rudest. 1.** discourteous. **2.** unrefined; crude.

ru'di·ment (roo'də mənt) *n.* basic thing to learn. **—ru·di·men'ta·ry** (-men'tə rē) *adj.*

rue (roo) *v.,* **rued, ruing.** regret. **—rue'ful,** *adj.*

ruff (ruf) *n.* deep full collar.

ruf'fi·an (ruf'ē ən) *n.* rough or lawless person.

ruf'fle (ruf'əl) *v.,* **-fled, -fling,** *n.* **—v. 1.** make uneven. **2.** disturb. **3.** gather in folds. **—n. 4.** break in evenness. **5.** band of cloth, etc., gathered on one edge.

rug (rug) *n.* floor covering.

Rug'by (rug'bē) *n.* English form of football.

rug'ged (rug'id) *adj.* **1.** roughly irregular. **2.** severe. **3.** strong.

ru'in (roo'in) *n.* **1.** destruction. **2.** (*pl.*) remains of fallen building, etc. **—v. 3.** bring or come to ruin or ruins. **—ru'in·a'tion,** *n.* **—ru'in·ous,** *adj.*

rule (rool) *n., v.,* **ruled, ruling. —n. 1.** principle; regulation. **2.** control. **3.** ruler (def. 2). **—v. 4.** control. **5.** decide in the manner of a judge. **6.** mark with ruler. **—rul'ing,** *n., adj.*

rul'er (roo'lər) *n.* **1.** person who rules. **2.** straight-edged strip for measuring, drawing lines, etc.

rum (rum) *n.* alcoholic liquor.

rum'ba (rum'bə, room'-) *n.* Cuban dance.

rum'ble (rum'bəl) *v.,* **-bled, -bling,** *n.* **—v. 1.** make long, deep, heavy sound. **—n. 2.** such sound.

ru'mi·nant (roo'mə nənt) *n.* **1.** cud-chewing mammal, as cows. **2.** cud-chewing.

ru'mi·nate' (-nāt') *v.,* **-nated, -nating. 1.** chew cud. **2.** meditate.

rum'mage (rum'ij) *v.,* **-maged, -maging.** search thoroughly.

rum'my (rum'ē) *n., pl.* **-mies.** card game.

ru'mor (roo'mər) *n.* **1.** unconfirmed but widely repeated story. **—v. 2.** tell as rumor.

rump (rump) *n.* **1.** hind part of animal's body. **2.** the buttocks.

rum'pus (rum'pəs) *n. Informal.* noise.

run (run) *v.,* **ran** (ran), **run, running,** *n.* **—v. 1.** advance quickly. **2.** be candidate. **3.** flow; melt. **4.** extend. **5.** operate. **6.** be exposed to. **7.** manage. **—n. 8.** act or period of running. **9.** raveled line in knitting. **10.** freedom of action. **11.** scoring unit in baseball.

run'a·round', *n. Informal.* evasive action or response.

run'a·way', *n.* **1.** fugitive. **2.** something that has broken away from control. **—adj. 3.** escaped. **4.** uncontrolled.

run'down', *adj.* **1.** weary. **2.** fallen into disrepair. **3.** not running because not wound.

run'down', *n.* short summary.

rung (rung) *n.* **1.** ladder step. **2.** bar between chair legs.

run'-in', *n.* confrontation.

run'ner, *n.* **1.** one that runs. **2.** messenger. **3.** blade of skate. **4.** strip of fabric, carpet, etc.

run'ner-up', *n.* competitor finishing in second place.

run'off', *n.* final contest held to break tie.

run'-of-the-mill', *adj.* mediocre.

runt (runt) *n.* undersized thing.

run'way', *n.* strip where airplanes take off and land.

rup'ture (rup'chər) *n., v.,* **-tured, -turing. 1.** break. **2.** hernia. **—v. 3.** break. **4.** cause breach of.

ru'ral (roor'əl) *adj.* of or in the country.

ruse (rooz) *n.* trick.

rush (rush) *v.* **1.** move with speed or violence. **—n. 2.** act of rushing. **3.** hostile attack. **4.** grasslike herb growing in marshes. **—adj. 5.** requiring or marked by haste.

rusk (rusk) *n.* sweet raised bread dried and baked again.

rus'set (rus'it) *n.* reddish brown.

Rus'sian (rush'ən) *n.* native or language of Russia. **—Russian,** *adj.*

rust (rust) *n.* **1.** red-orange coating that forms on iron and steel exposed to air and moisture. **—v. 2.** make or become rusty. **—rust'y,** *adj.*

rus'tic (rus'tik) *adj.* **1.** rural. **2.** simple. **—n. 3.** country person.

rus'ti·cate' (-ti kāt') *v.,* **-cated, -cating.** go to or live in the country.

rus'tle (rus'əl) *v.,* **-tled, -tling,** *n.* **—v. 1.** make small soft sounds. **2.** steal (cattle, etc.). **—n. 3.** rustling sound. **—rus'tler,** *n.*

rut (rut) *n., v.,* **rutted, rutting. —n. 1.** furrow or groove worn in the ground. **2.** period of sexual excitement in male deer, goats, etc. **—v. 3.** make ruts in. **4.** be in rut.

ru'ta·ba'ga (roo'tə bā'gə) *n.* yellow turnip.

ruth'less (rooth'lis) *adj.* without pity or mercy. **—ruth'less·ness,** *n.*

RV, recreational vehicle.

Rx, prescription.

rye (rī) *n.* cereal grass used for flour, feed, and whiskey.

S

S, s (es) *n.* nineteenth letter of English alphabet.

S, south, southern.

Sab·bath (sab′əth) *n.* day of religious observance and rest, observed on Saturday by Jews and on Sunday by most Christians.

sab·bat·i·cal (sə bat′i kal) *n.* paid leave of absence for study. —*adj.* 2. (*cap.*) of the Sabbath.

sa·ber (sā′bər) *n.* one-edged sword. Also, **sa′bre.**

sa·ble (sā′bəl) *n.* small mammal with dark-brown fur.

sab·o·tage′ (sab′ə täzh′) *n.*, *v.*, **-taged, -taging.** —*n.* 1. willful injury to equipment, etc. —*v.* 2. attack by sabotage.

sab·o·teur′ (-tûr′) *n.* person who sabotages.

sac (sak) *n.* baglike part.

sac·cha·rin (sak′ər in) *n.* sweet substance used as sugar substitute.

sac·cha·rine (-ər in, -ə rēn′) *adj.* overly sweet.

sa·chet′ (sa shā′) *n.* small bag of perfumed powder.

sack (sak) *n.* 1. large stout bag. 2. bag. 3. *Slang.* dismissal. 4. plundering. —*v.* 5. put into a sack. 6. *Slang.* dismiss. 7. plunder; loot.

sack′cloth′, *n.* coarse cloth worn for penance or mourning.

sac′ra·ment (sak′rə mant) *n.* rite in Christian church.

sa′cred (sā′krid) *adj.* holy. 2. regarded with reverence.

sac′ri·fice′ (sak′rə fīs′) *n.*, *v.*, **-ficed, -ficing.** —*n.* 1. offer of life, treasure, etc., to deity. 2. surrender of something for purpose. —*v.* 3. give as sacrifice. —**sac′ri·fi′cial** (-fish′əl) *adj.*

sac′ri·lege (-lijj) *n.* profanation of anything sacred. —**sac′ri·le·gious** (-lij′əs, -lē′jəs) *adj.*

sac′ris·tan (sak′ri stan) *n.* sexton.

sac′ris·ty (-ri stē) *n.*, *pl.* **-ties.** room in church, etc., where sacred objects are kept.

sac′ro·il′i·ac′ (sak′rō il′ē ak′, sā′krō-) *n.* joint in lower back.

sac′ro·sanct′ (sak′rō sangkt′) *adj.* sacred.

sac′rum (sak′rəm, sā′krəm) *n.*, *pl.* **sacra.** bone at rear of pelvis.

sad (sad) *adj.*, **sadder, saddest.** sorrowful. —**sad′den,** *v.*

sad′dle (sad′l) *n.*, *v.*, **-dled, -dling.** —*n.* 1. seat for rider on horse, etc. 2. anything resembling saddle. —*v.* 3. put saddle on. 4. burden.

sad′dle·bag′, *n.* pouch laid over back of horse or mounted over rear wheel of bicycle or motorcycle.

sad′ism (sā′diz əm, sad′iz-) *n.* sexual or other enjoyment in causing pain. —**sad′ist,** *n.* —**sa·dis′tic** (sə-dis′tik) *adj.*

sa·do·mas·o·chism (sā′dō mas′ə-kiz′əm) *n.* sexual or other enjoyment in causing or experiencing pain. —**sa′do·mas′o·chist′,** *n.*

sa·fa·ri (sə fär′ē) *n.* (in E. Africa) journey; hunting expedition.

safe (sāf) *adj.*, **safer, safest,** *n.* —*adj.* 1. secure or free from danger. 2. dependable. —*n.* 3. stout box for valuables. —**safe′ly,** *adv.* —**safe′keep′ing,** *n.*

safe′·con′duct, *n.* document authorizing safe passage.

safe′-de·pos′it, *adj.* providing safekeeping for valuables.

safe′guard′, *n.* 1. something that ensures safety. —*v.* 2. protect.

safe sex, sexual activity in which precautions are taken to avoid sexually transmitted diseases.

safety glass, shatter-resistant glass.

safety pin, pin bent back on itself with guard to cover point.

safety razor, razor with blade guard.

saf′flow·er (saf′lou′ər) *n.* thistle-like plant whose seeds yield cooking oil.

saf′fron (saf′rən) *n.* bright yellow seasoning.

sag (sag) *v.*, **sagged, sagging,** *n.* —*v.* 1. bend, esp. in middle, from weight or pressure. 2. hang loosely. —*n.* 3. sagging place.

sa′ga (sä′gə) *n.* heroic tale.

sa·ga′cious (sə gā′shəs) *adj.* shrewd. —**sa·gac′i·ty** (-gas′ə tē) *n.*

sage (sāj) *n.*, *adj.*, **sager, sagest.** —*n.* 1. wise person. 2. herb used in seasoning. —*adj.* 3. wise; prudent.

sage′brush′, *n.* sagelike, bushy plant of dry plains of western U.S.

sa′go (sā′gō) *n.* starchy substance from some palms.

sa·hib (sä′ib), *n.* (in colonial India) term of respect for European.

said (sed) *v.* pt. of SAY. —*adj.* named before.

sail (sāl) *n.* 1. sheet spread to catch wind to propel vessel or windmill. 2. trip on sailing vessel. —*v.* 3. move by action of wind. 4. travel over water. —**sail′or,** *n.*

sail′cloth′, *n.* fabric used for boat sails or tents.

sailfish

sail/fish/, n. large fish with upright fin.

saint (sānt), n. holy person. —**saint/hood,** n. —**saint/ly,** adj.

sake (sāk), n. 1. benefit. 2. purpose. 3. (sä/kē) rice wine.

sa·laam (sə läm/) n. 1. Islamic salutation. 2. low bow with hand on forehead.

sa·la·cious (sə lā/shəs) adj. lewd.

sal/ad (sal/əd), n. dish esp. of raw vegetables or fruit.

sal/a·man/der (sal/ə man/dər) n. small amphibian.

sa·la·mi (sə lä/mē) n. kind of sausage.

sal/a·ry (sal/ə rē) n., pl. **-ries.** fixed payment for regular work.

sale (sāl) n. 1. act of selling. 2. opportunity to sell. 3. occasion of selling at reduced prices. —**sales/man,** n. —**sales/la·dy, sales/wom/an,** n. fem. —**sales/per/son,** n. —**sales/people,** n.pl. —**sales/room/,** n.

sales/man·ship/, n. skill of selling a product or idea.

sa/li·ent (sā/lē ənt) adj. 1. conspicuous. 2. projecting. —n. 3. projecting part. —**sa/li·ence,** n.

sa/line (sā/lēn, -līn) adj. salty.

sa·li/va (sə lī/və) n. fluid secreted into mouth by glands. —**sal/i·var/y** (sal/ə ver/ē) adj. —**sal/i·vate** (-vāt/) v. —**sal/i·va/tion,** n.

sal/low (sal/ō) adj. having sickly complexion.

sal/ly (sal/ē) n., pl. **-lies,** v., **-lied, -lying.** —n. 1. sudden attack by besieged troops. 2. witty remark. —v. 3. make sally.

salm·on (sam/ən) n. pink-fleshed food fish of northern waters.

sal/mo·nel/la (sal/mə nel/ə) n., pl. **-nellae** (-nel/ē), **-nellas.** bacillus that causes various diseases, including food poisoning.

sa·lon/ (sə lon/; Fr. sä lôN/) n. 1. drawing room. 2. art gallery.

sa·loon/ (sə lōōn/) n. 1. place where intoxicating liquors are sold and drunk. 2. public room.

sal/sa (säl/sə, -sä) n. 1. Latin-American music with elements of jazz, rock, and soul. 2. sauce, esp. hot sauce containing chilies.

salt (sôlt) n. 1. sodium chloride, occurring as mineral, in sea water, etc. 2. chemical compound derived from acid and base. 3. wit. 4. Informal. sailor. —v. 5. season or preserve with salt. —**salt/y,** adj.

salt/cel/lar, n. shaker or dish for salt.

sal·tine/ (sôl tēn/) n. crisp, salted cracker.

salt lick, place where animals lick salt deposits.

salt of the earth, someone thought to embody the best human qualities.

salt/pe/ter (-pē/tər) n. potassium nitrate.

sa·lu/bri·ous (sə lōō/brē əs) adj. good for health. —**sa·lu/bri·ty,** n.

sal/u·tar/y (sal/yə ter/ē) adj. healthful; beneficial.

sal/u·ta/tion (sal/yə tā/shən) n. 1. greeting. 2. formal opening of letter.

sa·lute/ (sə lōōt/) v., **-luted, -luting,** n. —v. 1. express respect or goodwill, esp. in greeting. —n. 2. act of saluting.

sal/vage (sal/vij) n., v., **-vaged, -vaging.** —n. 1. act of saving ship or cargo at sea. 2. property saved. —v. 3. save from destruction.

sal·va/tion (sal vā/shən) n. 1. deliverance. 2. deliverance from sin.

salve (sav) n., v., **salved, salving.** —n. 1. ointment for sores. —v. 2. apply salve to.

sal/ver (sal/vər) n. tray.

sal/vo (sal/vō) n., pl. **-vos, -voes.** discharge of guns, bombs, etc., in rapid series.

sam/ba (sam/bə, säm/-) n., v., **-baed, -baing.** —n. 1. Brazilian dance of African origin. —v. 2. dance the samba.

same (sām) adj. 1. identical or corresponding. 2. unchanged. 3. just mentioned. —n. 4. same person or thing. —**same/ness,** n.

sam/ple (sam/pəl) n., adj., v., **-pled, -pling.** —n. 1. small amount to show nature or quality. —adj. 2. as sample. —v. 3. test by sample.

sam/pler, n. needlework done to show skill.

sam/u·rai/ (sam/ŏŏ rī/) n., pl. **-rai.** member of hereditary warrior class in feudal Japan.

san/a·to/ri·um (san/ə tôr/ē əm) n., pl. **-toriums, -toria** (-tôr/ē ə). sanitarium.

sanc/ti·fy/ (sangk/tə fī/) v., **-fied, -fying.** 1. make holy. 2. give sanction to. —**sanc/ti·fi·ca/tion,** n.

sanc/ti·mo/ni·ous (-mō/nē əs), adj. hypocritically devout.

sanc/tion (sangk/shən) n. 1. permission or support. 2. legal action by one state against another. —v. 3. authorize; approve.

sanc/ti·ty (sangk/ti tē) n., pl. **-ties.** 1. holiness. 2. sacred character.

sanc/tu·ar/y (-chŏŏ er/ē) n., pl. **-ies.** 1. holy place. 2. place of immunity from arrest or harm.

sanc′tum (-təm) n., pl. **-tums, -ta.** private place.

sand n. **1.** fine grains of rock. **2.** (pl.) sandy region. —v. **3.** smooth with sandpaper.

san′dal (san′dl) n. shoe consisting of sole and straps.

san′dal·wood′, n. fragrant wood.

sand′bag′, n. sand-filled bag used as fortification, ballast, or weapon.

sand′bar′, n. large mass of sand.

sand bar, bar of sand formed by tidal action.

sand′blast′, v. clean with blast of air or steam laden with sand.

sand′box′, n. receptacle holding sand for children to play in.

sand dollar, disklike sea animal.

sand′lot′, n. **1.** vacant lot used by youngsters for games. —adj. **2.** played in a sandlot.

sand′man′, n. figure in folklore who puts sand in children's eyes to make them sleepy.

sand′pa·per, n. **1.** paper coated with sand. —v. **2.** smooth with sandpaper.

sand′pip′er (-pī′pər) n. small shore bird.

sand′stone′, n. rock formed chiefly of sand.

sand′storm′, n. windstorm with clouds of sand.

sand′wich (sand′wich, san′-) n. **1.** two slices of bread with filling between. —v. **2.** insert.

sane adj., **saner, sanest.** free from mental disorder; rational.

sang-froid′ (Fr. sän frwa′) n. composure.

san·gri′a (sang grē′ə, san-) n. iced drink of red wine and fruit.

san·guin′a·ry (sang′gwə ner′ē) adj. **1.** bloody. **2.** bloodthirsty.

san′guine (-gwin) adj. **1.** hopeful. **2.** red.

san′i·tar′i·um (san′i târ′ē əm) n., pl. **-iums, -ia** (-ē ə). place for treatment of invalids and convalescents.

san′i·tar′y (-ter′ē) adj. of health.

sanitary napkin, pad worn to absorb menstrual flow.

san′i·ta′tion, n. application of sanitary measures.

san′i·tize′, v., **-tized, -tizing. 1.** free from dirt. **2.** make less offensive by removing objectionable elements.

san′i·ty, n. **1.** soundness of mind. **2.** good judgment.

San′skrit (san′skrit) n. extinct language of India.

sap (sap) n., v., **sapped, sapping.** —n. **1.** juice of woody plant. —n. Slang. fool. —v. **3.** weaken; undermine.

sa′pi·ent (sā′pē ənt) adj. wise.

sap′ling (sap′ling) n. young tree.

sap′phire (saf′ī̄r) n. deep-blue gem.

sar′casm (sär′kaz əm) n. **1.** harsh derision. **2.** ironical gibe. —**sar·cas′tic,** adj.

sar·co′ma (sär kō′mə) n., pl. **-mas, -mata** (-mə tə). type of malignant tumor.

sar·coph′a·gus (sär kof′ə gəs) n., pl. **-gi.** stone coffin.

sar·dine′ (sär dēn′) n. small fish.

sar·don′ic (sär don′ik) adj. sarcastic. —**sar·don′i·cal·ly,** adv.

sa·ri′ (sär′ē) n. length of cloth used as dress in India.

sa·rong′ (sə rông′) n. skirtlike garment.

sar′sa·pa·ril′la (sas′pə ril′ə) n. **1.** tropical American plant. **2.** soft drink flavored with roots of this plant.

sar·to′ri·al (sär tôr′ē al) adj. of tailors or tailoring.

SASE, self-addressed stamped envelope.

sash n. **1.** band of cloth usually worn as belt. **2.** framework for panes of window, etc.

sass (sas) Informal. —n. **1.** impudent back talk. —v. **2.** answer back impudently. —**sas′sy,** adj.

sas′sa·fras′ (sas′ə fras′) n. American tree with aromatic root bark.

Sa′tan (sāt′n) n. chief evil spirit; devil. —**sa·tan′ic** (sə tan′ik) adj.

satch′el (sach′əl) n. handbag.

sate (sāt) v., **sated, sating.** satisfy.

sat′el·lite′ (sat′l līt′) n. **1.** body that revolves around planet. **2.** subservient follower.

satellite dish, dish-shaped reflector, used esp. for receiving satellite and microwave signals.

sa′ti·ate′ (sā′shē āt′) v., **-ated, -ating.** surfeit.

sat′in (sat′n) n. glossy silk or rayon fabric. —**sat′in·y,** adj.

sat′ire (sat′ī̄r) n. use of irony or ridicule in exposing folly, etc. —**sa·tir′i·cal** (sə tir′i kəl), **sa·tir′ic,** adj. —**sat′i·rist** (sat′ər ist) n.

sat′i·rize′ (sat′ə rīz′) v., **-rized, -rizing.** subject to satire.

sat′is·fac′to·ry (sat′is fak′tə rē) adj. adequate. —**sat′is·fac′to·ri·ly,** adv.

sat′is·fy′ (-fī′) v., **-fied, -fying. 1.** fulfill desire, need, etc. **2.** convince. **3.** pay. —**sat′is·fac′tion** (-fak′shən) n.

sat′u·rate′ (sach′ə rāt′) v., **-rated, -rating.** soak completely.

Sat′ur·day (sat′ər dā′, -dē) n. seventh day of week.

Sat′urn (-ərn) n. sixth planet in order from the sun.

saturnine

sat/ur·nine/ (-ər nīn/) adj. gloomy.

sa/tyr (sā/tər, sat/ər) n. 1. woodland deity, part man and part goat. 2. lecherous person.

sauce (sôs) n. 1. liquid or soft relish. 2. stewed fruit.

sauce/pan/, n. cooking pan with handle.

sau/cer, n. small shallow dish.

sau/cy, adj., -cier, -ciest. impertinent. **—sau/ci·ly,** adv.

sauer/kraut/ (souⁱr/krout, souⁱ/ər-) n. chopped fermented cabbage.

sau/na (sô/nə) n. bath heated by steam.

saun/ter (sôn/tər) v., n. stroll.

sau/sage (sô/sij) n. minced seasoned meat, often in casing.

sau·té/ (sō tā/, sô-) v., -téed, -tée·ing. cook in a little fat.

sau·terne/ (sō tûrn/) n. sweet white wine.

sav/age (sav/ij) adj. 1. wild; uncivilized. 2. cruel. —n. 3. uncivilized person. **—sav/age·ly,** adv. **—sav/age·ry,** n.

sa·van/na (sə van/ə) n. grassy plain with scattered trees. Also, **sa·van/nah.**

sa·vant/ (sa vänt/) n. learned person.

save (sāv) v., saved, saving, prep., conj. —v. 1. rescue or keep safe. 2. reserve. —prep., conj. 3. except.

sav/ing, n. 1. economy. 2. (pl.) money put by. —prep. 3. except. 4. respecting.

sav/ior (sāv/yər) n. 1. one who rescues. 2. (cap.) Christ. Also, **sav/iour.**

sa/voir-faire/ (sav/wär fâr/) n. competence in social matters.

sa/vor (sā/vər) n., v. taste or smell.

sa/vor·y, adj., n., pl., -ories. —adj. 1. pleasing in taste or smell. —n. 2. aromatic plant.

sav/vy (sav/ē) n. practical understanding.

saw (sô) n., v. 1. toothed metal blade. —v. 2. cut with saw. **—saw/mill,** n. **—saw/yer** (sô/yər) n.

saw/buck/, n. 1. sawhorse. 2. Slang. ten-dollar bill.

saw/dust/, n. fine particles of wood produced in sawing.

saw/horse/, n. movable frame for supporting wood while it's sawed.

sax (saks) n. saxophone.

Sax/on (sak/sən) n. member of Germanic people who invaded Britain in the 5th–6th centuries.

sax/o·phone/ (sak/sə fōn/) n. musical wind instrument.

say (sā) v., said (sed), saying, n. —v. 1. speak; declare; utter. 2. de-

clare as truth. —n. 3. Informal. right to speak or choose.

say/ing, n. proverb.

SC, South Carolina. Also, **S.C.**

say/-so/, n., pl. -sos. Informal. personal assurance; word.

scab (skab) n., v., scabbed, scab-bing. —n. 1. crust forming over sore. 2. worker who takes striker's place. —v. 3. form scab. 4. work as scab. **—scab/by,** adj.

scab/bard (skab/ərd) n. sheath for sword blade, etc.

sca/bies (skā/bēz, -bē ēz/) n. infectious skin disease.

scad (skad) n. (usually pl.) great quantity.

scaf/fold (skaf/əld, -ōld) n. 1. Also, **scaf/fold·ing.** temporary framework used in construction. 2. platform on which criminal is executed.

scal/a·wag/ (skal/ə wag/) n. rascal.

scald (skôld) v. 1. burn with hot liquid or steam. 2. heat just below boiling. —n. 3. burn caused by scalding.

scale (skāl) n., v., scaled, scaling. —n. 1. one of flat hard plates covering fish, etc. 2. flake. 3. device for weighing. 4. series of measuring units. 5. relative measure. 6. succession of musical tones. —v. 7. remove or shed scales. 8. weigh. 9. climb with effort. 10. reduce proportionately. **—scal/y,** adj.

scal/lion (skal/yən) n. small green onion.

scal/lop (skol/əp, skal/-) n. 1. bivalve mollusk. 2. one of series of curves on a border. —v. 3. finish with scallops.

scalp (skalp) n. 1. skin and hair of top of head. —v. 2. cut scalp from. 3. buy and resell at inflated price.

scal/pel (skal/pəl) n. small surgical knife.

scam (skam) n., v., scammed, scamming. —n. 1. fraudulent scheme; swindle. —v. 2. cheat.

scamp (skamp) n. rascal.

scam/per, v. 1. go quickly. —n. 2. quick run.

scam/pi (skam/pē, skäm/-) n., pl. -pi. 1. large shrimp. 2. dish of scampi.

scan (skan) v., scanned, scanning. 1. examine closely. 2. glance at. 3. analyze verse meter.

scan/dal (skan/dl) n. 1. disgraceful act; disgrace. 2. malicious gossip. **—scan/dal·ous,** adj. **—scan/dal·mon/ger,** n.

scan/dal·ize/, v., -ized, -izing. offend; shock.

scan/ner, n. 1. person or thing that scans. 2. device that monitors selected radio frequencies and reproduces any signal detected. **3.** device that optically scans bar codes, etc., and identifies data.

scan'sion (skan'shan) *n.* metrical analysis of verse.

scant *adj.* barely adequate. Also, **scant'y**. —**scant'i•ly,** *adv.*

scape'goat' (skāp'gōt') *n.* one made to bear blame for others.

scar (skär) *n., v.,* **scarred, scarring.** —*n.* **1.** mark left by wound, etc. —*v.* **2.** mark with scar.

scar'ab (skar'ab) *n.* beetle.

scarce (skârs) *adj.,* **scarcer, scarcest. 1.** insufficient. **2.** rare. —**scar'ci•ty, scarce'ness,** *n.*

scarce'ly, *adv.* **1.** barely. **2.** definitely not.

scare (skâr) *v.,* **scared, scaring,** *n.* —*v.* **1.** frighten. —*n.* **2.** sudden fright.

scare'crow', *n.* object set up to frighten birds away from crops.

scarf (skärf) *n., pl.* **scarfs, scarves** (skärvz). band of cloth esp. for neck.

scar'i•fy' (skar'ə fī') *v.,* **-fied, -fy-ing.** loosen; cut.

scar'let (skär'lit) *n.* bright red.

scarlet fever, disease marked by fever and rash.

scar'y (skâr'ē) *adj.* **-ier, -iest.** causing fear.

scat (skat) *v.,* **scatted, scatting.** run off.

scath'ing (skā'thing) *adj.* bitterly severe.

scat'o•log'i•cal (skat'l oj'i kəl) *adj.* concerned with excrement or obscenity.

scat'ter (skat'ər) *v.* throw loosely about.

scat'ter•brain', *n.* person incapable of coherent thought.

scav'enge (skav'inj) *v.,* **-enged, -enging.** search for food.

sce•nar'i•o' (si närʹē ōʹ, -närʹ-) *n., pl.* **-ios.** plot outline.

scene (sēn) *n.* **1.** location of action. **2.** view. **3.** subdivision of play. **4.** display of emotion. —**scen'ic,** *adj.*

scen'er•y (sē'nə rē) *n.* **1.** features of landscape. **2.** stage set.

scent (sent) *n.* **1.** distinctive odor. **2.** trail marked by this. **3.** sense of smell. —*v.* **4.** smell. **5.** perfume.

scep'ter (sep'tər) *n.* rod carried as emblem of royal power. Also, **scep'tre.**

scep'tic (skep'tik) *n.* skeptic.

sched'ule (skej'ōōl, -ōōl; *Brit.* shed'yōōl, shej'ōōl) *n., v.,* **-uled, -uling.** —*n.* **1.** timetable or list. —*v.* **2.** enter on schedule.

scheme (skēm) *n., v.,* **schemed,**

scheming. —*n.* **1.** plan; design. **2.** intrigue. —*v.* **3.** plan or plot. —**sche•mat'ic** (ski mat'ik) *adj.*

scher'zo (skert'sō) *n., pl.* **-zos, -zi** (-sē). playful musical movement.

schil'ling (shil'ing) *n.* monetary unit of Austria.

schism (siz'əm, skiz'-) *n.* division within church, etc.; disunion.

schiz'oid (skit'soid) *adj.* having personality disorder marked by depression, withdrawal, etc.

schiz'o•phre'ni•a (skit'sə frē'nē ə) *n.* kind of mental disorder. —**schiz'o•phren'ic** (-fren'ik) *adj., n.*

schle•miel' (shlə mēl') *n. Slang.* awkward and unlucky person.

schlep (shlep) *v.,* **schlepped, schlepping,** *n. Slang.* —*v.* **1.** carry with great effort. —*n.* **2.** slow or awkward person. **3.** tedious journey.

schlock (shlok) *n. Informal.* inferior merchandise. —**schlock'y,** *adj.*

schmaltz (shmälts, shmôlts) *n. Informal.* sentimental art, esp. music. —**schmaltz'y,** *adj.*

schnapps (shnäps, shnaps) *n.* strong alcoholic liquor.

schol'ar (skol'ər) *n.* **1.** learned person. **2.** pupil. —**schol'ar•ly,** *adj.*

schol'ar•ship', *n.* **1.** learning. **2.** aid granted to promising student.

scho•las'tic (skə las'tik) *adj.* of schools or scholars.

school (skōōl) *n.* **1.** place for instruction. **2.** regular meetings of teacher and pupils. **3.** believers in doctrine or theory. **4.** group of fish, whales, etc. —*v.* **5.** educate; train. —**school'teach'er,** *n.*

schoon'er (skōō'nər) *n.* kind of sailing vessel.

schwa (shwä) *n.* vowel sound in certain unstressed syllables, as *a* in *sofa;* usually represented by ə.

sci•at'i•ca (sī at'i kə) *n.* neuralgia in hip and thigh. —**sci•at'ic,** *adj.*

sci'ence (sī'əns) *n.* systematic knowledge, esp. of physical world. —**sci'en•tif'ic** (-tif'ik) *adj.* —**sci'en•tif'i•cal•ly,** *adv.* —**sci'en•tist,** *n.*

science fiction, fiction dealing with space travel, robots, etc.

sci-fi (sī'fī') *n., adj. Informal.* science fiction.

scim'i•tar (sim'i tər) *n.* curved sword.

scin•til'la (sin til'ə) *n.* particle, trace of evidence.

scin'til•late' (-tl āt') *v.,* **-lated, -lating.** sparkle. —**scin'til•la'tion,** *n.*

sci'on (sī'ən) *n.* **1.** descendant. **2.** shoot cut for grafting.

scis'sors (siz'ərz) *n.pl.* cutting instrument with two pivoted blades.

scle•ro'sis (skli rō'sis) n. hardening, as of tissue.

scoff (skôf) v. jeer. —**scoff'er,** n.

scoff'law', n. person who flouts the law, as by ignoring traffic tickets.

scold (skōld) v. 1. find fault; reprove. —n. 2. scolding person.

sconce (skons) n. wall bracket for candles, etc.

scone (skōn, skon) n. small flat cake.

scoop (skōōp) n. 1. small deep shovel. 2. bucket of steam shovel, etc. 3. act of scooping. 4. quantity taken up. 5. Informal. earliest news report. —v. 6. take up with scoop. 7. Informal. best (competing news media) with scoop (def. 5).

scoot (skōōt) v. go swiftly.

scoot'er, n. low two-wheeled vehicle.

scope (skōp) n. extent.

scorch (skôrch) v. 1. burn slightly. —n. 2. superficial burn.

score (skōr) n., pl. **scores,** (for 3) **score,** v., **scored, scoring.** —n. 1. points made in game, etc. 2. notch. 3. group of twenty. 4. account; reason. 5. written piece of music. —v. 6. earn points in game. 7. notch or cut. 8. criticize. —**scor'er,** n.

scorn (skôrn) n. 1. contempt. 2. mockery. —v. 3. regard or refuse with scorn. —**scorn'ful,** adj.

scor'pi•on (skôr'pē ən) n. small venomous spiderlike animal.

Scot (skot) n. native or inhabitant of Scotland. —**Scot'tish,** adj., n.pl.

scotch (skoch) v. put an end to.

Scotch, adj. 1. (loosely) Scottish. —n. 2. (pl.) (loosely) Scottish people. 3. whiskey made in Scotland.

scot'-free', adj. avoiding punishment or obligation.

Scots (skots) n. English spoken in Scotland.

scoun'drel (skoun'drəl) n. rascal.

scour (skou°r) v. 1. clean by rubbing. 2. range in searching.

scourge (skûrj) n., v., **scourged, scourging.** —n. 1. whip. 2. cause of affliction. —v. 3. whip.

scout (skout) n. 1. person sent ahead to examine conditions. —v. 2. examine as scout.

scowl (skoul) n. 1. fierce frown. —v. 2. frown fiercely.

scrab'ble (skrab'əl) v., -**bled, -bling.** 1. scratch with hands, etc. 2. scrawl.

scrag (skrag) n. scrawny creature.

scrag'gly, adj., -**glier, -gliest.** shaggy.

scram (skram) v., **scrammed, scramming.** Informal. go away quickly.

scram'ble (skram'bəl) v., -**bling,** n. —v. 1. move with difficulty, using feet and hands. 2. mix together. —n. 3. scrambling progression. 4. struggle for possession.

scrap (skrap) n., adj., v., **scrapped, scrapping.** —n. 1. small piece. 2. discarded material. 3. Informal. fight. —adj. 4. discarded. 5. in scraps or as scraps. —v. 6. break up; discard. —**scrap'py,** adj.

scrap'book', n. blank book for clippings, etc.

scrape (skrāp) v., **scraped, scraping,** n. —v. 1. rub harshly. 2. remove by scraping. 3. collect laboriously. —n. 4. act or sound of scraping. 5. scraped place. 6. predicament. —**scrap'er,** n.

scratch (skrach) v. 1. mark, tear, or rub with something sharp. 2. strike out. —n. 3. mark from scratching.

scrawl (skrôl) v. 1. write carelessly or awkwardly. —n. 2. such bad handwriting.

scraw'ny (skrô'nē) adj., -**nier, -niest.** thin. —**scraw'ni•ness,** n.

scream (skrēm) n. 1. loud sharp cry. —v. 2. utter screams.

screech (skrēch) n. 1. harsh shrill cry. —v. 2. utter screeches.

screen (skrēn) n. 1. covered frame. 2. anything that shelters or conceals. 3. wire mesh. 4. surface for displaying motion pictures. —v. 5. shelter with screen. 6. sift through screen. 7. project on a screen.

screen'play', n. outline or full script of motion picture.

screw (skrōō) n. 1. machine part or fastener driving or driven by twisting. 2. propeller. 3. coercion. —v. 4. hold with screw. 5. turn as screw.

screw'ball', Slang. —n. 1. eccentric person. —adj. 2. eccentric.

screw'driv'er, n. tool for turning screws.

screw'y, adj., -**ier, -iest.** Slang. 1. crazy. 2. absurd.

scrib'ble (skrib'əl) v., -**bled, -bling,** n. —v. 1. write hastily or meaninglessly. —n. 2. piece of such writing.

scribe (skrīb) n. professional copyist.

scrim'mage (skrim'ij) n., v., -**maged, -maging.** n. 1. rough struggle. 2. play in football. —v. 3. engage in scrimmage.

scrimp (skrimp) v. economize.

scrip (skrip) n. certificate, paper money, etc.

season

script (skript) n. 1. handwriting. 2. manuscript.

Scrip′ture (skrip′chər) n. 1. Bible. 2. (l.c.) sacred or religious writing or book. —**scrip′tur·al,** adj.

scriv′ner (skriv′nər) n. scribe.

scrod (skrod) n. young codfish or haddock.

scrof′u·la (skrof′yə lə) n. tuberculous disease, esp. of lymphatic glands. —**scrof′u·lous,** adj.

scroll (skrōl) n. roll of inscribed paper.

scro′tum (skrō′təm) n., pl. **-ta** (-tə), **-tums.** pouch of skin containing testicles. —**scro′tal,** adj.

scrounge (skrounj) v., **scrounged, scrounging.** Informal. 1. beg or mooch. 2. search. —**scroung′er,** n.

scrub (skrub) v., **scrubbed, scrubbing,** n., adj. —v. 1. clean by rubbing. —n. 2. low trees or shrubs. 3. anything small or poor. —adj. 4. small or poor. —**scrub′by,** adj.

scruff (skruf) n. nape.

scruff′y (skruf′ē) adj. **scruffier, scruffiest.** untidy.

scrump′tious (skrump′shəs) adj. extremely pleasing; delicious.

scru′ple (skrōō′pəl) n. restraint from conscience.

scru′pu·lous (-pyə ləs) adj. 1. having scruples. 2. careful.

scru′ti·nize′ (skrōōt′n īz′) v., **-nized, -nizing.** examine closely. —**scru′ti·ny,** n.

scu′ba (skōō′bə) n. self-contained breathing device for swimmers.

scud (skud) v., **scudded, scudding.** move quickly.

scuff (skuf) v. mar by hard use.

scuf′fle n., v., **-fled, -fling.** —n. 1. rough, confused fight. —v. 2. engage in scuffle.

scull (skul) n. 1. oar used over stern. 2. light racing boat. —v. 3. propel with scull.

scul′ler·y (skul′ə rē) n., pl. **-leries.** workroom off kitchen.

scul′lion (-yən) n. kitchen servant.

sculp′ture (skulp′chər) n. 1. three-dimensional art of wood, marble, etc. 2. piece of such work. —**sculp′tor** (-tər) n. —**sculp′tress** (-tris) n.fem.

scum (skum) n. 1. film on top of liquid. 2. worthless persons.

scup′per (skup′ər) n. opening in ship's side to drain off water.

scurf (skûrf) n. 1. loose scales of skin. 2. scaly matter on a surface.

scur′ril·ous (skûr′ə ləs) adj. coarsely abusive or derisive.

scur′ry (skûr′ē, skur′ē) v., **-ried, -rying,** n., pl. **-ries.** hurry.

scur′vy (skûr′vē) n., adj., **-vier, -vi-**

-est. —n. 1. disease from lack of vitamin C. —adj. 2. contemptible.

scut′tle (skut′l) n., v., **-tled, -tling.** —n. 1. covered opening, esp. on flat roof. 2. coal bucket. —v. 3. sink intentionally. 4. scurry.

scut′tle·butt′ (-but′) n. Informal. rumor; gossip.

scythe (sīᵺ) n. curved, handled blade for mowing by hand.

SD, South Dakota. Also, **S.D.**

S. Dak., South Dakota.

SE, southeast.

sea (sē) n. 1. ocean. 2. body of salt water smaller than ocean. 3. turbulence of water. —**sea′board′, sea′shore′,** n. —**sea′coast′,** n. —**sea′port′,** n. —**sea′go′ing,** adj.

sea bass (bas) marine food fish.

sea′bed′, n. ocean floor.

sea′far′ing, adj. traveling by or working at sea. —**sea′far′er,** n.

sea′food′, n. edible marine fish or shellfish.

sea gull, n.

sea horse, small fish with beaked head.

seal (sēl) n., pl. **seals,** (also for 3) **seal,** v. —n. 1. imprinted device affixed to document. 2. means of closing. 3. marine animal with large flippers. —v. 4. affix seal to. 5. close by seal. —**seal′ant,** n.

sea legs, ability to adjust balance to motion of ship.

sea level, position of the sea's surface at mean level between low and high tides.

sea lion, large seal.

seam (sēm) n. 1. line formed in sewing two pieces together. —v. 2. join with seam.

sea′man, n., pl. **-men.** sailor.

seam′stress (-stris) n. woman who sews.

seam′y, adj., **-ier, -iest.** sordid.

sé′ance (sā′äns) n. meeting to attempt communication with spirits.

sea′plane′, n. airplane equipped with floats.

sea′port′, n. port for seagoing vessels.

sear (sēr) v. 1. burn. 2. dry up.

search (sûrch) v. 1. examine, as in looking for something. 2. investigate. —n. 3. examination or investigation. —**search′er,** n.

search′light′, n. device for throwing strong beam of light.

sea′shell′, n. shell of marine mollusk.

sea′sick′ness, n. nausea from motion of ship. —**sea′sick′,** adj.

sea′son (sē′zən) n. 1. any of four distinct periods of year. 2. best or usual time. —v. **3.** flavor with salt, spices, etc. —**sea'son·al,** *adj.*

sea·son·a·ble, *adj.* appropriate to time of year.

sea·son·ing, *n.* flavoring, as salt, spices, or herbs.

seat (sēt) *n.* **1.** place for sitting. **2.** right to sit, as in Congress. **3.** site; location. **4.** established center. —*v.* **5.** place on seat. **6.** find seats for.

seat belt, strap to keep passenger secure in vehicle.

seat'ing, *n.* **1.** arrangement of seats. **2.** material for seats.

sea urchin, small, round sea animal with spiny shell.

sea'way', *n.* waterway from ocean to inland port.

sea'weed', *n.* plant growing in sea.

sea'wor'thy, *adj.,* **-thier, -thiest.** fit for sea travel.

se·ba·ceous (si bā'shəs) *adj.* secreting a fatty substance.

seb'or·rhe·a (seb'ə rē'ə) *n.* abnormally heavy discharge from sebaceous glands.

se·cede (si sēd') *v.,* **-ceded, -ceding.** withdraw from nation, alliance, etc. —**se·ces'sion** (-sesh'ən) *n.*

se·clude (si klōōd') *v.,* **-cluded, -cluding.** locate in solitude. —**se·clu'sion,** *n.*

sec·ond (sek'ənd) *adj.* **1.** next after first. **2.** another. —*n.* **3.** one that is second. **4.** person who aids another. **5.** (*pl.*) imperfect goods. **6.** sixtieth part of minute or time of degree. —*v.* **7.** support; further. —*adv.* **8.** in second place. —**sec'ond·ly,** *adv.*

sec·ond·ar·y (-an der'ē) *adj.* **1.** next after first. **2.** of second rank or stage. **3.** less important.

sec·ond-guess', *v.* use hindsight in criticizing or correcting.

sec·ond·hand', *adj.* not new.

second nature, deeply ingrained habit or tendency.

sec·ond-rate', *adj.* of lesser or minor quality or importance.

second string, squad of players available to replace those who start a game.

second wind (wind) energy for renewed effort.

se·cret (sē'krit) *adj.* **1.** kept from knowledge of others. —*n.* **2.** something kept secret. —**se'cre·cy,** *n.*

sec're·tar'i·at (sek'ri târ'ē ət) *n.* group of administrative officials.

sec're·tar'y (-ter'ē) *n., pl.* **-taries. 1.** office assistant. **2.** head of department of government. **3.** tall writing desk. —**sec're·tar'i·al,** *adj.*

se·crete (si krēt') *v.,* **-creted, -cret-**

ing. 1. hide. **2.** discharge or release by secretion.

se·cre·tion (-krē'shən) *n.* **1.** glandular function of secreting, as bile or milk. **2.** product secreted.

se'cre·tive (sē'kri tiv, si krē'-) *adj.* **1.** disposed to keeping things secret. **2.** secretory. —**se'cre·tive·ly,** *adv.*

sect (sekt) *n.* group united in religious faith. —**sec·tar'i·an,** *adj., n.*

sec'tion (sek'shən) *n.* **1.** separate or distinct part. —*v.* **2.** divide.

sec'tor (sek'tər) *n.* **1.** plane figure bounded by two radii and an arc. **2.** part of combat area.

sec'u·lar (sek'yə lər) *adj.* worldly; not religious. —**sec'u·lar·ism,** *n.* —**sec'u·lar·ize',** *v.,* **-ized, -izing.**

se·cure (si kyŏŏr') *adj., v.,* **-cured, -curing.** —*adj.* **1.** safe. **2.** firmly in place. **3.** certain. —*v.* **4.** get. **5.** make secure. —**se·cure'ly,** *adv.*

se·cu·ri·ty (-kyŏŏr'i tē) *n., pl.* **-ties. 1.** safety. **2.** protection. **3.** pledge given on loan. **4.** certificate of stock, etc.

security blanket, something that gives feeling of security.

se·dan' (si dan') *n.* closed automobile for four or more.

se·date' (si dāt') *adj.* **1.** quiet; sober. —*v.* **2.** give sedative to. —**se·date'ly,** *adv.* —**se·da'tion,** *n.*

sed'a·tive (sed'ə tiv) *adj.* **1.** soothing. **2.** relieving pain or excitement. —*n.* **3.** sedative medicine.

sed'en·tar·y (sed'ən ter'ē) *adj.* characterized by sitting.

sedge (sej) *n.* grasslike marsh plant.

sed'i·ment (sed'ə mənt) *n.* matter settling to bottom of liquid. —**sed'i·men·ta·ry,** *adj.*

se·di·tion (si dish'ən) *n.* incitement to rebellion. —**se·di'tious,** *adj.*

se·duce (si dōōs', -dyōōs') *v.,* **-duced, -ducing. 1.** corrupt; tempt. **2.** induce to have sexual intercourse. —**se·duc'er,** *n.* —**se·duc'tion,** (-duk'shən) *n.* —**se·duc'tive,** *adj.*

see (sē) *v.,* **saw** (sô), **seen, seeing,** *n.* —*v.* **1.** perceive with the eyes. **2.** find out. **3.** make sure. **4.** escort. —*n.* **5.** jurisdiction of bishop.

seed (sēd) *n.* **1.** propagating part of plant. **2.** offspring. —*v.* **3.** sow seed. **4.** remove seed from.

seed'ling, *n.* plant grown from seed.

seed money, capital for beginning an enterprise.

seed'y, *adj.,* **seedier, seediest. 1.** having many seeds. **2.** shabby.

see'ing, *conj.* inasmuch as.

seek (sēk) v., **sought, seeking. 1.** search for. **2.** try; attempt.

seem (sēm) v. appear (to be or do).

seem·ing, adj. apparent.

seem·ly, adj., **-lier, -liest.** decorous. —**seem′age,** n.

seep (sēp) v. ooze; pass gradually. —**seep′age,** n.

seer (sēr) n. **1.** person who sees. **2.** prophet. —**seer′ess,** n.

seer·suck·er (sēr′suk′ər) n. crinkled cotton fabric.

see′saw′ (sē′sô′) n. **1.** children's sport played on balancing plank. —v. **2.** alternate, waver, etc.

seethe (sēth) v., **seethed, seething.** boil; foam.

see′-through′, adj. transparent.

seg·ment (seg′mənt) n. **1.** part; section. —v. **2.** divide into segments. —**seg·men′tal,** n. —**seg·men·ta′tion,** n.

seg·re·gate (seg′ri gāt′) v., **-gated, -gating.** separate from others. —**seg·re·ga′tion,** n.

se′gue (sā′gwā, seg′wā) v., **segued, segueing. 1.** continue at once with the next section, as in piece of music. **2.** make smooth transition. —n. **3.** smooth transition.

seine (sān) n., v., **seined, seining.** —n. **1.** kind of fishing net. —v. **2.** fish with seine.

seis·mic (sīz′mik, sīs′-) adj. of or caused by earthquakes.

seis·mo·graph′ (-mə graf′) n. instrument for recording earthquakes. —**seis·mog′ra·phy,** n.

seis·mol·o·gy (-mol′ə jē) n. science of earthquakes. —**seis·mo·log′i·cal,** adj. —**seis·mol′o·gist,** n.

seize (sēz) v., **seized, seizing. 1.** take by force or authority. **2.** understand.

seiz′ure (sē′zhər) n. **1.** act of seizing. **2.** attack of illness.

sel·dom (sel′dəm) adv. not often.

se·lect′ (si lekt′) v. **1.** choose. —adj. **2.** choice. **3.** exclusive. —**se·lec′tion,** n. —**se·lec′tive,** adj.

se·lect′man, n., pl. **-men.** town officer in New England.

self (self) n., pl. **selves** (selvz), adj. —n. **1.** person's own nature. **2.** personal advantage or interests. —adj. **3.** identical.

self′-ad·dressed′, adj. addressed for return to sender.

self′-as·ser′tion, n. expression of one's own importance, etc. —**self′-as·ser′tive,** adj.

self′-as·sur′ance, n. confidence in one's ability. —**self′-as·sured′,** adj.

self′-cen′tered, adj. interested only in oneself.

self′-con′fi·dence, n. faith in one's own judgment, ability, etc. —**self′-con′fi·dent,** adj.

self′-con′scious, adj. excessively aware of being observed by others; embarrassed or uneasy.

self′-con·tained′, adj. **1.** containing within itself all that is necessary. **2.** reserved in behavior.

self′-con·trol′, n. restraint of one's actions. —**self′-con·trolled′,** adj.

self′-de·fense′, n. **1.** act of defending oneself or one's property. **2.** plea that use of force was necessary in defending one's person.

self′-de·ni′al, n. sacrifice of one's desires.

self′-de·ter′mi·na′tion, n. right or ability to choose government or actions.

self′-ef·fac′ing, adj. keeping oneself in the background.

self′-ev′i·dent, adj. obvious.

self′-im′age, n. conception or evaluation of oneself.

self′-im·por′tant, adj. having or showing exaggerated sense of one's own importance.

self′-in′ter·est, n. one's personal benefit.

self·ish (sel′fish) adj. caring only for oneself. —**self′ish·ly,** adv.

self·less, adj. having little concern for oneself; unselfish.

self′-made′, adj. owing success entirely to one's own efforts.

self′-pos·sessed′, adj. calm; poised.

self′-pres·er·va′tion, n. instinctive desire to guard one's safety.

self′-re·spect′, n. proper esteem for oneself. —**self′-re·spect′ing,** adj.

self′-re·straint′, n. self-control.

self′-right′eous, adj. smugly convinced one is morally right.

self′same′, adj. identical.

self′-sat·is·fied′, adj. complacent.

self′-seek′ing, n. **1.** selfish seeking of one's own interests or ends. —adj. **2.** given to or characterized by self-seeking.

self′-serv′ice, adj. **1.** of a commercial establishment in which customers serve themselves. **2.** designed to be used without the aid of an attendant.

self′-serv′ing, adj. serving to further one's own interests.

self′-styled′, adj. so called only by oneself.

self′-suf·fi′cient, adj. able to supply one's own needs without external assistance.

sell (sel) v., **sold** (sōld), **selling. 1.** part with for payment. **2.** betray. **3.** be for sale. —**sell′er,** n.

sel′vage (sel′vij) n. finished edge on fabric.

se·man·tics (si man′tiks) *n.* study of meanings of words.

sem·a·phore (sem′ə fôr′) *n.* apparatus for signaling.

sem·blance (sem′bləns) *n.* **1.** appearance. **2.** copy.

se′men (sē′mən) *n.* male reproductive fluid.

se·mes·ter (si mes′tər) *n.* half school year.

semi-, prefix meaning half or partly.

sem·i·cir·cle (sem′i sûr′kəl) *n.* half circle. —**sem′·i·cir′cu·lar,** *adj.*

sem·i·co·lon (sem′i kō′lən) *n.* mark of punctuation (;) between parts of sentence.

sem·i·con·duc·tor *n.* substance, as silicon, with electrical conductivity between that of an insulator and a conductor.

sem·i·fi′nal, *adj.* **1.** of the next to last round in a tournament. —*n.* **2.** semifinal round or bout.

sem′i·nal (sem′ə nl) *adj.* **1.** of or consisting of semen. **2.** influencing future development.

sem·i·nar′ (-när′) *n.* class of advanced students.

sem·i·nar·y (-ner′ē) *n., pl.* **-ies.** school, esp. for young women or for divinity students.

Sem′i·nole (-nōl′) *n., pl.* **-nole, -noles.** member of American Indian people of Florida and Oklahoma.

sem·i·pre·cious (sem′ē-, sem′ī-) *adj.* of moderate value.

Se·mit′ic (sə mit′ik) *n.* **1.** language family of Africa and Asia, including Hebrew and Arabic. —*adj.* **2.** of Semitic languages or their speakers.

sem·i·tone (sem′ē-, sem′ī-) *n.* musical pitch halfway between two whole tones.

sem·o·li·na (sem′ə lē′nə) *n.* ground durum.

sen′ate (sen′it) *n.* legislative body, esp. (*cap.*) upper house of legislatures of United States, Canada, etc. —**sen′a·tor** (-i tər) *n.*

send (send) *v.,* **sent, sending. 1.** cause to go. **2.** have conveyed. **3.** emit. —**send′er,** *n.*

send′-off′, *n.* farewell demonstration of good wishes.

se·nile (sē′nīl) *adj.* feeble, esp. because of old age. —**se·nil·i·ty** (si-nil′ə tē) *n.*

sen·ior (sēn′yər) *adj.* **1.** older. **2.** of higher rank. **3.** denoting last year in school. —*n.* **4.** senior person.

senior citizen, person 65 years or over.

sen·ior·i·ty (sēn yôr′i tē) *n., pl.* **-ties.** status conferred by length of service.

se·ñor′ (se nyôr′) *n., pl.* **-ño·res**

(-nyôr′es). *Spanish.* **1.** gentleman. **2.** Mr. or sir. —**se·ño′ra,** *n.*

se·ño·ri′ta (se′nyō rē′tä) *n. Spanish.* **1.** Miss. **2.** young lady.

sen·sa′tion (sen sā′shən) *n.* **1.** operation of senses. **2.** mental condition from such operation. **3.** cause of excited interest.

sen·sa′tion·al, *adj.* **1.** startling; exciting. **2.** of senses or sensation.

sen·sa′tion·al·ism, *n.* use of sensational subject matter.

sense (sens) *n., v.,* **sensed, sensing.** —*n.* **1.** faculty for perceiving stimuli (sight, hearing, smell, etc.). **2.** feeling so produced. **3.** (*pl.*) consciousness. **4.** (*often pl.*) rationality; prudence. **5.** meaning. —*v.* **6.** perceive by senses.

sen·si·bil·i·ty (sen′sə bil′i tē) *n., pl.* **-ties. 1.** capacity for sensation. **2.** (*often pl.*) sensitive feeling.

sen·si·ble, *adj.* **1.** wise or practical. **2.** aware. —**sen′si·bly,** *adv.*

sen·si·tive, *adj.* **1.** having sensation. **2.** easily affected.

sen·si·tize (-tīz′) *v.,* **-tized, -tizing.** make sensitive.

sen′sor (sen′sôr, -sər) *n.* device sensitive to light, temperature, or radiation level that transmits signal to another instrument.

sen′so·ry (-sə rē) *adj.* of sensation or senses.

sen′su·al (sen′shōō əl) *adj.* **1.** inclined to pleasures of the senses. **2.** lewd. —**sen′su·al·i·ty** (-al′i tē) *n.* —**sen′su·al·ly,** *adv.*

sen′su·ous, *adj.* **1.** of or affected by senses. **2.** giving or seeking enjoyment through senses.

sen′tence (sen′tns) *n., v.,* **-tenced, -tencing.** —*n.* **1.** group of words expressing complete thought. **2.** judgment; opinion. **3.** assignment of punishment. —*v.* **4.** pronounce sentence upon.

sen·ten′tious (sen ten′shəs) *adj.* using maxims or pompous words.

sen′tient (sen′shənt) *adj.* having feeling. —**sen′tience,** *n.*

sen′ti·ment (-tə mənt) *n.* **1.** opinion. **2.** emotion. **3.** expression of belief or emotion.

sen′ti·men′tal (-men′tl) *adj.* expressing or showing tender emotion.

sen′ti·nel (sen′tn l, -tə nl) *n.* guard.

sen′try (sen′trē) *n., pl.* **-tries.** soldier on watch.

se′pal (sē′pəl) *n.* leaflike part of flower.

sep·a·rate (*v.* sep′ə rāt′; *adj.* sep′ər it) *adj., v.,* **-rated, -rating. 1.** keep, put, or come apart. —*adj.* (-rit) **2.** not connected; being apart. —**sep·a·ra'tion**, *n.* —**sep'a·ra·ble**, *adj.*

sep'a·ra·tist (-ə tist, -ə rā'-) *n.* advocate of separation.

sep'a·ra'tor, *n.* apparatus for separating ingredients.

se·pi·a (sē'pē ə) *n.* **1.** brown pigment. **2.** dark brown.

sep'sis (sep'sis). *n.* infection in blood. —**sep'tic** (-tik) *adj.*

Sept., September.

Sep·tem'ber (sep tem'bər) *n.* ninth month of year.

sep·tet' (sep tet') *n.* group of seven. Also, **sep·tette'**.

sep'ti·ce'mi·a (sep'tə sē'mē ə) *n.* blood poisoning.

septic tank, tank for decomposition of sewage.

sep'tu·a·ge·nar'i·an (sep'chōō ə jə närē ən) *n.* person 70 to 79 years old.

Sep'tu·a·gint (-jint) *n.* oldest Greek version of Old Testament.

sep'ul·cher (sep'əl kər) *n.* burial place. Also, **sep'ul·chre.** —**se·pul'chral** (sə pul'krəl) *adj.*

seq., **1.** sequel. **2.** the following.

se'quel (sē'kwəl) *n.* **1.** subsequent event. **2.** literary work, film, etc., continuing earlier one.

se'quence (-kwəns) *n.* **1.** succession; series. **2.** result.

se·ques'ter (si kwes'tər) *v.* **1.** seclude. **2.** seize and hold.

se'quin (sē'kwin) *n.* small spangle.

se·quoi'a (si kwoi'ə), *n.* very large tree of northwest U.S.

se·ra'glio (si ral'yō, -räl'-) *n.*, *pl.* **-glios.** harem.

ser'aph (ser'əf) *n.*, *pl.* **-aphs, -aphim** (-ə fim). angel of highest order. —**se·raph'ic** (sə raf'ik) *adj.*

sere (sēr) *adj.* withered.

ser'e·nade' (ser'ə nād') *n.*, *v.*, **-naded, -nading.** —*n.* **1.** music performed as compliment outside at night. —*v.* **2.** compliment with serenade.

ser'en·dip'i·ty (ser'ən dip'i tē) *n.* luck in making accidental discoveries.

se·rene' (sə rēn') *adj.* **1.** calm. **2.** fair. —**se·ren'i·ty** (-ren'ə tē) *n.*

serf (sûrf) *n.* **1.** person in feudal servitude. **2.** slave. —**serf'dom,** *n.*

serge (sûrj) *n.* stout twilled fabric.

ser'geant (sär'jənt) *n.* noncommissioned officer above corporal.

se'ri·al (sēr'ē əl) *n.* **1.** story, etc., appearing in installments. —*adj.* **2.** of serial. **3.** of or in series.

se'ries (sēr'ēz) *n.* things in succession.

ser'if (ser'if) *n.* smaller line used to finish off main stroke of letter.

ser'i·graph (ser'i graf) *n.* silk-screen print.

se'ri·ous (sēr'ē əs) *adj.* **1.** solemn. **2.** important.

ser'mon (sûr'pant) *n.* religious discourse.

ser'pent (sûr'pant) *n.* snake.

ser'pen·tine' (-pən tēn', -tīn') *adj.* **1.** like a snake. **2.** winding.

ser'rat·ed (ser'ā tid) *adj.* toothed; notched. Also, **ser'rate** (ser'it).

se'rum (sēr'əm) *n.*, *pl.* **serums, sera** (sēr'ə). **1.** pale-yellow liquid in blood. **2.** such liquid from animal immune to certain disease.

serv'ant (sûr'vənt) *n.* person employed at domestic service.

serve (sûrv) *v.*, **served, serving. 1.** act as servant. **2.** help. **3.** do official duty. **4.** suffice. **5.** undergo (imprisonment, etc.). **6.** hand out.

serv'ice (sûr'vis) *n.*, *v.*, **-iced, -icing.** —*n.* **1.** helpful activity. **2.** domestic employment. **3.** armed forces. **4.** act of public worship. **5.** set of dishes, etc. —*v.* **6.** keep in repair.

serv'ice·a·ble, *adj.* usable.

ser'vile (sûr'vil, -vīl) *adj.* slavishly submissive or obsequious. —**ser·vil'i·ty** (-vil'ə tē) *n.*

ser'vi·tor (sûr'vi tər) *n.* servant.

ser'vi·tude' (-tōōd', -tyōōd') *n.* bondage.

ses'a·me (ses'ə mē) *n.* small edible seed of tropical plant.

ses'sion (sesh'ən) *n.* **1.** sitting, as of court or class.

set (set) *v.*, **set, setting,** *n.*, *adj.* —*v.* **1.** put or place. **2.** put (broken bone) in position. **3.** arrange (printing type). **4.** pass below horizon. **5.** become firm. —*n.* **6.** group; complete collection. **7.** radio or television receiver. **8.** represented setting of action in drama. —*adj.* **9.** prearranged. **10.** fixed. **11.** resolved.

set'back', *n.* return to worse condition.

set·tee' (se tē') *n.* small sofa.

set'ter (set'ər) *n.* kind of hunting dog.

set'ting, *n.* **1.** surroundings. **2.** music for certain words.

set'tle (set'l) *v.*, **-tled, -tling. 1.** agree. **2.** pay. **3.** take up residence. **4.** colonize. **5.** quiet. **6.** come to rest. **7.** deposit dregs. —**set'tle·ment,** *n.* —**set'tler,** *n.*

set'-to' (-tōō') *n.*, *pl.* **-tos.** brief, sharp fight.

set·up', *n.* *Informal.* situation in detail.

sev'en (sev'ən) *n.*, *adj.* six plus one. —**sev'enth,** *adj.*, *n.*

sev·en·teen/, n., adj. sixteen plus one. —**sev/en·teenth/**, adj., n.

seventh heaven, bliss.

sev·en·ty/, n., adj. ten times seven. —**sev/en·ti/eth**, adj., n.

sev/er (sev'ər) v. separate; break off. —**sev/er·ance,** n.

sev/er·al (sev'ər al) adj. **1.** some, but not many. **2.** respective. **3.** various. —n. **4.** some.

se·vere/ (sə vēr') adj., -verer, -verest. **1.** harsh. **2.** serious. **3.** plain. **4.** violent or hard. —**se·vere/ly,** adv. —**se·ver/i·ty** (-ver'i tē) n.

sew (sō) v., **sewed, sewed** or **sewn, sewing.** join or make with thread and needle. —**sew/er,** n.

sew/age (sōō'ij) n. wastes carried by sewers.

sew/er (sōō'ər) n. conduit for waste water, refuse, etc.

sex (seks) n. **1.** character of being male or female. **2.** sexual intercourse. —**sex/u·al** (sek'shōō al) adj. —**sex/u·al·i·ty,** n.

sex/a·ge·nar/i·an (sek'sə jə när'ē-ən) n. person 60 to 69 years old.

sex chromosome, chromosome that determines individual's sex.

sex/ism, n. bias because of sex, esp. against women. —**sex/ist,** n., adj.

sex/tant (sek'stənt) n. astronomical instrument for finding position.

sex·tet/ (seks tet') n. group of six. Also, **sex·tette/.**

sex/ton (sek'stən) n. church caretaker.

sexual harassment, unwelcome sexual advances, esp. by a superior.

sexual intercourse, genital contact between individuals, esp. penetration of penis into vagina.

sexually transmitted disease, disease transmitted by sexual contact.

sex/y, adj., -ier, -iest. sexually interesting or exciting; erotic.

Sgt., Sergeant.

shab/by (shab'ē) adj., -bier, -biest. **1.** worn; wearing worn clothes. **2.** mean. —**shab/bi·ly,** adv.

shack (shak) n. rough cabin.

shack/le (shak'əl) n., v., -led, -ling. —n. **1.** iron bond for wrist, ankle, etc. —v. **2.** restrain.

shad (shad) n. kind of herring.

shade (shād) n., v., **shaded, shading.** —n. **1.** slightly dark, cool place. **2.** ghost. **3.** degree of color. **4.** slight amount. —v. **5.** protect from light.

shad/ow (shad'ō) n. **1.** dark image made by body intercepting light. **2.** shade. **3.** trace. —v. **4.** shade. **5.** follow secretly. —**shad/ow·y,** adj.

shad/ow·box/, v. go through mo-

tions of boxing without an opponent, as in training.

shad/y, adj., -ier, -iest. **1.** in shade. **2.** arousing suspicion.

shaft (shaft) n. **1.** long slender rod. **2.** beam. **3.** revolving bar in engine. **4.** vertical space.

shag (shag) n. **1.** matted wool, hair, etc. **2.** napped cloth.

shah (shä) n. (formerly) ruler of Persia (now Iran).

shake (shāk) v., **shook** (shŏŏk), **shaken, shaking,** n. —v. **1.** move with quick irregular motions. **2.** tremble. **3.** agitate. —n. **4.** act of shaking. **5.** tremor. —**shak/er,** n.

shake/down/, n. **1.** extortion, as by blackmail. **2.** thorough search.

shake/up/, n. Informal. organizational reform.

shak/y, adj., -ier, -iest. **1.** not firm; insecure. **2.** affected by fright.

shale (shāl) n. kind of layered rock.

shall (shal; unstressed shəl) v. **1.** am (is, are) going to. **2.** am (is, are) obliged or commanded to.

shal/lot (shal'ət) n. small onionlike plant.

shal·low (shal'ō) adj. not deep.

sham (sham) n. adj. v., **shammed, shamming.** —n. **1.** pretense or imitation. —adj. **2.** pretended. —v. **3.** pretend.

sham/ble, v., -bled, -bling, n. —v. **1.** walk awkwardly. —n. **2.** shambling gait. **3.** (pl.) scene of confusion.

shame (shām) n., v., **shamed, shaming.** —n. **1.** distress and guilt over wrong or foolish act. **2.** disgrace. —v. **3.** cause to feel shame.

shame/faced/ (-fāst') adj. bashful. **2.** showing shame.

sham·poo/ (sham pōō') v. **1.** wash (hair, rugs, or upholstery). —n. **2.** act of shampooing. **3.** soap, etc., for shampooing.

sham/rock (sham'rok) n. plant with three-part leaf.

shang·hai (shang'hī) v., -haied, -haiing. (formerly) abduct to serve as sailor.

shank (shangk) n. part of leg between knee and ankle.

shan/tung (shan'tung') n. silk.

shan/ty (shan'tē) n., pl. -ties. rough hut.

shape (shāp) n., v., **shaped, shaping.** —n. **1.** form. **2.** condition. —v. **3.** give form to; take form. **4.** adapt. —**shape/less,** adj.

shape/ly, adj., -ier, -iest. handsome in shape. —**shape/li·ness,** n.

share (shâr) n., v., **shared, sharing.** —n. **1.** due individual portion. **2.** portion of corporate stock. —v. **3.**

distribute. **4.** use, enjoy, etc., jointly. —**share′hold′er,** n.

share′crop′per, n. tenant farmer who pays as rent part of the crop.

shark (shärk) n. marine fish, often ferocious.

sharp (shärp) adj. **1.** having thin cutting edge or fine point. **2.** abrupt. **3.** keen. **4.** shrewd. **5.** raised in musical pitch. —adv. **6.** punctually. —n. **7.** musical tone one half step above given tone. —**sharp′en,** v. —**sharp′en·er,** n. —**sharp′ly,** adv. —**sharp′ness,** n.

sharp′shoot′er, n. skilled shooter.

shat′ter (shat′ər) v. break in pieces.

shat′ter·proof′, adj. made to resist shattering.

shave (shāv) v., **shaved, shaved** or **shaven, shaving,** n. —v. **1.** remove hair with razor. **2.** cut thin slices. —n. **3.** act of shaving.

shav′ings, n.pl. thin slices of wood.

shawl (shôl) n. long covering for head and shoulders.

she (shē) pron. **1.** female last mentioned. —n. **2.** female.

sheaf (shēf) n., pl. **sheaves.** bundle.

shear (shēr) v., **sheared, sheared** or **shorn, shearing.** clip, as wool.

shears, n.pl. large scissors.

sheath (shēth) n. **1.** case for sword blade. **2.** any similar covering.

sheathe (shēth) v., **sheathed, sheathing.** put into or enclose in sheath.

she·bang′ (shə bang′) n. Informal. organization or contrivance.

shed (shed) v., **shed, shedding,** n. —v. **1.** pour forth. **2.** cast (light). **3.** throw off. —n. **4.** simple enclosed shelter.

sheen (shēn) n. brightness.

sheep (shēp) n., pl. **sheep.** mammal valued for wool and meat.

sheep dog, dog trained to herd sheep.

sheep′fold′, n. enclosure for sheep.

sheep′ish, adj. embarrassed or ashamed.

sheer (shēr) adj. **1.** very thin. **2.** complete. **3.** steep. —v., n. **4.** swerve.

sheet (shēt) n. **1.** large piece of cloth used as bedding. **2.** broad thin layer or piece.

sheik (shēk) n. (Arab) chief.

shek′el (shek′əl) n. ancient Hebrew and modern Israeli monetary unit.

shelf (shelf) n., pl. **shelves** (shelvz). **1.** horizontal slab on wall, etc., for holding objects. **2.** ledge.

shelf life, period during which commodity remains fit for use.

shell (shel) n. **1.** hard outer covering. **2.** shotgun cartridge. **3.** explosive missile from cannon. **4.** light racing boat. —v. **5.** remove shell from. **6.** take from shell. **7.** bombard with shells.

shel·lac′ (shə lak′) n., v., **-lacked, -lacking.** —n. **1.** substance used in varnish. **2.** varnish. —v. **3.** coat with shellac.

shell′fish′, n. aquatic animal having shell.

shell shock, combat fatigue.

shel′ter (shel′tər) n. **1.** place of protection. —v. **2.** protect.

shelve (shelv) v., **shelved, shelving. 1.** put on shelf. **2.** lay aside. **3.** furnish with shelves. **4.** slope.

she·nan·i·gans (shə nan′i ganz) n.pl. Informal. mischief.

shep′herd (shep′ərd) n. **1.** person who tends sheep. —v. **2.** guide. —**shep′herd·ess,** n.

sher′bet (shûr′bit) n. frozen fruit-flavored dessert.

sher′iff (sher′if) n. county law-enforcement officer.

sher′ry (sher′ē) n., pl. **-ries.** fortified wine served as cocktail.

shib·bo·leth (shib′ə lith) n. peculiarity of pronunciation or usage that distinguishes a group.

shield (shēld) n. **1.** plate of armor carried on arm. —v. **2.** protect.

shift (shift) v. **1.** move about. **2.** change positions. —n. **3.** act of shifting. **4.** period of work.

shift′less, adj. resourceless or lazy.

shift′y, adj., **-ier, -iest.** devious.

shill (shil) n. person who poses as a customer to lure others.

shil·le·lagh (shə lā′lē, -lə) n. rough Irish walking stick or cudgel.

shil′ling (shil′ing) n. former British coin, 20th part of pound.

shil′ly-shal′ly (shil′ē shal′ē) v., **-lied, -lying.** hesitate or waste time.

shim′mer (shim′ər) v. **1.** glow faintly; flicker. —n. **2.** faint glow.

shin (shin) n. front of leg from knee to ankle.

shin′bone′, n. tibia.

shin·dig′ (shin′dig′) n. Informal. elaborate and usu. large party.

shine (shīn) v., **shone** (shōn) or (for 4) **shined, shining,** n. —v. **1.** give forth light. **2.** sparkle. **3.** excel. **4.** polish. —n. **5.** radiance. **6.** polish. —**shin′y,** adj.

shin′er, n. Informal. black eye.

shin′gle (shing′gəl) n., v., **-gled, -gling.** —n. **1.** thin slab used in overlapping rows as covering. **2.** (pl.) viral skin disease marked by blisters. —v. **3.** cover with shingles.

shin splints, painful condition of

shins associated with strenuous activity.

Shin/to (shin′tō) *n.* native religion of Japan.

ship (ship) *n., v.,* **shipped, shipping.** —*n.* **1.** vessel for use on water. —*v.* **2.** send as freight. **3.** engage to serve on ship. **4.** send away. —**ship/board/,** *n.* —**ship/mate/,** *n.* —**ship/ment,** *n.*

-ship, suffix meaning: **1.** state or quality, as *friendship.* **2.** position or rank, as *lordship.* **3.** skill or art, as *horsemanship.*

ship/shape/, *adj., adv.* in good order.

ship/wreck/, *n.* destruction of ship.

ship/wright/, *n.* carpenter for ship repair or construction.

ship/yard/, *n.* place where ships are built or repaired.

shire (shīr) *n.* county in Great Britain.

shirk (shûrk) *v.* evade (obligation).

shirr (shûr) *v.* **1.** gather (cloth) on parallel threads. **2.** bake (eggs).

shirt (shûrt) *n.* garment for upper body.

shirt/tail/, *n.* part of shirt below waistline.

shirt/waist/, *n.* tailored blouse.

shish/ ke-bab/ (shish′ kə bob′) cubes of meat broiled on a skewer.

shiv/er (shiv′ər) *v.* **1.** tremble as with cold. **2.** splinter. —*n.* **3.** quiver. **4.** splinter. —**shiv/er-y,** *adj.*

shoal (shōl) *n.* **1.** shallow part of stream. **2.** large number, esp. of fish.

shock (shok) *n.* **1.** violent blow, impact, etc. **2.** anything emotionally upsetting. **3.** state of nervous collapse. **4.** effect of electric charge. **5.** bushy mass of hair, etc. —*v.* **6.** strike with force, horror, etc. **7.** subject to electric shock

shock absorber, device for damping sudden rapid motion.

shock therapy, treatment for mental disorders using electricity.

shod/dy (shod′ē) *adj.* **-dier, -diest.** of poor quality. —**shod/di-ly,** *adv.*

shoe (shōō) *n., v.,* **shod** (shod), **shoeing.** —*n.* **1.** external covering for foot. **2.** shoelike machine part. —*v.* **3.** provide with shoes.

shoe/horn/, *n.* shaped object to assist in slipping on shoe.

shoe/mak/er, *n.* person who makes or mends shoes.

shoe/string/, *n.* very small amount of money.

shoe/tree/, *n.* device placed in shoe to hold its shape.

sho/gun (shō′gən) *n.* chief military

commander of Japan from 8th to 12th centuries.

shoo (shōō) *v.,* **shooed, shooing.** drive away by shouting "shoo."

shoo/-in/, *n.* one regarded as certain to win.

shoot (shōōt) *v.* **1.** hit or kill with bullet, etc. **2.** discharge (firearm, bow, etc.). **3.** pass or send rapidly along. **4.** emit. **5.** grow; come forth. —*n.* **6.** shooting contest. **7.** young twig, etc. —**shoot/er,** *n.*

shooting star, meteor.

shop (shop) *n., v.,* **shopped, shopping.** —*n.* **1.** store. **2.** workshop. —*v.* **3.** look at or purchase goods.

shop/lift/er, *n.* person who steals from shops while posing as customer.

shop/talk/, *n.* conversation about one's work or occupation.

shore (shōr) *v.,* **shored, shoring,** *n.* —*v.* **1.** prop. —*n.* **2.** prop. **3.** land beside water. **4.** land or country.

shorn (shôrn) *v.* pp. of **shear.**

short (shôrt) *adj.* **1.** not long or tall. **2.** rudely brief. **3.** scanty. **4.** inferior. **5.** crumbly, as pastry. —*adv.* **6.** abruptly. —*n.* **7.** anything short. **8.** (*pl.*) short, loose trousers. **9.** short circuit. —**short/en,** *v.*

short/age (shôr′tij) *n.* scarcity.

short/bread/, *n.* rich butter cookie.

short/cake/, *n.* rich biscuit topped with fruit and cream.

short/change/, *v.,* **-changed, -changing. 1.** give less than the correct change to. **2.** cheat; defraud.

short circuit, *Elect.* abnormal connection between two points in circuit.

short/com/ing, *n.* defect.

short/cut/, *n.* shorter way to goal.

short/en-ing (shôrt′ning) *n.* butter or other fat used to make pastry.

short/hand/, *n.* system of swift handwriting.

short/-hand/ed, *adj.* not having enough workers.

short/-lived/ (-līvd, -livd) *adj.* lasting only a short time.

short/ly, *adv.* in a short time.

short shrift, little attention or consideration.

short/-sight/ed, *adj.* lacking foresight.

short/stop/, *n. Baseball.* player or position between second and third base.

short/-tem/pered, *adj.* irascible.

short/wave/, *n.* radio frequencies used for long-distance transmission.

Sho-sho/ne (shō shō′nē) *n., pl.* **-ne, -nes.** member of an American Indian people.

shot (shot) *n., pl.* **shots** (or for 3), **shot.** **1.** discharge of firearm, bow, etc. **2.** range of fire. **3.** *(often pl.)* lead pellets. **4.** act or instance of shooting. **5.** person who shoots. **6.** heavy metal ball.

shot'gun', *n.* kind of smoothbore gun.

shot put, competition in which heavy metal ball is thrown for distance. —**shot'-put'ter,** *n.*

should (shŏŏd) *v.* pt. of **shall.**

shoul'der (shōl'dar) *n.* **1.** part of body from neck to upper joint of arm or foreleg. —*v.* **2.** push as with shoulder. **3.** take up as burden.

shout (shout) *v.* **1.** call or speak loudly. **2.** loud cry.

shove (shuv) *v.*, **shoved, shoving,** *n.* —*v.* **1.** push hard. **2.** hard push.

shov'el, *n., v.*, **-eled, -eling.** —*n.* **1.** implement with broad scoop and handle. —*v.* **2.** dig or clear.

show (shō) *v.*, **showed, shown** or **showed, showing.** —*v.* **1.** display. **2.** guide. **3.** explain. **4.** prove. **5.** be visible. —*n.* **6.** exhibition. **7.** acted entertainment. **8.** appearance.

show'case', *n., v.*, **-cased, -casing.** —*n.* **1.** setting for displaying something. —*v.* **2.** exhibit to best advantage.

show'down', *n.* decisive confrontation.

show'er (shou'ar) *n.* **1.** short fall of rain. **2.** any similar fall. **3.** bath in which water falls from above. —*v.* **4.** rain briefly. **5.** give liberally.

show'-off' (shō'-) *n.* person who seeks attention.

show'piece', *n.* something worthy of being exhibited.

show'place', *n.* place notable for its beauty or historical interest.

show'y, *adj.*, **-ier, -iest.** conspicuous; ostentatious.

shrap'nel (shrap'nl) *n.* shell filled with missiles.

shred (shred) *n., v.*, **shredded** or **shred, shredding.** —*n.* **1.** torn piece or strip. **2.** bit. —*v.* **3.** reduce to shreds.

shrew (shrōō) *n.* **1.** quarrelsome woman. **2.** small mouselike mammal. —**shrew'ish,** *adj.*

shrewd (shrōōd) *adj.* astute.

shriek (shrēk) *n.* **1.** loud shrill cry. —*v.* **2.** utter shrieks.

shrill (shril) *adj.* **1.** high-pitched; piercing. —*v.* **2.** cry shrilly.

shrimp (shrimp) *n.* small long-tailed edible shellfish.

shrine (shrīn) *n.* place for sacred relics.

shrink (shringk) *v.*, **shrank** (shrangk) or **shrunk** (shrungk), **shrunk** or **shrunken, shrinking.** **1.** draw back. **2.** become smaller.

shrink'age (shring'kij) *n.* **1.** act of shrinking. **2.** amount of shrinking.

shrinking violet, shy person.

shrink'-wrap', *v.*, **-wrapped, -wrapping,** *n.* **1.** seal in plastic film that when exposed to heat shrinks tightly around object. —*n.* **2.** plastic used to shrink-wrap.

shrive (shrīv) *v.*, **shrove** (shrōv) or **shrived, shriven** (shriv'an) or **shrived, shriving.** **1.** impose penance on. **2.** grant absolution to.

shriv'el (shriv'al) *v.*, **-eled, -eling.** wrinkle in drying.

shroud (shroud) *n.* **1.** burial gown or cloth. —*v.* **2.** hide from view.

shrub (shrub) *n.* woody perennial plant. —**shrub'ber•y,** *n.*

shrug (shrug) *v.*, **shrugged, shrugging,** *n.* **1.** move shoulders to show ignorance, indifference, etc. —*n.* **2.** this movement.

shtick (shtik) *n. Slang.* **1.** showbusiness routine. **2.** special interest, talent, etc. Also, **shtik.**

shuck (shuk) *n.* **1.** husk. **2.** shell. —*v.* **3.** remove shucks from.

shud'der (shud'ar) *v.* **1.** tremble, as from horror. —*n.* **2.** this movement.

shuf'fle (shuf'al) *v.*, **-fled, -fling.** **1.** drag feet in walking. **2.** mix (playing cards). **3.** shift. —*n.* **4.** shuffling gait. **5.** act of shuffling cards.

shuf'fle•board', *n.* game played on marked floor surface.

shun (shun) *v.*, **shunned, shunning.** avoid.

shunt (shunt) *v.* divert; sidetrack.

shut (shut) *v.*, **shut, shutting,** *adj.* —*v.* **1.** close. **2.** confine. **3.** exclude. —*adj.* **4.** closed.

shut'out', *n.* game in which one side does not score.

shut'ter, *n.* **1.** cover for window. **2.** device for opening and closing camera lens.

shut'tle (shut'l) *v.*, **-tled, -tling.** —*n.* **1.** device for moving thread back and forth in weaving. **2.** bus, plane, etc., moving between two destinations. —*v.* **3.** move quickly back and forth.

shut'tle•cock', *n.* feathered object hit back and forth in badminton.

shy (shī) *adj.*, **shyer** or **shier, shyest** or **shiest,** *v.*, **shied, shying,** *n., pl.* **shies.** —*adj.* **1.** bashful. **2.** wary. **3.** short. —*v.* **4.** start aside, as in fear. **5.** throw suddenly. —*n.* **6.** shying movement. **7.** sudden throw.

shy′ster (shī′stər) *n. Informal.* unscrupulous lawyer.

Si′a·mese′ twins (sī′ə mēz′, -mēs′) twins joined together by body part.

sib′i·lant (sib′ə lant) *adj.* 1. hissing. —*n.* 2. hissing sound.

sib′ling (sib′ling) *n.* brother or sister.

sib′yl (sib′əl) *n.* female prophet.

sic (sik) *v.*, **sicked, sicking.** —*v.* 1. urge to attack. —*adv.* 2. *Latin.* so (it reads).

sick (sik) *adj.* 1. ill; not well. 2. of sickness. 3. nauseated. —*n.pl.* 4. sick people. —**sick′en,** *v.*

sick′le (sik′əl) *n.* reaping implement with curved blade.

sick′ly, *adj.*, **-lier, -liest,** *adv.* 1. ailing. 2. faint; weak.

side (sīd) *n.*, *adj.*, *v.*, **sided, siding.** —*n.* 1. edge. 2. surface. 3. part other than front, back, top, or bottom. 4. aspect. 5. region. 6. faction. —*adj.* 7. at, from, or toward side. 8. subordinate. —*v.* 9. align oneself.

side′bar′, *n.* short news feature highlighting longer story.

side′board′, *n.* dining-room cupboard.

side′burns′, *n.pl.* short whiskers in front of ears.

side effect, *n.* often adverse secondary effect.

side′kick′, *n.* 1. close friend. 2. confederate or assistant.

side′light′, *n.* item of incidental information.

side′line, *n.*, *v.*, **-lined, -lining.** —*n.* 1. business or activity in addition to one's primary business. 2. additional line of goods. 3. line defining the side of an athletic field. —*v.* 4. remove from action.

side′long, *adj.*, *adv.* to or toward the side.

side′sad′dle, *adv.* with both legs on one side of a saddle.

side′show′, *n.* subordinate event or spectacle.

side′split′ting, *adj.* very funny.

side′step′, *v.*, **-stepped, -stepping.** avoid, as by stepping aside.

side′swipe′, *v.*, **-swiped, -swiping.** strike along side.

side′track′, *v.* divert.

side′walk′, *n.* paved walk along street.

side′ward (-ward) *adj.* toward one side. —**side′ward, side′wards,** *adv.*

side′ways′, *adj.*, *adv.* 1. with side foremost. 2. toward or from a side. Also, **side′wise′.**

sid′ing, *n.* short railroad track for halted cars.

si′dle (sīd′l) *v.*, **-dled, -dling.** move sideways or furtively.

SIDS (sidz) *n.* sudden infant death syndrome.

siege (sēj) *n.* surrounding of place to force surrender.

si·en′na (sē en′ə) *n.* yellowish- or reddish-brown pigment.

si·er′ra (sē er′ə) *n.* jagged chain of hills or mountains.

si·es′ta (sē es′tə) *n.* midday nap or rest.

sieve (siv) *n.*, *v.*, **sieved, sieving.** —*n.* 1. meshed implement for separating coarse and fine loose matter. —*v.* 2. sift.

sift (sift) *v.* separate with sieve.

sigh (sī) *v.* 1. exhale audibly in grief, weariness, etc. 2. yearn. —*n.* 3. act or sound of sighing.

sight (sīt) *n.* 1. power of seeing. 2. glimpse; view. 3. range of vision. 4. device for guiding aim. 5. interesting place. —*v.* 6. get sight of. 7. aim by sights. —**sight′less,** *adj.*

sight′ed, *adj.* not blind.

sight′read′ (rēd) *v.*, **-read** (-red′), **-reading.** perform without previous study.

sight′see′ing, *n.* visiting new places and things of interest. —**sight′se′er,** *n.* —**sight′see′,** *v.*

sign (sīn) *n.* 1. indication. 2. conventional mark, figure, etc. 3. advertising board. 4. trace. 5. omen. —*v.* 6. put signature to.

sig′nal (sig′nl) *n.*, *adj.*, *v.*, **-naled, -naling.** —*n.* 1. symbolic communication. —*adj.* 2. serving as signal. 3. notable. —*v.* 4. communicate by symbols. —**sig′nal·er,** *n.*

sig′nal·ly, *adv.* notably.

sig′na·to′ry (sig′nə tôr′ē) *n.*, *pl.* **-ries.** signer.

sig′na·ture (-nə chər) *n.* 1. person's name in own handwriting. 2. *Music.* sign indicating key or time of piece.

sig′net (sig′nit) *n.* small seal.

sig·nif′i·cance (sig nif′i kəns) *n.* 1. importance. 2. meaning. —**sig·nif′i·cant,** *adj.*

significant other, spouse or cohabiting lover.

sig′ni·fy′ (sig′nə fī′) *v.*, **-fied, -fying.** 1. make known. 2. mean. —**sig′ni·fi·ca′tion,** *n.*

Sikh (sēk) *n.* member of religion of India that rejects Hindu caste system. —**Sikh′ism,** *n.*

si′lage (sī′lij) *n.* fodder preserved in silo.

si′lence (sī′ləns) *n.*, *v.*, **-lenced, -lencing.** —*n.* 1. absence of sound. 2. muteness. —*v.* 3. bring to silence. —**si′lent,** *adj.*

si′lenc·er, n. device for deadening report of a firearm.

sil′hou·ette′ (sil′ōō et′), n., v., **-etted, -etting.** —n. **1.** filled-in outline. —v. **2.** show in silhouette.

sil′i·ca (sil′i ka) n. silicon dioxide, appearing as quartz, sand, flint, etc.

sil′i·cate (-kit, -kāt′) n. mineral consisting of silicon and oxygen with a metal.

sil′i·con (-kan, -kon′) n. abundant nonmetallic element.

sil′i·cone′ (-kōn′) n. polymer with silicon and oxygen atoms, used in adhesives, lubricants, etc.

sil′i·co·sis (-kō′sis) n. lung disease caused by inhaling silica.

silk (silk) n. **1.** fine soft fiber produced by silkworms. **2.** thread or cloth made of it. —adj. **3.** Also, **silk′en, silk/y.** of silk.

silk′worm′, n. caterpillar that spins silk to make its cocoon.

sill (sil) n. horizontal piece beneath window or door.

sil′ly (sil′ē) adj., **-lier, -liest. 1.** stupid. **2.** absurd. —**sil′li·ness,** n.

si′lo (sī′lō) n., pl. **-los.** airtight structure to hold green fodder.

silt (silt) n. **1.** earth, etc., carried and deposited by a stream. —v. **2.** fill with silt.

sil′ver (sil′var) n. **1.** valuable white metallic element. **2.** coins, utensils, etc., of silver. **3.** whitish gray color. —adj. **4.** of or plated with silver. **5.** indicating 25th anniversary.

sil′ver·fish′, n. wingless, silvery-gray insect that damages books, etc.

silver lining, prospect of hope or comfort.

silver nitrate, poisonous powder used in photography.

sil′ver-tongued′, adj. eloquent.

sil′ver·ware′, n. eating and serving utensils of silver or other metal.

sim′i·an (sim′ē an) n. **1.** ape or monkey. —adj. **2.** of apes or monkeys.

sim′i·lar (sim′a lar) adj. with general likeness. —**sim′i·lar′i·ty** (-lar′i tē) n. —**sim′i·lar·ly,** adv.

sim′i·le′ (-a lē′) n. phrase comparing two things using "like" or "as."

si·mil′i·tude′ (si mil′i tōōd′, -tyōōd′) n. likeness.

sim′mer (sim′ar) v. remain or keep near boiling.

si′mo·ny (sī′ma nē) n. buying or selling of ecclesiastical preferments.

sim·pa′ti·co′ (sim pä′ti kō′) adj. like-minded.

sim′per (sim′par) v. **1.** smile affectedly. —n. **2.** affected smile.

sim′ple (sim′pal) adj., **-pler, -plest.**

1. easy to grasp, use, etc. **2.** not complex. **3.** mentally weak. —**sim·plic′i·ty** (-plis′i tē) n.

simple interest, interest payable only on the principle.

sim′ple-mind′ed, adj. **1.** unsophisticated. **2.** mentally deficient.

sim′ple·ton (-tan) n. fool.

sim′pli·fy′ (-pla fī′) v., **-fied, -fying.** make simpler.

sim·plis′tic (-plis′tik) adj. foolishly or naïvely simple.

sim′u·late′ (sim′ya lāt′) v., **-lated, -lating.** imitate or feign.

si′mul·cast′ (sī′mal kast′), n., **-cast, -casted, -casting.** —n. **1.** program broadcast simultaneously on radio and television. —v. **2.** broadcast a simulcast.

si·mul·ta′ne·ous (-tā′nē as) adj. occurring at the same time.

sin (sin) n., v., **sinned, sinning.** —n. **1.** offense, esp. against divine law. —v. **2.** commit sin. —**sin′ner,** n. —**sin′ful,** adj. —**sin′ful·ly,** adv.

since (sins) adv. **1.** from then till now. **2.** subsequently. —conj. **3.** from time when. **4.** because.

sin·cere′ (sin sēr′) adj., **-cerer, -cerest.** honest; genuine. —**sin·cere′ly,** adv. —**sin·cer′i·ty** (-ser′i tē) n.

si′ne·cure′ (sī′ni kyoor′) n. job without real responsibilities.

si′ne di′e (sī′nē dī′ē), without fixing a day for future action.

si′ne qua non′ (sinä kwä nōn′) indispensable condition or element.

sin′ew (sin′yōō) n. **1.** tendon. **2.** strength. —**sin′ew·y,** adj.

sing (sing) v., **sang** (sang) or **sung** (sung), **sung, singing. 1.** utter words to music. **2.** make musical sounds. **3.** acclaim. —**sing′er,** n.

singe (sinj) v., **singed, singeing,** n. scorch.

sin′gle (sing′gal) adj., v., **-gled, -gling,** n. —adj. **1.** one only. **2.** unmarried. —v. **3.** select. —n. **4.** single thing. **5.** unmarried person.

single file, line of persons or things one behind the other.

sin′gle-hand′ed, adj. **1.** accomplished by one person. **2.** by one's own effort; unaided. —adv. **3.** by one person alone.

sin′gle-mind′ed, adj. having or showing a single aim or purpose.

sin′gly, adv. **1.** separately. **2.** one at a time. **3.** single-handed.

sing′song′, adj. monotonous in rhythm.

sin′gu·lar (sing′gya lar) adj. **1.** extraordinary. **2.** strange. **3.** denoting one person or thing. —n. **4.** singular number or form.

sin·is·ter (sin′ə stər) *adj.* threatening evil.

sink (singk) *v.*, **sank** (sangk) or **sunk** (sungk), **sunk** or **sunken**, **sinking**, *n.* —*v.* **1.** descend or drop. **2.** deteriorate gradually. **3.** submerge. **4.** dig (a hole, etc.). **5.** bury (pipe, etc.). —*n.* **6.** basin connected with drain.

sink′hole′, *n.* hole in rock through which surface water drains into underground passage.

sin′u·ous (sin′yōō əs) *adj.* winding.

si′nus (sī′nəs) *n.* cavity or passage in the skull.

sip (sip) *v.*, **sipped, sipping**, *n.* —*v.* **1.** drink little at a time. —*n.* **2.** act of sipping. **3.** amount taken in sip.

si′phon (sī′fən) *n.* **1.** tube for drawing liquids by gravity and suction to another container. —*v.* **2.** move by siphon.

sir (sûr) *n.* **1.** formal term of address to man. **2.** title of knight or baronet.

sire (sī°r) *n.*, *v.*, **sired, siring.** —*n.* **1.** male parent. —*v.* **2.** beget.

si′ren (sī′rən) *n.* **1.** mythical, alluring sea nymph. **2.** noise-making device used on emergency vehicles.

sir′loin (sûr′loin) *n.* cut of beef from the loin.

si′sal (sī′səl, sis′əl) *n.* fiber used in ropes.

sis′sy (sis′ē) *n.*, *pl.* **-sies.** effeminate or timid boy.

sis′ter (sis′tər) *n.* **1.** daughter of one's parents. **2.** nun. —**sis′ter·hood′**, *n.* —**sis′ter·ly**, *adj.*

sis′ter-in-law′, *n.*, *pl.* **sisters-in-law. 1.** sister of one's spouse. **2.** wife of one's brother.

sit (sit) *v.*, **sat** (sat), **sitting**, *n.* **1.** rest on buttocks. **2.** be situated. **3.** pose. **4.** be in session. **5.** seat.

sit·tar′ (si tär′) *n.* Indian lute.

sit′-down′, *n.* strike in which workers occupy their place of employment and refuse to work.

site (sīt) *n.* position; location.

sit′-in′, *n.* protest by demonstrators who occupy premises.

sitting duck, easy target.

sit′u·ate′ (sich′ōō āt′) *v.*, **-ated, -ating.** locate.

sit′u·a′tion (-ā′shən) *n.* **1.** location. **2.** condition. **3.** job.

six (siks) *n.*, *adj.* five plus one. —**sixth**, *adj.*, *n.*

six′teen′, *n.*, *adj.* ten plus six. —**six′teenth′**, *adj.*, *n.*

sixth sense, power of intuition.

six′ty, *n.*, *adj.* ten times six. —**six′ti·eth**, *adj.*, *n.*

siz′a·ble (sī′zə bəl) *adj.* fairly large. Also, **size′a·ble.**

size (sīz) *n.*, *v.*, **sized, sizing.** —*n.* **1.** dimensions or extent. **2.** great magnitude. **3.** Also, **sizing.** coating for paper, cloth, etc. —*v.* **4.** sort according to size. **5.** treat with sizing.

siz′zle (siz′əl) *v.*, **-zled, -zling**, *n.* —*v.* **1.** make hissing sound, as in frying. —*n.* **2.** sizzling sound.

skate (skāt) *n.*, *pl.* **skates** (or (for 3) **skate**, *v.*, **skated, skating.** —*n.* **1.** steel runner fitted to shoe for gliding on ice. **2.** roller skate. **3.** flat-bodied marine fish; ray. —*v.* **4.** glide on skates. —**skat′er**, *n.*

skate′board′, *n.* oblong board on roller-skate wheels.

ske·dad′dle (ski dad′l) *v.*, **-dled, -dling.** *Informal.* run away.

skein (skān) *n.* coil of yarn or thread.

skel′e·ton (skel′ə tən) *n.* bony framework of human or animal. —**skel′e·tal**, *adj.*

skeleton key, key that opens various simple locks.

skep′tic (skep′tik) *n.* person who doubts or questions. —**skep′ti·cal**, *adj.* —**skep′ti·cism** (-siz′əm) *n.*

sketch (skech) *n.* **1.** simple hasty drawing. **2.** rough plan. —*v.* **3.** make sketch of.

sketch′y, *adj.*, **-ier, -iest.** vague; approximate. —**sketch′i·ly**, *adv.*

skew (skyōō) *v.* turn aside; slant.

skew′er, *n.* **1.** pin for holding meat, etc., while cooking. —*v.* **2.** fasten with skewer.

ski (skē) *n.* **1.** slender board fastened to shoe for traveling over snow. —*v.* **2.** travel by skis.

skid (skid) *n.*, *v.*, **skidded, skidding.** —*n.* **1.** surface on which to support or slide heavy object. **2.** act of skidding. —*v.* **3.** slide on skids. **4.** slip.

skid row (rō) run-down urban area frequented by vagrants.

skiff (skif) *n.* small boat.

skill (skil) *n.* expertness; dexterity. —**skilled**, *adj.* —**skill′ful**, *adj.*

skil′let (skil′it) *n.* frying pan.

skim (skim) *v.*, **skimmed, skimming. 1.** remove from surface of liquid. **2.** move lightly on surface.

skim milk, milk from which cream has been removed.

skimp (skimp) *v.* scrimp.

skimp′y, *adj.*, **-ier, -iest.** scant.

skin (skin) *n.*, *v.*, **skinned, skinning.** —*n.* **1.** outer covering, as of body. —*v.* **2.** remove skin.

skin diving, underwater swimming with flippers and face mask, sometimes with scuba gear.

skin′flint′, *n.* stingy person.

skin′ny, *adj.,* **-nier, -niest.** very thin.

skin′ny-dip′, *v.,* **-dipped, -dipping,** *n. Informal.* swim in the nude.

skip (skip) *v.,* **skipped, skipping,** *n.* —*v.* **1.** spring; leap. **2.** omit; disregard. —*v.* **3.** light jump.

skip′per (skip′ər) *n.* **1.** master of ship. —*v.* **2.** act as skipper of.

skir′mish (skûr′mish) *n.* **1.** brief fight between small forces. —*v.* **2.** engage in skirmish.

skirt (skûrt) *n.* **1.** part of gown, etc., below waist. **2.** woman's garment extending down from waist. **3.** (*pl.*) outskirts. —*v.* **4.** pass around edge of. **5.** border.

skit (skit) *n.* short comedy.

skit′tish, *adj.* apt to shy; restless.

skiv′vy (skiv′ē) *n., pl.* **-vies. 1.** man's cotton T-shirt. **2.** (*pl.*) men's underwear consisting of T-shirt and shorts.

skul·dug′ger·y (skul dug′ə rē) *n., pl.* **-geries.** trickery.

skulk (skulk) *v.* sneak about.

skull (skul) *n.* bony framework around brain.

skull′cap′, *n.* brimless, close-fitting cap.

skunk (skungk) *n.* **1.** small, striped, fur-bearing mammal that sprays acrid fluid to defend itself. **2.** contemptible person.

sky (skī) *n., pl.* **skies.** region well above earth.

sky′cap′, *n.* airport porter.

sky′dive′, *v.,* **-dived, -diving.** make parachute jump with longest free fall possible. —**sky′div′er,** *n.*

sky′jack′, *v. Informal.* seize (aircraft) while in flight.

sky′light′ (-līt′) *n.* window in roof, ceiling, etc.

sky′line′, *n.* **1.** outline against sky. **2.** apparent horizon.

sky′rock′et, *n.* firework that rises into air before exploding.

sky′scrap′er, *n.* building with many stories.

sky′writ′ing, *n.* writing in sky formed by smoke from airplane.

slab (slab) *n.* broad flat piece of material.

slack (slak) *adj.* **1.** loose. **2.** inactive. —*adv.* **3.** slackly. —*n.* **4.** slack part. **5.** inactive period. —*v.* **6.** slacken. —**slack′ly,** *adv.*

slack′en, *v.* **1.** make or become slack. **2.** weaken.

slack′er, *n.* person who evades work.

slacks, *n.pl.* loose trousers.

slag (slag) *n.* refuse matter from smelting metal from ore.

slake (slāk) *v.,* **slaked, slaking.** allay (thirst, etc.).

sla′lom (slä′ləm) *n.* downhill ski race over winding course, around numerous barriers.

slam (slam) *v.,* **slammed, slamming,** *n.* —*v.* **1.** shut noisily. —*n.* **2.** this sound.

slam′mer, *n. Slang.* prison.

slan′der (slan′dər) *n.* **1.** false, defamatory spoken statement. —*v.* **2.** utter slander against.

slang (slang) *n.* informal, colorful language. —**slang′y,** *adj.*

slant (slant) *v.* **1.** slope. —*n.* **2.** slope. **3.** opinion.

slap (slap) *n., v.,* **slapped, slapping,** *n.* —*v.* **1.** strike, esp. with open hand. —*n.* **2.** such blow.

slap′dash′, *adj.* hasty and careless.

slap′hap′py, *adj.,* **-pier, -piest. 1.** befuddled. **2.** agreeably foolish.

slap′stick′, *n.* boisterous comedy with broad farce and horseplay.

slash (slash) *v.* **1.** cut, esp. violently and at random. —*n.* **2.** such cut.

slat (slat) *n., v.,* **slatted, slatting. 1.** thin narrow strip. —*v.* **2.** furnish with slats.

slate (slāt) *n., v.,* **slated, slating.** —*n.* **1.** kind of layered rock. **2.** dark bluish gray. **3.** list of nominees. —*v.* **4.** put in line for appointment.

slat′tern (slat′ərn) *n.* untidy woman. —**slat′tern·ly,** *adj.*

slaugh′ter (slô′tər) *n.* **1.** killing of animals, esp. for food. **2.** brutal killing of people, esp. in great numbers. —*v.* **3.** kill for food. **4.** massacre. —**slaugh′ter·house′,** *n.*

slave (slāv) *n., v.,* **slaved, slaving.** —*n.* **1.** person owned by another. —*v.* **2.** drudge. —**slav′er·y,** *n.*

slav′er (slav′ər) *v.* **1.** let saliva run from mouth. —*n.* **2.** saliva coming from mouth.

Slav′ic (slä′vik, slav′ik) *n.* **1.** language family that includes Russian, Polish, Czech, etc. —*adj.* **2.** of these languages and their speakers.

slav′ish (slā′vish) *adj.* **1.** without originality. **2.** servile.

slaw (slô) *n.* chopped seasoned raw cabbage.

slay (slā) *v.,* **slew** (slōō) **slain, slaying.** kill. —**slay′er,** *n.*

slea′zy (slē′zē) *adj.,* **-zier, -ziest.** shoddy or disreputable.

sled (sled) *n., v.,* **sledded, sledding.** —*n.* **1.** vehicle traveling on snow. —*v.* **2.** ride on sled.

sledge (slej) *n., v.,* **sledged, sledging.** —*n.* **1.** heavy sledlike vehicle. **2.** Also, **sledge′ham′mer.** large heavy hammer. —v. **3.** travel by sledge.

sleek (slēk) adj. **1.** smooth; glossy. —v. **2.** smooth. —**sleek'ly,** adv.

sleep (slēp) v., **slept** (slept), **sleeping,** n. —v. **1.** rest during natural suspension of consciousness. —n. **2.** state or period of sleeping. —**sleep'less,** adj. —**sleep'y,** adj.

sleep'er, n. **1.** person who sleeps. **2.** railroad car equipped for sleeping. **3.** raillike foundation support. **4.** unexpected success.

sleeping bag, warmly lined bag in which a person can sleep.

sleeping car, railroad car with sleeping accommodations.

sleet (slēt) n. hard frozen rain.

sleeve (slēv) n. part of garment covering arm. —**sleeve'less,** adj.

sleigh (slā) n. light sled.

sleight of hand (slīt) skill in conjuring or juggling.

slen'der (slen'dər) adj. **1.** small in circumference. **2.** scanty or weak.

sleuth (slōōth) n. detective.

slew (slōō) pt. of **slay.**

slice (slīs) n., v., **sliced, slicing.** —n. **1.** broad flat piece. —v. **2.** cut into slices. —**slic'er,** n.

slick (slik) adj. **1.** sleek. **2.** sly. **3.** slippery. n. **4.** oil-covered area. —v. **5.** smooth. —**slick'ness,** n.

slick'er, n. raincoat.

slide (slīd) v., **slid, sliding,** n. —v. **1.** move easily; glide. —n. **2.** act of sliding. **3.** area for sliding. **4.** landslide. **5.** glass plate used in microscope. **6.** transparent picture.

sliding scale, scale, as of prices, that varies with such conditions as the ability of individuals to pay.

slight (slīt) adj. **1.** trifling; small. **2.** slim. —v. **3.** treat as unimportant. —n. **4.** such treatment; snub.

slight'ly, adv. barely; partly.

slim (slim) adj., **slimmer, slimmest. 1.** slender. **2.** poor. —v. **3.** make or become slim. —**slim'ness,** n.

slime (slīm) n. **1.** thin sticky mud. **2.** sticky secretion. —**slim'y,** adj.

sling (sling) n., v., **slung** (slung). **slinging.** —n. **1.** straplike device for hurling stones. **2.** looped rope, bandage, etc., as support. —v. **3.** hurl. **4.** hang loosely.

sling'shot', n. Y-shaped stick with elastic strip between prongs, for shooting small missiles.

slink (slingk) v., **slunk** (slungk), **slinking.** go furtively. —**slink'y,** adj.

slip (slip) v., **slipped, slipping,** n. —v. **1.** move or go easily. **2.** slide accidentally. **3.** escape. **4.** make mistake. —n. **5.** act of slipping. **6.** mistake. **7.** undergarment.

slip cover, easily removable cover for piece of furniture.

slip'knot', n. knot that slips easily along cord.

slipped disk, abnormal protrusion of spinal disk between vertebrae.

slip'per, n. light shoe.

slip'per·y, adj. **1.** causing slipping. **2.** tending to slip.

slip'shod' (-shod') adj. careless.

slip'-up', n. mistake.

slit (slit) v., **slit, slitting,** n. —v. **1.** cut apart or in strips. —n. **2.** narrow opening.

slith'er (slith'ər) v. slide.

sliv'er (sliv'ər) n., v. splinter.

slob (slob) n. slovenly or boorish person.

slob'ber, v., n. slaver.

sloe (slō) n. small sour fruit of blackthorn.

sloe'-eyed', adj. **1.** having very dark eyes. **2.** having slanted eyes.

slog (slog) v., **slogged, slogging. 1.** plod heavily. **2.** work hard.

slo'gan (slō'gən) n. motto.

sloop (slōōp) n. kind of sailing vessel.

slop (slop) v., **slopped, slopping,** n. —v. **1.** spill liquid. —n. **2.** swill.

slope (slōp) v., **sloped, sloping,** n. —v. **1.** incline; slant. —n. **2.** amount of inclination. **3.** sloping surface.

slop'py, adj. -**pier,** -**piest. 1.** untidy. **2.** careless. —**slop'pi·ly,** adv.

slosh (slosh) v. splash.

slot (slot) n. narrow opening.

sloth (slôth) n. **1.** laziness. **2.** treeliving South American mammal. —**sloth'ful,** adj.

slot machine, gambling machine.

slouch (slouch) v. **1.** move or rest droopingly. —n. **2.** drooping posture. —**slouch'y,** adj.

slough, n. **1.** (slou) muddy area. **2.** (slōō) marshy pond or inlet. —v. **3.** (sluf) be shed. **4.** cast off.

slov'en (sluv'ən) n. untidy or careless person. —**slov'en·ly,** adj.

slow (slō) adj. **1.** not fast. **2.** not intelligent or perceptive. **3.** running behind time. —adv. **4.** slowly. —v. **5.** make or become slow.

slow burn, Informal. gradual build-up of anger.

slow'down', n. slackening of pace or speed.

slow motion, process of projecting or replaying film or television sequence so that action appears to be slowed down.

slow'poke', n. Informal. person who moves, works, or acts very slowly.

slow/-wit/ted, adj. slow to understand.

sludge (sluj) n. mud.

slue (slōō) v., **slued, sluing.** turn round.

slug (slug) v., **slugged, slugging,** n. —v. **1.** hit with fists. —n. **2.** slimy, crawling mollusk having no shell. **3.** bullet. **4.** counterfeit coin. **5.** hard blow, esp. with fist. —**slug/ger,** n.

slug/gard (slug/ərd) n. lazy person.

slug/gish, adj. inactive; slow.

sluice (slōōs) n. channel with gate to control flow.

slum (slum) n. squalid, overcrowded residence or neighborhood.

slum/ber (slum/bər) v., n. sleep.

slum/lord/, n. landlord of slum dwellings who charges exorbitant rents.

slump (slump) v. **1.** drop heavily or suddenly. —n. **2.** act of slumping.

slur (slûr) v., **slurred, slurring,** n. —v. **1.** say indistinctly. **2.** disparage. —n. **3.** slurred sound. **4.** disparaging remark.

slurp (slûrp) v. eat or drink with loud smacking noises.

slush (slush) n. partly melted snow.

slush fund, money used for illicit political purposes.

slut (slut) n. **1.** slatternly woman. **2.** sexually immoral woman.

sly (slī) adj., **slyer, slyest** or **slier, sliest. 1.** cunning. **2.** stealthy.

smack (smak) v. **1.** separate (lips) noisily. **2.** slap. **3.** have taste or trace. —n. **4.** smacking of lips. **5.** loud kiss. **6.** slap. **7.** taste. **8.** trace. **9.** small fishing boat. **10.** Slang. heroin.

small (smôl) adj. **1.** not big. **2.** not great in importance. **3.** ungenerous. —adv. **4.** in small pieces. —n. **5.** small part, as of back.

small fry. 1. young children. **2.** unimportant people.

small/-mind/ed, adj. petty or selfish.

small/pox/, n. contagious disease marked by fever and pustules.

small/-scale/, adj. **1.** of limited scope. **2.** being a small version of an original.

small talk, light conversation.

small/-time/, adj. not important.

smarm/y (smär/mē) adj., **-ier, -iest.** excessively flattering.

smart (smärt) v. **1.** cause or feel sharp superficial pain. —adj. **2.** sharp; severe. **3.** clever. **4.** stylish. —n. **5.** sharp local pain.

smart al/eck (al/ik) Informal. ob-

noxiously conceited and impertinent person. Also, **smart al/ec.**

smart bomb, air-to-surface missile guided by laser beam.

smart/en, v. improve in appearance.

smash (smash) v. **1.** break to pieces. —n. **2.** act of smashing.

smat/ter-ing (smat/ər ing) n. slight knowledge.

smear (smēr) v. **1.** rub with dirt, grease, etc. **2.** sully. —n. **3.** smeared spot. **4.** slanderous attack.

smell (smel) v. **1.** perceive with nose. **2.** have odor. —n. **3.** faculty of smelling. **4.** odor. —**smell/y,** adj., **-ier, -iest.**

smelt (smelt) n., pl. **smelts, smelt,** v. —n. **1.** small edible fish. —v. **2.** melt (ore or metal). —**smelt/er,** n.

smid/gen (smij/ən) n. very small amount. Also, **smid/gin, smid/geon.**

smile (smīl) v., **smiled, smiling,** n. —v. **1.** look pleased, amused, etc. **2.** look favorably. —n. **3.** smiling look.

smirch (smûrch) v. soil or sully. —n. **2.** stain.

smirk (smûrk) v. **1.** smile smugly or affectedly. —n. **2.** such a smile.

smite (smīt) v., **smote** (smōt), **smitten** (smit/n) or **smote, smiting. 1.** strike. **2.** charm.

smith (smith) n. worker in metal.

smith/er-eens/ (smith/ə rēnz/) n.pl. fragments.

smith/y (smith/ē, smith/ē) n., pl. **smithies.** blacksmith's shop.

smit/ten (smit/n) adj. very much in love.

smock (smok) n. long, loose overgarment.

smog (smog) n. smoke and fog.

smoke (smōk) n., v., **smoked, smoking.** —n. **1.** visible vapor from burning. —v. **2.** emit smoke. **3.** draw into mouth and puff out tobacco smoke. **4.** treat with smoke. —**smok/er,** n. —**smoke/less,** adj. —**smok/y,** adj.

smoke detector, alarm activated by presence of smoke.

smoke/house/, n. building in which meat or fish is cured with smoke.

smoke screen. 1. mass of dense smoke for concealment from enemy. **2.** something intended to deceive.

smoke/stack/, n. **1.** pipe for escape of smoke, combustion gases, etc. —adj. **2.** engaged in heavy industry, as steelmaking.

smol/der (smōl/dər) v. **1.** burn

without flame. **2.** continue, but suppressed. Also, **smoul/der.**

smooch (smōōch) n., v. *Informal.* kiss.

smooth (smōōth) adj. **1.** even in surface. **2.** easy; tranquil. —v. **3.** make smooth. —n. **4.** smooth place.

smooth/bore/, adj. (of gun) not rifled.

smor/gas·bord/ (smôr/gas bôrd/; *often* shmôr/-) n. buffet meal of assorted foods.

smoth/er (smuth/ər) v. suffocate.

smudge (smuj) n., v., **smudged, smudging.** —n. **1.** dirty smear. **2.** smoky fire. **3.** soil.

smug (smug) adj. self-satisfied.

smug/gle (smug/əl) v., **-gled, -gling. 1.** import or export secretly and illegally. **2.** bring or take secretly.

smut (smut) n. **1.** soot. **2.** smudge. **3.** obscenity. **4.** fungous disease of plants. —**smut/ty,** adj.

snack (snak) n. light meal.

snag (snag) n., v., **snagged, snagging.** —n. **1.** sharp projection. **2.** obstacle. —v. **3.** catch on snag.

snail (snāl) n. crawling, spiralshelled mollusk.

snake (snāk) n., v., **snaked, snaking.** —n. **1.** scaly limbless reptile. —v. **2.** move like snake. **3.** drag.

snap (snap) v., **snapped, snapping,** n., adj. —v. **1.** make sudden sharp sound. **2.** break abruptly. **3.** bite (at). **4.** photograph. —n. **5.** snapping sound. **6.** kind of fastener. **7.** *Informal.* easy thing. —adj. **8.** unconsidered.

snap/drag/on, n. plant with spikes of flowers.

snap/pish, adj. cross or irritable.

snap/py, adj., **-pier, -piest.** *Informal.* **1.** quick. **2.** stylish.

snap/shot/, n. unposed photograph.

snare (snâr) n., v., **snared, snaring.** —n. **1.** kind of trap. **2.** strand across skin of small drum. —v. **3.** entrap.

snarl (snärl) v., n. **1.** growl. **2.** tangle.

snatch (snach) v. **1.** grab. —n. **2.** grabbing motion. **3.** scrap of melody, etc. —**snatch/er,** n.

sneak (snēk) v. **1.** go or act furtively. —n. **2.** person who sneaks.

sneak/er, n. rubber-soled shoe.

sneak preview, preview of a motion picture, often shown in addition to an announced film.

sneer (snēr) v. **1.** show contempt. —n. **2.** contemptuous look.

sneeze (snēz) v., **sneezed, sneezing,** n. —v. **1.** emit breath suddenly

and forcibly from nose. —n. **2.** act of sneezing.

snick/er (snik/ər) n. derisive, stifled laugh. —**snick/er,** v. Also, **snig/ger.**

snide (snīd) adj., **snider, snidest.** derogatory in nasty, insinuating way.

sniff (snif) v. **1.** inhale quickly and audibly. —n. **2.** such an inhalation. Also, **snif/fle.**

snif/ter (snif/tər) n. pear-shaped glass for brandy.

snip (snip) v., **snipped, snipping,** n. —v. **1.** cut with small, quick strokes. —n. **2.** small piece cut off. **3.** cut. **4.** (pl.) large scissors.

snipe (snīp) n., v., **sniped, sniping.** —n. **1.** shore bird. —v. **2.** shoot from hidden position. —**snip/er,** n.

snip/pet (snip/it) n. small bit, scrap, or fragment.

snip/py, adj., **-pier, -piest.** sharp or curt, esp. in haughty way.

snit (snit) n. agitated state.

snitch (snich) *Informal.* v. **1.** steal; pilfer. **2.** turn informer; tattle. —n. **3.** informer.

sniv/el (sniv/əl) v. **1.** weep weakly. **2.** have a runny nose.

snob (snob) n. person overconcerned with position, wealth, etc. —**snob/bish,** adj. —**snob/ber·y,** n.

snoop (snōōp) *Informal.* v. **1.** prowl or pry. —n. **2.** Also, **snoop/er.** person who snoops.

snoot/y (snōō/tē) adj., **-ier, -iest.** *Informal.* snobbish; condescending.

snooze (snōōz) v., **snoozed, snoozing,** n. *Informal.* nap.

snore (snôr) v., **snored, snoring,** n. —v. **1.** breathe audibly in sleep. —n. **2.** sound of snoring.

snor/kel (snôr/kəl) n. **1.** tube through which swimmer can breathe while underwater. **2.** ventilating device for submarines.

snort (snôrt) v. **1.** exhale loudly and harshly. —n. **2.** sound of snorting.

snot (snot) n. *Informal.* **1.** nasal mucus. **2.** impudently disagreeable young person. —**snot/ty,** adj. **-tier, -tiest.**

snout (snout) n. projecting nose and jaw.

snow (snō) n. **1.** white crystalline flakes that fall to earth. —v. **2.** fall as snow. —**snow/drift/,** n. —**snow/fall/,** n. —**snow/flake/,** n. —**snow/storm/,** n. —**snow/y,** adj.

snow/ball/, n. **1.** ball of snow. —v. **2.** grow rapidly.

snow/board/, n. board for gliding on snow, resembling a wide ski.

snow/drop/, n. early-blooming plant with white flowers.

snow/man/, n. figure of person made of packed snow.

snow/mo·bile/ (-mə bēl/) n. motor vehicle for travel on snow.

snow/shoe/, n. racketlike shoe for walking on snow.

snow/suit/, n. child's warmly insulated outer garment.

snow tire, tire with deep tread.

snub (snub) v., **snubbed, snubbing,** n., adj. —v. 1. treat with scorn. 2. check or stop. 3. rebuke or slight. —adj. 4. (of nose) short and turned up.

snuff (snuf) v. 1. inhale. 2. smell. 3. extinguish. —n. 4. powdered tobacco.

snuf·fle (snuf/əl) v., **-fled, -fling,** n. sniff.

snug (snug) adj., **snugger, snuggest.** 1. cozy. 2. trim; neat.

snug/gle, v., **-gled, -gling.** nestle.

so (sō) adv. 1. in this or that way. 2. to such degree. 3. as stated. —conj. 4. consequently. 5. in order that.

soak (sōk) v. 1. wet thoroughly. 2. absorb. —**soak/er,** n.

so/-and-so/, n., pl. **so-and-sos.** person or thing not definitely named.

soap (sōp) n. 1. substance used for washing. —v. 2. rub with soap.

soap/box/, n. improvised platform on which speaker stands.

soap/stone/, n. variety of talc.

soar (sôr) v. fly upward.

sob (sob) v., **sobbed, sobbing,** n. —v. 1. weep convulsively. —n. 2. convulsive breath.

so/ber (sō/bər) adj. 1. not drunk. 2. grave. —v. 3. make or become sober. —**so/bri·e/ty** (sə brī/ĭ tē) n.

so/bri·quet/ (sō/brĭ kā/, -ket/) n. nickname.

so/-called/, adj. called thus.

soc/cer (sok/ər) n. game resembling football.

so/cia·ble (sō/shə bəl) adj. friendly. —**so/cia·bil/i·ty,** n.

so/cial (sō/shəl) adj. 1. devoted to companionship. 2. of human society. —**so/cial·ly,** adv.

so/cial·ism (-sha lĭz/əm) n. theory advocating community ownership of means of production, etc. —**so/cial·ist,** n. —**so/cial·is/tic,** adj.

so/cial·ite/ (-sha līt/) n. socially prominent person.

so/cial·ize/, v., **-ized, -izing.** 1. associate with others. 2. put on socialistic basis.

socialized medicine, system to provide nation with complete medical care through government subsidization.

social security, (often caps.) federal program of old age, unemployment, health, disability, and survivors' insurance.

social work, services or activities designed to improve social conditions among poor, sick, or troubled persons.

so·ci·e·ty (sə sī/ĭ tē) n., pl. **-ties.** 1. group of persons with common interests. 2. human beings generally. 3. fashionable people.

Society of Friends, Christian sect founded 1650; Quakers.

so/ci·o·ec·o·nom/ic (sō/sē ō-, -shē ō-) adj. pertaining to a combination of social and economic factors.

so/ci·ol/o·gy (sō/sē ol/ə jē, sō/shē-) n. science of social relations and institutions. —**so/ci·ol/o·gist,** n.

sock (sok) n. short stocking.

sock/et (sok/ĭt) n. holelike part for holding another part.

sod (sod) n. grass with its roots.

so/da (sō/də) n. 1. drink made with soda water.

soda cracker, crisp cracker.

soda fountain, counter at which ice cream, sodas, etc., are served.

soda water, water charged with carbonic dioxide.

sod/den (sod/n) adj. 1. soaked. 2. dull. —**sod/den·ness,** n.

so/di·um (sō/dē əm) n. soft whitish metallic element.

sodium bicarbonate, baking soda.

sodium chloride, salt.

sod/o·my (sod/ə mē) n. anal or oral copulation.

so/fa (sō/fə) n. couch with back and arms.

soft (sôft) adj. 1. yielding readily. 2. gentle; pleasant. 3. not strong. 4. (of water) free from mineral salts. 5. without alcohol. —**soft/en,** v.

soft/ball/, n. form of baseball played with larger, softer ball. 2. the ball used.

soft/-boiled/, adj. boiled only until the egg's yolk is partially set.

soft/-core/, adj. sexually provocative without being explicit.

soft drink, nonalcoholic drink.

soft/-heart/ed, adj. very sympathetic.

soft/-ped/al, v., **-aled, -aling.** make less obvious; play down.

soft sell, quietly persuasive method of selling.

soft soap, persuasive talk.

soft/ware/, n. programs for use with a computer.

sog/gy (sog/ē) adj., **-gier, -giest.** 1. soaked. 2. damp and heavy.

soi·gné/ (swän yā/; Fr. swa nyā/) adj. elegant. Also, **soi·gnée/.**

soil (soil) v. **1.** dirty. —n. **2.** spot or stain. **3.** sewage. **4.** earth; ground.

soi·rée (swä rā′) n. evening party.

so·journ v. (sō′jûrn, sō jûrn′) **1.** dwell briefly. —n. (sō′jûrn) **2.** short stay.

sol·ace (sol′is) n., v. comfort in grief.

so·lar (sō′lər) adj. of the sun.

solar cell, cell that converts sunlight into electricity.

so·lar·i·um (sə lâr′ē əm, sō–) n., pl. **-iums, -i·a** (-ē ə). glass-enclosed room for enjoying sunlight.

solar plexus, point on stomach wall just below sternum.

solar system, sun and all the celestial bodies revolving around it.

sol·der (sod′ər) n. **1.** fusible alloy for joining metal. —v. **2.** join with solder.

sol·dier (sōl′jər) n. **1.** member of army. —v. **2.** serve as soldier.

sole (sōl) n., v., **soled, soling,** adj. —n. **1.** bottom of foot or shoe. **2.** edible flatfish. **3.** put sole on. —adj. **4.** only. —**sole′ly,** adv.

sol·emn (sol′əm) adj. **1.** grave; serious. **2.** sacred. —**so·lem·ni·ty** (sə lem′ni tē) n. —**sol·emn·ly,** adv.

sol·em·nize (–nīz′) v., **-nized, -nizing.** observe with ceremonies.

so·lic·it (sə lis′it) v. **1.** entreat; request. **2.** lure; entice, as to a prostitute. **3.** solicit trade or sex.

so·lic·i·tor (-i tər) n. **1.** person who solicits. **2.** Brit. lawyer.

so·lic·it·ous, adj. anxious; concerned. —**so·lic·i·tude′,** n.

sol·id (sol′id) adj. **1.** having length, breadth, and thickness. **2.** not hollow. **3.** dense. **4.** substantial. **5.** entire. —n. **6.** solid body. —**so·lid′i·fy′,** v. —**so·lid′i·ty,** n.

sol·i·dar·i·ty (-i dar′i tē) n., pl. **-ties.** unanimity of attitude or purpose.

sol·id·ly, adv. **1.** so as to be solid. **2.** whole-heartedly; fully.

so·lil·o·quy (sə lil′ə kwē) n., pl. **-quies.** speech when alone. —**so·lil′o·quize′** (-kwīz′) v., **-quized, -quizing.**

sol·i·taire (sol′i târ′) n. **1.** card game for one person. **2.** gem set alone.

sol·i·tar·y (sol′i ter′ē) adj. **1.** alone. **2.** single. **3.** secluded. —**sol′i·tude′,** n.

so·lo (sō′lō) n., pl. **-los.** performance by one person. —**so′lo·ist,** n.

sol·stice (sol′stis, sōl′–) n. time in summer (June 21) or winter (Dec. 21) when sun is at its farthest from equator.

sol·u·ble (sol′yə bəl) adj. able to be dissolved. —**sol′u·bil′i·ty,** n.

so·lu·tion (sə lōō′shən) n. **1.** explanation or answer. **2.** dispersion of one substance in another. **3.** resulting substance.

solve (solv) v., **solved, solving.** find explanation of.

sol·vent (sol′vənt) adj. **1.** able to pay one's debts. **2.** causing dissolving. —n. **3.** agent that dissolves.

som·ber (som′bər) adj. **1.** gloomy; dark. —**som′ber·ly,** adv.

som·bre·ro (som brâr′ō) n., pl. **-ros.** tall, broad-brimmed hat.

some (sum; unstressed səm) adj. **1.** being an unspecified one or number. **2.** certain. —pron. **3.** unspecified number or amount.

—**Usage.** SOME is used in sentences that are affirmative: I'd like some milk. ANY is used instead of SOME with negative phrases or in questions: I don't want any milk. I never see any of my friends these days. Do you have any milk? But SOME can be used in questions when the answer is expected to be "yes": Can I have some milk, please?

some·bod·y (sum′bod′ē, -bud′ē, -bə dē) pron. some person. Also, **some′one′.**

some·day, adv. at some distant time.

some·how, adv. in some way.

som·er·sault (sum′ər sôlt′) n. heels-over-head turn of body.

some·thing, n. unspecified thing.

some·time, adv. **1.** at indefinite time. —adj. **2.** former.

some·times, adv. at times.

some·what, adv. to some extent.

some·where, adv. in, at, or to unspecified place.

som·nam·bu·lism (som nam′byə liz′əm, səm–) n. sleep-walking.

som·no·lent (som′nə lənt) adj. sleepy. —**som′no·lence,** n.

son (sun) n. male offspring.

so·nar (sō′när) n. method or apparatus for detecting objects in water by means of sound waves.

so·na·ta (sə nä′tə) n. instrumental composition.

song (sông) n. music or verse for singing. —**song′ster,** n. —**song′stress,** n.fem.

son·ic (son′ik) adj. of sound.

sonic boom, loud noise caused by aircraft moving at supersonic speed.

son′-in-law′, n., pl. **sons-in-law.** husband of one's daughter.

son·net (son′it) n. fourteen-line poem in fixed form.

so·no·rous (sə nôr′əs, son′ər əs)

adj. **1.** resonant. **2.** grandiose in expression. **—so·nor'i·ty,** *n.*

soon (sōōn) *adv.* in short time.

soot (sŏŏt, sōōt) *n.* black substance in smoke. **—soot'y,** *adj.*

soothe (sōōth) *v.,* soothed, soothing. calm; allay.

sooth'say'er (sōōth'sā'ər) *n.* person who predicts.

sop (sop) *n., v.,* sopped, sopping. **—n. 1.** something given to pacify. **—v. 1.** soak or dip in liquid.

so·phis'ti·cat·ed (sə fis'ti kā'tid) *adj.* **1.** worldly; not simple. **2.** complex; intricate. **—so·phis'ti·cate** (-kit) *n.* **—so·phis'ti·ca'tion,** *n.*

soph'ist·ry (sof'ə strē) *n., pl.* -ries. clever but unsound reasoning.

soph'o·more' (sof'ə môr') *n.* second-year high school or college student.

soph'o·mor'ic (-môr'ik) *adj.* intellectually immature.

so·po·rif'ic (sop'ə rif'ik) *adj.* **1.** causing sleep. **—n. 2.** soporific agent.

sop'py (sop'ē) *adj.,* -pier, -piest. **1.** drenched. **2.** sentimental.

so·pra'no (sə pran'ō) *n., pl.* -pranos. highest singing voice.

sor·bet' (sôr bā', sôr'bit) *n.* fruit or vegetable ice.

sor'cer·er (-sər ər) *n.* magician; wizard. Also, *fem.* **sor'cer·ess.** **—sor'cer·y,** *n.*

sor'did (sôr'did) *adj.* **1.** dirty. **2.** morally low.

sore (sôr) *adj.,* sorer, sorest, *n.* **—adj. 1.** painful or tender. **2.** grieved. **3.** causing misery. **4.** *Informal.* annoyed. **—n. 5.** sore spot.

sore'head', *n. Informal.* person who is easily annoyed.

sor'ghum (sôr'gəm) *n.* cereal used in making syrup, etc.

so·ror'i·ty (sə rôr'i tē) *n., pl.* -ties. club of women or girls.

sor'rel (sôr'əl) *n.* **1.** reddish brown. **2.** sorrel horse. **3.** salad plant.

sor'row (sor'ō) *n.* **1.** grief; regret; misfortune. **—v. 2.** feel sorrow. **—sor'row·ful,** *adj.*

sor'ry (sor'ē) *adj.* **1.** feeling regret or pity. **2.** wretched.

sort (sôrt) *n.* **1.** kind or class. **2.** character. **3.** manner. **—v. 4.** separate; classify. **—sort'er,** *n.*

sor'tie (sôr'tē) *n.* **1.** attack by defending troops. **2.** combat mission.

SOS (es'ō'es') call for help.

so'-so', *adj.* **1.** neither good nor bad. **—adv. 2.** tolerably.

sot (sot) *n.* drunkard.

sot'to vo'ce (sot'ō vō'chē) *adv.* in a low voice; softly.

souf·fle' (sōō flā') *n.* fluffy baked dish.

sough (sou, suf) *v.* **1.** rustle or murmur, as wind. **—n. 2.** act of soughing.

sought (sôt) *pt.* and *pp.* of **seek.**

soul (sōl) *n.* **1.** human spiritual quality. **2.** essential quality. **3.** person. **4.** Also, **soul music.** black popular music drawing on church influences. **—adj. 5.** of black customs and culture. **—soul'ful,** *adj.*

sound (sound) *n.* **1.** sensation affecting organs of hearing, produced by vibrations (**sound waves**). **2.** special tone. **3.** noise. **4.** inlet or passage of sea. **5.** make sound. **6.** say. **7.** give certain impression. **8.** measure depth of. **9.** examine. **—adj. 10.** healthy; strong. **11.** reliable. **12.** valid. **—sound'·proof',** *adj.* **—sound'ly,** *adv.*

sound barrier, abrupt increase in drag experienced by aircraft approaching speed of sound.

sound bite, brief, memorable statement excerpted for broadcast news.

sounding board, 1. thin board placed in musical instrument to enhance resonance. **2.** person whose reactions reveal acceptability of an idea.

sound'proof', *adj.* **1.** impervious to sound. **—v. 2.** make soundproof.

sound'track', *n.* band on motion-picture film on which sound is recorded.

soup (sōōp) *n.* liquid food of meat, vegetables, etc.

soup'y, *adj.,* -ier, -iest. **1.** resembling soup in consistency. **2.** dense. **3.** overly sentimental.

sour (sou⁰r) *adj.* **1.** acid in taste; tart. **2.** spoiled. **3.** disagreeable. **—v. 4.** turn sour. **—sour'ly,** *adv.*

source (sôrs) *n.* origin.

sour grapes, pretended disdain for something unattainable.

souse (sous) *v.,* soused, sousing, *n.* **—v. 1.** immerse. **2.** pickle. **—n. 3.** pickled food. **4.** *Slang.* drunkard.

south (south) *n.* **1.** point of compass opposite north. **2.** territory in this direction. **—adj., adv. 3.** toward, in, or from south. **—south'·er·ly** (suth'ər lē) *adj., adv.* **—south'ern** (suth-) *adj.* **—south'·ern·er,** *n.* **—south'ward,** *adj., adv.*

south'east', *n.* point or direction midway between south and east. **—south'east',** *adj., adv.*

south'paw', *n. Informal.* left-handed person.

south'west', *n.* point or direction midway between south and west. **—south'west',** *adj., adv.*

sou've·nir' (soo'və nēr') n. memento.

sov'er·eign (sov'rin, -ər in) n. **1.** monarch. **2.** (formerly) British gold coin worth one pound. —adj. **3.** of a sovereign; supreme. —**sov'er· eign·ty,** n.

so'vi·et' (sō'vē et', -it) n. **1.** (in the former USSR) governing body. —adj. **2.** (cap.) of the former USSR.

sow, v. (sō) **1.** plant seed. —n. (sou) **2.** female hog. —**sow'er,** n.

soy'bean' (soi'-) n. nutritious seed of leguminous plant.

soy sauce, salty sauce made from soybeans.

spa (spä) n. resort at mineral spring.

space (späs) n., v., **spaced, spacing.** —n. **1.** unlimited expanse. **2.** particular part of this. **3.** linear distance. **4.** interval of time. —v. **5.** divide into spaces. **6.** set at intervals.

space'craft' n., pl. **-craft.** vehicle for traveling in outer space.

spaced'-out', adj. Slang. dazed by or as if by drugs.

space heater, device for heating small area.

space'ship', n. rocket vehicle for travel between planets.

space shuttle, reusable spacecraft.

space station, manned spacecraft orbiting the earth and serving as base for research.

spa'cious (spä'shəs) adj. roomy.

spade (späd) n., v., **spaded, spading.** —n. **1.** tool with blade for digging. **2.** (pl.) suit of playing cards. —v. **3.** dig with spade.

spa·ghet'ti (spə get'ē) n. pasta in form of long strings.

span (span) n., v., **spanned, spanning.** —n. **1.** distance between extended thumb and little finger. **2.** space between two supports. **3.** full extent. **4.** team of animals. —v. **5.** extend over.

span'dex (span'deks) n. elastic synthetic fiber.

span'gle (spang'gəl) n., v., **-gled, -gling.** —n. **1.** small bright ornament. —v. **2.** decorate with spangles.

span'iel (span'yəl) n. kind of dog.

Span'ish (span'ish) n. language or people of Spain. —**Spanish,** adj.

Spanish fly, preparation of powdered green European beetles once used as aphrodisiac.

spank (spangk) v. **1.** strike on buttocks. **2.** such a blow.

spank'ing, adj. brisk; vigorous.

spar (spär) v., **sparred, sparring,** n. —v. **1.** box. **2.** bandy words. —n.

3. Naut. mast, yard, etc. **4.** bright crystalline mineral.

spare (spâr) v., **spared, sparing,** adj., **sparer, sparest.** —v. **1.** deal gently with. **2.** part with easily. —adj. **3.** kept in reserve. **4.** extra. **5.** lean.

spare'rib', n. cut of pork ribs.

spark (spärk) n. **1.** burning particle. **2.** flash of electricity. **3.** trace.

spar'kle (spär'kəl) v., **-kled, -kling,** n. —v. **1.** emit sparks. **2.** glitter. **3.** produce little bubbles. —n. **4.** little spark. **5.** brightness.

spark plug, device in internal-combustion engine that ignites fuel.

spar'row (spar'ō) n. small, common, hardy bird.

sparse, adj., **sparser, sparsest.** thinly distributed. —**spar'si·ty,** n.

Spar'tan (spär'tn) adj. austere.

spasm (spaz'əm) n. sudden involuntary muscular contraction.

spas·mod'ic (spaz mod'ik) adj. **1.** of spasms. **2.** intermittent.

spas'tic (spas'tik) adj. of or marked by spasms.

spat (spat) n. petty quarrel.

spate (spāt) n. sudden outpouring.

spa'tial (spā'shəl) adj. of or in space.

spat'ter (spat'ər) v., n. sprinkle in many fine drops.

spat'u·la (spach'ə lə) n. broad-bladed implement.

spawn (spôn) n. **1.** eggs of fish, mollusks, etc. —v. **2.** produce spawn.

spay (spā) v. neuter (female dog, cat, etc.).

speak (spēk) v., **spoke** (spōk), **spoken, speaking. 1.** talk. **2.** deliver speech.

speak'eas'y, n., pl. **-easies.** place selling alcoholic beverages illegally.

speak'er, n. person who speaks.

spear (spēr) n. **1.** long staff bearing sharp head. —v. **2.** pierce with spear.

spear'head', n. **1.** head of spear. **2.** leader. —v. **3.** lead.

spear'mint', n. aromatic herb.

spe'cial (spesh'əl) adj. **1.** particular in nature or purpose. **2.** unusual or unique. **3.** exceptional. **4.** special thing or person.

spe'cial·ize', v., **-ized, -izing.** study of work in special field. —**spe'cial· ist,** n. —**spe'cial·i·za'tion,** n.

spe'cial·ty, n., pl. **-ties.** field of special interest or competence.

spe'cie (spē'shē, -sē) n. coined money.

spe'cies (spē'shēz, -sēz) n. class of related individuals.

spe·cif'ic (spi sif'ik) adj. **1.** definite.

2. of a particular kind. **3.** peculiar to someone or something. —**spe•cif'i•cal•ly,** adv.

spec'i•fi•ca'tion (spes'ə fi kā'shən) n. **1.** act of specifying. **2.** detailed requirement.

specific gravity, ratio of density of substance to density of standard substance, water being the standard.

spec'i•fy', v., **-fied, -fying.** mention or require specifically.

spec'i•men (spes'ə mən) n. anything typical of its kind.

spe'cious (spē'shəs) adj. plausible but false or incorrect.

speck (spek) n. **1.** spot or particle. —v. **2.** spot.

speck'le, n., v., **-led, -ling.** —n. **1.** small spot. —v. **2.** mark with speckles.

specs (speks) n.pl. Informal. **1.** spectacles; eyeglasses. **2.** specifications (def. 2).

spec'ta•cle (spek'tə kal) n. **1.** anything presented to view. **2.** public display. **3.** (pl.) eyeglasses.

spec•tac'u•lar (-tak'yə lər) adj. dramatic; thrilling.

spec•ta'tor (spek'tā tər) n. observer.

spec'ter (spek'tər) n. ghost. Also, **spec'tre.** —**spec'tral** (-tral) adj.

spec'trum (-trəm) n., pl. **-tra** (-trə), **-trums.** band of colors formed when light ray is dispersed.

spec'u•late' (spek'yə lāt') v., **-lated, -lating. 1.** think; conjecture. **2.** invest at some risk. —**spec'u•la'•tion,** n. —**spec'u•la'tive** (-lā'tiv, -lə tiv) adj. —**spec'u•la'tor,** n.

speech (spēch) n. **1.** power of speaking. **2.** utterance. **3.** talk before audience. **4.** language. —**speech'less,** adj.

speed (spēd) n., v., **sped** (sped) or **speeded, speeding. 1.** swiftness. **2.** rate of motion —v. **3.** increase speed of. **4.** move swiftly. —**speed'y,** adj. —**speed'i•ly,** adv.

speed•om'e•ter (spē dom'i tər, spi-) n. device for indicating speed.

speed'well', n. plant having spikes of small flowers.

spe'le•ol'o•gy (spē'lē ol'ə jē) n. exploration and study of caves.

spell (spel) v., **spelled** or **spelt, spelling.** —v. **1.** give letters of in order. **2.** (of letters) form. **3.** signify. **4.** relieve at work. —n. **5.** enchantment. **6.** brief period.

spell'bound', adj. fascinated.

spe•lunk'er (spi lung'kər) n. person who explores caves.

spend (spend) v., **spent, spending.**

1. pay out. **2.** pass (time). **3.** use up. —**spend'er,** n.

spend'thrift', n. extravagant spender.

sperm (spûrm) n. male reproductive cell. —**sper•mat'ic** (-mat'ik) adj.

sper'ma•ce'ti (spûr'mə set'ē), n. waxy substance from large square-headed whale (**sperm whale**).

sper•mat'o•zo'on (spûr mat'ə-zō'ən, -on) n., pl. **-zoa** (-zō'ə), male reproductive cell.

sper'mi•cide' (spûr'mə sīd') n. sperm-killing agent.

spew (spyōō) v. **1.** vomit. **2.** gush or pour out.

sphere (sfēr) n. **1.** round ball. **2.** particular field of influence or competence. —**spher'i•cal,** adj.

sphe'roid (sfēr'oid) n. body approximately spherical.

sphinc'ter (sfingk'tər) n. muscle closing anus or other body opening.

sphinx (sfingks) n. figure of creature with human head and lion's body.

spice (spīs) n., v., **spiced, spicing.** —n. **1.** aromatic plant substance used as seasoning. —v. **2.** season with spice. —**spic'y,** adj.

spick'-and-span' (spik'ən span') adj. **1.** spotlessly clean. **2.** perfectly new.

spi'der (spī'dər) n. web-spinning insectlike animal with eight legs.

spiel (spēl, shpēl) n. Slang. high-pressure sales talk.

spiff'y (spif'ē) adj., **-ier, -iest.** Informal. smart; fine.

spig'ot (spig'ət) n. faucet.

spike (spīk) n., v., **spiked, spiking.** —n. **1.** large strong nail. **2.** stiff, pointed part. —v. **3.** fasten with spikes. **4.** frustrate or stop. —**spik'y,** adj., **-ier, -iest.**

spill (spil) v., **spilled** or **spilt, spilling. 1.** run or let run over. **2.** shed (blood). —**spill'age,** n.

spill'way', n. overflow passage.

spin (spin) v., **spun** (spun), **spinning. 1.** make yarn or thread from fiber. **2.** secrete filament. **3.** whirl. —n. **4.** spinning motion. **5.** short ride. **6.** Slang. particular viewpoint or bias.

spin'ach (spin'ich) n. plant with edible leaves.

spinal column, series of vertebrae forming axis of skeleton.

spinal cord, cord of nerve tissue extending through spinal column.

spin control, Slang. attempt to give a bias to news coverage.

spin'dle (spin'dl) n. **1.** tapered rod. **2.** any shaft or axis.

spin′dling, *adj.* tall and thin. Also, **spin′dly.**

spin doctor, *Slang.* press agent or spokesperson skilled in spin control.

spine (spīn) *n.* **1.** Also, **spinal column.** connected series of bones down back. **2.** any spinelike part. **3.** stiff bristle or thorn. —**spi′nal,** *adj.* —**spin′y,** *adj.*

spine′less, *adj.* weak in character.

spin′et (spin′it) *n.* small piano.

spinning wheel, device for spinning yarn or thread.

spin′-off′, *n.* by-product or secondary development.

spin′ster (spin′stər) *n. Usually Offensive.* unmarried woman, esp. elderly.

spi·ral (spī′rəl) *n., adj., v.,* **-raled, -raling.** —*n.* **1.** curve made by circling a point while approaching or receding from it. —*adj.* **2.** like or of spiral. —*v.* **3.** move spirally.

spire (spīr) *n.* tall tapering structure, esp. on tower or roof.

spi·re·a (spī rē′ə) *n.* common garden shrub. Also, **spiraea.**

spir′it (spir′it) *n.* **1.** vital force in humanity; soul. **2.** supernatural being. **3.** feelings. **4.** vigor. **5.** intent. **6.** (*pl.*) alcoholic liquor. **7.** (*cap.*) Holy Ghost. —*v.* **8.** carry off secretly. —**spir′it·ed,** *adj.*

spir·it·u·al (-choo əl) *adj.* **1.** of or in spirit; ethereal. **2.** religious. —*n.* **3.** religious song. —**spir′it·u·al·ly,** *adv.* —**spir·it·u·al′i·ty** (-al′i tē) *n.*

spir·it·u·al·ism, *n.* belief that spirits of dead communicate with living. —**spir′it·u·al·ist,** *n.*

spit (spit) *n., v.,* **spat** (spat) or **spit** (for 2 **spitted**), **spitting.** —*v.* **1.** eject from mouth. **2.** pierce. —*n.* **3.** saliva. **4.** *Informal.* image. **5.** rod for roasting meat. **6.** point of land.

spite (spīt) *n., v.,* **spited, spiting.** —*n.* **1.** malice; grudge. —*v.* **2.** annoy out of spite. —**spite′ful,** *adj.*

spit′fire′, *n.* person with fiery temper.

spit·toon′ (spi toon′) *n.* cuspidor.

splash (splash) *v.* **1.** dash water, etc. —*v.* **2.** act or sound of splashing. **3.** spot. —**splash′y,** *adj.*

splash′down′, *n.* landing of space vehicle in ocean.

splat (splat) *n.* sound made by splattering.

splat′ter, *v.* splash widely.

splay (splā) *v., adj.* spread out.

spleen (splēn) *n.* **1.** ductless organ near stomach. **2.** ill humor.

splen′did (splen′did) *adj.* gorgeous; superb; fine. —**splen′dor,** *n.*

splice (splīs) *v.,* **spliced, splicing,** *n.* —*v.* **1.** join, as ropes or boards. —*n.* **2.** union made by splicing.

splint (splint) *n.* **1.** brace for broken part of body. **2.** strip of wood for weaving. —*v.* **3.** brace with splints.

splin′ter, *n.* **1.** thin sharp fragment. —*v.* **2.** break into splinters.

split (split) *v.,* **split, splitting,** *n., adj.* —*v.* **1.** separate; divide. **2.** burst. —*n.* **3.** crack or breach. —*adj.* **4.** cleft; divided.

split′-lev′el, *adj.* **1.** having rooms on levels a half story apart. —*n.* **2.** split-level house.

split pea, dried green pea.

split personality, mental disorder in which person acquires several personalities.

splotch (sploch) *n., v.,* blot; stain.

splurge (splûrj) *n., v.,* **splurged, splurging.** —*n.* **1.** big display or expenditure. —*v.* **2.** be extravagant.

splut′ter (splut′ər) *v.* **1.** talk vehemently and incoherently. —*n.* **2.** spluttering talk.

spoil (spoil) *v.,* **spoiled** or **spoilt, spoiling.** —*v.* **1.** damage; ruin. **2.** become tainted. —*n.* **3.** (*pl.*) booty. **4.** waste material. —**spoil′age,** *n.*

spoil′sport′, *n.* person who spoils the pleasure of others.

spoils system, practice of filling nonelective public offices with supporters of victorious party.

spoke (spōk) *n.* bar between hub and rim of wheel.

spokes′man, *n., pl.* **-men.** person speaking for others. Also, *fem.,* **spokes′wom′an;** *masc.* or *fem.,* **spokes′per·son.**

sponge (spunj) *n., v.,* **sponged, sponging.** —*n.* **1.** marine animal. **2.** its light skeleton or an imitation, used to absorb liquids. —*v.* **3.** clean with sponge. **4.** impose or live on another. —**spong′er,** *n.*

sponge cake, light cake without shortening.

spon′sor (spon′sər) *n.* **1.** one that recommends or supports. **2.** godparent. **3.** advertiser on radio or television. —*v.* **4.** act as sponsor for. —**spon′sor·ship,** *n.*

spon·ta′ne·ous (spon tā′nē əs) *adj.* **1.** occurring naturally or without planning. **2.** impulsive. —**spon′ta·ne′i·ty,** *n.*

spontaneous combustion, ignition of a substance without heat from external source.

spoof (spoof) *n.* **1.** parody. **2.** prank. —*v.* **3.** make fun of lightly.

spook (spook) *n.* **1.** ghost. —*v.* **2.** frighten. —**spook′y,** *adj.*

spool (spool) *n.* cylinder on which something is wound.

spoon (spoon) *n.* **1.** utensil for stirring or taking up food. —*v.* **2.** lift in spoon. —**spoon′ful**, *n.*

spoon′bill′, *n.* large wading bird.

spoon′er·ism (spoo′nə riz′əm) *n.* inadvertent transposition of initial sounds of words.

spoon′-feed′, *v.*, **-fed, -feeding. 1.** feed in manner of infant. **2.** provide information in a simplified way.

spoor (spoor) *n.* trail of wild animal.

spo·rad′ic (spə rad′ik) *adj.* occasional; scattered.

spore (spôr) *n.* seed, as of ferns.

sport (spôrt) *n.* **1.** athletic pastime. **2.** diversion. **3.** person who shows sportsmanship. —*adj.* **4.** of or for sport. —*v.* **5.** play. —**sports′man**, *n.* —**sports′wear′**, *n.*

spor′tive, *adj.* playful.

sports car, small, high-powered car.

sports′man·ship′, *n.* ability to win or lose gracefully.

sport-utility vehicle, rugged vehicle with trucklike chassis, designed for occasional off-road use.

sport′y, *adj.*, **-ier, -iest.** flashy or showy.

spot (spot) *n.*, *v.*, **spotted, spotting,** *adj.* —*n.* **1.** blot. **2.** locality. —*v.* **3.** stain with spots. **4.** notice. —*adj.* **5.** made, done, etc., at once. —**spot′less**, *adj.* —**spot′ty**, *adj.*

spot check, random sampling or investigation. —**spot′-check′**, *v.*

spot′light′, *n.* **1.** intense light focused on person or thing, as on stage. **2.** intense public attention.

spouse (spous) *n.* husband or wife.

spout (spout) *v.* **1.** discharge (liquid, etc.) with force. **2.** utter insincerely. —*n.* **3.** pipe or lip on container.

sprain (sprān) *v.* **1.** injure by wrenching. —*n.* **2.** such injury.

sprat (sprat) *n.* herringlike fish.

sprawl (sprôl) *v.* **1.** stretch out ungracefully. —*n.* **2.** sprawling position.

spray (sprā) *n.* **1.** liquid in fine particles. **2.** appliance for producing spray. **3.** branch of flowers, etc. —*v.* **4.** scatter as spray. **5.** apply spray to. —**spray′er**, *n.*

spread (spred) *v.*, **spread, spreading,** *n.* —*v.* **1.** stretch out. **2.** extend. **3.** scatter. —*n.* **4.** extent. **5.** diffusion. **6.** cloth cover. **7.** preparation for eating on bread.

spread′-ea′gle, *adj.*, *v.*, **-gled, -gling.** —*adj.* **1.** suggesting form of eagle with outstretched wings. —*v.* **2.** stretch out in this position.

spread′sheet′, *n.* **1.** outsize ledger sheet. **2.** such a sheet simulated by computer software.

spree (sprē) *n.* frolic.

sprig (sprig) *n.* twig or shoot.

spright′ly (sprīt′lē) *adj.*, **-lier, -liest.** lively. —**spright′li·ness**, *n.*

spring (spring) *v.*, **sprang** (sprang) or **sprung** (sprung), **sprung, springing,** *n.*, *adj.* —*v.* **1.** leap. **2.** grow or proceed. **3.** disclose. —*n.* **4.** jump. **5.** natural fountain. **6.** season after winter. **7.** elastic device. —*adj.* **8.** of or for spring (def. 6). —**spring′time′**, *n.* —**spring′y**, *adj.*

spring′board′, *n.* flexible board used in diving and gymnastics. **2.** starting point.

spring fever, restless feeling associated with spring.

sprin′kle (spring′kəl) *v.*, **-kled, -kling,** *n.* —*v.* **1.** scatter in drops. **2.** rain slightly. —*n.* **3.** instance of sprinkling. **4.** something sprinkled.

sprint (sprint) *v.* **1.** run fast. —*n.* **2.** short fast run. —**sprint′er**, *n.*

sprite (sprīt) *n.* elf; fairy.

sprock′et (sprok′it) *n.* tooth on wheel for engaging with chain.

sprout (sprout) *v.* **1.** begin to grow; bud. —*n.* **2.** plant shoot.

spruce (sproos) *adj.*, **sprucer, sprucest,** *v.*, *n.* —*adj.* **1.** trim; neat. —*v.* **2.** make spruce. —*n.* **3.** cone-bearing evergreen tree.

spry (sprī) *adj.*, **spryer** or **sprier, spryest** or **spriest.** nimble.

spud (spud) *n.* **1.** spadelike tool. **2.** *Informal.* potato.

spume (spyoom) *n.* foam.

spunk (spungk) *n. Informal.* courage; spirit. —**spunk′y**, *adj.*

spur (spûr) *n.*, *v.*, **spurred, spurring.** —*n.* **1.** sharp device worn on heel to goad horse. **2.** spurlike part. —*v.* **3.** prick with spur. **4.** urge.

spu′ri·ous (spyŏŏr′ē əs) *adj.* not genuine. —**spu′ri·ous·ly**, *adv.*

spurn (spûrn) *v.* scorn; reject.

spurt (spûrt) *v.* **1.** gush or eject in jet. **2.** speed up briefly. —*n.* **3.** forceful gush. **4.** brief increase of effort.

sput′ter (sput′ər) *v.* **1.** emit violently in drops. **2.** splutter. —*n.* **3.** act or sound of sputtering.

spu′tum (spyoo′təm) *n.* spittle, esp. mixed with mucus.

spy (spī) *n.*, *pl.* **spies,** *v.*, **spied, spying.** —*n.* **1.** secret observer, esp. one employed by government. —*v.* **2.** watch secretly. **3.** sight.

spy glass, small telescope.

squab (skwob) *n.* young pigeon.

squab·ble (skwob′əl) *n.*, *v.*, **-bled,**

-**bling.** n. 1. petty quarrel. —v. 2. have squabble.

squad (skwod) n. small group.

squad car, police car.

squad/ron (-ran) n. unit in Navy, Air Force, etc.

squal/id (skwol/id) adj. dirty or wretched. —**squal/id·ly,** adv.

squall (skwôl) n. 1. strong gust of wind, etc. 2. loud cry. —v. 3. cry loudly. —**squall/y,** adj.

squal/or (skwol/ər) n. squalid state.

squan/der (skwon/dər) v. use or spend wastefully.

square (skwâr) n., v., **squared, squaring,** adj., **squarer, squarest,** adv. —n. 1. plane figure with four equal sides and four right angles. 2. anything square. 3. tool for checking right angles. 4. product of number multiplied by itself. 5. Slang. conventional, conservative, unimaginative person. —v. 6. make square. 7. adjust; agree. 8. multiply by itself. —adj. 9. being a square. 10. level. 11. honest. —adv. 12. directly. —**square/ly,** adv.

square dance, dance by sets of four couples arranged in squares.

square root, quantity of which a given quantity is the square.

squash (skwosh) v. 1. crush; suppress. —n. 2. game resembling tennis. 3. fruit of vinelike plant.

squat (skwot) v., **squatted** or **squat, squatting,** adj., n. —v. 1. sit with legs close under body. 2. settle on land illegally or to acquire title. —adj. 3. Also, **squat/ty.** stocky. —n. 4. squatting position.

squaw (skwô) n. Often Offensive. American Indian woman.

squawk (skwôk) n. 1. loud harsh cry. —v. 2. utter squawks.

squeak (skwēk) n. 1. small shrill sound. —v. 2. emit squeaks. —**squeak/y,** adj. —**squeak/er,** n.

squeal (skwēl) n. 1. long shrill cry. —v. 2. utter squeals.

squeam/ish (skwē/mish) adj. 1. prudish. 2. overfastidious.

squee/gee (skwē/jē) n. implement for cleaning glass surfaces.

squeeze (skwēz) v., **squeezed, squeezing,** n. —v. 1. press together. 2. cram. —n. 3. act of squeezing. 4. hug.

squelch (skwelch) v. 1. make a sucking noise. 2. silence. —n. 3. crushing retort.

squib (skwib) n. 1. short witty item. 2. hissing firecracker.

squid (skwid) n. marine mollusk.

squig/gle (skwig/əl) n. short, irregular curve or twist. —**squig/gly,** adj.

squint (skwint) v. 1. look with eyes partly closed. 2. be cross-eyed. —n. 3. squinting look. 4. cross-eyed condition.

squire (skwī°r) n., v., **squired, squiring.** —n. 1. country gentleman. 2. escort. —v. 3. escort.

squirm (skwûrm) v., n. wriggle.

squir/rel (skwûr/əl) n. bushy-tailed, tree-living rodent.

squirt (skwûrt) v. 1. gush; cause to gush. —n. 2. jet of liquid.

squish (skwish) v. 1. make gushing sound when squeezed. 2. squash (def. 1). —n. 3. squishing sound.

Sr., 1. Senior. 2. Sister.

SRO, 1. single-room occupancy. 2. standing room only.

SS, social security.

SST, supersonic transport.

St., 1. Saint. 2. Street.

stab (stab) v., **stabbed, stabbing,** n. —v. 1. pierce with pointed weapon. —n. 2. thrust with or wound from pointed weapon.

sta/bi·lize/ (stā/bə līz/) v., **-lized, -lizing.** make or keep stable.

sta/ble (stā/bəl) n., v., **-bled, -bling,** adj. —n. 1. building for horses, etc. —v. 2. keep in stable. —adj. 3. steady. —**sta·bil/i·ty,** n.

stac·ca/to (stə kä/tō) adj. Music. disconnected; detached.

stack (stak) n. 1. orderly heap. 2. (often pl.) book storage area. 3. funnel for smoke. —v. 4. pile in stack.

sta/di·um (stā/dē əm) n., pl. **-diums, -dia** (-ə). large open structure for games.

staff (staf) n., pl. **staves** (stāvz) or **staffs** (for 1, 3); **staffs** (for 2); v. —n. 1. stick carried as support, weapon, etc. 2. body of administrators or assitants. 3. set of five lines on which music is written. —v. 4. provide with staff.

staff/er, n. member of a staff.

stag (stag) n. 1. adult male deer. —adj. 2. for men only. —adv. 3. without a date.

stage (stāj) n., v., **staged, staging.** —n. 1. single step or degree. 2. raised platform. 3. theater. —v. 4. present on stage.

stage/coach/, n. horse-drawn public coach that traveled over fixed route.

stage/hand/, n. worker in theater who deals with props and scenery.

stage/struck/, adj. obsessed with desire to act.

stag/ger (stag/ər) v. 1. move unsteadily. 2. astonish. 3. arrange at intervals. —n. 4. staggering movement. **5.** (*pl.*) disease of horses, etc.

stag′ger•ing, *adj.* amazing.

stag′ing (stā′jing) *n.* scaffolding.

stag′nant (stag′nənt) *adj.* **1.** not flowing; foul. **2.** inactive. —**stag′nate** (-nāt) *v.*, **-nated, -nating.** —**stag•na′tion,** *n.*

staid (stād) *adj.* sedate.

stain (stān) *n.* **1.** discolored patch. **2.** kind of dye. —*v.* **3.** mark with stains. **4.** color with stain.

stainless steel, steel allied with chromium to resist rust.

stair (stâr) *n.* series of steps between levels. —**stair′case′, stair′way′,** *n.*

stair′well′, *n.* vertical shaft containing stairs.

stake (stāk) *n.*, *v.*, **staked, staking.** —*n.* **1.** pointed post. **2.** something wagered. **3.** (*pl.*) prize. **4.** hazard. —*v.* **5.** mark off with stakes. **6.** wager.

stake′out′, *n.* surveillance by police.

sta•lac′tite (stə lak′tīt) *n.* icicle-shaped formation hanging from cave roof.

sta•lag′mite (stə lag′mīt) *n.* cone-shaped deposit on cave floor.

stale (stāl) *adj.*, **staler, stalest,** *v.*, **staled, staling.** —*adj.* **1.** not fresh. —*v.* **2.** make or become stale.

stale′mate′ (-māt′) *n.* deadlocked position, orig. in chess.

stalk (stôk) *v.* **1.** pursue stealthily. **2.** walk in haughty or menacing way. —*n.* **3.** plant stem. —**stalk′er,** *n.*

stall (stôl) *n.* **1.** compartment for one animal. **2.** sales booth. **3.** (of airplane) loss of air speed. **4.** *Slang.* pretext for delay. —*v.* **5.** keep in stall. **6.** stop. **7.** lose necessary air speed. **8.** *Slang.* delay.

stal′lion (stal′yən) *n.* male horse.

stal′wart (stôl′wərt) *adj.* **1.** robust. **2.** brave. —*n.* **3.** stalwart person.

sta′men (stā′mən) *n.* pollen-bearing organ of flower.

stam′i•na (stam′ə nə) *n.* endurance.

stam′mer (stam′ər) *v.* speak with involuntary breaks or repetitions. —*n.* **2.** such speech.

stamp (stamp) *v.* **1.** trample. **2.** mark. **3.** put paper stamp on. —*n.* **4.** act of stamping. **5.** marking device. **6.** adhesive paper affixed to show payment of fees.

stam•pede′ (stam pēd′) *n.*, *v.*, **-peded, -peding.** —*n.* **1.** panicky flight. —*v.* **2.** flee in stampede.

stamping ground, favorite haunt.

stance (stans) *n.* way of standing.

stanch (stônch, stanch) *adj.* **1.**

staunch. —*v.* **2.** stop flow, esp. of blood.

stan′chion (stan′shən) *n.* upright post.

stand (stand) *v.*, **stood** (sto̅o̅d), **standing,** *v.* **1.** rise or be upright. **2.** remain firm. **3.** be located. **4.** be candidate. **5.** endure. —*n.* **6.** firm attitude. **7.** place of standing. **8.** platform. **9.** support for small articles. **10.** outdoor salesplace. **11.** area of trees. **12.** stop.

stand′ard (stan′dərd) *n.* **1.** approved model or rule. **2.** flag. **3.** upright support. —*adj.* **4.** being model or basis for comparison.

stan′dard-bear′er, *n.* leader of a cause.

stan′dard•ize′, *v.*, **-ized, -izing.** make standard.

standard time, civil time officially adopted for a region.

stand′-by′, *n.*, *pl.* **-bys,** *adj.* —*n.* **1.** chief support. —*adj.* **2.** substitute.

stand′-in′, *n.* substitute.

stand′ing, *n.* **1.** status or reputation. **2.** duration. —*adj.* **3.** upright. **4.** stagnant. **5.** lasting; fixed.

stand′off′, *n.* tie or draw; situation in which neither side has advantage.

stand′off′ish, *adj.* tending to be aloof.

stand′out′, *n.* one that is conspicuously superior.

stand′pipe′, *n.* vertical pipe into which water is pumped to obtain required pressure.

stand′point′, *n.* point of view.

stand′still′, *n.* complete halt.

stand′-up′, *adj.* **1.** erect. **2.** performing a comic monologue while standing alone before audience.

stan′za (stan′zə) *n.* division of poem.

sta′ple (stā′pəl) *n.*, *v.*, **-pled, -pling,** *adj.* —*n.* **1.** bracket-shaped wire fastener. **2.** chief commodity. —*v.* **3.** fasten with staple. —*adj.* **4.** basic. —**sta′pler,** *n.*

star (stär) *n.*, *adj.*, *v.*, **starred, starring.** —*n.* **1.** heavenly body luminous at night. **2.** figure with five or six points. **3.** asterisk. **4.** principal performer. **5.** famous performer. —*adj.* **6.** principal. —*v.* **7.** mark with star. **8.** have leading part. —**star′ry,** *adj.* —**star′dom,** *n.*

star′board′ (-bərd, -bôrd′) *n.* right-hand side of vessel, facing forward. —**star′board′,** *adj.*, *adv.*

starch (stärch) *n.* **1.** white tasteless substance used as food and as a stiffening agent. **2.** preparation from starch. —*v.* **3.** stiffen with starch.

stare (stâr) v., **stared, staring**, n. —v. 1. gaze fixedly. —n. 2. fixed look.

star·fish′, n. star-shaped marine animal.

star·gaze′, v., **-gazed, -gazing**. 1. gaze at stars. 2. daydream.

stark (stärk) adj. 1. utter; sheer. 2. bleak. 3. harsh. —adv. 4. utterly.

star·let (-lit) n. young movie actress.

star·light′, n. light emanating from the stars. —**star′lit′**, adj.

star·ling (-ling) n. small bird.

star·ry-eyed′, adj. overly romantic or idealistic.

start (stärt) v. 1. begin. 2. move suddenly. 3. establish. —n. 4. beginning. 5. startled movement. 6. lead. —**start′er**, n.

star·tle, v., **-tled, -tling**. disturb suddenly.

starve (stärv) v., **starved, starving**. 1. die or suffer severely from hunger. 2. kill or weaken by hunger. —**star·va′tion**, n.

stash (stash) v. 1. hide away. —n. 2. something hidden away. 3. hiding place.

stat (stat) n. statistic.

state (stāt) n., adj., v., **stated, stating**. —n. 1. condition. 2. pomp. 3. nation. 4. commonwealth of a federal union. 5. civil government. —adj. 6. ceremonious. —v. 7. declare. —**state′hood**, n. —**state′house**, n.

state′craft′, n. art of government.

state′less, adj. lacking nationality.

state′ly, adj., **-lier, -liest**. dignified.

state′ment, n. 1. declaration. 2. report on business account.

state of the art, most advanced stage.

state′room′, n. quarters on ship, etc.

states′man, n. person skilled in government. —**states′man·ship′**, n.

stat′ic (stat′ik) adj. 1. fixed; at rest. —n. 2. atmospheric electricity. 3. interference caused by it.

sta′tion (stā′shən) n. 1. place of duty. 2. depot for trains, buses, etc. 3. status. 4. place for sending or receiving radio or television broadcasts. —v. 5. assign place to.

sta′tion·ar′y (-shə ner′ē) adj. not moving; not movable; fixed.

sta′tion·er, n. dealer in stationery.

sta′tion·er·y (-sha ner′ē) n. writing materials.

sta·tis′tics (sta tis′tiks) n. science of collecting, classifying, and using numerical facts. —**stat′is·ti′cian** (stat′ə stish′ən) n.

stat′u·ar′y (stach′ŏŏ er′ē) n. statues.

stat′ue (stach′ōō) n. carved, molded, or cast figure.

stat·u·esque′ (-esk′) adj. like statue; of imposing figure.

stat·u·ette′ (-et′) n. little statue.

stat′ure (-ər) n. 1. height. 2. status from achievement.

sta′tus (stā′təs, stat′əs) n. 1. social standing. 2. present condition.

status quo (kwō) existing state.

status symbol, possession believed to indicate high social status.

stat′ute (stach′ōōt) n. law enacted by legislature. —**stat′u·to·ry** (-tōr′ē) adj.

statute of limitations, statute defining period within which legal action may be taken.

staunch (stônch) adj. 1. firm; steadfast; strong. —v. 2. stanch.

stave (stāv) n., v., **staved** (or (for 3) **stove** (stōv), **staving**. —n. 1. narrow strip of wood. 2. Music. staff. —v. 3. break hole in. 4. ward (off).

stay (stā) v. 1. remain; continue. 2. stop or restrain. 3. support. —n. 4. period at one place. 5. stop; pause. 6. support.

staying power, endurance.

STD, sexually transmitted disease.

std., standard.

stead (sted) n. 1. place taken by another. 2. advantage.

stead′fast′, adj. 1. fixed. 2. loyal.

stead′y, adj., **-ier, -iest**, v., **steadied, steadying**. —adj. 1. firmly fixed. 2. uniform; regular. 3. steadfast. —v. 4. make or become steady. —**stead′i·ly**, adv.

steak (stāk) n. slice of meat or fish.

steal (stēl) v., **stole** (stōl), **stolen, stealing**. 1. take wrongfully. 2. move very quietly.

stealth (stelth) n. secret action. —**stealth′y**, adj.

steam (stēm) n. 1. water in form of gas or vapor. —v. 2. pass off as or give off steam. 3. treat with steam, as in cooking. —adj. 4. operated by steam. 5. conducting steam. —**steam′boat′, steam′ship′**, n.

steam′er, n. 1. vessel moved by steam. 2. device for cooking, treating, etc., with steam.

steam′roll′er, n. 1. heavy vehicle with roller used for paving roads. —v. 2. crush, flatten, or overwhelm as if with steamroller.

steam shovel, machine for excavating.

steed (stēd) n. horse, esp. for riding.

steel (stēl) n. 1. iron modified with

carbon. —*adj.* **2.** of or like steel.
—*v.* **3.** make resolute.

steel wool', mass of woven steel, used for scouring and smoothing.

steep (stēp) *adj.* **1.** sloping sharply. **2.** exorbitant. —*v.* **3.** soak. **4.** absorb. —**steep'ly**, *adv.*

stee'ple (stē'pəl) *n.* **1.** lofty tower on church, etc. **2.** spire.

stee'ple·chase', *n.* horse race over obstacle course.

stee'ple·jack', *n.* person who builds or repairs steeples.

steer (stēr) *v.* **1.** guide; direct. —*n.* **2.** ox.

steer'age (-ij) *n.* part of ship for passengers paying cheapest price.

steg'o·saur' (steg'ə sôr') *n.* plant-eating dinosaur with bony plates along back.

stein (stīn) *n.* mug, esp. for beer.

stel'lar (stel'ər) *adj.* of or like stars.

stem (stem) *n.*, *v.*, **stemmed, stemming.** —*n.* **1.** supporting stalk of plant. **2.** ancestry. **3.** part of word not changed by inflection. **4.** *Naut.* bow. —*v.* **5.** remove stem of. **6.** originate. **7.** stop or check. **8.** make headway against.

stem'ware', *n.* glassware with footed stems.

stench (stench) *n.* bad odor.

sten'cil (sten'səl) *n.*, *v.*, **-ciled, -ciling.** —*n.* **1.** sheet cut to pass design through when colored over. —*v.* **2.** print with stencil.

ste·nog'ra·phy (-i rə fē) *n.* writing in shorthand. —**ste·nog'ra·pher**, *n.*

sten·to'ri·an (sten tôr'ē ən) *adj.* very loud.

step (step) *n.*, *v.*, **stepped, stepping.** —*n.* **1.** movement of foot in walking. **2.** distance of such movement. **3.** pace. **4.** footprint. **5.** stage in process. **6.** level on stair or ladder. —*v.* **7.** move by steps. **8.** press with foot.

step-, prefix showing relation by remarriage of parent. —**step'child**, *n.* —**step'son'**, *n.* —**step'daugh'ter**, *n.* —**step'par'ent**, *n.* —**step'fath'er**, *n.* —**step'moth'er**, *n.* —**step'brother**, *n.* —**step'sis'ter**, *n.*

step'lad'der, *n.* ladder with flat treads.

steppe (step) *n.* vast plain.

-ster, suffix meaning one who is, who is associated with, or one who makes or does.

ster'e·o (ster'ē ō', stēr'-) *n.*, pl. **-eos.** stereophonic sound or equipment.

ster'e·o·phon'ic (ster'ē ə fon'ik, stēr'-) *adj.* (of recorded sound) played through two or more speakers.

ster'e·o·type', *n.*, *v.*, **-typed, -typing.** **1.** idea, etc., without originality. **2.** simplified image of person, group, etc. —*v.* **3.** give fixed, trite form to.

ster'ile (ster'il; *esp. Brit.* -īl) *adj.* **1.** free from living germs. **2.** unable to produce offspring; barren. —**ste·ril'i·ty** (stə ril'i tē) *n.*

ster'i·lize', *v.*, **-lized, -lizing.** make sterile. —**ster'i·li·za'tion**, *n.* —**ster'i·liz'er**, *n.*

ster'ling (stûr'ling) *adj.* **1.** containing 92.5% silver. **2.** of British money. **3.** excellent.

stern (stûrn) *adj.* **1.** strict; harsh; grim. —*n.* **2.** hind part of vessel.

ster'num (stûr'nəm) *n.*, pl. **-na, -nums.** flat bone in chest connecting with clavicle and ribs.

ster'oid (stēr'oid, ster'-) *n.* any of a group of fat-soluble organic compounds.

stet (stet) *v.*, **stetted, stetting.** **1.** let it stand (direction to retain material previously deleted). **2.** mark with word "stet."

steth'o·scope' (steth'ə skōp') *n.* medical instrument for listening to sounds in body.

ste've·dore' (stē'vi dôr') *n.* person who loads and unloads ships.

stew (stōō, styōō) *v.* **1.** cook by simmering. —*n.* **2.** food so cooked.

stew'ard (stōō'ərd, styōō'-) *n.* **1.** person who manages another's affairs, property, etc. **2.** person in charge of supplies, food, etc., for ship, club, etc. **3.** domestic employee on ship or airplane. —**stew'ard·ship'**, *n.*

stick (stik) *v.*, **stuck** (stuk), **sticking.** —*v.* **1.** pierce; stab. **2.** thrust. **3.** cause to adhere. **4.** adhere. **5.** persist. **6.** extend. —*n.* **7.** small length of wood, etc.

stick'er, *n.* adhesive label.

stick'-in-the-mud', *n.* person who avoids change.

stick'ler, *n.* someone who insists on something difficult.

stick'pin', *n.* ornamental pin.

stick shift, manual transmission.

stick'y, *adj.*, **-ier, -iest. 1.** adhering. **2.** humid. —**stick'i·ness**, *n.*

stiff (stif) *adj.* **1.** rigid. **2.** not moving easily. **3.** formal. —**stiff'en**, *v.* **stiff'-necked'**, *adj.* obstinate.

sti'fle (stī'fəl) *v.*, **-fled, -fling. 1.** smother. **2.** repress.

stig'ma (stig'mə) *n.*, pl. **stig·ma·ta** (stig mä'tə, —**mas. 1.** mark of disgrace. **2.** pollen-receiving part of pistil. —**stig'ma·tize'**, *v.*

stile (stīl) *n.* set of steps over fence, wall, etc.

stiletto

sti·let·to (sti let′ō) n., pl. **-tos**, **-toes**. thin-bladed dagger.

still (stil) adj. **1.** motionless. **2.** silent. **3.** tranquil. —adv. **4.** as previously. **5.** until now. **6.** yet. —conj. **7.** nevertheless. —v. **8.** make or become still. —n. **9.** distilling apparatus. —**still′ness**, n.

still′born′, adj. born dead.

still life, picture of inanimate objects.

stilt (stilt) n. one of two poles enabling user to walk above the ground.

stilt′ed, adj. stiffly dignified.

stim′u·lant (stim′yə lant) n. food, medicine, etc., that stimulates briefly.

stim′u·late′ (-lāt′) v., **-lated, -lating. 1.** rouse to action. **2.** invigorate. —**stim′u·la′tion**, n.

stim′u·lus (-las) n., pl. **-li.** something that stimulates.

sting (sting) v., **stung** (stung), **stinging**, n. —v. **1.** wound with pointed organ, as bees do. **2.** pain sharply. **3.** goad. —n. **4.** wound caused by stinging. **5.** sharp-pointed organ. —**sting′er**, n.

stin·gy (stin′jē) adj., **-gier, -giest. 1.** miserly. **2.** scanty.

stink (stingk) v., **stank** (stangk) or **stunk** (stungk), **stunk, stinking**, n. —v. **1.** emit bad odor. —n. **2.** bad odor.

stint (stint) v. **1.** limit. —n. **2.** limitation. **3.** allotted task.

sti·pend (stī′pend) n. regular pay.

stip·ple (stip′əl) v., **-pled, -pling**, n. —v. **1.** paint or cover with tiny dots. —n. **2.** such painting.

stip′u·late′ (stip′yə lāt′) v., **-lated, -lating.** require as condition.

stir (stûr) v., **stirred, stirring**, n. —v. **1.** mix or agitate (liquid, etc.), esp. with circular motion. **2.** move. **3.** rouse; excite. —n. **4.** movement; commotion. **5.** Slang. prison.

stir′-cra′zy, adj. Slang. restless from long confinement.

stir′-fry′, v., **-fried, -frying.** fry quickly while stirring constantly over high heat.

stir′rup (stûr′əp, stir′-) n. looplike support for foot, suspended from saddle.

stitch (stich) n. **1.** complete movement of needle in sewing, knitting, etc. **2.** sudden pain. —v. **3.** sew.

stock (stok) n. **1.** goods on hand. **2.** livestock. **3.** stem or trunk. **4.** line of descent. **5.** meat broth. **6.** part of gun supporting barrel. **7.** (pl.) framework in which prisoners were publicly confined. **8.** capital or shares of company. **9.**

standard; common. **10.** of stock. —v. **11.** supply. **12.** store. —**stock′-brok′er**, n. —**stock′hold′er**, n.

stock·ade′ (sto kād′) n., v., **-aded, -ading.** —n. **1.** barrier of upright posts. —v. **2.** protect with stockade.

stock company, theatrical company acting repertoire of plays.

stock exchange, place where securities are bought and sold. Also, **stock market.**

stock′ing, n. close-fitting covering for foot and leg.

stocking cap, conical knitted cap with tassel or pompom.

stock′pile′, n., v., **-piled, -piling.** —n. **1.** stock of goods. —v. **2.** accumulate for eventual use.

stock′-still′, adj. motionless.

stock′y, adj., **-ier, -iest.** sturdily built.

stock′yard′, n. enclosure for livestock about to be slaughtered.

stodg·y (stoj′ē) adj., **-ier, -iest.** pompous and uninteresting.

sto·gy (stō′gē) n., pl. **-gies.** long, slender, cheap cigar.

sto·ic (stō′ik) adj. **1.** Also, **sto′i·cal.** not reacting to pain. —n. **2.** person who represses emotion.

stoke (stōk) v., **stoked, stoking.** tend (fire). —**stok′er**, n.

stole (stōl) n. scarf or narrow strip worn over shoulders.

stol′id (stol′id) adj. unemotional; not easily moved. —**sto·lid′i·ty**, n.

stom·ach (stum′ək) n. **1.** organ of food storage and digestion. **2.** appetite; desire. —v. **3.** tolerate.

stomp (stomp) v. tread or tread on heavily.

stone (stōn) n., pl. **stones** or (for 4) **stone**, adj., v., **stoned, stoning**, adv. —n. **1.** hard, nonmetallic mineral substance. **2.** small rock. **3.** gem. **4.** Brit. unit of weight = 14 pounds. **5.** stonelike seed. **6.** concretion formed in body. —adj. **7.** of stone. —v. **8.** throw stones at. **9.** remove stones from. —adv. **10.** entirely. —**ston′y**, adj.

Stone Age, prehistoric period before use of metals.

stoned, adj. Informal. **1.** drunk. **2.** drugged.

stone′wall′, v. be evasive or uncooperative.

stooge (stōōj) n. **1.** assistant to comedian. **2.** person acting in obsequious obedience.

stool (stōōl) n. seat without arms or back.

stool pigeon, Slang. decoy or informer.

stoop (stōōp) v. **1.** bend forward.

2. condescend. —n. 3. stooping posture. 4. small doorway or porch.

stop (stop) v., **stopped, stopping,** n. —v.1. cease; halt. 2. prevent. 3. close up. 4. stay. —n. 5. act, instance, or place of stopping. 6. hindrance.

stop′gap′, n., adj. makeshift.

stop′o′ver, n. temporary stop on journey.

stop′per, n. 1. plug. —v. 2. close with stopper. Also, **stop′ple**.

stop′watch′, n. watch with hand that can be stopped or started instantly.

stor′age (stôr′ij) n. 1. place for storing. 2. act of storing. 3. state of being stored. 4. fee for storing.

store (stôr) n., v., **stored, storing.** —n. 1. place where merchandise is kept for sale. 2. supply. —v. 3. lay up; accumulate. 4. put in secure place. —**store′keep′er,** n.

store′front′, n. small, street-level store.

store′house′, n. building for storage. —**store′room′,** n.

stork (stôrk) n. wading bird with long legs and bill.

storm (stôrm) n. 1. heavy rain, snow, etc., with strong winds. 2. violent assault. —v. 3. blow, rain, etc., strongly. 4. rage. 5. attack.

sto′ry (stôr′ē) n., pl. **-ries.** 1. fictitious tale. 2. plot. 3. newspaper report. 4. *Informal.* lie. 5. horizontal section of building.

stoup (stoōp) n. basin for holy water.

stout (stout) adj. 1. solidly built. 2. strong. 3. firm. —n. 4. dark ale.

stout′-heart′ed, adj. brave and resolute.

stove (stōv) n. apparatus for giving heat.

stow (stō) v. 1. put away, as cargo. 2. stow away, hide on ship, etc., to get free trip. —**stow′age,** n. —**stow′a•way′,** n.

strad′dle (strad′l) v., **-dled, -dling,** n. —v. 1. have one leg on either side of. —n. 2. straddling stance.

strafe (strāf, sträf) v., **strafed, strafing.** shoot from airplanes.

strag′gle (strag′al) v., **-gled, -gling.** stray from course; ramble. —**strag′gler,** n.

straight (strāt) adj. 1. direct. 2. even. 3. honest. 4. right. 5. *Informal.* heterosexual. —adv. 6. directly. 7. in straight line. 8. honestly. —n. 9. five-card consecutive sequence in poker. —**straight′en,** v.

straight′-arm′, v. deflect an opponent by pushing away with the arm held straight.

straight arrow, often righteously conventional person.

straight′a•way′, adv. at once. Also, **straight′way′.**

straight′edge′, n. bar with straight edge for use in drawing lines.

straight face, expression that conceals feelings, as when keeping a secret.

straight′for′ward, adj. direct; frank.

straight man, entertainer who acts as foil for comedian.

strain (strān) v. 1. exert to utmost. 2. injure by stretching. 3. sieve; filter. —n. 4. great effort. 5. injury from straining. 6. severe pressure. 7. melody. 8. descendants. 9. ancestry. 10. hereditary trait.

strained, adj. not natural.

strait (strāt) n. 1. narrow waterway. 2. (pl.) distress.

strait′en, v. 1. put into financial troubles. 2. restrict.

strait′jack′et, n. 1. garment of strong material designed to bind arms and restrain violent person. 2. anything that severely confines or hinders.

strait′-laced′, adj. excessively strict in conduct or morality.

strand (strand) v. 1. run aground. 2. leave helpless —n. 3. shore. 4. twisted component of rope. 5. tress. 6. string, as of beads.

strange (strānj) adj., **stranger, strangest.** 1. unusual; odd. 2. unfamiliar. —**strange′ly,** adv.

stran′ger (strān′jar) n. person not known or acquainted.

stran′gle (strang′gal) v., **-gled, -gling.** 1. kill by choking. 2. choke. —**stran′gu•la′tion** (-gya lā′shan) n.

stran′gle•hold′, n. restrictive force.

stran′gu•late′ (-gya lāt′) v., **-lated, -lating.** constrict.

strap (strap) n., v., **strapped, strapping.** —n. 1. narrow strip or band. —v. 2. fasten with strap.

strapped, adj. needing money.

strat′a•gem (strat′ə jəm) n. plan; trick.

strat′e•gy (strat′i jē) n., pl. **-gies.** 1. planning and direction of military operations. 2. plan for achieving goal. —**stra•te′gic** (stra tē′jik) adj. —**strat′e•gist,** n.

strat′i•fy (strat′ə fī′) v., **-fied, -fying.** form in layers. —**strat′i•fi•ca′tion,** n.

strat′o•sphere′ (-ə sfēr′) n. upper region of atmosphere.

stra′tum (strā′təm, strat′əm) n., pl. **-ta** (-tə), **-tums.** layer of material.

straw (strô) n. 1. stalk of cereal

grass. **2.** mass of dried stalks. **3.** tube for drinking.

straw/ber/ry (-ber'ē, -bə rē) n., pl. **-ries.** fleshy fruit of stemless herb.

straw boss, assistant foreman.

straw vote, unofficial vote taken to determine general trend of opinion.

stray (strā) v. **1.** ramble; go from one's course or rightful place. —adj. **2.** straying. —n. **3.** stray creature.

streak (strēk) n. **1.** long mark or smear. **2.** vein; stratum. —v. **3.** mark with streaks. **4.** flash rapidly.

stream (strēm) n. **1.** flowing body of water. **2.** steady flow. —v. **3.** move in stream. **4.** wave.

stream/er, n. long narrow flag.

stream/line/, adj., n., v., **-lined, -lining.** —adj. **1.** having shape past which fluids move easily. —n. **2.** streamline shape. —v. **3.** shape with streamline. **4.** reorganize efficiently.

street (strēt) n. public city road.

street/car/, n. public conveyance running on rails.

street smarts, shrewd awareness of how to survive in urban environment. —**street/-smart/,** adj.

street/walk/er, n. prostitute who solicits on the streets.

street/wise/, adj. possessing street smarts.

strength (strengkth, strength, strenth) n. **1.** power of body, mind, position, etc. **2.** intensity.

strength/en, v. make or grow stronger.

stren/u·ous (stren'yōō əs) adj. vigorous; active.

strep throat (strep) acute sore throat caused by streptococci.

strep/to·coc/cus (strep'tə kok'əs) n., pl. **-ci** (-sī, -sē). one of group of disease-producing bacteria.

stress (stres) v. **1.** emphasize. —n. **2.** emphasis. **3.** physical, mental, or emotional strain.

stretch (strech) v. **1.** extend; spread. **2.** distend. **3.** draw tight. —n. **4.** act of stretching. **5.** extension; expansion. **6.** continuous length.

stretch/er, n. **1.** canvas-covered frame for carrying sick, etc. **2.** device for stretching.

strew (strōō) v., **strewed, strewed** or **strewn, strewing.** scatter.

stri/at·ed (strī'ā tid) adj. furrowed; streaked. —**stri·a/tion** (-ā'shən) n.

strick/en (strik'ən) adj. **1.** wounded. **2.** afflicted, as by disease or sorrow.

strict (strikt) adj. **1.** exacting; severe. **2.** precise. **3.** careful. **4.** absolute. —**strict/ly,** adv.

stric/ture (strik'chər) n. **1.** adverse criticism. **2.** morbid contraction of body passage.

stride (strīd) v., **strode** (strōd), **stridden** (strid'n), **striding,** n. —v. **1.** walk with long steps. **2.** straddle. —n. **3.** long step. **4.** steady pace.

stri/dent (strīd'nt) adj. harsh in sound. —**stri/den·cy,** n.

strife (strīf) n. conflict or quarrel.

strike (strīk) v., **struck** (struk), **struck** or **strick·en** (strik'ən), **striking,** n. —v. **1.** deal a blow. **2.** hit forcibly. **3.** cause to ignite. **4.** impress. **5.** efface; mark out. **6.** afflict or affect. **7.** sound by percussion. **8.** discover in ground. **9.** encounter. **10.** (of workers) stop work to compel agreement to demands. **11.** strike out, Baseball. put or be put out on three strikes. —n. **12.** act of striking. **13.** Baseball. failure of batter to hit pitched ball. **14.** Bowling. knocking-down of all pins at once.

strik/ing, adj. **1.** conspicuously attractive or impressive. **2.** noticeable.

string (string) n., v., **strung** (strung), **stringing.** —n. **1.** cord, thread, etc. **2.** series or set. **3.** cord on musical instrument. **4.** plant fiber. —v. **5.** supply with strings. **6.** arrange in row. **7.** mount on string. —**stringed,** adj. —**string/y,** adj.

string bean, bean with edible pod.

strin/gent (strin'jənt) adj. very strict. —**strin/gen·cy,** n.

string/er (string/-) n. **1.** horizontal timber connecting upright posts. **2.** part-time news reporter.

strip (strip) v., **stripped, stripping,** n. —v. **1.** remove covering or clothing. **2.** rob. **3.** cut into strips. —n. **4.** long narrow piece.

stripe (strīp) n., v., **striped, striping.** —n. **1.** band of different color, etc. **2.** welt from whipping. —v. **3.** mark with stripes.

strip/ling (strip'ling) n. youth.

strip mine, mine in open pit. —**strip/-mine/,** v., **-mined, -mining.**

strip/tease/, n. act, as in burlesque, in which performer gradually removes clothing. —**strip/per,** n.

strive (strīv) v., **strove** (strōv), **striv·en** (striv'ən), **striving.** try hard; struggle.

strobe (strōb) n. electronic flash producing rapid bursts of light.

stroke (strōk) n., v., **stroked, stroking,** n. —v. **1.** rub gently. —n. **2.** act of stroking. **3.** blow. **4.** blockage or hemorrhage of blood vessel leading to brain. **5.** one complete movement. **6.** piece of luck, work, etc. **7.** method of swimming.

stroll (strōl) v. **1.** walk idly. **2.** roam.

stroll′er, n. chairlike carriage in which young children are pushed.

strong (strông) adj. **1.** vigorous; powerful; able. **2.** intense; distinct.

strong′-arm′, adj. **1.** involving physical force. —v. **2.** use physical force.

strong′box′, n. strongly made box for money.

strong′hold′, n. fortress.

stron′ti·um (stron′shē əm, -shəm, -tē əm) n. metallic chemical element.

strop (strop) n., v., **stropped, strop-ping.** —n. **1.** flexible strap. —v. **2.** sharpen on strop.

struc′ture (struk′chər) n. **1.** form of building or arrangement. **2.** something built. —**struc′tur·al,** adj.

stru′del (strōōd′l; Ger. shtrōōd′l) n. fruit-filled pastry.

strug′gle (strug′əl) v., **-gled, -gling,** n. —v. **1.** contend; strive. **2.** combat. —n. **3.** strong effort. **4.** combat.

strum (strum) v., **strummed, strum-ming.** play carelessly on (stringed instrument).

strum′pet (strum′pit) n. prostitute.

strut (strut) v., **strutted, strutting,** n. —v. **1.** walk in vain, pompous manner. —n. **2.** strutting walk. **3.** prop; truss.

strych′nine (strik′nīn, -nēn, -nīn) n. colorless poison.

stub (stub) n., v., **stubbed, stub-bing.** —n. **1.** short remaining piece. **2.** stump. —v. **3.** strike (one's toe) against something. —**stub′by,** adj.

stub′ble (stub′əl) n. **1.** short stumps, as of grain stalks. **2.** short growth of beard. —**stub′bly,** adj.

stub′born (stub′ərn) adj. **1.** unreasonably obstinate. **2.** persistent.

stuc′co (stuk′ō) n., pl. **-coes, -cos,** v., **-coed, -coing.** —n. **1.** plaster for exteriors. —v. **2.** cover with stucco.

stuck′-up′, adj. Informal. snobbishly conceited.

stud (stud) n., v., **studded, stud-ding.** —n. **1.** projecting knob, pin, etc. **2.** upright post. **3.** detachable button. **4.** collection of horses or other animals for breeding. **5.** stallion. —v. **6.** set or scatter with studs.

stu′dent (stōōd′nt, styōōd′-) n. person who studies.

stud′ied (stud′ēd) adj. deliberate.

stu′di·o (stōō′dē ō′, styōō′-) n., pl. **-dios.** **1.** artist's workroom. **2.** place equipped for radio or television broadcasting.

stud′y (stud′ē) n., pl. **studies,** v., **studied, studying.** —n. **1.** effort to learn. **2.** object of study. **3.** deep thought. **4.** room for studying, writing, etc. —v. **5.** make study of —**stu′di·ous** (stōō′dē əs, styōō′-) adj. —**stu′di·ous·ly,** adv.

stuff (stuf) n. **1.** material. **2.** worthless matter. —v. **3.** cram full; pack.

stuffed shirt, pompous, self-satisfied person.

stuff′ing, n. material stuffed in something.

stuff′y, adj., **-ier, -iest. 1.** lacking fresh air. **2.** pompous; pedantic.

stul′ti·fy (stul′tə fī′) v., **-fied, -fy-ing. 1.** cause to look foolish **2.** make futile.

stum′ble (stum′bəl) v., **-bled, -bling. 1.** lose balance. **2.** come unexpectedly upon.

stumbling block, obstacle.

stump (stump) n. **1.** lower end of tree after top is gone. **2.** any short remaining part. —v. **3.** baffle. **4.** campaign politically. **5.** walk heavily.

stun (stun) v., **stunned, stunning. 1.** render unconscious. **2.** amaze.

stun′ning, adj. strikingly attractive.

stunt (stunt) v. **1.** check growth. —n. **2.** performance to show skill, etc.

stu′pe·fy (stōō′pə fī′, styōō′-) v., **-fied, -fying. 1.** put into stupor. **2.** stun.

stu·pen′dous (stōō pen′dəs, styōō-) adj. **1.** amazing. **2.** immense.

stu′pid (stōō′pid, styōō′-) adj. having or showing little intelligence. —**stu·pid′i·ty,** n.

stu′por (-pər) n. dazed or insensible state.

stur′dy (stûr′dē) adj., **-dier, -diest. 1.** strongly built. **2.** firm.

stur′geon (stûr′jən) n. large fish of fresh and salt water.

stut′ter (stut′ər) v., n. stammer.

sty (stī) n., pl. **sties. 1.** pig pen. **2.** inflamed swelling on eyelid.

style (stīl) n., v., **styled, styling.** —n. **1.** particular kind. **2.** mode of fashion. **3.** elegance. **4.** distinct way of writing or speaking. —v. **5.** name. —**sty·lis′tic,** adj.

styl′ish, adj. fashionable.

styl′ist, n. person who cultivates distinctive style.

styl′ize, v., **-ized, -izing.** cause to conform to conventionalized form.

sty′lus (stī′ləs) n. pointed tool for writing, etc.

sty′mie (stī′mē) v., **-mied, -mying.** hinder or obstruct, as in golf.

styp′tic (stip′tik) adj. **1.** checking bleeding. —n. **2.** styptic substance.

Sty/ro·foam/ (stī′rə fōm′) n. Trademark. lightweight plastic.

suave (swäv) adj. polite and agreeable. —**suav′i·ty,** n.

sub-, prefix meaning under; below; beneath; less than.

sub′a·tom′ic, adj. of particles within an atom.

sub·com·mit′tee, n. committee appointed out of main committee.

sub·con′scious, adj. 1. existing beneath consciousness. —n. 2. ideas, feelings, etc., of which one is unaware. —**sub·con′scious·ly,** adv.

sub·con′ti·nent (sub kon′tn ant, sub′kon′-). n. large subdivision of continent.

sub′cul′ture, n. group with social, economic, or other traits distinguishing it from others within larger society.

sub′cu·ta′ne·ous, adj. beneath the skin.

sub′di·vide′ (sub′di vīd′, sub′di-vīd′) v., -vided, -viding. divide into parts. —**sub′di·vi′sion,** n.

sub·due′ (səb doo′, -dyoo′) v., -dued, -duing. 1. overcome. 2. soften.

sub·fam′i·ly (sub fam′ə lē, sub-fam′ə lē) n., pl. -lies. 1. category of related organisms within a family. 2. group of related languages within a family.

sub′head′, n. 1. heading of a subdivision. 2. subordinate division of a title.

sub′ject, n. (sub′jikt) 1. matter of thought, concern, etc. 2. person under rule of government. 3. noun or pronoun that performs action of predicate. 4. one undergoing action, etc. —adj. (sub′jikt) 5. being a subject. 6. liable; exposed. —v. (səb jekt′) 7. cause to experience. 8. make liable. —**sub·jec′tion,** n.

sub·jec′tive, adj. 1. personal. 2. from a particular point of view. —**sub′jec·tiv′i·ty,** n.

sub·join′ (səb join′) v. append.

sub′ju·gate′ (sub′jə gāt′) v., -gated, -gating. subdue; conquer. —**sub′ju·ga′tion,** n.

sub·junc′tive (səb jungk′tiv) adj. 1. designating verb mode of condition, impression, etc. —n. 2. subjunctive mode.

sub′lease′, n., v., -leased, -leasing. —n. (sub′lēs′) 1. lease granted by tenant. —v. (sub lēs′) 2. rent by sublease.

sub·let′ (sub let′, sub′let′) v., -let, -letting. 1. (of lessee) let to another person.

sub′li·mate′, v., -mated, -mating. n. —v. (sub′lə māt′) 1. deflect (bi-

ological energies) to other channels. 2. sublime. —n. (-mit, -māt′) 3. substance obtained in subliming.

sub·lime′ (sə blīm′) adj. n., v., -limed, -liming. —adj. 1. lofty; noble. —n. 2. that which is sublime. —v. 3. heat (substance) to vapor that condenses to solid on cooling. —**sub·lim′i·ty** (sə blim′i tē) n.

sub·lim′i·nal (sub lim′ə nl) adj. below threshold of consciousness.

sub′ma·chine′ gun, automatic weapon.

sub·ma·rine′, n. (sub′mə rēn′, sub′mə rēn′) 1. vessel that can navigate under water. —adj. (sub′mə rēn′) 2. of submarines. 3. being under sea.

sub·merge′ (səb mûrj′) v., -merged, -merging. plunge under water. —**sub·mer′gence,** n.

sub·merse′ (-mûrs′) v., -mersed, -mersing. submerge. —**sub·mer′sion** (-mûr′zhən, -shən) n., **sub·mers′i·ble,** adj.

sub·mis′sive, adj. yielding or obeying readily. —**sub·mis′sive·ly,** adv.

sub·mit′ (səb mit′) v., -mitted, -mitting. 1. yield; surrender. 2. offer for consideration. —**sub·mis′sion** (-mish′ən) n.

sub·nor′mal (sub nôr′məl) adj. of less than normal intelligence.

sub·or′di·nate, adj., n., v., -nated, -nating. —adj. (sə bôr′dn it) 1. of lower rank or importance. —n. (sə-bôr′dn it) 2. subordinate person or thing. —v. (-dn āt′) 3. treat as subordinate. —**sub·or′di·na′tion,** n.

sub·orn′ (sə bôrn′) v. bribe or incite to crime, esp. to perjury.

sub′plot′ (sub′plot′) n. secondary plot.

sub·poe′na (sə pē′nə, səb-), n., v., -naed, -naing. 1. summons to appear in court. —v. 2. serve with subpoena.

sub ro′sa (sub rō′zə) secretly.

sub·scribe′ (səb skrīb′) v., -scribed, -scribing. 1. promise contribution. 2. agree; sign in agreement. 3. contract to receive periodical regularly. —**sub·scrip′tion** (-skrip′shən) n.

sub′script (sub′skript) n. letter, number, etc. written low on line.

sub′se·quent (sub′si kwənt) adj. later; following.

sub·serv′i·ent (səb sûr′vē ənt) adj. 1. servile; submissive. 2. useful. —**sub·serv′i·ence,** n.

sub·side′ (səb sīd′) v., -sided, -siding. 1. sink; settle. 2. abate. —**sub·sid′ence,** n.

sub·sid′i·ar·y (-sīd′ē er′ē) adj., n., pl. -aries. —adj. 1. auxiliary. 2. subordinate. —n. 3. anything subsidiary.

sub/si·dy (-si dē) *n., pl.* **-dies.** direct pecuniary aid, esp. by government. **—sub/si·dize/**, *v.*, **-dized, -dizing.**

sub·sist/ (sab sist/) *v.* **1.** exist. **2.** live (as on food).

sub/soil/ (sub/soil/) *n.* layer of earth immediately underneath surface soil.

sub·son/ic, *adj.* of a speed below the speed of sound.

sub/stance (sub/stans) *n.* **1.** matter or material. **2.** density. **3.** meaning. **4.** wealth.

sub·stan/dard, *adj.* below standard; not good enough.

sub·stan/tial (sab stan/shal) *adj.* **1.** actual. **2.** fairly large. **3.** strong. **4.** of substance. **5.** prosperous.

sub·stan/ti·ate/ (-shē āt/) *v.,* **-ated, -ating.** support with evidence.

sub/stan·tive (sub/stan tiv) *n.* noun, pronoun, or word used as noun. **—adj. 2.** of or denoting substantive.

sub/sti·tute/ (sub/sti tōōt/, -tyōōt/) *v.,* **-tuted, -tuting,** *n.* **—v. 1.** put or serve in place of another. **—n. 2.** substitute person or thing.

sub/struc/ture (sub/struk/char) *n.* structure forming a foundation.

sub·sume/ (sab sōōm/) *v.,* **-sumed, -suming.** consider or include as part of something larger.

sub/ter·fuge/ (sub/tar fyōōj/) *n.* means used to evade or conceal.

sub·ter·ra/ne·an (-tə rā/nē ən) *adj.* underground.

sub/text/ *n.* underlying or implicit meaning.

sub/ti/tle, *n., v.,* **-tled, -tling.** **—n. 1.** secondary or subordinate title, as of book. **2.** text of dialogue, etc., appearing at bottom of motion picture screen, etc. **—v. 3.** give subtitles to.

sub/tle (sut/l) *adj.,* **-tler, -tlest. 1.** delicate; faint. **2.** discerning. **3.** skillful. **—sub/tle·ty,** *n.*

sub/to/tal (sub/tōt/l, sub tōt/-) *n., v.,* **-totaled, -totaling.** **—n. 1.** total of part of a group of figures. **—v. 2.** determine subtotal for.

sub·tract/ (sab trakt/) *v.* take from another; deduct. **—sub·trac/tion,** *n.*

sub·trop/i·cal, *adj.* bordering on tropics.

sub/urb (sub/ûrb) *n.* district just outside city. **—sub·ur/ban,** *adj.*

sub·ur/bi·a (-bē ə) *n.* **1.** suburbs or suburbanites collectively. **2.** life in the suburbs.

sub·vert/ (-vûrt/) *v.* overthrow; destroy. **—sub·ver/sion,** *n.* **—sub·ver/sive,** *adj., n.*

sub/way/ (sub/wā/) *n.* underground electric railway.

sub·ze/ro, *adj.* indicating lower than zero on some scale.

suc·ceed/ (sak sēd/) *v.* **1.** end or accomplish successfully. **2.** follow and replace.

suc·cess/ (-ses/) *n.* **1.** favorable achievement. **2.** good fortune. **3.** successful thing or person. **—suc·cess/ful,** *adj.*

suc·ces/sion (-sesh/ən) *n.* **1.** act of following in sequence. **2.** sequence of persons or things. right or process of succeeding another. **—suc·ces/sive,** *adj.*

suc·ces/sor, *n.* one that succeeds another.

suc·cinct/ (sak singkt/) *adj.* without useless words; concise.

suc/cor (suk/ar) *n., v.* help; aid.

suc/co·tash/ (suk/ə tash/) *n.* corn and beans cooked together.

suc/cu·lent (suk/yə lənt) *adj.* juicy. **—suc/cu·lence,** *n.*

suc·cumb/ (sa kum/) *v.* **1.** yield. **2.** die.

such (such) *adj.* **1.** of that kind, extent, etc. **—n. 2.** such person or thing.

suck (suk) *v.* **1.** draw in by using lips and tongue. **2.** absorb. **—n. 3.** act of sucking.

suck/er, *n.* **1.** one that sucks. **2.** fresh-water fish. **3.** *Informal.* lollipop. **4.** shoot from underground stem or root. **5.** *Informal.* gullible person.

suck/le, *v.,* **-led, -ling.** nurse at breast.

suck/ling (-ling) *n.* **1.** infant. **2.** unweaned animal.

su/crose (sōō/krōs) *n.* sugar obtained esp. from sugar cane or sugar beet.

suc/tion (suk/shan) *n.* tendency to draw substance into vacuum.

sud/den (sud/n) *adj.* abrupt; unexpected. **—sud/den·ly,** *adv.*

sudden death, overtime period in which tied contest is won after one contestant scores.

suds (sudz) *n.pl.* **1.** lather. **2.** soapy water. **—suds/y,** *adj.*

sue (sōō) *v.,* **sued, suing. 1.** take legal action. **2.** appeal.

suede (swād) *n.* soft, napped leather.

su/et (sōō/it) *n.* hard fat about kidneys, etc., esp. of cattle.

suf/fer (suf/ar) *v.* **1.** undergo (pain or unpleasantness). **2.** tolerate.

suf/fer·ance (-ans) *n.* **1.** tolerance. **2.** endurance.

suf·fice/ (sə fīs/) *v.,* **-ficed, -ficing.** be enough.

suf·fi·cient (fish/ənt) *adj.* enough.
—**suf·fi/cien·cy,** *n.*

suf·fix (suf/iks) *n.* element added to end of word to form another word.

suf·fo·cate/ (suf/ə kāt/) *v.,* **-cated, -cating.** kill or choke by cutting off air to lungs. —**suf·fo·ca/tion,** *n.*

suf·frage (suf/rij) *n.* right to vote.

suf·fuse/ (sə fyōōz/) *v.* overspread.

sug/ar (shŏŏg/ər) *n.* **1.** sweet substance, esp. from sugar cane or sugar beet. —*v.* **2.** sweeten with sugar. —**sug/ar·less,** *adj.* —**sug/ar·y,** *adj.*

sugar beet, beet with white root having high sugar content.

sugar cane, tall grass that is the chief source of sugar.

sug/ar·coat/, *v.* make more pleasant or acceptable.

sugar maple, maple with sweet sap.

sugar plum, candy.

sug·gest/ (səg jest/, sə-) *v.* **1.** offer for consideration or action. **2.** imply. —**sug·ges/tion,** *n.*

sug·gest/i·ble, *adj.* easily led or influenced. —**sug·gest/i·bil/i·ty,** *n.*

sug·ges/tive, *adj.* suggesting, esp. something improper.

su/i·cide/ (sōō/ə sīd/) *n.* **1.** intentional killing of oneself. **2.** person who commits suicide. —**su/i·cid/al,** *adj.*

su/i ge/ne·ris (sōō/ē jen/ər is, sōō/ī) being one of a kind.

suit (sōōt) *n.* **1.** set of clothes. **2.** legal action. **3.** division of playing cards. **4.** petition. **5.** wooing. —*v.* **6.** clothe. **7.** adapt. **8.** please.

suit/a·ble, *adj.* appropriate; fitting. —**suit/a·bil/i·ty,** *n.*

suit/case/, *n.* oblong valise.

suite (swēt) *n.* **1.** series or set, as of rooms or furniture. **2.** retinue.

suit/ing (sōō/ting) *n.* fabric for making suits.

suit/or (sōō/tər) *n.* wooer.

su/ki·ya/ki (sōō/kē yä/kē, sŏŏk/ē-, skē-) *n.* Japanese dish of meat and vegetables cooked in soy sauce.

sul/fate (-fāt) *n.* salt of sulfuric acid.

sul/fide (-fīd, -fid) *n.* sulfur compound.

sul/fur (-fər) *n.* yellow nonmetallic element.

sul·fur/ic (-fyŏŏr/ik) *adj.* of or containing sulfur. Also, **sul/fur·ous.**

sulfuric acid, corrosive liquid used in chemicals and explosives.

sulk (sulk) *v.* **1.** be sullen and aloof. —*n.* **2.** fit of sulking.

sulk/y, *adj.,* **-ier, -iest,** —*n.* **1.** sullen; ill-humored. —*n.* **2.** two-wheeled racing carriage for one person. —**sulk/i·ly,** *adv.*

sul/len (sul/ən) *adj.* **1.** silently ill-humored. **2.** gloomy.

sul/ly (sul/ē) *v.,* **-lied, -lying.** soil; defile.

sul/phur (-fər) *n.* sulfur.

sul/tan (sul/tn) *n.* ruler of Muslim country. —**sul/tan·ate/,** *n.*

sul·tan/a (-tan/ə) *n.* raisin.

sul/try (-trē) *adj.,* **-trier, -triest.** hot and close. —**sul/tri·ness,** *n.*

sum (sum) *n., v.,* **summed, summing.** —*n.* **1.** aggregate of two or more numbers, etc. **2.** total amount. **3.** gist. —*v.* **4.** total. **5.** summarize.

su/mac (sōō/mak, shōō/-) *n.* small tree with long pinnate leaves.

sum/ma·rize/ (sum/ə rīz/) *v.,* **-rized, -rizing.** make or be summary of.

sum/ma·ry (-rē) *n., pl.* **-ries.** *adj.* **1.** concise presentation of main points. —*adj.* **2.** concise. **3.** prompt.

sum·ma/tion (sə mā/shən) *n.* **1.** act of summing up. **2.** total.

sum/mer (sum/ər) *n.* **1.** season between spring and fall. —*adj.* **2.** of, like, or for summer. —*v.* **3.** spend summer. —**sum/mer·y,** *adj.*

sum/mer·house/, *n.* structure in garden to provide shade.

sum/mit (sum/it) *n.* highest point.

sum/mon (sum/ən) *v.* order to appear.

sum/mons, *n.* message that summons.

su/mo (sōō/mō) *n.* Japanese form of wrestling featuring extremely heavy contestants.

sump (sump) *n.* pit for collecting water, etc.

sump/tu·ous (sump/chōō əs) *adj.* revealing great expense; luxurious.

sun (sun) *n., v.,* **sunned, sunning.** —*n.* **1.** heat- and light-giving body of solar system. **2.** sunshine. —*v.* **3.** expose to sunshine.

Sun., Sunday.

sun/bathe/, *v.,* **-bathed, -bathing.** expose body to sunlight.

sun/belt/, *n. Informal.* southern and southwestern U.S.

sun/block/, *n.* substance that prevents most tanning.

sun/burn/, *n., v.,* **-burned** or **-burnt, -burning.** —*n.* **1.** superficial burn from sun's rays. —*v.* **2.** affect with sunburn.

sun/dae (sun/dā, -dē) *n.* ice cream topped with fruit, etc.

Sun/day (sun/dā, -dē) *n.* first day of week.

sun/der (sun/dər) *v.* separate.

sun/di/al, *n.* outdoor instrument for telling time by shadow.

sun′dry (sun′drē) *adj.*, *n.*, *pl.* **-dries.** —*adj.* **1.** various. —*n.* **2.** (*pl.*) small items of merchandise.

sun′fish′, *n.* fresh-water fish.

sun′flow′er, *n.* tall plant with yellow flowers.

sun′glass′es, *n.pl.* eyeglasses with tinted vision with tinted vision in bright sun.

sun′light′, *n.* light from sun.

sun′lit′, *adj.* lighted by the sun.

sun′ny, *adj.*, **-nier, -niest. 1.** with much sunlight. **2.** cheerful; jolly.

sun′rise′, *n.* ascent of sun above horizon. Also, **sun′up′.**

sun′roof′, *n.* section of automobile roof that can be opened.

sun′screen′, *n.* substance that protects skin from ultraviolet light.

sun′set′, *n.* descent of sun below horizon. Also, **sun′down′.**

sun′shine′, *n.* light of sun.

sun′spot′, *n.* dark spot on sun.

sun′stroke′, *n.* illness from overexposure to sun's rays.

sun′tan′, *n.* darkening of skin caused by exposure to sun.

sup (sup) *v.*, **supped, supping.** eat supper.

su′per (soo′pər) *n.* **1.** superintendent. —*adj.* **2.** very good; first-rate.

super-, prefix meaning above or over; exceeding; larger or more.

su′per·a·bun′dant, *adj.* exceedingly abundant.

su′per·an′nu·at′ed (-an′yoo ā′tid) *adj.* **1.** retired. **2.** antiquated.

su·perb′ (soo pûrb′, sə-) *adj.* very fine. —**su·perb′ly,** *adv.*

su′per·charge′, *v.*, **-charged, -charging. 1.** charge with abundant or excess energy, etc. **2.** supply air to (engine) at high pressure. —**su′per·charg′er,** *n.*

su′per·cil′i·ous (soo′pər sil′ē əs) *adj.* haughtily disdainful.

su′per·con·duc·tiv′i·ty, *n.* disappearance of electrical resistance in certain metals at extremely low temperatures. —**su′per·con·duc′tor,** *n.*

su′per·e′go, *n.* part of personality representing conscience.

su′per·fi′cial (soo′pər fish′əl) *adj.* **1.** of, on, or near surface. **2.** shallow, obvious, or insignificant. —**su′per·fi′ci·al′i·ty** (-fish′ē al′i tē) *n.*

su·per′flu·ous (soo pûr′floo əs) *adj.* **1.** being more than is necessary. **2.** unnecessary. —**su′per·flu′i·ty** (-floo′i tē) *n.*

su′per·high′way (soo′pər hī′wā, soo′pər hī′wā′) *n.* highway for travel at high speeds.

su′per·hu′man, *adj.* **1.** beyond what is human. **2.** exceeding human strength.

su′per·im·pose′, *v.*, **-posed, -posing.** place over something else.

su′per·in·tend′ (soo′pər in tend′, soo′prin-) *v.* oversee and direct. —**su′per·in·tend′ent,** *n.*, *adj.*

su·pe′ri·or (sə pēr′ē ər, soo-) *adj.* **1.** above average; better. **2.** upper. **3.** arrogant. —*n.* **4.** superior person. **5.** head of convent, etc. —**su·pe′ri·or′i·ty,** *n.*

su·per′la·tive (sə pûr′lə tiv, soo-) *adj.* **1.** highest kind; best. **2.** highest in comparison. —*n.* **3.** anything superlative.

su′per·man′ (soo′pər-) *n.*, *pl.* **-men.** person of extraordinary or superhuman powers.

su′per·mar′ket, *n.* self-service food store with large variety.

su′per·nat′u·ral, *adj.* **1.** outside the laws of nature; ghostly. —*n.* **2.** realm of supernatural beings or things.

su′per·no′va, *n.*, *pl.* **-vas, -vae** (-vē). nova millions of times brighter than the sun.

su′per·nu′mer·ar′y (-nōō′mə rer′ē, -nyōō′-) *adj.*, *n.*, *pl.* **-aries.** —*adj.* **1.** extra. —*n.* **2.** extra person or thing.

su′per·pow′er, *n.* large, powerful nation greatly influencing world affairs.

su′per·script′, *n.* letter, number, or symbol written high on line of text.

su′per·sede′ (-sēd′) *v.*, **-seded, -seding.** replace in power, use, etc.

su′per·son′ic, *adj.* faster than speed of sound.

su′per·star′, *n.* entertainer or sports figure of world renown.

su′per·sti′tion (-stish′ən) *n.* irrational belief in ominous significance of particular thing, event, etc. —**su′per·sti′tious,** *adj.*

su′per·store′, *n.* very large store that stocks wide variety of merchandise.

su′per·struc′ture, *n.* upper part of building or vessel.

su′per·vene′ (-vēn′) *v.*, **-vened, -vening.** come as something extra. —**su′per·ven′tion** (-ven′shən) *n.*

su′per·vise′ (-vīz′) *v.*, **-vised, -vising.** direct and inspect. —**su′per·vi′sion** (-vizh′ən) *n.* —**su′per·vi′sor,** *n.* —**su′per·vi′so·ry,** *adj.*

su′per·wom′an, *n.*, *pl.* **-women. 1.** woman of extraordinary or superhuman powers. **2.** woman who copes successfully with demands of career, marriage, and motherhood.

su·pine′ (soo pīn′) *adj.* **1.** lying on back. **2.** passive. —**su·pine′ly,** *adv.*

sup′per (sup′ər) *n.* evening meal.

sup·plant' (sə plant') v. supersede.

sup·ple (sup'əl) adj., **-pler, -plest.** flexible; limber. **—sup·ple·ly,** adv.

sup·ple·ment (sup'lə mənt) n. **1.** something added to complete or improve. —v. (-mĕnt') **2.** add to or complete. **—sup·ple·men'tal** (-mĕn'tl) v. adj. **—sup·ple·men'ta·ry,** adj.

sup·pli·cate' (sup'li kāt') v., **-cated, -cating.** beg humbly. **—sup'pli·ant** (sup'lē ənt), **sup'pli·cant,** n., adj.

sup·ply' (sə plī') v., **-plied, -plying,** n., pl. **-plies. 1.** furnish; provide. **2.** fill (a lack). —n. **3.** act of supplying. **4.** that supplied. **5.** stock. **—sup·pli'er,** n.

supply'-side', adj. of economic theory that reduced taxes will stimulate economic growth.

sup·port' (sə pōrt') v. **1.** hold up; bear. **2.** provide living for. **3.** uphold; advocate. **4.** corroborate. —n. **5.** act of supporting. **6.** maintenance; livelihood. **7.** thing or person that supports. **—sup·port'a·ble,** adj. **—sup·port'ive,** adj.

support group, group of people who meet regularly to support each other by discussing problems.

sup·pose' (sə pōz') v., **-posed, -posing. 1.** assume; consider. **2.** take for granted. **—sup·pos'ed·ly** (-pōz'zid lē) adv. **—sup'po·si'tion** (sup'ə zish'ən), n.

sup·pos·i·to·ry (sə poz'i tôr'ē), n., pl. **-ries.** solid mass of medication that melts on insertion into rectum or vagina.

sup·press' (sə pres') v. **1.** end forcibly; subdue. **2.** repress. **3.** withhold from circulation. **—sup·pres'·sion** (-presh'ən) n.

sup·pu·rate' (sup'yə rāt') v., **-rated, -rating.** form or discharge pus. **—sup'pu·ra'tion,** n.

su'pra (sōō'prə) adv. above, esp. in text.

su·prem'a·cist (sə prem'ə sist, sōō-) n. person who advocates supremacy of particular group.

su·preme' (sə prēm', sōō-) adj. chief; greatest. **—su·prem'a·cy** (-prem'ə sē) n. **—su·preme'ly,** adv.

sur·charge', n., v., **-charged, -charging.** —n. (sûr'chärj') **1.** extra or excessive charge, load, etc. —v. (sūr chärj', sûr'chärj') **2.** put surcharge on. **3.** overburden.

sure (shōōr, shûr) adj., **surer, surest. 1.** certain; positive. **2.** reliable. **3.** firm. **—sure'ly,** adv.

sure'fire', adj. Informal. certain to succeed.

sure'foot'ed, adj. not likely to stumble.

sure'ty (shōōr'i tē, shōōr'tē, shûr'-)

n., pl. **-ties. 1.** security against loss, etc. **2.** person who accepts responsibility for another.

surf (sûrf) n. **1.** waves breaking on shore. —v. **2.** ride on crest of wave while standing or lying on surfboard. **—surf'er,** n.

sur·face (sûr'fis) n., adj., v., **-faced, -facing.** —n. **1.** outer face; outside. —adj. **2.** superficial. —v. **3.** finish surface of. **4.** come to surface.

surf'board', n. board on which person rides in surfing.

sur·feit (sûr'fit) n. **1.** excess, esp. of food or drink. **2.** disgust at excess. —v. **3.** overeat; satiate.

surge (sûrj) n., v., **surged, surging.** —n. **1.** swelling or rolling movement of body. —v. **2.** rise and fall.

sur'geon (sûr'jən) n. person skilled in surgery.

surge protector, device to protect computer, etc., from damage by high-voltage electrical surges.

sur·ger·y (-jə rē) n., pl. **-geries.** treatment of disease, etc., by cutting and other manipulations. **—sur'gi·cal** (-ji kəl) adj.

sur·ly (sûr'lē) adj., **-lier, -liest.** rude; churlish. **—sur'li·ness,** n.

sur·mise' (v., sər mīz') **-mised, -mising,** n. (sər mīz', sûr'mīz) guess.

sur·mount' (sər mount') v. **1.** get over or on top of. **2.** overcome.

sur·name' (sûr'nām') n. family name.

sur·pass' (sər pas') v. **1.** exceed. **2.** transcend. **—sur·pass'ing,** adj.

sur·plice (sûr'plis) n. white, loose-fitting robe worn over cassock.

sur·plus (sûr'plus, -pləs) n. **1.** amount beyond that needed; excess. —adj. **2.** being a surplus.

sur·prise' (sər prīz', sə-) v., **-prised, -prising.** —v. **1.** come upon unexpectedly; astonish. —n. **2.** act of surprising. **3.** something that surprises. **4.** feeling of being surprised.

sur·re'al·ism (sə rē'ə liz'əm) n. art attempting to express the subconscious. **—sur·re'al·ist,** n., adj.

sur·ren'der (sə ren'dər) v. **1.** yield. **2.** act of yielding.

sur·rep·ti'tious (sûr'əp tish'əs) adj. stealthy; secret.

sur'ro·gate' (sûr'ə gāt', -git, sur'-) n. **1.** substitute. **2.** judge concerned with wills, estates, etc.

surrogate mother, woman who bears child for another couple.

sur·round' (sə round') v. **1.** encircle; enclose.

sur·round'ings, n.pl. environment.

sur'tax' (sûr'taks') n. additional tax, esp. on high incomes.

sur·veil·lance (sər vā′ləns) *n.* close watch.

sur·vey′, *v.* (sər vā′) **1.** view. **2.** measure or determine dimensions or nature of. —*n.* (sûr′vā) **3.** methodical investigation.

sur·vey′ing, *n.* science of making land surveys. **—sur·vey′or,** *n.*

sur·vive′ (sər vīv′) *v.*, **-vived, -viving. 1.** remain alive. **2.** outlive. **—sur·viv′al,** *n.* **—sur·vi′vor,** *n.*

sus·cep′ti·ble (sə sep′tə bəl) *adj.* apt to be affected. **—sus·cep′ti·bil′i·ty,** *n.*

su′shi (soo′shē) *n.* Japanese dish of rice cakes with raw fish, vegetables, etc.

sus·pect′, *v.* (sə spekt′) **1.** imagine to be guilty, false, etc. **2.** surmise. —*n.* (sus′pekt) **3.** one suspected. —*adj.* (sus′pekt) **4.** liable to doubt.

sus·pend′ (sə spend′) *v.* **1.** hang. **2.** keep temporarily inactive. **3.** refuse work to temporarily.

sus·pend′ers, *n.pl.* straps for holding up trousers.

sus·pense′ (sə spens′) *n.* uncertainty; anxiety.

sus·pen′sion, *n.* **1.** act of suspending. **2.** temporary inactivity. **3.** state in which undissolved particles are dispersed in fluid.

suspension bridge, bridge with deck suspended from cables.

sus·pi′cion (sə spish′ən) *n.* **1.** act or instance of suspecting. **2.** trace.

sus·pi′cious, *adj.* **1.** having suspicions. **2.** causing suspicion.

sus·tain′ (sə stān′) *v.* **1.** support; maintain. **—sus·tain′er,** *n.*

sus′te·nance (sus′tə nəns) *n.* **1.** food. **2.** maintenance.

su′ture (soo′chər) *n.*, *v.*, **-tured, -turing.** —*n.* **1.** stitch used to close wound. —*v.* **2.** join by suture.

SUV, *pl.* **SUVs.** sport-utility vehicle.

su′ze·rain·ty (soo′zə rin tē), *n.*, *pl.* **-ties.** sovereignty of one state over another.

svelte (svelt, sfelt) *adj.* gracefully slender.

SW, southwest.

swab (swob) *n.*, *v.*, **swabbed, swabbing.** —*n.* **1.** bit of cloth, etc., esp. on stick. —*v.* **2.** clean with swab.

swad′dle (swod′l) *v.*, **-dled, -dling.** bind with strips of cloth.

swag (swag) *n.* something fastened at each end and hanging down in the middle.

swag′ger, *v.* **1.** walk with insolent air. —*n.* **2.** swaggering gait.

Swa·hi′li (swä hē′lē) *n.* Bantu language of Africa.

swain (swān) *n.* male admirer.

swal′low (swol′ō) *v.* **1.** take into stomach through throat. **2.** assimilate. **3.** suppress. —*n.* **4.** act of swallowing. **5.** small graceful migratory bird.

swal′low·tail′, *n.* kind of butterfly.

swa′mi (swä′mē) *n.* Hindu religious teacher.

swamp (swomp) *n.* **1.** marshy ground. —*v.* **2.** drench with water. **3.** overwhelm. **—swamp′y,** *adj.*

swan (swon) *n.* large long-necked swimming bird.

swank (swangk) *adj.*, **swanker, swankest. 1.** stylish or elegant. **2.** pretentiously stylish. Also, **swank′y.**

swan song, final act or farewell appearance.

swap (swop) *v.*, **swapped, swapping,** *n.* trade.

swarm (swôrm) *n.* **1.** group of bees. **2.** fly off to start new colony. **3.** cluster; throng.

swarth′y (swôr′thē, -thē) *adj.*, **-ier, -iest.** (esp. of skin) dark.

swash′buck′ler (swosh′buk/lər) *n.* swaggering fellow. **—swash′buck′ling,** *adj.*

swas′ti·ka (swos′ti kə) *n.* emblem of Nazi Party.

swat (swot) *v.* **1.** *Informal.* —*v.* **1.** strike. —*n.* **2.** sharp blow. **—swat′ter,** *n.*

swatch (swoch) *n.* sample of material or finish.

swath (swoth) *n.* long cut made by scythe or mowing machine.

swathe (swoth, swäth) *v.*, **swathed, swathing,** *n.* —*v.* **1.** wrap closely. —*n.* **2.** bandage.

sway (swā) *v.* **1.** swing to and fro. **2.** influence or incline. —*n.* **3.** act of swaying. **4.** rule.

sway′back′, *n.* excessive downward curvature of the back, esp. of horses. **—sway′backed′,** *adj.*

swear (swâr) *v.*, **swore** (swôr), **sworn, swearing. 1.** affirm on oath; vow. **2.** use profane language. **3.** bind by oath.

sweat (swet) *v.*, **sweat** or **sweated, sweating.** —*v.* **1.** excrete moisture through pores. **2.** gather moisture. —*n.* **3.** secretion of sweat glands. **—sweat′y,** *adj.*

sweat′er, *n.* knitted jacket.

sweat gland, tubular gland in skin that secretes sweat.

sweat′pants′, *n.* pants of absorbent fabric.

sweat′shirt′, *n.* loose pullover of absorbent fabric.

sweat′shop′, *n.* manufacturing establishment employing workers at low wages, for long hours.

Swed'ish, *n.* language or people of Sweden. —**Swedish,** *adj.*

sweep (swēp) *v.,* **swept** (swept), **sweeping,** *n.* —*v.* **1.** move or clear with broom, etc. **2.** clear or pass over with forceful, rapid movement. —*n.* **3.** act of sweeping. **4.** extent.

sweep'ing, *adj.* of wide range or scope.

sweep'stakes', *n.* **1.** race for stakes put up by competitors. **2.** lottery.

sweet (swēt) *adj.* **1.** having taste of sugar. **2.** fragrant. **3.** fresh. **4.** pleasant in sound. **5.** amiable. —*n.* **6.** anything sweet. —**sweet'en,** *v.*

sweet'bread', *n.* thymus or pancreas, esp. of calf or lamb, used for food.

sweet'bri'er, *n.* fragrant wild rose.

sweet'en•er, *n.* substance, esp. a substitute for sugar, to sweeten food or drink.

sweet'heart', *n.* beloved.

sweet'meat', *n.* confection.

sweet pea, annual vine with fragrant blooms.

sweet pepper, mild-flavored bell-shaped pepper.

sweet potato, plant with sweet edible root.

sweet'-talk', *v.* cajole; flatter.

sweet tooth, liking or craving for sweets.

sweet' wil'liam (wil'yəm) low plant with dense flower clusters.

swell (swel) *v.,* **swelled, swelled** or **swollen, swelling,** *n., adj.* —*v.* **1.** grow in size, degree, force, etc. —*n.* **2.** act of swelling. **3.** wave. —*adj.* **4.** *Informal.* excellent.

swel'ter (swel'tər) *v.* perspire or suffer from heat.

swel'ter•ing, *adj.* **1.** suffering from heat. **2.** oppressively hot.

swerve (swûrv) *v.,* **swerved, swerving,** *n.* —*v.* **1.** turn aside. —*n.* **2.** act of swerving.

swift (swift) *adj.* **1.** moving with speed. **2.** prompt or quick. —*n.* **3.** small bird. —**swift'ly,** *adv.*

swig (swig) *n., v.,* **swigged, swigging.** *Informal.* —*n.* **1.** deep drink. —*v.* **2.** drink heartily.

swill (swil) *n.* **1.** moist garbage fed to hogs. —*v.* **2.** guzzle.

swim (swim) *v.,* **swam** (swam), **swum** (swum), **swimming,** *n.* —*v.* **1.** move in water by action of limbs, etc. **2.** be immersed. **3.** be dizzy. —*n.* **4.** act or period of swimming.

swimming hole, place with water deep enough for swimming.

swim'suit', *n.* bathing suit.

swin•dle (swin'dl) *v.,* **-dled, -dling,**

n. —*v.* **1.** cheat; defraud. —*n.* **2.** act of swindling; fraud.

swine (swīn) *n., pl.* **swine.** hog.

swing (swing) *v.,* **swung** (swung), **swinging,** *n.* —*v.* **1.** move to and fro around point. **2.** brandish. —*n.* **3.** act, way, or extent of swinging. **4.** progress. **5.** scope. **6.** suspended seat for swinging.

swing'er, *n. Slang.* **1.** person with modern attitudes. **2.** sexually uninhibited person.

swing shift, work shift from midafternoon until midnight.

swipe (swīp) *n., v.,* **swiped, swiping.** —*n.* **1.** sweeping blow. —*v.* **2.** deal such blow. **3.** *Informal.* steal.

swirl (swûrl) *v.,* whirl; eddy.

swish (swish) *v.* **1.** rustle. —*n.* **2.** swishing sound.

Swiss cheese (swis) firm, pale yellow cheese with holes.

switch (swich) *n.* **1.** flexible rod. **2.** device for turning electric current on or off. **3.** change. —*v.* **4.** whip with switch. **5.** shift; divert. **6.** turn (electric current) on or off.

switch'back', *n.* zigzag highway or railroad track arrangement for climbing steep grade.

switch'blade', *n.* pocketknife with blade released by spring.

switch'board', *n.* panel for controlling electric circuits.

swiv•el (swiv'əl) *n., v.,* **-eled, -eling.** —*n.* **1.** device permitting rotation of thing mounted on it. —*v.* **2.** rotate.

swiz'zle stick (swiz'əl) small wand for stirring mixed drinks.

swol'len (swō'lən) *adj.* pp. of **swell.**

swoon (swōōn) *v., n.* faint.

swoop (swōōp) *v.* **1.** sweep down upon. —*n.* **2.** sweeping descent.

sword (sôrd) *n.* weapon with blade fixed in hilt or handle.

sword'fish', *n.* marine fish with swordlike upper jaw.

syb'a•rite' (sib'ə rīt') *n.* person devoted to pleasure.

syc'a•more' (sik'ə môr') *n.* plane tree.

syc'o•phant (sik'ə fant, -fant', sī'kə-) *n.* flatterer; parasite.

syl•lab'i•cate' (si lab'i kāt') *v.,* **-cated, -cating.** divide into syllables. Also, **syl•lab'i•fy'** (-fī').

syl'la•ble (sil'ə bəl) *n.* single unit of speech.

syl'la•bus (sil'ə bəs) *n., pl.* **-buses, -bi** (-bī'). outline of course of study.

syl'lo•gism (sil'ə jiz'əm) *n.* three-part chain of logical reasoning.

sylph (silf) *n.* **1.** graceful woman.

2. imaginary being supposed to inhabit the air.

syl′van (sil′vən) *adj.* **1.** of forests. **2.** wooded.

sym•bi•o′sis (sim′bē ō′sis, -bī-) *n., pl.* **-ses** (-sēz) living together of two dissimilar organisms. —**sym′bi•ot′ic** (-ot′ik) *adj.*

sym′bol (sim′bəl) *n.* **1.** emblem; token; sign. **2.** thing that represents something else. —**sym•bol′ic** (-bol′ik), **sym•bol′i•cal,** *adj.* —**sym′bol•ize′,** *v.,* **-ized, -izing.**

sym′bol•ism, *n.* **1.** representing things by symbols. **2.** symbolic meaning.

sym′me•try (sim′i trē) *n., pl.* **-tries.** pleasing balance or proportion. —**sym•met′ri•cal** (si me′tri kəl) *adj.*

sym′pa•thize′ (-thīz′) *v.,* **-thized, -thizing. 1.** be in sympathy. **2.** feel or express sympathy.

sym′pa•thy (-thē) *n., pl.* **-thies. 1.** agreement in feeling; accord. **2.** compassion. —**sym′pa•thet′ic** (-thet′ik) *adj.*

sym′pho•ny (sim′fə nē) *n., pl.* **-nies. 1.** composition for orchestra. **2.** harmonious combination. —**sym•phon′ic** (-fon′ik) *adj.*

sym•po′si•um (sim pō′zē əm) *n., pl.* **-siums, -sia** (-zē ə) meeting to present essays on one subject.

symp′tom (simp′təm) *n.* sign or indication, esp. of disease. —**symp′to•mat′ic** (-mat′ik) *adj.*

syn′a•gogue′ (sin′ə gog′) *n.* **1.** assembly of Jews for worship. **2.** place of such assembly.

sync (singk) *n., v.,* **synced, syncing.** —*n.* **1.** synchronization. **2.** harmonious relationship. —*v.* **3.** synchronize.

syn′chro•nize′ (sing′krə nīz′) *v.,* **-nized, -nizing. 1.** occur at same time. **2.** show or set to show same time. —**syn′chro•ni•za′tion,** *n.* —**syn′chro•nous,** *adj.*

syn′co•pate′ (sing′kə pāt′, sin′-) *v.,* **-pated, -pating. 1.** *Music.* play by accenting notes normally unaccented. **2.** *Gram.* omit middle sound in (word). —**syn′co•pa′tion,** *n.*

syn′di•cate, *n., v.,* **-cated, -cating.** —*n.* (sin′də kit) **1.** combination of persons or companies for large joint enterprise. **2.** agency dealing in news stories, etc. —*v.* (sin′di kāt′) **3.** publish as syndicate.

syn′drome (sin′drōm, -drəm) *n.* characteristic group of symptoms.

syn′er•gism (sin′ər jiz′əm) *n.* joint action of agents so that their combined effect is greater than sum of individual effects.

syn′fu•el (sin′fyōō′əl) *n.* synthetic fuel.

syn′od (sin′əd) *n.* meeting of church delegates.

syn′o•nym (sin′ə nim) *n.* word meaning same as another. —**syn•on′y•mous** (si non′ə məs) *adj.*

syn•op′sis (si nop′sis) *n., pl.* **-ses** (-sēz). brief summary.

syn′tax (sin′taks) *n.* arrangement of words into sentences, etc.

syn′the•sis (sin′thə sis) *n., pl.* **-ses** (-sēz). **1.** combination of parts into whole. **2.** such whole.

syn′the•size′ (-sīz′) *v.,* **-sized, -sizing.** make by combining parts.

syn′the•siz′er, *n.* electronic, usu. computerized device for creating or modifying musical sounds.

syn•thet′ic (sin thet′ik) *adj.* **1.** produced artificially rather than by nature. **2.** of synthesis.

syph′i•lis (sif′ə lis) *n.* infectious venereal disease.

sy•ringe′ (sə rinj′, sir′inj) *n.* device for drawing in and ejecting liquids.

syr′up (sir′əp, sûr′-) *n.* sweet thick liquid. —**syr′up•y,** *adj.*

sys′tem (sis′təm) *n.* **1.** orderly assemblage of facts, parts, etc. **2.** plan. **3.** organization of body. —**sys•tem•at′ic** (-tə mat′ik) *adj.*

sys′tem•a•tize′ (-tə ma tīz′) *v.,* **-tized, -tizing.** arrange by system.

sys•tem′ic (si stem′ik) *adj.* affecting entire body.

systems analysis, study of data-processing needs of project.

sys′to•le′ (sis′tə lē′) *n.* regular contraction of the heart. —**sys•tol′ic** (si stol′ik) *adj.*

T

T, t (tē) *n.* twentieth letter of English alphabet.

tab (tab) *n., v.,* **tabbed, tabbing.** —*n.* **1.** small flap. **2.** tag. —*v.* **3.** furnish with tab.

Ta•bas′co (tə bas′kō) *n. Trademark.* pungent condiment sauce.

tab′by (tab′ē) *n., pl.* **-bies,** *adj.*

—*n.* **1.** striped or brindled cat. **2.** silk fabric. —*adj.* **3.** striped.

tab′er•nac•le (tab′ər nak′əl) *n.* **1.** temporary temple, esp. Jewish. **2.** church for large congregation.

ta′ble (tā′bəl) *n., v.,* **-bled, -bling. 1.** piece of furniture consisting of level part on legs. **2.** food. **3.**

tableau 320

company at table. **4.** compact arrangement of information in parallel columns. —v. **5.** postpone deliberation on. —**ta′bleau·cloth′,** n.

tab·leau′ (ta blō′, tab′lō) n., pl. **-leaux** (ta blōz′). picture.

ta′ble d′hôte′ (tä′bal dōt′, tab′al) meal fixed in courses and price.

ta′ble·land′, n. elevated, level region of considerable extent.

ta′ble·spoon′, n. **1.** large spoon in table service. **2.** tablespoonful.

ta′ble·spoon·ful′, n., pl. **-fuls.** quantity tablespoon holds, about ½ fluid ounce or 3 teaspoonfuls.

tab′let (tab′lit) n. **1.** pad of writing paper. **2.** small slab. **3.** pill.

table tennis, game resembling tennis, played on table with paddles and small hollow ball.

ta′ble·ware′, n. dishes, etc., used at table.

tab′loid (tab′loid) n. newspaper about half ordinary size.

ta·boo′ (tə bōō′, ta-) adj., n., pl. **-boos,** v. —adj. **1.** forbidden. —n. **2.** prohibition. —v. **3.** prohibit.

tab′u·late′ (tab′yə lāt′) v., **-lated, -lating.** arrange in table. —**tab′u·lar,** adj. —**tab′u·la′tion,** n.

ta·chom′e·ter (ta kom′i tər, tə-) n. instrument for measuring velocity.

tach′y·car′di·a (tak′i kär′dē ə) n. excessively rapid heartbeat.

tac′it (tas′it) adj. **1.** silent. **2.** implied. **3.** unspoken. —**tac′it·ly,** adv.

tac′i·turn′ (tas′i tûrn′) adj. inclined to silence. —**tac′i·tur′ni·ty,** n.

tack (tak) n. **1.** short nail with flat head. **2.** straight windward run of sailing ship. —v. **3.** fasten by tack. **4.** navigate by tacks.

tack′le, n., v., **-led, -ling.** —n. **1.** fishing equipment. **2.** hoisting apparatus. —v. **3.** undertake to deal with. —**tack′ler,** n.

tack′y, adj., **-ier, -iest.** **1.** Informal. shabby; dowdy. **2.** slightly sticky. **3.** in poor taste. —**tack′i·ness,** n.

ta′co (tä′kō) n. fried tortilla folded and filled with chopped meat, cheese, lettuce, etc.

tact (takt) n. skill in handling delicate situations. —**tact′ful,** adj. —**tact′less,** adj.

tac·ti′cian (tak tish′ən) n. person versed in tactics.

tac′tics (tak′tiks) n. **1.** maneuvering of armed forces. **2.** methods for attaining success. —**tac′ti·cal,** adj.

tac′tile (tak′til, -tīl) adj. of sense of touch. —**tac·til′i·ty** (-til′i tē) n.

tad (tad) n. Informal. **1.** small child. **2.** small amount or degree.

tad′pole (tad′pōl) n. larval form of frogs, toads, etc.

taf′fe·ta (taf′i tə) n. lustrous silk or rayon fabric.

taf′fy (taf′ē) n., pl. **-fies.** molasses candy.

tag (tag) n., v., **tagging.** —n. **1.** small paper, etc., attached as mark or label. **2.** game in which players chase and touch each other. —v. **3.** furnish with tag. **4.** touch in playing tag.

t′ai chi ch′uan (tī′ jē′ chwän′, chē′) n. Chinese system of meditative exercises. Also, **tai′ chi′.**

tail (tāl) n. **1.** appendage at rear of animal's body. **2.** something resembling this. **3.** bottom or rear part. —v. **4.** follow.

tail′gate′ (tāl′gāt′) n., v., **-gated, -gating.** —n. **1.** hinged board at back of vehicle. —v. **2.** drive too closely behind.

tail′light′, n. light at the rear of automobile, train, etc.

tai′lor (tā′lər) n. maker or mender of outer garments.

tail′pipe′, n. exhaust pipe at rear of motor vehicle.

tail′spin′, n. descent of airplane in steep spiral course.

tail′wind′ (-wind′) n. wind from directly behind.

taint (tānt) n. **1.** unfavorable trace. —v. **2.** contaminate.

take (tāk) v., **took** (tŏŏk), **taken, taking.** **1.** seize, catch, or embrace. **2.** receive; obtain. **3.** select. **4.** remove. **5.** deduct. **6.** conduct. **7.** travel by. **8.** occupy. **9.** assume. **10.** require.

take′off′, n. **1.** leaving of ground in leaping or flying. **2.** Informal. piece of mimicry.

take′out′, adj. **1.** intended to be taken from restaurant and eaten elsewhere. —n. **2.** food taken out from restaurant.

take′o′ver, n. act of seizing authority or control.

talc (talk) n. soft mineral, used for lubricants, etc. Also, **tal′cum.**

tal′cum powder (tal′kəm) powder for the skin made of purified talc.

tale (tāl) n. story or lie.

tal′ent (tal′ənt) n. natural ability.

tal′is·man (tal′is mən, -iz-) n. amulet.

talk (tôk) v. **1.** speak; converse. **2.** gossip. —n. **3.** speech; conversation. **4.** conference. **5.** gossip. —**talk′a·tive,** adj. —**talk′er,** n.

talk′ing-to′, n., pl. **-tos.** scolding.

tall (tôl) adj. **1.** of great height. **2.** of specified height.

tare

tal·low (tal′ō) *n.* **1.** suet. **2.** hardened fat for soap, etc.

tal·ly (tal′ē) *n.*, *pl.* **-lies**, *v.*, **-lied**, **-lying.** **1.** record of amounts. —*v.* **2.** record. **3.** match.

tal·ly·ho′ (-hō′) *interj.* cry in hunting on catching sight of fox.

Tal·mud (tāl′mŏŏd, tal′mad) *n.* collection of Jewish laws. —**Tal·mud′ic**, *adj.*

tal′on (tal′an) *n.* claw.

tam (tam) *n.* tam-o′-shanter.

ta·ma′le (ta mä′lē) *n.* Mexican dish of cornmeal, meat, red peppers, etc.

tam′a·rack′ (tam′a rak′) *n.* N American larch.

tam′a·rind (-a rind) *n.* tropical fruit.

tam′bou·rine′ (-ba rēn′) *n.* small drum with metal disks in frame.

tame (tām) *adj.*, **tamer**, **tamest**, *v.*, **tamed**, **taming.** —*adj.* **1.** not wild; domesticated. **2.** uninterestingly conventional. —*v.* **3.** domesticate. —**tame′ly**, *adv.* —**tam′er**, *n.*

tam′-o′-shan′ter (tam′a shan′tar) *n.* cap with flat crown.

tamp (tamp) *v.* force down or in. —**tamp′er**, *n.*

tam′per, *v.* meddle.

tam′pon (tam′pon) *n.* plug of cotton or the like for insertion into wound or body cavity to absorb blood.

tan (tan) *v.*, **tanned**, **tanning**, *n.*, *adj.* —*v.* **1.** convert into leather. **2.** make or become brown by exposure to sun. —*n.* **3.** light brown. Also, **tan′bark′.** bark used in tanning hides. —*adj.* **5.** light brown. —**tan′ner**, *n.* —**tan′ner·y**, *n.*

tan′dem (tan′dam) *adv.* **1.** one behind another. —*adj.* **2.** having one following behind another.

tang (tang) *n.* strong flavor.

tan′ge·lo′ (tan′ja lō′) *n.*, *pl.* **-los.** fruit that is a cross between grapefruit and tangerine.

tan′gent (tan′jant) *adj.* **1.** touching. —*n.* **2.** tangent line, etc. **3.** sudden change of course, thought, etc.

tan·gen′tial (-jen′shal) *adj.* **1.** touching. **2.** not relevant.

tan′ge·rine′ (tan′ja rēn′) *n.* looseskinned fruit similar to orange.

tan′gi·ble (tan′ja bal) *adj.* **1.** discernible by touch. **2.** real. **3.** definite. —**tan′gi·bil′i·ty**, *n.*

tan·gle (tang′gal) *v.*, **-gled**, **-gling**, *n.* —*v.* **1.** come or bring together in confused mass. **2.** involve. **3.** snare. **4.** *Informal.* come into conflict. —*n.* **5.** tangled state or mass.

tan′go (tang′gō) *n.*, *pl.* **-gos**, *v.*, **-goed**, **-going.** —*n.* **1.** Spanish-

American dance. —*v.* **2.** dance the tango.

tank (tangk) *n.* **1.** large receptacle for liquid or gas. **2.** armored combat vehicle on caterpillar treads. —**tank′ful**, *n.*

tank′ard (tang′kard) *n.* large cup.

tank′er, *n.* ship, truck, or airplane for transporting liquid bulk cargo.

tank top, sleeveless shirt.

tan′nin (tan′in) *n.* astringent compound used in tanning.

tan′ta·lize′ (tan′tl īz′) *v.*, **-lized**, **-lizing.** torment by prospect of something desired.

tan′ta·mount′ (tan′ta mount′) *adj.* equivalent.

tan′trum (tan′tram) *n.* noisy outburst of bad temper.

tap (tap) *v.*, **tapped**, **tapping.** —*n.* **1.** plug or faucet through which liquid is drawn. **2.** light blow. —*v.* **3.** draw liquid from. **4.** reach or pierce to draw something off. **5.** strike lightly.

tap dance, dance in which rhythm is audibly tapped out by toe or heel. —**tap′-dance′**, *v.* —**tap′-danc′er**, *n.*

tape (tāp) *n.*, *v.*, **taped**, **taping.** —*n.* **1.** narrow strip of flexible material. —*v.* **2.** furnish or tie with tape. **3.** record on tape.

tape deck, audio system component for playing tapes.

tape measure, tape marked for measuring. Also, **tape′line′.**

ta′per (tā′par) *v.* **1.** make or become narrower toward end. —*v.* **2.** gradual decrease. **3.** small candle.

tape recorder, electrical device for recording or playing back sound recorded on magnetic tape.

tap·es·try (tap′a strē) *n.*, *pl.* **-tries.** woven, figured fabric for wall hanging, etc.

tape′worm′, *n.* parasitic worm in alimentary canal.

tap′i·o′ca (tap′ē ō′ka) *n.* granular food from starch of tuberous plants.

ta′pir (tā′par, ta pēr′) *n.* tropical swineline animal.

tap′room′, *n.* barroom.

tap′root′, *n.* main, central root pointing downward and giving off small lateral roots.

tar (tär) *n.*, *v.*, **tarred**, **tarring.** —*n.* **1.** dark viscid product made from coal, wood, etc. **2.** sailor. —*v.* **3.** cover with tar. —**tar′ry** (tär′ē) *adj.*

tar′an·tel′la (tar′an tel′a) *n.* rapid, whirling southern Italian dance.

ta·ran′tu·la (ta ran′cha la) *n.* large hairy spider.

tar′dy (tär′dē) *adj.*, **-dier**, **-diest.** late. —**tar′di·ness**, *n.*

tare (târ) *n.* weed.

tar′get n. something aimed at.

tar′iff n. **1.** list of export or import duties. **2.** one such duty.

tar′nish (tär′nish) v. **1.** lose luster. **2.** sully. —n. **3.** tarnished coating or state.

ta′ro (tärō, târ′ō, tar′ō) n. tropical plant cultivated for edible tuber.

ta′rot (tarō, ta rō′) n. any of set of 22 playing cards used for fortune-telling.

tar·pau′lin (tär pô′lin, tär′pə lin) n. waterproof covering of canvas, etc.

tar′ra·gon′ (tar′ə gon′, -gən) n. plant with aromatic leaves used as seasoning.

tar′ry (tarē) v., -ried, -rying. **1.** stay. **2.** linger.

tart (tärt) adj. **1.** sour; acid. **2.** caustic. —n. **3.** pastry shell filled with fruit, etc. —**tart′ly**, adv.

tar′tan (tär′tn) n. cloth worn by natives of N Scotland, having criss-cross pattern.

tar′tar (tär′tər) n. **1.** hard deposit on teeth. **2.** savage, intractable person. —**tar·tar′ic** (-tar′ik, -tär′-) adj.

tartar sauce, mayonnaise sauce containing chopped pickles, onions, etc.

task (task) n. **1.** assigned piece of work. —v. **2.** put strain on.

task force, **1.** temporary group of armed units for carrying out specific mission. **2.** temporary committee for solving specific problem.

task′mas′ter, n. assigner of burdensome tasks.

tas′sel (tas′əl) n. fringed ornament hanging from roundish knot.

taste (tāst) v., tasted, tasting, n. —v. **1.** try flavor by taking in mouth. **2.** eat or drink a little of. **3.** perceive flavor. **4.** have particular flavor. —n. **5.** act of tasting. **6.** sense by which flavor is perceived. **7.** flavor. **8.** sense of fitness or beauty. —**taste′less**, adj.

taste bud, one of numerous small bodies, chiefly in tongue, that serve for sense of taste.

tast′y, adj., -ier, -iest. savory; tasting good. —**tast′i·ness**, n.

tat′ter (tat′ər) n. **1.** torn piece. **2.** (pl.) ragged clothing.

tat′tle (tat′l) v., -tled, -tling, n. —v. **1.** tell another's secrets. —n. **2.** chatter; gossip. —**tat′tler**, **tat′tle·tale**, n.

tat·too′ (ta tōō′) n. **1.** indelible marking on skin by puncturing and dyeing. **2.** design so made. **3.** military signal on drum, bugle, etc., to go to quarters. —v. **4.** mark by tattoo.

taunt (tônt, tänt) v. **1.** reproach insultingly or sarcastically. —n. **2.** insulting or sarcastic gibe.

taupe (tōp) n. dark gray usually tinged with brown, purple, yellow, or green.

taut (tôt) adj. tight; tense.

tau·tol′o·gy (tô tol′ə jē) n., pl. -gies. needless repetition. —**tau′to·log′i·cal** (-tl oj′i kal) adj.

tav′ern (tav′ərn) n. **1.** saloon. **2.** inn.

taw′dry (tô′drē) adj., -drier, -driest. gaudy; cheap.

taw′ny (tô′nē) adj., -nier, -niest. n. —adj. **1.** of a dark-yellow or yellow-brown color. —n. **2.** tawny color.

tax (taks) n. **1.** money regularly paid to government. **2.** burdensome duty, etc. —v. **3.** impose tax. **4.** burden. **5.** accuse. —**tax′a·ble**, adj. —**tax·a′tion**, n.

tax′i (tak′sē) n., v., taxied, taxiing. —n. **1.** taxicab. —v. **2.** go in taxicab. **3.** (of airplane) move on ground under its own power.

tax′i·cab′, n. automobile carrying paying passengers.

tax′i·der′my (tak′si dûr′mē) n. art of preserving and mounting skins of animals. —**tax′i·der′mist**, n.

tax′pay′er, n. person who pays tax.

tax shelter, financial arrangement that reduces or eliminates taxes due.

TB, tuberculosis. Also, **T.B.**

tbs., tablespoon. Also, **tbsp.**

T cell, cell involved in regulating immune system's response to infected or malignant cells.

tea (tē) n. **1.** dried aromatic leaves of Oriental shrub. **2.** beverage made by infusion of these leaves in hot water. **3.** similar beverage made by steeping leaves or flowers of other plants. **4.** afternoon meal. —**tea′cup′**, n. —**tea′ket′tle**, n. —**tea′pot′**, n.

teach (tēch) v., taught, teaching. impart knowledge to. —**teach′er**, n.

teak (tēk) n. East Indian tree with hard wood.

teal (tēl) n. **1.** any of certain small fresh-water ducks. **2.** greenish blue.

team (tēm) n. **1.** persons, etc., associated in joint action. —v. **2.** join in team. —**team′work′**, n. —**team′mate′**, n.

team′ster (-stər) n. driver of team.

tear (târ) v., tore (tôr), torn, tearing, n. —v. **1.** pull apart by force. **2.** distress. **3.** divide. **4.** lacerate. **5.** rend. —n. **6.** act of tearing. **7.** torn

place. **8.** (tēr) Also, **tear/drop/.**
drop of fluid secreted by eye duct.
　—**tear/ful** (tēr/-) adj.

tear gas (tēr) gas that makes eyes
smart and water.

tear/jerk/er (tēr/jûr/kər) n. Informal. sentimental story, etc.

tease (tēz) v., **teased, teasing,** n.
—v. **1.** annoy by raillery. —n. **2.**
person who teases. —**teas/er,** n.

tea/spoon/ n. small spoon. —**tea/-
spoon·ful/,** n., pl. **-fuls.**

teat (tēt, tit) n. nipple.

tech/ni·cal (tek/ni kal) adj. **1.** pertaining to skilled activity. **2.** considered in strict sense.

tech/ni·cal·i·ty (-kal/i tē) n., pl.
-ties. 1. technical point or detail. **2.**
technical character.

Tech/ni·col/or, n. Trademark. system of making color motion
pictures.

tech·nique/ (-nēk/) n. skilled
method. Also, **tech·nic/.**

tech·noc/ra·cy (-nok/rə sē) n., pl.
-cies. government by technological
experts.

tech·nol/o·gy (-nol/ə jē) n., pl.
-gies. 1. practical application of science. **2.** technological invention or
method. —**tech/no·log/i·cal** (-na-
loj/i kal) adj. —**tech·nol/o·gist,** n.

tech/no·thrill/er (tek/nō thril/ər) n.
suspense novel in which sophisticated technology is prominent.

ted/dy bear (ted/ē) stuffed toy
bear.

Te De/um (tā dā/əm) hymn of
praise and thanksgiving.

te/di·ous (tē/dē əs, tē/jəs) adj. long
and tiresome. —**te/di·um,** n.

tee (tē) n., v., **teed, teeing.** Golf.
—n. **1.** hard mound of earth at beginning of play for each hole. **2.**
object from which ball is driven.
—v. **3.** place on tee. **4.** strike from
tee.

teem (tēm) v. abound; swarm.

teens (tēnz) n.pl. years (13–19) of
ages ending in -teen. —**teen/ag/er,
teen,** n. —**teen/age/, teen/aged/,**
adj.

tee/ter (tē/tər) Informal. —v. **1.**
seesaw. **2.** walk unsteadily. —n. **3.**
seesaw.

teethe (tēth) v., **teethed, teething.**
grow or cut teeth.

tee·to/tal·er (tē tōt/l ər, tē/tōt/-) n.
person who does not drink alco-
holic beverages.

Tef/lon (tef/lon) n. Trademark.
polymer with nonsticking properties, used to coat cookware. —adj.
2. impervious to blame or criti-
cisms.

tel., 1. telegram. **2.** telegraph. **3.** telephone.

tel/e·cast/ (tel/i kast/) v., **-cast** or
-casted, -casting, n. —v. **1.** broadcast by television. —n. **2.** television
broadcast.

tel/e·com·mu/ni·ca/tions, n. science and technology of transmitting
information in the form of electromagnetic signals.

tel/e·con/fer·ence, n. conference of
participants in different locations
via telecommunications equipment.

tel/e·gen/ic (-jen/ik) adj. looking
good on television.

tel/e·graph/ (-graf/) n. **1.** electrical
apparatus or process for sending
message (**tel/e·gram/**). —v. **2.** send
by telegraph. —**te·leg/ra·pher** (ta-
leg/rə fər) n. —**tel/e·graph/ic,** adj.
—**te·leg/ra·phy** (tə leg/rə fē) n.

tel/e·mar/ket·ing, n. selling or advertising by telephone.

te·lep/a·thy (tə lep/ə thē) n. communication between minds without
sensory means. —**tel/e·path/ic**
(tel/ə path/ik) adj.

tel/e·phone/ (tel/ə fōn/) n., v.,
-phoned, -phoning. —n. **1.** electrical apparatus or process for transmitting speech. —v. **2.** communicate by telephone.

tel/e·pho/to, adj. of a lens producing large image of small or distant
object.

tel/e·scope/, n., v., **-scoped, -scop-
ing.** —n. **1.** optical instrument for
enlarging image of distant objects.
—v. **2.** force or slide one object into
another. —**tel/e·scop/ic** (-skop/ik)
adj.

tel/e·thon/ (-thon/) n. lengthy television broadcast, usu. to raise
money for charity.

tel/e·van/ge·list (tel/i van/jə list) n.
evangelist who conducts religious
services on television. —**tel/e·van/-
ge·lism** (-liz/əm) n.

tel/e·view/, v. view with a television receiver. —**tel/e·view/er,** n.

tel/e·vise/ (-vīz/) v., **-vised, -vising.**
broadcast by television.

tel/e·vi/sion, n. radio or electrical
transmission of images.

Tel/ex (tel/eks) n. Trademark. two-
way teletypewriter system.

tell (tel) v., **told** (tōld), **telling. 1.**
relate. **2.** communicate. **3.** say posi-
tively. **4.** distinguish. **5.** inform. **6.**
divulge. **7.** order. **8.** produce
marked effect. —**tell/ing,** adj.

tell/-all/, adj. thoroughly revealing.

tell/er, n. bank cashier.

tell/tale/, n. **1.** divulger of secrets.
—adj. **2.** revealing.

te·mer·i·ty (tə mer′i tē) n. rash boldness.

temp (temp) n. temporary worker.

tem·per, n. 1. state or habit of mind. 2. heat or passion. 3. control of one's anger. 4. state of metal after tempering. —v. 5. moderate. 6. heat and cool metal to obtain proper hardness, etc.

tem·per·a (tem′pər ə) n. technique of painting using media containing egg.

tem·per·a·ment (tem′pər ə mənt, -prə mənt) n. mental disposition.

tem·per·a·men·tal (-men′tl) adj. 1. moody or sensitive. 2. of one's personality.

tem·per·ance (tem′pər əns) n. 1. moderation. 2. total abstinence from alcohol.

tem·per·ate (tem′pər it) adj. moderate.

Temperate Zone, part of earth's surface lying between either tropic and nearest polar circle.

tem·per·a·ture (-pər ə chər, -prə-) n. degree of warmth or coldness.

tem·pest (tem′pist) n. 1. violent storm, commotion, or disturbance. —**tem·pes·tu·ous** (-pes′chŏŏ əs) adj. —**tem·pes·tu·ous·ly,** adv.

tem·plate (tem′plit) n. pattern, mold, etc., serving as gauge or guide in mechanical work.

tem·ple (tem′pəl) n. 1. place dedicated to worship. 2. flat area at side of forehead.

tem·po (tem′pō) n., pl. **-pos, -pi** (-pē). rate of speed.

tem·po·ral (tem′pər əl) adj. 1. of time. 2. worldly.

tem·po·rar·y (-pə rer′ē) adj. not permanent. —**tem·po·rar·i·ly,** adv.

tem·po·rize (-rīz′) v., **-rized, -riz·ing.** 1. delay by evasion or indecision. 2. compromise.

tempt (tempt) v. 1. entice. 2. appeal strongly. —**temp·ta′tion,** n. —**tempt′er,** n. —**tempt′ress,** n. fem.

tem·pur·a (tem pŏŏr′ə) n. Japanese deep-fried dish of vegetables or seafood.

ten (ten) n., adj. nine plus one.

ten·a·ble (ten′ə bəl) adj. defensible in argument. —**ten·a·bil′i·ty,** n.

te·na·cious (tə nā′shəs) adj. 1. holding fast. 2. retentive. 3. obstinate. 4. sticky. —**te·na′cious·ly,** adv. —**te·nac′i·ty** (-nas′i tē) n.

ten·an·cy (ten′ən sē) n., pl. **-cies.** holding; tenure.

ten·ant (-ənt) n. 1. one renting from landlord. 2. occupant.

Ten Commandments, precepts delivered to Moses on Mount Sinai.

tend (tend) v. 1. incline in action or effect. 2. lead. 3. take care of.

tend·en·cy (ten′dən sē) n., pl. **-cies.** 1. disposition to behave or act in certain way. 2. predisposition.

ten·den·tious (-den′shəs) adj. having or showing bias.

ten·der, adj. 1. soft; delicate; weak. 2. immature. 3. soft-hearted. 4. kind. 5. loving. 6. sensitive. —v. 7. present formally. 8. offer. —n. 9. something offered. 10. person who tends. 11. auxiliary vehicle or vessel. —**ten′der·ness,** n. —**ten′der·ize′,** v., **-ized, -izing.**

ten′der·foot′, n., pl. **-foots, -feet.** Informal. inexperienced person.

ten′der·heart′ed, adj. soft-hearted; sympathetic.

ten′der·loin′, n. 1. tender meat on loin of beef, pork, etc. 2. brothel district of city.

ten·di·ni·tis (ten′də nī′tis) n. inflammation of tendon.

ten·don (-dən) n. band of fibrous tissue connecting muscle to bone or part.

ten·dril (-dril) n. clinging threadlike organ of climbing plants.

ten·e·ment (-ə mənt) n. run-down apartment house.

ten·et (-it) n. principle, doctrine, dogma, etc.

Tenn., Tennessee.

ten·nis (-is) n. game of ball played with rackets (**tennis rackets**) on rectangular court (**tennis court**).

ten·on (-ən) n. projection inserted into cavity (**mortise**) to form joint.

ten·or (-ər) n. 1. continuous course or progress. 2. perceived meaning or intention. 3. male voice between bass and alto.

ten·pins, n. bowling game played with ten pins.

tense (tens) adj., **tenser, tensest,** v., **tensed, tensing.** —adj. 1. taut; rigid. 2. emotionally strained. —v. 3. make or become tense. —n. 4. verb inflection indicating time of action or state. —**tense′ly,** adv.

ten·sile (ten′səl, -sil, -sīl) adj. 1. of tension. 2. ductile.

ten·sion (-shən) n. 1. stretching or being stretched. 2. strain. 3. strained relations.

tent (tent) n. portable shelter, usually fabric.

ten·ta·cle (ten′tə kəl) n. long, flexible organ of octopuses, etc.

ten·ta·tive (-tə tiv) adj. in trial; experimental. —**ten′ta·tive·ly,** adv.

ten′ter·hook′ (-tər hŏŏk′) n. on **tenterhooks,** in suspense.

tenth (tenth) adj., n. next after ninth.

ten·u·ous (ten'yōō əs) adj. **1.** lacking a sound basis. **2.** thin, slender. **3.** rarefied. —**ten'u·ous·ly,** adv.

ten·ure (-yər) n. **1.** holding of something. **2.** assurance of permanent work.

te·pee (tē'pē) n. American Indian tent.

tep·id (tep'id) adj. lukewarm. —**te·pid'i·ty, tep'id·ness,** n.

te·qui·la (tə kē'lə) n. Mexican liquor.

term (tûrm) n. **1.** name for something. **2.** period, as of school instruction. **3.** (pl.) conditions of agreement or bargain. —v. **4.** name; designate.

ter·mi·nal (-mə nl) adj. **1.** at end; concluding. **2.** leading to death. —n. **3.** end or extremity. **4.** terminating point for trains, buses, etc. **5.** point of electrical connection. **6.** device for entering information into or receiving information from computer. —**ter'mi·nal·ly,** adv.

ter·mi·nate' (-nāt') v., **-nated, -nating. 1.** end or cease. **2.** occur at end. —**ter·mi·na'tion,** n.

ter·mi·nol·o·gy (-nol'ə jē) n., pl. **-gies.** terms of technical subject.

ter·mi·nus (-nəs) n. **1.** end. **2.** end of line for buses, trains, etc.

ter·mite (tûr'mīt) n. destructive woodeating insect.

tern (tûrn) n. gull-like aquatic bird.

ter·race (ter'əs) n., v., **-raced, -racing.** —n. **1.** raised level with abrupt drop at front. **2.** flat roof. **3.** open area connected with house. —v. **4.** make or furnish with terrace.

ter·ra cot'ta (ter'ə kot'ə) **1.** hard, usually unglazed earthenware. **2.** brownish red.

ter·ra fir'ma (fûr'mə) solid land.

ter·rain' (tə rān') n. area of land of specified nature.

ter·ra·pin (ter'ə pin) n. edible North American turtle.

ter·rar·i·um (tə râr'ē əm) n., pl. **-iums, -ia** (-ē ə) glass tank for raising plants or land animals.

ter·raz·zo (tə rät'sō, -razō) n. mosaic flooring composed of stone chips and cement.

ter·res·tri·al (tə res'trē əl) adj. of or living on earth.

ter·ri·ble (ter'ə bəl) adj. **1.** dreadful. **2.** severe. —**ter'ri·bly,** adv.

ter·ri·er (ter'ē ər) n. hunting dog.

ter·rif·ic (tə rif'ik) adj. **1.** excellent. **2.** terrifying. —**ter·rif'i·cal·ly,** adv.

ter·ri·fy (ter'ə fī') v., **-fied, -fying.** fill with terror.

ter·ri·to·ry (ter'i tôr'ē) n., pl. **-ries. 1.** region. **2.** land and waters of state. **3.** region not a state but having elected legislature and appointed officials. —**ter'ri·to'ri·al,** adj.

ter·ror (ter'ər) n. intense fear.

ter·ror·ism, n. use of violence and threats to obtain political demands. —**ter'ror·ist,** n.

ter·ror·ize', v., **-ized, -izing.** fill with terror. —**ter'ror·i·za'tion,** n.

ter·ry (ter'ē) n., pl. **-ries.** pile fabric with loops on both sides. Also, **terry cloth.**

terse (tûrs) adj. **1.** concise. **2.** curt; brusque. —**terse'ly,** adv.

ter·ti·ar·y (tûr'shē er'ē) adj. of third order or stage.

tes·sel·late' (tes'ə lāt') v., **-lated, -lating.** form mosaic pattern from small squares.

test (test) n. **1.** trial of or substance used to try quality, content, etc. **2.** examination to evaluate student or class. —v. **3.** subject to test.

tes·ta·ment (tes'tə mənt) n. **1.** legal will. **2.** testimony. —**tes'ta·men'ta·ry** (-men'tə rē) adj.

tes·tate (-tāt) adj. having left a valid will. —**tes·ta'tor,** n.

tes·ti·cle (-ti kəl) n. either of two male sex glands located in scrotum. Also, **tes·tis** (-tis).

tes·ti·fy (tes'tə fī') v., **-fied, -fying. 1.** give evidence. **2.** give testimony.

tes·ti·mo·ni·al (-mō'nē əl) n. written declaration certifying character, etc.

tes·ti·mo·ny (-nē) n., pl. **-nies. 1.** statement of witness under oath. **2.** proof.

tes·tos·ter·one (tes tos'tə rōn') n. male sex hormone.

test tube, small cylindrical glass container used in laboratories.

tes·ty (tes'tē) adj., **-tier, -tiest.** irritable. —**tes'ti·ly,** adv.

tet·a·nus (tet'n əs) n. infectious disease marked by muscular rigidity.

tête-à-tête (tāt'ə tāt', tet'ə tet') n. private conversation.

teth'er (teth'ər) n. **1.** rope, chain, etc., for fastening animal to stake. —v. **2.** fasten with tether.

tet·ra (te'trə) n., pl. **-ras.** small, brightly colored fish of tropical American waters.

tet·ra·he'dron (-hē'drən) n., pl. **-drons, -dra.** solid contained by four plane faces.

Tex., Texas.

text (tekst) n. **1.** main body of matter in book or manuscript. **2.** quotation from Scripture, esp. as subject of sermon, etc. —**tex'tu·al** (-chōō əl) adj. —**tex'tu·al·ly,** adv.

text/book/, *n.* book used by student to study.

tex/tile (teks/tīl, -til) *n.* 1. woven material. —*adj.* 2. woven. 3. of weaving.

tex/ture (teks/char) *n.* characteristic surface or composition. —**tex/tur-al,** *adj.*

thal/a-mus (thal/ə məs) *n.* part of brain that transmits and integrates sensory impulses.

tha-lid/o-mide (thə lid/ə mīd/) *n.* drug formerly used as sedative, found to cause fetal abnormalities.

thal/li-um (thal/ē əm) *n.* rare metallic element.

than (than, then; *unstressed* than, ən) *conj.* particle introducing second member of comparison.

thank (thangk) *v.* 1. express gratitude. —*n.* 2. (*usually pl.*) expression of gratitude. —**thank/ful,** *adj.* —**thank/less,** *adj.* —**thanks/giv/ing,** *n.*

Thanksgiving Day, festival in acknowledgment of divine favor, celebrated in U.S. on fourth Thursday of November and in Canada on second Monday of October.

that (that; *unstressed* that) *pron., pl.* **those** (thōz), *adj., adv., conj.* —*pron., adj.* 1. demonstrative word indicating the person, thing, etc., more remote. 2. one of two persons, etc., pointed out or mentioned before (opposed to **this**). 3. relative pronoun used as: **a.** subject or object of relative clause. **b.** object of preposition. —*adv.* 3. to that extent. —*conj.* 4. word used to introduce dependent clause or one expressing reason, result, etc.

thatch (thach) *n.* 1. rushes, leaves, etc., for covering roofs. —*v.* 2. cover with thatch.

thaw (thô) *v.* 1. melt. 2. remove ice or frost from. —*n.* 3. act or instance of thawing.

the (*stressed* thē; *unstressed before a consonant* thə, *unstressed before a vowel* thē) *def. article.* 1. word used, esp. before nouns, with specifying effect. —*adv.* 2. word used to modify comparative or superlative form of adjective or adverb.

the/a-ter (thē/ə tər, thē/-) *n.* 1. building for dramatic presentations, etc. 2. dramatic art. 3. place of action. Also, **the/a-tre.** —**the-at/ri-cal** (-a/tri kal) *adj.*

thee (thē) *pron. Archaic.* you.

theft (theft) *n.* act or instance of stealing.

their (thâr; *unstressed* thər) *pron.* 1. possessive form of **they** used before

noun. 2. (*pl.*) that which belongs to them.

theirs (thârz) *pron.* that which belongs to them.

the/ism (thē/iz əm) *n.* belief in one God. —**the/ist,** *n.*

them (them; *unstressed* thəm, əm) *pron.* objective case of **they.**

theme (thēm) *n.* 1. subject of discourse, etc. 2. short essay. 3. melody. —**the-mat/ic** (-mat/ik) *adj.*

them-selves/ (thəm selvz/, them/-) *pron.* emphatic or reflexive form of **them.**

then (then) *adv.* 1. at that time. 2. soon afterward. 3. at another time. 4. besides. 5. in that case. —*adj.* 6. being such at that time.

thence (thens) *adv.* 1. from that place or time. 2. therefore.

thence/forth/ (thens/fôrth/, thens/-fôrth/) *adv.* from that place or time on. Also, **thence/for/ward.**

the-ol/o-gy (-ol/ə jē) *n.* study of God and of God's relations to the universe. —**the/o-lo/gian** (-ə lō/jən, -jē ən) *n.* —**the/o-log/i-cal** (-loj/i kal) *adj.*

the/o-rem (thēr/əm, thēr/əm) *n.* 1. *Math.* statement embodying something to be proved. 2. rule or law, esp. one expressed by equation or formula.

the/o-ret/i-cal (thē/ə ret/i kal) *adj.* 1. in theory. 2. not practical. 3. speculative.

the/o-ry (thē/ə rē, thēr/ē) *n., pl.* **-ries.** 1. proposition used to explain class of phenomena. 2. proposed explanation. 3. principles. —**the/o-rist,** *n.* —**the/o-rize/,** *v.*

ther/a-py (ther/ə pē) *n., pl.* **-pies.** 1. treatment of disease. 2. psychotherapy. —**ther/a-pist** (-pist) *n.* —**ther/a-peu/tic** (-pyōo/tik) *adj.* —**ther/a-peu/tics,** *n.*

there (thâr; *unstressed* thər) *adv.* 1. in or at that place, point, matter, respect, etc. 2. to that place. —**there/a-bout/,** **there/a-bouts/,** *adv.* —**there-af/ter,** *adv.* —**there-by/,** *adv.* —**there/in/,** *adv.* —**there-to/,** *adv.* —**there-un/der,** *adv.*

there/fore/, *adv.* consequently.

there-of/, *adv.* of or from that.

there-on/, *adv.* 1. on that. 2. immediately after that.

there/up-on/, *adv.* 1. immediately after that. 2. because of that. 3. with reference to that.

there-with/, *adv.* with or in addition to that.

ther/mal (thûr/məl) *adj.* of heat.

ther/mo-dy-nam/ics (thûr/mō dī-nam/iks) *n.* science concerned with relations between heat and mechanical energy or work.

ther·mom/e·ter (thər mom/i tər) *n.* instrument for measuring temperature.

ther/mo·nu/cle·ar (thûr/mō-) *adj.* of nuclear-fusion reactions at extremely high temperatures.

ther/mo·plas/tic (thûr/mə-) *adj.* soft and pliable whenever heated, as some plastics, without change of inherent properties.

Ther/mos (thûr/məs) *n. Trademark.* container with vacuum between double walls for heat insulation.

ther/mo·sphere/ (thûr/mə sfēr/) *n.* region of upper atmosphere in which temperature increases continually with altitude.

ther/mo·stat/ (-mə stat/) *n.* device regulating temperature of heating system, etc. —**ther/mo·stat/ic,** *adj.*

the·sau/rus (thi sôr/əs) *n., pl.* **-sauruses, -sauri** (-sôr/ī). book of synonyms and antonyms.

these (thēz) *pron.* pl. of **this.**

the/sis (thē/sis) *n., pl.* **-ses** (-sēz). **1.** proposition to be proved. **2.** essay based on research.

thes/pi·an (thes/pē ən) *adj.* **1.** of dramatic art. —*n.* **2.** actor or actress.

they (#hā) *pron.* nominative plural of **he, she,** and **it.**

thi/a·mine (thī/ə min, -mēn/) *n.* vitamin B1. Also, **thi/a·min.**

thick (thik) *adj.* **1.** not thin. **2.** in depth. **3.** compact. **4.** numerous. **5.** dense. **6.** husky. **7.** slow-witted. —*adv.* **8.** so as to be thick. —*n.* **9.** something thick. —**thick/en,** *v.* —**thick/en·er,** *n.*

thick/et, *n.* thick growth of shrubs, bushes, etc.

thick/set/, *adj.* **1.** set closely; dense. **2.** with heavy or solid body.

thick/-skinned/, *adj.* not sensitive to criticism or contempt.

thief (thēf) *n., pl.* **thieves** (thēvz). person who steals. —**thieve,** *v.,* **thieved, thieving.** —**thiev/er·y** (thē/və rē) *n.*

thigh (thī) *n.* part of leg between hip and knee.

thigh/bone/, *n.* femur.

thim/ble (thim/bəl) *n.* cap to protect finger while sewing.

thin (thin) *adj.,* **thinner, thinnest,** *v.,* **thinned, thinning.** —*adj.* **1.** having little extent in one opposite sides; slender. **2.** lean. **3.** scanty. **4.** rarefied; diluted. **5.** flimsy. **6.** weak. —*v.* **7.** make or become thinner. —**thin/ner,** *n.* —**thin/ly,** *adv.*

thing (thing) *n.* **1.** inanimate object. **2.** entity. **3.** matter. **4.** item.

think (thingk) *v.,* **thought** (thôt),

thinking. 1. conceive in mind. **2.** meditate. **3.** believe. —**think/er,** *n.*

think tank, research organization employed to analyze problems and plan future developments.

thin/-skinned/, *adj.* sensitive to criticism or contempt.

third (thûrd) *adj.* **1.** next after second. —*n.* **2.** next after the second. **3.** any of three equal parts.

third/-class/, *adj.* of the lowest class or quality.

third degree, use of brutal measures by police (or others) in extorting information or confession.

third dimension, 1. thickness or depth. **2.** aspect that heightens reality.

third party, 1. party to case or quarrel who is incidentally involved. **2.** in two-party political system, usu. temporary party composed of independents.

third/-rate/, *adj.* distinctly inferior.

Third World, developing countries of Asia, Africa, and Latin America.

thirst (thûrst) *n.* **1.** sensation caused by need of drink. —*v.* **2.** be thirsty. —**thirst/y,** *adj.* —**thirst/i·ly,** *adv.*

thir/teen/ (thûr/tēn/) *n.,* *adj.* ten plus three. —**thir·teenth/,** *adj., n.*

thir/ty (thûr/tē) *n.,* *adj.* ten times three. —**thir/ti·eth,** *adj., n.*

this (this) *pron.,* *pl.* **these** (thēz). *adj.,* *adv.* —*pron.,* *adj.* **1.** demonstrative word indicating something as just mentioned, present, near, etc. —*adv.* **2.** to the indicated extent.

this/tle (this/əl) *n.* prickly plant.

thith/er (thith/ər, thith/-) *adv.* to that place, point, etc.

tho (thō) *conj., adv. Informal.* though.

thong (thông) *n.* **1.** strip of leather. **2.** sandal with strip of leather, etc., passing between first two toes.

tho/rax (thôr/aks) *n., pl.* **thoraxes, thoraces** (thôr ə sēz/). part of body between neck and abdomen. —**tho·rac/ic** (thô ras/ik) *adj.*

thorn (thôrn) *n.* sharp spine on plant. —**thorn/y,** *adj.*

thor/ough (thûr/ō, thur/ō) *adj.* complete. —**thor/ough·ly,** *adv.*

thor/ough·bred/ (-ō bred/, -ə bred/) *adj.* **1.** of pure breed. **2.** well-bred. —*n.* **3.** thoroughbred animal or person.

thor/ough·fare/, *n.* road, street, etc., open at both ends.

thor/ough·go/ing, *adj.* doing things thoroughly.

those (thōz) *pron., adj.* pl. of **that.**

thou (#hou) *pron.* you (now little

used except provincially, archaically, in poetry or elevated prose, in addressing God, and by the Friends).

though (t͟hō) *conj.* **1.** notwithstanding that. **2.** even if. **3.** nevertheless. —*adv.* **4.** however.

thought (thôt) *n.* **1.** mental activity. **2.** idea. **3.** purpose. **4.** regard.

thought′ful, *adj.* **1.** meditative. **2.** heedful. **3.** considerate.

thought′less, *adj.* **1.** showing lack of thought. **2.** careless; inconsiderate. —**thought′less·ly,** *adv.*

thou′sand (thou′zənd) *n., adj.* ten times one hundred. —**thou′sandth,** *adj., n.*

thrall (thrôl) *n.* **1.** person in bondage; slave. **2.** slavery; bondage.

thrash (thrash) *v.* **1.** beat thoroughly. **2.** toss wildly.

thread (thred) *n.* **1.** fine spun cord of flax, cotton, etc. **2.** filament. **3.** helical ridge of screw. **4.** connected sequence. —*v.* **5.** pass end of thread through needle's eye. **6.** fix beads, etc., on thread.

thread′bare′, *adj.* shabby.

threat (thret) *n.* expression of intent to harm.

threat′en, *v.* **1.** utter threats. **2.** look ominously close.

three (thrē) *n., adj.* two plus one.

three′-di·men′sion·al, *adj.* having or seeming to have depth as well as width and height.

three′fold′, *adj.* **1.** having three parts. **2.** three times as great.

three R's, reading, writing, and arithmetic.

three score, *adj.* sixty.

thresh (thresh) *v.* separate grain or seeds from a plant. —**thresh′er,** *n.*

thresh′old (thresh′ōld, -hōld) *n.* **1.** doorway sill. **2.** entrance. **3.** beginning; border.

thrice (thrīs) *adv.* three times.

thrift (thrift) *n.* frugality.

thrift shop, store that sells second-hand goods.

thrift′y, *adj.,* **-ier, -iest.** saving; frugal.

thrill (thril) *v.* **1.** affect with sudden keen emotion. **2.** vibrate. —*n.* **3.** sudden wave of keen emotion or excitement.

thrill′er, *n.* suspenseful play or story.

thrive (thrīv) *v.,* **thrived, thriving.** flourish.

throat (thrōt) *n.* passage from mouth to stomach or lungs.

throat′y, *adj.,* **-ier, -iest.** (of sound) husky; heavy.

throb (throb) *v.,* **throbbed, throbbing,** *n.* —*v.* **1.** beat violently or

rapidly. **2.** vibrate. —*n.* **3.** act of throbbing.

throe (thrō) *n.* **1.** spasm. **2.** (*pl.*) pangs.

throm·bo′sis (throm bō′sis) *n.* clotting of blood in circulatory system.

throne (thrōn) *n.* official chair of sovereign, bishop, etc.

throng (thrông) *n., v.* crowd.

throt′tle (throt′l) *n., v.,* **-tled, -tling.** —*v.* **1.** device controlling flow of fuel. —*v.* **2.** choke. **3.** check.

through (thrōō) *prep.* **1.** in at one end and out at other. **2.** during all of. **3.** having finished. **4.** by means or reason of. —*adv.* **5.** in at one end and out at other. **6.** all the way. **7.** to the end. **8.** finished. —*adj.* **9.** passing through.

through·out′, *prep.* **1.** in all parts of. —*adv.* **2.** in every part, etc.

throw (thrō) *v.,* **threw** (thrōō), **thrown, throwing,** *n.* —*v.* **1.** propel or cast. **2.** fell in wrestling. **3.** host. **4.** confuse. —*n.* **5.** act of throwing. —**throw′er,** *n.*

throw′a·way′, *adj.* **1.** to be discarded after use. **2.** notice distributed free.

throw′back′, *n.* **1.** setback or check. **2.** reversion to ancestral type.

thru (thrōō) *prep., adv., adj.* Informal. through.

thrush (thrush) *n.* **1.** migratory singing bird. **2.** fungal disease of mouth.

thrust (thrust) *v.,* **thrust, thrusting,** *n.* —*v.* **1.** push; shove. **2.** stab. —*n.* **3.** push; lunge. **4.** stab.

thru′way′ (thrōō′wā′) *n.* express providing direct route between distant areas.

thud (thud) *n., v.,* **thudded, thudding.** —*n.* **1.** dull striking sound. —*v.* **2.** make thudding sound.

thug (thug) *n.* violent criminal.

thumb (thum) *n.* **1.** short, thick finger next to the forefinger. —*v.* **2.** manipulate with thumb.

thumb′nail′, *n.* **1.** nail of thumb. —*adj.* **2.** brief and concise.

thumb′screw′, *n.* **1.** instrument of torture that compresses thumbs. **2.** screw turned by thumb and finger.

thumb′tack′, *n.* **1.** tack with large, flat head. —*v.* **2.** secure with thumbtack.

thump (thump) *n.* **1.** blow from something thick and heavy. —*v.* **2.** pound.

thump′ing, *adj.* **1.** exceptional. **2.** of or like a thump.

thun′der (thun′dər) *n.* **1.** loud noise accompanying lightning. —*v.* **2.** give forth thunder. **3.** speak

loudly. —**thun′der·ous,** adj.
—**thun′der·storm′,** n.

thun′der·bolt′, n. flash of lightning
with thunder.

thun′der·clap′, n. crash of thunder.

thun′der·cloud′, n. electrically
charged cloud producing lightning
and thunder.

thun′der·head′, n. mass of cumulus clouds warning of thunderstorms.

thun′der·struck′, adj. astonished.

Thurs., Thursday.

Thurs′day (thûrz′dā, -dē) n. fifth
day of week.

thus (ᵺus) adv. **1.** in this way. **2.**
consequently. **3.** to this extent.

thwack (thwak) v. **1.** strike hard
with something flat. —n. **2.**
thwacking blow.

thwart (thwôrt) v. frustrate.

thy (ᵺī) adj. Archaic. your.

thyme (tīm; spelling pron. thīm) n.
plant of mint family.

thy′mus (thī′məs) n. gland at base
of neck that helps produce T cells.

thy′roid (thī′roid) adj. of thyroid
gland.

thyroid gland, ductless gland near
windpipe, involved in controlling
metabolism and growth.

thy·self′ (ᵺī self′) pron. **1.** emphatic appositive to **thou** or **thee**.
2. substitute for reflexive **thee.**

ti·ar′a (tē är′ə, -âr′ə, -ârʹə) n.
woman's ornamental coronet.

Ti·bet′an (ti bet′n) n. native or language of Tibet. —**Tibetan,** adj.

tib′i·a (tib′ē ə) n., pl. -iae (-ē ēʹ)
-ias. bone from knee to ankle.

tic (tik) n. sudden twitch.

tick (tik) n. **1.** soft, recurring click.
2. bloodsucking mitelike animal. **3.**
cloth case of mattress, pillow, etc.
—v. **4.** produce tick (def. 1).

tick′er, n. **1.** one that ticks. **2.** telegraphic instrument that prints stock
prices and market reports, etc., on
tape (**ticker tape**). **3.** Slang. heart.

tick′et (-it) n. **1.** slip indicating
right to admission, transportation,
etc. **2.** tag. **3.** summons for traffic
or parking violation. —v. **4.** attach
ticket to.

tick′ing, n. cotton fabric for ticks
(def. 3).

tick′le, v., -led, -ling, n. —v. **1.**
touch lightly so as to make tingle
or itch. **2.** gratify. **3.** amuse. —n.
4. act of tickling. —**tick′lish,** adj.

tickler file, file for reminding user
at appropriate times of matters
needing attention.

tick′-tack-toe′ (tik′tak tō′) n. game
for two players, each trying to com-

plete row of three X's or three O's
on nine-square grid.

tidal wave, large, destructive ocean
wave produced by earthquake.

tid′bit′ (tid′bit′) n. choice bit.

tid′dly·winks′ (tid′lē wingks′) n.
game in which small disks are
snapped with larger disks into cup.

tide (tīd) n., v., tided, tiding. —n.
1. periodic rise and fall of ocean
waters. **2.** stream. —v. **3.** be
enough to get over difficult period.
—**tid′al,** adj.

tide′land′, n. land alternately exposed and covered by tide.

ti′dings (tī′dingz) n.pl. news.

ti′dy (tī′dē) adj., -dier, -diest, v.,
-died, -dying. —adj. **1.** neat; orderly. **2.** fairly large. —v. **3.** make
tidy. —**ti′di·ly,** adv.

tie (tī) v., tied, tying, n. —v. **1.**
bind with cord, etc. **2.** confine. **3.**
equal or be equal. —n. **4.** something used to tie or join. **5.** necktie.
6. equality in scores, votes, etc. **7.**
contest in which this occurs. **8.**
bond of kinship, affection, etc.

tie′-dye′ing, n. method of dyeing
with sections of garment bound so
as not to receive dye.

tie′-in′, n. link, association, or relationship.

tier (tēr) n. row or rank.

tie′-up′, n. **1.** undesired stoppage
of business, traffic, etc. **2.** connection.

tiff (tif) n. petty quarrel.

ti′ger (tī′gər) n. large striped Asian
cat. —**ti·gress,** n.fem.

tiger lily, lily with flowers of dull-orange color spotted with black.

tight (tīt) adj. **1.** firmly in place. **2.**
taut. **3.** fitting closely. **4.** impervious to fluids. **5.** stingy. —**tight′en,**
v. —**tight′ly,** adv. —**tight′ness,** n.

tight′-fist′ed, adj. stingy.

tight′-lipped′, adj. reluctant to
speak.

tight′rope′, n. taut wire or cable
on which acrobats perform.

tights, n.pl. close-fitting pants,
worn esp. by acrobats, etc.

tight′wad′, n. Slang. stingy person.

til′de (til′də) n. diacritical mark
(˜) placed over letter.

tile (tīl) n., v., tiled, tiling. —n. **1.**
thin piece of baked clay, etc., used
as covering. —v. **2.** cover with
tiles.

til′ing, n. **1.** operation of covering
with tiles. **2.** tiles collectively.

till (til) prep., conj. **1.** until. —v. **2.**
labor on to raise crops. **3.** plow.
—n. **4.** drawer in back of counter
for money. —**till·age,** n.

—**Usage.** TILL and UNTIL are used

interchangeably in speech and writing: *It rained till/until nearly midnight.* TILL is not a shortened form of UNTIL and is not spelled *'till.* 'TIL is usually considered a spelling error, though commonly used in business and advertising: *open 'til ten.*

till/er (til′ər), *n.* **1.** one that tills. **2.** handle on head of tiller.

tilt (tilt) *v.* **1.** lean; slant. **2.** charge or engage in joust. —*n.* **3.** act of tilting. **4.** slant.

tim/ber (tim′bər) *n.* **1.** wood of growing trees. **2.** trees. **3.** wood for building. **4.** wooden beam, etc. —*v.* **5.** furnish or support with timber.

tim/ber•line′, *n.* altitude or latitude at which timber ceases to grow.

timber wolf, large brindled wolf of forested Canada and northern United States.

tim/bre (tam′bər, tim′-) *n.* characteristic quality of a sound.

time (tīm) *n.*, *v.*, **timed, tim/ing.** —*n.* **1.** duration. **2.** period of time. **3.** occasion. **4.** point in time. **5.** appointed or proper time. **6.** meter of music. **7.** rate. —*v.* **8.** determine or record time. —**tim/er,** *n.*

time clock, clock with attachment that records times of arrival and departure of employees.

time′-hon′ored, *adj.* long valued or used; traditional.

time/keep′er, *n.* **1.** person who keeps time. **2.** timepiece, esp. as regards accuracy.

time/less, *adj.* eternal. **2.** referring to no particular time.

time line, 1. linear representation of events in the order in which they occurred. **2.** schedule.

time/ly, *adj.*, **-li•er, -li•est,** *adv.* —*adj.* **1.** opportune. —*adv.* **2.** opportunely.

time′-out′, *n.* brief suspension of activity, as in sports contest.

time/piece′, *n.* clock; watch.

times, *prep.* multiplied by.

time′-shar′ing, *n.* **1.** plan in which several people share cost of a vacation home. **2.** system in which users at different terminals simultaneously use a single computer.

time/ta/ble, *n.* schedule of times of departures, work completion, etc.

time/worn′, *adj.* **1.** showing the effects of long use. **2.** trite.

time zone, one of 24 divisions of globe coinciding with meridians at successive hours from observatory at Greenwich, England.

tim/id (tim′id) *adj.* **1.** easily alarmed. **2.** shy. —**ti•mid/i•ty,** *n.*

tim/ing (tī′ming) *n.* control of speed or occasion of an action, event, etc., so that it occurs at the proper moment.

tim/or•ous (tim′ər əs) *adj.* **1.** fearful. **2.** timid. —**tim/or•ous•ly,** *adv.*

tim/pa•ni (tim′pə nē) *n.pl.* kettledrums. —**tim/pa•nist,** *n.*

tin (tin) *n.*, *v.*, **tinned, tinning.** —*n.* **1.** malleable metallic element. —*v.* **2.** cover with tin. —**tin/ny,** *adj.*

tinc/ture (tingk′chər) *n.* medicinal solution in alcohol.

tin/der (tin′dər) *n.* inflammable substance. —**tin/der•box**′, *n.*

tine (tīn) *n.* prong of fork.

tin/foil′, *n.* tin or alloy in thin sheet, used as wrapping.

tinge (tinj) *v.*, **tinged, tinge/ing** or **tinging.** —*v.* **1.** impart trace of color, taste, etc., to. —*n.* **2.** slight trace.

tin/gle (ting′gəl) *v.*, **-gled, -gling,** *n.* —*v.* **1.** feel or cause slight stings. —*n.* **2.** tingling sensation.

tink/er (ting′kər) *n.* **1.** mender of pots, kettles, pans, etc. —*v.* **2.** do the work of a tinker. **3.** work or repair unskillfully or clumsily.

tin/kle (ting′kəl) *v.*, **-kled, -kling,** *n.* —*v.* **1.** make light ringing sounds. —*n.* **2.** tinkling sound.

tin plate, thin iron or steel sheet coated with tin.

tin/sel (tin′səl) *n.* **1.** glittering metal in strips, etc. **2.** anything showy and worthless.

tint (tint) *n.* **1.** color or hue. —*v.* **2.** apply tint to.

tin/tin•nab/u•la/tion (tin′ti nab′yə lā′shən) *n.* ringing or sound of bells.

ti/ny (tī′nē) *adj.*, **-nier, -niest.** very small.

-tion, suffix meaning action or process, result of action, or state or condition.

tip (tip) *n.*, *v.*, **tipped, tipping.** —*n.* **1.** small gift of money. **2.** piece of private information. **3.** useful hint. **4.** slender or pointed end. **5.** top. —*v.* **6.** give tip to. **7.** furnish with tip. **8.** tilt. **9.** overturn.

tip′-off′, *n. Slang.* hint or warning.

tip/ple, *v.*, **-pled, -pling.** drink alcoholic liquor. —**tip/pler,** *n.*

tip/ster (-stər) *n.* person who sells tips.

tip/sy, *adj.*, **-si•er, -si•est.** slightly intoxicated.

tip/toe′, *n.*, *v.*, **-toed, -toeing.** —*n.* **1.** tip of toe. —*v.* **2.** move on tiptoes.

tip/top′ (-top′, -top′) *n.* **1.** extreme top. **2.** situated at very top. **3.** *Informal.* of highest excellence.

token

ti'rade (tī'rād, tī rād') n. long denunciation or speech.

ti'ra.mi'su (tīr'ə mē'sōō) n. Italian dessert.

tire (tīr) v., **tired, tiring,** n. —v. **1.** exhaust strength, interest, patience, etc. —n. **2.** hoop of metal, rubber, etc., around wheel. —**tire'less,** adj. —**tire'some,** adj.

tired (tīrd) adj. **1.** exhausted; fatigued. **2.** weary. —**tired'ly,** adv.

tis'sue (tish'ōō) n. **1.** substance composing organism. **2.** light, gauzy fabric.

tissue paper, very thin paper.

ti'tan (tīt'n) n. person or thing of great size or power. —**ti.tan'ic** (tī-tan'ik) adj.

ti.ta'ni.um (tī tā'nē əm) n. corrosion-resistant metallic element.

tit for tat (tit' fər tat') equivalent given in retaliation, repartee, etc.

tithe (tīth) n. tenth part, paid to church.

ti'tian (tish'ən) n., adj. yellowish or golden brown.

tit'il.late' (tit'l āt') v., **-lated, -lating. 1.** tickle. **2.** excite agreeably.

tit'i.vate' (-ə vāt') v., **-vated, -vating.** make smart or spruce.

ti'tle (tīt'l) n., v., **-tled, -tling.** —n. **1.** name of book, picture, etc. **2.** caption. **3.** appellation, esp. of rank. **4.** championship. **5.** right to something. **6.** document showing this. —v. **7.** furnish with title.

tit'mouse' (tit'mous') n., pl. **-mice.** small bird with crest and conical bill.

tit'ter (tit'ər) n. **1.** restrained laugh. —v. **2.** laugh in this way.

tit'tle (tit'l) n. very small thing.

tit.u.lar (tich'ə lər, tit'yə-) adj. **1.** of or having a title. **2.** being so in title only. —**tit'u.lar.ly,** adv.

tiz'zy (tiz'ē) n., pl. **-zies.** Slang. dither.

TN, Tennessee.

TNT, trinitrotoluene.

to (tōō; unstressed tŏŏ, tə) prep. **1.** particle expressing point reached. **2.** sign of the infinitive. —adv. **3.** toward. **4. to and fro,** to and from place or thing.

toad (tōd) n. tailless, froglike amphibian.

toad'stool', n. fungus with umbrellalike cap.

toad'y, n., pl. **toadies,** v., **toadied, toadying.** —n. **1.** fawning flatterer. —v. **2.** be toady.

toast (tōst) n. **1.** words said before drinking to a person or event. **2.** sliced bread browned by heat. —v. **3.** propose as toast. **4.** make toast.

toast'er, n. appliance for toasting bread.

toast'mas'ter, n. person who introduces the after-dinner speakers or proposes toasts. —**toast'mis'tress,** n.fem.

toast'y, adj., **-tier, -iest.** cozily warm.

to.bac'co (tə bak'ō) n., pl. **-cos, -coes. 1.** plant with leaves prepared for smoking or chewing. **2.** the prepared leaves.

to.bac'co.nist (-bak'ə nist) n. dealer in tobacco.

to.bog'gan (tə bog'ən) n. **1.** long, narrow, flat-bottomed sled. —v. **2.** coast on toboggan.

to.day' (tə dā') n. **1.** this day, time, or period. —adv. **2.** on this day. **3.** at this period.

tod'dle (tod'l) v., **-dled, -dling.** go with short, unsteady steps, like a young child. —**tod'dler,** n.

tod'dy (tod'ē) n., pl. **-dies.** drink made of alcoholic liquor and hot water, sweetened.

to-do' (tə dōō') n., pl. **-dos.** Informal. fuss.

toe (tō) n. **1.** digit of foot. **2.** part covering toes. —**toe'nail',** n.

toe'hold', n. **1.** small niche that supports the toes. **2.** any slight advantage.

tof.fee (tô'fē) n. taffy.

to.fu (tō'fōō) n. soft cheeselike food made from curdled soybean milk.

to'ga (tō'gə) n. ancient Roman outer garment.

to.geth'er (tə geth'ər) adv. **1.** into or in proximity, association, or single mass. **2.** at same time. **3.** in cooperation.

to.geth'er.ness, n. warm fellowship.

togs, n.pl. Informal. clothes.

toil (toil) n. **1.** hard, exhausting work. —v. **2.** work hard.

toi'let (toi'lit) n. **1.** receptacle for excretion. **2.** bathroom. **3.** Also, **toi.lette'.** act or process of dressing.

toi'let.ry, n., pl. **-ries.** article or preparation used in grooming oneself.

toilet water, scented liquid used as light perfume.

to.kay' (tō kā') n. **1.** rich, sweet, aromatic wine. **2.** the variety of grape from which it is made.

toke (tōk) n., v., **toked, toking.** Slang. —n. **1.** puff on marijuana cigarette. —v. **2.** puff or smoke (marijuana).

to'ken (tō'kən) n. **1.** thing expressing or representing something else.

2. metal disk used as ticket, etc.
—*adj.* **3.** being merely a token;
minimal.

to/ken·ism, *n.* minimal conformity
to law or social pressure.

tole (tōl) *n.* enameled or lacquered
metal.

tol/er·a·ble (tol′ər ə bəl) *adj.* **1.** en-
durable. **2.** fairly good.

tol/er·ance (-əns) *n.* fairness toward different opinions, etc. —**tol/
er·ant,** *adj.* —**tol/er·ant·ly,** *adv.*

tol/er·ate/ (-ə rāt′) *v.,* **-ated, -ating.**
1. put up with. **2.** endure. —**tol/er·
a′tion,** *n.*

toll (tōl) *v.* **1.** sound bell slowly
and repeatedly. —*n.* **2.** payment, as
for right to travel. **3.** payment for
long-distance telephone call.

toll/booth/, *n.* booth where toll is
collected.

tom (tom) *n.* male of various animals.

tom/a·hawk/ (tom′ə hôk′) *n.* light
ax used by North American Indians.

to·ma·to (tə mā′tō) *n., pl.* **-toes.**
cultivated plant with pulpy, edible
fruit.

tomb (tōōm) *n.* burial place for dead
body; grave. —**tomb/stone/,** *n.*

tom/boy/ (tom′-) *n.* boisterous,
romping girl. —**tom/boy·ish,** *adj.*

tom/cat/, *n.* male cat.

Tom Col/lins (kol′inz) tall iced
drink containing gin, lemon or lime
juice, and carbonated water.

tome (tōm) *n.* large book.

tom/fool/er·y (tom/fōō/lə rē) *n., pl.*
-eries. foolish or silly behavior.

Tommy gun, type of submachine
gun.

tom/my·rot/, *n. Slang.* nonsense.

to·mor·row (tə môr′ō) *n.* **1.** day after this day. —*adv.* **2.** on day after
this day.

tom/-tom/, *n.* primitive drum.

ton (tun) *n.* **1.** unit of weight,
equal to 2000 pounds (**short ton**)
in U.S. and 2240 pounds (**long ton**)
in Great Britain. **2.** *Naut.* unit of
volume, equal to 100 cubic feet.

to·nal·i·ty (tō nal′i tē) *n., pl.* **-ties.**
1. relation between tones of musical
scales. **2.** the tones.

tone (tōn) *n., v.,* **toned, toning.**
—*n.* **1.** sound. **2.** quality of sound.
3. quality, etc., of voice. **4.** firmness. **5.** expressive quality. **6.** elegance; amenity. —*v.* **7.** give proper
tone to. —**ton/al,** *adj.*

tone/-deaf/, *adj.* unable to distinguish differences in musical pitch.

tongs (tôngz) *n.pl.* two-armed implement for grasping.

tongue (tung) *n.* **1.** organ on floor
of mouth, used for tasting, etc. **2.**
language. **3.** tonguelike thing.

tongue/-lash/ing, *n.* severe scolding.

tongue/-tied/, *adj.* unable to speak,
as from shyness.

tongue twister, sequence of words
difficult to pronounce rapidly.

ton/ic (ton′ik) *n.* **1.** invigorating
medicine. —*adj.* **2.** invigorating.

to·night/ (tə nīt′) *n.* **1.** this night.
—*adv.* **2.** on this night.

ton/nage (tun′ij) *n.* **1.** carrying capacity or total volume of vessel. **2.**
duty on cargo or tonnage. **3.** ships.

ton/sil (ton′səl) *n.* oval mass of tissue in throat.

ton/sil·lec/to·my (-sə lek′tə mē) *n.,
pl.* **-mies.** removal of tonsils.

ton/sil·li/tis (-lī′tis) *n.* inflammation
of tonsils.

ton·so/ri·al (ton sôr′ē əl) *adj.* of
barbers.

ton/sure (ton′shər) *n.* shaved part
of cleric's head.

too (tōō) *adv.* **1.** also. **2.** excessively.

tool (tōōl) *n.* **1.** mechanical instrument, as hammer or saw. **2.** exploited person; dupe. —*v.* **3.** decorate with tool.

toot (tōōt) *v.* sound horn.

tooth (tōōth) *n., pl.* **teeth** (tēth). **1.**
hard white structure attached to
jaw, used in chewing. **2.** projection,
as on comb or saw. —**tooth/ache/,**
n. —**tooth/brush/,** *n.* —**tooth/
paste/,** *n.* —**tooth/pick/,** *n.*

tooth and nail, with all one's
resources and energy.

tooth/some (-səm) *adj.* tasty.

tooth/y (tōō′thē, -thē) *adj.,* **tooth-
ier, toothiest.** having or displaying
conspicuous teeth.

top (top) *n., v.,* **topped, topping.**
—*n.* **1.** highest point, part, rank,
etc. **2.** lid. **3.** child's spinning toy.
4. separable upper part of clothing.
—*v.* **5.** put top on. **6.** be top of. **7.**
surpass.

to/paz (tō′paz) *n.* colored crystalline gem.

top brass, high-ranking officials.

top/coat/, *n.* light overcoat.

top/flight/ (-flīt′) *adj.* excellent.

top hat, man's tall silk hat.

top/-heav/y, *adj.* disproportionately
heavy at top.

top/ic (top′ik) *n.* subject of discussion or writing.

top/i·cal, *adj.* **1.** of or dealing with
matters of current interest. **2.** of
topics. **3.** pertaining to local area.

top kick, *Mil. Slang.* first sergeant.

top'mast', *n.* mast next above lower mast on sailing ship.

top'most, *adj.* highest.

top'-notch', *adj. Informal.* first-rate.

to·pog'ra·phy (tə pog'rə fē) *n., pl.* **-phies.** description of features of geographical area.

top'per, *n.* **1.** one that tops. **2.** *Slang.* top hat. **3.** short coat worn by women.

top'ping, *n.* sauce or garnish placed on food.

top'ple, *v.*, **-pled, -pling.** fall; tumble.

top'-se'cret, *adj.* extremely secret.

top'soil', *n.* fertile upper soil.

top'sy-tur'vy (top'sē tûr'vē) *adv., adj.* **1.** upside down. **2.** in confusion.

tor (tôr) *n.* hill.

To'rah (tôr'ə, tōr'ə) *n.* **1.** five books of Moses; Pentateuch. **2.** (*also l.c.*) whole Torah Scripture.

torch (tôrch) *n.* light carried in hand.

torch'bear'er, *n.* **1.** person who carries torch. **2.** leader in movement.

tor·e·a·dor' (tôr'ē ə dôr') *n.* bullfighter.

tor'ment' *v.* (tôr ment') **1.** cause great suffering to. —*n.* (tôr'ment) **2.** agony. —**tor·men'tor,** *n.*

tor·na'do (tôr nā'dō) *n., pl.* **-does, -dos.** destructive storm.

tor·pe'do (tôr pē'dō) *n., pl.* **-does,** *v.,* **-doed, -doing.** —*n.* **1.** self-propelled missile launched in water and exploding on impact. —*v.* **2.** strike with torpedo.

tor'pid (tôr'pid) *adj.* **1.** inactive; sluggish. **2.** dull; apathetic; lethargic. —**tor·pid'i·ty,** *n.*

tor'por (-pər) *n.* **1.** suspension of physical activity. **2.** apathy.

torque (tôrk) *n.* rotating force.

tor'rent (tôr'ənt) *n.* rapid, violent stream. —**tor·ren'tial** (tô ren'shal, tə-) *adj.* —**tor·ren'tial·ly,** *adv.*

tor'rid (tôr'id) *adj.* **1.** very hot. **2.** passionate.

tor'sion (tôr'shən) *n.* **1.** act of twisting. **2.** twisting by two opposite torques. —**tor'sion·al,** *adj.*

tor'so (tôr'sō) *n., pl.* **-sos, -si.** trunk of body.

tort (tôrt) *n. Law.* civil wrong (other than breach of contract or trust) for which law requires damages.

torte (tôrt) *n., pl.* **tortes.** rich cake, made with eggs and nuts.

tor'tel·li·ni (tôr'tl ēnē) *n.* (used with sing. or pl. v.) small ring-

shaped pieces of pasta filled with meat or cheese.

tor·til'la (tôr tē'ə) *n.* flat, round bread of Mexico, made from cornmeal or wheat flour.

tor'toise (tôr'təs) *n.* turtle.

tor'toise·shell', *n.* **1.** horny brown and yellow shell of certain turtles, used for making combs, etc. **2.** synthetic tortoiseshell. —*adj.* **3.** colored like tortoiseshell.

tor'tu·ous (tôr'chōō əs) *adj.* **1.** twisting; winding. **2.** indirect.

tor'ture (tôr'chər) *n., v.,* **-tured, -turing.** —*n.* **1.** infliction of great pain. —*v.* **2.** subject to torture.

To'ry (tôr'ē) *n., pl.* **-ries.** **1.** (*also l.c.*) conservative. **2.** American supporter of Great Britain during Revolutionary period. —**To'ry·ism,** *n.*

toss (tôs) *v.* **1.** throw or pitch. **2.** pitch about. **3.** throw upward. —*n.* **4.** throw or pitch.

toss'up', *n.* **1.** tossing of coin to decide something by its fall. **2.** *Informal.* even chance.

tot (tot) *n.* small child.

to'tal (tōt'l) *adj., n., v.,* **-taled, -taling.** —*adj.* **1.** entire. **2.** utter; outright. —*n.* **3.** total amount. —*v.* **4.** add up. —**to·tal'i·ty,** *n.*

to·tal·i·tar'i·an (tō tal'i târ'ē ən) *adj.* of centralized government under sole control of one party. —**to·tal·i·tar'i·an·ism,** *n.*

tote (tōt) *n.,* **toted, toting.** *Informal.* —*v.* **1.** carry or bear, as burden. —*n.* **2.** act or course of toting. **3.** that which is toted. **4.** tote bag.

tote bag, open handbag.

to'tem (tō'təm) *n.* object in nature assumed as emblem of clan, family, or related group.

totem pole, pole with totemic figures, erected by Indians of northwest coast of North America.

tot'ter (tot'ər) *v.* **1.** falter. **2.** sway as if about to fall.

tou'can (tōō'kan, -kän) *n.* large-beaked tropical American bird.

touch (tuch) *v.* **1.** put hand, finger, etc., in contact with something. **2.** come or be in contact. **3.** reach. **4.** affect with sympathy. **5.** refer to. —*n.* **6.** act or instance of touching. **7.** perception of things through contact. **8.** contact. —**touch'ing,** *adj.*

touch' and go', precarious condition.

touch'down', *n. Football.* act of player in touching ball down to ground behind opponent's goal line.

tou·ché' (tōō shā') *interj.* (used to acknowledge telling remark or rejoinder).

touched, adj. **1.** moved; stirred. **2.** slightly crazy; unbalanced.

touch'-me-not', n. yellow-flowered plant whose ripe seed vessels burst open when touched.

touch'stone', n. **1.** stone used to test purity of gold and silver by color produced when it is rubbed with them. **2.** any criterion.

touch'y, adj., **-ier, -iest. 1.** irritable. **2.** requiring tact. **—touch'i-ness,** n.

tough (tuf) adj. **1.** not easily broken. **2.** difficult to chew. **3.** sturdy. **4.** pugnacious. **5.** trying. **—**n. **6.** ruffian. **—tough'en,** v.

tou-pee' (tōō pā') n. wig or patch of false hair worn to cover bald spot.

tour (tŏŏr) v. travel or travel through, esp. for pleasure. **—**n. **2.** trip. **3.** period of duty. **—tour'ist,** n. **—tour'ism,** n.

tour de force' (tŏŏr' də fôrs') n., pl. **tours de force.** exceptional achievement.

tour'na-ment (tŏŏr'nə mənt, tûr') n. **1.** meeting for contests. **2.** contest between mounted knights. **3.** competition involving number of rounds. Also, **tour'ney.**

tour'ni-quet (tûr'ni kit, tŏŏr'-) n. bandlike device for arresting bleeding by compressing blood vessels.

tou'sle (tou'zəl, -səl) v. **-sled, -sling.** dishevel.

tout (tout) Informal. **—**v. **1.** solicit (business, votes, etc.) importunately. **2.** advertise. **3.** give tip on (race, etc.). **—**n. **4.** person who touts.

tow (tō) v. **1.** drag by rope or chain. **—**n. **2.** act of towing. **3.** thing towed.

to-ward' (tôrd, twôrd) prep. Also, **to-wards'. 1.** in direction of. **2.** with respect to. **3.** nearly.

tow'boat', n. boat for pushing barges.

tow'el (tou'əl, toul) n. cloth or paper for wiping.

tow'el-ing, n. fabric of cotton or linen used for towels.

tow'er (tou'ər) n. **1.** tall structure. **—**v. **2.** rise high.

tow'er-ing, adj. **1.** very high or great. **2.** violent; furious.

tow'head', n. (tō'hed') n. person with light-colored hair.

town (toun) n. **1.** small city. **2.** center of city. **—towns'man,** n. **—towns'wom'an,** n.fem. **—towns'peo'ple, towns'folk',** n.pl.

town house, one of group of similar houses joined by common side walls.

town meeting, meeting of voters of town.

town'ship, n. **1.** division of county. **2.** (in U.S. surveys) district 6 miles square.

tow'path' (tō'path') n. path along bank of canal or river.

tox-e'mi-a (tok sē'mē ə) n. blood poisoning resulting from presence of toxins in blood. **—tox-e'mic,** adj.

tox'ic (tok'sik) adj. **1.** of toxin. **2.** poisonous. **—tox-ic'i-ty,** n.

tox-i-col'o-gy (-si kol'ə jē) n. science of poisons.

toxic shock syndrome, rapidly developing toxemia.

tox'in (tok'sin) n. poisonous product of organism.

toy (toi) n. **1.** plaything. **—**v. **2.** play.

trace (trās) n., v., **traced, tracing. —**n. **1.** mark or track left by something. **2.** small amount. **—**v. **3.** follow trace of. **4.** find out. **5.** draw over lines of.

trac'er-y, n., pl. **-eries.** ornamental pattern of interlacing lines, etc.

tra'che-a (trā'kē ə) n., pl. **-cheae** (-kē ē'). air-conveying tube from larynx to bronchi.

tra-che-ot'o-my (-ot'ə mē) n., pl. **-mies.** operation of cutting into trachea to help person breathe.

track (trak) n. **1.** parallel rails for railroad. **2.** wheel rut. **3.** footprint or other mark left. **4.** path. **5.** course. **—**v. **6.** follow; pursue.

track'ball', n. computer input device for controlling pointer on screen by rotating ball set inside case.

track record, record of achievement or performance.

tract (trakt) n. **1.** region. **2.** brief treatise.

trac'ta-ble (trak'tə bəl) adj. easily managed. **—trac'ta-bil'i-ty,** n.

trac'tion (-shən) n. **1.** act or instance of pulling. **2.** adhesive friction.

trac'tor (-tər) n. vehicle for pulling farm machinery, etc.

trade (trād) n., v., **traded, trading. —**n. **1.** buying, selling, or exchange of commodities; commerce. **2.** exchange. **3.** occupation. **—**v. **4.** buy and sell. **5.** exchange. **—trad'er,** n. **—trades'man,** n.

trade'-in', n. goods given in trade or part payment for purchase.

trade'mark', n. name, symbol, etc., identifying brand or source of things for sale.

trade name, word or phrase

whereby particular class of goods is designated.

trade′-**off**′, *n.* exchange of one thing for another.

trade union, labor union.

trade wind (wind) sea wind blowing toward equator from latitudes up to 30° away.

tra·di′tion (trə dish′ən) *n.* 1. handing down of beliefs, customs, etc., through generations. 2. something so handed down. —**tra·di′tion·al**, *adj.* —**tra·di′tion·al·ist**, *n., adj.*

tra·duce′ (trə dōōs′, -dyōōs′) *v.*, **-duced, -ducing.** slander.

traf′fic (traf′ik) *n., v.,* **-ficked, -ficking.** —*n.* 1. traveling persons and things. 2. trade. —*v.* 3. trade.

traffic circle, circular roadway at multiple intersection.

traffic light, set of signal lights at intersection.

tra·ge′di·an (trə jē′dē ən) *n.* actor or writer of tragedy. —**tra·ge′di·enne′**, *n.fem.*

trag′e·dy (traj′i dē) *n., pl.* **-dies.** 1. serious drama with unhappy ending. 2. sad event. —**trag′ic**, *adj.*

trail (trāl) *v.* 1. draw or drag. 2. be drawn or dragged. 3. track. —*n.* 4. path. 5. track, scent, etc., left.

trail′blaz′er, *n.* pioneer.

trail′er, *n.* 1. van attached to truck for hauling freight, etc. 2. vehicle attached to car or truck with accommodations for living.

train (trān) *n.* 1. railroad locomotive with cars. 2. moving line of persons, vehicles, etc. 3. series of events, ideas, etc. 4. trailing part. —*v.* 5. instruct or undergo instruction. 6. make or get fit. 7. direct. —**train·ee′**, *n.* —**train′er**, *n.*

traipse (trāps) *v.,* **traipsed, traipsing.** *Informal.* walk aimlessly.

trait (trāt) *n.* characteristic.

trai′tor (trā′tər) *n.* 1. betrayer of trust. 2. person guilty of treason. —**trai′tor·ous**, *adj.*

tra·jec′to·ry (trə jek′tə rē) *n., pl.* **-ries.** curve described by projectile in flight.

tram (tram) *n. Brit.* streetcar.

tram′mel (tram′əl) *n., v.,* **-meled, -meling.** —*n.* 1. impediment to action. —*v.* 2. hamper.

tramp (tramp) *v.* 1. tread or walk firmly. 2. march. —*n.* 3. firm, heavy tread. 4. hike. 5. vagabond.

tram′ple, *v.,* **-pled, -pling.** step roughly on.

tram′po·line′ (tram′pə lēn′, -lin) *n.* cloth or rubber sheet attached to frame by springs for tumbling.

trance (trans) *n.* half-conscious or hypnotic state.

tran′quil (trang′kwil) *adj.* peaceful; quiet. —**tran′quil·ly**, *adv.* —**tran·quil′li·ty**, *n.* —**tran′quil·ize′**, *v.*

tran′quil·iz′er (-kwi lī′zər) *n.* drug to reduce tension.

trans-, prefix meaning across; through; on the other side; changing thoroughly; beyond or surpassing.

trans·act′ (tran sakt′, -zakt′) *v.* carry on business. —**trans·ac′tion**, *n.*

trans′at·lan′tic (trans′at lan′tik, tranz′-) *adj.* 1. passing across Atlantic. 2. on other side of Atlantic.

trans·ceiv′er (tran sēv′ər) *n.* radio transmitter and receiver combined.

trans·cend′ (tran send′) *v.* 1. go or be beyond. 2. excel.

trans·cend′ent, *adj.* 1. extraordinary. 2. superior; supreme.

tran′scen·den′tal (tran′sen den′tl, -san-) *adj.* beyond ordinary human experience.

trans′con·ti·nen′tal (trans′kon tin ən′tl) *adj.* across a continent.

trans·scribe′ (tran skrīb′) *v.,* **-scribed, -scribing.** 1. copy. 2. make recording of. —**tran·scrip′tion** (-skrip′shən), **tran′script**, *n.*

trans·duc′er (trans dōō′sər, -dyōō′, tranz′-) *n.* device that converts signal from one form of energy to another.

tran′sept (tran′sept) *n.* transverse portion of cross-shaped church.

trans·fer′, *v.,* **-ferred, -ferring,** *n.* —*v.* (trans fûr′, trans′fər) 1. convey, hand over, or transport. 2. be transferred. —*n.* (trans′fər) 3. means or act of transferring. —**trans·fer′a·ble**, *adj.* —**trans·fer′al**, *n.* —**trans·fer′ence**, *n.*

trans·fig′ure, *v.,* **-ured, -uring.** 1. transform. 2. glorify.

trans·fix′, *v.* 1. pierce. 2. paralyze with terror, etc.

trans·form′, *v.* change in form, nature, etc. —**trans′for·ma′tion**, *n.*

trans·form′er, *n.* device for converting electrical currents.

trans·fuse′ (-fyōoz′) *v.,* **-fused, -fusing.** 1. transmit, as by pouring. 2. transfer blood from one person to another. —**trans·fu′sion**, *n.*

trans·gress′ (trans gres′, tranz-) *v.* 1. go beyond limit. 2. violate law, moral code, etc. —**trans·gres′sion** (-gresh′ən) *n.* —**trans·gres′sor**, *n.*

tran′sient (tran′shənt, -zhənt, -zē-ənt) *adj.* 1. lasting or staying only a short time. —*n.* 2. transient person.

tran·sis′tor (tran zis′tər) *n.* small electronic device replacing vacuum tube.

trans•it (tran′sit, -zit) n. passage or conveyance.

tran•si•tion (tran zish′ən, -sish′-) n. passage from one condition, etc., to another. —**tran•si′tion•al,** adj.

tran•si•tive (tran′si tiv, -zi-) adj. (of verb) regularly accompanied by direct object. —**tran•si•tive•ly,** adv.

tran•si•to•ry (tran′si tôr′ē, -zi-) adj. 1. not enduring. 2. brief.

trans•late′ (trans lāt′, tranz-, trans′lāt, tranz′-) v., -**lated, -lating.** change from one language into another. —**trans•la′tion,** n. —**trans•lat′a•ble,** adj. —**trans•lat′or,** n.

trans•lit•er•ate′ (-lit′ə rāt′) v., -**ated, -ating.** change into corresponding characters of another alphabet or language.

trans•lu•cent (-lo̅o̅′sənt) adj. not transparent but transmitting light diffusely.

trans•mi•gra′tion, n. passage of soul into another body.

trans•mis′sion (-mish′ən) n. 1. act or process of transmitting. 2. something transmitted. 3. set of gears to transfer force between mechanisms, as in automobile. 4. broadcast.

trans•mit′ (-mit′) v., -**mitted, -mitting.** 1. send over or along. 2. communicate. 3. hand down. 4. cause or permit light, heat, etc., to pass through. 5. emit radio waves. —**trans•mit′ter,** n.

trans•mog•ri•fy′ (-mog′rə fī′) v., -**fied, -fying.** change in appearance or form; transform.

trans•mute′ (-myo̅o̅t′) v., -**muted, -muting.** change from one nature or form to another. —**trans•mut′a•ble,** adj. —**trans•mu•ta′tion,** n.

trans•na′tion•al, adj. going beyond national boundaries or interests.

trans•o′ce•an′ic, adj. across or beyond ocean.

tran′som (tran′səm) n. window above door.

trans•pa•cif′ic (trans′-) adj. passing across Pacific.

trans•par′ent (-pâr′ənt) adj. 1. allowing objects to be clearly seen through it. 2. frank. 3. obvious. —**trans•par′en•cy,** n.

tran•spire′ (tran spī′ər) v., -**spired, -spiring.** 1. occur. 2. give off waste matter, etc., from surface.

trans•plant′ v. (trans plant′) 1. remove and put or plant in another place. —n. 2. (trans′plant′) act of transplanting. 3. something transplanted. —**trans•plan•ta′tion,** n.

trans•port′ v. (trans pôrt′) 1. convey from one place to another. 2. enrapture. —n. (trans′pôrt) 3.

---

something that transports. —**trans′por•ta′tion,** n. —**trans•port′er,** n.

trans•pose′ (-pōz′) v., -**posed, -posing.** alter relative position, order, musical key, etc. —**trans•po•si′tion,** n.

trans•sex′u•al, n. 1. person with sexually altered genitals. 2. person feeling identity with opposite sex.

trans•ship′, v., -**shipped, -shipping.** transfer from one conveyance to another. —**trans•ship′ment,** n.

trans•sub•stan′ti•a′tion, n. (in the Eucharist) conversion of whole substance of bread and wine into body and blood of Christ.

trans•verse′ (trans vûrs′, tranz-; trans′vûrs, tranz′-) adj. 1. lying across. —n. 2. something transverse. —**trans•verse′ly,** adv.

trans•ves′tite (trans ves′tīt, tranz-) n. person who dresses like opposite sex.

trap (trap) n., v., **trapped, trapping.** —n. 1. device for catching animals. 2. scheme for catching a person unawares. 3. U-shaped section in pipe to prevent escape of air or gases. —v. 4. catch in or set traps.

tra•peze′ (tra pēz′, tra-) n. suspended bar used in gymnastics.

trap′e•zoid′ (trap′ə zoid′) n. foursided figure with two parallel sides.

trap′pings, n.pl. equipment or dress.

trap′shoot′ing, n. sport of shooting at clay pigeons hurled from trap.

trash (trash) n. rubbish. —**trash′y,** adj.

trau′ma (trou′mə, trô′-) n., pl. -**mata, -mas.** 1. externally produced injury. 2. experience causing permanent psychological harm. —**trau•mat′ic** (-mat′ik) adj.

tra•vail′ (tra vāl′, trav′āl) n. 1. toil. 2. labor pains.

trav′el (trav′əl) v., -**eled, -eling,** n. —v. 1. journey. 2. move. —n. 3. journeying. —**trav′el•er,** n.

trav•erse, v., -**ersed, -ersing,** n. —v. (tra vûrs′, trav′ərs) 1. pass over or through. —n. (trav′ərs, tra vûrs′) 2. act of traversing.

trav′es•ty (trav′ə stē) n., pl. -**ties,** v., -**tied, -tying.** —n. 1. literary burlesque. 2. debased likeness. —v. 3. make travesty of.

trawl (trôl) n. 1. fishing net dragged on bottom of water. —v. 2. fish with trawl. —**trawl′er,** n.

tray (trā) n. flat, shallow receptacle or container.

treach′er•y (trech′ə rē) n., pl. -**eries.** betrayal; treason. —**treach′er•ous,** adj.

tread (tred) v., **trod** (trod), **trodden** or **trod, treading,** n. —v. **1.** step, walk, or trample. **2.** crush. —n. **3.** manner of walking. **4.** surface meeting road or rail. **5.** horizontal surface of step. —**tread'er,** n.

trea·dle (tred′l) n. lever, etc., worked by foot to drive machine.

tread'mill', n. apparatus moved by treading on moving steps, as for exercise.

trea·son (trē′zan) n. violation of allegiance to sovereign or state.

treas·ure (trezh′ər) n., v., **-ured, -uring.** —n. **1.** accumulated wealth. **2.** thing greatly valued. —v. **3.** prize. **4.** put away for future use.

treas·ure-trove' (-trōv′) n. **1.** anything valuable that one finds. **2.** treasure of unknown ownership, found hidden.

treas·ur·y, n., pl. **-uries. 1.** place for keeping public or private funds. **2.** the funds. **3.** (cap.) government department that handles funds. —**treas'ur·er,** n.

treat (trēt) v. **1.** behave toward. **2.** deal with. **3.** relieve or cure. **4.** discuss. **5.** entertain. —n. **6.** entertainment. **7.** something special and enjoyable. —**treat'ment,** n.

trea·tise (trē′tis) n. writing on particular subject.

trea·ty (trē′tē) n., pl. **-ties.** formal agreement between states.

tre·ble (treb′al) adj., n., v., **-bled, -bling.** —adj. **1.** triple. **2.** of highest pitch or range. —n. **3.** treble part in music. —v. **4.** triple.

tree (trē) n., v., **treed, treeing.** —n. **1.** plant with permanent, woody, usually branched trunk. —v. **2.** drive up tree.

tre·foil (trē′foil, tref′oil) n. herb with leaf divided in three parts.

trek (trek) v., **trekked, trekking,** n. journey.

trel'lis (trel′is) n. lattice.

trem·ble (trem′bal) v., **-bled, -bling,** n. —v. **1.** quiver. —n. **2.** act or state of trembling.

tre·men·dous (tri men′das) adj. extraordinarily great.

trem·o·lo (trem′a lō′) n., pl. **-los.** vibrating effect on instrument or in voice.

trem'or (trem′ar, trē′mar) n. **1.** involuntary shaking. **2.** vibration.

trem'u·lous (trem′ya las) adj. **1.** trembling. **2.** fearful.

trench (trench) n. ditch or cut.

trench'ant (tren′chant) adj. **1.** incisive. **2.** vigorous.

trench coat, belted raincoat with epaulets.

trench'er, n. flat piece of wood on which meat is served or carved.

trench'er·man, n., pl. **-men.** person with hearty appetite.

trench foot, disease of feet due to prolonged exposure to cold and wet.

trench mouth, acute ulcerating infection of gums and mouth.

trend (trend) n. **1.** tendency. **2.** increasingly popular fashion.

trend'y, adj. **-ier, -iest.** Informal. following current fads.

trep·i·da·tion (trep′i dā′shan) n. fearful anxiety.

tres·pass (tres′pas, -pas) v. **1.** enter property illicitly. **2.** sin. —n. **3.** act of trespassing. —**tres'pass·er,** n.

tress (tres) n. braid of hair.

tres·tle (tres′al) n. supporting frame or framework.

tri-, prefix meaning three.

tri'ad (trī′ad, -ad) n. group of three.

tri·age' (trē äzh′) n. sorting victims to determine priority of medical treatment.

tri'al (trī′al) n. **1.** examination before judicial tribunal. **2.** test. **3.** attempt. **4.** state of being tested. **5.** source of suffering.

tri'an·gle (trī′ang′gal) n. figure with three straight sides and three angles. —**tri·an'gu·lar,** adj.

Tri·as'sic (trī as′ik) adj. pertaining to period of Mesozoic Era.

tribe (trīb) n. people united by common descent, etc. —**trib'al,** adj.

tribes'man, n., pl. **-men.** man belonging to tribe. —**tribes'wom'an,** n.fem.

trib·u·la'tion (trib′ya lā′shan) n. **1.** trouble. **2.** affliction.

tri·bu'nal (tri byoon′l, trī-) n. **1.** court of justice. **2.** place of judgment.

trib'une (trib′yoon, tri byoon′) n. **1.** person who defends rights of the people. **2.** rostrum.

trib'u·tar·y (trib′ya ter′ē) n., pl. **-taries,** adj. —n. **1.** stream flowing into larger body of water. —adj. **2.** flowing as tributary.

trib'ute (trib′yoot) n. **1.** speech or gift expressing gratitude or respect. **2.** tax paid to acknowledge subjugation.

trice (trīs) n. instant.

tri·cen·ten'ni·al (trī′sen ten′ē al) adj. tercentennial.

tri'ceps (trī′seps) n. muscle at back of upper arm.

trick (trik) n. **1.** artifice or stratagem. **2.** prank. **3.** knack. **4.** cards won in one round. —v. **5.** deceive

trickle   338

or cheat by tricks. —**trick′er·y,** n.
—**trick′ster,** n. —**trick′y,** adj.

trick·le (trik′əl) v., **-led, -ling,** n.
—v. **1.** flow in small amounts. —n.
2. trickling flow.

tri·col·or (trī′kul′ər) adj. **1.** of three
colors. —n. **2.** three-colored flag,
esp. of France.

tri·cus·pid (trī kus′pid) adj. having three cusps
or points, as tooth.

tri·cy·cle (trī′si kəl, -sik′əl) n.
child's vehicle with large front
wheel and two smaller rear wheels.

tri′dent (trīd′nt) n. three-pronged
spear.

tried (trīd) adj. tested; proved.

tri·en·ni·al (trī en′ē əl) adj. **1.** lasting three years. **2.** occurring every
three years. —n. **3.** period of three
years. **4.** third anniversary.

tri·fle (trī′fəl) n., v., **-fled, -fling.**
—n. **1.** article of small value. **2.**
trivial matter or amount. —v. **3.**
deal without due respect. **4.** act
idly or frivolously. —**tri′fling,** adj.

trig·ger (trig′ər) n. **1.** projecting
tongue pressed to fire gun. **2.** device to release spring. —v. **3.** precipitate.

tri·go·nom·e·try (trig′ə nom′i trē)
n. mathematical study of relations
between sides and angles of trian-
gles.

trill (tril) v. **1.** sing or play with vi-
bratory effect. —n. **2.** act or sound
of trilling.

tril·lion (tril′yən) n., adj. 1 followed by 12 zeroes.

tril·o·gy (tril′ə jē) n., pl. **-gies.**
group of three plays, operas, etc.,
on related theme.

trim (trim) v., **trimmed, trimming,**
n., adj., **trimmer, trimmest.** —v. **1.**
make neat by clipping, paring, etc.
2. adjust (sails or yards). **3.** dress
or ornament. —n. **4.** proper condition. **5.** adjustment of sails, etc. **6.**
dress or equipment. **7.** trimming.
—adj. **8.** neat. **9.** in good condition.
—**trim′ly,** adv. —**trim′mer,** n.

tri·ma·ran′ (trī′mə rän′) n. boat
with three hulls.

tri·mes·ter (trī mes′tər, trī′mes-) n.
1. period of three months. **2.** one of
three divisions of academic year.

trim′ming (trim′ing) n. something
used to decorate.

tri·ni·tro·tol·u·ene′ (trī nī′trō tol′-
yōō ēn′) n. high explosive, known
as TNT.

Trin′i·ty (trin′i tē) n. unity of Father, Son, and Holy Ghost.

trin′ket (tring′kit) n. **1.** bit of jewelry, etc. **2.** trifle.

tri·o (trē′ō) n., pl. **trios.** group of
three.

trip (trip) n., v., **tripped, tripping.**
—n. **1.** journey. **2.** stumble. **3.**
Slang. drug-induced event. —v. **4.**
stumble or cause to stumble. **5.**
slip. **6.** tread quickly. —**trip′per,** n.

tri·par·tite (trī pär′tīt) adj. **1.** divided into or consisting of three
parts. **2.** participated in by three
parties.

tripe (trīp) n. **1.** ruminant's stomach, used as food. **2.** Slang. worthless statements or writing.

tri·ple (trip′əl) adj., n., v., **-pled,**
-pling. —adj. **1.** of three parts. **2.**
three times as great. —n. **3.** Baseball. hit allowing batter to reach
third base. —v. **4.** make or become
triple. —**tri′ply,** adv.

tri′plet (trip′lit) n. one of three
children born at a single birth.

trip·li·cate (-li kit, -kāt′) adj. **1.** triple. —n. **2.** set of three copies.

tri′pod (trī′pod) n. three-legged
stool, support, etc.

trip′tych (trip′tik) n. set of three
panels side by side, with pictures
or carvings.

trite (trīt) adj., **triter, tritest.** commonplace; hackneyed.

tri′u·rate (trich′ə rāt′) v., **-rated, -rating,**
—v. **1.** to reduce to
fine particles or powder; pulverize.
2. (-ər it) triturated substance.

tri′umph (trī′əmf, -umf) n. **1.** victory. **2.** joy over victory. —v. **3.** be
victorious or successful. **4.** rejoice
over this. —**tri·um′phal,** adj. —**tri·**
um′phant, adj.

tri·um′vir (trī um′vər) n., pl. **-virs,**
-viri (-və rī′). Rom. Hist. any of
three magistrates exercising same
public function.

tri·um′vi·rate (-vər it, -və rāt′) n.
1. Rom. Hist. the office of triumvir.
2. government of three joint magistrates. **3.** association of three, as in
office.

triv′et (triv′it) n. device protecting
table top from hot objects.

triv′i·a (triv′ē ə) n. things that are
very unimportant.

triv′i·al, adj. trifling. —**triv′i·al·i·**
ty, n. —**triv′i·al·ly,** adv.

tro·chee (trō′kē) n. verse foot of
two syllables, long followed by
short. —**tro·cha′ic** (-kā′ik) adj.

trog·lo·dyte′ (trog′lə dīt′) n. **1.**
cave dweller. **2.** hermit.

troi′ka (troi′kə) n. **1.** Russian vehicle drawn by three horses. **2.** ruling
group of three.

troll (trōl) v. **1.** sing in rolling
voice. **2.** sing as round. **3.** fish
with moving line. —n. **4.** Music.
round. **5.** underground monster.

trol/ley (trol/ē) n. **1.** trolley car. **2.** pulley on overhead track or wire.

trolley bus, bus drawing power from overhead wires.

trolley car, electric streetcar receiving current from a trolley.

trol/lop (trol/əp) n. **1.** untidy or slovenly woman. **2.** prostitute.

trom/bone (trom bōn′, trom/bōn) n. brass wind instrument with long bent tube. —**trom/bon/ist,** n.

troop (trōōp) n. **1.** assemblage. **2.** cavalry unit. **3.** body of police, etc. —v. **4.** gather or move in numbers. **5.** walk, as if in a march.

troop/ship′, n. ship for conveyance of military troops; transport.

tro/phy (trō/fē) n., pl. **-phies. 1.** memento taken in hunting, war, etc. **2.** silver cup, etc., given as prize.

trop/ic (trop/ik) n. **1.** either of two latitudes (**tropic of Cancer** and **tropic of Capricorn**) bounding torrid zone. **2.** (pl.) region between these latitudes. —**trop/i•cal,** adj.

trop/o•sphere′ (trop/ə sfēr′, trō/pə-) n. lowest layer of atmosphere.

trot (trot) v., **trotted, trotting,** n. —v. **1.** go at gait between walk and run. **2.** go briskly. **3.** ride at trot. —n. **4.** trotting gait. —**trot/ter,** n.

troth (trôth, trōth) n. **1.** fidelity. **2.** promise.

trou/ba•dour′ (trōō/bə dôr′) n. medieval lyric poet of W Mediterranean area who wrote on love and gallantry.

trou/ble (trub/əl) v., **-bled, -bling,** n. —v. **1.** distress. **2.** put to or cause inconvenience. **3.** bother. —n. **4.** annoyance or difficulty. **5.** disturbance. **6.** inconvenience. —**trou/ble•some,** adj.

trou/bled, adj. **1.** emotionally or mentally distressed. **2.** economically or socially distressed.

trou/ble•mak′er, n. person who causes trouble.

troub/le•shoot′er, n. expert in eliminating causes of trouble.

trough (trôf) n. **1.** open boxlike container. **2.** long hollow or channel.

trounce (trouns) v., **trounced, trouncing,** beat severely.

troupe (trōōp) n. company of performers. —**troup/er,** n.

trou/sers (trou/zərz) n.pl. outer garment divided into two separate leg coverings.

trous/seau (trōō/sō, trōō sō′) n., pl. **-seaux, -seaus** (-sōz). bride's outfit.

trout (trout) n. freshwater game fish.

trow/el (trou/əl) n. **1.** tool for spreading or smoothing. **2.** small digging tool.

troy (troi) adj. expressed in troy weight.

troy weight, system of weights for precious metals and gems.

tru/ant (trōō/ənt) n. **1.** student absent from school without leave. —adj. **2.** absent from school without leave. —**tru/an•cy,** n.

truce (trōōs) n. suspension of military hostilities.

truck (truk) n. **1.** hand or motor vehicle for carrying heavy loads. —v. **2.** transport by or drive a truck. **3.** trade. —**truck/er,** n.

truck/le, v., **-led, -ling.** submit humbly.

truckle bed, trundle bed.

truc/u•lent (truk/yə lənt, trōō/kyə-) adj. aggressive. —**truc/u•lence,** n.

trudge (truj) v., **trudged, trudging,** n. —v. **1.** walk, esp. wearily. —n. **2.** tiring walk.

true (trōō) adj., **truer, truest. 1.** conforming to fact. **2.** real. **3.** sincere. **4.** loyal. **5.** correct. —**tru/ly,** adv. —**true/ness,** n.

true/-blue′, adj. staunch; true.

truf/fle (truf/əl) n. **1.** edible fungus. **2.** chocolate confection resembling truffle.

tru/ism (trōō/iz əm) n. obvious truth.

trump (trump) n. **1.** playing card of suit outranking other suits. **2.** the suit itself. —v. **3.** take with or play trump. **4.** fabricate.

trump/er•y, n., pl. **-eries.** nonsense; twaddle.

trum/pet (trum/pit) n. **1.** brass wind instrument with powerful, penetrating tone. —v. **2.** blow trumpet. **3.** proclaim. —**trum/pet•er,** n.

trun/cate (trung/kāt) v., **-cated, -cating.** shorten by cutting.

trun/cheon (trun/chən) n. club.

trun/dle (trun/dl) v., **-dled, -dling,** n. —v. **1.** roll, as on wheels. —n. **2.** small roller, wheel, etc.

trundle bed, low bed on casters, usually pushed under another bed when not in use. Also, **truckle bed.**

trunk (trungk) n. **1.** main stem of tree. **2.** box for clothes, etc. **3.** body of person or animal, excepting head and limbs. **4.** storage space in car. **5.** elephant's long flexible nasal appendage. **6.** pl. shorts.

trunk line, 1. major long-distance transportation line. **2.** telephone line between two switching devices.

truss (trus) v. **1.** bind or fasten. **2.** furnish or support with a truss.

—*n.* **3.** rigid supporting framework. **4.** apparatus for confining hernia.

trust (trust) *n.* **1.** reliance on person's integrity, justice, etc. **2.** confident hope. **3.** credit. **4.** responsibility. **5.** care. **6.** something entrusted. **7.** holding of legal title for another's benefit. **8.** combination of companies, often monopolistic, controlled by central board. —*v.* **9.** place confidence in. **10.** rely on. **11.** hope. **12.** believe. **13.** give credit.
—**trust′wor′thy,** *adj.*

trus·tee′, *n.* **1.** administrator of company, etc. **2.** holder of trust (def. 7).

trus·tee′ship, *n.* **1.** office of trustee. **2.** control of territory granted by United Nations. **3.** the territory.

trust fund, money, etc., held in trust.

trust territory, territory which United Nations has placed under administrative control of a nation.

trust′y, *adj.,* **-ier, -iest,** *n., pl.* **trust·ies.** —*adj.* **1.** reliable. —*n.* **2.** trusted one. **3.** trustworthy convict given special privileges.

truth (trōōth) *n.* **1.** true facts. **2.** conformity with fact. **3.** established fact, principle, etc. —**truth′ful,** *adj.*

try (trī) *v.,* **tried, trying. 1.** attempt. **2.** test. **3.** examine judicially. **4.** strain endurance, patience, etc., of.

try′ing, *adj.* annoying; irksome.

try′out′, *n. Informal.* trial or test to ascertain fitness for some purpose.

tryst (trist, trīst) *n.* **1.** appointment, as of lovers, to meet. **2.** the meeting. **3.** place of meeting. —*v.* **4.** meet.

tsar (zär, tsär) *n.* czar.

tset′se fly (tset′sē, tsēt′sē) African fly transmitting disease.

T′-shirt′, *n.* short-sleeved knitted undershirt. Also, **tee′-shirt′.**

tsp., teaspoon.

T square, T-shaped ruler used in mechanical drawing.

tub (tub) *n.* **1.** bathtub. **2.** deep, open-topped container.

tu′ba (tōō′bə, tyōō′-) *n.* low-pitched brass wind instrument.

tub′by (tub′ē) *adj.,* **-bier, -biest.** short and fat.

tube (tōōb, tyōōb) *n.* **1.** hollow pipe for fluids, etc. **2.** compressible container for toothpaste, etc. **3.** railroad or vehicular tunnel. —**tu·bu·lar** (-byə lər) *adj.* —**tub′ing,** *n.*

tu′ber (tōō′bər, tyōō′-) *n.* fleshy thickening of underground stem or shoot. —**tu′ber·ous,** *adj.*

tu′ber·cle (-kəl) *n.* small roundish projection, nodule, or swelling.

tu·ber·cu·lo′sis (-lō′sis) *n.* infectious disease marked by formation of tubercles. —**tu·ber′cu·lar, tu·ber′cu·lous,** *adj.*

tube′rose′ (tōōb′-, tyōōb′-) *n.* cultivated flowering plant.

tu′bule (-byool) *n.* small tube.

tuck (tuk) *v.* **1.** thrust into narrow space or retainer. **2.** cover snugly. **3.** draw up in folds. —*n.* **4.** tucked piece or part.

tuck′er, *n.* **1.** piece of cloth formerly worn by women about neck and shoulders. —*v.* **2.** *Informal.* tire; exhaust.

Tues., Tuesday. Also, **Tue.**

Tues′day (tōōz′dā, -dē, tyōōz′-) *n.* third day of week.

tuft (tuft) *n.* **1.** bunch of feathers, hairs, etc., fixed at base. **2.** clump of grasses, etc. —*v.* **3.** arrange in or form tufts. —**tuft′ed,** *adj.*

tug (tug) *v.,* **tugged, tugging,** —*v.* **1.** drag; haul. —*n.* **2.** act of tugging. **3.** tugboat.

tug′boat′, *n.* powerful vessel used for towing.

tug of war, 1. contest between teams pulling opposite ends of rope. **2.** struggle for supremacy.

tu·i′tion (tōō ish′ən, tyōō-) *n.* charge for instruction.

tu′lip (tōō′lip, tyōō′-) *n.* plant bearing showy, cup-shaped flowers.

tulle (tōōl) *n.* thin silk or rayon net.

tum′ble (tum′bəl) *v.,* **-bled, -bling,** *n.* —*v.* **1.** fall over or down. **2.** perform gymnastic feats. **3.** roll about; toss. —*n.* **4.** act of tumbling.

tum′ble-down′, *adj.* dilapidated.

tum′bler, *n.* **1.** drinking glass. **2.** performer of tumbling feats.

tum′ble·weed′, *n.* plant whose upper part becomes detached and is driven about by wind.

tum′brel (tum′brəl) *n.* farmer's cart that can be tilted to discharge its load. Also, **tum′bril.**

tu′mid (tōō′mid, tyōō-) *adj.* **1.** swollen. **2.** turgid; bombastic. —**tu·mes′cent** (-mes′ənt) *adj.*

tum′my (tum′ē) *n., pl.* **-mies.** *Informal.* stomach or abdomen.

tu′mor (tōō′mər, tyōō′-) *n.* abnormal swelling of cells in part of body. —**tu′mor·ous,** *adj.*

tu′mult (tōō′mult, -malt, tyōō′-) *n.* disturbance, commotion, or uproar. —**tu·mul′tu·ous** (-mul′chōō əs) *adj.*

tun (tun) *n.* large cask.

tu′na (tōō′nə, tyōō′-) *n.* large oceanic fish.

tun′dra (tōōn′drə, tōōn′-) *n.* vast, treeless, arctic plain.

tune (tōōn, tyōōn) *n., v.,* **tuned, tuning.** —*n.* **1.** melody. **2.** state of proper pitch, frequency, or condition.

3. harmony. —*v.* **4.** adjust to correct pitch. **5.** adjust to receive radio or television signals. —**tune′ful,** *adj.* —**tune′less,** *adj.* —**tun′er,** *n.*

tune′-up′, *n.* adjustment, as of motor, to improve working condition.

tung′sten (tung′stən) *n.* metallic element used for electric-lamp filaments, etc.

tu′nic (tōō′nik, tyōō′-) *n.* **1.** coat of uniform. **2.** ancient Greek and Roman garment. **3.** woman's upper garment.

tun′ing fork, steel instrument struck to produce pure tone of constant pitch.

tun′nel (tun′l) *n., v.,* **-neled, -neling.** —*n.* **1.** underground passage. —*v.* **2.** make tunnel.

tur′ban (tûr′bən) *n.* head covering made of scarf wound round head.

tur′bid (tûr′bid) *adj.* **1.** muddy. **2.** dense. **3.** confused.

tur′bine (tûr′bin, -bīn) *n.* motor producing torque by pressure of fluid.

tur′bo·jet′ (tûr′bō-) *n.* **1.** jet engine that compresses air by turbine. **2.** airplane with such engines.

tur′bo·prop′ (-prop′) *n.* **1.** turbojet with turbine-driven propeller. **2.** airplane with such engines.

tur′bot (tûr′bət) *n.* flatfish.

tur′bu·lent (tûr′byə lənt) *adj.* **1.** disorderly. **2.** tumultuous. —**tur′bu·lence,** *n.*

tu·reen′ (tōō rēn′, tyōō-) *n.* large covered dish for soup, etc.

turf (tûrf) *n.* **1.** covering of grass and roots. **2.** familiar area, as of residence or expertise.

tur′gid (tûr′jid) *adj.* **1.** swollen. **2.** pompous or bombastic. —**tur·gid′i·ty,** *n.* —**tur′gid·ly,** *adv.*

tur′key (tûr′kē) *n.* large, edible American bird.

turkey vulture, blackish brown New World vulture.

tur′mer·ic (tûr′mər ik) *n.* aromatic spice from Asian plant.

tur′moil (tûr′moil) *n.* tumult.

turn (tûrn) *v.* **1.** rotate. **2.** reverse. **3.** divert. **4.** depend. **5.** sour. **6.** nauseate. **7.** alter. **8.** become. **9.** use. **10.** pass. **11.** direct. **12.** curve. —*n.* **13.** rotation. **14.** change or point of change. **15.** one's due time or opportunity. **16.** trend. **17.** short walk, ride, etc. **18.** inclination or aptitude. **19.** service or disservice.

turn′a·bout′, *n.* change of opinion, loyalty, etc.

turn′coat′, *n.* renegade.

turning point, time at which decisive change takes place.

tur·nip (tûr′nip) *n.* fleshy, edible root of cabbagelike plant.

turn′off′, *n.* small road that branches off from larger one.

turn′out′, *n.* **1.** attendance at meeting, show, etc. **2.** output.

turn′o·ver, *n.* **1.** rate of replacement, movement, trade, etc. **2.** small pastry with filling.

turn′pike′ (-pīk′) *n.* **1.** barrier across road (**turnpike road**) where toll is paid. **2.** turnpike road.

turn′stile′, *n.* gate with revolving arms to allow people through one by one.

turn′ta′ble, *n.* rotating platform.

tur′pen·tine′ (tûr′pən tīn′) *n.* oil from resin from coniferous trees.

tur′pi·tude′ (tûr′pi tōōd′, -tyōōd′) *n.* depravity.

tur′quoise′ (tûr′koiz, -kwoiz) *n.* **1.** greenish-blue mineral used in jewelry. **2.** bluish green.

tur′ret (tûr′it, tur′-) *n.* **1.** small tower. **2.** towerlike gun shelter.

tur′tle (tûr′tl) *n.* marine reptile with shell-encased body.

tur′tle·dove′ (-duv′) *n.* small Old World dove.

tur′tle·neck′, *n.* **1.** high, close-fitting collar. **2.** garment with turtleneck.

tusk (tusk) *n.* very long tooth, as of elephant or walrus.

tus′sle (tus′əl) *v.,* **-sled, -sling.** fight; scuffle.

tus′sock (tus′ak) *n.* tuft of growing grass.

tu′te·lage (tōōt′l ij, tyōōt′-) *n.* **1.** guardianship. **2.** instruction.

tu′tor (tōō′tər, tyōō′-) *n.* **1.** private instructor. **2.** college teacher (below instructor). —*v.* **3.** teach. —**tu·to′ri·al** (-tôr′ē al) *adj.*

tut′ti-frut′ti (tōō′tē frōō′tē) *n.* ice cream, flavored with variety of fruits.

tu′tu′ (tōō′tōō′) *n.* short, full skirt worn by ballerina.

tux (tuks) *n. Informal.* tuxedo.

tux·e′do (tuk sē′dō) *n., pl.* **-dos.** semiformal jacket or suit for men.

TV, television.

twad′dle (twod′l) *n.* nonsense.

twain (twān) *adj., n. Archaic.* two.

twang (twang) *v.* **1.** sound sharply and ringingly. **2.** have nasal tone. —*n.* **3.** twanging sound.

tweak (twēk) *v.* **1.** seize and pull or twist. —*n.* **2.** sharp pull and twist.

tweed (twēd) *n.* coarse, colored wool cloth.

tweet (twēt) *n.* **1.** chirping sound. —*v.* **2.** chirp.

tweez′ers (twē′zərz) *n.pl.* small pincers.

twelve (twelv) n., adj. ten plus two. —**twelfth**, adj., n.

Twelve Step, of or based on program for recovery from addiction that provides 12 progressive levels toward attainment.

twen/ty (twen′tē) n., adj. ten times two. —**twen/ti·eth**, adj., n.

twerp (twûrp) n. Slang. insignificant or despicable person.

twice (twīs) adv. **1.** two times. **2.** doubly.

twid/dle (twid′l) v., **-dled, -dling. 1.** turn round and round, esp. with the fingers. **2.** twirl (one's fingers) about each other.

twig (twig) n. slender branch on tree.

twi/light/ (twī′līt/) n. light from sky when sun is down.

twill (twil) n. fabric woven in parallel diagonal lines.

twin (twin) n. either of two children born at single birth.

twine (twīn) n., v., **twined, twining. 1.** strong thread of twisted strands. —v. **2.** twist or become twisted together. **3.** encircle.

twinge (twinj) n., v., **twinged, twinging.** —n. **1.** sudden, sharp pain. —v. **2.** give or have twinge.

twin/kle (twing′kəl) v., **-kled, -kling,** n. —v. **1.** shine with light, quick gleams. —n. **2.** sly, humorous look. **3.** act of twinkling.

twin/kling, n. instant.

twirl (twûrl) v. **1.** spin; whirl. —n. **2.** a twirling.

twist (twist) v. **1.** combine by winding together. **2.** distort. **3.** combine in coil, etc. **4.** wind about. **5.** writhe. **6.** turn. —n. **7.** curve or turn. **8.** spin. **9.** wrench. **10.** spiral.

twist/er, n. Informal. tornado.

twit (twit) v., **twitted, twitting,** n. —v. **1.** taunt; tease. —n. **2.** Informal. fool.

twitch (twich) v. **1.** jerk. —n. **2.** quick jerky movement.

twit/ter (twit′ər) v. **1.** utter small, tremulous sounds, as bird. **2.** tremble with excitement. —n. **3.** twittering sound. **4.** state of excitement.

two (tōō) n., adj. one plus one.

two/-bit/, adj. Informal. inferior or unimportant.

two bits, Informal. 25 cents.

two/-faced/, adj. deceitful or hypocritical.

two/-fist/ed, adj. strong and vigorous.

two/fold/ adj. (-fōld′) **1.** having

two parts. **2.** twice as great. —adv. (-fōld′) **3.** in two-fold measure.

two/-ply/, adj. consisting of two layers, strands, etc.

two/some (-səm) n. pair.

two/-time/, v., **-timed, -timing.** Informal. be unfaithful to.

two/-way/, adj. **1.** allowing movement in two directions. **2.** involving two participants.

twp., township.

TX, Texas.

-ty, suffix meaning state or condition, as certainty.

ty·coon/ (tī kōōn′) n. businessperson having great wealth and power.

tyke (tīk) n. small child.

tympanic membrane, membrane separating middle from external ear.

tym/pa·num (tim′pə nəm) n. **1.** middle ear. **2.** tympanic membrane.

type (tīp) n., v., **typed, typing.** —n. **1.** kind or class. **2.** representative specimen. **3.** piece used in printing. **4.** such pieces collectively. —v. **5.** typewrite. —**typ/ist,** n.

type/cast/, n., v., **-cast, -casting.** cast (actor) exclusively in same kind of role.

type/script/, n. typewritten matter.

type/set/ter, n. **1.** person who sets type. **2.** machine for setting type. —**type/set/,** v. **-set, -setting.**

type/writ/er, n. machine for writing mechanically.

ty/phoid/ (tī′foid) n. infectious disease marked by intestinal disorder. Also, **typhoid fever.**

ty·phoon/ (tī fōōn′) n. cyclone or hurricane of western Pacific.

ty/phus (tī′fəs) n. infectious disease transmitted by lice and fleas.

typ/i·cal (tip′i kəl) adj. **1.** serving as a representative specimen. **2.** conforming to the characteristics of a particular group.

typ/i·fy/, v., **-fied, -fying.** serve as typical example of.

ty/po (tī′pō) n., pl. **-pos.** error in typography or typing.

ty·pog/ra·phy (tī pog′rə fē) n. **1.** art or process of printing. **2.** general character of printed matter.

ty·ran/no·saur/ (ti ran′ə sôr′, tī-) n. large dinosaur that walked upright.

tyr/an·ny (tir′ə nē) n., pl. **-nies. 1.** despotic abuse of authority. **2.** government or rule by tyrant. —**ty·ran/ni·cal** (tə ran′i kəl, tī-) adj. —**tyr/an·nize/,** v., **-nized, -nizing.**

tyr/rant (tī′rənt) n. oppressive, unjust, or absolute ruler.

ty/ro (tī′rō) n., pl. **-ros.** novice.

tzar (zär, tsär) n. czar.

U

U, u (yōō) *n.* twenty-first letter of English alphabet.

u·biq/ui·tous (yōō bik′wi təs) *adj.* simultaneously present everywhere.

ud/der (ud′ər) *n.* mammary gland, esp. of cow.

UFO (yōō′ef′ō′; *sometimes* yōō′fō) unidentified flying object.

ug/ly (ug′lē) *adj.*, **-lier, -liest. 1.** repulsive. **2.** dangerous.

u/ku·le/le (yōō′ka lā′lē) *n.* small guitar.

ul/cer (ul′sər) *n.* open sore, as on stomach lining. —**ul/cer·ous,** *adj.*
—**ul/cer·ate/,** *v.,* **-ated, -ating.**

ul/na (ul′nə) *n.* larger bone of forearm. —**ul/nar,** *adj.*

ul·te/ri·or (ul tēr′ē ər) *adj.* **1.** not acknowledged; concealed. **2.** later.

ul/ti·mate (-mit) *adj.* **1.** final; highest. **2.** basic. —**ul/ti·mate·ly,** *adv.*

ul/ti·ma/tum (-mā′təm, -mä′-) *n., pl.* **-tums, -ta** (-tə). final demand.

ultra-, prefix meaning beyond; on the far side of; extremely.

ul/tra·con·serv/a·tive (ul′trə kən-sûr′və tiv) *adj.* extremely conservative, esp. in politics.

ul/tra·fiche/ (-fēsh′) *n.* form of microfiche with images greatly reduced in size.

ul/tra·high/ frequency (ul′trə hī′) radio frequency between 300 and 3000 megahertz.

ul/tra·ma·rine/, *n.* deep blue.

ul/tra·sound/, *n.* application of sound above human hearing to medical diagnosis and therapy.

ul/tra·vi/o·let, *adj.* of invisible rays beyond violet in spectrum.

um/ber (um′bər) *n.* **1.** reddish brown. —*adj.* **2.** of or like umber.

umbilical cord (um bil′i kəl) cord-like structure connecting fetus with placenta, conveying nourishment and removing wastes.

um·bil/i·cus (-kəs) *n., pl.* **-ci** (-sī). navel. —**um·bil/i·cal,** *adj.*

um/brage (um′brij) *n.* resentment.

um·brel/la (um brel′ə) *n.* cloth-covered framework carried for protection from rain, etc.

um/laut (ōōm′lout) *n.* **1.** (in Germanic languages) assimilation in which vowel is influenced by following vowel. **2.** diacritical mark (¨) used over vowel to indicate umlaut.

ump (ump) *n., v.* umpire.

um/pire (um′pīēr) *n., v.,* **-pired, -piring.** —*n.* **1.** judge or arbitrator. —*v.* **2.** be umpire in.

ump/teen/ (ump′tēn′) *adj.* Infor-

mal. innumerable. —**ump/teenth/,** *adj.*

UN, United Nations.

un-, prefix indicating negative or opposite sense, as in *unfair, unwanted,* and *unfasten.*

un·a/ble (un ā′bəl) *adj.* lacking necessary power, skill, or resources.

un/ac·count/a·ble, *adj.* inexplicable. **2.** not responsible.

un/af·fect/ed, *adj.* **1.** without affectation. **2.** not concerned or involved.

u·nan/i·mous (yōō nan′ə məs) *adj.* completely agreed. —**u/na·nim/i·ty** (-nə nim′i tē) *n.*

un/as·sum/ing (un′-) *adj.* modest; without vanity.

un/at·tached/, *adj.* **1.** not attached. **2.** not engaged or married.

un/a·vail/ing, *adj.* not effective.

un/a·wares/, *adv.* not knowingly.

un·bal/anced, *adj.* **1.** out of balance. **2.** irrational; deranged.

un·bear/a·ble, *adj.* unendurable.

un/be·com/ing, *adj.* unattractive or unseemly.

un·bend/, *v.,* **-bent, -bending. 1.** straighten. **2.** act in genial, relaxed manner.

un·bend/ing, *adj.* rigidly formal or unyielding.

un·bid/den, *adj.* **1.** not commanded. **2.** not asked.

un·blush/ing, *adj.* showing no remorse; shameless.

un·bos/om, *v.* disclose (secrets, etc.).

un·bowed/ (-boud′) *adj.* **1.** not bent. **2.** not subjugated.

un·brid/led, *adj.* unrestrained.

un·bro/ken, *adj.* **1.** not broken. **2.** undisturbed. **3.** not tamed.

un·bur/den, *v.* **1.** free from burden. **2.** relieve one's mind, conscience, etc., by confessing.

un·called/-for/, *adj.* not warranted.

un·can/ny, *adj.* unnaturally strange or good.

un·cer/e·mo/ni·ous, *adj.* **1.** informal. **2.** rudely abrupt.

un·chart/ed, *adj.* not shown on map; unexplored.

un·clad/, *adj.* naked.

un/cle (ung′kəl) *n.* **1.** brother of one's father or mother. **2.** husband of one's aunt.

Uncle Sam (sam) United States government.

un/com·pro·mis/ing, *adj.* refusing to compromise; rigid.

un·con·cern', n. lack of concern; indifference.

un·con·di'tion·al, adj. absolute; without conditions or reservations.

un·con'scion·a·ble (-shən-) adj. not reasonable or honest.

un·con'scious, adj. **1.** lacking awareness, sensation, or cognition. **2.** not perceived at level of awareness. **3.** done without intent. —n. **4.** the unconscious, part of psyche rarely accessible to awareness but influencing behavior.

un·couth' (un kōōth') adj. rude; boorish.

unc'tion (ungk'shən) n. **1.** anointment with oil. **2.** soothing manner of speech.

unc'tu·ous (-chōō əs) adj. **1.** oily. **2.** overly suave.

un·cut' (un-) adj. **1.** not shortened; unabridged. **2.** not yet given shape, as a gemstone.

un·daunt'ed, adj. not discouraged.

un·de·mon'stra·tive, adj. reserved.

un'der (un'dər) prep., adj., adv. **1.** beneath; below. **2.** less than. **3.** lower.

under-, prefix meaning: **1.** below or beneath, as underbrush. **2.** lower in grade, as understudy. **3.** of lesser degree or amount, as underestimate.

un'der·a·chieve', v., -achieved, -achieving. perform below one's intellectual potential.

un'der·age', adj. being below legal or required age.

un'der·bel'ly, n., pl. -ies. **1.** lower abdomen. **2.** vulnerable area.

un'der·brush', n. low shrubs, etc., in forest.

un'der·car'riage, n. supporting framework underneath vehicle.

un'der·clothes', n.pl. underwear.

un'der·cov'er, adj. secret.

un'der·cur'rent, n. hidden tendency or feeling.

un'der·cut', v., -cut, -cutting. sell at lower price than.

un'der·de·vel'oped, adj. **1.** insufficiently developed. **2.** having relatively low living standards and industrial development.

un'der·dog', n. **1.** weaker contestant, etc. **2.** victim of injustice.

un'der·done', adj. not cooked enough.

un'der·es'ti·mate' (-māt') v., -mated, -mating. estimate too low.

un'der·ex·pose', v., -posed, -posing. expose (film) to insufficient light or for too short a period.

un'der·gar'ment, n. item of underwear.

un'der·go', v., -went, -gone, -going. experience; endure.

un'der·grad'u·ate (-it) n. college student before receiving first degree.

un'der·ground' adv. (un'dər·ground') adj. (-ground'). **1.** under the ground. **2.** secret. —n. (-ground') **3.** secret resistance army.

un'der·growth', n. underbrush.

un'der·hand', adj. sly; secret.

un'der·line', v., -lined, -lining. **1.** draw line under. **2.** stress.

un'der·ling' (-ling) n. subordinate.

un'der·mine' (un'dər mīn', un'dər·mīn') v., -mined, -mining. weaken or destroy, esp. secretly.

un'der·neath' (-nēth', -nēth') prep., adv. beneath.

un'der·pass', n. passage running underneath.

un'der·pin'ning, n. **1.** system of supports. **2.** foundation; basis.

un'der·priv'i·leged, adj. denied normal privileges of society.

un'der·score', v., -scored, -scoring. underline; stress.

un'der·sec're·tar'y, n., pl. -taries. government official subordinate to principal secretary.

un'der·signed', n. the undersigned, person signing document.

---

un·ack·now'ledged	un'con·trol'la·ble	un'ex·pect'ed
un'a·void'a·ble	un·cork'	un·fail'ing
un'a·ware'	un·cov'er	un·fail'ing
un'be·liev'a·ble	un·de·cid'ed	un·fair'
un·born'	un·de·clared'	un·faith'ful
un·bound'ed	un·de·feat'ed	un·fa·mil'iar
un·but'ton	un·de·ni'a·ble	un·fas'ten
un·cer'tain	un·doubt'ed	un·fit'
un·civ'il	un·dress'	un·fold'
un·clean'	un·due'	un'for·get'ta·ble
un·cloak'	un·du'ly	un'for·giv'a·ble
un·clothe'	un·e'qual	un·for'tu·nate
un·com'fort·a·ble	un·err'ing	un·friend'ly
un·com'mon	un·e'ven	un·god'ly

un'der-staffed', *adj.* having not enough workers.

un'der-stand', *v.*, **-stood, -standing. 1.** know meaning of. **2.** accept as part of agreement. **3.** sympathize. **—un'der-stand'ing**, *n.*

un'der-stand', *v.*, **-stated, -stating. 1.** state less strongly than facts warrant. **2.** set forth in restrained terms. **—un'der-state'ment**, *n.*

un'der-stud'y, *n.*, *pl.* **-studies.** substitute for performer.

un'der-take', *v.*, **-took, -taken, -taking. 1.** attempt. **2.** promise. **3.** arrange funerals.

un'der-tak'er, *n.* funeral director; mortician.

un'der-tak'ing, *n.* (un'dər tā'king, un'-dər tā'-) **1.** enterprise; task. **2.** promise.

un'der-the-coun'ter, *adj.* illegal; unauthorized.

un'der-tone', *n.* **1.** low tone. **2.** underlying quality. **3.** subdued color.

un'der-tow' (-tō') *n.* strong subsurface current moving opposite surface current.

un'der-wear', *n.* garments worn next to skin, under other clothing.

un'der-world', *n.* **1.** criminal element. **2.** land of the dead.

un'der-write' (un'dər rīt', un'dər-rīt') *v.*, **-wrote, -written, -writing.** guarantee, esp. expense.

un-do' (un dōō') *v.*, **-did, -done, -doing. 1.** return to original state. **2.** untie. **3.** destroy.

un-do'ing, *n.* **1.** reversing. **2.** ruin. **3.** cause of ruin.

un'du-late' (un'jə lāt', -dyə-) *v.*, **-lated, -lating.** have wavy motion or form. **—un'du-la'tion**, *n.*

un-dy'ing, *adj.* eternal; unending.

un-earned', *adj.* **1.** not earned by service. **2.** not deserved. **3.** (of income) derived from investments.

un-earth', *v.* discover.

un-earth'ly, *adj.* supernatural; weird.

un-eas'y, *adj.*, **-ier, -iest.** anxious.

un'e-quiv'o-cal, *adj.* not ambiguous.

un'e-vent'ful, *adj.* routine.

un'ex-cep'tion-al, *adj.* ordinary.

un-feel'ing, *adj.* lacking sympathy. **—un-feel'ing-ly**, *adv.*

un-flap'pa-ble (un flap'ə bəl) *adj.* not easily upset or panicked.

un-fledged' (-flejd') *adj.* **1.** lacking sufficient feathers for flight. **2.** immature.

un-found'ed, *adj.* not supported by evidence.

un-frock', *v.* deprive of ecclesiastical rank, authority, and function.

un-gain'ly (-gān'lē) *adj.* clumsy.

un'guent (ung'gwənt) *n.* salve.

un-hand', *v.* release from grasp.

un-hinge', *v.*, **-hinged, -hinging. 1.** take off hinges. **2.** make mentally unstable; unbalance.

uni-, prefix meaning one.

u'ni-corn' (yōō'ni kôrn') *n.* mythical horselike animal with one horn.

u'ni-form' (yōō'nə fôrm') *adj.* **1.** exactly alike. **2.** constant. *—n.* **3.** distinctive clothing of specific group. *—v.* **4.** put in uniform. **—u'-ni-form'i-ty**, *n.*

u'ni-fy' (-fī') *v.*, **-fied, -fying.** make into one. **—u'ni-fi-ca'tion**, *n.*

u'ni-lat'er-al, *adj.* one-sided.

un'im-peach'a-ble (un'im pē'chə-bəl) *adj.* above reproach.

un'in-hib'it-ed, *adj.* unrestrained by convention.

un'in-ter-est-ed, *adj.* not interested; indifferent. **—Usage.** See DISINTERESTED.

un'ion (yōōn'yən) *n.* **1.** uniting; combination. **2.** labor group for mutual aid on wages, etc. **—un'ion-ist**, *n.*; **—un'ion-ize'**, *v.*

Union Jack, British flag.

u-nique' (yōō nēk') *adj.* **1.** only. **2.** most unusual or rare. **—Usage.** UNIQUE is an adjective representing an absolute state that cannot exist

---

un·gra'cious
un·guard'ed
un·hap'py
un·heard'-of
un·ho'ly
un'in·tel'lig·i·ble
un'in·ter·rupt'ed
un·kind'
un·known'
un·lace'
un·law'ful
un·like'
un·like'ly
un·load'

un·lock'
un·mask'
un'mis·tak'a·ble
un·mor'al
un·nat'u·ral
un·nec'es·sar'y
un·pack'
un·pop'u·lar
un·rea'son·a·ble
un·roll'
un·screw'
un·shack'le
un·sight'ly
un·skilled'

un·tan'gle
un·true'
un·truth'
un·twist'
un·typ'i·cal
un·used'
un·u'su·al
un·veil'
un·wind'
un·wise'
un·worn'
un·wor'thy
un·wrap'
un·yoke'

in degrees. Therefore, it cannot be sensibly used with a limiting or comparative adverb such as "very," "most," or "extremely": *She has a* unique (not *"very unique"* or *"most* unique") *style of singing.*

u′ni·sex′ (yōō′nə seks′) *adj.* of type or style used by both sexes.

u′ni·son (-sən, -zən) *n.* agreement.

u′nit (yōō′nit) *n.* **1.** single entity. **2.** one of a number of identical or similar parts within whole.

U′ni·tar′i·an (yōō′ni târ′ē ən) *n.* **1.** member of Christian denomination asserting unity of God. —*adj.* **2.** concerning Unitarians or their beliefs.

u·nite′ (yōō nīt′) *v.,* **united, uniting.** join, make, etc., into one.

United Nations, organization of nations to preserve peace and promote human welfare.

u′ni·ty (yōō′ni tē) *n., pl.* **-ties. 1.** state of being one. **2.** agreement.

u′ni·ver′sal (yōō′nə vûr′səl) *adj.* **1.** of all; general. **2.** applicable or existing everywhere. —**u′ni·ver·sal′i·ty** (-sal′i tē) *n.*

Universal Product Code, standardized bar code.

u′ni·verse′ (-vûrs′) *n.* all things that exist, including heavenly bodies.

u′ni·ver′si·ty (-vûr′si tē) *n., pl.* **-ties.** institution composed of various specialized colleges.

un·kempt′ *adj.* untidy.

un·lead′ed (-led′id) *adj.* (of gasoline) free of pollution-causing lead.

un·less′ (un les′, ən-) *conj., prep.* except that.

un·let′tered, *adj.* illiterate.

un·mit′i·gat′ed, *adj.* **1.** not lessened. **2.** absolute.

un·nerve′, *v.,* **-nerved, -nerving.** deprive of courage, strength, or determination.

un·par′al·leled′, *adj.* without equal.

un·plumbed′, *adj.* not explored in depth.

un·prin′ci·pled, *adj.* without principles or ethics.

un·print′a·ble, *adj.* unfit for print, esp. because obscene.

un·rav′el, *v.,* **-eled, -eling. 1.** disentangle. **2.** solve.

un′re·con·struct′ed, *adj.* stubbornly maintaining beliefs considered out of date.

un′re·mit′ting, *adj.* not abating.

un·rest′, *n.* **1.** restless state. **2.** strong, almost rebellious, dissatisfaction.

un·ruf′fled, *adj.* calm.

un·ru′ly (un rōō′lē) *adj.* **-lier, -liest.** lawless.

un·sa′vo·ry, *adj.* morally objectionable.

un·sea′son·a·ble, *adj.* **1.** being out of season. **2.** inopportune.

un·seat′, *v.* **1.** dislodge from seat. **2.** remove from political office.

un·seem′ly, *adj.,* **-lier, -liest.** improper.

un·set′tle, *v.,* **-tled, -tling. 1.** cause to be unstable; disturb. **2.** agitate mind or emotions of.

un·sound′, *adj.* **1.** unhealthy. **2.** not solid. **3.** not valid. **4.** not secure.

un·spar′ing, *adj.* **1.** profuse. **2.** unmerciful.

un·speak′a·ble, *adj.* **1.** exceeding the power of speech. **2.** inexpressibly bad.

un·sta′ble, *adj.* **1.** unsteady. **2.** changeable. **3.** emotionally unsettled.

un·strung′, *adj.* nervously upset; unnerved.

un·sung′, *adj.* not celebrated, as in song; unappreciated.

un·ten′a·ble, *adj.* not defensible as true.

un·think′a·ble, *adj.* not to be imagined; impossible.

un·ti′dy, *adj.,* **-dier, -diest.** not tidy or neat. —**un·tid′i·ly,** *adv.*

un·tie′, *v.,* **-tied, -tying.** loosen or open (something tied).

un·til′ (un til′) *conj., prep.* **1.** up to time when. **2.** before. —Usage. See TILL.

un′to (un′tōō; *unstressed* -tə) *prep.* Archaic. to.

un·told′, *adj.* countless.

un·touch′a·ble, *adj.* **1.** beyond control or criticism. **2.** too vile to touch. —**un·touch′a·ble,** *n.*

un·to·ward′, *adj.* unfavorable or unfortunate.

un·well′, *adj.* ill or ailing.

un·wield′y, *adj.,* **-ier, -iest.** awkward to handle.

un·wit′ting, *adj.* not aware.

un·wont′ed (un wôn′tid, -wōn′-, -wun′-) *adj.* not habitual or usual.

up (up) *adv., prep., n., v.,* **upped, upping.** —*adv.* **1.** to higher place, etc. **2.** erectly. **3.** out of bed. **4.** at bat. —*prep.* **5.** to, toward, or in a higher place, etc. —*n.* **6.** rise. —*v.* **7.** increase.

up′-and-com′ing, *adj.* likely to succeed; promising.

up·beat′, *adj.* optimistic; happy.

up·braid′ (up brād′) *v.* chide.

up′bring′ing, *n.* care and training of children.

up'com'ing, adj. about to take place or appear.

up'coun'try, adj., adv. of, toward, or situated in the interior of a region.

up'date (up'dāt', up'dāt') v., **-dated, -dating.** modernize, esp. in details.

up·end', v. set on end.

up'-front', adj. **1.** invested or paid in advance. **2.** honest; candid.

up'grade' n., v., **-graded, -grading.** —n. (up'grād') **1.** upward incline. **2.** increase, rise, or improvement. —v. (up grād', up'grād') **3.** raise in position, quality, or value.

up·heav'al (up hēv'əl) n. **1.** sudden and great movement or change.

up'hill', adv. up a slope or incline.

up·hold', v., **-held, -holding.** support. —**up·hold'er,** n.

up·hol'ster (up hōl'stər, ə pōl'-) v. provide (furniture) with coverings, etc. —**up·hol'ster·er,** n. —**up·hol'ster·y,** n. maintenance.

up'keep', n. maintenance.

up'land (up'lənd, -land') n. elevated region.

up·lift' v. (up lift') **1.** improve; exalt. —n. (up'lift') **2.** improvement.

up·on' (ə pon', ə pôn') prep. on.

up'per, adj. higher.

up'per·case', adj. **1.** (of a letter) capital. —n. **2.** capital letter.

upper hand, controlling position; advantage.

up'pi·ty (up'i tē) adj. Informal. haughty, snobbish, or arrogant.

up'right', (up'rīt', up rīt') adj. **1.** erect. **2.** honest.

up'ris'ing (up'rī'zing, up rī'-) n. revolt.

up'roar', n. tumult; noise; din. —**up·roar'i·ous,** adj.

up·root', v. tear up by roots.

up'scale', adj. of or for people at upper end of economic scale.

up·set', v., **-set, -setting,** n., adj. —v. (up set') **1.** turn over. **2.** distress emotionally. **3.** defeat. —n. (up'set') **4.** overturn. **5.** defeat. **6.** (up set') **7.** disorderly. —adj. (up set') **6.** disorderly. **7.** distressed.

up'shot', n. final result.

upside down, **1.** with upper part undermost. **2.** in or into complete disorder. —**up'side-down',** adj.

up'stage', adv., adj., v., **-staged, -staging.** —adv. **1.** at or toward back of stage. —v. **2.** outdo professionally or socially.

up'stairs', adv., adj. on or to upper floor.

up'start', n. person newly risen to wealth or importance.

up'-to-date', adj. **1.** until present time; current. **2.** modern; latest.

up'ward (up'wərd) adv. to higher place. Also, **up'wards.** —**up'ward,** adj.

u·ra'ni·um (yŏŏ rā'nē əm) n. white, radioactive metallic element, important in development of atomic energy.

U'ra·nus (yŏŏr'ə nəs, yŏŏ rā'-) n. planet seventh in order from the sun.

ur'ban (ûr'bən) adj. of or like a city.

ur·bane' (ûr bān') adj. polite or suave. —**ur·ban'i·ty** (-ban'i tē) n.

ur'chin (ûr'chin) n. ragged child.

u·re'a (yŏŏ rē'ə, yŏŏr'ē ə) n. compound occurring in body fluids, esp. urine.

u·re'ter (yŏŏ rē'tər) n. duct that conveys urine from kidney to bladder.

u·re'thra (yŏŏ rē'thrə) n., pl. **-thrae** (-thrē), **-thras.** duct that conveys urine and, in males, semen.

urge (ûrj) v., **urged, urging,** n. —v. **1.** force, incite, or advocate. **2.** entreat. —n. **3.** desire; impulse.

ur'gent (ûr'jənt) adj. vital; pressing. —**ur'gen·cy,** n.

u'ri·nal (yŏŏr'ə nl) n. wall fixture used by men for urinating.

u'ri·nar'y (-ner'ē) adj. **1.** of urine. **2.** of organs that secrete and discharge urine.

u'ri·nate' (-nāt') v., **-nated, -nating.** pass urine. —**u'ri·na'tion,** n.

u'rine (yŏŏr'in) n. secretion of kidneys. —**u'ric** (yŏŏr'ik) adj.

urn (ûrn) n. vase or pot.

u·rol'o·gy (yŏŏ rol'ə jē) n. medical study of urinary or genitourinary tract. —**u·rol'o·gist,** n.

us (us) pron. objective case of **we.**

us'age (yŏŏ'sij, -zij) n. **1.** custom. **2.** treatment.

use, v., **used, using,** n. —v. (yŏŏz or, for pt. form of **5,** yŏŏst) **1.** do something with aid of. **2.** expend. **3.** make practice of. **4.** treat. **5.** accustom. —n. (yŏŏs) **6.** act or way of using. **7.** service or value. —**use'ful,** adj. —**use'less,** adj. —**us'er,** n.

us'er-friend'ly, adj. easy to operate or understand.

ush'er (ush'ər) n. person who escorts people to seats, as in theater.

u'su·al (yŏŏ'zhŏŏ əl) adj. **1.** customary. **2.** common. —**u'su·al·ly,** adv.

u·surp' (yŏŏ sûrp', -zûrp') v. seize without right. —**u·surp'er,** n.

u'su·ry (yŏŏ'zhə rē) n. lending

money at exorbitant rates of interest. —u/sur·er, *n.*

UT, Utah. Also, **Ut.**

u·ten/sil (yōō ten/sal) *n.* device, container, etc., esp. for kitchen.

u/ter·us (yōō/tar as) *n., pl.* -ter·i (-ta rī/) part of woman's body in which fertilized ovum develops. —u/ter·ine (-in) *adj.*

u·til/i·tar/i·an (yōō til/i târ/ē an) *adj.* of practical use.

u·til/i·ty, *n., pl.* -ties. **1.** usefulness. **2.** public service.

u/ti·lize/ (yōōt/l īz/) *v.,* -lized, -liz·ing. use. —u/ti·li·za/tion, *n.*

ut/most/ (ut/mōst/) *adj.* **1.** greatest. **2.** furthest.

U·to/pi·an (yōō tō/pē an) *adj.* impossibly perfect.

ut/ter (ut/ar) *v.* **1.** speak; say. —*adj.* **2.** complete; total.

ut/ter·ly, *adv.* completely; absolutely.

u/vu·la (yōō/vya la) *n., pl.* -las, -lae. small, fleshy part on soft palate.

V

V, v (vē) *n.* twenty-second letter of English alphabet.

VA, Virginia. Also, **Va.**

va/can·cy (vā/kan sē) *n., pl.* -cies. **1.** state of being vacant. **2.** vacant space or position.

va/cant (-kant) *adj.* **1.** empty. **2.** devoid. **3.** unintelligent.

va/cate (vā/kāt) *v.,* -cated, -cating. **1.** empty. **2.** annul.

va·ca/tion (vā kā/shan, va-) *n.* **1.** freedom from duty, business, etc. **2.** holiday. —*v.* **3.** take a vacation.

vac/ci·nate/ (vak/sa nāt/) *v.,* -nated, -nating. inoculate against disease. —vac/ci·na/tion, *n.*

vac·cine/ (vak sēn/) *n.* substance injected into bloodstream to give immunity.

vac/il·late/ (vas/a lāt/) *v.,* -lated, -lating. **1.** waver; fluctuate. **2.** be irresolute. —vac/il·la/tion, *n.*

va·cu/i·ty (va kyōō/i tē, va-) *n., pl.* -ties. **1.** emptiness. **2.** lack of intelligence. —vac/u·ous (vak/yōō as) *adj.* —vac/u·ous·ly, *adv.*

vac/u·um (vak/yōōm, -yōō am, -yam) *n.* space from which all matter has been removed.

vacuum bottle, bottle with double wall enclosing vacuum to retard heat transfer.

vacuum cleaner, apparatus for cleaning by suction.

vac/uum-packed/, *adj.* packed with as much air as possible evacuated before sealing.

vacuum tube, sealed bulb, formerly used in radio and electronics.

vag/a·bond/ (vag/a bond/) *adj.* **1.** wandering. —*n.* **2.** vagrant.

va·ga/ry (va gâr/ē, vā/ga rē) *n., pl.* -garies. capricious act or idea.

va·gi/na (va jī/na) *n., pl.* -nas, -nae. passage from uterus to vulva. —vag/i·nal (vaj/a nl) *adj.*

va/grant (vā/grant) *n.* **1.** homeless person with no job. —*adj.* **2.** wandering. —va/gran·cy, *n.*

vague (vāg) *adj.,* vaguer, vaguest. **1.** not definite. **2.** indistinct.

vain (vān) *adj.* **1.** futile. **2.** conceited. —vain/ly, *adv.*

vain/glo/ry, *n.* boastful pride. —vain·glo/ri·ous, *adj.*

va/lance (val/ans, vā/lans) *n.* drapery across top of window.

vale (vāl) *n.* valley.

val/e·dic·to/ri·an (val/i dik tôr/ē an) *n.* graduating student who delivers valedictory.

val/e·dic/to·ry (-tə rē) *n., pl.* -ries. farewell address, esp. one delivered at commencement.

va/lence (vā/lans) *n.* combining capacity of atom or radical. Also, va/len·cy.

val/en·tine/ (val/an tīn/) *n.* **1.** affectionate card or gift sent on February 14 (**Saint Valentine's Day**). **2.** sweetheart chosen on that day.

val/et (va lā/, val/it, val/ā) *n.* personal manservant.

val/iant (val/yant) *adj.* brave.

val/id (val/id) *adj.* **1.** sound; logical. **2.** legally binding. —val/i·date/, *v.* —va·lid/i·ty (va lid/i tē) *n.*

va·lise/ (va lēs/) *n.* traveling bag.

val/ley (val/ē) *n.* long depression between uplands or mountains.

val/or (val/ar) *n.* bravery, esp. in battle.

val/u·a·ble (-yōō a bal, -ya bal) *adj.* **1.** of much worth, importance, etc. —*n.* **2.** (*usually pl.*) valuable articles. —val/u·a·bly, *adv.*

val/u·a/tion (-yōō ā/shan) *n.* estimation or estimated value.

val/ue, *n., v.,* -ued, -uing. —*n.* **1.** worth or importance. **2.** equivalent or estimated worth. **3.** conception of what is good. —*v.* **4.** estimate worth of. **5.** esteem. —val/ue·less, *adj.*

valve (valv) *n.* device controlling flow of liquids, etc.

va·moose/ (va mōōs/) *v.,* -moosed, -moosing. *Slang.* leave hurriedly.

vamp (vamp) n. **1.** Slang. seductive woman. —v. **2.** improvise.

vam'pire (vam'pīr') n. **1.** corpse supposed to be reanimated and to suck blood of living persons. **2.** extortionist. **3.** Also, **vampire bat.** South and Central American bat.

van (van) n. **1.** vanguard. **2.** covered truck for moving furniture, etc. **3.** small closed trucklike vehicle.

van'dal (van'dl) n. person who willfully damages or destroys property. —**van'dal·ism,** n. —**van'dal·ize',** v., **-ized, -izing.**

Van·dyke' (van dīk') n. short, pointed beard.

vane (vān) n. **1.** weathervane. **2.** one of set of blades set diagonally on a rotor to move or be moved by fluid.

van'guard' (van'-) n. **1.** foremost part. **2.** leaders of a movement.

va·nil'la (va nil'ə, often -nel'ə) n. **1.** tropical orchid, whose fruit (**vanilla bean**) yields flavoring extract. **2.** the flavoring.

van'ish (van'ish) v. disappear.

van'i·ty (van'i tē) n., pl. **-ties.** **1.** vainness. **2.** makeup table. **3.** compact (def. 4).

van'quish (vang'kwish, van'-) v. conquer; defeat. —**van'quish·er,** n.

van'tage (van'tij) n. superior position or situation.

vap'id (vap'id) adj. insipid; dull.

va'por (vā'pər) n. **1.** exhalation, as fog or mist. **2.** gas.

va'por·ize', v., **-ized, -izing.** change into vapor. —**va'por·i·za'tion,** n. —**va'por·iz'er,** n.

var'i·a·ble (vâr'ē ə bəl) adj. **1.** changeable. **2.** inconstant. —n. **3.** something variable. —**var'i·a·bil'i·ty,** n. —**var'i·a·bly,** adv.

var'i·ance (-əns) n. **1.** divergence or discrepancy. **2.** disagreement.

var'i·ant, adj. **1.** varying. **2.** altered in form. —n. **3.** variant form, etc.

var'i·a'tion (-ā'shən) n. **1.** change. **2.** amount of change. **3.** variant. **4.** transformation of melody with changes in harmony, etc.

var'i·col'ored (vâr'i kul'ərd) adj. having various colors.

var'i·cose' (vâr'i kōs') adj. abnormally swollen, as veins.

var'i·e·gate' (vâr'ē i gāt', vâr'i-) v., **-gated, -gating.** **1.** mark with different colors, etc. **2.** vary.

va·ri'e·ty (va rī'i tē) n., pl. **-ties.** **1.** diversity. **2.** number of different things. **3.** kind; category. **4.** variant.

var'i·ous (vâr'ē əs) adj. **1.** of different sorts. **2.** several.

var'mint (vär'mənt) n. undesir-

able, usu. verminous animal. **2.** obnoxious person.

var'nish (vär'nish) n. **1.** resinous solution drying in hard, glossy coat. **2.** gloss. —v. **3.** lay varnish on.

var'y (vâr'ē) v., **varied, varying.** **1.** change; differ. **2.** cause to be different. **3.** deviate; diverge.

vas'cu·lar (vas'kyə lər) adj. of vessels that convey fluids, as blood or sap.

vase (vās, vāz, väz) n. tall container, esp. for flowers.

vas·ec'to·my (va sek'tə mē, və-) n., pl. **-mies.** surgery for male sterilization.

vas'sal (vas'əl) n. **1.** feudal holder of land who renders service to lord. **2.** subject, follower, or slave.

vast (vast) adj. immense; huge.

vat (vat) n. large container for liquids.

vaude·ville (vôd'vil, vōd'-, vô'də-) n. theatrical entertainment made up of separate acts.

vault (vôlt) n. **1.** arched ceiling or roof. **2.** arched space, chamber, etc. **3.** room for safekeeping of valuables. —v. **4.** build or cover with vault. **5.** leap. —**vault'ed,** adj.

vault'ing, adj. **1.** leaping. **2.** excessive.

vaunt (vônt, vänt) v. **1.** boast of. —n. **2.** boast.

VCR, videocassette recorder.

VD, venereal disease.

V'-Day', n. day of military victory.

VDT, video display terminal.

veal (vēl) n. flesh of calf as used for food.

vec'tor (vek'tər) n. **1.** quantity possessing both magnitude and direction. **2.** person or animal that transmits disease-causing organism.

veep (vēp) n. Informal. vice president, esp. of U.S.

veer (vēr) v. change direction.

veg'e·ta·ble (vej'tə bal, vej'i tə-) n. **1.** plant used for food. **2.** any plant.

veg'e·tar'i·an (vej'i târ'ē ən) n. person who eats only vegetable food on principle (**vegetarianism**). —adj. **2.** of or advocating vegetarianism. **3.** suitable for vegetarians.

veg'e·tate' (-tāt') v., **-tated, -tating.** **1.** grow as plants do. **2.** live dull, inactive life. —**veg'e·ta'tive,** adj.

veg'e·ta'tion, n. **1.** plants collectively. **2.** act or process of vegetating.

ve'he·ment (vē'ə mənt) adj. **1.** impetuous or impassioned. **2.** violent. —**ve'he·mence, ve'he·men'cy,** n.

ve'hi·cle (vē'i kəl) n. means of

transport, etc. —**ve·hic/u·lar** (-hik/-ya lar) *adj.*

veil (vāl) *n.* **1.** material concealing face. **2.** part of headdress, as of nun or bride. **3.** cover; screen. **4.** pretense. —*v.* **5.** cover with veil.

vein (vān) *n.* **1.** vessel conveying blood from body to heart. **2.** tubular riblike thickening, as in leaf or insect wing. **3.** stratum of ore, coal, etc. **4.** mood. —*v.* **5.** furnish or mark with veins.

Vel·cro (vel/krō) *n. Trademark.* fastening tape with opposing pieces of nylon that interlock.

vel/lum (vel/əm) *n.* parchment.

ve·loc/i·ty (və los/i tē) *n., pl.* **-ties.** speed.

ve·lour/ (və lŏōr/) *n.* velvetlike fabric used for clothing and upholstery.

vel/vet (vel/vit) *n.* fabric with thick, soft pile. —**vel/vet·y,** *adj.*

vel/vet·een/ (-vi tēn/) *n.* cotton fabric resembling velvet.

ve/nal (vēn/əl) *adj.* corrupt.

vend (vend) *v.* sell. —**ven/dor,** *n.*

ven·det/ta (ven det/ə) *n.* long, bitter feud.

vending machine, coin-operated machine for selling small articles.

ve·neer/ (və nēr/) *v.* **1.** overlay with thin sheets of fine wood, etc. —*n.* **2.** veneered layer of wood. **3.** superficial appearance.

ven/er·a·ble (ven/ər ə bəl) *adj.* worthy of reverence.

ven/er·ate/ (-ə rāt/) *v.,* **-ated, -ating.** revere. —**ven/er·a/tion,** *n.*

ve·ne/re·al (və nēr/ē əl) *adj.* relating to or caused by sexual intercourse.

ve·ne/tian blind (və nē/shən) window blind with horizontal slats.

venge/ance (ven/jəns) *n.* revenge.

venge/ful, *adj.* seeking vengeance.

ve/ni·al (vē/nē əl, vēn/yəl) *adj.* pardonable.

ven/i·son (ven/ə sən, -zən) *n.* flesh of deer used for food.

ven/om (ven/əm) *n.* **1.** poisonous fluid secreted by some snakes, spiders, etc. **2.** spite; malice. —**ven/om·ous,** *adj.*

ve/nous (vē/nəs) *adj.* **1.** of or having veins. **2.** of or being blood carried back to heart by veins.

vent (vent) *n.* **1.** outlet, as for fluid. **2.** expression. **3.** slit in garment. **4.** express freely.

ven/ti·late/ (ven/tl āt/) *v.,* **-lated, -lating. 1.** provide with fresh air. **2.**

submit to discussion. —**ven/ti·la/-tion,** *n.* —**ven/ti·la/tor,** *n.*

ven/tral (ven/trəl) *adj.* of or near belly; abdominal.

ven/tri·cle (ven/tri kəl) *n.* either of two lower cavities of heart.

ven·tril/o·quism/ (ven tril/ə kwiz/-əm) *n.* art of speaking so that voice seems to come from another source. —**ven·tril/o·quist,** *n.*

ven/ture (ven/chər) *n., v.,* **-tured, -turing.** —*n.* **1.** hazardous undertaking. —*v.* **2.** risk. **3.** dare. **3.** enter daringly. —**ven/ture·some** (-səm), **ven/tur·ous,** *adj.*

ven/ue (ven/yŏō) *n.* scene or locale of action or event.

Ve/nus (vē/nəs) *n.* second planet from sun.

Ve/nus's-fly/trap, *n.* plant with hinged leaves that trap insects.

ve·rac/i·ty (və ras/ə tē) *n.* truthfulness or accuracy. —**ve·ra/cious** (-rā/shəs) *adj.*

ve·ran/da (-ran/də) *n.* open porch. Also, **ve·ran/dah.**

verb (vûrb) *n.* part of speech expressing action, occurrence, existence, etc., as "saw" in the sentence "I saw Tom."

ver/bal (vûr/bəl) *adj.* **1.** of or in form of words. **2.** oral. **3.** of verbs. **ver/bal·ize/,** *v.,* **-ized, -izing.** express in words.

ver·ba/tim (vər bā/tim) *adv.* word for word.

ver·be/na (vər bē/nə) *n.* plant with long spikes of flowers.

ver/bi·age (vûr/bē ij) *n.* **1.** wordiness. **2.** manner of verbal expression.

ver·bose/ (vər bōs/) *adj.* wordy. —**ver·bos/i·ty** (-bos/i tē) *n.*

ver·bo/ten (vər bōt/n, fer-) *adj.* forbidden.

ver/dant (vûr/dnt) *adj.* green with vegetation. —**ver/dan·cy,** *n.*

ver/dict (vûr/dikt) *n.* decision.

ver/di·gris/ (vûr/di grēs/, -gris) *n.* green or bluish patina on some metals.

ver/dure (vûr/jər) *n.* **1.** greenness. **2.** green vegetation.

verge (vûrj) *n., v.,* **verged, verging.** —*n.* **1.** edge or margin. —*v.* **2.** border. **3.** incline; tend.

ver/i·fy/ (ver/ə fī/) *v.,* **-fied, -fying. 1.** prove to be true. **2.** ascertain correctness of. —**ver/i·fi/a·ble,** *adj.* —**ver/i·fi·ca/tion,** *n.* —**ver/i·fi/er,** *n.*

ver/i·si·mil/i·tude/ (-si mil/i tōōd/, -tyŏōd/) *n.* appearance of truth.

ver/i·ta·ble (-tə bəl) *adj.* genuine.

ver/i·ty (-tē) *n., pl.* **-ties.** truth.

ver·mi·cel·li (vûr/mi chel/ē, -sel/ē) n. pasta in long threads.

ver·mil/ion (vər mil/yən) n. 1. bright red. —adj. 2. of or like vermilion.

ver·min (vûr/min) n.pl. or sing. small, troublesome animals collectively. —ver·min·ous (-əs) adj.

ver·mouth/ (vər mōōth/) n. white wine flavored with herbs.

ver·nac/u·lar (vər nak/yə lar, -nak/-) adj. 1. (of language) used locally or in everyday speech. —n. 2. native speech. 3. language of particular group.

ver·nal (vûr/nl) adj. of spring.

ver·sa·tile (vûr/sə tl; esp. Brit. -tīl/) adj. doing variety of things well. —ver/sa·til/i·ty, n.

verse (vûrs) n. 1. line of poem. 2. type of metrical form, etc. 3. poem. 4. poetry. 5. division of Biblical chapter.

versed, adj. expert; skilled.

ver/si·fy/ (vûr/sə fī/) v., -fied, -fying. 1. treat in or turn into verse. 2. compose verses.

ver/sion (vûr/zhən, -shən) n. 1. translation. 2. account. 3. particular form.

ver/sus (vûr/səs, -səz) prep. in opposition or contrast to.

ver/te·bra (vûr/tə brə) n., pl. -brae, -bras. bone or segment of spinal column. —ver/te·bral, adj.

ver/te·brate (-brāt, -brāt/) adj. 1. having vertebrae. —n. 2. vertebrate animal.

ver/tex (vûr/teks) n., pl. -texes, -tices (-tə sēz/) highest point.

ver/ti·cal (vûr/ti kəl) adj. 1. perpendicular to plane of horizon. —n. 2. something vertical.

ver·tig/i·nous (vər tij/ə nəs) adj. 1. whirling. 2. affected with or liable to cause vertigo.

ver/ti·go/ (vûr/ti gō/) n., pl. -goes. dizziness.

verve (vûrv) n. vivaciousness, energy, or enthusiasm.

ver/y (ver/ē) adv., adj., -ier, -iest. —adv. 1. extremely. —adj. 2. identical. 3. mere. 4. actual. 5. true.

ves/i·cle (ves/i kəl) n. small sac in body.

ves/pers (ves/pərz) n. evening service.

ves/sel (ves/əl) n. 1. ship or boat. 2. container. 3. tube, as for blood.

vest (vest) n. 1. sleeveless garment worn under jacket. —v. 2. clothe or robe. 3. endow with powers, etc.

ves/tal (ves/tl) adj. chaste.

vest/ed, adj. held completely and permanently.

vested interest, special interest in a system, arrangement, or institution for personal reasons.

ves/ti·bule/ (ves/tə byōōl/) n. small room between entrance and main room.

ves/tige (ves/tij) n. 1. trace of something extinct. 2. slight trace of something. —ves·tig/i·al (ve stij/ē-al, -stij/əl) adj.

vest/ing, n. the granting to an employee of the right to pension benefits despite early retirement.

vest/ment, n. ceremonial garment.

vest/-pock/et, adj. conveniently small.

ves/try (ves/trē) n., pl. -tries. 1. room in church for vestments or for meetings, etc. 2. church committee managing temporal affairs.

vet (vet) n. Informal. 1. veterinarian. 2. veteran.

vetch (vech) n. plant used for forage and soil improvement.

vet/er·an (vet/ər ən) n. 1. person who has served in armed forces. 2. experienced person. —adj. 3. experienced.

vet/er·i·nar/i·an (-ə när/ē ən) n. veterinary practitioner.

vet/er·i·nar/y (-ner/ē) n., pl. -naries, adj. —n. 1. veterinarian. —adj. 2. of medical and surgical treatment of animals.

ve/to (vē/tō) n., pl. -toes, v., -toed, -toing. —n. 1. power or right to reject or prohibit. 2. prohibition. —v. 3. reject by veto.

vex (veks) v. 1. irritate. 2. worry. —vex·a/tion, n. —vex·a/tious, adj. —vexed, adj.

vi/a (vī/ə, vē/ə) prep. by way of.

vi/a·ble (vī/ə bəl) adj. 1. capable of living. 2. practicable; workable.

vi/a·duct/, n. long highway or railroad bridge.

vi/al (vī/əl, vīl) n. small glass container.

vi/and (vī/ənd) n. 1. article of food. 2. (pl.) dishes of food.

vibes (vībz) n.pl. Slang. something, esp. an emotional aura, emitted as if by vibration. 2. vibraphone.

vi/brant (vī/brənt) adj. 1. resonant. 2. energetic; vital. —vi/bran·cy, n.

vi/bra·phone/ (vī/brə fōn/) n. instrument like metal xylophone, with electrically enhanced resonance.

vi/brate (vī/brāt) v., -brated, -brating. 1. move very rapidly to and fro; oscillate. 2. tremble. 3. resound. 4. thrill. —vi·bra/tion, n. —vi/bra·tor, n.

vi·bra/to (vi brä/tō) n., pl. -tos. pulsating effect produced by rapid but slight alterations in pitch.

vi·bur'num (vī bûr'nəm) *n.* shrub bearing white flower clusters.

vic'ar (vik'ər) *n.* **1.** parish priest. **2.** representative of bishop.

vic'ar·age (-ij) *n.* residence or position of vicar.

vi·car'i·ous (vī kâr'ē əs, vi-) *adj.* **1.** done or suffered in place of another. **2.** substitute. —**vi·car'i·ous·ly,** *adv.*

vice (vīs) *n.* **1.** evil habit or fault. **2.** immoral conduct. **3.** vise. —*prep.* **4.** instead of.

vice-, prefix meaning deputy.

vice'-ad·mi'ral (vīs'-) *n.* commissioned officer ranking above rear admiral.

vice·ge'rent (-jēr'ənt) *n.* deputy to sovereign or magistrate.

vice president, officer next in rank to president. —**vice' pres'i·den·cy,** *n.*

vice'roy' (vīs'roi) *n.* ruler of country or province as deputy of sovereign.

vi'ce ver'sa (vī'sə vûr'sə, vīs', vī'sē) in opposite way.

vi'chys·soise' (vish'ē swäz', vē'shē-) *n.* cold cream soup of potatoes and leeks.

vi·cin'i·ty (vi sin'i tē) *n., pl.* -ties. neighborhood; nearby area.

vi'cious (vish'əs) *adj.* **1.** immoral; depraved. **2.** evil. **3.** malicious.

vi·cis'si·tude' (vi sis'i tōōd', -tyōōd') *n.* change, esp. in condition.

vic'tim (vik'təm) *n.* **1.** sufferer from action or event. **2.** dupe. **3.** sacrifice. —**vic'tim·ize',** *v.,* -ized, -izing.

vic'tor (vik'tər) *n.* winner. —**vic·to'ri·ous** (-tôr'ē əs) *adj.*

vic'to·ry (-tə rē) *n., pl.* -ries. success in contest.

vict'ual (vit'l) *n.* **1.** (*pl.*) food. —*v.* **2.** supply with victuals. —**vict'ual·er,** *n.*

vid·e·o' (vid'ē ō') *n.* **1.** of television. —*n.* **2.** videotape or videocassette.

vid·e·o'cas·sette', *n.* cassette containing videotape.

videocassette recorder, electronic device for recording and playing videocassettes.

vid'e·o·disc', disc on which pictures and sound are recorded for playback on TV set.

video game, electronic game played on screen or television set.

vid'e·o·tape', *n., v.,* -taped, -taping. —*n.* **1.** magnetic tape on which TV program, motion picture, etc., can be recorded. —*v.* **2.** record on this.

vie (vī) *v.,* vied, vying. contend for superiority.

view (vyōō) *n.* **1.** seeing or beholding. **2.** range of vision. **3.** landscape, etc., within one's sight. **4.** aspect. **5.** mental survey. **6.** purpose. **7.** notion; opinion. —*v.* **8.** see; look at. **9.** regard. —**view'er,** *n.*

view'find'er, camera part for viewing what will appear in picture.

view'point', *n.* **1.** place from which view is seen. **2.** attitude toward something.

vig'il (vij'əl) *n.* period of staying awake, esp. as watch.

vig'i·lant (-lənt) *adj.* **1.** wary. **2.** alert. —**vig'i·lance,** *n.*

vig'i·lan'te (-lan'tē) *n.* person who takes law into own hands.

vi·gnette' (vin yet') *n., v.,* -gnetted, -gnetting. —*n.* **1.** literary sketch. —*v.* **2.** make vignette of.

vig'or (vig'ər) *n.* **1.** active strength. **2.** energy. —**vig'or·ous,** *adj.*

Vi'king (vī'king) *n.* medieval Scandinavian raider.

vile (vīl) *adj.,* viler, vilest. **1.** very bad. **2.** offensive. **3.** evil. —**vile'ly,** *adv.* —**vile'ness,** *n.*

vil'i·fy' (vil'ə fī') *v.,* -fied, -fying. defame. —**vil'i·fi·ca'tion,** *n.*

vil'la (vil'ə) *n.* luxurious country residence.

vil'lage (vil'ij) *n.* small town. —**vil'lag·er,** *n.*

vil'lain (vil'ən) *n.* wicked person. —**vil'lain·ous,** *adj.* —**vil'lain·y,** *n.*

vil'lein (vil'ən, -ān) *n.* feudal serf.

vim (vim) *n.* vigor.

vin'ai·grette' (vin'ə gret') *n.* dressing, esp. for salad, of oil and vinegar, usu. with herbs.

vin'di·cate' (vin'di kāt') *v.,* -cated, -cating. **1.** clear, as from suspicion. **2.** uphold or justify. —**vin'di·ca'tion,** *n.* —**vin'di·ca'tor,** *n.*

vin·dic'tive (vin dik'tiv) *adj.* holding grudge; vengeful.

vine (vīn) *n.* creeping or climbing plant with slender stem.

vin'e·gar (vin'i gər) *n.* sour liquid obtained by fermentation. —**vin'e·gar·y,** *adj.*

vine'yard (vin'yərd) *n.* plantation of grapevines.

vin'tage (vin'tij) *n.* **1.** wine from particular harvest. **2.** grape harvest.

vint'ner (vint'nər) *n.* person who makes wine.

vi'nyl (vīn'l) *n.* type of plastic.

vi·o'la (vē ō'lə) *n.* stringed instrument resembling violin but slightly larger.

vi'o·late' (-lāt') *v.,* -lated, -lating. **1.** break or transgress. **2.** break through or into. **3.** desecrate. **4.**

rape. —**vi•o•la′tion,** n. —**vi•o•la′tor,** n.

vi•o•lent, adj. **1.** uncontrolled, strong, or rough. **2.** of destructive force. **3.** intense; severe. —**vi′o•lence,** n. —**vi′o•lent•ly,** adv.

vi•o•let (vī′ə lit) n. **1.** low herb bearing flowers, usually purple or blue. **2.** bluish purple.

vi•o•lin′ (vī′ə lin′) n. stringed instrument played with bow. —**vi′o•lin′ist,** n.

vi•o•lon•cel′lo (vē′ə lən chel′ō, vī′-) n., pl. -los. cello.

VIP (vē′ī′pē′) Informal. very important person.

vi′per (vī′pər) n. **1.** Old World venomous snake. **2.** malicious or treacherous person. —**vi′per•ous,** adj.

vi•ra•go (vi rä′gō, -rā′-) n., pl. -goes, -gos. shrewish woman.

vi′ral (vī′rəl) adj. of or caused by virus.

vir•gin (vûr′jin) n. **1.** person who has not had sexual intercourse. —adj. **2.** being or like virgin. **3.** untried; unused. —**vir′gin•al,** adj. —**vir•gin′i•ty,** n.

vir•gule (vûr′gyōōl) n. oblique stroke (/) used as dividing line.

vir•ile (vir′əl) adj. **1.** manly. **2.** vigorous. **3.** capable of procreation. —**vi•ril′i•ty,** n.

vi•rol•o•gy (vī rol′ə jē) n. study of viruses. —**vi•rol′o•gist,** n.

vir′tu•al (vûr′chōō əl) adj. **1.** such in effect, though not actually. **2.** simulated by computer.

virtual reality, realistic simulation by computer system.

vir′tue (vûr′chōō) n. **1.** moral excellence. **2.** chastity. **3.** merit. —**vir′tu•ous,** adj. —**vir′tu•ous•ly,** adv.

vir•tu•o•so (vûr′chōō ō′sō) n., pl. -sos, -si. person of special skill, esp. in music. —**vir′tu•os′i•ty** (-os′i tē) n.

vir′u•lent (vir′yə lənt, vir′ə-) adj. **1.** poisonous; malignant. **2.** hostile. —**vir′u•lence,** n.

vi′rus (vī′rəs) n. **1.** infective agent. **2.** corrupting influence. **3.** segment of self-replicating code planted illegally in computer program.

vi′sa (vē′zə) n. passport endorsement permitting foreign entry or immigration.

vis′age (viz′ij) n. **1.** face. **2.** aspect.

vis′-à-vis′ (vē′zə vē′) prep. **1.** in relation to. **2.** opposite.

vis′cer•a (vis′ər ə) n.pl. **1.** soft interior organs of body. **2.** intestines.

vis′count (vī′kount′) n. nobleman

ranking below earl or count. —**vis′count•ess,** n.fem.

vis′cous (vis′kəs) adj. sticky; gluey. Also, **vis′cid** (vis′id).

vise (vīs) n. device, usually with two jaws, for holding object firmly.

vis′i•ble (viz′ə bəl) adj. **1.** capable of being seen. **2.** perceptible or manifest. —**vis•i•bil′i•ty,** n.

vi′sion (vizh′ən) n. **1.** power or sense of sight. **2.** imagination or unusually keen perception. **3.** mental image of something imaginary.

vi′sion•ar•y (vizh′ə ner′ē) adj., n., pl. -ar•ies. —adj. **1.** fanciful. **2.** seen in vision. **3.** unreal. —n. **4.** seer of visions. **5.** bold or impractical schemer.

vis′it (viz′it) v. **1.** go to for purposes of talking, staying, etc. **2.** afflict. —n. **3.** act of visiting. **4.** stay as guest. —**vis′i•tor, vis′it•ant,** n.

vis•it•a′tion (-ə tā′shən) n. **1.** visit. **2.** bringing of good or evil, as by supernatural force.

vi′sor (vī′zər) n. front piece, as of helmet or cap.

vis′ta (vis′tə) n. **1.** extended view in one direction.

vis′u•al (vizh′ōō əl) adj. **1.** of or by means of sight. **2.** visible.

vis′u•al•ize′, v., -ized, -izing. **1.** make visual. **2.** form mental image of. —**vis′u•al•i•za′tion,** n.

vi′tal (vīt′l) adj. **1.** of life. **2.** living; energetic; vivid. **3.** giving or necessary to life. **4.** essential.

vi•tal′i•ty (-tal′i tē) n., pl. -ties. **1.** vital force. **2.** physical or mental vigor. **3.** power of continued existence.

vital signs, essential body functions, comprising pulse rate, body temperature, and respiration.

vital statistics, statistics concerning deaths, births, and marriages.

vi′ta•min (vī′tə min) n. food element essential in small quantities to maintain life. —**vi′ta•min′ic,** adj.

vi′ti•ate (vish′ē āt′) v., -ated, -ating. **1.** impair. **2.** invalidate.

vit′i•cul′ture (vit′i kul′chər, vī′ti-) n. cultivation of grapes.

vit′re•ous (vi′trē əs) adj. of or like glass.

vitreous humor, transparent gelatinous substance that fills eyeball.

vit′ri•fy′, v., -fied, -fying. change to glass.

vi•trine (vi trēn′) n. glass cabinet.

vit′ri•ol (vi′trē əl) n. **1.** glassy metallic compound. **2.** sulfuric acid. **3.** caustic criticism, etc. —**vit′ri•ol′ic** (-ol′ik) adj.

vi•tu′per•ate′ (vī tōō′pə rāt′, -tyōō′-)

vivacious
354

-, vi.) v., **-ated, -ating.** criticize harshly. —**vi·tu/per·a/tion,** n.

vi·va/cious (vi vā/shəs, vī-) adj. lively; animated. —**vi·vac/i·ty** (-vas/i tē) n.

viv/id (viv/id) adj. **1.** bright, as color or light. **2.** full of life. **3.** intense; striking. —**viv/id·ly,** adv.

viv/i·fy/, v., **-fied, -fying.** give life to.

viv/i·sec/tion (viv/ə sek/shən) n. dissection of live animal.

vix/en (vik/sən) n. **1.** female fox. **2.** ill-tempered woman.

vi·zier/ (vi zēr/, viz/yər) n. high official in certain Muslim countries.

vo·cab/u·lar/y (vō kab/yə ler/ē) n., pl. **-laries. 1.** words used by people, class, or person. **2.** collection of defined words, usually in alphabetical order.

vo/cal (vō/kəl) adj. **1.** of the voice. **2.** of or for singing. **3.** articulate or talkative. —n. **4.** vocal composition or performance. —**vo/cal·ize/,** v., **-ized, -izing.** —**vo/cal·i·za/tion,** n.

vocal cords, membranes in larynx producing sound by vibration.

vo/cal·ist (-kə list) n. singer.

vo·ca/tion (vō kā/shən) n. occupation, business, or profession. —**vo·ca/tion·al,** adj.

voc/a·tive (vok/ə tiv) adj. of or being grammatical case used to indicate one being addressed.

vo·cif/er·ate/ (vō sif/ə rāt/) v., **-ated, -ating.** cry noisily; shout. —**vo·cif/er·ous,** adj.

vod/ka (vod/kə) n. colorless distilled liquor.

vogue (vōg) n. **1.** fashion. **2.** popular favor.

voice (vois) n., v., **voiced, voicing.** —n. **1.** sound uttered through mouth. **2.** speaking or singing voice. **3.** expression. **4.** choice. **5.** right to express opinion. **6.** verb inflection indicating whether subject is acting or acted upon. —v. **7.** express or declare. —**voice/less,** adj.

voice box, larynx.

voice mail, electronic system that routes voice messages to appropriate recipients.

voice/-o/ver, n. voice of off-screen narrator or announcer.

void (void) adj. **1.** without legal force. **2.** useless. **3.** empty. —n. **4.** empty space. —v. **5.** invalidate. **6.** empty out. —**void/a·ble,** adj.

voile (voil) n. lightweight, semisheer fabric.

vol., volume.

vol/a·tile (vol/ə tl) adj. **1.** evaporating rapidly. **2.** explosive. **3.** rapidly changeable in emotion.

vol·ca/no (vol kā/nō) n., pl. **-noes, -nos. 1.** vent in earth from which lava, steam, etc., are expelled. **2.** mountain with such vent. —**vol·can/ic** (-kan/ik) adj.

vole (vōl) n. short-tailed stocky rodent.

vo·li/tion (vō lish/ən, və-) n. act or power of willing.

vol/ley (vol/ē) n. **1.** discharge of many missiles together. **2.** returning of ball before it hits ground. —v. **3.** hit or fire volley.

vol/ley·ball/, n. **1.** game in which large ball is volleyed back and forth over net. **2.** ball used in this game.

volt (vōlt) n. unit of electromotive force. —**volt/age,** n. —**volt/me/ter,** n.

vol/u·ble (vol/yə bəl) adj. glibly fluent. —**vol/u·bil/i·ty,** n.

vol/ume (vol/yōōm, -yəm) n. **1.** book. **2.** size in three dimensions. **3.** mass or quantity. **4.** loudness or fullness of sound.

vo·lu/mi·nous (və lōō/mə nəs) adj. **1.** filling many volumes. **2.** ample.

vol/un·tar/y (vol/ən ter/ē) adj. **1.** done, made, etc., by free choice. **2.** controlled by will. —**vol/un·tar/i·ly,** adv.

vol/un·teer/, n. **1.** person who offers self, as for military duty. **2.** worker forgoing pay. —v. **3.** offer for some duty or purpose.

vo·lup/tu·ous (və lup/chōō əs) adj. **1.** luxurious; sensuous. **2.** full and shapely. —**vo·lup/tu·ous·ly,** adv.

vom/it (vom/it) v. **1.** eject from stomach through mouth. **2.** eject with force. —n. **3.** vomited matter.

voo/doo (vōō/dōō) n. polytheistic religion deriving chiefly from African cults.

vo·ra/cious (vô rā/shəs) adj. greedy; ravenous. —**vo·ra/cious·ly,** adv. —**vo·rac/i·ty** (-ras/i tē) n.

vor/tex (vôr/teks) n., pl. **-texes, -tices** (-tə sēz/). whirling movement or mass.

vo/ta·ry (vō/tə rē) n., pl. **-ries.** worshiper; devotee.

vote (vōt) n., v., **voted, voting.** —n. **1.** formal expression of wish or choice, as by ballot. **2.** right to this. **3.** votes collectively. —v. **4.** cast one's vote. **5.** cause to go or occur by vote. —**vot/er,** n.

vouch (vouch) v. **1.** answer for. **2.** give assurance, as surety or sponsor.

vouch/er, n. document, receipt, etc., proving expenditure.

vouch·safe/, v., **-safed, -safing.** grant or permit.

wallboard

vow (vou) n. 1. solemn promise, pledge, or personal engagement. —v. 2. make vow.

vow·el (vou′əl) n. 1. speech sound made with clear channel through middle of mouth. 2. letter representing vowel.

voy·age (voi′ij) n, v., **-aged, -ag·ing.** —n. 1. journey, esp. by water. —v. 2. make voyage.

vo·yeur′ (vwä yûr′, vo ûr′) n. person who obtains sexual gratification by looking at sexual objects or acts. —vo·yeur′ism, n.

V.P., Vice President. Also, **VP.**

vs., versus.

VT, Vermont. Also, **Vt.**

vul·can·ize′ (vul′kə nīz′) v., **-ized, -izing.** treat rubber with sulfur and heat. —vul·can·i·za′tion, n.

vul·gar (vul′gər) adj. 1. lacking good breeding or taste. 2. obscene. 3. plebeian. 4. vernacular. —vul·gar′i·ty (-gar′i tē) n.

vul·ner·a·ble (vul′nər ə bəl) adj. 1. liable to physical or emotional hurt. 2. open to attack.

vul·ture (vul′chər) n. large, carrion-eating bird.

vul·va (vul′və) n., pl. **-vae, -vas.** external female genitals.

vy′ing (vī′ing) adj. competing.

W

W, w (dub′əl yŏŏ′, -yŏŏ) n. twenty-third letter of English alphabet.

W, west, western.

WA, Washington.

wack′y (wak′ē) adj., **-ier, -iest.** Slang. odd or irrational.

wad (wod) n., v., **wadded, wad·ding.** —n. 1. small soft mass. —v. 2. form into wad. 3. stuff.

wad·dle (wod′l) v., **-dled, -dling,** n. —v. 1. sway in walking, as duck. —n. 2. waddling gait.

wade (wād) v., **waded, wading.** —v. 1. walk through water, sand, etc. —n. 2. act of wading.

wa′fer (wā′fər) n. 1. thin crisp biscuit. 2. small disk of bread used in Eucharist.

waf·fle (wof′əl) n., v., **-fled, -fling.** —n. 1. batter cake baked in a double griddle (**waffle iron**). —v. 2. speak or write evasively.

waft (wäft, waft) v. 1. float through air or over water. —n. 2. sound, odor, etc., wafted.

wag (wag) v., **wagged, wagging,** n. —v. 1. move rapidly back and forth. —n. 2. act of wagging. 3. joker. —**wag′gish,** adj.

wage (wāj) n., v., **waged, waging.** —n. 1. pay; salary. 2. recompense. —v. 3. carry on (war, etc.).

wa′ger (wā′jər) n., v. bet.

wag·gle (wag′əl) v., **-gled, -gling,** n. wiggle.

wag·on (wag′ən) n. four-wheeled vehicle for drawing heavy loads.

wagon train, train of wagons and horses.

waif (wāf) n. homeless child.

wail (wāl) n. 1. long mournful cry. 2. sound like this. —v. 3. utter wails. —**wail′er,** n.

wain·scot (wān′skət, -skot, -skōt) n. woodwork lining wall.

waist (wāst) n. part of body be-

tween ribs and hips. —**waist′band′,** n. —**waist′line′,** n.

waist′coat′ (wes′kət, wāst′kōt′) n. Brit. vest.

wait (wāt) v. 1. stay in expectation. 2. be ready. 3. await. 4. wait on; serve. —n. 5. act of waiting. 6. delay. 7. ambush.

wait′er, n. man who waits on table. —**wait′ress,** n.fem.

waiting list, list of persons waiting, as for reservations or admission.

waive (wāv) v., **waived, waiving.** give up; forgo.

waiv′er, n. statement of relinquishment.

wake (wāk) v., **waked** or **woke** (wōk), **waked, waking,** n. —v. 1. stop sleeping; rouse from sleep. —n. 2. vigil, esp. beside corpse. 3. track or path, esp. of vessel.

wake′ful, adj. awake; alert.

wak·en (wā′kən) v. wake.

wale (wāl) n., v., **waled, waling.** —n. 1. mark left on skin by rod or whip. 2. vertical rib or cord in fabric. —v. 3. mark with wales.

walk (wôk) v. 1. go or traverse on foot. 2. cause to walk. —n. 3. act, course, or manner of walking. 4. distance walked. 5. sidewalk or path.

walk′a·way′, n. easy victory.

walk·ie-talk′ie (wô′kē tô′kē) n. portable radio transmitter and receiver.

walking stick, 1. stick used for support in walking. 2. insect with long twiglike body.

walk′out′, n. strike in which workers leave place of work.

wall (wôl) n. 1. upright structure that divides, encloses, etc. —v. 2. enclose, divide, etc., with wall.

wall′board′, n. artificial material used to make or cover walls, etc.

wal·let (wol′it) *n.* small flat case for paper money, etc.

wall·eye′ (wôl′-) *n.* **1.** condition in which eye or eyes are turned outward. **2.** N American freshwater food fish. Also, **walleyed pike.**

wall·flow′er, *n.* **1.** person who, because of shyness, remains at the side at a party. **2.** perennial plant with fragrant flowers.

wal·lop (wol′əp) *Informal.* —*v.* **1.** thrash or defeat. —*n.* **2.** blow.

wal·lop·ing, *adj. Informal.* **1.** very large. **2.** impressive.

wal·low (wol′ō) *v.* lie or roll in mud, etc.

wall·pa′per, *n.* decorative paper for covering walls and ceilings.

wal·nut′ (wôl′nut′, -nat) *n.* northern tree valued for edible nut.

wal·rus (wôl′rəs) *n.* large tusked mammal of Arctic seas.

waltz (wôlts) *n.* **1.** dance in triple rhythm. —*v.* **2.** dance a waltz.

wam·pum (wom′pəm) *n.* shell beads, formerly used by North American Indians as money.

wan (won) *adj.,* **wanner, wannest.** pale; worn-looking. —**wan′ly,** *adv.*

wand (wond) *n.* slender rod or shoot.

wan·der (won′dər) *v.* move aimlessly; stray. —**wan′der·er,** *n.*

wan·der·lust′, *n.* desire to travel.

wane (wān) *v.,* **waned, waning,** *n.* —*v.* **1.** (of moon) decrease periodically. **2.** decline or decrease. —*n.* **3.** decline or decrease.

wan·gle (wang′gəl) *v.,* **-gled, -gling.** bring out or obtain by scheming or underhand methods.

wan·na·be′ (won′ə bē′) *n. Informal.* one who aspires, often vainly, to emulate another's success or status.

want (wont) *v.* **1.** feel need or desire for. **2.** lack; be deficient in. —*n.* **3.** desire or need. **4.** lack. **5.** poverty.

want′ing, *adj., prep.* lacking.

wan·ton (won′tn) *adj.* **1.** malicious; unjustifiable. **2.** lewd. —*n.* **3.** lascivious person.

war (wôr) *n., v.,* **warred, warring.** —*n.* **1.** armed conflict. —*v.* **2.** carry on war.

war·ble (wôr′bəl) *v.,* **-bled, -bling,** *n.* —*v.* **1.** sing with trills, etc., as birds. —*n.* **2.** warbled song.

war′bler, *n.* small songbird.

ward (wôrd) *n.* **1.** division of city. **2.** division of hospital. **3.** person under legal care of guardian or court. **4.** custody. —*v.* **5. ward off,** repel or avert.

ward′en, *n.* **1.** keeper. **2.** administrative head of prison.

ward′er, *n.* guard.

ward heeler, minor politician who does chores for political machine.

ward′robe, *n.* **1.** stock of clothes. **2.** clothes closet.

ware (wâr) *n.* **1.** (*pl.*) goods. **2.** pottery. **3.** vessels for domestic use.

ware′house′, *n., v.,* **-housed, -housing.** —*n.* **1.** storehouse for goods. —*v.* (-houz′-, -hous′) **2.** store in warehouse.

war′fare′, *n.* waging of war.

war′head′, *n.* section of missile containing explosive or payload.

war′horse′, *n.* veteran of many conflicts.

war′like′, *adj.* waging or prepared for war.

war′lock′, *n.* male witch.

warm (wôrm) *adj.* **1.** having, giving, or feeling moderate heat. **2.** cordial. **3.** lively. **4.** kind; affectionate. —*v.* **5.** make or become warm. —**warmth,** *n.*

warm′-blood′ed, *adj.* having relatively constant body temperature that is independent of environment.

warmed′-o′ver, *adj.* **1.** reheated. **2.** stale; not new.

warm′heart′ed, *adj.* having emotional warmth.

war′mon′ger, *n.* person who advocates or incites war.

warn (wôrn) *v.* **1.** give notice of danger, evil, etc. **2.** caution. —**warn′ing,** *n., adj.*

warp (wôrp) *v.* **1.** bend out of shape; distort. —*n.* **2.** bend or twist. **3.** lengthwise threads in loom.

war·rant (wôr′ənt) *n.* **1.** justification. **2.** guarantee. **3.** document authorizing something. —*v.* **4.** authorize or justify. **5.** guarantee.

warrant officer, military officer between enlisted and commissioned grades.

war′ran·ty, *n., pl.* **-ties.** guarantee.

war′ren (wôr′ən) *n.* place where rabbits live.

war′ri·or (wôr′ē ər) *n.* soldier.

war′ship′, *n.* ship for combat.

wart (wôrt) *n.* small hard elevation on skin. —**wart′y,** *adj.*

war′y (wâr′ē) *adj.,* **-ier, -iest.** careful. —**war′i·ly,** *adv.*

was (wuz, woz; *unstressed* wəz) *v.* first and third pers. sing., past indicative of **be.**

wash (wosh) *v.* **1.** cleanse in or with water. **2.** flow over. **3.** carry in flowing. **4.** cover thinly. —*n.* **5.** act of washing. **6.** Also, **wash′ing.** clothes, etc., to be washed. **7.** liquid covering. **8.** rough water or air behind moving ship or plane. —**wash′a·ble,** adj. —**wash′bowl′,** n. —**wash′cloth′,** n.

Wash., Washington.

wash′board′, n. board to scrub clothes on.

washed′-out′, adj. **1.** faded. **2.** Informal. weary or tired-looking.

washed′-up′, adj. Informal. done for; having failed.

wash′er, n. **1.** machine for washing. **2.** flat ring of rubber, metal, etc., to give tightness.

wash′out′, n. **1.** destruction from action of water. **2.** Slang. failure.

wash′room′, n. public room with toilets.

wasn′t (wuz′ənt, woz′-) contraction of **was not.**

wasp (wosp) n. **1.** stinging insect. **2.** Slang. (cap. or caps.) white Anglo-Saxon Protestant.

wasp′ish, adj. irritable; snappish.

was′sail (wos′əl, wo säl′) n. drinking party.

waste (wāst) v., **wasted, wasting,** n., adj. —v. **1.** squander. **2.** fail to use. **3.** destroy gradually. **4.** become wasted. —n. **5.** useless expenditure. **6.** neglect. **7.** gradual decay. **8.** devastation. **9.** anything left over. —adj. **10.** not used. **11.** left over or worthless. —**waste′ful,** adj.

waste′land′, n. barren land.

wast′rel (wā′strəl) n. **1.** spendthrift. **2.** idler.

watch (woch) v. **1.** look attentively. **2.** be careful. **3.** guard. —n. **4.** close, constant observation. **5.** guard. **6.** period of watching. **7.** small timepiece. —**watch′band′,** n. —**watch′ful,** adj.

watch′dog′, n. **1.** dog that guards property. **2.** guardian, as against illegal conduct.

watch′man, n. person who keeps watch.

watch′tow′er, n. tower for guard.

watch′word′, n. **1.** password. **2.** slogan.

wa′ter (wô′tər) n. **1.** transparent liquid forming rivers, seas, lakes, rain, etc. **2.** liquid solution. **3.** liquid organic secretion. —v. **4.** moisten or supply with water. **5.** dilute. **6.** discharge water. —adj. **7.** of, for, or powered by water.

wa′ter·bed′, n. water-filled plastic bag used as bed.

water buffalo, domesticated Asian buffalo with curved horns.

water chestnut, aquatic plant with edible, nutlike fruit.

water closet, room containing flush toilet.

wa′ter·col′or, n. **1.** pigment mixed with water. **2.** painting using such pigments.

wa′ter·course′, n. **1.** stream of water. **2.** bed of stream.

wa′ter·cress′, n. plant that grows in streams and bears pungent leaves used in salad.

wa′ter·fall′, n. steep fall of water.

wa′ter·fowl′, n., pl. **-fowl, -fowls.** aquatic bird.

wa′ter·front′, n. part of city or town on edge of body of water.

water gap, transverse gap in mountain ridge.

wa′ter·ing place, resort to water or having mineral springs.

water lily, aquatic plant with showy flowers.

water line, one of series of lines on ship's hull indicating level to which it is immersed.

wa′ter·logged′, adj. filled or soaked with water.

wa′ter·mark′, n. **1.** mark showing height reached by river, etc. **2.** manufacturer's design impressed in paper. —v. **3.** put watermark in (paper).

wa′ter·mel′on, n. large sweet juicy fruit of a vine.

water moccasin, cottonmouth.

wa′ter·proof′, adj. **1.** impervious to water. —v. **2.** make waterproof.

water rat, aquatic rodent.

wa′ter·re·pel′lent, adj. repelling water but not entirely waterproof.

wa′ter·shed′, n. **1.** area drained by river, etc. **2.** high land dividing such areas. **3.** important point of division or transition.

water ski, short, broad ski for gliding over water behind boat. —**wa′ter·ski′,** v., **-skied, -skiing.** —**wa′ter·ski′er,** n.

wa′ter·spout′, n. tornadolike storm over lake or ocean.

water table, underground level beneath which soil and rock are saturated with water.

wa′ter·tight′, adj. **1.** constructed or fitted to be impervious to water. **2.** allowing no doubt.

wa′ter·way′, n. body of water as route of travel.

water wheel, wheel turned by water to provide power.

wa′ter·works′, n.pl. apparatus for collecting and distributing water, as for city.

wa′ter·y, adj. of, like, or full of water. —**wa′ter·i·ness,** n.

watt (wot) n. unit of electric power.

wat′tle (wot′l) n. **1.** flesh hanging

from throat or chin. **2.** interwoven rods and twigs.

wave (wāv), *n.*, *v.*, **waved, waving.** —*n.* **1.** ridge on surface of liquid. **2.** surge; rush. **3.** curve. **4.** vibration, as in transmission of sound, etc. **5.** sign with moving hand, flag, etc. —*v.* **6.** move with waves. **7.** curve. **8.** signal by wave. —**wav′y,** *adj.*

wave′length′, *n.* distance between two successive points in wave.

wa′ver (wā′vər) *v.* **1.** sway. **2.** hesitate. **3.** fluctuate.

wax (waks), *n.* **1.** yellowish substance secreted by bees. **2.** any similar substance. —*v.* **3.** rub with wax. **4.** (esp. of moon) increase. **5.** become. —**wax′en,** *adj.* —**wax′y,** *adj.*

wax museum, museum displaying wax effigies of famous persons.

wax myrtle, bayberry of southeastern U.S.

wax paper, paper made moisture-resistant by paraffin coating.

wax′wing′, *n.* small crested bird.

way (wā) *n.* **1.** manner; fashion. **2.** plan; means. **3.** direction. **4.** road or route. **5.** custom.

way′bill′, *n.* list of goods with shipping directions.

way′far′er, *n.* rover.

way′lay′ (wā′lā′, wā lā′) *v.* ambush.

way′-out′, *adj. Informal.* very unconventional.

ways and means, methods of raising revenue.

way′side′, *n.* **1.** side of road. —*adj.* **2.** beside road.

way′ward (-ward) *adj.* capricious.

we (wē) *pron.* nominative plural of I.

weak (wēk) *adj.* **1.** not strong; frail. **2.** deficient. —**weak′en,** *v.* —**weak′ness,** *n.*

weak′-kneed′, *adj.* yielding readily to opposition, pressure, or intimidation.

weak′ling (-ling) *n.* weak creature.

weak′ly, *adj.,* **-lier, -liest,** *adv.* —*adj.* **1.** sickly. —*adv.* **2.** in weak manner.

weal (wēl) *n. Archaic.* well-being.

wealth (welth) *n.* **1.** great possessions or riches. **2.** profusion. —**wealth′y,** *adj.*

wean (wēn) *v.* **1.** accustom to food other than mother's milk. **2.** detach from obsession or view.

weap′on (wep′ən) *n.* instrument for use in fighting.

weap′on·ry, *n.* weapons collectively.

wear (wâr) *v.,* **wore** (wôr), **worn,**

wearing, *n.* —*v.* **1.** have on body for covering or ornament. **2.** impair or diminish gradually. **3.** weary. **4.** undergo wear. **5.** last under use. —*n.* **6.** use of garment. **7.** clothing. **8.** gradual impairment or diminution. —**wear′a·ble,** *adj.*

wea′ri·some (wēr′ē səm) *adj.* **1.** tiring. **2.** tedious.

wea′ry, *adj.,* **-rier, -riest,** *v.,* **-ried, -rying.** —*adj.* **1.** tired. **2.** tedious. —*v.* **3.** tire. —**wea′ri·ly,** *adv.*

wea′sel (wē′zəl) *n.* small carnivorous animal.

weath′er (weth′ər) *n.* **1.** state of atmosphere as to moisture, temperature, etc. —*v.* **2.** expose to weather. **3.** withstand. —*adj.* **4.** of or on windward side.

weath′er-beat′en, *adj.* worn or marked by weather.

weath′er·ing, *n.* action of wind and water on exposed rock.

weath′er·ize′, *v.,* **-ized, -izing.** make secure against cold weather.

weath′er·proof′, *adj.* **1.** able to withstand all kinds of weather. —*v.* **2.** make weatherproof.

weath′er·vane′, *n.* device to show direction of wind.

weave (wēv) *v.,* **wove** (wōv), **woven** or **wove, weaving,** *n.* —*v.* **1.** interlace, as to form cloth. **2.** take winding course. —*n.* **3.** pattern or method of weaving. —**weav′er,** *n.*

web (web) *n.,* *v.,* **webbed, webbing.** —*n.* **1.** something woven. **2.** fabric spun by spiders. **3.** membrane between toes in ducks, etc. **4. the Web,** World Wide Web. —*v.* **5.** cover with web.

web′foot′, *n.* foot with webbed toes. —**web′foot′ed,** *adj.*

Web′ster (web′stər) *n. Informal.* a dictionary of the English language. Also, **Web′ster's.**

wed (wed) *v.,* **wedded, wedded** or **wed, wedding.** **1.** bind or join in marriage. **2.** attach firmly.

Wed., Wednesday.

wed′ding, *n.* marriage ceremony.

wedge (wej) *n.,* *v.,* **wedged, wedging.** —*n.* **1.** angled object for splitting. —*v.* **2.** split with wedge. **3.** thrust or force like wedge.

wed′lock, *n.* matrimony.

Wednes′day (wenz′dā, -dē) *n.* fourth day of week.

wee (wē) *adj.* tiny.

weed (wēd) *n.* **1.** useless plant growing in cultivated ground. —*v.* **2.** free from weeds. **3.** remove as undesirable. —**weed′y,** *adj.*

weeds (wēdz) *n.pl.* black clothes for mourning.

week (wēk) *n.* **1.** seven successive days. **2.** working part of week.

week/day/, *n.* any day except Sunday, or, often, Saturday and Sunday.

week/end/ (-end/, -end/) *n.* **1.** Saturday and Sunday. —*adj.* **2.** of or for weekend.

week/ly, *adj., adv., n., pl.* **-lies.** —*adj.* **1.** happening, appearing, etc., once a week. **2.** lasting a week. —*adv.* **3.** once a week. **4.** by the week. —*n.* **5.** weekly periodical.

weep (wēp) *v.,* **wept** (wept), **weeping. 1.** shed tears. **2.** mourn.

wee/vil (wē/vəl) *n.* beetle destructive to grain, fruit, etc.

weft (weft) *n.* threads interlacing with warp.

weigh (wā) *v.* **1.** measure heaviness of. **2.** burden. **3.** consider. **4.** lift. **5.** have heaviness. —**weigh/er,** *n.*

weight (wāt) *n.* **1.** amount of heaviness. **2.** system of units for expressing weight. **3.** heavy mass. **4.** pressure. **5.** burden. **6.** importance. —*v.* **7.** add weight to. —**weight/y,** *adj.* —**weight/less,** *adj.*

weir (wēr) *n.* **1.** dam in a stream. **2.** fence set in stream to catch fish.

weird (wērd) *adj.* **1.** supernatural. **2.** uncannily strange.

weird/o (wēr/dō) *n. Slang.* odd, eccentric, or abnormal person.

wel/come (wel/kəm) *n., v.,* **-comed, -coming.** —*n.* **1.** friendly reception. —*v.* **2.** receive or greet with pleasure. —*adj.* **3.** gladly received. **4.** given permission or consent.

weld (weld) *v.* **1.** unite, esp. by heating and pressing. —*n.* **2.** welded joint. —**weld/er,** *n.*

wel/fare/ (wel/fâr/) *n.* **1.** well-being. **2.** provision of benefits to poor.

well (wel) *adv., compar.* **better,** *superl.* **best,** *adj., n., v.* —*adv.* **1.** excellently; properly. **2.** thoroughly. —*adj.* **3.** in good health. **4.** good. —*n.* **5.** hole made in earth to reach water, oil, etc. **6.** source. **7.** vertical shaft. —*v.* **8.** rise or gush.

well/-advised/, *adj.* prudent.

well/-appoint/ed, *adj.* attractively furnished.

well/-be/ing, *n.* good or prosperous condition.

well/-born/, *adj.* of good family.

well/-bred/, *adj.* showing good manners.

well/-dis-posed/, *adj.* feeling favorable, sympathetic, or kind.

well/-done/, *adj.* **1.** performed accurately and skillfully. **2.** thoroughly cooked.

well/-found/ed, *adj.* having or based on good reasons, sound information, etc.

well/-ground/ed, *adj.* having good basic knowledge of a subject.

well/-heeled/, *adj.* prosperous.

well/-informed/, *adj.* having extensive knowledge.

well/-man/nered, *adj.* polite.

well/-mean/ing, *adj.* intending good. —**well/-meant/,** *adj.*

well/-nigh/, *adv.* nearly.

well/-off/, *adj.* **1.** in good or favorable condition. **2.** prosperous.

well/-round/ed, *adj.* desirably varied.

well/spring/, *n.* source.

well/-to-do/, *adj.* prosperous.

well/-worn/, *adj.* **1.** showing effects of extensive use. **2.** trite.

Welsh (welsh, welch) *n.* people or language of Wales.

welt (welt) *n.* **1.** wale from lash. **2.** strip around edge of shoe. **3.** narrow border along seam. —*v.* **4.** put welt on.

wel/ter (wel/tər) *v.* **1.** roll, as waves. **2.** wallow.

wen (wen) *n.* small cyst.

wench (wench) *n.* girl or young woman.

wend (wend) *v.,* **wended, wending.** *Archaic.* go.

went (went) *v.* pt. of **go.**

were (wûr; *unstressed* wər) *v.* past plural and pres. subjunctive of **be.**

weren't (wûrnt, wûr/ənt) contraction of **were not.**

were/wolf/ (wâr/wŏŏlf/, wēr/-, wûr/-) *n., pl.* **-wolves.** (in folklore) human turned into wolf.

west (west) *n.* **1.** point of compass opposite east. **2.** territory in this direction. —*adj. adv.* **3.** toward or from west. —**west/er-ly,** *adj. adv.* —**west/ern,** *adj.* —**west/ern-er,** *n.*

west/ern-ize/ (wes/tər nīz/) *v.,* **-ized, -izing.** influence with or convert to western ideas and customs.

west/ward (-ward) *adj.* **1.** moving or facing west. —*adv.* **2.** Also, **west/wards.** toward west. —*n.* **3.** westward part. —**west/ward-ly,** *adj., adv.*

wet (wet) *adj.,* **wetter, wettest,** *n., v.,* **wet** or **wetted, wetting.** **1.** covered or soaked with water. **2.** rainy. —*n.* **3.** moisture. —*v.* **4.** make or become wet.

wet blanket, one that dampens enthusiasm.

wet nurse, woman hired to suckle another's infant.

wet suit, close-fitting rubber suit worn for body warmth, as by scuba divers.

whack (hwak, wak) *Informal.* v. **1.** strike sharply. —n. **2.** smart blow.

whale (hwāl, wāl) n., pl. **whales** or **whale**, v., **whaled, whaling.** —n. **1.** large fishlike marine mammal. —v. **2.** hunt and kill whales.

whale/bone/, n. elastic horny substance in upper jaw of some whales.

wharf (hwôrf, wôrf) n., pl. **wharves.** structure for mooring vessels.

wharf/age, n. **1.** use of wharf. **2.** charge for such use.

what (hwut, hwot, wut, wot; *unstressed* hwət, wət) pron., pl. **what,** adv. —pron. **1.** which one? **2.** that which. **3.** such. —adv. **4.** how much. **5.** partly.

what•ev/er, pron. **1.** anything that. **2.** no matter what. —adj. **3.** no matter what.

what/not/, n. small open cupboard, esp. for knickknacks.

what/so•ev/er, pron., adj. whatever.

wheat (hwēt, wēt) n. grain of common cereal grass, used esp. for flour.

whee/dle (hwēd/l, wēd/l) v., **-dled, -dling.** influence by flattery.

wheel (hwēl, wēl) n. **1.** round object turning on axis. —v. **2.** turn on axis. **3.** move on wheels. **4.** turn.

wheel/bar/row, n. one-wheeled cart lifted at one end.

wheel/base/, n. Auto. distance between centers of front and rear wheel hubs.

wheel/chair/, n. chair mounted on wheels for use by persons who cannot walk.

wheeze (hwēz, wēz) v., **wheezed, wheezing,** n. —v. **1.** whistle in breathing. —n. **2.** wheezing breath.

whelp (hwelp, welp) n. **1.** young of dog, wolf, bear, etc. —v. **2.** bring forth whelps.

when (hwen, wen; *unstressed* hwən, wən) adv. **1.** at what time. —conj. **2.** at time that. **3.** and then.

whence (hwens, wens) adv., conj. from what place.

when•ev/er, adv. at whatever time.

where (hwâr, wâr) adv. **1.** in, at, or to what place? —conj. **2.** in what respect? —conj. **3.** in, at, or to what place. **4.** and there.

where/a•bouts/, adv. **1.** where. —n. **2.** location.

where•as/, conj. **1.** while on the contrary. **2.** considering that.

where•by/, conj. by what or which; under the terms of which.

where/fore/, adv. **1.** why; for what. —n. **2.** reason.

where•in/, conj. **1.** in what or in which. —adv. **2.** in what way or respect?

where•of/, adv., conj. of what.

where/up•on/, conj. **1.** upon which. **2.** at or after which.

wher•ev/er, conj. at or to whatever place.

where/with•al/ (-with ôl/, -with-) n. means.

whet (hwet, wet) v., **whetted, whetting.** sharpen. —**whet/stone/**, n.

wheth/er (hweth/ər, weth/-) conj. (word introducing alternative.)

whey (hwā, wā) n. watery part that separates out when milk curdles.

which (hwich, wich) pron. **1.** what one? **2.** the one that. —adj. **3.** what one of (those mentioned).

which•ev•er, pron. any that.

whiff (hwif, wif) n. **1.** slight puff or trace. —v. **2.** blow in whiffs.

while (hwīl, wīl) n., conj., v., **whiled, whiling.** —n. **1.** time. —conj. **2.** in time that. —v. **3.** pass (time) pleasantly.

whim (hwim, wim) n. irrational or fanciful decision or idea.

whim/per (hwim/pər, wim/-) v. **1.** cry softly and plaintively. —n. **2.** whimpering cry. —**whim/per•er**, n.

whim/sy (hwim/zē, wim/-) n., pl. **-sies.** fanciful idea; whim. —**whim/si•cal**, adj.

whine (hwīn, wīn) n., v., **whined, whining.** n. **1.** low complaining sound. —v. **2.** utter whines.

whin/ny (hwin/ē, win/ē) v., **-nied, -nying,** n., pl. **-nies.** neigh.

whip (hwip, wip) v., **whipped, whipping,** n. —v. **1.** strike repeatedly; flog. **2.** jerk; seize. **3.** cover with thread; overcast. **4.** beat (cream, etc.). **5.** move quickly; lash about. —n. **6.** instrument with lash and handle for striking. **7.** party manager in legislature.

whip/cord/, n. fabric with diagonal ribs.

whip/lash/, n. **1.** lash of whip. **2.** neck injury caused by sudden jerking of the head.

whip/per•snap/per (hwip/ər snap/-ər, wip/-) n. insignificant, presumptuous person, esp. young one.

whip/pet (hwip/it, wip/-) n. type of slender swift dog.

whip/poor•will/ (hwip/ər wil/, wip/-) n. nocturnal American bird.

whir (hwûr, wûr) v., **whirred, whirring,** n. —v. **1.** move with buzzing sound. —n. **2.** such sound.

whirl (hwûrl, wûrl) v. **1.** spin or turn rapidly. **2.** move quickly. —n.

3. whirling movement. **4.** round of events, etc. —**whirl'er,** n.

whirl'i·gig' (hwûr'lī gig', wûr'-) n. toy revolving in wind.

whirl'pool', n. whirling current in water.

whirl'wind' (-wind') n. whirling mass of air.

whisk (hwisk, wisk) v. **1.** sweep up. **2.** move or carry lightly. **3.** beat. —n. **4.** act of whisking. **5.** kitchen tool for beating.

whisk'er, n. **1.** (pl.) hair on man's face. **2.** bristle on face of cat, etc. Also, **whis'ky.**

whis'key (hwis'kē, wis'-) n. distilled alcoholic liquor made from grain or corn. Also, **whis'ky.**

whis'per (hwis'pər, wis'pər) v. **1.** speak very softly. —n. **2.** sound of whispering. **3.** something whispered. —**whis'per·er,** n.

whist (hwist, wist) n. card game.

whis'tle (hwis'əl, wis'-) v., **-tled, -tling.** —v. **1.** make clear shrill sound with breath, air, or steam. —n. **2.** device for making such sounds. **3.** sound of whistling.

whis'tle-blow'er, n. person who publicly discloses government or wrongdoing.

whistle stop, n. **1.** small town. **2.** short talk from rear platform of train during political campaign.

whit (hwit, wit) n. particle; bit.

white (hwīt, wīt) adj. **1.** of color of snow. **2.** having light skin. **3.** pale. —n. **4.** color without hue, opposite to black. **5.** Caucasian. **6.** white or light part. —**whit'en,** v.

white blood cell, nearly colorless blood cell of immune system.

white'-bread', adj. bland; conventional.

white'-col'lar, adj. of professional or office workers whose jobs usu. do not involve manual labor.

white elephant, useless, expensive possession.

white'fish', n. small food fish.

white gold, gold alloy colored white esp. by presence of nickel.

white goods, household linens.

white lie, harmless lie; fib.

white'wash', n. **1.** substance for whitening walls, etc. —v. **2.** cover with whitewash. **3.** cover up faults or errors of.

white water, frothy water, as in rapids.

whith'er (hwith'ər, with'-) adv., conj. Archaic. to what place.

whit'ing (hwī'ting, wī'-) n. small Atlantic food fish.

whit'low (hwit'lō, wit'-) n. inflammation on finger or toe.

Whit'sun·day (hwit'sun'dā, -dē,

-sən dā', wit'-) n. seventh Sunday after Easter.

whit'tle (hwit'l, wit'l) v., **-tled, -tling. 1.** cut bit by bit with knife. **2.** reduce. —**whit'tler,** n.

whiz (hwiz, wiz) v., **whizzed, whizzing,** n. —v. **1.** move with hum or hiss. —n. **2.** whizzing sound. **3.** person who is very good at something. Also, **whizz.**

who (hōō) pron. **1.** what person? **2.** the person that.

whoa (hwō, wō) interj. (stop!)

who·dun'it (-dun'it) n. detective story.

who·ev'er, pron. anyone that.

whole (hōl) adj. **1.** entire; undivided. **2.** undamaged. **3.** Math. not fractional. **4.** complete amount or extent. **5.** complete thing. —**whol'ly,** adv. —**whole'ness,** n.

whole'-heart'ed, adj. sincere.

whole'sale', n., adj., v., **-saled, -saling. 1.** sale of goods in quantity, as to retailers. —adj. **2.** of or engaged in wholesale. —v. **3.** sell by wholesale. —**whole'sal'er,** n.

whole'some (-səm) adj. beneficial; healthful. —**whole'some·ly,** adv.

whole'-wheat', adj. prepared with complete wheat kernel.

whom (hōōm) pron. objective case of **who.**

whom·ev'er, pron. objective case of **whoever.**

whoop (hwōōp, hwōōp, wōōp, wōōp; esp. for 2 hōōp, hōōp) n. **1.** loud shout or cry. **2.** gasping sound characteristic of whooping cough. —v. **3.** utter whoops.

whoop'ing cough (hōō'ping, hōōp'ing) infectious disease characterized by short, convulsive coughs followed by whoops.

whop'per (hwop'ər, wop'-) n. Informal. **1.** something uncommonly large. **2.** big lie.

whop'ping, adj. Informal. uncommonly large.

whore (hōr; often hōōr) n., v., **whored, whoring.** —n. **1.** prostitute. —v. **2.** consort with whores.

whorl (hwûrl, hwôrl, wûrl, wôrl) n. circular arrangement; spiral.

whose (hōōz) pron. possessive case of **who.**

who'so·ev'er, pron. whoever.

why (hwī, wī) adv., n., pl. **whys.** —adv. **1.** for what reason. —n. **2.** cause or reason.

WI, Wisconsin.

wick (wik) n. soft threads that absorb fuel and burn in candle, etc.

wick'ed (wik'id) adj. **1.** evil; sinful. **2.** naughty. —**wick'ed·ly,** adv.

wick'er, n. **1.** slender pliant twig.

—*adj.* **2.** made of wicker. —**wick′er·work′,** *n.*

wick′et (wik′it) *n.* **1.** small gate. **2.** framework in cricket.

wide (wīd) *adj.,* **wider, widest,** *adv.* —*adj.* **1.** broad. **2.** extensive. **3.** expanded. **4.** far. —*adv.* **5.** far. **6.** to farthest extent. —**wid′en,** *v.*

wide′-awake′ *adj.* **1.** fully awake. **2.** alert or observant.

wide′-eyed′, *adj.* with eyes open wide, in amazement or innocence.

wide′spread′, *adj.* occurring widely.

wid′ow (wid′ō) *n.* **1.** woman whose husband has died. —*v.* **2.** make widow of. —**wid′ow·er,** *n. masc.* —**wid′ow·hood,** *n.*

width (width, witth) *n.* **1.** breadth. **2.** piece of full wideness.

wield (wēld) *v.* **1.** exercise (power, etc.). **2.** brandish.

wie′ner (wē′nar) *n.* small sausage; frankfurter.

wife (wīf) *n., pl.* **wives** (wīvz). married woman. —**wife′ly,** *adj.*

wig (wig) *n.* artificial covering of hair for head.

wig′gle (wig′əl) *v.,* **-gled, -gling,** —*v.* **1.** twist to and fro; wriggle. —*n.* **2.** wiggling movement. —**wig′gly,** *adj.* —**wig′gler,** *n.*

wig′wag′ (wig′wag′) *v.,* **-wagged, -wagging,** —*v.* **1.** signal in code with flags, etc. —*n.* **2.** such signaling. **3.** message so sent.

wig′wam (-wom) *n.* American Indian dwelling.

wild (wīld) *adj.* **1.** not cultivated. **2.** uncivilized. **3.** violent. **4.** uninhabited. **5.** disorderly. —*adv.* **6.** wildly. —*n.* **7.** wilderness. —**wild′ly,** *adv.*

wild′cat′, *n., v.,* **-catted, -catting.** —*n.* **1.** large North American feline. —*v.* **2.** prospect independently. —*adj.* **3.** not called or sanctioned by labor union.

wil′de·beest (wil′də bēst′, vil′-) *n.* gnu.

wil′der·ness (wil′dər nis) *n.* wild or desolate region.

wild′-eyed′ *adj.* **1.** having a wild expression in the eyes. **2.** extreme or radical.

wild′fire′, *n.* outdoor fire that spreads rapidly and is hard to extinguish.

wild′flow′er, *n.* flower of plant that grows wild.

wild′-goose′ chase′, senseless search for something unobtainable.

wild′life′, *n.* animals living in nature.

wile (wīl) *n.* trick to fool or trap.

will (wil) *n.* **1.** power of conscious action or choice. **2.** wish; pleasure. **3.** attitude, either hostile or friendly. **4.** declaration of wishes for disposition of property after death. —*v.* **5.** decide to influence by act of will. **6.** consent to. **7.** give by will. —*auxiliary verb.* **8.** am (is, are) about to. **9.** am (is, are) willing to.

will′ful, *adj.* **1.** intentional. **2.** headstrong. Also, **wil′ful.**

wil′lies (wil′ēz) *n.pl.* nervousness.

will′ing, *adj.* **1.** consenting. **2.** cheerfully done, given, etc. —**will′ing·ly,** *adv.* —**will′ing·ness,** *n.*

will′-o′-the-wisp′ (wil′ə tħə wisp′) *n.* **1.** flitting, elusive light. **2.** something that fascinates and deludes.

wil′low (wil′ō) *n.* slender tree or shrub with tough, pliant branches.

wil′low·y, *adj.* **-lower, -lowest.** tall and slender.

wil′ly-nil′ly (wil′ē nil′ē) *adv.* willingly or unwillingly.

wilt (wilt) *v.* **1.** wither or droop. —*n.* **2.** wilted state.

wil′y (wī′lē) *adj.,* **-ier, -iest.** crafty.

wimp (wimp) *n. Informal.* weak, ineffectual person. —**wimp′y,** *adj.*

win (win) *v.,* **won** (wun), **winning,** *n.* —*v.* **1.** succeed or get by effort. **2.** gain (victory). **3.** persuade. —*n.* **4.** victory.

wince (wins) *v.,* **winced, wincing,** *n.* —*v.* **1.** shrink, as from pain or blow. —*n.* **2.** wincing movement.

winch (winch) *n.* **1.** windlass. **2.** crank.

wind (wind for 1–7; wīnd for 8–11), *n., v.,* **winded** (for 5–7) or **wound** (wound) (for 8–11), **winding.** —*n.* **1.** air in motion. **2.** gas in stomach or bowels. **3.** animal odor. **4.** breath. —*v.* **5.** make short of breath. **6.** change direction. **7.** roll into cylinder or ball. **8.** turn (handle, etc.). —**wind′y** (win′dē) *adj.*

wind′bag′ (wind′-) *n.* pompous talker.

wind′break′ (wind′-) *n.* shelter from wind.

wind′chill factor (wind′chil′) apparent temperature felt on exposed skin owing to combination of temperature and wind speed.

wind′ed (win′did) *adj.* breathless.

wind′fall′ (wind′-) *n.* **1.** something blown down. **2.** unexpected luck.

winding sheet (wīn′ding) shroud.

wind instrument (wind) musical instrument sounded by breath.

wind′lass (wind′ləs) *n.* drum mechanism for hoisting.

wind′mill′ (wind′-) *n.* mill operated by wind acting on vanes.

win′dow (win′dō) *n.* opening for

air and light, usually fitted with glass in frame.

window dressing, 1. art, act, or technique of decorating store display windows. **2.** something done solely to create favorable impression.

win′dow·pane′, *n.* pane of glass for window.

win′dow-shop′, *v.,* **-shopped, -shopping.** look at articles in store windows without making purchases. **—window shopper.**

wind′pipe′ (wind′-) *n.* trachea.

wind′shield′ (wind′-, win′-) *n.* glass shield above automobile, etc., dashboard.

wind′sock′ (wind′-) *n.* mounted cloth cone that catches wind to indicate wind direction.

wind′storm′ (wind′-) *n.* storm with heavy wind but little or no precipitation.

wind′surf′ing (wind′-) *n.* sport of riding on surfboard mounted with a sail. **—wind′surf′,** *v.* **—wind′surf′-er,** *n.*

wind′-swept′ (wind′-) *adj.* exposed to or blown by wind.

wind′up′ (wind′-) *n.* close; end.

wind′ward (wind′ward) *n.* direction from which wind blows.
—adj. 2. of, in, or to windward.

wine (wīn) *n., v.,* **wined, wining.**
—n. 1. fermented juice, esp. of grape. **2.** dark purplish red. **—v. 3.** entertain with wine. **—win′y,** *adj.*

win′er·y, *n., pl.* **-eries.** place for making wine.

wing (wing) *n.* **1.** organ of flight in birds, insects, and bats. **2.** winglike or projecting structure. **3.** flight. **4.** supporting surface of airplane. **—v. 5.** travel on wings. **6.** wound in wing or arm. **—wing′ed,** *adj.*

wing′ding′ *n.* Slang. noisy, exciting party.

wink (wingk) *v.* **1.** close and open (eye) quickly. **2.** signal by winking. **3.** twinkle. **—n. 4.** winking movement.

win′ner (win′ər) *n.* one that wins.

win′ning, *n.* **1.** (*pl.*) that which is won. **—adj. 2.** charming.

win′now (win′ō) *v.* **1.** free from chaff by wind. **2.** separate.

wi′no (wī′nō) *n., pl.* **-os.** person addicted to wine.

win′some (win′səm) *adj.* sweetly or innocently charming.

win′ter (win′tər) *n.* **1.** last season of year. **—adj. 2.** of, like, or for winter. **—v. 3.** pass winter. **4.** keep during winter. **—win′try,** *adj.*

win′ter·green′, *n.* creeping aromatic shrub.

wipe (wīp) *v.,* **wiped, wiping,** *n.*
—v. 1. rub lightly. **2.** remove or blot. **—n. 3.** act of wiping. **—wip′er,** *n.*

wire (wīʳr) *n., adj., v.,* **wired, wiring.** **—n. 1.** slender, flexible piece of metal. **2.** telegram or telegraph. **—adj. 3.** made of wires. **—v. 4.** bind with wire. **5.** *Elect.* install system of wires in. **6.** telegraph.

wire′less, *adj.* **1.** activated by electromagnetic waves rather than wires. **—n. 2.** *Brit.* radio.

wire service, agency that sends syndicated news by wire to its subscribers.

wire′tap′, *v.,* **-tapped, -tapping,** *n.* **—v. 1.** connect secretly into telephone. **—n. 2.** act of wiretapping.

wir′ing, *n.* system of electric wires.

wir′y, *adj.,* **-ier, -iest.** like wire; lean and strong. **—wir′i·ness,** *n.*

Wis., Wisconsin. Also, **Wisc.**

wis′dom (wiz′dəm) *n.* **1.** knowledge and judgment. **2.** wise sayings.

wisdom tooth, last tooth to erupt.

wise (wīz) *adj.* **1.** having knowledge and judgment. **2.** prudent. **3.** informed. **—n. 4.** way; respect.

wise′acre (-ā′kər) *n.* conceited, insolent person.

wise′crack′, *n.* **1.** smart or facetious remark. **—v. 2.** make or say as a wisecrack.

wish (wish) *v.* **1.** want; desire. **2.** bid. **—n. 3.** desire. **4.** that desired. **—wish′ful,** *adj.* **—wish′ful·ly,** *adv.*

wish′bone′, *n.* forked bone in front of breastbone in most birds.

wish′y-wash′y (wish′ē wosh′ē) *adj.* thin or weak.

wisp (wisp) *n.* small tuft. **—wisp′y,** *adj.*

wis·te′ri·a (wi stēr′ē ə) *n.* climbing shrub with purple flowers.

wist′ful (wist′fəl) *adj.* **1.** pensive. **2.** longing. **—wist′ful·ly,** *adv.*

wit (wit) *n.* **1.** power of combining perception with clever expression. **2.** person having this. **3.** (*pl.*) intelligence. **—v.** *Archaic.* know. **5.** **to wit,** namely.

witch (wich) *n.* **1.** woman thought to practice magic. **2.** ugly or mean old woman. **—witch′craft′,** *n.*

witch doctor, person in some cultures who uses magic esp. to cure illness.

witch′er·y, *n., pl.* **-eries. 1.** magic. **2.** charm.

witch ha′zel (hā′zəl) preparation for bruises, etc.

with (with, with) *prep.* **1.** accompanied by. **2.** using. **3.** against.

with·draw′ (with drô′, with-) *v.,*

-drew, -drawn, -drawing. **1.** draw back. **2.** retract. —**with•draw′al,** *n.*

with′ers, *n.pl.* part of animal's back just behind neck.

with•hold′ (with hōld′, with-) *v.,* -held, -holding. hold or keep back.

withholding tax, that part of employee's tax liability withheld by employer from wages.

with•in′ (with in′, with-) *adv.* **1.** inside; inwardly. —*prep.* **2.** in; inside of. **3.** at point not beyond.

with•out′, *prep.* **1.** lacking. **2.** beyond. —*adv.* **3.** outside. **4.** outwardly. **5.** lacking.

with•stand′ (with stand′, with-) *v.,* -stood, -standing. resist.

wit′less, *adj.* stupid.

wit′ness (wit′nis) *v.* **1.** see. **2.** testify. **3.** attest by signature. —*n.* **4.** person who witnesses. **5.** testimony.

wit′ti•cism′ (wit′ə siz′əm) *n.* witty remark.

wit′ting, *adj.* knowing; aware.

wit′ty, *adj.,* -tier, -tiest. showing wit. —**wit′ti•ly,** *adv.*

wiz′ard (wiz′ərd) *n.* magician. —**wiz′ard•ry,** *n.*

wiz′ened (wiz′ənd, wē′zənd) *adj.* shriveled.

wk., week.

w/o, without.

wob′ble (wob′əl) *v.,* -bled, -bling. move unsteadily from side to side. —**wob′bly,** *adj.*

woe (wō) *n.* grief or affliction. —**woe′ful,** *adj.* —**woe′ful•ly,** *adv.*

woe•be•gone′ (-bi gôn′) *adj.* showing woe.

wok (wok) *n.* Chinese cooking pan.

wolf (wŏŏlf) *n., pl.* **wolves** (wŏŏlvz), *v.* —*n.* **1.** wild carnivorous animal of dog family. —*v.* **2.** *Informal.* eat ravenously. —**wolf′ish,** *adj.*

wolf′hound′, *n.* kind of hound.

wolfs′bane′, *n.* poisonous plant.

wol′ver•ine′ (wŏŏl′və rēn′) *n.* North American mammal of weasel family.

wom′an (wŏŏm′ən) *n., pl.* **women** (wim′in). adult female human being. —**wom′an•hood,** *n.* —**wom′an•ly,** *adj.*

womb (wŏŏm) *n.* uterus.

wom′bat (wom′bat) *n.* burrowing, herbivorous Australian marsupial.

won′der (wun′dər) *v.* **1.** be curious about. **2.** marvel. —*n.* **3.** something strange. **4.** Also, **won′der•ment.** amazement.

won′der•ful, *adj.* **1.** exciting wonder. **2.** excellent.

won′drous, *adj.* **1.** wonderful. —*adv.* **2.** remarkably.

wont (wônt, wōnt, wunt) *adj.* **1.** accustomed. —*n.* **2.** habit.

—**wont′ed,** *adj.*

won′t (wōnt) contraction of **will not.**

woo (wŏŏ) *v.* seek to win, esp. in marriage. —**woo′er,** *n.*

wood (wŏŏd) *n.* **1.** hard substance under bark of trees. **2.** timber or firewood. **3.** (*often pl.*) forest. —*adj.* **4.** made of wood. **5.** living in woods. —*v.* **6.** plant with trees. —**wood′craft′,** *n.* —**wood′y,** *adj.*

wood′bine′ (-bīn′) *n.* any of various vines, as the honeysuckle.

wood′chuck′, *n.* bushy-tailed burrowing rodent. Also called **ground′hog′.**

wood′cut′, *n.* print made from a carved block of wood.

wood′ed, *adj.* covered with trees.

wood′en, *adj.* **1.** made of wood. **2.** without feeling or expression.

wood′land′ (-land′, -lənd) *n.* forest.

wood′peck′er, *n.* bird with hard bill for boring.

wood′pile′, *n.* stack of firewood.

wood′ruff (-rəf, -ruf′) *n.* fragrant plant with small white flowers.

wood′shed′, *n.* shed for storing firewood.

woods′man, *n.* person who works in woods.

woods′y, *adj.,* -ier, -iest. of or resembling woods.

wood′wind′ (-wind′) *n.* musical instrument of group including flute, clarinet, oboe, and bassoon.

wood′work′, *n.* wooden fittings inside building. —**wood′work′er,** *n.*

woof (wŏŏf, wŏŏf) *n.* **1.** yarns from side to side in loom. **2.** bark.

woof′er (wŏŏf′ər) *n.* loudspeaker to reproduce low-frequency sounds.

wool (wŏŏl) *n.* **1.** soft curly hair, esp. of sheep. **2.** garment, yarn, or fabric of wool. **3.** curly, fine-stranded substance. —**wool′en** or (*esp. Brit.*) **wool′len,** *adj., n.*

wool′gath′er•ing, *n.* daydreaming.

wool′ly, *adj.* **1.** of or resembling wool. **2.** confused or disorganized.

woolly bear, caterpillar with woolly hairs.

word (wûrd) *n.* **1.** group of letters or sounds that represents concept. **2.** talk or conversation. **3.** promise. **4.** tidings. **5.** (*pl.*) quarrel. —*v.* **6.** express in words. —**word′less,** *adj.*

word′age (wûr′dij) *n.* **1.** words collectively. **2.** number of words.

word′ing, *n.* way of expressing.

word of mouth, oral communication.

word/play/, n. witty repartee.

word processing, production of documents using computers.

word processor, computer program or system for word processing.

word/y, adj. **-i-er, -i-est.** using too many words. **—word/i-ness,** n.

work (wûrk) n. **1.** exertion; labor. **2.** task. **3.** employment. **4.** place of employment. **5.** materials on which one works. **6.** result of work. **7.** (pl.) industrial plant. **—adj. 8.** of or for work. **—v. 9.** do work. **10.** operate successfully. **11.** move or give. **12.** solve. **13.** excite. **14.** ferment. **—work/a-ble,** adj. **—work/er,** n.

work/a-day/ (wûr′kə dā′) adj. commonplace; uneventful.

work/a-hol/ic (-hô′lik) n. person who works compulsively.

work/horse/, n. **1.** horse used for heavy labor. **2.** person who works tirelessly.

work/house/, n. penal institution for minor offenders.

working class, social or economic class composed of workers.

work/load/, n. amount of work that machine or employee is expected to perform.

work/man, pl. **-men.** laborer.

work/man-like/, adj. skillful.

work/man-ship/, n. **1.** skill of workman. **2.** quality of work done.

work/out/, n. **1.** practice or test to maintain or determine physical ability or endurance. **2.** structured regime of physical exercise.

work/shop/, n. **1.** place where work is done. **2.** seminar.

work/sta/tion, n. **1.** work area for one person, as in office, usu. with electronic equipment. **2.** powerful small computer used for graphics-intensive processing.

work/up/, n. thorough medical diagnostic examination.

world (wûrld) n. **1.** earth; globe. **2.** particular part of earth. **3.** milieu. **4.** humanity. **5.** universe. **6.** great quantity.

world/-class/, adj. of the highest caliber.

world/ly, adj., **-li-er, -li-est. 1.** secular or earthly. **2.** devoted to affairs of this world; sophisticated; shrewd. **3.** of this world. **—world/li-ness,** n.

world/ly-wise/, adj. wise as to the affairs of this world.

world/-wea/ry, adj. blasé.

World Wide Web, system of exten-

sively interlinked documents: branch of the Internet.

worm (wûrm) n. **1.** small slender creeping animal. **2.** (pl.) intestinal disorder. **—v. 3.** move like worm. **4.** extract (secret) craftily. **5.** free from worms.

worm/wood/, n. bitter aromatic herb.

worn (wôrn) adj. exhausted; spent.

worn/-out/, adj. **1.** exhausted. **2.** destroyed by wear.

wor/ry (wûr′ē, wur′ē) v., **-ried, -ry-ing,** n., pl. **-ries. —v. 1.** make or feel anxious. **2.** seize with teeth and shake. **—n. 3.** anxiety. **4.** cause of anxiety. **—wor/ri-some,** adj.

worse (wûrs) adj. **1.** less good; less favorable. **—n. 2.** that which is worse. **—adv. 3.** in worse way. **—wors/en,** v.

wor/ship (wûr′ship) n., v., **-shiped, -shiping** or **-shipped, -shipping. —n. 1.** homage paid to God. **2.** rendering of such homage. **—v. 3.** render religious reverence to. **—wor/ship-er,** n. **—wor/ship-ful,** adj.

worst (wûrst) adj. **1.** least satisfactory; least well. **—n. 2.** that which is worst. **—adv. 3.** in the worst way. **—v. 4.** defeat.

wor/sted (wŏŏs′tid, wûr′stid) n. **1.** firmly twisted wool yarn or thread. **2.** fabric made of it.

worth (wûrth) adj. **1.** good enough to justify. **2.** having value of. **—n. 3.** excellence; importance. **4.** quantity of specified value. **—worth/less,** adj. **—worth/less-ness,** n.

worth/while/, adj. repaying time and effort spent.

wor/thy (wûr′thē) adj., **-thier, -thi-est,** n., pl. **-thies. —adj. 1.** of adequate worth. **2.** deserving. **—n. 3.** person of merit. **—worth/i-ly,** adv. **—wor/thi-ness,** n.

would (wŏŏd; unstressed wəd) v. past of **will** (defs. 8, 9).

would/-be/, adj. wishing, pretending, or intended to be.

wound (wŏŏnd) n. **1.** injury from external violence. **—v. 2.** inflict wound. **3.** grieve with insult or reproach.

wrack (rak) n. ruin.

wraith (rāth) n. ghost.

wran/gle (rang′gəl) v., **-gled, -gl-ing,** n. **1.** dispute. **—wran/gler,** n.

wrap (rap) v., **wrapped** or **wrapt, wrapping,** n. **—v. 1.** enclose; envelop. **2.** wind or fold about. **—n. 3.** shawl.

wrap/per, n. **1.** one that wraps. **2.** Also, **wrapping.** outer cover. **3.** long loose garment.

wrath (rath) *n.* **1.** stern or fierce anger. **2.** vengeance.

wreak (rēk) *v.* inflict.

wreath (rēth) *n.* circular band of leaves, etc.

wreathe (rēth) *v.,* **wreathed, wreathing.** encircle with wreath.

wreck (rek) *n.* **1.** anything reduced to ruins. **2.** destruction. **3.** person in poor state. —*v.* **4.** damage.

wreck/age, *n.* ruin or damage.

wreck/er, *n.* **1.** vehicle for towing wrecked automobiles. **2.** one that demolishes buildings.

wren (ren) *n.* small active bird.

wrench (rench) *v.* **1.** twist forcibly. **2.** injure by wrenching. —*n.* **3.** wrenching movement. **4.** tool for turning bolts, etc.

wrest (rest) *v.* **1.** twist violently. **2.** get by effort. —*n.* **3.** twist; wrench.

wres/tle (res'əl) *v.,* **-tled, -tling,** *n.* —*v.* **1.** contend with by trying to force other person down. —*n.* **2.** this sport. **3.** struggle. —**wres/tler,** *n.* —**wres/tling,** *n.*

wretch (rech) *n.* pitiable person.

wretch/ed, *adj.* **1.** pitiable. **2.** despicable. **3.** pitiful.

wrig/gle (rig'əl) *v.,* **-gled, -gling,** *n.* wiggle; squirm. —**wrig/gly,** *adj.*

wring (ring) *v.,* **wrung** (rung), **wringing,** *n.* —*v.* **1.** twist or compress. **2.** expel by wringing. **3.** clasp tightly. —*n.* **4.** twist or squeeze. —**wring/er,** *n.*

wrin/kle (ring'kəl) *n.,* *v.,* **-kled, -kling.** —*n.* **1.** ridge or furrow. —*v.* **2.** form wrinkles in. —**wrin/kly,** *adj.*

wrist (rist) *n.* joint between hand and arm.

writ (rit) *n.* **1.** formal legal order. **2.** writing.

write (rīt) *v.,* **wrote** (rōt), **written** (rit'n), **writing.** **1.** form (letters, etc.) by hand. **2.** express in writing. **3.** produce, as author or composer. —**writ/er,** *n.*

write/-in/, *n.* candidate or vote for candidate not listed on ballot but written in by voter.

write/-off/, *n.* something cancelled, as a debt.

writhe (rīth) *v.,* **writhed, writhing,** *n.* —*v.* **1.** twist, as in pain. —*n.* **2.** writhing movement. —**writh/er,** *n.*

wrong (rông) *adj.* **1.** not right or good. **2.** deviating from truth or fact. **3.** not suitable. **4.** under or inner (side). —*n.* **5.** evil; injury; error. —*v.* **6.** do wrong to. **7.** misjudge. —**wrong/do/er,** *n.* —**wrong/do/ing,** *n.* —**wrong/ful,** *adj.* —**wrong/ly,** *adv.*

wrong/head/ed, *adj.* misguided and stubborn.

wrought (rôt) *adj.* **1.** worked. **2.** shaped by beating.

wrought/-up/, *adj.* perturbed.

wry (rī) *adj.,* **wrier, wriest.** **1.** twisted; distorted. **2.** ironic. —**wry/ly,** *adv.* —**wry/ness,** *n.*

WV, West Virginia. Also, **W. Va.**

WWW, World Wide Web.

WY, Wyoming. Also, **Wyo.**

WYSIWYG (wiz'ē wig') *adj.* of or being computer display screen that shows text exactly as it will appear when printed.

X Y Z

X, x (eks) *n.* twenty-fourth letter of English alphabet.

X, motion-picture rating applied to sexually explicit films.

X chromosome, sex chromosome that determines femaleness when paired with another X chromosome.

xen/o•pho/bi•a (zen/ə fō'bē ə, zē'-nə-) *n.* fear or hatred of foreigners. —**xen/o•pho/bic,** *adj.*

xe•rog/ra•phy (zi rog'rə fē) *n.* copying process in which resins are fused to paper electrically.

Xe/rox (zēr'oks) *n.* **1.** *Trademark.* brand name for copying machine using xerography. —*v.* **3.** *(l.c.)* print or reproduce by Xerox.

Xmas (kris'məs; *often* eks'məs) *n.* Christmas.

X-rat/ed (eks'rā'tid) *adj.* sexually explicit; obscene.

x/-ray/, *n.* **1.** highly penetrating type of electromagnetic ray, used esp. in medicine. —*v.* **2.** photograph or treat with x-rays.

xy/lo•phone/ (zī'lə fōn') *n.* musical instrument of wooden bars, played with small hammers. —**xy/lo•phon/ist,** *n.*

Y, y (wī) *n.* twenty-fifth letter of English alphabet.

-y, suffix meaning: **1.** full of or like, as *cloudy.* **2.** inclined to, as *squeaky.* **3.** dear or little, as *kitty.* **4.** action of, as *inquiry.* **5.** quality or state, as *victory.*

yacht (yot) *n.* **1.** pleasure ship. —*v.* **2.** sail in yacht. —**yacht/ing,** *n.* —**yachts/man,** *n.*

ya/hoo (yä'hōō) *n.* coarse stupid person.

yak (yak) *n.,* *v.,* **yakked, yakking.** —*n.* **1.** long-haired Tibetan ox. **2.**

Slang. incessant idle or gossip talk. —*v.* **3.** *Slang.* gab; chatter.

yam (yam) *n.* edible potatolike root.

yam'mer (yam'ər) *v. Informal.* whine or chatter.

yank (yangk) *v.* **1.** pull suddenly; jerk. —*n.* **2.** sudden pull; jerk.

Yan'kee (yang'kē) *n.* native or inhabitant of the United States, northern U.S., or New England.

yap (yap) *v.,* **yapped, yapping,** *n.* **1.** yelp. **2.** chatter.

yard (yärd) *n.* **1.** linear unit (3 feet). **2.** long spar. **3.** enclosed outdoor area, used as a lawn, etc.

yard'age (yär'dij) *n.* amount in yards.

yard'arm', *n.* either of the yards of square sail.

yard'stick', *n.* **1.** measuring stick one yard long. **2.** criterion.

yar'mul.ke (yär'məl kə, -mə-, yär') *n.* cap worn by Jewish males during prayer.

yarn (yärn) *n.* **1.** many-stranded thread. **2.** story.

yar'row (yar'ō) *n.* plant with flat-topped clusters of white-to-yellow flowers.

yaw (yô) *v.* **1.** deviate. —*n.* **2.** deviation.

yawl (yôl) *n.* small sailboat.

yawn (yôn) *v.* **1.** open mouth wide involuntarily, as from sleepiness or boredom. —*n.* **2.** act of yawning.

Y chromosome, sex chromosome present only in males and paired with X chromosome.

ye (yē) *pron. Archaic.* **1.** you. **2.** the.

yea (yā) *adv., n.* yes.

year (yēr) *n.* period of 365 or 366 days. —**year'ly,** *adv., adj.*

year'book', *n.* **1.** book published annually with information on past year. **2.** commemorative book published as by graduating class.

year'ling (-ling) *n.* animal in its second year.

yearn (yûrn) *v.* desire strongly.

year'-round', *adj.* **1.** continuing, available, or used throughout the year. —*adv.* **2.** throughout the year.

yeast (yēst) *n.* yellowish substance, used to leaven bread.

yell (yel) *v.* shout loudly.

yel'low (yel'ō) *n.* **1.** color of butter, lemons, etc. —*adj.* **2.** of or like yellow. **3.** *Slang.* cowardly.

yellow fever, infectious tropical disease transmitted by mosquitoes.

yelp (yelp) *v.* **1.** give sharp, shrill cry. —*n.* **2.** such a cry.

yen (yen) *n. Informal.* desire.

yeo'man (yō'mən) *n.* **1.** petty officer in navy. **2.** independent farmer.

yes (yes) *adv., n.* expression of affirmation or assent.

ye.shi'va (yə shē'və) *n.* Orthodox Jewish school.

yes'-man', *n. pl.* **-men.** person who always agrees with superiors.

yes'ter.day (yes'tər dā', -dē) *adv., n.* day before today.

yet (yet) *adv.* **1.** so far; up to this (or that) time. **2.** moreover. **3.** still. **4.** nevertheless. —*conj.* **5.** but.

yew (yō) *n.* evergreen coniferous tree.

Yid'dish (yid'ish) *n.* German-based Jewish language.

yield (yēld) *v.* **1.** produce; give. **2.** surrender. **3.** give way. —*n.* **4.** that which is yielded; product.

yip (yip) *v.,* **yipped, yipping.** *Informal.* bark sharply.

yo'del (yōd'l) *v.,* **-eled, -eling.** **1.** sing with quick changes to and from falsetto. —*n.* **2.** song yodeled.

yo'ga (yō'gə) *n.* Hindu series of postures and breathing exercises practiced to attain physical and mental control and tranquillity.

yo'gi (yō'gē) *n.* Hindu who practices yoga.

yo'gurt (yō'gərt) *n.* custardlike food made from milk fermented by bacteria. Also, **yo'ghurt.**

yoke (yōk) *n., v.,* **yoked, yoking.** —*n.* **1.** piece put across necks of oxen pulling cart, etc. **2.** pair. —*v.* **3.** couple with, or place in, yoke.

yo'kel (yō'kəl) *n.* rustic.

yolk (yōk) *n.* yellow part of egg.

yon'der (yon'dər) *adj., adv. Archaic.* over there. Also, **yon.**

yore (yôr) *n.* time past.

you (yōō; *unstressed* yŏŏ, yə) *pron.* person or persons addressed.

young (yung) *adj.* **1.** in early stages of life, operation, etc. **2.** of youth. —*n.* **3.** young persons. **4.** young offspring. —**young'ish,** *adj.*

young'ster (-stər) *n.* child.

your (yŏŏr; *unstressed* yər) *pron., adj.* possessive of **you;** (without noun following) **yours.** —**Usage.** Do not confuse YOUR and YOU'RE. YOUR is the possessive form of "you": *Your book is overdue at the library.* YOU'RE is the contraction of "you are": *You're just the person we need for this job.*

you're (yŏŏr; *unstressed* yər) contraction of **you are.** —**Usage.** See YOUR.

your.self', *pron.* emphatic or reflexive form of **you.**

youth (yōōth) *n.* **1.** young state. **2.**

early life. **3.** young persons. **4.** young man. —**youth′ful,** adj.

yowl (youl) v., n. howl.

yo′-yo (yō′yō) n., pl. **-yos,** v., **-yoed, -yoing.** —n. **1.** spoollike toy spun out and reeled in by string looped on finger. —v. **2.** move up and down or back and forth.

yr., year.

yuc′ca (yuk′ə) n. tropical American plant.

yuck (yuk) interj. Slang. (exclamation of disgust or repugnance.) —**yuck′y,** adj.

yule (yōol) n. Christmas.

yule′tide″, n. Christmas season.

yum′my (yum′ē) adj., **-mier, -miest.** very pleasing, esp. to taste.

yup′pie (yup′ē) n. young, ambitious, and affluent professional who lives in or near a city.

Z, z (zē; esp. Brit. zed) n. twenty-sixth letter of English alphabet.

zaf′tig (zäf′tik, -tig) adj. Slang. (of a woman) pleasingly plump.

za′ny (zā′nē) n., pl. **-nies,** adj. **-nier, -niest.** —n. **1.** clown. **2.** fool. —adj. **3.** silly. —**za′ni•ness,** n.

zap (zap) v., **zapped, zapping.** Slang. kill or defeat.

zeal (zēl) n. intense ardor or eagerness. —**zeal′ous** (zel′əs) adj.

zeal′ot (zel′ət) n. excessively zealous person; fanatic. —**zeal′ot•ry,** n.

ze′bra (zē′brə) n. wild, striped horselike animal.

Zen (zen) n. Buddhist movement emphasizing enlightenment by meditation and direct, intuitive insight. Also, **Zen Buddhism.**

ze′nith (zē′nith) n. highest point.

zeph′yr (zef′ər) n. mild breeze.

zep′pe•lin (zep′ə lin) n. large dirigible of early 20th century.

ze′ro (zēr′ō) n., pl. **-ros, -roes. 1.** symbol (0) indicating nonquantity. **2.** nothing. **3.** starting point of a scale.

zero hour, starting time.

zero population growth, condition in which population remains constant because of equal number of births and deaths.

zest (zest) n. something adding flavor, excitement, etc. —**zest′ful,** adj.

zig′zag″ (zig′zag″) n., adj., adv., v., **-zagged, -zagging.** —n. **1.** line going sharply from side to side. —adj., adv. **2.** with sharp turns back and forth. —v. **3.** go in zigzag.

zilch (zilch) n. Slang. zero; nothing.

zil′lion (zil′yən) n. Informal. extremely large, indeterminate number.

zinc (zingk) n. bluish metallic element.

zinc oxide, salve made of zinc and oxygen.

zing (zing) n. **1.** sharp singing sound. —v. **2.** make such sound. —interj. **3.** (descriptive of such sound.)

zin′ni•a (zin′ē ə) n. bright, full-flowered plant.

Zi′on (zī′ən) n. **1.** Jewish people. **2.** Palestine as Jewish homeland. **3.** heaven as final gathering place of true believers.

Zi′on•ism, n. advocacy of Jewish establishment of state of Israel. —**Zi′on•ist,** n., adj.

zip (zip) v., **zipped, zipping,** n. Informal. —v. **1.** go very speedily. —n. **2.** energy.

ZIP code (zip) code numbers used with address to expedite mail.

zip′per, n. fastener with interlocking edges.

zip′py, adj., **-pier, -piest.** Informal. lively; smart.

zir′con (zûr′kon) n. mineral used as gem when transparent.

zir•co′ni•um (zûr kō′nē əm) n. metallic element used in metallurgy and ceramics.

zit (zit) n. Slang. pimple.

zith′er (zith′ər, zith′-) n. stringed musical instrument. Also, **zith′ern.**

zo′di•ac″ (zō′dē ak″) n. imaginary belt of heavens containing paths of all major planets, divided into twelve constellations.

zom′bie (zom′bē) n. reanimated corpse.

zone (zōn) n., v., **zoned, zoning.** —n. **1.** special area. —v. **2.** mark into zones. —**zon′al,** adj.

zonked (zongkt) adj. Slang. stupefied from or as if from alcohol or drugs.

zoo (zōō) n. place where live animals are exhibited.

zo•ol′o•gy (zō ol′ə jē) n. scientific study of animals. —**zo′o•log′i•cal** (-ə loj′i kal) adj. —**zo•ol′o•gist,** n.

zoom (zōōm) v. speed sharply.

zoom lens, camera lens allowing continual change of magnification without loss of focus.

zo′o•phyte″ (-fīt″) n. plantlike animal, as coral.

zuc•chi′ni (zōō kē′nē) n. cucumber-shaped squash.

zwie′back″ (zwī′bak″, -bäk′, swē′-) n. biscuit of dried, twice-baked bread.

zy′gote (zī′gōt) n. cell produced by union of two gametes. —**zy•got′ic** (-got′ik) adj.

Rules of Punctuation

1. **Period (.):** Ends a sentence which makes a statement or expresses a request, order or command. It is also used after most abbreviations.

2. **Question Mark (?):** Ends a sentence which asks a question.

3. **Exclamation Point (!):** Ends a sentence which expresses strong emotion or feeling.

4. **Colon (:):** Used (a) to introduce a formal or long direct quotation; (b) to introduce a long series of items or illustrations; (c) in the salutation of a formal letter.

5. **Semicolon (;):** Used (a) to separate long clauses of a compound sentence; (b) to separate independent clauses if the conjunction is omitted; (c) to separate long items in a series.

6. **Comma (,):** Used (a) to separate independent clauses connected by conjunctions *and, but, or, nor, for, yet, so*; (b) to separate a non-restrictive clause from the rest of the sentence; (c) to separate three or more words, phrases or clauses in a series; (d) to set off appositives and nouns in direct address; (e) to set off mild interjections; (f) to separate words in dates and addresses; (g) to introduce a direct quotation.

7. **Dash (—):** Used (a) to show a definite interruption or change of thought; (b) to indicate the omission of words, letters, or numbers.

8. **Apostrophe ('):** Used (a) in the possessive forms of nouns and indefinite pronouns; (b) to indicate the omission of one or more letters in contractions; (c) to form plurals of numbers or letters.

9. **Hyphen (-):** Used (a) to mark the break in an unfinished word at the end of a line; (b) between a prefix and a proper name or when the emphasis is on the prefix; (c) in fractions and in compound numerals from twenty-one to ninety-nine; (d) between the parts of certain compound words.

10. **Parentheses ( ):** Used to set off words, phrases, or clauses which are not basic to the main point of the sentence.

11. **Brackets ([ ]):** Used to indicate editorial explanation.

12. **Quotation Marks (" "):** Used (a) to enclose direct quotations; (b) to set off titles.

Rules of Spelling

No spelling rule should be followed blindly, for every rule has exceptions and words analogous in some forms may differ in others.

1. **Silent e dropped.** Silent *e* at the end of a word is usually dropped before a suffix beginning with a vowel: *abide, abiding; recite, recital.* **Exceptions:** Words ending in *ce* or *ge* retain the *e* before a suffix beginning with *a* or *o* to keep the soft sound of the consonant: *notice, noticeable; courage, courageous.*

2. **Silent e kept.** A silent *e* following a consonant (or another *e*) is usually retained before a suffix beginning with a consonant: *late, lateness; spite, spiteful.* **Exceptions:** *fledgling, acknowledgment, judgment, wholly,* and a few similar words.

3. **Final consonant doubled.** A final consonant following a single vowel in one-syllable words or in a syllable that will take the main accent when combined with a suffix is doubled before a suffix beginning with a vowel: *begin, beginning; occur, occurred.* **Exceptions:** *h* and *x (ks)* in final position; *transferable, gaseous,* and a few others.

4. **Final consonant single.** A final consonant following another consonant or a double vowel or diphthong or not in a stressed syllable is not doubled before a suffix beginning with a vowel: *part, parting; remark, remarkable.* **Exceptions:** An unaccented syllable does not prevent doubling of the final consonant, especially in British usage: *traveller* beside *traveler,* etc.

5. **Double consonants remain.** Double consonants are usually retained before a suffix except when a final *l* is to be followed by *ly* or *less.* To avoid a triple *lll,* one *l* is usually dropped: *full, fully.* **Exceptions:** Usage is divided, with *skilful* beside *skillful, instalment* beside *installment,* etc.

6. **Final y.** If the *y* follows a consonant, change *y* to *i* before all endings except *ing.* Do not change it before *ing* or if it follows a vowel: *bury, buried, burying; try, tries;* but *attorney, attorneys.* **Exceptions:** *day, daily; gay, gaily; lay, laid; say, said.*

7. **Final ie to y.** Words ending in *ie* change to *y* before *ing: die, dying; lie, lying.*

8. **Double and triple e reduced.** Words ending in double *e* drop one *e* before an ending beginning in *e,* to avoid a triple *e.* Words ending in silent *e* usually drop the *e* before endings beginning in *e* to avoid forming a syllable. Other words ending in a vowel sound commonly retain the letters indicating the sound. *Free-ed = freed.*

9. **ei or ie.** Words having the sound of *ē* are commonly spelled *ie* following all letters but *c;* with a preceding *c,* the common spelling is *ei.* Examples: *believe, achieve, besiege* but *conceit, ceiling, receive, conceive.* When the sound is *ā* the common spelling is *ei* regardless of the preceding letter. Examples: *eight, weight, deign.* **Exceptions:** *either, neither, seize, financier;* some words in which *e* and *i* are pronounced separately, such as *notoriety.*

10. **Words ending in c.** Before an ending beginning with *e, i,* or *y,* words ending in *c* commonly add *k* to keep the *c* hard: *panic, panicky.*

11. **Compounds.** Some compounds written as a unit bring together unusual combinations of letters. They are seldom changed on this account. *Bookkeeper, roommate.* **Exceptions:** A few words are regularly clipped when compounded, such as *full* in *awful, cupful,* etc.

Facts About the United States

State	Capital	Population	Area (sq. mi.)
Alabama	Montgomery	4,273,084	51,609
Alaska	Juneau	607,007	586,400
Arizona	Phoenix	4,428,068	113,909
Arkansas	Little Rock	2,509,793	53,103
California	Sacramento	31,878,234	158,693
Colorado	Denver	3,822,676	104,247
Connecticut	Hartford	3,274,238	5009
Delaware	Dover	724,842	2057
Florida	Tallahassee	14,399,985	58,560
Georgia	Atlanta	7,353,225	38,876
Hawaii	Honolulu	1,183,723	6424
Idaho	Boise	1,189,251	83,557
Illinois	Springfield	11,846,544	36,400
Indiana	Indianapolis	5,840,528	36,291
Iowa	Des Moines	2,851,792	56,290
Kansas	Topeka	2,572,150	82,276
Kentucky	Frankfort	3,883,723	40,395
Louisiana	Baton Rouge	4,350,579	48,522
Maine	Augusta	1,243,316	33,215
Maryland	Annapolis	5,071,604	10,577
Massachusetts	Boston	6,092,352	8257
Michigan	Lansing	9,594,350	58,216
Minnesota	St. Paul	4,657,758	84,068
Mississippi	Jackson	2,716,115	47,716
Missouri	Jefferson City	5,358,692	69,674
Montana	Helena	879,372	147,138
Nebraska	Lincoln	1,652,093	77,237
Nevada	Carson City	1,603,163	110,540
New Hampshire	Concord	1,162,481	9304
New Jersey	Trenton	7,987,933	7836
New Mexico	Santa Fe	1,713,407	121,666
New York	Albany	18,184,774	49,576
North Carolina	Raleigh	7,322,870	52,586
North Dakota	Bismarck	643,539	70,665
Ohio	Columbus	11,172,782	41,222
Oklahoma	Oklahoma City	3,300,902	69,919
Oregon	Salem	3,203,735	96,981
Pennsylvania	Harrisburg	12,056,112	45,333
Rhode Island	Providence	990,225	1214
South Carolina	Columbia	3,698,746	31,055

Facts About the United States (Continued)

State	Capital	Population	Area (sq. mi.)
South Dakota	Pierre	732,405	77,047
Tennessee	Nashville	5,319,654	42,246
Texas	Austin	19,128,261	267,339
Utah	Salt Lake City	2,000,494	84,916
Vermont	Montpelier	588,654	9609
Virginia	Richmond	6,675,451	40,815
Washington	Olympia	5,532,939	68,192
West Virginia	Charleston	1,825,754	24,181
Wisconsin	Madison	5,159,795	56,154
Wyoming	Cheyenne	481,400	97,914
Washington, D.C.	—	543,213	63
Total U.S.		**265,283,783**	**3,615,122**

Chief American Holidays

New Year's Day	January 1
Martin Luther King Day	January 15[1]
Inauguration Day	January 20
Lincoln's Birthday	February 12[2]
Washington's Birthday	February 22[2]
Good Friday	Friday before Easter
Memorial Day	May 30[3]
Independence Day	July 4
Labor Day	First Monday in September
Columbus Day	October 12[4]
Veterans Day	November 11
Election Day	Tuesday after first Monday in November
Thanksgiving Day	Fourth Thursday in November
Christmas Day	December 25

[1]officially observed on 3rd Monday in January
[2]officially observed as Presidents' Day on 3rd Monday in February
[3]officially observed on last Monday in May
[4]officially observed on 2nd Monday in October

Presidents of the United States

Name (and party)	Birth State	Born	Term	Died
George Washington (F)	Va.	1732	1789–1797	1799
John Adams (F)	Mass.	1735	1797–1801	1826
Thomas Jefferson (D-R)	Va.	1743	1801–1809	1826
James Madison (D-R)	Va.	1751	1809–1817	1836
James Monroe (D-R)	Va.	1758	1817–1825	1831
John Quincy Adams (D-R)	Mass.	1767	1825–1829	1848
Andrew Jackson (D)	S.C.	1767	1829–1837	1845
Martin Van Buren (D)	N.Y.	1782	1837–1841	1862
William Henry Harrison (W)	Va.	1773	1841–1841	1841
John Tyler (W)	Va.	1790	1841–1845	1862
James Knox Polk (D)	N.C.	1795	1845–1849	1849
Zachary Taylor (W)	Va.	1784	1849–1850	1850
Millard Fillmore (W)	N.Y.	1800	1850–1853	1874
Franklin Pierce (D)	N.H.	1804	1853–1857	1869
James Buchanan (D)	Pa.	1791	1857–1861	1868
Abraham Lincoln (R)	Ky.	1809	1861–1865	1865
Andrew Johnson (R)	N.C.	1808	1865–1869	1875
Ulysses Simpson Grant (R)	Ohio	1822	1869–1877	1885
Rutherford Birchard Hayes (R)	Ohio	1822	1877–1881	1893
James Abram Garfield (R)	Ohio	1831	1881–1881	1881
Chester Alan Arthur (R)	Vt.	1830	1881–1885	1886
Grover Cleveland (D)	N.J.	1837	1885–1889	1908
Benjamin Harrison (R)	Ohio	1833	1889–1893	1901
Grover Cleveland (D)	N.J.	1837	1893–1897	1908
William McKinley (R)	Ohio	1843	1897–1901	1901
Theodore Roosevelt (R)	N.Y.	1858	1901–1909	1919
William Howard Taft (R)	Ohio	1857	1909–1913	1930
Woodrow Wilson (D)	Va.	1856	1913–1921	1924
Warren Gamaliel Harding (R)	Ohio	1865	1921–1923	1923
Calvin Coolidge (R)	Vt.	1872	1923–1929	1933
Herbert Clark Hoover (R)	Iowa	1874	1929–1933	1964
Franklin Delano Roosevelt (D)	N.Y.	1882	1933–1945	1945
Harry S. Truman (D)	Mo.	1884	1945–1953	1972
Dwight D. Eisenhower (R)	Tex.	1890	1953–1961	1969

Presidents of the United States (Continued)

Name (and party)	Birth State	Born	Term	Died
John Fitzgerald Kennedy (D)	Mass.	1917	1961–1963	1963
Lyndon Baines Johnson (D)	Tex.	1908	1963–1969	1973
Richard Milhous Nixon (R)	Cal.	1913	1969–1974	1994
Gerald R. Ford (R)	Neb.	1913	1974–1977	
James Earl Carter, Jr. (D)	Ga.	1924	1977–1981	
Ronald Wilson Reagan (R)	Ill.	1911	1981–1989	
George H. W. Bush (R)	Mass.	1924	1989–1993	
William J. Clinton (D)	Ark.	1946	1993–	

F–Federalist; D–Democrat; R–Republican; W–Whig.

Distances Between U.S. Cities

	Atlanta	Chicago	Dallas	Denver	Los Angeles	New York	St. Louis	Seattle
Atlanta	—	592	738	1421	1981	762	516	2354
Boston	946	879	1565	1786	2739	184	1118	2831
Chicago	592	—	857	909	1860	724	251	1748
Cincinnati	377	255	870	1102	1910	613	550	2003
Cleveland	587	307	1080	1216	2054	458	558	2259
Dallas	738	857	—	683	1243	1391	547	2199
Denver	1421	909	683	—	838	1633	781	1074
Detroit	619	247	1045	1156	2052	486	463	1947
Kansas City	745	405	452	552	1360	1117	229	1626
Los Angeles	1981	1860	1243	838	—	2624	1589	956
Miami	614	1199	1405	1911	2611	1106	1123	2947
Minneapolis	942	350	860	840	1768	1020	492	1398
New Orleans	427	860	437	1120	1680	1186	609	2608
New York	762	724	1381	1633	2624	—	888	2418
Philadelphia	667	671	1303	1578	2467	95	841	2647
Pittsburgh	536	461	1318	1349	2157	320	568	2168
St. Louis	516	251	547	781	1589	888	—	1890
San Francisco	2308	1856	1570	956	327	2580	1916	687
Seattle	2354	1748	2199	1074	956	2418	1890	—
Washington, D.C.	547	600	1183	1519	2426	215	719	2562

Weights and Measures

Troy Weight

24 grains	=	1 pennyweight
20 pennyweights	=	1 ounce
12 ounces	=	1 pound

Avoirdupois Weight

$27\,^{11}/_{32}$ grains	=	1 dram
16 drams	=	1 ounce
16 ounces	=	1 pound
100 pounds	=	1 short hundredweight
20 short hundredweight	=	1 short ton

Apothecaries' Weight

20 grains	=	1 scruple
3 scruples	=	1 dram
8 drams	=	1 ounce
12 ounces	=	1 pound

Linear Measure

12 inches	=	1 foot
3 feet	=	1 yard
$5\,^{1}/_{2}$ yards	=	1 rod
40 rods	=	1 furlong
8 furlongs (5280 feet)	=	1 statute mile

Mariners' Measure

6 feet	=	1 fathom
1000 fathoms (approx.)	=	1 nautical mile
3 nautical miles	=	1 league

Apothecaries' Fluid Measure

60 minims	=	1 fluid dram
8 fluid drams	=	1 fluid ounce
16 fluid ounces	=	1 pint
2 pints	=	1 quart
4 quarts	=	1 gallon

Square Measure

144 square inches	=	1 square foot
9 square feet	=	1 square yard
$30\,^{1}/_{4}$ square yards	=	1 square rod
160 square rods	=	1 acre
640 acres	=	1 square mile

Cubic Measure

1728 cubic inches	=	1 cubic foot
27 cubic feet	=	1 cubic yard

Surveyors' Measure

7.92 inches = 1 link
100 links = 1 chain

Liquid Measure

4 gills = 1 pint
2 pints = 1 quart
4 quarts = 1 gallon
31 1/2 gallons = 1 barrel
2 barrels = 1 hogshead

Dry Measure

2 pints = 1 quart
8 quarts = 1 peck
4 pecks = 1 bushel

Wood Measure

16 cubic feet = 1 cord foot
8 cord feet = 1 cord

Angular and Circular Measure

60 seconds = 1 minute
60 minutes = 1 degree
90 degrees = 1 right angle
180 degrees = 1 straight angle
360 degrees = 1 circle

10 dekaliters = 1 hectoliter
10 hectoliters = 1 kiloliter

Weights

10 milligrams = 1 centigram
10 centigrams = 1 decigram
10 decigrams = 1 gram
10 grams = 1 dekagram
10 dekagrams = 1 hectogram
10 hectograms = 1 kilogram
100 kilograms = 1 quintal
10 quintals = 1 ton